ETHICS
Revised Edition

Ethics
Revised Edition

Volume 2
Genocide and democide — Power

Edited by

JOHN K. ROTH
Claremont McKenna College
Department of Philosophy and Religious Studies

SALEM PRESS, INC.
PASADENA, CALIFORNIA   HACKENSACK, NEW JERSEY

Editor in Chief: Dawn P. Dawson
Managing Editor: Christina J. Moose
Project Editor: R. Kent Rasmussen
Assistant Editor: Andrea Miller
Acquisitions Editor: Mark Rehn
Photograph Editor: Philip Bader
Research Assistant: Andy Perry
Production Editor: Kathy Hix
Graphics and Design: James Hutson
Layout: William Zimmerman

Library of Congress Cataloging-in-Publication Data

Ethics / edited by John Roth.— Rev. Ed.
   p. cm.
  Includes bibliographical references and index.
  ISBN 1-58765-170-X (set : alk. paper) — ISBN 1-58765-171-8 (vol. 1 : alk. paper) — ISBN 1-58765-172-6 (vol. 2 : alk. paper) — ISBN 1-58765-173-4 (vol. 3 : alk. paper)
  1. Ethics—Encyclopedias. I. Roth, John K.
  BJ63.E54 2004
  170'.3—dc22
                                            2004021797

First Printing

PRINTED IN THE UNITED STATES OF AMERICA

CONTENTS

Contents

CONTENTS

COMPLETE LIST OF CONTENTS

Volume 1

Volume II

Volume III

ETHICS
Revised Edition

Genocide and democide

DEFINITION: Intentional destruction of human groups based upon identifying characteristics that members of the groups are assumed to have

TYPE OF ETHICS: Human rights

SIGNIFICANCE: Modern political, social, and religious leaders agree that genocide and democide violate the most basic principles of international human rights.

Raphael Lemkin, a Polish jurist and scholar of international law, coined the term "genocide" during the early 1940's. The term later became a basis of international law, making it possible to try crimes of genocide before the International Criminal Court. In its narrowest sense, genocide is an intentional and systematic attempt to destroy an entire human group, based upon the nationality, ethnicity, race, or religion of the group's members. Since Lemkin's time, the meaning of the term has been expanded to encompass other defining human characteristics, such as sexual orientation or political affiliation. However, not all scholars accept these broader definitions, and legally such expansion is not permitted. To overcome these limitations, Rudolph Rummel coined the term "democide" during the 1990's to serve as a more inclusive label for governmental efforts to perpetrate mass murder. Estimates of the numbers of persons who were victims of genocide and democide during the twentieth century range from 170 to 210 million. These numbers are at least four times greater than the numbers of people killed while fighting wars during the last century.

DEFINITIONS

Although legalistic definitions of genocide are limited to definable groups, the concept includes the destruction of human groups through mass murder as well as the process of limiting procreation. Thus, genocide can be committed through efforts to sterilize a population to prevent the birth of future generations. Early eugenics movements had at their core, in the early twentieth century, the elimination of those whose genes were deemed inferior. The Nazis used such policies to begin massive sterilizations of the mentally and physically disabled as well as Jews and Roma/Sinti (Gypsies). The pattern of mass rape as practiced during the atrocities against Bosnians during the 1990's was officially codified as a form of genocide by the International Criminal Tribunal for the former Yugoslavia. Definitions of genocide are not based solely on nation-states or governments as perpetrators. Individuals and nongovernmental groups whose actions include the destruction of another group may also be found guilty of genocide.

Mass murders that clearly fit the criteria for genocide include the killing of Armenians by the Young Turks of the Ottoman Empire during World War I, the killing of Gypsies by Nazis during World War II, and the killing of Tutsis by Hutus in Rwanda in 1994.

While the term democide is broader in terms of target groups, the term is applied only to murders undertaken by governments or quasi-governmental bodies. Thus, a hate group that targets specific individuals for murder would technically not be guilty of democide. However, a government engaged in the same kind of crime would be guilty of democide. On the other hand, the term democide is not applied to the killing of soldiers during wars and the execution of persons lawfully convicted of capital crimes.

The list of mass murders that fit the definition of democide is extensive and includes the mass killing of political dissidents by Joseph Stalin in the Soviet Union and the mass murders committed under the rule of Mao Zedong in China. Many cases of democide are more often described as a genocide. For example, the Cambodian genocide of the mid-1970's fits the definition of democide but is usually referred to as a genocide. The targeted groups in the killing fields of Cambodia consisted largely of groups such as city dwellers and the educated. As that episode had Cambodians killing Cambodians on the basis of characteristics not identified within the narrow definition of genocide, it theoretically should not be identified as genocide but rather as democide. However, the killing of the Vietnamese by Cambodia's Khmer Rouge communists would be considered an instance of genocide.

REVERSAL OF MORALITY

The ethical issues involved in genocide and democide appear transparent at first glance. Both actions violate the principles underlying the major world religions and are also considered to be violations of international law. Individuals, groups, and nations involved in genocide and democide are considered guilty of violating the United Nations Convention on the Prevention and Punishment of the Crime of Genocide (1948) and the Universal Declaration of Human Rights (1948). Although no ethical or moral defense for the atrocities of mass murder, genocide, and democide exists, perpetrators of genocide often view their actions as moral and for the greater good. Moreover, few perpetrators of genocide and democide have been held accountable under international law and have thus acted with impunity. This apparent reversal of morality with its accompanying moral relativity raises questions as to how individuals and nations can move from general acceptance of ethical codes against killing to a moral position that justifies atrocity.

Doctors working for Germany's Nazi regime believed that they were engaged in a higher good by sterilizing and later "euthanizing" or killing patients who were regarded as incurable. These included epileptics, schizophrenics, alcoholics, people with mental disabilities, and a host of others labeled "useless eaters" and killed by starvation, lethal injection, gunshot, or poisonous gas. The regime justified its actions by arguing not only that patients would appreciate being spared future suffering but also that their extermination removed dangerous genetic infections that threatened the well-being of the people of Germany. The Nazi genocide of Jews, Gypsies, and other peoples was regarded as the removal of a tumor from the body of Germany, a Final Solution in dealing with Germany's "problem" groups. Thus, the Nazis and their supporters perceived their genocide as a valiant, courageous, and morally good action.

During World War II, the United States dropped atom bombs on the Japanese cities of Nagasaki and Hiroshima, killing more than 120,000 men, women, and children. The government rationale for these actions was that such destruction was horrible but necessary to save the lives of the Allied soldiers who would otherwise be needed to invade Japan. While the validity of this rationale has been debated, it represents a case in which the morality of democide may be unclear. If purely military targets in Japan had been selected for destruction, the resulting loss of life would not fit the criteria identified for democide. However, as Hiroshima and Nagasaki were civilian targets, the loss of life represents a case of democide. If similar bombs had been dropped on major population centers in England or the United States during the war, it most likely would not have been viewed as morally acceptable.

Centuries of genocide against indigenous populations have been justified through self-interest, primarily need for land and resources. The indigenous populations in North and South America, Australia, and Africa all experienced varying levels of physical as well as cultural genocide. Little is written about these groups, however, as the colonizers and conquerors have written most of the histories of their conquests.

AUTHORITARIAN LEADERS

Nations that commit genocide and democide are generally led by authoritarian rulers in totalitarian governments. Such governments and leaders may also have destructive ideologies and are thus more likely to commit atrocities than are governments of democracies. The rulers responsible for the most destructive genocides and democides are Joseph Stalin, Mao Zedong, and Adolf Hitler, who were all totalitarian leaders. Moreover, the members of societies ruled by such governments also tend to exhibit high degrees of conformity as well as obedience to authority. Such people may be willing to kill other people simply because obedience and conformity are considered to be their only appropriate ethical choices. During the Nuremberg Trials of Nazi war criminals held after Germany's defeat in World War II, many former Nazi officers tried to justify their crimes by claiming to have merely followed orders. Judges on the Nuremberg tribunal did not accept such defenses, but individual soldiers whose participation in the Holocaust may have been less pivotal were not tried in part because of this justification.

PATHS TO GENOCIDE AND DEMOCIDE

The practice of genocide and democide often begins slowly within a culture. Pre-genocidal cultures typically have histories of believing that members of certain groups or classes within their cultures are superior to members of other groups. During times of relative stability and prosperity such cultural populations may engage in limited prejudice, stereotyping, and discrimination. However, during times of economic or political crisis, latent hatreds can be revived and used by authoritarian leaders as a means to build solidarity and support within the dominant groups. What begins as prejudice and discrimination over time may evolve into a pattern of deliberate denial of civil rights. Thus, members of a targeted group may find they are denied such rights as employment, citizenship, or the ability to own property. If few objections are publicly voiced, the next step may be a move toward greater loss of fundamental human rights and finally loss of existence. Little outrage was expressed when Jews began losing their rights in Nazi Germany during the 1930's. That fact made it easier for the government to progress from laws prohibiting certain forms of work to loss of citizenship, then ghettoization, and finally deportation and death.

For human beings to move down such a path toward greater violence, a process of moral disengagement and exclusion must occur. It is difficult simply to kill a person whom one has known as an associate or neighbor. Propaganda helps a society advance step by step toward a policy of genocide. Such propaganda includes a vilifying of members of the target group as well as a dehumanization of the group. For example, during Germany's Holocaust, government propaganda denounced Jews as parasites who threatened Germany's well-being and equated Jews with rats and vermin. When human beings begin morally disengaging and finally excluding their neighbors from what is perceived as their moral realm, the process becomes complete. Human beings have less trouble killing people whom they perceive as not fitting within what they regard as traditional human boundaries, particularly if they regard those people as a threat. In Rwanda, for example, Hutus who killed their Tutsi neighbors during the mid-1990's regarded them not as fellow Rwandans but as dangerous aliens, whom they characterized as *inyenzi* (cockroaches). Euphemistic language also assists with this process of moral disengagement and exclusion. Germany's Nazi government did not tell German citizens that it was sending Jews and other people to their deaths in concentration camps; it simply told them that their Jewish neighbors were being "sent east."

BYSTANDERS

Bystanders—whether they be individuals, groups, or nations—can prevent genocide from developing if they raise protests early as a government moves down the path to genocide and democide. This raises serious questions about the ethics of those who stand by passively as a disenfranchised group becomes increasingly targeted for violence and genocide. As violence began in Rwanda, both outside nations and the United Nations distanced themselves from the developing genocide and proclaimed it to be an internal matter that was solely Rwanda's responsibility. For outside nations to label the events in Rwanda as genocide would have necessitated action. This inaction by a passive world that watched the horror unfold helped fuel the deaths of approximately 800,000 Tutsis over the course of one hundred days. By the time the United Nations finally sent international peacekeepers into Rwanda, the mass killings had ceased.

The longer bystanders wait to act as a genocide develops, the more difficult intervention becomes. When intervention occurs late, both the outside governments and their citizens must accept moral responsibility for their earlier inaction. Moreover, as time passes, bystanders tend to rationalize that the victims of a genocide deserve their fates in order to maintain their belief in a just and moral world.

DENIAL

The last step on the path of genocide and democide is denial that the mass killing ever occurred. Thus, the final assault on the victims is that their very memory is excised from history. Denial can take many forms. For example, the government of Turkey has consistently denied that it staged a genocide against its Armenian citizens during World War I. Instead, the government portrays the events of that period as an unfortunate effect of deportations of a internally dangerous population. Most modern Turkish citizens who deny the Armenian genocide are basing their denial not on a history of prejudice but rather on a history shaped by the Turkish victors. Thus, they are simply repeating what they and their parents have learned of the events during World War I in revisionist history.

Other instances of genocide such as the man-made famine in the Ukraine during the 1930's have been simply written off as unintended and accidental occurrences resulting from distant governmental policies. The deaths of large numbers of Native American groups in what is now the United States have often been dismissed simply as unintentional deaths resulting from disease and failure to adapt to life on reservations. Famine, disease, exposure, and other "natural causes" of death manufactured by governmental policies enable the distancing of responsibility and the denial of genocide. Other forms of denial clearly have at their base an agenda of hate. Holocaust denial is not a new phenomenon and is propagated by many white supremacist groups within the United States and around the world. Such forms of hate-based denial have at their core genocidal intent. Whatever the intent of those who deny specific instances of genocide or democide, whether out of ignorance or hate, such efforts at denial are ethically unjustifiable.

Linda M. Woolf

FURTHER READING

Barnett, Victoria. *Bystanders: Conscience and Complicity During the Holocaust.* Westport, Conn.: Greenwood Press, 2000. Examination of moral and ethical issues relating to bystanders during the Holocaust, particularly communities living within Nazi-occupied Europe.

Opotow, Susan, ed. "Moral Exclusion." *Journal of Social Issues* 46, no. 1 (1990). Special issue of the journal with articles exploring facets of moral exclusion, including the ability to exclude others from one's moral sphere during times of genocide and extreme destructiveness.

Rummel, Rudolph. *Death by Government.* New Brunswick, N.J.: Transaction, 1996. Excellent statistical and historical information concerning instances of twentieth century genocides and democide, from the Holocaust to the Soviet gulag state. Evaluates the role of power in the creation of democidal states and cultures.

Staub, Ervin. *The Psychology of Good and Evil.* New York: Cambridge University Press, 2003. Collection of Staub's seminal writings on all facets of genocide, including cultural preconditions, leaders, bystander behavior, rescue and altruistic behavior, and intervention.

Totten, Samuel, William Parsons, and Israel Charny, eds. *Century of Genocide: Eyewitness Accounts and Critical Views.* New York: Garland, 1997. Articles combining historical facts, scholarly analysis, and accounts of both survivors and witnesses of several genocides, including genocides of indigenous populations. The element of personal testimony enables readers to transcend the numbing effect resulting from the enormity of each genocide.

SEE ALSO: Bystanders; Concentration camps; Ethnic cleansing; Evil; Genocide, cultural; Genocide, frustration-aggression theory of; Holocaust; Lemkin, Raphael; Native American genocide; Pogroms; Rwanda genocide; United Nations Convention on the Prevention and Punishment of the Crime of Genocide.

Gewirth, Alan

IDENTIFICATION: American philosopher and educator

BORN: November 28, 1912, Union City, New Jersey

TYPE OF ETHICS: Human rights

SIGNIFICANCE: Gewirth proposed the principle of generic consistency—the principle of equal and universal human rights—and justified freedom and the ethical obligation to respect human rights.

The author of *Reason and Morality* (1978), *Human Rights: Essays on Justification and Applications* (1982), *The Community of Rights* (1996), and *Self-Fulfillment* (1998), Alan Gewirth is recognized as one of the most prominent ethicists of the late twentieth century. He has published over one hundred articles on moral, ethical, social, and political philosophy, the epistemology of René Descartes, and many other topics. He is well known for his work on the philosophical foundations and ethical implications of human rights. In the late 1970's, he proposed the idea that freedom and well-being are fundamental, universal human rights, a concept known as the principle of generic consistency (PGC), Gewirth's supreme principle of morality.

Gewirth claims that freedom and well-being are the foundation attributes necessary for all human action. They establish the common (generic) conditions for the successful exercise of free agency for the members of all cultures. Gewirth argues that all other rights can be derived from these two. He assumes that people in general act for purposes that they regard as being good—not necessarily morally good, but valuable. Thus people must be entitled to freedom and well-being. For consistency, people are bound by duty to not restrain others from obtaining freedom and well-being. In other words, it is an ethical requirement that every individual must allow the same human rights to every other individual. Some philosophers have used the PGC to analyze complex ethical questions, such as the attempt to determine human traits prior to birth.

One inference drawn from Gewirth's PGC is that people who violate the principle must either be using incorrect reasoning or be unethical persons. The principle also makes the transition of transforming fundamental, prudential rights into moral rights. However, many philosophers criticize and disregard the PGC because of these implications.

Gewirth is a strong advocate that self-fulfillment is a fundamental goal of human endeavor. Although many deem it to be an egotistical effort, Gewirth developed an ethical theory showing that self-fulfillment is based on the dignity of human beings and that human rights are essential to self-fulfillment, completing its interrelationship with the PGC. Self-fulfillment enhances the ethical and moral growth of not only an individual, but also of the society in which the individual resides.

Alvin K. Benson

FURTHER READING

Beyleveld, Deryck, and Alan Gewirth. *The Dialectical Necessity of Morality: An Analysis and Defense of Alan Gewirth's Argument to the Principle of Generic Consistency.* Chicago: University of Chicago Press, 1991.

Boylan, Michael, ed. *Gewirth.* Lanham, Md.: Rowman & Littlefield, 1999.

Regis, Edward. *Gewirth's Ethical Rationalism: Critical Essays with a Reply by Alan Gewirth.* Chicago: University of Chicago Press, 1984.

SEE ALSO: Consistency; Egotist; Epistemological ethics; Theory and practice.

al-Ghazālī

IDENTIFICATION: Persian philosopher
BORN: 1058, Ṭūs, Khurasan, Iran
DIED: December 18, 1111, Ṭūs, Khurasan, Iran
TYPE OF ETHICS: Religious ethics
SIGNIFICANCE: Al-Ghazālī is author of several widely read works on ethics, including *The Revival of Religious Sciences* (late eleventh century), *The Niche for Lights* (early twelfth century), and *The Incoherence of the Philosophers*

(late eleventh century), as well as an influential spiritual autobiography, *The Deliverer from Error* (early twelfth century). His mysticism also made Sufism more acceptable to conservatives.

Abū Ḥāmid al-Ghazālī (not to be confused with his younger brother, Ahmad Ghazālī) is best known for his writings on ethics, the proper foundations for ethics, and mysticism (which is, for al-Ghazālī, continuous with ethics). His work enjoys widespread respect, earning him the honorific title "the scholar among the inhabitants of the world." Unlike many other philosophers, who were happy to begin their reflections with reason or sense experience, al-Ghazālī placed great emphasis on the importance of the Qurʾān and the *Ḥadīth* (traditions) of the life of Muḥammad.

Al-Ghazālī was a successful and respected professor of theology at the most important college in the Seljuk empire, the Nizāmiyya, in Baghdad. In 1095, however, he suffered a severe personal crisis, left the Nizāmiyya, traveled throughout the Middle East, and eventually resettled in his ancestral home, Ṭūs. There, he wrote the many treatises that secured his enduring, central place in Islamic thought.

The crisis of 1095 was focal to al-Ghazālī's later thought. A superb logician, al-Ghazālī was not only able to construct impressive systematic theology but also was aware that intellectual argumentation about that which transcends the abilities of argumentation is built on a foundation of sand. Furthermore, the scholarly endeavors of orthodox legalists and theologians came to seem arid, even spiritually sterile, to al-Ghazālī, who appears to have felt an increasing sense of loss of the presence of God in these scholarly religious investigations. After carefully studying the works of numerous Sufis and understanding their principles intellectually, he appears to have had an epiphany in which those principles became experiential.

THE INCOHERENCE OF THE PHILOSOPHERS

The Incoherence of the Philosophers and the reply by Averroës (*The Incoherence of the Incoherence*) constitute one of the most famous philosophical exchanges in the Islamicate world and were also very widely discussed in medieval and Renaissance Europe. Al-Ghazālī attacked Avicenna, al-Fārābī, and Aristotle for logical inconsistencies in their work and for basing their systems of thought on rational argument alone, denying a central role for revelation and for the direct experience of God. Al-Ghazālī did not reject wholesale the conclusions of these philosophers, and he did not deny an important role for Aristotelian logic. Some of his conclusions about practical ethics, for example, do not differ from those of Aristotle. Further, although he did reject Neoplatonic emanation schemes entirely, he did so by perspicuously demonstrating their logical impossibility. Nevertheless, al-Ghazālī argued that the work of these philosophers was not built on a sound foundation; would lead the faithful astray in many matters; and, hence, ought to be abandoned in favor of an ethical system based on the Qurʾān, *Ḥadīth*, and experiential knowledge of God—a system that he provided in the *Revival*.

THE REVIVAL OF RELIGIOUS SCIENCES

Written in forty (the number symbolic of patient effort) chapters, the first section of the *Revival* concerns ʿIbādāt, or worship. The second section, on customs, might seem mundane to Western readers. It offers very practical guidance in such areas as diet, ways to serve food, child rearing, and so forth. (Much of al-Ghazālī's advice on child rearing strikes the modern reader as far ahead of its time.) In Islam, however, all aspects of life, even the most mundane, should be infused with reminders of divine will, and therefore these practical matters are part of religious sciences. The central chapter celebrates the Prophet and emphasizes the importance of the traditions of Muḥammad's life as the "good example" (Qurʾān, *sūra* 33:21) for ethical conduct. The third section examines vices and their sources, and the final section examines those things that lead to salvation (including virtues and their sources, as well as mystical love and longing).

Although Western modernity might see the topics of the *Revival* as diverse, al-Ghazālī clearly saw them as continuous, as necessary training in one's gradual development toward the highest possible perfection. The ultimate goal is experiential knowledge of God, which "can be reached only when the barriers in the heart precluding such achievement are removed." This essentially mystical goal requires practical ethical training so that the passions and excessive attachment to bodily pleasures can be curbed, and so that wisdom can be developed.

THE NICHE FOR LIGHTS

The relationship of this text to al-Ghazālī's other works has been highly controversial. The *Niche for Lights* is a commentary on the "Sūra of Light" (Qurʾān, 24:35), in which Allah is indicated as the purest Light, which inspired al-Ghazālī to develop a metaphysics of light that has remarkably strong affinities with Illuminationist Sufi doctrines. One refers to Light properly only when one indicates God, al-Ghazālī argued, and one uses "light" only analogically in all other instances. Only the Divine Light exists, and all in this phenomenal world is but a shadow cast by that light (comparison with Plato's allegory of the cave would not be farfetched). The ultimate good in human life is attainment of direct apprehension of Light and complete immersion in Light.

Thomas Gaskill

FURTHER READING

Abrahamov, Binyamin. *Divine Love in Islamic Mysticism: The Teachings of al-Ghazālī and al-Dabbāgh.* New York: RoutledgeCurzon, 2003.

Ghazālī, al-. *The Faith and Practice of Al-Ghazālī.* Translated by W. Montgomery Watt. London: George Allen & Unwin, 1967.

_____. *Imam Gazzali's "Iḥyā ʿUlūm-ud-Din."* Translated by Al-Haj Maulana Fazl-ul-Karim. 4 vols. Lahore, Pakistan: Sh. Muhammad Ashraf, 1993.

Rafiabadi, Hamid Naseem. *Emerging from Darkness: Ghazzali's Impact on the Western Philosophers.* New Delhi: Sarup & Sons, 2002.

Umaruddin, Muhammad. *The Ethical Philosophy of al-Ghazzālī.* Lahore, Pakistan: Muhammad Ashraf, 1970.

SEE ALSO: Averroës; Avicenna; Fārābī, al-; *Ḥadīth*; Sufism.

Gideon v. Wainwright

THE EVENT: U.S. Supreme Court decision holding that felony defendants are entitled to legal representation regardless of the crime with which they are charged, and that if such a defendant cannot afford an attorney, the court must appoint one

DATE: Ruling made on March 18, 1963

TYPE OF ETHICS: Legal and judicial ethics
SIGNIFICANCE: The Supreme Court ruled that forcing criminal defendants to represent themselves is a violation of the due process clause of the Fifth Amendment, as well as the right to counsel guaranteed in the Sixth Amendment.

Because of a 1942 Supreme Court decision, *Betts v. Brady*, the state was not required to appoint an attorney for Clarence Earl Gideon at the time of his first trial for robbery in Panama City, Florida, in 1961. Following the dictates of *Betts*, Florida provided counsel only to defendants accused of capital offenses, and Gideon, an impoverished individual of limited education, was forced to act as his own attorney. He was found guilty and sent to prison. While there, he penciled a petition to the Supreme Court to hear his claim that his constitutional rights had been violated. The Court agreed that, because he had been forced to appear without benefit of counsel, Gideon had been denied a fair trial. The Court ordered that

Gideon be allowed a new trial and a court-appointed attorney. At his second trial, Gideon was acquitted of all charges. He had demonstrated the power of a single individual to change the entire legal establishment.

Lisa Paddock

SEE ALSO: Accused, rights of; Attorney-client privilege; Bill of Rights, U.S.; Constitution, U.S.; Due process; Supreme Court, U.S.

Global warming

DEFINITION: Gradual increase of the earth's surface temperatures
TYPE OF ETHICS: Environmental ethics
SIGNIFICANCE: Global warming is a source of long-term but increasing danger to human beings and to all ecosystems on Earth that raises questions

Scientists take water samples from the sea, gathering data used to study global warming. (AP/Wide World Photos)

about the point at which future problems become present ethical concerns.

During the twentieth century, the earth's average surface temperature increased about 0.5 degree Celsius, arguably as a result of concurrent human generation of "greenhouse" gases. Furthermore, some environmental modeling indicates another 0.7 to 2 degrees Celsius of warming after the oceans reach equilibrium, plus a further 2 to 5 degrees by the year 2020 if no action is taken.

Even greater changes, however, occurred many times in the more remote past when no human activities could have caused them. Repeated glaciation and deglaciation in the last million years repeatedly exceeded the hypothesized changes without human influence, and the causes of glaciation are not thoroughly understood. The major environmental effects of global warming include the poleward shift of climatic belts, the sea level's rising as much as 6 meters by 2020, and drastically changed atmospheric and oceanic circulation. All these occurrences will disrupt present human activity. Thus, regulation or abolition of activities that may be responsible for warming, such as the burning of fossil fuels, is an ethical issue that has provoked proposals for action at both national and international levels. The prohibition of combustible fuels, for example, entails massive social and economic changes, which should not be undertaken lightly in view of substantial lack of consensus regarding the causes and future course of currently observed global warming.

Ralph L. Langenheim, Jr.

SEE ALSO: Bioethics; Earth and humanity; Ecology; Environmental ethics; Future generations; Greenhouse effect; Nature, rights of; Rain forests.

Globalization

DEFINITION: Process of increasing interconnections and linkages within societies and across international boundaries through improved communications and expanded world trade

TYPE OF ETHICS: International relations

SIGNIFICANCE: Because of the economic and social disparities that exist among between countries

and continents, the ethics of globalization are often debated in the international arena, and this debate focuses on who benefits from globalization and who loses.

The term "globalization" began gaining prominence during the mid-1980's as a description of the expansion of interrelated economic, social, and cultural activity beyond national borders to societies across national and international geographical boundaries. The interconnections and linkages that occur with globalization have removed barriers to free trade, which has resulted in an increased standard of living for many around the world along with increased life expectancies. At the same time, however, that phenomenon challenged traditional social, political, and economic structures.

Globalization has been brought about by reductions in transportation and communication costs, as well as dissolutions of artificial barriers to movements of trade, services, capital, and knowledge across borders. Specific trade agreements that most often draw attention in discussions of globalization are the General Agreement on Tariffs and Trade (GATT) and the North American Free Trade Agreement (NAFTA).

PROCESS OF GLOBALIZATION

The process of globalization has been brought about by the creation of new international organizations such as the World Bank, the International Monetary Fund (IMF), and the World Trade Organization (WTO). The World Bank and the IMF were established at Bretton Woods, New Hampshire, in 1944. Known as the Bretton Woods Institutions, the two organizations seem similar but have clear differences. The IMF was established to create stability in international trade and provide temporary financial assistance to countries in financial crises. The World Bank was created to eliminate poverty through reconstruction and development. The three organizations, taken together, attempt to regulate and provide stability to the global economic and trade environment, in the hope of furthering globalization and creating opportunities for globalization for all countries in the world.

The benefits of globalization include open markets, positive competition, increased use of technology, and the potential to enrich many people, espe-

Thousands of Filipinos march in Manila on September 13, 2003, as part of coordinated protests throughout the developing world against the developed world's globalization policies. The worldwide "Global Day of Action" coincided with a ministerial meeting of the World Trade Organization in Cancun, Mexico. (AP/Wide World Photos)

cially the poor. Globalization has reduced the sense of isolation felt by many in the developing world. The expansion and increased use of technology have provided access to knowledge and information that before was limited to only the wealthiest countries.

Globalization has also increased the types and frequency of interactions among peoples of varied cultures. People from all over the world meet together to a much greater extent than they had in the past, and they consequently begin to influence each other as well as begin to understand each other. This global culture has let to the creation of new identities and new forms of literature, music, and art.

While globalization has clear benefits, it has not succeeded in reducing poverty as was promised; in fact, the gap between the haves and the have nots in developing countries is widening. Globalization has also not provided for stability in developing nations. Latin American and Asia are two good examples

of how financial crises can affect the entire global economy. In addition, globalization has had negative effects on the environment, with many poor countries using precious environmental resources in the name of development. The "sustainable development" movement is an attempt to preserve the environment while at the same time providing for development opportunities.

ETHICS ISSUES

The ethics of globalization ultimately centers around two questions: Who benefits from globalization? Who loses from globalization? Political leaders are continually having to consider their economic and social priorities between serving their own people and working to benefit the welfare of citizens in countries other than their own. For those whose interests lie in the health and environmental movements, ethical principles such as autonomy, beneficence, nonmalfeasance, justice, utility, and stewardship are important to the discussion of the ethics of globalization. For others, global ethics must support social equity and cultural diversity, as well as developing common global goals.

Global ethics cannot be discussed without some reference to the role of morality. However, this further complicates the discussion, since one has to ask "whose morality"? Many people are looking to the religious communities of the world to provide some answer to this question. In a publication entitled *Our Creative Diversity*, published in 1995 by the World Commission on Culture and Development, the United Nations, and UNESCO, the commission lists several elements of a global civic culture that could provide the framework for a global ethical code, including human rights and responsibilities, the peaceful resolution of conflicts, democracy and civic governance, the protection of minorities, fairness of negotiation, and intergenerational equity.

Nongovernmental organizations (NGOs) are calling for global ethics that emerge from a process of discussion and debate from global grassroots movements. These organizations proved to be quite powerful when they worked together to protest the WTO meetings in Seattle, Washington, and in the campaign against the World Bank and the IMF. Their ability to join together across continents allowed for an understanding of shared values and objectives. The production of common statements of protest and organized actions begins to set the stage for a discussion on global ethics. The question now is who will facilitate this process and take responsibility for the ensuing debate.

Robin Sakina Mama

FURTHER READING

Bello, Walden, Shea Cunningham, and Bill Rau. *Dark Victory: The United States, Structural Adjustment, and Global Poverty.* London: Pluto Press, 1994.

Berberoglu, Berch. *Globalization of Capital and the Nation-State: Imperialism, Class Struggle, and the State in the Age of Global Capitalism.* Lanham, Md.: Rowman & Littlefield, 2003.

Dunning, John H., ed. *Making Globalization Good: The Moral Challenges of Global Capitalism.* New York: Oxford University Press, 2003.

Gerle, Elisabeth. *In Search of a Global Ethics: Theo-logical, Political, and Feminist Perspectives.* Lund, Sweden: Lund University Press, 1995.

Hurrell, Andrew, and Ngaire Woods, eds. *Inequality, Globalization, and World Politics.* New York: Oxford University Press, 1999.

Kung, Hans, and Karl Josef Kaschel, eds. *A Global Ethic: Declaration of the World's Religions.* London: Continuum, 1993.

Monshipouri, Mahmood, et al., eds. *Constructing Human Rights in the Age of Globalization.* Armonk, N.Y.: M. E. Sharpe, 2003.

Singer, Peter. *One World: The Ethics of Globalization.* New Haven, Conn.: Yale University Press, 2002.

Stiglitz, Joseph E. *Globalization and Its Discontents.* New York: W. W. Norton, 2002.

SEE ALSO: Agribusiness; Developing world; International justice; International law; International Monetary Fund; Multinational corporations; Outsourcing; World Trade Organization.

Gluttony

DEFINITION: Overindulgence in food and drink
TYPE OF ETHICS: Personal and social ethics
SIGNIFICANCE: Traditionally one of the seven deadly sins, gluttony is a self-destructive form of behavior, morally objectionable on the grounds both of social propriety and of the imperative to self-preservation. In modern society, gluttony is quickly becoming an endemic social problem as irresponsible eating and exercise habits become one of the major causes of death in the United States.

Since classical antiquity, gluttony has been regarded as a reprehensible individual choice; however, both the motivation and the degree of social censure have varied. In ancient Rome, the vomitoria were viewed as the ultimate symbol of decadence (the *Satyricon* of Petronius), but in general, overindulgence for sheer hedonistic pleasure inspired more envy than disdain.

During the Middle Ages, gluttony came under heavy censure, partly because the overindulging individual was incapacitated, but primarily because of the awareness that excessive consumption by a few denied food to those in need. Gluttony was counted

Gluttony as a Competitive Sport

In the early twenty-first century—a period when health care professionals are warning of an epidemic of obesity in the United States and are campaigning for more sensible eating habits—competitive eating has reached new levels of popularity. Since Nathan's hot dog stand at Coney Island, New York, began an annual eating contest in 1916, Americans have associated eating competitions with modest numbers of frankfurters, pies, and watermelon slices. Today, however, eating contests have reached unprecedented levels of volume, vulgarity, and publicity, and some people are seriously arguing that competitive eating should be regarded as a "sport." Meanwhile, competitors such as these have captured the public imagination:

- A young 145-pound Japanese man whose records include eating more than 20 pounds of food in a single sitting

- A 380-pound American who has eaten—on different occasions—15 burritos in 8 minutes, 9.5 pounds of peas in 12 minutes; 49 doughnuts in 8 minutes, and 12 pounds of cheesecake (containing 37,000 calories) in 6 minutes

- A slender 36-year-old American woman who has eaten 432 oysters in 10 minutes, 7.75 pounds of stuffed duck and turkey in 10 minutes, and 23 pulled-pork sandwiches in 10 minutes

Apart from the obvious health hazards that such eating stunts pose, the growing popularity of the contests raises questions about both the ethics and the aesthetics of conspicuous consumption. In an e-mail message to the *Los Angeles Times*, Michael Strober, the director of the Eating Disorders Program at UCLA's Neuropsychiatric Institute, suggested that competitive eating might represent, at least for some participants, a means of channeling clinical disturbances of eating behavior, such as binge eating, into socially acceptable behavior.

among the seven deadly sins on the strength of Paul's censure of "those whose god is their belly" (Phil. 3:19).

From the Renaissance onward, the religious and social censure of gluttony gradually became muted; gluttony even received an ironic apology from François Rabelais in the course of his overall attack on the

vestiges of medieval philosophy and ethics (*Gargantua*, 1552). In the eighteenth and nineteenth centuries, gluttony became increasingly regarded as a purely medical problem, and by the late twentieth century, the term "gluttony" was generally replaced by "eating disorder," "compulsive eating," "compulsive drinking," and "alcoholism," reflecting a sense that overindulgence in food and drink (including alcohol) is involuntary and is thus outside the sphere of moral or ethical choice.

D. Gosselin Nakeeb

SEE ALSO: Greed; Laziness; Psychology; Sin; Temperance.

God

DEFINITION: Supreme supernatural being
TYPE OF ETHICS: Religious ethics
SIGNIFICANCE: If God exists, and if human conceptions of God are at all accurate, God's existence would necessarily entail the existence of a universal objective moral law. However, in the absence of conclusively accepted evidence supporting either of those two conditions, religious belief and practice are largely, if not wholly, matters of faith, and morality is a matter of personal conviction.

All persons of sound mind have in some way answered, though few may have asked, the question "Why be moral?" The typically philosophical question is "What is the good?" The answers to both questions have attempted to lay the cornerstone for a moral life. One common answer centers on humanity within the context of the world. "The good," or "being moral," is defined in terms of the natural world. Here, natural sciences and anthropocentric disciplines are used to discover the moral life.

A second response to the seldom-asked question "Why be moral?" is God—solely God. God is good, God's acts are moral acts. God's acts define morality. From this perspective, theology and philosophy are the primary disciplines that provide insight into the moral life.

A third customary response maintains that there is no fundamental contradiction between God and God's creation. Many believers in God, therefore, combine the first two answers to one of life's most fundamental questions. God is good. God has created a good world. God has created humanity as part of the world in such a way that humans are to live in the manner that God has required of them. Consequently, the natural sciences, social sciences, philosophy, and theology can all contribute to the moral life. Although this more unified approach to morality is most inclusive, avoiding both the abstractions of an intellectually isolated theology and a narrow thoroughgoing naturalism, the remainder of this article focuses on the concept of God and the moral life.

GOD AND HUMAN MORALITY

There are at least three ways in which God's actions can be relevant for human morality. These three relationships constitute the main theological theories of ethical objectivism. First, God's actions and commandments define what is right. Whatever God commands is moral simply because God commands it. The weakness of this view is that whatever a person understands God to do or to command would be considered moral, including, for example, war, infanticide, and human sacrifice. This would magnify God's power, but at great cost to God's morality. Another way in which God and ethics might be related is for morality to be determined independently of God. All of God's actions and commandments would still be morally correct, but their morality would be determined externally to God. The problem with this view is that morality is determined prior to and separately from God. Thus, God is rendered dependent and limited. Moreover, the identity and nature of this unrivaled moral power is unknown.

The third view holds that God's actions correspond to the good. It is not that any arbitrary act of God defines moral actions or that the good is externally delimited, but that every act of God reveals God's character as the good God who created the good world and continues to act without self-contradiction. God has revealed God's own nature in creating and sustaining a moral world. The difficulty with this view is that one must explain how persons who believe that there is no God, and how persons with radically divergent ideas about God, can nevertheless lead highly moral lives. This complaint appears answer-able, however, by the third response to the initial question: Humans should be moral because God has created them in the cosmos in such a way that they are to live in the manner for which they have been created. Thus, the sciences, philosophy, and theology can all contribute to the moral life that builds upon God as the source and foundation of morality.

VARYING NOTIONS OF GOD

Different notions of God lead to different moral decisions. According to the priestly theology of the Pentateuch, Moses justifies many of ancient Israel's civil laws by citing the acts of Yahweh, the God of Israel. At Yahweh's direction Moses taught, "You shall be holy, for I the LORD your God am holy. . . . When you reap the harvest of your land, you shall not reap to the very edges of your field, or . . . strip your vineyard bare; . . . you shall leave them for the poor and the alien: *I am the LORD your God.* . . . You shall not cheat in measuring length, weight, or quantity. You shall have honest balances and honest weights: *I am the LORD your God, who brought you out of the land of Egypt. You shall keep all my statutes:* . . . *I am the LORD*" (Lev. 19). Although it is the case that many of Israel's laws are related to other religions and nations, its ethical justifications are not cultural, political, or philosophical but historical and, preeminently, theological.

Although not identified as God, Plato's "form of the good" functions in his ethics as God. At the pinnacle of his philosophical hierarchy rests "the good" in relation to which all other objects exist (both ideals and sensible objects) and must properly live. The good is the source of all moral principles. This functional apotheosis of the good, conjoined with the primacy of his ideals or forms (they are nonphysical, nonspatial, nontemporal, and beyond the sensible world), leads Plato to distrust the material world even to the point of rejecting most physical pleasures and advocating a philosopher king rather than a popularly chosen ruler.

In another example, according to the Gospel of Luke, Jesus of Nazareth understands God as generous and forgiving toward all persons. Jesus consciously roots his moral teachings in his concept of God. "Bless those who curse you, pray for those who abuse you. . . . If you love those who love you, what credit is that to you? For even sinners love those who love them. . . . But love your enemies, do good, and lend, expecting nothing in return. Your reward will be great, and you will be children of the Most High; for he is kind to the ungrateful and the wicked. Be merciful, just as your Father is merciful" (Luke 6:27-36).

By definition, beliefs about God influence the ethics of those who believe that God exists. Nevertheless, a system of ethics and human behavior are not identical. Research has shown that behavior is less predicated upon theological beliefs than upon perceived threats and authority, and upon the central object of one's trust and loyalty.

Paul Plenge Parker

FURTHER READING

Cahn, Steven M., and David Shatz, eds. *Questions About God: Today's Philosophers Ponder the Divine.* New York: Oxford University Press, 2002.

Gustafson, James M. *Ethics from a Theocentric Perspective.* 2 vols. Chicago: University of Chicago Press, 1981-1984.

Hare, John E. *God's Call: Moral Realism, God's Commands, and Human Autonomy.* Grand Rapids, Mich.: W. B. Eerdmans, 2001.

Moltmann, Jurgen. *The Crucified God.* Translated by R. A. Wilson and John Bowden. New York: Harper & Row, 1974.

Niebuhr, H. Richard. *Radical Monotheism and Western Culture.* New York: Harper & Row, 1970.

Plato. *The Republic.* Translated by Desmond Lee. 2d ed. New York: Penguin Books, 2003.

Stassen, Glen H. "Social Theory Model for Religious Social Ethics." *Journal of Religious Ethics* 5 (Spring, 1977): 9-37.

SEE ALSO: Anthropomorphism of the divine; Deism; Divine command theory; Ethical monotheism; Good, the; Human nature; Jesus Christ; Objectivism; Pantheism; Religion.

Godparents

DEFINITION: Persons who take on special responsibilities when they sponsor candidates for baptism or initiation into Christian life
TYPE OF ETHICS: Family issues
SIGNIFICANCE: Godparents fulfill a historical custom in the ethical and religious education of the newly initiated that expands family and spiritual ties.

In the Christian tradition, godparents take responsibility for the religious and ethical educations of the newly baptized or newly initiated whom they are sponsoring. The history of godparenting is thus coextensive with the history of Christian baptism, originating in the early practices of the Church. Serving as godparents is considered an honor, a significant responsibility, and a spiritual bond with the godchildren—who may be infants, children, or adult—and their families.

Although specific practices vary by denomination, godparents traditionally assume several responsibilities for their godchildren. They sponsor the children for baptism, the rite of initiation into the Christian religion (for this reason, godparents are also known as sponsors), and represent the witness of the faith community. Second, they help instruct the children in the religious and ethical doctrines of the faiths into which they are baptized. Finally, they help form and educate their godchildren throughout their spiritual lives.

To fulfill these responsibilities, it is usually required that godparents be active, adult church members who are able to exemplify the faith to their godchildren in both words and practice. Godparents assume the duty of assisting the parents in the religious education of the godchildren, and they assume full responsibility for that duty if the parents cannot fulfill it. For these reasons, preferred godparents are those who can form close, lifelong relationships with their godchildren and be available to them at all the important stages of life.

Godparents also often give their godchildren religious gifts at baptism, send cards on religious anniversaries, teach prayers and customs, and suggest names for infant godchildren. Their chief gift, however, is perhaps to pray for their godchildren. It is commonly thought to be ideal if the same godparent can sponsor a godchild for both baptism and confirmation.

Howard Bromberg

SEE ALSO: Character; Christian ethics; Gossip; Morality; Parenting; Responsibility; Role models.

Golden mean

DEFINITION: Ethical principle that virtue consists of
    following a course of moderation between ex-
    tremes
DATE: Articulated between 335 and 323 B.C.E.
TYPE OF ETHICS: Classical history
SIGNIFICANCE: The golden mean is based on a model
    of human experience in which extremity of any
    kind is to be avoided and stability and comfort in
    the world are positive ethical goods.

The ethical doctrines of Aristotle are expounded in
three major works: the *Nicomachean Ethics*, the
Eudemian Ethics, and the *Great Ethics*, or *Magna
Moralia*. The *Nicomachean Ethics* is considered
to be Aristotle's most mature work on the subject of
ethics. In the *Nicomachean Ethics*, a work divided
into ten "books" of roughly similar length (approximately 20 pages), Aristotle addresses the issue of human conduct and raises and attempts to answer the
question: "What is the good life?" In book 6 of the
Nicomachean Ethics, Aristotle gives one of the most
typically Greek answers to this question of ethics and
in so doing makes use of the compromise position
that he took in philosophy generally.

The golden mean, which has also been called the
"doctrine of the mean" and the "Aristotelian mean,"
is the ideal that Greeks customarily sought as a guide
to their daily lives, both public and private. It followed naturally that Aristotle associated ethics with
the state—not with religion, as Christianity subsequently taught. Thus, the *Nicomachean Ethics* has
been viewed as a fundamentally political work.

Aristotle argues from the premise that human beings occupy an intermediate position in the hierarchy
of living forms: Human lives are not as good as those
of gods, but they are (or at least can be) better than the
lives of other animals and plants. He seeks a theory of
the human good that not only accords with this assumption but also explains it: Humans want to know
what it is that makes their lives occupy this intermediate position. The best good for a human being, according to Aristotle, must be something that no other
animal or plant can achieve.

VIRTUES OF CHARACTER

To fully understand Aristotle's defense of the virtues of character—the skills that enable humans to
listen to reason—it is necessary to see how they are
connected to the preeminent virtue: practical wisdom. In book 2 of the *Nicomachean Ethics*, Aristotle
states that he undertakes his present project for a
practical purpose: for humans not to contemplate
truths about what virtue is, but to become good people. In this spirit, Aristotle then introduces the notion
of a mean: Such bodily virtues as strength and health
are destroyed by deficiency and excess (too much or
too little exercise, too much or too little eating), and
the same holds of such virtues of the soul as temperance and courage. For example, to be courageous
means not to fear everything and avoid every danger,
nor must humans be without fear and accept every
risk; to be temperate one must not pursue every pleasure, and one must not go to the opposite extreme of
pursuing none. Aristotle points out that the mean for
one person in one situation will differ from the mean
for someone else in a different situation. The idea is
that there is not some one correct amount of anger,
for example. Instead, when one aims at the mean, one
must aim at something that is for him or her neither
too great nor too little: It must be the appropriate
amount of anger, fear, or appetite at this time, in relation to this person, and so on.

To be virtuous, people must aim their actions and
feelings at a mean between deficiency and excess. In
the same way that a good craftsman attempts to produce something from which nothing should be taken
away and to which nothing need be added, so humans
should strive for something equally appropriate to
the situations in which they find themselves. Finding
this intermediate path is difficult, according to Aristotle, because there are so many different ways to un-
der- or overshoot one's target. Striking the mean in
one's actions and feelings is a task that requires practical reason. Thus, when Aristotle defines ethical virtue, he describes it as a state concerned with choice,
since a mean is relative to the individual as determined by reason, the reason by which the practically
wise person would determine it.

Echoes of this formulation run throughout Aristotle's discussion of the virtues—to exercise the virtues is to follow reason; his doctrine of the mean is
the guiding principle behind his classification of virtues and vices. To possess an ethical virtue is to know
how to strike the mean. Consequently, there are two
kinds of character defects: One may regularly do and
feel either too much or too little. Every such virtue is

therefore to be understood by comparing it with its corresponding vice.

Whether or not Aristotle's claims are true, it has been argued that they do provide a workable standard for decision making. Nearly the whole of book 6 of the *Nicomachean Ethics* is devoted to the study of two kinds of virtues: practical wisdom and theoretical wisdom. Aristotle is saying that either of these should be the target toward which the reasonable person aims. Thus, the "right" amount in actions and feelings will be whatever amount best contributes to the fullest expression of these two rational skills. Aristotle's entire discussion may be viewed as contributing in one way or another to an understanding of what he maintains are the two highest human virtues.

Genevieve Slomski

FURTHER READING

De Geus, Marius. *The End of Over-Consumption: Towards a Lifestyle of Moderation and Restraint.* Utrecht, the Netherlands: International Books, 2003.

Hans, James S. *The Golden Mean.* Albany: State University of New York Press, 1994.

Hardie, W. F. R. *Aristotle's Ethical Theory.* 2d ed. New York: Oxford University Press, 1980.

Hutchinson, D. S. *The Virtues of Aristotle.* New York: Routledge & Kegan Paul, 1986.

Kraut, Richard. *Aristotle on the Human Good.* Princeton, N.J.: Princeton University Press, 1989.

Moravcsik, J. M. E., ed. *Aristotle: A Collection of Critical Essays.* Garden City, N.Y.: Anchor Books, 1967.

Urmson, J. O. "Aristotle's Doctrine of the Mean." In *Essays on Aristotle's Ethics*, edited by Amelie O. Rorty. Berkeley: University of California Press, 1980.

SEE ALSO: Aristotelian ethics; Aristotle; Excellence; Mādhyamaka; *Nicomachean Ethics*.

Golden rule

DEFINITION: Ethical principle that advises that one should treat others as one wants to be treated

TYPE OF ETHICS: Theory of ethics

SIGNIFICANCE: The golden rule includes both an ide-alist and a practical component. It asserts that there is a fundamental human nature which entitles all people to the same level of dignity and respect, and it also assumes that the life of each individual will be made better if everyone agrees to abide by a law founded on this assumption, whether the assumption itself is true or not.

The injunction that one should treat others as one wants to be treated is known as the "golden" rule because it is often said to be of unparalleled value as a fundamental ethical principle. Testimony to the value that human beings have accorded this principle is found in its long and rich history, a history that includes, but is not limited to, its appearance in Confucianism (sixth century B.C.E.), Buddhism (fifth century B.C.E.), Jainism (fifth century B.C.E.), Zoroastrianism (fifth century B.C.E.), Hinduism (third century B.C.E.), Judaism (first century B.C.E.), Christianity (first century C.E.), and Sikhism (sixteenth century C.E.).

The golden rule has been formulated both negatively (do *not* do to others what you would not want done to yourself) and positively (do unto others what you would have them do unto you). The negative formulation seems to be the older of the two, being the version endorsed in Confucianism, Buddhism, Jainism, and Zoroastrianism; nevertheless, it has been argued that the positive formulation is superior to the negative formulation because the former includes a call to beneficence that is lacking in the latter. This criticism of the negative version does not withstand scrutiny, however, for neglect is certainly one of the things that an individual might want to avoid and thus—in keeping with the negative formulation—would be something an individual should not do to others.

A more serious problem said to afflict both versions of the golden rule is that neither provides a basis for distinguishing between virtuous and nonvirtuous wants. Thus, an individual who wants to be debased or subjugated is enjoined by the golden rule to debase and subjugate others. For this reason, it has been thought that the golden rule cannot serve as a fundamental principle of morality, since its just application is possible only if one already has some independent means for distinguishing between morally good and morally corrupt behavior.

LOVE THY NEIGHBOR

Because of this concern, it has sometimes been suggested that a close cousin of the golden rule—Love thy neighbor as thyself—is a superior fundamental moral principle. The superiority of the call to love one's neighbor as oneself is thought to reside in the concept of love, a concept that specifies that one's wants should be directed toward the welfare of oneself and others. By virtue of its focus upon the welfare of the beloved, the call to extend the same love to oneself and others prohibits acting upon wants that are unjustifiably damaging. In fairness to the golden rule, however, it should be pointed out that applicability of loving one's neighbor as oneself presupposes both that people do love themselves and that this self-love can be used as a model for attitudes toward others. While these presuppositions might seem reasonable, it is worth noting that the possibility of nonvirtuous self-directed wants that drives the objection against the golden rule poses similar problems for the aforementioned presuppositions of the call to love thy neighbor as thyself.

It was also concern over the problem of corrupt wants that led Immanuel Kant to distinguish his own first moral principle, the categorical imperative, from the golden rule. One version of Kant's categorical imperative states that one should act only according to that maxim (rule of action) that one can, at the same time, will to be a universal law. The difference between the golden rule and the categorical imperative is found, according to Kant, in the fact that one can always treat others as if they shared one's wants, corrupt or otherwise; however, it is not possible consistently to will the universalization of corrupt behavior. To illustrate the difference between the two principles, Kant points out that many individuals would gladly agree to receive no assistance from others and thereby—in accordance with the golden rule—be relieved of the duty to assist others. Willing that such mutual neglect be universal would be irrational, however, because it would involve willing that no human being ever render assistance to others, a policy that would undermine the very existence of the human race. In this way, says Kant, the categorical imperative excludes corrupt wants that the golden rule allows to stand.

Even if the problem of nonvirtuous wants and related problems do show that the golden rule cannot generate an ethical system by itself, however, the rule is still deserving of its rich history insofar as it can serve as a ready test of the impartiality of some proposed plan of action.

James Petrik

FURTHER READING

Allinson, Robert E. "The Confucian Golden Rule: A Negative Formulation." *Journal of Chinese Philosophy* 12 (Spring, 1985): 305-315.

Blackstone, W. T. "The Golden Rule: A Defense." *The Southern Journal of Philosophy* 3 (Winter, 1965): 172-177.

Gewirth, Alan. "The Golden Rule Rationalized." *Midwest Studies in Philosophy* 3 (1978): 133-147.

Gould, James A. "The Not-So-Golden Rule." *The Southern Journal of Philosophy* 1 (Fall, 1963): 10-14.

Ivanhoe, Philip J. "Reweaving the 'One Thread' of the Analects." *Philosophy East and West* 40 (January, 1990): 17-33.

Kant, Immanuel. *Groundwork for the Metaphysics of Morals.* Edited and translated by Allen W. Wood. New Haven, Conn.: Yale University Press, 2002.

Pike, E. Royston. *Ethics of the Great Religions.* London: C. A. Watts, 1948.

Rawls, John. *A Theory of Justice.* Rev. ed. Cambridge, Mass.: Belknap Press of Harvard University Press, 1999.

Rost, H. T. D. *The Golden Rule: A Universal Ethic.* Oxford, England: George Ronald, 1986.

Wattles, Jeffrey. *The Golden Rule.* New York: Oxford University Press, 1996.

SEE ALSO: Impartiality; Kant, Immanuel; Sidgwick, Henry; Universalizability.

The Good

DEFINITION: That which one ought to do

TYPE OF ETHICS: Theory of ethics

SIGNIFICANCE: The good is the total of all positive morality: actions one is required to take, qualities which are considered virtuous, and constructive, full, or otherwise admirable ways to live one's life. It names a presence of moral right rather than a mere absence of moral wrong.

Plato spoke of a kind of trinity of forms: the good, the true, and the beautiful. Each of these corresponded to the perfection of a faculty in humanity. The beautiful was the perfect object of the faculty of judgment. The true was the perfect object of the faculty of the intellect, and the good was the perfect object of the faculty of the will. In Platonic metaphysics, moreover, these three forms enjoy a kind of consubstantiality. In later natural-law thinking, goodness, truth, and beauty were coextensive with being itself.

In the theodicy of Saint Augustine, furthermore, this becomes crucial, since that father of the Church overcame the metaphysical implications of the existence of evil by denying real being to evil: Evil does not enjoy substantial existence but subsists in a kind of parasitic relation to the good. Evil is the absence of a good where a good should be. In the will, this situation amounts to a choice of a lesser good over a greater good.

In these ways, metaphysical notions of goodness interact with ethical conceptions of the good. Classical philosophers as well as patristic and Scholastic theologians held that the human will must always will a good; in reality, there are only goods to be willed.

Aristotle analyzed the nature of goods by distinguishing between intrinsic and nonintrinsic goods (often called instrumental goods). Intrinsic goods are valuable for their own sake, while nonintrinsic goods are sought for the sake of some intrinsic good. Aristotle further noted that among intrinsic goods, one good will be a *summum bonum*, or ultimate good. The *summum bonum* for Aristotle (and for Saint Thomas Aquinas) was happiness—*eudaimonia*—and the activity/state most associated with the achievement of this end was philosophical contemplation for Aristotle and beatitude (with the attendant beatific vision) for Saint Thomas. On account of this divergence, Aristotelian ethics are designated as natural eudaimonism and Thomistic ethics as supernatural, or theological, eudaimonism.

For both Aristotle and Thomas Aquinas, the *summum bonum* served as an architectonic principle that was capable of ordering all other lesser goods in relationship to it. This Aristotelian-Thomistic approach combines eudaimonism with a natural-law approach that conceives of a fixed and universally shared human essence. Each subordinate faculty of humanity has its own teleology—its specific purpose or end (that is, its own good)—but the ends of these are ordered to the final end of humanity.

NATURAL LAW AND THE GOOD

This natural-law approach to morality upholds a strict objectivity in ethics, for while a man might pervert his nature by ignoring the promptings of his conscience and his reason, that would in no way alter the nature of his true good. Ethical pluralists deny that there is a *summum bonum* for humankind; there are only individual choices of goods in accordance with hierarchies of value created by individual tastes and commitments.

The distinction between ethical objectivists and ethical subjectivists in regard to goodness is vital. Subjectivists maintain that there is no activity of persons or state of being that is inherently good unless it produces an appropriate subjective response in the individual. An objectivist, however, claims that some human activities or states of being are inherently good, apart from any subjective response that they may produce in the subject.

Classical hedonism of both the rational school, associated with Epicurus, and the so-called irrationalist school (or Cyrenaic school), associated with Aristippus of Cyrene, claimed pleasure as the inherent good for humanity. In the more sophisticated versions of hedonism, the concept of pleasure is so expanded as to come close to the multifaceted concept of *eudaimonia*.

In modern times, in both the act utilitarianism of Jeremy Bentham and the rule utilitarianism of John Stuart Mill, pleasure is the good for humanity, which position has caused many scholars to treat utilitarianism as a special form of hedonism. Classical hedonism developed its social aspects by building up its theory from the individual's interests, needs, and desires, while utilitarianism, with its central criterion of "the greatest good for the greatest number," begins with an inherently social perspective.

Both Mill and Bentham defined the good as pleasure, but they differed so radically in their definitions of pleasure that it has been standard practice among philosophers to refer to Bentham's quantitative theory of pleasure as hedonistic utilitarianism and to Mill's qualitative theory of pleasure as eudaimonistic utilitarianism.

599

THE NATURALISTIC FALLACY

There was, perhaps, no more significant development in the modern search for the good than G. E. Moore's demonstration of the so-called naturalistic fallacy. Having demonstrated that no natural property can be designated as the good, Moore went on to claim that goodness must be a nonnatural property inhering in good acts.

Analytical philosophers of the Anglo-American tradition accepted Moore's proof that the good could not be a simple natural property, but they rejected his notion that it constituted a nonnatural property, electing instead to assume that the term was used differently in different contexts, indicating quite different natural properties or combinations of natural properties.

Pragmatists such as John Dewey agreed with the analytical philosophers concerning the nature of the good, but they were led to their conclusions by ontological rather than linguistic considerations. Given his commitment to situational ethics and to the ultimate plasticity of human nature, Dewey envisioned the good as varying with historical circumstances and cultural contexts.

Noncognitivist ethicians have interpreted the good in terms of their special linguistic approaches. Emotivists have held the term "good"—like all positive ethical language—to express a positive emotional response to ethical actions in the world: "Charity is good" is translated as an emotional approval of charity. Imperativists hold that ethical statements are overt or covert commands, and "Charity is good," for them, means "Perform charitable deeds." Finally, emoto-imperativists see a term such as "good" as combining a command function with emotional responses.

David Hume's explication of the is/ought problem also must be seen as vital for an understanding of the difficulties that modern ethical philosophers have had with the concept of the good. With the discovery that prescriptive ("ought") conclusions cannot be derived from descriptive ("is") premises, the conception of the good was put under an inordinate strain. Always implicit in the concept of the good had been the notion of "that which one ought to do." With the is/ought dichotomy, this aspect of the concept of the good was forever divorced from the more substantive contents of its various alternative definitions.

Sir Karl Popper noted that the definition of the good as "that which one ought to do" cannot be expanded to accommodate any substantive content beyond that meaning.

In contrast to the consequentialistic tradition in ethics, the great countertradition of formalism arose, defining the good not in view of the consequences of particular acts, but in respect to the form of the ethical judgments that choose those acts. Cicero may be seen as the originator of formalism, with his unique ethical theory that derived from the academics of the late Platonic school, the peripatetics of the late Aristotelian school, and the stoics. In Ciceronian moral philosophy, the *summum bonum* was equated generally with virtue and specifically with the virtue of *honestum*, or right doing.

IMMANUEL KANT

Immanuel Kant, whose ethical thought seems to have been influenced by Cicero and the stoics, is the very epitome of a formalist ethician. Although Kant believed that a properly virtuous person would ultimately enjoy acting morally and would achieve happiness thereby, these considerations were unnecessary for the essential goodness of his or her actions. The goodness of an action rests in its meeting the formal criterion of the categorical imperative: An action whose implicit maxim can become a universalizable law for all moral agents is a good action. Any action not in accord with that standard is a morally impermissible action.

For Kant, furthermore, it is not meritorious to do the correct action because one desires some benefit from that action. A merchant who keeps honest weights and measures because such a practice is good for his business is not acting in a morally good manner. To be morally virtuous, Kant would maintain, an action must be done for the sake of the moral law. That is why Kant could term his ethical system a "deontology"—a science of duty.

In contrast to the absolutist moral claims of Kantian formalism, the various forms of ethical relativism have descriptive definitions of the good. In individual ethical relativism, nothing is held to be right or wrong for the individual person except that which he or she truly believes to be right or wrong. Cultural ethical relativism holds that good actions are those approved by one's culture and that evil actions are those condemned by one's culture. Finally, the relativism of situational ethics defines the good in terms of the judgments of one's historical era and so forth.

Divine command morality, one of the less fashionable byways of ethical theory, must be acknowledged as having a formalistic account of the good, for the goodness of acts consists in their being done in response to divine command alone.

The history of ethical philosophy may well be said to be the history of the changing notions of goodness, and that history is a tormented one indeed. In the earliest days of ethical theory, Aristotle found it necessary to abandon Plato's form of the good because, attractive as that concept was, it seemed to bear no real relationship to human ethics. Aside from possible mystical experience, humans do not seem to have access to the form of the good; thus, it could have no real bearing upon ethical theory.

Aristotle's abandonment of the form of the good led to great alterations in agathokakological theory—the philosophy of good and evil. While Plato ascribed evil to ignorance—Socrates stated repeatedly that to know the good is to do the good—Aristotle added *akrasia* (weakness of the will) to the causes of evil. Aristotle did not deny the role that the Socratic/Platonic concept of evil arose from ignorance, but he held that notion to be inadequate to encompass all evil. Some men know the good, Aristotle believed, but lack the force of will and character to pursue it.

In late Judaism and early Christianity, the concept of the free will (*liberum arbitrium*) and its role in the selection or rejection of the greater good came to play a predominant part. The notion that one may know the good, have the strength of will to do it, and yet deliberately reject it entered theological ethics. Freely chosen evil—the "Mystery of Iniquity"—came not merely to supplement the concepts of ignorance and *akrasia* as wellsprings of evil but to dominate them. Evil done from ignorance or *akrasia* in this view would be true moral evil only if the ignorance or *akrasia* were itself culpable, and that culpability requires that, at the end of the chain of moral causation, a free choice must have been the basis of all else that followed.

In part, concerns of theodicy—the theological/philosophical investigation of divine justice—fueled the Judeo-Christian development of the concept of freely chosen evil. How is it just that God punishes sin if an individual could not act otherwise? Freely chosen evil was the answer that was proposed. In addition, Judeo-Christian demonology, with the figure of Satan/Lucifer, contributed to the need for a new explanation for the rejection of the good, for by traditional doctrine, Lucifer was the highest of all created minds and, as an angel, lacked a lower nature—thus, ignorance and *akrasia* are excluded as explanations for his evil.

For Kant also, the question of freely chosen evil became a fundamental problem in his ethical theory. In the *Foundations of the Metaphysics of Morals* (1895) and the *Critique of Practical Reason* (1873), Kant seemed to speak as if deliberately chosen evil were possible. Already, however, there were problems, for true freedom—the autonomous will—was possible only when the will made a law for itself, and that law could only be the categorical imperative.

Finally, in *Religion Within the Bounds of Reason Alone* (1838), Kant repudiated the notion of freely chosen evil, maintaining that there could be no "devilish minds." Despite Kant's conclusion, however, it is unclear that the notion of human free will—the *liberum arbitrium*, the free choice between good and evil—can be maintained without the concept of freely chosen evil. Furthermore, as hard and soft determinists contest with one another, it is uncertain that moral responsibility can be maintained in the absence of the *liberum arbitrium*. In this way, the very question of the ability freely and knowingly to reject the good ties into the most basic issues in ethics, such as free will and the existence of moral responsibility.

There is, perhaps, no concept so central to every aspect of ethical philosophy as the concept of goodness. What distinguishes ethical philosophies from one another most often are their differing visions of the good. They are further distinguished by their handling of the brute fact of human rejection of the good. What is the good? Why do people find it attractive? How are some able to reject the good? These are among the three most crucial questions in the ethical sphere.

Patrick M. O'Neil

FURTHER READING

Aristotle. *Nicomachean Ethics*. Translated and edited by Roger Crisp. New York: Cambridge University Press, 2000. Explores the nature of the good, which Aristotle defines as leading a fully human existence or flourishing (*eudaimonia*).

Brandt, Richard B. *A Theory of the Good and the Right*. Rev. ed. Foreword by Peter Singer. Amherst, N.Y.: Prometheus Books, 1998. The good is seen as the object of rational desire.

Carson, Thomas L., and Paul K. Moser, eds. *Morality and the Good Life*. New York: Oxford University Press, 1997. An excellent anthology of significant, mainly contemporary, moral philosophy. The first two sections are "Concepts of Goodness" and "What Things Are Good?"

Hinde, Robert A. *Why Good Is Good: The Sources of Morality*. New York: Routledge, 2002. Written by a biologist, this book attempts a truly interdisciplinary genealogy of morality, combining anthropology, evolutionary biology, psychology, and philosophy to determine the origins of ethical ideas and conduct.

Hobbes, Thomas. *Leviathan*. Edited by Richard Tuck. Rev. student ed. New York: Cambridge University Press, 1996. Rational prudence is seen as the basis of morality, and ethical egoism is defended as the true moral philosophy.

Kant, Immanuel. *Groundwork for the Metaphysics of Morals*. Edited and translated by Allen W. Wood. New Haven, Conn.: Yale University Press, 2002. The good will (proper moral intention to obey the moral law) is seen as the source of all ethical good.

Mill, John Stuart. *Utilitarianism*. Edited by George Sher. 2d ed. Indianapolis: Hackett, 2001. The greatest good—defined as a kind of eudaimonistic pleasure—for the greatest number is seen as the standard of the good action for moral agents.

Oates, Whitney Jennings, ed. *Stoic and Epicurean Philosophers: The Complete Extant Writings of Epicurus, Epictetus, Lucretius, Marcus Aurelius*. New York: Modern Library, 1957. The stoic notions of virtue and the Epicurean idea of pleasure as the highest good for humanity may be found in a number of different representatives of these schools who have been assembled in this anthology.

Plato. *The Republic*. Translated by Desmond Lee. 2d ed. New York: Penguin Books, 2003. The form of the good is introduced and explicated.

SEE ALSO: *Beyond Good and Evil*; Epicurus; God; Hedonism; Intrinsic good; Life, meaning of; Morality; Teleological ethics; Truth; Value; Virtue ethics; Wickedness.

Good samaritan laws

DEFINITION: Taking their name from the New Testament story of the Good Samaritan, laws specifying that, under normal circumstances, health care professionals and other people attempting to provide help during an emergency cannot be sued for damages inadvertently caused by their efforts

DATE: First enacted during the 1980's

TYPE OF ETHICS: Legal and judicial ethics

SIGNIFICANCE: Good samaritan laws afford a measure of legal protection for emergency medical professionals and for passersby who decide to get involved in emergency situations. They are founded in the beliefs that it would be unjust to punish someone for making a good faith effort to help people in need, and that such efforts should be encouraged as a matter of public policy.

Some people refuse to stop and help injured accident victims because they fear being sued for improper action. Much of the fear is generated by misunderstanding and by misinterpretation of the laws. Good samaritan laws have helped to alleviate some of these fears. Essentially, good samaritan laws protect from lawsuit emergency medical services personnel (and, in some cases, private citizens), as long as they act in good faith and to the best of their abilities. Mistreatment, gross negligence, and abandonment are not included in this protection.

Thus, these good samaritan laws attempt to ensure that anyone who voluntarily helps an injured or ill person at a scene is not legally liable for error or omissions in rendering good faith emergency care. The provision of the Massachusetts General Law c111C, section 14, which is typical of that of many other states, reads: "No emergency medical technician who in the performance of his duties and in good faith renders emergency first aid or transportation to an injured or incapacitated person shall be personally in any way liable as a result of rendering such aid or as a result of transporting such person to a hospital or other safe place."

Jane A. Slezak

SEE ALSO: Charity; Disability rights; Human rights; Physician-patient relationship; Right to life.

Goss v. Lopez

THE EVENT: U.S. Supreme Court decision holding that states must provide some elements of due process of law in school disciplinary proceedings that can result in suspension

DATE: Ruling made on January 22, 1975

TYPE OF ETHICS: Civil liberties

SIGNIFICANCE: *Goss* established that, since disciplinary proceedings in public schools have the power to deprive students of a state-provided right to education, they must be conducted in accordance with the basic principles of due process.

During a period of unrest in the Columbus, Ohio, school system, Dwight Lopez was a student at Central High School. He was suspended from school for ten days for allegedly participating in a demonstration in the school cafeteria. There was some physical damage to the lunch room. Lopez received no hearing prior to his suspension. He later testified that he himself had not participated in the disturbance.

In a 5-4 decision written by Justice Byron R. White, the Supreme Court held that Lopez and the other nine suspended appellants were entitled to a hearing prior to suspension so that the charges against them could be assessed. The state of Ohio's argument that it was constitutionally entitled not to offer public education at all and could thus manage the system as it pleased was rejected by the Court; having established the system and given the public rights in it, Ohio could not deprive people of due process by later depriving them of that right. The dissenting justices in this case argued that the penalty was too insignificant to warrant a hearing.

Robert Jacobs

SEE ALSO: Bill of Rights, U.S.; Due process; *Gault, In re*; Supreme Court, U.S.

Gossip

DEFINITION: Rumors or talk of a personal, sensational, or intimate nature regarding other persons who are not present

TYPE OF ETHICS: Personal and social ethics

SIGNIFICANCE: Although gossip is generally regarded as an unethical behavior, it can serve positive social functions.

The word "gossip" comes from Old English *godsibb*, meaning a person related to one in God, or a godparent. Before the nineteenth century, the word "gossip" signified friendship. Because the amounts of gossip usually increase as the amounts of firm information on other people decrease, the information provided during gossip is founded primarily on speculation. It is in part because of this speculation that gossip is typically considered an unethical behavior and prohibited by most religious teachings and secular rules. Jewish law, for instance, generally forbids gossip and contends that gossip is a means by which personal honor is stolen. Passages in the Old Testament books of Leviticus, Exodus, Psalms, and Proverbs condemn the spreading of information, whether true or false, against someone in private.

Although by modern standards gossip is considered undesirable, it serves several positive social functions. For example, it is a means by which social rules and norms and limits on personal behavior can be communicated to new members without direct confrontations. It also allows members of groups to make comparisons with other members to put their own problems in perspective and gain moral compasses on their own behavior. Finally, gossip allows people to share intimacies that promote social bonding, which in turn helps to build sustainable communities.

The question of whether gossip may be considered ethical may be answered by asking questions such as these: Are the remarks that people say or hear about others the kinds of things that they would not want said about themselves? Are people saying things with the intent of harming other people's reputations? Are the remarks being made for personal gain? Are the remarks betraying personal confidences or spreading sensitive information? If the answers to any of these are yes, then the gossip is probably unethical.

T. Steuart Watson
Tonya S. Butler

SEE ALSO: Buddhist ethics; Cell-phone etiquette; Cheating; Confidentiality; Etiquette; Internet chat rooms; Jewish ethics; Journalistic ethics; Privacy.

Gratitude

DEFINITION: Appreciation or thankfulness

TYPE OF ETHICS: Personal and social ethics

SIGNIFICANCE: The appropriate expression of gratitude may be considered a virtue, while ingratitude may be considered a vice.

Humankind is constantly preoccupied with equitable exchange. Gratitude is the heart's internal indicator when the tally of gifts outweighs exchanges. Gratitude is a moral value that helps regulate the "give and take" of human encounters. Gratitude is a universally recognized virtue. The Roman poet Cicero called it the "mother of all virtue." Seneca, an ancient Stoic, stated, "There was never any man so wicked as not to approve of gratitude and detest ingratitude." When the ancient Chinese sage Confucius was asked to summarize his ethics in one word, he replied, "Reciprocity." "Reciprocity" implies a sense of gratitude that arises when goods received go beyond what was deserved. The consensus of sages and philosophers is that people have a moral duty to keep fresh the memory of good things done for them.

As is often the case, moral injunctions serve to counter a trend in human nature that would otherwise remain unchecked. Prophets and moralists have found it necessary to counter the selfish and ungrateful tendency in human nature. Social critic Christopher Lasch, in his *Culture of Narcissism* (1978), has called attention to the dangers of a society that fails to maintain an "attitude of gratitude" as a core value. When the individual's "expectation of entitlement" becomes the group norm, gratitude is destroyed and the fabric of society is weakened. Gratitude is imperative for group survival and cohesion.

Many Christian theologians have argued that gratitude is the obligatory response of the believing person to the grace and goodness of God's creation and redemption. Saint Paul writes, "In everything give thanks." One's metaphysical and political commitments may, however, shape one's perceptions of life in such a way that "gratitude," rather than being a virtue, may be judged to be a form of self-deception or even a subtle coalition with one's oppressors. For example, Jean-Paul Sartre argues that life is essentially absurd and inchoate, prompting one who is "authentic" to have a fundamental attitude of "nausea" toward life. Karl Marx, an economic determin-

ist, implied that the individual has a moral obligation to feel ingratitude toward society when that society fails to fairly meet the needs of all.

ASIAN SYSTEMS OF BELIEF

In many forms of Asian thought, the status of gratitude is ambiguous, since gratitude requires a certain dualism between "benefactor" and "recipient" that may not apply in Asian systems. In much of Asian thought, the goal of life is to transcend the smallness of the finite self. As the devotee comes to identify with the impersonal absolute, the concept of "giving and receiving" becomes vacuous. The enlightened Hindu devotee may say, "One to me is loss or gain, One to me is fame or shame, One to me is pleasure, pain." Thus, gratitude may assume a different meaning in Asian thought.

Buddhists, who hold steadfastly to the doctrine of "no-self," staunchly express gratitude to the noble Buddha who taught the path of "no-self." In the Daoist perspective, good and evil lose their absolute character to such a degree that the concept of gratitude may become irrelevant. If both faces of fortune are greeted with equal countenance, the concept of gratitude becomes equivocal.

The book *Twelve Steps and Twelve Traditions* by Bill Wilson, a cofounder of Alcoholics Anonymous, states, "Action expresses more gratitude than words." Retroactively, gratitude is expressed through thankful remembrances, verbal expressions, and thank-you notes. Proactively, gratitude is expressed through charitable deeds that are performed without thought of reward. Alcoholics Anonymous (AA) meetings often focus on the topic of "gratitude" since the inculcation of this attitude is believed to be not only morally desirable but also necessary for peace of mind and high-quality sobriety. AA teaches that gratitude is the key to happiness and recovery, thus implying a moral imperative to be grateful.

Friedrich Nietzsche believed that gratitude was usually a disguise for covert interests. To have a person's gratitude is to have that person's loyalty. Sacrifice to the gods was never purely to express gratitude but to appease or ward off other evils. The "slave" who serves the "master" above the call of duty secretly expects a boon, not merely the master's gratitude. If gratitude is expressed with the motive of eliciting more gifts from God or any other superior agent, it becomes a form of mercantilism or spiritual materialism.

Nietzsche did, however, recognize a higher gratitude that makes possible a noble expression based on strength and true generosity of spirit. Similarly, Fyodor Dostoevski saw a dynamic connection between gratitude and human freedom. In the "Legend of the Grand Inquisitor," in *The Brothers Karamazov* (1912), he allegorized that when God calls to humanity he must do so in an ambiguous form in order to maintain humanity's nobility. If God were to appear to humans with all of his power, glory, and gifts, humans would be awed with gratitude and would have no choice but to obey. God, however, wanted human obedience and gratitude to be freely given. Hence the ambiguous nature of God's gifts and communications. This ambiguity dampens humanity's gratitude while preserving its freedom.

Joseph Amato, in his *Guilt and Gratitude* (1982), argues that the concept of gratitude is based on an older worldview that assumes a "limited good and the age-old struggle against scarcity." This older worldview taught that humankind was dependent on material things. In a world of "scarcity," gifts are deeply appreciated. To give generously was noble. Amato argues that the concept of gratitude requires a worldview based on scarcity of goods. There is a new "worldview" emerging, however, which says that the good is unlimited and that happiness can be achieved on Earth. A new ethics of gratitude is implied in this view. This challenges the old understanding of gratitude as based on sacrifice and limitation. Gratitude no doubt will continue to be a socially desirable attitude but will have high moral value only when intentions to posture, control, or placate the benefactor are absent. Correlatively, the only gift that can evoke the highest form of gratitude is one that is truly given without expectation that the recipient be obliged or perhaps even capable of repaying the gift.

Paul August Rentz

FURTHER READING

Amato, Joseph A. *Guilt and Gratitude*. Westport, Conn.: Greenwood Press, 1982. Through the perspective of "tragic optimism," this work establishes a new ethics of gratitude.

Dostoevski, Fyodor. *The Brothers Karamazov*. Translated by Richard Pevear and Larissa Volokhonsky. New York: Farrar, Straus, and Giroux, 2002.

Leddy, Mary Jo. *Radical Gratitude*. Maryknoll, N.Y.: Orbis Books, 2002.

McCloskey, Mary A. "Gratitude." In *Encyclopedia of Ethics*, edited by Lawrence C. Becker and Charlotte B. Becker. 2d ed. Vol. 1. New York: Routledge, 2001.

McConnell, Terrance. *Gratitude*. Philadelphia: Temple University Press, 1993.

Nietzsche, Friedrich. *On the Genealogy of Morals*. Edited and translated by Walter Kaufmann. New York: Vintage Books, 1967.

SEE ALSO: Confucius; Dostoevski, Fyodor; Etiquette; Generosity; Humility; Marx, Karl.

Gray Panthers

IDENTIFICATION: Public advocacy group that combats discrimination based on age

DATE: Founded in 1970

TYPE OF ETHICS: Civil rights

SIGNIFICANCE: Gray Panthers was the first national organization to bring old and young people together to address discrimination based on age.

In 1970, a woman named Maggie Kuhn joined several friends to address two concerns. They wanted to change the laws that permitted forced retirement at age sixty-five, because they knew many people older than that who had much to contribute, and they wanted to join younger people in actively opposing the Vietnam War. From these concerns came a group called the Consultation of Older and Younger Adults for Social Change, whose name was later changed to Gray Panthers.

The name of the Gray Panthers is a humorous takeoff on Black Panthers, a militant nationalist group for African Americans. Gray Panthers, whose motto is "Age and Youth in Action," is unlike many other advocacy groups for older people in that it does not set up or feed on competition between old and young people. It advises that by valuing its youngest and oldest citizens, society can become more just and humane. Through national publications and local seminars, the members of Gray Panthers work for improved media sensitivity to age, regulation of the nursing-home and hearing-aid industries, affordable and adequate housing for all, innovative concepts for jobs and work emphasizing the involvement of people of all ages, and an increased emphasis on intergenerational association.

Cynthia A. Bily

SEE ALSO: Ageism; American Association of Retired Persons; Health care allocation; Retirement funds.

Greed

DEFINITION: Excessive desire to acquire things; avarice

TYPE OF ETHICS: Beliefs and practices

SIGNIFICANCE: Traditionally one of the seven deadly sins, greed is often described both as a personal moral failing and as a sign of societal corruption or decline.

Greed occurs at all levels of human endeavor, and it can occur at the individual or the group level. Donald Worster documents the "greed is good" mentality in the rise of agribusiness. In its greed for short-term profits, it has followed a "slash-and-burn" policy of economic development that has wreaked environmental destruction and bequeathed future generations a legacy of worsening soil erosion, water shortage, dust bowl conditions, and extinction of wildlife.

Greed may also characterize the workings of government. Robert Lekachman stated the liberal argument that the administration of U.S. president Ronald Reagan was motivated by greed. Reagan's administration purportedly engaged in an enthusiastic and massive redistribution of wealth and power that further enriched the already rich, such as "greedy dabblers in oil, gas and coal properties." All this was at the expense of the working poor, minorities, and welfare families.

ORIGINS OF GREED

In Western systems of belief, greed is a sin. The biblical concept of Original Sin states that individuals are born as sinners; sin is rooted in human nature.

Rather than viewing greed as an inherent trait or motive, other explanations have looked to the environment. Psychoanalyst Erich Fromm believed that parents are shaped by society to mold their children in a manner consistent with society's values. Fromm viewed American society as passing through a series of stages. One of these was the "hoarding character," which was obsessed with accumulating, holding, and retaining things. In this vein, Ray Porter observed that the noble and virtuous intentions of the Constitution and Bill of Rights, Christian religion, and the capitalist economy actually fostered a mentality of greed that led to widespread destruction of the environment. The right to own and accumulate private property and do with it whatever one wanted was seen as legitimate self-interest. The view that humankind was created in God's image and had a soul led to the view that plants and animals were subordinate to human purposes. The Scriptures and the Protestant ethic encouraged people to control and exploit nature to their profit. Economics contributed the belief that the source of all that was of value was labor. Nature had no intrinsic value until it was exploited for products and wealth—a "greed is good" mentality.

GREED AND ETHICS

Greed is a sin—that is, a thought, motive, or desire that results in evil behavior because of a wrong attitude toward God. Greed rests in opposition to the eternal law of God and results in alienation from him and possible ruin and destruction. The Old and New Testaments of the Bible contain numerous references to the sinfulness of greed.

The list of the seven deadly sins has been common since the time of Thomas Aquinas. One of these sins is gluttony, which is listed in *Roget's Thesaurus* and *Webster's Collegiate Dictionary* as a synonym for greed. Gluttony/greed and the other sins were considered to be root causes of actions or failures to act that constitute serious sins or which are the inevitable source of other sins. They are considered to be deadly because they are directly opposed to virtue.

SOLUTIONS

Both the Bible and modern writers agree that greed is bad and potentially destructive to the individual and to society. Both also agree that greed needs to be replaced by contentment with a modest style of living. The Bible extols individuals to "Keep your lives free from the love of money and be content with what you have" (Heb. 13:5). "Godliness with contentment is great gain. For we brought nothing into the world and we can take nothing out of it. But if we have food and clothing we will be content with that" (1 Tim. 6:6-10).

Psychologist Burrhus F. Skinner believed that people must reduce their consumption, especially of nonessential luxuries that are falsely believed to be necessary for a satisfying life. "The assignment is to somehow induce people to take the future into account and live simpler lives, consuming less and moving less . . . we need to arrange immediate consequences which will induce people to act in ways which have consequences that are ultimately constructive."

John A. Nevin believes that it is necessary to emphasize the increasingly aversive conditions under which humankind lives and target those responsible: industries seeking short-term profits at the expense of long-term well-being; religions that encourage overpopulation to maintain and increase their membership; and, ultimately, each overavid consumer.

Laurence Miller

FURTHER READING

Childs, James M., Jr., *Greed: Economics and Ethics in Conflict*. Minneapolis: Fortress Press, 2000.

Fromm, Erich. *To Have or to Be?* New York: Harper & Row, 1976.

Knitter, Paul F., and Chandra Muzaffar, eds. *Subverting Greed: Religious Perspectives on the Global Economy*. Maryknoll, N.Y.: Orbis Books, 2002.

Lekachman, Robert. *Greed Is Not Enough*. New York: Pantheon Books, 1982.

Nicolaus, Robert H. "B. F. Skinner Talks About Energy." *Behaviorists for Social Action Journal* 3, no. 2 (1982): 22-24.

Robertson, A. F. *Greed: Gut Feelings, Growth, and History*. Malden, Mass.: Blackwell, 2001.

Schumacher, E. F. *Small Is Beautiful*. New York: Harper & Row, 1973.

Worster, Donald. *The Wealth of Nature: Environmental History and the Ecological Imagination*. New York: Oxford University Press, 1993.

SEE ALSO: Corporate compensation; Exploitation; Gluttony; Laziness; Needs and wants; Professional athlete incomes; Profit economy; Selfishness.

Green parties

DEFINITION: Diverse political parties that are most widely known for promoting environmental issues

DATE: First organized during the 1980's

TYPE OF ETHICS: Environmental ethics

SIGNIFICANCE: Greens were the first political parties promoting environmental issues to win seats in national legislatures.

Green parties, or Greens, make environmental issues the focus of their political goals. They criticize the social, political, and economic structures and policies of industrialized countries as the causes of the environmental crisis. Greens consider environmental, economic, social, and political problems to be interrelated and global. Because of this relationship, Greens variously espouse grassroots democracy, social justice and equality, peace, and small-scale economics. They often oppose capitalism, the construction of nuclear power plants, and the testing and production of nuclear weapons.

Most Green parties were established during the 1980's in industrialized countries and became active in every Western European country, as well as in Australia and New Zealand. West Germany's Green Party (*die Grünen*), one of the most powerful Green parties, in 1983 became the first to win seats in a national legislature. Support for the Greens was strongly linked with active involvement in social movements. The majority of voters supporting the German Green party in 1983 were active in the ecology, antinuclear, or peace movements. Green parties have also won seats in Austria, Belgium, Finland, Luxembourg, the Netherlands, Romania, Sweden, Switzerland, and the European Parliament.

In the United States, the Association of State Green Parties (ASGP), later the Green Party, was formed after the presidential elections of 1996. The first Green statewide officeholder was Audie Bock, who was elected to the California Assembly in 1999, and the Green Party's choice to run Ralph Nader as its presidential candidate in 2000 arguably changed the outcome of that election.

Marguerite McKnight
Updated by the editors

SEE ALSO: Environmental ethics; Environmental movement; Nader, Ralph; Social justice and responsibility.

Greenhouse effect

DEFINITION: Increase in the earth's surface temperature caused by the absorption of reflected infrared radiation by atmospheric "greenhouse gases"

TYPE OF ETHICS: Environmental ethics

SIGNIFICANCE: The greenhouse effect poses a potential danger to all human life and societies, as well as other species. It raises the issue of the extent of each individual person's and corporation's ethical responsibility to alleviate a threat to the species and to the planet.

The "greenhouse gases"—water vapor and small amounts of carbon dioxide, methane, nitrous oxide, ozone, and chlorofluorocarbons—absorb reflected infrared radiation, thus raising the atmospheric temperature. Without this increase, the earth's mean surface temperature would be about 15 degrees Celsius rather than the observed 17.3 degrees Celsius (approximate); therefore, the "greenhouse effect" makes the earth habitable. The warming primarily results from absorption and restricted diffusion rather than reflection and is more properly referred to as the "atmospheric effect."

Human production of carbon dioxide, chlorofluorocarbons, nitrous oxide, and ozone may have caused the global warming that has been noted since industrialization. Atmospheric carbon dioxide is increasing about 0.3 percent annually, an increase closely paralleling rates of fuel consumption. Some scientists predict doubled atmospheric carbon dioxide by the year 2080. Chlorofluorocarbons, which are entirely of industrial origin, are increasing by 5 percent per year. Actions to control greenhouse gas emissions include attempts to restrict fossil fuel combustion, which generates carbon dioxide, and reforestation and forest preservation, which remove carbon dioxide from the atmosphere. An international agreement made in 1987 required the halving of chlorofluorocarbon emissions in thirty-one countries by the next century.

Ralph L. Langenheim, Jr.

The Greenhouse Effect

Clouds and atmospheric gases such as water vapor, carbon dioxide, methane, and nitrous oxide absorb part of the infrared radiation emitted by the earth's surface and reradiate part of it back to the earth. This process effectively reduces the amount of energy escaping to space and is popularly called the "greenhouse effect" because of its role in warming the lower atmosphere. The greenhouse effect has drawn worldwide attention because increasing concentrations of carbon dioxide from the burning of fossil fuels may result in a global warming of the atmosphere.

Scientists know that the greenhouse analogy is incorrect. A greenhouse traps warm air within a glass building where it cannot mix with cooler air outside. In a real greenhouse, the trapping of air is more important in maintaining the temperature than is the trapping of infrared energy. In the atmosphere, air is free to mix and move about.

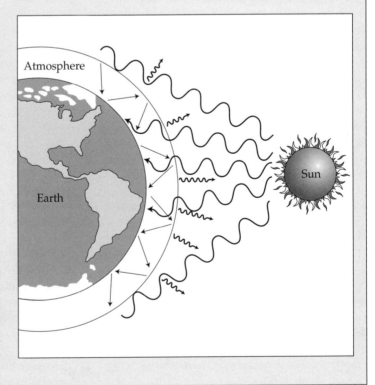

SEE ALSO: Clean Air Act; Earth and humanity; Global warming; Nuclear energy; Pollution; Rain forests.

Greenpeace

IDENTIFICATION: International organization dedicated to the protection of the environment

DATE: Founded in 1971

TYPE OF ETHICS: Environmental ethics

SIGNIFICANCE: Greenpeace helped introduce the practice of organized interference with environmentally destructive activities, including governmental activities. The group helped extend the principles of civil disobedience to the environmental movement.

In 1971 Jim Bohlen, Paul Cote, and Irving Stowe formed the Don't Make a Wave Committee, in Vancouver, Canada, and it sent a protest vessel, the *Rainbow Warrior*, to Amchitka in the Aleutian Islands to provoke publicity regarding nuclear testing at that site. An attempt to disrupt the test failed, but the resultant publicity established Greenpeace, the new name of the group, as a major factor in environmental activism. Also, no further tests were held at that site.

Among the notable continuing campaigns of Greenpeace is the attempted disruption of French nuclear tests at Mururoa in the South Seas. This effort led to violence on the high seas when French agents sank the *Rainbow Warrior* in Auckland Harbor, New Zealand, killing one activist. In 1973, Greenpeace began expanding from antinuclear activity to general environmental protest. Interference with sealing and whaling in the St. Lawrence estuary and on the high seas, also involving physical conflict at sea, became prominent. The organization also spread to Europe, the United States, Argentina, and elsewhere, initiating numerous acts of protest and physical interference with such activities as waste disposal.

SEE ALSO: Civil disobedience; Earth and humanity; Ecology; Environmental movement; Green parties; Nature, rights of.

Sailors from a French naval vessel prepare to board the Rainbow Warrior *in September, 1995, when the Greenpeace ship attempted to enter the restricted zone around the South Pacific's Mururoa atoll, where the French were planning to test nuclear weapons. The French later sank the* Rainbow Warrior. *(AP/Wide World Photos)*

Griswold v. Connecticut

THE EVENT: U.S. Supreme Court decision striking down a Connecticut law that prohibited both the use of contraceptives and counseling about contraception

DATE: Ruling made on June 7, 1965

TYPE OF ETHICS: Sex and gender issues

SIGNIFICANCE: *Griswold* has significant free speech implications, but its primary intent and effect are to affirm the existence of a constitutionally guaranteed right to privacy and explicitly to extend the protections afforded by that right to the conduct of one's marriage. It places a limit upon the state's ability to regulate the intimate details of citizens' private lives.

The Planned Parenthood League's executive director (Griswold) and medical director (Buxton) knowingly violated a Connecticut statute that prohibited the giving of counsel to any person for the purpose of preventing conception. After being convicted in the Connecticut courts, Griswold and Buxton appealed to the U.S. Supreme Court, which overturned the Connecticut birth control law as unconstitutional. Justice William O. Douglas, writing the majority opinion, held that a right to privacy is implied in the Bill of Rights, that the marriage "right of privacy [was] older than the Bill of Rights . . . ," and that the state could not invade its freedoms.

Concurring opinions by the court emphasized that the due process clause of the Fourteenth Amendment incorporated the Bill of Rights against any intrusion by state governments. Justices Hugo Black and Potter Stewart dissented on the grounds that the Bill of Rights does not explicitly list a right of privacy, stating that this law did not violate any specific provision of the Constitution and that the high court had no right to invalidate state laws simply because those laws were "capricious or irrational."

Stephen D. Livesay

SEE ALSO: Birth control; Due process; Privacy; Sexual revolution; Supreme Court, U.S.

Grotius, Hugo

IDENTIFICATION: Dutch philosopher who wrote *On the Law of War and Peace* (*De iure belli ac pacis libri res*, 1625)
BORN: April 10, 1583, Delft, Holland
DIED: August 28, 1645, Rostock, Mecklenburg
TYPE OF ETHICS: Personal and social ethics
SIGNIFICANCE: Grotius pioneered the early modern concept of the secular international society whose members should interact according to an international law based upon norms.

Living in a world embroiled in sectarian religious wars that were both civil and international, Hugo Grotius sought to provide a model for international

relationships that was grounded in natural, God-given guidelines that were fully secular in that they could be learned and understood by unaided reason alone. Any unity in Christian revelation had disintegrated in the success of the Reformation movements, and thus only the action of human reason might lead to certain guidelines. This was essentially an extension of the Renaissance era's program of uncovering the natural truth of classical pagan ethics.

A Dutch Protestant, Grotius believed in the divine ordering of the universe. God's preferences for human behavior were embedded from Creation in what Grotius calls "divine law," which is manifested in God's revelations to people. This is a law that demands a "very high degree of moral perfection" and is associated with the Jewish and Christian moral and ethical systems. Natural law, on the other hand, is also an expression of God's will, but it is discernible through the exercise of human reason alone and requires a rather lower ethical and moral bar than that for God's Chosen or saved peoples. People assent to the first through faith and to the second by what Grotius called the "exercise of Right Reason" and "common consent of mankind."

International relations, especially matters of war and peace, should be carried out according to the natural law that applies to all people and nations at all times. This was Grotius's "primary law of nations." Custom and written agreements constituted a "secondary law," or positive law, that may or may not have been in synch with natural law. To be just and command the obedience of Christians, human-made laws must be based in the natural law established by God. By extension, states' interactions should also conform to the norms embodied in and derived from natural law.

Grotius recognized that the conduct of war was a legitimate activity of a state, but he insisted that just as there were wars acceptable under natural law, there were those that could not be justified, and states and their soldiers had to conform to norms rooted in natural law to be justified in their conduct of hostilities. In important ways he adjusted St. Augustine's comments on just wars and justifiable combat. By grounding these in the same natural law according to which nations should interact among themselves, he laid the groundwork for the modern agreements, such as the Geneva Conventions, that regulate the conduct of war.

Joseph P. Byrne

FURTHER READING

Onuma, Yasuaki, ed. *A Normative Approach to War: Peace, War, and Justice in Hugo Grotius.* New York: Oxford University Press, 1993.

Sotirovich, William Vasilio. *Grotius' Universe: Divine Law and a Quest for Harmony.* New York: Vantage Press, 1978.

Walzer, Michael. *Just and Unjust Wars: A Moral Argument with Historical Illustrations.* 3d ed. New York: Basic Books, 2000.

SEE ALSO: Christian ethics; Geneva conventions; International law; Jewish ethics; Just war theory; Lying; Natural law; Natural rights; Nussbaum, Martha.

Group therapy

DEFINITION: Simultaneous psychotherapeutic treatment of several clients under the leadership of therapists who try to facilitate helpful interactions among group members

DATE: Term coined in 1932

TYPE OF ETHICS: Psychological ethics

SIGNIFICANCE: In addition to abiding by the same ethical strictures that bind all psychotherapists, group therapists must take special care not to aid one member of the group at the expense of another member. Moreover, all members of therapy groups are morally obligated to hold confidential everything that occurs within group sessions.

Typically, therapy groups consist of three to twelve members who meet once per week for twelve to an unlimited number of weeks. Formats of group therapy differ widely depending on the approach taken by the therapist, but all forms provide an opportunity for members to interact with other members and to learn from these interactions with the help of the therapist.

Compared to individual therapy, group therapy provides a fuller social context in which an individual can work out social problems. Thus, group therapy affords a unique laboratory for working out interpersonal relationships. Members interact in a setting that is more representative of real life than is individual therapy.

Group therapy was developed over the first three decades of the twentieth century by several innovative mental health professionals. The term was coined by Jacob Moreno, also associated with the invention of psychodrama, at a psychiatric conference in 1932. The practice first became popular during World War II, when there were too few therapists available to treat all the psychological casualties of war. Many experienced therapists, however, have come to believe that group therapy has a number of advantages beyond the efficient use of a therapist's time (and lower cost to the individual).

One additional advantage of group therapy is that it encourages members to recognize quickly that they are not the only ones who feel the way they do; it gives them the opportunity to derive comfort, encouragement, and support from others who have similar, perhaps more severe, problems. This recognition tends to raise each member's expectations for improvement, an important factor in all forms of treatment. In addition, members have an opportunity to see themselves as others see them and to obtain more honest feedback about their behavior than they receive elsewhere in everyday life. They receive this feedback not only from the leader but also from other members, whose insights and observations can be very beneficial.

Members also have opportunities to try alternative responses when old ones prove ineffective. Thus, they can actually practice new behaviors in addition to talking about them. Further, members can learn vicariously by watching how others behave and can explore attitudes and reactions by interacting with a variety of people, not only the therapist. Also, members often benefit from feeling that they are part of a group, from getting to know new people, from expressing their own points of view, and from becoming emotionally intimate with others. The group experience may make members less guarded, more willing to share feelings, and more sensitive to other people's needs, motives, and messages. Members may also experience increased self-esteem as a result of helping other members.

Group therapy poses several potential disadvantages. First, some people, because of insecurities or distrustfulness, may be unsuited to group therapy or may need individual therapy before they can function well in a group setting. Second, in some groups, the therapist's attention may be spread too thin to give each member the attention that he or she needs. Third, the pressure to conform to group rules may limit the therapy process. Fourth, some people may desire more confidentiality than a group can afford or may desire individual attention.

Some types of problems are more appropriate for group than individual therapy. Such problems include substance abuse, eating disorders, child abuse, problems with intimacy, compulsive behaviors (such as gambling), hypochondriasis, narcissism, and post-trauma adjustment (such as post-divorce adjustment or recovering from the effects of sexual victimization). Also, group therapy is a popular form of personal growth therapy; thus, groups are often composed of individuals who are essentially normal but who want to grow or develop more fully.

TYPES OF GROUP THERAPY

Some forms of group therapy currently in existence are sensitivity training or encounter groups, which promote personal growth by encouraging members to focus on their immediate relationships with other members; assertiveness training, in which leaders demonstrate specific ways of standing up for one's rights in an assertive but not aggressive manner; psychodrama, in which an individual acts out dramatic incidents resembling those that cause problems in real life; family therapy, in which two or more family members work as a group to resolve the problems of each individual family member (for example, school phobia in an eight-year-old) and to create harmony and balance within the family by helping each family member better understand the family's interactions and the problems they create; marriage encounter, in which couples explore themselves and try to expand and deepen their marriage relationships; and self-help groups such as Alcoholics Anonymous, Parents Without Partners, Synanon, and Weight Watchers, which often function within a specified structure but without a trained or formal leader.

People most likely to benefit from group therapy are those who can communicate thoughts and feelings and who are motivated to be active participants. Poor candidates are those who are withdrawn, uncommunicative, combative, antisocial, or so depressed or unreachable that they are likely to frustrate other group members.

Lillian M. Range

FURTHER READING

Bowen, Murray. *Family Therapy in Clinical Practice.* New York: Jason Aronson, 1978.

Brabender, Virginia. *Introduction to Group Therapy.* New York: Wiley, 2002.

Haley, Jay, and Lynn Hoffman. *Techniques of Family Therapy.* New York: Basic Books, 1967.

Kline, William B. *Interactive Group Counseling and Therapy.* Upper Saddle River, N.J.: Merrill/Prentice Hall, 2003.

Lieberman, Morton A., Irvin D. Yalom, and Matthew B. Miles. *Encounter Groups: First Facts.* New York: Basic Books, 1973.

Minuchin, Salvador. *Families & Family Therapy.* Cambridge, Mass.: Harvard University Press, 1974.

Napier, Augustus, with Carl Whitaker. *The Family Crucible.* New York: Harper & Row, 1978.

Satir, Virginia. *Conjoint Family Therapy.* Rev. ed. Palo Alto, Calif.: Science and Behavior Books, 1967.

Yalom, Irvin D. *The Theory and Practice of Group Psychotherapy.* 4th ed. New York: Basic Books, 1995.

SEE ALSO: Behavior therapy; Family therapy; Personal relationships; Psychology; Therapist-patient relationship.

Guilt and shame

DEFINITION: Painful emotions resulting from self-evaluation either as moral transgressor (guilt) or as morally inadequate in the judgment of others (shame)

TYPE OF ETHICS: Personal and social ethics

SIGNIFICANCE: Along with outrage or anger at others' transgressions, guilt and shame are the most visceral and immediate aspects of a person's moral judgment and experience. They play crucial roles in motivating people to avoid moral transgressions.

An individual is "objectively" guilty if he or she is responsible for violating a standard of conduct prescribed by an authority, which violation renders the individual liable to compensation for the transgression. The violated standard may be a law, a rule of group morality, or a principle of the individual's own conscience. The subjective condition of "feeling guilty" is the sense of having committed an immoral act for which one is answerable to the authority of one's own conscience. Although the compensation to which one feels bound because of this transgression can take a variety of forms (punishment, repayment, being forgiven, and so forth), subjective guilt always involves the sense that one must do or suffer something in order to rectify a moral wrong that one has committed. As defined, the sense of being guilty is not identical with feeling empathic pain for those harmed by the violation. It is also not fear of repercussion or fear of punishment or the sense of having "made a mistake."

A person may be "objectively" guilty of acting against the law or the morals of others and yet not feel guilty. This occurs when such transgressions are not contrary to personal conscience. A person also may be objectively innocent of violating the law or group morality and yet feel guilty. This occurs if the individual violates the dictates of conscience even though the conduct is allowed by the law or others' morals.

SHAME

Shame is the sense that one is a failure because one is regarded as such in the eyes of others. In feeling moral shame, one is thinking of and endorsing a moral condemnation by others (either real or imagined) of some specific fault, which occasions a global sense of one's own moral inadequacy. One is "shamed" by others into being "ashamed of" one's whole self. In feeling guilt, one condemns oneself and does so only for a specific misdeed. This difference between shame and guilt is evident in the way each varies in intensity. Guilt varies as a function of the grievousness of the misdeed and the degree of responsibility of the agent.

A sense of full responsibility for doing something horribly wrong should elicit a severe sense of guilt. A sense of less responsibility for doing something that is regarded as less grievous should elicit a less severe sense of guilt. Moral shame varies in degree as a function of the esteem in which the others who are condemning the self are held. Those who are held in low regard should elicit little or no shame in the individual whom they morally disparage. Those who are

held in high esteem should elicit much shame if they are regarded as being critical (even if what they are morally condemning is regarded by the individual as trivial).

Both guilt and shame play crucial roles in moral motivation. Guilt motivates one to make compensation for wrongs done, by submitting to punishment and/or by making satisfaction for harm caused. Doing either assuages the painful feeling of being guilty by partially "undoing" the wrong. Because guilt is a painful emotion, people are motivated to avoid experiencing it in the first place; that is, to avoid committing the wrongs that cause them to feel guilty. By shame, people are motivated to correct moral defects that they take others to be criticizing in them. This correction serves to assuage the pain of shame by eliminating its cause. It also serves to reestablish good relations with those who are regarded as being critical. Again, because shame is a painful emotion, people are motivated to avoid experiencing it in the first place; that is, to avoid acting in ways that cause them to be ashamed. Thus, people take account of and anticipate the moral judgments of them by others and "adjust" themselves accordingly.

Guilt and shame have closely related origins. When wrongdoing and punishment by parents become sufficiently linked in a child's mind, the mere thought of having done wrong will elicit the associated pain, as in guilt. Parental punishment also establishes a linkage between pain and negative evaluation of the self by others. Hence, the very thought of disapproval of oneself by "significant" others will come to elicit the associated pain, as in shame.

Whether an individual is more prone to guilt or to shame depends upon whether the wrongs done by the person as a child or the disapproval by others of those wrongs was emphasized by the parents. This emphasis varies across cultures. Some societies emphasize the individual's sense of responsibility for wrongdoing (so-called "guilt societies"), while others emphasize the individual's sense of what others think of the individual's wrongdoing (so-called "shame societies").

Experiencing the appropriate degree of either shame or guilt on the occasion of moral wrongdoing or failure is rational and constitutive of being a moral person. Shame and guilt become irrational, however, when they are unwarranted by the occasion in which they are experienced. Irrational shame and guilt become pathological when they are persistently experienced even after their irrationality is acknowledged.

Mark Stephen Pestana

FURTHER READING

Cavell, Stanley. "The Avoidance of Love: A Reading of *King Lear*" and "Othello and the Stake of the Other." In *Disowning Knowledge in Seven Plays of Shakespeare*. Updated ed. New York: Cambridge University Press, 2003.

Morris, Herbert. *Guilt and Shame*. Belmont, Calif.: Wadsworth, 1971.

_____. *On Guilt and Innocence: Essays in Legal Philosophy and Moral Psychology*. Berkeley: University of California Press, 1976.

Piers, Gerhart, and Milton B. Singer. *Shame and Guilt: A Psychoanalytic and a Cultural Study*. New York: W. W. Norton, 1971.

Tangney, June Price, and Rhonda L. Dearing. *Shame and Guilt*. New York: Guilford Press, 2002.

Taylor, Gabriele. *Pride, Shame, and Guilt: Emotions of Self-Assessment*. New York: Oxford University Press, 1985.

SEE ALSO: Bystanders; Conscience; Forgiveness; Freud, Sigmund; Jurisprudence; Moral education; Moral responsibility; Passions and emotions; Punishment.

The Gulag Archipelago

IDENTIFICATION: Book by Aleksandr Solzhenitsyn (1918-   )

DATE: *Arkhipelag GULag, 1918-1956: Opyt khudozhestvennogo issledovaniya*, 1973-1975 (*The Gulag Archipelago, 1918-1956: An Experiment in Literary Investigation*, 1974-1978)

TYPE OF ETHICS: Modern history

SIGNIFICANCE: Solzhenitsyn's *The Gulag Archipelago* examines the history of the penal system established in the Soviet Union after the Russian Revolution and brought to light the cruelties inflicted upon millions of political prisoners.

The word "gulag" derives from the Russian acronym for the Chief Administration of Collective Labor Camps, which was established in the Soviet Union after the Russian Revolution of 1918. An archipelago is an extensive group of islands, such as exists in the Arctic Ocean off the coast of Siberia. It was in these bitterly cold regions that collective labor camps were built to house more than ten million inmates. In 1973, Aleksandr Solzhenitsyn, a Russian novelist, began publishing a three-volume history of those camps called *The Gulag Archipelago, 1918-1956: An Experiment in Literary Investigation*. Although banned in his own homeland, Solzhenitsyn's work was smuggled to the West, was translated, became a bestseller, and led to the author's expulsion from Soviet territory in 1974. The three published volumes were based on letters, documents, and the experiences of 227 eyewitnesses, including those of the author, who spent eight years in the camps.

HISTORY

Soviet labor camps were first established by Vladimir Lenin, leader of the Russian communists during the revolution, to reeducate and punish enemies of the Communist Party. After Lenin's death in 1924, Joseph Stalin took power and sent millions of Soviet citizens to the camps for "crimes against the state." In a chapter titled "The History of Our Sewage Disposal System," Solzhenitsyn explores Stalin's legal and ethical motivations for carrying out a reign of terror that lasted from 1927 until the dictator's death in 1953. Under the Soviet constitution, written by the dictator himself, any "counterrevolutionary" activity was punishable by ten years of slave labor or even death. Any actions "injurious to the military might" of the Soviet Union, any "intention" to do injury, and any "attempt to weaken state power" could get a citizen thrown into the Gulag.

Other crimes included attempts at armed rebellion, providing aid to the "international bourgeoisie" or capitalist class, espionage, suspicion of espionage, and contacts "leading to suspicion to engage in espionage," including more easily witnessed criminal acts such as "subversion of industry, transport, and trade" by failing to achieve and produce as much as was expected of loyal citizens. One could also be punished for failing to denounce people whom one suspected of having committed any of these crimes. Solzhenitsyn received an eight-year sentence for violating the law against weakening the state by criticizing its leaders. He had criticized Stalin's military leadership in a "private" letter to a fellow army officer, but since all mail was opened and read by secret police agents, nothing was truly private. The communist judge sent Solzhenitsyn to a labor camp in Siberia. While in the Gulag, he heard many stories of suffering, death, and other horrors, and he pledged to write about those experiences so that they would never be forgotten.

ETHICAL PRINCIPLES

Inside the camps, the most vicious criminals were in charge. According to Stalinist ethics, political prisoners had no human rights because they were inferior beings and enemies of the state. Refusal to obey orders or attempts to avoid work meant immediate death. Millions died from twenty-hour days in gold mines or in clearing forests in 60-degrees-below-zero weather. Inmates were not expected to survive, so they were fed inadequate, miserable food, frequently nothing more than watery potato or "fish" soup and a moldy crust of bread once a day.

The camps were built and maintained according to the ethics of pure force. Stalin's word became law, and his only motive became increasing his own power. "To choose one's victims, to prepare one's plans minutely, to slake an implacable vengeance, and then to go to bed . . . there is nothing sweeter in the world," he wrote. The methods of force that he used included torture and psychological terror. The only way to avoid immediate death at the hands of the police was to confess to everything and to submit to the absolute power of the torturers. Stalinist ethics were based on one principle: Stalin and the party were right, and everything else was wrong. Even children as young as twelve could be executed for crimes against the state, usually upon no more proof than a confession elicited after the child had been subjected to days of continuous questioning, without sleep, in an isolated cell.

The ethics of the Gulag inmates demanded the destruction of all human feeling and trust. Survival depended upon finding meaning in circumstances that evoked only horror, hatred, and degradation. Yet, as Solzhenitsyn discovered, many inmates did survive. He attributed survival inside the camps to a prisoner's strength of character before he entered the system. The people who surrendered and died or became informers were those who "before camp had not been enriched by any morality or by any spiritual upbringing." Survival demanded a "steadfast faith" in the human spirit or in some religious ethic. People who had found meaning in life before becoming victims of the terrorists could put up with the worst conditions, while those without a philosophy of life surrendered to despair and died horrible deaths. For Solzhenitsyn, this was the lesson of the Gulag: Know how to live and you will survive any conditions within or without the camps.

Leslie V. Tischauser

FURTHER READING

Bloom, Harold, ed. *Alexandr Solzhenitsyn*. Philadelphia: Chelsea House, 2001.

Bullock, Alan. *Hitler and Stalin: Parallel Lives*. New York: Alfred A. Knopf, 1992.

Conquest, Robert. *The Great Terror: A Reassessment*. New York: Oxford University Press, 1990.

_____. *Kolyma: The Arctic Death Camps*. New York: Viking Press, 1978.

Fireside, Harvey. *Soviet Psychoprisons*. New York: W. W. Norton, 1979.

Mahoney, Daniel J. *Aleksandr Solzhenitsyn: The Ascent from Ideology*. Lanham, Md.: Rowman & Littlefield, 2001.

Medvedev, Roy A. *Let History Judge*. Rev. and exp. ed. Edited and translated by George Shriver. New York: Columbia University Press, 1989.

Solzhenitsyn, Aleksandr I. *The Gulag Archipelago, 1918-1956: An Experiment in Literary Investigation*. Translated by Thomas P. Whitney. 3 vols. New York: Harper & Row, 1974-1978.

Tucker, Robert C. *Stalin in Power: The Revolution from Above, 1928-1941*. New York: W. W. Norton, 1990.

SEE ALSO: Concentration camps; Solzhenitsyn, Aleksandr; Soviet psychiatry; Stalin, Joseph; Torture.

H

Ḥadīth

DEFINITION: Traditions of the life and sayings of the
  Prophet Muḥammad
DATE: Developed during the seventh to ninth
  centuries
TYPE OF ETHICS: Religious ethics
SIGNIFICANCE: The actions and decisions of Muḥammad, as related in the *Ḥadīth*, are seen as exemplary in Islamic ethics and are, in many traditions,
  legally binding in those instances in which there
  are not specific Quranic injunctions.

The first source of ethical guidance in Islam is the
Qurʾān and its exegesis. One text, however rich, cannot supply guidance in the particulars of all matters,
though, and so great importance usually is placed on
the traditions of the actions and statements (way of
life, or *sunna*) of the Prophet Muḥammad. The importance of *Ḥadīth* is further grounded in the Qurʾān,
which enjoins the faithful to look to Muḥammad's
example for guidance. There is a broad range of subjects of *Ḥadīth*, from those that have or are alleged to
have mystical import, to those concerned with proper
worship, to those that deal with the most everyday
matters such as manner of dress.

There has also been a broad range of approaches
to the use of *Ḥadīth*. In many Islamic legal traditions,
Ḥadīth is second only to the Qurʾān in authority and
is legally binding. Very often, it is seen as ethically
regulative, especially in matters of worship but not
always in more mundane matters. There has also
been persistent critique of the use of *Ḥadīth* as innovative or unreliable, although such critique tends to
be a minority position.

The question of which *Ḥadīth* to accept as authentic became a central concern in Islamic legal and
ethical thought because the *Ḥadīth* could determine
the community's acceptable range of behavior. Thus
arose the science of analysis of *isnād*, the chain
of transmission of *Ḥadīth* in which the authenticity
and accuracy of each stage of the transmission is ex-

amined. The major collections of *Ḥadīth* were assembled in the ninth century, with the collections by
Abū ʿAbdallāh Muḥammad al-Bukhārī and Abū al-
Ḥusayn Muslim ibn al-Ḥallār most often accepted as
authoritative. The elections of *Ḥadīth* were at the
core of the curriculum at many of the medieval
madrasas (roughly equivalent to modern colleges).
The importance of *Ḥadīth* was also a major impetus to serious, scholarly research into history in the
Islamicate world, since the soundness of the chain of
transmission of *Ḥadīth* cannot be determined without
accurate facts about the history of the transmitters.

Many Sufis often employ controversial *Ḥadīth*
with less concern for *isnād* than for transcendent or
mystical meaning of the *Ḥadīth*. Ibn ʿArabī, for example, reported the *Ḥadīth* that God had revealed to
Muḥammad that God was a hidden jewel, who created the world so that he could be known. Ibn ʿArabī
then argued against the independent reality of the
phenomenal world, which is merely a mirror of God.

Thomas Gaskill

SEE ALSO: Bukhārī, al-; Ghazālī, al-; Islamic ethics;
Muḥammad; Qurʾān; Sharīʿa; Sufism.

al-Ḥallāj

IDENTIFICATION: Persian mystic
BORN: c. 858, Ṭūr (now in Iran)
DIED: March 26, 922, Baghdad (now in Iraq)
TYPE OF ETHICS: Religious ethics
SIGNIFICANCE: Al-Ḥallāj's life, his teachings in *The
  Tawasin* (early tenth century), and his execution
  and martyrdom were central to the development
  of Sufism.

Abū al-Mughīth al-Ḥusayn ibn Manṣūr al-Ḥallāj has
often been called the martyr of mystical love, because he paid the highest price for his devotion to loss
of the ego in pure, unconditional love of God. His
burning desire for extinction of the self is reflected in

his verse, "Kill me, oh, my trustworthy friends." He is best known for proclaiming, in a state of mystical ecstasy, *"anā'l-ḥaqq." Al-ḥaqq* literally means "the truth" (often in the sense of "true reality"), but is also one of the names of God. *Anā'* is the first-person singular pronoun. This led many to interpret al-Ḥallāj as a pantheist (reading *anā'l-ḥaqq* as "I am God"), which led to his particularly gruesome execution. Al-Ḥallāj's surviving works and the work of Louis Massignon (*The Passion of Ḥallāj*) make clear that the charge was false. Al-Ḥallāj's calm and steadfastness in love of God throughout his execution ensured his later role in much of Sufism as a martyr. Following his execution, most of his disciples fled from Iraq to the more tolerant northeast, where they energized Khurasani and Central Asian Sufism.

Thomas Gaskill

SEE ALSO: Ahiṁsā; *Bhagavadgītā*; God; Moral status of animals; Nonviolence.

Hammurabi's code

IDENTIFICATION: Set of 282 specific laws regulating the social and economic behavior of the people of Babylon
DATE: Established between 1792 and 1750 B.C.E.
TYPE OF ETHICS: Legal and judicial ethics
SIGNIFICANCE: The code of Hammurabi was one of the earliest and most thorough attempts in history to set up a harmonious social order based on individual rights backed by the gods and the state.

Hammurabi (ruled c. 1792-1750 B.C.E.) was the sixth king of an Amorite (Semitic) dynasty ruling over the city-state of Babylon and one of the most important rulers of ancient times. He united all the city-states of Mesopotamia under his rule and, in time, created a huge empire. As an effective, pragmatic administrator, he desired to establish order by setting up standardized rules of moral conduct and ensuring that people would accept decisions made by courts rather than seek to avenge wrongs on the spur of the moment without restraint.

In order to establish a uniform system of justice and create something approaching universal law applicable to varying cultures from formerly independent city-states, Hammurabi used existing laws and court decisions, and he added new laws as different situations arose. Earlier Mesopotamian law codes, antedating Hammurabi's code by one to three centuries, indicate that the great Babylonian king consulted precedent and that his code rested on a widespread ancient Near Eastern legal tradition. Three previous Near Eastern codes are the Code of Ur-nammu (founder of the third dynasty of Ur c. 2060 B.C.E.); the Code of Lipit-Ishtar (c. 1870 B.C.E.); and the Laws of Eshnunna (promulgated c. nineteenth century B.C.E.)

INSCRIPTION

After all the laws and judgments had been collected, they were inscribed on several stelae, which were set up in public in various cities of the empire. Officials were appointed by the king to mete out the prescribed penalties to violators of the law.

A single copy of the Code of Hammurabi was first discovered in the winter of 1901-1902 at Susa, the capital of ancient Elam. The recovered stele is an eight-foot-tall block of black diorite. The upper part displays a relief, or carving, depicting Hammurabi receiving the commission to write the law from the god of justice, the sun god Shamash. This commission provided significant legitimization of the code by showing the world that the gods were behind the establishment of the code and that they desired, as well as expected, mortals to behave according to its principles. There is no hint in the code itself, however, of the concept of *imitatio dei* (the requirement to be holy because God is holy) as the rationale for moral behavior.

The inscription on the stele was divided into three parts: a prologue, the code itself, and an epilogue at the bottom of the stone slab. The epilogue added extra incentive for obedience by reinforcing the promise of rewards to those who obeyed the laws and punishment to those who disobeyed.

ETHICAL PRINCIPLES

Hammurabi proclaimed that he issued his code on divine authority in order to "establish law and justice in the language of the land, thereby promoting the welfare of the people." The main ethical principle upon which the code rested was that "the strong shall not injure the weak." Individuals were not permitted to take the law into their own hands.

An important consideration for modern interpreters of the code, however, centers on how one defines such terms as "justice" and "injury to the weak." One striking feature of the code is that it was not strictly egalitarian in its application of punishments; the law differed according to the social status of the offender. Aristocrats were not punished as harshly as commoners, and commoners were not punished as harshly as slaves. Still, slaves had rights and received some protection under the law.

The code also rested on the conviction that punishment should fit the crime. Like the Law of Moses in ancient Israel, Hammurabi's code employed the *lex talionis*, "an eye for an eye, and a tooth for a tooth," and it may be the oldest law code in the ancient Near East to prescribe this system. It operated, however, only among equals. An aristocrat who destroyed the eye of a commoner or slave could pay a fine instead of losing his own eye. As long as the criminal and victim shared the same social status, however, the latter could demand exact retribution.

In an attempt to guarantee a fair trial and a just verdict, the code forbade a judge to change his verdict once a decision had been rendered. Any judge who did so was heavily fined and deposed. There were no public prosecutors in Hammurabi's day, so individuals brought their own complaints before the court and produced supporting documentation or witnesses. In cases of murder, the accuser had to prove the defendant guilty. Any accuser who failed to do so was put to death. This severe measure was designed to prevent frivolous, groundless cases from clogging the courts and wasting the time of defendants.

Hammurabi's code displays an understanding of the difference between accidental deed and malicious intent, but it does not seem to attach to this principle the same importance afforded it by the later Mosaic code.

CIVILIZATION AND MORAL CONTINUITY

Hammurabi's code addressed what it considered to be unethical behavior in a wide variety of situations, demonstrating a significant moral continuity between ancient and modern civilization. The concept of strict accountability is evident in all the laws.

The code mandated consumer protection. Merchants and businessmen had to guarantee the quality of their goods and services. No one was exempt. A house builder whose careless work resulted in the collapse of a house and the death of its inhabitants was himself put to death. A merchant who tried to increase the interest rate on a loan forfeited the entire loan amount. A surgeon whose patient died during an operation was executed. A surgeon whose patient lost an eye during treatment had his fingers cut off—a punishment that no doubt proved inconvenient to his future career.

Crime was a serious problem in Mesopotamian urban life, so the code ordered that exacting measures be taken against criminals. Burglars caught in the act were put to death on the spot. Anyone caught looting a burning building was thrown into the fire. Such penalties were intended to stamp out crime as well as limit the cycle of violence that sometimes resulted from private vengeance.

Hammurabi's code gave careful attention to marriage and family relationships. Proved adultery with a married woman incurred the death penalty for both participants. The wife was expected to be rigorously faithful, and the husband had virtually absolute power over his household. By the standards of the time, however, certain "rights" of women were set forth in this code for the first time. Husbands who abused their wives without cause had to pay a penalty in silver. If a wife proved herself innocent of charges of adultery, she could take her dowry and leave her husband.

There is debate over how often, if ever, the penalties and provisions of Hammurabi's code were actually carried out. Contemporary legal documents are scanty and silent on the issue, but there is no question that the code greatly influenced the behavior of the civilizations and the people of the Near East long after the fall of Babylonia. It provided the backdrop against which Moses revealed the law to Israel. The Law of Moses contains many similarities and parallels to Hammurabi's code. While it was not the first law code in history, the Code of Hammurabi was the most comprehensive in the world until the Byzantine emperor Justinian ordered the compilation of the *Corpus Juris Civilis* about 550 C.E.

Andrew C. Skinner

FURTHER READING
Cook, Stanley A. *The Laws of Moses and the Code of Hammurabi.* London: A. and C. Black, 1903.

Driver, Godfrey R., and John C. Miles, eds. *The Babylonian Laws.* 2 vols. Oxford, England: Clarendon Press, 1952.

Harper, Robert F., ed. *The Code of Hammurabi, King of Babylon About 2250 B.C.* Chicago: University of Chicago Press, 1904. Reprint. Holmes Beach, Fla.: Wm. W. Gaunt, 1994.

Hoare, Frederick R. *Eight Decisive Books of Antiquity.* Freeport, N.Y.: Books for Libraries Press, 1969.

Martin, W. J. "The Law Code of Hammurabi." In *Documents from Old Testament Times*, edited by David Winton Thomas. New York: Harper, 1961.

Mendenhall, George E. *Law and Covenant in Israel and the Ancient Near East.* Pittsburgh: Biblical Colloquium, 1955.

VerSteeg, Russ. *Early Mesopotamian Law.* Durham, N.C.: Carolina Academic Press, 2000.

SEE ALSO: Capital punishment; Constitutional government; Criminal punishment; Ethical monotheism; Hebrew Bible; Homicide; Jewish ethics; Law; Magna Carta; Moses; Ten Commandments.

Hare, R. M.

IDENTIFICATION: English philosopher
BORN: March 21, 1919, Backwell, near Bristol, Somerset, England
DIED: January 29, 2002, Ewelme, Oxfordshire, England
TYPE OF ETHICS: Modern history
SIGNIFICANCE: In such works as *The Language of Morals* (1952), *Freedom and Reason* (1963), *Applications of Moral Philosophy* (1972), *Moral Thinking* (1981), *Essays in Ethical Theory* (1989), and *Essays on Political Morality* (1989), Hare attempted to argue that all moral judgments are commands rather than factual propositions, without sacrificing the normative force of such judgments.

R. M. Hare's moral theory, called "universal prescriptivism," was based on the idea that moral judgments are universalizable prescriptions. Like the noncognitivist, he stressed the commending or evaluating function of value statements. Therefore, at least part of what it means to say "*x* is right" is "*x* is to be commended," or "one ought to do *x*." Hare also thought, however, unlike the noncognitivist, that moral statements are meant both to guide choices through a veiled appeal to universal principles and to assert on rationally testable grounds that something is the case. He agreed with G. E. Moore that naturalistic theories are fallacious but differed in his account of the reason for this.

Hare's work was one of the most eclectic efforts in contemporary moral philosophy, for his view had certain definite affinities with utilitarianism (in the idea that the basic human good is to maximize rational preferences that embody prescriptions), with existentialist ethics (in his suggestion that one makes a "decision of principle" when one chooses a particular action), with Kantian ethics (in connection with his universalizability thesis), and with emotivism (in his focus on the logic of the language of morals). On the practical side of moral philosophy, Hare showed an unusual philosophical interest in problems related to moral education and moral decision making.

R. Douglas Geivett

SEE ALSO: Cognitivism; Emotivist ethics; Existentialism; Kantian ethics; Language; Metaethics; Moore, G. E.; Ought/can implication; Prescriptivism; Unamuno y Jugo, Miguel de; Will.

Harm

IDENTIFICATION: Physical or mental damage done to others
TYPE OF ETHICS: Theory of ethics
SIGNIFICANCE: An important consequence of wrongdoing, harm is often argued a necessary prerequisite to certain charges of wrongdoing or to set limits on the conduct that the state can legitimately criminalize.

The term "harm" in ethics, as in ordinary language, appears in both noun and verb form. Although vague, ambiguous, and reflecting contested value judgments, the term has a number of discernable meanings in ethics.

Use of the noun "harm" is typically limited to refer to any diminution from an entity's good, welfare, function or well-being. To cause harm, one must at least cause such diminution. It is, however, often said that harm can only occur to something that not only has a good or function but is also sentient or has interests. Hence, one might harm a person or animal but one cannot directly harm (one can merely damage) a knife or tool. One might still cause harm in a derivative sense to a knife or tool, by damaging something that someone takes an interest in. Some also extend harm to refer nonderivatively to purported harms to certain inanimate entities like the environment. Persons employing such extensions almost always aim to invoke some of the moral objection that they view as warranted by harm to sentient beings.

In verb form, "harm" can be used minimally to mean simply to cause harm. In this sense, inanimate objects, natural events, and people engaging in nonobjectionable conduct can harm others. To say that one has harmed another in ethics is, however, often to make a more serious moral charge of wrongdoing. Hence, only appropriate subjects of moral criticism—such as persons, agents, or groups—can so harm another. To harm another in this morally laden sense, one must also typically negligently, recklessly, knowingly, or intentionally cause foreseeable harm to another by violating another's rights. Hence, one cannot harm another, in this morally laden sense, by such actions as giving birth to someone who happens to undergo a traumatic death later in life, attempting but failing to cause harm, voting, benefiting from a contract freely entered into, or failing to return another's love. One does not harm another in this sense by failing to provide a benefit where no special duty is owed.

JOHN STUART MILL'S HARM PRINCIPLE

Perhaps the best-known use of "harm" in ethics appears in John Stuart Mill's harm principle, which asserts that the state can only legitimately criminalize conduct, or otherwise coerce individuals, to prevent them from harming others. In elaborating this principle, Mill explicitly excludes both purported moral corruption and offenses to others' moral or religious sensibilities as relevant cases of harm. Others theorists have, however, used harm to include these latter phenomena and have thought that such harms must be taken into account when deciding what laws, norms or state actions are legitimate or good.

Robin Bradley Kar

FURTHER READING

Feinberg, Joel. *Harm to Others*. Oxford, England: Oxford University Press, 1984

Mill, John Stuart. *On Liberty, and Other Essays*. Edited by John Gray. New York: Oxford University Press, 1998.

SEE ALSO: Collective guilt; Ethical Principles of Psychologists; Experimentation; Milgram experiment; Mill, John Stuart; *On Liberty*.

Hart, H. L. A.

IDENTIFICATION: English legal philosopher
BORN: July 18, 1907, Harrogate, England
DIED: December 19, 1992, Oxford, England
TYPE OF ETHICS: Legal and judicial ethics
SIGNIFICANCE: Hart defended a distinctively modern version of legal positivism—the view that law can be accounted for in neutral sociological terms, without adverting to moral criteria.

H. L. A. Hart was the most influential Anglo-American legal philosopher of his generation and, arguably, of the twentieth century. He wrote on a wide range of topics, including punishment, the nature of obligation, the illegitimacy of criminally enforcing popular morality, and the role of excuses and causality in morality and law. He is, however, best known for his legal positivist account of what law is. Against natural law theorists, who believed that law is inextricably bound up with moral standards, Hart argued that there is no necessary connection between law and morality. Hart thought this separation critical for the meaningful moral criticism of law.

Drawing on advances in linguistic philosophy, Hart nevertheless argued that prior legal positivists—such as John Austin—who sought to offer similarly neutral, descriptive accounts of law had failed to distinguish between legal systems and situations of gunmen writ large. For Austin, law consisted in sovereign orders, habitually obeyed and backed by coercive threats, but such accounts fail to distinguish between following commands and being coerced. To cure this defect, Hart analyzed social rules as involving widespread attitudes (the "internal point of view") toward standards as offering both internal guides to conduct and grounds for criticizing deviations. To Hart, Austinian accounts of law also reduced too many phenomena to the criminal law model, thus obfuscating the way law allows people to vary their normative relations with one another—as in the law of contracts, trusts, and estates. Hart dubbed rules of the latter kind "power-conferring rules."

For Hart, law is distinctive in that it combines primary rules of conduct with secondary, power-conferring rules, including a "rule of recognition," which allows officials to identify the law. Law consists in the complex social situation in which a group of officials takes up the internal point of view toward a rule of recognition, which in turn specifies primary rules of conduct for citizens, who typically obey (for any number of reasons).

Hart later clarified that he is an inclusive legal positivist: Rules of recognition are social conventions that can require employing moral criteria. This clarification was meant to deflect Ronald Dworkin's modern natural law criticisms—namely, that interpreting the law often involves employing moral standards. The clarification nevertheless exposed Hart to Joseph Raz's exclusive legal positivist criticism that any such reference to moral criteria would prevent law from providing independent practical guidance, as law purportedly claims. That such prominent legal philosophers define their positions partly in response to Hart's testifies to Hart's continuing centrality to modern jurisprudence.

Robin Bradley Kar

FURTHER READING

Cane, Peter. *Responsibility in Law and Morality.* Portland, Oreg.: Hart, 2002.

Hart, H. L. A. *The Concept of Law.* 2d ed. Oxford, England: Oxford University Press, 1994.

———. *Punishment and Responsibility.* Oxford, England: Oxford University Press, 1968.

SEE ALSO: Ayer, A. J.; Comte, Auguste; Emotivist ethics; Language; Law; Negligence.

Hartshorne, Charles

IDENTIFICATION: American philosopher and theologian

BORN: June 5, 1897, Kittanning, Pennsylvania

DIED: October 9, 2000, Austin, Texas

TYPE OF ETHICS: Religious ethics

SIGNIFICANCE: Credited with reviving interest in religious ethics among philosophers, Hartshorne was a proponent of process theology—the theory that God is not an absolute but constantly changes in response to events affecting humanity. From his theories of religion, Hartshorne argued for a rational, relative view of ethics.

Despite his prolific publications, Charles Hartshorne was a little-known philosopher of theology. He challenged the traditional view of God as being omnipotent or omniscient while recognizing the existence of God. In more than twenty books and one hundred articles, Hartshorne argued that God suffered and celebrated with his creations as they traveled through life. Hartshorne found the origins of his theories in the work of Harvard philosopher Alfred North Whitehead for whom he worked as an assistant during the 1920's.

Hartshorne is credited with reviving interest in religious philosophy. As a first step, he applied mathematics to develop sixteen proofs of the existence of God. Arguing that God existed placed Hartshorne beyond the mainstream of philosophers. He then postulated a dipolar view of God. At one pole, the abstract God is unchanging and absolute. The concrete pole is a God who perfectly suffers with his creations.

Late in his life, Hartshorne published many of the writings he had completed but stored away. One of these works was *Omnipotence and Other Theological Mistakes* (1984), which he published when he was more than eighty years old. Hartshorne also developed an expertise in ornithology, specializing in natural selection among birds. In *Born to Sing: An Interpretation and World Survey of Bird Song* (1973), he argued that some birds like to sing simply for the joy of it, even when not in mating season or when threatened.

Despite the volume of his writing, Hartshorne was troubled that his theories did not attract the attention of his peers. However, by the time he died in 2000, he was able to see that his theories were being debated in a reenergized discipline. His writings on ethical issues, such as abortion, attracted less attention. These arguments were marked by rational, less emotional, views of ethical behavior.

John David Rausch, Jr.

SEE ALSO: Derrida, Jacques; God; Niebuhr, H. Richard; Niebuhr, Reinhold; Religion; Tillich, Paul; Whitehead, Alfred North.

Hasidism

DEFINITION: Form of emotional Jewish mysticism originating in eighteenth century Poland
TYPE OF ETHICS: Religious ethics
SIGNIFICANCE: Hasidism rejects an intellectual, scholarly model of religious practice and instead insists that true worship is simply the joyous recognition of the immanence of God in all of creation.

Modern Hasidism is based on the teachings of the eighteenth century Jewish leader Baal Shem Tov, who was born Israel ben Eliezer. His relatively uncomplicated message of joyful worship appealed to the predominantly uneducated peasant populations of eastern Europe. Many Jews abandoned the rabbinical, intellectual traditions of Talmudic study to embrace Hasidism's emotionalism. Hasidism stressed God's mercy, the goodness inherent in human beings, the universality of God leading to the spiritual unity of God and humanity, and the joyfulness of religious experience, which frequently found expression in music and dance.

Despite the opposition of Talmudists who, in 1781, pronounced Hasidism heretical, the popularity of the anti-intellectual movement peaked during the early nineteenth century. While less numerous in the twenty-first century, Hasidic communities remain an active force in modern Judaism, and Hasidism has broader influence in both the Jewish and gentile worlds principally through Hasidic composers, artists, and philosophers, including, notably, composer Ernest Bloch and Yiddish writer Isaac Bashevis Singer. Through the works of philosopher Martin Buber, Hasidism has also influenced twenty-first century life, notably, through the adoption of Buber's system of collective farming known as the *kibbutz*.

Mary E. Virginia

SEE ALSO: Buber, Martin; *I and Thou*; Jewish ethics; Kabbala; *Tzaddik*; Wiesel, Elie.

Hate

DEFINITION: Personal or social antipathy toward others
TYPE OF ETHICS: Personal and social ethics
SIGNIFICANCE: Hate is a primary cause of conflict between individuals, groups, and nations. Its moral status varies wildly in different contexts, from the Christian view that hatred is sinful to Friedrich Nietzsche's frank admiration of the great haters who brought about the slave revolt in morality.

Most people understand hate, or hatred, as an emotion felt by one individual for another that is characterized by animosity and sometimes is accompanied by the desire to see the hated person suffer. This highly personal understanding of hate is, however, relegated almost entirely to laypersons; scholars have given it not only moral but also metaphysical, sociological, psychological, and criminological significance.

To the early Greek philosopher Empedocles, hate was a metaphysical reality, one of two forces of change in the universe, the other being love. Empedocles explains all natural objects in terms of four basic material elements—fire, earth, air, and water—which combine and decombine in a cyclical process of production and decomposition. Love is responsible for the attraction between elements and for whatever order and stability the universe possesses. Love is in constant conflict with hate, its cosmic opposite. As the cycle of change unfolds, love is superseded by hate in its turn, and disorder and decay appear in direct proportion to the hate unleashed by the progression of this cycle. The universe is the scene of constant creation and destruction as the dyadic conflict between love and hate proceeds.

SPINOZA AND NIETZSCHE

Baruch Spinoza gives hate a prominent place in his *Ethics* as a fundamental emotion and determinant of human behavior. People love what arouses joy in them, while they hate what arouses sorrow; likewise, one loves the person who "affects with joy a thing which we love" but hates him if "we imagine that he affects it with sorrow." Love and hate, the respective responses to joy and sorrow, are psychological constants in the deterministic natural order of which humans are a part, acting as the determinants of the nature of all relationships with others, whether they be individuals, classes of individuals, or entire nations. So strong are these emotions that one may hate an entire class or nation of people because one of its members has done one an injury. Hatred induces "anger," the desire to injure those one hates; when one's hatred and anger toward others are mutual and result in an injury being done to one, one develops the desire for vengeance against those who have injured one. Hatred also exists in other forms—"indignation," hatred of those who injure others, and "envy," hatred of another's good fortune.

For Friedrich Nietzsche, hate exists primarily as *ressentiment* (resentment), the vengeful, jealous hatred that reveals the weakness of those who perceive their own self-respect to be threatened by their superiors. The early Christians resented the Romans because of their paganism and their power. Resentment is what was directed by the "herd," the masses of nineteenth century Europeans, who were bound to one another by mediocrity and conformity, against the noble individual who dared to be different, who determined for himself what his values would be, and who used the life-giving energy provided by his animal instincts to create a superior life characterized by the mastery of those instincts. Consequently, resentment of others, according to Nietzsche, is beneath the dignity of the noble man; if he does experience hatred, it spends itself quickly and is over before it "poisons" him. Hatred festers in the souls of the weak and powerless, who spend whatever creative energies they possess cultivating plans for revenge.

The Nietzschean view of hatred as a psychosocial phenomenon is reflected in the attitudes of twentieth century thinkers, who have made it the object of not only philosophical reflection but also psychological, sociological, and criminological research. Samuel Tenenbaum, in *Why Men Hate* (1947), adopts a distinctly Nietzschean view of hatred: "Hate warps and stultifies the soul. It consumes the individual and fills him with suspicion and distrust. . . . The world becomes a giant conspiracy, where men and women, instead of living normal lives, connive and plot." The twentieth century saw hatred erupt as animosity to-

ward various racial, ethnic, and religious groups, often culminating in open warfare.

OTHER VIEWS

Jeffrie Murphy, in *Forgiveness and Mercy* (1988), acknowledges several varieties of hatred: simple hatred, which is dislike for someone for some "nonmoral objectionable quality," such as being a bore; moral hatred, which consists of hatred of someone because of the person's association with an immoral cause, such as Nazism; and, finally, malicious hatred, which consists of the desire to injure another for the purpose of gaining some competitive advantage. Only the last variety of hatred is morally objectionable, but Murphy also argues for the existence of "retributive hatred."

Retributive hatred is hatred that is motivated by justifiable anger over an unjustifiable wrong, for which the wronged party rightfully expects and is entitled to some form of retribution. No matter how justifiable it is, however, Murphy does not favor acting upon retributive hatred. Moral humility demands that one recognize one's own limitations of knowledge and virtue, lest one's hatred drive one to excessive vengeance. In addition, retribution is often either impossible or too costly, and one's own moral decency imposes constraints upon one's desire for revenge. For these reasons, although retributive hatred is a proper response to a genuine wrong, it can be dangerous and should be subjected to "reflective restraint."

Barbara Forrest

FURTHER READING

Beck, Aaron T. *Prisoners of Hate: The Cognitive Basis of Anger, Hostility, and Violence*. New York: Perennial, 2000.

Berrill, Kevin T., and Gregory M. Herek, eds. *Hate Crimes: Confronting Violence Against Lesbians and Gay Men*. Newbury Park, Calif.: Sage, 1992.

Goldberg, Jane G. *The Dark Side of Love: The Positive Role of Negative Feelings*. New Brunswick, N.J.: Transaction, 1999.

Hamm, Mark. *American Skinheads: The Criminology and Control of Hate Crime*. Westport, Conn.: Praeger, 1993.

Kaufmann, Walter, ed. "Empedocles." In *Thales to Ockham*. Vol. 1 in *Philosophic Classics*. Englewood Cliffs, N.J.: Prentice-Hall, 1968.

Moss, Donald, ed. *Hating in the First Person Plural:*

Psychoanalytic Essays on Racism, Homophobia, Misogyny, and Terror. New York: Other Press, 2003.

Murphy, Jeffrie G., and Jean Hampton. *Forgiveness and Mercy.* New York: Cambridge University Press, 1988.

Nietzsche, Friedrich. *On the Genealogy of Morals.* Edited and translated by Walter Kaufmann. New York: Vintage Books, 1967.

Spinoza, Benedictus de. *Ethics.* Edited and translated by G. H. R. Parkinson. New York: Oxford University Press, 2000.

Tenenbaum, Samuel. *Why Men Hate.* New York: Beechhurst Press, 1947.

SEE ALSO: Bigotry; Cruelty to animals; Genocide, Frustration-aggression theory of; Hate crime and hate speech; Hitler, Adolf; Racism; Revenge; Sexual stereotypes.

Hate crime and hate speech

DEFINITION: Criminal acts and offensive speech directed against individuals because of their race, ethnicity, religion, sexual orientation, or other group affiliations

TYPE OF ETHICS: Human rights

SIGNIFICANCE: The impact and control of hate crimes and hate speech have become significant public policy concerns and raise a variety of ethical questions that may not be obvious.

Since the early 1980's, nearly every U.S. state has passed some type of hate-crime law, and many local governments and other agencies (especially schools and universities) have attempted to regulate hate speech in some manner. These laws and regulations have engendered several important ethical issues. One issue that has arisen is the question of what kinds of groups should be included within hate-crime and hate-speech protections. Although categories such as race, ethnicity, and religion are virtually always included, there has been considerable debate over other categories, such as those pertaining to sexual orientation and gender.

By 2003, approximately sixteen states had hate-crime laws that did not include crimes committed on the basis of sexual orientation. In addition, one of the primary impediments to the enactment of federal hate-crime legislation has been the question of whether to include sexual orientation. This is a significant issue because research has shown that sexual-orientation-based crimes are almost as common as those based on race and religion. Critics, however, assert that including sexual orientation in hate-crime laws will amount to an official government endorsement of homosexuality, which they oppose because they believe that homosexuality is morally or spiritually wrong. On the other hand, proponents of inclusion claim that when laws address other kinds of bigoted acts but not those motivated by sexual orientation, they send the implicit message that violence against gays and lesbians is acceptable.

By late 2003, gender was included in the hate-crime statutes in nineteen states. Opponents of inclusion have voiced several concerns. Among other things, they claim that gender-based violence is significantly different in character than crime based on categories such as race and religion, and some fear that if all cases of sexual assault and domestic violence eventually become hate crimes, that development will obscure other kinds of bigotry. Conversely, other critics claim that crimes against women will no longer receive adequate attention if they are subsumed under the rubric of hate crime. However, those who wish to include gender claim that these concerns are unwarranted, and that gender-based crimes are very much like those based on more traditional hate-crime categories.

Aside from questions about which groups to include in hate-crime and hate-speech protections, the other major ethical dilemma that has arisen is how to protect people from violent or offensive attacks, while at the same time protecting the freedoms of expression and association. For example, should college students be permitted to hang Confederate or Nazi flags in their dorm windows if other students find such displays offensive? Should there be efforts to regulate the content of Web sites created by white supremacist and other extremist groups? Should people be punished for burning crosses? Answers to such questions are not obvious, and the questions have inspired both debate and legal controversies.

Phyllis B. Gerstenfeld

FURTHER READING

Gerstenfeld, Phyllis B. *Hate Crimes: Causes, Controls, and Controversies.* Thousand Oaks, Calif.: Sage, 2004.

Holzer, Henry Mark, ed. *Speaking Freely: The Case Against Speech Codes.* Studio City, Calif.: Second Thoughts Books, 1994.

Lederer, Laura, and Richard Delgado, eds. *The Price We Pay: The Case Against Racist Speech, Hate Propaganda, and Pornography.* New York: Hill & Wang, 1995.

SEE ALSO: Bigotry; Genocide, frustration-aggression theory of; Genocide and democide; Hate; Homophobia; Ku Klux Klan; Lynching; Racism; Sexual abuse and harassment; Violence.

Head Start

IDENTIFICATION: Comprehensive U.S. developmental program of educational, social, and health services for disadvantaged children
DATE: Founded in 1965
TYPE OF ETHICS: Children's rights
SIGNIFICANCE: Head Start was designed to break the cycle of poverty by enabling children from low-income families, as well as their parents, to improve their intellectual development, self-esteem, and physical and mental health.

Created as a result of the Economic Opportunity Act of 1964, Head Start emerged as a social-action program at a time in history when social and political forces, as well as intellectual traditions in the social sciences, had begun to focus on the problem of poverty. The program developed out of the civil rights era and the War on Poverty, the revival of scientific interest in the role of the environment in human development, and the design of educational-intervention efforts for economically disadvantaged children. The lines of its development converged amid an alliance of child-development experts and social policy makers, under whose auspices Head Start grew from an idea to a proposal and finally to an active program. Head Start provides a broad range of services to children and their families. Play, group, and individual activities with both direct and indirect instruction are offered, as well as medical and dental care.

Genevieve Slomski

SEE ALSO: Bilingual education; Child labor legislation; Children's rights; Children's television; Godparents; Moral education; United Nations Declaration of the Rights of the Child.

Health care allocation

DEFINITION: Distribution of health care resources to specific areas and to certain individuals in need of particular procedures
TYPE OF ETHICS: Bioethics
SIGNIFICANCE: Health care allocation raises questions of societal obligation and individual rights to health care, as well as values inherent in specific treatment choices.

The allocation of scarce resources is an issue central to every political party, every government, and every organization and company. Whether to allocate 2 percent or 10 percent of the gross national product to health care, rather than defense, or education, or housing, or whatever other particular need is most pressing, is a decision that is central to the type of government and the values of those in power. Once a health care budget is established, the choices become progressively less global and more oriented to the individual recipient of health care. Although the values inherent in the original budget decisions can still be found, they are often less visible than the physician's personal opinions or the assessment of medical or social utility found in specific allocation decisions. Certain salient issues include the need to balance ethical concerns with economic realities, the need to allocate scarce health resources, the call for heightened accountability, and the impact of various policies on vulnerable populations.

MACRO- VS. MICROALLOCATION

Are patients individuals or members of populations? Should health care be regulated as part of the public good? Given a set amount of resources—funding, personnel, equipment, and so forth—to dedicate to health care, a particular system must then

625

determine the allocation to different areas of health care. Preventive medicine, health care promotion, research, medical education, the physical establishment of new facilities, and technological advancement all compete for resources dealing with the treatment of injured and ill patients. This system-wide form of decision making, along with the initial allotment of resources, is usually considered macro-allocation. The macro level concerns the scope and design of basic health care institutions: the delivery and financing of personal medical services that comprise acute care, including the system of high-technology hospital and clinic, support staff, research institutions, and public health programs involved in prevention.

Macro decisions generally determine the kinds of health care services that exist in society, who will receive them and on what bases, who will deliver them, and the distribution of financial burdens. In contrast, the individual determination of eligibility for a given procedure or selection of patients for treatment is called microallocation. Allocation in general is inextricably linked with societal and individual perceptions of justice. A society that considers inequities in health to be unjust, as opposed to unfortunate, will allocate a proportionately greater amount of its resources to mitigate health differences. If a society deems it a pity but not unjust that some people enjoy better health care than others, it will not feel such a societal obligation to correct these differences.

THEORIES OF JUSTICE

Distributive justice establishes principles for the distribution of scarce resources in circumstances in which demand outstrips supply and rationing must occur. Needs are to be considered in terms of overall needs and the dignity of members of society. Aside from the biological and physiological elements, the social context of health and disease may influence a given problem and its severity. Individual prejudices and presuppositions may enlarge the nature and scope of the disease, creating a demand for health care that makes it even more difficult to distribute scarce resources for all members of society. Principles of fair distribution in society often supersede and become paramount to the concerns of the individual. Questions about who shall receive what share of society's scarce resources generate controversies about a national health policy, unequal distributions of

advantages to the disadvantaged, and rationing of health care.

Similar problems recur with regard to access to and distribution of health insurance, medical equipment, and artificial organs. The lack of insurance as well as the problem of underinsurance constitutes a huge economic barrier to health care access in the United States. Tom L. Beauchamp and James F. Childress have pointed out that the acquired immunodeficiency syndrome (AIDS) crisis has presented dramatic instances of the problems of insurability and underwriting practices, where insurers often appeal to actuarial fairness in defending their decisions, while neglecting social justice. Proposals to alleviate the unfairness to those below the poverty line have been based on charity, compassion, and benevolence toward the sick rather than on claims of justice. The ongoing debate over the entitlement to a minimum of health care involves not only government entitlement programs but also complex social, political, economic, and cultural beliefs.

Decisions concerning the allocation of funds will dictate the type of health care that can be provided for which problems. Numerous resources, supplies, and space in intensive care units have been allocated for specific patients or classes of patients. A life-threatening illness, of course, complicates this decision. In the United States, health care has often been allocated by one's ability to pay rather than other criteria; rationing has at times been based on ranking a list of services or one's age. There are several theories of justice with regard to health care, some of which overlap, and others of which have different possible methods of distribution applicable to the overall concept. Three of the most general theories are the egalitarian, the libertarian, and the utilitarian.

EGALITARIAN THEORIES

Egalitarian theories of distributive justice advocate either the equal distribution of goods and resources to all people or the provision of equality of opportunity in obtaining care. Equal distribution has the major drawback of ignoring differences in health needs in a given population. For example, treatments appropriate to reasonably healthy individuals would certainly not be appropriate for people with diabetes or epilepsy, much less kidney disease or cancer.

Equality of opportunity emphasizes distribution of resources in accordance with what each individual person needs in order to function at a "normal" level. "Normal" in this sense is usually taken to mean that level that is species-typical. The assumption made is that no one should be denied medical treatment on the basis of undeserved disadvantaging properties such as social class, ability to pay, or ill health. The questions of what constitutes need and what constitutes an undeserved disadvantage, however, make the application of this theory very complicated. For example, does a person with a disfiguring feature, such as a birthmark or scar, need to have plastic surgery in order to enjoy the same social benefits as others?

Problems also arise when a particular system does not have enough resources to provide for all. At what level is it necessary to provide these resources? The range goes from the treatment of common diseases and injuries to the provision (at least theoretically) of heart and liver transplants to anyone who shows a need.

LIBERTARIAN AND UTILITARIAN THEORIES

Libertarian theories of justice, when applied to health care, challenge the concept of health care as a right. If something is a right, society has an obligation to provide it to all people. Libertarians contend that justice results from allowing a society to participate in voluntary exchanges to obtain what they need; in other words, a free-market economy. A person is entitled to health care in proportion to his or her ability to exchange that which has been rightfully acquired. Any redistribution of resources, such as taxing the wealthy to fund health care for the poor, is inherently unjust, because it denies the wealthy the right to use that which they fairly gained. These theories tend to ignore the fact that extreme wealth can give the rich the power to deny the poor the ability to exercise their rights freely.

Utilitarian theories focus on the principle of the greatest good for the greatest number. If *x* dollars could provide food for fifty starving people or open-heart surgery for one, that money should be devoted to food. Utilitarians think that the government is responsible for enacting laws that promote the general public's happiness and that the legislature is responsible for inducing people to act in socially desirable ways through a system of incentives and disincentives. They feel that the law should focus on equality of opportunity for all people and that property rights should be protected because the security of property

is crucial to attaining happiness. The problem with utilitarian systems in general is that they tend to lose sight of the individual in favor of the entire population as a whole.

TWO-TIERED SYSTEMS

Many modern health systems are the results of a two-tiered philosophy. On the first level, a minimum of health care is provided to every person in a society, without regard to wealth or class. On the second level, goods are obtained on the basis of individual decisions and ability to pay. This is usually considered a fair compromise in the United States' health care system. Debate will always exist regarding where the tiers separate, and what decent minimum should be provided for all. There is a lack of consensus on principles for allocating resources.

Margaret Hawthorne
Updated by Marcia J. Weiss

FURTHER READING

Beauchamp, Tom L., and James F. Childress. *Principles of Biomedical Ethics*. 5th ed. New York: Oxford University Press, 2001.

Beauchamp, Tom L., and LeRoy Walters, eds. *Contemporary Issues in Bioethics*. 4th ed. Belmont, Calif.: Wadsworth, 1994.

Danis, Marion, Carolyn Clancy, and Larry R. Churchill, eds. *Ethical Dimensions of Health Policy*. New York: Oxford University Press, 2002.

Garrett, Thomas M., Harold W. Baillie, and Rosellen M. Garrett. *Health Care Ethics: Principles and Problems*. Englewood Cliffs, N.J.: Prentice-Hall, 1989.

Greenberg, Warren. *Competition, Regulation, and Rationing in Health Care*. Ann Arbor, Mich.: Health Administration Press, 1991.

Roemer, Milton I. *National Health Systems of the World*. New York: Oxford University Press, 1991.

VanDeVeer, Donald, and Tom Regan, eds. *Health Care Ethics: An Introduction*. Philadelphia: Temple University Press, 1987.

Veatch, Robert M., ed. *Medical Ethics*. Boston: Jones & Bartlett, 1989.

SEE ALSO: Acquired immunodeficiency syndrome (AIDS); Ageism; Cost-benefit analysis; Distributive justice; Holistic medicine; Illness; Medical bills of rights; Medical ethics; Medical insurance.

Hebrew Bible

IDENTIFICATION: Foundational scripture for Judaism and the basis for the Christian Old Testament

TYPE OF ETHICS: Religious ethics

SIGNIFICANCE: The ethics of the Hebrew Bible are bound up in the sacred story of the ancient Israelites, in which divine implications are at the heart of social actions. Ancient Israelis saw themselves as God's family, a metaphor that forms the basis for ethics in the three Abrahamic monotheisms, in which human beings are socially responsible as well as individually free. The primary ethics of ancient Israel are social justice and mercy, which are indivisible with the commandment to love God unconditionally.

In the religion of the Hebrew Bible, human beings are socially responsible and free to choose. In many religious traditions, the human drama is only part of the vast cosmos. In biblical religion, however, human history is the divine arena and human social action is the center of meaning. At the heart of the concept of monotheism is a god who is intimately related to the acts and feelings of human beings; thus human ethics comes to surpass the sacrificial model of worship. The Hebrew Bible, or Tanakh, is the foundational scripture for Judaism, which became the Old Testament for Christians, and which was also one of the major influences on the formation of the Qur'ān, the sacred text of Islam.

The three Abrahamic monotheisms—Judaism, Christianity, and Islam—ground their ethical assumptions and challenges in a familial relationship between the biblical god and his people. The biblical story is basically one of family, and from these family dynamics, the central characteristics of biblical ethics is formed.

The Hebrew Scriptures, treated devotionally as a single text, constitute a collection, or library, that extends over a millennium of events, ideas, and literary forms. Tanakh is an acronym for the three categories of books in the Bible: Torah, law; Nebiim, prophets; and Kesubim, writings. Each of these categories—law, prophets, and writings—exemplifies a key element of biblical ethics. They can be characterized in these ways: Ethics in Torah is embedded in the narratives of the patriarchs, in the covenantal relationship that ensures devotion to god and to fam-

ily. Ethics in the Prophets is also twofold: devotion to god and social responsibility as worship. Ethics in the writings, in particular the wisdom writings, is also grounded in devotion to god, but without the emphasis on expectations for god's intervention in history, or divine meaning in family or ethnic histories.

TORAH: THE ANCIENT STORIES

Torah is made up mostly of three cycles of stories: tales of the origins of Earth and people; founding tales of the patriarchs, Abraham, Isaac, and Jacob; and the story of the Exodus, the return of the people from slavery to the promised land of Israel. These cosmogonic tales—or myths of origin—generate the basis of biblical ethics, that worship is based in a covenant, or contract, of loyalty toward god and enacted in family or community. Throughout the stories runs a deep thread of human frailty and God's judgment and forgiveness. Some of the ancient stories, particularly in Genesis or Judges, would be difficult to comprehend ethically if they were not understood in the context of the uncompromising devotion to the god of Israel and human relationships as the echo of that devotion to the divine. Otherwise, stories such as the sacrifice of Jephthah's daughter (Judges 11), or even the testing of Abraham (Genesis 22), would make little sense to modern readers.

RITUAL AND ETHICAL LAW CODES

Attached to these sacred stories are law codes, such as the pre-monarchial (before the tenth century B.C.E.) Covenant Code (Exodus 20:22-23:33), perhaps the oldest set of biblical laws, in which appears the "eye for eye, tooth for tooth" sense of justice. It has many parallels to the Code of Hammurabi of the Babylonians. These are case laws (casuistic law), or specific legal questions with an if/then form:

> When a man seduces a virgin who is not engaged to be married, and lies with her, he shall give the bride-price for her and make her his wife. But if her father refuses to give her to him, he shall pay an amount equal to the bride-price for virgins (Exodus 22:16-17).

Although women had some protections under Israelite law, the laws favored patriarchal values—women were subject to the authority, or even ownership, of men. Nevertheless, the Covenant Code also reveals compassion for widows, orphans, servants, outsiders, and even beasts. The Deuteronomic Code (Deuteronomy 12-26) is perhaps the "Book of the Law" referred to as discovered in the temple during the reign of Josiah (622 B.C.E.), setting off a reform including centralized worship in Jerusalem. The Holiness Code in Leviticus (17-26) is a priestly concern that lists prohibitions on worship, on sex and daily life for individuals to keep the people of Israel pure, in order to set them apart from their neighbors, the Canaanites. Thus, their purity is bound up also in exclusivism.

TEN COMMANDMENTS (DECALOGUE)

The law codes collected in Torah are attributed traditionally to Moses, the deliverer of his people from Egypt. The Decalogue in particular is tied to a story of Moses ascending the Mountain of God and receiving two tablets of law written by the finger of God. According to the story, Moses descended the mountain only to find his people worshiping a golden calf. Enraged, he smashed the tablets, then ground the golden calf to powder, mixed it with water, and made the people drink it. He then ascended the mountain again, and God again prepared two tablets of law.

It is notable that the story emphasizes the violation of cultic regulations rather than social morality. These apodictic, or unconditional, laws of the Decalogue cover the two crucial aspects of ancient Israelite life: the way to worship God (religious obligations) and the way people should treat one another. Often the Decalogue is emblematic for universally accepted moral behavior; however, the religious obligations belong to a particular way of conceptualizing the divine, and the social obligations may have left room for ownership of human beings in their ancient forms. Modern traditions have shifted their ways of reading the laws or their understanding of the ancient laws. For example, the commandment against killing may have originally been a law forbidding murder of a member of one's own community, but not forbidding the killing of outsiders, as in warfare. Not only is it difficult to determine what it may have meant historically, modern communities are divided about what the law means for moral behavior today.

THE PROPHETS

Ancient Israel conceived of ultimate reality as a family relationship, of God as father or husband, and the people as wayward sons or unfaithful wives. Around 750 B.C.E., Amos went to the northern kingdom of Israel to utter profound oracles spoken with the authority of Yahweh (God). Amos claimed that Yahweh had said, "I hate and despise your feast days," meaning that cultic regulations were not sufficient for worship. Instead, he said, "Let justice roll down like waters, and righteousness like a mighty stream."

Amos's words became a touchstone for Martin Luther King, Jr., as he cited them in his "Letter from Birmingham Jail," marking the Civil Rights movement. Thus, beginning with Amos, the writing prophets (Nebiim), insisted that worshipping God was embedded in moral behavior toward one another. Some of the prophets, notably Hosea, were equally interested in cultic purity, the exclusive worship of Yahweh, uncontaminated by the symbols and practices of the gods of the neighbors—including some Israelites who practiced religion outside the parameters of pure Yahwism.

WISDOM LITERATURE AND STORIES

Two sorts of wisdom writings are represented in the biblical canon: conventional wisdom (such as found in Proverbs), which tends to be practical and answers questions about human behavior, and speculative wisdom (as found in Ecclesiastes), which raises questions about human meaning. The Book of Job is the masterpiece of speculative wisdom; it is an ethical departure from the major thrust of biblical moral principles, as wisdom in the Book of Job is not concerned with Israel's history or God's intervention in human affairs; rather, the wisdom writings of the sages is concerned with a search for the moral order of the natural world.

The concern with God's justice, called theodicy, asks, why is there suffering? Beginning with a folktale form, God and Ha-satan (who is a servant of God in this book) hold a contest over Job's unswerving loyalty to God. Everything is stripped from Job: his riches, his animals, his children (who are marks of his wealth, the blessings that had been heaped upon him), even his health. His friends make the case that Job must have caused the misfortune. However, Job was a blameless and upright man.

629

Job angrily accuses God, demanding an explanation. God answers out of the whirlwind, with startling, poetic grandeur. He does not justify his ways to humanity, but rather the God of Job is beyond human reason and justification. The poem places God as the maker of nature rather than the maker of social justice. It is likely that the conclusion to Job, in which he gets all his wealth restored and more, is a pious addition to a troubling wisdom writing suggesting the mysteries of God are beyond the realm of the social good.

Stories and rituals, which may seem on the surface to have little to do with ethics and morality, are the source and sustenance of a biblical worldview that posits a god who acts in history for the moral benefit of humans, and humans, whose historical activities have metaphysical meaning. Ethics arise from social order, ritual protections, and the deep stories (or myths) that illuminate those social and ritual activities. Sacred story in the age of the patriarchs is the basis of biblical ethics; social ethics in the age of the prophets is a means to worship.

Lynda Sexson

FURTHER READING

Douglas, Mary. *Leviticus as Literature*. Oxford, England: Oxford University Press, 2000. In this book, and in *In the Wilderness: The Doctrine of Defilement in the Book of Numbers* (Rev. ed. Oxford: Oxford University Press, 2001), anthropologist Douglas brilliantly challenges readers to reconsider the concepts of cleanness and pollution, to reimagine the literary structures of Leviticus and Numbers.

Niditch, Susan. *Ancient Israelite Religion*. New York: Oxford University Press, 1997. There are many competent introductions to biblical religion; this one has a particularly lucid chapter on "The Legal and Ethical Dimension."

_____. *War in the Hebrew Bible: A Study in the Ethics of Violence*. New York: Oxford University Press, 1993. Insightful study that places ethical questions of biblical warfare and violence in the cultural contexts of ancient Israel.

Schwartz, Regina M. *The Curse of Cain: The Violent Legacy of Monotheism*. Chicago: University of Chicago Press, 1997. Examines biblical narratives in their historical contexts, exposing the exclusivism and violence toward others that has influence on contemporary social attitudes and behaviors.

SEE ALSO: Jewish ethics; Talmud; Ten Commandments; Torah; *Tzaddik*.

Hedonism

DEFINITION: Philosophical belief that pleasure is the highest good
TYPE OF ETHICS: Theory of ethics
SIGNIFICANCE: Classical hedonism and its descendants are full-fledged philosophical systems that argue that the rational pursuit of pleasure as the greatest good is a positive moral virtue. Hedonism can also name the rejection of rationality and constraint and the unfettered license of desire. This latter practice is commonly thought of as either immoral or amoral.

From the Greek word *hīdonī*, meaning "pleasure," hedonism is the ethical theory that maintains that pleasure is the highest good. The term is also sometimes used to refer to the psychological theory that all human behavior is motivated by the desire for pleasure or the avoidance of pain. This second view is properly designated "psychological hedonism" (a theory about the way things *are*) in order to distinguish it from ethical hedonism (a theory about the way things *ought* to be or about what things are good). The English philosopher Jeremy Bentham, in his *Introduction to the Principles of Morals and Legislation* (1789), espoused both of these views when he wrote, "Nature has placed mankind under the guidance of two sovereign masters, pain and pleasure. It is for them alone to point out what we ought to do, as well as to determine what we shall do."

PSYCHOLOGICAL HEDONISM

Many ethical hedonists point to the purported fact of psychological hedonism in support of their ethical position, but is it a fact? Only if an adherent admits the possibility of a human action not being motivated by the desire for pleasure can psychological hedonism be a factual or empirical claim. Since the adherent cannot admit an exception because he or she equates motivation with desire for pleasure, however, then the claim is not a factual one; it provides no information.

Philosophers opposed to hedonism have noted that persons who deliberately seek pleasure fail to find it, while, paradoxically, they find pleasure when they seek other things as their end and obtain those other things. This has been called the "hedonistic paradox."

Further, if psychological hedonism is true and all human actions *are* motivated by a desire for pleasure, then the ethical hedonist's admonition that people *ought* to seek pleasure is unnecessary.

Ethical hedonists also support their position in other ways. One of these is by claiming that hedonism is true by definition. Examples of this approach can be seen in John Locke, who defined "good" as that which "is apt to cause or increase pleasure," and in Baruch Spinoza, who defined it as "every kind of pleasure." John Stuart Mill has also been said to define "good" as the "desirable" and the "desirable" as what is desired, which happens to be pleasure.

This definitional approach is criticized by those who insist that there are things other than pleasure that are intrinsically good and some pleasurable things that are intrinsically bad. Further, G. E. Moore has argued that such attempts to define "good" commit the naturalistic fallacy; that is, they purport to define the indefinable, especially to define a moral entity in terms of a natural one.

THE ANCIENT GREEKS

Aristippus founded an early school of hedonism known as the Cyrenaics, so named for his birthplace, Cyrene. This Greek philosopher, a follower of Socrates, claimed that one's way of life should be one of as much pleasure as possible, even if followed by pain, but that one should maintain control of the pleasures as opposed to being a slave to them.

The Greek philosopher Epicurus on the contrary, maintained that practical wisdom weighs pleasures against pains, choosing pleasures that are accompanied by the least pain and pains that are accompanied by the most pleasure. Mental pains were especially to be avoided. The Epicureans believed that the fear of death or fear of the gods could be dispelled by the study of atomistic philosophy.

MODERN ENGLISH PHILOSOPHERS

Bentham supported his quantitative hedonism (that is, one that claims that all pleasures are sensual and hence comparable quantitatively) with a "hedonistic calculus." The calculus allows the computation of specific values of pleasures in terms of their intensity, duration, certainty (how likely to be realized), propinquity (nearness or remoteness), fecundity (likelihood of being followed by more pleasures), purity (chance of *not* being followed by pain), and extent (number of persons affected by them). Bentham provided his students with a ditty to help them remember:

John Stuart Mill, Bentham's young friend and protégé, rejected Bentham's quantitative hedonism for a qualitative one, holding that pleasures differ in kind as well as quantity. "Human beings have faculties more elevated than the animal appetites, and when once made conscious of them, do not regard anything as happiness which does not include their gratification." "Better to be a human being dissatisfied than a pig satisfied; better to be a Socrates dissatisfied than a fool satisfied. And if the fool, or the pig, are of a different opinion, it is because they only know their own side of the question. The other party to the comparison knows both sides."

Mill, in his attempt to raise hedonism from the level of a "pig philosophy," may have espoused a view that abandoned hedonism. If the amount of pleasure ceases to be definitive, and if the only judges qualified to make qualitative judgments must exercise "higher-than-pig" judgments, it seems that Mill is guilty of either circular reasoning (with respect to his choice of judges) or of introducing criteria other than pleasure as being intrinsically good (in his appeal to qualitative differences).

Hedonism has had a long and continuing history in varied forms. As long as philosophers and others ask questions about what is intrinsically valuable or good, hedonism will no doubt remain a popular answer.

Ruth B. Heizer

FURTHER READING

Broad, C. D. *Five Types of Ethical Theory.* 1930. Reprint. London: Routledge & K. Paul, 1962.

Feldman, Fred. *Utilitarianism, Hedonism, and Desert: Essays in Moral Philosophy.* New York: Cambridge University Press, 1997.

Frankena, William K. *Ethics.* 2d ed. Englewood Cliffs, N.J.: Prentice-Hall, 1973.

Oates, Whitney Jennings, ed. *Stoic and Epicurean*

Philosophers: The Complete Extent Writings of Epicurus, Epictetus, Lucretius, Marcus Aurelius. New York: Modern Library, 1957.

Rudebusch, George. *Socrates, Pleasure, and Value.* New York: Oxford University Press, 1999.

Sahakian, William S. *Systems of Ethics and Value Theory.* New York: Philosophical Library, 1963.

Tännsjö, Torbjörn. *Hedonistic Utilitarianism.* Edinburgh: Edinburgh University Press, 1998.

Taylor, Paul W. *Principles of Ethics: An Introduction.* Encino, Calif.: Dickenson, 1975.

Watson, John. *Hedonistic Theories from Aristippus to Spencer.* Bristol, Avon, England: Thoemmes Press, 1993.

Wheelwright, Philip. *A Critical Introduction to Ethics.* 3d ed. New York: Odyssey Press, 1959.

SEE ALSO: Bentham, Jeremy; Cyrenaics; Epicurus; Existentialism; Good, the; Human nature; Sidgwick, Henry; Utilitarianism.

Hegel, Georg Wilhelm Friedrich

IDENTIFICATION: German philosopher
BORN: August 27, 1770, Stuttgart, Württemberg (now in Germany)
DIED: November 14, 1831, Berlin, Prussia (now in Germany)
TYPE OF ETHICS: Politico-economic ethics
SIGNIFICANCE: The author of *The Phenomenology of Spirit* (*Die Phänomenologie des Geistes*, 1807) and *The Philosophy of Right* (*Grundlinien der Philosophie des Rechts*, 1821), Hegel was one of the most influential philosophers of the nineteenth century. He put forward an idealist teleological model of history in which all of reality was coming to know and understand itself, and history would eventually end in a world of absolute knowledge, perfect justice, and total social harmony.

Georg Wilhelm Friedrich Hegel's central ethical beliefs include a moral requirement of each person to recognize fully each other person's unique dignity and contribution to the social totality, and the insight that freedom is a property of societies rather than individuals, so that until everyone is free, no one is truly free. The political and ethical dimensions of his philosophy grow out of his understanding of mind and dialectic.

In Hegel's philosophy, mind (*Geist* in the original German) is defined as "absolute consciousness." "Absolute," in this usage, means "absolved" of relations to objects outside consciousness. As absolute consciousness, mind is consciousness of consciousness itself. The opposite concept, "relative consciousness," is so called because it relates to objects outside itself.

LOGIC AND DIALECTIC

Logic is traditionally understood to consist of unchanging rules that govern thought. Hegel's logic is different. He sees the rules of thought in terms of mind as absolute consciousness. Absolute consciousness, as Hegel understands it, is a process in which mind continuously realizes itself, moving from potential to actual self-knowledge. The laws of thinking that concern Hegel are the steps in this process. The resulting "logic in motion" is called dialectic. It proceeds in a three-step pattern that repeats itself, in spiral form, on ever-higher levels of consciousness.

Hegel's philosophy is known for its difficulty, but anyone who has entered a hall of mirrors can retrace the basic steps of Hegelian dialectic:

Step 1: I become conscious of some object outside my consciousness, for example a stone.

Step 2: I become conscious of my consciousness of the stone.

Step 3: I become conscious of self-consciousness in my consciousness of my consciousness of the stone.

Step 1 (repeated at higher level): The consciousness of self-consciousness just realized becomes the new object of my consciousness. What was consciousness is now distanced from it, no longer consciousness in immediacy, but its object.

Step 2 (repeated at higher level): I become conscious of my consciousness of this new object.

Step 3 (repeated at higher level): I become conscious of self-consciousness in my consciousness—and so on.

The self-consciousness that keeps appearing in this spiral of self-reflection is occasioned by an object outside consciousness (the stone) but is not dependent on it as a specific object. Any other object would do as well. This self-consciousness is also occasioned by an individual "I" but is not dependent on any specific person. Anyone will do. Consider the hall of mirrors. Each individual sees his or her own image reflected, but the pattern of reflection, determined by the mirrors and the unchanging laws of optics, remains the same no matter who is reflected. Consciousness of consciousness always has the same form and content, regardless of which specific individual happens to be "reflecting."

The pure self-consciousness that appears in this spiraling reflection is the phenomenon Hegel refers to when he speaks of mind. The highest level of consciousness occurs when the individual becomes conscious of the universal aspect of this pure self-consciousness, recognizes it as mind, and realizes that this recognition is not so much an individual recognizing mind as it is mind recognizing itself. The individual is an instrument used by mind to come to itself.

The spiraling steps of Hegelian dialectic have names. The first is called "thesis," the second "antithesis," and the third "synthesis." The movement continues as the synthesis becomes the thesis of the next dialectical round.

Thesis and antithesis oppose but do not destroy each other. The synthesis conserves their opposition at a higher level of awareness, in which the condition that held thesis and antithesis together in opposition is discovered to be their underlying unity.

This can be illustrated by reconsidering the stone used above as an example of an object "outside consciousness." This object is not left behind in the dialectical steps that follow, but is taken along. What changes is the perception of its nature. At a higher level—from the point of view of absolute consciousness—it is seen that the stone did not enter consciousness through the individual's sense perception, but was in the consciousness from the beginning. What really happened—again, from the Hegelian position of absolute consciousness—is that mind concealed or negated itself with respect to the stone so that the individual consciousness could discover it as an object outside its own consciousness, thus occasioning the dialectical process of progressively greater self-consciousness, in which mind comes to itself.

Ultimately, for Hegel, nothing is truly outside absolute consciousness: All that is, is mind. This is the fundamental tenet of German idealism.

PHILOSOPHY OF HISTORY AND POLITICAL PHILOSOPHY

The dialectical process in which mind realizes itself as absolute consciousness is, for Hegel, not an abstract principle. It is the meaning of history. Hegel's concept of history is Eurocentric. He believed that history realized itself more perfectly in Europe than elsewhere. Western history begins, Hegel taught, with the Judaic teaching of monotheism, the first awakening of mind to its own oneness. The rest of Western history is interpreted as a process in which mind achieves progressively higher levels of self-awareness, finally approaching full development in Germanic civilization, Hegel believed, the first to completely exclude slavery and conceive of universal freedom.

The bloody French Revolution and slavery in the United States convinced Hegel that democracy would not lead to freedom. History, as the increasing self-realization of mind, must lead to ever-increasing freedom—not for individuals to pursue happiness, but for the state to institute laws integrating culture, religion, and politics into a rational, harmoniously functioning national unity.

Hegel's philosophy influenced conservative and revolutionary political theory. Hegel used it to justify the Prussian State (a centralized monarchy, enlightened, perhaps, in comparison to others, but an authoritarian regime with police-state tactics all the same). His philosophy also, however, provided the background for the theory of socialistic democracy developed by Karl Marx.

Ted William Dreier

FURTHER READING

Hegel, Georg Wilhelm Friedrich. *Elements of the Philosophy of Right.* Edited by Allen W. Wood. Translated by H. B. Nisbet. New York: Cambridge University Press, 1991.

_____. *The Phenomenology of Spirit.* Translated by A. V. Miller. Oxford, England: Oxford University Press, 1977.

Heidegger, Martin. *Hegel's Phenomenology of the Spirit.* Bloomington: Indiana University Press, 1988.

Inwood, M. J. *A Hegel Dictionary.* Malden, Mass.: Blackwell, 1992.

Kaufmann, Walter, ed. *Hegel: Texts and Commentary.* Garden City, N.Y.: Doubleday, 1966.

Peperzak, Adriaan T. *Modern Freedom: Hegel's Legal, Moral, and Political Philosophy.* Boston: Kluwer Academic, 2001.

Pippin, Robert B. *Hegel's Idealism: The Satisfactions of Self-Consciousness.* New York: Cambridge University Press, 1989.

_____. *Idealism as Modernism: Hegelian Variations.* New York: Cambridge University Press, 1997.

Taylor, Charles. *Hegel.* Cambridge, England: Cambridge University Press, 1975.

Williams, Robert R., ed. *Beyond Liberalism and Communitarianism: Studies in Hegel's "Philosophy of Right."* Albany: State University of New York Press, 2001.

Wood, Allen W. *Hegel's Ethical Thought.* Cambridge, England: Cambridge University Press, 1990.

SEE ALSO: Alienation; Bradley, F. H.; Existentialism; Idealist ethics; Ideology; Marx, Karl; *Phenomenology of Spirit*; Tragedy; Work.

Heidegger, Martin

IDENTIFICATION: German philosopher
BORN: September 26, 1889, Messkirch, Germany
DIED: May 26, 1976, Messkirch, West Germany
TYPE OF ETHICS: Modern history
SIGNIFICANCE: Heidegger's philosophy, espoused in his *Being and Time* (*Sein und Zeit*, 1927), subsumed the discipline of ethics wholly within the discipline of ontology, or the study of being.

Martin Heidegger studied at the University of Freiburg under Edmund Husserl, whom he succeeded as professor of philosophy in 1928. For Heidegger, the basic questions of ethics, such as "What is good?" and "What is it that one ought to do?" are subsumed in the prior ontological question "What is?" Heidegger found, however, that the traditional formulation of the ontological question "What is being?" failed to explicitly thematize the dimension of *meaning*. The leading question in Heidegger's thought, as opposed to traditional ontology, became "What is the *meaning* of being?" The Greek words used by Plato and Aristotle that are commonly translated as "being" and "truth," had meanings, Heidegger showed, that had been neglected by the tradition. The Greek words for being (*einai, ousía*) mean "presence"; the central word for truth (*aletheia*) means "discovered."

Discovering these early meanings for being and truth marked the beginning, not the end, of Heidegger's search for the meaning of being. Why was "presence" the first name for being in the Western tradition? Had not this tradition always taught that "presence" was a mode of time, and that being was essentially timeless, outside the real of history? Is time the original and necessary context for asking about the meaning of "being?" This final question was the question of *Being and Time*, Heidegger's first major publication.

Ted William Dreier

SEE ALSO: Arendt, Hannah; Existentialism; Levinas, Emmanuel; Personal relationships; Sartre, Jean-Paul; Unamuno y Jugo, Miguel de.

Heroism

DEFINITION: Overcoming of significant danger or difficulty in order to help others or act for the common good
TYPE OF ETHICS: Personal and social ethics
SIGNIFICANCE: Heroism as a label is reserved for actions of extraordinary virtue or nobility. It connotes moral admirability of the highest order.

Anxiety is a primary human emotion and is existential; that is, it is a basic, normal part of existence. Anxiety is a pervasive, unpleasant feeling of apprehension, menace, threat, or fear that is produced by a dangerous or difficult situation. Thus, heroism involves the consideration of the advantages and disadvantages of several alternative courses of action that may present a danger or threat to the self and that elicit anxiety and the subsequent choice of a course of action that confronts that danger and anxiety, that is indicated by practical reason, and that promotes the general well-being and common good.

HEROISM AND COURAGE

Courage is widely listed as a synonym for heroism. Courage is certainly a necessary component of

The Components of Heroism

- One particular act is performed rather than another.

- That act is perceived as risky or dangerous to the actor's well-being. To perceive no peril in what one does is not to act heroically. The peril may involve injury or death, economic loss, loss of prestige, ostracism, or censure. The act is likely to be accompanied by feelings of fear or anxiety. The danger involved in performing the act may be formidable enough that most people in the same situation would find it difficult to perform the act.

- The actor believes that performing the act is worth the risk that it entails.

- The decision to perform the act is reasoned and rational, rather than foolish or reckless. A person playing Russian roulette who backs down, afraid to pull the pistol's trigger, is acting wisely, not cowardly.

- The actor is not coerced into performing the act by threats of a punishment more feared than performing the act itself. A soldier who destroys an enemy tank after being ordered to do so or be summarily executed is not acting heroically.

- The act has a purpose or goal that is believed to be important and worthwhile. Heroism is a virtue that is exhibited through goal-directed behavior that benefits the general well-being and public good.

heroism; heroism could not exist without courage. Yet courage lacks a component that heroism possesses. Courage has been called a "self-regarding" virtue because it may primarily serve the purpose of the courageous individual. Heroism, in contrast, represents an "other-regarding" virtue because the welfare of others and the common good are the central considerations. Heroic acts are noble and virtuous in that they are necessarily intended to promote the general well-being of others or the common good. Because heroic individuals can be relied on when the common good is threatened, heroism is a highly prized commodity.

One can exhibit acts of courage without being heroic, however, if the act does not positively affect the general well-being or the common good. A criminal who executes a daring bank robbery, may be courageous but certainly not heroic.

Cowardice is the opposite of heroism. The coward is beset by excessive fears that prevent him or her from acting on his or her practical reasoning in situations in which it would be reasonable to act. The coward therefore avoids actions that he or she might otherwise perform and is thus incapacitated.

HEROISM AND ETHICS

Heroism is an ethical act of the highest order. Through it, the actor affirms the essence of his or her being and serves humanity in the face of elements that conflict with this affirmation of the self. Since the beginning of the history of Western thought, heroism has been considered to be noble and virtuous. In Plato's *Republic*, it is the unreflective quest for that which is noble. Aristotle believed that heroism led a person to act for the sake of what was noble, which was the purpose of virtue. Heroism is to be praised because it allows one to achieve one's potential.

Thomas Aquinas continued this thought. He often refers to courage, but it would seem that what he says describes heroism rather than courage. For him, courage/heroism was a strong mind that was able to overcome whatever blocked the path to the highest good. Courage/heroism, along with wisdom, temperance, and justice, were the four cardinal virtues.

These themes carry through to modern times. A noteworthy example is F. Scott Peck's famous book *The Road Less Travelled* (1978). To Peck, life is difficult because it continually presents problems that demand confrontation and solution. This fact can make life a painful process, but this is also where life achieves meaning. Problems call forth and create the resources that allow people to solve them. By solving problems, people grow mentally and spiritually. In order to foster the growth of the human spirit, it is necessary to solve problems. When this process incorporates actions that serve the common good and general welfare, human mental and spiritual growth attain high levels.

Laurence Miller

Fᴜʀᴛʜᴇʀ Rᴇᴀᴅɪɴɢ

Cofer, Charles N., and Mortimer H. Appley. *Motivation: Theory and Research*. New York: Wiley, 1964.

Darling-Smith, Barbara, ed. *Courage*. Notre Dame, Ind.: University of Notre Dame Press, 2002

Miller, William Ian. *The Mystery of Courage*. Cambridge, Mass.: Harvard University Press, 2000.

Moran, Charles. *The Anatomy of Courage*. Boston: Houghton Mifflin, 1967.

Nisters, Thomas. *Aristotle on Courage*. New York: Peter Lang, 2000.

Peck, M. Scott. *The Road Less Travelled*. New York: Simon & Schuster, 1978.

Tillich, Paul. *The Courage To Be*. 2d ed. Introduction by Peter J. Gomes. New Haven, Conn.: Yale University Press, 2000.

Wallace, James D. "Cowardice and Courage." In *Studies in Ethics*, edited by N. Rescher. Oxford, England: Basil Blackwell, 1973.

Sᴇᴇ ᴀʟsᴏ: Courage; Narrative ethics; Role models; Schindler, Oskar.

Hindu ethics

Dᴇꜰɪɴɪᴛɪᴏɴ: Ethical systems derived from the Hindu religion and Vedic texts

Tʏᴘᴇ ᴏꜰ ᴇᴛʜɪᴄs: Religious ethics

Sɪɢɴɪꜰɪᴄᴀɴᴄᴇ: Hindu ethics postulates that moral virtue is ultimately rewarded by liberation from a cycle of repeated reincarnations and the achievement of a paradise beyond the mundane world. It sees personal and spiritual well-being as fundamentally interdependent.

Hindu ethics is based on the premise that ethical life is the means to spiritual freedom. Hinduism has behind it a philosophy that is not only a religious doctrine but also a complex web of moral principles. It offers practical guidance, rites, prayers, festivals, and social structures, all aimed at securing social harmony and God realization (direct experience of God). Since God is the embodiment of truth and justice, right action is the means to experience God realization.

Hindu ethical philosophy has been evolving for four thousand years. Its sources are the Vedas, the oldest known literature in the world. Hindu ethics differ from much of Western ethics in perceiving a direct link between social and spiritual life. Greek philosophy is a "pursuit of truth for its own sake," based on reason and the intellect, in which the wise, the lawmakers, direct people to create a moral society. Hindu ethics is primarily concerned with right action as a means to religious fulfillment.

Vᴇᴅɪᴄ Lɪᴛᴇʀᴀᴛᴜʀᴇ

The Vedas are hymns and rites that glorify the Vedic gods, who are representatives of the divine power of the Supreme God. They deal with personal issues, universal concerns, and theories of creation. Hinduism teaches that reading or listening to the Vedas enlivens the connection between the individual and the Creator. Vedic writings are fundamental to Hinduism.

The *Ṛg Veda* and the *Atharva Veda*, the hymns of the Vedas, are quite specific about actions that can be seen as righteous and moral. Honesty, rectitude, friendship, charity, nonviolence (Ahiṁsā, a moral principle that attracted considerable attention when it was espoused by Mohandas K. Gandhi), truthfulness, modesty, celibacy, religious worship, and purity of heart are all listed as desirable and necessary virtues. The *Ṛg Veda* also cites bad intentions, swearing, falsehood, gambling, egoism, cruelty, adultery, theft, and injury to life as sinful actions.

The *Bhagavadgītā*, a central text of Hinduism, gives very specific ethical advice. It consists of a dialogue between Lord Kṛṣṇa, an incarnation of one of the three major gods of Hinduism, and Arjuna, a noble warrior. Arjuna is unable to go into battle because his opponents are also his kinsmen. He appeals for help. Lord Kṛṣṇa states that the correctness of the action should be the primary consideration when doing something. He advises Arjuna always to act in accordance with dharma (ethical living). Furthermore, he says, if Arjuna could experience the divine, his actions would spontaneously reflect absolute wisdom and purity, and therefore all dilemmas would evaporate. In this instance, the right course of action is to fight.

There are numerous stories in Hindu literature about morality and how best to behave. Deities advise and guide. In the *Rāmāyana*, the hero, Rāmā, is the embodiment of dharma, teaching the values of obedience, respect, and duty. The later writings of the

On the first day of Hinduism's Kumbh Mela festival, millions of Hindus bathe themselves at the confluence of the Ganges, Jamuna, and Saraswati Rivers, near Allahabad in India. According to Hindu beliefs, the rivers' sacred waters wash away sins. (AP/Wide World Photos)

Purāṇas, specific to Śiva and Viṣṇu, advocate worship and devotion as a means to liberation.

The Upaniṣads embrace the concept of God as an impersonal Supreme Being, *Brāhmin*. The verses state that divinity is everywhere, that the individual is indeed *Brāhmin* itself—"Ahum Brahmmasmi" ("I am the totality"). The Upaniṣads reaffirm that *mokṣa* ("liberation") is the goal of life. To achieve liberation, it is necessary to follow a strict code of ethical and spiritual discipline. Austerity, chastity, silence, and solitude lead the soul forward, while self-restraint, self-sacrifice, and compassion free one from greed and anger.

SOCIAL LIFE

Hinduism asserts that, just as there is order in the universe, human life can be equally harmonious and orderly. Human society should express the divine purpose. All people belong to social castes determined by character, natural inclinations, and function in society. These castes consist of *Brāhmins* (the wise), *Kṣatriyas* (warriors), *Vaiśyas* (merchants), and *Śūdras* (laborers). Within each caste, the individual can achieve perfection, and the whole system promotes spiritual progress.

Hindu thought divides life into four twenty-five-year stages, giving specific ethical advice for each. The first stage is for learning, the second is the time of the householder, the third is a time for meditation and study of the scriptures, and the final stage is one of renunciation of the outer life. This sequence should ultimately end in liberation, the goal of life. Members of a family should always follow their duty. Children should respect and obey their parents' wishes. Husbands and wives ought to be loving and respectful, advising their families and teaching moral values.

Many Hindu practices derive from the belief that *Brāhmin*, the divine, is all-pervading. If divinity is everywhere, then everything must be respected. Nature is not separate from humanity; therefore, animals are revered, particularly cows. Gandhi defended this as a "practical application of the belief of oneness, and therefore the sacredness of life."

The importance given to spiritual life in India creates the interdependence between the mystical and the practical. Ethics is central to Hinduism, improving the present and ultimately freeing the individual from the cycle of birth and death. Hinduism, with all its complexity, has unity at the heart of its diversity. Its goals are to raise the quality of life, ensure spiritual awakening, and fulfill humanity's destiny.

Catherine Francis

FURTHER READING

Berry, Thomas. *Religions of India*. New York: Bruce Publishing, 1971.

Mahesh Yogi, Maharishi. *On the Bhagavad-Gita*. Harmondsworth, England: Penguin Books, 1969.

Perrett, Roy W. *Hindu Ethics: A Philosophical Study*. Honolulu: University of Hawaii Press, 1998.

Radhakrishnan, Sarvepalli. *Eastern Religions and Western Thought*. New York: Oxford University Press, 1959.

Ravi, Illa. *Foundations of Indian Ethics*. New Delhi: Kaveri Books, 2002.

Sharma, I. C. *Ethical Philosophies of India*. Edited and revised by Stanley M. Daugert. New York: Harper & Row, 1970.

Shearer, Alaister, and Peter Russell, trans. *The Upanishads*. New York: Harper & Row, 1978.

SEE ALSO: Ahiṁsā; Aśoka; *Bhagavadgītā*; Buddhist ethics; Caste system, Hindu; Jain ethics; Karma; Nirvana; Poona Pact; Sikh ethics; Upaniṣads.

Hippocrates

IDENTIFICATION: Greek physician
BORN: c. 460 B.C.E., Greek island of Cos
DIED: c. 377 B.C.E., Larissa, Thessaly (now in Greece)
TYPE OF ETHICS: Bioethics
SIGNIFICANCE: Hippocrates is traditionally credited

with the authorship of a collection of about sixty treatises on medicine and medical ethics, including the Hippocratic oath. This body of writings both created a standard of professional etiquette for the physician and formed the basis of the Western tradition of medical ethics.

Although Hippocrates has traditionally enjoyed the reputation of being the father of Greek medicine, little is known about him. Only a few references to him by contemporary or near-contemporary authors exist. According to these references, he came from the island of Cos, off the southwestern coast of Asia Minor, and was a teacher of medicine. He was a member of the Asclepiads, a family or guild of physicians that traced its origins to the god of healing, Asclepius. For reasons that are not clear, Hippocrates came to be idealized after his death, and he became the subject of an extensive biographical tradition. Four short biographies exist, together with a collection of spurious epistles that are attributed to Hippocrates. They assert that Hippocrates learned medicine from his father, who was also a physician. He is supposed to have taught medicine in Cos (which later boasted a famous school of medicine) and to have traveled throughout Greece, dying at an advanced age at Larissa in Thessaly, in northern Greece. Many of the biographical details recorded in these later works must be regarded as legendary.

A large collection of about sixty medical treatises, the Hippocratic Corpus, came to be attributed to Hippocrates after his death. Most were written during the late fifth or fourth centuries B.C.E., but some were composed much later. The works are anonymous and are marked by differences in style. Even in antiquity it was recognized that not all of them were genuine, and attempts were made to determine which were written by Hippocrates. There is no reliable tradition that attests the authenticity of any of the treatises, and the internal evidence is inconclusive. Most modern scholars believe that none of them can be attributed with certainty to Hippocrates.

HIPPOCRATIC MEDICAL ETHICS

The ethical or deontological treatises of the Hippocratic Corpus (*The Physician, Precepts*, and *Decorum*, dates unknown) constitute the earliest writings on medical etiquette. They define the professional duties that should be expected of Greek physicians.

Most of these principles of etiquette are the product of common sense. They recognize that certain types of conduct are inherently detrimental to the practice of medicine. Physicians should behave in a manner that will add dignity to their profession. Thus, they should look healthy and not be overweight. They should be gentlemen, cheerful and serene in their dealings with patients, self-controlled, reserved, decisive, and neither silly nor harsh. They should not engage in sexual relations with patients or members of their households. They are to be sensitive to the fees they charge, should consider the patient's means, and should on occasion render free treatment.

The Hippocratic Oath

I will look upon him who shall have taught me this Art even as one of my parents.

I will share my substance with him, and I will supply his necessities, if he be in need.

I will regard his offspring even as my own brethren, and I will teach them this Art, if they would learn it, without fee or covenant.

I will impart this Art by precept, by lecture, and by every mode of teaching, not only to my own sons but to the sons of him who has taught me, and to disciples bound by covenant and oath, according to the Law of Medicine.

The regimen I adopt shall be for the benefit of my patients according to my ability and judgment, and not for their hurt or for any wrong.

I will give no deadly drug to any, though it be asked of me, nor will I counsel such, and especially I will not aid a woman to procure abortion.

Whatsoever house I enter, there will I go for the benefit of the sick, refraining from all wrongdoing or corruption, and especially from any act of seduction, of male or female, of bond or free.

Whatsoever things I see or hear concerning the life of men, in my attendance on the sick or even apart therefrom, which ought not to be noised abroad, I will keep silence thereon, counting such things to be as sacred secrets.

Many of these precepts are meant to preserve the reputation of the physician, which (in the absence of medical licensure) was his most important asset in building and maintaining a medical practice.

THE HIPPOCRATIC OATH

The best-known, though most puzzling, of the Hippocratic writings is the so-called Hippocratic oath. The oath is characterized by a religious tenor. It begins with an invocation of the healing gods Apollo and Asclepius and includes a pledge to guard one's life and art "in purity and holiness." It is divided into two parts: the covenant, which is a contract between the teacher and his pupil; and the precepts, which defines the duty of the physician to his patients. The oath prohibits, among other things, dispensing a deadly drug, performing an abortion, and practicing surgery (or at least lithotomy).

Several stipulations of the oath are not consonant with ethical standards prevalent elsewhere in the Hippocratic treatises, while some practices prohibited by the oath (induced abortion, euthanasia, and surgery) were routinely undertaken by Greek physicians. It is difficult, moreover, to find a context in which to place the oath. Although it was traditionally attributed (like the other Hippocratic treatises) to Hippocrates, it is anonymous. It has been dated as early as the sixth century B.C.E. and as late as the first century of the Christian era (when it is first mentioned). Most scholars assign it to the fifth or fourth century B.C.E., making it roughly contemporaneous with Hippocrates. It has been suggested that it was administered to students who were undertaking a medical apprenticeship, but there is no evidence that it ever had universal application in the Greek world. Greek and Roman physicians were not required to swear an oath or to accept and abide by a formal code of ethics. To be sure, ethical standards appear in the Hippocratic Corpus, but no one knows how widespread these standards were among medical practitioners in antiquity. The oath appealed to Christian physicians, however, who in late antiquity took over its precepts and infused them with new meaning. It was later adopted by Christian, Jewish, and Muslim physicians as a covenant by which physicians could govern their practices.

There have been a number of attempts to explain away the problem passages of the oath or to attribute it to an author whose views represented those of a group that lay outside the mainstream of medical ethics as described in the Hippocratic Corpus. The most notable is the attempt by Ludwig Edelstein to demonstrate that the oath originated in the Pythagorean community. Parallels can be found outside Pythagoreanism for even the most esoteric injunctions of the oath, however, and its Pythagorean origin cannot be said to have been conclusively proved.

THE INFLUENCE OF HIPPOCRATIC ETHICS

The medical-ethical treatises of the Hippocratic Corpus have exercised great influence on the formulation and development of Western medical ethics. In establishing not only guidelines for the physician's deportment but also standards of professional obligation, they created both the basis of Greek medical ethics and an ideal of what the physician ought to be. Even in the rapidly changing field of bioethics, their influence continues to be felt to the present day.

Anne-Marie E. Ferngren
Gary B. Ferngren

FURTHER READING

Cantor, David, ed. *Reinventing Hippocrates*. Burlington, Vt.: Ashgate, 2002.

Carrick, Paul. *Medical Ethics in Antiquity: Philosophical Perspectives on Abortion and Euthanasia*. Boston: Reidel, 1985.

Edelstein, Ludwig. *Ancient Medicine: Selected Papers of Ludwig Edelstein*. Edited by Owsei Temkin and C. Lilian Temkin. Translated by C. Lilian Temkin. Baltimore: Johns Hopkins University Press, 1967.

Hippocrates. *Hippocrates*. Translated by W. H. S. Jones and Paul Potter. 8 vols. New York: Putnam, 1923-95.

Sigerist, Henry E. *Early Greek, Hindu, and Persian Medicine*. Vol. 2 in *A History of Medicine*. Edited by Ludwig Edelstein. New York: Oxford University Press, 1961.

Temkin, Owsei. *Hippocrates in a World of Pagans and Christians*. Baltimore: Johns Hopkins University Press, 1991.

SEE ALSO: American Medical Association; Bioethics; Confidentiality; Medical bills of rights; Medical ethics; Medical research; Mental illness; Physician-patient relationship; Professional ethics.

Hiring practices

DEFINITION: Methods used by employers to hire new personnel

TYPE OF ETHICS: Business and labor ethics

SIGNIFICANCE: The late twentieth century saw a significant increase in government oversight of hiring practices, pressure on employees by special interest groups, and greater efforts to develop fair hiring practices within private companies.

During the last two decades of the twentieth century, hiring processes of private American entities came under increasing supervision by the federal government and various special interest or pressure groups in society. In addition, the presence of human resource departments within companies and their role in the hiring process became more evident and influential in the workforce. All signs pointed to greater efforts by employers to bring ethics into their hiring practices.

However, the task of incorporating ethical processes into hiring is not easy for several reasons. One of the biggest obstacles to ethical hiring practices is the simple fact that different people are sometimes not in agreement as to what constitutes an ethical decision. However, the difficulties that employers face in their attempts to bring ethical behavior to the hiring process should not stop them from trying to bring it about. Companies may not succeed to the extent that they wish when it comes to bringing ethical choices in the hiring process, but even a small amount of success is better than no success at all.

In contemplating how to incorporate ethical behavior into the hiring process, several issues need to be kept in mind. First, it has to be a major goal for employers. This means that its presence has to be foremost in the minds of employers as something they desire to achieve. However, companies must also be honest and demonstrate integrity in the hiring process. This implies that they clearly indicate to future employees what their reasons are for choosing one candidate over others. Employers must also be aware of their need to conform to the law when making employment decisions. The federal government has made it clear that it intends to provide equal employment opportunities to its citizens, and it is important that there be compliance with all legal provisions relating to hiring practices.

Employers must also be careful not to be influenced in the hiring process by subjective reasons and avoid any projection of personal gain. Perhaps one of the best ways to answer the question of whether employers have been successful at incorporating ethical behavior into the hiring process is to ask what an outside committee reviewing the employer's actions might indicate about how it made its choice regarding an employment position.

William E. Kelly

Further Reading

Berenbeim, Ronald. "What Is Ethical? An American View." *Vital Speeches of the Day* 68, no. 18 (July 1, 2002): 549.

Brown, Fred. "Ethics vs. Law." *Quill* 88, no. 9 (October-November, 2000): 6.

Coates, Joseph F. "Updating the Ten Commandments." *Futurist* 37, no. 3 (May-June 2003): 68.

Militello, Frederick, and Michael Schwalberg. "Ethical Conduct: What Financial Executives Do to Lead." *Financial Leadership* 1911 (January-February, 2003): 49.

Sniderman, Joe. "When Good Hiring Is a Challenge." *Nation's Business* 87, no. 4 (April, 1999): 10.

"White House Defends Faith-Based Hiring." *Christian Century* 120, no. 15 (July 26, 2003): 16.

See also: Biometrics; Business ethics; College applications; Downsizing; Equal pay for equal work; Fear in the workplace; Labor-Management Relations Act; Merit; Resumés; Wage discrimination; Work.

Hiroshima and Nagasaki bombings

THE EVENTS: U.S. dropping of atom bombs on two Japanese cities during World War II

DATES: August 6 and 9, 1945

TYPE OF ETHICS: Military ethics

SIGNIFICANCE: The ethics of choosing to use a weapon of mass destruction to attack the civilian residents of two densely populated cities have been debated ever since the close of World War II. The philosophical issue revolves around whether it was acceptable to kill tens of thousands of inno-

cents in order to prevent the deaths of hundreds of thousands or even millions more by bringing the war to a swift conclusion. A further practical issue concerns whether it is in fact true that use of the atom bomb ultimately saved so many lives.

The unleashing of atomic weapons on Hiroshima and Nagasaki profoundly shaped the nature of international relations in the post-World War II era. These bombs, so lethal and used only twice in history, have forced humankind to examine critically the nature of modern warfare, especially within the context of "just war theory."

The development of the atom bomb by the U.S. government during World War II is generally regarded as one of the greatest technological and engineering achievements of modern times. What was particularly noteworthy about the atom bomb was the sheer scale of its ability to kill and devastate. Drawing upon the insights and efforts of the most brilliant physicists, mathematicians, and chemists of the nineteenth and twentieth centuries, scientists and engineers were able to liberate the cataclysmic power of the atom, harnessed in a single bomb that had the destructive impact of almost twenty kilotons of conventional explosives.

Ethical Context

Using a weapon of such magnitude raised serious ethical issues, especially as they related to an idea that can be traced back to the ancient Greeks: just-war theory. Considered down through the centuries by such thinkers as Aristotle, Cicero, and Saint Augustine, just-war theory involves the essential notion that war, though intrinsically evil, can be justified morally if certain conditions exist. Although the theory consists of several components, particularly relevant to the bombing of Hiroshima and Nagasaki are the ideas of proportionality and discrimination.

Proportionality refers to the idea that a warring power should not use any means over and above what is necessary to achieve victory. By late July, 1945, according to most military historians, Japan's military situation was desperate. From March onward, Japan suffered almost daily bombings by American B-29 bombers armed with incendiary bombs. Such bombing runs resulted in almost 190,000 deaths from fires and asphyxiation in six major Japanese cities. In addition, the U.S. Navy was taking steps to implement a

full-scale blockade of Japan. After the war, the U.S. Strategic Bombing Survey maintained that such tactics would have eventuated in Japan's surrender by approximately November 1, 1945, without the use of atom bombs.

Those who advocate that the dropping of atom bombs was a proportional response in the war make two points. First, while the bomb that fell on Hiroshima immediately killed 78,000 people and the one that fell on Nagasaki killed 70,000 people, the use of the bombs prevented a large-scale land invasion of the Japanese mainland. While estimates vary, some speculate that total American and Japanese casualties would have approached one million because of the determination of the Japanese people. Hence, the atom bombings, while gruesome, actually prevented

more deaths in the immediate future. A second line of argument holds that given the conduct of the Japanese military during the war—for example, the surprise attack on the U.S. fleet at Pearl Harbor, the Bataan "Death March," and the brutal treatment of Allied prisoners-of-war—the dropping of the atom bombs was a morally justifiable and proportional action.

The concept of discrimination maintains that in the conduct of war, every effort should be made to prevent civilians from suffering the potentially brutal fate of soldiers. The force unleashed by an atom bomb is such that it devastates everything in its wake: combatants, noncombatants, military outposts, hospitals, crops, and so forth. It must be pointed out, however, that the distinction between civilians and soldiers already had been blurred by more conventional weapons in use during the war. The fires ignited by incendiaries dropped from American planes over Hamburg and Dresden resulted in tens of thousands of civilian deaths. Moreover, Dresden was bombed although it was primarily a cultural center, not a significant military target. Similarly, toward the end of the war, German V-1 and V-2 rockets fell indiscriminately throughout England, resulting in thousands of civilian casualties.

Also apropos of discrimination, some military strategists argued that since many civilians were engaged in supporting a nation's capacity to wage war through their jobs as farmers, machinists, seamstresses, and technicians, the distinction between civilian and military no longer obtained. Indeed, British pilots were explicitly ordered to bomb working-class neighborhoods during their runs in order to reduce both the Nazi war effort and civilian morale. In the conduct of the war, "civilian" deaths increasingly became a regrettable, but accepted, component of modern warfare.

ETHICS OF SCIENCE

After the detonation of atom bombs, the avowed neutrality of science was questioned. For example, because something is theoretically and practically possible (nuclear fission), especially something so powerful as atomic energy, must it be developed? If scientists develop something novel, can they guarantee control of its use? After witnessing the awesome energy released in the first explosion of a nuclear device in New Mexico in July, 1945, some of the scientists working on the bomb's development argued that Japanese officials should be privy to a demonstration of the bomb's power rather than experiencing an actual bombing. Their views were summarily dismissed by the military as impractical.

A final aspect of the ethics of the atom bombing of Hiroshima and Nagasaki concerns utilitarian logic. This model of decision making argues that people must rationally calculate the perceived costs and benefits of pursuing certain actions. From this perspective, the investment of more than $1 billion and four years of intense work by tens of thousands of workers and scientists (the bomb's costs) almost guaranteed that the bomb would be used once it was developed (its perceived benefit, shortening the war). No one could have perceived, however, the immense eco-

nomic, political, and social costs associated with the Cold War after "The Bomb," and people still debate whether the decision to drop atom bombs on Hiroshima and Nagasaki was a benefit at all.

Craig M. Eckert

FURTHER READING

Boyer, Paul. *By the Bomb's Early Light: American Thought and Culture at the Dawn of the Atomic Age*. New York: Pantheon, 1985. Reprint. Chapel Hill: University of North Carolina Press, 1994.

Catholic Church National Conference of Catholic Bishops. *The Challenge of Peace: God's Promise and Our Response*. Washington, D.C.: Office of Public Services, United States Catholic Conference, 1983.

Gilpin, Robert. *American Scientists and Nuclear Weapons Policy*. Princeton, N.J.: Princeton University Press, 1962.

Howard, Michael, ed. *Restraints on War*. New York: Oxford University Press, 1979.

Lackey, Douglas P. *Moral Principles and Nuclear Weapons*. Totowa, N.J.: Rowman & Allanheld, 1984.

Sherwin, Martin J. *A World Destroyed: Hiroshima and Its Legacies*. Foreword by Robert J. Lifton. 3d ed. Stanford, Calif.: Stanford University Press, 2003.

VanDeMark, Brian. *Pandora's Keepers: Nine Men and the Atomic Bomb*. Boston: Little, Brown, 2003.

SEE ALSO: Atom bomb; Dresden firebombing; Just war theory; Manhattan Project; Military ethics; Unconditional surrender.

Hitler, Adolf

IDENTIFICATION: German political leader
BORN: April 20, 1889, Braunau am Inn, Austro-Hungarian Empire (now in Austria)
DIED: April 30, 1945, Berlin, Germany
TYPE OF ETHICS: Politico-economic ethics
SIGNIFICANCE: Hitler initiated the Holocaust against European Jewry, perhaps the single most traumatic event in modern history. As a result, he has come to symbolize the ultimate evil for many, al-

though others think of him as insane rather than evil. Hitler was, moreover, an extremely charismatic figure in his heyday, and his theories of racial and national destiny combined to form a powerfully twisted ethic that continues to attract many people.

It does little good to insist that Adolf Hitler and his Nazi Party were without a system of ethics; to do so demonizes Hitler and perpetuates the unfortunate myth that the Nazi period may be explained by the German nation having temporarily lost its collective mind. The more difficult truth is that a great many German people identified a system of morality in the Nazi party that corresponded with their own.

Adolf Hitler's system of ethics was based upon the twin foundations of race and nationalism. His combination of these traditions in German political life was both of great help to him in his quest for

power and of inestimable force in the drive toward the Holocaust. Believing that might made right, Hitler promoted this ethic within his party—and later his state—with a ruthless zealotry.

ORIGINS

The variety of anti-Semitism that Hitler found in Vienna in the period of 1907 to 1913 was both populist and German nationalist—best described by the German word *volkisch*. Hitler was greatly influenced by the mayor of Vienna, Karl Lüger, who combined vehement anti-Semitism and the political strength to dominate Viennese politics to a degree that Hitler admired. In fact, Hitler, in an uncharacteristic display of humility, described Lüger in his book *Mein Kampf* as the last great German born in Austria.

Another great influence on Hitler's intellectual development in Vienna was the leader of the Pan-German movement, Georg von Schönerer. Schön-

Surrounded by the trappings of the Nazi Party, Adolf Hitler addresses a party meeting in 1938. (Library of Congress)

erer's movement appealed to Hitler on both a racial and a national level. Like Hitler, Schönerer believed that the unification of all German-speaking peoples was an imperative and blamed Germans of Jewish extraction for standing in the way of unification.

In German history, as well, there were many influences on Hitler's thought. Figures as diverse as Martin Luther, Frederick the Great, Houston Stewart Chamberlain, and, most famously, Richard Wagner contributed to Hitler's ideas of race and the destiny of the German people. Their ideas about authority, nationalism, race, and the romantic ideals of war, sacrifice, and destiny all influenced Hitler in ways that many historians have identified as seminal.

RACE

Essentially, Hitler believed that the German race could only succeed if it were "pure." *Mein Kampf* is filled with statements such as "the originally creative race died out from blood poisoning." Hitler blamed the Jews for the apparent dissipation of "pure German stock," particularly in Austria, where he first was introduced to anti-Semitism. Hitler's variety of anti-Semitism differed from that of Lüger and Shönerer, though, in that Hitler insisted that religion had nothing to do with it; race, not religion, was what made Jews different and dangerous in Hitler's mind.

The implications of this idea are grim. If Jews are considered dangerous because of their religion, they can at least convert. This is what happened in a great many cases previous to Hitler. If, as Hitler thought, Jews are dangerous because of their race, there can be no conversion. Extermination is the logical answer in Hitler's convoluted and hateful system of thought. Because he believed that the "parasite" of European Jewry was threatening the strength and virtue (Hitler employed a great deal of sexual imagery in his discussions on this subject) of the German nation, Hitler thought it justifiable to "eradicate the parasite."

NATIONALISM

The second foundation for Hitler's system of thought was nationalism. Considering himself a student of history, Hitler was influenced by a kind of skewed Hegelianism, identifying cycles of world leadership and seeing a sort of dialectical pattern of struggle and destiny in assuming that leadership. Further influenced by the Franco-Prussian War (1870-1871) and the unification of Germany (1871),

and filled with a patriotism that only an envious noncitizen can muster (Hitler was not a German citizen), Hitler came to the conclusion that it was Germany's turn to act as leader of the world. There was no room in the world for Jews, intellectuals, socialists, or liberals.

Much of the intolerance contained in Hitler's nationalism can be traced to the traditions of German Romanticism. The romantic imagery found in Hitler's anti-Semitism was also present in his thought on questions of nationalism (race and nationalism were inexorably tied in his mind). Shunning Christianity as "a religion for cowards," he saw Germany's true heritage in the pagan spectacle of the operas of Richard Wagner. The antirationalism of the Romantic period, as filtered through the German experience, served to create a religion of nationality and race in Hitler's mind, with himself as messiah (Hitler spoke at length about Providence's intentions for him), that was as compelling to the true believer as any other religion could be.

ZEALOTRY

Hitler's religion of blood and nation was compelling to many Germans in large part because of the power it promised. The hate that Hitler felt, his dreams of dominion, could not be fulfilled without both power and an ethic that sanctioned the use of power in ways that most people would describe as morally reprehensible. Hitler worshipped power, and his system of thought relied on it heavily. On reading *Mein Kampf*, one cannot help but be struck by the number of times Hitler wrote the equivalent of "might makes right." Hitler admired the Marxists' tactics of violence and intimidation, preferring to use converted communists as street fighters because they shared his zealotry. His greatest scorn for the liberal parties of his day concentrated on "the weakness of will inherent in parliamentary government."

IMPLICATIONS

Hitler and his millions of followers believed that his vision allowed, even compelled, them to shun questions of everyday ethics. His vision established a new system of ethics defined by race and the nation, utterly devoid of moral restraint. The outcome of this system of thought was, inevitably, the Holocaust.

Robert A. Willingham

FURTHER READING

Bullock, Alan. *Hitler: A Study in Tyranny.* Rev. ed. New York: Harper & Row, 1962.

Fest, Joachim C. *Hitler.* Translated by Richard and Clara Winston. New York: Harcourt Brace Jovanovich, 1974.

Flood, Charles B. *Hitler: The Path to Power.* Boston: Houghton Mifflin, 1989.

Giblin, James Cross. *The Life and Death of Adolf Hitler.* New York: Clarion Books, 2002.

Heiden, Konrad. *Der Fuehrer: Hitler's Rise to Power.* Translated by Ralph Manheim. Boston: Houghton Mifflin, 1944.

Hitler, Adolf. *Mein Kampf.* 1925-1926. Translated by Ralph Manheim. Boston: Houghton Mifflin, 1999.

Kershaw, Ian. *Hitler.* London: Longman, 1991.

McDonough, Frank. *Hitler and the Rise of the Nazi Party.* New York: Pearson/Longman, 2003.

Von Maltitz, Horst. *The Evolution of Hitler's Germany.* New York: McGraw-Hill, 1973.

Waite, Robert G. L. *The Psychopathic God: Adolf Hitler.* New York: Basic Books, 1977.

SEE ALSO: Anti-Semitism; Concentration camps; Dictatorship; Evil; Fascism; Genocide and democide; Holocaust; Nazism; Racial prejudice; Stalin, Joseph; Tyranny.

Hobbes, Thomas

IDENTIFICATION: English political philosopher
BORN: April 5, 1588, Westport, Wiltshire, England
DIED: December 4, 1679, Hardwick Hall, Derbyshire, England
TYPE OF ETHICS: Enlightenment history
SIGNIFICANCE: Hobbes was the most prominent seventeenth century English advocate of political absolutism. Author of *De Cive* (1642), *Leviathan: Or, The Matter, Form, and Power of a Commonwealth* (1651), and *De Homine* (1658), he deduced his theories of morality, including his political ethics, from a mechanistic, materialist understanding of reality.

Thomas Hobbes was a proponent of natural rights and monarchical absolutism, although he was dis-

trusted by both Cromwellian republicans and supporters of the Stuart monarchy. As a student at Magdalen College, Oxford University, Hobbes rejected the ethics and methodological perspectives of Aristotelianism, medieval Scholasticism, and Christian philosophy. The moral political philosophy expressed in Hobbes's works was grounded in the methodology of mathematical argumentation, empirical science, and secularism. Hobbes's mechanistic and materialist explanation of existence, including political ethics, was sharply criticized by seventeenth century ecclesiastical leaders for having suggested an agnostic or atheistic metaphysical foundation.

In Hobbes's political philosophical works, moral behavior was scientifically explained and logically reduced to corporal matter in motion. Moral judgments were made in reference to two types of human movements or endeavors: appetites, or motions toward material objects perceived to be desirable; and aversions, or motions away from material objects perceived to be harmful. Hobbes's pessimistic interpretation of human nature, in conjunction with his "resolutive compositive" method, reduced political morality to an individual's most basic fears and passions (for example, fear of violent death and the desire for possessions). In contrast to classical Greek and medieval Christian moral political philosophy, in Hobbes's thought, reason was not the faculty that guided and constrained the passions. Knowledge (or "scientific reason") and power were the prescribed means to fulfill each individual's subjective desires.

Hobbes considered ethics to be an essential field of philosophy and natural rights as the critical subject of ethics. Hobbes's political philosophical works, particularly *Leviathan*, conveyed a moral theory that was focused on the natural right of self-preservation and governmental legitimacy linked to the protection of human life. Although all people were in agreement about the critical value of self-preservation, Hobbes's ethical relativism or nominalism articulated the position that there were no universal objective or absolute moral, political, or spiritual truths. Individuals named or evaluated the moral worth of particular acts based upon the consequences of such acts to their self-interests. *Leviathan* expressed the political theory that sovereign political authority and governmental legitimacy were based on a social contract (government by "institution") or superior physical coercion (government by "acquisition"). The prescribed commonwealth was conceived as the highly centralized rule of an absolute sovereign—preferably, an absolute monarch.

Mitchel Gerber

SEE ALSO: *Leviathan*; Locke, John; Machiavelli, Niccolò; Social contract theory; *Two Treatises of Government*.

Holistic medicine

DEFINITION: Approach to medicine that treats the whole person as a unity rather than isolating, attending to, or diagnosing only parts of the whole

TYPE OF ETHICS: Bioethics

SIGNIFICANCE: Holistic approaches to medicine usually emphasize noninvasive procedures, patient education, and nontraditional or non-Western practices such as acupuncture, homeopathy, and yoga. Advocates of such an approach see it as ethically admirable, because it humanizes the patient, whereas they believe mainstream medicine often treats patients as mechanical systems or objects.

Holistic health practitioners regard patients as whole persons, teaching health maintenance, offering a wide choice of cures, and freely sharing expert knowledge. Holistic practitioners accept as valid knowledge from prescientific ages, as well as psychological and spiritual knowledge that is accessible to everyone. Therefore, for the holistic practitioner, the best possible health care makes use of ancient as well as modern healing arts from a variety of cultures. It treats people as psychological and spiritual beings as well as bodies and educates them in the care of their own psychological and physical health. Therefore, holistic health maintenance and disease curing typically involve teaching the patient actively to change habits of nutrition, exercise, and self-reflection.

In contrast, mainstream medicine is based on the premise that physical science is the most authoritative field of knowledge, though it can only be understood by trained experts such as medical doctors. Therefore, the mainstream physician offers the best possible care by acting as an expert authority, dispensing diagnoses and treatments of bodily diseases with the help of new technologies that are the fruits of science.

Laura Duhan Kaplan

SEE ALSO: Fairness and Accuracy in Reporting; Faith healers; Health care allocation; Illness; Medical ethics; Medical research.

Holocaust

THE EVENT: Systematic murder by the Nazi regime of six million Jews, as well as Gypsies, homosexual men, political and religious dissenters, the mentally ill, and others

DATE: 1933-1945

TYPE OF ETHICS: Human rights

SIGNIFICANCE: The Holocaust stands as an evil of incomprehensible, unimaginable scope and horror. Since it occurred, ethics has striven to comprehend how it could have happened and what meaning it holds for systematic formulations of morality.

Referring to their regime as the Third Reich, Adolf Hitler and his Nazi Party ruled Germany from 1933 to 1945. The Holocaust happened during those years. It was Nazi Germany's planned total destruction of the Jewish people and the actual murder of nearly six million of them. That genocidal campaign—the most systematic, bureaucratic, and unrelenting the world has seen—also destroyed millions of non-Jewish civilians. They included Gypsies (Roma and Sinti), Slavs, Jehovah's Witnesses, Freemasons, homosexuals, the mentally retarded, the physically handicapped, and the insane. The Nazis believed that their threat to the Third Reich approached, though it could never equal, the one posed by Jews.

In the German language, this unprecedented destruction process became known euphemistically as *die Endlösung*—the "final solution." The Hebrew word *Shoah*, which means catastrophe, is also used to name it, but the term "Holocaust" most commonly signifies the event. That word has biblical roots. In the Septuagint, a Greek translation of the Hebrew Bible, the Hebrew word *olah* is translated as *holokauston*. In context, *olah* means that which is offered

Estimated Numbers of Jews Killed During the Holocaust

Country	Jewish populations		
	Pre-Holocaust	Deaths	Percent who died
Poland	3,300,000	3,000,000	90
Baltic countries	253,000	228,000	90
Germany/Austria	240,000	210,000	90
Protectorate of Bohemia and Moravia	90,000	80,000	89
Slovakia	90,000	75,000	83
Greece	70,000	54,000	77
Netherlands	140,000	105,000	75
Hungary	650,000	450,000	70
SSR White Russia	375,000	245,000	65
SSR Ukraine*	1,500,000	900,000	60
Belgium	65,000	40,000	60
Yugoslavia	43,000	26,000	60
Romania	600,000	300,000	50
Norway	1,800	900	50
France	350,000	90,000	26
Bulgaria	64,000	14,000	22
Italy	40,000	8,000	20
Luxembourg	5,000	1,000	20
Russia (RSFSR)*	975,000	107,000	11
Denmark	8,000	—	—
Finland	2,000	—	—
Totals	*8,861,800*	*5,933,900*	*67*

*Germany did not occupy the entire territories of these republics.

up. It refers to a sacrifice, often specifically to "an offering made by fire unto the Lord." Such connotations make "Holocaust" a problematic term for the devastation it names. The word's religious implications seem inappropriate, even repulsive, to many people, including many Jews. Still, Holocaust remains the term that is most widely used.

Nazi Germany's system of concentration camps, ghettos, murder squadrons, and killing centers took more than twelve million defenseless human lives.

Between five and six million of them were Jewish, including approximately one million children under the age of fifteen. Although not every Nazi victim was Jewish, the Nazi intent was to rid Europe, if not the world, of Jews. Hitler went far in meeting that goal. Although Europe's Jews resisted the onslaught as best they could, by the end of World War II, two-thirds of European Jews—and about one-third of Jews worldwide—were dead. The vast majority of the Jewish victims came from Eastern Europe. More than half of them were from Poland; there, the German annihilation effort was 90 percent successful. At Auschwitz alone—located in Poland, it was the largest of the Nazi killing centers—more than one million Jews were gassed.

How did the Holocaust happen and why? Those questions are both historical and ethical. Their implications are huge. As Elie Wiesel, Jewish survivor of Auschwitz and winner of the 1986 Nobel Peace Prize, has rightly said of Birkenau, the major killing area at Auschwitz: "Traditional ideas and acquired values, philosophical systems and social theories—all must be revised in the shadow of Birkenau."

HISTORY

Hitler became chancellor of Germany on January 30, 1933. He soon consolidated his power through tyranny and terror. Within six months, the Nazis stood as the only legal political power in Germany,

Hitler's decrees were as good as law, basic civil rights had been suspended, and thousands of the Third Reich's political opponents had been imprisoned.

Emphasizing the superiority of the German people, Nazi ideology was anti-Semitic and racist to the core. The Nazis affirmed that German racial purity must be maintained. Building on precedents long-established by Christianity's animosity toward Jews, the Nazis went further and vilified Jews as the most dangerous threat to that goal. Here it is important to underscore that Jews are not, in fact, a race but a people unified by memory and history, culture, tradition, and religious observances that are widely shared. Any person of any race can become Jewish through religious conversion. Nevertheless, Nazi ideology defined Jewish identity in biological and racial terms.

German law established detailed conditions to define full and part-Jews. To cite three examples, if one had three Jewish grandparents, that condition was

Starved concentration camp prisoners who died while being moved by train from one camp to another in 1945. (National Archives)

Death Camps in Nazi-Occupied Territories During the Holocaust

Source: Yitzhak Arad, ed., *The Pictorial History of the Holocaust* (New York: Macmillan, 1990).

determined, paradoxically, not by blood but by their membership in the Jewish religious community. Once these Nazi classifications were in effect, the identity they conferred was irreversible.

Defining Jewish identity was crucial for identifying the population targeted by the Nazis' anti-Semitic policies. Those policies focused first on segregating Jews, making their lives intolerable, and forcing them to leave Germany. Between 1933 and the outbreak of World War II in September, 1939, hundreds of decrees, such as the Nuremberg Laws of September, 1935, deprived the Third Reich's Jews of basic civil rights. When Jews tried to emigrate from German territory, however, they found few havens. In general, doors around the world, including those in the United States, were opened reluctantly, if at all, for Jewish refugees from Hitler's Germany.

World War II began with Germany's invasion of Poland on September 1, 1939. With the notable exception of its failure to subdue England by air power, the German war machine had things its own way until it experienced reversals at El Alamein and Stalingrad in 1942. By the end of that year, 4 million Jews had already been murdered.

As Hitler's forces had advanced on all fronts, huge numbers of Jews, far exceeding the 600,000 who lived in Germany when Hitler took control, came under Nazi domination. For a year after the war began, Nazi planning had still aimed to enforce massive Jewish resettlement, but there were no satisfactory ways to fulfill that intention. Other tactics had to be found. The Holocaust did not result from a detailed master plan that timed and controlled every move in advance. When one step reached an impasse, however, the next was always more drastic, because the Nazis did not deviate from their basic commitment: Somehow the Jews had to be eliminated.

In the spring of 1941, as plans were laid for the invasion of the Soviet Union, Hitler decided that special mobile killing units—*Einsatzgruppen*—would follow the German army, round up Jews, and kill them. In the fateful months that followed, a second prong of attack in Germany's war against the Jews

sufficient to make one fully Jewish. If one had only two Jewish grandparents and neither practiced Judaism nor had a Jewish spouse, however, then one was a *Mischlinge* (mongrel) first-class. A person with only a single Jewish grandparent would be a *Mischlinge* second-class. The identity of one's grandparents was became operational as well. Instead of moving killers toward their victims, it would bring victims to their killers.

Utilizing a former Austrian military barracks near the Polish town of Oświęcim, the Germans made their concentration camp of Auschwitz operational in June, 1940, when 728 Polish prisoners were transferred there. By the summer of 1941, the original camp (Auschwitz I) had been supplemented by a much larger camp at nearby Birkenau (Auschwitz II). Within the next year—along with five other sites in occupied Poland (Chelmno, Belzec, Sobibor, Treblinka, and Majdanek)—Auschwitz-Birkenau became a full-fledged killing center. Auschwitz "improved" killing by employing fast-working hydrogen cyanide gas, which suppliers offered in the form of a deodorized pesticide known as Zyklon B. Efficiency at Auschwitz-Birkenau was further improved in 1943 when new crematoria became available for corpse disposal. Optimum "production" in this death factory meant that thousands of Jews could be killed per day. When *Schutzstaffel* (SS) leader Heinrich Himmler ordered an end to the systematic killing at Auschwitz in late 1944, his reasoning was not based entirely on the fact that Soviet troops were nearby. For all practical purposes, he could argue, the "final solution" had eliminated Europe's "Jewish problem."

With Hitler's suicide on April 30, 1945, and the subsequent surrender of Germany on May 7, a chapter ended, but the history and the legacy of the "final solution" continue. Everyone who lives after Auschwitz is affected by the Holocaust. Everyone, moreover, ought to be affected particularly by the ethical problems and moral challenges left in its wake.

ETHICAL PROBLEMS AND MORAL CHALLENGES

Ethics clarifies what people should and should not do. It explores differences between what is right, just, and good and what is wrong, unjust, and evil. What Nazi Germany did to the European Jews clearly belongs in the latter categories. Thus, the most crucial moral problem posed by the Holocaust is that no moral, social, religious, or political constraints were sufficient to stop Nazi Germany from unleashing the "final solution." Only when military force crushed the Third Reich did the genocide end.

David Rousset, a French writer who endured German concentration camps, understated the case, but he was surely correct when he said simply, "The exis-tence of the camps is a warning." Two aspects of that warning are especially challenging.

First, the Holocaust warns about the depth of racism's evil. It shows that racism's destructive "logic" ultimately entails genocide. If one takes seriously the idea that one race endangers the well-being of another, the only way to remove that menace completely is to do away, once and for all, with everyone and everything that embodies it. If most forms of racism shy away from such extreme measures, Nazi Germany's anti-Semitism did not. The Nazis saw what they took to be a practical problem: the need to eliminate "racially inferior" people. Then they moved to solve it.

Consequently, the Holocaust did not result from unplanned, random violence. It was instead a state-sponsored program of population elimination made possible by modern technology and political organization. As Nazi Germany became a genocidal state, its anti-Semitic racism required a destruction process that needed and got the cooperation of every sector of German society. The killers and those who aided and abetted them directly—or indirectly as bystanders—were civilized people from a society that was scientifically advanced, technologically competent, culturally sophisticated, and efficiently organized. These people were, as Holocaust scholar Michael Berenbaum has noted, "both ordinary and extraordinary, a cross section of the men and women of Germany, its allies, and their collaborators as well as the best and the brightest."

Teachers and writers helped to till the soil in which Hitler's virulent anti-Semitism took root; their students and readers reaped the wasteful harvest. Lawyers drafted and judges enforced the laws that isolated Jews and set them up for the kill. Government and church personnel provided birth records to document who was Jewish and who was not. Other workers entered such information into state-of-the-art data processing machines. University administrators curtailed admissions for Jewish students and dismissed Jewish faculty members. Bureaucrats in the Finance Ministry confiscated Jewish wealth and property. Postal officials delivered mail about definition, expropriation, denaturalization, and deportation.

Driven by their biomedical visions, physicians were among the first to experiment with the gassing of *lebensunwertes Leben* (lives unworthy of life).

Scientists performed research and tested their racial theories on those branded subhuman or nonhuman by German science. Business executives found that Nazi concentration camps could provide cheap labor; they worked people to death, turning the Nazi motto, *Arbeit macht frei* (work makes one free), into a mocking truth. Stockholders made profits from firms that supplied Zyklon B to gas people and from companies that built crematoria to burn the corpses. Radio performers were joined by artists such as the gifted film director Leni Riefenstahl to broadcast and screen the polished propaganda that made Hitler's policies persuasive to so many. Engineers drove the trains that transported Jews to death, while other officials took charge of the billing arrangements for this service. Factory workers modified trucks so that they became deadly gas vans; city policemen became members of squadrons that made the murder of Jews their specialty. As the list went on and on, so did the racially motivated destruction of the European Jews.

HANS MAIER

Short of Germany's military defeat by the Allies, no other constraints—moral, social, religious, or political—were sufficient to stop the "final solution." Accordingly, a second Holocaust warning is the challenge that no one should take human rights for granted. To make that warning more personal, consider Hans Maier. Born on October 31, 1912, the only child of a Catholic mother and Jewish father, he considered himself an Austrian, not least because his father's family had lived in Austria since the seventeenth century. Hans Maier, however, lived in the twentieth century, and so it was that in the autumn of 1935 he studied a newspaper in a Viennese coffeehouse. The Nuremberg Laws had just been passed in Nazi Germany. Maier's reading made him see that, even if he did not think of himself as Jewish, the Nazis' definitions meant that in their view he was Jewish. By identifying him as a Jew, Maier would write later on, Nazi power made him "a dead man on leave, someone to be murdered, who only by chance was not yet where he properly belonged."

When Nazi Germany occupied Austria in March, 1938, Maier drew his conclusions. He fled his native land for Belgium and joined the Resistance after Belgium was swept into the Third Reich in 1940. Arrested by Nazi police in 1943, Maier was sent to Auschwitz and then to Bergen-Belsen, where he was liberated in 1945. Eventually taking the name Jean Améry, by which he is remembered, this philosopher waited twenty years before breaking his silence about the Holocaust. When Améry did decide to write, the result was a series of remarkable essays about his experience. In English, they appear in a volume entitled *At the Mind's Limits: Contemplations by a Survivor on Auschwitz and Its Realities.* "Every morning when I get up," he tells his reader, "I can read the Auschwitz number on my forearm. . . . Every day anew I lose my trust in the world. . . . Declarations of human rights, democratic constitutions, the free world and the free press, nothing," he went on to say, "can lull me into the slumber of security from which I awoke in 1935."

In *The Cunning of History: The Holocaust and the American Future* (1987), Richard L. Rubenstein echoes Améry's understanding. "Does not the Holocaust demonstrate," he suggests, "that there are absolutely no limits to the degradation and assault the managers and technicians of violence can inflict upon men and women who lack the power of effective resistance?" Rubenstein's outlook may be debatable, but he believes that "the dreadful history of Europe's Jews had demonstrated that *rights do not belong to men by nature.*" If Rubenstein is correct, then, practically speaking, people can expect to enjoy basic rights such as those proclaimed by the Declaration of Independence—life, liberty, and the pursuit of happiness—only within a political community that honors and defends those rights successfully.

John K. Roth

FURTHER READING

Améry, Jean. *At the Mind's Limits: Contemplations by a Survivor on Auschwitz and Its Realities.* Translated by Sidney Rosenfeld and Stella P. Rosenfeld. Bloomington: Indiana University Press, 1980. These reflections by a survivor of the Holocaust consider the status of human rights and responsibility after Auschwitz.

Banki, Judith H., and John T. Pawlikowski, eds. *Ethics in the Shadow of the Holocaust: Christian and Jewish Perspectives.* Franklin, Wis.: Sheed & Ward, 2001. Anthology examining the moral causes and effects of the Holocaust, focusing especially on Jewish-Christian relations. Also includes sections on medical ethics in the wake of

Nazi experiments and modern socio-economics as seen through the lens of Nazi business executives.

Browning, Christopher R. *Ordinary Men: Reserve Police Battalion 101 and the Final Solution in Poland.* New York: HarperCollins, 1992. One of the most important case studies to emerge from Holocaust scholarship, Browning's book examines how a unit of ordinary German men became a killing squadron that produced extraordinary inhumanity.

Garrard, Eve, and Geoffrey Scarre, eds. *Moral Philosophy and the Holocaust.* Burlington, Vt.: Ashgate, 2003. Anthology combining philosophical, historical, and cultural analysis. Examines moral issues raised during the Holocaust, as well as its current moral and political implications and the portrayal of the Holocaust in contemporary culture.

Haas, Peter J. *Morality After Auschwitz: The Radical Challenge of the Nazi Ethic.* Philadelphia: Fortress Press, 1988. Arguing that the Nazis had their own understanding of morality, Haas analyzes how their "idealism" led many people to accept genocide as tolerable and even routine.

Hallie, Philip P. *Lest Innocent Blood Be Shed: The Story of the Village of Le Chambon and How Goodness Happened There.* New York: Harper & Row, 1979. Written by an important moral philosopher, this book investigates how and why the people in the French village of Le Chambon risked their lives to rescue some five thousand Jews.

Hatley, James. *Suffering Witness: The Quandary of Responsibility After the Irreparable.* Albany: State University of New York Press, 2000. Hatley theorizes the nature and extent of our responsibility in the face of the inconceivable and irreparable horror of the Holocaust. Arguing from a Levinasian perspective, he discusses the difficulty, the necessity, and the rewards of acting as a witness to that horror.

Hilberg, Raul. *The Destruction of the European Jews.* 3d ed. 3 vols. New Haven, Conn.: Yale University Press, 2003. Hilberg's book is an unrivaled study of the bureaucratic process of destruction that the Nazis directed toward the Jews of Europe. The author's reflections on the Holocaust's consequences contain important ethical content.

Rittner, Carol, and John K. Roth, eds. *Different Voices: Women and the Holocaust.* New York: Paragon House, 1993. Drawing on the memoirs of Holocaust victims, historical studies, and philosophical and religious reflections, this volume discusses moral dilemmas created by the Holocaust's impact on women.

Rubenstein, Richard L., and John K. Roth. *Approaches to Auschwitz: The Holocaust and Its Legacy.* Atlanta: John Knox Press, 1987. The authors show how religious conflict and racism intensified the anti-Semitism that led to Auschwitz. This study also focuses on the roles played by the churches, industry, and the professions during the Nazi era.

Wiesel, Elie. *Night.* Translated by Stella Rodway. New York: Bantam Books, 1982. The winner of the 1986 Nobel Peace Prize describes his experiences in Auschwitz and Buchenwald. In this classic, one of the most famous Holocaust memoirs, Wiesel repeatedly asks disturbing moral and religious questions.

SEE ALSO: Anti-Semitism; Choiceless choices; Concentration camps; Fascism; Genocide, Frustration-aggression theory of; Genocide and democide; Hitler, Adolf; Lemkin, Raphael; Nazism; Schindler, Oskar; War.

Holy war

DEFINITION: Presence, in a situation of war, of a "sanctifying" principle that transfers religious righteousness to the acts of participants in violence

DATE: Concept developed during the medieval era

TYPE OF ETHICS: Religious ethics

SIGNIFICANCE: Going beyond the broader secular ethical question of justifying "morally just" wars fought to defeat evil and injustice, the concept of holy war relies on God as the highest authority justifying war against a religious enemy.

Wars involving intense religious animosities have been fought in almost every period of recorded history. However, when it comes to the ethical implications of the concept of "holy war," important distinctions must be made. Political wars involving enemies of different religions do not necessarily involve levels of institutionalization of individual "holy warriors'" committed to religiously motivated warfare.

Although examples of holy war have occurred in other civilizations, the most commonly cited phenomena come from the experiences of Islam and Christianity. In both cases, one can find, according to the specific junctures of otherwise political warring actions, forms of religiously institutionalized "sanctification" bestowed on holy warriors. The ethical content of such institutionalization, however, varies between the two dominant prototypes.

MEDIEVAL CHRISTIANITY AND THE CRUSADES

Saint Augustine and other fathers of the early Christian church held that God stood behind certain wars, if their cause could be considered morally just and aimed at destroying evil. Defense of what can be seen as morally "right," however, did not necessarily mean service to a higher religious cause. These earliest searches for a possible "ethical" justification for some wars, therefore, fell short in a number of ways of the technical phenomenon of holy war. They did not, for example, imply an acceptance of warring in the name of religious principles.

The Christian concept of "sanctification" of warfare in the name of religion dates from the eleventh century, when Pope Gregory VII, adding to the less specific suggestions of the ninth century pope Leo IV (in 853) and the eleventh century pope Leo IX (in 1053), assured Christians that death in war against a religious enemy freed the holy warrior from the consequences of his past sins. From the beginning in 1095 of the Christian Crusades to regain the Holy Land of Palestine from Islam, there was a linkage between the existing institution of knighthood and formal military orders whose fighting members were devoted to the Crusades as a spiritual calling. Historically, various orders—such as the Knights Templar and Knights Hospitaliers—would continue even after the formal period of Crusades to the Holy Land.

Holy Wars in History

POLITICAL-RELIGIOUS WARS APPROVED BY RELIGIOUS AUTHORITIES

1618-1648	Thirty Years' War in Europe
1690	William II, Protestant king of Orange, defeats England's Roman Catholic king James in Ireland
1880-1900	Mahdist Uprising in the Sudan
1947-1948	Muslim-Hindu strife in the wake of Indian and Pakistani independence

HOLY WARS SANCTIFIED BY RELIGIOUS AUTHORITIES

800-1000	Frankish Knights' war to convert pagans east of former Roman imperial borders
1095-1099	First Crusade to the Holy Lands
1147-1149	Second Crusade
1189-1192	Third Crusade, following Saladin's recapture of Jerusalem
1202-1204	Fourth Crusade
1208	Albigensian Crusade by Pope Innocent II against Christian heretics
1212	Children's Crusade
1217-1221	Fifth Crusade (in Egypt)
1228-1229	Sixth Crusade (a truce makes possible partial Christian control in Jerusalem)
1248-1254	Seventh Crusade (Saint Louis—King Louis IX—travels to Egypt)
1270	Eighth Crusade (Saint Louis dies in Tunisia)
1271-1272	Ninth Crusade
1291	Fall of Acre, last Christian stronghold in the Holy Lands

Another aspect of Church "sanctification" of violence in the name of religion that did not disappear with the passing of a particular historical era was the holy war against Christian heretics proclaimed by the Third Lateran Council in the year 1179. Fighters in what was to be known as the Albigensian Crusade, launched by Pope Innocent III in 1208, would receive the same papal indulgences that were granted to those who had served in the Crusades against the Muslims of the Near East.

HOLY WAR IN ISLAMIC LAW

The Islamic religion, in its "classical" theological origins, identifies two domains: the Dar al Islam (domain of Islam) and the Dar al Harb (domain of war). This is a concept that has often been interpreted as a necessarily continuous state of war between Islam and any representative of non-Islamic belief. Along with this general concept of the hostile separation of the world between Islamic believers and nonbelievers, a more specific term emerged that would be rife with presumptions of ethical obligations falling on individual Muslim believers: jihad. Jihad is not one of the five formal Pillars of the Faith, but an individual conscience-binding obligation on believers (fard).

Although it is not uncommon to see jihad translated as "holy war," one comes closer to the ethical core of this concept through examination of Islamic legal discussions of the term. The first striking observation is that—in contrast to Christian equivalents to holy war—jihad is taken to be a society-wide ethical obligation. Its legal meaning—although clearly extending into the realm of physical struggle to extend the "borders" of the Dar al Islam—includes a sense of effort, in a variety of forms, to strengthen the bases of the Islamic faith. Indeed, the broadest possible legal and ethical sense of individual effort—*ijtihad*, deductive effort to reach balanced decisions—suggests not religious war per se but "individual application" to protect the essential principles of the faith.

This observation notwithstanding, there is considerable evidence suggesting that, at almost every stage of military conflict associated with Islamic expansionism, believers were exhorted to consider their physical struggle to be service in holy war. Although an oft-quoted speech attributed to the first caliph, Abū Bakr, during the early seventh century probably refers to the spirit of later ages, this meaning predominates: "If any people holds back from fighting the holy war for God, God strikes them with degradation."

On the Islamic as well as the Christian side, it was during the period of the Crusades that an individual ethical dedication to holy war took on its most nota-

ble attributes. Much more modern, and even late-twentieth and early twenty-first century phenomena in both cultures, however, contain elements of dedication to holy war in varying degrees.

MODERN BLENDS OF POLITICAL AND RELIGIOUS ETHICS

The twentieth century saw many cases in which individual dedication to what is essentially a political cause brought about levels of religious ethical devotion that were close to what has been defined as holy war. Among Asian religions, for example, the concept of *kamikaze* (divine wind) pushed Japanese military pilots to undertake suicidal missions to serve the emperor-god in World War II.

Other manifestations of the "mixed" application of religious fervor and essentially political violence approach, but do not fully correspond to, holy war in the ethical sense of the term. Irish Roman Catholic underground forces opposing Protestant domination of Northern Ireland include—as do Protestant "fighting brotherhoods"—a form of spiritual bonding in their secret Irish Republican Army (IRA). Like members of Islamic radical organizations declaring "war" against the state of Israel or, increasingly, against the effects of what they consider to be corrupt secular governments in several Islamic countries, the Irish Catholics have aimed more at the establishment of alternative political regimes. Nevertheless, in some cases, the religious "sanctification" of such struggles (including Muslim-Hindu strife in parts of India beginning during the 1990's) brings them close to the category of holy wars.

ESCALATING ISLAMIC INTERPRETATIONS OF HOLY WAR

Various circumstances emerged in the late twentieth century that gave rise to vigorous reinterpretations of the Islamic concept of Holy War. Deterioration of political and economic conditions in several Islamic countries spawned a variety of movements that began to use jihad as a rallying point against perceived enemies of Islam. Some of these movements aim at deposing what they see as corrupt secular governments in their own modern nation states. Others claim to defend the whole of the Islamic world against a general enemy represented by the presumed infidel Western world. Although the Islamic reform movement that overthrew the shah of Iran in 1979 involved more than jihad as a motivating force, it did contain both of these (internal and external) elements.

When "normal" political channels for representing religiously based movements fail, rising militancy in reaction can lead to the adoption by Islamic warriors known as mujahiddeen of violent methods presumably justified by religion. This happened in Algeria in 1991, when elections that should have allowed an Islamic party to join the government were effectively canceled. Algeria's subsequent experience of more than a decade of continuous violence—mainly in the form of terrorist attacks against both political targets and anonymous victims—tended to cloud distinctions between fanatical opposition politics and calls for holy war.

The al-Qaeda terrorists who flew hijacked airliners into the World Trade Center and the Pentagon are believed to have seen themselves as heroes in a holy war against the United States. (AP/Wide World Photos)

Another example of what one could call internally directed holy war grew out of political and economic grievances in Egypt during the 1970's. When Egypt's secular regime arrested thousands of demonstrators, organized militants under a number of names, including Islamic jihad, carried out the 1981 assassination of President Anwar Sadat. Both violent underground and overt activities involving religious discontent continued to mount over the ensuing decades. Some groups refer to continuation of the status quo in Egypt and elsewhere as reverting to the pre-Islamic "Age of Ignorance" and call for "flight" (*hijra*) within Islamic territory to escape and regroup for a concerted religious struggle.

In this case, which refers to the model provided by traditional accounts of the Prophet Muḥammad's flight to Medina to confront his enemies in Mecca, many holy war polemists draw on writings by famous spiritual leaders, such as Sayyid Qutb, who was martyred in Egypt during the 1960's. Whether Qutb's intention was to incite actual methods of holy war to achieve the assumed pristine goals of Islam, many of his revolutionary ideas were appropriated by underground movements, not only in Egypt, but beyond its borders. Both the Islamic jihad movement and Hamas (meaning "zeal," or "ardour") in Israeli-occupied areas of Palestine, for example, have used Qutb's ideas to justify terrorist attacks against Israel, even though Qutb made few, if any, references to the specific circumstances affecting the plight of Palestinians. Like Algerian and Egyptian exponents of violence within particular national settings in the name of religion, the Hamas and Islamic jihad movements claim that only a religiously based mass movement can succeed in overcoming perceived injustices that have not been adequately addressed by their secular political leaders.

Other religiously motivated movements have also used the concept of holy war to support forceful actions against presumed threats, both political and moral, coming from outside the Islamic world. Until several terrorist attacks against U.S. interests at home and abroad culminated in the September 11, 2001, disasters attributed to Osama bin Laden's al-Qaeda organization, the most outstanding model of mujahiddeen operations against a foreign enemy of Islam appeared in the 1980's in Afghanistan. There religious militants bore arms against the "infidel" Soviet presence in their lands. Ironically, the non-Muslim West, especially the United States, supported what they perceived to be the anti-Soviet focus of Afghanistan's mujahiddeen forces. Only later, when the extremist Islamic Taliban movement took over in Afghanistan and not only harbored, but encouraged, al-Qaeda in its operations against what it considered as the "illegitimate" Saudi government as well as the "infidel" West, did the threat of cross-border holy war become alarming.

Whether in real practical, or mainly theoretical, terms, early twenty-first century linkages involving Islamic religio-political causes in countries as far apart as Indonesia (where the Jamaa Islamiyyah, or Islamic Society, supported antigovernment and anti-Western campaigns of violence), Palestine, and Western-occupied Afghanistan and Iraq have given new global meaning to the phenomenon of holy war.

Byron D. Cannon

FURTHER READING

Abraham, Antoine J. *The Warriors of God.* Bristol, Ind.: Wyndam Hall Press, 1989.

Armstrong, Karen. *Holy War: The Crusades and Their Impact on Today's World.* New York: Doubleday, 1991.

Brundage, James A., ed. *The Crusades, Holy War and Canon Law.* Aldershot, England: Variorum, 1991.

Esposito, John L. *Unholy War.* New York: Oxford University Press, 2002.

Keppel, Gilles. *Jihad: The Trail of Political Islam.* Cambridge, Mass.: Belknap Press, Harvard University, 2002.

Khadduri, Majid. *War and Peace in the Law of Islam.* Baltimore: Johns Hopkins University Press, 1955.

Lyons, Malcolm C. *Saladin: The Politics of the Holy War.* Cambridge, England: Cambridge University Press, 1982.

SEE ALSO: Abū Bakr; Islamic ethics; Jihad; Just war theory; Religion; Religion and violence; War.

Homeland defense

DEFINITION: Government preparations for the defense of a nation against foreign enemies during peacetime

TYPE OF ETHICS: Military ethics

SIGNIFICANCE: The September 11, 2001, attacks on the United States underscored the vulnerability of the nation's territory to terrorism and lifted homeland defense from an abstract concept to a subject of public consciousness, while raising questions about some of the methods used to implement homeland defense.

During the twentieth century, the United States relied primarily on its Navy and Air Force to defend its territory against possible enemy attack during peacetime. During the two World Wars, when the bulk of American military troops served overseas, the country relied on a combination of state militia, civilian law enforcement agencies, and some federal military troops to defend the homeland from enemy raiders and saboteurs.

The terrorist attacks of September 11, 2001, vividly demonstrated a threat against which traditional military forces were ill-prepared. Instead of the kinds of conventional military forces that were considered threats, the most dangerous threats to the United States came from a combination of terrorist and criminal forces. Potential targets included civilian populations, segments of the economic infrastructure, computer networks, and other vulnerable areas not considered traditional military targets. After the September 11 attacks were made using hijacked commercial airliners, possible future weapons appeared to include everything from toxic germs and computer viruses to nuclear bombs. To counter such threats, President George W. Bush created a new cabinet-level Department of Homeland Security that would combine federal, state, and local resources to protect the United States from future terrorist attacks.

The concept of Homeland Defense raised few new ethical questions. Defense of the homeland is one of the primary purposes of government, and no nation is expected to ignore homeland defense. However, the methods employed to implement homeland defense can and do raise ethical problems, most of which stem from preventive methods of battling terrorism. For example, the racial profiling of possible

Members of the U.S. Marine Corps' Chemical-Biological Incident Response Force demonstrate anthrax cleanup techniques in Washington, D.C., a few weeks after the September 11, 2001, terrorist attacks on the United States. (AP/Wide World Photos)

terrorists and the detaining of suspects have raised questions over racism, individuality, and the concept that a person is innocent until proven guilty in a court of law. After 2001, fear of terrorist attacks led to increased use of government surveillance and intrusion of privacy. Civil libertarians have raised concerns over the erosion of what they see as fundamental rights of privacy, whereas security specialists worry about terrorists using the very openness and freedom of the nation as a tool to attack it.

Barry M. Stentiford

FURTHER READING

Campbell, Geoffrey, A. *Vulnerable American Overview: National Security Library of Homeland Security.* San Diego, Calif.: Lucent Books, 2004.

Cordesman, Anthony H. *Terrorism, Asymmetric Warfare, and Weapons of Mass Destruction: Defending the U.S. Homeland.* New York: Praeger, 2001.

Stentiford, Barry M. *The American Home Guard: The State Militia in the Twentieth Century.* College Station: Texas A&M Press, 2002.

SEE ALSO: Accused, rights of; Biochemical weapons; Chemical warfare; Electronic surveillance; Limited war; Military ethics; National security and sovereignty; North Atlantic Treaty Organization; Terrorism.

Homeless care

DEFINITION: Public responsibility for the welfare and care of homeless persons
TYPE OF ETHICS: Human rights
SIGNIFICANCE: The question of the responsibility that society takes for its homeless members is an important part of the larger ethical debate about society's responsibilities to the disadvantaged.

One of the most enduring and controversial issues from Franklin D. Roosevelt's New Deal policies of the 1930's and 1940's to George W. Bush's so-called Compassionate Conservatism of the early twenty-first century has been about what should be the level of government assistance to homeless people. The issue has been rancorous because of a fundamental dichotomy in American society. On one hand, the judicial system has historically favored property rights over human rights, and both laissez-faire economics and Calvinist religious traditions have emphasized individualism and self-reliance. On the other hand, Americans have always considered themselves generous and unselfish, with a record of government aid to the poor dating back to the early nineteenth century.

Social Darwinists have claimed that poverty is a historical constant, and that therefore any government assistance to the poor is a futile waste of resources. Most modern Americans, however, acknowledge that society bears some responsibility for those without homes.

THE ETHICAL ISSUES

Does government have an ethical obligation to provide for the needs of all its citizens from cradle to grave? Is there a danger that massive federal expenditures, such as free housing, will destroy the work ethic? Will the higher taxes likely to be needed for such spending increases aggravate the class animosity between those who pay for benefits and those who receive them? These are just some of the questions connected to the issue of government responsibility for the homeless, and each question leads to more. Like most ethical concerns, there are a few consensual answers or absolute truths so the debate will continue.

On one point there is nearly universal agreement: The homeless lead a miserable existence. They are likely to be found in dangerous and unsavory neighborhoods, largely because the affluent refuse to allow them to come near them. People without homes are easily victimized. Many suffer physical, mental, and emotional problems, which make it even more difficult for them to protect themselves. They enjoy no safety, shelter, or security on an ongoing basis, and many are reluctant to seek assistance from police. Government statistics on hate crime indicate that eighteen homeless people were murdered in the United States in 2001. Some attackers killed homeless people because they saw themselves as vigilantes ridding the world of undesirable people, while others committed the crimes for thrills.

Many would argue that the federal government does have an ethical obligation to provide adequate housing to all the nation's citizens. The framers of both the Declaration of Independence and the U.S. Constitution believed in the concept of natural rights. As espoused by Enlightenment era philosophers John Locke and Jean Jacques Rousseau, and echoed by Thomas Jefferson and James Madison, natural rights theory held that God gave people certain rights, such as the right to life. Therefore, government has a moral requirement to provide, when necessary, the basic means of life. The ethics embraced by the Judeo-Christian religious tradition stressed charity and generosity toward others. Socialist and communist political ideology also embraced the idea of government-provided housing.

However, other people equally concerned with ethics have held that there is no such government responsibility.

Adam Smith and others supported laissez-faire economics, which stressed minimalist government and rugged individualism. Thomas Malthus and other Social Darwinists taught that there would always be poor and homeless people and any form of government assistance was both futile and counterproductive. The United States has always held sacred the concept of self-made and self-reliant persons, and such persons would never dream of asking the government for housing or any other form of assistance. Also, the judiciary has historically held in high esteem the property rights of all owners. Until the 1930's, the judiciary was critical of federal welfare programs. Many social commentators, such as former president Herbert Hoover, believed that federally provided housing would help not only to destroy the work ethic but would be an unconstitutional intrusion of big government.

OTHER ISSUES

If there were a universal consensus that homelessness is a problem not to be tolerated, other issues of an ethical nature would arise. Once it is conceded that is government's job to house the poor, then the question would arise of whether government is also responsible for providing food, medicine, utilities, and transportation. How ethical would it be to heavily tax hardworking and productive citizens to provide benefits for idle, nonproductive citizens? Is the core belief of the welfare state that by nature people are incompetent to provide for their own needs? Are people poor and homeless because of their own failures and inadequacies. or are they victimized by capitalism and the wealthy? All these and many other ethical concerns would remain to be addressed.

Homelessness remains a paradoxical issue. Despite vast sums spent by various government entities and substantial assistance from the private sector, the numbers and problems of the homeless remained staggering in the early twenty-first century. Government aid has clearly alleviated the problem and assisted millions who would otherwise be homeless. However, it appeared that no amount of money would totally redress the situation.

Thomas W. Buchanan

FURTHER READING

Hombs, Mary Ellen, and Mitch Snyder. *Homelessness in America: A Forced March to Nowhere.* Washington, D.C.: Community for Creative Non-Violence, 2001.

Newman, Katherine S. *No Shame in My Game: The Working Poor in the Inner City.* New York: Vintage Books, 2000.

Rossi, Peter H. *Down and Out in America: The Origins of Homelessness.* Chicago: University of Chicago Press, 1989.

Tucker, William. *The Excluded Americans: Homelessness and Housing Policies.* Washington, D.C.: Regnery Gateway, 1990.

White, Richard W. *Rude Awakenings: What the Homeless Crisis Tells Us.* San Francisco: ICS Press, 1992.

SEE ALSO: Charity; Communitarianism; Distributive justice; Entitlements; Institutionalization of patients; Poverty; Service to others; Welfare programs; Welfare rights.

Homicide

DEFINITION: Killing of one human being by another
TYPE OF ETHICS: Legal and judicial ethics
SIGNIFICANCE: Legal systems generally treat homicide as a particularly heinous crime, requiring the most severe punishment, but they also allow for justifications and mitigating factors such as self-defense, lack of intent, or insanity.

All modern societies regard the premeditated murder of another human as a crime; the research of various ethologists working amongst a large number of species suggests, however, that it is not uncommon for an animal to play an active role in taking the life of another member of its own species. For example, black widow spiders are named for killing their mates, and chimpanzees have been reported to kill members of their own troops. Such observations may suggest that members of the species *Homo sapiens* have from time to time killed one another for as long as humans have existed. Furthermore, no matter how antisocial or repulsive such behavior may seem, it would be inappropriate to label such action as criminal or homicidal, since such labels introduce the notion of legality.

Additionally, while the origin of such actions may prompt ethical and moral concerns, various social and natural scientists have discussed the evolutionary advantage of such behavior while addressing kin selection and the origin of altruism. A review of anthropological literature suggests that various human societies have sanctioned the killing of humans in certain specific situations, including suicide, infanticide, war, and euthanasia. Although both activities are legally acceptable, some in the United States have called abortion murder, while others have said the same thing about capital punishment.

HISTORICAL BACKGROUND

Regarding human behavior and the origin and evolution of society, an action did not become criminal until it was covered by a law prohibiting it that prescribed a punishment for it. Crime is generally considered to be an assault against the state or government because it disrupts public order and disturbs social tranquillity. According to fragments of a clay tablet recovered from what was Sumer, the earliest legal prohibitions were prepared by approximately 2000 B.C.E.

The Code of Lipit-Ishtar was established during the eighteenth century B.C.E. and represents the first documented attempt to codify the laws governing human behavior. Specifically, the code outlined the rights and privileges of all members of Sumerian society. Similar codified laws representing a Babylonian dynasty of 1200-1700 B.C.E. are referred to as Hammurabi's code, and like those that preceded them, they outline the legal and social contract between members of society and society. These codes established courts, fines, and penalties, as well as the rights and obligations of each member of society. As is true of present laws, the early laws reflected the values of their time, and therefore, they incorporated the notion of an "eye for an eye." For example, a portion of Hammurabi's code states, "If a man destroys the eye of another man, he shall have his destroyed." Elsewhere it states, "If a man breaks the bone of another man, he shall have his like bone broken." Certainly a notable homicide for some was that of Abel by his brother Cain, which is discussed in the book of Genesis in the Bible.

Throughout the Western world, criminal violations are classified as those perpetrated against a person (such as kidnapping and rape), those against property (such as robbery), and those against the state (such as treason). Furthermore, they are classified as felonies and misdemeanors based upon society's perception of the severity of each crime and thus the penalty associated with it. In the United States, felonies carry a sentence of at least one year in prison, while misdemeanors are punishable by jail terms of less than a year or by a fine, or both. In the West, traditionally, the three major felonies are murder, arson, and sexual assault, although other crimes such as kidnapping and bank robbery have been added in some countries.

HOMICIDE IN THE UNITED STATES

In the United States, murder is practically the only capital felony, or one that authorizes the death penalty for its perpetration. Under special circumstances, however, a homicide may not be considered a crime. Specifically, in cases involving self-defense, or when a homicide is carried out to prevent the commission of a further serious felony, the perpetrator may not be prosecuted. Homicides are classified as those that are premeditated, those involving manslaughter, and those caused by negligence.

The most serious type of homicide is that which is planned in advance or is premeditated. The least serious homicide is one caused by carelessness or resulting from a negligent act. Manslaughter is defined as a homicide resulting from recklessness or a violent emotional outburst. By convention, homicide rates are reported as the number per 100,000 population, although not all countries distinguish among murder, manslaughter, and negligent homicide.

The homicide rate for various countries from 1940 to 1970 are shown in the accompanying table in five-year increments. Because of the effect of population size, the number of such deaths is also reported. For example, for Australia, the rate jumps from 0.46 to 0.90 between 1940 and 1955, while the increase in the number of deaths is only 50. This is because of the relatively small population of Australia. This should be kept in mind while noting the smallest five-year difference in the number of deaths in the United States (147 between 1950 and 1955), which is nearly three times the difference in number for Australia between 1940 and 1955.

It is clearly demonstrated by the table that the homicide rate for each country has remained relatively stable (Australia's shows the greatest rate of change—from 0.46 in 1940 to 2.38 in 1970), while there is a notable difference between countries (the lowest thirty-year average is that of England, at 0.70, while the highest is that of the United States, at 5.79). Such intercountry differences may be attributed to cultural differences and a society's attitudes toward the value of human life, the availability of weapons, and accepted techniques for resolving interpersonal conflict.

Turhon A. Murad

FURTHER READING

Archer, Dane, and Rosemary Gartner. *Violence and Crime in Cross-National Perspective.* New Haven, Conn.: Yale University Press, 1984.

Daly, Martin, and Margo Wilson. *Homicide.* New York: Aldine de Gruyter, 1988.

Fox, James Alan, and Jack Levin. *The Will to Kill: Making Sense of Senseless Murder.* Boston: Allyn and Bacon, 2001.

Geberth, Vernon J. *Practical Homicide Investigation.* 2d ed. New York: Elsevier, 1990.

Robbins, Sara, ed. *Law: A Treasury of Art and Literature.* New York: Hugh Lauter Levin, 1990.

Samaha, Joel. *Criminal Law.* St. Paul, Minn.: West, 1983.

SEE ALSO: Abortion; Assassination; Capital punishment; Death and dying; Euthanasia; Genocide and democide; Infanticide; Life and death; Lynching; Suicide assistance.

Homophobia

DEFINITION: Fear and hatred of nonheterosexual people

TYPE OF ETHICS: Civil rights

SIGNIFICANCE: Homophobia may be seen as immoral in itself, and it also causes people to commit immoral acts, from discrimination to hateful speech to acts of violence including murder. Those who subscribe to a moral system that labels homosexuality as wrong would object to the very term homophobia on the ground that it pathologizes their beliefs.

Derived from the Greek *homos*, meaning "same," and *phobikos*, meaning "having a fear of and/or aversion for," the term "homophobia" was popularized by George Weinberg in 1972 in his book *Society and the Healthy Homosexual*. Other terms that have been used include: "homophilephobia," "homoerotophobia," "homosexphobia," "homosexophobia," "homosexism," "homonegativism," "lesbian-" and "gay-hatred" or "-hating," and "sexual orientationalism" (giving a parallel structure with "racism," "sexism," and "classism"). "Biphobia" is the fear and hatred of those who love and sexually desire both males and females, and it can include prejudice and acts of discrimination against bisexual people.

"Heterosexism" (a close ally to homophobia) is the system of advantages bestowed on heterosexuals. It is the institutional response to homophobia that assumes that all people are or should be heterosexual and therefore excludes the needs, concerns, and life experiences of lesbians, gay males, and bisexuals. At times subtle, heterosexism is a form of oppression by neglect, omission, and/or distortion, whereas its more active ally—homophobia—is oppression by intent and design.

Heterosexism forces lesbians, gay males, and bisexuals to struggle constantly against their own invisibility and makes it much more difficult for them to integrate a positive identity. This is not unlike the situation of a Jew or a Muslim in a predominantly Christian country, a wheelchair user in a town with only stepped entrances to buildings, or a Spanish-speaking visitor in a country in which Spanish is not spoken.

Homophobia and heterosexism (like all forms of oppression) operate on four distinct but interrelated levels: the personal, the interpersonal, the institutional, and the societal (or cultural).

The personal level refers to an individual's belief system (bias or prejudice). Forms of personal homophobia include the beliefs that sexual minorities (gay males, lesbians, and bisexuals) either deserve to be pitied as unfortunate beings who are powerless to control their desires or should be hated; that they are psychologically disturbed or genetically defective; that their existence contradicts the "laws" of nature; that they are spiritually immoral, infected pariahs who are disgusting—in short, that they are generally inferior to heterosexuals.

Personal heterosexism, the belief that everyone is

or should be heterosexual, is in operation, for example, when parents automatically assume that their children are heterosexual and will eventually marry a person of the other sex.

The interpersonal level is manifested when a personal bias affects relations among individuals, transforming prejudice into its active component—discrimination.

Interpersonal homophobia includes name calling or joke telling intended to demean or defame sexual minorities; verbal and physical harassment and intimidation as well as more extreme forms of violence; the withholding of support; rejection; abandonment by friends and other peers, coworkers, and family members; and the refusal of landlords to rent apartments, shop owners to provide services, insurance companies to extend coverage, and employers to hire on the basis of actual or perceived sexual identity.

Interpersonal heterosexism occurs, for example, when teachers assume that all their students are heterosexual and teach only the contributions of heterosexuals. This leaves sexual minorities without a legacy and sense of history.

INSTITUTIONAL HOMOPHOBIA

The institutional level refers to the ways in which governmental agencies, businesses, and educational, religious, and professional organizations systematically discriminate on the basis of sexual orientation. Sometimes laws, codes, or policies actually enforce such discrimination.

Institutional homophobia includes "sodomy laws" that remain on the books in many states to punish people engaging in same-sex sexual activity; "anti-gay rights laws," such as the prototype Colorado Constitution Ballot Amendment 2 (approved by 53 percent of the voters on November 3, 1992) prohibiting equal protection under the law on the basis of sexual orientation; state and municipal policies restricting gay, lesbian, and bisexual people from serving as foster and adoptive parents and making it more difficult for them to win custody of their own children in the courts; military policy excluding gays, lesbians, and bisexuals; the doctrines of some religious denominations that oppose homosexuality; the classification of homosexuality as a "disordered condition" according to the American Psychiatric Association until 1973 and the American Psychological Associa-

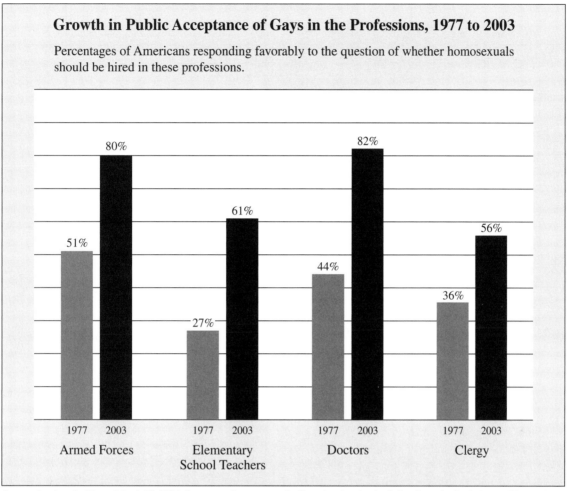

Growth in Public Acceptance of Gays in the Professions, 1977 to 2003

Percentages of Americans responding favorably to the question of whether homosexuals should be hired in these professions.

	1977	2003
Armed Forces	51%	80%
Elementary School Teachers	27%	61%
Doctors	44%	82%
Clergy	36%	56%

Source: Los Angeles Times, March 30, 2004. Summary of responses of polls undertaken by the Gallup Organization in June, 1977, and May, 2003.

tion until 1975; and school policies clearly stipulating that same-sex couples may not attend proms and other social functions.

Institutional heterosexism includes religious and governmental sanction of the marriages of only heterosexual couples; companies providing employee benefits only to "legally" married spouses and children; the heterosexual bias on government, business, and community groups' printed forms when listing only the categories "single," "married," and "divorced" in reference to relationship status; municipal, state, and national governments giving special tax benefits to heterosexually married couples; medical policy permitting only "blood relatives" or spouses certain hospital visitation rights; and school

dances designed specifically to encourage the socialization of males with females, and vice versa.

The societal (or cultural) level refers to the social norms or codes of behavior that, although not expressly written into law or policy, nevertheless work within a society to legitimize oppression. Societal homophobia includes the stereotypes of sexual minorities that are taught in the culture, ranging from their alleged predatory appetites, to their physical appearance, to the possible "causes" of their desires. It also includes active attempts to falsify historical accounts of same-sex love—through censorship, deletion, half-truths, and the altering of pronouns signifying gender—making accurate reconstruction extremely difficult.

An example of societal heterosexism is evident whenever the only positive and satisfying relationships portrayed in the media are heterosexual. This is not unlike media portrayals of white people, especially in the United States during the 1950's and 1960's, which excluded positive images of people of color.

Gay, lesbian, and bisexual people are not immune to the destructive effects of homophobia, biphobia, and heterosexism. Internalized homophobia and biphobia occur when gay, lesbian, and bisexual people incorporate or "internalize" society's negative notions of homosexuality or bisexuality and of gay, lesbian, and bisexual people, thus inhibiting their ability to establish a positive self-identity or to form close and intimate relationships. This internalization may result in the denial of one's sexual and emotional attractions on the conscious or unconscious level to oneself and others; overachievement as a bid for acceptance; contempt for the more open and "obvious" members of the lesbian, gay, or bisexual community; attempts to alter or change one's sexual orientation; projection of prejudice onto another minority group (reinforced by society's already existing prejudices); delayed or retarded emotional or cognitive development; attempts to "pass" as heterosexual, sometimes marrying someone of the other sex to gain social approval; increased fear and withdrawal from friends and relatives; conflicts with the law; unsafe sexual practices and other destructive risk-taking behaviors, including substance abuse; and suicidal ideation, attempts, and completion.

Warren J. Blumenfeld

FURTHER READING

Blumenfeld, Warren J., ed. *Homophobia: How We All Pay the Price.* Boston: Beacon Press, 1992.

Blumenfeld, Warren J., and Diane Raymond. *Looking at Gay and Lesbian Life.* Boston: Beacon Press, 1993.

Comstock, Gary David. *Violence Against Lesbians and Gay Men.* New York: Columbia University Press, 1991.

DeCecco, John P., ed. *Bashers, Baiters, and Bigots: Homophobia in American Society.* New York: Harrington Park Press, 1985.

Fone, Byrne. *Homophobia: A History.* New York: Picador, 2001.

Herek, Gregory M, ed. *Stigma and Sexual Orientation: Understanding Prejudice Against Lesbians, Gay Men, and Bisexuals.* Thousand Oaks, Calif.: Sage, 1998.

Hutchins, Loraine, and Lani Kaahumanu, eds. *Bi Any Other Name: Bisexual People Speak Out.* Boston: Alyson, 1991.

Moss, Donald, ed. *Hating in the First Person Plural: Psychoanalytic Essays on Racism, Homophobia, Misogyny, and Terror.* New York: Other Press, 2003.

Pharr, Suzanne. *Homophobia: A Weapon of Sexism.* Inverness, Calif.: Chardon Press, 1988.

SEE ALSO: Gay rights; Hate crime and hate speech; Homosexuality; Oppression; Sexism; Sexual stereotypes; Stonewall Inn riots.

Homosexuality

DEFINITION: Disposition to feel romantic love for, and to have sexual relations with, persons of one's own sex

TYPE OF ETHICS: Sex and gender issues

SIGNIFICANCE: In modern Western societies, homosexuality is often seen as both a set of practices and a fundamental category of identity. As a result, both individual acts or behaviors and the character of the person as a whole are made the subject of moral judgments. The appropriate content of such judgments is a matter of ongoing controversies that increasingly bring traditional religious values into conflict both with reformist religious movements and with secular egalitarian governmental and social values.

The human body, like the bodies of many animal species, cannot perpetuate itself by itself. Human reproduction requires the union of sperm and egg cells. When this union is initiated within the body of the female of the species, the involvement of the nervous system, especially the brain, results in an awareness of sensory pleasure. Social behavior is enhanced as a result of sexual sensory input into the central nervous system, especially if there is emotional input of care, gentleness, esteem, trust, and increased well-being associated with the outward physical actions. Some people perform heterosexual activities with their own sex; this is the case with homosexuals. Various disciplines such as psychology, psychiatry, theology, philosophy, sociology, anthropology, and the biological and medical sciences have attempted to gather information in order to understand homosexuality better.

HISTORY

The early legal codes of Mesopotamia do not mention homosexual acts, except for the provision in the code of Hammurabi (1726 B.C.E.) that concerns sons adopted by palace eunuchs. David Greenberg, in *The Construction of Homosexuality* (1988), comments that while some scholars have claimed that the second millennium B.C.E. Hittite law provided for male homosexual marriages, this concept is now found only in the writings of the nonspecialist. At about the same time in Babylon, there was an *Almanac of Incantations*, which contains prayers that bless the love of a man for a man as well as that of a man for a woman and a woman for a man. It is not easy to be sure about homosexuality in very ancient papyri from Egypt. Greenberg was unable to find any basis for a claim that new pharaohs were masturbated and sodomized by priests. It was believed, however, that homosexual intercourse with a god would be a great blessing.

Two fragmented manuscripts from the Sixth Dynasty, about 2272-2178 B.C.E., describe a conspiracy to obstruct a court hearing involving a homosexual relationship between a top royal administrator and his military general. In the Eighteenth Dynasty, a set of religious and mortuary spells called the *Book of the Dead* has the deceased proclaiming the absence of homosexual activity in his life, and a copy of the book prepared for women indicates the existence of lesbianism. The Hebrews address homosexuality, but there is much controversy over dating and interpretation. Homosexuality within Sodom and Gomorrah seems to be implied, and the suggestion of inhospitality as the chief sin of Sodom and Gomorrah could easily include homosexual rape.

Overt homosexuality seems to have been a part of life among the Greeks by the early part of the sixth century B.C.E. Kenneth James Dover, in *Greek Homosexuality* (1989), refers to homosexual expressions that were included in graffiti on the rocks of a Spartan colony, Thera; these graffiti may even be from the

seventh century B.C.E. There seem to be no elements of homosexuality in the poetry from the seventh century B.C.E., even though there are explicit heterosexual references. By the sixth century B.C.E., lesbian poetry from Sparta did exist, as did many indications of male homosexuality. Images on many vases depict every level of intimacy between males, including the touching of genitals.

The period between 570 and 470 B.C.E. seems to be the great age of erotic vase painting. Plays that date from 425 to 388 B.C.E. used homosexuality as material for humor, but this use seemed to decline after the mid-fourth century B.C.E. in Greece. Plato's philosophical writings extol homosexuality. There exists, however, a copy of a trial that dates to 346 B.C.E. in which a citizen of Athens, a politician, was prosecuted for prostituting himself to another man.

THE MIDDLE AGES AND LATER

During the Middle Ages, King Charles V promulgated the *Constitutio Criminalis Carolina* (1532) which punished homosexuality with death by fire. Jonathan Katz, in *Gay American History* (1976), reports that approximately one percent of the erotic Peruvian pottery that dates from 100-1200 C.E. depicts lesbianism. The writings of a Franciscan friar in 1565 refer to sodomy and lesbianism in Mexico. In writing between 1742 and 1750, missionaries of the Moravian church, a German Protestant denomination, describe the Native Americans of Pennsylvania, New York, and North Carolina as decent in public, yet committing unnatural sins in private. The term "berdache" was used for the homosexual male in some Native American tribes.

As early as 1924, prohomosexual organizations existed in the United States. The Chicago Society for Human Rights received its charter as a nonprofit organization on December 10 of that year. This group published two issues of "Friendship and Freedom" and, later, the monthly homosexual emancipation magazine *One*. Various novels and plays appeared that depicted homosexuals as a misjudged and misunderstood minority. In England, Radclyffe Hall wrote *The Well of Loneliness* (1928), which was published in New York after it was banned in England.

In California in 1948, Henry Hay founded the Mattachine Society, a homosexual emancipation organization for males. Two years after attending a meeting of the one-year-old lesbian organization the Daughters of Bilitis in San Francisco in 1956, Barbara Gittings founded the first East Coast chapter. She was the first editor of its periodical, *The Ladder*, which began publication in 1963. In 1961, Illinois led the way for a number of states to decriminalize homosexual activity in private between two consenting adults. In the summer of 1969, customers at the Stonewall Inn, a homosexual bar on Christopher Street in New York, rebelled against a police raid. This event is considered to mark the beginning of group rebellion, the beginning of the "Gay Rights" movement.

ETHICAL PRINCIPLES AND ISSUES

It is basic that every person be free to make decisions regarding sexual activity within the realm of others' rights. To make a free decision requires that the person has attained maturity and an appropriate level of knowledge. The acquisition of pertinent facts regarding homosexual behavior and reasoned reflection on its outcomes should precede one's decision at all levels of sexual intimacy. One's actions should also, at all times, respect the dignity of life.

Ethical issues in the area of homosexuality fall into one of two categories. They are either microcosmic, related to the concerns and care of the individual or a small unit of society, or they are macrocosmic, related to society on a large scale.

Allowing a person the freedom to make personal choices is one of the highest forms of respect. Some say that this microcosmic approach is the only sensible one. Each person may have programmed limits of freedom that are the result of genes, early family relationships, and cultural relationships. The uniqueness of the human nervous system makes possible an unusual awareness that seems to transcend the physical.

At the macrocosmic level, a society's treatment of minority or marginalized segments of its population is often a significant yardstick for measuring the justice or enlightenment of that society as a whole. Homosexuals, often the object of extremely strong opinions and feelings on the part of a heterosexual majority, are at risk of persecution unless a society takes explicit measures to prevent such treatment.

HEALTH CARE ALLOCATION

In Europe and the United States, late-nineteenth century physicians began to say that homosexuality was a problem for them to treat rather than something for judges, lawyers, and legislators to address. Karl Heinrich Ulrichs, impressed with the discovery that the early human embryo contained both male and female organs, then lost one set as development continued in the uterus, began using the term "third sex." Psychiatry, especially, began treating people who wanted to be helped. Some states in the United States adopted compulsory sterilization for homosexuals. Some homosexuals during the early twentieth century sought castration to stem unwanted homosexual desires.

The rise of the acquired immunodeficiency syndrome (AIDS) during the 1980's put the homosexual issue firmly into the health care realm. The medical world had not only the problem of dealing with the human immunodeficiency virus (HIV) but also that of treating the many health problems related to a suppressed immune system in the human: pneumonia, AIDS-related cancers such as Kaposi's sarcoma, and various types of brain involvement. Homosexual men are at particularly great risk of contracting AIDS.

RESEARCH

Psychological studies show that environmental influences, especially parental relationships before age two, may irreversibly determine a person's sexual identity. Sigmund Freud suggested that people who react negatively to homosexuals are exhibiting "reaction formation"; there is a desire but the superego forbids its expression. The transmission of this prohibition happened at an early age, but this does not explain the origin of the primary prohibition. Even though research into homosexuality continues, in 1975 the American Psychological Association deleted the word "homosexuality" from its *Diagnostic and Statistical Manual of Mental Disorders*.

Many religions attest the perversity of homosexual activities. To Jews, moral law and natural law are products of the one God, and nature clearly seems to intend that human males and females should engage in sexual relations only with each other. Not only Judaism and Christianity but also Islam and Zoroastrianism condemn homosexual actions. In the Hindu civilization, the Laws of Manu impose only a mild penance for homosexual conduct.

Sociological inquiry into homosexuality has attempted to find out how the homosexual stigma has produced dramatic consequences for these individuals. A landmark paper by Mary McIntosh, "The Homosexual Role," which was published in *Social Problems* in 1968, states that only when the homosexual person sees himself or herself in terms of a social category does that person start to act in terms of that role. The homosexual role is not universal, even though homosexual experiences are. In 1978, Barry Adam presented the results of his study in *The Survival of Domination: Inferiorization and Daily Life.* He shows that gays have restricted opportunities, their lives are dominated by unacceptance, and their mental lives are devalued. Not all sociologists, however, consider homosexuality an issue of social concern that is worth their research time and effort.

Anthropological studies on homosexuality are sparse and do not give a clear picture. In most societies, however, sexual activity takes place in private. In 1976, Gwen Broude and Sarah Greene, in their article "Cross-Cultural Codes on Twenty Sexual Attitudes and Practices," published in *Ethnology,* suggested that little homosexuality is reported because it is not customary to do so. Information on the frequency of homosexuality is given for only 70 of 186 societies in the Human Relations Area File's Standard Sample, and there are only 42 reports on attitudes toward homosexuality. Native reluctance to share such information with Western, white anthropologists has been reported. Many anthropologists have been men, so questions on lesbian activities have been prevented by norms of propriety. If sex is a part of religious ritual, that can be a further reason for secrecy.

Scientific research has shown that hormones, chemicals circulating in the blood, have a profound effect upon sexuality, but human sexual activity is not totally controlled by hormones and cycles, as it is in many animals. In 1982, Christine de LaCoste-Utamsing and Ralph Holloway reported, in *Science,* the presence of sexual dimorphism in the part of the brain called the corpus callosum.

In 1985, a sexually dimorphic nucleus, or area that consists of a collection of nerve cell bodies (gray matter) surrounded by the white matter of the brain, was reported in the hypothalamus, a primitive part of the

brain that functions in eating as well as in reproductive activities. In 1991, Simon LeVay published in *Science* the results of his study of forty-one human brains. Six were from heterosexual women, sixteen were from heterosexual men, one was from a bisexual man, and eighteen were from homosexual men. Four nuclei in the anterior part of the hypothalamus (interstitial nuclei 1, 2, 3, and 4) were studied. Differences were found only in the interstitial nuclei 3 in these postmortem brains. Nucleus 3 was twice the size in the homosexual men compared to its size in the heterosexual men. The size of this nucleus in the homosexual men was about equal to that found in the heterosexual women. The sample size used in this study was small. Also, it is not known whether nucleus 3 was larger at birth, became larger in early childhood, or became larger as the result of homosexual activity. The last possibility is important to consider, because the projections, or dendrites, from

Homosexuality in Broadway Dramas

Although often obliquely presented, homosexuality surfaced on the American stage as early as the 1920's. Gay elements pervaded such plays as Lillian Hellman's *The Children's Hour* (1934) and plays by Tennessee Williams, including *The Glass Menagerie* (1944), *A Streetcar Named Desire* (1947), *Cat on a Hot Tin Roof* (1955), and *Suddenly Last Summer* (1958). However, it was not until the late 1960's that gay themes became more overt in dramatic productions. In 1967, New York State officially lifted its edict banning homosexuality from the stage. That edict had long violated the First Amendment rights of both authors who wished to write about life's realities and audiences who wished to see such plays.

In 1968, one year after the New York ban was lifted, Mart Crowley's overtly homosexual play, *Boys in the Band,* opened on Broadway. A quarter century later, Jonathan Tolins's *The Twilight of the Golds* (1993) presented audiences with the ethical dilemma of a homophobic family whose daughter's unborn fetus tests positive for the "gay gene," raising thorny questions about whether to abort the fetus. The play asked the question of whether being gay is so horrible that it justifies killing an unborn infant. Meanwhile, other thoughtful dramatic presentations on screen as well as on stage have posed complex ethical questions and helped to cast homosexuality in a context related to issues many families with homosexual members confront.

pyramidal cells in the cortex of young mammals increase with sensory input.

Some studies of the sexual preferences of twins have shown a high correlation between them. In one study, 52 percent of identical twins were homosexual, compared with 22 percent of fraternal twins and 11 percent of adopted brothers. Again, the sample size is small (only 161 sets of twins).

NATURE OF HOMOSEXUALITY

Science has not shed definitive light on the physical basis of homosexuality, although biologists tend to look to genetics for an answer. History seems to indicate that homosexuality was a part of ancient civilizations, but it was especially banned by the Hebrew religious code, which separated homosexuals from others who were called pagans. The Hebrew evaluation of homosexuality was adopted by the Christian community, and especially, by the Roman Catholic Church, which holds that each person can be respected even though the actions of the homosexual person are difficult to judge and are not approved. There have always been those who have been both heterosexual and homosexual in their activities. The members of the "gay movement" want homosexuality to be a way of life that is accepted and considered equal to heterosexuality in every way.

ETHICAL DECISION MAKING

This activity involves both content and process. For the individual, there needs to be a clear understanding of the preference to seek sexual pleasure with the same sex and the performance of the action at whatever level of intimacy it may be. One needs to reflect upon the effect of sexual sensory input into the central nervous system, and especially the human brain, with its ability to remember, imagine, and affect the entire person. The process might also include answering some of the following questions. How do my actions relate to the dignity of my personhood? Do my actions show responsible stewardship of the human species? Does this pleasure ensure my future health and well-being? Do my actions promote the common good?

PUBLIC POLICY

Greenberg relates governmental laws regarding homosexual activity to the rise of capitalism. The development of the political power of the working class resulted in the state's assuming a greater role in civil society. As the industrial revolution continued, educational requirements for jobs increased. The public education of both male and female children caused children to be considered asexual. By 1885, the law put English children into a category that was out of the sexual reach of adults. In the United States, statutory penalties for homosexual activity were enacted. For example, the 1881 *Revised Statutes for the State of Indiana*, section 100 of chapter 32, states,

> Whoever commits the abominable and detestable crime against nature, by having carnal knowledge of a man or a beast, or who, being male, carnally knows any man or any woman through the anus, and whoever entices, allures, instigates or aids any person under the age of twenty-one years to commit masturbation or self-pollution, is guilty of sodomy, and, upon conviction thereof, shall be imprisoned in the State prison not more than fourteen years nor less than two years.

Between 1880 and 1890 the number of people in prison in the United States for homosexual activity increased 350 percent compared to a 25 percent increase in population.

During the 1970's, attempts were made to change public policies on this matter in the United States. On June 7, 1977, in Dade County, Florida, a referendum to ban discrimination regarding housing, employment, and public accommodations based on a person's public statements regarding affectual or sexual preference failed to pass. A similar bill in New York City had been defeated in the city council by a vote of twenty-two to nineteen on May 23, 1974. Many laws that favor professed homosexuals did pass, however, especially in Washington, D.C., and San Francisco, California. In many situations, no questions are asked regarding one's sexual preference, and during the early years of the twenty-first century, San Francisco and other major cities were even openly condoning gay marriages.

Rose Ann Bast
Updated by the editors

FURTHER READING

Ball, Carlos A. *The Morality of Gay Rights: An Exploration in Political Philosophy.* New York:

Routledge, 2003. This book is simultaneously an analysis of current debates in gay rights and a demonstration that these debates are an important component of contemporary political and legal philosophy.

Dover, K. J. *Greek Homosexuality.* Cambridge, Mass.: Harvard University Press, 1989. This well-researched book contains a section of analyzed photographs of art objects to support the statements made.

Foucault, Michel. *The History of Sexuality.* Translated by Robert Hurley. New York: Vintage, 1990. Foucault famously argues that, while homosexual behavior has of course always occurred, the homosexual person—that is, homosexuality as a fundamental category of identity—was an invention of the nineteenth century.

Greenberg, David F. *The Construction of Homosexuality.* Chicago: University of Chicago Press, 1988. An extensive treatment of ancient and modern homosexuality. There are 113 pages of references at the end of the book.

Horgan, John. "Eugenics Revisited." *Scientific American* 268 (June, 1993): 122-131. Twin studies are reported to have found about 50 percent predisposition to male or female homosexuality, but these findings are disputed.

Katz, Jonathan. *Gay American History.* New York: Thomas Y. Crowell, 1976. This is an unique documentary—a collection of passages organized under the topics of trouble, treatment, women, Native/gay Americans, and resistance, with an introduction to each section.

LeVay, Simon. "A Difference in Hypothalamic Structure Between Heterosexual and Homosexual Men." *Science* 253 (August 30, 1991): 1034-1037. This report is very technical. It is the original report of a difference between an area of the brain in heterosexual and homosexual men.

Mirkes, Renée. "Science, Homosexuality, and the Church." *Ethics and Medics* 17 (June, 1992): 1-3. This article gives a view of the Roman Catholic Church's approach to homosexuality.

Plummer, Kenneth, ed. *The Making of the Modern Homosexual.* Totowa, N.J.: Barnes & Noble, 1981. This collection of eight articles by different authors ends with an appendix that suggests a research format for doing one's own research and a listing of research sources.

SEE ALSO: Acquired immunodeficiency syndrome (AIDS); *Dronenburg v. Zech*; Gay rights; Hammurabi's code; Homophobia; National Gay and Lesbian Task Force; Stonewall Inn riots.

Honesty

DEFINITION: Fair and truthful conduct, free from deception or fraud

TYPE OF ETHICS: Personal and social ethics

SIGNIFICANCE: Honesty is the one virtue most commonly subjected to situational ethics. While dishonest acts that cause harm are generally treated as clear ethical violations, dishonest acts that protect the happiness of others may be condoned or even recommended, and honesty itself is often deemed embarrassing or even morally questionable depending on its context.

As a virtue, honesty belongs to the ethical *genus* of justice. Other concepts relative to honesty are dignity, uprightness, fidelity to the truth, and chastity in words and actions. Because they harm other people, the opposites of honesty are generally condemned; among those opposites are lying, dishonesty, sham, covetousness, unscrupulousness, inaccuracy, treachery, and infidelity in words and actions.

DISHONESTY, SOCIETY, AND INDIVIDUALS

All groups, including the family, the clan, and the larger society as a whole, must practice honesty, for to do otherwise would undermine the group by destroying mutual confidence. Subsequently, the group would disintegrate. Treachery of any kind can flourish between hostile groups but never within a group, for it scatters people and breaks down groups.

Dishonesty is a type of war in disguise. Unless honesty and truth are observed and practiced by people, no one can trust anyone else and no one can know what to expect from others. Society would then fragment and—as Thomas Hobbes mentioned long ago—revert to a "state of nature," a war of one against all and all against all. Life, Hobbes said, would become "solitary, poor, nasty, brutish, and short." Another philosopher held that falsehood was the worst of "evils" because its negative consequences—including the end of society—would be so great.

Many types of dishonesty exist. One type involves lying in an attempt to deceive, and prevarication is probably the most effective form of lying. Prevarication is the attempt to leave a false impression by using words that in some other sense might be true. The best example of prevarication is the case of the two diplomats who promise that their two countries will remain at peace so long as they stand upon "this earth." Immediately after such agreement, both diplomats go to a private place to remove their shoes and pour the sand out of them. Thus can a lie be told with words that are technically "true" but are false in context.

A lie can be told without words—by means of gestures or silence. A forger lies with the pen, a medical quack with fraudulent prescriptions, a smuggler by "expert" packing, and the pickpocket with his hands. Robbers and thieves are also, in a sense, liars, for they are dishonest when they take money or goods that rightfully belong to someone else. Such lies and dishonesty in effect break the implied promise that civilized people make to one another to be truthful and to cause no harm.

In addition to harming others, the dishonest one also hurts himself or herself. The liar's attacks on society wear it down, and as society "loses," so, too, do its individuals. Furthermore, dishonesty tears away at the character of the offender. Once the dishonest one is caught in a crime or even a simple lie, society damns him, and no one will ever believe him again, not even when he speaks the truth. Additionally, many dishonest people eventually start to believe their own lies or justify their crimes, whatever those crimes may be. Someone, for example, might steal goods and "justify" it by saying, "The rich owe me this much" or "Society owes me at least this much." When such thinking occurs, internal honesty is replaced by internal dishonesty and self-deceit. Since inner truthfulness is a key to moral growth and personal vigor, the dishonest person throws away his or her chances to achieve that growth and vigor.

DEVELOPING A PHILOSOPHY OF HONESTY

First, the question of relativism must be resolved, and one type of relativism involves recognition that different cultures have differing customs and mores. Different cultures may also have different moral values. One need look no further than Eskimo society. The men not only practice polygamy but also share their wives with male guests, for such behavior is considered the proper sign of hospitality. Furthermore, a dominant male might also have access to all other men's wives. Eskimos also practice infanticide, with female newborns being most likely to be killed. Eskimo society also approves of leaving old people, who have ceased to be productive, out in the snow to die. While American laypersons might be shocked by such practices, relativists are not. They argue that there is no standard "right" and "wrong" and that moral rules vary from society to society. In other words, cultural relativists challenge the view that there are universal moral truths.

Despite the arguments described above, many thinkers remain critical of relativism. First, critics contend that relativists confuse what people simply believe or want with objective truth. For example, if nations make war to enslave other people, is that war justified simply because the aggressive nation believes that it is? During the World War II era, Nazi Germans had elaborate reasons to justify the murder of millions of Jews. Were such exterminations justified simply because the Nazis thought that they were? Similarly, in some societies of the past, people believed that the world was flat, but does that mean that there is no objective truth in geography? No. Similarly, there are objective truths in moral philosophy, and honesty is one of them.

Cultural relativism's "big brother" is relativism in general. Some thinkers hold that there should be no fixed principles to guide human words and actions. According to them, everything is relative and ethical decisions must be rendered on a case-by-case basis. The idea that all is relative is, however, a fixed principle. Everything is not relative, and certain ethics *should* be obeyed by all. An ethical philosophy of honesty, for example, allows but few examples wherein it is "right" to be dishonest or to lie.

The case of the "inquiring murderer," however, does bedevil a thinker: Jane Doe sees a man running down the street on a dark, rainy night. As the man turns a corner and disappears, a second man rushes up. Jane notices that the second man is carrying a gun at just the moment when he asks Jane, "Which way did he go?" Should Jane tell the truth? That course might lead to the murder of another human being. Here, one must conclude that no, in this case Jane should lie because saving a human life outweighs Jane's responsibility to tell the truth to an armed man.

Said another way, one duty that Jane owes humanity is greater than another. Thus, there are times when honesty and dishonesty are relative, but those cases are few and far between. Only a person's strongest powers of reason can discern the rare occasions when it is correct to be dishonest.

PHILOSOPHY OF IMMANUEL KANT

Exceptions aside, honesty in most avenues of life is still the best policy. One really needs to look no further than the philosophy of Immanuel Kant to justify that policy. Kant held that there were certain absolute rules—called "categorical imperatives"—that were not relative and that did not change no matter what the circumstances. Basically, his imperatives called for people to think, speak, and act only in ways that would be acceptable if they were mandated as universal laws to be followed by all people everywhere; that is, people should ask, before they decide on an action, should my behavior become a universal law? Thus, is it permissible for one to steal the money or goods of another? No, because if everyone became a thief, civilized society would crumble. Is it permissible to lie (except in a life-threatening emergency such as that of the aforementioned Jane Doe)? No, because if lying became a universal law, the war of all against all would start. Kant's imperatives would also ban such acts as armed robbery, murder, adultery, incest, and so on. Except for certain moral dilemmas, Kant's system seems to work well as a general guide for determining honesty: Tell the truth, do not rob or steal, do not kill others, do not physically or mentally assault others, and so on.

Kant's lines of reasoning are as follows: You should take only those actions that conform to rules that you are willing to adopt as universal laws. If you are dishonest, you are announcing that universal dishonesty is permissible. The last point is absurd, however, because it is a self-defeating proposition. If all people were liars, cheats, and thieves, people would stop trying to believe one another, and it would do no good to be a dishonest liar, because one would not be believed. Therefore, it is best not to lie, cheat, or steal.

Kant's categorical imperatives seem even more correct if one considers other philosophical doctrines. For example, some thinkers still hold that religion is the key to truthfulness, honesty, and right action: Simply do what God commands. Such a view does little, however, to guide atheists or agnostics. Kant's imperatives do.

The utilitarian philosophy is also unacceptable as a replacement for Kant's imperatives. The three founders of utilitarian thought—David Hume, Jeremy Bentham, and John Stuart Mill—and their followers held that people should be guided by the principle of happiness and the greatest good for the greatest number. To make people happy was the greatest good, and questions about honesty and dishonesty would become the servants of the greatest good; that is, dishonesty could be practiced if it made people happier. To give Hume, Bentham, and Mill their due, all three were reformers who were trying to make English law and society more just, but their philosophy falters on the issue of dishonesty. For example, consider the person who breaks into a home and steals most of the family's treasures, including jewelry, televisions, personal computers, microwave oven, and money. The thief next distributes the goods to his many friends. If one were a strict, no-exceptions-allowed utilitarian, one would have to conclude that the theft was acceptable because the thief made more people happy than unhappy.

Utilitarianism in its extreme form is hedonism, a philosophy that justifies behavior based on how people "feel." If what one "feels" is the criterion for action, then all is allowed—even dishonesty. Additionally, other virtues might well disappear if they conflict with hedonism, virtues including, but not limited to, justice, the rights of other human beings, and truthfulness.

HONESTY AND DISHONESTY IN MODERN AMERICAN SOCIETY

Although many millions of Americans are most likely honest in all their endeavors, if one looks at public life, one must conclude that it is a rare public official who tells the truth. Scandal has been the order of the day for decades. In the Cold War era, for example, some individuals in the state department, the military, and the Central Intelligence Agency (CIA) were dishonest with the American people in striving to make them terrified of the Soviet Union, which was only a regional power at best. During the Vietnam War, the same agencies were regularly dishonest in what they told the people. Then, when the Gulf War was being fought during the 1990's, generals "managed" the news about the war, leaving an impression that the American victory was greater than it really was. It was only later that investigators discovered, for example, that "friendly fire" killed many soldiers and that American missiles had not been as accurate as the generals had said. As the turn of a new century neared, many Americans became so jaded that they took it for granted that the government would be dishonest and would lie about most military matters.

Dishonesty is also rampant in American internal affairs and has been for decades. By 1952, despite his own best efforts, President Harry Truman's administration became hopelessly corrupt; that fact helped the Republicans retake the Oval Office, but the Dwight D. Eisenhower administration had its scandals, too. President John F. Kennedy contributed to the trend of dishonesty among public figures. He received the Pulitzer Prize for *Profiles in Courage* (1955). The problem? He did not write it. His staff, headed by Theodore Sorensen, did. Next, President Lyndon B. Johnson did his best with the internal War on Poverty, but he lied about the shooting war in Vietnam. One need say little about the Richard M. Nixon administration except one word—Watergate. On and on the trend goes. During the 1992 political cam-

paign, president-to-be Bill Clinton was less than candid about certain matters in his private life. His immediate predecessors, Ronald Reagan and George Bush, were no better; both became mired in the "Irangate" arms-for-hostages scandal.

Dishonesty also flourished in Congress, especially during the 1980's, as one scandal after another occurred. For example, in their bank, members of Congress regularly engaged in the practice of check "kiting." In their post office, other irregularities occurred. In their restaurant, members of Congress charged but refused to pay their bills—this while voting themselves such massive pay raises that they could disengage themselves altogether from the concerns of the lower and middle classes. Even though some dishonest members of Congress were "retired" after the scandals, many of the guilty returned to Washington to continue their corrupt careers. Sex scandals, racism, gender discrimination—all these ills can also be laid at the feet of Congress, and all such ills have an aspect of dishonesty about them.

In the modern United States, it is not only politicians who are dishonest. Before he left office in 1961, President Eisenhower warned about the development of the "military-industrial" complex. Indeed, the alliance between the military and big business grew by leaps and bounds, and dishonesty flourished as many defense contractors defrauded the government. Worse, many businesspeople seemed to lose whatever honesty they might have had. During the 1980's and 1990's, for example, Americans had to watch the spectacle of the savings and loans scandals. For decades, taxpayers will pay billions of dollars and therefore be punished for the criminal acts of a handful of dishonest bankers.

Religionists are also numerous among the dishonest. In front of a television audience that numbered millions of people, Protestant fundamentalist Jimmy Swaggert thundered against sin and actually laughed heartily about all the awful tortures that sinners would receive when they all went to Hell. He said that shortly before he was caught more than once be-

U.S. marshals escort former televangelism superstar Jimmy Bakker away from his attorney's office after he was arrested for fraud in 1989. (AP/Wide World Photos)

ing unfaithful to his wife by frequenting prostitutes. Jim Bakker was a "man of God" who built a ministry of millions of both people and dollars, only to be convicted later of fraud and sent to prison. Yet Protestants were not the only guilty religionists. Newspapers reported one case after another of Roman Catholic priests who molested children or adults, while Jewish rabbis heading schools that received federal and state money enrolled imaginary students to receive more money.

In almost any field that one surveys, dishonesty exists, and society is in danger of decline as trust is increasingly lost. Worse, when the young see the dishonest behavior of preachers, lawyers, physicians, politicians, and so on, they come to believe that dishonesty is acceptable. When those children grow into young adults, they may become corrupted by tempting situations wherein they must choose between honesty and dishonesty.

CONCLUSIONS

All people who wish to live ethically must understand the consequences of dishonesty. First, it threatens all of society. If dishonesty becomes widespread enough, civilization itself will decline. Second, dishonesty also threatens the dishonest person by slowly working to destroy that person's character, integrity, and honor. It may well be time to reembrace Kant and to declare that of his categorical imperatives, the imperative that demands honesty is one with the greatest reason on its side. Dishonesty can never become universal or "natural" law, because it is self-defeating in the end.

James Smallwood

FURTHER READING

Cabot, Richard C. *Honesty.* New York: Macmillan, 1938. After providing several chapters on the nature of honesty, this study focuses on honesty and dishonesty in various career fields, including education, science, industry, and government.

_____. *The Meaning of Right and Wrong.* Rev. ed. New York: Macmillan, 1936. Like Cabot's *Honesty*, this volume discusses similar themes, including dishonesty and its harmful consequences to all.

Johnson, Larry, and Bob Phillips. *Absolute Honesty: Building a Corporate Culture That Values Straight Talk and Rewards Integrity.* New York: American Management Association, 2003. Written in response to the high-profile corporate scandals of the early twenty-first century, this book approaches honesty from a practical standpoint. Recommends policies and procedures for ensuring the honesty and integrity of employees at every level of a corporation.

Greider, William. *Who Will Tell the People: The Betrayal of American Democracy.* New York: Simon & Schuster, 1992. A journalist rather than a trained philosopher, Greider nevertheless subjected Americans to an honesty "test" and found that fraud, deception, and dishonor were rife in American life—including a less-than-ethical national government, giant corporations driven by greed, and bankers who stole money from their own depositors.

Payne, Robert. *The Corrupt Society: From Ancient Greece to Present-Day America.* New York: Praeger, 1975. Although he wrote almost twenty years ago, Payne focused on dishonesty through history while emphasizing frauds and falsehoods in modern American life. Payne dedicated this book to President Richard Nixon.

Rachels, James. *The Elements of Moral Philosophy.* 3d ed. Boston: McGraw-Hill, 1999. This author surveys topics such as morality, honesty, and relativism in ethical philosophy. He also examines religion, utilitarianism, and the social contract and discusses them in relation to ethics.

Riley, Sue Spayth. *How to Generate Values in Young Children: Integrity, Honesty, Individuality, Self-Confidence, and Wisdom.* Washington, D.C.: National Association for the Education of Young Children, 1984. Although this volume targets the parents and teachers of young children, all would benefit from examining it. Spayth's subtitle expresses the most important themes that the book discusses.

Taylor, A. E. *The Problem of Conduct: A Study in the Phenomenolgy of Ethics.* New York: Macmillan, 1901. Dishonesty and "the liar" are Taylor's topics. He points out, among other things, the absurdity of the liar, who must assume that everyone else is honest and truthful.

SEE ALSO: Cheating; Corporate scandal; Corruption; Lying; Orwell, George; Perjury; Relativism; Situational ethics; Truth; Utilitarianism; Watergate scandal.

Honor

DEFINITION: Consciousness of self-worth and corresponding code of behavior thought particularly appropriate to individuals whose self-esteem is grounded in their ancestry and breeding

TYPE OF ETHICS: Personal and social ethics

SIGNIFICANCE: A worldly and exclusive ethic, honor was particularly compatible with traditional, hierarchical societies in which allegiance was directed to individuals rather than to an impersonal state governed by abstract law.

Honor is an elusive term whose meaning has undergone considerable change from antiquity to the present. It refers to a personal sense of worth and dignity as well as to a corresponding code of behavior or standard of conduct expected by one's peers. Honors are marks of approbation or recognition bestowed by virtue of one's actions in accordance with such codes and standards.

Some social scientists contend that honor is universal, found in virtually all societies. Some scholars refer to "primal honor," as evident in pagan and Indo-European societies, signifying a code of behavior that emphasized valor, the reputation of family and group with which the individual identified, male virility and ferocity, and loyalty. Primal honor, as the term suggests, was archetypal and universal, the moral property of the whole community and consequently neither class-based nor elite-based. Above all, it valued the opinion of others as a gauge of self-esteem and worth. It was, however, an exclusively masculine property. Presumably, the more traditional the society, the more visible would be the qualities of primal honor.

Literary scholars and historians are more inclined to confine honor to Western civilization, as an ethic first evident in antiquity, altered in the Middle Ages, and subsequently transformed during the Renaissance and later. Honor's primal qualities were transmuted by the medieval Roman Catholic Church in the cult of chivalry that elevated the lady. When applied to the lady, honor referred to purity or chastity. Nevertheless, if a lady's honor was impugned, it remained a man's responsibility to defend it. Renaissance humanists joined learning, manners, and civility to the earlier code and produced, especially in the Anglo-Saxon tradition, a more reified code of honor. With its emphasis upon inner worth along with external expressions of respect and esteem, this more elevated variety of honor was exclusive, as opposed to primal honor's alleged universality. The historian Jacob Burckhardt referred to the Renaissance concept of honor as "an enigmatic mixture of conscience and egoism."

In medieval England, an honor was originally a large estate granted by the crown. It was a physical property that was the outward sign of a man's dignity and was heritable. While honor's meaning was subsequently translated from land to character, its heritability was retained, as was its elitist associations. Honor was a quality associated with the hereditary ruling elite and was to be emulated. Thomas Hobbes referred to honor as "the opinion of power." Edmund Burke considered honor a quality "to be found in the men the best born, and the best bred, and in those posses'ed of rank which raises them in their own esteem, and in the esteem of others, and posses'ed of hereditary settlement in the same place, which secures with a hereditary wealth, a hereditary inspection." Honor, then, was a peculiarly aristocratic quality.

While some critics of the Scottish Enlightenment professed that honor was universal, the examples they provided of its operation were invariably drawn from the world of privilege. Even such critics of honor as William Paley, who saw it as an instrument of social control, defined honor as an aristocratic code that "regulates the duties *betwixt equals.*"

THE "MAN OF HONOR"

Insofar as a man of honor sought the rewards of approbation, honor was a worldly ethic that was often at odds with the ascetic or other-worldly aspirations sometimes associated with a higher morality. The man of honor subscribed to a code distinct from and sometimes in conflict with the laws of God or the laws of his country. A sensitivity to personal reputation was foremost, and, especially in early modern European history, the "point of honor" became the duel, despite condemnation of the practice by both Church and state law.

Many theorists from the Renaissance to the Enlightenment sought to reconcile honor with public virtue, particularly in the form of benevolence. For such theorists as Adam Smith, Baron de Montesquieu, and David Hume, aristocratic honor was necessary for the preservation and transmission of liberty. Nevertheless, the association of honor with traditional societies that valued privilege and patronage resulted in its attenuation and further transformation once those traditional societies were replaced by the modern industrial state.

The French Revolution's assault upon the old regime's world of privilege implied a rejection of the code of aristocratic honor that had been linked with monarchy, the king having been the "fount of honor." The quality that had once been personal, however, having been associated with serving the monarch, came to be associated with serving the impersonal nation. Hence, in the nineteenth and twentieth centuries, the concept of national honor became prominent. It was not an altogether new concept, since varieties of collective honor persisted when men of rank identified with their families or clans. Moreover, while honor as a personal ethic characteristic of elites was being weakened, the collective honor associated with those elites was strengthened.

When aristocracies controlled their nations, national honor was a projection of their personal honor. In the nineteenth and twentieth centuries, the concept of national honor acquired mass appeal, as the nation displaced the individual as the object of loyalty. Numerous statesmen appealed to national honor in the diplomacy of the countries they represented, and the phrase "peace with honor" was frequently used to justify a particular policy or arrangement. It has been invoked by such disparate figures as British prime ministers Benjamin Disraeli, after the Congress of Berlin in 1879, and Neville Chamberlain, when he returned from his meeting with Adolf Hitler at Munich in 1938. In seeking to conclude the Vietnam War, President Richard Nixon and Secretary of State Henry Kissinger claimed to bring peace with honor.

Abraham D. Kriegel

FURTHER READING

Best, Geoffrey. *Honour Among Men and Nations: Transformations of an Idea.* Toronto: University of Toronto Press, 1981.

O'Neill, Barry. *Honor, Symbols, and War.* Ann Arbor: University of Michigan Press, 1999.

Peristiany, J. G. *Honour and Shame: The Values of a Mediterranean Society.* Chicago: University of Chicago Press, 1966.

Pitt-Rivers, Julian. "Honor." In *The International Encyclopedia of the Social Sciences*, edited by David L. Sills. Vol. 6. New York: Macmillan, 1968-1991.

Spierenburg, Pieter. *Men and Violence: Gender, Honor, and Rituals in Modern Europe and America.* Columbus: Ohio State University Press, 1998.

Watson, Curtis. *Shakespeare and the Renaissance Concept of Honor.* Princeton N.J.: Princeton University Press, 1960.

Wyatt-Brown, Bertram. *Southern Honor: Ethics and Behavior in the Old South.* New York: Oxford University Press, 1982.

SEE ALSO: Bushido; Chivalry; Choiceless choices; Dignity; Elitism; Integrity; Self-love; Self-respect.

Honor systems and codes

DEFINITION: Obligations that members of groups—such as students—accept by taking oaths binding them to follow group rules without external compulsion

DATE: First student honor code adopted at the University of Virginia in 1842

TYPE OF ETHICS: Personal and social ethics

SIGNIFICANCE: Honor codes establish principles of behavior within certain social contexts, but such principles may conflict with universal theories of ethics based upon deontological or utilitarian concepts of morality.

By pledging to follow a code of honor, members of a group expect to be trusted on the basis of their oaths to carry out certain obligations under any circumstances. For instance, the medieval code of chivalry and the Bushido, the code of Samurai warriors, both maintained that vassals should remain loyal to their lords. Failure to live up to such fealty was considered the highest form of disgrace. Similarly, the young men of many North American Indian societies took oaths never to retreat in the face of danger, and the *mafioso* (men of honor) are sworn to a code of silence about the criminal activities of their brethren.

Students sworn to college and university honor codes accept responsibility for the academic integrity of their classrooms. They pledge to uphold the

---

Academic Honor Codes on the Web

The Web site of the Center for Academic Integrity (www.academicintegrity.org) offers links to Web sites of more than one hundred member colleges and universities that have honor systems. Most of these sites offer the complete texts of the institutions' honor codes and explanations of their enforcement policies. Among the types of information found on these pages are detailed definitions of cheating, plagiarism, collusion, and other offenses, as well as descriptions of the positive behaviors that students are expected to exhibit.

---

codes by conducting themselves honestly in all grading activities and by reporting any violations of fellow students (under nontoleration clauses). Faculty members recognize student honor codes by not proctoring exams and allowing students to adjudicate by themselves any charges of cheating. Under some university honor codes, students found guilty of academic dishonesty, no matter what the violation, are punished by expulsion. Single sanctions for all degrees of cheating rest upon the idea that what is being punished is not merely a particular violation of classroom rules, but the breaking of one's pledge to the code itself.

Nontoleration clauses and single-sanction punishments are two ethically controversial features of academic honor codes. Turning in classmates for violations may appear to be a kind of betrayal, while single-sanctions punish both trivial and serious violations with the same severity. Around the turn of the twenty-first century, extensive cheating scandals at honor code schools and at the U.S. military academies raised questions about the effectiveness of strict honor codes. In response, many universities have adopted "modified" honor systems, which do not necessarily require reporting violations and that offer a variety of punishments.

Bland Addison

FURTHER READING

Gould, David B. L. *A Handbook for Developing and Sustaining Honor Codes*. Atlanta, Ga.: Council for Spiritual and Ethical Education, 1999.

McCabe, Donald L., L. K. Trevino, and K. D. Butterfield. "Academic Integrity in Honor Code and Non-Honor Code Environments." *Journal of Higher Education* 70 (1999): 211-234.

SEE ALSO: Applied ethics; Character; Cheating; Chivalry; College applications; Ethical codes of organizations; Honesty; Honor; Loyalty oaths; Perjury; Professional ethics; Promises.

Huineng

IDENTIFICATION: Chinese Buddhist monk
BORN: 638, Southwest Guangdong, China
DIED: 713, Guangdong, China
TYPE OF ETHICS: Religious ethics
SIGNIFICANCE: The sixth patriarch of Chinese Chan (Japanese, Zen) Buddhism, Huineng taught that liberation consisted not in overcoming desire but in not producing it in the first place.

Both the life and thought of Huineng are recounted in records that are legendary and polemical, so certainty about either is impossible. It is likely, however, that Huineng came from an impoverished family and went to the East Mountain in 674 to study Chan with Hongren, quickly gaining enlightenment. Huineng succeeded his master at Hongren's death, becoming the sixth patriarch. He emphasized that enlightenment came all at once. Subsequent to enlightenment, one engaged in various exercises to develop what had been born or discovered. Huineng was monistic but did not care to elaborate that monism. Consequently, he believed that good and evil, while contradictory, are only temporal realities. Behind that dualism lay a unity out of which the enlightened person acted. The implication of this idea is that acts are not so much right or wrong as measured by some standard as they are in harmony or out of harmony with the unity of things. Differently put, since there is no difference between oneself and others, one harms oneself if one harms others. If one realizes that there is no self, one will produce no desire.

Paul L. Redditt

SEE ALSO: Bodhidharma; Buddhist ethics; Dōgen; Zen.

Human Genome Project

IDENTIFICATION: International project launched by the U.S. National Institutes of Health and Department of Energy whose goal was to build a complete sequence map of the entire human genome, locating all the genes on their respective chromosomes

DATE: Begun in 1990

TYPE OF ETHICS: Bioethics

SIGNIFICANCE: While the potential for good held out by the project is vast, it is recognized that firm legal, ethical guidelines for the use of human genetic information must be established and enforced.

The Human Genome Project began in 1990 with the goal of better understanding the human genetic makeup and providing a free database to be used for the common good of everyone. The project released its first draft of the human genome sequence in February, 2001. The chemical structure of each gene sequence provides scientists with the necessary information to identify which genes are associated with specific human traits and with diseases such as cancer, diabetes, cardiovascular, arthritis, Alzheimer's, deafness, and blindness. Through ethical use of the human genome information, the hope is that serious diseases will be treated more effectively and eventually eliminated through the development of new drugs and gene therapy.

Although the results of the Human Genome Project are based on the principles of science and technology, the project itself is permeated with complex ramifications related to politics, public opinion, public relations, economics, and ethics. Issues of genetic privacy, genetic discrimination, and genetic determinism arise. One fundamental question that has

André Rosenthal of Germany's Human Genome Project explains genome sequencing at a press conference in June, 2000. (AP/Wide World Photos)

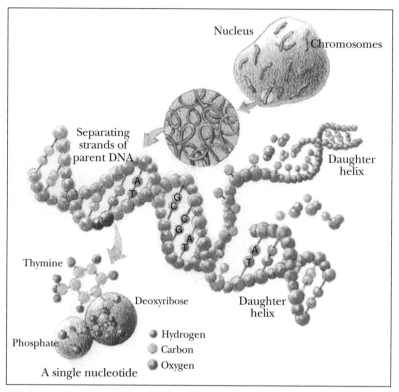

This illustration from the Human Genome Program of the Department of Energy shows the basic context of DNA replication from the cellular nucleus, which contains the chromosomes, to the separation of DNA strands and their replication at the molecular and atomic levels into daughter helixes. (U.S. Department of Energy Human Genome Program, http://www.ornl.gov/hgmis.)

Genetic information derived from the Human Genome Project is expected to help future researchers gain a better understanding of the human system, including particular organs, tissues, and the complete chemistry of life. As this progress continues, scientists and ethicists have pointed out that legal and ethical guidelines must be established, updated, and enforced to prevent the misuse of human genetics from leading to the abuse of human beings. The U.S. Department of Energy and the National Institutes of Health have devoted about 5 percent of their annual Human Genome Project funding toward studying and dealing with the ethical, legal, and social issues associated with the availability of human genetic information. Positive benefits of Human Genome research must be maximized, while social, economic, and psychological harm must be minimized.

Alvin K. Benson

arisen is who should be genetically tested to determine his or her risk for contracting a debilitating disease and what should be done to prevent the misuse of such information. People undergoing genetic testing might face significant risks by jeopardizing their employment or insurance status. Since the process involves genetic information, such risks could also be easily extended to other family members. Confidentiality and privacy of an individual's genetic formation must be protected.

Other ethical concerns raised by the project include human cloning and the possible manipulation of genes to produce superior traits. Animal cloning has proven to be inefficient and often produces animals with debilitating conditions. Many scientists and physicians strongly believe that it would be unethical to attempt human cloning.

FURTHER READING

Munson, Ronald. *Outcome Uncertain: Cases and Contexts in Bioethics*. Belmont, Calif.: Thomson/Wadsworth, 2003.

Sulston, John, and Georgina Ferry. *The Common Thread: A Story of Science, Politics, Ethics and the Human Genome*. New York: Bantam, 2002.

Zilinskas, Raymond A., and Peter J. Balint, eds. *The Human Genome Project and Minority Communities: Ethical, Social, and Political Dilemmas*. Westport, Conn.: Praeger, 2000.

SEE ALSO: Bioethics; Biotechnology; Cloning; Exploitation; Genetic engineering; Genetic testing; Medical research; Science; Technology; UNESCO Declaration on the Human Genome and Human Rights.

Human nature

DEFINITION: General inherent character or innate disposition of humankind

TYPE OF ETHICS: Theory of ethics

SIGNIFICANCE: All ethical theories take a stance, whether explicit or implicit, on human nature. Some are based in a model of humanity's inherent virtues, which must be cultivated. Some are based in a model of humanity's inherent vices or sinfulness, which must be overcome or redeemed. Some hold that there is no human nature, and any attempt to assert one does violence to those whose characters do not conform to the model of humanity being put forward.

The question of "human nature" figures prominently in ethical theory. There is a broad consensus that, for all practical purposes, ethics must take into account the basic facts of human nature. Otherwise, it will be inefficient and ineffective. Although moral philosophers agree on the centrality of human nature to ethics, they do not agree on its meaning.

DEFINITIONS

Some definitions of human nature seek to identify the essential qualities and universal characteristics that all people have in common. Here it is necessary to distinguish between human nature and animal nature. While all people, by nature, have physical needs such as air, food, sleep, and an imperative to survive, these exigencies are by no means uniquely human. In addition, some distinctly human attributes or features, such as art, culture, creativity, cruelty, and historical consciousness, are by no means universal. Plenty of people lack a disposition toward creativity, a personality capable of torture, or a historical sense of themselves in relation to their ancestors and progeny.

Further complicating the problem of definition is the fact that human nature is a subject of study in numerous academic disciplines, each of which has a different approach. Philosophers must consider the views of psychologists, anthropologists, economists, criminologists, theologians, and sociobiologists, and reconcile the ways in which they understand and use the term "human nature." Another problem is the challenge posed by skeptics, such as Hannah Arendt, Jean-Paul Sartre, and Richard Rorty, who deny, on various grounds, that there is such a thing as human nature. Skeptical claims rest on defining the term in a way that emphasizes its universal aspects (for which exceptions provide falsification) or emphasizing the importance of environmental influences (which serves to downplay the innate dimension of human personality). The varieties of usage and the many existing definitions create a problem of ambiguity. A useful working definition of human nature is "the general inherent character or innate disposition of humankind."

PERENNIAL QUESTIONS

Since ancient times, debates about human nature have revolved around the most basic questions of philosophy. Are humans essentially spiritual beings or primarily physical and rational beings? Are people basically good? Are human actions determined or does free will exist? To what extent are humans influenced by heredity and environment? Does human nature change? Are women significantly different from men? Although often posed as false dilemmas, these questions help define the parameters of the debate. Responses to these complex questions result in varying approaches to ethics.

Most controversial, perhaps, is the tension that exists between spiritualism and secularism. For those who regard humans as essentially spiritual creatures, it follows that ethics should help bring out humans' divine nature or promote their religious/spiritual welfare. Those who hold such a view believe that it is appropriate for ethical teachings to present people with the highest ideals. Religions call upon their adherents to master their natures. Moral responsibility implies that through knowledge, self-discipline, and will, people can control their desires, passions, and moods. Unfortunately, the variety of religious beliefs gives rise to conflicting prescriptions of right action. For those who embrace a secular view, religious ethical ideals lead to frustration and failure because they seem more appropriate for angels than for humans. Emphasizing spiritual values is illusory, often distracting people from the urgent problems of this world. For those who believe that humans embody souls, however, emphasizing the ephemeral, materialistic aspects of life neglects that which is truly important.

A belief in the basic goodness of people generates a moral outlook that is optimistic and trusts people to behave ethically. David Hume observed that humans are distinguished by their capacity for benevolence. People have sympathetic feelings that stem from the consciousness that others experience pleasure and pain. Social theorists Jean-Jacques Rousseau and Karl Marx and humanistic psychologists Carl Rogers and Abraham Maslow all believed that humans are basically good, and they attributed human evil entirely to societal influences.

Rousseau and Marx regarded people as communitarian, and they sought to re-create society in a way that would bring out moral goodness. The humanist psychologists held that to be human is to have virtually unlimited potential for growth, and they called for freedom to promote self-actualization. Thomas Hobbes and Jonathan Edwards, however, denied the inherent goodness of people. Hobbes regarded people as fundamentally selfish, and Edwards saw people as morally depraved—deserving of hellfire and damnation. To control evil human impulses, both thinkers called for restraint to prevent human negativity from manifesting immoral behavior.

The vast majority of ethicists believe in free will. If actions are determined, people cannot be held morally responsible. Nevertheless, many metaphysicians, theologians, psychologists, and scientists argue for determinism in ways that would have dramatic ramifications for ethics as well as for education, law, and criminal justice. Arguments for determinism come in many forms: divine foreknowledge or fate, Sigmund Freud's claim that early childhood experience determines the basis of adult personality, B. F. Skinner's claim that human behavior is explainable in terms of operant conditioning, and scientific claims that "biology is destiny" and that "genes hold culture on a leash." If one accepts any of these theories, then one must reexamine the ethical principles of human accountability, autonomy, and choice. Moreover, these determinist theories also have various implications for the ongoing nature/nurture controversy.

Gender also raises interesting questions. Influenced by Stoic philosophy, some early Christian theologians, such as Tertullian, Saint Augustine, and John Chrysostom, based a belief in women's moral inferiority on Eve's sin of tasting the forbidden fruit in the Garden of Eden. Many feminists, such as Betty Friedan, argue that aside from the obvious physiological distinctions, the differences between men and women are caused by cultural factors and that conceptions of femininity are essentially social constructs. Motivated by an activist agenda for political and social change, the feminist movement emphasizes the environmental factors in shaping sex roles. Attributing gender differences to human nature makes permanent change less likely, since it is far easier to change society than it is to alter nature.

Carol Gilligan, showing that Lawrence Kohlberg's model of moral development has been misapplied to females, argues that the sexes conceptualize moral problems differently. Gilligan explains that the male-dominated culture idealizes the moral values of autonomy, independence, and impartial justice. Women, who tend to stress such communitarian values as caring, relationships, and responsibilities to others, are unfairly held to a male standard. Hence, they are judged to be less developed morally rather than appreciated for communicating "in a different voice." A parallel view in traditional Judaism carries this idea further in claiming that women are, by nature, more gentle, caring, and refined than men, and that therefore they require fewer laws to regulate their behavior.

LEADING THEORIES

Perceptions of human nature lie at the heart of several important ethical theories. Ethical egoism asserts that only self-interest is intrinsically good and that a person ought to do that which is in his or her self-interest. This follows directly from psychological egoism, which claims that human beings are so constituted that they act only in ways that promote their (perceived) interest. The operative principle here is that "ought implies can." If one accepts this descriptive claim, then a practical moral system must appeal to a person's self-interest. An ethics based on altruism would be contrary to human nature and would therefore fail. Many cite the collapse of the Soviet Union to illustrate this point.

The egoist view is shared by Thomas Hobbes and Ayn Rand and is supported by capitalist economic theory. Sophisticated versions of ethical egoism attempt to create a moral order by channeling the natural motivative force toward self-interest in a way that is beneficial for society as a whole. Those with an "enlightened self-interest" recognize their personal interest in the welfare of society. It is noteworthy that although religions preach altruism, they all appeal to self-interest by promising rewards and threatening punishments.

Hedonism is another moral theory that makes a normative claim based on a descriptive claim. Ethical hedonism asserts that happiness (that is, the presence of pleasure and the absence of pain) is the sole intrinsic good, and thus one always ought to do that which will promote the greatest happiness. This follows from the claim of psychological hedonism that humans are constituted in such a way that they always pursue pleasure and avoid pain. The fundamental tenet of Epicurus's moral teaching is that pleasure is the standard by which every good and every right action is evaluated.

Similarly, the British utilitarians Jeremy Bentham and John Stuart Mill considered hedonism to be the primary law of human nature, and their ethical writings stress the need to maximize pleasure and minimize pain. In their theory, hedonism is distinguished from egoism by its commitment to the universalist value of taking everyone's happiness into account. Simply pursuing one's own happiness is selfish and unethical. Defending hedonism, Mill's version of utilitarianism emphasized the distinctly human capacity to develop and refine one's tastes and preferences, and he underlined the importance of pursuing the "higher pleasures."

Ethical theories that regard humans as basically rational creatures make appeals to reason to motivate people to right action. Some major theories, such as those of Aristotelian and Kantian ethics, objectivism, and natural law, rely on humans' power of reason to lead them to universal moral truth. Theories such as subjectivism and relativism, however, discount the power of reason. They are also based on the belief that humans are characterized by individuality and diversity. This belief leads to a denial of absolute, objective, and universal values and points instead to the importance of personal feelings, tolerance, and cultural influences. Many proponents of these beliefs deny that there is such a thing as universal human nature.

Hume, an outspoken subjectivist, believed that human reason is limited. He was a skeptic who recognized the unlikelihood of uncovering the ultimate qualities of human nature, yet he also thought that careful observation of human behavior could lead to some knowledge about human nature. His empirical approach led him to emphasize passions or feelings

as the source of voluntary actions. In *A Treatise of Human Nature* (1739) he wrote: "Reason is and ought only to be the slave of the passions, and can never pretend to any other office than to serve and obey them." Hume argued that feelings of benevolence and sympathy are universal tendencies of human nature. People have a natural concern for the welfare of others, just as they care about themselves. He recognized self-love as a powerful principle of human nature, but he rejected Hobbes's sweeping claims for psychological egoism.

Hume also incorporated hedonism into his theory. He identified good with pleasure and evil with pain, establishing happiness as the moral standard for judging behavior. Moreover, he gave a central role to utility (defined as "usefulness" or the "tendency to ulterior good") in assessing right and wrong. By combining a number of motivating factors into his theory, Hume avoided the trappings of reducing human nature to a single, dominant drive.

Another nonreductionist theory was developed by the American philosopher John Dewey, who sought to base morality on a scientific understanding of the human being. For Dewey, morality involves the relationship between human nature and the social environment. He describes human nature as an unorganized mass of reflexes and impulses that are shaped by the social forces of habit, custom, and institutions. Because human nature is a part of nature, morality is linked with the natural sciences. Likewise, because people interact with others in social settings, morality is linked with the social sciences. Dewey held that people live in a social world characterized by change and that people have the ability to restructure their social environment and change human nature. Ethics entails making choices, and Dewey advocated conscious, reflective conduct that would lead to growth and improve the world. Through education, it is possible to encourage those habits that foster creative problem solving and intelligence.

An important, ambitious theory of human nature that presents a challenge to moral philosophy is E. O. Wilson's sociobiology, which he defines as "the systematic study of the biological basis of all forms of social behavior in all kinds of organisms, including man." Drawing upon genetics, population biology, ethology, and entomology and interpreting them all in terms of Darwinian evolutionary theory, Wilson sees genetic survival as the overriding aim of life.

681

Morality is subordinated to this goal, because the cultural development of higher ethical values will not overcome the power of genetic evolution.

Wilson incorporates such phenomena as love, altruism, aggression, and religion into his theory and insists that a practical system of ethics must conform to that theory. For example, he considers altruism to be "disguised genetic selfishness." Sociobiology remains highly controversial. It rocks the premises of both religious and secular ethics by questioning the view that humans are the only rational animal as well as the claim that humans have a morally distinct status. Moreover, sociobiology can be construed to justify the status quo or to offer a rationale for Social Darwinism. Wilson's own interpretation argues for tolerance, cooperation, diversity, peace, and environmentalism, but these lofty (and voguish) values do not necessarily follow from his descriptive claims.

CONCLUSION

The many theories touched upon here have something to teach. While most of them identify some aspect or truth about human nature, sweeping reductionist claims to validity generate exceptions or contradictions that are not easily resolved. For example, a stubborn proponent of egoism or sociobiology must really stretch to redefine all acts of altruism as ultimately selfish. The many competing theories and the different approaches to ethics that follow from them underscore the difficulty of reducing human nature to a single factor or tracing it to some given set of causes. This is because reality does not easily conform to theory or handy categorizations. People are not uniform, and their priorities, interests, and values are legitimately diverse. The numerous perceptions in circulation lend credence to the conclusion that there may be a variety of human natures, just as there are a variety of personality types.

While it may contradict the claims of hedonism, not everyone pursues a life of happiness. Some people shun physical comfort or emotional and intellectual pleasures and instead choose to endure suffering and hardship. A soldier, artist, or religious devotee may rationally pursue a lifestyle characterized by sacrifice and pain, without any desire or hope for happiness. Similarly, while many people live according to the principles of sociobiology, many do not. It is hardly unusual to encounter people who have no interest in having children; or who are kinder to strangers than they are to their own relatives; or who consider cats, whales, or jewelry more important than people.

The existence of diverse human natures is not only evident among people or groups of people on a macro level, it is also observable on a micro level. Individuals, over time, demonstrate a combination of drives that support several theories in a limited way rather than inclusively. For example, a man may be motivated by self-interest as a consumer; by aggression, self-sacrifice, and selfless devotion to strangers as a soldier; by altruism and generosity as a father; by piety when performing religious rituals; and by some combination of these characteristics in his professional career. Moreover, the same man may act with reckless disregard for his health, family, religious beliefs, and career while intoxicated or angry.

Human diversity and intricacy on both the individual level and the group level make the task of articulating universal generalizations about human nature extremely problematic. Thus far, the complexity of the human experience lends itself neither to a clear and convincing theory of human nature nor to a moral philosophy upon which most people agree. The questions surrounding human nature remain unresolved. For this reason, the study of human nature continues to be a fascinating and open field for speculation and research.

Don A. Habibi

FURTHER READING

Berry, Christopher J. *Human Nature*. Atlantic Highlands, N.J.: Humanities Press International, 1986. An informative survey of how the concept of human nature shapes political theory and how all moral and social doctrines make claims about human nature.

Carruthers, Peter. *Human Knowledge and Human Nature*. New York: Oxford University Press, 1992. Examines human nature as it pertains to epistemology. Carruthers defends empiricism in conjunction with innate knowledge and realism by examining the historical roots of contemporary debates on the nature of knowledge.

Derrida, Jacques. "The Ends of Man." In *Margins of Philosophy*. Translated by Alan Bass. Chicago: University of Chicago Press, 1982. Derrida's most important critique of the concepts of humanism and human nature; begins and ends with the question of who gets to define the human, and who gets excluded when such definitions are created.

Dewey, John. *Human Nature and Conduct*. Vol. 14 in *The Collected Works: The Middle Works*, edited by Jo Ann Boydston Carbondale: Southern Illinois University Press, 1985. Analyzing the interaction between psychology and ethics, Dewey focuses on the social power of habit. Individual human nature is an unorganized mass of impulses that comes to be shaped by the social environment. By reconstructing society, people can change human nature. Social institutions such as education can promote habits that constitute intelligence and growth.

Hobbes, Thomas. *Leviathan*. Edited by Richard Tuck. Rev. student ed. New York: Cambridge University Press, 1996. Hobbes bases his political and moral philosophy on the presupposition that all humans are equal in the sense that they are all vulnerable to being murdered while they sleep. Reduces "human nature" to this vulnerability and implicitly rejects any more substantive definitions or claims.

Hume, David. *A Treatise of Human Nature*. London: Everyman, 2003. Hume's masterpiece follows his conception of philosophy as the inductive science of human nature. His observations of human thinking and behavior lead him to a nonreductionist ethical theory that combines benevolence, sympathy, self-love, hedonism, custom, and justice.

Mandler, George. *Human Nature Explored*. New York: Oxford University Press, 1997. A comprehensive analysis of the concept of human nature, incorporating evolutionary and genetic theory, psychology, social and political philosophy, and philosophy of mind.

Wilson, Edward O. *On Human Nature*. Cambridge, Mass.: Harvard University Press, 1978. A readable and thought-provoking synthesis based on Wilson's theory of sociobiology. His consideration of evidence is somewhat uneven, since he gleans information from academic studies ranging from anthropology to zoology.

SEE ALSO: Altruism; Anthropological ethics; Communitarianism; Edwards, Jonathan; Egoism; Epicurus; Hedonism; *Human Nature and Conduct*; Social Darwinism.

Human Nature and Conduct

IDENTIFICATION: Book by John Dewey (1859-1952)
DATE: Published in 1922
TYPE OF ETHICS: Modern history
SIGNIFICANCE: *Human Nature and Conduct* fostered a positive, liberal view of human nature, proposed that philosophy should provide practical service to humanity, and reemphasized the role of creative intelligence in controlling events.

The American philosopher John Dewey bared many of his seminal ideas in *Human Nature and Conduct*. Drawing on themes found in Charles Darwin's *On the Origin of Species* (1859), one of the modern world's most influential studies, Dewey defined human beings as creatures within the natural order who, like members of other species, were obliged to adapt continually to one another and to their environments in order to survive. In this context, Dewey argued that past philosophies had been too abstract and too concerned with constructing intellectual systems to serve humanity's practical needs.

Much like his fellow American philosopher William James, Dewey also believed that truth was what happened to an idea and therefore, that truth changed over a period of time. For Dewey, life began and ended in human experience; in other words, humans who used appropriate methods could successfully negotiate life's confusing, obscure, and indeterminate situations. The key to coping with such problems, Dewey insisted, was using insight to define problems, establishing a set of possible solutions, determining the likely consequences of each possibility, and then evaluating the best possibility through observation and experiment.

These flexible steps, which produced what Dewey called "warranted assertibilities," were, he believed, as relevant to social reform as they were to laboratory science. The purpose of warranted assertibilities and the inquiries of which they were a part was changing specific situations. Ideas, in short, were instruments. Humankind, like other species, had no fixed natural end; therefore, events could be shaped by open-ended, democratized inquiry and the freeing of human intelligence. The greater the number of human alternatives, the freer humans could become.

In *Human Nature and Conduct*, Dewey championed both naturalism and instrumentalism, upon which he elaborated later in his many writings. As a reformer, he earned international esteem for the fresh directions that he advocated in education and in the democratization of social and political institutions—a democratization that he regarded as essential to human adaptability and the problem-solving play of the human intellect.

Clifton K. Yearley

SEE ALSO: Bradley, F. H.; Darwin, Charles; Human nature; James, William; Peirce, Charles Sanders; Pragmatism; Relativism.

Human rights

DEFINITION: Body of rights believed to belong fundamentally to all persons

TYPE OF ETHICS: Human rights

SIGNIFICANCE: Advocates of human rights believe that those rights exist independently of their recognition by any legal or political authority. Indeed, the purpose of the concept of human rights is to provide an apolitical moral principle that will form the basis for efforts to protect those people who are not protected, or who are harmed, by their own sovereign governments.

The idea of human rights as a field of study and as a body of legal rights and obligations is a relatively recent phenomenon that has grown out of ancient roots and faces two timeless problems. The fundamental problems facing the enterprise are, first, what to recognize as a human right, and, second, and even more troublesome, how to guarantee the protection of such rights once they have been recognized. These problems have been part of the political and social life of human beings for all time. How does one protect people from the unjust and sometimes brutal treatment of their fellows? Many governments throughout the ages have devised legal systems to reduce, mitigate, and relieve injustices committed by citizens or subjects against one another, but how does one protect the citizens or subjects of a country from their own government? These timeless and fundamental problems continue to face governments in both their domestic and their foreign affairs.

From the standpoint of ethics, human rights serve as a statement of the aspirations of peoples and governments toward ideals that are not always attained in practice and that at times lead to contradiction and conflict. Human rights represent an effort by governments, international agencies, and nongovernmental (NGO) advocacy groups to overcome the harsher aspects of political life within and between countries.

Although considerable progress was made in recognizing human rights during the twentieth century, the fact that they are referred to as human rights rather than legal rights reminds one how far modern practices are from stated ideals and aspirations. Moreover, the pursuit of human rights objectives involves hard choices about whether members of the international community may, how they should, and even whether they can punish the most egregious offenders of human rights, which are often governments that can claim and defend traditional rights of sovereignty against external scrutiny and encroachment.

HISTORY

The notion of human rights is a relatively recent innovation in the history of political thought, tracing its roots to the social contract thinkers, such as Thomas Hobbes and John Locke, who insisted during the seventeenth and eighteenth centuries that individuals possess certain natural rights that serve as the very foundation of political order and that may not be legitimately revoked by governments. This revolutionary concept served as the foundation upon which the great statements of individual rights and liberties—the American Declaration of Independence and the French Declaration on the Rights of Man—were based.

If the concept of natural rights is relatively new, the notions that individuals deserved dignity and respect and that particular citizens of particular cities were invested with certain rights were ancient. The ancient Greek polis, for example, recognized that its citizens had certain rights and privileges that were denied to aliens, while also recognizing that the polis and its individual members might have obligations to aliens, but whatever rights or privileges a citizen or subject enjoyed by custom, tradition, or statute were potentially subject to revision. The rights, in other words, were conventional in nature. They could be granted or taken away. They did not inhere in individual persons. Indeed, whatever rights citizens or even aliens might have were ultimately overshadowed by their duties to the state and to their fellow citizens or subjects. So it was later in Rome. A Roman citizen might have a right to suffrage and a means of political participation through the tribunes in republican Rome, but the empire's constitutional shift to monarchy saw these rights substantially altered. Rights came and went with the vagaries of politics and constitutions.

In the ancient world, the emergence of the Stoic and the Christian conceptions of human equality and dignity foreshadowed a more universal and abiding conception of rights. Both the Stoics and the Christians believed in the divine origin of creation. Both believed that human beings were endowed by that creator with a basic equality and that virtue rather than vice, mercy rather than severity, and charity rather than cruelty were the standards of upright living, whether for the ruler or the ruled. Yet still the concept of rights rested on convention and was rooted in the tumultuous, changing, and unreliable world of politics, where brutality was often respected as greatly as clemency was admired.

In Europe, after the eclipse of Roman domination, Christianity gradually gained ascendancy. The rulers as well as the ruled operated within a system of duties and responsibilities defined by Christianity itself. Customary and canonical restraints helped to prevent outrages against humanity, but the rough and tumble of political competition was never really fully tamed, and centuries of contention over the proper roles of the church and state in moral and temporal affairs culminated in the brutal wars of religion during the sixteenth and seventeenth centuries, following the Protestant Reformation. Roman Catholic and Protestant monarchs and princes gradually recognized that a new order resting on the sovereignty of states would be necessary to quell the sectarian violence. States would create their own rules and regulations without outside interference. They would treat their citizens as they pleased, without regard to any "higher law" that a church might assert. They would be the ultimate sovereigns.

It was at this time, then, that Hobbes and Locke asserted the conception of natural rights, offering to ground the newfound virility of the independent and sovereign state on a principle that would recognize the rights of its people. Their notion did not find wide support among the monarchs of their own time, who were just then enjoying the unlimited powers associated with the rule of an absolute sovereign, but in time the conception of natural rights took root. Modern experiments with democratic regimes founded on the principle emerged, and with them came regimes that were committed to a universal conception of human rights.

RIGHTS AND CONSTITUTIONALISM

Realization of this broader conception of human rights was hampered, however, by the very international system that made it possible for certain governments to develop constitutions that were rooted in conceptions of natural and human rights. Democratic regimes resting on such principles found themselves in contention with authoritarian regimes that either did not recognize such principles or only paid them lip service. Even the democratic regimes often failed to live up to their own standards. Nevertheless, democratic states during the late nineteenth and early twentieth centuries made the first international efforts to protect human rights by pursuing the gradual abolition of slavery and beginning to enforce anti-slave-trading measures. Similarly, during the early part of the twentieth century, governments in Europe took interest in protecting minority populations and promoting the development of humanitarian law, especially to protect vulnerable groups in time of war.

Human rights today, as in the past, can only be effectively guaranteed by individual governments that agree to respect them. The international system is still composed, even in the twenty-first century, of sovereign states that have exclusive legal control over their own territories and citizens. There is no world government or authority higher than the governments of states that can impose human rights obligations, although some regional systems for protection of human rights have developed, particularly in Europe. Rather, governments, at their sole discretion, may agree voluntarily to develop domestic legislation guaranteeing human rights or to sign international agreements promising to respect them.

Nevertheless, the twentieth century witnessed a veritable explosion of human rights activity, much of which was given impetus by the horrible atrocities witnessed during two global wars. First, after World War I, the League of Nations, gingerly and without great success, and then, after World War II, the United Nations (U.N.), with greater effectiveness, addressed the problems of collective insecurity, war, and abuse of human rights. Governments determined the pace of progress in these endeavors, since the League of Nations and the United Nations lacked sovereignty and possessed only those authorities and mandates that had been granted to them by their member states. Nevertheless, especially since World War II, the world has witnessed a proliferation of U.N.-related human rights agreements by which governments sought to recognize, promote, and guarantee the development of human rights. Most of the guarantees, however, are very fragile, and continue to call upon governments as the principal mechanisms through which human rights are protected.

UNITED NATIONS ACTIVITY IN HUMAN RIGHTS

Article 1(3) of the U.N. Charter stipulates that one of the purposes of the United Nations is "to achieve international cooperation . . . in promoting and encouraging respect for human rights and for fundamental freedoms for all without distinction as to race, sex, language, or religion." Numerous additional references to human rights are made in the Charter. The Charter also stipulates in Article 2(1), however, that "the Organization is based on the principle of the sovereign equality of all its Members," and in Article 2(&) that "Nothing contained in the present Charter shall authorize the United Nations to intervene in matters which are essentially within the domestic jurisdiction of any state."

Protection of human rights may be a fundamental purpose of the United Nations, but state sovereignty serves as a fundamental organizing principle. States, not the United Nations, would do the determining about how human rights would be encouraged and protected, although they agreed to pursue these ends jointly and separately. To this end, U.N. member states created a Human Rights Commission that would report to the Economic and Social Council (ECOSOC). In short, the U.N. Charter reflected the still rather ambiguous status of human rights. They became a priority for governmental attention, but governments preferred to protect their sovereign prerogatives. Hence, governments paradoxically remained, as they had for centuries, the chief guarantors, as well as the chief violators, of human rights.

Despite setbacks, much progress in recognizing, if not in fully protecting, human rights has been made. The U.N. General Assembly, on the recom-

mendation of the Human Rights Commission, adopted the Universal Declaration of Human Rights in 1948. This declaration, though not legally binding, did articulate the full range of human rights that states proclaimed should be respected, including the rights to life, liberty, security of person, nationality, and equal protection under and nondiscrimination before the law, and freedom from slavery and torture, freedom of religion, of political preference, and of movement, to name only a few of the most important provisions. Subsequent human rights treaties sought to provide legally binding protections, while many governments incorporated the declaration in whole or in part into their constitutions.

Not all governments that have taken these steps are known for their scrupulous adherence to human rights principles, while many others have not signed the most important conventions—the Covenant on Civil and Political Rights and the Covenant on Economic and Social Rights—which were adopted by the U.N. General Assembly in 1966 and entered into force for the signatories in 1976. Numerous treaties dealing with more specific issues have also been promulgated, including international agreements on refugees, stateless persons, elimination of racial discrimination, the political rights of women, the rights of children, and the rights of migrant workers. Added to this are numerous regional treaties, the most important and effective of which is the European Convention on Human Rights.

Like all past efforts at protecting individual rights and liberties, U.N. activity has faced the question of how to enforce human rights standards given the prevailing standard of state sovereignty. In general, formal international enforcement mechanisms remain rather weak, with states taking the leading role through their domestic systems in protecting human rights standards through domestic legal institutions. Informal pressure through private diplomatic channels, NGO advocacy groups, and the public media does, however, often lead to better state compliance with human rights standards.

ETHICAL CONSIDERATIONS

To a large extent, human rights standards remain guidelines for how governments *should* behave, rather than legal descriptions about how they actually *do* behave. Moreover, human rights often posit potentially contradictory standards. Human rights obligations may require states to ensure that their people receive adequate nutrition, security of person, and a rudimentary education while at the same time calling for popular political participation, free elections, and freedom of speech. In a very poor country plagued by civil war, however, achieving stability may be incompatible with modern democratic norms. Governments are concerned primarily with survival and only secondarily with reform.

Human rights are most regularly and routinely violated in countries where meeting the most basic needs of people is most difficult. These governments may well subscribe to international human rights treaties, but if domestic political circumstances are not favorable, compliance with them is doubtful. Some human rights treaties bow to this reality, granting states the right to derogate from certain human rights obligations once due notice and explanations are provided. The U.N. Covenant on Civil and Political Rights, for example, allows governments, during times of national emergency, to revoke or curtail rights to privacy, liberty, security of person, peaceable assembly, and political activities. Other rights, however, such as freedoms of religion, thought, and conscience, as well as prohibitions against slavery and torture, remain obligatory at all times.

What should be done with those governments that routinely shock the conscience of humanity by brutalizing their own citizens? An ethical dilemma is created here, since the principle of sovereignty imposes a duty of nonintervention in the affairs of states. A state may have a legal right to intervene to protect its own citizens from human rights abuses at the hands of other governments, but what right does it have to do this on behalf of another state's citizens? Under current international mechanisms, such an intervention would have to be conducted under U.N. auspices and justified, not by recourse to human rights, as such, but as a matter constituting a threat to international peace and security.

These questions have been faced in several modern civil war situations, including Iraq's treatment of Kurds and Shīʿites, Serbian treatment of Muslims in Bosnia, and in Somalia. In cases in which a country's population is facing genocide or disaster threatens large numbers of people, strong and quick action is required to save life. In all such situations, the problem that emerges is whether and how force should be used to achieve human rights objectives.

One consideration that must be taken into account is the circumstances surrounding the threat to life. Does the threat exist because of the deliberate policy of the government or because of the government's inability to cope with disaster? In Somalia, the situation involved anarchy produced by the lack of any effective government. Humanitarian intervention in that case was relatively easy to justify and to accomplish. The issue is considerably more complicated and dangerous when governments undertake deliberate genocidal or persecutory policies. How much killing should the international community resort to in order to prevent killing? What severity of economic pressure should be imposed to prevent persecution or ensure nondiscrimination? What degree of force will be effective? Is any degree of potential force or pressure likely to succeed?

Enforcement of international law and human rights in conflict situations sometimes presents very painful ethical and prudential choices. This explains in part the international indecision about how to deal with ethnic cleansing in Bosnia, where the use of force to achieve human rights objectives raises a series of thorny questions. In the case of Iraq, a more determined U.N. response to Iraqi government persecution of its own people was made possible by its clearly illegal invasion of neighboring sovereign, Kuwait, and by the cease-fire obligations it agreed to in the aftermath of its expulsion from Kuwait by coalition forces.

There are relatively few cases in which the courses of action open to governments, international agencies, and private groups are so stark. In most instances, the ethical questions for international human rights policy turn on how to apply the right amounts of persuasion, diplomacy, and publicity to realize humanitarian objectives. The humane treatment of prisoners, for example, is constantly monitored by the International Committee for the Red Cross and Amnesty International. By pursuing quiet modes of diplomacy or by publicizing human rights violations, such groups can bring pressure to bear on governments to comply with more acceptable human rights practices. These informal efforts, together with ongoing attempts to convince governments to ratify and comply with international human rights agreements, hold out hope that human rights will in fact one day become legal rights widely protected by governments.

Robert F. Gorman

FURTHER READING

Brownlie, Ian, ed. *Basic Documents on Human Rights*. 2d ed. Oxford, England: Clarendon Press, 1981. This valuable resource includes the texts of the most important international and regional human rights agreements.

Buergenthal, Thomas. *International Human Rights in a Nutshell*. St. Paul, Minn.: West, 1988. This user-friendly reference book describes the essential contents of regional and international human rights agreements, ranging from the U.N. Charter and U.N. Declaration and Covenants to European, inter-American, and African documents on human rights.

Donnelly, Jack. *Universal Human Rights in Theory and Practice*. Ithaca, N.Y.: Cornell University Press, 1989. This philosophical inquiry into the meaning of human rights and the policy contexts in which human rights operate is both thoughtful and realistic, especially in distinguishing between human rights and legal rights.

Ellis, Anthony, ed. *Ethics and International Relations*. Manchester, England: Manchester University Press, 1986. This compilation of papers and essays addresses a range of ethical issues in international relations, including questions of citizenship, asylum, intervention, human rights, and humanitarian aid.

Falk, Richard. *Human Rights and State Sovereignty*. New York: Holmes & Meier, 1981. In this provocative work, a prominent and innovative proponent of human rights takes on the issue of sovereignty as the most critical issue in effective enforcement of human rights agreements.

Forsythe, David. *Human Rights and World Politics*. Lincoln: University of Nebraska Press, 1983. A readable, generally realistic treatment of the international and domestic contexts of human rights protection. It distinguishes between formal and informal efforts to protect human rights.

Gibney, Mark, ed. *Open Borders? Closed Societies? The Ethical and Political Issues*. New York: Greenwood, 1988. This collection of articles addresses questions concerning rights and duties surrounding asylum, refugee resettlement, and assistance. The contributions explore the ethical and political obligations that arise between peoples and states in international relations.

Hannum, Hurst, ed. *Guide to International Human Rights Practice*. 3d ed. Ardsley, N.Y.: Transnational, 1999. This volume contains numerous articles exploring the actual means by which NGOs and advocacy groups can lobby effectively for the advancement of human rights.

Henkin, Louis. *The Rights of Man Today*. Boulder, Colo.: Westview, 1978. A well-written and reasonably compact treatment of the historical development and current significance of human rights.

Monshipouri, Mahmood, et al., eds. *Constructing Human Rights in the Age of Globalization*. Armonk, N.Y.: M. E. Sharpe, 2003. Anthology of essays that look at the struggle over the definition of "human rights," and the political consequences of that struggle. Interrogates what the editors call the "human rights regime" and the political powers that strive to control it.

Owen, Nicholas, ed. *Human Rights, Human Wrongs: The Oxford Amnesty Lectures, 2001*. New York: Oxford University Press, 2003. Collects a series of lectures given at Oxford University by some of the most important moral thinkers of our time. Includes lectures by Tzvetan Todorov, Peter Singer, Susan Sontag, Gayatri Chakravorty Spivak, Gitta Sereny, Michael Ingatieff, Eva Hoffman, and Geoffrey Bindman.

SEE ALSO: Amnesty International; Bill of Rights, U.S.; Dignity; Human Rights Watch; International justice; International law; Natural rights; Rights and obligations; Universal Declaration of Human Rights.

Human Rights Watch

IDENTIFICATION: Independent, nonprofit human rights advocacy organization
DATE: Founded in 1978
TYPE OF ETHICS: Human rights
SIGNIFICANCE: Human Rights Watch is one of the largest and most influential advocacy organizations that documents abuses of political, social, and economic rights around the world.

Human Rights Watch is an organization predicated on the idea that human rights are universal, applying equally to all individuals. The organization is concerned with traditional political rights, as well as broader social and economic rights. The mission of the organization is to document and publicize rights violations, whether they are committed by state or nonstate actors, in order to shame and hold the rights violators publicly accountable.

Human Rights Watch was established in 1978 as Helsinki Watch, an organization that focused narrowly on tracking Soviet and Eastern European compliance with human rights commitments made by those regions' governments in the 1975 Helsinki Accords. Over its first decade, the organization and its mission steadily expanded. During the 1980's, a series of regional "watch committees," such as America's Watch, arose. In 1988, these watch committees were brought together and the overall organization was renamed Human Rights Watch.

By the first years of the twenty-first century, Human Rights Watch was the largest human rights organization based in the United States, with nearly two hundred full-time staff members and an annual budget of approximately twenty million dollars. It accepted no public money and raised all its funds from private donations. Headquartered in New York City, Human Rights Watch also maintained permanent offices in Washington, D.C., San Francisco, Los Angeles, London, Moscow, Brussels, and Hong Kong.

ACTIVITIES

Human Rights Watch is often compared to Amnesty International; however it deals with a broader set of issues than the latter organization and carries out its advocacy by different means. While Amnesty International focuses mainly on physical abuses—such as political imprisonment, torture, and killings—Human Rights Watch addresses a much broader set of rights. Human Rights Watch concerns itself with such issues as press freedom, discrimination, the conduct of war, the use of land mines, fair labor practices, and social and cultural rights.

Human Rights Watch also pursues a different methodology than that of Amnesty International. While the latter organization mobilizes its membership to lobby directly on behalf of individual human rights victims, Human Rights Watch seeks to document and publicize patterns of abuses. The intent is to shine a bright light on abuses, to shame and embarrass abusers, and, by extension, to deter potential future abusers. In pursuit of this strategy, Human Rights Watch conducts fact-finding missions, pub-

lishes extensive reports, and then works with governments and international organizations to build pressure for change.

Beyond its publications and topical reports, Human Rights Watch has provided expert testimony in international war crimes trials, played a lead role in a coalition of organizations drafting a treaty to ban the use of child soldiers, and, along with other organizations in the International Campaign to Ban Landmines, won the 1997 Nobel Peace Prize.

David Carleton

FURTHER READING

Hannum, Hurst, ed. *Guide to International Human Rights Practice.* 3d ed. Ardsley, N.Y.: Transnational, 1999.

Lawson, Edward, comp. *Encyclopedia of Human Rights.* Edited by Mary Lou Bertucci. 2d ed. Washington, D.C.: Taylor & Francis, 1996.

Welch, Claude E., Jr. *NGO's and Human Rights: Promise and Performance.* Philadelphia: University of Pennsylvania Press, 2000.

World Report 2003. New York: Human Rights Watch, 2003.

SEE ALSO: Amnesty International; Human rights; Natural rights; Rights and obligations; SALT treaties; Universal Declaration of Human Rights.

Humane Society of the United States

IDENTIFICATION: Advocacy group devoted to the alleviation of animal suffering

DATE: Founded in 1954

TYPE OF ETHICS: Animal rights

SIGNIFICANCE: The Humane Society of the United States was founded to counteract the conservatism its founders believed was then inhibiting the effectiveness of other animal welfare societies, such as the American Humane Association and the Society for the Prevention of Cruelty to Animals.

During the 1940's, legislation was passed requiring the provision of animals for research laboratories by federally supported humane societies. Initially, the

The Humane Society and Elephant Ethics

By the turn of the twenty-first century, animal rights organizations were focusing increasing attention on zoos. Of particular concern was the welfare of captive elephants, which require great amounts of space and costly and difficult care. Many public zoos acknowledged their inability to provide adequate space and conditions to keep their elephants physically and mentally healthy and were giving animals with health problems to other zoos with better facilities. In May, 2004, however, the directors of the Detroit Zoo decided to give away its elephants for another reason. One of largest public zoos in the United States, the Detroit Zoo already provided a spacious facility for its two Indian elephants. However, its directors concluded that Detroit's cold climate was not good for elephants and that the elephants would do better in a more spacious animal sanctuary. Wayne Pacelle, the chief executive officer of the Humane Society of the United States, applauded the Detroit Zoo's decision. He pointed out that the zoo was the first with spacious grounds and adequate care to give up its elephants for ethical reasons and expressed the hope that other zoos would follow Detroit's example.

American Humane Association (AHA), led by president Robert Sellar, vigorously opposed these "pound seizure laws." With Sellar's death, however, a new conservative leadership was elected to the AHA. Frustrated by the ineffectiveness of their organization, three key AHA personnel, all appointees of Sellar, formed a new association, the Humane Society of the United States (HSUS). Dedicated to the alleviation of suffering in domestic and wild animals, the HSUS polices animal research centers, zoos, and the entertainment industry. Furthermore, the HSUS opposes all hunting sports and calls for a drastic reduction in the use of animals in biomedical experiments.

The society also lobbies for the strengthening and extension of legislation protecting animals. Public education related to the inherent rights of animals and human responsibility in securing those rights is furthered through a division within the society, the National Association for the Advancement of Humane Education.

Mary E. Virginia

SEE ALSO: Animal research; Animal rights; Cruelty to animals; Moral status of animals; Society for the Prevention of Cruelty to Animals.

Humanism

DEFINITION: Philosophy based on the freedom, responsibility, and rationality of human beings, and the centrality of human values
TYPE OF ETHICS: Personal and social ethics
SIGNIFICANCE: Humanism is embraced by those who believe in human nature and who seek a secular, nonsupernatural value system, or a universalist, nonsectarian religion. It is attacked by those who reject the idea that all humans have a common nature or values and who are therefore suspicious of the supposedly universal values put forward in the name of Humanism. It is also rejected by sectarian religious movements.

Although it has classical and Renaissance roots, modern Humanism is a child of the European Enlightenment. Elsewhere—for example, in India, Japan, and China—it appears in some forms of Buddhism (Theravāda Buddhism, Zen) and Confucianism. Among Humanism's modern antecedents were "natural religion," Deism, "free thought" and "the religion of humanity" (proposed by the nineteenth century French sociologist Auguste Comte).

The development of natural science, of liberal democracy, and of secular society marked the institutional context of Humanism. Nineteenth century social reform in the United States and democratic socialism in England and Europe reinforced the move toward a human-centered philosophy. Critical studies—for example, the "higher criticism" of scripture, archeology, and comparative religious scholarship—encouraged a skeptical view of transcendent and supernatural bases for ethics and politics. With the advent of Darwinism and the development of modern biology, sociology, and psychology, the stage was set. Thus, during the early decades of the twentieth century, modern Humanism appeared as both a secular philosophy of living and a religious movement.

The term "Humanism" was not always used. For example, American pragmatism and instrumentalism were both naturalistic and humanistic. Explicit use of the term in its modern form appeared with the emergence of a "religion without god" in the thought of three twentieth century Unitarian ministers: John H. Dietrich, Curtis Reese, and Charles Francis Potter. While they and a few of their colleagues in Unitarianism and the Ethical Culture Societies were moving toward a "religious" Humanism, a secular expression of the same notion was appearing in the work of naturalistic philosophers such as Roy Wood Sellars and John Dewey. Both threads came together with the publication of *The Humanist Manifesto* (1933).

A second *Manifesto* (1973) and *A Secular Humanist Declaration* (1981) expanded but did not alter the meaning of the 1933 document. Signed by some thirty-five philosophers and religious leaders, *The Humanist Manifesto* marked the entry of an independent explicit Humanism into the Western world. Before that, Humanism had been attached to existing movements, such as Christian Humanism and Socialist Humanism, or had other names, such as Ethical Culture and Free Religion. With the founding of The American Humanist Association (1941) and The North American Committee for Humanism (1982), Humanism as a philosophy of living was formally established. After World War II, similar developments in Great Britain, Netherlands, Belgium, France, Germany, and India led, in 1952, to the organization of the International Humanist and Ethical Union, which had its headquarters in Utrecht, Netherlands.

PHILOSOPHICAL BASES

Humanism rests, philosophically, on two classical notions: the sophist Protagoras's belief that "man is the measure of all things" and the poet Lucretius's naturalistic interpretation of life and world. In these two root ideas, the career of modern Humanism was foreshadowed. The human-centered feature of Humanism appears in its commitment to human responsibility and freedom. Denying the mistaken view that Humanism is merely the arrogant replacement of God by the human person, freedom and responsibility require human beings to acknowledge their obligation to judge, choose, and act and their opportunity to make a difference to themselves and the world around them.

Human beings, thus, are autonomous moral agents (for example, see the ethics of Immanuel Kant).

From this view flows the commitment to democracy as the social and political expression of agency, to education as the method of developing competence as an agent, and to science as the outcome of organized intelligence. From this view, too, flows Humanism's skepticism about God and the gods, a skepticism rooted in a rejection of authoritarianism at least as much as in a theological argument about the existence or nonexistence of an all-powerful and all-knowing Being.

From classical Humanism comes modern Humanism's acknowledgment of the interdependence of all beings as well as an appreciation of the beauties and harmonies of the world. At the same time, a tragic note is heard, since Humanists are sensitive to the fact that the world is as precarious as it is dependable and that experience is as surprising (for good or ill) as it is predictable. Thus, Humanist agency is admittedly finite as human insight, and human existence itself is finite. A stoic quality, therefore, attaches to Humanism, a sense of acceptance of the givenness of the world and of the uncontrollable in nature and the individual. Admittedly, the Enlightenment notion of "progress" interpreted the direction of history as ultimately positive, and early twentieth century Humanism interpreted "evolution" as confirming that direction. Post-World War II Humanist thought, particularly because of its Existentialist inspiration, is likely to acknowledge the darker sides of both the individual and the world.

Finally, agency and creativity evolve on the basis of human rationality—the ability to make and understand distinctions, to grasp connections and consequences, and to draw sensible conclusions. Institutionally, this appears as Humanism's commitment to science. It also appears in the celebration of human powers, which it owes to Renaissance Humanism, the move from naturalistic appreciation to Humanist aesthetic sensibility. Overall, then, Humanism is a philosophy of living that views the human person as a rational agent living in a world that both supports and limits him or her. Instead of bemoaning fate or escaping to another and more secure world—a supernatural or transnatural world—the Humanist accepts, enjoys, and works within the constraints that he or she acknowledges as given with the givenness of being.

Howard B. Radest

FURTHER READING

Bullock, Alan. *The Humanist Tradition in the West.* New York: W. W. Norton, 1985.

Cooper, David E. *The Measure of Things: Humanism, Humility, and Mystery.* New York: Oxford University Press, 2002.

Derrida, Jacques. "The Ends of Man." In *Margins of Philosophy.* Translated by Alan Bass. Chicago: University of Chicago Press, 1982.

Dewey, John. *A Common Faith.* New Haven, Conn.: Yale University Press, 1991.

Ericson, Edward L. *The Humanist Way.* New York: Continuum, 1988.

Grayling, A. C. *Meditations for the Humanist: Ethics for a Secular Age.* New York: Oxford University Press, 2002.

Halliwell, Martin, and Andy Mousley. *Critical Humanisms: Humanist, Anti-humanist Dialogues.* Edinburgh: Edinburgh University Press, 2003.

Lamont, Corliss. *The Philosophy of Humanism.* 7th ed., rev. and enl. New York: Continuum, 1990.

Radest, Howard B. *The Devil and Secular Humanism.* New York: Praeger, 1990.

Sartre, Jean-Paul. "Existentialism Is a Humanism." In *Existentialism from Dostoevsky to Sartre,* edited and translated by Walter Kaufmann. Rev. and expanded ed. New York: New American Library, 1975.

Storer, Morris B., ed. *Humanist Ethics.* Buffalo, N.Y.: Prometheus, 1980.

SEE ALSO: Atheism; Comte, Auguste; Dewey, John; Enlightenment ethics; Existentialism; Kantian ethics; Marx, Karl; Pragmatism; Progressivism; Sartre, Jean-Paul.

Hume, David

IDENTIFICATION: English philosopher
BORN: May 7, 1711, Edinburgh, Scotland
DIED: August 25, 1776, Edinburgh, Scotland
TYPE OF ETHICS: Enlightenment history
SIGNIFICANCE: The most famous and influential proponent of skepticism in the modern era, Hume worked to free ethics from a metaphysical basis rooted either in religion or in natural law. His most important works include *A Treatise of Human Nature* (1739-1740), *An Enquiry Concerning Human Understanding* (1748), and *An Enquiry Concerning the Principles of Morals* (1751).

In his philosophy and in his theory of ethics—or morals, the term he preferred—David Hume was the complete empiricist. That is, he denied the validity of any knowledge that existed outside the realm of sensory experience. His ideas and writings were diametrically opposed to the teachings of the established church, which maintained that a vast body of metaphysical knowledge existed that could be revealed to humankind only by the grace of God. This was the basis for the formulation of Christian ethics, which were considered eternal.

The philosophers of the Enlightenment had in many ways created a similar metaphysical world of science or nature and had charged humankind with the task of discovering its secrets. For Hume, no knowledge for which there was no antecedent sense impression could claim any validity.

A TREATISE OF HUMAN NATURE

This seminal work has had a profound effect on the development of Western philosophy in many areas: on the evolution of human institutions, on the limitations of knowledge, and on changing moral values. The book is, in a sense, Hume's only work, since all of his subsequent writings were either related to or were reworkings of parts of the original work. Divided into three parts, "Of the Understanding," "Of the Passions," and "Of Morals," the book consists essentially of two parts: one examining how knowledge comes into being and another focusing on the relationship of knowledge to the development of ethics or morals.

AN ENQUIRY CONCERNING HUMAN UNDERSTANDING

The basic theme of the *Enquiry*, a reworking of the first part of *A Treatise of Human Nature*, is that all opinions, all theories, and all knowledge, in order to be validated, must be submitted to the test of experience. The idea of unknowable substance has no empirical justification in either the spiritual or the material sense. Hume posited the validity of causality. A given cause has always been followed by a given effect. Only custom, repeated experience, and familiarity, however, make it possible to ascertain the development of the effect. Were the knowledge or theory not in the mind, it would not exist. Hume anticipates the relativity of the nineteenth century when he asserts that the opposite of every fact remains possible and that no amount of deductive reasoning from first principles can determine in advance what course nature actually will follow.

AN ENQUIRY CONCERNING THE PRINCIPLES OF MORALS

To free ethics or morals of their religious bases, Hume first had to attack the religious establishment, which he did in a subtle but devastating manner. So fearful were his supporters of the reaction to his work that *An Enquiry Concerning the Principles of Morals* was published posthumously. In his *Essay on Miracles*, published in 1748, Hume stated that a miracle in the sense of a supernatural event as a sign of the divinity cannot possibly be established. Rather than constituting evidence of moral and spiritual value, such events are characteristic of sorcery or wizardry.

Once he had stripped away the religious connection, Hume developed his theory of ethics or morals on the basis of pleasure, pain, and utility. It was useless to reason that virtue was "natural" and vice was "unnatural," since both were "natural." Reason is equally useless. Perfectly inert, it can never be the source of so active a principle as conscience or a sense of morality. The solution devolves on the individual. Inherent in all humans are basic feelings or instincts toward family, neighbors, and society. Turning inward, one tends to project oneself into another's situation and to imagine how one would feel under certain circumstances. Happiness in others creates joy, while misery generates sorrow. In other words, conduct is good in proportion to its capacity for producing happiness; conversely, conduct is evil in proportion to its capacity to produce pain. The result of the first is virtue; the result of the second is vice. The greater the pleasure or joy, the greater its utility. It is left to the cognitive and reasoning facilities of humankind to create from these myriad pleasure-pain-utility experiences a coherent ethical code.

Limiting the hedonistic application of this system of ethics and morals based on pain and pleasure was Hume's concept of justice. This was not arrived at by nature but by human conventions. Of all the animals, humans alone suffer a great disparity between their

David Hume. (Library of Congress)

wants and their means of satisfying them. Stability of possession, transference by consent, and the performance of promise are the three fundamental laws of nature. Society is necessary for human existence, and society in the name of justice doles out the rewards that may seem capricious but upon which the peace and security of human society depend.

IMPLICATIONS FOR ETHICAL CONDUCT

The implications of Hume's thought are threefold. First, Hume broke the individual's tie with God and transferred it to society. Punishment and rewards were immediate, not confined to the hereafter. Second, Hume invited human society to create its own system of ethics. Third, rather than being static, based on values created by other societies in other times, ethics and morality are organic and ever-changing. Since ethics are subjective, it is society that determines their applicability.

Nis Petersen

FURTHER READING

Baillie, James. *Routledge Philosophy Guidebook to Hume on Morality.* New York: Routledge, 2000.
Flage, Daniel. *David Hume's Theory of Mind.* New York: Routledge, 1990.

Hume, David. *Dialogues Concerning Natural Religion*. Edited by Norman K. Smith. Indianapolis: Bobbs-Merrill, 1981.

_____. *Enquiries Concerning Human Understanding and Concerning the Principles of Morals*. 3d ed. Oxford, England: Clarendon Press, 1975.

_____. *A Treatise of Human Nature*. London: Everyman, 2003.

Merrill, Kenneth R., and Robert W. Shahan, eds. *David Hume: Many-Sided Genius*. Norman: University of Oklahoma Press, 1976.

Passmore, John Arthur. *Hume's Intentions*. 3d ed. London: Duckworth Press, 1980.

Russell, Bertrand. "David Hume." In *A History of Western Philosophy*. New York: Simon & Schuster, 1972.

Russell, Paul. *Freedom and Moral Sentiment: Hume's Way of Naturalizing Responsibility*. New York: Oxford University Press, 2002.

SEE ALSO: Christian ethics; Enlightenment ethics; Hobbes, Thomas; Skepticism; Smith, Adam; State of nature; Utilitarianism; Voltaire.

Humility

DEFINITION: Self-deprecation, modesty, or submission; lack of egoism or arrogance

TYPE OF ETHICS: Personal and social ethics

SIGNIFICANCE: Humility may be based in a belief in one's inferiority or simply in one's lack of superiority rooted in the equality of all. Its ethical status is very different in different value systems: Individualist and nonegalitarian systems despise humility, while those for whom pride is a sin esteem humility as one of the greatest goods.

Humility is a disposition of character that is usually acquired through training. It consists of an inner attitude of low self-esteem that motivates an outward pattern of deferential behavior. Humble persons are not self-assertive, since they do not pridefully suppose that they possess much merit of their own. Their sense of inferiority leads them to defer respectfully to the wishes of those whom they regard as superior.

To be sure, the term "humility" sometimes is used in other ways. For example, the feminist Sara Ruddick (in her *Maternal Thinking*), after saying that humility is an important virtue for mothers to have, then reveals that she thinks it consists in recognizing that one cannot control everything. Her usage is potentially misleading because she is equating humility with the mere absence of something contrary to it.

Every society regards at least some degree of humility as desirable in at least some of its members. Parents often want their children to be humble toward them, and many customers prefer to be served by humble salespersons. Societies differ greatly, however, in the degree to which they think this trait of character ought to pervade life. Some prize humility highly and advocate it for everyone; others think that inferior members of the community should be humble but that superior ones should recognize their own merits proudly.

In the Judeo-Christian tradition, humility is assigned a prominent place among the qualities that all human beings ought to cultivate in themselves. Although Christianity does not classify humility as one of the cardinal virtues, it nevertheless continually commends humility, and Saint Thomas Aquinas described humility as the foundation of all other human virtues.

This stress on humility comes about because one of the most distinctive features of the Judeo-Christian tradition is the vast moral difference it sees between God and human beings. God is described not only as all-powerful and all-knowing but also as supremely good. He is the one faultless being. Moreover, he is quick to become angry at those who fail to show him respect. To heighten the contrast between the human and the divine, human beings are regarded as utterly contemptible in their sinful weakness and moral corruption. They are seen as deserving no credit for any good qualities that they may possess, since these come entirely as gifts from God. Pride is considered to be the fundamental vice, because it involves a declaration of self-worth apart from God. Thus, the Judeo-Christian view is that human beings should recognize their lack of any independent worth and should seek to walk humbly before God, desiring that in all things his will, not theirs, be done.

ANCIENT GREEK PHILOSOPHERS

The ancient Greek outlook is substantially different. Although believing that their gods were powerful and that it was dangerous to fail to show them respect, the Greeks did not consider their gods to be morally superior. Indeed, according to the Greek myths, every type of misbehavior of which mortals are capable was engaged in by the gods. Far from regarding all human beings as corrupt and contemptible, the Greeks thought that only some of them (especially the non-Greeks) were so. They believed that humans of the better type sometimes can manage on their own to be temperate, courageous, and wise, and are entitled to be proud of such great deeds as they occasionally succeed in performing.

In his *Nicomachean Ethics*, Aristotle lists many moral virtues, each of which he interprets as an intermediate (or "golden mean") between two vices, one of excess and the other of deficiency. With regard to self-appraisal, he sees one extreme as overweening pride, or boastfulness (the vice of having an excessively favorable opinion of oneself), and at the other extreme, he places humility (the vice of being deficient in favorable opinion of oneself). For him, the balanced, correct attitude is proper pride. Thus, he sees constant groveling before the gods as a sign of faulty character; people show excellence, he thinks, who have merits of their own and do not hide this from themselves or anyone else.

Aristotle seems to have supposed that the habit of appraising one's own merits accurately should always be cultivated. Some Judeo-Christian thinkers might agree with this recommendation, but they embrace a view of human nature that is different from Aristotle's, and so they think that accuracy dictates an abysmally low appraisal of all merely human qualities. Yet surely accuracy is not quite what one should be seeking here.

Consider someone whose humility is admirable; someone, for example, who displays extraordinary courage in a good cause or unusually energetic devotion to helping the unfortunate, and who then brushes aside praise, sincerely denying that what has been done was in any way remarkable. In such a person, this self-deprecation is inaccurate, since what was done really was outstanding. Yet here this self-deprecation makes the individual's character more admirable, for courage or devotion combined with such humility is even better than courage or devotion without it. An element of self-deception is thus to be welcomed; it is admirable to have trained oneself to underrate one's own merits to some extent.

Why is it deemed to be admirable that people should cultivate an inaccurate humility, rather than strict accuracy in self-appraisal? Surely it is because inflated self-estimates are so widespread and troublesome that society needs to fight against them very forcefully. To set up accuracy in self-appraisal as one's goal would not be sufficiently forceful. Stronger than that as a defense against the pressing dangers of overweening pride is the requirement that one should underrate oneself. Inaccurate humility, because of its social utility, thus rightly comes to be valued above accurate self-appraisal.

Stephen F. Barker

FURTHER READING

Aristotle. *Nicomachean Ethics*. Translated and edited by Roger Crisp. New York: Cambridge University Press, 2000.

Bowra, C. M. *The Greek Experience*. Cleveland: World, 1957.

Driver, Julia. "The Virtues of Ignorance." *Journal of Philosophy* 86. (July, 1989): 373-384.

"The Gospel According to Matthew." In *New American Standard Bible*. Reference ed. Nashville, Tenn.: Holman, 1981.

Häring, Bernard. *The Law of Christ*. Translated by Edwin G. Kaiser. Vol. 1. Westminster, Md.: The Newman Press, 1961.

Richards, Norvin. *Humility*. Philadelphia: Temple University Press, 1992.

SEE ALSO: Aristotelian ethics; Christian ethics; Jewish ethics; *Nicomachean Ethics*; Pride.

Hunger

DEFINITION: Desire or need for food

TYPE OF ETHICS: Human rights

SIGNIFICANCE: Hunger is one of the fundamental physical needs of all people. On an individual level, it can motivate crime and self-destructive bouts of consumption. On a social or global level, hunger stands for some as both symbol and consequence of the unequal distribution of wealth and resources and as a grounds for the moral condemnation of social and economic systems.

Hunger is as old as history. More than 15 percent of the world's people are malnourished in even the best of years, and this situation has existed throughout recorded history. In bad years, up to 67 percent of the world's people may suffer from malnutrition. Hunger is an ordinary part of life for many people, even in developed nations such as the United States. Millions of people do not get either enough food or enough nourishing food, and the results are disease and death. Globally, 50 percent of malnourished children in poor countries die before reaching the age of five. Countless others become physically or mentally handicapped for life because of malnutrition.

Hunger is deadly during famines. Throughout history, famines have afflicted one area or another every few years. The principal causes of famine are drought, floods, plant disease, and war. Of these causes, drought is the most frequent.

DROUGHTS AND FLOODS

In 3500 B.C.E., the Egyptians documented the first famine to be recorded, which was caused by drought and a plague of locusts. The death rate was extremely high, but no accurate estimates of the number of lives lost are available. The Romans documented the second known drought in 436 B.C.E. Thousands of Roman citizens threw themselves into the Tiber River so that they would not have to face starvation. Many early civilizations believed that famines were punishments sent by God.

Mohandas K. Gandhi once said, "If God should appear to an Indian villager it would be as a loaf of bread." Five of the ten deadliest known famines have occurred in India. Most were caused by the failure of the monsoon rains, which caused drought and crop failure. One of the worst famines in Indian history occurred in 1865, when the monsoons failed to arrive.

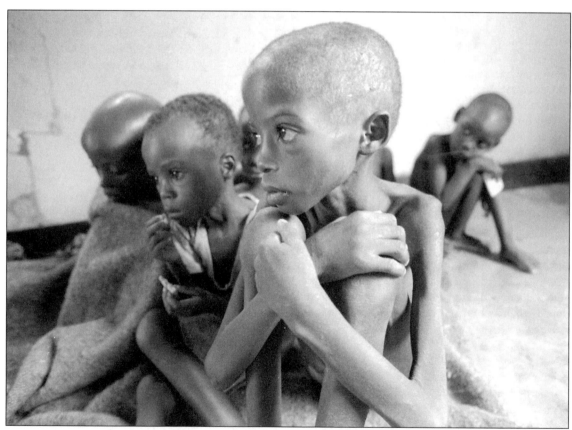

Severely malnourished Rwandan orphans waiting to be fed in a refugee camp in Zaire in early 1997. Already an endemic problem throughout tropical Africa, hunger takes a particularly heavy toll on the continent's millions of refugees. (AP/Wide World Photos)

India was a British colony at the time, but Great Britain decided to export the extra food that was produced in India rather than send it to the areas that were affected by the famine. The reason that the British gave was that the people in the affected areas could not pay for the food, whereas hungry people in other countries could. Ten million people ultimately died. The monsoon rains failed again between 1876 and 1878, killing 5 million people. A three-year drought that occurred in China between 1876 and 1879 killed more than 13 million people. Tragedy struck again in the Calcutta region of India in 1943 and 1944, killing 1.5 million people.

During the early 1970's and again in 1984, drought plagued many African nations. The Sahel nations lost more than a million people during the 1970's, and eastern and Southern Africa lost more than 1.5 million people throughout the 1980's because of drought.

Archaeologists believe that droughts have caused the collapse of whole civilizations. About 4,500 years ago, a great civilization arose in the Indus River valley. Drought caused this civilization, whose major cities were Harappa and Mohenjo-daro, to vanish by 1700 B.C.E. In the southwestern United States, the civilization of the Cliff Dwellers may have ended as a result of drought in approximately 1300.

Although the lack of rainfall is the major cause of famine, too much rain can also be disastrous. China has suffered hundreds of famines because of floods of the Yellow River. These disasters are so common that the Chinese have nicknamed the river "China's Sorrow." In 1889, as many as 2 million people died in floods, and between 1929 and 1930, the river claimed another 2 million lives. People died in such large numbers that they were buried in mass graves called "ten-thousand-man holes." Women and children were sold to obtain food, and cannibalism spread rapidly. Hurricanes also cause floods that cause famines in many nations.

PLANT DISEASES

Plants suffer from diseases just as humans do. Plant diseases can wipe out crops, causing famine and starvation. Perhaps the most famous example of such a famine occurred in Ireland during the 1840's, when a fungus wiped out most of the crop of potatoes, which were the staple food of the Irish. The resulting famine claimed more than a million lives.

Ireland was a British colony at the time, but the British expended little effort to help Ireland. In fact, Irish peasants who could not pay their rent were thrown out into the cold and left to starve in ditches. Many perished, and others tried to escape by migrating. The emigrants were so weak when they boarded ships leaving the country that these ships became known as "coffin ships" because so many people died on board of sickness and starvation before reaching America, England, or Australia. More than a million Irish emigrated because of the "Great Hunger."

WAR

Drought, flood, and plant diseases have caused tremendous suffering, but the hunger and famine caused by war are even more horrifying because they are avoidable.

The people of Russia, the largest country in the world, have suffered often because of famines caused by humankind. One of the worst such famines occurred between 1921 and 1922. World War I was the cause of this tragedy. When many Russians went off to war, beginning in 1914, agricultural production dropped sharply, and by 1920, food was scarce. A drought hit the Volga River valley in 1920. By 1921, much farmland looked like desert land, and 30 million Russians went hungry. People made bread out of tree leaves, dirt, and water, and they ate cooked grass. Civil war made it difficult to send donated food to the affected areas, and ultimately 5 million people died from hunger. More Russians were killed by the famine than were killed in World War I.

During the Biafra civil war in Nigeria between 1967 and 1970, more than a million people, mostly women and children, died of starvation when federal forces withheld food from rebels to force them to stop trying to secede from Nigeria. It is not uncommon for governments to use famine as a weapon of war. The Ethiopian government used such tactics in its war against Eritrea, and they have also been used in Mozambique and Angola. The results were that thousands of people died.

EFFECTS OF HUNGER

People who lack food lose weight and grow weak. Many become so weak that they die of diarrhea or other simple ailments. This weakened condition is called marasmus. Children who have some food but not enough suffer from kwashiorkor, or malnutrition.

One symptom of kwashiorkor is edema, which manifests as a swollen stomach, puffy face, and swollen arms and ankles. Hair and skin often take on an orange or white color. Those who survive kwashiorkor often suffer lifelong mental and physical handicaps. In addition, when the human body is weakened by hunger, it cannot fight off disease. During most famines, survivors crowd together into relief centers to wait for food, creating the potential for epidemics of influenza, measles, cholera, dysentery, typhus, pneumonia, and tuberculosis.

Worse yet are the effects of skyrocketing crimes during droughts, floods, wars, and famines. Desperate people loot, steal, and kill to secure goods that are not otherwise available to them. They may sell stolen goods to purchase food. Women may prostitute themselves for food or sell their children for a meal. Children may band together to obtain food by looting. Violence may break out near food distribution centers, creating panic and anarchy, as occurred in Somalia in 1992. Adaptation to hunger can lead to desperate responses such as cannibalistic murder, which would not be practiced under other circumstances.

Crops are not the only things to be destroyed; livestock often die in record numbers during prolonged famines. Those that do not die may be killed for food. In addition, seed reserved for planting may be eaten to avoid starvation. This lowers agricultural production levels and makes returning to a normal way of life extremely difficult.

CONCLUSIONS

The English philosopher Thomas Hobbes noted that people are inherently selfish, mean, and aggressive. History demonstrates that, when they are hungry, parents will take food from the mouths of their own children. The Chinese have argued that if a child dies, it is easy to make another, but an older person who dies is more difficult to replace. During the Italian famine of 450, known as "Dufresnoy," parents allegedly ate their children. Well-fed people are likely to be content; are less likely than hungry people to be angry, hostile, and aggressive; and are less inclined to engage in desperate behavior that may cause harm to others. Therefore, it is in the interest of humankind to reduce or eliminate hunger. A world without hunger would be a safer place for everyone.

Dallas L. Browne

FURTHER READING

Byron, William, ed. *The Causes of World Hunger.* New York: Paulist Press, 1982.

Lappe, Frances Moore, and Joseph Collins. *World Hunger: Twelve Myths.* New York: Grove Press, 1986.

Lucas, George R., Jr., and Thomas Ogletree, eds. *Lifeboat Ethics: The Moral Dilemmas of World Hunger.* New York: Harper & Row, 1976.

McCormick, Peter. *When Famine Returns: Ethics, Identity, and the Deep Pathos of Things.* Heidelberg, Germany: C. Winter, 2003.

McCuen, Gary E. *World Hunger and Social Justice.* Hudson, Wis.: Author, 1986.

Rau, Bill. *From Feast to Famine: Official Cures and Grassroots Remedies to Africa's Food Crisis.* London: Zed Books, 1991.

Schwartz-Nobel, Loretta. *Starving in the Shadow of Plenty.* New York: Putnam, 1981.

Toton, Suzanne C. *World Hunger: The Responsibility of Christian Education.* Maryknoll, N.Y.: Orbis Books, 1982.

SEE ALSO: Charity; Duty; Famine; Generosity; Genetically modified foods; Morality; Vegetarianism.

Ḥusayn

IDENTIFICATION: Grandson of the Prophet Muḥammad

BORN: January, 626, Medina, Arabia (now in Saudi Arabia)

DIED: October 10, 680, Karbalāʾ, Iraq

TYPE OF ETHICS: Religious ethics

SIGNIFICANCE: The death of Ḥusayn was one of the formative events in Shīʿa Islam, and its annual remembrance is the most important occasion in Shīʿa communal life.

Ḥusayn and Ḥasan were the sons of ʿAlī ibn Abī Ṭālib, the cousin of Muḥammad, and Fāṭima, Muḥammad's daughter. Following Muḥammad's death, leadership of the Islamic community passed to, in order, Abū Bakr, ʿUmar, ʿUthmān, and ʿAlī. This succession was not without controversy: the "party of ʿAlī" (*shīʿat ʿAlī*; later, simply the Shīʿa) had always held that ʿAlī should be *khalīf*, or leader, of the community. The assassination of ʿAlī in 661 led to a convulsive dispute.

ʿAlī was succeeded by Muʿāwiyya, of the Umayya family (whom many mistrusted as outwardly converting to Islam only for selfish gain). Although Ḥasan relinquished his claims to the khalifate (and died c. 670, some claim of poisoning), his younger brother Ḥusayn gathered the *shīʿat ʿAlī* to challenge Muʿāwiyya. Ḥusayn and most of his party were killed by Muʿāwiyya's troops at Karbala. Shiʿa Muslims recognize that as the martyrdom of Ḥusayn, and their annual public remembrance serves as a visceral reminder that human lives belong only to God and are to be surrendered to his service.

Thomas Gaskill

SEE ALSO: Abū Bakr; Fāṭima; Muḥammad; Shīʿa.

Hussein, Saddam

IDENTIFICATION: Authoritarian president of Iraq from 1979 to 2003
BORN: April 28, 1937, Tikrit, Iraq
TYPE OF ETHICS: Human rights
SIGNIFICANCE: Hussein brutally suppressed internal opposition in his own country and led it into three devastating wars before international intervention ended his regime.

Saddam Hussein liked images that portrayed him with a sword in hand. A nominal Muslim, he apparently viewed the Islamic religion as a list of rules about external behaviors and demonstrated little concern for humanistic values such as altruism or human brotherhood. Indeed, he gave every indication of being proud of using violence to exact revenge and maintain power. He even spoke favorably about the methods of Adolf Hitler and Joseph Stalin.

Hussein experienced a harsh and deprived childhood. He was raised without a father in an inhospitable part of Iraq where members of rival ethnic, religious, and tribal groups constantly fought one another. After moving to the capital city, Baghdad, in 1955, he joined the radical Baath Party, which endorsed violent means to achieve socialism and Arab nationalism. Rising rapidly within the party, he participated in a failed attempt to assassinate the military president of Iraq in 1959. After the Baath Party took over the government in a *coup d'état* in 1968, Hussein gained power by controlling Iraq's infamous security agencies. In 1979, he was installed as president.

SUPREME LEADER

Hussein's first act as president was to purge the party of every person suspected of disloyalty to him. During the twenty-four years of his rule, all antigovernment dissent—no matter how trivial—was punished as treasonous. The regime commonly used torture to exact confessions. Although a few elections were held for the national assembly, as president, Hussein had the power to override the assembly's decisions. For reasons such as this, social scientists classify his regime as totalitarian. Many Iraqi citizens, nevertheless, supported Hussein because of his progressive social policies designed to improve education and help the poor.

Hussein wanted to make Iraq the dominant military and economic power in the Persian Gulf. In 1980, he ordered the invasion of Iran with the purpose of annexing the oil-rich province of Khuzistan. Lasting eight years and resulting in the deaths of perhaps a million people, the war accomplished nothing. During the conflict, Hussein brutally suppressed an Iranian-backed Kurdish insurrection and gassed the village of Halubjah, killing about five thousand civilians. In 1990, Hussein ordered the invasion of Kuwait, giving him control over a fifth of the world's oil supplies. In 1991, a large international coalition, led by the United States, ousted Iraqi troops from Kuwait, but left Hussein in power.

Between 1991 and 2003, the United Nations passed several resolutions that prohibited Iraq from acquiring weapons of mass destruction (WMD). Hussein never fully complied with United Nations demands for inspection, although the evidence suggests that he probably stopped development of the WMDs. In 2003, the United States, in coalition with Great Britain and a few other countries, used his noncooperation as a basis for invading Iraq and overthrowing his regime. Scholars and philosophers disagreed about whether this preemptive action could be justified by just-war theory. In December, 2003, Hussein was finally captured, and plans were made to

Saddam Hussein shortly after his capture by U.S. troops in December, 2003. (AP/Wide World Photos)

put him on trial for crimes against human rights. In April, 2004, it was announced that he would be tried by an Iraqi court.

Thomas Tandy Lewis

FURTHER READING

Coughin, Con. *Saddam: King of Terror.* New York: HarperCollins, 2002.

Karsh, Efrain, and Inari Rautsi. *Saddam Hussein: A Political Biography.* New York: Grove/Atlantic, 2002.

Munthe, Turi, ed. *The Saddam Hussein Reader.* New York: Thunder's Mouth Press, 2002.

SEE ALSO: Biochemical weapons; Dictatorship; Intervention; Iraq; Islamic ethics; Just war theory; Moral equivalence; Torture; Tyranny; Violence.

Hypnosis

DEFINITION: State of consciousness, achieved through techniques of induction, in which a person is unusually open to suggestion

TYPE OF ETHICS: Psychological ethics

SIGNIFICANCE: Because hypnosis gives the appearance of yielding control of one's behavior and mind and conforming to the wishes of the hypnotist, a potential for abuse is perceived.

Although the eighteenth century Viennese physician Franz Anton Mesmer no doubt hypnotized some of his patients ("mesmerism"), the concept of hypnosis was unknown before the work of the English physician James Braid. Braid invented the term "hypnosis" and conducted the first scientific studies of hypnotism. Braid devised numerous techniques for inducing the hypnotic state and extensively studied the psychological factors involved. Braid and the British physicians John Elliotson and James Esdaile made extensive use of hypnosis in their medical practices as an adjunct to surgery. Esdaile, for example, reported more than three hundred cases in which he performed major operations on unanesthetized but hypnotized patients who apparently experienced no pain.

The psychoanalyst Sigmund Freud found that hypnosis could be used to relieve symptoms of neurotic and abnormal behavior. Freud repudiated hypnosis as a therapeutic tool, however, because it could only relieve symptoms; it revealed nothing about the causes of the behavior.

Modern interest in hypnosis has passed from the physician and psychoanalyst to the experimental psychologist. Psychology's concern with hypnotism involves understanding its nature and mechanisms. Clark L. Hull's 1933 book *Hypnosis and Suggestibility* was the first systematic attempt to apply modern psychological methods to hypnosis, and Ernest R. Hilgard (b. 1904) and others added significantly to the understanding of this phenomenon.

ETHICAL ISSUES OF HYPNOSIS

The aforementioned characteristics of the hypnotic state raise the question of whether the hypnotized person becomes unduly dependent upon, controlled by, or influenced by the hypnotist. While in the hypnotic state, could the person be persuaded by an

Characteristics of the Hypnotized State

1. Planfulness ceases. Hypnotized subjects do not wish to initiate activities; instead, they prefer to be given suggestions by the hypnotist.

2. Attention becomes more than usually selective. Subjects attend to what the hypnotists command and ignore other events.

3. Enriched fantasy is readily produced. Unreal events, not unlike dreams, can be experienced easily.

4. Reality testing is reduced and reality distortion is accepted. Altered perceptions of the real world can be produced and believed; for example, talking with an imagined person believed to be sitting in a chair.

5. Suggestibility is increased. Subjects willingly agree to cooperate with the induction technique in order to be hypnotized. Some increase in suggestibility—but less than is commonly assumed—also appears to follow.

6. Posthypnotic amnesia is often present. Some subjects, if instructed to do so, will forget most of what occurs during the hypnotic suggestion. When prearranged signals are given, memories are restored. Also, a signal introduced during hypnotic suggestion, when given posthypnotically, may cause the previously hypnotized person to carry out a prearranged action even though the person has no memory of having been given the instruction.

7. Responsiveness to hypnotic induction varies. About 5 to 10 percent of people cannot be hypnotized at all, a similar percentage are easily hypnotized, but most people fall in between the two extremes. What appears to be the best predictor of susceptibility to being hypnotized is the degree to which a person enjoys daydreaming, can produce vivid mental images, and has a rich imagination.

Source: Rita L. Atkinson et al. *Introduction to Psychology* (1993).

unethical hypnotist to engage in behaviors that he or she otherwise would not perform? Is it possible to induce, for example, irrational, antisocial, criminal, unethical, immoral, or self-destructive behaviors such as impulsively buying a new car, robbing a bank, committing murder, injuring oneself, committing suicide, or having sex with one's hypnotherapist?

The consensus firmly states that hypnosis cannot induce or persuade a person to do anything that he or she would not otherwise do. The belief otherwise undoubtedly arises from the misconception that hypnosis is a condition induced in the person by the hypnotist.

In fact, the hypnotist acts simply as a facilitator, guiding and teaching the person how to think and what to do to produce a particular behavior within the person's capabilities. The person is responsible for and decides whether to perform that behavior. Before a behavior can occur, the person must be willing and able to produce it.

Therefore, the question of ethics is really a pseudoethical issue. The hypnotist is not doing anything to which the person does not consent and cannot compel a person to commit an act that is repugnant to that person or beyond his or her capabilities. As Roy Udolf cogently observed, antisocial and self-destructive behavior can and has been obtained in hypnotized persons, but the hypnotist cannot induce the hypnotized person to commit those acts. The person had decided to do so already. An unethical hypnotist could, however, facilitate the performance of that act. For example, a hypnotist could make a criminal less nervous and more self-assured during the commission of a crime.

Laurence Miller

FURTHER READING

Atkinson, Rita L., et al. *Introduction to Psychology.* 11th ed. New York: Harcourt Brace Jovanovich, 1993.

Gregory, Richard L., ed. *The Oxford Companion to the Mind.* New York: Oxford University Press, 1987.

Hilgard, Ernest R. *The Experience of Hypnosis.* New York: Harcourt, Brace & World, 1968.

Hilgard, Josephine R. *Personality and Hypnosis: A Study of Imaginative Involvement.* 2d ed. Chicago: University of Chicago Press, 1979.

Moss, C. Scott. *Hypnosis in Perspective.* New York: Macmillan, 1965.

Udolf, Roy. *Handbook of Hypnosis for Professionals.* New York: Van Nostrand Reinhold, 1981.

Weitzenhoffer, Andre M. *The Practice of Hypnotism.* 2d ed. New York: John Wiley & Sons, 2000.

SEE ALSO: Behavior therapy; Biofeedback; Epistemological ethics; Freud, Sigmund; Pain; Psychology.

Hypocrisy

DEFINITION: Feigning to be what one is not, assuming a false appearance of virtue or religion, "posturing"
TYPE OF ETHICS: Personal and social ethics
SIGNIFICANCE: Acts of hypocrisy are generally thought of as immoral in themselves, but they are also taken to impugn the character of the hypocrite, such that all of his or her other actions are rendered suspect as well.

Hypocrisy—pretending to have more virtue than one actually possesses—is, in one manner of speaking, the exact opposite of a moral and ethical philosophy, for its practitioners are liars, deceivers, and manipulators. People living according to a just ethical standard must exercise care, for hypocrites can copy the attitudes and behaviors of "good" people and will try to control the good for their own self-centered gain.

HYPOCRITICAL BEHAVIOR

The words "hypocrite" and "hypocrisy" connote the very dispositions and characters of people who are immoral or amoral but who hide their relative immorality with the appearance of morality. The hypocrite "undervalues" noble ideals and is ruled by inferior passions; he or she is inclined to do "bad" things rather than "good" things. He or she is totally corrupt and is a willful liar yet always presents the image of a virtuous person.

In their worship, religious people worldwide pray, lament, and make promises to their gods. Too often, they promptly forget those promises as they scurry to make money, showing little love, little mercy, little trust, little kindness, no brotherhood, and no forgiveness. Many people who call themselves Christians, Muslims, Jews, and so forth are curiously unmoved by the suffering of others.

To find religious hypocrites, one need not look beyond religious leaders. In the United States alone, the 1980's and 1990's witnessed many religious scandals. The Christian televangelist Jimmy Swaggert, a married parent, in preaching to his flock, often condemned sinners and showed much glee as he sadistically described their suffering in the "pits" of Hell for all eternity. Later, he was photographed patronizing a prostitute who later claimed that he was a "pervert." The televangelist then tearfully repented on his television show. Later, Swaggert was again caught patronizing a prostitute, but he continued his television show, the main purpose of which seemed to be to beg for money; the same man had earlier ruined another preacher by making references to the other's bad character.

Jimmy Bakker, another televangelist, famed for the development of a religious theme park, was eventually imprisoned because he misappropriated contributions from the faithful. Although several pentecostal leaders appeared to have attracted the largest news headlines, Roman Catholic priests have not been immune to criticism. In recent years, many priests have helped women commit adultery and have engaged in various sex crimes, including the molestation of children.

The world's hypocrites come not only from the realm of religion but from all "walks" of life. During the 1970's, as the United States faced the Watergate scandal, President Richard Nixon, in a nationwide television broadcast, righteously proclaimed that he was not a "crook"; this event occurred shortly before he resigned rather than face impeachment proceedings. Later, during the 1980's and 1990's, bankers all across the land lied to cover up their part in the savings and loan scandals, with many still lying just before authorities indicted, convicted, and sentenced them to very light terms in white collar prisons. Additionally, during the 1990's, many members of Congress showed "self-righteous indignation" upon learning that their "bank" was under investigation; shortly thereafter, it was proved that many of them were overdrawn and in arrears (check "kiting" is a crime, and common folk most likely would have been prosecuted).

Even the world of sports has its own kind of hypocrisy. A former football star of the University of Oklahoma's Sooners made television appearances on behalf of the "Just Say No" campaign against drugs. Additionally, he spoke on many occasions to youth groups—all this shortly before he was found guilty and sent to prison for the illegal use of drugs.

CONCLUSION

The dangers that the hypocrite poses are largely self-evident. The hypocritical politician "looks out for number one." While bespeaking the public interest, he or she may "sell out" to special interest groups and, if found out, will likely scream about assaults on his or her good character. The hypocritical religious leader will use—for selfish purposes—the very foundations of religious faith. Even the action of the aforementioned hypocritical football star had the negative effect of affecting young people's views of the adult world, in which leaders and "stars" too often are consummate liars—to the detriment of society.

James Smallwood

FURTHER READING

Eck, Marcel. *Lies and Truth.* Translated by Bernard Murchland. New York: Macmillan, 1970.

Evans, Donald. *Faith, Authenticity, and Morality.* Toronto: University of Toronto Press, 1980.

Fingarette, Herbert. *Self-Deception.* New York: Humanities Press, 1969.

Goleman, Daniel. *Vital Lies, Simple Truths: The Psychology of Self-Deception.* New York: Simon & Schuster, 1985.

Grant, Ruth W. *Hypocrisy and Integrity: Machiavelli, Rousseau, and the Ethics of Politics.* Chicago: University of Chicago Press, 1997.

Martin, Mike W. *Self-Deception and Morality.* Lawrence: University Press of Kansas, 1986.

Newman, Jay. *Fanatics and Hypocrites.* Buffalo, N.Y.: Prometheus Books, 1986.

Spiegel, James S. *Hypocrisy: Moral Fraud and Other Vices.* Grand Rapids, Mich.: Baker Books, 1999.

Trilling, Lionel. *Sincerity and Authenticity.* Cambridge, Mass.: Harvard University Press, 1971.

Wittgenstein, Ludwig. *Culture and Value: A Selection from the Posthumous Remains.* Translated by Peter Winch. Edited by Georg Henrik von Wright, Heikki Nyman, and Alois Pichler. Rev. 2d ed. Cambridge, Mass.: Blackwell, 1997.

SEE ALSO: Cheating; "Everyone does it"; Honesty; Lying; Self-righteousness; Televangelists.

I

I and Thou

IDENTIFICATION: Book by Martin Buber (1878-1965)

DATE: *Ich und Du*, 1923 (*English translation*, 1937)

TYPE OF ETHICS: Modern history

SIGNIFICANCE: Buber's work views reality as fundamentally social, consisting of interpersonal relationships. These relationships are defined in moral action and are expressed in the symbiotic kinship of humankind and nature.

Buber's central question of the meaning of humanness is expressed in his recurring word *Wesen* (essence, being, nature), as understood in terms of two primary word pairs: "I-You" and "I-It." The I-You relationship is total involvement of self and other in intimacy, sharing, empathy, caring, openness, and trust. The I-It relationship consists of self viewing other in abstract terms, resulting in possession, exploitation, and distrust. The I-It pair permits the self to objectify the other, creating a state of manipulative dependency, and the I-You pair encourages an atmosphere of interdependence, permitting growth and respect. Only through genuine I-You encounters do people discover their humanity and, by mutually affirming and confirming one another, come face to face with the Eternal Thou.

Realistically, Buber recognized that every I-You can become an encounter, and in his poetic *Sprachdenken* ("thinking in terms of language"), he counseled that one's essential humanity is lost if one treats every You (animate and inanimate) as an It (acts of hate, killing, vandalism). "Without It man cannot live; but he who lives with It alone, is not a man." In the area of religion, Buber insisted that any religious form that is not in the category of I-You is illicit or at least nonreligious. Thus, he was critical of Jewish Halachah (religious orthopraxy) and Christian sacraments; he believed that the nature and essence of God are not restricted to doctrines and dogmas. Buber's classic statement on essentials is essentially existential.

Zev Garber

SEE ALSO: Buber, Martin; Friendship; Hasidism; Personal relationships.

Austrian philosopher Martin Buber, the author of I and Thou. *(Library of Congress)*

Ibn al-ʿArabī

IDENTIFICATION: Arab philosopher

BORN: July 28, 1165, Murcia, Valencia (now in Spain)

DIED: November 16, 1240, Damascus, Ayyūbid Empire (now in Syria)

TYPE OF ETHICS: Religious ethics

SIGNIFICANCE: In such works as *Meccan Revelations* (thirteenth century) and *Gems of Wisdom* (1229), Ibn al-ʿArabī put forward a systematic philosophical account of Sufism. Still widely influential in modern practice, his work is often seen as the creative zenith of Sufism.

Ibn al-ʿArabī's work captured the devotional spirit of earlier Sufism, gave it sophisticated and original philosophical expression, and, in so doing, both gave it new force and made it more acceptable to more conservative Muslims. His singular obsession was with *waḥdat al-wujūd* (perhaps, "the unity of Being"). He argued that God is the only true reality (*al-ḥaqq*) and the inner nature of all things; the phenomenal world is a manifestation or mirror of that reality. God, considered as manifestation, is creation (*al-khalq*)—a claim that has led to controversies about whether Ibn al-ʿArabī was a pantheist. Annihilation or immersion of the soul (*fanāʾ*) in the real unity of Being is, he argued, the ultimate human good. Humans occupy a special position in the cosmos because they are able to know God both in his phenomenal nature through sense perception and in his inner nature by achieving *fanāʾ*. One who has perfected all the potentials of the soul is the Perfect Man, who, in Ibn al-ʿArabī's thought, is exemplified by Muḥammad.

Thomas Gaskill

SEE ALSO: Maimonides, Moses; Muḥammad; Sufism.

Ibn Gabirol

IDENTIFICATION: Arab philosopher and poet

BORN: c. 1020, probably Málaga, Caliphate of Córdoba (now in Spain)

DIED: c. 1057, probably Valencia, Kingdom of Valencia (now in Spain)

TYPE OF ETHICS: Religious ethics

SIGNIFICANCE: Considered one of the greatest poets of the "Golden Age" of Spanish Jewry (ninth century through twelfth century), Ibn Gabirol was also an important philosopher: He introduced Neoplatonism into Europe and strongly influenced the Christian Scholasticism of the Middle Ages. He is author of *The Source of Life* (eleventh century).

Orphaned early in life and raised in Saragossa, Ibn Gabirol devoted much of his life to the pursuit of wisdom (philosophy), in which he found solace from his serious physical ailments and his squabbles with wealthy patrons and town elders, which caused him great mental anguish. His *The Source of Life* (*Fons vitae*) is more Neoplatonic than Aristotelian, more religious than theological. It holds that the purpose of human life is for the soul to commune with the upper world, and it emphasizes knowledge and contemplation rather than action. The subjects of *The Source of Life* are three: God, or pure spiritual substance; divine will, which is separate from the essence of God; and universal matter and universal form, which, in combination, produce universal reason. The universe is a gradual series of emanations of substances, and the farther a substance is from the source of all, the more material and corporeal it becomes.

The gradation of substances is unified by the divine will, which permeates the whole series of gradations. In this point, Ibn Gabirol departs from classical Neoplatonism, which teaches the system of emanations in a mechanical way that is totally alien to the Jewish idea of creation. The human soul, an emanation of the world-soul, is eternal, but, in uniting with the body in the corporeal world, it is lowered from its pristine purity. The soul retains its desire to return to its source, however, and this is accomplished in two ways: through knowledge of the divine will as it extends into matter and form, and apart from matter and form; and by reason, by means of which the soul unites with world reason and ultimately attaches to the "source of life." Ibn Gabirol's long philosophical poem *Keter Malkhut* (*The Kingly Crown*, 1911) is addressed to the human intellectual aspiration to discover God ("I flee from You, to You") and praises figuratively the attributes of God. This classic poem is included in the High Holiday services of Ashkenazic and Sephardic Jews.

Zev Garber

SEE ALSO: Jewish ethics; Kabbala.

Ibn Khaldūn

IDENTIFICATION: Arab philosopher
BORN: May 27, 1332, Tunis, Tunisia
DIED: March 17, 1406, Cairo, Egypt
TYPE OF ETHICS: Religious ethics
SIGNIFICANCE: Ibn Khaldūn was the first and one
of the greatest practitioners of the philosophy of
history. His mammoth work *The Muqaddimah*
(1375-1379) lays out a philosophical analysis
of, and foundation for, the methodology of historical research and writing, and it constitutes the
earliest known work in the theory of social and
cultural history. Ibn Khaldūn also developed a
system of political ethics that he hoped would
benefit society and aid in the development of civilizations.

Born into a family of scholars and government officials, Ibn Khaldūn lost his family in 1349 to the bu-
bonic plague. After the completion of his formal
studies, he became a roving ambassador, serving a
series of rulers in North Africa and Moorish Spain.
At the same time, he began collecting material for his
Kitāb al-ᶜibar, or universal history, which he completed in 1382. The most important part of this work
was its "Prolegomena," or introduction, which made
an attempt to establish a purpose for history.

Disturbed by the decline of the Muslim states and
Muslim civilization, Ibn Khaldūn sought to find reasons for it, after which he set forth a series of ethical
principles that he believed must be followed to reverse the decline. Although he was a good Muslim,
Ibn Khaldūn introduced the concept of natural causality. He believed that society was the creation and
the responsibility of human beings. Ibn Khaldūn believed that social organization, and especially the
state, was the key to improved individual welfare and
the refinement of civilization. He held that rulers
should develop ethical political principles such as
placing the welfare of society before individual ag-
grandizement, ameliorating taxes, infusing the state
with a sense of purpose, and avoiding unnecessary
wars. Ibn Khaldūn spent the final years of his life
in Cairo, where he was a Muslim judge and a professor.

Nis Petersen

FURTHER READING
Enan, Mohammad Abdullah. *Ibn Khaldun: His Life
and Work*. Lahore, India: Muhammad Ashraf,
1969.
Lacoste, Yves. *Ibn Khaldun*. London, England: Verso,
1984.

SEE ALSO: Islamic ethics; Politics.

Ideal observer

DEFINITION: Person or being who has an ideal degree
of nonmoral knowledge and the ability rationally
to comprehend and analyze that knowledge
TYPE OF ETHICS: Theory of ethics
SIGNIFICANCE: The model of the ideal observer is
used by some rationalist ethical systems to think
about or define the nature of the good. It is anath-
ema to systems based on emotion or moral sentiment rather than reason, as well as to those epistemological models that hold prejudice or
perspective to be constitutive of knowledge.

The idea of an ideal observer emerged in the eighteenth century in the work of British moralists such
as Francis Hutcheson, David Hume, and Adam
Smith. These writers emphasized the importance of
full information and impartiality in moral judgment,
and they considered the approval of an observer with
such characteristics to define moral truth. For the
British moralists, such approval depended on the existence of certain moral sentiments, such as benevolence and sympathy.

By the twentieth century, the ideal observer, which
had come to be thought of as mainly self-interested,
was used to provide naturalistic theories of moral
judgment and moral truth. For example, Richard
Brandt has defined a person's own good as what that
person would want if he or she had full information
and had reflected on it in the appropriate way. Some
philosophers, such as John Rawls, have also defined
moral rightness in terms of the idea of self-interested,
impartial observers.

Eric H. Gampel

SEE ALSO: Good, the; Hume, David; Nussbaum, Martha; Smith, Adam.

Idealist ethics

DEFINITION: Ethical system, such as Plato's, based on the proposition that perfect forms and values actually exist in the world, or an ethical system, such as those of the German Romantics, based on the proposition that the nature and structure of the self's experience constitutes the necessary beginning and central object of all philosophical inquiry

TYPE OF ETHICS: Theory of ethics

SIGNIFICANCE: Platonic idealism counts moral concepts among the universal, unchanging Forms studied by philosophers: Under this type of idealism, one is ethically obligated to determine the nature of those absolute and eternal values and then to act in conformity with them. Kantian and post-Kantian idealism are characterized by the so-called "Copernican turn" inward, in which the self is placed at the center of the philosophical system: Under this type of idealism, moral principles are deduced transcendentally by examining the properties of human subjectivity and drawing conclusions based upon the nature of reason and the structure of phenomenological experience.

Most proponents of idealist ethics view values as unchanging, timeless realities. Values are real existents. The efficacy of values is situated in an ongoing, vital interrelationship between the uniqueness of a person's value experiences, on the one hand, and the harmonious totality of life, often termed the "Universal Self" or "Absolute," on the other hand. The ethics of human behavior are governed by immutable universal moral laws that are binding on all persons. These laws are known through the exercise of human reason.

HISTORY

The early Greek originator of idealist ethics, Plato posited a world of absolutes consisting of eternal Ideas or Forms, on the basis of which to formulate ethical concepts. These Forms include "goodness," "justice," and "virtue," which Plato discussed respectively in *Protagoras*, *Republic*, and *Meno*. Plato's assumption that the ethical quality of human life is governed by the person's obligation to form a rational moral personality, succinctly stated in the maxim "All virtue is knowledge," is present in the views of his disciples regarding ethical behavior. The Christian Platonist Saint Augustine viewed human behavior as governed by a priori absolutes (that is, absolutes that exist prior to experience and can therefore be discovered by reason alone): the right direction of love, for example.

During the Enlightenment, a new kind of idealism was developed by Immanuel Kant. Kant's German Idealism influenced other German Romantic thinkers, notably Georg Wilhelm Friedrich Hegel, as well as American Transcendentalists such as Ralph Waldo Emerson. Like Plato, Kant believed in an objective reality, which he referred to as the noumenal realm, and he differentiated it from the reality experienced by human beings, the phenomenal realm. Kant argued, however, that the only way to know anything about noumena was to examine the structure of one's experience of phenomena and to make rational deductions based upon that structure. He referred to this strategy as "transcendental deduction."

Kantian ethics, as with all of Kant's philosophical system, was ultimately concerned with determining the nature of human freedom, and Kant argued forcefully that acting in accordance with a universal moral law, a law that has noumenal and not mere phenomenal existence, is the only way to achieve freedom, because it is the only way to act neither randomly, based upon capricious internal desires, nor according to purely external impositions. Hegel also employed a strategy of transcendental philosophy, but instead of examining the structure of experience from the outside, he attempted to engage in a transcendental philosophy from a first-person point of view. Hegel's species of idealism embraced absolute ideals, but not immutable ideals, because he believed that philosophy, society, and all of reality, exist fundamentally as a process of historical evolution. So for Hegel values do change over time, and their universality is as much an aspect of those changes as it is contained within their final form.

More modern idealists, such as Josiah Royce and Alfred North Whitehead, continued the Platonic tradition of founding ethical considerations on absolute, presumed permanent ideals. Royce's student Herman Harrell Horne applied idealist ethics to education in his *This New Education* (1931), which was reminiscent of an earlier American idealist's work: that of William T. Harris, editor of *The Journal of Speculative Philosophy* and post-Civil War spokesperson for the neo-Hegelians of the St. Louis, Missouri, Philosophical Society. Of Plato's impact on the subsequent development of Western philosophy, Whitehead wrote: "The safest general characterization of the European philosophical tradition is that it consists of a series of footnotes to Plato."

PRINCIPLES OF IDEALIST ETHICS

Platonic idealist ethics originates in human comprehension of and adherence to the Platonic ideational forms of the "good": justice, knowledge, and virtue. Enunciated in the *Republic* by Plato's allegory of the metals, the just society is an idealized one in which rulers, guardians (those who enforce rulers' decisions), farmers, and crafts-people harmoniously coexist by internalizing the four cardinal virtues of wisdom, courage, temperance, and justice, the latter defined as a state of human affairs in which each contributes to society according to the predetermined limits of his function.

Kantian idealist ethics originates in a dedication to obeying a universal and universalizable law that has the form of law as such, regardless of its content. This is necessary both because only considerations of formal structure can yield a truly objective law—everyone will disagree about moral laws based on their content—and because only universal laws discovered and willed through pure practical reason are constitutive of human freedom rather than constituting a form of constraint. The universal law exists as much within the reasoned reflection of the self as it does in the external noumenal world. Therefore, for Kant, to act morally is to be free, and to be free is to act morally. Any other course of action makes one either a slave to one's desires or a slave to external impositions.

Nineteenth century philosophy was largely post-Kantian philosophy, in the sense that almost all major philosophers saw themselves as either refuting or completing Kant's system, and sometimes doing both at once. Hegel, in particular, took Kantian idealism and rendered it historical, teleological, and collective. In his *Phenomenology of Spirit (Die Phänomenologie des Geistes*, 1807), Hegel used dialectical logic to perform a transcendental deduction, much as Kant did. Hegel's deduction, however, very quickly broke with Kant, when it was discovered that remaining focused on the level of the single individual would make it impossible to achieve objective

knowledge. Only when a self-conscious mind interacts with another self-conscious mind, discovers and confronts desire in itself and its counterpart, and goes on to create social structures based on what it has learned through its confrontations, Hegel argued, can it discover an absolute moral law. If for Kant such a law was a pure formal construct deduced through individual detached reason, for Hegel absolute morality existed only through collective, intersubjective, historical practice in the world.

Idealist ethics accents the principle that human self-realization occurs within a societal context providing development and nurture; morality or ethical behavior is, however, often essentially ideational in nature. Hence, for many idealists the ethics through which human lives are lived results not from sensory experience but from cognitive deliberation. For others, though, the distinction between perception and cognition is at best a problem and at worst a misunderstanding of the nature of the mind.

IDEALIST ETHICS: AN APPRAISAL

During the late nineteenth century and throughout the twentieth century, principles of idealist ethics were on the defensive. Realist Bertrand Russell saw in idealist ethics a failure to distinguish between a person's perceptual act and the separately existing content, or "sense datum," of that act, a weakness attributed to the British empiricist George Berkeley's statement *esse est percipi* ("to be is to be perceived"). In *Religion and Science* (1936), Russell viewed ethical values as totally subjective and hence unknowable: "What science cannot discover, mankind cannot know." Positivists and pragmatists have disagreed with the idealist accent on the pivotal place of the ideal or the spiritual in determining the criteria for ethical behavior. Linguistic philosophy finds ambiguities in the technical terms of idealist ethics; existentialists and phenomenologists take exception to the Platonist assumption that there exists in the universe a normative, prescriptive, intelligible or spiritual reality, independent of the sensory world, as the source of ethics.

While idealist ethics are on the wane in Western culture, support for the principles of idealist ethics—indeed, advocacy of those principles—has not diminished. Claiming Plato's *Republic* as "*the* book on education," Allan Bloom argues for a return to the "essential being" of idealist ethics through a "common concern for the good" in *The Closing of the American Mind* (1987). Moreover, Kantian philosophy still sets the agenda for much of the Western canon. Philosophers must either agree or disagree with elements of Kant's system; ignoring it is all but impossible. It is difficult, then, to view idealist ethical concerns and their underlying rich tradition as absent in the modern world.

Malcolm B. Campbell
Updated by the editors

FURTHER READING

Boucher, David, ed. *The British Idealists*. New York: Cambridge University Press, 1997.

Bubner, Rüdiger. *The Innovations of Idealism*. Translated by Nicholas Walker. New York: Cambridge University Press, 2003.

Foster, John. *The Case for Idealism*. Boston: Routledge & Kegan Paul, 1982.

Hoernle, R. F. A. *Idealism as a Philosophy*. New York: George H. Doran, 1927.

Hösle, Vittorio. *Objective Idealism, Ethics, and Politics*. Notre Dame, Ind.: University of Notre Dame Press, 1998.

Kant, Immanuel. *Lectures on Ethics*. Edited by Peter Heath and J. B. Schneewind. Translated by Peter Heath. New York: Cambridge University Press, 2001.

Plato. *The Republic*. Translated by Desmond Lee. 2d ed. New York: Penguin Books, 2003.

Sprigge, T. L. S. *The Vindication of Absolute Idealism*. Edinburgh: University of Edinburgh Press, 1983.

Urban, W. M. *The Intelligible World*. New York: Macmillan, 1929. Reprint. Westport, Conn.: Greenwood Press, 1977.

Vesey, Godfrey, ed. *Idealism, Past and Present*. New York: Cambridge University Press, 1982.

SEE ALSO: Emerson, Ralph Waldo; *Foundations of the Metaphysics of Morals*; Hegel, Georg Wilhelm Friedrich; Kant, Immanuel; Plato; Platonic ethics; *Republic*; Russell, Bertrand; Transcendentalism; Whitehead, Alfred North.

Identity theft

DEFINITION: Appropriation of another person's confidential information for the purpose of committing theft or fraud

TYPE OF ETHICS: Legal and judicial ethics

SIGNIFICANCE: Identity theft is a crime that not only may rob victims of their possessions and access to their own private accounts but also may damage their reputations, credit ratings, and freedom by causing them to be accused of unethical or criminal behavior.

Identity theft is a major violation of ethical norms. It confronts its victims with the unenviable task of proving negative truths: that they themselves are not criminals and did not behave in an unethical manner. Passage of the Identity Theft Deterrence Act in 1998 made it a federal crime to use another person's means of identification either to commit or to aid unlawful activity.

Impersonation for profit is an age-old crime. The book of Genesis in the Bible records how Jacob pretended to be his brother Esau and tricked their father into giving him his brother's birthright. In sixteenth century France, an imposter claiming to be Martin Guerre persuaded Guerre's wife to accept him. He was exposed only after the true Martin Guerre returned home after a long absence. The prizewinning 1990 play and 1993 film *Six Degrees of Separation* fictionalized the adventures of a young man who deceived wealthy New Yorkers into believing he was the son of a famous actor.

SOURCES OF PERSONAL DATA

With the advent of credit cards, computers, and the Internet in the late twentieth century, theft of personal information became easier to perpetrate than it had ever been in the past, and its consequences became more serious. Thieves seeking identification documents steal other people's wallets and purses or intercept mail containing financial data. By searching through trash, a practice known as "dumpster diving," criminals may even find discarded preapproved credit card applications. Some careless people throw away documents containing such information as their Social Security, bank account, and credit card numbers.

Another technique that identity thieves use for obtaining confidential information is pretext calls, a technique colloquially termed "phishing." They call victims claiming that banks or credit card companies need to confirm personal information, such as critical account numbers. An ingenious variation on "phishing" uses e-mail, headed with the logo of an established company, to request that updated identification data be sent to the thieves' Internet addresses.

By posing as prospective employers or landlords, thieves can acquire credit reports displaying vital identification numbers. Corrupt employees with access to credit records have been known to sell clients' names and Social Security numbers for sums as low as twenty dollars. A surprising amount of personal material is available on the Internet, sometimes placed there by the unsuspecting victims themselves. Information brokers advertise their willingness to provide confidential records for a fee; the service is legal and valuable for creditors seeking absconding debtors or wives tracking husbands who have abandoned them, but when identification data are sold to a criminal, the result may be disastrous for the target.

USES OF IDENTIFYING DATA

The impersonal nature of the Internet makes it particularly attractive to identity thieves. Only a card number and its expiration date are needed to order easily resalable merchandise. Armed with another person's name and valid Social Security number, an impersonator can change addresses on existing accounts and ask credit companies to send new cards.

When addresses are thus changed, the victims may not discover the unauthorized charges being made on their accounts for months or years. If thieves alter the means of verifying account holders' identities—such as by changing the maiden names of the account holders' mothers—the victims will not even be able to access their own accounts to find out if fraud is occurring.

By using victims' Social Security numbers, identity thieves can open new credit card accounts; take out loans; open new bank accounts to issue bad checks; and purchase automobiles, furniture, and jewelry, without ever paying for anything with their own money. People who always pay their bills on time, and thus have clear credit reports, are particularly desirable targets for identity theft. Older persons with mortgage-free homes are equally attractive to thieves, who may use personal data to obtain mortgages on the true owners' homes and then abscond with the money advanced on the loans.

REACTIONS TO IDENTITY THEFT

Some identity theft victims first learn of their problems when their checks bounce, they are denied loans, or collection agencies call, demanding immediate repayment of debts they never incurred. First awareness of trouble for some may even occur with police officers arriving to

Poster unveiled in Portland, Oregon, in early 2004 to heighten public awareness of the dangers of identity theft. (AP/Wide World Photos)

eBay and E-mail "Phishes"

By the year 2004, the online auction site eBay had expanded to become one of the most popular and prosperous e-businesses on the World Wide Web. With literally millions of dollars changing hands through auction sales every day, the online site's huge membership list presented a tempting target to identity theft specialists. A popular scam among such criminals was to send eBay members official-looking e-mail containing messages similar to this one:

> During our regular update and verification of the accounts, we couldn't verify your current information. Either your information has changed or it is incomplete. As a result, your access to bid or buy on eBay has been restricted. To start using your eBay account fully, please update and verify your information by clicking below.

Containing the familiar four-color eBay logo and coming from what appeared to be authentic eBay e-mail addresses, such messages could be very persuasive, making recipients who feared losing their eBay privileges very nervous. Recipients who followed instructions by clicking on the links provided were then taken to equally authentic-looking Web pages. Most recipients would not know how to tell that the ostensibly authentic eBay URL addresses to which they were directed actually hid the identity thieves' real URL addresses. However, savvy eBay members—who knew that eBay itself pledged *never* to ask for confidential information—knew something was wrong when they were asked to reveal their user passwords, credit card numbers, and sometimes even their ATM PIN numbers.

serve arrest warrants for crimes committed through the false use of their names.

The discovery that a thief has misused one's identity is always a major shock. Victims' reactions may include anger, rage, disbelief, denial, and feelings of shame and embarrassment. Nearly 80 percent of people who report identity theft to the Federal Trade Commission (FTC) have no idea how the thieves acquired their personal information. Many such persons blame themselves for their misfortune.

Protestations of innocence are greeted with skepticism by banks and merchants, who may suspect that their customers are simply trying to evade paying their legitimate debts. As one sufferer complained,

victims of identity theft are assumed guilty until proven innocent, but criminals, when apprehended, are assumed innocent until proven guilty. Criminals are entitled to a public defender, while victims have to hire lawyers at their own expense. Proving one's innocence to every creditor is an arduous and expensive process that can take years to accomplish.

Despite passage of the Identity Theft Deterrence Act in 1998, the problem continued to increase throughout in the United States. In 2002, the Federal Trade Commission's hot line for fraud recorded 162,000 complaints of identity theft in 2002—an 88 percent increase over the previous year's total of 86,000 complaints. In September, 2003, the FTC reported that more than 27 million people had suffered misuse of personal information over the previous five years. More than one-third of the victims, nearly ten million people, had experienced such misuse in the preceding year alone. The cost to banks and other businesses in that year exceeded $47 billion. Individual victims reported spending thousands of dollars of their own money to clear their names. Despite the magnitude of financial losses caused by identity theft, victims have insisted that the worst aspects of the crime are the shock, emotional stress, time lost, damaged credit reputation, and feelings of having been personally violated.

Milton Berman

FURTHER READING

Bianco, Katalina M. *Identity Theft: What You Need to Know.* Chicago: CCH, 2001.

Hammond, Robert J., Jr. *Identity Theft: How to Protect Your Most Valuable Asset.* Franklin Lakes, N.J.: Career Press, 2003.

Henderson, Harry. *Privacy in the Information Age.* New York: Facts On File, 1999.

ID Theft: When Bad Things Happen to Your Good Name. Washington, D.C.: Federal Trade Commission, 2002.

Lane, Carol A. *Naked in Cyberspace: How to Find Personal Information Online.* 2d ed. Medford, N.J.: CyberAge Books/Information Today, 2002.

O'Harrow, Robert, Jr. "Identity Crisis." *Washington Post Magazine*, Sunday, August 10, 2003, pp. 14ff.

SEE ALSO: Biometrics; Computer crime; Computer databases; Computer misuse; Confidentiality; Fraud; Information access; Resumés; Telemarketing; Victims' rights.

Ideology

DEFINITION: Any set of beliefs and values or a set of false ideas used to conceal reality

TYPE OF ETHICS: Theory of ethics

SIGNIFICANCE: If ideology is false consciousness, social critics believe there is an ethical imperative on the part of those who see clearly to reveal the truth to those caught within ideology. If all beliefs are ideological, critics believe there is an ethical imperative on the part of all people to understand the way in which their particular beliefs relate to current power structures and struggles. In either case, the question of the extent to which ethics itself is ideological—the extent to which it is an instrument of political power and social control—is a pressing one.

The French savant Antoine Destutt de Tracy can be credited for coining the term "ideology" in 1795. For Destutt de Tracy, ideology had a neutral value signifying only ideas and ideals. In the history of its development, ideology has acquired two distinct senses. In a general sense, it applies to any set or system of ideas, whether they are philosophical, political, theological, or ethical. In a more critical sense, ideology refers to any false set of ideas used by the dominant classes to control the subordinate classes.

Approaching ethics from an ideological point of view means to inquire into the relationship between ethics and social classes. Ideological critique presupposes a conflictual model of society in which dominant social classes and subordinate or oppressed social classes struggle for power and autonomy.

THE MARXIST TRADITION

The Marxist tradition has given more prominence to ideology in its social and ethical analysis than to any other theory. Karl Marx partly derived his concept of ideology from his intellectual mentor, the German philosopher Georg Wilhelm Friedrich Hegel, who, in his philosophy of history, set forth the claim that human history moves forward by the "Cunning of Reason," independent of any individual human awareness. From Ludwig Feuerbach, a critic of Hegel, Marx appropriated the idea that theological, moral, and metaphysical beliefs stem from the wishful projections of human psychology. Marx, however, deepened Feuerbach's position and asserted the sociological roots of ideology.

In his 1859 preface to a *Contribution to a Critique of Political Economy*, Marx summarized his historical method. He utilized a structural approach that divided society into "structure" and "superstructure." By structure, he meant the economic and social relations generated by the productive sphere. By superstructure, Marx referred to the state, its juridical-legal system, and the cultural realm of morality, religion, art, and philosophy—in short, ideology.

Marx believed that the form of the economic foundation of the state determined the form and content of the state's ideological superstructure. For example, in a capitalist society, the laws protect private property and moral norms justify the disparity between the rich and poor. In an earlier work called the *German Ideology*, Marx criticized the ideological nature of German philosophy for its justification of the Prussian state. There also appears the metaphysical claim that the material conditions of life determine forms of social consciousness.

In *Das Kapital*, Marx claims that capitalism generates a form of illusory consciousness that Marx names "commodity-fetishism." By commodity-fetishism, Marx means the false belief that commodities exchange on the basis of intrinsic value. In reality, values are extrinsic to the commodities and are based on ratios of social labor. In the *Critique of the Gotha Programme*, Marx refers to morality as ideological nonsense and calls the modern liberal ideas of equality and justice "bourgeois" and "ideological." Nevertheless, Marx was not beyond inveighing moral dictums against the exploitative and alienating features of capitalism like a Hebrew prophet.

Later Marxists followed the lines of thought opened up by Marx. Antonio Gramsci, founder of the Italian Communist Party, formulated the concept of hegemony to express the ideological forces of the modern bourgeois state. Hegemony refers to the power and authority attained and maintained by the ruling classes through the coercive apparatus of the state and through the consent gained by the cultural institutions of civil society. Louis Althusser, a French communist philosopher, developed the idea of ideological state apparatus. Briefly put, in order for society to maintain the status quo, it must also reproduce the fundamental economic social relations, that is, reproduce workers who submit to the bourgeois social control. This submission is made possible by ideological state apparatuses such as schools and churches, which express the ideas of the ruling classes. Jürgen Habermas stressed the notion of legitimation as the acceptance of a social system by the members of that society.

MAX WEBER AND KARL MANNHEIM

In the sociology of knowledge tradition, intellectuals sensitive to the crisis of relativism and skeptical of human rationality developed similar notions of ideology critique parallel to those of the Marxists. Max Weber linked certain religious tendencies to affinities with different social classes. He also set forth the idea of a theodicy of legitimation for the privileged and a theodicy of compensation for the oppressed. For Weber, ideology meant the consciousness of an epoch. Thus, ideology entailed ethical relativism.

Karl Mannheim showed how Christianity provided an ideology for the dominant classes and utopias for the oppressed. He also believed that there was a need for a class of individuals freed from any social class loyalty. These he found among academic intellectuals, the so-called free-floating intelligentsia. Sociology in general studies how social structures coerce individual human behavior and morality.

Several questions are raised by an ideological approach. How do social classes develop forms of consciousness containing particular ideologies? What role do ideologies play in social change? Does not the claim that ethics is ideological lead to ethical skepticism and ethical relativism?

Michael R. Candelaria

FURTHER READING

Althusser, Louis. *Lenin and Philosophy, and Other Essays.* Translated by Ben Brewster. Introduction by Fredric Jameson. New York: Monthly Review Press, 2001.

Eagleton, Terry. *Ideology: An Introduction.* New York: Verso, 1991.

Freeden, Michael. *Ideology.* Oxford, England: Oxford University Press, 2003.

Gramsci, Antonio. *Selections from the Prison Notebooks of Antonio Gramsci.* Edited and translated by Quintin Hoare and Geoffrey Nowell Smith. New York: International, 1999.

Lukacs, Georg. *History and Class Consciousness: Studies in Marxist Dialectics.* Translated by Rodney Livingstone. Cambridge, Mass.: MIT Press, 1983.

Marx, Karl, and Friedrich Engels. *The Marx-Engels Reader.* Edited by Robert C. Tucker. 2d ed. New York: W. W. Norton, 1978.

Weber, Max. *The Protestant Ethic and the Spirit of Capitalism.* Translated by Talcott Parsons. Introduction by Anthony Giddens. New York: Routledge, 2001.

Žižek, Slavoj. *The Sublime Object of Ideology.* New York: Verso, 1997.

_____, ed. *Mapping Ideology.* New York: Verso, 1995.

SEE ALSO: Capitalism; Communism; Critical theory; Hegel, Georg Wilhelm Friedrich; Marxism; Theory and practice; Weber, Max.

Illness

DEFINITION: Lack of health; presence of disease
TYPE OF ETHICS: Bioethics
SIGNIFICANCE: An accepted definition of illness defines the parameters of the responsibilities of medical professionals, patients, and society in the treatment of both healthy and ill people.

During the twentieth century, particularly after World War II, advances in medicine took place so rapidly that the health care profession ballooned. With this expansion has come consistently increasing, often unattainable, expectations about what can and should be treated by the medical profession.

It is impossible to focus on a particular definition or viewpoint of illness without looking at its counterpart, health. Some people hold that illness is simply lack of health, but any definition of health is controversial. The World Health Organization (WHO) in 1946 offered this definition: "Health is a state of complete physical, mental and social well-being." It is easy to see why this is controversial. This definition places in opposition to health such states as grief as well as such social problems as racial oppression and poverty. Simultaneously, by classifying these things as health problems, it obligates the health care profession to broaden its scope to include them. Many people have taken issue with the WHO definition of health, but no one has yet been able to formulate one that is any more widely accepted.

Views of Health and Illness

There are three predominant views of the concepts of health and illness. The first, the empirical view, proposes that the health of any organism is determined by whether that organism functions the way it was designed by nature to function. Illness, then, is any situation or entity that hinders the ability of the organism to function in the way in which nature intended. Proponents of this view point out that this definition is equally applicable to plants, animals, and humans. An organism is determined to be ill or healthy without reference to symptoms subject to interpretation by either the patient or the evaluator.

Another view of health and illness holds that health is that which is statistically normal, and illness is that which is statistically deviant. The problem with this view is that it ends up classifying many things society sees as positive traits, such as extreme intelligence or strength, as illness. Proponents, however, point out that what nature intended for a specific organism is often determined by statistical evidence.

The third view is that of normativism. Normativists believe that the concepts of health and illness incorporate cultural and societal values, because what is viewed as illness depends on what the particular culture considers desirable or undesirable. For example, in seventeenth century America, there was a "disease" called drapetomania, which caused otherwise content slaves in the South to have the uncontrollable urge to escape. The designation of illness also depends on the ability or willingness of a society to recognize a situation as undesirable. A society without writing would not be likely to consider dyslexia an impairment.

The normative view is especially prevalent (and compelling) in the field of mental health. The designation of what is a disease is a product of the culture of the time. For example, in the nineteenth century, women who enjoyed sexual intercourse were considered mentally dysfunctional, while in the twentieth century, the opposite is true. Certain factions, such as advocates for alcoholics, have fought long and hard to have their particular problems labeled as disease. Others, such as homosexuals, have fought equally hard to keep themselves from being so labeled.

Implications of Definitions

Why is the label of illness so desirable or undesirable? When a particular set of symptoms or problems is labeled as an illness, its presence carries with it certain properties of the "sick role." Behaviors that would otherwise be seen as unacceptable or immoral are excused. Responsibility is diminished, both for actions and for inaction. The label of illness also carries with it, however, a certain stigma, that of the necessity to strive for a cure. This is why groups such as homosexuals have fought it so strenuously.

On a more general level, definitions of health and illness define the boundaries and obligations of the medical profession. It is reasonably clear that ideas about health care needs follow the line of ideas about health. The current conception of health care in Western society, the medical model, tends to support the paternalism of health care professionals as interventionists who relieve patients of their responsibility to care for themselves. A nonmedical model, however, tends to emphasize individual responsibility for health.

Disease vs. Illness

Most people consider the terms "disease" and "illness" to be synonymous. Some, however, separate illness into a subcategory of disease. This separation bridges the gap between the empirical and the normative definitions of health. Disease is seen as simply the impairment of natural function, as in the empirical view. Illnesses are diseases that incorporate normative aspects in their evaluations. An illness is a disease whose diagnosis confers upon its owner the special treatment of the sick role. Not all diseases are illnesses. Diseases such as sickle-cell anemia may not impair the health of the individual, and thus do not incur the sick role.

Generally accepted definitions of health, illness, and disease are becoming more necessary as the health care profession grows. Until society clarifies these concepts, health care will be called upon to mitigate every problem society has, not only the enormous number it is traditionally expected to solve.

Margaret Hawthorne

FURTHER READING

Beauchamp, Tom L., and LeRoy Walters, eds. *Contemporary Issues in Bioethics.* 6th ed. Belmont, Calif.: Thomson/Wadsworth, 2003.

Boorse, Christopher. "On the Distinction Between Disease and Illness." *Philosophy and Public Affairs* 5 (Fall, 1975): 49-68.

Callahan, Daniel. "The WHO Definition of 'Health.'" *The Hastings Center Studies* 1, no. 3 (1973): 77-88.

Caplan, Arthur L. "The Concepts of Health and Disease." In *Medical Ethics*, edited by Robert M. Veatch. Boston: Jones & Bartlett, 1989.

Engelhardt, H. Tristam, Jr. "Health and Disease: Philosophical Perspectives." In *Encyclopedia of Bioethics*, edited by Warren T. Reich. Rev. ed. Vol. 2. New York: Macmillan, 1995.

Foucault, Michel. *The Birth of the Clinic: An Archaeology of Medical Perception*. Translated by A. M. Sheridan Smith. 1973. Reprint. New York: Vintage Books, 1994.

McGee, Glenn, ed. *Pragmatic Bioethics*. 2d ed. Cambridge, Mass.: MIT Press, 2003.

Macklin, Ruth. "Mental Health and Mental Illness: Some Problems of Definition and Concept Formation." *Philosophy of Science* 39 (September, 1972): 341-364.

SEE ALSO: Diagnosis; Health care allocation; Holistic medicine; Medical ethics; Medical insurance; Mental illness; Physician-patient relationship.

Immigration

DEFINITION: Flow into countries of people seeking to change their nationalities

TYPE OF ETHICS: Politico-economic ethics

SIGNIFICANCE: Governments regulate by force who may leave their territories and especially who may settle within their borders. Border controls designed to exclude unwanted immigrants may be viewed as legitimate forms of collective or communal self-determination, but critics argue that they often violate the individual right to freedom of movement and the ideal of equal economic opportunity for all.

During the 1990's, the U.S. government took unprecedented and costly measures to prevent migrants in search of greater economic opportunities from illegally crossing its long border with Mexico. The federal Immigration and Naturalization Service (INS) almost tripled its budget, doubled the size of its Border Patrol, and created a border of fences, cameras, and policing by helicopters. Concerns with security eventually led to further steps to close the border. Nations in the European Union have taken similar measures. However, it is unclear how effective various efforts at border control have been.

Although millions of illegal migrants were arrested throughout the world and returned to their countries of origin, there were still at least six million illegal immigrants in the United States and more than three million in Western Europe at the beginning of the twenty-first century. The cost in human suffering is also high. Every year, hundreds of migrants die trying to enter what critics of strict border controls call "fortress Europe and America." The moral question raised is what justifies governments' effort to exclude ordinary people who seek to improve their lives.

THE COMMUNAL RIGHT TO EXCLUDE

The communitarian philosopher Michael Walzer argues that communities have a right to determine the rules governing their cooperation and with whom to exchange the goods of their cooperation, including membership. He compares political communities to clubs, noting that within clubs existing members choose the new members and that no one has a right to join a club. Another aspect of the analogy is that people have the right to leave their clubs and so they have a right to emigrate. Walzer adds that political communities are also similar to families. The children of citizens are automatically citizens, and states typically give preference to would-be immigrants who are genetically related to its existing citizens. For Walzer, the right to exclude is not absolute: He argues that all states should take in some political refugees since every person has the right to belong to some political community.

There are many reasons that citizens may have for

wishing to exclude other people from entering their countries. Walzer stresses the danger of immigrants undermining a national culture and a shared way of life. Other grounds for exclusion are limiting population growth, protecting the environment and resources, shielding native workers from wage depression and increased competition for scarce jobs, and preventing an overburdening of welfare programs, public education, and other social services.

Critics of restrictive border policies contest the view that admitting many immigrants with different cultural backgrounds threatens national unity. They point out that cultural blending is common and that, at any rate, a multicultural society enriches the lives of its citizens. This latter view was challenged in the United States after the terrorist attacks of September 11, 2001, heightened public fears of Muslims living in the country.

On their account, national unity can be based on respect for individual rights and need not include a deep sharing of specific cultural values. They also argue that immigration contributes to economic growth and that many immigrants take jobs that natives find undesirable. A final perceived benefit of immigration is that it counteracts the shrinking or graying of the native populations of many Western nations.

ARGUMENTS FOR OPEN BORDERS

Proponents of open borders typically argue that even if more immigration does not benefit the receiving country, this does not necessarily warrant exclusion. Some utilitarian moral philosophers argue that the state must impartially balance the interests of its citizens against the interests of immigrants. Liberal human rights theorists maintain that individuals have a right to freedom of movement, arguing that just as people should be able to move from one city in the United States to another—whether or not their movement benefits the communities—so they should be able to move across borders. Egalitarian liberals hold

European immigrants sailing to the United States in 1906. (Library of Congress)

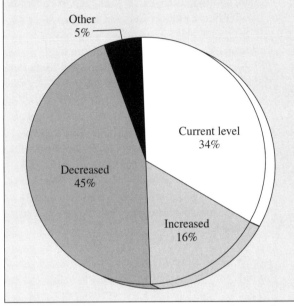

Public Opinion on U.S. Immigration Levels in 2004

In January, 2004, a CBS News/New York Times poll asked a cross-section of Americans whether legal immigration into the United States should be kept at its current level, increased, or decreased.

Other
5%

Current level
34%

Decreased
45%

Increased
16%

Source: Roper Center for Public Opinion Research. Figures reflect responses of 1,022 adults surveyed in January, 2004.

for professional workers, a preference that has become more extensive in recent years.

The active recruitment of immigrants with valuable professional skills has led to a "brain drain" from some developing countries to Western societies. Some countries of the developing world have lost anywhere from 25 percent to 75 percent of their highly skilled workers, including engineers, scientists, and physicians. It is generally held that professionals from these nations should not be denied the right to emigrate from their home countries; however, some ethicists have also argued that it would be appropriate to impose exit taxes to be paid by the hiring agencies to compensate for the economic loss to the sending countries and to reimburse them for their educational costs. Increasingly, professional immigrants view it as their duty to establish networks with professionals in their countries of origin and to promote local businesses and educational developments.

Harry van der Linden

FURTHER READING

Barry, Brian, and Robert E. Goodin, eds. *Free Movement: Ethical Issues in the Transnational Migration of People and of Money.* University Park: Pennsylvania State University Press, 1992.

Capaldi, Nicholas, ed. *Immigration: Debating the Issues.* Amherst, N.Y.: Prometheus Books, 1997.

Carens, Joseph. "Aliens and Citizens: The Case for Open Borders." *Review of Politics* 49, no. 2 (1987): 251-73.

Dummett, Michael. *On Immigration and Refugees.* London: Routledge, 2001.

Isbister, John. *The Immigration Debate.* West Hartford, Conn.: Kumarian Press, 1996.

Stalker, Peter. *The No-Nonsense Guide to International Migration.* London: Verso, 2001.

Walzer, Michael. *Spheres of Justice.* New York: Basic Books, 1983.

SEE ALSO: Citizenship; Communitarianism; Diversity; Immigration Reform and Control Act; Population Connection; Population control; Refugees and stateless people; Rorty, Richard; Zero-base ethics.

that closing borders to immigrants from the developing world is unjust because mere location of birth should not determine one's chances for economic success. As the liberal philosopher Joseph Carens puts it, keeping economic immigrants out by force makes citizenship in Western democracies a modern variant of feudal privilege.

IMMIGRATION POLICY STANDARDS

During the late eighteenth and nineteenth centuries, the United States placed few restrictions on immigration other than excluding the seriously ill, the criminally convicted, and certain non-Western populations. National origin quotas were adopted in 1921 and the Border Patrol emerged in 1924. Congress abolished this quota system in 1965 with the understanding that it was racist and replaced it by a system of preferences for relatives of citizens and permanent residents. Congress also reserved immigration slots

Immigration Reform and Control Act

IDENTIFICATION: Federal law designed to ease social and economic problems caused by illegal immigration

DATE: Passed in 1986

TYPE OF ETHICS: Politico-economic ethics

SIGNIFICANCE: With the Immigration Reform and Control Act (IRCA), the U.S. government attempted for the first time to punish the employers of illegal immigrants, not only the illegals themselves, recognizing both as lawbreakers contributing to a national problem.

Authored by Senator Alan Simpson, the Immigration Reform and Control Act was passed after emotional debate in Congress. Nearly everyone recognized that immigration policy needed to be overhauled, but many opponents felt that the proposed law was designed specifically to keep out Hispanics and other people of color. The act had three main goals. Illegal immigrants already in the United States lived in fear of being found and deported; therefore, they were easily exploited by unscrupulous employers who paid unfair wages. Under the terms of the act, illegal aliens who came forward to register were granted amnesty and could eventually apply for citizenship.

The act also further increased funding for Immigration and Naturalization Service (INS) to turn back illegals at the borders. Later years showed this attempt to be very successful. Finally, the act made it more difficult for illegals to be hired for work in the United States; it was hoped that this would discourage them from attempting to come in the first place. Employers were now required to document that new employees were legally eligible for work in the United States.

Cynthia A. Bily

SEE ALSO: Citizenship; Immigration.

Immortality

DEFINITION: Eternal life

TYPE OF ETHICS: Theory of ethics

SIGNIFICANCE: Many people believe that ethical grounds such as the demand for moral perfection, the justice of the universe, the value of the individual, and the goodness of God support or require belief in the immortality of the human soul.

Immanuel Kant, in his *Critique of Practical Reason* (1788), argued for the immortality of the soul along the following lines.

> We are morally obligated to achieve moral perfection, a complete correspondence between our intentions and the moral law. Anything we are obligated to do is something we can do. But we cannot achieve moral perfection in this life. So given that moral perfection is obligatory, an infinite life during which moral perfection can be attained must be postulated.

In effect, Kant claims that the moral law requires as a corollary the immortality of the soul.

Kant's argument has several questionable aspects. Some people, claiming that morality is solely a matter of societal opinion or individual feeling, will reject outright the idea of a moral law and therefore will not be moved by Kant's argument. Even objectivists in ethics may claim that Kant's argument does not prove the existence of immortality, since it does not prove an objective moral law. Optimists about human nature may say that if people can control themselves in any given case, they may also be able to control themselves in every case, and therefore moral perfection in this life is possible even though it is difficult.

Others may question whether people are obligated to be morally perfect. Does the moral law require people to be perfect as well as to do their duty? If people are not obligated to achieve moral perfection but only to strive to achieve it, there is no need to postulate immortality. Those who think that they have independent grounds against the belief in immortality may say that no one is obligated to be morally perfect, since it is not possible to achieve such perfection in a single lifetime. Finally, it may be asked why achieving moral perfection requires postulating immortality rather than an extremely long afterlife.

Other moral arguments for immortality clearly rest on religious assumptions. Some appeal to a divine recompense, as follows: "In this life, the virtuous are not always rewarded, and the vicious are not always punished. Since God is just and powerful, however, there is an eternal life in which each receives his or her just recompense." No doubt, many people are motivated by a desire to avoid Hell and reach Heaven. Others worry that raising questions about immortality will undermine the motivation to act morally. They think that if there is no ultimate recompense, it is irrational for people to do what is right when it conflicts with their self-interest.

It is a mistake, however, to assume that moral behavior cannot be rational unless it promotes one's own welfare. If rational behavior instead only promotes one's ends, then since one can have altruistic ends, one can behave rationally without promoting one's own welfare. Thus, moral behavior that is not rewarded in this life can be rational even if it is not rewarded in a future life. A major motive for moral behavior is concern for other people, respect for their value. This kind of motivation does not depend on immortality, and this kind of concern is an important part of a fully human life; therefore, it is not irrational.

THE RELEVANCE OF GOD

The recompense argument is based on the assumption that God exists. To accept God's existence on faith is to accept immortality on faith. To the extent that God's existence is not proved, the future life based on it is not proved. Granting God's existence, would divine recompense take an eternity? Even if it would, would God balance the scales of justice? Some people maintain that God's goodness would require this, but that conclusion does not follow. Even if a just God regards human mortality as bad, that does not mean that God should or would end it. To do so may require God to sacrifice something he regards as more important. God's overall best plan for the universe may include this evil as well as others. The evil of human mortality may be a necessary part of a greater good.

Some claim that a good and powerful God would guarantee human immortality because people are such valuable beings, full of infinite potentialities, or because God would not disappoint those in whom he has instilled a desire for immortality. These reasons are not convincing.

It is a mistake to think that humans cannot be valuable if they are not permanent. Many things, such as good health, are valuable even though they cannot last forever. It also seems clear that Socrates and Mohandas K. Gandhi were valuable individuals even though they did not last forever. From the claim that humans are worthy of being immortal, it does not follow that humans are immortal.

The idea that a good God would not disappoint those in whom he has inspired a natural desire for immortality also does not stand scrutiny. Does this desire come from God or from society? Many Hindus and Buddhists do not desire immortality. They strive to avoid being reborn, because they believe that blessedness involves a complete extinction of the individual. Even assuming that the desire for personal immortality were universal, it is clear that a good God would not necessarily satisfy every human desire.

Gregory P. Rich

FURTHER READING

Ducasse, C. J. *A Critical Examination of the Belief in a Life After Death.* Springfield, Ill.: Charles C Thomas, 1961.

Edwards, Paul, ed. *Immortality.* Amherst, N.Y.: Prometheus Books, 1997.

Flew, Antony. "Immortality." In *The Encyclopedia of Philosophy*, edited by Paul Edwards. Vol. 4. New York: Macmillan, 1972.

Hick, John. *Death and Eternal Life.* San Francisco: Harper & Row, 1980.

Lamont, Corliss. *The Illusion of Immortality.* Introduction by John Dewey. 5th ed. New York: Frederick Continuum, 1990.

Wainwright, William J. *Philosophy of Religion.* Belmont, Calif.: Wadsworth, 1988.

SEE ALSO: Christian ethics; Death and dying; God; Kant, Immanuel; Life, meaning of; Life and death; Religion.

Impartiality

DEFINITION: Absolute or relative freedom from prejudice or bias; fairness

TYPE OF ETHICS: Theory of ethics

SIGNIFICANCE: Impartiality is a central concept in several ethical theories that otherwise differ significantly. Many theorists assert that an ethics without impartiality is impossible. Others assert that to deny the fact of human partiality and assert a commitment to radical impartiality is to falsify the nature of the way people's minds and moral judgments actually work.

The concept of impartiality is suggested by various early writings and is implied by the Golden Rule of Jesus, which states that you should do unto others as you would have others do unto you. The idea of freedom from prejudice, even from prejudice toward oneself, however, occurs most often in ethical writing after 1700. David Hume claims that impartiality prevails when making moral judgments. Socially useful acts are approved. In "The Standard of Taste" (1757), Hume asserts that people accept as their own "the judgments of an impartial observer." Immanuel Kant, putting forward a very different theory from that of Hume, also stresses impartiality. He claims that duty is the same for all people. John Stuart Mill, developing a utilitarian ethical theory, asserts that utilitarianism requires one to be strictly impartial.

This concept of impartiality also occurs in writings of the twentieth century. In *The Moral Point of View* (1958), Kurt Baier states that the same rules should pertain to all. He asserts that we must adopt an impartial viewpoint. John Rawls, in *A Theory of Justice* (1971), urges a "veil of ignorance" where the rules of society are established by individuals who do not know what their own position will be in the society. In this approach, the rules that are developed will be impartial and fair to all.

Rita C. Hinton

SEE ALSO: Hume, David; Kant, Immanuel; Mill, John Stuart; Rawls, John; *Theory of Justice, A.*

In vitro fertilization

DEFINITION: Physiological union of sperm and ovum outside the female's body

DATE: First human born through in vitro fertilization on July 25, 1978

TYPE OF ETHICS: Bioethics

SIGNIFICANCE: In vitro fertilization permits the separation of the genetic from the gestational role of motherhood. It makes technically possible a range of practices that raise serious ethical questions, including surrogate motherhood, sex selection, and other types of genetic screening or manipulation.

The term's origins are unknown, since the terms *in vitro* ("in glass") and "fertilization" have long been used in science. Attempts at in vitro fertilization (IVF) were reported as early as 1878 but were not confirmed until M. C. Chang reported successful pregnancies from rabbit ova that had been fertilized externally and placed in foster wombs. After scientists mastered the preliminary steps to human IVF, Patrick C. Steptoe and Robert G. Edwards reported a tubal pregnancy in 1976. In 1978, Steptoe and Edwards conducted the first IVF procedure to lead to a successful human birth.

In 1995, 2.1 million married couples in the United States were infertile. IVF and related technologies show promise for 10 to 15 percent of those who do not respond to other treatments. The government reported about five thousand births from IVF worldwide by 1988.

NONCOITAL PARENTHOOD

The Roman Catholic Church and some non-Catholic theologians oppose all noncoital reproductive techniques, including artificial insemination, because they separate the marital and the reproductive functions of love. Others see nothing problematic about achieving human parenthood "artificially," since control over the environment intrinsically defines human nature. A middle position admits that IVF's artificiality may harm marriage but holds that the overall benefits provided by parenthood outweigh those harms for some couples.

Similar secular objections are that IVF's artificiality will affect society's conception of humanness and will lead to the objectification of all embryos and of women. Others worry about its psychological effects on the parents and children. Most consider the reproductive technologies to be no more of an "interference with nature" than is any other medical procedure.

Many IVF programs do not accept unmarried or lesbian women. Although many would argue that children should be raised in traditional families, this screening singles out IVF and makes physicians the moral arbiters for society. Some allege that IVF reinforces, without examination, societal views that women must provide husbands with a genetically related child in order to achieve full womanhood.

THE EMBRYO'S STATUS

When a single embryo is implanted to produce a live birth, IVF closely resembles coital conception. For those who believe that human life and personhood begin at implantation or later, the embryo's status presents few problems. For those who believe that human life and personhood begin at conception, however, IVF can be problematic, especially when it is used to study embryonic development or contraception. Does using embryos in research to provide a cure for diabetes or Parkinson's disease constitute unauthorized experimentation on unborn children? Even as a substitute for normal conception, IVF results in greater "wastage" of embryos because of more failures to implant and more miscarriages.

Because "harvesting" ova is expensive and invasive, women are often hormonally induced to produce several ova. Often, physicians implant multiple embryos to increase the chances of live births; this procedure increases the possibility of multiple births or selective abortion if too many embryos are implanted. Alternatively, because cryogenic preservation is possible after fertilization, some physicians

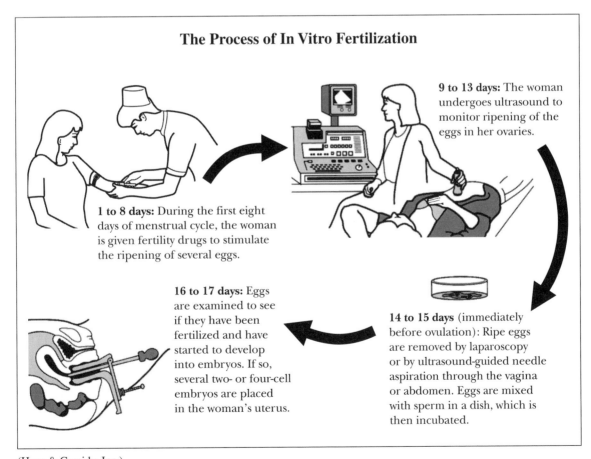

The Process of In Vitro Fertilization

9 to 13 days: The woman undergoes ultrasound to monitor ripening of the eggs in her ovaries.

1 to 8 days: During the first eight days of menstrual cycle, the woman is given fertility drugs to stimulate the ripening of several eggs.

16 to 17 days: Eggs are examined to see if they have been fertilized and have started to develop into embryos. If so, several two- or four-cell embryos are placed in the woman's uterus.

14 to 15 days (immediately before ovulation): Ripe eggs are removed by laparoscopy or by ultrasound-guided needle aspiration through the vagina or abdomen. Eggs are mixed with sperm in a dish, which is then incubated.

(Hans & Cassidy, Inc.)

Birth of Louise Brown

On July 25, 1978, Louise Brown, the first baby conceived outside a human mother's body in a laboratory dish, was born to Gilbert and Lesley Brown. The Browns were childless, because Lesley's fallopian tubes were blocked with adhesions and had to be surgically removed. Consequently, eggs from her ovaries could not migrate down the tubes, which prevented their possible fertilization and uterine implantation. To overcome this biological problem, physicians Patrick Steptoe and R. G. Edwards used in vitro technology. An egg surgically removed from the mother was combined with ejaculated sperm from the father in a laboratory dish to induce conception, or fertilization. The fertilized egg was then implanted into the mother's uterus, where its development culminated in the birth of Louise Joy Brown.

Among the most widely publicized events of its era, Louise's birth helped to turn the tide of public sentiment. The issue of in vitro fertilization (IVF) had been publicly debated with increasing fervor in the mid-1970's. Many feared the technologization of the reproductive process due to its potential miscarriages and abuses, and articles heralding a potential cure for infertility ran alongside articles decrying IVF's potential monstrosities. Louise Brown and her parents put a human face on IVF, however, and garnered popular support for the procedure.

implant embryos one at a time. Should excess frozen embryos be allowed to "die" or be donated to other infertile couples? A wealthy couple's 1983 death raised the issue of whether their frozen embryos should become their heirs. What happens if a couple divorces? A judge facing the issue awarded "custody" to the mother who wanted the embryos implanted. In 1992, the Tennessee Supreme Court reversed that decision, declaring that the embryos were neither property nor persons but an interim category entitled to respect because of their potential for human life; it held that both parents had rights to decide the embryos' fate prior to implantation but that the father's right not to be a genetic parent outweighed the mother's desire to donate the embryos.

All the government commissions examining the embryo's status adopted this interim category, recommending that experimentation be allowed until the fourteenth day of development and that the embryo be "treated with respect" but not accorded full rights of personhood.

Experimental Technique

As soon as IVF live births demonstrated success, "infertility centers" sprouted around the country. Since humans were only the fourth species that demonstrated success with IVF, some people accused scientists of rushing to experiment on women before properly studying IVF in animals. During the 1980's, many infertility "specialists" were inadequately trained and promised overgenerous results. Although there are no apparent problems, negative effects on the children of IVF cannot, as the DES tragedy demonstrated, be ruled out until the test group is larger and reaches reproductive age. Moreover, the long-term effects of superovulating women are unknown.

A de facto federal moratorium on funding IVF has resulted in no regulatory research to demonstrate the efficacy or safety of IVF and no development of guidelines; most research is connected with commercial interests. Moreover, IVF is expensive and has a low rate of successful pregnancies (an average rate of 10 to 15 percent per procedure during the late 1990's); some question making these expenditures to overcome infertility when resources are needed to care for or adopt living children and for research into avoiding the causes of infertility. Distributive justice concerns are also raised; even if covered by health insurance, which often declares IVF too experimental, IVF will not be affordable for most couples. At the beginning of the twenty-first century, IVF procedures alone could cost as much as nine thousand dollars in the United States, and the costs of drugs and donor eggs could easily raise the total cost to more than fifty thousand dollars.

Possible Uses of IVF

As with artificial insemination, IVF makes the donation of gametes possible; this possibility raises questions of the advisability of separating the genetic from the other roles of parenthood, including the possibility of detrimental effects on the children's identities. In fact, through surrogacy, the gestational mother need be neither the biological mother nor the intended mother. IVF is used to treat both male and female infertility. Some people question the reliance on using surgery on the woman to overcome the husband's low sperm count, particularly in the light of the dearth of research on the causes of and cures for male infertility. Preimplantation genetic testing of the embryo can be accomplished harmlessly, thus raising the advisability of genetic screening, including sex selection.

Ileana Dominguez-Urban

FURTHER READING

Bonnicksen, Andrea L. *In Vitro Fertilization: Building Policy from Laboratories to Legislatures.* New York: Columbia University Press, 1989.

Dyson, Anthony. *The Ethics of IVF.* New York: Mowbray, 1995.

Elias, Sherman, and George J. Annas. *Reproductive Genetics and the Law.* Chicago: Year Book Medical, 1987.

Gosden, Roger. *Designing Babies: The Brave New World of Reproductive Technology.* New York: W. H. Freeman, 1999.

McCartan, M. Karen. "A Survey of the Legal, Ethical, and Public Policy Considerations of In Vitro Fertilization." *Journal of Law, Ethics, and Public Policy* 2 (1986): 695-731.

Robertson, John A. "In the Beginning: The Legal Status of Early Embryos." *Virginia Law Review* 76, no. 3 (April 1, 1990): 437-517.

Sherwin, Susan. *No Longer Patient: Feminist Ethics and Health Care.* Philadelphia, Pa.: Temple University Press, 1992.

Smith, George P. "Assisted Noncoital Reproduction: A Comparative Analysis." *Boston University International Law Journal* 8, no. 1 (Spring, 1990): 21-52.

U.S. Congress. Office of Technology Assessment. *Infertility: Medical and Social Choices.* Washington, D.C.: Government Printing Office, 1988.

SEE ALSO: Genetic engineering; Life and death; Medical ethics; Right to life; Stem cell research; Surrogate motherhood.

Incest

DEFINITION: Sexual intercourse or sexual activity between close relatives

TYPE OF ETHICS: Sex and gender issues

SIGNIFICANCE: Incest is taboo in most societies. Usually, incest between a child and an adult relative is considered especially heinous. Sibling incest, while still taboo, is usually judged to be more pathological than criminal.

Incest seems to be a growing problem. In the United States, at least, reported cases of incest were on the rise during the 1990's. Prior to the 1970's, incest seemed to be kept hidden. Increasingly, however, victims and their protectors began speaking out, and the public and legal authorities became more aware of the problem than ever before.

The "typical" offender in incest cases is the father (in approximately 90 percent of the reported cases), and the victim is usually his daughter. Fully 97 percent of all reported cases of parent-offspring incest involve father-daughter couplings or arousing sex "play." Only 3 percent of the perpetrators are female. When incest involves the father and the son, as it does in approximately 7 percent of reported cases, the young male has a second issue to grapple with—that of the father's bisexuality or homosexuality. Men who take sexual advantage of young relatives typically suffer from low self-esteem brought on by physical, mental, and, sometimes, sexual abuse that they suffered as children.

Many reasons for forbidding incest have been offered. Society has been "told," for example, that incestuous relations are likely to produce mentally and physically defective offspring. Although modern geneticists have learned that that fear is unfounded, laypersons still fear incest for this reason. Another reason to forbid incest involves family stability: Incest could create chaos in the family by causing jealousies and the exchanging of, or confusion about, roles, which could cause the family to become "organizationally dysfunctional." Such a family would not survive as a unit, and if enough families engaged in the practice, society itself would break down. Hence, a ban or taboo on the practice becomes a "functional prerequisite" for society.

Another reason to avoid incest exists. Many authorities emphasize the psychological harm done to victims. The "crime" is so heinous that victims are often sworn to secrecy, becoming in a sense "responsible" not only for the act but also for keeping the family together by not talking. Fighting such strains, victims emerge with poor self-esteem and related psychological problems. As time passes, most victims cannot engage in "age-appropriate" play, and they tend to develop few outside interests. Some create discipline problems at home and at school. Furthermore, incest teaches some victims that if they like someone, they should act out their feelings sexually.

APPARENT EXCEPTIONS

Some scholars have begun to question the "negative only" view of incest. One study, for example, cited an investigator who studied twenty brother-sister marriages that occurred in one state. The investigator reported that the couples, all of whom were living in middle-class suburbia, led fruitful lives and were happily raising their offspring as normal human beings. Another case involved a twenty-eight-year-old married middle-class woman who regularly visited her old widowed father to clean his house and cook for him. The two regularly had sex because the woman had promised her mother that she would "take care of Dad."

Another case involved a nineteen-year-old college coed. When she was preparing a research paper for a class in abnormal psychology, she had a severe anxiety attack that required hospitalization. She had just read that incest was a taboo, a heinous crime; in apparent innocence, she had been having sex with her father and three brothers since she was thirteen. Her analyst reported that she had had to take over the domestic duties of the family upon the death of her mother and that she had "assumed" that sex was part of her "responsibility" because men "needed it." Furthermore, the analyst reported that the coed seemed well adjusted, happy, and guilt-free—until she went to the college library and read about the "horrors" of incest.

Such cases led some experts to talk of "functional" incest, which makes possible a shift in traditional family "roles" that enables the family to continue as a unit rather than to disintegrate. One scholar analyzed 425 published case studies of incest from America and Europe and identified 93 as "nonpathological" cases in which incest was a "functional" response that allowed the families to stay together.

One researcher recounted the story of a family in South America whose members had been shunned by their community because some family members engaged in prostitution and others engaged in bootlegging. The ostracism eventually resulted in incestuous relations among as many as forty family members and created a monstrous problem for those exploring the family genealogy. One man had relations with his mother, who bore his daughter. Years later, he had relations with his daughter, who then had a daughter. He thus became father, brother, and mate to his first daughter and grandfather, father, brother, and mate to his second daughter. In this case, however, incest did not mean disintegration of the family; in fact, the family members handled the cross-generational and sibling incest quite well. The family stayed together, and the individual members seemed well adjusted and happy.

Such cases should be regarded as exceptions. In most cases of incest, tragedy and suffering result; incest usually tears a family asunder, partly because of the behavior itself and partly because of the learned aversion to incest.

James Smallwood

FURTHER READING

Hamer, Mary. *Incest: A New Perspective.* Malden, Mass.: Blackwell, 2002.

Herman, Judith Lewis, with Lisa Hirschman. *Father-Daughter Incest.* 1981. Reprint. Cambridge, Mass.: Harvard University Press, 2000.

Maisch, Herbert. *Incest.* Translated by Colin Bearne. New York: Stein & Day, 1972.

Renshaw, Domeena C. *Incest.* Boston: Little, Brown, 1982.

Rush, Florence. *The Best-Kept Secret.* Englewood Cliffs, N.J.: Prentice-Hall, 1980.

Russell, Diana E. H. *The Secret Trauma: Incest in the Lives of Girls and Women.* Rev. ed. New York: Basic Books, 1999.

Starcke, Carl Nicolai. *The Primitive Family in Its Origin and Development.* Chicago: University of Chicago Press, 1976.

Stern, Curt. *Principles of Human Genetics.* San Francisco: W. H. Freeman, 1973.

Storr, Anthony. *Human Destructiveness.* 2d ed. London: Routledge, 1991.

Wilson, Edward O. *On Human Nature.* Cambridge, Mass.: Harvard University Press, 1978.

SEE ALSO: Child abuse; Family; Rape; Sexual abuse and harassment; Sexuality and sexual ethics; Taboos; Victims' rights.

Income distribution

DEFINITION: Distribution of various forms of income among members of society and their families
TYPE OF ETHICS: Politico-economic ethics
SIGNIFICANCE: The consumption opportunities and senses of self-worth of individuals are strongly affected by the individuals' incomes and their views concerning the fairness of how society's total wealth is distributed.

The incomes of most Americans take the form of salaries paid by employers, interest and dividends from investments, rents on properties, and profits from businesses. Most income revenue comes from the private sector, but a significant share also comes from government sources. Incomes are also distributed and redistributed within individual family households, and unpaid household services performed by family members constitute important nonmarket forms of real income.

BUSINESS INCOME

Most incomes paid by business are wage payments for labor services. In addition, firms make income payments for interest, rent, and dividends. Business profits constitute income for business owners, even if those profits are plowed back into the businesses.

Businesses pay out money in order to obtain labor and other productive services. They also make rental payments to obtain productive land, buildings, and equipment. Moreover, they pay interest and dividends in order to obtain funds that finance capital investments. Firms attempt to maximize profits and thus are motivated to pay as little as possible to obtain needed services. However, in order to compete with rival firms to obtain workers and other services, they must pay competitive wages. The individual worker's freedom of job choice is the most effective protection against workplace unfairness. Dissatisfied workers can always quit and go elsewhere or even start their own businesses. Employers experiencing

heavy turnovers in employees have an incentive to pay higher salaries to make their jobs more attractive to their workers.

Incomes from business are affected by taxation and by the activities of labor unions. Unions tend to display more concern for fairness than employers. A common union policy is seniority, a system wherein the workers who are employed the longest are given special consideration in pay and promotion decisions and protection against layoffs. However, seniority systems may work against efficiency and unfairly place younger workers at a disadvantage.

PRODUCTIVITY ETHICS

The most widely accepted economic theory of incomes from business is that each supplier of productive services receives payment equal to the value of its marginal product—in the simplest case, the value of additional output that results from adding that individual's services. To many economists, this seems eminently fair: Each person takes from the economy an amount of goods and services equivalent to the value that person contributes. Furthermore, the system promotes a high level of economic productivity. Workers and wealth-owners shop around for opportunities that yield them the best incomes. In the process, their services flow into highly productive outlets. Workers have incentives to improve their productivity through extra training and harder work. Investors have incentives to obtain information about the profitability of various firms. Firms look for employees whose work helps generate the highest possible profits. This process leads both workers and employers into efficient patterns of production.

Evidence that labor incomes reflect differences in productivity comes from the higher pay that goes, on average, to persons with more education, more experience, and greater on-the-job supervisory responsibility. These variables account for much of the earnings differentials involving women and members of ethnic minorities. Young persons and others entering the labor market for the first time usually have low productivity and consequently receive low pay. Recent immigrants to the United States are particularly vulnerable to initially low incomes.

INCOME DISTRIBUTION IN THE FAMILY

To assess the morality of market income distribution, one must be aware of the second system of income distribution, which is the family. In 2001, about 135 million Americans were employed. Many of the remaining 150 million people—particularly the 65 million people under sixteen years of age—were household members with those employed. Their incomes depended partly on the incomes received by other members of their households and partly on the nonmarket ways in which incomes were divided among members of the household. Families also provide other methods of rewarding virtues such as kindness, loyalty, altruism, optimism, and creativity that are not always rewarded in the business world.

INCOME FROM GOVERNMENT

The third principal source of income is government. In the United States, about one sixth of employed persons work for some level of government. Fairness is a more significant factor in government employment. Workers qualify for government civil service positions by taking examinations, and the rules for pay and promotion are publicly known. In the United States, government jobs have helped to improve opportunities for women, members of minorities, and persons with disabilities. However, excessive concern with providing employment can mean that efficiency is sacrificed and government offices overstaffed.

Governments also pay large amounts of income in the form of transfer payments: old-age pensions, unemployment compensation, disability benefits, and other income supplements for the poor. In 2000, one-eighth of personal income received by Americans came from transfer payments. In addition to cash incomes, government provides or subsidizes services such as medical care, education, and housing. People earn their government Social Security benefits by paying wage taxes while they are employed. Others earn interest from government bonds by lending money to the government. However, need rather than earning is the basis for government income programs for poor persons.

Government payments combine concerns for fairness with political expediency. For example, the first generation of Social Security retirement beneficiaries received far more than actuarial calculations would have warranted during the brief time the program had been in place. Conversely, working-age adults in the twenty-first century were paying much higher Social Security taxes than their parents had.

Medical benefits under Medicare and Medicaid have been the causes of a chronic political battleground. Before the federal welfare reforms of the 1990's, some opponents of government welfare programs argued that welfare benefits would subsidize irresponsible child-bearing.

WHAT IS FAIR?

The productivity ethics position is that individuals should receive rewards equal to their contributions to national output. However, this approach has led to wide disparities in income. In the year 2000, the one-fifth of American families with the lowest incomes received only 4.3 percent of the nation's aggregate income, while the top one-fifth of the population received 47.4 percent. The productivity standard is most obviously inappropriate for children, the elderly, and persons with disabilities, who cannot be expected to be very productive.

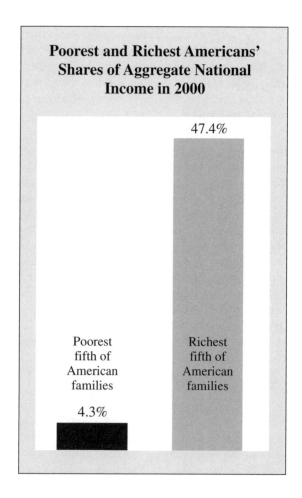

Poorest and Richest Americans' Shares of Aggregate National Income in 2000

Even in a free-market economy, incomes do not always match productivity. In every sizable workplace there are always some workers at who are extremely competent and reliable and others at the same pay level who are lazy, careless, or troublesome. Employers often have only imperfect knowledge of these differences among their employees. At the same time, workers often have imperfect knowledge of alternative job opportunities that might be open to them. Imperfect matching between incomes and productivity may arise from monopoly conditions and from union activities that exclude people from certain occupations.

The market standard for "productivity" equates it with anything people are willing to pay for—even illegal drug dealers, pimps, and pornographers. Hence, the morality of income distribution depends partly on the morality of the activities from which people derive their incomes.

There is much potential injustice in property incomes. Some people accumulate wealth by hard work and frugality and invest it wisely. However, much wealth is transmitted from one generation to another through inheritance or family gifts and reflects no particular merit on the part of the recipients. At best, the recipients of such wealth are called on to exercise skill and responsibility in the way their wealth is managed. The belief that an egalitarian society should not allow the accumulation of unearned wealth across generations has been the chief argument in favor of the estate tax, which imposes a tax on already taxed income prior to its inheritance.

Another possible standard of fairness is equality. Because someone needs to do the work in every society, and because there needs to be an incentive to do it, a complete equality standard has never been very practical. However, many people feel that income distribution in a free-market economy is unduly unequal and is particularly unfair to children. In 2000, American households below the poverty income line accounted for nearly one-sixth of all children, and nearly 30 percent of black and Hispanic children.

CHILDREN

The potential of individual people to achieve high-paying jobs depends greatly on their family backgrounds. Some children grow up in stable two-parent households that provide well for their nutrition, medical care, and education. Others live with parents who

have little education or job skills. Differences in intellectual capacity, physical fitness, and attractiveness can also affect earning capacity.

Poverty among able-bodied working-age adults often results from their life-style choices—drug and alcohol abuse, dishonesty, irresponsible pregnancies, violence, and neglect of their educations. However, large numbers of children are innocent victims of their parents' poor choices. Marital status is a good indicator of life-style choice. In 2000, married-couple households had median incomes about double those of female-headed households.

Concern for children leads inevitably to the idea that fairness requires equality of opportunity. Government programs and charitable efforts to provide for children's basic needs have the support of a large majority of the American people. In the early twenty-first century, the enormous disparities in public schools were a particular focal point for such concern.

GOVERNMENT MEASURES

Much of what government does displays its concern for changing income distribution. Income fairness has been a major consideration in government policies to end discrimination based on gender and ethnic identity. In this regard, the armed forces have set particularly high standards for fairness—for taking care of service members and in providing excellent schooling for children of military families.

A modified version of the equality standard is that each person has the same basic material needs—for food, clothing, shelter, medical care—and the society should provide for these.

Traditionally, many economists have favored progressive tax systems, which impose higher tax rates on persons with higher incomes. In 2000, the top 25 percent of American income receivers—those with incomes of $55,000 and higher—provided 84 percent of total U.S. income tax revenues. However, much government revenue comes from other types of tax that are not progressive.

Several moral objections have been raised against the principle of structuring taxes for the purpose of income redistribution. Taxation, by its nature, involves coercion. Taxation can impose heavy compliance costs and other forms of excess burden. Like all government actions, taxation reflects political expediency. All government measures are bent to serve powerful special interests. Moreover, taxation does not in itself raise the incomes of the poor.

At the beginning of the twenty-first century, much government redistribution came through transfer payments. Poverty among older Americans has been greatly reduced by Social Security, Medicare and Medicaid, and need-based supplements. Federal, state, and local governments provide extensive safety-net programs aimed at children. Their effectiveness is often impaired, however, by parental delinquency or indifference.

INTERNATIONAL DIMENSIONS

A broader question involves the enormous differences in incomes across the regions of the world. Efforts to remedy these by government foreign aid programs over the last half of the twentieth century proved relatively unsuccessful. Low-income countries generally have low incomes because their productivity is low. The reasons for low productivity often reflect defective legal and political environments as well as purely economic considerations. Well-meaning gestures from benefactor nations sometimes make matters worse. For example, donating food to a low-income nation may depress its local agricultural prices and thereby weaken its domestic agricultural sector.

Paul B. Trescott

FURTHER READING

Bauer, Peter. *From Subsistence to Exchange and Other Essays*. Princeton, N.J.: Princeton University Press, 2000. Offers a powerful critique of redistributionism with an international perspective.

Blocker, H. Gene, and Elizabeth H. Smith, eds. *John Rawls' Theory of Social Justice*. Athens: Ohio University Press, 1980. Includes several valuable commentaries on the relevance of Rawls to issues of income distribution, particularly those by Tom Beauchamp and John Schaar.

Friedman, Milton, and Rose Friedman. *Free to Choose*. New York: Avon Books, 1979. Nobel laureate Friedman critiques government pursuit of equality and welfare state measures.

Lindblom, Charles. *The Market System: What It Is, How It Works, and What to Make of It*. New Haven, Conn.: Yale University Press, 2001. Simple and readable presentation of the economics of in-come distribution, with an emphasis on the short-comings of market economies.

Sen, Amartya. *On Ethics and Economics*. New York: Basil Blackwell. A Nobel Prize-winning economist criticizes lack of ethical awareness on part of economists.

Sowell, Thomas. *The Quest for Cosmic Justice*. New York: Free Press, 1999. An African American economist, Sowell is critical of the "injustice" arguments directed at free markets.

Symposium on Intergenerational Mobility in *Journal of Economic Perspectives* 16, no. 3 (Summer, 2002): 3-66. Four excellent articles on how "unfair" differences in income can flow from parents to children.

SEE ALSO: Corporate compensation; Distributive justice; Equal pay for equal work; Minimum-wage laws; Nozick, Robert; Poverty; Poverty and wealth; Professional athlete incomes; Taxes; Wage discrimination.

Incommensurability

DEFINITION: State that develops when it is impossible to measure competing choices against a common denominator

TYPE OF ETHICS: Theory of ethics

SIGNIFICANCE: The difficulty of choosing rationally between choices that cannot be evaluated on the same scale can raise special ethical problems.

Situations involving incommensurability frequently occur in everyday life. For example, parents must often choose between putting their careers on hold in order to raise their children at home and sending their children to day-care centers while continuing to work. Faced with such decisions, individuals may try to make their decisions on the basis of cost-benefit analyses. Can people, however, place a value on raising their children at home and plug it into an equation opposite the value of their working? Early nineteenth century British philosopher Jeremy Bentham's theory of utility calculus requires similar quantifications of all goods in order to determine how to maximize utility.

By contrast, theories of incommensurability argue that the values of some goods are *not* interchangeable. An economist might assign monetary values to a person's career and the time the person spends with a child and compare them accordingly, but for many people such values cannot be measured in financial terms. Incommensurability can therefore be understood as a problem of translation, conversion, or compensation, as no amount of praise for the book that a mother writes during a year that here child is in day care might compensate her for the experiences that she does not share with her child. Aristotle's claim that no amount of one virtue can compensate for a lack of another challenged Plato's theory that all goods are ultimately instantiations, or reflections, of one essential good.

Problems of incommensurability also arise in political debates, typically when inherently valuable goods are at stake. For example, when considering whether a certain parcel of land is more valuable as a wildlife reserve or as an oil field, environmentalists are apt to object to conceptualizing the value of nature in financial terms.

Nick Smith

SEE ALSO: Aristotle; Bentham, Jeremy; Choice; Choiceless choices; Cost-benefit analysis; Moral equivalence; Utilitarianism.

Index librorum prohibitorum

IDENTIFICATION: Now-defunct list of books forbidden by the Roman Catholic Church
DATES: 1559-1966
TYPE OF ETHICS: Arts and censorship
SIGNIFICANCE: Members of the Roman Catholic Church were forbidden, except in special circumstances, from reading or even possessing books included in the *Index librorum prohibitorum*, on the theory that such works were harmful to the faith and morals of practicing Catholics, and that it was the function of the church to protect its members from such moral harm.

The *Index librorum prohibitorum* was never intended to be an exhaustive catalog of forbidden literature.

Index Librorum Prohibitorum Time Line

1557	First *Index librorum prohibitorum* is drawn up by the Congregation of the Inquisition, under Pope Paul IV but never published.
1559	First *Index* is published, in larger and more extensive format than that compiled in 1557.
1571	Pope Pius V establishes special "Congregation of the Index" to oversee list and revise it as necessary.
1664	*Index* begins to list books and authors alphabetically.
1753	Pope Benedict XIV develops detailed rules to be followed in future *Index* compilations.
1757	Under Benedict, *Index* is revised extensively and cleared of previous errors.
1897	Pope Leo XII's *Officiorum ac munerum* outlines censorship duties for diocesan bishops that include control of literature judged contrary to faith or morals. *Index* begins growing less prominent in hierarchical Church affairs.
1917	Pope Benedict XV transfers charge of the *Index* to the Holy Office.
1948	Final edition of the *Index*, with 4,100 entries, is published.
1966	*Index* is abolished after Vatican Council II and becomes a historic document for Roman Catholicism. However, Church officials retain the authority to prohibit future books that constitute a threat to the faith or morals of Catholics.

Rather, it represented those works condemned by the Roman Catholic Church in response to specific requests from people around the world. The majority of works included in the *Index* were theological in nature. During the first century (1559 to 1649) of its four centuries of existence, 469 texts appeared in the *Index*; in its second century, 1,585 were added; in its third, 1,039 were added; and in its final century, 1,585 were added.

By the time the *Index* was suppressed in June,

1966, it contained 4,126 entries. Some entries denoted specific titles, whereas others designated authors with Latin notations such as *omnia opera dramatica* ("all dramatic works" [forbidden]) or, the most severe censure, *opera omnia* ("all works" [forbidden]). Among those whose writings were forbidden were such notables as Émile Zola (all works), Stendhal (all love stories), Samuel Richardson (*Pamela: Or, Virtue Rewarded*, 1740), Laurence Sterne (*A Sentimental Journey Through France and Italy*,1768), Edward Gibbon (*The History of the Decline and Fall of the Roman Empire*, 1776-1788), and the complete works of British philosophers Thomas Hobbes and David Hume. Only four American authors (whose writings were theological in nature) were ever listed on the *Index*.

Robin G. Hanson

SEE ALSO: Art; Art and public policy; Book banning; Censorship; Christian ethics; Library Bill of Rights.

Individualism

DEFINITION: Theory that individual human beings are the fundamental units of reality and value
TYPE OF ETHICS: Personal and social ethics
SIGNIFICANCE: In Western culture, liberal individualism is the dominant mode of understanding society, history, and one's role within society and history. In ethics, individualist moral systems are founded upon the values and subjective experiences of the individual, and they valorize the rights of the individual and autonomist virtues above all else. Individualism opposes or marginalizes collective and communitarian theories of history and ethics, as well as other-centered virtues, such as nurturing, consensus-building, or responsibility to the community.

At the core of most debates about human nature, ethics, and politics is the debate about the power and value of the individual. In analyzing human nature, individualists emphasize that individuals have the power to control their own thoughts and actions and therefore to form their own characters by their choices. In ethics, individualists emphasize the value and potential of each individual, and so they encour-

age self-reliance, independence, and the quest for each person to realize his or her own unique self. In politics, individualists encourage laissez-faire—that is, leaving individuals free to pursue their own ends—and therefore they encourage free enterprise and limited government. In each area, individualists oppose the collectivist idea that individuals are molded by or subordinate to larger social groups.

HISTORY

Individualist ideas predate the use of the term "individualism." Early in the modern era, Thomas Hobbes and John Locke argued that political power begins with individuals and is consequently transferred to governments. They opposed the traditional idea that power naturally resides with an aristocracy or monarchy and is imposed on individuals. Government exists to serve its citizens, not vice versa. A gradual decentralization of power followed the rise of individualist ideas, giving rise to more democratic political institutions and free market economic institutions.

A highlight year for individualism was 1776, for in that year the United States of America was founded explicitly on individualist political ideas and Adam Smith published *The Wealth of Nations*, an influential description and defense of the free market system of economic individualism.

Alexis de Tocqueville is usually credited with the first use of the term "individualism," in his *Democracy in America* (1835-1839). He used "individualism" to describe the American character to which he had had mixed reactions; while he admired the energy and vitality of American individualism, he also feared that it would eventually degenerate into atomic selfishness.

F. A. Hayek has noted that the Saint-Simonians (named for Claude Saint-Simon), the founders of modern socialism, used "individualism" to describe the free-market, competitive society they opposed.

INDIVIDUALISM AND EGOISM

Individualism in ethics is associated with egoism, the theory that each individual's life is his or her highest value. Individuals are ends in themselves, not servants or slaves to the needs or interests of others. In order to survive and prosper, individuals need to think and act independently; therefore, self-reliance, initiative, pride, and courage in the face of disapproval are encouraged as virtues. Individualism thus is opposed to collectivism in ethics, the theory that larger social groupings are more important than the individuals who make them up and that individuals have a duty to sacrifice for the benefit of the group, whether the group be class, race, tribe, family, or nation. Individuals recognize the great value of cooperation but emphasize that cooperative social groups exist solely for the benefit of the individuals that participate in them; individuals do not exist to serve the group.

POLITICS

Individualism has important implications for economics and politics. Economically, valuing independence of thought and action translates into encouraging economic independence. Independence does not mean that individuals live as hermits. Rather, in a society based on the division of labor, it means providing for one's needs by producing the value-equivalent of what one needs and trading with others for mutual benefit.

Politically, valuing independence translates into recognizing and protecting individual spheres of autonomy. Individual autonomy can be violated in three broad ways: killing, assault (including slavery and kidnapping), and theft. Therefore, protecting individual autonomy means protecting individuals' lives, liberties, and property. The social institution established for this purpose is government, and to prevent abuses, political power will be decentralized as much as possible and limited to protective functions.

Thus, individualism encourages the decentralization of both political and economic power. The foundation of political authority resides in the individual citizens, and the power of government is limited to serving individuals' need for autonomy. Along with political decentralization goes economic decentralization: Economic power resides in individual ownership of property, and investment and consumption decisions remain in individual hands. Individualism is thus associated with limited government and free enterprise.

HUMAN NATURE

All the above depends on an analysis of human nature. To support individualism in ethics and politics, individuals must be both capable and worthy of autonomy. This leads to the three most fundamental

debates about human nature between individualists and collectivists:

1. Whether only individuals exist and groups are only aggregates of individuals, or social groups are organic wholes of which individuals are only dependent fragments.

2. Whether individuals are born cognitively and morally *tabula rasa* ("blank slate") or are born with the inherently destructive elements (for example, with Christian Original Sin or a Freudian id) and therefore require strict social constraints.

3. Supposing that individuals are born *tabula rasa*, either they have the capacity to create their own characters and destinies by controlling their own thoughts and actions or they are formed and controlled by the social groups to which they belong.

The second and third issues raise the complex of nature versus nurture versus free will issues, and it is in the resolution of these issues of human nature that the fate of individuals lies.

Stephen R. C. Hicks

FURTHER READING

Bellah, Robert N., et al. *Habits of the Heart: Individualism and Commitment in American Life.* Rev. ed. Berkeley: University of California Press, 1996.

Hayek, Friedrich A. "Individualism: True and False." In *Individualism and Economic Order.* Chicago: University of Chicago Press, 1980.

Macpherson, C. B. *The Political Theory of Possessive Individualism: Hobbes to Locke.* Oxford, England: Oxford University Press, 1988.

Rand, Ayn. *The Virtue of Selfishness: A New Concept of Egoism.* New York: New American Library, 1964.

Santoro, Emilio. *Autonomy, Freedom, and Rights: A Critique of Liberal Subjectivity.* Boston: Kluwer Academic, 2003.

Tocqueville, Alexis de. *Democracy in America.* In *"Democracy in America" and Two Essays on America.* Translated by Gerald E. Bevan. Introduction by Isaac Kramnick. London: Penguin, 2003.

SEE ALSO: Capitalism; Communitarianism; Egoism; Free enterprise; Freedom and liberty; Self-interest; Socialism.

Industrial research

DEFINITION: Technical inquiry and experimentation to develop new products, new manufacturing technologies, or more profitable and efficient techniques for creating and distributing commodities

TYPE OF ETHICS: Scientific ethics

SIGNIFICANCE: Industrial research raises a host of ethical issues involving fair employment practices, intellectual property rights, environmental responsibility, industrial espionage, workplace safety, and government oversight.

During the mid-twentieth century, the sociologist Robert Merton stated the norms of the scientific research community: communality, organized skepticism, originality, universality, and disinterestedness. To these should be added self-motivation, an openness in sharing results, and a readiness to change when objective evidence calls for it. To some degree, all these ethical norms are challenged by the practice of industrial research. The discussion that follows identifies some of these challenges, both to the individual and to the corporation.

THE INDIVIDUAL SCIENTIST

People with research degrees (usually doctorates) in the sciences are accustomed from their university experience to being their own bosses in choosing and executing research projects. In industry, by contrast, they are assigned a research problem and must report regular progress to a boss who reports to a higher boss, on up to the research director, with results appearing not in professional journals, but only in internal reports. The problem is less acute in very large, research-oriented companies, where the projects are correspondingly larger and more interesting. In companies with very small research operations, the problems can be depressingly trivial (for example, it is difficult to care how to lengthen the time it takes cornflakes to become soggy in milk). It is also less uncomfortable for graduates without university research training to be trained in a particular company's laboratory and absorb the company's goals with the training. Nevertheless, nearly all industrial researchers occasionally feel that they are compromising true science and must find their own way to be comfortable with this.

RESEARCH PRACTICES WITHIN CORPORATIONS

Companies must make money to survive. The problem for their research divisions, then, is to do as wide-ranging and complete research as possible within budgetary restraints. The urge to cut off research projects that do not pay off quickly must be resisted, as must the urge to stop a successful project the instant a product becomes possible. A more pernicious ethical problem is that of actually doing the research. Chemical procedures have sometimes been made up out of whole cloth, because "we know that's how they'd come out anyhow," and products have been represented as research breakthroughs that were nothing of the kind. Patent policy is worth mentioning: American firms customarily claim patent protection not only for a specific invention, the patent's subject, but also for any similar device or process that can be related to it, thus closing out research efforts by other firms. A topic that is too large to deal with here is the ethical handling of animals in industrial laboratories.

RELATIONS WITH OTHER CORPORATIONS

All companies examine competitors' products with the idea of improving their own or claiming a share of the market. So long as this practice does not infringe patents, it is legitimate. What is not legitimate is deliberate industrial espionage—hiring a firm to place a person on the competitor's payroll to ferret out secrets of process or formulation that can be obtained in no other way. Equally unethical is the hiring away of key employees to exploit their privileged knowledge. Some firms have explicit policies that forbid this practice; many require professional employees to sign contracts that forbid their working for a competitor for a specified time after leaving the company. A separate issue of marketing that touches on the research side is that of firms that compete, not by improving manufacturing and distribution processes to reduce costs, but by blitzing competitors with a steady flow of new products. A weak firm can be driven out of business by such practices.

RESPONSIBILITY TO CUSTOMERS

Customers need to know a great many things that only the industrial research laboratories can tell them—for example, about product safety. The Food and Drug Act was passed in 1906 to ensure the purity of foods and the safety and efficacy of drugs; even so, many errors have been made that have stemmed from careless, if not unethical, practices: the pediatric syrup of sulfa drugs marketed during the late 1930's that used toxic ethylene glycol as solvent; the grossly teratogenic drug thalidomide, which was withdrawn from the market during the 1960's; diethylstilbestrol (DES), which is carcinogenic in women even to the second generation; and a host of other drugs and food additives, some quietly taken off the market when studies that should have been done in the original research showed unacceptable side effects. Environmental effects should be investigated (although these cannot always be anticipated): for example, pesticide residue toxicity, chlorofluorocarbon depletion of the ozone layer, and so forth. Finally, customers need to know that new research products are genuine innovations: Could the ingredients of a new two-drug pill have been prescribed separately more cheaply? Will this new research-hyped cosmetic really make one sixteen years old again? Do automotive gimmicks such as rectangular headlights or hideaway headlights make a car safer or mechanically superior? Although some of these examples border on marketing and salesmanship, many relate to the research laboratory.

CONCLUSION

As the foregoing discussion indicates, industrial research deviates in many respects from pure research. Nearly all these points of deviation call for ethical decisions. No attempt has been made here to say what decisions should be made; the purpose of this article is descriptive rather than prescriptive.

Robert M. Hawthorne, Jr.

FURTHER READING

Amato, Ivan. "The Slow Birth of Green Chemistry." "Can the Chemical Industry Change Its Spots?" and "Making Molecules Without the Mess." *Science* 259 (March 12, 1993): 1538-1541.

Blevins, David E. "University Research and Development Activities: Intrusion into Areas Unattended? A Review of Recent Developments and Ethical Issues Raised." *Journal of Business Ethics* 7 (September, 1988): 645-656.

Carboni, Rudolph A. *Planning and Managing Industry-University Research Collaborations.* Westport, Conn.: Quorum Books, 1992.

Kornhauser, William. *Scientists in Industry: Conflict and Accommodation.* Berkeley: University of California Press, 1962.

Krimsky, Sheldon. *Science in the Private Interest: Has the Lure of Profits Corrupted Biomedical Research?* Lanham, Md.: Rowman & Littlefield, 2003.

Vagtborg, Harold. *Research and American Industrial Development.* New York: Pergamon Press, 1976.

Wilks, Stephen. "Science, Technology, and the Large Corporation." *Government and Opposition* 27, no. 2 (Spring, 1992): 190-212.

SEE ALSO: Business ethics; Environmental ethics; Marketing; Product safety and liability; Science; Weapons research.

Inequality

DEFINITION: Absence of an ethical entitlement of all people to the same legal, civil, economic, and social rights
TYPE OF ETHICS: Theory of ethics
SIGNIFICANCE: Although most people would agree that some forms of inequality are immoral, there is considerable ethical disagreement over how to distinguish just and unjust forms of inequality.

Inequality is a subject of concern in many areas of ethics, including politico-economic ethics, legal and judicial ethics, and business and labor ethics. A number of widely affirmed ethical principles address the issue of inequality. These include equality of opportunity, equality before the law, and the principle of treating people with equal concern and respect. Each principle represents an attempt to specify a kind of inequality that is regarded as unjust. For example, equality of opportunity is usually understood as precluding racial, religious, sexual, and ethnic discrimination for positions in business, government, and education.

Most ethicists argue that inequalities that arise from differences in race, religion, sex, or ethnicity are unjust inequalities. For example, people denied jobs at a corporation because of their religious beliefs are being treated unjustly: Religious beliefs are generally regarded as irrelevant to determining a person's qualifications as an employee in a secular organization. Long-standing moral and legal practices affirm the injustice of such forms of inequality.

Some argue that the best way to distinguish just from unjust inequality is to focus on the link between the forms of inequality and the choices that people make. According to this view, inequalities that result from unchosen differences, such as sexual inequality, are unjustified. By contrast, if two employees have equal opportunities for success on their jobs, the one who works harder may be said to deserve more income than the other. The fact that the other person earns less money is not necessarily unjust. Such a situation distinguishes inequalities that result from choices made by persons who have equal opportunities from those who do not. On this view, the first type of inequality is acceptable; the second is unjust.

There is much controversy about how to distinguish inequalities that reflect choice and inequalities that are beyond a person's control. The issue is complicated if one considers the role of luck in a person's chances for success in life. For example, people do not choose their own natural talents. Likewise, no child chooses the economic status of his or her parents. On the other hand, people can make choices about whether and how to develop the natural talents that they do have. However, there is little agreement among ethicists on such matters as the point at which ambition and effort matter more than luck for determining whether inequalities are just or unjust, whether society has an obligation to compensate inequalities that are not chosen, and whether affirmative action policies are a just means of eliminating racial inequalities.

Jon Mahoney

FURTHER READING

Dworkin, Ronald. *Sovereign Virtue: The Theory and Practice of Equality.* Cambridge, Mass.: Harvard University Press, 1999.

Hurrell, Andrew, and Ngaire Woods, eds. *Inequality, Globalization, and World Politics.* New York: Oxford University Press, 1999.

Rousseau, Jean-Jacques. "Discourse on the Origin and Foundations of Inequality Among Mankind." In *"The Social Contract" and "The First and Second Discourses,"* edited by Susan Dunn. New Haven, Conn.: Yale University Press, 2002.

Sen, Amartya. *Inequality Reexamined.* Cambridge, Mass.: Harvard University Press, 1992.

SEE ALSO: Affirmative action; Caste system, Hindu; Discrimination; Distributive justice; Equal pay for equal work; Equality; Feminist ethics; Gender bias; Wage discrimination.

Infanticide

DEFINITION: Intentional killing of human infants
TYPE OF ETHICS: Children's rights
SIGNIFICANCE: Arguments over what constitutes human life permeate abortion debates and flow over into the issue of infanticide. A key point in the debate concerns when human beings become persons with protected rights. Infanticide also has ethical implications for the broader issue of euthanasia.

If the question is asked whether killing a neonate (newborn) or infant human is equivalent to killing an older child or adult, the answer is yes—according to the law. However, in most past societies, and some modern societies in certain parts of the world, the distinction is not as clear. Leading modern ethicists, bioethicists, and sociobiologists continue seriously to debate under what, if any circumstances, infanticide may be justified.

Many sociobiologists point to the fact that killing even normal infants in particular circumstances, such as overpopulation, is common to most primates and is part of the complexities of intergroup reactions or reproductive strategies. Among prehistoric human societies, infanticide was used to help ensure the survival of older siblings. Infants with severe physical or mental handicaps rarely survived childhood. Even in the modern world, there is a strong medical and economics-driven argument that newborn babies with severe disabilities pose intolerable burdens on the scarce resources of both their families and society at large. Moreover, it is also argued that because infants with such disabilities may be doomed to short and painful existences, it is inhumane not to perform euthanasia (mercy killing).

REAL PEOPLE

In the debate over abortion, it is argued that the fetus is not a real person with an independent identity. Rationalizers of infanticide argue that a newborn is no different, and life and death issues should be under the jurisdiction of the biological parents. Furthermore, it is argued that a newborn human is a primitive creature with no self-concept, lacking the self-sufficiency and will to survive found in other mammals. In fact as the well-known ethicist and animal-rights activist Peter Singer pointed out, in his landmark study *Animal Liberation* (1975), humans eat a wide variety of life-forms that are much more advanced than human infants. Therefore, to argue against infanticide as being unethical is mere hypocrisy. Singer is joined by bioethicist Michael Tooley, who defined fifteen characteristics of personhood, all of which neonates lack. Although infants are clearly human beings, Tooley argued that they do not begin to become persons until the age of three months. Thus killing a baby younger than three months old clearly does not equate to killing an actual person.

PRO-INFANTICIDE PHILOSOPHERS

Neither Plato nor Aristotle, as is true of most ancient Greek philosophers, found anything wrong with infanticide of defective and unwanted newborn babies. Much like modern bioethicists, some major philosophers such as John Locke (who viewed human infants as being born into the world as "blank tablets" lacking personhood) and Immanuel Kant (who defined persons as beings that are conscious of themselves and able to consider themselves as themselves) approved of infanticide. In addition, the utilitarianism of Jeremy Bentham stressed the principle of the greatest good for the greatest number as well as the principle of avoiding pain and seeking pleasure. Consequently utilitarianism could be used to justify euthanasia of infants with serious birth defects or killing of infants merely to benefit the larger social unit.

ARGUMENTS FOR AND AGAINST INFANTICIDE

Some cultural historians have pointed to infanticide as a concern primarily within the Judeo-Christian and Islamic world. Nevertheless, until the late twentieth century, the fact that few questions were asked when infants died is an indication that Western societies tacitly accepted infanticide. Poverty and illegitimacy were major causative factors of infanticide. Infants abandoned to foundling homes generally received death sentences through neglect. Many unwanted infants in their parents' home fell victim to neglect so severe that it amounted to passive infanticide. Infanticide thus appears to have been an integral part of the human experience throughout the ages and not merely an aberration.

There are strong arguments for the notion that people actually protect their own lives by valuing life in general. In *Abortion and the Ways We Value Human Life* (1999), Jeffrey Reiman points to a natural human love for infants produced by evolution—an impulse exemplified by the attention and protectiveness given to infants even by strangers. Such love is necessary for human infants to survive precisely because human babies are the most helpless infants among all mammals. Likewise, respect for the development of humans from neonates to adults is needed for human survival. An example of this value of life is supported by the care devoted to the disposal of human corpses.

CRIMES AGAINST HUMANITY

Ethicists and historians point to euthanasia programs conducted by Nazi Germany under Adolf Hitler to eliminate people with mental and physical disabilities. Since such practices were condemned as crimes against humanity at the Nuremberg trials, a turn toward euthanasia would resurrect horrors of the past. Because older persons suffering from severe dementia or Alzheimer's disease may also be said to lack personhood and self-awareness, they too could be included in euthanasia programs.

Another argument against infanticide is that it victimizes the defenseless. Democratic societies provide individuals with rights precisely to protect the weak from being harmed by the strong. Worldwide, those suffering most from infanticide are female babies. Permitting infanticide is thus also contrary to the goal of redressing gender inequalities. Moreover, many historians would argue that the fact that infanticide pervades human history does not justify the practice. The institution of slavery also pervades human history, but few would argue that this fact justifies the institution.

Irwin Halfond

FURTHER READING

McMahan, Jeff. *The Ethics of Killing: Problems at the Margins of Life.* New York: Oxford University Press, 2002.

Petrinovich, Lewis. *Human Evolution, Reproduction, and Morality.* Cambridge, Mass.: MIT Press, 1998.

Piers, Maria. *Infanticide*. New York: W. W. Norton, 1978.

Reiman, Jeffrey. *Abortion and the Ways We Value Human Life*. Lanham, Md.: Rowman & Littlefield, 1999.

Singer, Peter. *Rethinking Life and Death*. New York: St. Martin's Press, 1996.

Tooley, Michael. *Abortion and Infanticide*. Oxford, England: Oxford University Press, 1983.

SEE ALSO: Abortion; Birth control; Birth defects; Children's rights; Death and dying; Euthanasia; Homicide; "Playing god" in medical decision making; Right to die; Singer, Peter.

Infomercials

DEFINITION: Paid commercials that mimic the lengths and formats of conventional television programs and are typically designed to sell specific products

DATE: First broadcast during the mid-1980's

TYPE OF ETHICS: Media ethics

SIGNIFICANCE: The dramatic rise in infomercial broadcasting at the end of the twentieth century posed ethical questions regarding truth in advertising and the blurring of lines between commercial and noncommercial television programming.

The two- to four-minute television commercials for household gadgets that entrepreneur Ron Popeil began broadcasting during the mid-1950's are often considered precursors of modern infomercials, which typically devote thirty minutes or more to promoting a single product or line of products. In 1984, the administration of President Ronald Reagan relaxed federal guidelines limiting the time that television stations could devote to advertising, paving the way for lengthier and more detailed on-air sales pitches. Later that same year, the HerbaLife company aired a sixty-minute advertisement for its diet products that is commonly regarded as the first true infomercial. Infomercials then proliferated rapidly throughout the rest of the decade and into the 1990's, fueled by budget cuts that forced local television stations to increase their advertising revenues.

Infomercials are frequently designed to mimic news programs, talk shows, or public service announcements, creating the illusion that the information they present meets journalistic standards of credibility and objectivity. Infomercial advertisers are often accused of utilizing these formats to reinforce outrageous claims and sell shoddy merchandise to consumers who are sometimes emotionally or intellectually vulnerable. Critics of this practice cite laws against deceptive advertising as well as the ethical tradition of the regulated market economies of Western nations, which holds that businesses and advertisers should not mislead consumers by lying or misrepresenting facts.

Defenders of infomercials argue that according to the dictates of the free market, infomercial producers and broadcasters have a fiduciary obligation to maximize profits that supersedes their obligation to consumers, that the disclaimers commonly included in these programs provide sufficient notification to viewers as to their content, and that consumers must assume at least partial responsibility for distinguishing between news and advertising.

Michael H. Burchett

SEE ALSO: Advertising; Children's television; Consumerism; Marketing.

Information access

DEFINITION: Ability to obtain, utilize, and disseminate information, especially personal information, stored on computers

TYPE OF ETHICS: Media ethics

SIGNIFICANCE: The advent of one integrated set of technologies, the computer network, to both store and transmit information, renders information both less secure and more easily exploited or disseminated once it has been accessed, by an order of magnitude. As a result, new ethical principles are required to arbitrate and safeguard the traditional right to privacy in the Information Age.

The ability to store and exchange computerized information about individuals raises ethical questions about access to that information. Who should have access to personal information? Does the right of the government to know take precedence over an individual's right to privacy? What kind of information should not be kept or shared? Complicating these issues is the tendency to accept information obtained from a computer as totally accurate. Given authorized access, how can the information be verified as accurate? Do people have a right to examine information pertaining to them?

RISE OF INFORMATION TECHNOLOGY

Since World War II, computer and communications technologies have combined to produce a major influence on Western society. The first generation of electronic computers had thousands of vacuum tubes, required huge amounts of electricity for power and cooling, and cost so much that only governments and very large corporations could afford them. The development of the transistor, the integrated circuit, and the microprocessor led to generations of ever-more-affordable computers. By the 1980's, computer technology had reached virtually every level of the economic infrastructure. Computers became repositories for criminal and tax records, health and employment records, and credit and financial information. The communications revolution parallels the computer revolution. Satellites and fiber-optic lines have made possible the almost instant transmission of data between geographically distant computers.

The first two decades of computer technology progressed without much public discussion of ethical issues. By 1965, the Federal Bureau of Investigation (FBI) had begun to develop the National Crime Information Center as a central repository of criminal arrest records. That same year, the proposed idea of centralizing government records of individual citizens in a National Data Center was met with strong opposition in Congress. Debate over the National Data Center focused national attention for the first time on the issue of invasion of privacy as people began to fear the prospect of an Orwellian all-seeing, all-knowing government becoming reality.

In *Menard v. Mitchell*, a landmark 1971 federal case, the U.S. Supreme Court ruled that a "compelling public necessity" had to be proved before an individual's arrest record could be widely disseminated. Legislation by Congress followed. The Privacy Act of 1975 regulated the use of criminal justice information, and the Freedom of Information Act of 1977 gave individuals the right to access nonclassified government records.

Ethical Questions Posed by Information Technology

What is the moral status and nature of ethics presented by artificial intelligence?

Are machines capable or being moral, or, should human beings be considered moral machines?

What is humanity's moral relationship with high-tech information technology, and what obligations does each owe to the other?

What can be done about the "digital divide" between the haves and have nots in access to computers and the Internet?

What moral issues arise from the impact of computers on work, the family, church, and other social institutions?

Should "bad" information technology be prohibited?

Is it possible for hackers and other "deviant" users of information technology to be considered ethical?

THE PRIVATE SECTOR

The first attempt to regulate the retail credit industry's use of personal credit information had come with the Fair Credit Reporting Act of 1969. By the 1980's and 1990's, however, personal information had become a lucrative commodity driving a huge industry. The two largest credit bureaus maintained separate databases of more than 150 million files, which they made available to banks, credit card companies, and virtually any other business willing to pay for the service. Many people believed that the protection of the Fair Credit Reporting Act was no longer adequate. Reports by the news media and consumer advocates documented cases of individuals being victimized by false and ruinous credit information. A 1991 Consumer Union study found inaccuracies in nearly half the records it sampled.

Smaller companies specialized in providing demographic and consumer information to direct marketing firms. For a small monthly fee, customers had access to detailed information on millions of households, including address, telephone number, property ownership, and legal records. Manufacturers often routinely sold information taken from cards returned by consumers for product warranty registration to direct marketers, who used it to target potential customers more accurately.

PROSPECTS FOR REGULATION

Because access to personal information has reached virtually every level of modern society, regulation by a single law or agency is impossible. Federal and state governments struggle to sort out the questions of access versus privacy and enact appropriate legislation, while some critics question the government's ability to regulate itself. By 1982, U.S. government computers contained more than 3.5 billion personal files. The FBI continues to build a database of the arrest records of 25 million people, whether or not their arrests resulted in convictions.

During the 1970's, the National Security Agency (NSA) and International Business Machines (IBM) developed the Data Encryption Standard (DES) to ensure secure transmission of classified information over telephone and data lines. Data or conversations that are transmitted between two points are encrypted with a mathematical key. In 1993, the introduction of a DES integrated circuit chip, to be made available in commercial products, led the Clinton administration to support its widespread use. Privacy advocates hailed the advent of the DES chip but worried that a new standard with government control of the keys could trigger abuses of wiretapping and that computer hackers might be able to duplicate the new standard's classified algorithm.

Meanwhile, groups such as the Consumer Union and the American Civil Liberties Union, as well as individual citizens, continued to press for protection against abuses by both the government and the private sector.

SUMMARY

The ethics of information access began with the issue of privacy versus the government's right to acquire knowledge for the public good but expanded as businesses began to perceive their access to personal information as part of their right to do business in a free-market economy.

Some social analysts claim that the Information Age has brought a change in values to modern society, where the benefits and convenience of free access to information outweigh the individual's right to privacy. It has even been proposed that since an individual's personal information is a commodity with commercial value, that person should be compensated with a royalty whenever the information is sold.

The Industrial Revolution was welcomed as an unmixed blessing to humankind for many years before society began to consider such ethical issues as child labor and pollution. The Information Age has brought sweeping changes to society at a much faster pace. Sorting out the ethics of information access and creating systems for control is a slow process, with much opportunity for abuse in the meantime, because the very concepts of information and privacy are being redefined by this rapidly developing technology.

Charles E. Sutphen

FURTHER READING

Allen, Dennis. "Ethics of Electronic Information." *Byte* 17 (August, 1992): 10.

Begley, Sharon, et al. "Technology: The Code of the Future." *Newsweek* 121 (June 7, 1993): 70.

Hoerr, John, et al. "Privacy." *Business Week*, March 28, 1988, 61-68.

Hunter, Richard. *World Without Secrets: Business, Crime, and Privacy in the Age of Ubiquitous Computing.* New York: J. Wiley, 2002.

Lacayo, Richard. "Nowhere to Hide." *Time* 138 (November 11, 1991): 34-40.

Marchand, Donald A. *The Politics of Privacy, Computers, and Criminal Justice Records: Controlling the Social Costs of Technological Change.* Arlington, Va.: Information Resources Press, 1980.

Mossberger, Karen, Caroline J. Tolbert, and Mary Stansbury, eds. *Virtual Inequality: Beyond the Digital Divide.* Washington, D.C.: Georgetown University Press, 2003.

Roszak, Theodore. *The Cult of Information.* New York: Pantheon Books, 1986.

Spinello, Richard A. *CyberEthics: Morality and Law in Cyberspace.* 2d ed. Boston: Jones and Bartlett, 2003.

Wayner, Peter. "Clipped Wings? Encryption Chip Draws Fire." *Byte* 18 (July, 1993): 36.

SEE ALSO: American Civil Liberties Union; Arrest records; Computer databases; Computer technology; Confidentiality; Freedom of Information Act; Identity theft; Orwell, George; Privacy.

Inside information

DEFINITION: Confidential knowledge possessed or obtained by people in positions of power or with privileged access to information within a company, organization, or government

TYPE OF ETHICS: Media ethics

SIGNIFICANCE: Inside information can be put to many uses with ethical implications. It can be used to profit the person who possesses or obtains it, it can be passed on to authorities or to a public whose interest in such knowledge is arguably legitimate, or it can be used to harm, or violate the privacy of, individuals, companies, or organizations. All of these uses are the subject of ethical codes and many are subject to legal regulation as well.

Confidential information that derives from the fulfillment of professional or civic duties is a valuable commodity. Misappropriation of such knowledge is a common occurrence in the banking and securities industry, where frequent opportunity exists to convert one's knowledge into a monetary profit through the buying and selling of stocks about which one has secret information. The Securities and Exchange Commission explicitly prohibits such practices and vigorously prosecutes violators.

Media professionals, too, have access to information that is proprietary in nature and that has the potential for misuse. The wide scope of the First Amendment and the privileges guaranteed to the press therein, however, preclude the existence of both a regulatory body and legal restrictions designed to control the use of information. Therefore, the press, as with other questions of conduct, is obliged to address the ethical issues on a situational basis, weighing circumstances along with values, loyalties, and journalistic principles.

Two central issues exist regarding the issue of inside information: how the information is obtained and how it is used. In regard to the securing of information, journalists are morally obligated to remain objective and uncompromised and to respect the boundaries of legal as well as ethical codes. Because a journalist's primary obligation is to distribute information, however, even these simple tenets must be weighed in the light of a situation's defining circumstances. *The New York Times*, for example, in the publication of the Pentagon Papers (the documents that exposed the illegal activities of the Nixon administration during the 1972-1973 Watergate Affair), knowingly accepted stolen materials in the light of what the editors reasoned was a greater moral good—the exposition of a governmental effort to misrepresent the realities of the Vietnam War.

The second question concerns how inside information can be ethically used by media professionals. The code of ethics of the Society of Professional Journalists states that journalists who use their professional status as representatives of the public for selfish or other unworthy motives violate a high trust. A vigorous and effective press relies on the public trust, so it is incumbent upon journalists to use information humanely, intelligently, and ethically. This process involves questioning the motives of both the reporter and the source of the information, any obligation that may be created on the part of the journalist in exchange for the information, and the nature of the relationship in which the information became known.

That the public interest is best served by making known everything that is knowable is a journalistic standard that justifies much of what is presented as news. When journalists become the recipients of confidential information, however, an ethical dilemma arises that challenges this utilitarian philosophy and the accompanying assertion that an action is just as long as it achieves the greatest good for the greatest number. The debate lies in an opposing belief that people are not to be treated as a means to a journalistic end. A corollary to this principle is that the journalist should not allow himself or herself to be so treated, which may well be the case when publishing information "leaked" from confidential sources. Journalists, therefore, are morally obligated to seek out competing perspectives and confirming information and to question whether they are being used by someone whose interest is counter to the public interest, such as a campaign worker who might provide information about an opponent's sexual history.

Journalists must also inquire about their own motives for pursuing confidential information. During the 1970's, Bob Woodward and Carl Bernstein of *The Washington Post* were guilty of unethical conduct when they sought to lure information from grand jurors hearing evidence on the Watergate case who were sworn to secrecy. Even though a corrupt administration was eventually driven from office partly as a result of their investigation of the Watergate break-in, they did not foresee this event at the time, and the means they employed to obtain information violated ethical codes.

OBLIGATIONS OF REPORTERS

A second ethical question raised by the use of inside information relates to the obligation it establishes on the part of the reporter. Does the journalist incur responsibility toward the informant when he or she has taken risks to provide the information? If he or she has broken the law to do so, does the reporter assume culpability as well? Such concerns refer again to the principle that people are to be treated with respect and not as a means to an end, and also begin to encroach into other ethical problems for journalists, those of source-reporter confidentiality and the use of anonymous sources.

Finally, the issue of respecting the nature of the relationship in which confidential information is learned presents yet another ethical challenge. Reporters, as representatives of the public trust, frequently find themselves privy to sensitive information that they are obligated to preserve in respect to their roles as journalists. Even seemingly insignificant violations of the public trust, such as providing friends with advance notice of an upcoming sale to be advertised in the local paper, are unethical by intention regardless of the consequences.

The press, by nature, is not governed by a concise, explicit code of professional conduct. The ethics codes that do exist offer guidelines for performance and not absolute standards of behavior. Journalists and other media professionals, therefore, are encouraged to weigh situational factors along with their principles of duty in a thoughtful, critical effort to determine the ethical use of inside information.

Regina Howard Yaroch

FURTHER READING

Bain, George. "The Subtleties of Inside Information." *Mclean's* 102 (May, 1989): 48.

Black, Jay, Bob Steele, and Ralph Barney. *Doing Ethics in Journalism: A Handbook with Case Studies.* Greencastle, Ind.: Sigma Delta Chi Foundation and the Society of Professional Journalists, 1993.

Christians, Clifford G., et al. *Media Ethics: Cases and Moral Reasoning.* 5th ed. New York: Longman, 1998.

Day, Louis A. *Ethics in Media Communications: Cases and Controversies.* Belmont, Calif.: Wadsworth, 1991.

Donaldson, Thomas, and Patricia Werhane. "Introduction to Ethical Reasoning." In *Case Studies in Business Ethics*, edited by Thomas Donaldson and A. R. Gini. Englewood Cliffs, N.J.: Prentice-Hall, 1990.

SEE ALSO: Confidentiality; Insider trading; Intellectual property; Journalistic ethics; News sources; Pentagon Papers; Privacy.

Insider trading

DEFINITION: Use of information not available to the public to guide decisions to buy or sell publicly traded securities

TYPE OF ETHICS: Business and labor ethics

SIGNIFICANCE: Federal laws regulating insider trading in the United States are designed to create a level playing field for all investors, on the theory that for the stock market to be fair, it must in principle be both equally accessible and equally unpredictable to all participants.

Insider trading has been prohibited in the United States since the passage of the Securities Exchange Act of 1934, whose Section 10(b) laid down restrictions. The federal regulations on securities were designed to prevent corporate executives, directors, attorneys, accountants, investment bankers, and other "insiders" from using their positions to gain unfair advantages in the market trading of their corporations' securities. To buy or sell securities on the basis of confidential information or to recommend trading to others on that basis constitutes a violation of federal securities regulations, potentially subjecting violaters to both criminal prosecution by the Security and Exchange Commission (SEC) and civil lawsuits by injured investors.

Over the years, the SEC and the courts developed a detailed description of insider trading in numerous individual cases, most notably in the U.S. Supreme

Court's decisions in *United States v. Chiarella* (1980) and *Dirks v. Securities and Exchange Commission* (1983). Insider trading became widely publicized during the 1980's, when two prominent financiers, Ivan Boesky and Michael Milken, were convicted of numerous securities violations, sentenced to prison, and fined more than $700 million.

No formal definition of insider trading was written into federal law until 2002, when the U.S. Congress passed the Sarbanes-Oxley Act. That law spelled out the conditions constituting lawful and unlawful insider trading and established ground rules for legal insider trading. These rules required dealers to file insider transactions, electronically, within two business days to the SEC and to post the transactions on their companies' Web sites within one day of filing the information with the SEC. Under previous legislation, insider traders had at least forty-one days to report their transactions, making it nearly impossible to detect abuses until well after damage was done. For example, executives of the failing Enron corporation did not report they had sold off most of their own stock in the company in 2001 until after the company's collapse was made public. By the end of the calendar year, the value of the company's stock fell from more than eighty-one dollars per share to virtually nothing.

W. Jackson Parham, Jr.
Updated by the editors

FURTHER READING

Lu Shen-Shin. *Insider Trading and the Twenty-Four Hour Securities Market: A Case Study of Legal Regulation in the Emerging Global Economy.* Hanover, Mass.: Christopher, 1999.

SEE ALSO: Corporate scandal; Inside information; Profit taking; Retirement funds; Stewart, Martha; White-collar crime.

Institutionalization of patients

DEFINITION: Involuntary confinement in mental health facilities of mentally ill individuals
TYPE OF ETHICS: Psychological ethics
SIGNIFICANCE: The involuntary institutionalization of people who are deemed to be mentally ill cre-

ates a conflict between the ethical values of personal autonomy on one hand and beneficence or care on the other. The question is when it is appropriate to violate the wishes of individuals for their own good. This question is made much more complicated by the fact that what has counted as mental illness and as legitimate grounds for institutionalization has changed significantly over time, which can cause any given standard to seem more arbitrary than it otherwise might.

Religions teach that the least among us deserve aid and comfort. To apply this rule to the mentally ill often requires some degree of forced institutionalization. To fulfill the ethical rule not to restrict liberty without good cause means to allow people to live on the streets and to conduct costly court hearings. Many solutions to the problem of the seriously mentally ill have been tried, but all are flawed.

A HISTORY OF INSTITUTIONALIZATION

Various societies at various times have attempted to find humane solutions to the problem of mentally ill persons. Many homeless mentally ill persons wandered the towns and roads of the American colonies. In 1752, Benjamin Franklin influenced the Pennsylvania colony legislature to open the first mental hospital in the thirteen colonies. During the mid-nineteenth century, many people hailed Dorothea Dix as a great reformer because her efforts on the behalf of the homeless mentally ill resulted in the creation of thirty mental hospitals that soon were filled with patients. Placing people in mental hospitals deprived them of liberty. Common law principles allowed the taking of a person's liberty only if that person was dangerous to himself or herself or the community, required due process, and maintained that a defendant was innocent until proved guilty. Application of the common law rules could have stopped physicians from attempting to treat the mentally ill.

In 1849, the Association of Medical Superintendents of American Institutions for the Insane (now the American Psychiatric Association) appointed a well-known expert, Isaac Ray, to draft a model law for involuntary confinements. He proposed that the involuntary confinement of the deranged for treatment be treated as a medical decision without legal formalities. After several years, most states accepted

741

Ray's idea. During the nineteenth century and the first half of the twentieth century, the states constructed many large mental asylums. In the United States in 1963, 679,000 persons were confined in mental hospitals, whereas only 250,000 were confined in state and federal prisons. From the medical viewpoint, confinement in mental institutions represented an opportunity to "help" those suffering from a disease.

THE DEINSTITUTIONALIZATION MOVEMENT

By the 1950's, many critics, including the well-known psychiatrist Thomas Szasz, attacked the involuntary confinement of the mentally ill unless the patients were dangerous to themselves or others. For Szasz, mental illness was a myth, a name for problems in living rather than a medical condition correctable by medical action. He proposed the deinstitutionalization of mental patients and the dismantling of community mental health centers. Szasz pointed to misuses of psychiatry in the former Soviet Union to institutionalize and "treat" political prisoners.

Patients' rights advocates who sued hospitals to release patients and improve conditions joined forces with fiscal conservatives who recommended the release of patients to more cost-effective community care. Judges forced mental hospitals to use more stringent criteria for involuntary admissions, to grant extensive rights to patients, to stop exploiting patients economically, and to improve conditions. The "need for treatment" criterion was rejected, and only the mentally ill who were a danger to themselves or others or were gravely disabled could be confined involuntarily and then only by means of a judicial decision. By 1984, the mental hospital population had dropped to roughly 125,000.

The courts also granted mental patients basic rights. Mental patients were to be treated as normal human beings, they were not to be embarrassed by disclosure of their patient status, and they were to be paid for work done in the institutions. They had a right to refuse most extreme treatments, such as shock therapy. Their rights included absolute access to an attorney and qualified rights for free communication. The restrictions on commitment and the new rights for mental patients made it more expensive and difficult to commit patients and more expensive to keep them. Mental hospitals had partially supported themselves by the unpaid labor of the patients, but this was now forbidden.

The theory behind deinstitutionalization was that community mental health facilities such as halfway houses would replace the large asylums, but legislatures did not fund adequate numbers of the new centers and communities resisted having the facilities in their midst. Outpatient care using chemotherapy was initiated, but most patients did not use such services. Deinstitutionalization freed patients but did not improve their overall welfare. Many freed patients moved to the streets and endured terrible conditions. Some had children on the streets. Citizens complained about the activities of mental patients in their neighborhoods. The argument that the mentally ill should have the same legal protection as criminals is flawed. The consequences of confinement and freedom for each group of persons and for society are different.

Today, state laws specify the procedures for involuntary confinement of the mentally ill. The normal grounds for such confinement are that the patient is a danger to self or others or is gravely disabled. As patients' loss of liberty increases through longer confinements, the courts play a larger role and patients have more due process rights. The state must provide an appointed attorney if one is requested and must allow jury trials.

TREATMENT AND A CLASH OF VALUES

A second factor that acted together with court rulings to promote the deinstitutionalization of the mentally ill was the discovery of powerful antipsychotic drugs during the 1950's. Chemotherapy treated symptoms but did not cure the mentally ill, and it often produced very unpleasant side effects. Because most patients could function as long as they took their medication, it made it possible to release many of them. Many patients improved during confinement because of therapy and drugs, won release, stopped taking their medication, and then relapsed.

Ironically, once the patients' rights advocates won the deinstitutionalization battle, they then attacked forced chemotherapy. Psychotherapists argued that chemotherapy liberated the mind from delusions. A majority of state courts granted patients rights to refuse chemotherapy, while the federal courts applied a "need-for-treatment" analysis and left the decisions in the hands of psychiatrists. As chemotherapy declined, hospital stays became longer and the use of physical restraints increased.

The basic institutionalization issue involves deciding which profession and which set of ethical values will control the treatment and confinement of the mentally ill. The patients' rights attorneys see themselves as being in conflict with arrogant physicians who deprive patients of civil rights. In fact, most therapists do tend to overdiagnose mental illness. The idea that judging a sick person to be well is more to be avoided than judging a well person to be sick is built into the medical model. Therapists are wary of public criticism and of lawsuits triggered by the violent acts of a few dangerous released mental patients, and they view involuntary confinement and treatment as being ethically required to protect patients and the public.

Leland C. Swenson

FURTHER READING

Appelbaum, Paul S. "The Right to Refuse Treatment with Antipsychotic Medications: Retrospect and Prospect." *American Journal of Psychiatry* 145 (April, 1988): 413-419.

Bartol, Curt R., and Anne M. Bartol. *Psychology and American Law.* Belmont, Calif.: Wadsworth, 1983.

Brooks, Alexander D. *Law, Psychiatry, and the Mental Health System.* Boston: Little, Brown, 1974.

Foucault, Michel. *Madness and Civilization: A History of Insanity in the Age of Reason.* Translated by Richard Howard. 1965. Reprint. New York: Vintage Books, 1988.

Lickey, Marvin E., and Barbara Gordon. *Medicine and Mental Illness: The Use of Drugs in Psychiatry.* New York: W. H. Freeman, 1991.

Roleff, Tamara L., and Laura K. Egendorf, eds. *Mental Illness: Opposing Viewpoints.* San Diego, Calif.: Greenhaven Press, 2000.

Schwitzgebel, Robert L., and R. Kirkland Schwitzgebel. *Law and Psychological Practice.* New York: Wiley, 1980.

Swenson, Leland C. *Psychology and Law for the Helping Professions.* Pacific Grove, Calif.: Brooks/Cole, 1993.

SEE ALSO: Consent; Lobotomy; Mental illness; Psychology; Right to die; Sterilization of women; Therapist-patient relationship.

Integration

DEFINITION: Incorporation as equals of the members of different groups, especially races, within an organization, institution, or society

TYPE OF ETHICS: Race and ethnicity

SIGNIFICANCE: The Civil Rights movement of the 1950's and 1960's in the United States helped bring about both a federal policy and eventually a general societal ethic of racial integration, replacing and stigmatizing previous segregationist practices and policies. The appropriate parameters of that ethic are still being debated, in relation to such practices as affirmative action and school busing.

A racially integrated society would be one in which African Americans can participate in all aspects of national life without being handicapped by their color. In such a society, there should be no neighborhood where an African American could not reside simply because of being black; no hotel, restaurant, or other public facility that an African American could not use on equal terms with whites; no school that an African American child could not attend because of being black; no kind of vocational training, university education, or line of work from which an African American would be barred because of being black; and no public office for which an African American could not contend. In an integrated society, whites would see African Americans not as pariahs but as fellow Americans, fellow veterans, coworkers, and neighbors. By the turn of the twenty-first century, the goal of a racially integrated society, despite much progress, was only half achieved; the role that public policy should play in creating a more racially integrated society was still a matter of lively debate.

ETHICAL AND LEGAL PRINCIPLES

Those who discuss the ethics of integration are dealing with the ethics of public policy rather than (as is the case, to some extent, with prejudice and racism) the morality of private behavior. The promotion of racial integration has been seen by its proponents as essential to the realization of an important value in public policy ethics: that of equality under the law regardless of race or color. This principle had first been publicly recognized in the United States by the Fourteenth Amendment to the Constitution (ratified in 1868), which mandated that every state guarantee its citizens the equal protection of the laws. Liberals tend to be more optimistic about the possibilities for achieving greater racial equality through government-sponsored integration; conservatives tend to perceive a conflict between government-mandated integration and other cherished American values.

Signposts of progress during these years (which witnessed the flowering of the Civil Rights movement) included the gradual desegregation of the American military, which began with President Harry S. Truman's executive order in 1948; the Supreme Court decision of 1954, which struck down the constitutionality of segregated schools; the admission of African Americans into southern state universities; the Civil Rights Act of 1964, which established the right of equal access to public accommodations and banned discrimination in employment; the Voting Rights Act of 1965; the Supreme Court decision of 1967 that overturned state laws against black-white intermarriage; and the federal fair housing law of 1968. By 1990, many of these changes had achieved general acceptance; efforts to integrate employment, schools, and housing, however, continued to arouse controversy.

AFFIRMATIVE ACTION CONTROVERSY

By the late 1970's, affirmative action, in which the presence or absence of a fixed percentage of African Americans in a business, government department, or university is used to determine whether that institution discriminates, had become the chief tool by which the federal government tried to open up opportunities for African Americans. In 1975, in the book *Affirmative Discrimination*, the white sociologist Nathan Glazer condemned the application of this policy in both private businesses and government employment. Glazer argued that affirmative action undermines respect for merit and encourages ethnic and racial divisiveness; unlike many liberals, he denied that the underrepresentation of African Americans in a particular job or profession is necessarily evidence of discrimination. Some African American conservatives believe that affirmative action stigmatizes as inferior those African Americans who do gain entrance to prestigious universities or get good jobs. Yet other thinkers—white as well as African American—argue that many employers would hire no African Americans at all if they were not prodded to do so by the existence of a numerical goal.

SCHOOL INTEGRATION AND THE SUPREME COURT

In *Brown v. Board of Education*, in 1954, the Supreme Court declared that officially enforced school segregation by race (then found mostly in the southern states) violated the Fourteenth Amendment to the Constitution. In a 1968 decision, the Supreme Court exerted pressure on southern school boards to end segregation more quickly; in a 1971 decision, *Swann v. Board of Education*, the Court held that school busing—the transportation of children out of their neighborhoods for schooling—might be an appropriate tool for achieving desegregation.

During the 1960's, the question arose of what to do about the de facto racial segregation of the schools, based on neighborhood racial patterns rather than on the law, found in many northern cities. In 1973, the Supreme Court ordered, for the first time, a northern school district (Denver, Colorado) to institute a desegregation plan. In 1974, however, the Court, in a sudden shift, banned (in the decision *Milliken v. Bradley*) busing for integration purposes across city-suburban boundaries. In general, the Court has ordered steps toward ending de facto segregation only when evidence exists that local authorities have deliberately rigged school district boundaries to keep the races apart.

INTEGRATION OF ELEMENTARY AND SECONDARY SCHOOLS

Ever since 1954, people have argued about how necessary integration of the races in the classroom is to providing equal educational opportunities for African American children. During the 1980's, even some maverick conservative African American thinkers, such as Thomas Sowell and Robert Woodson had their doubts. Woodson argued that a neighborhood school, even if it is exclusively African American, can become a valuable focus of neighborhood pride for low-income city dwellers; Sowell pointed nostalgically to a high-quality African American secondary school of the pre-1954 era of segregation, Dunbar High School in Washington, D.C. (Critics stress how atypical Dunbar was.)

Integrationist scholars, however, argue that forcible exclusion from the company of white schoolchildren stigmatizes and psychically wounds African American children; the African American journalist Carl Rowan thinks that such exclusion is psychically wounding even if it results from white flight to the suburbs rather than government edict. White liberal political scientist Gary Orfield suggests that racial integration of the schools is necessary if African American children are to have greater access to information about jobs and other opportunities; white liberal education writer Jonathan Kozol contends, like many African American thinkers, that all-African American public schools are more likely than integrated ones to be starved of money by legislatures that are beholden to white-majority electorates.

INTEGRATION VS. PARENTAL RIGHTS

Although the compulsory busing of children into schools predominantly of the other race may be necessary to achieve racial integration in some cases, it does severely limit the rights of parents, thereby causing some resentment. The Supreme Court's 1974 ban on busing across city-suburban boundaries means that the most bitter white foes of school integration could often shield their children from it by moving to the suburbs; even if this decision were overturned, achieving complete racial integration of the schools in defiance of segregated neighborhood patterns would be both a herculean task and a politically controversial one.

The rights of parents over their children are, as the African American philosopher Bernard R. Boxill points out, by no means absolute. There is a societal interest in promoting interracial harmony, Boxill suggests, that perhaps should be allowed to prevail over the wish of bigoted white parents to preserve their children from all contact with African American children. Rejecting the notion (found in the writings of African American conservative Glenn Loury) of an unresolvable tension between integrationist goals and individual rights, Boxill also argues that government can use inducements as well as penalties to promote integration, in education and in other areas.

To promote integration of the schools while keeping busing to a minimum, some local school authorities have instituted so-called magnet schools. By placing elementary and secondary schools with above-average endowment in facilities and curricula in the middle of African American neighborhoods, authorities hope to persuade, rather than force, white parents to accept racial integration of the schools. Yet because funds are limited, the number of magnet schools that can be established is also limited; inevi-

tably, some African American schoolchildren remain in all-African American schools, and some white parents cannot get their children into magnet schools. The magnet school solution is not perfect.

ACHIEVING HOUSING INTEGRATION

By 1990, neither the federal Fair Housing Act of 1968 nor the many state and local laws banning discrimination in the sale or rental of housing had solved the problem of racially segregated neighborhoods. One troublesome issue that arises with respect to housing integration is the tension between individual rights and the goal of keeping a neighborhood integrated over time. Many whites are reluctant to live in a neighborhood or an apartment complex when the percentage of African American residents exceeds a certain number. To prevent wholesale evacuation by whites, so-called benign quotas have been introduced limiting the African American influx in the interest of stable integration. Benign quotas have been used by realtors in the Chicago suburb of Oak Park and by the management of the Starrett City apartment complex in New York City; in the latter case, the constitutionality of benign quotas was challenged during the 1980's.

Another difficult question is whether poor as well as middle- or upper-income African Americans should be given the chance to live in the prosperous and mostly white suburbs. White suburbanites who might tolerate the occasional prosperous African American homeowner as a neighbor would almost certainly oppose the building of public housing projects in suburbia; yet it is the poorer African American who might benefit most from the greater employment opportunities found in the suburbs. In Chicago, the Gautreaux program attempted to circumvent the problem by settling small numbers of carefully selected poor African American families in prosperous white suburbs.

Nathan Glazer, in a 1993 magazine essay, argued that only an extremely intrusive government could make racially integrated neighborhoods remain racially integrated over time. Bernard Boxill contends, however, that not every action that is beyond the penalties of law is necessarily moral, and that government, if it cannot force whites to stay in integrated neighborhoods, can at least offer inducements for them to do so.

Paul D. Mageli

FURTHER READING

Boxill, Bernard R. *Blacks and Social Justice.* Totowa, N.J.: Rowman & Allanheld, 1984.

Conti, Joseph G., and Brad Stetson. *Challenging the Civil Rights Establishment: Profiles of a New Black Vanguard.* Westport, Conn.: Praeger, 1993.

Glazer, Nathan. *Affirmative Discrimination: Ethnic Inequality and Public Policy.* New York: Basic Books, 1975.

Graglia, Lino A. *Disaster by Decree: The Supreme Court Decisions on Race and the Schools.* Ithaca, N.Y.: Cornell University Press, 1976.

Hacker, Andrew. *Two Nations: Black and White, Separate, Hostile, Unequal.* New York: Scribner, 2003.

Kozol, Jonathan. *Savage Inequalities: Children in America's Schools.* New York: Crown, 1991.

Lagemann, Ellen Condliffe, and LaMar P. Miller, eds. *"Brown v. Board of Education": The Challenge for Today's Schools.* New York: Teachers College Press, 1996.

Massey, Douglas S., and Nancy A. Denton. *American Apartheid: Segregation and the Making of the Underclass.* Cambridge, Mass.: Harvard University Press, 1993.

Molotch, Harvey. *Managed Integration: Dilemmas of Doing Good in the City.* Berkeley: University of California Press, 1972.

Schnell, Izhak, and Wim Ostendorf, eds. *Studies in Segregation and Desegregation.* Burlington, Vt.: Ashgate, 2002.

SEE ALSO: Affirmative action; Civil Rights Act of 1964; Civil Rights movement; King, Martin Luther, Jr.; Racial prejudice; Racism; Segregation.

Integrity

DEFINITION: Consistent adherence to moral, intellectual, professional, or artistic principles despite temptation to abandon them

TYPE OF ETHICS: Personal and social ethics

SIGNIFICANCE: Integrity is an important personal characteristic in ethical systems based on virtue and moral character.

The etymology of the word "integrity" reveals its relationship to the Latin *integritas*, meaning "soundness, health, unimpaired condition," and to the English "integral," meaning "necessary for completeness" and "made up of parts forming a whole." On the assumption that this etymological relationship is relevant within a moral context, integrity as a moral virtue may be identified as early as the fourth century B.C.E. in Plato's ethical theory. The Platonic soul is tripartite, consisting of reason (intellect), spirit (feelings), and passion (desire). The harmonious interaction of these three parts, with reason dominant over the other two, is central to human virtue. The virtues corresponding to the correct exercise of each of these three parts are, respectively, wisdom, courage, and self-control, which together constitute the virtue of justice. A person in whom either spirit or passion is out of control is both morally and psychologically impaired, existing in a state of moral fragmentation. In such a case, the tripartite soul is splintered, making the person less than morally whole or complete. If justice is the harmonious interaction of the three parts of the soul, then Platonic justice is Platonic integrity, and Plato's understanding of integrity simultaneously serves as the benchmark for subsequent Western ethical theory and presages the development of modern moral psychology.

If integrity is defined as the willingness to abide by and defend one's principles, whether they are artistic, intellectual, professional, or moral, it is evident that the first three kinds of integrity are rooted in a more fundamental moral integrity, since without the latter, one cannot be relied on to retain and to act on whatever other principles one holds. The definition of integrity entails that, because of deeply held beliefs and commitments, there are some things that one is unwilling to do, an unwillingness that may persist even under extreme circumstances.

The artist whose artistic identity and principles are rooted in her originality might refuse to produce tasteless but lucrative popular art, even if this refusal means a life of relative poverty. A scholar, to preserve his intellectual integrity, may refuse to publish anything that will not make a genuine, worthwhile contribution to his discipline, even if he might advance professionally with more frequent but less qualitative publication. The businessperson, faced with the temptation to compromise important professional principles, declines to do so in the interest of both personal and corporate integrity. Moral integrity, which is at once more fundamental and more comprehensive, requires that an individual refuse to abandon important moral principles even when it is advantageous to do so and that the content of these principles be such that reasonable people would recognize them as moral. Moral steadfastness on behalf of manifestly sound moral principles entitles one to the esteem of others as an honorable person who maintains a high degree of consistency between principle and behavior when faced with the temptation to do otherwise.

In modern ethical theory, the discussion of integrity has centered more on its importance than on its definition. Emphasis on moral traits such as integrity is a defining feature of ethical systems based on personal virtue, in which individual moral character assumes primary importance and moral evaluation focuses on persons rather than (or in addition to) actions. For consequentialist ethical systems such as utilitarianism, however, actions and consequences rather than persons are the primary object of moral evaluation. The latter system is more typical of modern ethical theory, while the former is more traditional, dating back to the Greeks and Romans, and especially to Stoicism, in which personal character assumes a centrally important place. This difference reflects the modern tendency to distinguish between an individual's personal character and that individual's actions and to regard actions as being morally more important than character, since they have direct or indirect consequences for the well-being or harm of others.

Bernard Williams, in *Utilitarianism: For and Against* (1987), underscores the traditional importance of integrity by making it a focal point in his criticism of utilitarianism, according to which an action that increases the totality of human well-being is moral, regardless of the motives or character of the agent. Williams argues that one of the chief flaws in utilitarianism is that it constitutes an attack upon personal integrity by dismissing as unimportant the deeply held commitments from which emanate a person's most significant actions. Utilitarianism, which by its nature mandates taking into account only the consequences of actions, requires that one disregard personal convictions in favor of doing what ensures, on balance, an acceptable utilitarian outcome of greater good than harm. How one feels about one's action is irrelevant. Integrity is a strong component of moral conviction, however, and conviction is an im-

portant source of action. Williams argues that alienating a person from strongly held convictions by requiring that they be disregarded is unreasonable and unfair, amounting to the destruction of much of what constitutes the agent's identity.

Alasdair MacIntyre, in *After Virtue: A Study in Moral Theory* (1984), argues for a reintegration of character and action, contending that since personal virtue is an important determinant of actions, character is therefore an essential component of any complete moral context. To separate character and action is to displace virtues such as integrity from this context, making comprehensive moral judgments impossible. Such a separation destroys the "unity" or wholeness—integrity in the Platonic sense—of an individual life. A person's life, to be of genuine moral significance, must be one in which a set of virtues, firmly held and consistently acted upon, unifies the various roles that the individual occupies, and confers upon that individual a corresponding set of obligations. Such a life requires integrity (in both the ancient and modern senses), which is intelligible only in relation to a more universal good.

Finally, integrity is a characteristic for which one bears special individual responsibility, as enunciated by Aleksandr Solzhenitsyn upon receiving the Nobel Prize in Literature: "And the simple step of a simple courageous man is not to take part in the lie, not to support deceit. Let the lie come into the world, even dominate the world, but not through me."

Barbara Forrest

FURTHER READING

Blustein, Jeffrey. *Care and Commitment: Taking the Personal Point of View.* New York: Oxford University Press, 1991.

Cox, Damian, Marguerite La Caze, and Michael P. Levine. *Integrity and the Fragile Self.* Burlington, Vt.: Ashgate, 2003.

Grant, Ruth W. *Hypocrisy and Integrity: Machiavelli, Rousseau, and the Ethics of Politics.* Chicago: University of Chicago Press, 1997.

McFall, Lynne. "Integrity." In *Ethics and Personality: Essays in Moral Psychology*, edited by John Deigh. Chicago: University of Chicago Press, 1992.

MacIntyre, Alasdair. *After Virtue: A Study in Moral Theory.* 2d ed. Notre Dame, Ind.: University of Notre Dame Press, 1984.

Plato. "Phaedrus." In *The Collected Dialogues of Plato*, edited by Edith Hamilton and Huntington Cairns. 1961. Reprint. Princeton, N.J.: Princeton University Press, 1984.

Solzhenitsyn, Alexander. *"One Word of Truth . . . ": The Nobel Speech on Literature, 1970.* London: Bodley Head, 1972.

Williams, Bernard. "A Critique of Utilitarianism." In *Utilitarianism: For and Against*, edited by Bernard Williams and J. J. C. Smart. Cambridge, England: Cambridge University Press, 1987.

SEE ALSO: Character; Cheating; Consequentialism; Honor; Stoic ethics; Utilitarianism; Virtue ethics.

Intellectual property

DEFINITION: Ideas, devices, techniques, or representations whose ownership and control by their creators is recognized and enforced by law

TYPE OF ETHICS: Legal and judicial ethics

SIGNIFICANCE: Accepted public policy thinking holds that society has an interest in assigning ownership of ideas or expression for a limited duration. The initial right to profit from a creation motivates people to create things, while eventual transference of ownership to the public domain allows for the expansion and development of the initial ideas or expression in ways not envisioned by their creator, to society's benefit.

Society has a vested interest in encouraging useful inventions and artistic creations. Modern legal theory treats the ideas, designs, texts, images, or musical compositions of such persons as their private intangible property and allows them to restrict the use of this intellectual property for a set time or until certain events occur. Intellectual property law generally recognizes four forms of intellectual property: trade secrets, patents, copyrights, and trademarks. Inventors are considered to have the right to keep their invention trade secrets if it is practicable for them to do so but are encouraged to disclose fully their inventions in return for the exclusive rights provided by the issuance of a patent to practice their inventions for a fixed period of time.

Authors, artists, and composers generally can claim a copyright for their work, which will prevent others from using their ideas or reproducing or performing their creative work without permission, for which they may then receive a fee or royalty. A trademark is a word or symbol that a manufacturer can use to distinguish its products from those of its competitors. In effect, a trademark allows a firm to profit from its (intangible) reputation for quality or reliability. The owner of intellectual property is free to sell it to another or to grant a license for its use. Unauthorized use of intellectual property is called infringement. Plagiarism, the intentional misrepresentation of an idea or creation as one's own, is considered a serious breach of ethical behavior in almost every area of creative endeavor.

HISTORY

In ancient times, no formal protection was given to inventors, who had to resort to secrecy to prevent others from using their inventions. In the absence of printing presses and high-speed communication, there was little point in forbidding others to copy a work. In the Middle Ages, ideals of personal modesty encouraged anonymous authorship. It is only with the rise of capitalism and economic competition that the notion of intellectual property entered into legal and ethical thinking.

A monopoly is an individual or group that has been awarded an exclusive right to conduct a business or practice a profession. Since monopolies can demand a higher price for goods and services than can businesses that have competition, the existence of monopolies is generally considered undesirable unless required in a given area for the public good. The development of patent and copyright law is usually considered to begin with the English Statute of Monopolies of 1623, which in general was an attempt to eliminate monopolies but excepted patents on inventions and methods as necessary means of encouraging the development of industry. The Constitution of the United States expressly grants to the federal government the right to issue patents and copyrights "to promote the progress of science and the useful arts."

ETHICAL PRINCIPLES

Underlying the general concept of intellectual property is the notion that an individual is entitled to compensation for the products of his or her labor. In the case of inventions, there is the additional question of the inventor's right to privacy. In most legal systems, someone who develops a new process or recipe for, say, a long-lasting paint, is under no obligation to share the process with the public. He and his heirs may treat it as a trade secret forever. If anyone else, however, were to discover the process by any legitimate means, such as chemically analyzing a can of paint that had been purchased, he or she would be free to manufacture and sell the identical product at a lower price. In applying for a patent on this process, the inventor, in effect, enters into a contract with society in which secrecy is abandoned in return for the exclusive right to control the use of the process for a fixed number of years. Very few individuals could afford to be authors, composers, or filmmakers if anyone who wished to could make multiple copies of their works and sell them freely.

ETHICAL PROBLEMS

The question of where to draw the line between individuals' rights to their intellectual property and the welfare of the public has not been fully resolved. Some countries, including the United Kingdom, refuse on humanitarian grounds to issue patents for medicines. Many countries permit the suppliers of military hardware to infringe the patent rights of inventors, possibly with a provision for compensation but without advance permission, when such an act is justified by the requirements of national security. Even the existence of public libraries in effect deprives authors of the revenue they might otherwise gain from the readers of their books. The development of computer networks allows, in effect, many persons to use the same copy of a copyrighted program.

There are also possible conflicts between the rights of authors, artists, and composers and the rights of subsequent owners of a copyright. Many governments recognize as moral rights of creative individuals the rights of attribution, or recognition as being the creator of one's own work, and of integrity, or having one's work presented as a whole or in an acceptable abridgment, even though the work may have been purchased or performed for pay. It can also, of course, be argued that allowing the owners of intellectual property greater control over the form in which it is disseminated could increase their profits and thus ultimately benefit the creators.

Donald R. Franceschetti

FURTHER READING

Alderson, Wroe, Vern Terpstra, and S. J. Shapiro, eds. *Patents and Progress.* Homewood, Ill.: Richard D. Irwin, 1965.

Bentley, Lionel, and Spyros M. Maniatis, eds. *Intellectual Property and Ethics.* London: Sweet & Maxwell, 1998.

Dratler, Jay, Jr. *Intellectual Property Law: Commercial, Creative, and Industrial Property.* New York: Law Journal Seminars-Press, 1991.

Miller, Arthur R., and Michael H. Davis. *Intellectual Property.* 2d ed. St. Paul, Minn.: West, 1990.

Moore, Adam D. *Intellectual Property: Moral, Legal, and International Dilemmas.* Lanham, Md.: Rowman & Littlefield, 1997.

Rosenberg, Peter D. *Patent Law Basics.* New York: Clark Boardman Callaghan, 1992.

Strong, William S. *The Copyright Book: A Practical Guide.* Cambridge, Mass.: MIT Press, 1981.

SEE ALSO: Business ethics; Constitution, U.S.; Copyright; Freedom of expression; Internet piracy; Plagiarism; Property.

Intelligence testing

DEFINITION: Measurement of human intelligence
TYPE OF ETHICS: Bioethics
SIGNIFICANCE: Intelligence testing raises ethical concerns involving potential cultural bias of tests as well as the differential treatment of people based on their test results.

Alfred Binet and his colleagues first devised tests to assess the mental abilities of French children during the 1890's. A child's "mental age," divided by chronological age, gave an "intelligence quotient" (IQ). Binet thought that IQ scores could be improved through education, but many British psychologists insisted that intelligence was hereditary. Data on this issue were gathered by Cyril Burt, but some of his data were later shown to have been fabricated. American psychologists modernized Binet's tests but applied them, with considerable bias, against African Americans and immigrants.

Despite early claims that the tests measure "in-

Alfred Binet, inventor of one of the earliest intelligence tests. (National Library of Medicine)

nate intelligence," careful studies show that educational influences are strong and that most early studies were flawed. In particular, a fifteen-point average difference between unselected whites and African Americans disappears when comparison is made between samples matched by social status, family income, and similar factors. African Americans who have attended good schools and have had similar advantages achieve higher scores than do students from disadvantaged backgrounds regardless of race.

Test bias occurs because the test is given in a particular language and because it assumes a middle-class cultural environment; the results are therefore biased against the poor and against those who speak a different language. More subtle bias includes questions about activities that are common to middle-class white males, thus discriminating against females and blacks. Bias-free exams are difficult to write.

Proponents of eugenics have advocated favorable treatment of high-IQ individuals and unfavorable treatment (including sterilization) of low-IQ sub-

jects. Since test results can be modified by education and are subject to bias, such proposals have lost much favor since about 1940.

Eli C. Minkoff

SEE ALSO: Eugenics; Genetic counseling; Genetic testing; Psychology.

Intention

DEFINITION: Purpose or aim of an action; that which is intended

TYPE OF ETHICS: Theory of ethics

SIGNIFICANCE: Agents typically must intend to do something or be directed toward a certain intended state of affairs in order to be morally responsible for their actions.

The idea of the intentionality of action is commonly atrributed to Aristotle's *On the Soul* (335-323 B.C.E.). Aristotle's theory was transmitted through late medieval to modern philosophy primarily by Thomas Aquinas and William of Ockham. In the nineteenth and early twentieth centuries, intentionalism was associated with Franz Brentano's 1874 work *Psychology from an Empirical Standpoint* and his 1889 *The Origin of Our Knowledge of Right and Wrong*. Modern moral philosophy in the intentionalist tradition includes the work of, among others, G. E. M. Anscombe, Robert Audi, Roderick M. Chisholm, Donald Davidson, Joseph Margolis, and Richard Taylor.

An agent's intention is what the agent intends to do. It is the possibly nonexistent state of affairs that the agent assumes as the purpose or goal of action, toward which the action is directed. Some examples of intentions are to help another person, to perfect one's abilities, to achieve a career objective, and to move a finger.

It is standardly agreed that agents are not morally responsible for their actions unless they intend to do them. Behavior performed entirely without intention is not action or doing in the philosophically correct sense of the word, but something that a person suffers or undergoes. Doing something unintentionally, when there is no negligence or overriding obligation to determine the likely effects of an action, is often considered to render a person morally blameless for bad consequences. Agents are sometimes praised or blamed even for their unrealized or failed intentions, as a reflection of their moral attitudes and inclinations.

The main division in moral philosophy between deontological and consequentialist ethics can be drawn in terms of the role that intention is thought to play in moral evaluation. For the deontologist, having a good or morally approved intention, usually one that intends an action because it is prescribed by duty, is the most important factor in ethical conduct, regardless of the consequences. Consequentialists are unconcerned with the state of mind with which an action is undertaken, except insofar as it leads to good consequences, which are often understood as whatever maximizes happiness. Although the concept of intentionality does not resolve the dispute between these two types of moral philosophy, the fact that their disagreement can be characterized in terms of intentions indicates the importance of the concept of intentions to moral theory.

Dale Jacquette

FURTHER READING

Anscombe, G. E. M. *Intention.* 2d ed. Oxford, England: Blackwell, 1963. Reprint. Cambridge, Mass.: Harvard University Press, 2000.

Bratman, Michael. *Intention, Plans, and Practical Reason.* Cambridge, Mass.: Harvard University Press, 1987.

Gustafson, Donald F. *Intention and Agency.* Dordrecht, Netherlands: D. Reidel, 1986.

Meiland, Jack W. *The Nature of Intention.* London: Methuen, 1970.

Mohanty, Jitendranath. *The Concept of Intentionality.* St. Louis: W. H. Green, 1972.

Naffine, Ngaire, Rosemary Owens, and John Williams, eds. *Intention in Law and Philosophy.* Burlington, Vt.: Ashgate/Dartmouth, 2001.

Ryan, Thomas Arthur. *Intentional Behavior: An Approach to Human Motivation.* New York: Ronald Press, 1970.

SEE ALSO: Aristotle; Consequentialism; Deontological ethics; Desire; Kant, Immanuel; Practical reason; Responsibility; Thomas Aquinas.

International Covenant on Civil and Political Rights

IDENTIFICATION: Legally binding promise by signatory nations to ensure civil and political rights within their sovereign territory
DATE: Adopted on December 16, 1966; took effect on March 23, 1976
TYPE OF ETHICS: Civil rights
SIGNIFICANCE: The covenant represents a practical attempt to enforce the principles advocated in theory by the Universal Declaration of Human Rights.

For years after the 1948 Universal Declaration of Human Rights, the United Nations struggled to prepare treaties that would oblige nations to guarantee the rights and freedoms described in the declaration. In 1966, two covenants were presented: the International Covenant on Civil and Political Rights, and the International Covenant on Economic, Social, and Cultural Rights.

Those nations who are party to the Covenant on Civil and Political Rights have agreed to guarantee to all individuals under their jurisdiction certain basic rights. No distinctions are made because of race, color, sex, language, national origin, and so on. The rights and freedoms guaranteed under this covenant include the right to life and liberty, freedom from slavery, freedom from torture or inhuman punishment, freedom from arbitrary detention, the right to travel freely, and the freedom of thought and religion. Furthermore, the covenant guarantees protection for ethnic, religious, and linguistic minorities, and guarantees that no one may be forced to testify against himself or herself. Signatory nations found to be in violation of this covenant may be held accountable by the United Nations.

Cynthia A. Bily

SEE ALSO: Civil Rights movement; Commission on Civil Rights, U.S.; International law; League of Nations; UNESCO Declaration on the Human Genome and Human Rights; United Nations; United Nations Declaration of the Rights of the Child; United Nations Declaration on the Rights of Disabled Persons; Universal Declaration of Human Rights.

International Criminal Court

IDENTIFICATION: Permanent court established in The Hague, Netherlands, by the international community

DATE: Founded in 2002

TYPE OF ETHICS: Human rights

SIGNIFICANCE: The International Criminal Court (ICC) is the first standing international court designed specifically to prosecute individuals for war crimes and crimes against humanity. Its mission is to prosecute egregious criminals who enjoy impunity in their home countries and further to refine and articulate international laws of war and laws promoting human rights.

Creation of the International Criminal Court culminated a century of developments in international criminal law. While there has always been a belief that certain crimes are of such a hideous nature that their prosecution demands an international response, the political will to develop a serious legal institution to confront these crimes was long lacking. Prior to the establishment of the ICC, the only courts in which war criminals and other politically powerful criminals could be prosecuted were domestic courts or ad hoc tribunals—temporary courts convened only to prosecute a particular individuals or groups for crimes occurring at specific times and places. While such courts have had some success, their influence has been sharply limited by their inherently transitory nature. Other international courts, such as the International Court of Justice and the infrequently used Permanent Court of Arbitration, deal only with grievances among states and do not handle claims regarding individuals.

To address this issue, a large number of states convened in Rome to draw up plans for a court that would fill this gap in international law. Founded by the resulting Rome Statute of 2003, the ICC is designed as a standing body that can prosecute certain crimes almost anywhere in the world.

CONTROVERSY AND JURISDICTION

The ICC is not without its critics. In particular, the United States has been a strong opponent of the court, fearing that its own citizens may become targets of politically motivated prosecutions and that it may lose some of its independence to an unaccountable international power. In 2002, the U.S. government took the unprecedented step of removing its signature from the Rome Statute. In addition, it pressured smaller nations to sign agreements that would prevent them from sending Americans to the ICC, should the court seek to prosecute them. This policy has, in turn, met with stiff resistance from other countries throughout the world and from the European powers in particular, who see the court as an important first step in the creation of a more peaceful and just world order.

The ICC cannot pursue cases against anyone it wishes. For a prosecution to be authorized, the crimes must either take place in states that are party to the treaty or involve accused persons who are citizens of one of those states. In a novel development in international criminal law, domestic courts may first elect to investigate and prosecute accused criminals and then, if they are unable or unwilling to pursue the case, the ICC's own prosecutors may take over the prosecutions—a process known as "complementary jurisdiction."

The ICC has special jurisdiction over several types of crimes: war crimes, as defined by the Geneva Conventions; genocide; crimes against humanity, such as slavery, mass rape, ethnic cleansing, and apartheid; and aggression. The last crime is notoriously vague, and the treaty delays any prosecutions for aggression until the concept can be adequately defined.

ETHICAL ISSUES

The ICC faces a great number of ethical issues. At its founding, the hope was that an international judicial body would be better able to provide justice for many people who have been unable to find it in their home countries. Some of the most egregious crimes in history have been committed by powerful leaders, such as Adolf Hitler and Joseph Stalin, whose power placed them beyond traditional forms of legal accountability.

However, according to some critics, it is unclear whether it is practical to make political leaders subjects of ICC prosecutions. Tyrant who face possible international criminal trials are likely to hold onto power much longer if abdication means that they may face humiliating trials in The Hague and lengthy imprisonments. By contrast, if such rulers were instead offered immunity from prosecution and relatively comfortable retirements, they might be more easily persuaded to give up power without committing additional crimes or causing further suffering. Such a benefit, critics contend, is more concrete than any abstract notions of "justice" that the ICC can provide.

CRITICISMS

Some critics have contended that the justice that international courts apply will be biased in favor of the interests of wealthy and powerful countries and those countries' provincial value systems. The leadership of weaker states with difficult domestic problems and substantial civil strife may be unable to meet the standards of stable Western democracies. Some critics contend that it is unfair to hold such states to standards that they cannot possibly meet. Further, when the powerful states commit criminal acts, their governments are likely to possess the political clout to stop prosecution of their leaders. Thus, the court is not likely to provide justice for all, but rather will simply be another forum in which the powerful bully the weak.

However, the court's defenders have insisted that without some legal accountability for international criminals, victims will be forced to find justice outside of the law. They argue that resorting to vigilante justice will only prolong and deepen the bloodshed already caused. By providing a public record of the atrocities committed by the powerful, the ICC should provide the closure necessary for societies to move forward. Additionally, the court may deter powerful would-be criminals by publicly reminding them that they are not beyond the reach of the law.

Regardless of whether the ICC proves to be a success, its creation marks a turning point in the moral and ethical thinking of much of the world. For the first time, the vast majority of the world's nations have accepted that large-scale human suffering is not only a matter for local authorities but is always a concern for all of humanity.

Aaron Fichtelberg

FURTHER READING

Bassiouni, M. Cerif, ed. *The Statute of the International Criminal Court: A Documentary History.* Ardsley, N.Y.: Transnational, 2002.

Cassese, Antonio, et al. *The Rome Statute of the International Criminal Court: A Commentary.* Oxford, England: Oxford University Press, 2002.

Frye, Alton. *Toward an International Criminal Court? A Council Policy Initiative.* Washington, D.C.: Brookings Institution, 2000.

Sadat, Lelia. *The International Criminal Court and the Transformation of International Law.* Ardsley, N.Y.: Transnational, 2002.

Sewall, Sarah B., and Carl Kaysen, ed. *The United States and the International Criminal Court.* New York: Rowman & Littlefield, 2000.

SEE ALSO: Dictatorship; Geneva conventions; Genocide and democide; Hitler, Adolf; International justice; International law; Nuremberg Trials; Stalin, Joseph; War crimes trials.

International justice

DEFINITION: System established by sovereign nations to resolve disputes and punish offenders of international law; or principles of just and equitable treatment of nations and individuals applied to geopolitical analysis and activism

TYPE OF ETHICS: Legal and judicial ethics

SIGNIFICANCE: The concept of international justice transcends the parochial interests of individual nations in the name of larger concerns such as human rights or simply stable international relations. As a result, it is often based in universal, egalitarian or humanist moral systems, and it has the potential to threaten the sovereignty of individual nations.

The term "international justice" has three connotations. First, it refers to the mechanisms by which governments seek to fairly and legally resolve disputes among themselves. Second, it refers to the formal and informal systems by which governments are punished for wrongdoing. Finally, and more broadly, it has in recent years been used to call for a more fair allocation of global resources among nations.

Ethical considerations surrounding all these connotations are conditioned by the lack of centralized and completely effective mechanisms by means of which international justice can be effected. The international system is built on the principle of national sovereignty, which requires coordination of state policies to attain justice, rather than a system of subordination under which countries submit to a global authority exercising ultimate and binding jurisdiction over them. As sovereigns, nation-states are the highest authorities and are beholden to no higher authority unless they voluntarily concede by treaty to limit their sovereignty. Conflict in such a system is an ever-present threat. The achievement of order and justice, then, is accomplished by mutual accommodation, negotiation, political maneuvering, and sometimes through the use of collective force. Ethical constraints are not irrelevant in this system, but they are typically subordinated to political interest.

LEGAL RESOLUTION OF DISPUTES

Assuming that governments prefer to resolve disputes peacefully, rather than through conflict or force, numerous options are available to them, including political mechanisms such as direct bilateral negotiation, third-party mediation and conciliation, and legal mechanisms such as arbitration and adjudication. Political solutions are very common means of resolving international disputes. Arbitration and adjudication are less common at the international level. Disputes between citizens or business interests of two countries are quite common, however, and these are often resolved by the domestic courts of the involved countries or by mixed claims commissions that have been established by treaty.

When a legal dispute arises between two governments, they may choose to seek arbitration and adjudication to avoid conflict. When seeking arbitration, governments agree to submit the legal issue to an ad hoc panel of experts composed of members proposed by each of the countries involved and whose final judgment is accepted in advance as binding both parties to the dispute. Arbitration has been practiced for centuries by nations, and its roots go back at least as far as the ancient Greeks in the fifth century B.C.E. In modern times, states created the Permanent Court of Arbitration, which was established by the Hague Peace Conference of 1899 but has been resorted to only infrequently since World War I.

In addition to arbitration, states may seek to adjudicate disputes through standing courts, such as the International Court of Justice (ICJ) at the international level, or through various regional courts, such as the European Court of Justice. The sole international court, the ICJ, lacks compulsory jurisdiction over states, which means that no state is required, unless it consents to do so, to bring cases before the court or to appear in court to defend itself from suits brought against it by other states. Fewer than a third of the members of the United Nations recognize the ICJ's jurisdiction as compulsory. Once governments agree to the ICJ's jurisdiction, however, they are bound to abide by its decisions. Enforcement of court decisions, however, has not been completely satisfactory or effective. The ICJ operates, then, in a less than perfect environment in which states are not required to submit disputes to it and, even in those rare cases when they do, there is no guarantee that its judgments will be honored.

PUNISHING WRONGDOERS

Given its weak legal structures, international justice is often conducted either through collective punishment of offending states or by the self-help of individual governments. Members of the United Nations are required by the U.N. Charter to resolve disputes peacefully. Aggressor states that violate this obligation may be punished by the United Nations through the collective application of economic sanctions and even force. If the United Nations cannot agree to punish an aggressor, however, the injured state is left to defend itself. It may do so by recourse to the traditional laws of retaliation. Ultimately, the success of all such collective and individual efforts depends on the cooperation of powerful states. When powerful states are on the side of justice, justice can be done. If they are not, or if powerful states actively flout international law, the only prevailing justice is that of the strongest.

Apart from the legal resolution of disputes and the use of force to punish aggressor states, international justice is increasingly used to refer to the fair distribution of global resources. Significant inequities currently prevail among nations. This leads many poorer countries to call for a fairer international economic order. In many of the poorest countries, however, wealth is equally badly distributed. The ethical claim of the elite in such a country to an entitlement to greater access to international wealth for their nation rests on shaky ground. There exists no current legal principle by which wealthy states must transfer wealth to poorer ones, and even where ethical considerations demand it, as in the case of famine or disaster, the claim of a wealthy elite in a poor country to have absolute control over the internal allocation of foreign aid lacks justification.

CONCLUSION

The achievement of international justice depends to a very large extent on the voluntary cooperation of governments and peoples. Governments often do cooperate to mutual advantage. They often resolve disputes peacefully and help each other in time of need, but there is no world government to ensure that they do so. They do so out of a sense of either political interest or legal or ethical obligation. A government's first obligation is to its own people's security and prosperity. At the international level, its obligation to the security and prosperity of other nations is governed by traditional friendships and ties, by voluntarily accepted treaty and legal norms, and by prudence and expediency.

Robert F. Gorman

FURTHER READING

Bennett, A. LeRoy. *International Organizations: Principles and Issues.* 6th ed. Englewood Cliffs, N.J.: Prentice Hall, 1995.

Broomhall, Bruce. *International Justice and the International Criminal Court: Between Sovereignty and the Rule of Law.* New York: Oxford University Press, 2003.

Henkin, Louis, et al. *Right v. Might: International Law and the Use of Force.* 2d ed. New York: Council on Foreign Relations Press, 1991.

Hurrell, Andrew, and Ngaire Woods, eds. *Inequality, Globalization, and World Politics.* New York: Oxford University Press, 1999.

Jessup, Philip. *The Price of International Justice.* New York: Columbia University Press, 1971.

Kaplan, Morton, and Nicholas Katzenbach. *The Political Foundations of International Law.* New York: Wiley, 1961.

Tucker, Robert. *The Inequality of Nations.* New York: Basic Books, 1977.

SEE ALSO: Arbitration; Conflict resolution; Globalization; Human rights; International Criminal Court; International law; Intervention; Power; Sanctions; Sovereignty; Universal Declaration of Human Rights.

International Labour Organisation

IDENTIFICATION: Specialized agency of the League of Nations, and later of the United Nations, that attempts to improve global working conditions and standards of living

DATE: Founded in 1919

TYPE OF ETHICS: Business and labor ethics

SIGNIFICANCE: Formation of the International Labour Organisation (ILO) served to recognize and legitimize the ethical ideals of international labor groups.

As a result of lobbying by international labor unions and the governments of several countries, the Treaty of Versailles, which ended World War I, recognized the International Labour Organisation. Its declarations and resolutions were not, however, made enforceable.

During the Great Depression, the ILO encouraged governments to plan for the reemployment of workers and to develop relief and unemployment insurance schemes. The United States joined the ILO in 1934. Other countries had delayed joining; some also dropped their membership.

The ILO was the first specialized agency to be affiliated with the United Nations, which was created in 1946. It took on a more proscribed role, with some of its concerns delegated to other agencies. Its membership also changed, including many more developing rather than industrialized countries. The ILO became more of a statistical and information center that also provided technical assistance to developing countries. It turned its attention more to problems of poverty and social conditions rather than narrow labor issues. The agency is concerned with international disparities in the treatment of workers, and it attempts to prevent exploitation. As part of that program, it promotes relatively free immigration and emigration of workers. The ILO is unique among intergovernmental agencies in that member states send representatives not only from their governments but also from worker and employer groups.

A. J. Sobczak

SEE ALSO: American Federation of Labor; Employee safety and treatment; Fair Labor Standards Act;

Globalization; Knights of Labor; League of Nations; United Nations; Universal Declaration of Human Rights.

International law

DEFINITION: Body of obligatory customs, conventions, rules, and principles by which governments of nation-states order their interrelations

TYPE OF ETHICS: International relations

SIGNIFICANCE: International law seeks to minimize international conflict, to promote cooperation among nations, and to protect individuals victimized by their own nations or caught in the middle of hostilities between nations.

Unlike domestic systems of law, in which supreme legislative, executive, and judicial organs make, enforce, and interpret law, international law has developed between and among rather than above states in international relations. Possessing sovereignty, these states alone can make international law, and when they do so, it is of their voluntary accord rather than under the compulsion of any higher authority. This lack of a higher authority above states leads potentially to a system of anarchy in which evils of unspeakable proportions can be committed. Governments have, since the earliest dawn of civilizations, attempted to limit their sovereign prerogatives in an effort to avoid anarchy, preserve harmony in their interrelations, and promote the welfare of their respective populations. Even when cooperation broke down and war occurred, governments recognized a need to limit their behavior, protect innocent life, and curb the excessive brutality associated with violent war. They did so by devising systems of international law.

HISTORY

The roots of international law can be traced back at least to the times of the ancient Greeks and Romans, who developed principles of interstate law to govern diplomatic exchanges, treaties, the legal status of aliens, usages in war, and principles of citizenship and asylum. These ancient states saw the benefits of reciprocity—that is, of treating citizens and representatives of other nations with decorum and respect so that similar treatment would be accorded

their own citizens and representatives by other states. Much of this law was based in custom, but some was established by statute and treaty.

The Roman conceptions of *jus civile*, *jus gentium*, and *jus naturalae* established the foundation on which international law is today based. The *jus civile*, or law of cities, concerned the rules distinct to each city of the Roman Empire based on its own customs and traditions. The *jus gentium*, or law among nations, was the law that applied to citizens of all states in their relations to one another. The *jus naturalae*, or the natural law, comprised those overarching principles in nature that human reason could discern regardless of national affiliation. The closer the *jus civile* and *jus gentium* approximated the *jus naturalae*, the more perfect they became.

THE MIDDLE AGES AND BEYOND

During the Middle Ages in Europe, Christian moral principles served as a means of inhibiting the excesses of governments against their subjects and against other governments. Rules of war called for the protection of civilians and noncombatants, humane and fair treatment of prisoners, and even proscribed conflict during certain seasons and on certain days. Laws of diplomatic immunity persisted and developed. Rules for acquiring and disposing of territory gradually developed.

With the onset of the Protestant Reformation and the resulting religious wars in Europe, however, the princes and monarchs of Europe ultimately found it necessary to establish clear rules regarding state rights and duties. At the Peace of Westphalia in 1648, they determined that states were sovereign, equal, and independent; the sovereign within a particular territory had exclusive control over it and the right to determine its laws and its religion. No sovereign was obliged to abide by any treaty or rule that he or she did not explicitly and voluntarily accept or recognize. These principles continue to serve as the basis of modern international law, although governments in the intervening centuries have shed themselves of monarchs and in many instances adopted republican government.

As the Industrial Revolution, commercial expansion, and colonial competition grew, governments found the need to recognize both customary and treaty principles in order to promote a degree of cooperation and to curb excessive conflict. In the twentieth century, states agreed that force should not be used to settle international disputes, unless used in self-defense or under the aegis of a collective authority such as the United Nations. In addition, governments increasingly developed rules to protect aliens living, traveling, and working in foreign lands. States undertook the responsibility to protect aliens at a level commensurate to that enjoyed by their own citizens. Should the host state fail in this responsibility, an injured alien could, after exhausting available local remedies, appeal to his or her country of nationality to file a claim against the host government to obtain redress for the injury.

TWENTY-FIRST CENTURY ETHICAL PRINCIPLES AND ISSUES

As noted earlier, most international law is made and observed by states out of reciprocal self-interest. Once states make promises to one another in treaties, they are obliged to honor them, and in the vast majority of cases they do. If states should fail to honor their treaty or customary legal obligations, however, the injured parties may seek judicial remedies, or failing this, they may seek to punish offending states through sanctions or other retaliatory measures. When engaging in such retaliation, governments are obliged to observed the principle of proportionality, which means that they can take actions of roughly similar kind and degree against a state committing a prior wrong. Excessive retaliation is itself considered wrong.

During the twentieth century, with the emergence of guerrilla wars, total wars, and nuclear weaponry, the old distinction between civilian and combatant was blurred in practice. The customary laws of war, in turn, have often been disregarded, and many innocent lives have been lost. The Geneva Red Cross Conventions and Protocols have been promulgated to reassert the distinction between combatants and noncombatants and to preserve the rights of prisoners of war.

In addition, since World War II, governments have increasingly adopted a wide range of human rights declarations and treaties in order to define more clearly the respective rights and responsibilities of individuals and states under international law. Such agreements include the Universal Declaration of Human Rights, the Genocide Convention, and the Conventions on Civil and Political and Economic and Social Rights. Thus, although states remain the principal subjects of international law, they increasingly recognize the need to protect, usually through domestic legal mechanisms, the human rights of their respective citizens. In turn, individuals can be held directly accountable for a variety of international crimes, including war crimes, piracy, genocide, counterfeiting, and slave trading.

International law represents one of the means by which governments have countered the anarchic tendencies of international relations and thereby remained conscious of their legal and ethical obligations to one another and to their own citizens as well as to aliens.

Robert F. Gorman

FURTHER READING

Akehurst, Michael. *A Modern Introduction to International Law.* 6th ed. New York: Routledge, 1992.

Brierly, James. *The Law of Nations.* 6th ed. New York: Oxford University Press, 1963.

Broomhall, Bruce. *International Justice and the International Criminal Court: Between Sovereignty and the Rule of Law.* New York: Oxford University Press, 2003.

Corbett, Percy. *The Growth of World Law.* Princeton, N.J.: Princeton University Press, 1971.

Jessup, Philip C. *A Modern Law of Nations.* New York: Macmillan, 1948.

Kaplan, Morton, and Nicholas Katzenbach. *The Political Foundations of International Law.* New York: Wiley, 1961.

Lynch, Cecelia, and Michael Loriaux, eds. *Law and Moral Action in World Politics.* Minneapolis: University of Minnesota Press, 2000.

Rubin, Alfred P. *Ethics and Authority in International Law.* New York: Cambridge University Press, 1997.

Von Glahn, Gerhard. *Law Among Nations: An Introduction to Public International Law.* 7th ed. Boston: Allyn and Bacon, 1996.

SEE ALSO: Deterrence; Genocide and democide; Grotius, Hugo; Human rights; International Criminal Court; International justice; Intervention; Natural law; Sanctions; Sovereignty; War crimes trials.

International Monetary Fund

IDENTIFICATION: Organization that monitors the health of the world economy by lending money to countries facing balance-of-payment problems

DATE: Founded in December, 1945

TYPE OF ETHICS: International relations

SIGNIFICANCE: Ethical debates have arisen over the question of whether the International Monetary Fund's (IMF) free enterprise policies promote the welfare of the global poor, enhance democratic decision making, and protect the world's natural environment.

The International Monetary Fund, along with the World Bank, was first conceived in 1944 at the United Nations conference held in Bretton Woods, New Hampshire. Conference delegates believed an international agency was necessary to promote balance and growth in international trade. The IMF makes temporary loans to nations facing economic or financial crises. Since the Thatcher-Reagan era of the 1980's, the IMF has increasingly insisted that debtor nations adhere to free-market policies (known as "the Washington consensus"). Nations receiving IMF loans often must agree to structural adjustment programs (SAP), which may require eliminating tariffs and restrictions to the flow of capital and implementing policies of fiscal austerity and privatization.

Advocates of market liberalization such as the IMF, as well as defenders of protectionist policies, generally agree that ethical fairness means that the rich have some degree of obligation to help the worst-off, but they differ on the short- and long-term economic measures that best guarantee such assistance. Since IMF loans are made under stipulations that may cause short-term hardships, IMF policies raise ethical questions. The free market may improve economic efficiency and undercut bureaucratic graft in the developing world, but austerity policies may also force declines in wages and increase unemployment. While personal suffering may only be a short-term consequence of market adjustments, critics argue that it is morally unacceptable to force such hardship upon those least able to bear it

RICH VS. POOR NATIONS

The power that rich industrialized nations exercise over developing nations through the IMF raises other ethical debates. The vast imbalance of power between the IMF and client countries means that the latter are sometimes pressured to accept loan conditions in conflict with the will of the nation or its traditional values. Critics charge that such "conditionality" in effect gives the IMF undue influence upon the democratic determination of domestic policy. Furthermore, IMF negotiations are often cloaked in secrecy out of legitimate concern that required loan conditions might provoke domestic unrest, but this lack of transparency subverts the citizen's right to know government plans. Similarly, the liberalization of financial markets (removing barriers to the flow of investment) may undermine the power of a nation to control its own economic development. Defenders of globalization and the IMF argue that greater global equality and prosperity rests upon extending free trade practices across the world.

Bland Addison

FURTHER READING

Blustein, Paul. *The Chastening: Inside the Crisis That Rocked the Global Financial System and Humbled the IMF.* New York: Public Affairs, 2001.

Singer, Peter. *One World: The Ethics of Globalization.* New Haven, Conn.: Yale University Press, 2002.

Stiglitz, Joseph E. *Globalization and Its Discontents.* New York: W. W. Norton, 2002.

SEE ALSO: Agribusiness; Business ethics; Developing world; Ecology; Globalization; International law; Outsourcing; World Trade Organization.

International Organization of Consumers Unions

IDENTIFICATION: Global non-governmental organization that seeks to protect and expand the rights of consumers

DATE: Founded in 1960

TYPE OF ETHICS: Business and labor ethics

SIGNIFICANCE: The International Organization of Consumers Unions (IOCU) is the main vehicle through which national and regional consumers' groups share information and coordinate action.

Headquartered in The Hague, Netherlands, the International Organization of Consumers Unions is affiliated with 175 national and local consumer organizations in sixty-eight countries. Its purpose is to bring together the efforts and results of these smaller organizations to increase the power of consumers worldwide. Specifically, the IOCU has worked on such issues as the safety and effectiveness of infant formulas, and the safe distribution and use of pesticides.

The IOCU gathers and shares published information from its affiliates; provides a forum for further sharing of information and problems; encourages nations to cooperate with one another in testing product safety and in sharing the results of these tests; and studies and interprets local, national, and international laws relating to consumers. Because it works closely with the United Nations and other international bodies but not with any individual national governments, the IOCU can be an important advocate for consumers in developing nations. These consumers have sometimes been deceived or coerced into buying products that have been judged too dangerous or ineffective for sale in the developed nations where they were manufactured. Working with the United Nations, the IOCU offers consumer education and protection programs in developing nations.

Cynthia A. Bily

Red Cross workers cleaning buckets at a prison in northern Afghanistan, where the organization fed starving prisoners and greatly improved conditions in early 2002. In the Muslim world, the Red Cross is known as the "Red Crescent." (AP/ Wide World Photos)

SEE ALSO: Consumerism; Globalization; Product safety and liability; Public interest; United Nations; World Trade Organization.

International Red Cross

IDENTIFICATION: Charitable organization created in Switzerland to ameliorate the horrors of war by providing relief to its victims

DATE: Created in 1863

TYPE OF ETHICS: International relations

SIGNIFICANCE: Through the Geneva Conventions with which it is closely associated, the Red Cross has helped develop the concept of combatants adhering to ethical standards of conduct during military conflicts.

In 1859, the sight of wounded soldiers suffering on the battlefield after the Battle of Solferino in Italy so horrified a young Swiss businessman named Jean Henri Dunant that he wrote an impassioned book, *A Memory of Solferino* (1862), in which he called for the creation of an army of volunteers to treat the wounded and for the establishment of international conventions under which such an army would function. In 1863, a committee of five prosperous citizens of Geneva, Switzerland, took up Dunant's ideas and arranged an international conference that led to the first Geneva Convention on the treatment of wounded soldiers. The committee, which became known as the International Committee of the Red Cross because of the badge it adopted for its volunteers, initiated further conferences that produced additional conventions.

The Geneva Conventions established rules for the humane conduct of war in an attempt to alleviate the horrors of warfare. These rules included provisions facilitating the treatment of wounded soldiers by recognizing both the wounded and the medical personnel treating them as neutral. Later rules called for the humane treatment of prisoners of war, civilians affected by war, victims of civil wars, and political prisoners.

Although the central purpose of the Red Cross was to introduce ethical standards into military conflicts, some observers criticized its efforts on ethical grounds, arguing that by making the conduct of war more humane, the Red Cross was also making war more acceptable and thus encouraging rather than discouraging war. Some critics, including the noted English nurse Florence Nightingale, also said that providing a volunteer army of nurses and other medical personnel also made war easier for combatants by relieving their military authorities of medical responsibilities and freeing up their resources.

However, in the twentieth century, especially after World War I, there was general acceptance of the importance of the relief work carried out by the Red Cross under the Geneva Conventions. Ethical debates did arise, however, over how best to enforce the conventions, and the Red Cross, which generally preferred private communication to public denunciations, was criticized for not speaking out publicly against the treatment of the Jews by Nazi Germany during World War II.

Debates also arose over the political use of relief, especially during the Nigerian civil war during the late 1960's, and over the treatment of combatants in guerrilla wars. Historically, the approach of the Red Cross has generally been one of neutrality. The Red Cross does not judge the merits of conflicts; instead, it encourages humane treatment of all those affected by such conflicts.

Dunant, the founder of the International Red Cross, shared the first Nobel Peace Prize in 1901, and the organization itself received the award in 1917, 1944, and 1963.

Sheldon Goldfarb

FURTHER READING

Haug, Hans, et al. *Humanity for All: The International Red Cross and Red Crescent Movement.* Berne, Switzerland: Henry Dunant Institute, Paul Haupt, 1993.

Hutchinson, John F. *Champions of Charity: War and the Rise of the Red Cross.* Boulder, Colo.: Westview Press, 1996.

Moorehead, Caroline. *Dunant's Dream: War, Switzerland, and the History of the Red Cross.* London: HarperCollins, 1998.

SEE ALSO: Geneva conventions; Human rights; Limited war; Military ethics; Nobel Peace Prizes; War; World Health Organization.

Internet chat rooms

DEFINITION: Internet forums in which strangers engage in live and usually unsupervised discussions

TYPE OF ETHICS: Personal and social ethics

SIGNIFICANCE: The anonymity and undisciplined nature of online chat rooms exempts their participants from the responsibility to adhere to normal social and legal mores, and makes gullible, immature, and inexperienced participants vulnerable to deceptive and unethical practices.

Anonymous chat lacks ethical boundaries, a sense of place, and social rules. Private individuals and public authorities—sometimes even police officers—are lured into public displays of immoral behavior and such acts of deception as providing false identities and setting up entrapment schemes. So many married people have been known to flirt with strangers over the Internet that growing numbers of divorces have been fueled by online affairs.

Emotionally unstable people try to live out their fantasies by exaggerating their personal attributes and hiding their true selves from those they deceive and seek to exploit. Neurotics play roles, criminals try to recruit collaborators, and sexual exhibitionists find ready audiences. Racist, sexist, and homophobic speech is uncensored. Sexual predators and those entrapping predators offer pornographic images and statements. The types of legal protections from gov-

Surreptitious Advertising

Is it ethical for companies to promote their own products by having their employees enter chat room discussions to rave about their products, without revealing their connections with the companies? This very question was posed to Rabbi Asher Meier, the author of the online column *The Jewish Ethicist*. He answered by citing the Torah, which forbids putting "a stumbling block before the blind." Failing to reveal one's true identity in a chat room discussion is, in effect, leaving other participants "blind." This practice is not only unethical in Jewish law, but also violates the American Marketing Association's code of ethics, which counsels against "sales promotions that use deception or manipulation."

ernment intrusion that are ordinarily provided to mail, telephone conversations, and face-to-face conversations are generally not extended to Internet chat rooms, instant messaging, and e-mail, making online communications ripe for official abuse.

Despite the possibilities for unethical behavior on Internet chat rooms, the actual incidence of improper activity may be less common than has been thought. An AT&T WorldNet study conducted in 2004 found that the online behavior of most people who use the Internet online is the same as their behavior in everyday life. Early twenty-first century studies of young people who had been raised on the Internet found that they question assumptions they are asked to accept by those they meet online. The young people were constructing their own rules for online behavior and etiquette, making ethical judgments about message content, critically evaluating and responding to improper behaviors they encountered and dispensing online discipline for those who behave improperly in chat rooms.

Gordon Neal Diem

FURTHER READING

Tapscott, Don. *Growing up Digital: The Rise of the Net Generation.* New York: McGraw-Hill, 1998.
Turkle, Sherry. *Life on the Screen: Identity in the Age of the Internet.* New York: Simon and Schuster, 1995.

SEE ALSO: Child abuse; Computer misuse; Confidentiality; Electronic mail; Electronic surveillance; Gossip; Identity theft; Personal relationships; Pornography; Sexual abuse and harassment.

Internet piracy

DEFINITION: Unauthorized duplication and distribution of copyrighted materials taken from computer networks, usually to avoid paying for the use of commercially licensed materials such as music, motion pictures, photographs, computer software, and texts

TYPE OF ETHICS: Business and labor ethics

SIGNIFICANCE: Internet piracy is considered unethical because it prevents creators from being able to profit fairly from their works or regulate their use and distribution. The growing practice of Internet piracy raises issues concerning the ethical assumptions presupposed by intellectual property, fair use, and copyright laws.

Perhaps no new technology has created a more daunting challenge to traditional notions of intellectual property rights and their relationship to personal privacy than the popularity and ready availability of file-sharing mechanisms on the Internet. Internet use worldwide skyrocketed in the 1990's, as did the use of free and easily accessible computer software that allows users to make and share digital copies of music, video, and other media.

A significant portion of the material that was being exchanged in the early years of the twenty-first century consisted of illegally pirated works, copies of commercially recorded music, software, and similar materials originally created and distributed for profit. Encryption technology that might prevent unauthorized duplication of digitized materials was not able to keep pace with the software allowing users to "rip," or digitally duplicate, copyrighted materials via the Internet. Industry estimates in the late 1990's put the number of computer users exchanging pirated music, not to mention other commercial electronic media, in the tens of millions.

THE PIRACY PHENOMENON

In 1997, a small group of college students developed and made available free of charge on the Internet a software program that allowed its users to easily "rip" copies of music from compact discs and upload them to centralized storage servers. Other users could then access the servers to download the illegally copied music without charge. Initially used only by a handful of music enthusiasts, word of Napster's capabilities spread rapidly, and by 1999, Napster's developers estimated that their program had been downloaded about sixty million times. If even only a small fraction of Napster's users were robbing the entertainment industry of potential revenues, the courts viewed its existence as a potential disaster for the music industry. Consequently, Napster was shut down by a U.S. federal court injunction in 2002.

However, by that time, similar renegade file-sharing systems were proliferating the Internet. Some of these systems allowed users to swap not only music with ease but also a range of other types of digitized files—computer software, games, and full texts of books. In contrast to Napster, the new systems were decentralized, not requiring the use of central servers for storage of pirated material. Consequently, illegal piracy became more difficult to trace back to its sources. Identifying and attempting to shut down even a small fraction of the users of pirated files proved impractical if not impossible. Despite government and entertainment industry campaigns to inform users of the unethical and illegal use of Internet file-sharing systems, Web-based piracy continued to grow even after Napster's highly publicized court battles.

FAIR USE AND BIG BUSINESS

Many online file sharers have claimed that theirs is a victimless crime, asserting that they are merely sharing duplicated materials for their own personal use. Some have even argued that online file sharing actually leads to increased sales of music, games, and video materials because it increases exposure for commercial artists. However, representatives of the entertainment industry vehemently disagree. The Recording Industry Association of America (RIAA), a music industry trade group, attributed to the popularity of online piracy a significant plunge in music sales in the years following the proliferation of Internet file-sharing programs. In 2001, sales of compact discs (CDs) in the United States dropped 6.4 percent, and the following year, they plunged another 8.7 per-

cent. During the same period, the number of Internet users who admitted downloading ever more music while buying less of it outnumbered those who claimed downloading led them to buy more music by a two-to-one margin.

Both the entertainment and software industries tend to regard virtually *all* unauthorized duplication of their products as acts of piracy. However, certain considerations complicate the issue. The copyright laws of most countries, including the United States, provide for the "fair use" of protected artistic and intellectual materials. In other words, it is legal for those who own copyrighted copies of music, movies, and in some cases computer software, to duplicate them for their own private use—provided they do not share their "personal" copies with others. It is legal for a person who has purchased a collection of compact discs to make CD collections of their favorite songs, provided they do not share the copies that they make. The ethical and legal problem lies in what constitutes "sharing" such copies. Surely, giving a friend a copy of one's "personal" CD would infringe on copyright. Nonetheless, if one makes a "personal" copy of a song and plays it in the presence of a visiting friend, does this infringe on the rights of the copyright holder to profit from the friend's hearing the music?

Privacy advocates strongly oppose what they see as the entertainment industry's draconian efforts to invade personal privacy by limiting "fair use." They also warn against allowing software companies to have almost absolute control over their software's source code, pointing out that in many cases this limits the individual's rights to fair personal use and impedes the natural course of technological progress.

A HAPPY MEDIUM?

In 2003, the RIAA sued major Internet service providers Verizon and Earthlink, demanding that they turn over the names of their customers known to download or exchange copyrighted media files. However, in reality such lists only allowed the RIAA to verify the names of Internet subscribers from whose computers illegal file exchanges had occurred. They could not verify which particular members of these households had been sharing pirated materials because no electronic mechanism exists that can pinpoint exact violators. In one highly publicized case, the RIAA sent a letter threatening a sizeable lawsuit against a grandfather whose name appeared on a list of Internet accounts from which illegal downloads had allegedly been made. In truth the computer owner's grandson, who only visited his home occasionally, was actually downloading pirated music on the family computer. Privacy advocates view the RIAA's efforts at enforcing their rights as copyright holders as displaying an unethical disregard for personal privacy rights when taken to this extreme. They place the responsibility for preventing piracy on the entertainment companies themselves, suggesting that they develop and market new ways of copy-proofing their products rather than playing Big Brother and haphazardly attempting to target individual copyright violators. They maintain that although copyright infringement takes place on a widespread basis on the Internet, targeting individuals has a serious cost—the potential sacrifice of personal privacy and the significant risk of punishing the undeserving.

Gregory D. Horn

FURTHER READING

Graham, Jefferson. "Privacy vs. Internet Piracy." *USA Today*, June 6, 2003.

Hart-Davis, Guy. *Internet Piracy Exposed*. London: Sybex Press, 2001.

Manes, Stephen. "Copyright Law: Ignore at Your Own Peril." *PC World*, September, 2003, 182.

Monk, Bill. "Listen to Impartial Advice." *Computer Weekly*. July 29, 2003, 16.

Willcox, James K. "Where Have All the CDs Gone?" *Sound and Vision*, June, 2003, 87-89.

SEE ALSO: Computer crime; Computer misuse; Computer technology; Copyright; Intellectual property; Napster; Plagiarism; Song lyrics.

Intersubjectivity

DEFINITION: Communicative interaction or struggle between two or more conscious minds

TYPE OF ETHICS: Theory of ethics; beliefs and practices

SIGNIFICANCE: Intersubjectivity is a key concept in several influential theories of communication, knowledge, and desire. Ethical theories that focus on intersubjectivity emphasize the importance of one's ability to understand the points of view of others, to recognize the validity of their projects, and to negotiate conflicts between their desires and one's own.

Whereas subjectivism makes truth and knowledge dependent upon an individual knower, and objectivism holds that truth exists independently from any subjective state of mind, intersubjectivity makes the objective validity of truth depend upon the consensus of a community of subjects. In so doing, intersubjectivity avoids the relativism of subjectivism without granting to truth a status independent of the human mind. Intersubjectivity has been used as a heuristic concept to aid in the formulation of solutions for two thorny issues. First, how is meaning determined? Second, what is the foundation for the possibility and validity of ethics?

THE PROBLEM OF MEANING

Charles Sanders Peirce established pragmatism as a philosophical method for determining meaning and truth. Two elements stand out in his pragmatic theory. First, the conception of an object consists of the conception of its effects. Second, truth is indefinite. Truth is that upon which the ultimate community of investigators would agree. The ultimate community of investigators constitutes the intersubjective precondition for the possibility of meaning and of science.

In addition to pragmatism, Peirce also developed a theory of semiotics, the science of the interpretation of signs. He rejected the traditional philosophy of consciousness that interpreted knowledge in terms of a two-place relationship—the object in the world and its mental representation. Semiotic theory introduces a third element; that is, a sign not only stands for something in the world but is also addressed to an interpreter. The three-place relationship is essentially intersubjective. Signs have meaning only within the intersubjective framework of an interpretation community. The traditional role of the subject of knowledge is replaced by the interpretative community. Subjectivity is replaced by intersubjectivity. Signs can represent only if they are related to the intersubjective world of interpreters, and only those assertions are true that would be reaffirmed by an indefinite community.

Jürgen Habermas, influenced by the pragmatism of Peirce and his semiotic theory, formulated discourse ethics. Discourse ethics emphasizes the use theory of meaning. Meaning consists of a threefold relationship—what is meant, what is said, and the way it is used. Use theory builds on the third element and focuses on the interactive contexts of communication in which expressions function. These contexts were called "language games" by Ludwig Wittgenstein. Language games include the totality of linguistic expressions and nonlinguistic activities. The analysis of language games discloses the intersubjectively shared backgrounds of the forms of life and lifeworlds that influence the meaning and function of language.

Meanings of symbols, therefore, are never subjective but always intersubjective. Symbolic meaning does not derive validity from private interpretation but from intersubjective agreement.

Because of the interconnectedness of language and lifeworld, intersubjectivity is fixed in ordinary language. Interactive communication and agreement between human beings make social life possible.

Habermas also rejects the traditional concept of the subject understood as an ego. The subject is a community of investigators. For Habermas, the moral subject, as a subject of action, cannot even be conceived apart from communicative interaction with other human beings.

KARL-OTTO APEL

Karl-Otto Apel, a German philosopher, insisted that language and intersubjective agreement make meaningful ethical judgments possible. Apel held that the intersubjective community of investigators is the precondition for the possibility and validity of objectively valid ethics. Apel maintained, along with Immanuel Kant, the necessity for universal preconditions for the possibility and validity of ethics. Unlike Kant, however, he did not find these "transcendental" conditions in the consciousness of the solitary individual; following Peirce, Apel located them in the discursive ethical community.

Apel conceptualized this idea by utilizing a synthesis between transcendental idealism and historical materialism. From idealism, he postulated the normative and ideal presupposition of the "ideal communication community." The ideal communication community functions as an imaginary hypothetical

community free from inequality and unjust constraints. From materialism, he derived the "real communication community" as a given historical society in which real conflict and inequality exist. The dialectical relationship existing between the ideal communication community and the real communication community is characterized as an antagonism between the ideal and the factual. Notwithstanding its antagonistic character, this dialectical relationship results in the conceptualization of the discursive community as the precondition for both the ethical community as a moral subject and, at the same time, the discursive community as the object of ethical action. In this manner, Apel avoids the extremes of subjectivism and objectivism. In Apel's thought, ethics is made possible because of the search for mutual understanding that occurs intersubjectively between persons in conversation.

The heuristic model of the communication community functions in the same way as Wittgenstein's concept of the language game. In either case, consensus functions as a regulative principle. Truth and knowledge arise from communicative action under rule-governed institutions. It is this communicative interaction that makes the objective validity of ethics possible.

Michael R. Candelaria

FURTHER READING

Apel, Karl-Otto. *Towards a Transformation of Philosophy.* Translated by Glyn Adey and David Frisby. London: Routledge & Kegan Paul, 1980.

Cannon, Bob. *Rethinking the Normative Content of Critical Theory: Marx, Habermas, and Beyond.* New York: Palgrave, 2001.

Habermas, Jürgen. *Communication and the Evolution of Society.* Translated by Thomas McCarthy. Boston: Beacon Press, 1979.

Hohler, T. P. *Imagination and Reflection—Intersubjectivity: Fichte's "Grundlage" of 1794.* Martinus Nijhoff Philosophy Library 8. Boston: Martinus Nijhoff, 1982.

Husserl, Edmund. *Cartesian Meditations: An Introduction to Phenomenology.* Translated by Dorion Cairns. The Hague: Martinus Nijhoff, 1988.

Peirce, Charles. *The Essential Peirce: Selected Philosophical Writings.* Edited by Nathan Houser and Christian Kloesel. 2 vols. Bloomington: Indiana University Press, 1992-8.

Simms, Karl, ed. *Ethics and the Subject*. Atlanta: Rodopi, 1997.

Williams, Robert R. *Hegel's Ethics of Recognition*. Berkeley: University of California Press, 1997.

SEE ALSO: Kantian ethics; Peirce, Charles Sanders; *Phenomenology of Spirit*; Pragmatism; Sartre, Jean-Paul; Wittgenstein, Ludwig.

Intervention

DEFINITION: Activity undertaken by a state that coercively interferes in the domestic affairs of another state

TYPE OF ETHICS: International relations

SIGNIFICANCE: Intervention may be motivated by national interest, humanitarian concern, or both. It is often excused, or even mandated, when it seems primarily to be in the interests of the human rights of people being abused or neglected by their own government. Less apparently altruistic instances of intervention are often seen as examples of real-politik and therefore of questionable moral status.

Theoretically, no state has the right to interfere in the domestic affairs of another sovereign state. Such an act is a contradiction of the principles of sovereignty and therefore an attack on the very system on which the freedom of nations rests. Intervention comes in many forms: propaganda; espionage; discriminatory economic policies; and support or denial of support to governments or subversive movements in domestic crises, especially where such foreign support might prove to be decisive. The most notorious form, however, is military intervention.

It is not always easy to determine the morality of

U.S. Navy admiral Leighton Smith, commander of the North Atlantic Treaty Organization military mission in Bosnia in 1995, talks to reporters about the handover of power from United Nations to NATO forces. A map of Bosnia is in the background. (AP/Wide World Photos)

intervention, and where interventionist activities are concerned, morality may not always be the highest value. Instead, what matters most is the relationship of morality, power, and knowledge, which, when gainfully exploited, in its contemplative stage may be called wisdom and in its active phase may be called justice. Unfortunately, more often than not, this is not the case. During most of the Cold War, for example, intervention was undertaken on behalf of issues of national power far more often than because of poverty, tyranny, or exploitation. During that period, any action against the communist or imperialist threat, especially if it was successful, was considered by the interventionist power to be moral by definition, or else merely a problem of techniques.

Olusoji A. Akomolafe

SEE ALSO: Covert action; Espionage; Iraq; Kosovo; Peacekeeping missions; Realpolitik; Sovereignty; Vietnam War.

Intrinsic good

DEFINITION: Value that something has in itself, as opposed to its value based on its usefulness or what it can bring about
TYPE OF ETHICS: Theory of ethics
SIGNIFICANCE: Intrinsic good or intrinsic value is a crucial component of many philosophical systems and theories of morality, which see it as the very basis of value. Other, more skeptical, philosophies see the concept of intrinsic good as an obfuscation of the true (relational or historical) nature of value and therefore believe they have an ethical obligation to attack those systems that employ it.

The concept of intrinsic good goes back to Aristotle's notion of "the good" as that for the sake of which one chooses all other things. The contrast is with extrinsic good, which is understood as something that is good only because it brings about something else that is intrinsically good. Standard candidates for intrinsic goods are pleasure and happiness; pluralist theories include such things as friendship and virtue. G. E. Moore introduced a useful test for intrinsic goodness and a theory about its nature. For example,

to see whether music is intrinsically good, Moore would have one imagine a universe with only music in it—and therefore with no listeners to enjoy the music—and consider whether the universe seems a better one than a universe without any music. If the universe with music in it does seem better, music is intrinsically valuable; if not, music is valuable only because of its effects, such as its effects on listeners. Moore also argued that intrinsic goodness is an objective, nonnatural property and that rightness can be defined in terms of it.

Eric H. Gampel

SEE ALSO: Aristotle; Derrida, Jacques; Good, the; Intuitionist ethics; Moore, G. E.; Nietzsche, Friedrich; Utilitarianism; Value.

Intuitionist ethics

DEFINITION: Any of several ethical systems based, variously, in sensory perception, rational understanding, or considered judgment
TYPE OF ETHICS: Theory of ethics
SIGNIFICANCE: Intuitionist ethics seeks to justify or ground moral beliefs by demonstrating that they derive from a fundamental human faculty. The precise nature of that faculty, different in different versions of intuitionist ethics, will have profound implications for the theory and practice of moral judgment.

According to one version of intuitionist ethics, normal people can simply see the truth about at least some moral matters. In this view, the intuition that something is right or good is not just a hunch or a feeling. Instead, it is an immediate awareness, something like the awareness that three-sided plane figures have three angles. Thinking carefully about a particular act leads one simply to see that the act would be right. In this view, the judgment that this act would be right is self-evident—that is, knowable without reliance on further evidence. In a similar way, some intuitionists claim that some general moral principles are self-evident in the same way that mathematical axioms are self-evident.

The analogy with geometry and mathematics is, however, problematic. "Any three-sided plane figure has three angles" is self-evident, but "Always tell the truth" is not self-evident. General moral principles, unlike geometric principles, have exceptions, and therefore they cannot be self-evident in the same way. In the case of particular moral judgments, one cannot be sure that there is no hidden aspect of the situation that will make the judgment incorrect. Thus, such particular moral judgments also lack the self-evidence of geometric principles.

Some intuitionists think of "seeing" as looking instead of as understanding. For them, moral intuitions are like perceptions of colors as opposed to apprehensions of axioms. One objection to this approach is that perceiving requires a sense organ, and it does not seem that people have a moral sense organ. It seems clear, however, that seeing moral qualities only requires some means, not necessarily anything like "a moral eye or a moral nose."

Moral disagreement within societies, between societies, and across time periods presents a more serious problem for intuitionist ethics. How can one be sure that one is perceiving right and wrong if there is so much disagreement about them? Disagreement about what is red would raise serious questions about one's power to detect color qualities, and the same seems true about the power to detect moral qualities.

Intuitionists may respond that some people have a faulty moral faculty. Such people may be biased or lack relevant experiences, such as knowing what it is like to be without enough food to eat. The idea is that, just as some people suffer from color blindness, some people suffer from moral blindness. Unlike the case of color blindness, there is no agreed-upon test for determining moral blindness. Intuitionists may emphasize the "intuitions" of "normal moral observers" or "moral experts" and discount the "intuitions" of everyone else. Then, however, the difficulty is to say what a moral expert is, without making a moral judgment that rests on intuition.

Also responding to the problem of moral disagreement, other intuitionists claim that there is not really that much disagreement. For example, one culture may leave older people to die in the cold while another culture cares for older people. Yet both cultures may be trying to do what they think is good for older people and merely have different factual beliefs about what that is. All the same, it seems that people may agree on all "the facts" of abortion and still disagree about whether the fetus has a right to life.

OBLIGATIONS

Some intuitionists may try to lessen moral disagreement by talking about *prima facie* obligations. A *prima facie* obligation to keep promises, for example, is an obligation to keep promises unless there is an overriding moral reason not to keep them. This approach does away with some disagreement, but disagreement remains, since different intuitionists have different lists of *prima facie* obligations.

If having an intuition is supposed to guarantee that one has determined the truth, then what are the criteria for determining that one has actually had an intuition? Disagreeing parties may be equally certain that they are right. If intuition is a "seeing to see," something like a conviction, then how can it provide a solid foundation for moral judgments?

This appeal to intuition is not an appeal to one's general beliefs, but instead an appeal to one's considered beliefs, beliefs that one has arrived at after a process of rationally considering alternatives. These beliefs are not supposed to be self-evident; one checks them against one's other beliefs and against the considered beliefs of others. Beliefs that pass this test become part of the basis for testing other beliefs.

This approach makes justification largely a matter of "coherence" among beliefs. If this approach can avoid a vitiating circularity, can it avoid a built-in bias in favor of traditional beliefs? Might not traditional prejudices survive the process of testing beliefs? In any case, the problem of disagreement remains, since two incompatible sets of beliefs may be equally coherent.

Gregory P. Rich

FURTHER READING

Curnow, Trevor. *Wisdom, Intuition, and Ethics.* Brookfield, Vt.: Ashgate, 1999.

Donagan, Alan. *The Theory of Morality.* Chicago: University of Chicago Press, 1977.

Garner, Richard T., and Bernard Rosen. *Moral Philosophy: A Systematic Introduction to Normative Ethics and Meta-ethics.* New York: Macmillan, 1967.

Hudson, W. D. *Ethical Intuitionism.* New York: St. Martin's Press, 1967.

Ross, William D. *The Right and the Good.* New ed. New York: Oxford University Press, 2002.

Shaw, William H. "Intuition and Moral Philosophy." *American Philosophical Quarterly* 17, no. 2 (April, 1980): 127-34.

Stratton-Lake, Philip, ed. *Ethical Intuitionism: Re-evaluations*. New York: Oxford University Press, 2002.

SEE ALSO: Epistemological ethics; Metaethics; Moore, G. E.; Moral-sense theories; Naturalistic fallacy; Plato.

Invasion of privacy

DEFINITION: Exposure of one's personal life or information, especially by the media

TYPE OF ETHICS: Civil liberties

SIGNIFICANCE: Charges of invasion of privacy represent a clash between two fundamental civil liberties: the right to privacy and the right to freedom of the press. Generally speaking, the press is given more leeway to present the intimate details of the lives of public figures than those of private individuals, because the former are considered to have ceded some portion of their privacy rights voluntarily when they entered public life.

In 1890, two Boston lawyers, Samuel D. Warren and Louis D. Brandeis, published an article on the right to privacy in the *Harvard Law Review*. The article deplored the sensationalistic tactics used by the press at that time, which violated the average person's notions of privacy. Gradually, during the next century, such invasions of privacy were incorporated into an articulated concept in tort law. The earliest kind of privacy invasion was known as appropriation, the use of another's name or likeness for commercial purposes without that person's consent. Two other types of invasion of privacy—intrusion upon another person's seclusion and placing a person in a false light—developed later.

A last kind of invasion of privacy—the one to which Warren and Brandeis referred—is the publication of private information about a person. Today, if such information is newsworthy or is a matter of public record, the media may publish it. Since opinions differ regarding what is newsworthy, however, this type of invasion of privacy remains most vexing for citizens and media alike. Generally, though—supermarket tabloids notwithstanding—because the right of privacy is now recognized by law, the media can no longer publish whatever it wishes to without consequence.

Jennifer Eastman

SEE ALSO: Accuracy in Media; Biometrics; Drug testing; Fairness and Accuracy in Reporting; Journalistic ethics; Libel; Photojournalism; Privacy; Tabloid journalism; Telemarketing.

Iraq

IDENTIFICATION: Predominantly Arab Middle Eastern nation that has experienced an unusual amount of conflict and suffering

TYPE OF ETHICS: Modern history

SIGNIFICANCE: The modern history of Iraq has been afflicted by tyrannical leaders, abuses of human rights, religious and ethnic hostilities, power struggles among rival clans, and disastrous wars.

Situated in the northwest of the Persian Gulf, Iraq stands in the heart of western Asia. Except for a portion of the Shatt al-Arab (River of the Arabs), its national boundaries are generally arbitrary. A lack of common bonds for a national union has been one of the great problems of the country. Early in the twenty-first century, Iraq's proven oil reserves were surpassed only by those of Saudi Arabia. Until the disastrous war over Kuwait in 1991, which was followed by more than a decade of economic sanctions, the Iraqi population enjoyed a moderately high living standard.

ETHNIC AND RELIGIOUS CONFLICT

Almost 80 percent of Iraq's 22.6 million people are Arabs—people who speak the Arabic language and share a common Arab culture. The Kurds, the other major ethnic group, constitute about 17 percent of the population. The Kurds speak their own language, which is related to Persian, and most of them live in the mountainous regions of northern Iraq, next to Kurdish regions of Turkey and Iran. Having a strong sense of nationalist identity, they have long desired a separate country, to be called Kurdistan, an idea that the Iraqi government has long opposed. In

1988, the Iraq government used poison gas against Kurdish villages.

Small groups of other minorities are scattered throughout the country. Turkmen make up about 2 percent, while Iranians, Assyrians, Lurs, and Armenians each have less than 1 percent. Almost 3 percent of the people belong to various Christian churches. Before 1948, Iraq had about 150,000 Jews, but since then, forced emigration has reduced their numbers to about nine thousand. Except for Jews, small ethnic minorities have generally been tolerated so long as they have not opposed official government policies.

About 97 percent of Iraqis are Muslims—followers of the Islamic religion. Almost all Kurds and one third of the Arabs are Sunnī Muslims, who accept the orthodox Sunnī interpretations of the Qurʾān. The government has traditionally been controlled by Sunnī Muslims. Approximately two-thirds of the Arabs are Shiʿites, who have different views of Islam and look to Ali as Muḥammad's true successor. Located primarily in the country's south, they have separatist tendencies. Their 1991 rebellion against the central government was brutally suppressed.

A VIOLENT POLITICAL CULTURE

Conquered by the Ottoman Turks in 1515, Iraq was part of the Ottoman Empire until 1917. Great Britain then administered the country as a League of Nations mandate until 1932. During the first year after independence, Iraq's army massacred Assyrian Christians. A bloody *coup d'état* of 1936 added to political instability, and a series of eight military governments ruled the country until 1941, when the British returned in force. With Iraqi self-rule in 1945,

Iraqi Kurds who suffered under Saddam Hussein's "Arabization" policies celebrate as they enter the city of Khanaqin in Northern Iraq on April 10, 2003. Khanaqin was the first city in the region to fall to coalition forces after Iraqi government forces retreated. (AP/Wide World Photos)

chaotic conditions allowed the Kurds to form a short-lived Kurdish Republic, which was brutally suppressed by the national army.

In the post-World War II years, Prime Minister Nuri al-Said shared power with the regent for the young king Faisal II. Iraqis fought in the Arab-Israeli War of 1948, which intensified anti-Zionist and anti-Western attitudes among the population. During the Suez Crisis of 1956, al-Said's refusal to condemn Great Britain and France infuriated Arab nationalists. Two years later, a group of left-wing military officers, led by General Abdul Karim Kassim, took over in a coup, killing both al-Said and the young king. The new regime executed scores of politicians and officers who had been connected with the monarchy. Democratic institutions were abolished. In 1961, attempts to suppress Kurdish nationalists led to a guerrilla war.

In 1963, a left-leaning group of military officers seized power in a coup, executing Kassim and his close associates. The new president, Colonel Abdul Salam Arif made an alliance with the Baath Party, a radical organization endorsing violence in pursuit of socialism, Arab nationalism, and anti-Western policies. In November, 1963, President Arif staged a successful anti-Baath coup. The next year, Baath members failed in an attempt to assassinate Arif, but in 1968, Baathist officers seized power in a violent coup.

IRAQ SINCE 1968

Between 1968 and 1979, Colonel Ahmad Hassan al-Bakr was president of Iraq as well as chairman of the Revolutionary Command Council. Real power, however, was firmly in the hands of his assistant, Saddam Hussein, who controlled the internal security apparatus. When Bakr resigned in 1979, probably for health reasons, Hussein was quickly installed as president. Hussein's first act was to purge the Baath Party of senior officers suspected of disloyalty, making it clear that opposition would not be tolerated. Most historians agree that Hussein's regime became one of the most violent and repressive in the modern history of the Middle East.

Hussein led his country into three destructive wars. In 1980, he ordered the invasion of Iran, apparently with the goal of annexing an oil-rich Iranian province where Arabs were in the majority. The destructive conflict lasted eight years. Two years later, Hussein's army occupied the oil-rich kingdom of Kuwait. In the Gulf War of 1991, a massive U.S.-led co-alition forced the Iraqis to leave the small country. The United Nations passed numerous resolutions authorizing inspectors to determine whether Iraq was developing weapons of mass destruction (WMD). When Hussein failed fully to comply, a coalition of the United States, Britain, and a few other countries invaded Iraq and ended Hussein's regime. Observers debated about whether the coalition's preemptive war met the usual criteria of a just war.

Following Hussein's overthrow, coalition authorities appointed an Iraqi governing council, with representatives from the major religious and ethnic communities. The council was given the difficult task of producing a democratic constitution by the summer of 2004. Kurds wanted to gain independence, while Shi'ites and Sunnīs disagreed about how political leaders should be chosen. Numerous Iraqis bitterly resented the continued presence of foreign military forces, and some expressed their discontent with sniper attacks and terrorist bombings. Meanwhile, coalition inspectors failed to find any WMDs, the major reason given for intervention. Americans and British citizens became increasingly dissatisfied with the costs of the occupation.

Thomas Tandy Lewis

FURTHER READING

Bengio, Ofra. *Saddam's Word: Political Discourse in Iraq*. New York: Oxford University Press, 2002.

Hakim, Sahib. *Human Rights in Iraq*. London: Middle East Watch, 1992.

Makiya, Kanan. *Republic of Fear: The Politics of Modern Iraq*. Berkeley: University of California Press, 1998.

Miller, John, and Aaron Kenedi, ed. *Inside Iraq: The History, the People, and the Modern Conflicts of the World's Least Understood Land*. New York: Marlowe, 2002.

Shawcross, William. *Allies: The United States, Britain, Europe, and the War in Iraq*. New York: Perseus, 2004.

Tripp, Charles. *A History of Iraq*. Cambridge, England: Cambridge University Press, 2002.

Vaux, Kenneth. *Ethics and the Gulf War*. Boulder: Westview Press, 1992.

SEE ALSO: Biochemical weapons; Chemical warfare; Hussein, Saddam; Intervention; Israeli-Palestinian conflict; National security and sovereignty.

Is/ought distinction

DEFINITION: Distinction drawn in moral philosophy between prescriptive (value) statements and descriptive (empirical) statements in neither being verifiable nor representing a definable body of knowledge

TYPE OF ETHICS: Theory of ethics

SIGNIFICANCE: The distinction between "is" statements and "ought" statements is crucial to ethics, since it differentiates between statements that can be true or false on the one hand and articulations of subjective unverifiable judgments on the other.

One of the oldest continuing debates in moral philosophy concerns the relationship of "prescriptive" statements (about what one *ought* to do) to "descriptive" statements (about what one *is* doing). Descriptive statements are defined as statements of fact that refer to events or properties that are obtained through the experiences of the senses and therefore are verifiable—that is, they can be categorized as true or false.

Since descriptive statements are empirical in nature, they are thought collectively to form a body of "scientific" knowledge. An example of such a statement is "The water is hot." Both the subject and the predicate in this sentence can be verified; the liquid in question can be tested as to its composition, while its temperature can be measured and compared to accepted conventions of hot and cold. Once the sentence is analyzed, its truthfulness will either be affirmed or denied, but in either case, a concrete "fact" will have been established.

Prescriptive statements, however, do not always seem to proceed from the same empirical foundations, and it is not always possible to verify their truth or falsehood as one would verify that of a descriptive statement. Again, consider an example: "One ought never to cheat." Here, no actual event is necessarily referred to; thus, there is nothing concrete to verify as either true or false. Instead, the statement seems to express an attitude about a possible course of action—in this case, to assert disapproval. The debate in moral philosophy, however, is whether such statements have any relation at all to empirical facts and thus form a body of "knowledge" similar to that of descriptive statements. About this there remains much disagreement.

THE DISTINCTION'S ORIGINS

The origin of the modern philosophical debate about the nature of prescriptive statements is traditionally ascribed to the eighteenth century British philosopher David Hume. In his *Treatise of Human Nature* (1740), Hume criticized previous philosophers who attempted to draw prescriptive conclusions from descriptive premises. Since for Hume the two types of statements have fundamentally different natures, he considered it impossible to derive the former from the latter. Statements of value, in other words, were not reducible to statements of fact.

Hume's critique was challenged later in the eighteenth century by Immanuel Kant, who, in his *Fundamental Principles of the Metaphysics of Morals* (1785), attempted to avoid the trap of moral relativism that seemed to ensue from Hume's position. While Kant agreed that statements of value could not be derived from statements of fact, prescriptive statements could nevertheless be verified if they were derived from a universal moral principle that could be shown to be self-evidently true. Kant's categorical imperative ("I am never to act otherwise than so that I could also will that my maxim should become a universal law") represented one attempt to frame such a universal moral principle and thus allow prescriptive statements in general to form a body of knowledge.

MODERN DEBATE

More recent attempts to either affirm or resolve the is/ought distinction have led to the formation of a number of schools of thought. In the main, those who make such attempts fall into two major groups: the cognitivists, who claim that prescriptive statements do form a recognizable body of knowledge, and the noncognitivists, who deny such a possibility. Cognitivists further subdivide into two separate schools: naturalists (such as Jeremy Bentham and R. B. Perry) believe that prescriptive statements are simply different forms of factual statements that are, like any scientific fact, empirically verifiable. Such verification may occur through analyzing those acts that happen in accord with particular prescriptive principles (Are such acts consistent with established ethical norms?) or by observing the consequences of those acts (Have they led to desirable results?). In either case, the naturalist asserts that such observation takes place on the level of the senses and thus value statements themselves are considered to be facts.

The nonnaturalists (such as David Ross and G. E. Moore) differ, seeing prescriptive statements as unique forms in themselves, which cannot be reduced to the level of scientific fact. Values may be considered to be true or false, but they must be verified not according to the observations of sense experience, but instead by direct appeal to moral intuition, to a universal value-principle, or to a set of properties that define intrinsic moral value. This appeal to universals has led to the nonnaturalist position's also being defined as intuitionism.

In addition, G. E. Moore, in his monumental work *Principia Ethica* (1903), framed a critique of the naturalist position based on what he termed the naturalistic fallacy. Moore claimed that naturalistic statements attempt to equate value properties with empirical properties as if statements about each conveyed the same kind of meaning. ("Gandhi is a good man" as being no different from "The ball is green"). Since it can be shown, said Moore, that such statements are not the same, naturalistic statements are inherently fallacious.

Noncognitivists (such as Charles Stevenson and A. J. Ayer) continued Moore's critique of naturalism but extended it to include all cognitivist theories in general. Both naturalism and nonnaturalism are thought by this group to be incorrect in claiming that prescriptive statements can in any way be proved to be true or false. Rather, prescriptive statements communicate a person's attitudes about a particular event, property, or course of action and attempt to convince others to agree. Since attitudes are not verifiable, they cannot be considered true or false, and, since attitudes are not intrinsic value-properties (as nonnaturalism asserts), there can be no such thing as a body of moral knowledge.

More recently, noncognitivism itself has come into question from a variety of directions. Philippa Foote has claimed that when one examines how one actually uses prescriptive statements, no "logical gap" exists between one's observation of facts and one's moral evaluation of them. Also, Mortimer Adler has proposed his own form of cognitivism by distinguishing between "natural desires" (which he calls "needs") and "acquired desires" (called "wants"). Since what one needs is by definition good for one, and since one cannot do the opposite and not desire what one needs, one may thus construct an imperative that is self-evidently true. Having done this, one

may then observe specific actions and measure them empirically according to one's established norm—a process that allows prescriptive statements to be verifiable and to form a body of knowledge after all.

Robert C. Davis

FURTHER READING

Adler, Mortimer. *Ten Philosophical Mistakes.* New York: Macmillan, 1985.

Dancy, Jonathan, ed. *Normativity.* Malden, Mass.: Blackwell, 2000.

Edwards, Paul, ed. *The Encyclopedia of Philosophy.* New York: Macmillan, 1967.

Ferm, Vergilius, ed. *Encyclopedia of Morals.* New York: Greenwood Press, 1969.

Hocutt, Max. *Grounded Ethics: The Empirical Bases of Normative Judgments.* New Brunswick, N.J.: Transaction, 2000.

Jones, W. T. *A History of Western Philosophy.* 2d ed. 5 vols. New York: Harcourt, Brace & World, 1969-75.

Taylor, Paul, ed. *Problems of Moral Philosophy: An Introduction to Ethics.* 3d ed. Belmont, Calif.: Wadsworth, 1978.

SEE ALSO: Cognitivism; Hume, David; Intuitionist ethics; Kantian ethics; Moore, G. E.; Naturalistic fallacy; Prescriptivism.

Islamic ethics

DEFINITION: Ethics of the monotheistic religion that is the dominant faith in the Middle East and the religion of more than one billion adherents worldwide

DATE: Founded in seventh century C.E.

TYPE OF ETHICS: Religious ethics

SIGNIFICANCE: Islam unites the spiritual and temporal, setting forth the ethical and moral principles that have become the precepts by which the world's Muslims live.

The Islamic faith centers around the Qur'ān (also spelled Koran), which Muslims consider the word of Allah as revealed in the seventh century to Muḥammad, an affluent seventh century Arabian merchant who become the religion's founder and only prophet, through the archangel Gabriel. Muslims consider the ethical and behavioral precepts set forth in the Qur'ān to be the word of God (Allah) and, therefore, to be infallible.

Muslims are also guided by the Sunna and the *Ḥadīth*, collections of precepts and acts attributed to the Prophet Muḥammad and gathered after his death in 632 C.E. Based on oral traditions, the *Ḥadīth* and the Sunna provide temporal and spiritual guidance. They differ from the Qur'ān in being attributed to the Prophet, rather than to Allah, so they are not considered infallible and are subject to interpretation.

THE SPIRITUAL AND THE TEMPORAL

Muslims view life as a mere moment along the unimaginably long line of infinite time. Earthly existence is a prelude to life in the hereafter, the quality of which will be determined by the believers' adherence to the rules set forth in the Qur'ān and by their actions as dictated by this holy work. When the world comes to an end, a final judgment will occur. The obedient will be rewarded and the disobedient punished in grotesque ways. Those who die in defense of Islam are promised particularly lustrous afterlives.

The Qur'ān, quite remarkably to most non-Muslims, deals with such mundane matters as proper methods of cooking, bathing, brushing one's teeth, and defecating. However, while details of the temporal and corporeal aspects of everyday life are of great importance to Muslims, their importance never overshadows that of the spiritual.

The ethical codes of Islamic communities are clearly articulated. Most acts of Muslims fall into three categories: the morally acceptable, the morally neutral, and the morally unacceptable. Acts specifically forbidden by the Qur'ān include murder, cheating, sexual offenses, gambling, drinking liquor, and eating pork. All these prohibitions touch more on the temporal than on the spiritual. Infractions of these codes, such as theft, are severely punished on the second offense. While thieves may be lashed or incarcerated for their first offenses, the penalty they face for second offenses is having their right hands chopped off. Such penalties are rarely imposed in the most secular modern Islamic nations, such as Turkey, but in more traditional nations, they are practiced.

Followers of Islam need not shun earthly pleasures. However, they are commanded not to violate the moral and ethical codes necessary for their communities to function smoothly. Polygamy is accepted by Islam, but adultery and homosexuality are not. Both offenses were still punishable by death in a number of Islamic countries in the early twenty-first century.

FIVE PILLARS OF ISLAM

Islam is based upon five underlying precepts known as "pillars." The first and most important pillar is *shahadah*, accepting Allah as the one true god and Muḥammad as his Prophet. Indeed, the Arabic word *muslim* means one who submits. Unquestioning submission to the word of Allah and the precepts of Muḥammad are fundamental to accepting Islam.

The second pillar, *salah*, is closely tied to submission. It requires Muslims to pray five times at prescribed hours every day, prostrating themselves on prayer mats, with their heads bowed, and, facing toward the holy city of Mecca while praying. After praying, believers are to rise with their hands cupped behind their ears so that they might better hear the words of Allah. The washing of the head, forearms, hands, and feet frequently accompanies *salah* when it takes place within a mosque—a building devoted to Islamic worship.

Westerners may question the ethics of requiring such unquestioning adherence to any religious philosophy, but Islam demands total submission. In Muslim communities, a *muezzin*, or holy man, summons people to prayer, beginning in the early morning and continuing through the day until the final call to prayer at bedtime.

The third pillar is *zakah*, the giving of alms, initially a tax determined by Muslim communities based on specific assets. These alms were originally used to aid the poor, to help travelers and converts to Islam, and to buy freedom for slaves. In addition to *zakah*, Muslims practice *sadaqah*, or voluntary contribution. Islam has no moral strictures against the accumulation of wealth, but it both encourages and mandates sharing wealth with the less fortunate. The overlap between religion and politics is evident in this precept. Muslims are expected ethically to care about fellow human beings. The ethical question is not one of whether accumulating wealth is acceptable but how the wealth that is accumulated can best be used.

The fourth pillar of Islam is *sawm*, or fasting during the daylight hours through the entire month of Ramadan. Ritual fasting is viewed as an act of spiri-

Muslims gather for prayers before a mosque in India. Although India is a predominantly Hindu nation, it has more than 100 million Muslim citizens, who make it one of the largest Muslim nations in the world. (Library of Congress)

tual cleansing as well as an act of submission to the will of Allah. Some Muslim countries punish and even imprison people who do not observe *salah* and *sawm*, although strict interpretations of these precepts are less vigorously enforced in modern Islamic countries, largely because they pose ethical and legal questions about the interrelationship between religion and government. In some Muslim contexts, however, strict enforcement prevails.

Finally, there is the precept of the *hajj*, or the pilgrimage of Muslims to Mecca, the city in which Muḥammad received his revelations from Allah. All Muslims, with exception of those with severe disabilities, are expected to visit Mecca at least once during their lifetimes.

One might question the ethical validity of imposing these precepts and the strict set of rules that characterize Islam upon the diverse populations that accept the faith. The justification for this is the acceptance of the one underlying precept that colors significantly all the others: *shahadah*. After accepting this precept, no Muslim has a defensible justification for failing to yield to the will of Allah and for accepting the faith unconditionally.

ECONOMICS AND USURY

Muslims are not discouraged from engaging in profitable enterprises and from becoming rich. Muḥammad, after all, was a rich merchant. Indeed, the richer that individual Muslims become, the more the Islamic community benefits from their affluence, collecting *zakah* to be put to fruitful uses. Islam considers the desire to make money a God-given desire, not unlike sexual desire, which is also, in Islamic eyes, God-given. However, Islam imposes implacable ethical codes upon either form of desire. Just as sexual desire must be controlled and not used to the detriment or exploitation of anyone, so is material desire expected to result in ethical acts such as charitable giving.

The one economic practice to which Islam is most stalwartly opposed on ethical grounds is usury—the lending of money at high rates of interest. The Qur'ān and the other holy books of Islam strictly prohibit usury. Before the rise of Islam in Arabia, it was not uncommon for Arabs to lend money at exorbitant rates of interest. If borrowers defaulted on loans, the amount of money or goods owed was doubled. These draconian lending practices led to the total economic destruction of many borrowers. Such practices are completely opposed to the ethical strictures of Islam.

WOMEN AND ISLAM

When Islam was established, the status of women in Arabia was low. Women were considered objects, mere chattels whose main purpose, beyond child bearing, was to serve the pleasure of men. Women had few rights, little protection, and virtually no independence. Under Islam, this situation changed. Muḥammad outlawed the casual, uncommitted relationships that were common between men and women at that time, replacing them with laws that articulated rules for both the polygamous marriages that Islam countenances and for divorce.

Although it may not seem so to modern Westerners, Muḥammad's codification of male-female relationships represented a major step forward for seventh century Arabian women, whose unethical treatment and vulnerability to moral violations such as rape and incest was inimical to Islamic ethics. Muḥammad decreed that women could own property and be able to inherit. These changes accorded women a previously unheard-of legal status. Ethically, women, who existed at the pleasure of men and who had been inconsequential members of society, were now accorded their rights as humans, even though they did not share equal social status with men.

Muslim women were governed by stringent rules of conduct and could be punished severely for transgressions, especially for sexual indiscretions. Those found guilty of adultery could be stoned to death, as often happened. Even at the beginning of the twenty-first century, women were still punished in this fashion in parts of Africa and in Saudi Arabia.

The *Hadīth* require women to dress in loose clothing that masks their bodily contours. Muslim women in many Islamic societies are required to wear a *burqu'*, a floor-length head piece that covers the entire female body, with only a slit left open for the eyes. In Iran and other Islamic countries, women have been severely punished for not wearing the *burqu'* or for not covering their bodies sufficiently. Islamic women in many countries, however, have begun voicing serious objections to Islamic dress codes.

The prescriptions and proscriptions of the Qur'ān are designed to assure morality in Islamic societies, often by removing temptation. Men and women cannot intermingle freely in public. Men worship in the mosque, whereas women usually worship at home. If women are occasionally admitted into the mosque, they worship in rooms apart from those used by men.

In more developed Islamic countries, women are encouraged to seek higher education and to enter the professions. Coeducational facilities, however, do not exist. Islamic women are encouraged to study medicine because in most Islamic countries male physicians are legally forbidden to treat female patients. One may question the ethics of withholding from one gender the professional services of someone of another gender, but Muslims adhere strictly to the separation of the sexes.

JIHAD

After the terrorist attacks on the World Trade Center and the Pentagon on September 11, 2001, many Westerners became concerned with the Islamic notion of jihad, which is usually translated "holy war." However, attacks such as those, which were planned and executed by radical Islamic fundamentalists, have not been sanctioned by more centrist groups of Muslims.

A literal translation of the Arabic term *jihad* actually means something similar to "making an effort on the pathway of God." Most Muslims regard jihad as the efforts of individuals to act in ways that exemplify the demands of holy laws as they are outlined in Islam's holy books. Muslims strive through jihad to achieve ethical perfection on an individual basis. According to the precepts of Islam, an offensive jihad can be led only by someone on a level with Muḥammad, and most Muslims deny that any such person exists, although the Saudi leader of al-Qaeda, Osama bin Laden, apparently regarded himself as qualified to meet that mandate. Lacking a leader of Muḥammad's stature, Islam can engage only in a defensive jihad without violating the ethical precepts of the religion.

From time to time, some Islamic rulers have called their wars jihad, focusing their hostilities on people they identify as nonbelievers. Such leaders have generally represented the fringe elements of Islam and have been shunned by the vast central core of Muslims.

R. Baird Shuman

FURTHER READING

Brown, David. *A New Introduction to Islam*. Maiden, Mass.: Blackwell Publications, 2004.

Cook, Michael. *Commanding Right and Forbidding Wrong in Islamic Thought*. Cambridge, England: Cambridge University Press, 2000.

Ernst, Carl W. *Following Muhammad: Rethinking Islam in the Contemporary World.* Chapel Hill: University of North Carolina Press, 2003.

Esposito, John L., ed. *The Oxford History of Islam.* New York: Oxford University Press, 1999.

Hashmi, Sohail H., ed. *Islamic Political Ethics: Civil Society, Pluralism, and Conflict.* Princeton, N.J.: Princeton University Press, 2002.

Nasr, Seyyed Hossein. *Islam: Religion, History, and Civilization.* San Francisco: HarperSanFrancisco, 2003.

Ojeda, Auriana. *Islamic Fundamentalism.* San Diego: Greenhaven Press, Thomson/Gale, 2003.

Weirs, Walter M. *Islam.* New York: Baron's Educational Series, 2000.

SEE ALSO: Abū Bakr; Abū Ḥanīfah; Būkhārī, al-; Fāṭima; Jihad; Muḥammad; Qurʾān; Shīʿa; Sufism; Sunnīs.

Isolationism

DEFINITION: Foreign policy or attitude toward foreign affairs designed to maximize a nation's autonomy and minimize obligations or entanglements by abstaining as much as possible from alliances and other international relations

TYPE OF ETHICS: International relations

SIGNIFICANCE: On a theoretical level, isolationism raises the question of the extent to which the well-being of people in other nations, including those suffering from human rights abuses or unjust wars, should be the concern of a given government. On a practical level, it may be unclear whether the effect of isolationism is to benefit or to harm a nation's own citizenry.

Taken together with such major concepts as neutrality and the Monroe Doctrine and such lesser ones as nonintervention, recognition of de facto governments, and equality of trade opportunity, isolationism was one element of a larger policy of U.S. independence on the international stage. George Washington's declaration of as "little political connections as possible" and Thomas Jefferson's admonition of "no entangling alliances" did not preclude a different course from being adopted when the United States reached maturity. George Washington's Farewell Address constituted a foreign policy of independence, not one of isolationism. His primary concern was to keep the operations of the government immune from foreign intrigue and the decisions of the people free from alien domination.

Bill Manikas

SEE ALSO: Jefferson, Thomas; Manifest destiny; Monroe Doctrine; Sovereignty.

Israeli-Palestinian conflict

IDENTIFICATION: Long-standing dispute about the right to occupy a small piece of land in the Middle East

DATE: First armed conflict began in 1948

TYPE OF ETHICS: Modern history

SIGNIFICANCE: After the founding of the state of Israel in 1948, the Israelis fought against Palestinians and neighboring Arab nations in five bloody and destructive wars. During the early twenty-first century, the ongoing conflict still presented a major threat to international peace.

After Palestine's Jewish people rebelled against Roman imperial rule in 70 C.E., most of them were forcibly expelled from their homes in the province of Judea, which was part of Palestine. Throughout the ensuing centuries, Jews dreamed of one day returning to the original homeland of their ancestors, which they called Zion. By the eighth century, however, Arabic-speaking Muslims were firmly entrenched throughout the entire region. In the late nineteenth century, Jews of Central and Eastern Europe, faced with growing European anti-Semitism, organized the Zionist movement, which called on Jews everywhere to return to Palestine. Most Zionists were idealists who believed that the then sparsely settled region had enough room for both Jews and Arabs to live together in peace.

THE FOUNDING OF MODERN ISRAEL

During the early decades of the twentieth century, waves of Jewish immigrants flowed into Israel. Arabs living in the area were alarmed to see them arrive, and periodically members of the two groups

fought each other. After World War II, revelations about the Jewish Holocaust in Europe produced great support for Zionism among Western Europeans and Americans. In November, 1947, a special commission of the United Nations (U.N.) called for the creation of separate Jewish and Arab states and proposed an international status for Jerusalem, with free access to persons of all religions. Jewish settlers at that time were willing to accept the borders proposed by the commission, but virtually all the Arabs in the Middle East adamantly opposed the notion of creating a Jewish state.

On May 14, 1948, Jewish leaders in Palestine declared the establishment of the independent state of Israel. The declaration referred to the spiritual connection between the Jewish people and the land of Israel and provided a framework for a democratic system of government. It also promised religious freedom for members of all minority groups, called for peaceful relations with neighboring Arab countries, and recognized the right of all Jews to settle in Israel. Both the United States and the Soviet Union gave quick diplomatic recognition to the new state.

Meanwhile, Israel's Arab neighbors—Jordan, Egypt, Syria, Lebanon, and Iraq—quickly declared war and invaded Israel. The bitter fighting of this first Arab-Israeli war resulted in many thousands of deaths, including massacres such as one at Deir

Yassin. However, Israel prevailed and annexed one-third more land than had been provided for in the original U.N. partition plan. Truce agreements were finally signed in early 1949, but the Arab states still refused to recognize Israel's right to exist. Continued animosities later led to the Suez War of 1956, the Six-Day War of 1967, the Yom Kippur War of 1973, and Israel's invasion of Lebanon in 1982.

MORAL CLAIMS TO THE LAND

Israelis have cited several arguments to justify their right to live in Israel. Many conservative Jews base their claims on the Bible, which explicitly says that God has allocated the Promised Land to the Hebrew people, that is, the Jews. Liberal Jews, in contrast, have argued that they have purchased most of Israel's land, and that they will provide additional compensation for land to displaced Palestinians once a final settlement is made. Most Israelis further con-tend that there are many Arab countries in which the Palestinians might live, but only one place in the world reserved for Jews.

Arab-speaking Palestinians believe that the state of Israel is founded on unjust aggression. They argue that their ancestors were living and working in Palestine for more than a thousand years, until Jewish invaders forcibly took over. They demand, moreover, the return of their land and homes, not monetary compensation. Many of them compare Zionists to the Christian crusaders of the Middle Ages, who were eventually expelled from Palestine.

One of the most controversial issues relates to why more than a half-million Palestinians became refugees in 1948-1949. The Israelis deny Palestinian assertions that the refugees were forced out of Israel. Rather, they argue that the refugees left of their own accord in order to make it easier for Israel's Arab enemies to kill Jews within Israel. Regardless of which

Masked Palestinians in the militant Islamic Jihad demonstrate in the Gaza Strip in early January, 2004, to protest the Israeli government's killing of their top commander a week earlier. (AP/Wide World Photos)

claims are true, by the end of the twentieth century, the number of Palestinian refugees had grown to about four million. Large numbers of them have been living in squalid camps, and many have joined extremist groups that advocate violence, including terrorism against civilians, as a means of repossessing their homeland.

THE DIFFICULT QUEST FOR PEACE

Scholars of the Israeli-Palestinian conflict generally agree that peace can be achieved only if both sides make painful concessions. While seeking a solution to the conflict in 1967, the U.N. Security Council passed Resolution 242, which called for Arab recognition of Israel's right to exist in exchange for Israel's withdrawal from territories occupied during the Six-Day War. The basic idea was described as "land for peace." The two antagonists, however, disagreed about whether the resolution meant "all" or "some" of the occupied land. Each side blamed the other for intransigence

After 1967, moments of hopeful concessions were typically followed by periods of intensified violence. In the Camp David Accords of 1979, Egypt recognized Israel, while the latter promised eventually to accept limited autonomy for the Palestinians in the West Bank and Gaza regions. However, the Palestine Liberation Organization (PLO) continued to call for Israel's destruction, and Israel constructed increasing numbers of Jewish settlements in the West Bank. Hope reappeared when the Israeli government and the PLO in 1993 made secret agreements in Oslo, Norway, that envisioned peaceful coexistence and a gradual transition to an elected Palestinian government with authority over most of the West Bank and Gaza.

Extremists on both sides prevented full implementation of the Oslo agreements. Palestinian groups, such as Hamas, began sponsoring a series of suicide bombers, who blew up crowded buses and stores. The Israeli government responded by destroying homes and assassinating radical leaders. In 2000, Israelis elected as prime minister Ariel Sharon, a former military commander with strong Zionist convictions. The Palestinian government demanded an end to new settlements, while Sharon refused to make any concessions until all acts of terrorism ended. Meanwhile, growing unemployment and despair encouraged angry young Palestinians to volunteer for suicide missions.

Thomas Tandy Lewis

FURTHER READING

Dershowitz, Alan. *The Case for Israel*. New York: John Wiley & Sons, 2003.

La Guardia, Anton. *War Without End: Israelis, Palestinians, and the Struggle for a Promised Land*. New York: St. Martin's Press, 2002.

Reich, Walter. *A Stranger in My House: Jews and Arabs in the West Bank*. New York: Henry Holt, 1984.

Said, Edward, ed. *Blaming the Victims: Spurious Scholarship and the Palestinian Question*. New York: W. W. Norton, 2001.

Schulze, Kirsten. *The Arab-Israeli Conflict*. New York: Pearson Education, 1999.

Smith, Charles. *Palestine and the Arab-Israeli Conflict: A History with Documents*. New York: Bedford/St. Martin's Press, 2000.

Wasserstein, Bernard. *Israelis and Palestinians: Why Do They Fight? Can They Stop?* New Haven, Conn.: Yale University Press, 2003.

SEE ALSO: Anti-Semitism; Holocaust; Iraq; Islamic ethics; Jewish ethics; Jihad; Religion and violence; Zionism.

J

Jackson, Jesse

IDENTIFICATION: African American cleric and civil rights leader

BORN: October 8, 1941, Greenville, South Carolina

TYPE OF ETHICS: Civil rights

SIGNIFICANCE: A prominent civil rights spokesman and director of an organization dedicated to creating job opportunities, Jackson ran for president of the United States in 1984 and 1988, when he created controversies over racial and religious remarks that he made.

Jesse Jackson grew up in South Carolina during the era of rigid racial segregation. Because of his bitter experiences with racism and discrimination, he joined the Civil Rights movement and rose to become an assistant to Martin Luther King, Jr., in the Southern Christian Leadership Conference. The Civil Rights movement had a moral and ethical basis because of the historical mistreatment of southern blacks. After King's assassination in 1968, Jackson founded Operation PUSH, a Chicago-based organization whose goal was self-help and economic development. As a Christian minister, Jackson stressed moral values and often advocated boycotting businesses that engaged in discriminatory hiring and promoting practices. He regarded these matters as ethical issues, especially since employers practiced racial discrimination but wanted African American business.

In 1984 Jackson ran in the Democratic primaries for president of the United States. His appeal crossed racial lines and had a populist ring to it, reaching out to farmers, union workers, the working class, and the dispossessed in addition to the middle class. However, he created controversy for himself with remarks he made confidentially to a reporter, when he alluded to Jews as "Hymies" and New York City as "Hymietown." The reporter published the remarks in his newspaper the next day. As a minister, Jackson came under severe criticism for ethical misconduct in making the statements and his failure to apologize immediately. His critics also wanted him to renounce Nation of Islam leader Louis Farrakhan, an ardent but controversial supporter of Jackson's presidential bid. Farrakhan himself called Judaism a "gutter religion." Jackson then faced an ethical dilemma because Farrakhan had provided personal protection for him during his 1984 political

Jesse Jackson marches in a June, 2003, demonstration intended to discourage the Federal Communications Commission from relaxing restrictions on media ownership. (AP/ Wide World Photos)

campaign. When Jackson ran for president again in the 1988 Democratic primaries, he hired a Jew as his campaign manager, blunting criticisms that he was anti-Semitic.

In January, 2001, Jackson's morals and ethics were again tested after it was publicly revealed that he had fathered a baby out of wedlock and outside his marriage. This revelation appears to have done irreparable damage to his reputation as a Christian minister. Nevertheless, he continued to lead Operation PUSH after a vote of confidence from the board of directors, and he remained active in Chicago politics.

Mfanya D. Tryman

FURTHER READING

Barker, Lucius J., and Ronald W. Walters, eds. *Jesse Jackson's 1984 Presidential Campaign*. Urbana: University of Illinois Press, 1989.

Cavanaugh, Thomas, and Lorn Foster. *Jesse Jackson's Campaign: The Primaries and the Caucuses*. Washington, D.C.: Joint Center for Political Studies, 1984.

Reed, Adolph L. *The Jesse Jackson Phenomenon*. New Haven, Conn.: Yale University Press, 1986.

Timmerman, Kenneth R. *Shakedown: Exposing the Real Jesse Jackson*. Chicago: Regnery, 2002.

Tryman, Mfanya Donald. "Jesse Jackson's Campaigns for the Presidency: A Comparison of the 1984 and 1988 Democratic Primaries." In *Blacks and the American Political System*, edited by Huey L. Perry and Wayne Parent. Gainesville: University Press of Florida, 1995.

SEE ALSO: Adultery; Anti-Semitism; Apologizing for past wrongs; Boycotts; Civil Rights movement; Farrakhan, Louis; King, Martin Luther, Jr.; Nation of Islam; Song lyrics.

Jain ethics

DEFINITION: Religious tradition indigenous to India focusing on mystical insight leading to spiritual liberation and total nonviolence

TYPE OF ETHICS: Religious ethics

SIGNIFICANCE: The central Jain principle of ahiṁsā, or nonviolence, became important to a number of later philosophies, among them Mohandas K. Gandhi's philosophy of nonviolent political action.

The Jains constitute less than 1 percent of the population of modern India, but their modern and historical importance in the country far exceeds their numbers. The founder of the Jain faith, Vardhamānŭ Mahāvīra (called the *Jina*, or "conqueror") lived in what is now Bihar in north central India. He was roughly contemporaneous with the Buddha (both lived in the sixth century B.C.E.), and Jainism and Buddhism have many similarities. Central to Jainism is the principle of ahiṁsā, or nonviolence, which might be considered its primary contribution to ethics.

HISTORY AND CHARACTER OF JAINISM

It is probable that Jainism was a continuation of ancient aboriginal traditions of north-central India rather than a radical innovation of its "founder," Mahāvīra. The Jina himself is known as the twenty-fourth *tīrthaṅkara*, or "ford-maker" (that is, builder of a bridge between the mundane world and the world of the spirit). He was, however, responsible for organizing the Jaina saṅgha (community), which was notable for its inclusion of both men and women and its refusal to accept caste distinctions. Although Jainism was never a missionary religion per se, it spread from its homeland in Bihar along the trade routes and eventually acquired powerful converts such as the emperor Chandragupta Maurya.

Like Buddhism, Jainism was in some measure a populist response to the elite character of Vedic religion. It was preached not in Sanskrit, which few could understand, but in *prakrits*, or local dialects. Education, which was restricted to the few in Vedicism, was encouraged as a key antidote to the suffering caused by ignorance. Jains were therefore from the beginning a highly literate community, which they remain today.

In 79 C.E., the Jaina community split into two main sects, the *Digambara* ("sky-clad," or naked) and the *śvetāmbara* ("white-clad"). As well as differing in dress, the two groups differ in their definition of the Jaina canon, which is, given this tradition's emphasis on literacy, an extensive one. They also differ in the disciplines and austerities that they recommend; the Digambara is the more rigorous sect.

The Jaina conception of the universe basically emphasizes change rather than stasis and rejects the personified deities of Vedicism (the system of faith ancestral to modern Hinduism). The central theological component of the Jaina system is the *jīva*, which can be roughly translated as "soul." *Jīvas* are immortal, but they become entangled in worldly attachments that must be shed in order for them to escape the cycle of rebirth and attain *mokṣa* ("liberation").

The attainment of liberation is a difficult task that is pursued most diligently by Jaina monks and nuns, who strive to be *nirgrantha*, or "free from bonds." Abandonment of all property is the first prerequisite, accompanied by the taking of vows. During parts of the year, monks wander from place to place, begging for their food, meditating, and studying. Along with abstaining from causing injury to any life-form, monks and nuns commit to a life of chastity, honesty, and service. These are also the ideals to which laypersons of the Jaina community aspire.

JAINISM AS A WAY OF LIFE

All Jains try to cultivate the "three jewels" of "right faith," "right knowledge," and "right conduct." Among the elements of Jainism most characteristic of the Jaina lifestyle is the principle of ahiṁsā (nonviolence). This is translated in everyday life into total vegetarianism, a dietary habit shared by other communities in India such as those of the high-caste Hindus and Buddhists. In addition to vegetarianism, however, the Jains' characteristic concern for the protection of all life-forms is expressed in their support for veterinary hospitals, animal shelters, and means of livelihood that do not injure life. The Jaina community in India, which is unequivocally pacifistic in terms of military matters, influenced Mohandas K. Gandhi to develop his famous methods of nonviolent noncooperation.

Ahiṁsā as a principle stems from the notion that all life-forms contain *jīvas*, or souls, which are striving for liberation in their own unique ways. The path of an ant or a cow, for example, is different from the path of a human but equally valuable. This basically relativistic stance is expressed in such Jaina traditions as the use of brooms to sweep the path as one walks (to avoid stepping on small life-forms) and covering one's mouth with a cloth (to avoid inhaling insects). Because of ahiṁsā, agricultural occupations are essentially closed to Jains, involving as they do turning the earth, which may kill worms and other creatures dwelling in the soil. The ultimate aim of the

Jains is to live lightly on the earth, doing as little harm as possible.

Jain communities are generally quite well-to-do and support temples that are among the finest monuments of the subcontinent. Their iconography concerns key figures from the history of the Jaina tradition and various mystic symbols and designs. There are no deities in the Hindu sense, but ritual offerings are made at various Jaina sites.

Twenty-first century Jains are found primarily in the states of Gujarat and Rajasthan in western India, where they tend to live in urban environments. Despite their small numbers, they are prominent in education, the media, business, and the professions.

Cynthia Keppley Mahmood

FURTHER READING

Chatterjee, A. K. *A Comprehensive History of Jainism*. 2d rev. ed. 2 vols. New Delhi: Munshiram Manoharial, 2000.

Dundas, Paul. *The Jains*. New York: Routledge, 1992.

Jain, D. C., and R. K. Sharma, eds. *Jaina Philosophy, Art, and Science in Indian Culture*. 2 vols. Delhi: Sharada, 2002.

Jaini, Padmanabh S. *The Jaina Path of Purification*. Berkeley: University of California Press, 1979.

Matilal, Bimal Krishna. *The Central Philosophy of Jainism*. Ahmedabad, India: L. D. Insititute of Indology, 1981.

SEE ALSO: Ahiṁsā; Buddhist ethics; Hindu ethics; Karma; Nirvana; Vardhamāna.

James, William

IDENTIFICATION: American philosopher
BORN: January 11, 1842, New York, New York
DIED: August 26, 1910, Chocorua, New Hampshire
TYPE OF ETHICS: Religious ethics
SIGNIFICANCE: The most famous American pragmatist, James put forward an ethics founded upon humanity's freedom of choice. His most important works include *The Principles of Psychology* (1890), *The Varieties of Religious Experience: A Study in Human Nature* (1902), *Pragmatism: A New Name for Some Old Ways of Thinking* (1907), and *A Pluralistic Universe* (1909).

From 1873 to 1907, William James taught anatomy and physiology, psychology, and then philosophy at Harvard University. The first distinguished American psychologist, he won international recognition for his philosophy of "pragmatism" and "pluralism." James believed that ethics rests on the free choice to be moral; that is, to see life as better lived within a moral framework. That conviction, of course, can never be proved or refuted by factual evidence. Even so, the choice empowers a person to make specific ethical decisions, in defense of which a person may gather reasons. Since each person is free to make choices, a moral philosophy must be constructed from the study of widespread ethical choices.

James thought that over the course of time, certain ethical principles had taken precedence over others. These principles could be used to construct a unified moral system. Although not appealing directly to Christian (or, more broadly, religious) teachings, James nevertheless made room for explicitly religious systems. On an individual level, James thought that ethics consisted of adjudicating the conflict between duty and inclination. His solution was that individuals should perform the duties that led to a more becoming life or made life worth living.

Paul L. Redditt

SEE ALSO: Conversion of one's system of beliefs; Determinism and freedom; Duty; *Human Nature and Conduct*; Morality; Peirce, Charles Sanders; Perry, R. B.; Pluralism; Pragmatism; Royce, Josiah.

Japanese American internment

THE EVENT: Involuntary relocation of Japanese Americans and Japanese residents of the western United States to internment camps during World War II

DATE: 1942-1946

TYPE OF ETHICS: Modern history

SIGNIFICANCE: Japanese Americans were interned en masse in concentration camp-style relocation centers, based strictly on their national origin without due process of law. Although upheld as legal by the U.S. Supreme Court, this wartime practice has since been the subject of extended moral debate and national embarrassment.

On December 7, 1941, the Japanese Empire made a surprise attack on the United States naval base at Pearl Harbor in Hawaii. This action led to a declaration of war by the United States against Japan the next day.

Before 1941, an anti-Orientalist movement existed on the West Coast of the United States. The attack on Pearl Harbor intensified this regional animosity and provided an opportunity to rid the region of this unwanted race. Suspicion ran high against the Japanese living in the United States. Many leaders were arrested, and many others endured personal attacks and violence. Both American-born (Nisei) and Japanese-born (Issei) people of Japanese descent were considered threats simply because of their national origin.

EXECUTIVE ORDER 9066

The California Joint Immigration Committee; the U.S. Army, represented by General John L. DeWitt; the Pacific congressional delegation; and other anti-Japanese organizations recommended that President Franklin D. Roosevelt evacuate the Japanese population. On February 19, 1942, Roosevelt responded with Executive Order 9066, which authorized the secretary of war, or any military commander designated by him, to establish military areas and exclude therefrom any and all persons. DeWitt, commander of the Western Defense Command, became the person responsible for the evacuation under the executive order. This was unfortunate because he was extremely prejudiced against the Japanese.

On March 2, 1942, DeWitt issued Public Proclamation Number One, which defined the West Coast exclusion zone. The western halves of Washington, Oregon, and California became Military Area Number One. All persons of Japanese ancestry living in that area would be relocated in the interest of military necessity. This left opponents of mass evacuation defenseless and brought no opposition from public or civilian leaders, who were forced to accept military authority. It also afforded those of Japanese ancestry a brief period of voluntary relocation. Only a few thousand took this opportunity to move, and they were faced with anti-Japanese feelings wherever they went.

The Wartime Civilian Control Authority (WCCA), a military organization, and the War Relocation Authority (WRA), a civilian agency created by executive order on March 18, 1942, were established to aid

Members of a Japanese American family sharing a barracks room at the Granada relocation center in southeastern Colorado. (National Archives)

in the movement of the evacuees. The WRA had the authority to provide for the relocation of evacuees in appropriate places and to provide for their needs and activities. Milton S. Eisenhower was the WRA's director for the first three months. Both he and his successor, Dillon S. Myer, attempted to find a just way to relocate the Japanese Americans, which won them gratitude from that community. Millions of dollars in property and belongings were lost, however, by the Japanese Americans who were forced to relocate.

After the failure of the voluntary relocation, Eisenhower realized that some form of detention on federally managed, army-guarded land was necessary. In making the decision on internment, the WRA faced the constitutional question of whether it had the legal authority to detain American citizens without bringing charges against them. The Fifth Amendment to the Constitution guaranteed every citizen the rights of life, liberty, and property with due process

of law. The WRA thought, however, that it was justified in forgoing this amendment during wartime as a necessity for national security. The court system supported the relocation argument by virtue of the words "war necessity." Although the United States was at war with Italy and Germany, only a few people of these nationalities were detained.

By late May, 1942, almost 112,000 Japanese Americans were in assembly centers. They were forced from their homes with only what they could carry with them. Assembly centers were hastily set up at fairgrounds, racetracks, and stadiums with barbed wire placed around them. The evacuees spent between six weeks and six months at these temporary centers, until the relocation camps were completed.

RELOCATION CENTERS

A total of 117,116 people were evacuated to assembly or relocation centers or came under some phase of the evacuation program between March 2 and October 31 of 1942. This included 151 persons transferred from the Territory of Alaska to the custody of the WCCA and 504 babies who were born to mothers in assembly areas. Another 1,875 persons were sent from the Territory of Hawaii—1,118 to relocation centers and 757 to Justice Department internment camps. More than 70,000 were American citizens.

Life in the relocation centers was difficult at first. Many families were crowded into hastily erected barracks; living conditions were poor, and supplies were short. After the relocation authorities finally had the logistics worked out, conditions gradually improved. During 1943 and 1944, violence broke out and demonstrations were conducted in the camps to protest the treatment of the internees.

Early in 1943, the situation regarding the Japanese Americans lightened somewhat. Secretary of War Henry L. Stimson announced plans to form a Japanese American combat team made up of Nisei volunteers from the mainland and Hawaii. This unit served with distinction throughout the war. Director Myer wrote a letter to Stimson asking for an immediate relaxation in the West Coast Exclusion Zone, but Stimson rejected it. On March 20, 1943, Myer took the first step in decentralizing the relocation program by authorizing project directors to issue leave permits in cases in which leave clearance had previously been granted by the Washington office.

Finally, on December 17, 1944, the War Department announced the revocation of the West Coast mass exclusion orders of 1942, and the next day Myer announced that all relocation centers would be closed by June 30, 1946. On March 20, 1946, Tule Lake Segregation Center, the last of the WRA centers, was officially closed.

After the war, the government permitted the internees to file claims for losses during internment. The ceilings were low in relationship to the property losses and certainly did not cover the personal humiliation and suffering endured by the internees. In October, 1990, after many years of debate, U.S. Attorney General Dick Thornburgh presented the first reparation checks of $20,000 to those interned during World War II. The government finally admitted that it had been wrong.

Larry N. Sypolt

FURTHER READING

Collins, Donald E. *Native American Aliens, Disloyalty, and the Renunciation of Citizenship by Japanese Americans During World War II*. Contributions in Legal Studies 32. Westport, Conn.: Greenwood Press, 1985.

Hosokawa, Bill. *Nisei: The Quiet Americans*. Rev. ed. Boulder: University Press of Colorado, 2002.

Irons, Peter. *Justice at War.* New York: Oxford University Press, 1983.

Kashima Tetsuden. *Judgment Without Trial: Japanese American Imprisonment During World War II*. Seattle: University of Washington Press, 2003.

Myer, Dillon S. *Uprooted Americans: The Japanese Americans and the War Relocation Authority During World War II*. Tucson: University of Arizona Press, 1971.

U.S. Army. Western Defense Command and Fourth Army. *Final Report: Japanese Evacuation from the West Coast, 1942*. Washington, D.C.: Government Printing Office, 1943.

SEE ALSO: American Civil Liberties Union; Apologizing for past wrongs; Bigotry; Concentration camps; Hiroshima and Nagasaki bombings; Loyalty; Military ethics; Reparations for past social wrongs.

Jealousy

DEFINITION: Hostility toward rivalry or unfaithfulness and the predisposition to suspect rivalry or unfaithfulness; envy.

TYPE OF ETHICS: Personal and social ethics

SIGNIFICANCE: Jealousy is often judged on aesthetic rather than explicitly moral grounds: It is deemed to be an unattractive emotion as much as or more than a strictly sinful one.

Jealousy begins at about the age of two and develops rapidly during the preschool years. An early form of jealousy is sibling rivalry, which consists of feelings of resentment toward a brother or sister. Sibling rivalry is typical between brothers and sisters in a family.

Sibling rivalry is typically higher in cases of same-sex siblings than in cases of opposite-sex siblings. It is also typically higher in cases of smaller age differences; that is, sibling rivalry occurs more between siblings that are less than two years apart than it does between siblings that are more than three years apart. In the former case, the closeness in age probably heightens competition; siblings may prefer the same friends, the same toys, and the same activities. Sibling rivalry is also higher when the siblings have the same interests, and lower when they have different interests. In other words, sibling rivalry may be greater when two sisters are strongly inclined toward mathematics than when one is inclined toward mathematics and the other toward literature. Some sibling rivalry is typical in families, and it often is the first type of jealousy the child experiences.

Jealous feelings are typically caused by insecurity, such as when parents decrease the amount of warmth and attention they give the child and increase the number of prohibitions imposed on the child. Toddlers may show evidence of jealousy by doing such things as wedging themselves between mother and father as they are hugging, hitting a brother whom the mother just kissed, or asking "When are we taking the new baby back to the hospital?" These actions and comments reflect the small child's jealousy.

Parents can minimize the sting of jealousy and sibling rivalry by taking some specific steps. First, they can introduce firstborns early to their new role as "big sister" or "big brother." Telling the child beforehand that a new brother or sister is coming and involving the child in the pregnancy will lessen the impact of sibling rivalry. Second, parents can encourage and reward firstborns for helping in the care of the new baby. Although close supervision is necessary, even young children can be involved in the care of an infant. Third, parents can diminish jealousy and sibling rivalry by discussing the new baby as a person. Examples of helpful comments to a first child are, "She likes her bath, doesn't she?" and, "Look, he's calling you." Fourth, parents can diminish sibling rivalry and jealousy, and foster better relationships between siblings, by refraining from comparing children and, instead, recognizing and valuing each child as an individual. Thus, though some sibling rivalry may be inevitable, it can be increased or decreased by how parents handle the situation.

A later form of jealousy is sexual jealousy, which can occur in a marriage or a sexual relationship, chipping away at the foundations of trust and love that hold the two people together. In relationships in which jealousy occurs, it is sometimes extremely difficult to resolve the problem, because explanations are turned away as untrue and even exacerbate the jealousy.

MONOGAMY AND JEALOUSY

In the United States, the single greatest reason for sexual jealousy is the commonly held standard of sexual exclusivity in monogamous relationships. Most jealousy centers on the belief that the other person is sexually interested in or involved with another person. Typically, one partner plays the role of the jealous one and the other plays the role of the accused.

Other forms of jealousy are nonsexual. Generally, when anything threatens to weaken the relationship bond, jealousy can occur. The result is often possessiveness, which can be either reassuring or suffocating. Feelings of jealousy make a relationship less rewarding and lower the individual's self-esteem.

Jealousy in a relationship can result in several different scenarios. In some cases, the jealousy becomes pervasive, and adults wind up fighting in all related and tangential areas. In other cases, the jealousy represents a more deeply embedded conflict: The partners are in effect denying the deeper conflict by emphasizing the jealousy. In still other cases, the jealousy may play a positive role in the relationship, serving to bring the partners closer together. The beneficial effects, however, are often short-lived.

Adults sometimes act to maximize jealousy in a relationship. They may play intentional games that are aimed at increasing their partners' jealousy. Their hidden agenda in this situation may be to increase their own feelings of security by causing their partners to feel less secure. When surveyed, about 54 percent of adults describe themselves as jealous. Highly jealous people are frequently dependent. They may also harbor feelings of inadequacy and be concerned about sexual exclusiveness.

Jealousy has been successfully treated with systematic desensitization, a technique that involves encouraging the person to relax deeply and then introducing scenarios that are slightly jealousy-provoking. Then, as the person becomes adept at relaxing in these situations, additional scenarios are introduced that are slightly more jealousy-provoking. This process continues until the person has no more feelings of jealousy. This counter-conditioning process is based on the fact that it is impossible to be jealous and highly relaxed at the same time; the two feelings are mutually exclusive.

Lillian M. Range

FURTHER READING

Clanton, Gordon, and Lynn G. Smith, eds. *Jealousy.* Englewood Cliffs, N.J.: Prentice-Hall, 1977.

Kristjánsson, Kristján. *Justifying Emotions: Pride and Jealousy.* New York: Routledge, 2002.

Mathes, E. W., H. E. Adams, and R. M. Davies. "Jealousy: Loss of Relationship Rewards, Loss of Self-Esteem, Depression, Anxiety, and Anger." *Journal of Personality and Social Psychology* 48 (June, 1985): 1552-1561.

Minnet, A. M., D. L. Vandell, and J. W. Santrock. "The Effects of Sibling Status on Sibling Interaction: Influence of Birth Order, Age Spacing, Sex of Child, and Sex of Sibling." *Child Development* 54 (August, 1983): 1064-1072.

Turner, Samuel M., Karen S. Calhoun, and Henry E. Adams, eds. *Handbook of Clinical Behavior Therapy.* 2d ed. New York: Wiley, 1992.

SEE ALSO: Envy; Passions and emotions; Psychology; Sexuality and sexual ethics.

Jefferson, Thomas

IDENTIFICATION: American philosopher and politician

BORN: April 13, 1743, Shadwell, Goochland (now Albemarle) County, Virginia

DIED: July 4, 1826, Monticello, Albemarle County, Virginia

TYPE OF ETHICS: Enlightenment history

SIGNIFICANCE: One of the Founders of the United States, Jefferson served as the nation's third president, wrote the Declaration of Independence, founded the University of Virginia, and worked both publicly and privately to increase and ensure civil rights, public education, religious liberty, and democratic government.

The oldest son of Peter Jefferson and Jane Randolph, Thomas Jefferson was born on the frontier of Virginia. He studied at the College of William and Mary and was admitted to the Virginia Bar, but he chose not to practice law. He inherited approximately 10,000 acres of land, which freed him from having to earn a living. Jefferson served as a Virginia legislator, delegate to the Continental Congress, author of the Declaration of Independence, governor of Virginia, and commissioner to France.

While governor, Jefferson championed freedom of religion and conscience, state-supported public education, and gradual emancipation. He suggested the principles, including the subsidization of public education and the prohibition of slavery, for the Northwest Ordinance, which organized the Northwest Territory. Upon Jefferson's return from France in 1789, George Washington appointed him secretary of state. Jefferson left the Washington administration and formed the opposition Democratic Republican Party during the administration of John Adams. Jefferson was elected president of the United States in 1800 and 1804. In 1803 he purchased the Louisiana Territory. A principal problem of his administrations was the defense of neutral rights on the seas during the Napoleonic Wars. He used the policy of economic coercion in that struggle.

Robert D. Talbott

SEE ALSO: Church-state separation; Civil rights and liberties; Declaration of Independence; Human rights; Nature, rights of; Sedition Act of 1798.

Jesus Christ

IDENTIFICATION: Religious teacher

BORN: c. 6 B.C.E., Bethlehem, Judaea (now in Palestine)

DIED: 30 C.E., Jerusalem (now in Israel)

TYPE OF ETHICS: Religious ethics

SIGNIFICANCE: Jesus Christ was the originator of Christianity, which regards him as the son of God. He taught that love is the supreme value and that sin may be redeemed through sincere repentance.

Jesus taught ethics in the context of first century Judaism, which had both the (Old Testament) Scriptures and a long tradition of interpretation. He based his teaching on Scripture and sometimes used basic principles of reason to refute opposing interpretations.

Jesus' method and message often clashed with those of other Jewish scholars, as when he violated the detailed commandments of their venerated tradition of scriptural interpretation in order to keep the spirit of the original scriptural commandment. For this he was condemned by many Pharisees, who were teacher-scholars. In one incident, Jesus taught that eliminating human suffering on the Sabbath did not violate the spirit of the command that Israel rest on that day (Matt. 12:10-13). He condemned those who scrupulously donated one-tenth of their property to the point of counting grains of spice yet overlooked the "weightier" matters of the law, such as justice, mercy, and faithfulness (Matt. 23:22). He also condemned as hypocritical teachers who allowed religious duty to cover violations of the spirit of the law, such as those who taught that property "dedicated" to God need not be used to care for one's parents (Mark 7:11-13).

JESUS' MORAL PRECEPTS

Jesus focused on attitudes as the sources of action: From the heart come sins such as theft, murder, and envy (Mark 7:21-22). Thus, murder is wrong, but so are anger and contempt. Adultery is wrong, but so is lust (Matt. 5:22, 28).

Jesus taught that love should dominate one's inward attitudes. Insofar as all morality can be summed up, it can be reduced to the command to love God and others. To Jesus, love was a commitment to the good of another regardless of that person's attitudes or actions toward one. It should extend even to one's enemies, since God loves even those who are evil. Doing to others what one would want them to do to one (Matt. 7:12), the "golden rule," requires service to others and excludes apathy and self-centeredness. The conviction that God actively loves people in this way can give believers courage and dispel anxiety (Matt. 8:26; 6:26, 30).

Jesus showed that a leader should exemplify this loving attitude by seeking to serve, not by trying to dominate or to gain wealth or fame. More than once he reproved the apostles who sought exalted positions, and he himself washed his disciples' feet as an example of humble service (John 13:5). He regarded his very life as a sacrifice for human sin that would al-low righteousness to be graciously attributed to those who sought forgiveness from God. Humble confession and faith in God's gracious forgiveness provide access to divine mercy for moral failure.

A person who loves others and believes that God is loving can be free from concern about personal rights. The response to a slap on the cheek, a lawsuit, or the compulsion to carry another's load can be turning the other cheek, giving up more than the plaintiff asked for, and voluntarily carrying a load an extra distance (Matt. 5:38-42). After all, life is short, and someday everyone will be confronted with the absolute rule of God.

The rule of God creates paradoxes that defy conventional moral wisdom. The meek, not the assertive, will inherit the earth (Matt. 5:5). Those who try to exalt themselves will be humbled, whereas those who humble themselves will be exalted. Those who sacrifice for the good of others will find happiness themselves.

JESUS' WAY OF LIFE

Jesus motivated people with rewards, but not always the sort that would appeal to a selfish person. Those who do such things as love their enemies and lend expecting nothing in return will receive a "great reward" and will be true "sons of the Most High" (Luke 6:35). Jesus also said that people will generally give back what one gives them and more; "shaken down, pressed together, and running over" (Luke 6:38). Although this should motivate people to do good, they should be willing to "take up the cross," a symbol of complete renunciation of personal or worldly gain. The mature person acts out of pure love for others and a desire to emulate a morally pure and altruistic God.

Jesus voluntarily lived in poverty, but he did not condemn ownership. He advocated the compassionate use of private wealth: Those with means should be quick to share with those in need. Herein lies a profound difference between Jesus' teaching and various types of communism, which seek to eliminate private ownership as the solution to society's fundamental problems.

Jesus rejected insurrection as a means to effect change and was a disappointment to those who sought political or military deliverance for Israel. He did not confront the Roman methods of taxation or slavery, but in the ancient world he was radical regarding the treatment of women, as Paul Jewett shows in *Man as Male and Female* (1975). While living in a society that treated women little better than animals, he treated women with seriousness and dignity. He allowed them to follow his itinerant band and to serve tables, a function previously reserved for men. Domestic chores provided material for a number of parables. He confronted the double standard that allowed men but not women to divorce on a pretense; furthermore, he affirmed marriage as a lifelong commitment, breakable only in the case of serious sexual sin.

Jesus' ethics were moderate in that he advocated neither asceticism nor indulgence, neither legalism nor license. Yet he was passionate about righteousness and even chased officially sanctioned profiteers out of the Jerusalem temple with a hastily improvised scourge (John 2:15). He lived and taught devotion to God as expressed in a life of self-sacrificing love.

Brian K. Morley

FURTHER READING

Briggs, Charles Augustus. *The Ethical Teaching of Jesus*. New York: Charles Scribner's Sons, 1904.

Bruce, A. B. *The Training of the Twelve*. 4th ed. New Canaan, Conn.: Keats, 1979.

New American Standard Bible. Reference ed. Nashville, Tenn.: Holman, 1981.

Scott, Ernest F. *The Ethical Teaching of Jesus*. 1924. Reprint. New York: Macmillan, 1936.

Spohn, William C. *Go and Do Likewise: Jesus and Ethics*. New York: Continuum, 1999.

Stalker, James. *The Ethic of Jesus According to the Synoptic Gospels*. New York: Hodder & Stoughton, 1909.

Stassen, Glen H., and David P. Gushee. *Kingdom Ethics: Following Jesus in Contemporary Context*. Downers Grove, Ill.: InterVarsity Press, 2003.

SEE ALSO: Asceticism; Bonhoeffer, Dietrich; Christian ethics; Divine command theory; God; Messianism; Moses; Pacifism; *Summa Theologica*; Ten Commandments.

Jewish ethics

DEFINITION: Ethical traditions and systems of religious Judaism

TYPE OF ETHICS: Religious ethics

SIGNIFICANCE: Jewish ethics was the first to define morality in the context of a covenant or sacred contract that is equally binding upon both humans and God, and therefore to see God as not only the source of morality but also as a subject of moral obligation. It is founded upon an understanding of moral law as something to be interpreted and debated rather than univocally pronounced and automatically followed.

Jewish ethics is based on the premise that the Jewish people are in a covenant relationship with God. This covenant demands that society be organized and personal lives be conducted in accordance with God's revelation. As a result, Jewish ethics has generally been understood to be a matter of *imitatio Dei* and to have as its characteristic form legal discourse. Thus, Jewish ethical literature moves between two poles. On one hand, it stresses adherence to a certain life-regimen as spelled out in Jewish law (*halachah*), while on the other, it calls for the cultivation through this lifestyle of character traits, attitudes, and intentions that help the individual to be more godlike.

Although the earliest literature of Rabbinic Judaism (from the first century through the seventh century) is devoted almost exclusively to developing Jewish law, the importance of proper attitude and intention is not ignored. The late Mishnaic book *Pirqe Avot* ("Chapters of the Fathers"), edited in the third century, is a collection of moral aphorisms stressing the importance of honesty and selflessness in dealing with others and the need to act responsibly in the world.

These attitudes are given more formal recognition in the Talmuds (from the fifth century through the seventh century). Made up largely of real and hypothetical case law, the Talmudic literature not only illustrates how the letter of the law is to be understood and applied but also recognizes that there is a moral duty that goes beyond what the law requires. This extra-legal duty is referred to as *lifnim mishurat hadin* ("beyond the edge of the law"). In some instances (*Baba Metzia* 30b, for example), the Babylonian Talmud seems to regard such going beyond the call of duty to be not merely supererogation but an expectation that rests on all Jews.

MIDDLE AGES

During the Middle Ages, Jewish ethics took three different forms: the further development of Jewish law, philosophical speculation on the nature of the moral life, and the cultivation of humility and other beneficial character traits. The first was largely a result of the practical application of received Jewish law to new situations. In this connection, rabbis from the eighth century on created a large literature devoted to identifying and understanding the principles and values that were to guide them in their legal deliberations. Despite the diversity of situations, certain common principles seem to emerge from the practical application of Rabbinic law: the overriding imperative to protect human life; the importance of avoiding even the appearance of idolatry; and the values of sexual modesty, education, and child rearing.

Philosophical speculation on the nature of morality began in earnest among Jewish scholars with the rise of philosophical schools in the Islamic world. For the most part, Jewish philosophers from the ninth century on adopted the major philosophical principles and conclusions of Islamic scholars and applied them more or less directly to Judaism. Early writers such as Saadia Gaon in his *Book of Beliefs and Opinions* stressed that God's word as given in the Hebrew Scripture and interpreted by the rabbis is the only reliable source of truth.

Since God's law is fully known and since people have free will, Saadia argues, each individual bears full responsibility for acting in accord with God's word. Subsequent Judeo-Arabic philosophers, influenced by Arabic Neoplatonism, claimed that the true reward of the soul lay in contemplating the divine.

Jewish men, many wearing prayer shawls, pray in front of the Western, or "Wailing," Wall in Jerusalem's Old City during the annual priestly blessing in April, 2004. The wall is the holiest site in Judaism and many Jews believe in making pilgrimages to Jerusalem three times a year. (AP/Wide World Photos)

Adherence to Jewish law was the necessary first step in directing the soul toward a fuller apprehension of the divine. This line of thought reached its culmination in the Jewish neo-Aristotelians such as Moses ben Maimon (also known as Maimonides). In his *Eight Chapters*, Maimonides argues that actualizing the potential of the rational soul depends on proper discipline of the body and that such a discipline is precisely what is spelled out in the *halachah*.

Finally, pietistic writings attempted to instill in the readers moral sensitivity beyond mere obedience to the *halachah* and the contemplation of its principles. In some cases, these writings take the form of ethical wills, testimonies bequeathed to children by dying parents or relatives. These wills usually stress the importance of study, humility, and charity. In other cases, whole sects appeared that encouraged members to practice a life that was holier than that lived by the majority of the Jewish population. The Hasidai Ashkenaz of thirteenth century northern Germany is such a group. Its view of the moral life is spelled out in *Sefer Hasidim*. Similar ideas seemed to have influenced the Hasidic movement that sprang up in Eastern Europe during the mid-eighteenth century. Many early Hasidic stories presume that true virtue stems from the intention of the soul and at times may even run counter to the formal demands of *halachah*. The ethical writings of Hasidism have influenced such modern Jewish moral philosophers as Martin Buber, Abraham Joshua Heschel, and Elie Wiesel.

Modern Judaism

In modern times, Jewish ethical speculation has again drawn heavily on the philosophical currents of the day. Modern Jewish movements (Orthodoxy, Conservative Judaism, and Reform Judaism), which have their roots in nineteenth century Germany, have been heavily influenced by the writings of Immanuel Kant. Modern Jewish thought has argued that simply following the letter of Jewish law out of habit is not sufficient. Instead, one must choose to abide by the *halachah* purely for its own sake or because it is one's duty to conform to God's will. More recently, Reform and Conservative rabbis in particular have struggled to identify the rational and universal ideals behind the *halachah* as a basis for approaching ethical dilemmas posed by new technologies.

Peter J. Haas

Further Reading

Dorff, Elliot N. *Love Your Neighbor and Yourself: A Jewish Approach to Modern Personal Ethics*. Philadelphia: Jewish Publication Society, 2003.

Dorff, Elliot N., and Arthur Rosett. *A Living Tree: The Roots and Growth of Jewish Law*. Albany, N.Y.: SUNY Press, 1988.

Kellner, Menahem Marc, ed. *Contemporary Jewish Ethics*. New York: Sanhedrin Press, 1978.

Luz, Ehud. *Wrestling with an Angel: Power, Morality, and Jewish Identity*. Translated by Michael Swirsky. New Haven, Conn.: Yale University Press, 2003.

Novak, David. *Jewish Social Ethics*. New York: Oxford University Press, 1992.

Samuelson, Norbert M. *An Introduction to Modern Jewish Philosophy*. Albany, N.Y.: SUNY Press, 1989.

Siegel, Seymour, ed. *Conservative Judaism and Jewish Law*. New York: Rabbinical Assembly, 1977.

Spero, Shubert. *Morality, Halakha and the Jewish Tradition*. New York: KTAV, 1983.

See also: Anti-Semitism; Buber, Martin; Ethical monotheism; Hasidism; Hebrew Bible; *I and Thou*; Moses; Religion; Talmud; Ten Commandments; Torah.

Jihad

Definition: Arabic term for a holy war fought in behalf of Islam as a religious duty

Type of ethics: Religious ethics

Significance: In the late twentieth century the jihad began gaining increased international attention as Muslim groups and individuals used arms to oppose Israel, the West, and even other Muslims.

Islam is an exclusivist religion, and its followers are obligated to protect its principles against adversaries and to broaden the religion's boundaries. Such efforts have drawn many communities into armed conflict. During the centuries of expansion after the founding of Islam in the seventh century, the new religion spread across North Africa, into Spain, Yugoslavia, and eastern and central Asia, and as far east as

Indonesia. While Islam's spread into Mesopotamia and Persia resulted in Muslim military control and many willing converts to the religion, its spread into India resulted in conflict. There Hinduism was put on the defensive, and Buddhism was all but obliterated.

In 732 Charles Martel thwarted Islam's drive into Western Europe at the Battle of Tours. More important, the Christian Crusades of the eleventh and twelfth centuries pitted European Christians against Muslims in Palestine, and resulted in continued Muslim hegemony there. In that struggle jihad became an ethical obligation, in effect, a sixth principle, or "pillar" of Islam. During the fall of the Byzantine Empire in 1453, the capital city, Constantinople, fell to Muslims and became the seat of the Ottoman Empire until that empire's own fall after World War I. During the subsequent spread of Western European colonial rule into the Middle East, Muslim lands came under the control of non-Muslim countries. Nevertheless, Muslim scholars concluded that unless Islam was prohibited jihad was not permissible.

In 1948, Middle Eastern Muslims opposed the creation of the modern state of Israel in what was then called Palestine. Their efforts to recapture Israel in the so-called Six-Day War in 1967 ended in an embarrassing defeat. Chief among their losses was control over Jerusalem, the site of the third holiest sanctuary in Islam. Muslim militants called faithful Muslims to jihad to regain control over the city and other land taken by Israel. Israel's supporters were then portrayed as suitable targets for jihad. Some Muslims hailed the terrorist attacks on the Pentagon and World Trade Center on September 11, 2001, as appropriate recompense for American actions hostile to Islam. The U.S.-led war in Iraq begun in 2003 simply fueled that fire for many Muslims.

Muslims have long warred against one another. One Muslim reaction to European colonialism was to attempt to copy Western powers by adopting technology and by establishing Western-type democratic states that tolerate all religions. In Iran that attempt met disaster in the overthrow of the government of the shah and establishment of a strict Muslim state governed according to the Qurʾān. The Taliban established the same type of government in Afghanistan, and many observers thought that similar developments could occur in other Muslim countries.

Paul L. Redditt

FURTHER READING

Cole, Juan. *Sacred Space and Holy War: The Politics, Culture, and History of Shiʿite Islam.* London: I. B. Tauris, 2002.

Denny, Frederick Mathewson. *An Introduction to Islam.* 2d ed. New York: Macmillan, 1994.

Esposito, John L. *The Islamic Threat: Myth or Reality?* New York: Oxford University Press, 1999.

Keppel, Gilles. *Jihad: The Trail of Political Islam.* Cambridge, Mass.: Belknap Press of Harvard University Press, 2002.

Ojeda, Auriana. *Islamic Fundamentalism.* San Diego: Greenhaven Press, Thomson/Gale, 2003.

SEE ALSO: Islamic ethics; Israeli-Palestinian conflict; Just war theory; Muḥammad; Qurʾān; Religion and violence; Terrorism.

Journalistic entrapment

DEFINITION: Use of an undercover investigation to lure subjects into compromising or illegal acts they would not otherwise commit

TYPE OF ETHICS: Media ethics

SIGNIFICANCE: Reporters investigating wrongdoing may inadvertently or intentionally corrupt innocent people or cause the commission of crimes that would not otherwise have occurred.

Investigative journalism was propelled into prominence during the 1970's as a result of the Watergate scandal uncovered by *The Washington Post*, the leaking of the Pentagon Papers to *The New York Times*, and the general adversarial tone that characterized the relationship between government and the media throughout the Vietnam War. In subsequent years, technological advancements and the proliferation of broadcast shows that relied on videotape footage to document undercover findings swelled both the number and the scope of such investigations. Issues subject to such treatments have included home and commercial lending practices, nursing home care, governmental corruption, abortion practices, and military information confirmation.

The Federal Bureau of Investigation (FBI) and other law enforcement agencies frequently use undercover operations to expose criminal wrongdoing. Their activities, unlike those in journalism, are subject to explicit guidelines and legal restrictions that help to establish the line between legitimate investigative work and coercing or abetting in the commission of a crime. For journalists, however, that line is largely one of interpretation because of the broad latitude and significant freedoms offered by the First Amendment. It is incumbent upon journalists, therefore, to wrestle with a number of ethical considerations, such as the morality of devising an enticement for illegal activity and the awareness that reporters themselves may become, if even indirectly, agents of wrongdoing.

Industry misgivings about the practice exist, as revealed in the Pulitzer Prize committee's reluctance to recognize stories that rely on undercover investigations because of their deceptive nature. The usage continues, however, because of the journalistic belief that news organizations have an overriding obligation to distribute information to a democratic society and a moral responsibility to consider society's needs, thereby providing the greatest good for the greatest number of people. This approach, with its emphasis on consequences, accepts the belief that the end justifies the means. Therefore, the media's "watchdog role" in preserving and protecting the public interest—a good and moral end—is justified in its aggressive pursuit of certain undercover investigations. Because the journalism profession also professes a strong commitment to accuracy and truthfulness, however, any use of deception must be carefully weighed.

INTEGRITY OF THE PRESS

Recognizing that integrity is its greatest asset, the press is especially vigilant in upholding standards that do not erode or detract from its credibility, including the use of deception. Because codes of ethics among the media are more advisory than mandatory, however, much of the decision is left to interpretation by individual journalists who adjudge the specifics of individual situations. The long-standing reliance on consequential reasoning has typically emphasized the social benefit derived from an undercover investigation. For example, a series entitled "Abortion Profiteers" by the *Chicago Sun-Times* in November, 1978, relied on information obtained by reporters who, obscuring their identity as journalists, went to

work for several outpatient abortion clinics where gross negligence as well as medical misconduct had been reported. The articles resulted in a number of new state laws regulating outpatient abortion clinics, the closing of two of the four clinics under investigation (one of them permanently), and the imprisonment of one doctor. Several other doctors left the state.

It was agreed by the editors and reporters involved that the overwhelming benefit to the community of such an investigation outweighed the price of the deception. Another case involving a different publication, however, reveals that a positive outcome is not the only measure in weighing the ethical considerations of going undercover. In 1988, *Newsday* conceived and planned—but did not execute—an undercover investigation designed to confirm the suspected practice of real estate "steering," a method of maintaining racially segregated neighborhoods by directing potential buyers only to those areas already populated by people of the same race. After a year of preliminary work, management decided that the operation was logistically untenable and that the same information could be obtained through other methods, such as interviews with buyers and real estate records. Anthony Marro, the editor at the time, also questioned the existence of probable cause, wondering if the appropriate level of presumed bad conduct merited the use of entrapment techniques.

The Society of Professional Journalists, whose code of ethics is widely invoked by individual journalists and news organizations, in 1993 introduced a new approach to ethical decision making that combined the long-used consequential reasoning with an effort to examine a number of other factors, such as the characteristics of the situation, as well as journalistic values, loyalties, and professional principles. In addition, the new code set forth a number of conditions, all of which must be met to justify deceptive information-gathering strategies:

1. The information sought must be of profound importance.

2. Other alternatives have been exhausted.

3. The reporter is willing to make public the deception.

4. Excellence has been pursued through full allocation of the news organization's resources.

5. The harm prevented by the deception outweighs the harm of the deception.

793

6. Conscious, thoughtful, moral, ethical, and professional deliberations have been made.

In addition, the revised code outlined specific rationalizations that do not meet ethical standards and may not be used to justify the use of deception. These include

1. Winning a prize.
2. Beating the competition.
3. Saving costs or time.
4. Others have "already done it."
5. The subjects, themselves, are unethical.

Out of concern for their role as protectors of the public interest, journalists avoid concrete rules regarding the use of deception and undercover operations. They maintain the right to use such tactics ethically and morally on a situational basis when a greater good is served and when other methods have been exhausted.

Regina Howard Yaroch

FURTHER READING

Black, Jay, Bob Steele, and Ralph Barney. *Doing Ethics in Journalism: A Handbook with Case Studies*. Greencastle, Ind.: Sigma Delta Chi Foundation and the Society of Professional Journalists, 1993.

Bovee, Warren G. "The End Can Justify the Means—But Rarely." *Journal of Mass Media Ethics* 6, no. 3 (1991): 135-145.

"Cases and Commentaries: The Norfolk Abortion Case." *Journal of Mass Media Ethics* 5, no 2. (1990): 136-145.

Christians, Clifford G., et al. *Media Ethics: Cases and Moral Reasoning*. 5th ed. New York: Longman, 1998.

Dufresne, Marcel. "To Sting or Not to Sting?" *Columbia Journalism Review* 30 (May/June 1991): 49-51.

Englehardt, Elaine E., and Ralph D. Barney. *Media and Ethics: Principles for Moral Decisions*. Belmont, Calif.: Wadsworth Thomson Learning, 2002.

McQuail, Denis. *Media Accountability and Freedom of Publication*. Oxford, England: Oxford University Press, 2003.

SEE ALSO: Internet chat rooms; Journalistic ethics; News sources; Photojournalism; Tabloid journalism.

Journalistic ethics

DEFINITION: Formal and informal professional codes of conduct governing the practice of journalism

TYPE OF ETHICS: Media ethics

SIGNIFICANCE: Journalistic ethics seeks to balance the public's right to know with the moral responsibility of individual journalists to be truthful, objective, and fair both in their reporting and in their work to uncover and develop information. Moreover, because the First Amendment dictates that the press be virtually unregulated by the government and legal system, there is a greater than average need for journalists to regulate themselves.

Unlike doctors and lawyers, journalists do not control who may practice in their field or police their own ranks; neither do they prescribe a body of knowledge with which those entering the field must be familiar. In this sense, journalists do not fit within the traditional definition of a "profession." Nevertheless, responsible journalists—like members of these other professions—do adhere to a set of occupational principles, many of which are addressed in the ethical code (the "Code") of Sigma Delta Chi, the Society of Professional Journalists.

RESPONSIBILITY AND FREEDOM OF THE PRESS

The first three sections of the professional code concern what many journalists regard as their occupational imperative: to observe a constitutional mandate to serve the public's right to know. Such a right is not, in fact, explicitly stated in the Constitution and has been discounted by such eminent legal authorities as former Chief Justice Warren Burger. Other media critics point to abuses—such as invasion of privacy and interference with the right to a fair trial—stemming from overzealous pursuit of the journalistic mission. Still, courts have consistently upheld the media's First Amendment rights, which are regarded as so central to the nation's democratic principles that they can overcome—as they did during the 1971 "Pentagon Papers" case, *United States v. New York Times Company*—a countervailing concern as compelling as national security.

The Pentagon Papers case illustrates the code's precept that "[journalists] will make constant effort to assure that the public's business is conducted in public and that public records are open to public inspection." Other, less august, journalistic exercises, such as traffic reports and celebrity gossip, illustrate not so much the public's right to know as its need or desire to know. In such contexts, there is perhaps less justification for the kind of aggressive, sometimes invasive techniques employed by journalists.

ACCURACY, FAIRNESS, AND OBJECTIVITY

It would seem fundamental—and the professional code takes it for granted—that one of a journalist's primary duties is to report truth rather than falsehoods. Yet the news business has always been plagued with so-called "yellow journalism," which distorts or exaggerates facts in order to create sensationalism and attract consumers. In this sense, the blatant jingoism of William Randolph Hearst's papers during the 1890's is not unrelated to attempts on the part of modern television broadcasters to dramatize news through fictionalized "reenactments." Public skepticism about television news rose to new levels during the 2004 U.S. Presidential campaign, when CBS News was accused of using falsified documents to cast doubt on President Bush's service record in the National Guard during the 1970's.

Another method by which journalists can take liberties with the truth is through misattribution or misquotation. Although the plaintiff in *Westmoreland v. Columbia Broadcasting System* (1984), General William C. Westmoreland, commander of United States troops in Vietnam during the late 1960's, ultimately lost his libel action against CBS, the defendant clearly played fast and loose with the truth by deliberately misrepresenting a damaging cable regarding the deadly Tet offensive as Westmoreland's. In 1990, however, the Supreme Court permitted psychoanalyst Jeffrey Masson to proceed with his lawsuit against *New Yorker* magazine writer Janet Malcolm because her allegedly purposeful misquotation of him (for example, that he intended to turn the Freud Archives into "a place of sex, women, fun") could be libel.

Ironically, it was Malcolm herself, in her book about the relationship between convicted murderer Jeffrey MacDonald and his journalist/chronicler Joe McGinniss, who pinpointed one of the primary reasons that journalists sometimes violate the ethical imperative of fairness emphasized in the code: "The moral ambiguity of journalism lies not in its texts but in the relationships out of which they arise—relationships that are invariably and inescapably lopsided."

Malcolm's contention is that McGinniss insinuated himself into MacDonald's confidence in order to obtain exclusive information and then betrayed him by writing a damning portrait of him. Seen in this light, MacDonald is just as culpable as the reporter who fails to protect the confidentiality of his sources. If this evaluation is accurate—and if Jeffrey Masson's allegations about Malcolm are accurate—then clearly both McGinniss and Malcolm have violated the code's tenet that "Journalists at all times will show respect for the dignity, privacy, rights and well-being of people encountered in the course of gathering and presenting the news."

Just as MacDonald and Malcolm could be accused of not playing fair, they could also stand accused of bias, of failing to observe the journalistic objectivity that the code requires. They could, alternatively, be seen to be overcompensating for the intimate access they had to their respective subjects. The code states that "Journalists must be free of obligation to any interest other than the public's right to know." The most obvious interpretation of this precept is that journalists should not compromise their integrity by accepting payoffs. It can also be seen, however, to apply to situations such as McGinniss's and Malcolm's and to journalist-celebrities, who can themselves influence and even become the stories they cover.

Most ethical principles espoused in the code are simply restatements of common sense and courtesy. Because of the media's ability to influence and shape society, however, it is of particular importance that purveyors of news take seriously not only their First Amendment rights but also their moral obligations.

Carl Rollyson

FURTHER READING

Adams, Julian. *Freedom and Ethics in the Press.* New York: R. Rosen Press, 1983.

Elliott, Deni, ed. *Responsible Journalism.* Beverly Hills, Calif.: Sage, 1986.

Englehardt, Elaine E., and Ralph D. Barney. *Media and Ethics: Principles for Moral Decisions.* Belmont, Calif.: Wadsworth Thomson Learning, 2002.

Fink, Conrad C. *Media Ethics: In the Newsroom and Beyond.* New York: McGraw-Hill, 1988.

McQuail, Denis. *Media Accountability and Freedom of Publication.* Oxford, England: Oxford University Press, 2003.

Merrill, John C., and Ralph D. Barney, eds. *Ethics and the Press: Readings in Mass Media Morality.* New York: Hastings House, 1975.

Olen, Jeffrey. *Ethics in Journalism.* Englewood Cliffs, N.J.: Prentice-Hall, 1988.

See also: Accuracy in Media; Libel; News sources; Pentagon Papers; Privacy; Tabloid journalism.

Judicial conduct code

Definition: Ethical rules adopted in most American jurisdictions to govern the conduct of judges
Type of ethics: Legal and judicial ethics
Significance: The Model Code of Judicial Conduct seeks to preserve the integrity and independence of judges by prohibiting them from being influ-

enced by family, social, political, or other relationships in the conduct of their official business.

Since the early twentieth century the American Bar Association (ABA) has attempted to develop guidelines for judicial conduct. The ABA adopted the Canons of Judicial Ethics in 1924 and the Model Code of Judicial Conduct in 1972. The ABA substantially amended this code in 1990, and a significant number of states adopted the amended code to regulate the conduct of judges in their jurisdictions.

In some cases the code requires that judges disqualify themselves from participation in cases in which their impartiality might reasonably be questioned. In addition, the code prohibits conduct that might otherwise be classified as private or personal when such conduct risks undermining the integrity of the judiciary. For example, judges are prohibited from belonging to organizations that practice inappropriate discrimination on the basis of race, sex, religion, or national origin. In general, the code requires that judges conduct their nonjudicial affairs in such a way as to minimize conflicts with their judicial obligations.

Timothy L. Hall

See also: Adversary system; American Inns of Court; Attorney misconduct; Jurisprudence; Law; Legal ethics; Professional ethics; Supreme Court, U.S.

The Ethics of Socializing

Questions about the ethical conduct of judges in the United States reached the highest level in early 2003, when Supreme Court justice Antonin Scalia drew criticism for spending too much time socializing with power brokers and other high-level government officials. In the past, Supreme Court justices commonly acted as legal advisers to presidents. However, during the late twentieth century, greater sensitivity to the need for maintaining the separation of powers effectively ended that practice. Journalists, legal experts, and members of special interest groups all began questioning the propriety of justices becoming too friendly with people who might have important interests in cases that reach the Supreme Court. Justice Scalia was criticized especially strongly for spending too much time socialized with Vice President Dick Cheney. The Sierra Club was especially uneasy about Scalia's going on a hunting trip with Cheney only three weeks after the Supreme Court agreed to hear a case concerning Cheney's energy task force. It was believed that the negative attention that Scalia was drawing caused judges at all levels throughout the United States to review their own conduct.

Jung, Carl

Identification: Swiss psychologist
Born: July 26, 1875, Kesswil, Switzerland
Died: June 6, 1961, Küsnacht, Switzerland
Type of ethics: Modern history
Significance: The founder of analytical psychology, Jung approached ethical questions as medical problems concerning the mind. He believed mental health could be cultivated by bringing disturbing elements of the unconscious self to consciousness.

Jung studied medicine in Basel and psychiatry in Zurich. He collaborated for a time with Sigmund Freud but founded his own school of analytical psychology

Carl Jung. (Library of Congress)

in 1914. Jung's theory of the conscious personality, or ego, differentiates between the extroverted, or outgoing, personality, and the introverted, or inward-turning type. Both types of conscious personality are influenced by the unconscious self, which has two levels: the personal and the collective.

The personal unconscious includes knowledge that is too obvious to become conscious, together with repressed ideas and emotions that are too painful for conscious thought. The personal unconscious grows through individual experience, but the way it grows, Jung believed, is conditioned by the collective unconscious, which is common to all people.

The personal unconscious is found to include elements such as the old wise man and the earth mother, which appear, with variations, in dreams and myths all over the world. Jung called these elements archetypes and considered them inherited structures of the collective unconscious that condition the ways in which experience enters consciousness.

SEE ALSO: Freud, Sigmund; Psychology; Psychopharmacology.

Jurisprudence

DEFINITION: Philosophy of law
TYPE OF ETHICS: Legal and judicial ethics
SIGNIFICANCE: Jurisprudence is concerned with the nature and derivation of legal principles. It seeks both to understand why specific laws exist in specific forms, and to ascertain how they should be changed to better conform with a given social system or the requirements of justice.

Jurisprudence is the science of law; namely, that science that seeks to ascertain the principles on which legal rules are based, in order to not only classify those rules in their proper order and to show their relationships, but also to settle the manner in which new or doubtful cases should be brought under the appropriate rules. When a new or doubtful case arises out of two or more equally applicable rules, it is the function of jurisprudence to consider the ultimate effect if each rule were to be applied to an indefinite number of similar cases and to choose the rule that, when so applied, would produce the greatest advantage to the community.

Jurisprudence forms the basis for precedents, which provide the foundation for most judicial decision making, since most judges use the doctrine of *stare decisis* ("let the decision stand") to make future decisions based on precedents formed from past decisions. Jurisprudence, defined as the philosophy of law, deals with the legal reasoning behind the making of law and the decisions that judges make. Therefore, it has an overwhelming impact on society.

According to the nineteenth century English philosopher John Austin, there are two basic philosophies of jurisprudential reasoning, or patterns of jurisprudential thought. These philosophies of jurisprudential reasoning are analytical jurisprudence (known as positive law) and normative jurisprudence. Analytical jurisprudence studies the law as it actually is. It seeks to interpret, clarify, classify, and arrange in a legally systematic order actual legal concepts and doctrines. According to the analytical theory of jurisprudence, concepts of morality are totally distinct from one another. To legal positivists, such as Austin, the law is a matter of what is simply laid down, or posited, by the legislature, regardless of its moral status. A speed limit is an example of a positive law.

The other school, or pattern of jurisprudential thought, is normative jurisprudence, which concerns what the law should be. It subjects legal doctrines to moral evaluation and criticism in the name of social reform and justice. According to this theory, concepts of law and justice are equally related. For example, laws related to the constitutional principles that ban the use of cruel and unusual punishment, unreasonable searches and seizures, and denial of equal protection under the law, which cry out for moral interpretation, are more likely to be solved under the theory of normative jurisprudence than they are under the theory of analytical jurisprudence. One example of this can be found in *Brown v. Board of Education* (1954), which overturned the 1896 *Plessy v. Ferguson* decision.

The doctrine of *stare decisis* and the theory of analytical jurisprudence would have upheld the decision that the separate-but-equal theory of segregation was constitutional. Upon much criticism and examination of the moral and ethical issues involved in segregation, however, the U.S. Supreme Court overturned precedent, declaring that the U.S. Constitution is color-blind and that all U.S. citizens are entitled to equal protection before the law, regardless of the color of their skin. Some legal philosophers will say that moral, societal, and ethical evolution cried out for the overturning of the antiabortion laws of all fifty states, as was done in *Roe v. Wade*, an example of normative jurisprudence that gave women equal rights under the law. Normative jurisprudence is much more activist than is analytical jurisprudence, and judges who practice it create more law according to the needs of the particular case than do judges who adhere to the analytical philosophy of jurisprudence.

There are several other schools of jurisprudential thought that influence judges in their reasoning, from U.S. Supreme Court justices to county court judges. They are the natural law theory, the historical conception theory of law, the sociological conception school of jurisprudence, the realist conception theory of law, the economic conception theory of law, and the critical conception school of jurisprudence. The natural law theory states that law is ordained by nature. Higher principles exist independent of human experience. Natural law exists as an ideal condition that is either inherent in human nature or is derived from a divine source. Just as ethical standards transcend legal standards, natural law transcends human notions of what is right and just.

The historical school of jurisprudence defines law as an embodiment of society's customs. Historical jurisprudence asserts that customs are the chief manifestation of the law and that law evolves with social development. Sociological conception jurisprudence defines law in terms of present human conduct. The law, according to sociological jurisprudence, is the sum of what the lawbooks permit and what human nature provides. A realist conception of justice is that the law is only what is actually enforced. For example, if a speed limit is 55 miles per hour, that is technically the law. If the police do not pull people over unless they are driving 65 miles per hour, however, then, to the legal realist, the law is not 55 miles per hour but 65 miles per hour.

The economic conception of law is that the U.S. Constitution is merely an economic document that was written to ensure citizens economic freedom from the government. Therefore, every decision must be looked at in the light of how a law or statute or judicial decree will affect the economic freedom of the citizens. The critical conception of jurisprudence is involved with literary criticism and is not as publicized or as frequently used in jurisprudential decision making as are the other types of jurisprudence.

All these forms of jurisprudential reasoning are used by every judge, but most judges have a particular pattern or philosophy that guides their decision making. The ethical dilemmas involved in jurisprudence involve determining which applications of which concepts of jurisprudence allow that judge to fulfill his or her moral and vocational responsibilities to society while defining the standards that the society's members must meet when interacting with one another.

Amy Bloom

FURTHER READING

Bodenheimer, Edgar. *Jurisprudence: The Philosophy and Method of the Law.* Rev. ed. Cambridge, Mass.: Harvard University Press, 1974.

Cotterrell, Roger. *The Politics of Jurisprudence: A Critical Introduction to Legal Philosophy.* 2d ed. London: LexisNexis UK, 2003.

Dworkin, R. M. *A Matter of Principle.* Cambridge, Mass.: Harvard University Press, 1985.

Hart, H. L. *Essays in Jurisprudence and Philosophy.* Oxford, England: Oxford University Press, 1984.

Murphy, Jeffrie G. *Philosophy of Law: An Introduction to Jurisprudence.* Rev ed. Boulder, Colo.: Westview Press, 1990.

SEE ALSO: Brandeis, Louis D.; Constitutional government; Hart, H. L. A.; Law; Supreme Court, U.S.

Jury system

DEFINITION: Legal institution in which criminal or civil trials are decided by a group of citizens rather than judges or other professional court officers

TYPE OF ETHICS: Legal and judicial ethics

SIGNIFICANCE: The modern American jury system is founded in the notion that a person's peers are the best equipped to judge that person's actions, and that justice is best served when it is adjudicated by fellow citizens rather than imposed from above by an agent of the government.

Some hard historical data show how important a well-functioning jury system is to the encouraging of ethical behavior. The verdict in the famous Los Angeles, California, police brutality case involving the videotaped beating of black motorist Rodney King sparked an explosion of riots that lasted five days and set new records in terms of the number of casualties and the amount of damage; there were 60 dead, 2,383 injured, at least $1 billion in damage to property, and at least 20,000 residents lost jobs as a result of the business closings that followed. Some people argue that the riots were a rebellion that was akin to the Boston Tea Party and that it was unethical neglect of the problems of the underclass in Los Angeles that provided the powder keg that was ignited by the spark of the jury's verdict. The tragic riots focused much more attention on these problems.

Law is often complex and abstract. The jury system serves to forestall the potential injustice of a large or remote government. A jury of one's peers, to which U.S. citizens are constitutionally entitled, often prevents the law from running roughshod over people in situations that could not have been foreseen by the legislators who, often decades earlier, created the law. At the point of application of law, the jury can work justice in the particular case. Jury nullification is the jury's refusal to apply an unethical law. A jury can see people in court and adjust its views based on the equities it observes.

A major ethical issue surrounding the jury system is how representative of the larger community a jury should be. Many people believe that the verdict leading to the riots in the King case was the result of the facts that no African Americans were on that jury and that King was African American. During the *voir dire*, lawyers for each side have a limited power to prevent some people from serving on the jury without even showing why they may not serve. Lawyers have the right to remove any juror by showing cause (for example, that a juror is related to the accused). Lawyers use many psychological profiles involving stereotypes to remove potential jurors without cause. This may be unethical, because some discriminatory stereotypes are used in this process.

JURORS

Jurors are drawn from ordinary life. Therefore, the jury system is also a check and balance against unethical elitism in a democracy. This is why some states make jurors with extraordinary qualifications (such as a law degree) ineligible for jury duty. The jury system is used in both criminal prosecutions and civil suits. Usually, a unanimous verdict is needed to avoid a hung jury, but some states have allowed a nearly unanimous verdict to be decisive in some civil suits.

The jury system is part of an adversary system in which two sides clash and thereby, according to theory, provide the best picture of the whole truth by presenting both sides of the issue. Some countries use an inquisitorial system that uses judges or panels of authorities as investigators. The adversary system is often emotional and messy, but it provides a powerful incentive for each side to present its story. With this greater incentive comes a greater chance for the jury to hear the whole truth.

SEE ALSO: Accused, rights of; Adversary system; Erroneous convictions; Judicial conduct code; Jurisprudence; Law.

Just war theory

DEFINITION: Primarily Christian philosophy offering criteria for determining when it is just to wage war and how wars should be fought

TYPE OF ETHICS: Military ethics

SIGNIFICANCE: Just war theory attempts to prevent and limit wars by providing universal guidelines for ethically correct ways to resolve conflicts between states.

Moral considerations in the conduct of war can be found in the earliest records of warfare. The first systematic attempt to set forth universal rules of warfare—based on natural law—was proposed by the Roman statesman Cicero during the first century B.C.E. During the fourth century C.E. the North African theologian St. Augustine agreed that morality was "written in the heart" and synthesized rational and biblical arguments for reconciling the evil of killing with the demands for peace and justice. The thirteenth century theologian St. Thomas Aquinas summarized the classic rationale for declaring war and articulated moral guidelines for conduct in war. Building upon this philosophical tradition, Hugo Grotius published the first comprehensive exposition of international law in 1625, providing the foundation for subsequent international agreements to limit warfare, such as the modern Geneva Conventions. By the early twenty-first century, the just war tradition had evolved into a theory resting on a few core principles.

Thomas Aquinas identified three reasons for justifying going to war. First, and most important, there must be a just cause. The principal idea here is that there are times when certain injustices, such as unprovoked attacks or human rights violations, are so egregious that to not go to war would be a greater evil. Second, only the proper authority—states, not individuals—can declare war. Third, just wars are waged only with right intentions, such as the desire for just peace or promoting a greater good.

Three other bases for a just war have been added to those articulated by Thomas Aquinas. First, in order not to waste lives recklessly, a war should have a reasonable chance of success. Second, the principle of proportionality should apply; it states that the harm caused by war should not exceed the harm that provokes it. Finally, war should be a last resort, taken only when nonviolent means fail.

ACCEPTABLE CONDUCT IN WAR

The numerous guidelines for acceptable conduct in war can be grouped into two basic categories. The principle of discrimination specifies the legitimate targets of war and provides guidelines for the proper treatment of noncombatants and the defenseless. Pertinent to this principle, the "doctrine of double effect" states that killing civilians is excusable if military action against a genuine military target leads to unavoidable civilian loss—so-called "collateral damage"—and civilians themselves are not specifically targeted. The second major principle is a second kind of proportionality. The general idea here is to minimize destruction and suffering, especially by limiting the types of weapons used.

Just war theory holds that only wars fought for proper reasons and waged in the right way are just. Satisfying these criteria, however, is rarely clear-cut. Perhaps the best that just war theory can offer is to determine the degree to which any given war is just.

Paul J. Chara, Jr.

FURTHER READING

Elshtain, Jean Bethke, ed. *Just War Theory: Readings in Social and Political Theory.* New York: New York University Press, 1991.

Phillips, Robert L., and Duane L. Cady. *Humanitarian Intervention: Just War vs. Pacifism.* Lanham, Md.: Rowman & Littlefield, 1996.

Regan, Richard, J. *Just War: Principles and Cases.* Washington, D.C.: Catholic University of America Press, 1996.

Teichman, Jenny. *Pacifism and the Just War.* New York: Basil Blackwell, 1986.

Walzer, Michael. *Just and Unjust Wars: A Moral Argument with Historical Illustrations.* 3d ed. New York: Basic Books, 2000.

SEE ALSO: Augustine, Saint; Conscientious objection; Grotius, Hugo; Holy war; Jihad; Limited war; Military ethics; Peacekeeping missions; Realpolitik; War.

Justice

DEFINITION: Fundamental moral principle or ideal according to which each person should receive the treatment he or she deserves

TYPE OF ETHICS: Theory of ethics

SIGNIFICANCE: A concept of justice or moral desert is arguably the foundation of ethical judgment, and it underpins all legal and social systems in which a punishment or reward is designed to fit the actions or character of the person receiving it.

Such words as fairness, equality, honesty, equity, integrity, and lawfulness, which are sometimes used as synonyms for justice, indicate the social order that is connoted by the term. In common speech, justice indicates both right relationships among people and a correct social norm—that is, one that establishes a course of expected conduct.

The roots of the modern Western view of justice can be traced to the Hebrew Bible, on one hand, and to Greek philosophy, on the other. Many social reformers, in particular, have been influenced by the Hebrew prophets. Thus, for example, the Martin Luther King, Jr., memorial in Montgomery, Alabama, is inscribed with the words of the eighth century B.C.E. prophet Amos: ". . . until justice rolls down like waters, and righteousness like a mighty stream" (Amos 5:24). In the Hebrew Bible, justice (*tsedaqah*) is a quality of God. God delights in it and wishes it for his people. The laws of God make clear his nature and his will. If the people do as he has commanded, then they too will be just. Thus, *tsedaqah* indicates a right relationship between the people and God. It indicates proper balance or right order. The fruits of justice are peace and abundance. The Hebrew prophets especially emphasized the social dimension of *tsedaqah* by claiming that a right relationship with God is possible only when people act justly toward one another. According to the prophet Amos, this meant that God would not revoke punishment from a society that allowed the righteous to be sold for silver and the poor to be trampled into the dust of the earth (Amos 2:6-7).

EARLY WESTERN PHILOSOPHERS

The oldest surviving Western writings that examine the nature of justice are those of the Greek philosopher Plato. Although Plato raised questions concerning justice (*dikaiosyne*) in several dialogues, his fullest treatment of the subject is found in the *Republic*. In that work, one of the characters, Thrasymachus, defines justice as the interest of the stronger—namely the ruling class—as expressed in society's laws. As in the case of the Hebrew prophets, justice in this context indicates correct relationships among people. Since according to Thrasymachus the activity of rulers is governed by self-interest, however, and the obedience of the subjects is dictated by their weaker position, for him just subjects are those who obey the rulers of the state. Thus, Thrasymachus closely identifies justice with civil power, and since the rulers formulate the laws of the state, he also equates justice with civil lawfulness.

Socrates, the protagonist of the *Republic*, however, counters by claiming that justice is not only good for rulers but is also good "for its own sake." He does this, first, by arguing that rulers do not always act in their own self-interest. According to Socrates, states exist precisely because people are not self-sufficient. In an ideal state, the rulers would be those who would act always for the good of the state, at all times putting its interests ahead of their own. The good unites the state, while the bad divides it. A good state, like a good person, contains the four cardinal virtues of wisdom, bravery, temperance, and justice. Justice, for Socrates, means that each person in the state performs his or her proper function. Thus, justice provides the right balance or harmony among the parts. To Socrates, the unjust person is dominated by the appetites and emotions, whereas the just person is controlled by reason. The unjust state would be governed by a despot; the just state would be ruled by a philosopher-king.

The views of justice advocated by Thrasymachus and Socrates have been represented many times in the history of Western philosophy. The positive law theory of justice holds that justice depends on authority, agreement, or convention. For example, the social contract advocated by Thomas Hobbes in *Leviathan* (1651) closely connects justice with civil law. Hobbes imagined life without laws to be akin to a war in which each person seeks his or her own advantage, "a war as if of every man against every man." Out of their fear of anarchy and in order to preserve themselves, then, people agree in common to hand power over to the state, or Leviathan, which has coercive power and can enforce its laws. A just person, ac-

801

cording to Hobbes, is one who follows the laws of the state.

Like Socrates, John Locke held to a natural rights theory of justice. In *Concerning the True Original Extent and End of Civil Government*, he wrote that the law of nature taught that all people were equal and independent, and that "no one ought to harm another in his life, health, liberty or possessions." It was the duty of the state to protect people's natural rights. While Locke agreed with Hobbes in thinking that people willfully entered into a compact and thus formed the state, sovereignty, he thought, ultimately remained with the people. The purpose of the laws and the duty of rulers should be to represent and execute the will of the people. If the legislative or executive powers should betray their trust, they then should be counted as unjust and should be deposed.

One of the characters of the *Republic*, Glaucon, hints at but does not elaborate on a third view of justice; namely, that it is a social convention. According to this view, as developed by advocates such as David Hume and John Stuart Mill, justice is what promotes the welfare of society. It depends upon society, and it is a social product rather than a natural right. Justice is the basis of rights and laws, which are either just or unjust insofar as they promote the social good. Thus, this view of justice is sometimes called the social good theory of justice, and its proponents are perhaps most concerned with questions of how to perceive and identify the common good.

James M. Dawsey

FURTHER READING

Adamiak, Richard. *Justice and History in the Old Testament*. Cleveland, Ohio: J. T. Zubal, 1982.

Adler, Mortimer J. *Six Great Ideas—Truth, Goodness, Beauty, Liberty, Equality, Justice: Ideas We Judge By, Ideas We Act On*. New York: Macmillan, 1981.

Allen, Sir Carleton Kemp. *Aspects of Justice*. London: Stevens, 1958.

Feinberg, Joel. *Rights, Justice, and the Bounds of Liberty*. Princeton, N.J.: Princeton University Press, 1980.

O'Manique, John. *The Origins of Justice: The Evolution of Morality, Human Rights, and Law*. Philadelphia: University of Pennsylvania Press, 2003.

Rawls, John. *Justice as Fairness: A Restatement*. Edited by Erin Kelly. Cambridge, Mass.: Belknap Press, 2001.

_____. *A Theory of Justice*. Rev. ed. Cambridge, Mass.: Belknap Press of Harvard University Press, 1999.

Tillich, Paul. *Love, Power, and Justice: Ontological Analyses and Ethical Applications*. New York: Oxford University Press, 1972.

Vallentyne, Peter, ed. *Equality and Justice*. New York: Routledge, 2003.

SEE ALSO: Fairness; Hobbes, Thomas; *Leviathan*; Locke, John; Platonic ethics; *Republic*; Social justice and responsibility.

K

Kabbala

DEFINITION: Tradition of esoteric Jewish mysticism

TYPE OF ETHICS: Religious ethics

SIGNIFICANCE: The Kabbala, an occult formulation of the doctrines of the Jewish religion, is intended to supply a focus in contemplation, leading to a state of mystical awareness.

The Kabbala, an occult body of mystical teachings in the Jewish religion, focuses primarily on the notions of creation, revelation, and redemption. These teachings were usually surrounded by secrecy, and they were transmitted orally or in a highly veiled literature that proceeds by hints rather than by explicit declarations. The secrecy surrounding the Kabbala stems from the belief that its ideas were too subtle for the average mind. The Kabbalists, moreover, believed that their doctrines endowed certain individuals with mystical powers by which they might control nature itself. Those who sought to study the Kabbala were, therefore, screened to be certain that they would not invoke their powers too casually or for dishonorable ends. Only a chosen few in each generation were worthy of being the recipients of the wisdom of the Kabbala.

Sources of the Kabbala have been traced not only to the doctrines and literature of Judaism but also to a wide variety of cultures with which the Jewish people had come into contact in their dispersion. These influences include Persian, Neoplatonic, and neo-Pythagorean elements entering Judaism during the Hellenistic period. Christian and Gnostic themes were introduced somewhat later, as were borrowings from Muslim sectarianism following the emergence of Islam. This mixture of elements explains the difficulty that scholars have found in elucidating the Kabbala's sources. The Kabbala itself became one of the spiritual sources of the popular mysticism known as Hasidism, which flourished in the eighteenth and nineteenth centuries, especially in eastern Europe.

THE DOCTRINE OF CREATION

All Jewish mysticism has attempted to reinterpret the literal account of creation rendered in the book of Genesis. The mystics maintain that the account in Genesis does not sufficiently emphasize the transcendence of God. The reinterpretation has generally taken form as a demiurgic theory. In such a theory, God himself, who is boundless, infinite, and transcendent, did not perform the material act of creating the world. This was the work of a lesser spirit, or demiurge, who was brought into existence by God for this particular purpose. As the conception of God's transcendence developed, one demiurge seemed insufficient to express the sense of imposing distance between divinity and the material world. The remoteness of God from the world was intensified, therefore, by adding other intermediaries and thus forming a chain from God to matter in links of increasing materiality.

A second problem in the biblical account of creation, according to the Jewish mystics, concerns matter. If God is accepted as infinite, all must be contained within God. The question then arises, however, whether matter exists outside God. This issue was finally resolved by a theory that God, prior to creation, was actually infinite. To a make room for creation, however, he voluntarily contracted or limited himself. Some excess of spiritual substance overflowed into the space from which God had removed himself, and this excess, or emanation, provided both the demiurgic intermediaries and the matter out of which the world was created. Because all substance is thus ultimately an overflowing of God's substance, Kabbala is a pantheistic doctrine (the doctrine or belief that God is not a personality, but that all laws, forces, and manifestations of the self-existing universe are God). The completed series of emanations also served the purpose of providing the route by which the human ascending spirit might reach the heights of divinity.

803

THE DOCTRINE OF REVELATION

After the first destruction of the Temple at Jerusalem, and particularly after its second destruction, the scriptures served as a focus for the religious devotion of the Jews. Their state no longer existed; their culture had been destroyed. All that remained was their belief in God and his word. If the Jewish religion were to endure, it seemed necessary that not only the content of revelation but also even its physical form should be considered inviolate and unchangeable. The level on which mystics interpreted revelation to serve their purpose was highly symbolical. To make this interpretation possible, the Kabbalists developed letter and number symbolism of great variety, complexity, and obscurity.

THE DOCTRINE OF REDEMPTION

The Kabbalists maintained and even intensified the traditional Jewish view of redemption. In the Kabbalistic view, salvation of the individual was of little significance. It entered only as a means to the greater end of the salvation of humankind. This would come about through the agency of a messiah and the Davidic line, who would lead the Jews in triumph to the Holy Land and inaugurate a reign of truth, justice, and mercy. The ideal of salvation is thus the establishment of an earthly paradise of human life, raised to its highest humanity. Other elements clouded this doctrine at various times in the history of mystical messianism. In general, however, the Kabbalistic view of redemption was an extreme form of traditional messianism. Attempts to calculate the exact date of the coming of the messiah were widespread. The coincidence of various calculations in fixing on dates close to each other inspired a wave of messianic movements.

Genevieve Slomski

FURTHER READING

Bokser, Ben Zion. *From the World of the Cabbalah.* New York: Philosophical Library, 1954.

Heschel, Abraham Joshua. *God in Search of Man: A Philosophy of Judaism.* New York: Farrar, Straus and Cudahy, 1955.

Idel, Moshe. *Kabbalah: New Perspectives.* New Haven, Conn.: Yale University Press, 1988.

Ruderman, David B. *Kabbalah, Magic, and Science.* Cambridge, Mass.: Harvard University Press, 1988.

Scholem, Gershom. *Origins of the Kabbalah.* Edited by R. J. Zwi Werblowsky. Translated by Allan Arkush. Philadelphia, Pa.: Jewish Publication Society, 1987.

Steinsaltz, Adin. *Opening the "Tanya": Discovering the Moral and Mystical Teachings of a Classic Work of Kabbalah.* Translated by Yaacov Tauber. San Francisco: Jossey-Bass, 2003.

SEE ALSO: Hasidism; Jewish ethics; Messianism; Talmud; Torah.

Kant, Immanuel

IDENTIFICATION: German philosopher
BORN: April 22, 1724, Königsberg, Prussia (now Kaliningrad, Russia)
DIED: February 12, 1804, Königsberg, Prussia (now Kaliningrad, Russia)
TYPE OF ETHICS: Enlightenment history
SIGNIFICANCE: In *Foundations of the Metaphysics of Morals* (*Grundlegung zur Metaphysik der Sitten*, 1785), *The Metaphysics of Morals* (1797), and especially the *Three Critiques* (1781-1790), Kant synthesized rationalism and empiricism into a single philosophical system that stood as the culmination of Enlightenment thought. He argued for the existence of a universal and objective moral law, the categorical imperative, which had the form of law as such and therefore transcended any individual human concern or value.

Late in his life, after his revolutionary work in epistemology, Kant first presented his mature moral philosophy in *Foundations of the Metaphysics of Morals*. Here, Kant developed his influential idea that human beings as rational agents are "autonomous," or have the capacity for moral self-government. For Kant, autonomy means that, as rational beings, people set their own standards of conduct, as distinct from the demands made by their desires, and are able to decide and act on these standards. On the basis of a complex argument, Kant concluded that autonomy is possible only if the will is guided by a supreme principle of morality that he called the "categorical imperative." Kant viewed this imperative as the product of reason and as the basis for determining moral duties. He expressed it in three basic formulations.

THE FORMULA OF UNIVERSAL LAW

"Act only according to that maxim by which you can at the same time will that it should become a universal law." Kant defined a maxim as a subjective principle on which a person intends to act, and a universal law as a principle that applies to everyone. Therefore, his formula of universal law demands that one act only on maxims that one can rationally will that everyone adopt. Kant provided the following example of how to use the formula: Suppose that a person must borrow money for a personal need and knows that he is unable to repay it. Is it morally permissible for him to act on the maxim of falsely promising to pay back a loan in order to get the loan? The formula tells that the person may act on the maxim if he can rationally will its universalization. The person cannot rationally will this because it would mean that people would no longer trust promises to repay loans, including his own. Kant added that the immorality of the maxim is clear in that the person really wants people to keep their promises so that he can be an exception to the rule for this one occasion.

THE FORMULA OF HUMANITY

"Act so that you treat humanity, whether in your own person or in that of another, always as an end and never as a means only." For Kant, "humanity" refers to people's uniquely human characteristics, their rational characteristics, including autonomy and the capacity to understand the world and to form and pursue life-plans. Thus, his formula of humanity demands that people always act so that they respect themselves and others as beings with a rational nature.

In *Foundations of the Metaphysics of Morals*, Kant used the formula of humanity to argue for a variety of duties to oneself and others. According to Kant, respect for rational nature in oneself implies that one ought not to destroy or deny one's intellectual and moral capacities through suicide, drug abuse, lying, self-deception, or servility. It also implies that one must further one's own rational nature by developing one's natural talents and striving to be-

Immanuel Kant. (Library of Congress)

come virtuous. Respect for rational nature in others requires that one not harm them and that one uphold their individual liberty, but Kant discussed these duties as part of his legal and political philosophy. More exclusive ethical duties to others include the duty to contribute to the flourishing of rational nature in others through beneficence and the duty to refrain from arrogance, defamation, ridicule, and other activities that deny people's humanity.

THE FORMULA OF THE REALM OF ENDS

"All maxims . . . ought to harmonize with a possible realm of ends." This formula shows that the two previous formulas are interconnected. (Kant held them all to be equivalent, but this has not been widely accepted.) Kant described the realm of ends as a harmony between human beings, resulting from each acting only on maxims that can become universal laws. It is a harmony of ends in that its members, by acting only on universalizable maxims, act only on maxims that can meet everyone's consent; thus, they respect one another as rational self-determining agents, or ends in themselves. It is also a harmony of ends in that people will seek to further one another's individual ends.

Mᴏʀᴀʟ Vɪsɪᴏɴ

Kant held that people must mirror the realm of ends in their moral choices and actions, and that it is humanity's duty to bring about this ideal. He viewed the French Revolution and the Enlightenment as steps in the right direction; argued for a worldwide league of democratic states as a further step toward the realm of ends; and claimed, moreover, that the religious institutions of his time must embrace the ideal, setting aside their historically evolved differences. Kant maintained that moral philosophy must not formulate new duties, but should only clarify the moral principle operative in "common moral reason" in order to help ordinary persons more adequately resist immoral desires. Kant's clarification went beyond these confines, however, and it ended with an inspiring moral vision of the realm of ends as the purpose of history, the kingdom of God on Earth, and the ultimate individual and collective vocation.

Harry van der Linden

Fᴜʀᴛʜᴇʀ Rᴇᴀᴅɪɴɢ

Aune, Bruce. *Kant's Theory of Morals*. Princeton, N.J.: Princeton University Press, 1979.

Banham, Gary. *Kant's Practical Philosophy: From Critique to Doctrine*. New York: Palgrave Macmillan, 2003.

Hill, Thomas E., Jr. *Dignity and Practical Reason in Kant's Moral Theory*. Ithaca, N.Y.: Cornell University Press, 1992.

Kant, Immanuel. *Critique of Practical Reason*. Edited and translated by Lewis W. Beck. 3d ed. New York: Maxwell Macmillan, 1993.

_____. *Critique of Pure Reason*. Translated by Norman Kemp Smith. Introduction by Howard Caygill. Rev. 2d ed. New York: Bedford/St. Martins, 2003.

_____. *Critique of the Power of Judgment*. Edited by Paul Guyer. Translated by Paul Guyer and Eric Matthews. New York: Cambridge University Press, 2000.

_____. *Groundwork for the Metaphysics of Morals*. Edited and translated by Allen W. Wood. New Haven, Conn.: Yale University Press, 2002.

Kerstein, Samuel J. *Kant's Search for the Supreme Principle of Morality*. New York: Cambridge University Press, 2002.

Paton, H. J. *The Categorical Imperative: A Study in Kant's Moral Philosophy*. Philadelphia: University of Pennsylvania Press, 1971.

Sullivan, Roger J. *Immanuel Kant's Moral Theory*. Cambridge, England: Cambridge University Press, 1989.

Timmons, Mark, ed. *Kant's "Metaphysics of Morals": Interpretive Essays*. New York: Oxford University Press, 2002.

Sᴇᴇ ᴀʟsᴏ: Autonomy; Consistency; Deontological ethics; Duty; Enlightenment ethics; *Foundations of the Metaphysics of Morals*; Kantian ethics; Post-Enlightenment ethics; Practical reason; Transcendentalism.

Kantian ethics

Dᴇғɪɴɪᴛɪᴏɴ: Moral system put forward by, or modeled after that of, Immanuel Kant

Tʏᴘᴇ ᴏғ ᴇᴛʜɪᴄs: Enlightenment history

Sɪɢɴɪғɪᴄᴀɴᴄᴇ: Kantian ethics are concerned with the determination of an absolute and universal moral law and with the realization or modeling of an ideal society characterized by the mutual respect and harmonious coexistence of all moral agents.

The term "Kantian ethics" is commonly used to refer to the ethics of Immanuel Kant, as set forth in his *Foundations of the Metaphysics of Morals* and other moral writings of the 1780's and 1790's. The term is also frequently used to refer to later moral theories that are similar to Kant's ethics but contain modifications in response to its perceived shortcomings. Three important examples are the moral theories of Hermann Cohen, John Rawls, and Jürgen Habermas.

Iᴍᴍᴀɴᴜᴇʟ Kᴀɴᴛ

The ultimate purpose of moral rules, Kant argued, is to make possible his ideal society, the "realm of ends," which has two main aspects: All its members respect one another as self-determining agents who pursue different individual ends, and they seek to promote one another's ends. Kant believed that this moral ideal would evolve if everyone followed the fundamental principle of his ethics: the "categorical imperative." This imperative demands that one act only on those personal policies of conduct ("maxims") that one can rationally will to become universal laws or principles that guide everyone's conduct. According to Kant, obedience to the categorical imperative implies respect for others as self-determining beings with different individual ends; in acting only on maxims that can become universal laws, one acts only on principles to which others can rationally consent, and thus one upholds their right to legislate their own moral rules and pursue their own individual ends.

Kant also argued that general obedience to the categorical imperative would bring about universal mutual promotion of individual ends (as the other aspect of the realm of ends) because the imperative prohibits refusing to assist others. The reason for this prohibition is that one cannot rationally will that everyone adopt a maxim of not assisting others in the pursuit of their individual ends, for in such a world one would lack the assistance of others as a means for realizing one's own happiness.

Attempts to overcome the shortcomings of Kant's ethics, while preserving its strengths, have led to such influential examples of Kantian ethics as the moral theories of Hermann Cohen, John Rawls, and Jürgen Habermas. The most significant shortcomings are the following: The categorical imperative does not offer a sufficient criterion for determining universal laws, Kant failed to provide an adequate justification of the categorical imperative, he described moral agents as isolated legislators of universal laws, and he failed to address satisfactorily how the realm of ends can be institutionalized.

HERMANN COHEN

During the later part of the nineteenth century, Kant's philosophy regained in Germany the great influence it had had during his own lifetime. This resurgence is known as neo-Kantianism, and one of its most important representatives is Hermann Cohen, who transformed Kant's ideal of the realm of ends into a democratic socialist ideal. Cohen held that human agents can only arrive at universal laws, or approximations thereof, if all people become decision makers or colegislators in their institutions. Thus, Cohen argued that the realm of ends requires for its

realization not only political democracy, as Kant himself claimed, but also democracy in the workplace. Moreover, Cohen held that workplace democracy, in order to be effective, requires workers' ownership of productive property. Cohen also maintained that these democratic socialist proposals were necessary for realizing the aspect of the realm of ends that all of its members promote one another's individual ends.

JOHN RAWLS

A second main philosophical movement of renewed interest in Kant's ethics and corresponding attempts to improve his ethics occurred during the 1970's and 1980's. The American philosopher John Rawls and the German philosopher Jürgen Habermas are the two major figures of this movement. Rawls's primary concern is to argue for principles of justice that create a political society in accord with the realm of ends. More specifically, he argues for an extensive liberal welfare state based on the principles of justice that all persons must have equal political and civil liberties and that social and economic inequalities must be corrected to the greatest benefit of the least advantaged. Rawls holds that rational agents will opt for these principles of justice once their situation of choice, the "original position," is made impartial by a "veil of ignorance" that makes them temporarily forget about all the specific facts concerning themselves and their society. Whether this innovative transformation of the categorical imperative—the veil forces one to opt for principles that are acceptable to all—justifies Rawls's two principles of justice, and whether it can more generally be used to justify and explicate Kantian moral rules, are questions that have generated much debate.

JÜRGEN HABERMAS

The basic principle of the "discourse ethics" of Jürgen Habermas is a clear modification of the categorical imperative. The principle is that for a norm to be valid it must be accepted in a practical discussion by all those who are affected by the norm. The participants in the practical discourse must then also foresee the consequences of the general observance of the norm for the realization of the particular interests of each of them. This view that moral norms must be constructed by communities engaged in free practical discourse implies that the good society must be fundamentally democratic; unlike Cohen and Rawls, however, Habermas has been somewhat vague and hesitant about the specific institutional ramifications of his Kantian ethics.

Harry van der Linden

FURTHER READING

Habermas, Jürgen. *Moral Consciousness and Communicative Action.* Translated by Christian Lenhardt and Shierry Weber Nicholsen. Cambridge, Mass.: MIT Press, 1990.

Kant, Immanuel. *Groundwork for the Metaphysics of Morals.* Edited and translated by Allen W. Wood. New Haven, Conn.: Yale University Press, 2002.

Kerstein, Samuel J. *Kant's Search for the Supreme Principle of Morality.* New York: Cambridge University Press, 2002.

Rawls, John. *Justice as Fairness: A Restatement.* Edited by Erin Kelly. Cambridge, Mass.: Belknap Press, 2001.

_____. *Political Liberalism.* New York: Columbia University Press, 1993.

_____. *A Theory of Justice.* Rev. ed. Cambridge, Mass.: Belknap Press of Harvard University Press, 1999.

Van der Linden, Harry. *Kantian Ethics and Socialism.* Indianapolis: Hackett, 1988.

Willey, Thomas E. *Back to Kant: The Revival of Kantianism in German Social and Historical Thought, 1860-1914.* Detroit, Mich.: Wayne State University Press, 1978.

SEE ALSO: Autonomy; Consistency; Deontological ethics; Enlightenment ethics; *Foundations of the Metaphysics of Morals*; Kant, Immanuel; Post-Enlightenment ethics; Rawls, John; *Theory of Justice, A.*

Karma

DEFINITION: Spiritual and ethical force generated by a person's actions

TYPE OF ETHICS: Religious ethics

SIGNIFICANCE: In Eastern religious traditions, karma is the motive force determining the transmigration of souls in successive incarnations: One's next life will be better or worse depending on the good or evil of one's actions in this life. In modern Western culture, the term is used in a more general and secular sense to mean good luck or fortune earned through good deeds, or bad luck which is deserved as a result of malfeasance.

The word karma is a Sanskrit term meaning "action," "deed," or "work." By extension, it also came to mean the results of one's deeds and the law of retribution according to which one reaps what one sows.

The term karma does not appear in its extended sense in the oldest hymns of the Hindu scriptures. Nevertheless, the idea does appear that evil deeds have consequences that one would want to avoid. Furthermore, a person could obtain forgiveness from the god Varuṇa. The early hymns also taught continued personal existence beyond death, sometimes in an undifferentiated state, but sometimes with good men going to Heaven and others to a sort of hell.

In the Upaniṣads (composed roughly between the eighth and fifth centuries B.C.E.), Hindu speculation arrived at the conclusion that if one did not reap all that one had sown in this lifetime, one would inherit those uncompensated aftereffects in a future life. The cycle of rebirths came to be understood as the condition from which salvation was necessary. Furthermore, the law of karma was held to operate automatically; it was independent of the efforts of any god.

In its fully developed form, the law of karma is held to explain such phenomena as premature death (the result of misdeeds committed earlier in one's life or in a previous life), child prodigies (the child continues to develop skills already learned in a previous life), and differences in socioeconomic status (karma determines the caste into which one is born). In a moral universe, everything that happens to a person is earned; nothing is accidental or in any other way undeserved. In short, one determines one's own fate, in this and future lives.

Over time, Hindus developed several paths by which to escape the cycle of rebirth. The most important were enlightenment, work, love and devotion, and meditation, which also could be a method employed in other paths. The *Bhagavadgītā* (variously dated between the fifth and first centuries B.C.E.) dealt with the relationship between karma and one's caste duty. Simply put, it was the duty of each person to fulfill his or her role, even if the person found that role distasteful. Failure to do so would entangle one more tightly in the cycle of rebirth. Actions undertaken out of a desire for reward would also lead to rebirth. Hence, the ideal was to perform one's duties to society without desiring to reap the benefits of one's actions. Such detached behavior would build up no karma, particularly if it were combined with other methods of salvation. Thus, one could escape from the cycle of rebirth.

KARMA IN BUDDHIST ETHICS

Buddhism retained from Hinduism the ideas of karma and reincarnation but denied the existence of a permanent soul that could be reincarnated. Instead, Theravāda Buddhists argued that everything in the phenomenal world was temporary, passing in and out of existence every instant. Furthermore, nothing originated from itself; rather, everything originated from something that had existed previously. This transitoriness was not random, however; discrete streams of karma held one's flashes of existence together in a continuum and separate from other streams of karma. An analogy often used by Buddhists was the passing of a flame from one candle to another. In that process, the second flame is neither identical to nor completely different from the first. Thus, a "person" could commit good or bad deeds and experience the rewards or punishments appropriate to each. Furthermore, over time a person could "use up" all acquired karma and pass into nirvana.

Buddhists were not oblivious to the logical difficulties implicit in this view. On one hand, if things passed completely out of existence before being replaced by others, it would appear that anything could cause anything, a conclusion that Buddhists denied. On the other hand, if something connected the flashes of existence, that something would at least resemble a permanent soul. Various Buddhist schools debated the nature of that resemblance, with several Mahāyānist thinkers returning to monistic thinking.

Buddhists generally hold that three factors regulate the acquiring of karma: the intention of the person committing an act; physical actions, including speech; and the abiding effects of the action. A person's karma may be changed by subsequent good deeds performed by the person or (in popular Buddhism) by someone else (for example, a monk or a Buddha) acting on that person's behalf.

KARMA IN JAIN ETHICS

Jainism held that the life force, or *jīva*, within a person is pure and intelligent but can be clouded by karma, which Jains (like some Hindu schools) understood as a subtle form of matter that attaches itself to the *jīva*. Virtuous acts color the *jīva* only slightly, while vices darken and weigh it down. Even the unintentional harming of a lower form of life results in the accumulation of karma. Hence, Jains are strict vegetarians and make every effort to avoid stepping on or breathing in even the tiniest insects. Release from rebirth is possible only if one ceases to acquire new karma and removes the karma already present by means of physical austerity and meditative concentration.

Paul L. Redditt

FURTHER READING

Bstan-dzin Rgya-mtsho [Fourteenth Dalai Lama]. *The Meaning of Life: Buddhist Perspectives on Cause and Effect*. Edited and translated by Jeffrey Hopkins. Rev. ed. Boston: Wisdom, 2000.

Chakraborty, Aparna. *Karma, Freedom, and Responsibility*. New Delhi: Kaveri Books, 1998.

Glasenapp, Helmuth von. *The Doctrine of Karman in Jain Philosophy*. Edited by Hiralal R. Kapadia. Translated by G. Barry Gifford. Rev. ed. Fremont, Calif.: Asian Humanities Press, 2003.

Herman, A. L. *An Introduction to Indian Thought*. Englewood Cliffs, N.J.: Prentice-Hall, 1976.

Hume, Robert Ernest, trans. *The Thirteen Principal Upanishads*. 2d rev. ed. New York: Oxford University Press, 1983.

King, Winston L. *In the Hope of Nibbana: An Essay on Theravada Buddhist Ethics*. LaSalle, Ill.: Open Court, 1964.

Saddhatissa, H. *Buddhist Ethics*. London: Allen & Unwin, 1970.

Zimmer, Heinrich. *Philosophies of India*. Edited by Joseph Campbell. Princeton, N.J.: Princeton University Press, 1967.

SEE ALSO: *Bhagavadgītā*; Bodhidharma; Buddha; Buddhist ethics; Caste system, Hindu; Fatalism; Hindu ethics; Jain ethics; Śaṅkara; Vedānta.

Keller, Helen

IDENTIFICATION: American social activist
BORN: June 27, 1880, Tuscumbia, Alabama
DIED: June 1, 1968, Westport, Connecticut
TYPE OF ETHICS: Civil rights
SIGNIFICANCE: One of the most influential women of the twentieth century, Keller published many books and devoted her life to helping blind and deaf people.

At the age of eighteen months, Helen Keller suffered a severe illness that left her blind and deaf. She could not communicate with other people. When Helen was eight years old, her parents hired a teacher, Anne Sullivan, from the Perkins Institution for the Blind. Sullivan taught Helen a manual alphabet and finger-spelled the names of various objects. Within two years, Helen learned to read and write in braille. At age ten, Helen learned to speak by feeling the vibrations of Sullivan's vocal cords.

In 1890, Anne Sullivan accompanied Helen Keller to Radcliffe College. Four years later, Helen graduated cum laude and began writing essays on the rights of the disabled. She lectured worldwide and gained the support of famous people on improving the rights of people with disabilities. Her publications include *The Story of My Life* (1903), *The World I Live In* (1908), *Out of the Dark* (1913), *Helen Keller's Journal* (1938), and *Teacher: Anne Sullivan Macy* (1955). Helen Keller was an activist for the rights of people with disabilities until her death in 1968.

Noreen A. Grice

SEE ALSO: Americans with Disabilities Act; Disability rights; United Nations Declaration on the Rights of Disabled Persons.

Kevorkian, Jack

IDENTIFICATION: American pathologist
BORN: May 26, 1928, Pontiac, Michigan
TYPE OF ETHICS: Bioethics
SIGNIFICANCE: A medical doctor who has advocated the creation of a medical specialty ("obitiatry") for suicide assistance, organ harvesting, and experimentation on the moribund, Kevorkian per-

sonally assisted in the suicide of scores of terminally ill patients. Media coverage of his actions and ideas galvanized public debate on the issue of physician-assisted suicide.

Jack Kevorkian's career-long focus on death—from trying to ascertain its onset in patients' eyes to trying to salvage some benefit from it—has alienated him from the medical establishment. Kevorkian advocated cadaver blood transfusions and lobbied along with death-row inmates for execution by lethal injection because it would be more merciful and would permit organ donation and experimentation under irreversible anesthesia. Kevorkian wrote various journal articles promoting his controversial ideas, but his objectives were repeatedly frustrated, and he turned his attention to patients who desired euthanasia.

No Regrets

In a telephone interview with a Pontiac, Michigan, reporter in April, 2004, Dr. Jack Kevorkian said, "There is no doubt that I expect to die in prison." Although he reaffirmed a promise that he had made earlier in affidavits, that he would assist in no more suicides if he were to be released, he expressed no regrets for what he had done or what had happened to him, saying, "I knew what I was doing."

In response to a letter-writing campaign to secure Kevorkian's early release, prosecutor David Gorcyca, who had led Oakland County's successful prosecution of Kevorkian in 1999, said that Kevorkian should be treated no differently than any other convicted prisoner. "He flouted the law and baited, no, begged me, on national TV to prosecute him. . . . Now he has to suffer the penalty."

Source: Detroit Free Press, April 11, 2004.

In 1989, Kevorkian developed a saline drip by means of which a severely disabled person could activate a lethal drug, and he marketed this machine on talk shows. Kevorkian later developed another "suicide machine" that used carbon monoxide, which he used after his medical license was revoked and he no longer had access to prescription drugs. On Novem-

Jack Kevorkian with his "suicide machine." (AP/Wide World Photos)

ber 22, 1998, CBS's *60 Minutes* aired a video tape of Kevorkian injecting a patient named Thomas Youk with a lethal drug. The broadcast triggered renewed debate not only about the legality and morality of assisted suicide, but about journalistic ethics as well. Three days later, Kevorkian was arrested and charged with murder. He was convicted of second-degree murder in 1999 and sentenced to ten to twenty-five years in prison.

Kevorkian assisted in the deaths of at least 130 people. The media attention and controversy surrounding him throughout the 1990's made his name a household word. Besides questioning the propriety of assisted suicide, critics condemn Kevorkian's lack of medical experience with living patients; his brief relationships with the suicides; and the fact that many of the suicides were not terminally ill but merely in pain or afraid of advancing physical or mental disability, and possibly depressed. The number of people contacting him for assistance or openly endorsing his actions, however, demonstrates substantial dis-

satisfaction with available options for the terminally and chronically ill.

Ileana Dominguez-Urban
Updated by the editors

SEE ALSO: Abortion; Bioethics; Death and dying; Dilemmas, moral; Euthanasia; Homicide; Right to die; Suicide; Suicide assistance.

Kierkegaard, Søren

IDENTIFICATION: Danish philosopher and theologian
BORN: May 5, 1813, Copenhagen, Denmark
DIED: November 11, 1855, Copenhagen, Denmark
TYPE OF ETHICS: Religious ethics
SIGNIFICANCE: Widely regarded as the founder of existentialism, Kierkegaard focused throughout his writings on the situation of the concrete individual who must choose how to live without the ben-

efit of objective criteria upon which to base that choice. His most famous works include *Either/Or: A Fragment of Life* (*Enten-Eller*, 1843), *Fear and Trembling* (*Frygt og Bæven*, 1843), and *Concluding Unscientific Postscript* (*Afsluttende uvidenskabelig Efterskrift*, 1846).

In a span of only thirteen years, from 1842 to 1855, Søren Kierkegaard authored a richly varied, challenging, and copious body of works. These include philosophical and theological treatises, novels, literary criticism, psychological investigations, social analysis, devotional literature, polemical pamphlets, and a literary autobiography. Despite the diverse character of his writings, many of the same themes and concerns run through all of them. In particular, Kierkegaard was concerned by what he saw as the growing tendency to discount the significance of the individual person's existence and to focus instead on large-scale social and historical phenomena. He regarded this trend as closely related to the tendency to overvalue knowledge and undervalue ethical endeavor.

PSEUDONYMOUS AUTHORSHIP

Most of the best-known of Kierkegaard's writings were published not under his own name but under those of his fictional creations. These were not mere pen names to keep secret Kierkegaard's role as author. Instead, Kierkegaard presented the main options for human existence by creating ideally consistent representatives of the "stages on life's way" and then letting them speak for themselves. That way, the reader does not simply learn about the various forms of existence as a removed observer. Rather, the reader imaginatively enters into the worlds of the various pseudonyms and gets a feel for what it is to exist as they exist.

Kierkegaard identifies three main forms, or stages, of existence: the aesthetic, the ethical, and the religious. His classic presentation of the aesthetic and ethical stages is his first major work, *Either/Or*. The first volume of this monumental book contains a variety of essays by an unknown aesthete who lives for pleasure, amusement, stimulation, and, above all, the avoidance of boredom. The volume ends on a dark note, with the copied pages of another aesthete describing the cynical seduction and abandonment of a young woman. The second volume, depicting ethical existence, consists of two very lengthy letters

from a lower-court judge and family man, Judge William, to the aesthete of volume 1 encouraging the aesthete to change his ways and adopt an ethical form of existence. By placing these two volumes before his readers, Kierkegaard sought to force a choice: either choose to live for pleasure, amusement, success, and so forth, or choose to devote yourself to doing the right thing and fulfilling your duties. The point is not simply to learn about these forms of existence but to choose which to live. By using pseudonyms and disappearing from the scene, Kierkegaard refuses to tell the reader which way he or she should choose.

Kierkegaard considerably complicates the issue of existential choice in subsequent pseudonymous works. In *Fear and Trembling*, the pseudonymous author, John of Silence, intensely examines the story of Abraham and Isaac from the book of Genesis. Abraham's readiness to sacrifice his son at the command of God shows the difference between ethical and religious existence, a difference that Judge William had effectively denied. Subsequent pseudonymous works, notably *Philosophical Fragments* (*Philosophiske Smuler*, 1844) and *Concluding Unscientific Postscript* by Johannes Climacus, distinguish between two types of religious existence: the immanent, in which the divine is believed to be within each person; and the transcendent, which views fallen humans as radically alienated from the divine and in need of divine assistance to gain salvation. Climacus identifies this latter form of religion as the Christian. While Climacus denies that he himself is a Christian, he is fascinated by Christianity and stresses the paradoxical nature of its central claims. He sharply criticizes modern philosophical and theological attempts to diminish that paradoxicality so as to assimilate Christianity to comfortable ways of thinking and being.

NON-PSEUDONYMOUS WRITINGS

At the last moment before its publication, Kierkegaard added a brief statement to the end of *Concluding Unscientific Postscript* admitting responsibility for the whole pseudonymous authorship and explaining his unusual form of writing. He expected at this point to stop writing and become a pastor, a position for which he was already fully trained. Instead, he commenced a second and distinctive career as an author. Most of the works in this "second authorship" were written under his own name and from an explicitly Christian point of view. In *Works of*

Love, he develops a Christian ethic that is grounded in Jesus' command to love one's neighbor.

By showing how radical this ethical demand is, Kierkegaard set the stage for an increasingly acrimonious confrontation with the Danish Lutheran Church. In the writings from the last years of his life, Kierkegaard asserted that the Danish church systematically diluted Christianity as part of an implicit deal with the social status quo: In return for good pay and high social status for pastors, "official Christianity" (which Kierkegaard referred to as "Christendom") legitimates the social order and avoids causing the sorts of disturbances occasioned by the radical demands of genuine Christianity. While Kierkegaard first stated these charges in books such as *Practice in Christianity*, he eventually addressed a broader audience by writing letters to the editor of a major Copenhagen newspaper and then producing a publication of his own, *The Instant*. Shortly after publishing the ninth issue of *The Instant* and at the height of his battle with the Danish Lutheran Church, Kierkegaard fell ill and was taken to a hospital, where he died some weeks later.

George Connell

FURTHER READING

Davenport, John J., and Anthony Rudd, eds. *Kierkegaard After MacIntyre: Essays on Freedom, Narrative, and Virtue*. Chicago: Open Court, 2001.

Dooley, Mark. *The Politics of Exodus: Søren Kierkegaard's Ethics of Responsibility*. New York: Fordham University Press, 2001.

Kirmmse, Bruce. *Kierkegaard in Golden Age Denmark*. Bloomington: Indiana University Press, 1990.

Lowrie, Walter. *A Short Life of Kierkegaard*. Princeton, N.J.: Princeton University Press, 1942.

Mackey, Louis. *Kierkegaard: A Kind of Poet*. Philadelphia: University of Pennsylvania Press, 1971.

Malantschuk, Gregor. *Kierkegaard's Thought*. Translated by Edna Hong and Howard Hong. Princeton, N.J.: Princeton University Press, 1971.

Rudd, Anthony. *Kierkegaard and the Limits of the Ethical*. New York: Oxford University Press, 1993.

Taylor, Mark. *Kierkegaard's Pseudonymous Authorship*. Princeton, N.J.: Princeton University Press, 1975.

SEE ALSO: Altruism; Communitarianism; *Either/Or*; Existentialism; Love; Subjectivism; Unamuno y Jugo, Miguel de; Value.

al-Kindī

IDENTIFICATION: Arab philosopher
BORN: c. 800, Kufa, south of Karbala, Iraq
DIED: 866, Baghdad, Iraq
TYPE OF ETHICS: Religious ethics
SIGNIFICANCE: The first major Arab philosopher, Al-Kindī provided the first systematic philosophical expression of ethics and moral psychology in Arabic, and he was influential in Islamic and medieval European philosophy.

Al-Kindī, "the philosopher of the Arabs," argued that the soul is immaterial and is analogous to divine substance. The appetites and passions have their source in the material body and can lead a person into excessive love of physical pleasures. To avoid that development, the soul must be purified through the quest for truth and the rigorous study of philosophy. As the soul is thus further actualized, it can come to rule rationally over the lower faculties. If the virtuous soul has not been sufficiently purified here in the lower world, it will require further purification in the sphere of the moon and in those spheres beyond the moon before it is sufficiently cleansed to be able to partake in the intellectual apprehension of God (the bliss toward which all people should aim).

Al-Kindī drew upon the work of Neoplatonic and Pythagorean predecessors and, as is common for later Islamicate thinkers such as al-Fārābī, intermingled the metaphysics and moral psychology of both Plato and Aristotle. His work was important in medieval European attempts to understand Aristotle's *De Anima*.

Thomas Gaskill

SEE ALSO: Fārābī, al-; Islamic ethics.

King, Martin Luther, Jr.

IDENTIFICATION: American civil rights leader
BORN: January 15, 1929, Atlanta, Georgia
DIED: April 4, 1968, Memphis, Tennessee
TYPE OF ETHICS: Race and ethnicity
SIGNIFICANCE: As founding president of the Southern Christian Leadership Conference (SCLC), a post he held from 1957 until he died in 1968, King was the major American spokesperson for nonviolent social change and racial equality. He was recipient of the 1964 Nobel Peace Prize.

Influenced chiefly by the Indian liberator Mohandas K. Gandhi and the southern black evangelical tradition, King combined nonviolent activism and Christian theology in his ethic of social change. He maintained throughout his public career that he was not seeking to change only laws but also attitudes, so that people of all races and classes could live in the Beloved Community, a concept borrowed from social gospel advocate Walter Rauschenbusch.

Central to King's philosophy was an ethic of love drawn largely from traditional Christian morality and combined with a strong reformist mission. King openly challenged the acquiescence of both blacks and whites. It was time for change, he believed, because the status quo was perpetuating wrong behavior that was harming all races, but meaningful change would come only by ethical means. "Returning hate for hate," he affirmed, "multiplies hate, adding deeper darkness to a night already devoid of stars. Darkness cannot drive out darkness; only love can do that."

THE LOVE ETHIC AND THE HIGHER LAW

By love, King meant more than a positive feeling. Drawing upon the rich linguistic heritage of the Greeks, he defined love not in terms of *eros* (romantic love) or even *philos* (brotherly love), but *agape*, a word used in the New Testament to mean unselfish, redemptive love. Like Gandhi, King believed that love is a potent force in human relations, capable of effecting reform without crushing the opponent. The real "enemy" in this view is not a group of people but a system that exploits both the oppressor and the oppressed. People should love their enemies, he said, because "love is the only force capable of transforming an enemy into a friend."

After years of studying the ideas of Rauschenbusch, Reinhold Niebuhr, Karl Marx, Gandhi, Jean-Paul Sartre, and others, King developed a synthesis of Christianity and Gandhian nonviolence that satisfied his longing for a method "that would eliminate social evil." He found in Gandhi's thought what he could not find elsewhere, and the result was a synthesis: "Christ furnished the spirit and the motivation and Gandhi furnished the method."

Ambiguities had to be resolved in real situations. One that King often faced was the question of breaking segregationist laws without appearing to oppose rule under law, a particularly frustrating issue in the Birmingham campaign of 1963. Jailed for defying a federal injunction, he was criticized by several local clergymen who characterized him as an outside agitator. Although he rarely responded to criticism, this time he felt compelled to answer in what is called his "Letter from a Birmingham Jail." Of all people, he felt, clergymen should most readily understand that his actions were consistent with the prophetic tradition of leaving one's home to carry God's message.

Martin Luther King, Jr. (Library of Congress)

He could not be an outsider, because "injustice anywhere is a threat to justice everywhere"; he was violating the injunction on the same grounds used in the thirteenth century by Saint Thomas Aquinas to denounce laws that were contrary to God's higher law. "A just law is a man-made code that squares with the moral law or the law of God." Ethics and the legal codes that enforce public morality were thus linked to the moral order of creation.

ELEMENTS OF NONVIOLENT ETHICS

The higher moral law was one of the four main components of King's social ethics. The second, the principle of reconciliation, went beyond law to the level of community. To damage society permanently was contradictory, in his view. Just as God in Christian theology is a reconciler, so the social reformer must seek reconciliation. All sides in the confrontation must emerge with dignity and confidence that their interests will be protected in the new society.

Third, King believed that resistance by public officials or private citizens to social justice was only the surface manifestation of deeper evil. Reforms could not in themselves destroy that evil. For every pharaoh lying dead on the seashore—in a popular analogy to the Old Testament Exodus from Egypt—others will arise. The final victory over evil lies in the eschatological future. In that sense, King's social ethic combined a vision of the final victory of good with the necessity of confronting specific societal flaws with confidence that even partial victories are important.

No ethical principle was more basic to King's nonviolent ethics than was the concept of redemptive suffering. He knew that even the most limited gains in the Civil Rights movement would come with difficulty. Freedom would never be granted voluntarily. It had to be taken, and suffering would often result. Making frequent allusions in sermons and speeches to Christ's suffering on the cross, King compared the nonviolent struggle against racism to the redemptive suffering of the Judeo-Christian tradition. Suffering in a righteous cause would expose evil to public consciousness, as Gandhi had done with British oppression in India, and offer an alternative model of behavior. "Recognizing the necessity for suffering," wrote King, "I have tried to make of it a virtue." This did not

mean that King invited martyrdom, but it did suggest an approach to morality that recognized the persistence of evil despite dedicated opposition.

King's ethics demanded adherence to nonviolence based on the prophetic tradition. Although he was not primarily an original thinker, King infused nonviolent theory with a new intellectual integrity and created an effective grassroots movement to apply and test its viability in social reform efforts, international relations, and personal living. The nonviolent social ethics he articulated required discipline and the willingness to suffer for a good higher than that of one's personal safety or comfort.

Thomas R. Peake

FURTHER READING

Ansbro, John J. *Martin Luther King, Jr.: The Making of a Mind.* Maryknoll, N.Y.: Orbis Books, 1982.

Colaiaco, James A. *Martin Luther King, Jr.: Apostle of Militant Nonviolence.* New York: St. Martin's Press, 1988.

Deats, Richard. *Martin Luther King, Jr., Spirit-Led Prophet: A Biography.* Foreword by Coretta Scott King. New York: New City Press, 2000.

Hanigan, James P. *Martin Luther King, Jr., and the Foundations of Nonviolence.* Lanham, Md.: University Press of America, 1984.

Morris, Aldon D. *The Origins of the Civil Rights Movement: Black Communities Organizing for Change.* New York: Free Press, 1984.

Moses, Greg. *Revolution of Conscience: Martin Luther King, Jr., and the Philosophy of Nonviolence.* Forward by Leonard Harris. New York: Guilford Press, 1997.

Peake, Thomas R. *Keeping the Dream Alive: A History of the Southern Christian Leadership Conference from King to the Nineteen-Eighties.* New York: P. Lang, 1987.

Watley, William D. *Roots of Resistance: The Nonviolent Ethic of Martin Luther King, Jr.* Valley Forge, Pa.: Judson Press, 1985.

SEE ALSO: Bigotry; Christian ethics; Civil disobedience; Civil rights and liberties; Civil Rights movement; Evers, Medgar; Gandhi, Mohandas K.; Jackson, Jesse; Mandela, Nelson; Nonviolence.

Knights of Labor

IDENTIFICATION: Universal national labor union working to promote social reform
DATE: Founded in December, 1869
TYPE OF ETHICS: Business and labor ethics
SIGNIFICANCE: The Knights of Labor was the first national union to seek economic justice for unskilled labor by promoting a classless society in which each worker would also be an entrepreneur.

Established originally as a secret league, the Knights of Labor experienced tremendous growth when it became an open organization during the 1880's through the efforts of Terence Powderly, its grand master workman from 1879 to 1893. With the exception of professional workers, the Knights melded all labor, regardless of sex, race, creed, national origin, or skill level, into a single disciplined army that would check the power of concentrated wealth that, according to the Knights, was degrading labor.

The Knights of Labor believed that labor could regain its moral worth if it received a proper share of the wealth that it created and adequate leisure time to enjoy the blessings of a civilized society. The Knights sought to check the power of corporations through legislation to secure safe working conditions, equal pay for the sexes, an eight-hour day, a national banking system, public lands for settlers, weekly pay in full, the substitution of arbitration for strikes, and the abolition of contract labor and child labor. The Knights declined after 1886 when many skilled workers who desired less utopian reform joined the newly organized American Federation of Labor.

Stephen D. Livesay

SEE ALSO: American Federation of Labor; Executive Order 10988; International Labour Organisation; National Labor Union.

Kohlberg, Lawrence

IDENTIFICATION: American psychologist
BORN: October 25, 1927, Bronxville, New York
DIED: c. January 17, 1987, Boston, Massachusetts
TYPE OF ETHICS: Modern history

SIGNIFICANCE: In *Essays on Moral Development* (1981), Kohlberg put forward an influential theory of moral development based on the premise that morality is a cognitive ability that develops in stages. Application of Kohlberg's model has been controversial, because it lends itself to categorizing specific individuals or entire classes of people, such as women or the uneducated, as morally inferior to others based on the stage of development they are deemed to occupy.

While serving as professor of education and social psychology at Harvard University, Kohlberg refined his theory of moral development. He forced a rethinking of traditional ideas on moral development by asserting that one's maturity in moral decisions develops as one thinks about moral issues and decisions. With cognitive growth, moral reasoning appears, and moral reasoning allows children to gain control over their moral decision-making process. From approximately four years of age through adulthood, a person experiences six stages of development that are divided into three levels.

Because it is a cognitive developmental process, moral reasoning is taught using scenarios of moral dilemmas, causing students to justify the morality of their choices. Upon reaching cognitive maturity, a person will use reason to fashion an ethic of justice that is consistent with universal principles of justice and use it to satisfy the moral dilemma. For Kohlberg, moral judgment is the key ingredient in morality, taking precedence over other noncognitive factors. Some critics, notably Carol Gilligan, have challenged Kohlberg's system on the grounds that it seems to privilege values—such as detached, objective justice—more likely to be found in men, while it denigrates the moral values—such as caring and a desire to find solutions to moral problems that will benefit all parties—more commonly found in women in contemporary patriarchal society.

Stephen D. Livesay
Updated by the editors

SEE ALSO: Dilemmas, moral; Feminist ethics; Is/ought distinction; Justice; Moral education.

Kosovo

IDENTIFICATION: Province in southwestern Serbia

TYPE OF ETHICS: International relations

SIGNIFICANCE: In 1999, the North Atlantic Treaty Organization (NATO) conducted a massive bombing campaign against strategic targets throughout Serbia in order to force the Serbian government to stop its military operations against ethnic Albanians living in Kosovo.

During the 1990's, the province of Kosovo had a population of about two million people, of whom more than 90 percent were ethnic Albanians. Ethnic conflict between Serbs and Albanians in the province had roots deep in the past. After the Turkish Ottoman Empire conquered Serbia in the fifteenth century, its forces drove many Serbs out of the southwestern portion of the country and allowed Albanians to settle there. After Kosovo won its independence from the Ottoman Empire early in the twentieth century, Serbia, with the support of the European powers, annexed it as a province. From 1918 into the twenty-first century, Serbia remained part of the federation of Yugoslavia.

With the fall of communism throughout Eastern Europe during the late 1980's and early 1990's, nationalistic Serbs demanded an end to Kosovo's autonomous status. Albanians, in contrast, called for either full independence or annexation to neighboring Albania. In 1989, the Serbian government, led by strongman Slobodan Milošević placed Kosovo under military rule and abolished its parliament. The province's Albanian leaders then declared independence and established an underground government. Meanwhile, the Yugoslav federation was breaking apart,

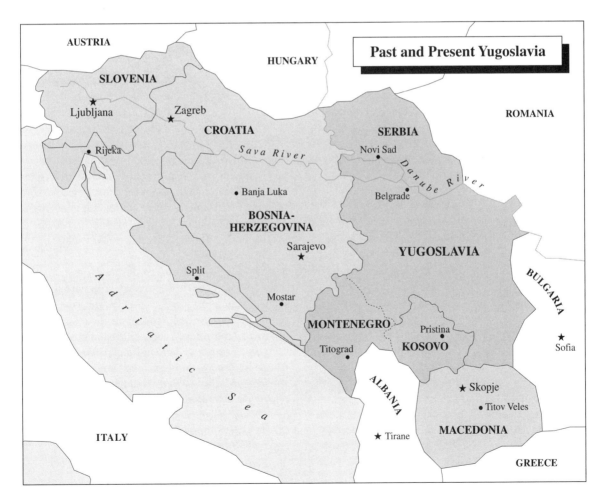

Orthodox Christians in Podgorica, Montenegro, march in March, 2004, to pay tribute to Serb victims of ethnic violence in neighboring Kosovo. (AP/Wide World Photos)

and by 1992 only two republics, Serbia and Montenegro, remained in the federation.

INTERVENTION TO STOP ETHNIC VIOLENCE

In 1995, thousands of Serb refugees from Croatia moved into Kosovo. Militant Albanian separatists formed the Kosovo Liberation Army (KLA) and began conducting guerrilla operations against Serb forces. In March, 1998, Milošević ordered a massive crackdown against Albanian separatists. By December, Serbian troops were destroying Albanian villages. During that year, more than 400,000 Albanians became refugees, most of them fleeing to Albania.

U.S. president Bill Clinton and many European leaders accused the Serbian government of practicing "ethnic cleansing." In late 1998, Western leaders threatened Milošević with a campaign of air strikes unless his government would agree to a peaceful settlement. Milošević refused to make adequate concessions. On March 24, 1999, NATO forces began to

bomb bridges, roads, and additional targets of military value. Milošević responded with intensified attacks on Albanian villages, which in turn led to more bombings. On June 2, a special International Criminal Tribunal announced indictments of Milošević and four other Serbian officials for war crimes.

On June 3, Milošević finally agreed to negotiate an end to the fighting, and six days later, the two sides agreed to terms for a settlement. The next day, the United Nations Security Council authorized a fifty-thousand-man peacekeeping force to supervise the return of an estimated 780,000 Albanian and Serb refugees. However, ethnic fighting in Kosovo continued. Over the next several years, the KLA made revenge attacks against Serbs and other non-Albanians, creating new refugees. Although the NATO operation of 1999 had successfully stopped an instance of ethnic cleansing, it also demonstrated the inherent difficulties and frustrations associated with attempts by outsiders to end long-standing ethnic conflicts.

Thomas Tandy Lewis

FURTHER READING

Clark, Wesley K. *Waging Modern War: Bosnia, Kosovo, and the Future of Conflict.* New York: Public Affairs, 2001.

Ignatieff, Michael. *Virtual War: Kosovo and Beyond.* New York: Henry Holt, 2000.

Judah, Tim. *Kosovo: War and Revenge.* New Haven: Yale University Press, 2002.

SEE ALSO: Bosnia; Concentration camps; Ethnic cleansing; Peacekeeping missions; Refugees and stateless people; War crimes trials.

Ku Klux Klan

IDENTIFICATION: White supremacist organization dedicated to racial segregation and the subjugation of people of color and other minorities

DATE: Founded in 1866

TYPE OF ETHICS: Race and ethnicity

SIGNIFICANCE: Persistent conflicts over the Ku Klux Klan highlight the tension between the competing moral principles of freedom of speech and assembly on one hand and racial tolerance on the other.

Few ethicists celebrate or condone the activities of the Ku Klux Klan; there is, however, a legal debate about how best to control these activities without unduly infringing on individual freedom.

The Klan initially appeared toward the end of 1865 as a social club for former Confederate soldiers, who adopted the hooded sheet as their uniform. Members of the Klan wore masks to disguise their identity. The Klan gained notoriety during the Reconstruction period (1865-1877) for harassing recently freed African Americans who tried to exercise their newly won privilege of voting. Cross-burning on the property of the African Americans and their white Republican political allies was one form of harassment that the Klan practiced; whipping was another. By 1877, when conservative white Democrats had wrested control of southern state governments from the coalition of African Americans and white Republicans, Klan activity had subsided. By 1900, when African Americans had been effectively deprived of the right to vote in most southern states, the Klan had effectively disappeared as an organization; it had lost its reason for being.

THE SECOND KLAN

In 1915, a new national organization was formed, which took the name and the distinctive costume of the old Ku Klux Klan. The leadership of this new organization viewed Jews, Roman Catholics, and immigrants as posing a danger to America that was equal to, if not greater than, that presented by African Americans. Although the Klan in the South did take part in outrages against African Americans in the immediate post-World War I years, the principal targets of the Klan in the North and the Midwest were the Roman Catholic Church, Jews, and all immigrants from southern and eastern Europe. It also claimed to enforce the traditional small-town virtues of alcoholic abstinence and Victorian sexual morality against all deviants. During this time, the Klan received much backing from Protestant ministers. It spread rapidly for a while throughout the Midwest and the Northwest but went into a sharp decline after the leader of the Indiana Klan was convicted, in 1926, of the rape of a young white woman. During the Great Depression (1929-1941), what remained of the Klan was eclipsed in importance by various other hate groups.

THE THIRD KLAN AND THE HATE SPEECH VS. FREE SPEECH DEBATE

There was a revival of the Ku Klux Klan during the 1950's and 1960's in the South. This revival was sparked by the 1954 Supreme Court decision *Brown v. Board of Education*, which mandated racial integration of the schools, and by the African American drive for voting rights in Mississippi and Alabama during the early 1960's. Many police officials condoned or cooperated with the Klan. The Klan was implicated in the deaths of three civil rights workers in Mississippi in 1964, military officer Lemuel Penn in 1964, and white civil rights worker Viola Liuzzo in 1965. After 1954, three main Klan organizations were formed: the Knights of the Ku Klux Klan; the United Klans of America; and the Invisible Empire, Knights of the Ku Klux Klan.

Toward the end of the 1960's, Klan influence in the South began to wane. Vigorous prosecution of Klan crimes by the Federal Bureau of Investigation, under federal civil rights statutes, reduced its power. As African Americans, protected by federal registrars after the passage of the Voting Rights Act of 1965, more and more came to exercise their right to vote, the once-common collusion between the Klan and local police became somewhat less frequent.

The Ku Klux Klan spread to the North during the 1970's and 1980's, as racial tensions spread across the country. The possibility that white males might lose jobs or promotions as a result of affirmative action policies was one Klan selling point. Klansmen practiced violence and intimidation, not only against African Americans but also, for a while, against post-1975 Indochinese refugee fishermen who had settled in the Gulf Coast states. Many Klansmen also opposed Mexican immigration; hostility to the Roman Catholic Church, however, was no longer emphasized.

Fading Popularity of the Klan

During the 1980's, the reputation of the Ku Klux Klan was probably worse than it had ever been. The association of the Klan with acts of violence was one mark against it. Other elements that limited the spread of Klan ideas were the adoption by the Klan of anti-Semitism and the organization's close association with the neo-Nazi movement. Condemnation of the Klan appeared even in the pages of the conservative religious magazine *Christianity Today*; the author of the article was appalled not only by the Klan's hatred of African Americans but also by its insistence that Jesus Christ was not a Jew. The Klan and its rituals seemed more and more limited to the South, although hate groups with similar ideas did arise in the North. When ex-Klansman David Duke ran for the offices of Louisiana state legislator, senator from Louisiana, and governor of Louisiana, in 1989, 1990, and 1991, respectively, he soft-pedaled his past activity in the Klan; he won only the first election.

The Klan and the Issue of Free Speech

In June, 1990, two white youths in St. Paul, Minnesota, burned a cross at the home of an African American family that had moved into a previously all-white neighborhood; the city of St. Paul immediately passed a law banning cross-burning. In June, 1992, this law was overturned by the U.S. Supreme Court. In Georgia, a law banning the wearing of masks—a traditional practice among Klansmen—was struck down by the courts in May, 1990, as a violation of the Klan's right to free speech.

At that time, controversy erupted in the racially tense town of Kansas City, Missouri, when the Mis-

souri Knights of the Ku Klux Klan tried to broadcast a program on local cable television. Mayor Emmanuel Cleaver, an African American man, opposed this idea as likely to cause trouble; so did many other people in Kansas City. In June, 1988, the city passed a law that would have kept the Klan off cable television. In May, 1989, however, a federal district court ruled against the city. Despairing of a Supreme Court victory, the city eventually allowed the Klan the right to broadcast in Kansas City; the first episode of the Klan cable program was broadcast on April 3, 1990.

Among white liberals, the issue of whether the Klan should be allowed free speech proved to be divisive during the 1980's. Some urged that the white-sheeted hate group's right to propagate its views be curbed. Other liberals, such as Nat Hentoff, while by no means accepting Klan viewpoints, insisted that the First Amendment to the Constitution guaranteed the right to propagate even views that most people consider to be evil.

When Klan activity led to violence and intimidation, the courts during the 1980's sometimes assessed penalties against it. In Alabama, when an African American woman's young son was killed by Klansmen during the early 1980's, a white civil rights lawyer, Morris Dees, successfully sued the Alabama branch of the United Klans of America. The courts, by holding the organization responsible for the murder, effectively bankrupted the organization. In 1983, a court decision ordered the Klan to cease its harassment of Vietnamese refugee fishermen who plied their trade off the Gulf Coast of Texas.

Paul D. Mageli

Further Reading

Alderman, Ellen, and Caroline Kennedy. "Freedom of Speech: *Missouri Knights of the Ku Klux Klan v. Kansas City*." In *In Our Defense: The Bill of Rights in Action*. New York: Morrow, 1991.

Becker, Verne. "The Counterfeit Christianity of the Ku Klux Klan." *Christianity Today* 28 (April 20, 1984): 30-35.

Chalmers, David. *Backfire: How the Ku Klux Klan Helped the Civil Rights Movement*. Lanham, Md.: Rowman & Littlefield, 2003.

George, John, and Laird Wilcox. *Nazis, Communists, Klansmen, and Others on the Fringe: Political Extremism in America*. Buffalo, N.Y.: Prometheus Books, 1992.

Hentoff, Nat. *Free Speech for Me—But Not for Thee: How the Right and the Left Relentlessly Censor Each Other.* New York: HarperCollins, 1992.

Kronenwetter, Michael. *United They Hate: White Supremacist Groups in America.* New York: Walker, 1992.

Levin, Jack, and Jack McDevitt. *Hate Crimes: The Rising Tide of Bigotry and Bloodshed.* New York: Plenum Press, 1993.

Pascoe, Elaine. *Freedom of Expression: The Right to Speak Out in America.* Brookfield, Conn.: Millbrook Press, 1992.

Quarles, Chester L. *The Ku Klux Klan and Related American Racialist and Antisemitic Organizations: A History and Analysis.* Jefferson, N.C.: McFarland, 1999.

Stanton, Bill. *Klanwatch: Bringing the Ku Klux Klan to Justice.* New York: Weidenfeld, 1991.

SEE ALSO: Bigotry; First Amendment; Hate crime and hate speech; Jesus Christ; Lynching; Racism; Segregation.

Kūkai

IDENTIFICATION: Japanese Buddhist monk
BORN: Saeki Mao; July 27, 774, Byōbugaura, Sanuki Province, Japan
DIED: April 22, 835, Mt. Kōya, Japan
TYPE OF ETHICS: Religious ethics
SIGNIFICANCE: Kūkai founded the Shingon school of Japanese Buddhism, teaching that there are ten rungs on the ladder of spiritual development that leads to true Buddhahood.

Kūkai entered university studies in Confucian classics at age eighteen but converted to Buddhism and in 804 made a two-year trip to China to learn about esoteric Buddhism. Its "secrets," which were transmitted from master to pupil, were available to anyone dedicated enough to master them. Kūkai subsumed all types of Buddhism under a ladder of ten spiritual rungs: the physical rung of food and sex; morality typical of lay Buddhism; deliverance from underworlds; realization that there is no soul; attainment of Theravādist disinterest; sharing the secret of liberation with others; meditation on the emptiness of things; seeing the true way of salvation; perceiving the Buddhahood of everything; and enlightenment.

Philosophically, Kūkai's system was monistic, with the ultimate Buddha manifesting in the form of Mahāvairochana (Japanese, Dainichi), the Great Sun. Other Buddhas and bodhisattvas were emanations. A person uncovers his or her innate Buddhahood through meditating, repeating formulas, and performing hand gestures. Despite the esoteric nature of his rituals, Kūkai's Buddhism appealed to the laity. Some Shingon adherents believe that he exists in the Heaven of the Satisfied, from which he will return with Maitreya, the future Buddha, and many people make pilgrimages to his tomb. After Kūkai's death, the Japanese bestowed on him the title Kōbō Daishi (Great Teacher of Karma).

Paul L. Redditt

SEE ALSO: Buddha; Buddhist ethics; Four noble truths.

L

Labor-Management Relations Act

IDENTIFICATION: Federal law that attempted to check the power given to labor unions under the National Labor Relations Act of 1935 by specifying a set of unfair union practices

DATE: Became law on August 22, 1947

TYPE OF ETHICS: Business and labor ethics

SIGNIFICANCE: The Labor-Management Relations Act sought to limit the power of labor partly to find a balance between labor interests and business interests and partly out of political fears that linked labor unions with communism.

After the passage of the National Labor Relations Act (Wagner Act) in 1935, manufacturers began a decade-long media blitz to convince the public and Congress of the evils of the new state of industrial relations. Manufacturers extolled the virtues of the free enterprise system and blamed the Wagner Act for allowing an unregulated growth of organized labor and producing the social and industrial unrest of post-World War II America. Probusiness Republicans turned the Democrats out of office in 1946 and promptly amended the Wagner Act, detailing six unfair labor practices and monitoring officials of labor organizations.

Changes in the law included outlawing the closed shop, prohibiting unions from participating in secondary strikes, allowing for an eighty-day injunction for emergency disputes, and requiring union officials to renounce any Communist Party affiliation or belief. This legislation provided a necessary balance between the interests of business and labor and proved the viability of the American system of government to keep its traditional economic institutions intact while meeting the current needs of all of its people.

SEE ALSO: American Federation of Labor; Executive Order 10988; National Labor Relations Act.

Land mines

DEFINITION: Antipersonnel and antivehicle weapons buried below the surface of the ground that explode when disturbed

TYPE OF ETHICS: Military ethics

SIGNIFICANCE: Difficult to detect and disarm, unexploded land mines can continue to pose threats to humans and animals for decades after military conflicts end.

During the twentieth century, victim-triggered land mines became increasingly popular with military strategists, partly because technological advances facilitated both the mass production and the ease of delivery of the weapons. A single aircraft pilot, for example, could create an extensive minefield by dropping thousands of land mines in one overhead pass, peppering fields, hills, and streambeds. Military strategists used antipersonnel mines to defend borders in regions where they lacked sufficient troops to provide human defenses, or to channel enemy troops into more strategic zones. In some cases, civilians themselves mined the lands around their homes to protect themselves from enemies intent on "ethnic cleansing."

Long after a military conflict ends, the land mines that are laid down during the fighting retain the ability to detonate and kill. Local residents often do not know the locations or boundaries of nearby minefields. Sometimes, refugees returning to their homes must travel along paths containing hidden mines. Because land mines cannot discriminate between combatants and civilians, they often kill or injure more people engaged in ordinary pursuits—such as trekking home, farming, or foraging—than they have killed or injured during the conflicts in which they are deployed. Typically, an unwitting farmer or child steps on a mine and is badly injured; if no one hears the explosion, the victim may bleed to death before help arrives. Even if a victim survives an initial blast, a systemic infection from the mud and flesh driven into the victim's body may prove fatal. Survivors need surgeons trained to amputate limbs, medicine to control their pain, prostheses to replace their missing limbs, and physical therapy to regain their physical functions. Civilians—especially children—living near minefields must be educated as to where it is unsafe to work or play.

After the Vietnam War, a groundswell of moral outrage against the use of land mines occurred, culminating in the Ottawa Treaty of 1999. That treaty prohibits the production, use, transfer, and stockpiling of antipersonnel mines. However, at the beginning of the twenty-first century, neither the United States, Russia, nor China had signed the document.

The primary virtue of an international ban is that antipersonnel land mines now belong to a category of unacceptable weapons. The stigma associated with deploying such weapons means that their use is much less likely in the future. It also legitimizes requests for support of programs for land-mine victims and their families.

The loss of limbs and lives, the ruin of lands, and the social and economic disruption of entire communities are global problems. Humanitarians argue that military groups responsible for placement of the mines should be held accountable, since the indiscriminate, disproportionate, and persistent nature of antipersonnel mines violates international conventions regarding acceptable weapons. Accountability implies that reparations for damages should be paid. In general, governmental responses have been inadequate with respect to postconflict problems caused by land mines, especially in developing countries.

Tanja Bekhuis

FURTHER READING

McGrath, Rae. *Landmines and Unexploded Ordnance: A Resource Book*. London: Pluto Press, 2000.

Monin, Lydia, and Andrew Gallimore. *The Devil's Gardens: A History of Landmines*. London: Pimlico, 2002.

SEE ALSO: Chemical warfare; Child soldiers; Ethnic cleansing; Human Rights Watch; Limited war; Mercenary soldiers; Military ethics; Scorched-earth policies; War; War crimes trials.

Mohammad Saber, an Afghan boy who lost both legs when he stepped on a land mine while collecting scraps of firewood for his family. According to a United Nations agency, as many as ten million land mines remained buried in Afghanistan during the late 1990's. (AP/Wide World Photos)

Language

DEFINITION: Any systematic means of communication or representation employing signs with conventionalized meanings

TYPE OF ETHICS: Theory of ethics

SIGNIFICANCE: The relationship of language to meaning and truth is a central concern for many philosophers, and the need to ground meaningful inquiry in a specific theory of language is no less pressing in ethics than in the other philosophical disciplines. Moreover, the rise of deconstruction and related disciplines has led many thinkers to endow the everyday use of language with a new and unprecedented level of ethical significance.

Since the modern division of ethics into normative ethics and metaethics, the latter study has concentrated almost exclusively on the meaning of ethical terminology, its nature, and the rules of its interrelationships. The concern of ethics with language is scarcely a modern phenomenon, and even in the dialogues of Plato, Socrates challenges his interlocutors with demands for precision in their use of terms such as good, just, right, piety, and virtue.

As modern metaethics analyzes contemporary language, there are vital divisions in ethical thought that depend entirely on particular approaches to ethical language. Moral (or ethical) realism maintains that ethical statements make truth claims and that ethical terms signify real properties and relationships. In addition, ethical information is seen as enjoying an objectivity that transcends culture, class, gender, and other categories.

Realism has suffered, however, under the criteria utilized by the school of logical positivism for verifiability, confirmation, and so forth in the twentieth century. In the wake of the decline of positivism, a renewed interest in moral realism has appeared, but serious problems remain regarding the relation of the moral to the nonmoral and regarding the explanatory role that moral propositions have in understanding the world. In regard to the latter, it is clearly the case that one can understand certain events and individuals in history better by understanding their morality, but it is not certain that one need know more than the empirical fact that those individuals simply believed in a particular moral code and acted upon it.

NONCOGNITIVISM

Noncognitivism has arisen as a way around imputing facticity and truth-value to moral statements. The three forms of noncognitivistic ethics are emotivism, imperativism, and emoto-imperativism.

Emotivism constitutes a grouping of theories that are metaevaluative in nature. Throughout the full range of axiology (the study of values), those theories deny that moral, aesthetic, economic, or other sorts of evaluations convey information or are susceptible of truth-value analysis.

Emotivism portrays ethical statements as mere emotional utterances, in line with the attempt of logical positivism to eliminate truth claims from all nonempirical statements. Early emotivists included

philosophers such as A. J. Ayer, Charles L. Stevenson, John L. Austin, and, later, Paul Edwards and Margaret MacDonald.

R. M. Hare's theory of prescriptivism has been claimed by many thinkers, including C. L. Stevenson, to be a form of near-emotivism, although this analysis is in dispute.

Imperativism espouses the position that all ethical language is imperative in character. Obviously, much ethical language is overtly and undeniably imperative—for example, "Thou shalt not kill" or "Remember thou keep holy the Lord's Day." In imperativist theory, however, even ethical statements that have the outward form of factual claims are only disguised commands: "Murder is evil" equates to "Do not commit murder," and "Theft is blameworthy" amounts to "Don't steal." Furthermore, because they are commands, they have no informational import and are not susceptible of any truth-claims, since a command can never be true or false.

Since there was no inherent contradiction between the emotivistic and the imperativistic interpretations, a third school evolved that combined both theories into a single supertheory. Emoto-imperativism maintains that any ethical utterance is actually an emotional response, a command, or both simultaneously. Thus, "murder is immoral" can be rendered as "Murder—ugh!," "Do not murder," or "Murder—ugh!—do not commit it."

On the cognitive side of the debate, ethical naturalism interpreted ethical language in terms of nonmoral empirical meanings. A clear example of ethical naturalism is Thomas Hobbes's assertion that to say that a thing is good has the simple meaning that the speaker likes that thing. As one of several alternative theories, one might hold "good" to mean that which would be desired for its own sake by any normal person with knowledge and experience of it, as Jeremy Bentham asserted.

G. E. Moore's discovery of the naturalistic fallacy has been seen by many as fatally undermining ethical naturalism, and that is certainly the case if there is any attempt in the particular ethical theory to imply a conjunction of the specific empirical content of the good and the notion that the good is "that which one ought to do." Without this prescriptive linkage, however, the naturalistic fallacy leaves ethical naturalism unscathed.

INTUITIONISM

Intuitionism has a long history in ethics, dating back at least to the moral philosophy of Lord Shaftesbury, but in modern ethical thought, it has especially been viewed as a possible solution to the metaethical enigmas surrounding ethical language.

The heart of intuitionism holds that ethical statements can be justified without being derived from other types of statements. This noninferential justification of moral judgments has often led intuitionists to call them "self-evident," but in any case, the clear import of modern intuitionism has been to avoid many of the epistemological pitfalls that have beset other theories of ethical language. Some intuitionists have gone so far as to assert a faculty of moral intuition as a source for all ethical judgments.

Despite the concern of ancient and medieval ethical philosophy with precision of language, it is modern philosophy that has made language one of the central concerns of ethics. Undoubtedly, David Hume's is/ought problem has been the source of much of this concern.

"Hume's Law"—the rule that one cannot deduce a prescriptive conclusion from descriptive premises—had the necessary effect of radically cleaving the empirical sphere of facts from the sphere of values. This radical divorcement of is and ought forced a search for new meanings in ethical language, together with the search for an epistemology of ethics that confines ethical terminology within the parameters of general philosophy of language, logic, and truth theory.

Patrick M. O'Neil

FURTHER READING

Ayer, A. J. *Language, Truth, and Logic.* London: V. Gollancz, 1936. Reprint. Introduction by Ben Rogers. London: Penguin, 2001.

Belfrage, Bertil. "Berkeley's Theory of Emotive Meaning." *History of European Ideas* 7 (1986): 643-649.

Carnap, Rudolph. *Philosophy and Logical Syntax.* 1935. Reprint. New York: AMS Press, 1979.

Derrida, Jacques. *Margins of Philosophy.* Translated by Alan Bass. Chicago: University of Chicago Press, 1982.

Edwards, Paul. *The Logic of Moral Discourse.* Glencoe, Ill.: Free Press, 1955.

Smith, R. Scott. *Virtue Ethics and Moral Knowledge:* *Philosophy of Language After MacIntyre and Hauerwas.* Burlington, Vt.: Ashgate, 2003.

Stevenson, Charles L. *Ethics and Language.* New Haven, Conn.: Yale University Press, 1960.

_____. *Facts and Values.* New Haven, Conn.: Yale University Press, 1963.

Stroll, Avrum. *The Emotive Theory of Ethics.* Berkeley: University of California Press, 1954.

Wittgenstein, Ludwig. *Philosophical Investigations.* 3d ed. Translated by G. E. M. Anscombe. Malden, Mass.: Blackwell, 2001.

SEE ALSO: Deconstruction; Derrida, Jacques; Emotivist ethics; Epistemological ethics; Fact/value distinction; Hare, R. M.; Is/ought distinction; Moral realism; Naturalistic fallacy; Postmodernism; Value.

Laozi

IDENTIFICATION: Chinese philosopher
BORN: 604 B.C.E., Quren, State of Chu, China
DIED: Sixth century B.C.E., place unknown
TYPE OF ETHICS: Classical history
SIGNIFICANCE: One of the three principal teachers of what later became known as Daoism, and supposed author of the *Dao De Jing*, Laozi ("Old Master Lao," or Lao Tze in Wade-Giles) is commonly considered to be the founder of the Daoist religion. Daoism calls on its adherents to achieve order in society and harmony in personal life by withdrawing from society, ceasing to strive, and seeking contentment without worldly fame.

Basic facts about the life of Laozi are difficult to verify. Although he is traditionally believed to have lived in the sixth century B.C.E., the earliest information regarding his life and work is found in the works of a Chinese historian of the second century B.C.E. According to this source, Laozi was a native of a small village in the south of China in a state then called Chu, which corresponds roughly to the modern-day region of eastern Henan.

It is said that Laozi served as an official historian to the royal house of Zhou and became well known for his versatile learning. He has been associated with the Li clan, a family whose existence is historical fact, but it seems that this connection was created during the Han Dynasty, several centuries after Laozi supposedly lived. At this time, the Li clan decided to adopt him as their ancestor, a practice that was common among noble families who wished to relate themselves to heroes of China's past. Some scholars contend that Laozi is a wholly fictitious person, posited by later generations of his followers who wished to ascribe various writings of Daoism to a single source.

DAO DE JING

The document attributed to Laozi, the *Dao De Jing*, or the *Way and Its Power*, is the oldest text of the Chinese mystical tradition. Known also as the *Laozi* after its alleged author, it is a short text of about five thousand Chinese characters. The work is probably not as old as tradition holds it to be. It was most likely compiled from various aphorisms that emerged during China's Warring States period, around 250 B.C.E. Scholars dispute whether it is the product of a single mind or simply a collection of adages drawn from several ancient sources. The *Dao De Jing* can be read in various ways: as a philosophical handbook on how to live prudently in the world, as a discourse on the ways of politics, as a treatise on military strategy, and as a religious tract. Chinese scholars have written hundreds of commentaries on it. A body of popular belief and religious ritual emerged from it that continues to be practiced as one of the major religions of China today.

Laozi believed that genuine knowledge of and insight into the nature of things could be obtained only through mystic intuition. He maintained that all things were composed of two opposite aspects, a kind of unity of contradiction, and much of his teaching inverted the generally assumed order of things. He said, for example, that "the softest thing in the universe overcomes the hardest" and that "seeing the small is insight, yielding to force is strength."

POPULAR DAOISM

The debate about Laozi's life derives from the context in which Daoist thinking gained popularity. The fourth and third centuries B.C.E., a period of anxiety caused by social disturbance and upheaval in China, fostered conditions that were particularly favorable to the development of philosophical and religious reflection. Some people saw Confucianism as the answer to the chaos. This school of thought maintained that social harmony derived from the fulfillment of mutual responsibilities in a clearly defined hierarchical system. Others believed that Legalism, which promoted meticulously enforced and stringent laws, was the solution for disorder.

Both of these philosophies were rejected by the Daoists. They argued that the salvation of both individuals and society could not be attained by rigorous loyalty to social codes or laws, but rather by pursuing retirement from the world as a means of mastering it. The aim, they taught, was to preserve and increase one's vital energy by recourse to various disciplines, including contemplation of the Way (Dao) as well as proper diet, breathing, and exercise. This did not exclude work, for the *Dao De Jing* assumes that work is necessary. Rather, work was to be done without rivalry, so that desire, competition, and those motivations that produce conflict would be avoided.

LEGACY OF LAOZI

Later Daoists ascribed a religious connotation to the mystical aspects of the original doctrine of Daoism. The impersonal and infinite force beneath nature became transformed into individual finite human souls, which, after death, became powerful spirits. Many important Chinese gods (of rain, fire, medicine, agriculture, and the kitchen) arose in the Daoist school. The popular Daoism of later times increasingly emphasized magical aspects that typically became attractive when daily life seemed hopelessly difficult. Particularly drawn to this form of Daoist thinking were Chinese peasants who lived on a narrow economic margin where hard work and skill were not always sufficient to guarantee even survival. As a consequence, the average person began to associate Daoism with the world of spirits who had to be placated and appeased. Increasingly, Daoists were expected to select lucky days for such important events as funerals and weddings. A fear of death emerged. This debasement of Daoism in its popular form departs significantly from the teachings of such early philosophical Daoists as Laozi.

Margaret B. Denning

FURTHER READING

Fung Yu-lan. *A History of Chinese Philosophy*. Vol. 1. Translated by Derk Bodde. Princeton, N.J.: Princeton University Press, 1983.

Hansen, Chad. *A Daoist Theory of Chinese Thought:*

A Philosophical Interpretation. New York: Oxford University Press, 2000.

Lao Tze. *Treatise on Response and Retribution.* Translated by D. T. Suzuki and Paul Carus. Edited by Paul Carus. LaSalle, Ill.: Open Court, 1973.

Lao Tzu. *Tao Te Ching: A Book About the Way and the Power of the Way.* Translated by Ursula K. Le Guin and J. P. Seaton. Boston: Shambhala, 1997.

Legge, James, trans. *"The Tao Te Ching of Lao Tzu" and "The Writings of Chuang Tzu, Books 1-17."* Vol. 1 in *The Sacred Books of China: The Texts of Taoism.* 1891. Reprint. New York: Dover, 1962.

Wang Pi. *Commentary on the Lao Tzu.* Translated by Ariane Rump and Wing-tsit Chan. Honolulu: University of Hawaii Press, 1979.

SEE ALSO: Confucian ethics; Confucius; Daoist ethics; Zhuangzi.

Law

DEFINITION: Body of rules enacted by a recognized authority that governs the conduct of the members of a given society, culture, or religion

TYPE OF ETHICS: Legal and judicial ethics

SIGNIFICANCE: There is no necessary or logical correspondence between secular law and morality, but most societies strive to a greater or lesser extent to craft their laws in such a way as to create such a correspondence. The perception that a law is unjust or immoral may be grounds to disobey that law. The laws of a given religion are generally speaking beyond question by adherents of that religion, although they may be open to interpretation.

Law is that which is laid down, ordained, or established. It is a body of rules of action prescribed by a controlling legal authority and having binding legal force. It is a written code of rules that must be obeyed by citizens, or those citizens will be subject to sanctions or legal consequences. Law is a solemn expression of the will of the supreme power of the state. Law is different from ethics. Ethics have been defined by former Supreme Court Justice Potter Stewart as "knowing the difference between what you have a right to do and what is the right thing to do."

Ethics involve following not only the letter of the law but also its spirit. Ethics are not codified in books. They are that which is moral. Ethics deal not only with conduct but also with motives and character.

Ethics constitute a higher standard than that of law; law dictates the minimum standards of behavior required of a person by society, whereas ethics go beyond what is required. Law comes from principles of morality; morality does not descend from law. Morality is that which pertains to character; it governs conduct not by legislative action or by force but by conscience and a desire to adhere to general principles of right conduct. Morality is a strict belief or conviction in the mind that is independent of legal proof or positive law. Law is essential to preserve society; ethics and morality are essential to sustain it at a higher level.

ETHICS, LAW, AND MORALITY

Ethics are concerned with human values. Often, these values are reflected in jurisprudence and in laws. Legal theory has always concerned itself with morality. Two legal philosophers who wrote a great deal concerning the relationship between law and ethics were Saint Thomas Aquinas, who founded the natural law theory of jurisprudence, and John Austin, who helped establish legal positivism. Theirs are two very different views of law, but both men stressed that law is subject to criticism from a moral point of view, and both believed that there are standards by which it may be properly judged.

Thomas Aquinas, in his *Treatise on Law*, says that "Law is nothing else than an ordinance of reason for the common good, promulgated by him who has the care of the community." He views law as something that is established for the good of all. Austin, however, sees the law as a social element that can be used for good or bad, and that can be exploited as a power tool by those in authority. Austin appears to be more realistic in his assessment of the possibility of the use of law by some to suppress others, since history has demonstrated that law is capable of doing good but has great capacity for evil. It can settle disputes and provide security, and it can lead to and enforce slavery. Law does not necessarily serve the common good and is not necessarily designed to do so. Austin recognizes that law can be good, if it is just and is derived from the laws of nature, as opposed to the laws that are framed by humankind. He says, "unjust human laws are a perversion of the ideal of law, which is given by right reason and the law of nature."

Thomas Aquinas taught that human laws are just when they serve the common good. Laws that distribute burdens fairly, show no disrespect for God, and do not exceed the lawmaker's authority are good laws. When laws fail to satisfy these conditions, however, they are unjust. Then, according to Thomas Aquinas, they do not "bind in conscience." One is morally bound to obey just laws but not unjust laws. Unjust laws should be obeyed only when circumstances warrant it or "in order to avoid scandal or disturbance." Human law does not automatically merit respect, and its legitimate claim to obedience depends on moral and ethical considerations that are independent of human law.

THE MORAL BASIS OF LAW

The role of law in enforcing morality is another ethical dilemma in the relationship between law and ethics. Conduct, the immorality of which involves serious rights violations (such as rape and murder), is obviously a proper object of state regulation and laws. The real conflict between law and ethics, however, involves state regulation of conduct that is not unjust or harmful in the sense of committing serious rights violations, but instead is regarded as immoral by the public, such as laws that prohibit sodomy between private consenting adults or laws criminalizing cohabitation. Should the mere fact that the majority of society's members and their elected representatives view such conduct as immoral serve as sufficient ground for making such conduct against the law?

Democratic societies such as the United States are supposed to allow the majority to have its way. Sometimes, however, liberty-maximizing societies will not be pure democracies and will place severe limits on the will of the majority in order to protect the rights of the individual, as does the Bill of Rights of the U.S. Constitution. Thus, a full moral discussion of the legitimacy of using the law to regulate private behavior that is judged to be immoral by a majority of citizens will mandate, at the very least, a moral theory of justified state coercion, and a moral theory of basic rights will be accorded to citizens in a just society. John Stuart Mill, in his treatise *On Liberty*, claims that the only purpose that justifies a society in coercing any of its members is to prevent harm to others.

Law has an interaction with moral opinion. Laws governing sexual conduct and drug usage confront the ethical issues head-on. What are the rights of the individual in relationship to society? What rights may the collective social body claim to the individual? When people form a society, how are the respective rights of both the individual and society at large to be structured? The general consensus is that both the individual and the society at large have rights that each must recognize, yet what those rights are and what boundaries restrict their invocation are matters of continuing struggle.

The struggle expresses itself in a number of ways, the most significant of which is the conflict between the individual conscience and the law. Should morality be legislated and enforced by law? When law and conscience conflict, which one should be obeyed? Laws seem to originate from moral convictions. Since it is morally wrong to take someone else's life without justification, murder is illegal. It is by no means clear, however, that all moral convictions of a society, even those of a majority in a democracy, should be enforced by judicial sanctions. Should moral opposition to prostitution and abortion, for example, result in laws prohibiting such activity?

Which moral convictions should be incorporated into the legal code? Who decides which moral convictions are allowed to be incorporated into law: judges, the people, or both? Should the law concern itself with traditionally private immorality (such as homosexual acts) unless the behavior is offensive to public order and decency or exposes to the ordinary citizen something that is offensive or injurious? Is an established code of morality essential to preserving social order, even at the expense of private acts? Should individual liberty and personal choice be limited simply by the moral feelings and convictions of others?

PRINCIPLES OF LAW AND ETHICS

Many great legal philosophers have debated these ideas. H. L. A. Hart, professor of jurisprudence at Oxford University, in 1959 published a detailed view of his theory of the relationship of law and morality in his treatise *Law, Liberty, and Morality*, in which he concluded that there was almost no legitimacy in making certain conduct illegal or criminal unless the conduct was harmful to others. The immorality of an action was not sufficient to make it illegal. Hart believed that "there must be a realm of private morality and immorality which is not the law's business."

Several principles are often used in the legal enforcement of morality as justification for limiting the freedom of individuals. There are the "harm" principles, which state, as did John Stuart Mill, that behavior should be prohibited only if it harms someone. There is the "offense" principle, which states that behavior should be coercively prohibited if it is publicly offensive to others, and there is the "principle of legal moralism," which holds that behavior should be punished simply because it is immoral. This perception that it is the responsibility of the law to enforce morality is used to justify the regulation of sexual and reproductive conduct, such as homosexuality and abortion. Joel Feinberg, in his essay "Hard Cases for the Harm Principle" (1973), holds that in order to characterize the kind of behavior that society is justified in controlling, the harm principle must be supplemented with a carefully drafted version of the offense principle.

There is a conflict between the individual conscience and the law. If one person believes that abortions are always morally wrong, but the law permits abortions under any circumstance, should that person attempt to prohibit women from obtaining legally permissible abortions? When the conscience and the law conflict, which takes priority? Conscience is an individual's convictions regarding what actions are right and wrong, morally good or bad. When a person's moral convictions lead him or her to object to abortion, or to a particular military position taken by the country, that person is also opposed to legal sanctions of abortion or that military position. A law is a rule of conduct prescribed by a properly constituted governing authority, enforced by sanctions, and justified by a mandate to legislate for the public benefit. A law is a rule of conduct that is "on the books."

Given these principles of conscience and law, a fundamental question arises. When a person is morally convinced that he or she ought to do one thing, yet a legally constituted authority directs otherwise, what is that person to do when the two courses of action are at odds with each other?

People faced with these choices can obey the law; follow their consciences and suffer the legal consequences because they conflict with the law; or follow neither of the previous choices, thus choosing to obey the law or follow personal conscience as the particular circumstances require. The third alternative seems to require specifying principles in terms of which the decision is made in any given instance to obey the law or follow one's conscience.

Another set of moral questions about the law is derived from the realization that law is not only a set of rules used to govern society but also a profession. Lawyers, people trained in the law who give legal advice and assistance in legal matters, have certain responsibilities as advocates that may at least appear to conflict with larger responsibilities as a whole. For example, if a defense lawyer makes the best defense for his client and obtains freedom for him, even when he is both guilty and a danger to society, the ethical question is whether this is morally justifiable. As the defendant's advocate, the lawyer must work for the client's best interests. As a citizen, however, does the lawyer not owe the best interests of society concern and attention as well? Some people would argue that it is the job of the adversary system to aim at justice and the common good, and that the lawyer's job is merely to play a part in the system, aiming not at justice but rather at vigorous advocacy of the side to which the lawyer has been assigned. Is this a valid moral defense or simply a retreat from social responsibility?

CONCEPTS OF JURISPRUDENCE

Several different philosophies guide the rule of law as interpreted by the judiciary system, as opposed to the laws that are created by legislatures and elected officials. These are the patterns of jurisprudence, or legal reasoning, which create legal standards of behavior that are as important as the statutes themselves, because they set precedents for others to follow in the enforcement of the law.

There are legal philosophers who are deeply skeptical of both doctrinal analysis and moral evaluation of the law, who see those approaches to law as so infected by prejudices in the status quo as to make them little more than covert political activity. These writers often follow the lead of "legal realism," which can be defined as the idea that law is simply a prediction of what the courts will decide, and suggest bringing such advocacy into the open and accepting an overtly political conception of the courts and the law, law being simply the exercise of power. The jurisprudential movement known as the "economic analysis of law," which encourages judges to decide cases in such a way as to ensure that economic freedom and wealth are protected and expanded, is a free-market version of the realist philosophy.

"Critical legal study," which advocates interpreting the law in ways that will assist the disadvantaged and exploited, is a socialist version of the same perspective. None of these versions, however, can exist without moral values and moral theory, because it is impossible to justify the importance of caring about whether a person has been exploited or oppressed unless moral values and moral theory have been imposed. After all, exploitation is simply a kind of unjust treatment. Thus, it appears that normative jurisprudence, the moral evaluation of law and the legal profession, will have important tasks to perform as long as human beings seek to regulate their conduct through the use of law.

Normative jurisprudence deals with the appraisal of law and the moral issues that law generates. Human law can be made and changed by deliberate decisions. What direction should those decisions take? Law claims the authority to lay down rules and enforce them. Are its claims warranted? Can people legitimately refuse to comply? Things are done in the name of the law that are not normally justifiable; people interfere in other people's lives, depriving them of goods, liberty, even life itself. How, if at all, can these practices be defended?

"Analytical jurisprudence" is the form of jurisprudence that questions the fundamental nature of law. What is law? How is it part of a system? How can a decision be made according to the law when the law is unclear? How is the law like or unlike moral standards? Analytical and normative questions concerning law are closely related.

LAW AND MORALITY

The law speaks of rights and responsibilities; duties and obligations; fairness, justice, and justification: Does this mean that the law inevitably contains or satisfies moral standards? Ideas about the essential nature of law have emphasized either its connections with or its separation from morality: Which view is right? Law is a social fact. Laws are commands. By its very nature, however, law is connected with morality. There are legal obligations that are moral obligations, but not all moral obligations are legal obligations, and the constant ethical struggle and changes

in the law represent attempts to determine which obligations should be legal obligations and should be sanctioned by law enforcement and the courts. Are there proper limits to the reach of the law? Are there areas of human conduct that are, in principle, properly beyond legal sanction? Is there a point at which it is correct to say that, notwithstanding the morality and the social preferences and spiritual values and the sensibilities of the public, the suppression of certain actions by law is not the business of the government and must be left up to each individual to determine what is moral and ethical conduct?

From time to time, the facts of a particular legal case raise issues that force people to go beyond precedent, beyond statute, and even beyond the task of constitutional interpretation. The facts of a case may take one to that area where law and philosophy intersect, where one finds lawyers thinking like philosophers and philosophers reasoning like lawyers. As the ethical issues and underlying principles that form American law and jurisprudence evolve, it becomes ever clearer that these cases play a very important role in what American society is to be and what values and standards of conduct it will set for its citizens. In trying to answer such difficult questions, the profession of law and the discipline of philosophy have much to offer each other as they combine to form and reflect the ethical, legal, and economic standards of American society.

Amy E. Bloom

FURTHER READING

Baird, Robert M., and Stuart E. Rosenbaum, eds. *Morality and the Law*. Buffalo, N.Y.: Prometheus Books, 1988. A textbook containing the writings of the legal philosophers H. L. A. Hart, Patrick Devlin, Joel Feinberg, and Erich Fromm, among others. Highly informative in referring to the different varieties of legal philosophy.

Cane, Peter. *Responsibility in Law and Morality*. Portland, Oreg.: Hart, 2002. An examination of law and ethics, both as academic disciplines and as practical activities. Explores the relationship between moral philosophy and legal philosophy, as well as the impact of theory upon practice.

Davis, Philip, ed. *Moral Duty and Legal Responsibility*. New York: Appleton-Century-Crofts, 1966. An excellent book that compares the actual legal responsibilities of citizens under law with moral duties. Usually, the legal duties are less binding on human behavior than are the moral duties, since moral duties constitute a higher standard.

Kipnis, Kenneth, ed. *Philosophical Issues in Law.* Englewood Cliffs, N.J.: Prentice-Hall, 1977. A book, containing Supreme Court cases and writings from legal philosophers, that comments on not only judicial decisions but also the philosophy applied to the decisions.

Lyons, David. *Ethics and the Rule of Law.* New York: Cambridge University Press, 1984. A treatise on the relationship between morality and the law. It details how moral judgment affects the law and how it applies to the rule of law by judges as well as legislatures.

Wasserstrom, Richard A., ed. *Morality and the Law.* Belmont, Calif.: Wadsworth, 1971. Part of the Basic Problems in Philosophy series, this volume contains the writings of legal scholars (such as John Stuart Mill's *On Liberty*) as well as treatises that discuss other applications of morality and law, such as morality in criminal law, treason, and the Model Penal Code.

SEE ALSO: Adversary system; Conscience; Due process; Hammurabi's code; Hart, H. L. A.; Jurisprudence; Legal ethics; Morality; Punishment.

Lawyer for the situation

DEFINITION: Lawyer representing multiple parties engaged in a joint endeavor or seeking an amicable settlement who is not partisan for any of those parties

TYPE OF ETHICS: Legal and judicial ethics

SIGNIFICANCE: Advocacy of a counsel for the situation, rather than a counsel for a given party thereto, represents one side in an ongoing debate over the scope of ethically proper relationships between lawyers and clients.

During the 1916 confirmation hearings on Louis D. Brandeis's nomination to the Supreme Court, opponents alleged that Brandeis was an unscrupulous lawyer who was unfit for the high court. Another Boston lawyer, Sherman Whipple, testified about his 1907 conversation with Brandeis on a bankruptcy matter in which the bankrupt party believed that Brandeis had favored his creditors. Brandeis informed Whipple that he had not represented the bankrupt party personally but had agreed to act fairly and equitably in everyone's interests. Asked whom he represented, Brandeis had replied that he "was counsel for the situation."

In contrast, the prevailing ethical model of a partisan advocate acting zealously and with absolute loyalty to a single client frowns upon a lawyer with divided loyalties, since no one "may serve two masters." Proponents, such as Yale law professor Geoffrey C. Hazard, Jr., argue that a lawyer for the situation can often act more efficiently, with less acrimony, and with a greater insight than is possible with separate representation. Lawyers often represent family members and business associates with largely harmonious interests when relations among them are cooperative rather than adversarial. Although tensions remain, the concept's official recognition has increased since it was publicized in 1916. The 1983 Model Rules of Professional Conduct recognize that a lawyer may "act as intermediary between clients" under strict limitations.

Ileana Dominguez-Urban

SEE ALSO: Adversary system; Brandeis, Louis D.; Law; Legal ethics.

Laziness

DEFINITION: Disinclination toward physical or mental exertion

TYPE OF ETHICS: Personal and social ethics

SIGNIFICANCE: The deadly sin of sloth is a species of laziness connoting disinclination to do the will of God or work toward salvation. Laziness more generally may have moral consequences if it is a persistent character trait, but it may also name a passing mood, in which case it is generally thought to be morally neutral.

Acedia ("sloth") was one of the seven deadly sins of medieval ethical tracts, which were termed deadly not because they were necessarily mortal, or unforgivable, but because they were deemed singularly attractive. Acedia is a lack of diligence in the love of

God, which may in turn lead to a lack of diligence in performing good works and an inclination toward inactivity.

The idea that idleness is inherently sinful is a post-Reformation one that is tied to the notion that economic prosperity is a sign that a person is one of God's elect. The popular moral literature of the eighteenth and nineteenth centuries is exemplified by William Hogarth's industrious apprentice, who marries the boss's daughter, and the idle apprentice, who is hanged at Tyburn.

The concept of laziness as a character defect is almost absent from early twenty-first century ethical thought; lazy behavior is viewed as the product of physical or mental illness. Disinclination toward exertion frequently accompanies depression, a complex of physiological and mental symptoms triggered by the perception that the situation is hopeless and effort will not change it. To the extent that it avoids futile effort, such inactivity is biologically adaptive.

Attitudes toward inactivity vary widely from culture to culture. The Western attitude that effort expended toward accumulating goods in excess of what is needed for survival is virtuous is far from universal, and the contempt of nineteenth century Europeans for "lazy, shiftless natives" reflects a narrow moral outlook. Avoidance of effort within a social context is damaging in a cooperative enterprise (such as marriage), however, because it deprives others of the fruits of their labors, and is generally censured.

Martha Sherwood-Pike

SEE ALSO: Anger; Envy; Gluttony; Greed; Lust; Pride; Sin.

Leadership

DEFINITION: Responsibility for making decisions that direct the actions of others

TYPE OF ETHICS: Theory of ethics

SIGNIFICANCE: Persons in positions of leadership have special responsibilities to behave ethically, both because their actions may have important consequences for the lives of others, and because they are expected to adhere to higher standards than those whom they lead.

There has always been a concern in society regarding leadership and ethics. Perhaps this is due to the recognition of the importance between the two concepts if society is to improve and bring about a certain amount of justice to individuals. Failure in an attempt to develop ethical forms of leadership may have disastrous consequences throughout the world. Individuals, countries, and future generations might suffer immeasurably as a result of leaders who avoid ethical issue. One need only look at the havoc brought throughout the world as a result of authoritarian political leaders of the twentieth century who showed little or no concern for the concept of ethical behavior.

The early twenty-first century has seen many examples of unethical behavior within the American business world that have contributed to public loss of confidence in the national economic system. The negative ramifications of this loss of confidence were felt by investors throughout the world. However, one can also find examples of beneficial results of other leaders who obviously were motivated by ethics. It is thus evident that ethics plays an important role in society. Attempting to practice ethical conduct obviously has its rewards, but unethical conduct has its faults.

IMPORTANCE OF LEADERSHIP

The ties between leadership and ethics are important for a number of reasons. For example leaders are often evaluated on the basis of their perceived ethical judgments. A simple lack of ethics therefore could result in poor evaluations by the leaders' followers. Ethics are also important because of the expectations that followers have of their leaders. Ethical behavior is something that leaders must understand as an unwritten requirement for their positions of authority. To enter into leadership positions without such an expectation contradicts an inherent requirement of the position. A lack of ethical behavior on the part of leaders may bring about negative effects on society, such as mistrust in organizations or general mistrust of a particular culture. This mistrust could also affect other parts of the organization or other entities with which it has contact over time.

Although it is generally hoped that all individuals in American society behave ethically, society expects higher standards of behavior from its leaders than it does from their followers. This is true for several reasons. For example, leaders within the public arena take oaths of office, pledging faithfully to obey and execute the law. Also, the actions of leaders, both public and private, typically affect larger numbers of people than the actions of ordinary people. When leaders engage in unethical conduct, they may hurt much larger numbers of people than nonleaders can hurt. Finally, leaders are usually expected to set examples for those who are led by them.

Laudatory though ethical behavior is, it does not come without costs. There may be a political cost. For example, judges who dismiss criminal cases because of the improper conduct of the police may not be reelected when citizens in their communities next have the opportunity to vote for judicial offices. There also may be financial costs, including possible loss of jobs. Such losses might negatively affect not only the politician, but also the politician's family. There may also be personal costs in the form of social ostracism by former friends as well as one's neighbors.

Leaders are also often faced with moral dilemmas when they face difficult public issues. This often comes about when they realize that even though their actions may be legal, they may be considered by some to be unethical. For example, abortion or artificial birth control may be viewed as unethical by a certain prominent religious group in this country. Nevertheless, both types of activity are legal in the United States. No matter what the political leader does about these activities, some group will be opposed to the particular public action.

A number of characteristics associated with leaders may affect their image as ethical. For example, a perception of honesty in a leader would tend to enhance that person's favorable image. In addition, a leader who works for the betterment of the majority, yet adequately protects individual minority rights, may also be perceived as ethical. Finally, leaders whose efforts result in improved societies without enriching the leaders might be considered ethical.

Potential future leaders may be made aware of the importance of ethical issues by a number of sources. For example, they should realize what happens to leaders who do not measure up to accepted ethical codes. Any ethical failings that result in leaders being dismissed from office should make other leaders understand what might happen to them if they behave similarly. Leaders can also be informed about attitudes toward particular activities in terms of their relationship to ethical conduct as a result of public

opinion surveys. How one's behavior is projected in the media may also serve a guide to better ethical behavior.

William E. Kelly

FURTHER READING
Covey, Stephen R. *Principle-Centered Leadership.* New York: Simon & Schuster, 1992.
Militello, Frederick, and Michael Schwalberg. "Ethical Conduct: What Financial Executives Do to Lead." *Financial Leadership* 1911 (January-February, 2003): 49.
Pareto, Vilfredo. *The Rise and Fall of the Elites.* Totowa, N.J.: Bedminster Press, 1968.
Pina-Cabral, João de, and Antónia Pedroso de Lima, eds. *Elites: Choice, Leadership, and Succession.* New York: Berg, 2000.

SEE ALSO: Corporate responsibility; Dictatorship; Dilemmas, moral; Messianism; Milgram experiment; Obedience; Paternalism; Power; Role models.

League of Nations

IDENTIFICATION: Council of world powers created to promote international cooperation, peace, and security
DATES: Began formal operations January 10, 1920; officially dissolved April 18, 1946
TYPE OF ETHICS: International relations
SIGNIFICANCE: The League of Nations was the first organization of its kind in modern history. Its effort to prevent war failed, but the experience of the league in the interwar period provided important lessons for the world's major governments in creating the United Nations as a successor organization.

The idea of a league of nations gained currency during World War I in large part because of the enormous human losses caused by the war and the belief of many leaders that only an international organization could prevent the recurrence of such a terrible cataclysm. Woodrow Wilson is credited with promoting the idea of the league, because of the call in his Fourteen Points for the creation of "a general association of nations." There were others, how-

U.S. president Woodrow Wilson boards the ship taking him to Europe, where he helped persuade delegates to the Paris Peace Conference to create the League of Nations. However, despite Wilson's championing of the League, the United States never joined the international organization. (AP/Wide World Photos)

ever, whose influence generated support for an international association of peace-loving states, notably President William H. Taft in the United States, Sir Edward Grey and Lord Robert Cecil in Great Britain, and Field Marshall J. C. Smuts in South Africa. In several allied and neutral countries during World War I, organizations were formed to enlist support for a postwar world organization. Nevertheless, special credit does belong to Wilson because of his leadership at the Paris Peace Conference in 1919 in drafting the Covenant of the League of Nations. The League covenant was incorporated into the Treaty of Versailles, which was adopted at Paris in 1919.

The central purpose of the league was to promote international peace and security. It sought to achieve this end by means of a variety of techniques, of which the most notable was a system for the peaceful settlement of disputes between states and for taking col-lective action against those nations that committed aggressive war. Other important objectives of the league were economic and social cooperation, disarmament, and national self-determination.

ORGANIZATION OF THE LEAGUE

There were three principal organs of the league: an assembly in which each member was represented; a council that was to be composed of representatives of the United States, Great Britain, France, Italy, and Japan as permanent members plus four others elected by the General Assembly; and a permanent Secretariat headed by a Secretary General. The assembly met annually beginning in September. Assembly decisions required a unanimous vote, thus giving every member a veto. In practice, members who disagreed with the majority often abstained, permitting many decisions to be taken by consensus. During the life of the league, sixty-three states were members, seventeen members withdrew from the assembly, and one, the Soviet Union, was expelled.

Because the United States declined to join the league, it never joined the council. The number of elected members was increased first to six and later to nine. The council generally met four times a year. While the scope of discussion in the assembly encompassed any issue of international affairs, the council confined its discussion to political problems. Decisions in the council required a unanimous vote, though if the subject was a dispute that was likely to lead to conflict, the parties in contention could not participate in the vote.

The principal purpose of the league was to resolve disputes between states and keep the peace. This responsibility was spelled out in Articles 10 to 17 of the covenant, which embodied what has become known as the idea of collective security. According to Article 10, each member undertook "to respect and preserve as against external aggression the territorial integrity and existing political independence of all Members of the League." Members were to settle their disputes peacefully, and under the provision of Article 16, league members were committed to join in common action against any state that went to war without observing the procedures for peaceful settlement specified in the covenant. Economic sanctions were to be the principal, though not necessarily exclusive, form of sanctions used to bring an aggressor state to heel.

LEGACY OF THE LEAGUE

Although the league is remembered primarily for its political activities, it also made major contributions of a social, scientific, economic, and humanitarian nature. These include work in controlling drug trafficking, protection of women, child welfare, abolition of slavery, and support for refugees. In the political realm, the league is considered to have been a failure, as indicated by the outbreak of World War II less than two decades after World War I.

In fact, the political contributions of the league were significant. Some of its major successes came during the 1920's: settlement of the Swedish-Finnish dispute over the Aland Islands, settlement of the Polish-German frontier dispute in Upper Silesia, and prevention of war between Greece and Bulgaria in 1925. Germany's entrance into the league in 1926 was an important step in the reconstruction of Europe. That step was linked to the signing of treaties known as the Locarno Pact, which guaranteed the inviolability of the Franco-German frontier and the demilitarization of the Rhineland.

The league's political accomplishments were, however, outweighed by its failures, particularly during the 1930's. A major blow to the league's prestige resulted from its inability to act against Japan when that country invaded Manchuria in September, 1931. The Lytton Commission, created by the League Council, determined that Japan was guilty of aggression. The only consequence of the league's investigation was Japan's withdrawal from the organization. The league's first major test of collective security was a failure.

Even more fateful for the league were the half-hearted economic sanctions imposed upon Italy to stop Benito Mussolini's invasion of Ethiopia in 1935. Because oil was not included in the embargo, the sanctions failed to stop the Italian dictator, and in July the assembly abandoned the sanctions. This blow to League prestige proved to be fatal. Within the next three years, Nazi Germany embarked upon a campaign of aggression that the league was powerless to stop. The Rhineland was remilitarized in violation of the Versailles Treaty (1936), Austria was annexed (1938), Czechoslovakia was occupied (1938-1939), and Poland was invaded (1939). The expulsion of the Soviet Union for its war against Finland was the league's last action, but that action reflected the organization's impotence rather than its efficacy.

FAILURE

Several explanations have been advanced to account for the political failure of the League of Nations. The first was the absence of the United States as a member. Without American involvement, economic and military sanctions were very difficult to institute. Second, the decision-making rules of the league made it difficult for the organization to take strong and decisive measures. Third, there were legal loopholes in the covenant that permitted members to evade their responsibilities. Fourth, the league lacked teeth; that is, it did not have military forces at its disposal to use against an aggressor. Fifth, the great powers that dominated the league were unwilling to subordinate their national interests to their commitments under the covenant.

Students of international organization are still divided in their general evaluation of the league: Did it fail because it was too weak or did it attempt to accomplish more than was possible in a world of sovereign states? Whatever the answer, there was enough faith in the principles of the league to make a second effort. The United Nations was organized in such a way as to overcome what many believed to be the flaws of the league. The Security Council of the United Nations has enforcement power that the League of Nations never possessed.

Joseph L. Nogee

FURTHER READING

Cecil, Robert, Viscount. *A Great Experiment*. New York: Oxford University Press, 1941.

Kuehl, Warren F., and Lynne K. Dunn. *Keeping the Covenant: American Internationalists and the League of Nations, 1920-1939*. Kent, Ohio: Kent State University Press, 1997.

Riches, Cromwell A. *The Unanimity Rule and the League of Nations*. Baltimore: Johns Hopkins University Press, 1933. Reprint. New York: AMS Press, 1971.

Schiffer, Walter. *The Legal Community of Mankind: A Critical Analysis of the Modern Concept of World Organization*. New York: Columbia University Press, 1954.

Walters, Francis P. *History of the League of Nations*. New York: Oxford University Press, 1969.

Zimmern, Alfred E. *The League of Nations and the Rule of Law*. New York: Russell & Russell, 1969.

SEE ALSO: Conflict resolution; International justice; International law; Treaty of Versailles; United Nations.

League of Women Voters

IDENTIFICATION: American voter education and advocacy organization

DATE: Founded in 1920

TYPE OF ETHICS: Sex and gender issues

SIGNIFICANCE: The League of Women Voters was founded on the principle that democratic government requires political responsibility on the part of its citizenry. It therefore encourages all members of the public to become as informed and politically active as possible.

The League of Women Voters is a direct descendant of the women's suffrage movement. At its jubilee convention in 1919, the National American Women's Suffrage Association, which was the leading women's suffrage organization, voted to dissolve itself because of the final ratification of the Nineteenth Amendment and to form a new body to be known as the League of Women Voters. The amendment enfranchised women in all federal elections. Ratification was completed in 1920, and the league was formally launched at a convention in Chicago.

Although many of the league's organizational principles and bylaws were not clear at that point, the new organization was based on several principles that have been maintained throughout its history. The purpose of the league was to educate the public in general and women in particular regarding public issues by preparing and distributing information and encouraging political participation. Until 1946, the center of the league's internal organization lay in relatively autonomous state associations similar to those that had been so successful during the struggle for women's suffrage. There was considerable disunity. In 1946, the league reorganized itself into a membership association of individuals rather than a federation of state associations. By 1992, it had some 125,000 members in 1,350 chapters all over the United States.

The major thrust of the league's activities continues to be voter education. At the local level, league chapters study issues, distribute information, and sponsor "candidates' nights" at which local political candidates appear and discuss the issues and their candidacies. At the national level, the League of Women Voters has been very active in arranging presidential campaign debates and in attempting to establish debating rules that enhance the quality and educational value of the discussion. The league, although nonpartisan, has never shied away from taking positions on national issues; for example, the league supported American foreign aid during the 1940's and 1950's, and the recognition of China during the 1960's. The league continues to be a force for the rational study of public issues and for moderation in politics.

Robert Jacobs

SEE ALSO: Campaign finance reform; Civil rights and liberties; Democracy; Equal Rights Amendment; Suffrage; Welfare programs.

Legal ethics

DEFINITION: Standards of moral and professional behavior governing members of the legal professions

TYPE OF ETHICS: Legal and judicial ethics

SIGNIFICANCE: American legal ethics evolved with the growth of the country, resulting finally in the American Bar Association's 1983 Model Rules of Professional Conduct.

Ethics are a mixture of honesty, decency, manners, and etiquette. They are not rules or laws imposed by others; rather, they are personal, internal mechanisms arrived at through self-evaluation and self-knowledge. Legal ethics are also internal individual beliefs. In the narrowest sense, legal ethics concern professional conduct. More broadly, they encompass the moral lives of lawyers and their behavior toward clients, courts, and colleagues. Legal ethics are fraught with the potential for conflict, as members of the legal profession can find themselves with conflicting loyalties.

Lawyers are taught that loyalty to a client should be foremost; personal interests and the interests of others should be relegated to second place. Lawyers should counsel their clients on the best way to use the law to their advantage and, if necessary, how to escape or mitigate its effect. Conflict often arises between the public trust a lawyer owes as an officer of the court and the loyalty owed the client. A lawyer may have to make a decision whether to report a client's improper behavior to the court and put public trust first or to counsel the client to cease and put the client first. In some cases, conscientiously and loyally representing a client may lead to civil disobedience or to the public impression that a lawyer is unethical and unprincipled.

ETHICS AND COMMON LAW

In addition to being personal, legal ethics derive from discussion and meeting with other members of the legal profession and agreement as to what is expected and accepted behavior. This tradition is found in English common law. King Edward I of England decreed in 1292 that the Court of Common Pleas was to choose lawyers and students to take part in court business and that these individuals were to live together under the supervision of the court. Also in the thirteenth century, the Inns of Court were established. True inns, they became places for people studying and practicing the law to live and work together under the supervision of judges. From this community, through discussion, came a set of professional mores guiding those engaged in the law and setting certain ethical behaviors and standards. American law and ethics followed the English pattern for a time.

As the United States expanded westward, however, and as the nation's commercial enterprises diversified, new types of knowledge and expertise were needed. This knowledge had to come from experience rather than from books or from the court itself. At the same time, the tradition of spending evenings with colleagues at the end of a day in court—a time for discussing mutually accepted rules and self-government—was becoming a thing of the past. Because there was less internal pressure to be faithful to established legal principles, ethical problems began to arise more frequently, and there was a growing movement urging the state to begin regulating the practice of law. Yet the rapidly increasing complexity of American law made it obvious to many observers that those who knew the legal system best—the lawyers themselves—would have to be the ones to develop new ethical guidelines or rules of professional conduct. In 1836, one of the first extensive considerations of American legal ethics was published by University of Maryland professor David Hoffman. His *Fifty Resolutions in Regard to Professional Ethics* dealt with etiquette and ethics and attempted to discourage behavior that would reflect badly on the legal profession.

WRITTEN RULES

Pennsylvania judge George Sharswood's written lectures on professional deportment, *The Aims and Duties of the Profession of the Law* (1854), noted the differences between professional and personal ethics and served as the basis for the Code of Professional Ethics, enacted by the Alabama state bar in 1887. Alabama's was the first state bar to enact such a code. The American Bar Association's Canons of Professional Ethics, also drawing heavily on Sharswood, were promulgated in 1908. By 1920 the canons had been adopted by all but thirteen of the state bar associations, although not without modification.

The canons were detailed, dealing with the positive obligations of a lawyer, such as the duty to represent the poor and indigent. They were largely hortatory in nature, intended as professional rules rather than public laws. By 1969 the original thirty-two canons had grown to forty-seven, supported by more than fourteen hundred interpreting opinions, often lacking coherence and consistency.

The American Bar Association (ABA) recognized the shortcomings of the canons. It sought rules that would exhort lawyers to uphold the highest standards of justice upon which the country's legal system was based, that would weed out those whose standards could damage the reputation of all, and that would provide standards for new lawyers. The Code of Professional Responsibility was therefore adopted, amended as needed, by all state bar associations except California, which adopted its own similar rules. The code had three parts: canons, expressing standards of professional conduct; ethical considerations, setting aspirational objectives toward which all should strive; and disciplinary rules, setting the minimum standards of conduct to avoid disciplinary action. Supreme Court decisions in the 1970's that addressed legal advertising and fees, as well as continuing problems with the ethical considerations, necessitated a new document.

In 1983 the American Bar Association produced the final version of the Model Rules of Professional Conduct. By the early 1990's most state bar associations had adopted the model rules, sometimes with substantial revision. The model rules focus more on mandatory guidelines for the legal profession than on moral considerations.

Bar association grievance committees have the ability to investigate complaints and, if necessary, refer the complaint to the court for further action. Disbarment may be recommended if a lawyer is found untrustworthy to advise and act for clients or if the lawyer's conduct reflects on the dignity and reputation of the court and the legal profession. Disciplinary codes cannot replace ethics and personal ethical behavior. They can only make it difficult for those guilty of unethical behavior to continue in the practice of law.

Elizabeth Algren Shaw

FURTHER READING

Applbaum, Arthur Isak. *Ethics for Adversaries: The Morality of Roles in Public and Professional Life*. Princeton, N.J.: Princeton University Press, 1999.

Kronman, Anthony T. *The Lost Lawyer: Failing Ideals of the Legal Profession*. Cambridge, Mass.: Harvard University Press, 1993.

Linowitz, Sol M., and Martin Mayer. *Betrayed Profession: Lawyering at the End of the Twentieth Century*. New York: Charles Scribner's Sons, 1994.

Rhode, Deborah L. *In the Interests of Justice: Reforming the Legal Profession*. New York: Oxford University Press, 2001.

_____, ed. *Ethics in Practice Lawyers' Roles, Responsibilities, and Regulation*. New York: Oxford University Press, 2000.

Salkin, Patricia E., ed. *Ethical Standards in the Public Sector: A Guide for Government Lawyers, Clients, and Public Officials*. Chicago: Section of State and Local Government Law, American Bar Association, 1999.

Schrader, David E. *Ethics and the Practice of Law*. Englewood Cliffs, N.J.: Prentice Hall, 1988.

Simon, William H. *The Practice of Justice: A Theory of Lawyers' Ethics*. Cambridge, Mass.: Harvard University Press, 1998.

SEE ALSO: Adversary system; American Inns of Court; Attorney-client privilege; Attorney misconduct; Code of Professional Responsibility; Codes of civility; Judicial conduct code; Jurisprudence; Law; Personal injury attorneys.

Leibniz, Gottfried Wilhelm

IDENTIFICATION: German philosopher
BORN: July 1, 1646, Leipzig, Saxony (now in Germany)
DIED: November 14, 1716, Hanover (now in Germany)
TYPE OF ETHICS: Enlightenment history
SIGNIFICANCE: A leading Protestant philosopher of the Enlightenment, Leibniz attempted, in such works as *Theodicy: Essays on the Goodness of God, the Freedom of Man, and the Origin of Evil*

(*Essais de Théodicée sur la bonté de Dieu, la liberté de l'homme et l'origine du mal*, 1710) and *New Essays Concerning Human Understanding* (*Nouveaux essais sur l'entendement humain*, written 1704; published 1765), to reconcile faith and reason.

A "universal genius"—mathematician, scientist, diplomat, historian, ecumenist, and philosopher—Leibniz was "the pathfinder of the German Enlightenment." For the last forty years of his life, he worked for the House of Hanover, principally as the royal librarian. A devout Lutheran, Leibniz, in an age of increasing determinism and materialism, strove to envision a worldview that was rational, hopeful, and spiritual. Reality for Leibniz was composed of an infinite number of individual spiritual substances ("monads," from the Greek word meaning "one"), arranged in an ascending order of consciousness from nearly nothing to God ("the Supreme Monad"). Created by God, this is "the best of all possible worlds," since in it an infinite being chose to honor the limitations of finitude. So-called evils (material, mental, or moral) contribute to the ultimate good of the universe. This intelligent and benevolent world is rational, and all things in it exhibit a pre-established harmony, or "unity." Such a universe invites ethical action that is both personal and social, both thoughtful and charitable.

C. George Fry

SEE ALSO: Enlightenment ethics; Idealist ethics; Religion.

Lemkin, Raphael

IDENTIFICATION: Polish legal scholar and political activist

BORN: June 24, 1900, Bezwodne, Russian Empire (now in Belarus)

DIED: August 28, 1959, New York, New York

TYPE OF ETHICS: Human rights

SIGNIFICANCE: Lemkin is credited with coining the word "genocide"; his vigorous efforts to have genocide recognized as a crime under international law facilitated the passage of the United Nations Convention on the Prevention and Punishment of the Crime of Genocide in 1948.

Raphael Lemkin began formulating his legal theories about the annihilation of national, religious, and racial groups when he was a law student in post-World War I Poland. Sensitized to organized mass persecution as a young Jewish child in Imperial Russia, he developed an intellectual interest in government-condoned killing as a university student, when he learned that there was no legal basis for prosecuting the perpetrators of the 1915 massacre of Armenians in Turkey. Lemkin's formal support for the codification of laws against acts of mass killing began in 1933 when he unsuccessfully urged adoption of an international treaty that was to punish acts of mass killing, at a meeting of the Legal Council of the League of Nations in Madrid, Spain.

Lemkin spent the ensuing years in private legal practice and was forced to flee Poland in 1939, when Germany invaded the country. After immigrating to the United States, Lemkin taught at several universities and served as a legal expert for the U.S. War Department. Profoundly influenced by the cruelty of the Nazi wartime policies in occupied Europe, Lemkin continued to write and solidify his ideas on the codification of punishment for crimes against humanity. He also served as a legal consultant to the chief U.S. prosecutor at the Nuremberg Trials.

Lemkin defined the word "genocide," which combines the Greek word *genos* (race) and the Latin *cide* (killing), as a deliberate destruction of a racial, ethnic, religious, or political group. He first used the word in his 1944 book, *Axis Rule in Occupied Europe*.

Myrna L. Goodman

SEE ALSO: Genocide, frustration-aggression theory of; Genocide and democide; Holocaust; Rwanda genocide; United Nations Convention on the Prevention and Punishment of the Crime of Genocide; Wiesel, Elie.

Lenin, Vladimir Ilich

IDENTIFICATION: Russian political leader

BORN: Vladimir Ilich Ulyanov; April 22, 1870, Simbirsk, Russia

DIED: January 21, 1924, Gorki, Soviet Union

TYPE OF ETHICS: Modern history

SIGNIFICANCE: One of the most influential political figures of the twentieth century, Lenin founded the Soviet Union, creating a national government based on the theories of Karl Marx and setting an example for others to do likewise.

V. I. Ulyanov Lenin was one of the most influential political leaders of modern history. His significance was both theoretical and practical. His two more significant theoretical contributions revolved around his theory of imperialism and his conception of the Communist Party. His practical contribution was as the maker and sustainer of one of the great revolutions of modern history.

LENINISM IN THEORY

Lenin's theory of "imperialism, the highest stage of capitalism," attempted to address the principal problem confronting Marxism during the last years of the nineteenth century and the early years of the twentieth century. Simply put, the advanced industrial powers appeared to have avoided many of the debilitating contradictions that Marx had predicted would cause the final crisis in the fourth stage in his theory of the historical process—capitalism. Marx believed that the anticipated crisis of capitalism would inevitably trigger a worker revolution, thereby advancing history to its fifth and culminating stage of history—socialism. Conversely, however, without the crisis of capitalism, there could be no revolution.

Drawing upon the thought of several other European Marxist and English liberal theorists, Lenin posited that the advanced industrial economies had temporarily avoided the contradictions central to Marxist theory by expanding their economies to engulf the entire globe. In doing so, the capitalists had been able to secure cheap labor and raw materials, as well as markets for products and outlets for surplus capital. This process had allowed the capitalists to derive "superprofits," which had, in turn, been partly used to bribe the workers in the advanced industrial countries and thereby postpone the inevitable crisis and revolution. Lenin referred to this expansion of the industrial economies to a global scale as "imperialism."

Lenin went on to maintain, however, that imperialism could not last in perpetuity but would inevitably be overcome by its own contradictions and give way to socialism as Marx had originally predicted. In

the broadest sense, Lenin argued that once the industrial economies had expanded to engulf the entire world, the contradictions that Marx had anticipated would eventually be activated. Monopolies and states would violently compete for global domination, with weaker competitors being driven from the field. Lenin further theorized that the imperial states would fight wars for the distribution of colonies and semicolonies, conflicts that would devastate both winners and losers.

Ultimately, the decline in superprofits and the costly international conflicts would force the capital-

Vladimir Ilich Lenin. (Library of Congress)

ists to withdraw first some, and eventually all, of the material and political concessions made earlier to the workers in the advanced industrial countries. This, combined with the suffering caused by the imperialist wars, would yield a dramatic increase in societal tension. Thus, the final crisis of capitalism would emerge, resulting in the eventual but inevitable overthrow of capitalism by the workers of the industrial states and the entry into history's culminating stage of socialism.

Lenin's other principal theoretical contribution to the Marxist movement was his conception of the Communist Party and its role as an agent to advance the historical process. Marx had expressed optimism that the workers of the advanced industrial countries would acquire both the impetus and organizational skills necessary to make the proletariat revolution merely by experiencing the deteriorating socioeconomic conditions within mature capitalist systems. Lenin, however, disagreed. He acknowledged that the workers would be aware of their increasingly miserable conditions and would, periodically and spontaneously, rise in revolt against their oppressors. Lenin maintained, however, that this nonrational impulse to revolt was not, in itself, motivated or guided by any understanding of the historical significance of the action.

For Lenin, only the "conscious" individuals in society, those who had studied the flow of history as interpreted by Marx and his successors, could understand where their particular society had been and currently was in the flow of history. Only these conscious people were capable of understanding where society was inevitably going and, perhaps most important, assessing the current revolutionary tasks confronting their society as it traversed the road of history. On this basis Lenin defined the Communist Party as composed of those individuals who had gained "consciousness" and were prepared to dedicate their lives on a full-time basis to promoting the revolution and advancing the historical process.

Lenin charged the party with the task of preparing for the moment when the impulse for a spontaneous outburst by the masses against local conditions fully ripened. When that outburst finally occurred, the party would seize the leadership of the revolt and channel it into action that would meaningfully advance the historical process. In short, the party alone was incapable of successfully making a revolution, while the masses alone, without guidance from the party, would similarly be incapable of taking historically meaningful action. Together, however, the masses, led by the party, would be the agents of history.

PLANNING COMMUNISM

Based upon these considerations, Lenin posited two missions for the party. The long-range mission was to educate the masses so that they might eventually acquire consciousness. Until that long-term goal was achieved, the immediate task of the party was to lead the masses. Since only the party knew what was appropriate policy and proper action for the unconscious masses, the party had a responsibility to guide or, if necessary, coerce the masses into proper action. Thus, although the means to move the masses along lines determined to be appropriate by the party might be manipulative, ruthless, or cruel, in Lenin's eyes, the party knew what was ultimately in the best interests of society. In short, for Lenin, the goal of future societal fulfillment via entry into the stage of socialism justified whatever means were deemed necessary to advance society in that direction.

Finally, since Lenin conceived of the party as being critical to historically significant action, he felt that the party's decision-making process must not be paralyzed by internal division and indecisiveness. To avoid that danger, Lenin argued that the party must employ the decision-making principle of "democratic-centralism." Lenin believed that all party members shared a common commitment to advancing the historical process under the leadership of the party. Thus, Lenin maintained that, with respect to specific policy questions confronting the party, the members of the party should be free to exchange opinions frankly prior to a decision having been made. Once a final decision was made by the party leadership, however, Lenin required all party members to defer to their common commitment to the party as the instrument of history, unreservedly accept that decision, and enthusiastically work toward its implementation. Any further dissent regarding the announced decision would constitute a breach of party discipline. Henceforth, discussion could center only on the manner in which the decision would be implemented.

While Lenin hoped that the principle of democratic-centralism would unite diversity of opinion and freedom of expression with resolute, united action, in fact, the principle was fraught with difficulties. In reality, any decision and its manner of implementation are much more closely intertwined than the principle of democratic-centralism allowed. Moreover, while in principle the party rules provided for the democratic election of its leadership, in reality leadership recruitment into the party hierarchy soon came to be based upon co-option by the incumbents. Overall, in practice, the democratic element of democratic-centralism yielded to the centralizing component.

Finally, connecting his conception of the party with his theory of imperialism, Lenin came to believe that it would be easier to start a revolution in the less industrially developed countries than in the advanced capitalist states, although he believed that the revolutionary momentum would be more difficult to sustain in these countries. This conclusion would shape Lenin's views regarding the nature and timing of the revolutionary process in Russia.

LENINISM IN PRACTICE

Armed with these theoretical concepts, Lenin made his practical contribution to history—as the maker of the Bolshevik Revolution and the founder of the Soviet Union. In Lenin's eyes, World War I, the first of the anticipated imperialist wars, offered a unique opportunity to advance the historical process internationally. He believed that if the Russian proletariat could seize power, that act would have profound consequences for the entire international system. He argued that Russia was a semicolony, exploited by the advanced industrial powers. Thus, a successful Russian proletariat takeover would disrupt the entire global economy upon which imperialism was based. Moreover, a successful revolution in Russia would signal the overthrow of what many in Europe regarded as the system's most reactionary state.

Finally, in the largest sense, a successful takeover by Russian workers would provide a heroic example for the workers of the advanced industrial economies to emulate. In short, a revolution in Russia, even a democratic one, would serve as the "spark" that would ignite the pyres of revolution in the advanced industrial countries and yield a quantum leap in the historical process. Based upon these considerations, Lenin moved decisively to capitalize upon the revolutionary situation in Russia in 1917; in the autumn, he employed the party to seize power on behalf of the Russian workers.

It soon became obvious that the proletariat of the developed industrial countries would fail to advance history by following the Russian example, overthrowing the existing capitalist order, and resolutely moving toward the final Marxist stage of socialism. Prior to taking power, Lenin had suggested that under these circumstances the Russian workers should launch a revolutionary war designed to liberate the European workers from their capitalist overlords. After taking power, however, Lenin realistically recognized that the new Soviet state lacked the resources to launch such a war of liberation. Moreover, to do so would jeopardize the revolutionary gains that had already been made. Therefore, Lenin decided that the foremost priority for the new Soviet regime would be to protect the revolutionary gains already made in Russia; only insofar as those gains would not be jeopardized would the Soviet Union attempt to spread revolution abroad.

Within Russia itself, however, retaining power was far from certain. The new Soviet regime was immediately confronted by a series of challenges emanating from both within and outside Soviet-controlled territory. Externally, the Soviets were threatened by counterrevolutionaries, national separatists, and the troops of foreign powers. Internally, a variety of noncommunist elements challenged the authority of the Communist Party of the Soviet Union (CPSU).

WAR COMMUNISM

To defeat these challenges, Lenin launched what became known as the period of War Communism. Between 1918 and 1921, he orchestrated a series of campaigns at various levels that were designed to suppress ruthlessly all internal challenges to the monopoly rule of the CPSU, while simultaneously increasingly centralizing the party itself at the expense of interparty democracy. Similarly, Lenin aggressively mobilized Russia's economic resources, although at the expense of such early policies as worker control over industry. Finally, Lenin oversaw the formation of the Red Army and, under his overall leadership, that instrument was used to crush the counterrevolutionaries and national separatists. In the eyes of many party members, however, many of the measures taken during the period of War Communism constituted an abandonment of the ideals of the revolution and were justifiable only as temporary expedients necessary to retain communist control in Russia. Finally, by late 1920, it appeared that the enemies of the Soviet regime had been routed and that the CPSU had successfully retained power.

Organized elements within the party now began to emerge, calling themselves by such names as the Workers Opposition and the Democratic Centralists, arguing that with the passage of the initial period of threat to the revolution, the party could now turn its attention to realizing the ideals of the revolution, ideals that had been compromised during the period of War Communism. Indeed, the issue of the future of the party and the revolution came to a head at the Tenth CPSU Congress in 1921. Here, Lenin not only successfully defeated the platforms presented by the party dissenters but also resolutely moved to drive them from the party hierarchy and permanently ban factionalism from the party.

CRUSHING OPPOSITION

Fatefully for the future of the CPSU, Lenin opted to sustain and intensify the bureaucratic, centralized, and authoritarian character that the party had increasingly assumed during the period of War Communism. Moreover, he intensified the campaign to crush any opposition to the CPSU monopoly rule over the Soviet Union. Finally, under Lenin's leadership, the party continued its relentless campaign to penetrate and exercise control over all elements of Soviet society. Thus, although with the inauguration of the New Economic Policy in 1921 the regime retreated from some of the extreme economic measures taken during the period of War Communism, the foundations and character of the Soviet sociopolitical, totalitarian system were firmly established by Lenin and his lieutenants.

Although, in his final months of life, Lenin may have had some regrets concerning the direction that the Soviet Union and the CPSU had taken under his leadership, everything that Lenin did during these formative years was consistent with the theoretical approach that he had formulated prior to the takeover in 1917. The ends—the advancement of the historical process—justified any means utilized in pursuit of that goal. Lenin's goal had been to make and consolidate a revolution in Russia led exclusively by the Communist Party. With enormous determination and ruthlessness, Lenin had succeeded in attaining his objective.

Howard M. Hensel

FURTHER READING

Chamberlin, William H. *The Russian Revolution 1917-1921*. 2 vols. New York: Grosset & Dunlap, 1965.

Daniels, Robert V. *The Conscience of the Revolution*. New York: Simon & Schuster, 1969.

Fischer, Louis. *The Life of Lenin*. New York: Harper & Row, 1964.

Lenin, Vladimir Il'ich. *Lenin on Politics and Revolution*. Edited by James E. Connor. New York: Pegasus, 1968.

Meyer, Alfred G. *Leninism*. New York: Praeger, 1962.

Pannekoek, Anton. *Lenin as Philosopher: A Critical Examination of the Philosophical Basis of Leninism*. Rev. ed. Edited by Lance Byron Richey. Milwaukee, Wis.: Marquette University Press, 2003.

Schapiro, Leonard. *The Origin of the Communist Autocracy*. 2d ed. Cambridge, Mass.: Harvard University Press, 1977.

White, James D. *Lenin: The Practice and Theory of Revolution*. New York: Palgrave, 2001.

SEE ALSO: Class struggle; Communism; Marx, Karl; Marxism; Socialism; Stalin, Joseph.

Leopold, Aldo

IDENTIFICATION: American scientist and writer
BORN: January 11, 1887, Burlington, Iowa
DIED: April 21, 1948, near Baraboo, Sauk County, Wisconsin
TYPE OF ETHICS: Environmental ethics
SIGNIFICANCE: Leopold was responsible for the establishment of the first U.S. Wilderness Area. His *A Sand County Almanac* (1949) put forward the "Land Ethic," which placed humanity within, rather than in charge of, the ecosystem.

Aldo Leopold's boyhood was dominated by sports and natural history. After completing one year of postgraduate work in forestry at Yale, Leopold spent fifteen years with the U.S. Forest Service in Arizona and New Mexico. There, he developed the idea of preserving large, ecologically undisturbed areas for ecological preservation; in 1924, he precipitated the establishment of the first U.S. forest Wilderness Area in the Gila National Forest of New Mexico. In 1933, he became professor of wildlife management at the

University of Wisconsin. In 1934 he became a member of the federal Special Committee on Wildlife Restoration. He was a founder of the Wilderness Society in 1935.

Leopold made a family project of restoring the ecosystem to its original condition on an abandoned farm he had purchased near Baraboo, Wisconsin. His posthumous publication relating to this experience, *A Sand County Almanac*, has become an environmentalist classic, and the farm has become a research center, the Leopold Reserve. Four of Leopold's five children became prominent, environmentally oriented scientists. Three of them, Starker, Luna, and Estella, became members of the National Academy of Sciences. His son Carl became an established research scientist, and his daughter Nina became director of the Leopold Reserve.

Ralph L. Langenheim, Jr.

SEE ALSO: Conservation; Deep ecology; Ecology; Environmental movement; Exploitation; Muir, John; National Park System, U.S.; Nature, rights of; Wilderness Act of 1964.

Leviathan

IDENTIFICATION: Book by Thomas Hobbes (1588-1679)
DATE: Published in 1651
TYPE OF ETHICS: Enlightenment history
SIGNIFICANCE: *Leviathan* is a rational, systematic study and justification of natural rights, sovereignty, and state absolutism. In it, Hobbes claimed logically to deduce a theory of ethics and politics from scientific and mathematically verifiable facts about human nature.

The moral language utilized by Hobbes in his *Leviathan* was expressed by the precise vocabulary of geometry, empirical science, and physics. The mathematical and scientific study of politics adopted by Hobbes did not incorporate a value-free or ethically neutral perspective. Hobbes's political ethical theory was grounded in a causal-mechanical and materialistic metaphysical theory. Hobbes's mechanistic scientific model was explanatory of all existence, since the universe consisted of interconnected matter in mo-

tion. This complex political theory and set of ethical arguments were deduced from Hobbes's pessimistic interpretation of human nature in the context of an original, or primitive, condition.

It was in this highly unstable, anarchic, and violent state of nature that individuals competitively pursued their self-interests. Hobbes depicted with bleak realism "the life of man solitary, poor, nasty, brutish, and short." The political ethics in *Leviathan* were justified primarily by the natural human egoistic motivation of fear of violent death, and secondarily by the passions for power and material possessions. Therefore, self-preservation was the most fundamental natural right and was the central reason for individuals to leave the state of nature and enter into commonwealths.

Hobbes's articulation of the normative egalitarian principle of universal natural rights was expressed in conjunction with his radical rejection of the principle of the divine right of kings. Hobbes's rejection of moral objectivism was articulated in conjunction with his moral relativism, which claimed that the diverse corporeal natures of individuals were explanatory of the multiplicity of value judgments. Moral judgments were identified by a particular individual's appetites and aversions, or mechanical movements toward or away from material objects. There was no *summum bonum*, or universal absolute common good, although the common evil to be avoided was violent death.

Hobbes expressed a political theory of authority that was justified by means of scientific, rational, and logical arguments, in lieu of traditional theories of political legitimacy based upon convention, theology, or the divine right of kings. Citizens of Hobbes's prescribed commonwealth were bound by a social contract or by the superior power of the sovereign to obey all the government's commands, regardless of the moral content of such commands or the intention of the sovereign. Hobbes's core assumption of the natural insecurity of human life was linked to his prescription of an absolute monarchy or a highly centralized parliamentary body as the most desirable form of government.

Mitchel Gerber

SEE ALSO: Hobbes, Thomas; Locke, John; Machiavelli, Niccolò; Social contract theory; *Two Treatises of Government*.

Levinas, Emmanuel

IDENTIFICATION: Philosopher and Jewish adult educator
BORN: January 12, 1906, Kaunas, Lithuania
DIED: December 25, 1995, Paris, France
TYPE OF ETHICS: Theory of ethics
SIGNIFICANCE: Levinas argued that ethics is the basis of philosophy, and that responsibility to others is the basis of ethics.

Emmanuel Levinas found most philosophers of his day overly occupied with trying to articulate the ultimate nature of "Being"—the reality that lies beyond everyday life. In his view, philosophers should focus instead on the most important concern of everyday life: How people should relate to one another. He himself asked such questions as how can a person respond to the suffering of others, which other people deserve one's response, and how can one balance one's responses to different people in ways that achieve justice.

For Levinas, ethics rests on the absolute responsibility that each person has to respond to the face of the Other. In *Time and the Other* (1987) Levinas argued that humans are social beings. They know themselves through their responses to others, not through their relationships with Being or with ultimate reality. In *Totality and Infinity: An Exercise on Exteriority* (1969), he argue that one does not need to know who people "really" are in order to respond to them. In fact, he wrote that it is impossible fully to know another person, even one's own spouse or children. The best anyone can do is to reach out toward others and grow as others continue to surprise one.

Levinas's ethical writings for educated Jewish readers reflect his World War II experiences. In *Difficult Freedom: Essays on Judaism* (2d ed. 1976), he describes a stray dog in the German camp in which he was imprisoned. The dog was in a sense more human than his guards, for it responded to the prisoners as if they were human beings. Elsewhere, Levinas argued that he was within his rights not to forgive philosopher Martin Heidegger for his Nazi Party affiliation, because of the great crimes perpetrated by the Nazi party during the Holocaust.

Laura Duhan Kaplan

FURTHER READING
Critchley, Simon. *The Ethics of Deconstruction: Derrida and Levinas*. Edinburgh: Edinburgh University Press, 1992.
Levinas, Emmanuel. *Ethics and Infinity*. Pittsburgh: Duquesne University Press, 1985.

SEE ALSO: Derrida, Jacques; Heidegger, Martin; Other, the.

Libel

DEFINITION: Defamation of a person or group by means of writing or visual images
TYPE OF ETHICS: Media ethics
SIGNIFICANCE: To be libelous, defamatory material must generally be both malicious and untrue, and it must be shown to cause actual harm. It must therefore be deemed to be morally indefensible in order to be legally prosecutable. In the United States, libel is one of the few classes of speech not protected by the First Amendment.

Libel is often confused with slander, which is oral defamation rather than written or visual defamation. One's good reputation is usually among one's most valuable possessions. Since libel, by definition, damages the reputation of another, it does serious harm and thus is clearly unethical.

Criminal libel is the malicious publishing of durable defamation. In common law and under most modern criminal statutes, criminal libel is a misdemeanor (an infraction usually punishable by a year or less in prison) rather than a felony (a more serious infraction punishable by more than a year in prison). Libel is also a tort, a noncontractual and noncriminal wrongdoing. Libel is thus grounds for a civil lawsuit in which one may seek to recover money to compensate for the damage that the libel has caused to one's reputation. Truth, however, is a defense against libel, and even if the damage is caused by a false claim, if the damaged person is a public figure, then one must show malice (intent to harm) or a reckless disregard for the truth in order to prove libel. Honest mistakes do not constitute libel against public figures. Civil lawsuits against libel and punishment for criminal libel are both limited by the First Amendment of the Constitution. This was the upshot of the landmark Supreme Court case *New York Times Co. v. Sullivan* (1964) and its progeny. This landmark case was designed to preserve the vigor and variety of public debate in a democracy, balancing democracy against serious harms to reputations in order to avoid a chilling effect on the exercise of the constitutional right of free speech.

Sterling Harwood

SEE ALSO: Censorship; Freedom of expression; Journalistic ethics; Lying; *New York Times Co. v. Sullivan*.

Liberalism

DEFINITION: Philosophy holding that human liberty is of paramount importance and rejecting the notion that set values should control the conduct of one whose conduct affects no one else

TYPE OF ETHICS: Politico-economic ethics

SIGNIFICANCE: The impact of liberalism on ethics has been profound. According to this philosophy, ethics is a means of resolving disputes created by competing individual goals, protecting one's ability to choose one's own values, rather than serving as a standard that espouses one set of values over another.

In 1869, the British political philosopher John Stuart Mill wrote an essay entitled "On Liberty," which many have come to regard as one of the primary sources of liberalistic thought. In that essay, Mill wrote that the only freedom deserving of the name is that of pursuing one's own good in one's own way, so long as one does do not attempt to deprive others of their pursuits. In the nineteenth century England in which Mill lived, there was a struggle between increasing religious strictness and the rebellion that accompanied that strictness. Mill believed that society should not impose its values on anyone, because it is in society's best interest to preserve personal liberty. This belief was based on the theory that individuals who have the freedom to be spontaneous and follow their own desires will naturally form a progressive and happy society.

THE IDEAL OF INDIVIDUAL SOVEREIGNTY

Liberalism seeks to protect the ability of individuals to live according to their own judgments. It is neutral with regard to the content of those judgments, resting on the notion that a self-governed life is good in and of itself. Thus, normative ethics in a liberal society are geared to improving the individual and resolving the disputes caused by competing desires, while at the same time maximizing individual freedom.

Moral standards prescribing what is right and wrong are inconsistent with liberalism in its purest sense, as they interfere with the ability of individuals to explore and develop their own beliefs. Accordingly, the concept of normative ethics, those prescribing good habits and duties, necessarily gives way to a sort of situational ethics. Individuals must have the freedom to decide when their conduct harms others, or the very ideal of individual sovereignty is compromised.

CLASSICAL VS. MODERN LIBERALISM

In its early stages, liberalism was associated with a laissez-faire approach to government. This was largely because government was generally viewed as an oppressor of the individual. The form of liberalism promoting this pro-individualist theory of government is sometimes called classical liberalism. In its modern form, however, liberalism is more commonly associated with increased government involvement in societal matters. It promotes the imposition of societal mechanisms that foster both social and economic equality, with the aim of giving the individual meaningful life choices. This change in liberal philosophy is sometimes known as the Great Switch.

Some philosophers have difficulty reconciling modern liberalism with the premise of classical liberalism. For example, societal laws concerning equal treatment, compulsory education, and publicly supported social welfare programs require an interventionist state and thus interfere, to at least some extent, with individual liberty. However, such laws are seen by liberal thinkers as a necessary means to achieve the end of individual sovereignty. In other words, unless individuals are given equal opportunities, only the privileged can maximize the benefits of individual sovereignty.

LIBERALISM AND ETHICS

According to liberalistic thought, the overarching ethical principle is that of individual freedom. Thus, the only ethical model that is consistent with this principle is one that does not impose any particular value system. Whereas traditional ethics often praise selfless acts and condemn those motivated alone by self-interest, liberal thinkers believe that the natural selfish desires of human beings will ultimately lead to progress and happiness for all of society's members. The question thus becomes whether any principles that do not presuppose any particular vision of the good life can be found.

Philosopher Ayn Rand advocated what she called "rational" self-interest. Under this approach, the individual must adopt certain character traits, or virtues, that help one develop a rational approach to making judgments about one's own life. For example, virtues such as integrity—consistently acting in accordance with one's beliefs—and honesty ensure a rational approach to self-governance. Thus, ethics that provide for development of the self ensure that the principle of individual sovereignty has the desired result on society as a whole. In other words, ethical obligations are generally owed to the self rather than to others. The major ethical dilemma posed by liberalism is the development of a principle by which conflicting individual conduct can be resolved.

Sharon K. O'Roke

FURTHER READING

Barzun, Jacques. *From Dawn to Decadence: Five Hundred Years of Cultural Life, 1500 to the Present.* New York: HarperCollins, 2000.

Berlin, Isaiah. *Four Essays on Liberty.* New York: Oxford University Press, 1979.

Bramsted, E. K., and K. J. Melhuish, eds. *Western Liberalism: A History in Documents from Locke to Croce.* London: Methuen, 1978.

Freeden, Michael. *The New Liberalism: An Ideology of Social Reform.* Oxford, England: Clarendon Press, 1978.

Gray, John. *Liberalism.* Minneapolis: University of Minnesota Press, 1986.

Merquior, J. G. *Liberalism Old and New.* Boston: Twayne Publishers, 1991.

Mill, John Stuart. *On Liberty and Other Essays.* New York: Oxford University Press, 1959.

Rand, Ayn. *The Virtue of Selfishness.* New York: New American Library, 1964.

Rawls, John. *A Theory of Justice.* Cambridge, Mass.: Harvard University Press, 1971.

Sandel, Michael J. *Liberalism and the Limits of Justice.* Cambridge, England: Cambridge University Press, 1982.

SEE ALSO: Campaign finance reform; Common good; Communitarianism; Conservatism; Democracy; Libertarianism; Mill, John Stuart; Niebuhr, Reinhold; Political liberty; Rorty, Richard; *Two Treatises of Government.*

Libertarianism

DEFINITION: Political movement advocating absolute personal liberty and the severe limitation or elimination of government

TYPE OF ETHICS: Theory of ethics

SIGNIFICANCE: Libertarianism treats individual autonomy as the highest good. As a result, libertarians are commonly on the left wing in terms of civil rights and on the right wing in matters of economics and public policy.

The libertarian movement consists of a diverse group of individuals who are united in the view that any social or political institution is wrong if it interferes with individuals' control over their own lives. Libertarians defend property rights, the free-market economy, and the full range of civil freedoms, including the rights to abortion, freedom of speech and the press, sexual freedom, and the use of drugs and alcohol.

Libertarianism should be placed on the political spectrum in contrast to conservatism, modern liberalism, and totalitarianism. Conservatives are generally in favor of more economic freedoms but fewer civil freedoms; conservatives typically favor antiabortion, antidrug, antisodomy, and some censorship laws. Modern liberals are generally in favor of more civil freedoms but fewer economic freedoms; modern liberals typically favor compulsory wealth-redistribution schemes and increased regulation of business. Totalitarians reject liberty in the economic and civil realms. In contrast to these three major political movements, libertarians claim to advocate both civil and economic liberty consistently.

HISTORY

Libertarian theory has roots in the history of modern political and economic thought. It draws on elements of the classical liberal tradition in politics, as exemplified in such thinkers as John Locke. Some libertarians emphasize classical liberalism's contractarian tradition, while others emphasize its natural rights tradition. Modern philosophers Robert Nozick and John Hospers are representative of these positions. Libertarianism also draws upon the anarchist tradition of the nineteenth century. Murray Rothbard, usually acknowledged as the founder of modern libertarianism, is a major representative of this tradition.

In economics, libertarianism has drawn inspiration from the "Austrian" school of economics, most notably from the work of Ludwig von Mises and Nobel laureate F. A. Hayek, and from the "Chicago" school of economics, most notably from the work of Nobel laureates Milton Friedman and James Buchanan.

JUSTIFICATIONS FOR LIBERTY

Libertarians disagree among themselves about how to justify the claim that liberty is the fundamental social value. Some believe that political liberty is an axiom: The value of liberty is self-evident and therefore not in need of justification. Most libertarians, however, offer arguments for liberty.

The most common argument starts with the premise that values are subjective. No individual's values are more right than any other's. The only universal points that can be made about values is that individuals have them, and in order to pursue their values, individuals need to be free of coercion by other individuals. Consequently, the only universal social principle is that the initiation of the use of force by one individual against another is wrong.

Other libertarians justify liberty via social contract arguments. Supposing a Hobbesian or Lockean state of nature, contractarians argue that rational individuals with conflicting interests would agree upon a set of legal constraints that would limit each individual's liberties only to the extent necessary to leave all other individuals at liberty. Therefore, rational individuals would voluntarily contract to institutionalize in their society the broad principle that the initiation of force is wrong.

A third group of libertarians justifies liberty by first arguing for universal and objective moral principles. Appealing to Aristotelian self-realization teleology, Lockean natural rights, or Kantian duties to treat others as ends in themselves, such libertarians derive the conclusions that using force against individuals is immoral and, accordingly, that only political liberty is compatible with their broader moral framework.

As much as these proposed justifications of liberty differ, all libertarians reach the same conclusion: Individuals must be left free to do what they wish with their own lives and property.

ROLE OF THE STATE

Libertarians also disagree among themselves about the extent of the role of the state in promoting liberty. The state is a coercive institution, and states have regularly used their coercive power to violate individuals' liberties through arbitrary laws, the sanctioning of various forms of slavery, compulsory taxation, compulsory military drafts, and so on. Reacting to these facts, libertarians fall into two major groups. One group, the anarchists, argues that the state is an inherently evil institution that should be abolished. The other major group, the "minarchists," allows that the state can play a limited role in promoting liberty.

Minarchist libertarians are divided into two subgroups. Some minarchists agree with the anarchists that the state is an evil, but unlike the anarchists they believe it to be a necessary evil: The state can be valuable in protecting the liberties of some individuals, but this value must be balanced against the inevitable abuses of the state's coercive power to violate individuals' liberties.

Other minarchists argue that the state is an inherently good institution, as long as its coercive power is constitutionally limited to defensive purposes and these limits are enforced strictly. In either case, minarchist libertarians agree that the state's functions should not extend beyond basic police, military, and judicial functions, and that these functions should be funded through voluntary mechanisms, not compulsory taxation. Anarchist libertarians reject any role for the state and argue that even the minarchist state functions can and should be supplied by private, voluntary protection agencies.

In the political realm, however, libertarians agree that they can set aside foundational disputes about the justification of liberty and the scope of the state in order to work together for a goal on which they do agree: the reduction of the current scope of the state.

Stephen R. C. Hicks

FURTHER READING

Carey, George W., ed. *Freedom and Virtue: The Conservative/Libertarian Debate*. Wilmington, Del.: Intercollegiate Studies Institute, 1998.

Lomasky, Loren. *Persons, Rights, and the Moral Community*. New York: Oxford University Press, 1987.

Machan, Tibor, ed. *The Libertarian Reader*. Totowa, N.J.: Rowman & Littlefield, 1982.

Nozick, Robert. *Anarchy, State, and Utopia*. New York: Basic Books, 1974.

Rasmussen, Douglas, and Douglas den Uyl. *Liberty and Nature: An Aristotelian Defense of Natural Order*. LaSalle, Ill.: Open Court, 1991.

Rothbard, Murray. *For a New Liberty: The Libertarian Manifesto*. Rev. ed. New York: Collier, 1978.

Sacks, Jonathan. *The Politics of Hope*. London: Jonathan Cape, 1997.

Santoro, Emilio. *Autonomy, Freedom, and Rights: A Critique of Liberal Subjectivity*. Boston: Kluwer Academic, 2003.

Von Mises, Ludwig. *Liberalism: A Socio-Economic Exposition*. Translated by Ralph Raico. Edited by Arthur Goddard. Mission, Kans.: Sheed Andrews & McMeel, 1978.

SEE ALSO: Anarchy; Conservatism; Free enterprise; Freedom and liberty; Individualism; Liberalism; Social contract theory.

Library Bill of Rights

IDENTIFICATION: Document of the American Library Association that sets forth policies on intellectual freedom meant to be followed by all U.S. libraries

DATE: Adopted on June 18, 1948

TYPE OF ETHICS: Arts and censorship

SIGNIFICANCE: The Library Bill of Rights is designed to protect the rights of all citizens to free and equal access to information and creative expression. Some provisions of the document may be controversial, especially the insistence (reaffirmed in 1996) that people of all ages should have access to the same materials.

The original text of the Library Bill of Rights was drawn up by Forrest Spaulding. It was adopted for the American Library Association (ALA) at the ALA Council in San Francisco. Subsequently, the ALA Committee on Intellectual Freedom was established to recommend any steps necessary to protect the rights of library users in accordance with the Bill of Rights of the United States and the Library Bill of Rights. Through discussion and approved emendation by members of the ALA Committee on Intellectual Freedom and by the membership of the ALA, the document was adopted on June 18, 1948, and amended in 1961 and 1980.

The six basic policies that make up the Library Bill of Rights are summarized as follows: (1) library materials should be chosen for the interest and enlightenment of all people in the community; (2) libraries should provide materials that represent all points of view on issues and concerns; (3) censorship should be challenged; (4) libraries should cooperate with those concerned with resisting the abridgement of free expression and free access to ideas; (5) rights of individuals to use libraries should not be denied based on "origin, age, background, or views"; and (6) meeting rooms of libraries should be available to community groups regardless of the beliefs and affiliations of their members.

Robin G. Hanson

SEE ALSO: Book banning; Censorship; Computer misuse; Freedom of expression; *Index librorum prohibitorum*; Intellectual property; Pornography; Song lyrics.

Life, meaning of

DEFINITION: Notion that human experience as such has a purpose, significance, or value which explains or grounds it, and which could provide guidance as to how one ought to live one's life

TYPE OF ETHICS: Personal and social ethics

SIGNIFICANCE: If life were determined either to have or to lack a definite and comprehensible meaning, that determination would have profound consequences for all of ethical theory and practice.

Albert Camus's *The Myth of Sisyphus* (1942) opens with this claim: "There is but one truly serious philosophical problem, and that is suicide." According to

Camus, judging whether life is worth living represents the most basic of all philosophical problems. Questions about the meaning of one's life are by no means confined to philosophers. Indeed, wondering why one is here and whether anything will come from what one is doing are familiar and pervasive activities. Ethicists offer a variety of responses ranging from the religious ("God provides a meaning for life and everything else"), to the existentialist ("I can give my life meaning"), to the nihilist ("There is no ultimate meaning to life or anything").

MEANING OF THE QUESTION

As with many philosophical inquiries, it is worthwhile to clarify the meaning of the question being asked: "What is the meaning of life?" It is easy to imagine such a question being asked by a severely depressed individual seeking psychological counseling or guidance, but this is not the context for the philosopher's concern.

The philosopher (or any reflective individual) comes to inquire about the meaning of life as a natural consequence of being self-conscious and rational. As people mature, they learn to make observations, generalize, offer explanations and predictions, and so on. Being rational means looking for explanations in terms of rules, principles, and theories, which are established by reason and by empirical methodologies. Being self-conscious involves awareness of one's rationality. Once one becomes aware of one's own rational nature and outlook, it is tempting to turn that rational outlook inward and seek an answer to the question "Why am I here?" in much the same way that one seeks an answer to the question "Why is that mountain here?" Another way of expressing the philosopher's question, then, is as follows: "Why am I self-conscious? What is the purpose of my self-awareness?"

This interpretation of the question about the meaning of life can be represented as "What is the meaning of my life?" Other questions about the meaning of life could focus on all life, or all animal life, or selected groups of human life, or all intelligent life, and so on. The philosophical question about the meaning of life, however, focuses on the meaning of an individual human life.

The reflective inquirer recognizes this principle: When one is wondering about the meaning of life, the most one can legitimately wonder about is the meaning of one's own life. One is not in a position to know the meaning of another person's life or to place a value on another's life.

TRANSCENDENTAL RESPONSES

There are two sorts of responses to the question about the meaning of an individual's life. One sort of response seeks an answer in something transcendental, or beyond this world. By far the most prevalent views of this sort are religious, and they are too numerous and varied to review here. Some nonreligious, mystical views about the meaning of life also invoke a transcendental and nonrational reality.

Transcendental explanations are not satisfying to skeptics, who ask for direct and obvious evidence of nonevident realities. The transcendental view that the meaning of an individual life (along with the sense of the whole universe) must lie outside the universe is subject to Ludwig Wittgenstein's criticism in *Tractatus Logico-Philosophicus* (1921) that things that are claimed by their very nature to be beyond the experiences of this world are among the things about which we are incapable of clear and meaningful discourse: "What we cannot speak about we must pass over in silence."

There are responses to the question about the meaning of life that do not ultimately rely on appeals to transcendental realities. In addition, there are a variety of types of nontranscendental responses. For example, positivists argue that the meaning of life is a question without an answer, because potential answers are not subject to independent verification or refutation; as a consequence, the meaning of life must remain a permanent mystery. Hedonists argue that the meaning of life is determined by the pleasures enjoyed in this life. Nihilists argue that there are no enduring values of any kind, no sense to anything, including one's own life; they often cite the prevalence of natural disasters, wars, and pettiness as evidence supporting their own view. While these responses differ widely, they share a common emphasis on the evidence of this world as that which determines what, if any, meaning attaches to life.

The most prevalent philosophical view of this type traces its history from Socrates in ancient Greece to Jean-Paul Sartre and other modern existentialists. What existentialists have in common is an emphasis on the actions of an individual in this world as the primary determinant of the meaning of that individual's life. Existentialists generally believe that how one lives one's life shows what one thinks of oneself. Because existentialists emphasize individual choices and human actions, their views are categorized as generally nontranscendental, although many existentialists accept the existence of transcendental realities.

THE EXAMPLE OF SOCRATES

The life of Socrates is often cited as an early example of existentialism. Most of what is commonly believed about the life and death of Socrates can be traced to four Platonic dialogues: *Euthyphro*, *Apology*, *Crito*, and *Phaedo* (for example, see Romano Guardini's *The Death of Socrates*, 1970). In the *Euthyphro*, Socrates is shown inquiring into the nature of piety. The situation is that the elder Socrates meets the youth Euthyphro at the city courthouse. Socrates is there to respond to charges of impiety and corruption of youth. Euthyphro, who is there to file questionable murder charges against his father, claims to understand the true nature of piety. Socrates' subsequent examination of Euthyphro's exaggerated claim is filled with irony and can be viewed as illustrating the character of Socrates as well as the general nature of Socratic inquiry. Socrates shows each of Euthyphro's definitions of piety to be deficient or confused, yet Euthyphro persists in his naïve belief that whatever is pleasing to the gods is holy and presumably proceeds to press charges against his father.

The *Apology* recounts the trial of Socrates. More of Socrates' irony and sharp wit are revealed, as Socrates mocks his politically powerful accusers while offering carefully reasoned defenses against each of the charges. Socrates is found guilty by a narrow majority of the 500 judges and is offered the opportunity to suggest an alternative to the death penalty proposed by the accusers. Socrates facetiously considers a series of alternative penalties, ranging from public support for his inquiries to a very minor fine, taking the opportunity once again to ridicule accusers and judges. Socrates is sentenced to death and takes the opportunity to make a final speech in which he re-

Engraving of Socrates taking hemlock by the eighteenth century French artist Louis Pierre Boitard. (Library of Congress)

peats his faith in the divine voice that warns him of exaggerations and other wrongs, imagines an afterlife filled with interrogations of ancient heroes, and asks his friends to punish his sons if they claim to know things that they do not know.

The *Crito* depicts Socrates' brief stay in jail awaiting execution. Socrates refuses opportunities to escape as inconsistent with his beliefs and continues to make philosophical inquiries about the nature of justice and other issues. The death scene is depicted in the *Phaedo*. On the day that Socrates is given the poison hemlock, he is visited by a group of friends, and they discuss the meaning of life and death. Socrates' dying words to his friend Crito were: "I owe a debt to Asclepius [the Greek god of healing]; do not forget to pay it."

The Socrates that emerges from these dialogues is an individual entirely dedicated to a search for truth (especially with regard to ethical matters), determined to expose popular views as exaggerated and confused, capable of great irony and insight, and subject to the divine guidance of an inner voice. Socrates clearly reflects the basic existentialist outlook in the *Crito*: What one does shows what kind of person one is. Socrates is not the kind of person who acts against his beliefs and breaks the laws. The existentialist credo found in Socrates can be stated as follows: One's life shows what one thinks of oneself. Socrates urges people to think highly of themselves.

THE PROBLEM OF SOCRATES

Socrates presents challenges to traditional views about justice, piety, and goodness but offers no positive account of his own about these ethical concerns other than the example of his own life. Yet Socrates' life is essentially unique—Socrates hears and obeys a divine inner voice. Socrates cannot say, "Be like me; get an inner voice." Socrates can give no account of his divine voice, and even he regards the fact that he hears this voice as mysterious.

In Friedrich Nietzsche's *Twilight of the Idols* (1889), another problem with Socrates is elaborated. On most ethical matters Socrates remained an inquiring skeptic, yet with regard to the value of life, Socrates became dogmatic, as best reflected in his dying judgment that life is worthless: "To live—that means to be sick a long time; I owe a debt to Asclepius, the savior." Nietzsche argues that the value of life can be estimated or judged neither by the living, for they constitute an interested and biased party, nor by the dead, because they are not talking. Therefore, Nietzsche argues, the problem of determining the meaning of life is a problem of will, not one of reason.

THE EXISTENTIALIST VIEW

The existentialist view is that each individual is responsible for beliefs held and actions selected, including whether to regard Socrates as a heroic seeker of truth, an eccentric teacher, or a corrupter of youth. Jean-Paul Sartre's *Existentialism* (1946) presents a clear explication of the fundamental tenets of existentialism, including the following: human existence precedes essence; subjectivity must be the starting point of any inquiry; some freedom of action exists; and in choosing who one becomes as an individual, one is choosing how to regard humanity. Part of the human condition is the predicament of choice—choosing one's emerging character. Sartre's existentialism carries a two-sided message: One has freedom and a burden of choice with regard to the kind of person one chooses to become. Sartre's advice is not unlike that of Socrates: Think highly of yourself. Of course, the existentialist leaves the specific interpretation of the word "highly" in the phrase "think highly" to the individual.

A recurrent theme in existentialist writings is that individuals can give meaning to their lives. While it is not possible to state precisely the particular meaning of an individual's life, it is possible to suggest what meaning an individual gave to life by an elaborate tale or story, as found in novels, for example. Indeed, the novels of Jean-Paul Sartre and Albert Camus are often cited as examples of existentialist literature, as are the works of Fyodor Dostoevski and Leo Tolstoy.

This existentialist notion that certain things (such as how one values life) show themselves or make themselves manifest is consistent with the positivist critique of ethical language as meaningless. Ludwig Wittgenstein's *Tractatus Logico-Philosophicus* makes this distinction explicit: there are things that cannot be put into words, these things make themselves manifest, and an example of something that makes itself manifest is "There are laws of nature" (ironically put in words).

The results of positivist attacks on ethical language include an eruption of all kinds of artistic endeavors meant to illustrate existentialist notions about enduring the human condition, choosing in the face of an absurd existence, accepting the responsibilities of choice, and so on. As a consequence, there now exists a substantial body of existentialist literature, philosophy, and art, which makes this area of philosophical inquiry unique in its multidisciplinary approach to the question of what it means to be a person. The appeal of an existentialist outlook is partly the focus on one's entire life rather than on a specific aspect of life such as one's physical attributes or intellectual abilities.

Existentialists typically place great emphasis on human choice and action, shifting the focus of the question about the meaning of life from reason to will. Existentialists would accept the usefulness of high-sounding ethical pronouncements (such as "The unexamined life is not worth living" or "To thine own self be true") but would argue that how one chooses to live in accordance with those and other maxims is the crucial issue—not the maxims themselves.

An existentialist ethical view might be encapsulated in words such as these: Become a voice that comforts and encourages, a hand that guides and assists, an eye that sees and reflects, a face that does not turn away, a person whose life shows what a person can become. Ultimately, however, it is not the words that matter. What matters is the comforting, encouraging, guiding, assisting, and so on.

In summary, there are two basic ways to understand questions about the meaning of life. One can think of the meaning of life in terms of what God can make it or in terms of what one can make it oneself.

J. Michael Spector

FURTHER READING

Bstan-dzin Rgya-mtsho [Fourteenth Dalai Lama]. *The Meaning of Life: Buddhist Perspectives on Cause and Effect*. Edited and Translated by Jeffrey Hopkins. Rev. ed. Boston: Wisdom, 2000. A series of lectures delivered in 1984 in which the Dalai Lama attempts to answer the question of whether life has meaning and how it should be lived.

Camus, Albert. *The Myth of Sisyphus*. Translated by Justin O'Brien. Introduction by James Wood. London: Penguin, 2000. A persuasively written argument against suicide and nihilism, and a powerful expression of the existentialist belief that individuals can give their lives meaning.

Fabry, Joseph B. *The Pursuit of Meaning*. Boston: Beacon Press, 1968. A clear explication of logotherapy, a psychological theory that takes philosophical questions about the meaning of life seriously by conceiving of individual answers as a form of therapy.

Guardini, Romano. *The Death of Socrates: An Interpretation of the Platonic Dialogues—Euthyphro, Apology, Crito, and Phaedo*. Translated by Basil Wrighton. Cleveland: World Publishing, 1967. This volume presents a translation of the four Platonic dialogues that deal with the death of Socrates, along with a running commentary and interpretation.

James, William. *The Varieties of Religious Experience*. London: Collins, 1968. This classic by one of America's most noted pragmatists represents the rich variety of religious practices and contains insightful discussions about religious views of the meaning of life.

Martin, Michael. *Atheism, Morality, and Meaning*. Amherst, N.Y.: Prometheus Books, 2002. An extended defense of atheism as possibly encompassing a meaningful existence, as well as an attack upon traditional notions of Judeo-Christian religions as a practical source of meaning.

Nietzsche, Friedrich. *Twilight of the Idols*. Translated by R. J. Hollingdale. Harmondsworth, England: Penguin Books, 1968. A critical analysis of the lives of Socrates and Jesus Christ as well as an attack on dogmatic attitudes about causality and free will.

Sartre, Jean-Paul. *Existentialism and Humanism*. Edited and translated by Phillip Mairet. Brooklyn, N.Y.: Haskell House, 1977. A clear and concise statement of the primary tenets of existentialism.

Wittgenstein, Ludwig. *Tractatus Logico-Philosophicus*. Translated by D. F. Pears and B. F. McGuinness. Introduction by Bertrand Russell. New York: Routledge, 2001. A carefully reasoned explanation of the limits of language, with implications for the inexpressibility of major ethical concerns including the meaning of life.

SEE ALSO: *Being and Nothingness*; Camus, Albert; Character; Dostoevski, Fyodor; Existentialism; Immortality; Life and death; Platonic ethics; Sartre, Jean-Paul; Socrates; Will.

Life and death

DEFINITION: Presence or withdrawal of the ineffable motive force that differentiates animate from inanimate matter

TYPE OF ETHICS: Bioethics

SIGNIFICANCE: Decisions regarding life and death are usually thought to be the most important and most difficult of all ethical issues. Specific definitions of life and death may determine the parameters of one's legal, ethical, economic, and personal obligations.

Since humans do the defining, all life is defined from the standpoint of human life. Definitions of life reflect the complexity of human life and the various cultural contexts within which the definitions are sought. Definitions of life and death therefore symbolize the concerns of the individuals seeking a definition as well as the culture that supports their search.

Definitions of life and death not only manifest the values and concerns of individuals and society but also determine who lives in that society. If a definition of death, for example, focuses on the irreversible loss of consciousness, then those who have irreversibly lost consciousness are no longer part of that human society because they are no longer considered human. If a definition of human life makes the possession of human DNA equal to being human, then every organism with human DNA is part of that human society.

Definitions also focus on one aspect of human existence rather than another. The word "death," for example, may refer to dying, the death event, or the time after the moment of death. People who say, "I am afraid of death" usually mean that they fear dying. Others, who say they look forward to death, usually mean an afterlife. Today, many people use "death" as it is used in this article to refer to the point at which a living entity changes from a living to a nonliving state.

The focus of modern Western society is on the biological nature of life and death; therefore, its ethical concern is with the biological aspects of life and death. This concern will be the focus of this article.

DEFINING LIFE AND DEATH

No society can exist without explicit or implicit definitions of life and death. People must know when someone is dead. Without such knowledge, wills could not be probated, burial could not take place, leadership positions in business and politics could not be clearly defined, and life-support systems could not be removed. Without clear definitions of human life and death, one would consider a thing (a cadaver) to be a human person. To treat things as human is not only an intellectual error but also an ethical one.

Western society has had, and still has in many situations, both implicit and explicit definitions of life and death. A person who steps off a curb and is run over by a truck is alive when he or she steps off the curb and dead afterward. One can point to a living person before the event and a corpse after the event. One "knows" both life and death in this situation. Since people need official recognition of what they know intuitively, common law developed a definition of death. In common law, death as the cessation of life is determined by "a total stoppage of the circulation of the blood." People's intuitive judgment and society's legal definition were adequate until modern technologies altered the ability to extend life.

In modern industrial societies, acute death, such as occurs in a truck accident, does not happen often. Most people die slowly, die old, and balance on the edge of death for a long time. The end of life today more properly may be described as "living-dying," because it is an extensive period of time during which individuals know that they will die and usually act differently in the light of this knowledge. This "living-dying" phase of life results in experiences and relationships that never have been dealt with in cultures that do not possess the technological ability to produce such a phase of life. This phase is not present when one is run over by a truck: one moment one is alive, the next one is dead.

Things are different today not only for those in the "living-dying" phase of their life but also for those who are "patients"—those who are ill but will probably get better. A significant number of patients will recover only if they receive a living human organ to replace one of their dead ones. The ability to transplant organs such as the heart, liver, and lungs leads modern society to deal with life and death in a different way. This ability produces a culture whose new definitions of death challenge the human view of life and ultimately determine who is human and who is not.

REDEFINING LIFE AND DEATH

Since death is basically the cessation of life, a definition of death is also a definition of life. If one examines the corpse of an individual run over by a truck, one might notice that, although the person is dead, some parts of her or him are still alive. The heart may be beating and thus may be alive. The hair, fingernails, and many cells are also alive. If someone who was unaware of the person's death examined these human parts, that person would not know whether they came from a live human or a dead human. It could be said, therefore, that human death is a process in which it takes a long time for everything human to die. Yet society treats human death as an event. The laws and customs surrounding dying and death seek to mark a point before which the person is alive and after which the person is dead. Obviously, something more than cellular death is needed to indicate when a person is dead.

A medical doctor declares a person dead based on certain criteria. Modern criteria are the result of centuries of experience. A doctor who declares someone dead is saying that experience has shown that when certain criteria are fulfilled, this dead human will never again be a living human.

Commonsense observations that the person was dead in the truck accident are officially confirmed by someone who has the authority to do so, and after that confirmation has been made, people begin to then treat the corpse in a different way.

For most of human history, commonsense observation was the only way to tell the difference between life and death. Part of that observation involved determining whether the person was breathing or not and whether his or her blood was flowing. The breath and the flow of blood were considered the criteria for life and death. Blood and breath, or spirit, are still central to many cultures' views of life. Commonsense observation told people that when their breath was gone, their life was gone. Common sense also demonstrated that if one lost a large quantity of blood, one's breathing stopped and one was dead. Certainly, human life was not only blood and breath, but without blood and breath one was not human.

The history of science has also been the history of challenging commonsense observations. The discovery of the human circulatory system and the invention of the stethoscope were challenges to commonsense observation. The discovery of the way in which the blood circulates demonstrated that when the heart stops pumping, there is effectively no blood; when the lungs stop functioning, there is no more breath. Commonsense observations were augmented by new scientific discoveries and inventions that showed that the previous criteria were ways of knowing that certain essential organs were dead. These criteria now were linked with certain places of death, such as the heart and/or lungs. People now believed that once these organs were dead, a corpse would never again be human.

Commonsense observation might lead one to believe that the lungs and the heart are not moving, whereas a stethoscope might indicate that they are. One no longer had to use a mirror held to a person's nose to know whether breathing had stopped; one did not have to see the loss of blood to know that the heart had stopped. The heart could stop for other reasons and still be dead. One could hear whether it was making noise and was alive. One could listen to the lungs to hear whether there was breath; if not, the person was considered dead. With the advent of the stethoscope, technology began to augment, and sometimes contradict, commonsense observations.

DEATH AND MODERN TECHNOLOGY

Modern technologies continue to augment and to defy commonsense observations, but the sequence of determining a death is the same: Certain criteria indicate that part of the human is dead; experience has shown that once these criteria are fulfilled, that person will never be alive again.

Because humans developed the ability to keep the heart and lungs alive, former commonsense observations about death were challenged. Many investigators were led to conclude that if the brain were dead, the human would never again be alive. Since for most of human history the life of the organs was identical with the life of the human organism, the challenge of developing new criteria included determining new definitions of death, such as those that focused on the brain.

The meaning and definition of life were always concerns for philosophers and theologians. Scientists usually viewed these definitions as too abstract for scientific investigation because they could not be quantified and subjected to experimentation. To many biologists, it made no difference whether they were operating on a human heart or a pig's heart. A muscle was a muscle. A primary model for many scientists working with human anatomy is that of the machine. They speak of human parts in the same way that a mechanic would speak of automobile parts. The realization that these parts form a conscious, willing, and loving machine is of little consequence to scientists using this model. This model's implicit definition of life seems to be that human life is equal to the efficient operation of the parts, which is indicated by the flow of blood and breath. Death occurs when there is an irreversible stopping of blood and breath; that is, when one of the parts no longer functions, the machine is dead.

When one views the human being from a perspective other than that of the machine model, one arrives at different definitions. Robert Veatch, in *Death, Dying, and the Biological Revolution* (1989), provides an excellent summary of two modern definitions.

OTHER DEFINITIONS

One definition is that death is the irreversible loss of the capacity for bodily integration and social interaction. Death occurs when the entire brain is dead. The criteria for determining that the brain is dead are that there are no spontaneous movements, breathing, or reflexes and that such unreceptivity and lack of response are confirmed by a flat electroencephalogram. These same criteria might be met by someone who was suffering from hypothermia or who was taking a central nervous system depressant, so these possibilities must be ruled out before death is determined. It could be that a person whose heart and lungs were functioning with the aid of machines would be declared dead using this definition. For those accustomed to linking death with the circulation of vital body fluids, to remove the person from the machine would necessitate the ethical decisions associated with euthanasia. For those who accept this definition of death, however, to continue to treat the person as if he or she were alive would be unethical.

Another definition of death is that death is the irreversible loss of consciousness or the capacity for social interaction. Notice that the capacity for bodily integration does not have to be irreversible according to this definition. If one's neocortex is dead, one has lost consciousness and cannot communicate with others. The easiest way to determine whether this is the case is with an electroencephalogram. Common sense is certainly challenged here, because a person

in the living-dying phase of life could be breathing without a machine and still be considered dead.

In both of these definitions, human life is understood to be more than mere biological functions. The first definition assumes that both the biological function of spontaneous blood and breath circulation are necessary to be human, as is an ability to interact with others. If these are not present, then human life is absent. The second definition goes further; it says that consciousness and social function are uniquely human. If both are absent, then human life is absent.

The initial commonsense definition led to legal definitions of death. The new definitions also led to legal definitions. The common law definition was gradually redefined with the advent of the new technologies and discoveries. The most famous definition for legal purposes was that of the President's Commission for the Study of Ethical Problems in Medicine and Biomedical and Behavioral Research. The commission rejected the vague general definitions mentioned above for a more specific and biological definition, suggesting that the following definition be used in laws throughout the country: "An individual who has sustained either (1) irreversible cessation of circulatory and respiratory functions, or (2) irreversible cessation of all functions of the entire brain, including the brain's stem, is dead."

REFINING DEFINITIONS OF LIFE AND DEATH

Definitions reflect the questions of persons and societies. These modern definitions reflect the concerns of the modern age: rational analysis and reductionism for the purpose of technological control. Other cultures have defined human life and death in terms of other concerns. Many times, the human life known and analyzed by the five senses was seen as limited in the face of something that transcended ordinary life. The sensual reality might be the spirit, or breath, but this sensual reality was a manifestation of a deeper reality that connected human beings with their past, present, and future. It has been called soul and *atman*. Many terms from many cultures attempt to define life and death. Modern arguments about definitions of life and death in Western culture are arguments about who human beings are and what they will become. Old views of life and death are no longer valid. Commonsense observation is insufficient. New views are still to be discovered. Modern definitions do not match human experience. Inevitably, there will be confusion as people search for definitions that reflect their experience and improve the quality of life in the face of its inevitable end.

CONFUSION AS A HOPEFUL SIGN

Modern popular literature uses four phrases that reflect definitional confusion: brain death, heart death, right to life, and right to death. The first two phrases reflect the difficulty experienced by many people who attempt to understand definitions of life and death. The last two phrases reflect attempts to argue for definitions within the political arena. Most people understand life and death not with the formal definitions stated here but within the parameters of "television-speak"; many decisions concerning social policy are made not by professionals but by the political process. These two phrases reflect the two major social constraints to definitions of life and death: the demand for simplicity in a very complex affair, and the unwillingness to change ideas about a very personal reality.

Modern Western society communicates through the media. The media need short and simple phrases to describe something. Such phrases show how one must think in using this technology.

To use the phrases "brain death" and "heart death" as many reporters do is to suggest that there are two different kinds of death. This is inaccurate. A person is either dead or alive. To say that someone is "heart dead" is to refer to common, primitive definitions of death. To say that a person is "brain dead" indicates that the brain comes into the judgment about death—nothing more. The use of "heart death" and "brain death" to refer to the death of the person also gives the impression that a human being is identified with the heart and/or brain. Such an identification implicitly supports a materialistic view of the person that is not accepted by many philosophers.

The supporters of the "right to life" and those of the "right to die" use modern "rights" language to argue about life and death. They know what they do not want society to do. Right-to-life supporters do not want human life maximized in such a way that large groups of people who are defective, or perhaps lack full consciousness, will find themselves defined out of the human race. Right-to-die supporters do not want human life minimized in such a way that if any of a person's organs is alive, society would be obliged to sustain that person's life. Rights mean obligations.

Right-to-life supporters say that society is obliged to sustain human life under any circumstances. Right-to-die supporters say that society is obliged to allow an individual to choose a particular mode of death rather than experience a slow death of various organs. Most arguments about rights to life and death deal with the issue of euthanasia rather than the issue of definitions of death. The euthanasia issue concerns whether one may ethically hasten the death of someone in the living-dying phase of life. Definitions of death seek to determine whether a person is dead. These are two different issues.

Confusion and argument about definitions of life and death indicate that Western culture is undergoing significant change. They indicate that people are aware of the change that is taking place, thinking about it, and offering arguments for one side or the other. Being aware of these definitions means being aware of what arguments are offered and taking one's place in the conversation, not the confusion.

Nathan R. Kollar

FURTHER READING

Chidester, David. *Patterns of Transcendence.* Belmont, Calif.: Wadsworth, 1990. A review of the concepts of death and life in various world cultures and religions.

Gervais, Karen Grandstrand. *Redefining Death.* New Haven, Conn.: Yale University Press, 1986. A review and critique of all the major definitions of death according to their methodologies.

Goldberg, Steven. "The Changing Face of Death: Computers, Consciousness, and Nancy Cruzan." *Stanford Law Review* 43 (February, 1991): 659-684. An extension of the life-death debate into the area of artificial intelligence. The changes in the legal definition of death are shown to occur as science progresses.

Heinegg, Peter, ed. *Mortalism: Readings on the Meaning of Life.* Amherst, N.Y.: Prometheus Books, 2003. An anthology of essays arguing for the finitude of human existence and examining the consequences of that finitude.

Searle, John. *The Rediscovery of the Mind.* Cambridge, Mass.: MIT Press, 1992. A review of the arguments that identify the human person with the brain.

Veatch, Robert M. *Death, Dying, and the Biological Revolution: Our Last Quest for Responsibility.*

Rev. ed. New Haven, Conn.: Yale University Press, 1989. An exploration of the philosophical, ethical, legal, and public policy consequences of the radical changes in the definitions of death and life.

SEE ALSO: Bioethics; Brain death; Death and dying; Homicide; Immortality; Life, meaning of; "Playing god" in medical decision making; Right to die; Right to life; Suicide.

Lifeboat ethics

DEFINITION: Concept that likens the ethical principles of living on Earth with those of sharing an overcrowded lifeboat
DATE: Concept developed during the 1970's
TYPE OF ETHICS: Environmental ethics
SIGNIFICANCE: Lifeboat ethics is a neo-Malthusian response to human population growth, overpopulation, and hunger that advocates the denial of food aid to starving peoples.

Garrett Hardin, who first articulated the concept of lifeboat ethics during the 1970's, employed three metaphors to explain the idea. First, he described he relatively few truly affluent nations as living in well-stocked lifeboats, while the much more numerous poor nations' populations continuously fall out of their own overcrowded lifeboats, while hoping to board affluent lifeboats. As in real overcrowded lifeboats, Hardin argues that it is suicidal to help the poor, even if a lifeboat has extra room, as the affluent have a primary obligation to provide for their own future generations.

Hardin's second metaphor is the tragedy of the commons, a term used historically for shared pasturelands using for grazing livestock. Open to all livestock raisers, commons lands invited overuse and consequent destruction. Hardin sees modern immigration—which moves poor people to food—and the World Food Bank—which moves food to the poor—as forms of commons lands. The former accelerates environmental destruction in affluent countries, while the latter leads to exhaustion of the environment.

Hardin's third metaphor is what he calls the ratchet effect. When population increases in poor countries lead to crises, the humanitarian food aid that pours into the countries spurs further population increases, setting up vicious cycles. Food aid thus ultimately contributes to enormous population crashes and untold suffering. Hardin's conclusion challenges altruistic practices and employs a utilitarian approach: Withholding food aid will prevent massive global starvation and suffering in the future.

ASSESSMENT

Lifeboat ethics requires a careful assessment of the premises and facts. Hardin assumes that Earth's human population is close to the planet's biological carrying capacity. However, no one actually knows what that capacity really is. World population has historically risen geometrically without the massive starvation that Hardin's theory should expect. Moreover, starvation may have political or economic causes, as it is often occurs in countries involved in wars or beset by irresponsible governments.

The degradation of arable land, overfishing, and global climate change present real threats to the future of the ability of the earth to feed its increasing human population. Moreover, some argue that food aid reinforces governmental irresponsibility in poor nations. Among the countertheories is the cornucopian argument of Julian Simon, which suggests that technological innovations will keep up with population increases, forestalling a crash. Sharing modern technology, and not merely giving food, could become a moral obligation of the affluent.

Ethical responses to lifeboat ethics include the problem of distributive justice, a much discussed difficulty with utilitarianism. While Hardin believes that survival overrides justice, Peter Singer argues that affluent nations have an obligation to ameliorate world suffering. Singer and others also argue that eating meat—which is generally done mostly by the affluent—is unethical, as well as inefficient, as the food given to livestock could be better used to feed the hungry poor. Others treat food aid as supererogatory, an optional as opposed to an obligatory action.

Kristen L. Zacharias

FURTHER READING
Boucher, Douglas M. *The Paradox of Plenty: Hunger in a Bountiful World*. Oakland, Calif.: Institute for Food and Development Policy, 1999.

Lappe, Frances Moore, Joseph Collins, and Peter Rosset. *World Hunger: Twelve Myths.* Emeryville, Calif.: Grove Press, 1998.

Lucas, George R., Jr., and Thomas W. Ogletree, eds. *Lifeboat Ethics: The Moral Dilemmas of World Hunger.* New York: HarperCollins, 1976.

SEE ALSO: Agribusiness; Distributive justice; Famine; Future-oriented ethics; Hunger; Malthus, Thomas; Mercy; Population control; Triage; Utilitarianism; Zero-base ethics.

Lifestyles

DEFINITION: Typical behavior patterns or modes of living of specific individuals, groups, or cultures

TYPE OF ETHICS: Beliefs and practices

SIGNIFICANCE: Lifestyle choices reflect the fundamental values of the people making them, but the term "lifestyle" is most commonly applied only to unusual or distinctive values and choices. The lifestyle of the mainstream can become invisible in its ubiquity.

Everyone, either consciously or unconsciously, subscribes to some set of values and beliefs. A lifestyle is a person's active expression of his or her values and beliefs. People tend to inherit the lifestyles of those who are important to them and then individualize those lifestyles. Lifestyles are learned by experience.

Lifestyles may be divided into two significant sets. The first set consists of Eastern and Western lifestyles, which are based on the beliefs and values of two different parts of the world. The second set consists of the modern, conservative, liberal, and fundamentalist lifestyles, which are based on various ways in which people respond to modern life. An understanding of these lifestyles allows one to understand those values and beliefs that condition one's ethical choices. Many commentators would be quick to add that the world is moving into a postmodern age, which will generate significant change. Such significant change is always accompanied by an increase in the number of alternative lifestyles that are available in a given area. Alternative lifestyles offer people new ways of life and challenge the way of life of the majority in a given area. Alternative lifestyles should not be mistaken for fads, which last only for a short time, such as a year or two. Alternative lifestyles usually exist for at least a generation before they die out or become the lifestyle of the majority.

EASTERN AND WESTERN LIFESTYLES

Eastern lifestyles are represented by the religions or philosophies of Hinduism, Buddhism, Daoism, Confucianism, and Shintōism. These lifestyles are very much oriented toward nature and tend to view time as a series of recurrent cycles. They also tend to de-emphasize the will of the individual and the role of choice. Western lifestyles are represented by the related religions of Judaism, Christianity, and Islam. Western lifestyles tend to emphasize history and time, believing that the world began at a specific point in time. Western thought is generally dualistic (right or wrong, yes or no), whereas Eastern thought is generally unified (right and wrong, yes and no). Western thought also tends to emphasize choice and the will of the individual.

In the middle of the seventeenth century, new ideas initiated a new set of beliefs and values that can be called "the modern." In this case, modern does not mean contemporary. The modern lifestyle affirms most of the beliefs and values of the Western lifestyle. It adds to the Western lifestyle, however, the belief that the mind (reason) is the only instrument that should be used to examine and evaluate the nature of reality. This view constitutes a rejection of the roles of the supernatural and of religious traditions in providing models for behavior and belief. In the modern view, one should analyze how other people act and determine what nature requires. Only if actions are consistent with natural requirements should they become behavioral norms. As the sciences that grew out of modern thought developed, the importance of universal objective norms was minimized; more emphasis was placed on the pluralism of norms and, therefore, ways of living.

The liberal lifestyle accommodated itself to pluralism. The ideas of progress and rationality were central to this lifestyle. Life was viewed as an adventure that, because of the sciences, would continually improve. It was thought that the discoveries of the sciences should be used to improve the quality of life and to develop new behavioral norms.

The conservative lifestyle, however, did not wish to operate on the basis of the ideas of progress, pluralism, and scientific rationality. Instead, conservatism reflected a lifestyle that emphasized hierarchy, order, tradition, and religion. The old was held to be more important than the new. The most important values and beliefs were those that had been inherited from religion.

The fundamentalist lifestyle is based upon the religion (Eastern or Western) within which it is practiced. The Christian fundamentalist lifestyle generally reflects many of the beliefs of the modern in its belief in the literal truth of the Bible and the conviction that the end of the world will come soon. Christian fundamentalism rejects the modern's view of the supernatural by holding to the belief that God regularly intervenes in the world. Some other forms of fundamentalism—Islamic fundamentalism, for example—can be thought of more accurately as reflecting a conservative lifestyle. Although many people view fundamentalism in general as a violent lifestyle that rejects democracy and seeks to reorganize society on the basis of religion, that is not always the case. Each form of fundamentalism must be examined in its own religious, cultural, and national context.

ALTERNATIVE LIFESTYLES

Alternative lifestyles are united in that they respond to the lifestyles that dominate the cultures in which they occur. Each alternative lifestyle rejects all or part of these dominant lifestyles and promotes a different set of beliefs and behavioral norms.

Nathan R. Kollar

FURTHER READING

Chaney, David. *Lifestyles*. New York: Routledge, 1996.

Lande, Nathaniel. *Mindstyles, Lifestyles*. Los Angeles: Price/Stern/Sloan, 1976.

Mitchell, Arnold. *The Nine American Lifestyles*. New York: Macmillan, 1983.

Plummer, Kenneth. *Intimate Citizenship: Private Decisions and Public Dialogues*. Seattle: University of Washington Press, 2003.

Postman, Neil. *Technopoly: The Surrender of Culture to Technology*. New York: Alfred Knopf, 1992.

Shove, Elizabeth. *Comfort, Cleanliness, and Convenience: The Social Organization of Normality*. New York: BERG, 2003.

Smart, Ninian. *Worldviews: Crosscultural Explorations of Human Beliefs*. New York: Scribner's, 1983.

SEE ALSO: Conservatism; Liberalism; Religion.

Limited war

DEFINITION: Combat undertaken by a government that deliberately limits the extent of its military action against its enemy

TYPE OF ETHICS: Military ethics

SIGNIFICANCE: Limited war theory attempts to apply ethical considerations of justice and fairness in the political-military arena.

A government's limitations in war may be expressed in terms of the power and types of weapons it uses, the geographical areas that it targets for attack, the specific segments of the enemy's military structure it targets, the techniques that it employs to minimize harm to noncombatants, its reluctance to seek help from its allies, or how long it will pursue its objectives. In addition to the traditional legitimizations of war as a means of self-defense and a method of defending the public good, many countries have come to perceive a moral obligation to respond to blatant violations of human rights, especially in the light of the various genocidal events of the last century. However, such a "nobility of cause" makes it even more morally pressing to avoid excessive destruction and human casualties. This limitation is usually decided out of ethical considerations such as the inequality of the military capacity of the combatants.

The just war theory, which is closely allied to limited war theory, was designed to determine when a war is morally justifiable (*jus ad bellum*) and what limitations should be placed on the ways in which wars are waged (*jus in bello*). The criterion pertaining to *jus in bello* is commonly called proportionality—the insistence that the estimated collateral destruction inflicted and the costs (in lives and materials) must be proportional to the anticipated good that will result from the military engagement. Many ethicists and religious leaders have pointed out that in the modern nuclear age, in which weapons of mass destruction threaten to obliterate much of the planet, the limitation of proportionality is essential in any military engagement.

Proportionality also includes the shielding of noncombatants from harm, ensuring that they can never be considered targets of attack. When the United States began to invade Iraq in 2003, the American leaders delineated eight specific objectives. In the light of these objectives and the American assertion that its military action was a war of liberation and not one of conquest, great efforts were made to avoid targeting the Iraqi infrastructure, since it would be vital in postwar rebuilding. The so-called American "shock and awe" air campaign, unsurpassed in its focus and magnitude, was highly successful in keeping the number of civilian casualties low and damage to the Iraqi infrastructure minimal.

One of the clearest examples of limited war in modern history was the Falkland Islands War of early 1982, in which Great Britain resisted Argentina's unilateral seizure of the islands. During that war, which last only seventy-two days, Britain limited its military response to the region immediately around the islands themselves and never even hinted that it might attack the Argentine mainland, although it had the force to do so. The British thus limited the duration of the conflict, its geographical focus, and the weapons that it used.

Mara Kelly Zukowski

FURTHER READING

Elshtain, Jean Bethke, ed. *Just War Theory: Readings in Social and Political Theory.* New York: New York University Press, 1991.

Gacek, Christopher M. *The Logic of Force: The Dilemma of Limited War in American Foreign Policy.* New York: Columbia University Press, 1994.

O'Brien, William V. *The Conduct of Just and Limited War.* New York: Praeger Press, 1981.

Phillips, Robert L., and Duane L. Cady. *Humanitarian Intervention: Just War vs. Pacifism.* Lanham, Md.: Rowman & Littlefield, 1996.

Teichman, Jenny. *Pacifism and the Just War.* New York: Basil Blackwell, 1986.

Walzer, Michael. *Just and Unjust Wars: A Moral Argument with Historical Illustrations.* 3d ed. New York: Basic Books, 2000.

SEE ALSO: Biochemical weapons; Dresden firebombing; Geneva conventions; Genocide and democide; Israeli-Palestinian conflict; Jesus Christ; Just war theory; Mutually assured destruction; Peacekeeping missions; Sanctions; War.

Lincoln, Abraham

IDENTIFICATION: President of the United States during the Civil War

BORN: February 12, 1809, near Hodgenville, Kentucky

DIED: April 15, 1865, Washington, D.C.

TYPE OF ETHICS: Politico-economic ethics

SIGNIFICANCE: Lincoln led the American people in an effective political response to the ethical problems posed by slavery.

Slavery was the major moral issue affecting American politics in the early and mid-nineteenth century. Although Lincoln grew up in areas of Indiana and Illinois in which most people were friendly to slavery and hostile to African Americans, Lincoln himself said that he always opposed the institution. He insisted, however, that opponents of slavery had to accept the fact that the U.S. Constitution protected slavery in states where it already existed. In 1837, as a member of the Illinois legislature, Lincoln voted against a motion condemning abolitionist societies and placed on record his condemnation of slavery as morally offensive. To preserve his political future in abolitionist-hating Illinois, he also stated that he rejected demands for the immediate end of slavery because the institution was constitutionally protected.

Lincoln opposed expansion of slavery, hoping that confining it to existing areas would eventually lead to its extinction. When serving as a congressman during the Mexican War, he voted for the Wilmot Proviso that would exclude slavery from any territory acquired from Mexico. The Kansas-Nebraska Act of 1850, which opened new areas to slavery, infuriated Lincoln, who proceeded to lead antislavery Illinois Whigs into the newly forming Republican Party.

While debating Stephen A. Douglas during his campaign for an Illinois senatorial seat in 1858, Lincoln rejected leaving decisions on slavery to residents of the territories, arguing that doing so would treat slavery and liberty as equally acceptable. He insisted that slavery was morally wrong and that black people were human beings having the right not to be enslaved. Citing the Declaration of Independence, Lincoln mocked Douglas for interpreting it to read that all men were created equal except Negroes.

As president, Lincoln showed continual growth in his understanding of how an antislavery position could be effective within the American political system. During the months preceding his inauguration, he reaffirmed his objection to slavery's expansion, rejecting the proposed Crittenden Compromise in Congress that would have guaranteed Southerners the right to export slavery to all land south of the Missouri Compromise line. When the slave states that remained with the Union during the Civil War rejected his proposal to emancipate slaves and compensate their owners, Lincoln strongly supported passage of the Thirteenth Amendment abolishing slavery throughout the country. Using his war powers, President Lincoln issued the Emancipation Proclamation, freeing slaves in territories rebelling against the Union.

While he was growing up in racist Illinois, Lincoln originally doubted the ability of African Americans to become fully functioning citizens, but in 1865, shortly before his death, he denounced the Unionist legislature in Louisiana for refusing to extend the suffrage to black soldiers who had fought for the Union.

Milton Berman

FURTHER READING

Kennealy, Thomas. *Abraham Lincoln*. New York: Lipper Viking, 2003.

Miller, William Lee. *Lincoln's Virtues: An Ethical Biography*. New York: Alfred A. Knopf, 2002.

SEE ALSO: Constitution, U.S.; Declaration of Independence; Emancipation Proclamation; Right and wrong; Slavery.

Lobbying

DEFINITION: Organized efforts by individuals and members of groups to influence public officials—particularly legislators—to pursue their own political agendas

TYPE OF ETHICS: Politico-economic ethics

SIGNIFICANCE: Lobbying is a fundamental and constitutionally protected democratic political right that may influence the content and direction of public policy. It is ethically controversial because of the inequalities in the resources that lobbying forces bring to the process in their attempts to influence government decision making.

Found most predominantly in democratic societies, lobbying is a political activity in which individuals or groups make direct appeals to officials in the legislative and executive branches of government to support legislation and regulations favoring their own interests. The process takes its name from the lobbies of buildings, such as the federal government's Capitol rotunda, in which the "lobbyists" traditionally gather in their attempts to get the attention of the legislators passing through the buildings.

CONSTITUTIONAL PROTECTION

Within the United States, lobbying is protected under the First Amendment's guarantee that citizens have the right to "petition their government." As a constitutionally protected right, lobbying is difficult to regulate and would be impossible to abolish without a constitutional amendment directly and explicitly forbidding such activity.

Lobbying activity is also supported by such other First Amendment guarantees as freedom of speech, freedom of the press, and the right to assemble. Freedom of speech allows lobbyists to voice their opinions on policy to politicians. Freedom of the press allows lobbying organizations to produce printed materials to distribute to the media, politicians, or the general public. Freedom of assembly permits lobbying organizations to gather their members in protest, or support, of public policies.

Despite its constitutional protections and importance in democratic society, lobbying has not been without controversy. Lobbying is about the pursuit and exercise of political influence. Many people, especially those who see themselves as marginalized within the system, have advocated regulating lobbying in order to achieve a more equable balance of power within the lobbying environment and to prevent corruption.

At the national level, attempts to regulate lobbying have never gone further than the Federal Regulation of Lobbying Act of 1946. That simple piece of legislation stipulated that anyone paid to serve as a lobbyist must register with the clerk of Congress. The law itself is weak, however, because it requires only those who call themselves "lobbyists" to register. People who do the same things that lobbyists do but call themselves something else—such as lawyers or public relations specialists—do not need to register under the law. Indeed, the great majority of people engaged in lobbying do not register. However, for legal regulation of lobbying to go any further would invite constitutional challenges. In the early twenty-first century, there was no indication that the American system of lobbying would change in the near future, if ever.

ETHICAL IMPLICATIONS

As a form of political activity, lobbying is not, in and of itself, unethical. In fact, one could argue that to lobby is an important exercise of one's constitutional rights. However, ethical dimensions of lobbying may enter into its practice in several ways.

The tools used by lobbyists can be ethical or unethical. For example, money or other gifts may be offered to influence politicians. During the nineteenth century, lobbyists frequently offered scarcely concealed bribes. Through the twentieth century and into the twenty-first, otherwise legal campaign contributions used in tandem with lobbying efforts have been seen by many to exert corrupting and unethical influences. "Buying votes" is the term often used when connecting lobbying and campaign contributions.

In lobbying, the timely and persuasive dissemination of information is critical. Therefore, the use of knowingly false or misleading information may be unethical. Under the intense pressure of pursuing political goals, some of which may have extreme consequences, lobbying organizations may be tempted to disseminate information that inflates the merits of their cases. This would clearly be unethical, and a high price in loss of credibility may be paid by such organizations. Credibility and a good reputation are invaluable assets to lobbyists. With credibility comes respect on the part of listener, as respected lobbyists are more likely to be believed, trusted, and rewarded.

Some critics of lobbying are bothered by the inherent social inequalities found in its practice. Lobbying requires time, education, and money. Organizations that represent the poor, children, or other marginalized groups can face severe disadvantages

against competing lobbying forces that may be much better funded.

Finally, conflicts of interest may arise. Politicians may be lobbied by organizations in which they have vested interests. For example, a politician may own stock in a lobbying corporation. That situation presents a conflict of interest that may lead to an inherently unethical action on the politician's part. Many states have laws designed to reduce this problem, but their effects have been mixed. In some states, such as Texas, incumbent state senators are permitted to serve outside clients as lobbyists and lobby their own colleagues. Because of the possibilities for conflicts of interest that such practices may create, similar behavior was outlawed at the national level during the nineteenth century.

Steve Neiheisel

FURTHER READING

Berry, Jeffrey M. *The Interest Group Society*. New York: Addison-Wesley, 1996.

Cigler, Allan J., and Burdett A. Loomis. *Interest Group Politics*. Washington, D.C.: Congressional Quarterly Press, 2002.

Eagleton, Thomas F. "Lobbying." In *Issues in Business and Government*. Englewood Cliffs, N.J.: Prentice-Hall, 1991.

Schlozman, Kay Lehman, and John T. Tierney. *Organized Interests and American Democracy*. New York: Harper & Row, 1986.

Wolf, Alvin. *Lobbies and Lobbyists: In Whose Best Interest?* Boston: Allyn & Bacon, 1976.

SEE ALSO: American Association of Retired Persons; Bribery; Business ethics; Conflict of interest; Congress; Corruption; Critical theory; Ethics in Government Act; Nader, Ralph; World Trade Organization.

Lobotomy

DEFINITION: Destruction of tissue in the frontal lobes of the brain, or severing of the connection between those lobes and the rest of the brain

DATE: First performed on human patients in 1935

TYPE OF ETHICS: Bioethics

SIGNIFICANCE: The use of lobotomy to treat mental disorders raises ethical questions as to the relative cost and benefits of the procedure, the possibility of destroying a personality, and the adequacy of the evidence supporting the technique. In the popular imagination and judgment, lobotomy has come to stand for all forms of psychosurgery.

The lobotomy is based on the biomedical model of mental illness, which posits that mental disorders are caused by abnormalities in brain structure. If this is the case, surgically treating the brain should cure the disorder. The field that does so is called psychosurgery.

The antecedent of the lobotomy was the prefrontal leukotomy, which was invented by the Portuguese neurosurgeon António Egas Moniz in 1935. In this procedure, a surgical device called a leukotome was inserted through a hole into the frontal lobe and rotated, destroying whatever nerve tissue it contacted. The prefrontal leukotomy was replaced by the prefrontal lobotomy, which was developed by the American neurosurgeons Walter Freeman and James Watts in 1937. The limitation of the prefrontal leukotomy was that it did not permit precise determination of the area to be cut. In the prefrontal lobotomy, larger holes were drilled into both sides of the skull, after which a leukotome was inserted and precisely moved in a sweeping motion through the frontal lobe.

The prefrontal lobotomy was in turn replaced by the transorbital lobotomy, which was developed by Freeman in 1948. A knife was inserted through the top of the eye socket into the brain and then swung back and forth. This procedure was quick and efficient and could be performed as an office procedure.

The inspiration for these surgical procedures came from data presented by Carlyle Jacobsen that showed a marked change in the level of emotionality of a chimpanzee following destruction of a large part of the frontal lobe of the cerebral cortex. Formerly, the chimpanzee was highly emotional and obstinate. After the operation, the animal appeared calm and cooperative. Egas Moniz believed that this technique could be used on humans to relieve anxiety and other hyperemotional states. Egas Moniz claimed great success in alleviating extreme states of emotionality, and his work aroused worldwide interest, excitement, and practice. Psychosurgical techniques were seen as quick and effective methods for alleviating certain common mental disorders that could not be treated effectively and rapidly by other means, and as providing a partial solution to the problem of overcrowding in mental hospitals.

From 1936 to 1978, about 35,000 psychosurgical operations were performed in America, with perhaps double that number worldwide. Egas Moniz was awarded the Nobel Prize for Physiology or Medicine in 1949 in recognition of his work. The Nobel citation states: "Frontal leukotomy, despite certain limitations of the operative method, must be considered one of the most important discoveries ever made in psychiatric therapy, because through its use a great number of suffering people and total invalids have been socially rehabilitated."

ETHICAL ISSUES

Contrast Egas Moniz's Nobel citation, however, with David L. Rosenhan and Martin E. P. Seligman's assessment of the lobotomy in their 1989 textbook *Abnormal Psychology*: "Moreover, there is the danger that physicians and patients may become overzealous in their search for a quick neurological cure . . . the disastrous history of frontal lobotomies . . . should serve as a warning."

In fact, Rosenhan and Seligman were correct and the Nobel Prize citation was wrong. The leukotomies and lobotomies were a disaster. Their sorry history is rife with ethical violations involving their rationale and the evidence that was used to justify their use on humans.

Within three months of hearing Jacobsen's account, Egas Moniz performed leukotomies. He did so despite the lack of clear evidence from animal experimentation to justify the procedure. Egas Moniz conducted no animal experimentation himself; in addition, his reading of the scientific literature to support his beliefs was spotty and selective, and he ignored contradictory evidence. Furthermore, there was a large animal and human literature that clearly demonstrated a range of serious side effects and deficits produced by lesions to the frontal lobe, such as apathy, retarded movement, loss of initiative, and mutism. With no supporting evidence, Egas Moniz insisted that these side effects were only temporary, when in fact they could be permanent. Egas Moniz's initial report on twenty patients claimed a cure for seven, lessening of symptoms in six, and no clear effect in the rest. An impartial review of these cases concluded, however, that only one of the twenty cases provided enough information to make a judgment.

There is also the question of whether it is ethical to destroy brain tissue as a means of treating cognition and action. Proponents of psychosurgery argue that newer techniques avoid the frontal lobes, the procedure is based upon a good understanding of how the nervous system functions, side effects are minimal, its use is much more strictly monitored and regulated, and it is undertaken only as a treatment of last resort.

Opponents of psychosurgery, however, argue that it is an ethically and morally unacceptable procedure of dubious value for several reasons. First, there are surprisingly few ethical or legal guidelines regulating psychosurgery. Second, psychosurgery has been used to treat a wide variety of disorders, such as schizophrenia, depression, obsessive-compulsive disorder, acute anxiety, anorexia nervosa, attention deficit disorder, uncontrollable rage or aggression, substance abuse and addictions, homosexual pedophilia, and intractable pain. Psychosurgery is performed with the belief that the specific locations in the nervous system that are associated with the above disorders are known and that surgically altering them will in turn alter the particular behavior. Opponents of psychosurgery argue, first, that such knowledge does not in fact exist and that the assumption that these behaviors are tied to specific locations in the brain has not been proved. Second, opponents argue, careful examination of the literature reveals psychosurgery to be an unpredictable, hit-or-miss procedure. Third, the destruction of brain tissue cannot be reversed, and undesirable side effects, which also cannot be reversed, are unavoidable.

Laurence Miller

FURTHER READING

Kleinig, John. *Ethical Issues in Psychosurgery.* London: Allen & Unwin, 1985.

Marsh, F. H., and Janet Katz, eds. *Biology, Crime, and Ethics: A Study of Biological Explanations for Criminal Behavior.* Cincinnati: Anderson, 1985.

Pressman, Jack D. *Last Resort: Psychosurgery and the Limits of Medicine.* New York: Cambridge University Press, 1998.

Rodgers, Joann E. *Psychosurgery: Damaging the Brain to Save the Mind.* New York: HarperCollins, 1992.

Valenstein, E. S. *Great and Desperate Cures.* New York: Basic Books, 1986.

_____, ed. *The Psychosurgery Debate.* San Francisco: W. H. Freeman, 1980.

SEE ALSO: Bioethics; Institutionalization of patients; Mental illness; Psychology.

Locke, John

IDENTIFICATION: English philosopher
BORN: August 29, 1632, Wrington, Somerset, England
DIED: October 28, 1704, Oates, Essex, England
TYPE OF ETHICS: Enlightenment history
SIGNIFICANCE: The author of *An Essay Concerning Human Understanding* (1690) and *Two Treatises of Government* (1690), Locke was one of the most influential of all Enlightenment political theorists. He is credited with creating the fundamental ideas which later formed the basis of the American Declaration of Independence and the U.S. Constitution. In the realms of philosophy of mind and ethics, Locke's blending of empiricism and theism was equally influential.

Locke is known for his political writings (the *Two Treatises of Government* are the basis for the principles used in the American and British constitutions) and for his epistemology, which is the central focus of *An Essay Concerning Human Understanding*. He never wrote a work devoted specifically to ethics, but he did develop a fairly clear stand on the nature of ethics. His *An Essay Concerning Human Understanding* is the most important of his works in terms of his ethical views, but *Two Treatises, Some Thoughts Concerning Education* (1693), and *The Reasonableness of Christianity* (1695) also contain some of his ideas on the subject.

Locke came from the non-Anglican Protestant community in England, learning as a child the virtues of Calvinist simplicity but little of the harsh, judgmental aspect of that sect. He was educated at Oxford University, but he moved away from the then-fashionable Scholasticism and, under the influence of Robert Boyle, began to study practical science. He chose medicine as his specialty and worked with the famous Thomas Sydenham. He never took his degree or practiced medicine (the former was not required for the latter at that time), but the influence of his training would remain with him.

After completing a diplomatic mission in 1665, Locke returned to Oxford and immersed himself in the writings of René Descartes. Two years later, the earl of Shaftesbury, a school friend, invited Locke to become his personal physician and live with him. Locke proved to be as much secretary as doctor, helping his patron with such projects as the Constitution for the Carolinas. He was also elected a fellow of the Royal Society.

In 1675, Locke began a long visit to France both for his health and to expand his study of Descartes. He returned home in 1679 only to face political problems when his patron, Shaftesbury, was accused of treason. Although he was acquitted, Shaftesbury fled to Holland in 1681, and Locke, who had held some minor government posts under Shaftesbury's influence, found it best to follow his example. After

John Locke. (Library of Congress)

Monmouth's Rebellion (1685), Locke was branded a traitor, and the English government demanded his extradition. The Dutch paid little attention to the matter, however, and Locke still lived quietly, continuing work on what was to be *An Essay Concerning Human Understanding*. He returned home after the Glorious Revolution of 1688 and increasingly divided his time between London, where he served as a commissioner of appeals, and Oates, the Essex home of his friends Sir Francis and Lady Masham. It was in this comfortable, supportive home that Locke, during the 1690's, was at his most prolific, though his *Essay* and *Two Treatises* had been in development for years.

ETHICAL VIEWS

Like Thomas Hobbes and some other philosophers, Locke defined good as that which gives, or is conducive to, pleasure. His is a very individualistic view, for it allows no room for altruistic pleasure. He also asserted that there were no inborn attitudes, including ethical principles. As an empiricist, Locke, whom most students know for his assertion that the mind is at birth a *tabula rasa*, or blank slate, on which experience writes, logically concluded that ethical principles must be learned. He also asserted that such ethical principles were as logical and scientific as mathematics, but he was never able to prove his case.

Unlike most strict empiricists, however, Locke was also a theist. The natural laws of ethics, he asserted, could be learned deductively and hence applied to all human beings. They also came to people as revelation. Thus, natural law and divine law were the same. The importance of the former was that it was accessible to all, not only to mystics and those who believed in their pronouncements of God's messages. Theism also influenced Locke's ethics in another way. When he had to consider why an individual would follow ethical principles, especially when another course of action might seem more conducive to his or her pleasure, Locke fell back on the fear of ultimate punishment. Whatever the potential for short-term pleasure, failure to observe the laws of ethics would result in long-term suffering.

IMPLICATIONS FOR ETHICAL CONDUCT

Despite the inconsistencies that other philosophers have pointed out in his ethical views, Locke's ideas have been consistently popular. This seems to be because, for most people, inconsistent beliefs are common, and Locke's positions are much like those of a typical modern Western person. Modernism has produced liberal Christianity, in which the believer is encouraged to select those principles that seem to fit his or her observations of life and produce happiness. While not exactly Locke's view, the view of liberal Christianity is close enough to encourage a continuing interest in his writings. Students are more likely to start reading his work because of his importance in political philosophy and epistemology than because of his ethics, but as they discover his ethical views and find them congenial, they will keep them in the public view.

Fred R. van Hartesveldt

FURTHER READING

Colman, John. *John Locke's Moral Philosophy.* Edinburgh: Edinburgh University Press, 1983.

Cranston, Maurice. *John Locke: A Biography.* London: Longmans, 1957.

Locke, John. *Two Treatises of Government.* Edited by Peter Laslett. New York: Cambridge University Press, 1988.

Milton, J. R., ed. *Locke's Moral, Political, and Legal Philosophy.* Brookfield, Vt.: Ashgate, 1999.

Seliger, Martin. *The Liberal Politics of John Locke.* London: Allen & Unwin, 1968.

Swabey, William Curtis. *Ethical Theory: From Hobbes to Kant.* New York: Philosophical Library, 1961.

Yolton, John W. *John Locke: Problems and Perspectives.* London: Cambridge University Press, 1969.

_____. *John Locke and the Way of Ideas.* Bristol, England: Thoemmes Press, 1993.

SEE ALSO: Descartes, René; *Enquiry Concerning the Principles of Morals, An*; Epistemological ethics; Intuitionist ethics; Justice; Natural law; Rawls, John; Shaftesbury, third earl of; Social contract theory; State of nature; *Two Treatises of Government.*

Lotteries

DEFINITION: Government-run operations involving chance selections in which people buy numbered tickets, and cash awards are granted based on numbers being drawn by lot

TYPE OF ETHICS: Politico-economic ethics

SIGNIFICANCE: Once almost universally rejected as ethically unacceptable, lotteries and other forms of state-supported gambling have become major sources of revenue for U.S. states reluctant to raise taxes; they have also created new ethical challenges for governments.

Until the late twentieth century, a widespread American ethos rejected state support for any form of gambling. Objections were based mainly on Protestant Christian beliefs, which held that gambling itself was morally wrong. Political jurisdictions with majorities or substantial minorities of Roman Catholic voters tended to be more tolerant of some forms of gambling. Forms of gambling based on contests depending partly on skill—such as betting on horse racing—generally had better chances of public acceptance. By contrast, lotteries and casino gambling—which depend on pure luck—were slower to gain acceptance. Even without an absolutist moral stance, the dominant American attitude still rejected state-supported gambling out of a fear that such support would give a stamp of approval to an unwise or savory practice.

By the last third of the twentieth century, Americans were becoming more tolerant of gambling. While casino gambling had long been associated almost exclusively with the state of Nevada, other states became willing to experiment with it to add new sources of tax revenue. The state of New Hampshire started its lottery in 1964. Lotteries then spread slowly to other states, but the trend gained speed as states found they were facing revenue losses as they competed with states with lotteries.

Lotteries could be acceptable only when an absolute moral standard condemning gambling was replaced by a standard closer to utilitarianism. Challenges to the utilitarian ethical arguments as a proper moral mode of argument are well known, especially for those who attack utilitarianism on absolutist religious grounds, but they lead to only one kind of ethical debate. Other debates occur even within utili-

Frank and Shirley Capaci of Wisconsin pose with their ticket in the Powerball lottery in May, 1998. The winners of the largest lottery prize to that date, they received a lump-sum payment of $104.3 million. Had they opted for annual payments instead, they would have collected $7.7 million per year for twenty-five years, for a total of $192.5 million. (AP/Wide World Photos)

a non-lottery state faces competition from neighboring lottery states.

ARGUMENTS AGAINST LOTTERIES

Opponents challenge state-sponsored gambling on grounds of hidden social costs as individuals, especially with low incomes, gamble away money that should properly be used to care for their dependents. For those low-income individuals succumbing to a gambling addiction, the state may be encouraging the impoverishment of families, especially poor families with children. Gambling may even be associated with other social problems, such as alcoholism and drug addiction. By supporting gambling, the state may seem to encourage other maladies. Above all, by supporting gambling, the state may promote get-rich-quick attitudes that contribute to eroding the work and savings ethics badly needed in any society. Opponents clearly see state-sponsored gambling as having deleterious social consequences.

Opponents bolster their arguments with statistics tending to show that the welfare cost of treating the victims may outweigh the revenue gain. Such statistics require complicated calculations and are frequently challenged by gambling's proponents, who have continued to argue that the urge to gamble is so widespread that gambling will occur whether the state sponsors it or not.

These ethical arguments frequently lead to another debate over the size of government. Opponents of large governments tend to argue that governments are more likely to be kept small if they must receive all their revenue from taxes. Because lotteries provide additional, nontax, revenue, they thus may encourage overly large governments.

Lottery revenues are not guaranteed and may fall after the novelty interest in lotteries wears off or if excessive numbers of states begin to use lotteries. If the enlarged government's programs become seen as entitlements, then those programs may be difficult to eliminate—or even trim—after lottery revenues subside. Taxes may then have to be raised to support the

tarianism, particularly when state sponsorship is an alternative to taxation.

Proponents of state-sponsored gambling argue that the propensity to gamble is so widespread that it will flourish without state sponsorship, as it has historically, even in the face of rigorous state prohibition. Given this fact, proponents argue that the state should at least cash in on a practice that will continue in any event. Gambling may even be seen as a boon providing funds for education or other welfare activities that cannot be provided given a public reluctance to raise taxes. This argument is strengthened any time programs. Since states often rely on regressive taxes, the tax burden on low-income individuals may be even more severe as they are caught in a scissors-like situation in which their taxes go up as their state benefits go down.

For all these reasons, ethical debates over lotteries and other forms of state-sponsored gambling are likely to continue to dominate public discussion over lotteries.

Richard L. Wilson

FURTHER READING

Borg, Mary O., Paul M. Mason, and Stephen L. Shapiro. *The Economic Consequences of State Lotteries*. New York: Greenwood Publishing Group, 1991.

Cook, Philip J., and Charles T. Clotfelter. *Selling Hope: State Lotteries in America*. Cambridge, Mass.: Harvard University Press, 1991.

Douglas, Andrew. *The National Lottery and Its Regulation: Process, Problems, and Personalities*. New York: Continuum, 2002.

Duxby, Neil. *Random Justice: On Lotteries and Legal Decision Making*. New York: Oxford University Press, 2003.

Mason, John Lyman, Michael Nelson, and Richard C. Leon. *Governing Gambling*. New York: Twentieth Century Fund, 2001.

Nibert, David. *Hitting the Lottery Jackpot: State Government and the Taxing of Dreams*. New York: Monthly Review Press, 2000.

Von Hermann, Denise. *The Big Gamble: The Politics of Lottery*. Boulder, Colo.: Praeger, 2003.

SEE ALSO: Betting on sports; Luck and chance; Native American casinos; Taxes; Vice; Will.

Love

DEFINITION: Attraction, attachment, or devotion to another person; affection

TYPE OF ETHICS: Theory of ethics

SIGNIFICANCE: Love may be seen to raise issues of, or even create, moral responsibilities between individuals. For some ethical systems, notably Christianity, love in itself is a morally admirable and possibly obligatory act.

Philosophers have treated a number of issues connected with love: the nature and value of romantic love, the distinction between *agape* and *eros*, the motivation of those who love, self-love, friendship, the possibility of altruistic love, and the nature of caring, compassion, benevolence, and sympathy.

ROMANTIC LOVE

Most philosophers have been critical of romantic love. Stendhal claims that in passion-love, lovers "find" perfections in their beloved that are not really there. José Ortega y Gasset believes that in love the lover's attention becomes fixed solely on the beloved. All else that formerly absorbed the lover is eliminated from consciousness; therefore, the rest of the world does not exist for the lover. Ernest Becker, in *The Denial of Death* (1974), claims that romantic love is but another example of the basic human drive for heroism. Each person in a love relation endows the other with godlike qualities so that each can feel cosmically justified. In *The Second Sex* (1949), Simone de Beauvoir criticizes "orthodox patriarchal romantic ideology," in which a woman is to find her identity and value solely in her beloved's superiority and independence. Romantic love, she writes, makes a woman servile and devoid of self-respect; the woman is "pitiful, insecure, dependent, and powerless through her loving."

Not all philosophers, however, have been so negative about romantic love. Robert Solomon states that love is an ordinary but spectacular emotion. Ethel Spector Person argues that though romantic love can be harmful, it can also be enriching. It can liberate people from old habits, give them hope, move them to enlarge their possibilities, and incite them to transcend their self-centered concerns.

AGAPE AND EROS

The classic description of *eros*-love is contained in Plato's dialogue *Symposium*. Plato characterizes love as a desire for pure beauty. One does not love others because of their beautiful qualities but because they are instances of, and point to, "the Beautiful itself." Moreover, those who love pure beauty do so in order to satisfy a self-directed desire—the desire to know beauty, not just for the moment, but forever. The receiving character of this love, which it has in common with sexual love, has been contrasted with the giving character of *agape* love. *Agape* love is said to bestow worth on its object instead of being derived from its object's worth, and it is said to exclude self-love, unlike *eros*, which is essentially self-love. From this it is inferred by some that only divine love is agapic, because only it is nonacquisitive and entirely other-directed; others, however, assert that some human love is agapic.

A number of questions arise about these descriptions of *agape* and *eros*. Are the two as mutually exclusive as they are sometimes claimed to be? Is all human love erotic? Is *agape* always a better love than *eros*? Is the element of self-sacrifice in *agape* love appropriate to women's experience, which is said by some twentieth century feminists to contain too little self-regard; too much self-surrender, especially toward men; and insufficient concern for self-development?

DUTY AND EMOTION

Should people love because they desire to be loving or because they believe that it is their duty to do so? Immanuel Kant and Søren Kierkegaard side with the latter alternative on the grounds that desire and emotion are capricious—they change easily, and people have little control over them. Moreover, Kant said, for any action to have moral worth, including a loving one, it must be motivated by a sense of duty. Other philosophers, including many twentieth century feminists, side with the first alternative. Desire and emotion are not so capricious as Kant and Kierkegaard thought, and the feature of love that gives it moral worth is its emotion—the acceptance felt by a beloved or the sympathy felt by a sufferer. Some writers characterize the duty approach as masculine because it conceives love as rational and impersonal, and the emotion approach as feminine because of its appeal to feeling and connectedness.

CARING

There is a rich philosophical literature that describes the nature of caring and similar phenomena. Caring is said to involve receptivity, which is depicted as "feeling with" the one who is cared for. The carer is attentive to the other, absorbed in the other, and aware of the other's thoughts, feelings, and facial expressions. Sensitivity to the cared for's situation is present; so also is a sense of "we-ness." For some, the essence of caring is the attitude of wanting to help the cared-for grow. For others, the essence of caring is

the sense of being present with the other. Distinctions are drawn between caring and other states with which it is sometimes confused, such as being submerged in the other without the awareness that the other is a separate person.

THE POSSIBILITY OF ALTRUISTIC LOVE

For psychological, social, and religious reasons, some people have wondered whether other-directed love is possible. Imagination may make one think one loves when in fact one does not, emotionally distant parents may produce children who are unable to connect, competitive capitalism may make people feel alienated from one another, an emphasis on sexuality may make people strive for nothing but sexual satisfaction, and sin may make people irremediably self-centered. In *Being and Nothingness* (1943), French philosopher Jean-Paul Sartre asserts that separateness and opposition are at the core of human relations, including love. Love is impossible, he says, because both the one who loves and the one who is loved are trying to get something from the other, and neither is able to do so. Sartre graphically portrays these ideas in his well-known play *No Exit*. Others believe that separateness can be overcome by certain sorts of "interpersonal oneness," such as Martin Buber's I-Thou relation, and that the obstacles to love can be met with a social or religious transformation.

Clifford Williams

FURTHER READING

Evans, Mary. *Love: An Unromantic Discussion*. Malden, Mass.: Blackwell, 2003.

Gilligan, Carol. *The Birth of Pleasure*. New York: Alfred A. Knopf, 2002.

Kierkegaard, Søren. *Works of Love*. Translated by Howard Hong and Edna Hong. Princeton, N.J.: Princeton University Press, 1995.

Noddings, Nel. *Caring: A Feminine Approach to Ethics and Moral Education*. Berkeley: University of California Press, 1984.

Nygren, Anders. *Agape and Eros*. Translated by Philip S. Watson. New York: Harper & Row, 1969.

Nussbaum, Martha C. *Love's Knowledge: Essays on Philosophy and Literature*. New York: Oxford University Press, 1990.

Ortega y Gasset, José. *On Love: Aspects of a Single*

Theme. Translated by Toby Talbot. New York: Meridian Books, 1957.

Person, Ethel Spector. *Dreams of Love and Fateful Encounters: The Power of Romantic Passion.* New York: W. W. Norton, 1988.

Singer, Irving. *The Nature of Love.* 3 vols. Chicago: University of Chicago Press, 1984-1987.

Solomon, Robert. *Love: Emotion, Myth, and Metaphor.* Garden City, N.Y.: Anchor Press, 1981.

SEE ALSO: *Being and Nothingness*; Benevolence; Compassion; Feminist ethics; Friendship; *I and Thou*; Kierkegaard, Søren; Passions and emotions; Plato; *Second Sex, The*; Self-love.

Loyalty

DEFINITION: Dedication or commitment to a person, cause, country, or ideal

TYPE OF ETHICS: Personal and social ethics

SIGNIFICANCE: Loyalty is generally seen as a virtue regardless of its content, but it can also be judged to be misplaced or misguided, in which case it can be more ethically ambiguous.

In the Old Testament, God's first commandment to Moses on Mount Sinai requires the uncompromising loyalty of the Israelites: "I am the Lord thy God, which have brought thee out of the land of Egypt, out of the house of bondage. Thou shalt have no other gods before me." Thus, loyalty to God becomes the paramount duty of Judaism and, subsequently, Christianity, in which it is reaffirmed by Jesus: "Thou shalt love the Lord thy God with all thy heart, and with all thy soul, and with all thy mind." Jesus also acknowledges earthly loyalties, however, requiring one to "render therefore unto Caesar the things which are Caesar's" and to "love thy neighbor as thyself."

Loyalty was the essence of the ancient Greek *eusebia*, or "piety," meaning devotion to the gods but encompassing devotion to parents, friends, country, and anything else worthy of respect and veneration. Loyalty as such is specifically discussed by neither Plato nor Aristotle, even though both philosophers devote much attention to other virtues, defining them and subjecting them to exacting philosophical scru-

tiny. Yet *eusebia* was important not only to them but to all Greeks, constituting the heart of Greek citizenship. The greatest example of Greek loyalty was Socrates, who refused to repudiate his beloved Athens even when its laws punished him unjustly, just as he refused to repudiate philosophy, which he believed was the only means of leading Athenians to the moral truth that would restore the city's integrity. Choosing death at the hands of the state for refusing to give up philosophy, he preserved his loyalty to both.

Aristotle likewise attests the importance of loyalty in the *Nicomachean Ethics*: "It is also true that the virtuous man's conduct is often guided by the interests of his friends and of his country, and that he will if necessary lay down his life in their behalf." He also considers the problem of conflicting loyalties:

> A . . . problem is set by such questions as, whether one should in all things give the preference to one's father and obey him . . . and similarly whether one should . . . show gratitude to a benefactor or oblige a friend, if one cannot do both. . . . That we should not make the same return to everyone, nor give a father the preference in everything . . . is plain enough; but since we ought to render different things to parents, brothers, comrades, and benefactors, we ought to render to each class what is appropriate and becoming.

For Aristotle, specific loyalties are rooted in one's relationships with others, and the obligations attendant upon these loyalties are determined by the nature of these relationships.

Loyalty as piety is preserved in the Roman *pietas*, encompassing reverence for the gods and those to whom natural relationships bind one—family, countrymen, and all of humankind. "Natural" loyalties, springing from kinship to fellow humans, entail "natural duties" that are consonant with these loyalties. Since such kinships are part of the natural order, any violation of these duties transgresses natural moral law. *Pietas* reflects the Stoic belief in a cosmopolitan loyalty to all people by virtue of natural human kinship and obligation to God.

In the Middle Ages, loyalty was exemplified in the "fealty" owed by a vassal to his lord and by the lord to his king. Also included in the concept of fealty was the reciprocal obligation of the king to his subjects. The desire to depose rulers who violated this obligation led to the distinction between loyalty to the *office* of the king and loyalty to the *person* of the king. The Magna Carta constituted a statement that loyalty to the office did not require loyalty to the person; conversely, disloyalty to the person did not signify disloyalty to the office.

Modern Views

The transition to the modern world, which engendered a new political entity, the "nation-state," resulted in loyalty's becoming a predominantly political virtue, from which sprang both the fanatical, nationalistic loyalty of fascism and communism and the pluralistic loyalties of democracy. Despite attempts to transcend national loyalties through organizations such as the United Nations, loyalty in the modern sense is associated with both benign patriotism and radical nationalism, in which loyalty is often interpreted as a call to military aggression. Even in democratic countries, national loyalty is often considered the highest political virtue. The Alien and Sedition Acts of 1798 and the Sedition Act of 1918 were attempts by the U.S. Congress to mandate loyalty by outlawing all publications that were considered defamatory or seditious. Uncertainty about the national loyalty of some Americans led to the internment of Japanese Americans during World War II and to the "blacklisting" of people suspected of subversive activities during the McCarthy era, from 1950 to 1954.

Among philosophers, only Josiah Royce has given loyalty sustained critical scrutiny. Royce's dismay at "that ancient and disastrous association" between loyalty and war prompted him to write *The Philosophy of Loyalty* (1908), in which he defines loyalty as "the willing and practical and thoroughgoing devotion of a person to a cause." The cause to which one declares loyalty becomes the plan for one's life, which, combined with the personal gratification of serving this cause, makes life meaningful. Lest loyalty be construed as being consistent with devotion to an evil cause, Royce stipulates that genuine loyalty respects the loyalties of others and forbids actions that destroy them or prevent their being acted upon. Royce refers to respect for the loyalties of others as "loyalty to loyalty."

Barbara Forrest

Further Reading

Aristotle. *Nicomachean Ethics*. Translated and edited by Roger Crisp. New York: Cambridge University Press, 2000.

Baron, Marcia. *The Moral Status of Loyalty.* Dubuque, Iowa: Kendall/Hunt, 1984.

Konvitz, Milton R. "Loyalty." In *Dictionary of the History of Ideas: Studies of Selected Pivotal Ideas*, edited by Philip P. Wiener. Vol. 3. New York: Charles Scribner's Sons, 1973.

Ladd, John. "Loyalty." In *The Encyclopedia of Philosophy*, edited by Paul Edwards. Vol. 5. New York: Macmillan, 1972.

Plato. "Apology." In *The Collected Dialogues of Plato*, edited by Edith Hamilton and Huntington Cairns. 1961. Reprint. Princeton, N.J.: Princeton University Press, 1984.

Royce, Josiah. *The Philosophy of Loyalty*. Introduction by John J. McDermott. Nashville, Tenn.: Vanderbilt University Press, 1995.

Trotter, Griffin. *On Royce.* Belmont, Calif.: Wadsworth/Thomson Learning, 2001.

See also: Character; Christian ethics; Friendship; Gangs; Jewish ethics; Loyalty oaths; Nationalism; Patriotism; Royce, Josiah; Sedition; Trustworthiness.

Loyalty oaths

Definition: Formal and solemn pledges to support and defend a country, government, or leader

Type of ethics: Legal and judicial ethics

Significance: In the United States positive oaths (or affirmations) of future loyalty are obligatory in numerous situations, despite widespread beliefs that such requirements infringe upon individual freedom and contradict the principles of liberty they are ostensibly designed to protect.

Throughout recorded history, governments and leaders have utilized loyalty oaths as a means of consolidating power and punishing nonconformists. In England, after the Protestant Reformation, such oaths had the effect of restricting the legal rights of Roman Catholics and other religious dissidents. In colonial America, citizens were typically required to take oaths to support and defend the commonwealth. Some oaths included the additional responsibility pledge to report political dissidents to the government. During the American Revolution, the Continental Congress and individual state legislatures mandated that citizens pledge allegiance to the U.S. government. Loyalists and Quakers refusing to make this pledge were punished with exile and confiscation of property.

THE IDEA OF LOYALTY

Unconditional loyalty to governments, regardless of the morality of the governments' actions, has often resulted in great evil. The most obvious example occurred in Nazi Germany under Adolf Hitler. On the other hand, democratic societies appear to benefit from a patriotism that is checked by a critical spirit and sound ethical convictions. In his classic work *A Philosophy of Loyalty* (1908), Josiah Royce argued that loyalty to good causes is the most basic of virtues. Recognizing the evils of intolerance and fanaticism, however, Royce insisted that individuals should have the freedom to choose their own objects of loyalty without coercion. His philosophy envisioned the desirability of a pluralistic society that promotes reasonable patriotism while tolerating a broad diversity of dissident voices.

In the Anglo-American tradition, loyalty oaths were based on an invocation to God as a witness to truth. In common law, therefore, the oaths of atheists were considered invalid. However, as culture became increasingly secular, individuals were given the option of making simple affirmations of loyalty without reference to any religious beliefs. Only a small minority of citizens objects to making nonreligious affirmations of general loyalty to their country. However, members of some law-abiding groups, including the Jehovah's Witnesses, refuse on religious grounds to affirm allegiance to any secular government.

ETHICAL ARGUMENTS

Critics of mandatory loyalty oaths, such as Benjamin Franklin and Supreme Court justice Hugo L. Black, commonly argue that such oaths are pernicious because of their chilling effect on the free expression of unorthodox ideas, their tendency to engender divisions of opinion, and their susceptibility to abuse. Almost everyone admits that the oaths themselves do not restrain subversive actions because disloyal persons are apt to lie about their true intentions. Moreover, to punish those guilty of treasonable and other illegal behavior, it is not necessary to require oaths.

Proponents nevertheless believe that loyalty oaths have the positive function of encouraging a healthy spirit of patriotism and national unity. They further observe that loyalty oaths used in the United States after the 1960's have not included pledges to support particular policies or political ideas. Proponents of the oaths thus find it difficult to understand why good citizens would not gladly proclaim loyalty to a democratic country that allows peaceful means to change laws and policies.

CONSTITUTIONALLY APPROVED MANDATES

The U.S. Constitution requires the president, members of Congress and state legislatures, and all executive and judicial officers to pledge by oath or affirmation to support it. Following this model, Congress has mandated that members of the armed forces, naturalized citizens, and employees in sensitive governmental positions must also pledge or affirm their allegiance to the United States. Most jurists interpret these requirements to be consistent with the First Amendment's guarantees of freedom of religion, speech, and association.

In *Cole v. Richardson* (1972), the U.S. Supreme Court upheld legislation requiring positive oaths or affirmations of loyalty so long as they are not unduly vague and do not infringe on constitutional freedoms. The Court's decision allowed oaths to include a pledge to oppose the forceful overthrow of the government. However, a minority of the justices who voted on that case argued that requiring such a pledge was unconstitutional because it might be interpreted in ways that restrict freedom of speech and association. The majority, however, found the pledge acceptable, because the Constitution does not guarantee any right to advocate or endorse the overthrow of the government by violence or other illegal means.

The Supreme Court does not permit public schools to require children to pledge their allegiance to flag and country. In contrast, *Cole* upheld the constitutionality of requiring adults to pledge loyalty as a condition of public employment. However, in 1994 a federal appeals court ruled that these requirements violated the Restoration of Religious Freedom Act of

1993, because the government could not show that loyalty oaths served a compelling objective. However, the decision was based on a federal statute that later lapsed and became unenforceable, which means that courts in the future may not utilize that decision as a precedent.

UNCONSTITUTIONAL MANDATES

Jurists distinguish between positive oaths to support one's country and negative oaths to refrain from particular acts and associations. One variant of negative oaths, called "test oaths," makes reference to the past rather than the future. After the Civil War, for instance, Congress and state legislatures required public officials and lawyers to swear oaths pledging that they had never supported the Confederacy. Such oaths were required for holding public office and for working in certain professions. In the *Test Oath Cases* (1867), the Supreme Court found that such retroactive test oaths were unconstitutional because they imposed legislative punishments for acts not illegal when performed.

Because of fears of communism after World War II, most U.S. states required teachers and other public employees to sign loyalty oaths that included pledges of nonassociation with the Communist Party or another subversive organization. In 1949, thirty-one professors of the University of California were fired for refusing to take one such oath. During the 1960's, however, the Supreme Court held that almost all requirements for negative oaths were unconstitutional. In one of its most notable decisions, *Keyishian v. Board of Regents* (1967), the Court recognized the importance of academic freedom in higher education and proscribed loyalty statutes that unduly restrict teachers' speech in their classrooms.

Thomas Tandy Lewis

FURTHER READING

Benson, Larry. *The Loyalty Oath Controversy: A Bibliography.* Monticello, Ill.: Vance Bibliographies, 1990.

Gardner, David. *The California Oath Controversy.* Berkeley: University of California Press, 1967.

Hyman, Harold. *To Try Men's Souls: Loyalty Tests in American History.* Westport, Conn.: Greenwood Press, 1982.

Macintyre, Alastair. *Is Patriotism a Virtue?* Lawrence: University Press of Kansas, 1984.

Pauley, Matthew. *I Do Solemnly Swear: The President's Constitutional Oath: Its Meaning and Importance to Our History.* Lanham, Md.: University Press of America, 1999.

Royce, Josiah. *The Philosophy of Loyalty.* Introduction by John J. McDermott. Nashville, Tenn.: Vanderbilt University Press, 1995.

SEE ALSO: Academic freedom; Art and public policy; Drug testing; Loyalty; McCarthy, Joseph R.; Professional ethics; Royce, Josiah.

Luck and chance

DEFINITION: Unpredictable and uncontrollable events and forces that may shape events favorably or unfavorably

TYPE OF ETHICS: Theory of ethics

SIGNIFICANCE: If the unpredictable, uncontrollable forces that shape events can affect the ethical status of people who experience it, then this type of luck is called moral luck.

Ordinary luck is a concept familiar to nearly everyone. The role that luck plays within the realm of ethics can best be illustrated by a hypothetical contrast:

Bert is normally a careful driver and rarely backs his car out of his driveway without first looking. One morning, however, he is distracted by something that he hears on the radio and backs out without looking. As a result, he fails to see a small child running across his driveway, and his car strikes and kills the child.

Carol is another a careful driver who rarely backs out of her driveway without looking. One morning she, too, is distracted by something she hears on the radio, and she backs out without looking. However, no child is running across her driveway, and nothing bad happens as a result of her momentary carelessness.

Those who believe moral luck is present in these examples would affirm that, other things being equal, Bert is more to blame morally for backing out of his driveway without looking than is Carol for doing exactly the same thing. Those who hold this position would appeal to the ways these facts would be treated in a court of law. While there would be harsh penalties for Bert, Carol's penalties would be relatively mild. To the extent that the law is based upon considerations of ethics, moral luck seems defensible.

Not everyone is convinced that moral luck is possible. Some philosophers are convinced that unpredictable forces can never affect a peron's moral or ethical status. An example is the great German philosopher Immanuel Kant. One who shares Kant's point of view would react to the example by holding that both Bert and Carol are to blame for backing out without looking, as nothing about their states of mind or actions is relevantly different. Carol may happen to be lucky that no child runs across her driveway, but opponents of moral luck would see nothing morally significant in this fact. If Bert is to be judged harshly for what he does, there is no reason to judge Carol any less harshly. They both act in identical ways, and their acts grew out of identical motives.

In many ways people's lives are affected by chance. Some philosophers have pointed out that a person's very existence is a matter of luck. The reason is that many people die without producing offspring. However, every time a new human being comes into existence, it means that not one of that person's thousands of ancestors died without producing offspring, a statistical fact that is incredibly improbable.

The ethical character of each human being has been shaped by parents and other early influences. The extent to which these have been positive moral influences is likewise a matter of luck, as is the extent to which people have been spared from temptations to engage in wrongdoing.

Gregory F. Mellema

FURTHER READING

Mellema, Gregory. "Moral Luck and Collectives." *Journal of Social Philosophy* 38 (1997): 145-152.
Statman, Daniel, ed. *Moral Luck.* Albany: State University of New York Press, 1993.

SEE ALSO: Altruism; Determinism and freedom; Inequality; Karma; Lotteries; Moral luck; Morality.

Lust

DEFINITION: Intense sexual desire, or, by extension, a nonsexual desire that resembles sexual desire in its intensity

TYPE OF ETHICS: Personal and social ethics

SIGNIFICANCE: Lust may be defined as excessive desire which is not held in check by reason, or which otherwise defeats the sovereignty of the individual. By that definition, lust is, traditionally, one of the seven deadly sins.

Injunctions against lust, in the sense of sexual activity outside marriage (also called "lechery" in the Middle Ages), figure prominently in the Old and New Testaments of the Bible. The Jewish tradition emphasizes the harmfulness of lust in its disruption of a family-centered social structure. It presents marriage as being handed down to humankind from the time of Adam and Eve, and being further reinforced by the Ten Commandments of Moses and other divine revelation. The New Testament, while suggesting that more individual freedom of choice and forgiveness of repentant transgressors is permitted, assumes that the sexual behavioral norms of Jewish tradition are still very much in effect. The letters of the apostle Paul set the stage for a Christian tradition that makes sexual abstinence a good in itself. This finds parallels in the monastic movements of many of the world's religions.

From a societal standpoint, "lust" is a term of opprobrium for sexual activity that disrupts the social structure—above all, extramarital sex. For the individual, however, sexual behavior may be perceived as "lust" if it is performed without love and respect, even within the confines of marriage. All such loveless sex has been designated as a form of "lust"—hence, one of the seven deadly sins—from the early Middle Ages onward. In a modern context, "lust" in this sense is replaced by such terms as "using" one's sexual partner and "sexual harassment."

D. Gosselin Nakeeb

SEE ALSO: Buddhist ethics; Christian ethics; Daoist ethics; Desire; Jewish ethics; Promiscuity; Sexuality and sexual ethics; Sin.

Luther, Martin

IDENTIFICATION: German Protestant reformer

BORN: November 10, 1483, Eisleben, Saxony (now in Germany)

DIED: February 18, 1546, Eisleben, Saxony (now in Germany)

TYPE OF ETHICS: Religious ethics

SIGNIFICANCE: Perhaps the most significant figure in the second millennium of Christianity, Luther initiated the Protestant Reformation by criticizing what he saw as corrupt and inappropriate practices of the Roman Catholic Church.

Only in modern Christian ethics is an artificial line drawn between religious doctrine and its practical application—Luther himself recognized no such boundary. His career as a reformer was imbued with the notion of ethics as an outgrowth of Christian faith, as it was with the faith that made ethics both possible and valid. Indeed, one could say that Luther's reforming activity was first occasioned by ethical concerns, since it was corrupt practice on the part of the Roman church that first led him to consider the possibility of corrupt doctrine. The preaching of indulgences in German churches in order to raise funds for papal building projects and for the purchasing of German bishoprics, along with traffic in relics and hastily recited masses for the dead, seemed to Luther to be symptoms of a larger spiritual decay—a decay that he was convinced would swiftly be reversed if those in authority knew of its existence. It was only when the authorities refused to alter these practices that Luther began to realize that a more fundamental change was needed, after which his career as a reformer started to take shape.

JUSTIFICATION BY FAITH

At the same time, Luther was undergoing a spiritual crisis of his own that would have a profound effect on his ethical thought. The medieval Church taught that, while salvation was to be obtained through Christ, the individual Christian could assist his or her own cause through participation in the sacraments of the church. Luther's time as an Augustinian monk was largely spent in such acts, but with no sense of spiritual relief. It was only when he began a study of the Scriptures—in particular, the Epistles to the Romans and the Galatians—in preparation for his teaching at the University of Wittenberg that he came upon the doctrine that would free him from his spiritual trials and start a theological revolution: "The just shall live by faith" (Rom. 1:17). It became Luther's contention that salvation could not be gained by any human effort but was solely a gift of God. All that was required to be "justified" was faith, which was itself a gift of God. Nothing else mattered, since nothing else was effective.

At the same time, Luther was not willing to give up good works, but it was clear that his ethics would have to occupy a new place in his system. This problem was worked out in several of his early works, including "Treatise on Good Works" and "On Christian Liberty," both written in 1520. The gist of Luther's maturing ethic is best summarized in a sentence from "On Christian Liberty": "Good works do not make a man good, but a good man does good works." Following the biblical writings of Paul and James, Luther asserted that Christian faith had to be enacted, both out of gratitude for what God had done for the believer and so that God could continue His perfecting work. It was Luther, anticipating John Wesley, who first suggested a doctrine of "sanctification." Furthermore, Luther's doctrine of the "priesthood of all believers" declared that all Christians were responsible for doing good works, not only the members of the clergy and the cloister, who were called to lives of "higher righteousness."

LIVING FOR OTHERS

What works should the justified Christian do? Luther's definition of ethical behavior was, like his doctrine, taken directly from biblical models. The redeemed believer was to give no thought to his or her own needs, which had already been fulfilled through faith, but was to give himself or herself up wholly for the benefit of others, in the same way that Jesus Christ himself took no thought of his own interests, giving himself wholly for humankind. Although Luther's ethic contained practical elements—he recommended marriage and the public education of youth—at bottom it was primarily existential: "I will give myself as a Christ to my neighbor, just as Christ offered himself to me." The nature of ethical behavior was to be seen in self-sacrifice, through which Christ would be revealed in acts of service, as he had been revealed in the ultimate service of the cross.

SECULAR AUTHORITY

Luther did make specific ethical prescriptions that had to do with the nature of secular authority. As with everything else, Luther's politics were based on his doctrine: God has ordained two spheres of authority, or two "kingdoms"—one internal and moral, over which the Church was to have authority; and the other external, to be ruled by the "sword." Both were divinely ordained, the latter on the basis of Paul's dictum that everyone was to be subject to secular authority (Rom. 13:1).

With this belief as his starting point, Luther remonstrated with both rulers and their subjects. Rulers, he said, were not to stray outside their ordained boundaries into religious and moral legislation but were to concentrate on restraining, convicting, and punishing sinful behavior in their own sphere. That this was necessary was occasioned, Luther believed, by the fact that, although truly justified Christians had no need of such authority, most Christians were not yet in so spiritual a state but were still enslaved by sin, and thus were prone to disobedience and chaos. Rulers were needed to maintain order.

Subjects were to obey their rulers in all things. (Luther included in this injunction justified Christians, who ought to remain obedient for the sake of their weaker neighbors.) The difficulty arose when rulers became corrupt: Was there any point at which despotic rulers could be legally resisted? Luther's answer was a cautious and provisional yes, since the ultimate authority over both "kingdoms" was God, and no ruler could compel his subjects to disobey God in their obedience to the ruler. Again, Luther's foundation was biblical: "We must obey God rather than men" (Acts 5:29). Luther's insistence on the divine foundation of secular rule, however, led him to counsel obedience even to corrupt rulers so long as there was any doubt about the proper response. It was on this basis that Luther opposed the Peasants' Revolt of 1525, even though he affirmed the legitimacy of the peasants' grievances. Such opposition, while consistent with his overall ethic, cost him much support among his early followers.

One reason why Luther consistently opposed the overthrow of secular authority by oppressed subjects was that he was convinced that God himself would end the rule of any authority that was mired in corruption, as he had in biblical times. Thus, Luther's political ethic, like the rest of his thought, was grounded in his personal confidence that God would ultimately set all things right, since nothing lay outside his power.

Robert C. Davis

FURTHER READING

Bainton, Roland. *Here I Stand: A Life of Martin Luther.* New York: Abingdon-Cokesbury Press, 1950.

Dillenberger, John, ed. *Martin Luther: Selections from His Writings.* New York: Anchor Books, 1962.

Lage, Dietmar. *Martin Luther's Christology and Ethics.* Lewiston, N.Y.: E. Mellen Press, 1990.

Luther, Martin. *A Compend of Luther's Theology.* Edited by Hugh T. Kerr. Philadelphia: Westminster Press, 1966.

_____. *Luther's Works.* Edited by Jaroslav Pelikan. Saint Louis: Concordia, 1955-1986.

McKim, Donald K., ed. *The Cambridge Companion to Martin Luther.* New York: Cambridge University Press, 2003.

Todd, John. *Luther: A Life.* New York: Crossroad, 1982.

SEE ALSO: Bonhoeffer, Dietrich; Christian ethics; Jesus Christ; Politics; Private vs. public morality; Religion; Revelation; Supererogation; *Utopia.*

Lying

DEFINITION: Making a false statement with the intention of misleading another person

TYPE OF ETHICS: Personal and social ethics

SIGNIFICANCE: Lying is most often judged along a spectrum, from bearing false witness against another person, prohibited by the Ten Commandments, to telling "little white lies," which is often deemed to be harmless and therefore permissible.

Although there is little sustained philosophical or religious discussion of the issue of lying and its consequences for society, there is some embryonic discussion of the ethics of lying, particularly in connection with the issues of truth and sin.

Influenced by Manichaean beliefs that pitted

good against evil and truth against lies, Saint Augustine provided Catholic orthodoxy with the judgment that lying jeopardizes one's relationship with God, because God is truth and all lying is a form of blasphemy. Although Augustine holds that the teaching of false doctrine is the worst type of lying, he was opposed to lying in all its forms.

A great scholar in the fields of law, the classics, theology, and history, Hugo Grotius was arrested for his anti-Calvinist views on tolerance and politics. Sentenced to life in prison, he arranged a clever escape and fled to France and Sweden, where he proceeded to write his most famous legal work, *On the Law of War and Peace* (1625). His confrontation with Dutch Protestant internecine battles and the ruse he used in making his escape from jail may have led him to modify his theological opinions about lying. He argued eruditely that lying was permissible when directed toward children, the insane, thieves, and unrighteous persons, as well as when it was done for the public good.

Immanuel Kant's reliance on pure reason obviated any appeal to emotional or pragmatic reasons to excuse lying. Kant argued that a lie always harms humankind because it "vitiates the source of law itself." This deontological view does not excuse any form of lie even in a life-threatening situation.

CONTEMPORARY VIEWS OF LYING: SISSELA BOK

The 1979 work *Lying: Moral Choice in Public and Private Life* by Sissela Bok is the first major, systematic philosophical study of the ethics of lying. Bok's contribution to the debate is her superb, detailed intellectual discussion of the taxonomy of lying. She analyzes "white lies," false excuses, inauthentic justifications, lies in a crisis, lies to liars, lies to enemies, lies for the public good, lies to protect peers and clients, deceptive social science research, lies to the sick and dying, and the effects of lying on both the liar and the person who is deceived.

Reflecting the contemporary lack of any single authority, Bok marshals new categories of lying and analyzes them with an eclectic set of criticisms. She defines lying not as a sin or as an untruth but as "a false statement made to another person with the intention to mislead." Bok emphasizes the consequences of lying: The deceived person becomes distrustful of the liar and, by extension, the society that allows lies to be disseminated without any barriers.

The liar loses both self-respect and a sense of reality as he or she continues to become absorbed in a system of transmitting lies to retain power or authority. From this point of view, lying harms not only the individual but also the community.

Bok partially shifts the responsibility for exposing and correcting the problems of lying from the individual to society. After all, she argues, how can an individual change the whole structure of a medical, legal, or business system that values sales, bottom-line income, and success more than it does honesty? How can an individual change misleading advertising, deceptive social science research, deceitful pharmaceutical claims, and fallacious government reports and regulations? These fraudulent activities contribute to the destruction of moral values, the loss of respect for authority, and the proliferation of individual despair in the pursuit of justice.

Bok is not an absolutist: She finds that there may be a need for certain types of lying. Like Grotius, she believes that one may lie to a terrorist or a criminal, or lie in other life-threatening circumstances. Lying to protect the innocent is not Bok's only exemption. She also allows provisionally for certain white lies. Lying to protect someone's feelings or to avoid a painful situation can be justified, but only as a last resort. One must always look at the overall context. Will one white lie lead to many more, cumulatively creating more distrust in and harm for the one who is deceived?

Bok has extended the significance of lying to all personal relations. She has also warned of the danger of the pressure to lie that derives from such institutions as the government and from such professions as the law, medicine, and business. She has called for the discussion of ethical standards in all institutions, and especially in the field of medicine. To see the act of lying as an authentic issue—separate from its relationship to sin or the individual's responsibility—is a major accomplishment. Bok concludes that without the active support of society and its institutions to correct the problem of lying, the individual will not be able to overcome the need and the temptation to lie.

Richard Kagan

FURTHER READING

Bailey, F. G. *The Prevalence of Deceit*. Ithaca, N.Y.: Cornell University Press, 1991.

Bok, Sissela. *Lying: Moral Choice in Public and Private Life.* 2d ed. New York: Vintage Books, 1999.

Goldberg, M. Hirsh. *The Book of Lies: Schemes, Scams, Fakes, and Frauds That Have Changed the Course of History and Affect Our Daily Lives.* New York: Morrow, 1990.

Kincher, Jonni. *The First Honest Book About Lies.* Minneapolis, Minn.: Free Spirit, 1992.

Nyberg, David. *The Varnished Truth: Truth Telling and Deceiving in Ordinary Life.* Chicago: University of Chicago Press, 1993.

Smyth, John Vignaux. *The Habit of Lying: Sacrificial Studies in Literature, Philosophy, and Fashion Theory.* Durham, N.C.: Duke University Press, 2002.

SEE ALSO: Augustine, Saint; Buddhist ethics; Cheating; Five precepts of Buddhism; Fraud; Honesty; Hypocrisy; Ten Commandments; Trustworthiness; Truth.

Lynching

DEFINITION: Unlawful killing of a person by a mob, usually by hanging

TYPE OF ETHICS: Human rights

SIGNIFICANCE: Lynching became a common form of racial violence in the American South, especially in the wake of the U.S. Civil War. Defenders claimed that lynching was used to protect the virtue of white women. In reality, however, it was used to keep African Americans in fear for their lives.

The term "lynching" comes from Captain William Lynch, a captain in the Virginia militia during the American Revolution. Lynch and his men sought to rid Pittsylvania County of Loyalists, Americans who supported the British during the war, and subjected them to trials before a hastily assembled court. Lynch said that the tribunal was justified because no other legal authority existed in the county, so citizens had the right to create their own system of justice and carry out its punishments. The court was said to practice "lynch law," and by the 1830's, that term was applied to instances in which mobs took the law into their own hands without waiting for legal authorization.

Lynching was common on America's western frontier during the nineteenth century, but no statistics are available concerning how many people were killed by this form of mob action. After the end of the Civil War and the abolition of slavery in 1865, lynching was most common in the southern United States, where it became a frequent occurrence, especially between 1882 and 1930. During that period, a total of 4,761 lynchings took place in the United States, 90 percent of them in the states of the Old Confederacy. Of the victims, 3,386 (71 percent) were African American and 1,375 (29 percent) were white. Half of these killings were carried out with the help of local police, and in 90 percent of the other cases, local legal and judicial authorities gave their approval. No member of any lynch mob was ever arrested or punished for participating in these crimes.

RATIONALES FOR LYNCHING

Defenders of lynching—and these included most southern white political, business, and community leaders—argued that fear of such deadly violence alone prevented African American men from raping white women. Ben Tillman defended lynching and announced that, although he was governor of South Carolina, he would still "lead a mob to lynch a man who had ravished a white woman. I justify lynching for rape, and before almighty God, I am not ashamed of it." Lynching from this perspective was ethically justified because it protected the purity and honor of a physically weak population, white women, from the violent attacks of sex-crazed fiends, African American men.

This rationale has come to be seen in recent years as a cultural denial of a deeper truth. Fear of white women being raped by African American men was used to obscure or displace attention from the fact that it was actually white men who had an established, institutionally sanctioned history of raping African American women in the South. Slave owners had routinely raped their slaves. In only 23 percent of southern lynchings was the victim even accused of rape.

More lynchings, 28 percent, happened because of minor infractions of social customs, such as a black man's simply talking to a white girl or whistling at her from across the street, than because of violent

Richard Wright on the Emotional Impact of Lynching

Richard Wright, the author of *Native Son* (1940) and *Black Boy* (1945), observed that lynch mobs could strike anywhere, anytime, and for any reason. Lynching was part of a reign of terror imposed by the white majority to keep African Americans subjugated. "The things that influenced my conduct as a Negro," Wright wrote about violence against African Americans, "did not have to happen to me directly. I needed but to hear of them to feel their full effects in the deepest layers of my consciousness."

sexual crimes attributed to the victim. Therefore, it appears that lynch law was used more as a way of maintaining white supremacy than as a way of punishing criminals. The real purpose of lynching was to maintain white supremacy by making all African Americans aware of the terrible penalty that could be imposed upon them for breaking the southern code of racial ethics.

ANTILYNCHING LEGISLATIVE EFFORTS

A campaign to end lynching by declaring it a federal crime instead of a state crime began in 1930. Two groups, both composed of white southerners—the Association of Southern White Women for the Prevention of Lynching and the Atlanta-based Commission on Interracial Cooperation—called upon the Congress of the United States to pass an antilynching bill. Both organizations believed that through education and public pressure, a majority could be found to give the Federal Bureau of Investigation jurisdiction over cases in which local authorities had failed to protect victims of mob violence. Thirty people had been lynched that year, and a particularly brutal incident in Sherman, Texas, in which a retarded African American youth was slowly burned to death changed the hearts of enough congressmen and senators for the bill to win passage. However, though the House of Representatives approved the measure, the Senate did not. Instead, Senator Thomas Heflin of Alabama led a successful filibuster against the bill. Heflin made his position quite clear: "Whenever a Negro crosses this dead line between the white and Negro races and lays his black hand on a white woman he deserves to die."

Southern white leaders raised the constitutional issue of states' rights. States had always been responsible for enforcing criminal laws, and these leaders believed that that power should not be reduced. Raising any crime to a federal level would only lead to the creation of an all-powerful national police force that could threaten the freedoms of Americans everywhere. Arguments favoring local control helped to defeat later attempts to outlaw lynching through federal law, while masking the racially motivated intentions of its defenders.

That race and not constitutional issues lay behind opposition to antilynching legislation was demonstrated by events that occurred during the debate on lynching legislation in Congress in 1935. The horrible lynching of Claude Neal in Florida, in which a white mob cut off the victim's fingers and toes and forced him to eat his own flesh before mutilating his body with a hot poker and hanging it from a tree, received national attention. Still, the Senate did not act; southerners killed the bill with a six-day filibuster. One opponent denounced the legislation for promoting federal interference in local affairs, while another defended the lynchers because Neal had allegedly raped his white girlfriend, though she denied it, and "the virtue of white women must be defended, at any cost." Not even a separate bill calling for a national committee to research the problem of lynching survived the Senate debate.

Lynchings were significantly reduced by the late 1930's to an average of fifteen per year, and by the 1940's, such mob-inspired murders had almost disappeared. Yet during the 1950's, two black men were killed in Mississippi for violating the southern racial code. Fourteen-year-old Emmett Till was brutally killed apparently simply because he had talked to a white woman. The last officially recognized lynching happened in Mississippi in 1959, when Mack Charles Parker was hanged by a mob for allegedly raping a white girl. Apparently, no recorded lynchings have taken place since then, though a young African American, chosen at random, was mutilated and murdered by the Ku Klux Klan in Mobile, Alabama, in 1981. The decline in lynching is attributed to increased press coverage and public awareness of the crime, plus progress in federal protection of civil rights.

ETHICAL PRINCIPLES

The ethics of lynching was summarized in a long speech by Senator Allan J. Ellender of Louisiana in January of 1938. Again a horrible incident—a case in which two African Americans had been blowtorched to death by a Texas mob—had led to the introduction of an antilynching bill in Washington. Ellender led the fight against the bill and celebrated the South's long battle to subjugate blacks in which "lynch law" played a prominent part. "It was costly: it was bitter, but oh, how sweet the victory."

Leslie V. Tischauser
Updated by the editors

FURTHER READING

Brundage, W. Fitzhugh, ed. *Under Sentence of Death: Lynching in the South.* Chapel Hill: University of North Carolina Press, 1997.

Hall, Jacquelyn Dowd. *Revolt Against Chivalry: Jessie Daniel Ames and the Women's Campaign Against Lynching.* New York: Columbia University Press, 1979.

Kluger, Richard. *Simple Justice: The History of "Brown v. Board of Education" and Black America's Struggle for Equality.* New York: Alfred A. Knopf, 1976.

McGovern, James R. *Anatomy of a Lynching: The Killing of Claude Neal.* Baton Rouge: Louisiana State University Press, 1982.

Raper, Arthur. *The Tragedy of Lynching.* New York: Arno Press, 1969.

Smead, Howard. *Blood Justice: The Lynching of Mack Charles Parker.* New York: Oxford University Press, 1986.

Wells-Barnett, Ida B. *On Lynchings.* Amherst, N.Y.: Humanity Books, 2002.

SEE ALSO: Bigotry; Hate crime and hate speech; Homicide; Ku Klux Klan; Law; Racial prejudice; Racism.

M

McCarthy, Joseph R.

IDENTIFICATION: U.S. senator best remembered for leading communist witch hunts during the 1950's

BORN: November 14, 1908, Grand Chute, near Appleton, Wisconsin

DIED: May 2, 1957, Bethesda, Maryland

TYPE OF ETHICS: Politico-economic ethics

SIGNIFICANCE: While chairing a Senate committee investigating alleged communist agents in the federal government, McCarthy gained notoriety for his tactics of attacking witnesses and making unsubstantiated allegations; his name became synonymous with unethical behavior.

Republican senator Joseph R. McCarthy of Wisconsin sought to rid the nation of what he saw was communist infiltration of the administrations of both Harry S. Truman and Dwight D. Eisenhower. He also sought to uncover what he saw was a communist takeover of such major cultural institutions as the motion picture industry. He saw the nation as being threatened by sinister communist agitators quietly seeking to undermine American values by secretly gaining control of key national institutions.

McCarthy's use of the phrase "card-carrying member of the Communist Party" publicly raised ethical concerns about both the objects of his attacks and the nature of his tactics themselves. On one hand, McCarthy's allegations made citizens worry about the possibly unethical behavior of the leaders of key American institutions. On the other hand, his failure to substantiate any of his allegations ultimately ignited charges that he was wantonly destroying the lives and careers of innocent people in order to further his political career.

McCarthy's primary targets were initially many of the architects of the New Deal who had been in public service during the administrations of Franklin D. Roosevelt and Harry S. Truman. He singled out for criticism successive secretaries of state in those administrations—George C. Marshall and Dean Acheson. Thanks, in part, to the publicity he gained from making these charges, McCarthy won reelection to the Senate in 1952.

McCarthy next launched attacks against officials in the newly installed Eisenhower administration. McCarthy's notoriety crested in the fall of 1953 when he began investigating alleged communist infiltration of the ranks of U.S. Army officers and civilian leaders. During televised month-long hearings the following spring, McCarthy appeared before the nation primarily as a bullying interrogator of witnesses. These investigations, which quickly became known as the Army-McCarthy hearings, swayed public opinion against him and led to a growing public distrust of his numerous unproven allegations.

The following fall, possibly due in part to a voter backlash against McCarthy and his tactics, the Republicans did poorly in the off-year elections and lost control of the Senate. With the change in party control of the Senate, McCarthy was forced to relinquish chairmanship of his investigating committee. His public career hit bottom on December 2, 1954, when the Senate, by a 67-22 vote, censured him for behavior "contrary to Senate traditions."

McCarthy's tactics of bullying interrogation coupled with unsubstantiated allegations left a legacy of unethical behavior in public life. Hence, for one to be branded with the label "McCarthyism" or for using "McCarthy tactics" is to be charged with engaging in unethical persecution of another person.

FURTHER READING

Doherty, Thomas. *Cold War, Cool Medium: Television, McCarthyism, and American Culture*. New York: Columbia University Press, 2003.

Ranville, Michael. *To Strike at a King: The Turning Point in the McCarthy Witch-Hunts*. Ann Arbor, Mich.: Momentum Books, 1997.

Reeves, Thomas C. *The Life and Times of Joe Mc-Carthy: A Biography.* Lanham, Md.: Madison Books, 1997.

Schrecker, Ellen. *Many Are the Crimes: McCarthyism in America.* New York: Little, Brown and Company, 1998.

Robert E. Dewhirst

SEE ALSO: Academic freedom; Cold War; Communism; Loyalty; Loyalty oaths.

Machiavelli, Niccolò

IDENTIFICATION: Italian political theorist
BORN: May 3, 1469, Florence (now in Italy)
DIED: June 21, 1527, Florence (now in Italy)
TYPE OF ETHICS: Renaissance and Restoration history
SIGNIFICANCE: One of the first early modern thinkers to distinguish between private and public morality, Machiavelli sought in *The Prince* (*Il principe*, 1532) to provide rulers with guidelines for attaining and maintaining authority. "Machiavellianism" has come to mean the belief that power is the ultimate good, or even the only good, and that any method for obtaining it is justified.

The ideas of Niccolò Machiavelli have been associated with the darker side of politics. To be Machiavellian has for centuries meant to be willing to do anything in the quest for power. Machiavelli has been viewed as a political devil, advising leaders to embrace the arts of treachery, force, and cruelty in order to be successful. These notions derive almost wholly from his work *The Prince*, and although they have persisted, they are exaggerations of the substance of Machiavelli's ideas. Machiavelli also wrote plays, poetry, and histories. His most expansive work was *Discourses on the First Ten Books of Titus Livius* (1636). In it, the breadth of Machiavelli's political thinking may be seen, and especially his high regard for republican government.

HISTORY

For good or ill, it was *The Prince* that, as Count Carlo Sforza said, "made Machiavelli famous and infamous." Although it is unfair to say that Machiavelli was a preacher of treachery and evil, there is some truth in these perceptions of Machiavellian ethics. Moreover, there is an inheritance from Machiavelli's ideas that has deeply influenced political thinking into the modern era. Because of this influence of *The Prince*, it must be the focus of any discussion of Machiavellian ethics.

Machiavelli grew up in the Florence of Lorenzo de Medici. He was disheartened by his city's decline following the French invasion of 1494. During the period of the Republic (1494-1512), Machiavelli, as second chancellor, was intimately involved with diplomatic relations involving France, Germany, the papacy, and other Italian states. When the Medici retook the city in 1512, Machiavelli was tried for treason and exiled to San Casciano. While he was in exile, he devoted his life to writing, yet he sought a return to public life. Around 1513, Machiavelli wrote *The Prince* and dedicated it to Lorenzo di Medici. Although they had been enemies in the past, Machiavelli hoped that Lorenzo would be impressed by the work and employ his skilled advice. Machiavelli's work went unnoticed in his lifetime, but the succinct power of *The Prince*, a condensation of

Niccolò Machiavelli. (Library of Congress)

Excerpt from Machiavelli's
The Prince

From this circumstance, an argument arises: Whether it is better to be loved rather than feared, or the opposite. The answer is that one would like to be both one and the other; but since they are difficult to combine, it is more secure to be feared than loved, when one of the two must be surrendered. For it may be said of men in general that they are ingrates, fickle, deceivers, evaders of danger, desirous of gain. So long as you are doing good for any of them they are all yours, offering you their blood, goods, lives, children, when any real necessity for doing so is remote, but turning away when such need draws near, as I have remarked. The prince who relies wholly on their words, and takes no other precautions, will come to ruin. Friendships gained at a price and not founded on greatness and nobility of soul, are indeed purchased but never possessed; and in times of need cannot be drawn upon.

Machiavelli's thought regarding rulership, outlasted both its purpose and the Medici.

THE PRINCE

If it has been unfair to say that *The Prince* and its interpretations accurately portray the depth of Machiavelli's thinking, it is equally fair to say that he meant every word of what he wrote. In *The Prince*, Machiavelli states that he will not speak of republics, for here he has a single purpose. *The Prince* discusses how principalities are won, held, and lost. It is a primer that tells how a single ruler may gain and maintain power. Machiavelli emphasized how power is garnered in a corrupt and dangerous political environment such as the one that existed in Renaissance Italy. In such treacherous times, a prince required special skills to control the state. This, the purpose of *The Prince*, accounts for the work's narrow focus and tone. The book stresses the need for rulers to develop clear objectives and pursue them vigorously and boldly. They must be willing to resort to illicit behavior in the interest of self-survival. Although Machiavelli does affirm certain principles (for example, avoid dependence on others, establish a citizen mili-

tia), he advises princes to be flexible in carrying out their policies.

MACHIAVELLI'S IDEAS

Machiavelli's attention to the mechanics of government in *The Prince* made political and military affairs paramount. He separated these from religious, moral, or social considerations, except as these might be politically expedient. The purpose of the state is to preserve power, and the one criterion of evaluation is success. Machiavelli was indifferent regarding whether a policy was brutal or treacherous, but he was aware that such qualities might affect the success of policy. Hence, Machiavelli preferred that policy be perceived as honorable and fair, but he emphasized that one should never risk failure for moral considerations.

In *The Prince*, Machiavelli openly discussed the advantages of skillful immorality. He was not immoral; instead, he advised princes to embrace political amorality, which encouraged virtuous behavior among subjects but accepted a rulership that transcended morality. This double standard for rulers and subjects is a hallmark of Machiavellian ethics. Machiavelli never advised cruelty for its own sake, but attempted political objectivity. This unabashed objectivity did not make him a devil, but he did exaggerate the quest for power and confuse the objectives of politics with the game itself.

PRINCIPLES

Machiavelli's ideas were precursors to many modern political attitudes. He addressed human nature, rulership, the character of the state, and the role of popular government. His observations about skillful policy were based on the assumption that the primary human motivations are selfish and egoistic. Machiavelli assumed that government derives from human weakness and the need to control the conflict that grows out of human self-interest. People are naturally aggressive, and the role of the state is to provide security.

This perspective on human nature led Machiavelli to emphasize the role of lawgiver and ruler. He argued that moral and civic virtues grow out of law and government; they are not inherent in human nature. The ruler represents the law and implements morals but is above morality. For this reason, the ruler must be both a "lion and a fox." When necessary, a ruler must disguise the real intent of policy by controlling outward appearances. At other times, a ruler will have no recourse but to use brute force. Force must be used discreetly and effectively, but the ruler cannot flinch when the preservation of the state is at stake. Machiavelli argued that a ruler should be both loved and feared but stated that it is difficult to have it both ways. Thus, if one cannot be both loved and feared, it is better to be feared that to be loved. The ruler must have the virtues of strength and vision, and the flexibility to adapt to the whims of fortune.

Machiavelli was a national patriot, and he defined the state in terms of a personal identification of the citizens with the state. This idea accounts for Machiavelli's preference for popular government, whenever practical. He disliked noble classes because they were divisive and because noble class interests often clashed with those of the state. Machiavelli disdained the use of mercenary armies and encouraged a standing army of citizens who were willing to die for their country. Machiavelli believed that the goal of the state was to preserve national integrity and property, and he suggested that no state can survive without popular support.

Machiavelli was a realist, a skeptic, a patriot, a populist, and an adviser to tyrants, and his vision profoundly influenced political thinking. Even the meaning of the state as a sovereign institution appears to have originated with him. Unfortunately, Machiavellian ethics makes power the primary goal of politics, while moral, economic, and social forces are only factors to be controlled in the power game.

Anthony R. Brunello
Thomas Renna

FURTHER READING

Berlin, Isaiah. "The Question of Machiavelli." *New York Review of Books* 17 (November 4, 1971): 20-37.

Cassirer, Ernst. *The Myth of the State.* New Haven, Conn.: Yale University Press, 1973.

Coyle, Martin, ed. *Niccolò Machiavelli's "The Prince": New Interdisciplinary Essays.* New York: Manchester University Press, 1995.

Gilbert, Felix. *Machiavelli and Guicciardini.* Princeton, N.J.: Princeton University Press, 1965.

Machiavelli, Niccolò. *The Prince.* Edited and translated by Angelo M. Codevilla. New Haven, Conn.: Yale University Press, 1997.

Machiavelli, Niccolò, and Francesco Guicciardini. *The Sweetness of Power: Machiavelli's "Discourses" and Guicciardini's "Considerations."* Translated by James V. Atkinson and David Sices. De Kalb: Northern Illinois University Press, 2002.

Mansfield, Harvey C. *Machiavelli's Virtue.* Chicago: University of Chicago Press, 1996.

Skinner, Quentin. *Machiavelli: A Very Short Introduction.* Rev. ed. New York: Oxford University Press, 2000.

SEE ALSO: Cruelty; Dirty hands; Political realism; Politics; Power; Realpolitik; Tyranny.

MacIntyre, Alasdair

IDENTIFICATION: Scottish moral philosopher
BORN: January 12, 1929, Glasgow, Scotland
TYPE OF ETHICS: Modern history
SIGNIFICANCE: One of the most significant moral philosophers of the second half of the twentieth century, MacIntyre wrote *After Virtue* (1981) in an attempt to summarize the history of Western moral thinking to date, to explain the quandaries of the modern moral landscape, and to synthesize a new approach to ethical theory that will address and resolve those quandaries.

In *After Virtue*, Alasdair MacIntyre analyzes theories of morality with regard to culture and states that virtue is found within the community, in its *ethos*, or character, and not in the individual alone. He argues that the Enlightenment abandoned the belief in a divine origin of morality and overemphasized the individual. This leads, says MacIntyre, to a breakdown of the triad of ethics: "man-as-he-happens-to-be," "man-as-he-would-be-if-he-realized-himself," and a divine system of rules to be followed. Such grounding of morality in human nature can produce moral relativism. MacIntyre is looking for a balance between the utilitarian concept of morality as usefulness and the relativism of different social norms. This question of the individual and the society is addressed in MacIntyre's book *A Short History of Ethics* (1966), in which he asserts that morality emerges out of human history rather than out of human nature.

This conception places ethical decisions beyond the limits of individuals. MacIntyre believes that valid moral principles reflect what rational people would accept collectively as good for the individual, regardless of the individual's place in society.

James A. Baer

SEE ALSO: Aristotle; Communitarianism; Comparative ethics; Nietzsche, Friedrich; Relativism; Virtue; Virtue ethics.

Mādhyamaka

DEFINITION: School of thought in Buddhism based on moderation

TYPE OF ETHICS: Religious ethics

SIGNIFICANCE: Mādhyamaka Buddhism teaches that all worldly thought and beliefs are ultimately contradictory, and that the true path to nirvana entails recognition that the truth transcends anything that can be thought rationally or put into words.

Mādhyamaka is a school of thought within Buddhism that derives from the notion of "one who follows the middle way." It was begun by the scholar and theologian Nāgārjuna, who lived during the period from 150 to 250 C.E. in India, and it is one of four central Buddhist schools. Mādhyamaka Buddhism spread throughout eastern Asia and is known by various other names, including *sanronshu* in Japan, *sanlun zong* in China, and *dbu-ma-pa* in Tibet.

HISTORY

Born in southern India in the second century, Nāgārjuna was the author of several philosophical treatises. His central contribution was the idea of *śūnyatā*, or "emptiness," meaning the recognition that everything in this world, including human beings, is devoid of reality. His argument contradicted other contemporary philosophies of India, which looked on things as having substance in and of themselves. Nāgārjuna proposed that everything is defined or given meaning in terms of everything else. He called this contextualization of reality *pratītya-samutpāda*, or "interdependent co-arising." Recognition of the illusoriness of human perceptions of reality and the mutual dependency of things in the

world is a first step toward true understanding, wrote Nāgārjuna and his major disciple Āryadeva.

In the so-called Middle Period of Mādhyamaka, eight Indian scholars wrote commentaries on the work of Nāgārjuna. During this period, Mādhyamaka split into two schools, the Prāsaṅgika and the Svātantrika. This distinction was primarily based on different logical and rhetorical methods for establishing the truths of Mādhyamaka Buddhism.

During the Later Period, scholars integrated aspects of other schools of thought in Indian Buddhism into Mādhyamaka. Mādhyamaka thought also spread to Tibet, China, and Japan, and more commentaries and treatises were written by scholars in those areas.

PHILOSOPHY

Although there are many complexities in the arguments presented by various thinkers within Mādhyamaka Buddhism, some general trends stand out. Primary among these is the recognition that reality is one and whole, and the human perception of separable "things" in the world is based on artificially cutting up that single reality through rationality and language. Nothing actually exists in and of itself, and attachment to the notion of the reality of self and world is a basic source of human suffering. Nonattachment to the illusory notions of self and world is liberation, or nirvana.

The meditative techniques emphasized in the Chan (Zen) tradition in China and Japan are focused on releasing the individual from the suffering that comes from attachment to atomized, hence false, conceptions of self and world. They seek to bring perception beyond the constraining rationalism of language, which is delusory in its fragmentation of reality.

ETHICS

One might suppose that rejecting the reality of perceived things and selves in the world and declaring everything "empty" of meaning could lead to a moral nihilism in which no action is any more meaningful or better than any other action. This was not, however, the interpretation of at least some of the key thinkers in Mādhyamaka Buddhism. Nāgārjuna recognized that although everything was devoid of reality on an ultimate or philosophical level, on a pragmatic level people have no choice but to live fully in the world, however faultily defined it may be. Nāgārjuna believed the ideal to be that of the *bodhi-*

sattva, or "enlightened being," who lives in the world and pursues a moral path but is aware of the ultimate insubstantiality of mundane reality.

The "Middle Way" of Mādhyamaka is a path of moderation between rejecting the world as illusion and accepting the world as fully real and substantive. One tentatively accepts reality as it is, creating meaning through moral action, while realizing all the time that there is no ultimate grounding behind the reality in which one lives. The Japanese sage Dōgen, founder of the Sōtō school of Zen Buddhism, said, "Before Enlightenment, carrying firewood. After Enlightenment, carrying firewood." The point is that one pursues daily activities in the world, but one's perception of them, one's mind, has changed. Although Dōgen is not properly considered part of Mādhyamaka Buddhism, this popular insight identifies clearly the position of the Mādhyamaka Buddhist with regard to action and philosophy.

Cynthia Keppley Mahmood

FURTHER READING

Candrakīrti. *Four Illusions: Candrakīrti's Advice for Travelers on the Bodhisattva Path.* Translated by Karen C. Long. New York: Oxford University Press, 2003.

Huntington, C. W. *The Emptiness of Emptiness: An Introduction to Early Indian Mādhyamika.* Honolulu: University of Hawaii Press, 1989.

Nagao, Gajin. *The Foundational Standpoint of Madhyamika Philosophy.* Translated by John P. Keenan. Albany: State University of New York Press, 1989.

Nāgārjuna. *The Philosophy of the Middle Way.* Translated by David J. Kalupahana. Albany: State University of New York Press, 1986.

Nishitani, Keiji. *Religion and Nothingness.* Translated by Jan Van Bragt. Berkeley: University of California Press, 1982.

Streng, Frederick J. *Emptiness: A Study in Religious Meaning.* Nashville, Tenn.: Abingdon Press, 1967.

Thupten Jina. *Self, Reality, and Reason in Tibetan Philosophy: Tsongkhapa's Quest for the Middle Way.* New York: RoutledgeCurzon, 2002.

Tuck, Andrew P. *Comparative Philosophy and the Philosophy of Scholarship: On the Western Interpretation of Nagarjuna.* New York: Oxford University Press, 1990.

SEE ALSO: Bodhisattva ideal; Buddha; Buddhist ethics; Dōgen; Five precepts of Buddhism; Four noble truths; Nirvana; Zen.

Magna Carta

IDENTIFICATION: Grant of rights and privileges conceded by King John to English barons
DATE: Signed on June 15, 1215
TYPE OF ETHICS: Legal and judicial ethics
SIGNIFICANCE: The Magna Carta dealt with the grievances of feudal lords, but succeeding ages have used its language as a guarantee of the rights of all British citizens to freedom under the law and judgment by peers.

The Magna Carta, or Great Charter, is an English document that granted privileges and liberties that were to become the cornerstones of English constitutional government. It became a symbol of resistance to oppression, and many future generations looked upon it to formulate protection against their own threatened liberties. Earlier kings of England had issued charters and granted concessions to their barons. The difference between those charters and the Magna Carta was that the former were granted by the kings whereas the Magna Carta was demanded by the barons under threat of civil war.

The English kings before John were Norman and Angevin rulers who centralized the government, demanded increased taxation, and expanded feudal and judicial systems as a means of political control. Consequently, when John succeeded his brother Richard I in 1199, he was able to exploit his subjects. John was unskilled in waging war, and when he lost all of his continental possessions except Aquitaine to Philip II of France, his barons sought redress of their wrongs.

John had demanded military service or large amounts of money in lieu of it, sold offices, favored friends, arbitrarily increased taxes, and shown little respect for feudal law, breaking it when it suited him. King John also took the Church's possessions and was excommunicated by Pope Innocent III in 1209. It was 1213 when John finally sought peace with the Church. In 1214, John returned from France in total defeat. His barons met with him and refused to serve him or pay for not serving in the military. The barons began to prepare for war against John, if he did not confirm their liberties.

THE BARONS' REVOLT

In May of 1215, the barons formally renounced their allegiance to the king. John made concessions to the Church and granted London the freedom to elect its own mayor, hoping to gain support. John offered arbitration, but the barons refused. John finally agreed to grant the laws and liberties that the barons had demanded. They agreed to meet on June 15, at a place called Runnymede.

The barons came with a prepared list of demands, the Articles of the Barons. After the king had agreed to the terms, they were reduced to the form of a charter. King John finally affixed his royal seal to them on June 15, 1215. It was the custom to affix a seal instead of signature to royal documents.

The original charter was not carefully organized. It was later divided into sixty-three parts. These clauses can be divided into several groups, each dealing with specific issues.

The first of these groups concerns the Church, stating that it is to be free. The King must not interfere in the matters and offices of the Church. Two more groups deal with feudal law pertaining to those holding land directly from the crown, tariff reliefs, and those who are subtenants. A particularly large group deals with law and justice. No man was to be imprisoned without lawful judgment of his peers or by the law of the land.

Another group of clauses relates to towns, trade, and free movement for merchants. The conduct of royal officials is the subject of other clauses, while still others deal with the administration of the royal forest. Immediate issues were also mentioned, such as the recalling of foreign mercenaries, the returning of lands that had been seized unlawfully, and King John's compliance with the charter. If he failed to live up to his agreement, the council of twenty-five barons had the power to wage war against him.

REVISIONS AND ADDITIONS

Although King John swore an oath to abide by the terms of the Magna Carta, he had Pope Innocent III annul it on August 24, 1215, on the ground that it had been enacted by force. Civil war followed. King John died in November, 1216, and was succeeded by his nine-year-old son, Henry III. The advisers of young Henry accepted the reforms of the Magna Carta in good faith. Reissues of the charter were granted in 1216, 1217, and 1225. The charter had been accepted by the government, to be used for guidance. Certain provisions, however, were omitted from the reissues. In 1216, the restraints and demands made against King John did not need to be retained. John's granting of freedom of elections in the Church was ignored, even though the declaration that the Church "should be free" remained. Also absent was the provision for a review of the king's performance by the twenty-five barons.

The 1217 Charter added provisions for suppressing the anarchy that was still prevalent in several districts, amended a few details of the original Charter that had proved to be defective or objectionable, and addressed new problems that had surfaced since the first charter. The final revision of the Magna Carta, which was made in 1225, contained only slight variations from the 1217 version.

The reissue of the Magna Carta in 1225 took the place that it still retains among the fundamental laws of England. It is this version that is always cited in editions of the statutes, courts of law, Parliament, and classical law books.

The Magna Carta is viewed as the cornerstone of the English Constitution. Before the close of the Middle Ages, it had been confirmed thirty-eight times. Edward I, with his confirmation in 1297, placed the Magna Carta on the statute books, and it remains there today. The declaration that statutes that are contrary to the Magna Carta are null and void carries a similarity to the language of the U.S. Constitution. The principle that no person shall be deprived of life, liberty, or property without due process of law was not merely a bargain between a king and barons. It was meant for free people in every age.

Larry N. Sypolt

FURTHER READING

Danziger, Danny, and John Gillingham. *1215: The Year of the Magna Carta*. London: Hodder & Stoughton, 2003.

Holt, James C., ed. *Magna Carta and the Idea of Liberty*. New York: John Wiley & Sons, 1972.

_____. *The Making of Magna Carta*. Charlottesville: University Press of Virginia, 1965.

Howard, A. E. Dick. *Magna Carta: Text and Com-*

mentary. Rev. ed. Charlottesville: University Press of Virginia, 1998.

McKechnie, William Sharp. *Magna Carta: A Commentary on the Great Charter of King John*. Glasgow: James Maclehose & Sons, 1905.

Thorne, Samuel E., et al. *The Great Charter*. New York: Pantheon Books, 1965.

SEE ALSO: Bill of Rights, U.S.; Civil rights and liberties; Due process; English Bill of Rights; Freedom and liberty; Freedom of expression; Hammurabi's code; Loyalty; Tyranny.

Maimonides, Moses

IDENTIFICATION: Jewish philosopher
BORN: Moses ben Maimon; March 30, 1135, Córdoba (now in Spain)
DIED: December 13, 1204, Cairo, Egypt
TYPE OF ETHICS: Medieval history
SIGNIFICANCE: The most influential Jewish thinker of the Middle Ages, Maimonides wrote extensively on philosophy, science, and medicine. Although he wrote no works on ethics per se, ethical issues permeate all of his philosophical writings, notably *Mishneh Torah* (1185) and *Guide of the Perplexed* (1190).

Maimonides, who was certainly the greatest intellectual figure to arise from the Sephardic (Iberian) Jewish tradition, was one of the most respected and influential Jewish thinkers in all of history. He is known chiefly for his commentaries on Jewish law and the origins of ethical behavior, but he also wrote works on general philosophy, medicine, and astronomy. His writings sparked controversy, but he came to be regarded as preeminent among Jewish philosophers and (by some) as the spiritual descendant of the biblical lawgiver Moses.

HIS LIFE

Maimonides was born in 1135 in Córdoba, in Islamic Spain. His family was wealthy, his father a notable intellectual and judge in a rabbinical court. Recognizing his son's brilliance, Maimonides' father personally tutored him in Jewish law. Maimonides was born at the end of the "golden age" of Jewish

Spain, a time of relative religious tolerance when the richness of Islamic thought intersected with Jewish and Christian traditions, drawing also on newly rediscovered Greek and Latin texts.

When Maimonides was about thirteen, the relative peace and tolerance in Spain ended abruptly with the ascendancy of the Almohad Islamic sect, whose fanaticism included the forced conversion of Jews to Islam. Maimonides' family was forced to flee Córdoba, settling in 1160 in the Moroccan city of Fez—which, as the center of the Almohad movement, was an odd choice.

In 1165, life in Fez became intolerable, so Maimonides' family moved first to Palestine and finally to Egypt. There, Maimonides' father died and Moses joined his brother David in the jewelry trade. When his brother died in a shipwreck, Maimonides supported himself as a physician, quickly rising to prominence as physician to the sultan, Saladin, and his vizier, al-Afdal. Thereafter, he practiced medicine, lectured to medical colleagues at a Cairo hospital, served as spiritual adviser to the local Jewish community, and wrote extensively on medicine, astronomy, and philosophy. He married late in life; fathered a son, Abraham (who also became a notable scholar); and died in 1204. It is likely that his varied life of surviving religious persecution, engaging in international commerce, and practicing medicine added a dimension of common sense and practicality to Maimonides' philosophical writings, enhancing his ability to communicate with a wide audience.

MISHNEH TORAH

Maimonides did not write books on ethics, as such, but wrote extensively on Jewish law, in which the distinction between law and ethics is unimportant. Probably his most significant legal work was the *Mishneh Torah*, which was completed in 1185 in Egypt and was written in Hebrew, unlike his other important writings, which were in Arabic. It consists of fourteen books and is widely regarded as among the most splendid and significant works of Jewish literature. The book attempts a systematic compilation of all Jewish law; rather than dwelling on points of contention or scholarly refinements, however, it tries to go to the heart of the issues, presenting the law in a clear and practical fashion.

Maimonides believed that the law was closely connected to logic, a prejudice that produced clarity in his presentation. The influence of Aristotle, which was very much a factor in Jewish intellectual activity at that time, was everywhere apparent. Perhaps it was the Greek influence that enabled Maimonides to go beyond the conservativism of contemporary Talmudic scholarship and to place his own distinctive imprint on his work.

The section of the work dealing with "character traits" deals explicitly with ethical matters and shows the clearest Aristotelian focus. It is based on the notion that right actions are congruent with good character and the idea of a God-like mean. Thus, in matters of ethics, the wise man emulates the deity in following the mean course: that course of action that avoids all extremes that might reflect humanity's natural inclinations. The nobility of character that makes such action possible also dictates a lack of interference with others and renders an orderly society possible. This general precept leads in a natural way to a number of secondary conclusions, including the importance of speaking kindly, of paying attention to one's own health, and even of suppressing truth to the extent that it may inflict injury on others.

GUIDE OF THE PERPLEXED

Unquestionably the best-known of Maimonides' writings, the *Guide*, completed in 1190, was also his last important work. Written in Arabic, it was translated into Hebrew and Latin. It attempted a synthesis of Hebrew religion and classical philosophy, an attempt that evidently succeeded, judging from the work's enormous authority in subsequent Jewish (and Christian) religious thought, and from the fact that it was immediately assailed by some contemporaries as heretical. The perplexity in the title refers to inconsistencies or tensions between the rabbinical and the classical philosophical traditions. The intended audience was, presumably, urbane Jewish intellectuals (who were literate in Arabic). The purpose of the work is clearly theoretical, but, interestingly, the portions dealing with ethical matters can operate on a distinctly practical level. Thus, the purpose of the law is the health of both body and soul, the health of the soul is a question of character, and good character is associated with right actions. Right actions, as discussed earlier, proceed from adherence to the mean and from the exercise of kindness.

John L. Howland

FURTHER READING

Fox, Marvin. *Interpreting Maimonides: Studies in Methodology, Metaphysics, and Moral Philosophy.* Chicago: University of Chicago Press, 1990.

Gerber, J. S. *The Jews of Spain: A History of the Sephardic Experience.* New York: Free Press, 1992.

Heschel, A. J. *Maimonides.* New York: Farrar, Straus & Giroux, 1982.

Kreisel, Howard. *Maimonides' Political Thought: Studies in Ethics, Law, and the Human Ideal.* Albany: State University of New York Press, 1999.

Maimonides, Moses. *Ethical Writings of Maimonides.* Translated by Raymond L. Weiss and Charles E. Butterworth. New York: Dover, 1983.

_____. *A Maimonides Reader.* Edited by Isadore Twersky. New York: Behrman House, 1972.

Weiss, Raymond L. *Maimonides' Ethics: The Encounter of Philosophic and Religious Morality.* Chicago: University of Chicago Press, 1991.

SEE ALSO: Altruism; Ibn al-ʿArabī; Jewish ethics; Torah.

Malcolm X

IDENTIFICATION: American religious leader and social activist

BORN: Malcolm Little; May 19, 1925, Omaha, Nebraska

DIED: February 21, 1965, New York, New York

TYPE OF ETHICS: Modern history

SIGNIFICANCE: Malcolm X advocated employing "any means necessary" to bring about a world of human rights and universal brotherhood based on truth, equality, righteousness, peace, justice, and freedom. One of the most important figures of the Civil Rights and Black Power movements, Malcolm X inspired many militant activists and helped to spark important debates over the relative merits of violent and nonviolent protest.

Appalled at the racial discrimination that was widely practiced in predominantly Christian America, Malcolm X chastised Christianity as unethically enslaving African Americans through its teaching that the oppressed should focus on Heaven, where they will

Malcolm X. (Library of Congress)

reap rewards and their wrongs will be righted, instead of doing something about their deprivation here on Earth. He taught that Islam could bring about true brotherhood because of the "color-blindness" of Muslims.

Distancing himself from the "turn-the-other-cheek" philosophy of Christianity, Malcolm advocated the "fair exchange" of an "eye for an eye, a tooth for a tooth, a head for a head, and a life for a life," if that was what it took to obtain human rights for African Americans and to create an egalitarian society of true human brotherhood. Just as love should be reciprocated, so should enmity. He believed that violent confrontation was necessary to defend the weak (women and children) against the strong (the Ku Klux Klan) but saw it as ethically wrong to form an African American Ku Klux Klan, since it "threatens the brotherhood of man." He was convinced that confrontation based on moral tactics succeeds only when the system one is dealing with is moral. In 1964, he formed Muslim Mosque, Incorporated, to give a spiritual basis to the correcting of the vices that destroy the moral fiber of society, and founded the

Organization of Afro-American Unity, a nonreligious, nonsectarian group intended to unite African Americans in the goal of attaining human rights.

I. Peter Ukpokodu

SEE ALSO: Civil Rights movement; Discrimination; Farrakhan, Louis; Human rights; King, Martin Luther, Jr.; Nation of Islam; Nonviolence; Violence.

Malthus, Thomas

IDENTIFICATION: English economist
BORN: February 13, 1766, the Rookery, near Dorking, Surrey, England
DIED: December 23, 1834, Claverton, Bath, England
TYPE OF ETHICS: Enlightenment history
SIGNIFICANCE: Responding to the demand for revision of England's Poor Laws, Malthus advocated limitations on human reproduction in *An Essay on the Principle of Population, as It Affects the Future Improvement of Society* (1798). His *Principles of Political Economy* (1820) encouraged private and public spending as a palliative for a lagging economy, thereby anticipating the 1930's economic system of John Maynard Keynes.

Contrary to the philosophers Jean-Jacques Rousseau and William Godwin, who professed the inherent goodness and perfectibility of humanity, Malthus argued that poverty could not be abolished, because of the inevitability of population growth consistently exceeding the food supply. While population grew geometrically, according to Malthus, resources grew arithmetically. Thus, population increases always would be checked by famine, disease, and war. Practical application of Malthusian theory occurred in the renovation of English Poor Laws. Believing that poverty was encouraged by the old system, which allowed people to live in their homes with community aid, thereby encouraging them to have many children, Malthus advocated workhouses in which the poor would be forced to live and work in conditions sufficiently bad to keep out all but the most desperate. Because of steadily rising food production rates brought about by increasingly sophisticated agricultural techniques, Malthusian predictions of

891

food shortages—on an international scale—have failed to manifest. Yet mounting ecological devastation—frequently caused by exploitative agricultural practices—the poor distribution of food, and unprecedented, unchecked population growth in the twentieth century, as well as predicted population growth in the twenty-first century, will undoubtedly result in a Malthusian ceiling.

Mary E. Virginia

SEE ALSO: Environmental ethics; Famine; Lifeboat ethics; Pollution; Population control.

Mandela, Nelson

IDENTIFICATION: South African social activist and statesman

BORN: July 18, 1918, Mvezo, Umtata district, Transkei, South Africa

TYPE OF ETHICS: Human rights

SIGNIFICANCE: After emerging with dignity from nearly three decades of political imprisonment, Mandela helped end South Africa's oppressive apartheid system and became the nation's first fully democratically elected president.

Before Nelson Mandela was sentenced to life imprisonment during the early 1960's, his struggle for freedom for black people in the Republic of South Africa led him first as a member of the African National Congress to advocate nonviolent acts of civil disobedience. However, after the Sharpeville massacre in 1960, in which South African police killed 69 peaceful demonstrators and wounded another 178, Mandela persuaded the African National Congress (ANC) to change its tactics to include acts of violent sabotage because peaceful protest had proven ineffective against overwhelming governmental force. Following a government raid on the headquarters of Umkhonto We Sizewa (Spear of the People), the military arm of the ANC that Mandela cofounded, the five-year jail term he was serving for leaving the country without permission and for inciting workers to strike was changed to life imprisonment.

IMPRISONMENT

During the years he was imprisoned, Mandela spent many hours at hard labor. Nevertheless, he managed to be of help to many of his fellow prisoners. However, his time in solitude was especially valuable because it gave him opportunities to read, meditate, and write. The hours he spent alone in his cell deepened and clarified his thinking about his cause and contributed to making him South Africa's most important African nationalist leader.

International concern for Mandela's situation grew steadily and was accompanied by pressure for his release and for an end to apartheid. Some countries

Former U.S. president Bill Clinton (right) and South African president Nelson Mandela look out of a window of Section B, Cell no. 5 at the Robben Island prison in South Africa on March 27, 1998. Mandela spent 18 of his 27 years in prison in the small cell. (AP/ Wide World Photos)

imposed painful economic sanctions against South Africa. The government responded several times during the 1970's and 1980's by offering Mandela his freedom—but only on the condition that he renounce his principles and tactics. He refused all such offers and told President P. W. Botha that only a truly free man could agree to such an arrangement.

In view of the mounting economic consequences of international sanctions against South Africa, Botha's successor, President Frederik W. de Klerk, arranged a series of secret meetings with Mandela to work out a mutually acceptable solution to the problem of making a transition from apartheid to a free and democratic society. Success came in 1990, when sanctions were lifted against the ANC, which promised to avoid violence, and Mandela was released from prison. For their achievement, Mandela and de Klerk shared the Nobel Peace Prize.

When South Africa held its first universal free elections in 1994, the ANC won in a landslide and the new parliament elected Mandela president of the country. Mandela's prompt call for reconciliation after taking office and his determination to ensure fairness for all the nation's people helped make the radical transition peaceful. However, the challenges that he faced were enormous: to extend the benefits previously enjoyed only by a minority of South Africa's population to its deprived majority. This meant great changes in every aspect of South African life: provisions for such basic necessities as housing, food, and water; education of children and adults; amendments and corrections in laws and methods of transferring land ownership; transformations in health care; and expanded electric power and telephone service. In addition, the growing acquired immunodeficiency syndrome (AIDS) epidemic, unemployment, waste and corruption within the government, and the need to reconstruct South African business and industry required close attention.

Not all these problems were solved during Mandela's four-year term as president. Nevertheless, Mandela presided over a comparatively united country in which progress was made on all fronts. He continued his concern for peace and justice not just at home but wherever in the world human rights were

American Feelings Toward Mandela

After Nelson Mandela completed his term as president of South Africa in 1998, the Chicago Council on Foreign Relations asked a cross-section of Americans to express their feelings about him on a thermometer scale.

Other 6%

31-49 degrees 5%

0-30 degrees "Cool" 13%

76-100 degrees "Warm" 26%

50 degrees "Neutral" 25%

51-75 degrees 25%

Source: Roper Center for Public Opinion Research. Figures reflect responses of 1,507 adults surveyed in the fall of 1998.

threatened. He helped mediate Indonesia's dispute with its East Timor independence movement and Libya's resolution of its responsibility for the 1988 terrorist downing of a Pan Am jetliner over Lockerbie, Scotland. He also helped Iran, Syria, Jordan, Israel, Palestine, and the United States in several attempts to make a durable peace in the Middle East.

RETIREMENT

After Mandela retired from the presidency in 1999, he continued to work for children's welfare through two foundations he created. He also went on missions to bring peace and reconciliation to various parts of the world and spoke out on issues about which he felt strongly. For example, in 2002 and 2003, he condemned American military intervention in Iraq as a threat to world peace. In 2003 he also sponsored a large-scale rock concert that featured world-famous performers who donated their time to raise money to combat AIDS in Africa.

Because of Mandela's achievements as a revolutionary, his courageous work in transforming South Africa into a free and democratic country, and his wisdom, integrity, and moral stature as a champion of world peace and justice, many people have ranked him among the most important statesmen of the twentieth century.

Margaret Duggan

FURTHER READING

Mandela, Nelson. *Long Walk to Freedom: The Autobiography of Nelson Mandela.* Boston: Little, Brown, 1994.

_____. *Nelson Mandela Speaks: Forging a Democratic, Nonracial South Africa.* Edited by Steve Clark. New York: Pathfinder, 1993.

Rasmussen, R. Kent. "Nelson Mandela." In *Modern African Political Leaders.* New York: Facts On File, 1998.

Sampson, Anthony. *Mandela: The Authorized Biography.* New York: Knopf, 1999.

SEE ALSO: African ethics; Apartheid; King, Martin Luther, Jr.; Nobel Peace Prizes; South Africa's Truth and Reconciliation Commission; Tutu, Desmond.

Manhattan Project

IDENTIFICATION: Research and development program established by the U.S. War Department to create a superexplosive utilizing the process of nuclear fission

DATE: Established in June, 1942

TYPE OF ETHICS: Scientific ethics

SIGNIFICANCE: The Manhattan Project created the first atom bombs and the only such bombs ever to

Workers at the Trinity test site in New Mexico prepare to raise the first prototype atom bomb to the top of a one-hundred-foot tower for detonation on July 16, 1945. (AP/Wide World Photos)

be used against human targets. The morality both of creating and of employing those weapons has been a matter of debate ever since.

In 1939, physicists in the United States learned of Nazi Germany's attempts to develop a fission bomb of unprecedented power and alerted President Franklin D. Roosevelt to the situation in a letter written by Albert Einstein. Given the brutality of the Nazis, the ramifications of such a weapon were frightening. On December 6, 1941, the president directed the Office of Scientific Research and Development to investigate the possibility of producing a nuclear weapon. The head of the office, Vannevar Bush, reported back in early 1942 that it probably would be possible to produce sufficient fissionable uranium or plutonium to power such a weapon. Accomplishing that task was by far the greatest obstacle to building an atom bomb.

In strict secrecy, in June of 1942, the Army Corps of Engineers established the Manhattan Engineer District, a unit devoted to building the bomb. On September 17, then-colonel Leslie R. Groves was appointed to head the entire effort (plan and organization), which by this time was called simply the Manhattan Project. Groves was promoted to general shortly thereafter. Physicist J. Robert Oppenheimer directed the scientific group that was responsible for actually designing the weapon.

By 1944, the Project was spending one billion dollars per year—a situation that some people believed was out of control. Project scientists detonated a prototype bomb in New Mexico on July 16, 1945, producing an energy yield that was beyond their expectations. Two more bombs were readied and dropped in early August, and Japan surrendered soon after. At the time, only some contributing scientists protested the use of the atomb bomb against a live target. Qualms were dispelled by the thought that Germany and Japan would have used it if they had developed it. As the effects of the new weapon became more fully appreciated, however, many began to feel remorse.

Andrew C. Skinner
Updated by the editors

SEE ALSO: Atom bomb; Cold War; Hiroshima and Nagasaki bombings; Union of Concerned Scientists; Weapons research.

Manichaeanism

DEFINITION: Proselytizing, gnostic, universal religion
DATE: Founded around 240 C.E.
TYPE OF ETHICS: Religious ethics
SIGNIFICANCE: Most famous as a species of absolute dualism, Manichaeanism espoused a belief in the ability of the human soul to redeem itself and transcend the corruption of worldly matter.

Manichaeanism was founded and organized by the Persian Mani, who was born on April 12, 216 C.E., in the province of Babylon (modern Iraq). Drawing on evidence such as the Turfan texts, discovered in Chinese Turkestan in 1904 and 1905, which contain portions of Mani's "bible," the Mani Codex, and on Manichaean literature, scholars accept the tradition that Mani's mother was a noble and that Mani was artistic, well educated, and multilingual. His father was an Elkesaite, a member of a Jewish-Christian religious movement that practiced baptism, purifications, and food taboos, all of which the mature Mani rejected. At the ages of twelve and twenty-four, Mani reported visions of a heavenly twin that persuaded him to abandon the Elkesaites and to proclaim his own doctrine publicly.

THE SPREAD OF MANICHAEANISM

Expelled by the Elkesaites and persecuted by the Persian regime, Mani fled for a time to India. In either March, 242, or April, 243, however, the Persian emperor Shapur I recalled Mani, sanctioned his religious views, and permitted him to preach throughout Persia. Having gathered a handful of converts, including his father, Mani thereafter rapidly won adherents within Shapur's realm before his rivals, in cooperation with a new emperor, imprisoned and martyred him in 277.

Manichaean missionaries, even before Mani's death, had begun spreading their religion into Egypt and the Roman colonies of North Africa (where the young Augustine of Hippo was a convert), as well as across Central Asia. In Persia's eastern provinces, in fact, Manichaeans thrived until the tenth century, when their enemies drove them eastward into Samarkand, Turkestan. There, when the Uighur Turks conquered eastern Turkestan, Manichaeanism became the official religion until that area, in turn, was decimated by the Mongols in the thirteenth century.

Meanwhile, during the fourth century, Manichaean influences in the West had reached their peak in Sicily, southern Gaul (France), and Spain.

Manichaeans subsequently penetrated China in 696 and, despite persecutions during the ninth century, their doctrines persisted there, clandestinely, for another five hundred years. In medieval Europe, in large part because of the hostile fifth century writings of Augustine, "manichaean" was a pejorative term applied by Christian theologians to heretical sects such as the Paulicians, the Cathars, the Bogomils, and the Albigensians, whose dualism or gnosticism resembled Manichaeanism. In sum, for roughly a thousand years and across much of the Northern Hemisphere, Manichaean beliefs and ethical practices won many converts and were exposed to the scrutiny of learned people and their governments.

MANICHAEAN BELIEFS AND ETHICS

Mani acknowledged that his religion was ecumenical, or all-encompassing, by design, and he openly drew upon a variety of philosophical and religious beliefs, including Judaism, Zoroastrianism, Greek philosophy, Chaldean astrology, Buddhism, Daoism, and Christianity.

Mani's primary objective was the salvation of men's souls (women were excluded as unredeemably corrupt) through personal acquisition of deeply experienced special knowledge, or *gnosis* (Greek for "wisdom"). For Manichees there were, at creation, two separate worlds. One world was paradisaical, suffused by the light of God, goodness, and beauty. In the present, however, humans lived in another world, a world of darkness, or evil, whose matter, although containing some mixtures of light, was corrupted almost totally. Human beings themselves were corrupt products of the mating of demons amid evil's partial triumph over light.

That some of God's light remained mingled in the battle between light and evil and that it could still be discovered in man nevertheless offered Manichaeans hope of salvation. An elite—the elect or *perfecti*—therefore could be saved if they carefully, at times painfully, lived their lives in search of the light within them. Finding light, they also discerned the nature of reality and of the past, present, and future of the universe. Their souls were destined for the kingdom of light. Manichees whose vows were incomplete—hearers—were destined for reincarnation.

Manichaeanism demonstrated an attractive tolerance for other faiths. Jesus, Buddha, Zarathustra, and Laozi, for example, were important figures from whom Manichees believed Mani was descended or reincarnated. Their writings or sayings formed parts of Manichaean liturgies and literature. Strict and benevolent personal and social behavior were stressed, particularly among the five classes of Manichaean clergy. Prayer was expected four times a day. Taxes were levied to support temples and clergymen. Monogamy was prescribed. Violence, including suicide, was denounced. Fasting was expected once a week and for thirty days at the spring equinox. Believing that humans ate living entities, including plants and fruits, for whom tears were in order, Manichees were supposed to be strict vegetarians.

ETHICAL IMPLICATIONS

Manichaeanism, in a harsh world of savagely conflicting regimes and faiths, was a religion of hope and redemption, the key to which was gaining inner wisdom. With a well-ordered clergy, temple observances, rites, and strict rituals, it provided a culturally rich and secure framework for hopeful, benign, and tolerant living that deplored violence and avoided warfare.

Clifton K. Yearley

FURTHER READING

Asmussen, Jes P. *Manichaean Literature.* Delmar, N.Y.: Scholars' Facsimiles & Reprints, 1975.

Campbell, Joseph. *Creative Mythology.* Vol. 4 in *The Masks of God.* New York: Penguin Books, 1976.

_____. *Occidental Mythology.* Vol. 3 in *The Masks of God.* New York: Penguin Books, 1976.

Eliade, Mircea. *A History of Religious Ideas.* Translated by Willard R. Trask. Chicago: University of Chicago Press, 1985.

Heuser, Manfred, and Hans-Joachim Klimkeit. *Studies in Manichaean Literature and Art.* Boston: Brill, 1998.

Noss, John. *Man's Religions.* 7th ed. New York: Macmillan, 1984.

Welburn, Andrew, comp. *Mani, the Angel, and the Column of God: An Anthology of Manichaean Texts.* Edinburgh: Floris, 1998.

SEE ALSO: Augustine, Saint; Buddhist ethics; Christian ethics; Daoist ethics; Evil; Human nature; Vegetarianism.

Manifest destiny

DEFINITION: Political doctrine holding that the entire North American continent was intended by God or Providence to become the territory of the United States

DATE: Term coined in 1845

TYPE OF ETHICS: International relations

SIGNIFICANCE: The doctrine of manifest destiny was referred to most explicitly in congressional debates of 1845 and 1846, but it shaped U.S. foreign and domestic policy throughout the nineteenth century.

The notion of manifest destiny has come to be associated with the policy espoused by President James Monroe in the Monroe Doctrine, but the phrase itself was coined later, by John L. O'Sullivan in the July-August 1845 issue of *United States Magazine and Democratic Review*. During that year, the merits of expansionist policies were the subject of debate, as the United States attempted to lay claim to the territories of Oregon and Texas.

Proponents of manifest destiny such as O'Sullivan held that the United States had a moral right, and indeed a religious obligation, to occupy and develop these lands. Opponents saw this attitude not only as heretical but also as potentially self-destructive, since it was possible for the still young nation to annex more territory than it could control and defend. Later historians, aware of the full extent of the genocide of Native Americans perpetrated in the name of manifest destiny, have raised more direct questions about the ethical effects of the doctrine.

Whatever its moral status, however, the conviction that the United States was destined to possess North America largely became reality during the nineteenth century. French claims to North America vanished with the Louisiana Purchase of 1803. Spanish claims received settlement in the Adams-Onis Transcontinental Treaty of 1819, after which Spain's lands contiguous to the United States came under the control of an independent Mexico. Russia's claim to Oregon Country was withdrawn as part of an 1824 Russian-American agreement. British claims to Oregon Country disappeared in a treaty signed in 1846. In addition, by 1848, Mexico's claims to Texas, New Mexico, and California were no more.

Bill Manikas
Updated by the editors

SEE ALSO: International law; Isolationism; Monroe Doctrine; Racism; Sovereignty.

Mapplethorpe, Robert

IDENTIFICATION: American photographer

BORN: November 4, 1946, New York, New York

DIED: March 9, 1989, Boston, Massachusetts

TYPE OF ETHICS: Arts and censorship

SIGNIFICANCE: Mapplethorpe was an important and controversial artist whose work has been exhibited in museums and galleries worldwide. He was one of a small group of photographers and performance artists at the center of battles in the United States over censorship and public funding for the arts during the late 1980's and early 1990's.

The work of the late photographer Robert Mapplethorpe, who frequently depicted homoerotic and sadomasochistic subjects, excited controversy throughout his career. With a slick and sophisticated style, Mapplethorpe often juxtaposed underground, subculture matter with classical composition. A 1989 exhibition of Mapplethorpe's photographs in Washington, D.C., which was partly funded by a grant from the National Endowment for the Arts, provoked a conservative campaign to halt government subsidies for what some considered to be "obscene" works.

After an emotional debate, Congress enacted restrictions on National Endowment for the Arts grants that did not fully satisfy either side, although they were milder than many in the art world had feared they would be. Meanwhile, a Mapplethorpe exhibition at the Cincinnati Contemporary Art Center led to the first trial of an art museum and its director on obscenity charges. Against the odds, the defendants were acquitted by a jury that decided that Mapplethorpe's photographs were the work of a serious artist.

Genevieve Slomski

SEE ALSO: Art; Art and public policy; Censorship; Freedom of expression.

Marcus Aurelius

IDENTIFICATION: Roman emperor

BORN: Marcus Annius Verus; April 26, 121, Rome

DIED: March 17, 180, Sirmium, Pannonia (now in Serbia) or Vindobona (now Vienna, Austria)

TYPE OF ETHICS: Classical history

SIGNIFICANCE: Marcus Aurelius is remembered as much for his Stoic philosophy, recorded in the *Meditations* (c. 171-180), as for his rule of the Roman Empire. His personal honor and nobility are perhaps best attested to by the fact that, in a time and place notorious for utterly ruthless imperial politics, he insisted on honoring a perceived commitment to his adoptive brother to share the throne. The brothers became the first fully equal joint emperors in the history of the empire.

While ruling the Roman Empire during its greatest period, Marcus Aurelius practiced a simple, even austere personal lifestyle based on a sincere belief in Stoic philosophy, which emphasized the overwhelming importance of spiritual and intellectual values over physical or material pleasures. Noted publicly for his restraint, modesty, and nobility, Marcus Aurelius devoted many of his private hours to writing his *Meditations*, which contained the essence of his version of Stoic ethics. The core of his ethical beliefs may be summed up in a few basic rules: forgive others for their wrongs; be aware of the harm done to people by their own bad actions; avoid judging others; be conscious of your own faults; consider that you cannot know the inner thoughts of others; avoid anger, for life is brief; anger and grief can be worse than actual physical harm; and kindness and friendship are best for all. Although these rules are hardly revolutionary in theory, they assumed and retain importance because they were held by a Roman emperor.

Michael Witkoski

SEE ALSO: Augustine, Saint; Stoic ethics.

Marketing

DEFINITION: Promotion, sale, and distribution of commodities

TYPE OF ETHICS: Business and labor ethics

SIGNIFICANCE: Marketing in modern society entails identifying potential consumers, persuading them to purchase one's products, and designing, modifying, manufacturing, or providing those products with the target market in mind. All these practices require ethical decisions to be made, about everything from invasions of privacy to honesty in advertising to fairness in pricing.

Various personal, societal, and environmental factors have led to an increased awareness of ethics in business practices. Frequently, this awareness is focused on marketing activities. Continual publicity about businesses involved with unethical marketing practices such as price fixing, unsafe products, and deceptive advertising has led many people to believe that marketing is the area of business in which most ethical misconduct takes place.

MARKETING AND ETHICS

Broadly speaking, "ethics" implies the establishment of a system of conduct that is recognized as correct moral behavior; it concerns deciphering the parameters of right and wrong to assist in making a decision to do what is morally right. "Marketing eth-

---

Marketers' Code of Ethics

The American Marketing Association's code of ethics requires members to accept responsibility for their actions by making sure that their decisions, recommendations and actions serve their customers, organizations, and society. The professional conduct of marketers is to be guided by the basic rule of ethics not knowingly to do harm, adherence to relevant laws and regulations, accurate representation of their qualifications, and practice of the association's code of ethics.

The code itself lays down specific guidelines under the headings of honesty and fairness, rights and duties of parties in the marketing exchange process, product development and management; promotions; distribution; pricing; and marketing research.

The full text of the code can be found at www.marketingpower .com/live/content175.php

ics" is the application of ethical evaluation to marketing strategies and tactics. It involves making judgments about what is morally right and wrong for marketing organizations and their employees in their roles as marketers.

The American Marketing Association (AMA) is the major international association of marketers. It has developed a code of ethics that provides guidelines for ethical marketing practices. Marketers who violate the tenets of the AMA code risk losing their membership in this prestigious and influential association.

Marketing is involved with a variety of ethical areas. Although promotional matters are often in the limelight, other ethical areas deserving attention relate to marketing research, product development and management, distribution, and pricing.

The area of marketing that seems to receive most scrutiny with respect to ethical issues is promotion. Because advertising, personal selling, and other promotional activities are the primary methods for communicating product and service information, promotion has the greatest visibility and generally has the reputation of being one of the most damaging areas of marketing. Misleading and deceptive advertising, false and questionable sales tactics, the bribing of purchase agents with "gifts" in return for purchase orders, and the creation of advertising messages that exploit children or other vulnerable groups are some examples of ethical abuses in promotional strategy.

MARKETING RESEARCH, DEVELOPMENT, AND MANAGEMENT

Marketing research can aid management in understanding customers, in competing, and in distribution and pricing activities. At times, however, it has been criticized on ethical grounds because of its questionable intelligence-gathering techniques; its alleged invasion of the personal privacy of consumers; and its use of deception, misrepresentation, and coercion in dealing with research participants and respondents.

Potential ethical problems in the product area that marketing professionals can face involve product quality, product design and safety, packaging, branding, environmental impact of product and packaging, and planned obsolescence. Some marketers have utilized misleading, deceptive, and unethical practices in their production or packaging practices by making unsubstantiated and misleading claims about their products or by packaging in a way that appeals to health-conscious or environmentally concerned shoppers. Ethical behavior involves using safe and ethical product development techniques, providing a product quality that meets customers' product specifications, using brand names that honestly communicate about the product, and using packaging that realistically portrays product sizes and contents.

Planned obsolescence represents an ongoing ethical question for marketers. Consumers are critical of it for contributing to material wear, style changes, and functional product changes. They believe that it increases resource shortages, waste, and environmental pollution. Marketers, on the other hand, say that planned obsolescence is responsive to consumer demand and is necessary to maintain sales and employment.

DISTRIBUTION AND PRICING

Many of the potential ethical problems in distribution are covered by laws such as those contained in the Robinson-Patman Act. Nevertheless, distribution involves some ethical issues that merit scrutiny. Deciding the appropriate degree of control and exclusivity between manufacturers and franchised dealers, weighing the impact of serving unsatisfied market segments where the profit potential is slight (for example, opening retail stores in low-income areas), and establishing lower standards in export markets than are allowed in domestic markets are examples of some distribution cases that have significant ethical implications.

Since pricing is probably the most regulated aspect of a firm's marketing strategy, virtually anything that is unethical in pricing is also illegal. Some of the primary ethical issues of pricing are price discrimination, horizontal/vertical price fixing, predatory pricing, price gouging, and various misleading price tactics such as "bait-and-switch" pricing, nonunit pricing, and inflating prices to allow for sale markdowns.

SOCIAL RESPONSIBILITY

It seems tenable to suggest that the areas of marketing ethics and social responsibility should be seen as concomitant. If marketing is authentically concerned with meeting consumer needs and concerns, it should also entail carefully evaluating how decisions impact and affect consumer expectations and quality of life.

Bait-and-Switch Techniques

Bait-and-switch advertising is the practice of advertising a product or service that the seller knows will not be reasonably available when consumers respond to the ad. When a consumer expresses a desire to buy the advertised product, the seller explains that it is not available for some reason—perhaps it has sold out—then apologizes and offers another product, one that has a higher price or a higher profit margin. After going to the trouble of seeking out advertised products, customers are often willing to accept alternatives, even if they are more expensive, particularly if the sellers are good at making the alternatives appear to be good deals.

Used car dealers are notorious for bait-and-switch techniques. A common ploy for a dealer is advertising a single vehicle at a bargain price that brings in many potential buyers. If the advertised vehicle actually exists, it is likely to be sold quickly, allowing the dealer to say, in all honesty, that the lot has sold all its advertised vehicles and then turn the customers' attention to more expensive vehicles. If the advertised vehicle does *not* exist, the dealer may say exactly the same thing, with the same results. In either case, the practice is unethical and may even be illegal.

Marketing activities can have significant societal and environmental ramifications. The rise of ecological consciousness among consumers gives social responsibility increasing stature. Consumers now are very concerned about whether the products or services they buy cause air or water pollution, landfill expansion, or depletion of natural resources. Recognizing this increased ecological concern of consumers, many companies are reevaluating the ways in which they produce and package their products and are considering the alteration of other areas of their marketing mix.

John E. Richardson

FURTHER READING

Boone, Louis E., and David L. Kurtz. *Contemporary Marketing, 1999*. Rev. 9th ed. Fort Worth, Tex.: Dryden Press, 1999.

Bovée, Courtland L., and John V. Thill. *Marketing*. New York: McGraw-Hill, 1992.

Davidson, D. Kirk. *The Moral Dimension of Marketing: Essays on Business Ethics*. Chicago: American Marketing Association, 2002.

Evans, Joel R., and Barry Berman. *Marketing*. 5th ed. New York: Macmillan, 1992.

Laczniak, Gene R., and Patrick E. Murphy. *Ethical Marketing Decisions: The Higher Road*. Boston: Allyn & Bacon, 1993.

Milne, George R., and Maria-Eugenia Boza. *A Business Perspective on Database Marketing and Consumer Privacy Practices*. Cambridge, Mass.: Marketing Science Institute, 1998.

Richardson, John E., ed. *Annual Editions: Business Ethics*. 5th ed. Guilford, Conn.: Dushkin, 1993.

_____. *Annual Editions: Marketing 93/94*. 15th ed. Guilford, Conn.: Dushkin, 1993.

Schlegelmilch, Bodo B. *Marketing Ethics: An International Perspective*. Boston: International Thomson Business Press, 1998.

Smith, N. Craig, and John A. Quelch. *Ethics in Marketing*. Homewood, Ill.: Richard D. Irwin, 1993.

SEE ALSO: Advertising; Boycotts; Business ethics; Industrial research; Information access; Multinational corporations; Resumes; Sales ethics; Telemarketing.

Marriage

DEFINITION: Formalized union, traditionally of members of the opposite sex, governed by the customs of a specific society

TYPE OF ETHICS: Beliefs and practices

SIGNIFICANCE: Marriage is commonly both a religious sacrament and a social institution with economic, educational, and other functions crucial to the maintenance of modern societies. Thus, the institution and anyone entering into it are enmeshed in an extensive network of moral functions, rights, and obligations.

In Western societies steeped in the Judeo-Christian tradition, marriages are monogamous, conjoining one member of each sex, but there are also polygamous cultures in which one male marries more than one wife (polygyny) or one female marries more than one husband (polyandry). Whatever its form, marriage provides a sanctioned context for mating and initializes the basic family unit.

PATRIARCHAL HERITAGE

In Western societies, there is a strong patristic heritage that still influences marital laws and customs. Even in ancient cultures with no roots in Judaism there was a deeply ingrained, patriarchal bias. For example, in pre-Christian Rome, fathers had supreme authority, including the right to dispose of the property and even the lives of their wives and children.

In many ancient societies, including that of Rome, marriage involved tradition rather than law per se. Marriages were arranged by family patriarchs, particularly in cultures with stratified classes based on birthright and inheritance. Marriages of convenience were prevalent and often involved the endogamous union of close relatives to preserve social rank and family property. The emphasis in such marriages was on the bride's social rank, dowry, childbearing potential, and domestic management skills. As a result, male infidelity, even when officially condemned, was widely practiced; under an infamous double standard, however, no such sexual freedom was granted to wives. Moreover, vestiges of Roman law and custom geared to male primacy have remained in Western law, going unchallenged until the twentieth century.

RELIGIOUS AND CIVIL SANCTIONS

During the Middle Ages, the Roman Catholic Church became the principal agent of change in those geographic areas formerly under Roman domination. Basing its arguments on scriptural prohibitions against sex outside marriage, the Church sought to modify the rules of courtship and marriage and vigorously condemned both fornication and adultery. The Church gave marriage a sacramental status and, technically, made it binding for life.

The Church also kept records of marriages, births, baptisms, and deaths until civil records were instituted, making all but baptismal and confirmation records redundant. Strongly influenced by the Church, criminal and civil law reflected both Christian ideology and its collateral Roman legacy. Civil codes made it extremely difficult to obtain divorces in secu-

lar courts, while criminal laws exacted harsh penalties for adultery.

In most Western countries, it has become possible to marry outside the purview of any church, in a civil ceremony that is legally binding but precludes any religious sanctions. Those who marry in a religious ceremony must obtain civil authorization, however, and the service itself must conform to law. In the United States, marriage is treated as a legal contract, but it differs from normal contractual agreements in that it cannot be dissolved without judicial arbitration. Although laws have gradually been liberalized to make divorce easier to obtain, the legal right to divorce may be inhibited by conflicting religious doctrines that, for many people, take precedence over legal rights.

RELATIONSHIP TO THE FAMILY

Because marriage was traditionally undertaken to provide generational continuity in name, blood, and property, it cannot be separated from the concept of family. Prior to the modern industrial and technological revolutions, in a more sparsely populated, less mobile world, many families took the form of extended families, in which the family patriarch held both dominion and roof over not only his children but also his grandchildren and even his great-grandchildren. The nuclear family, consisting only of parents and their immediate children, eventually displaced the extended family as the norm in the more industrialized areas of the world.

The concept of marriage has also undergone modification. Beginning with the suffrage movement, women sought to achieve many rights and prerogatives that both tradition and law granted exclusively to men. Vigorously advanced was the idea of marriage as an equal partnership, with all rights equitably shared by husband and wife. Most laws governing such matters as property and the custody of children now reflect the principle of joint ownership and responsibility.

MODERN PROBLEMS

The emancipation of women has raised new moral and legal issues that are yet to be resolved. An example is the notion of conjugal rape, an idea that is alien to much conventional thinking about marriage. Legal redress in cases of spouse abuse has been difficult because law enforcement agencies still tend to view marriage problems as private matters. The battered wife, though not exclusively a new phenomenon, is relatively new to public awareness.

Closely linked to the concept of procreation, marriage has traditionally sanctioned only heterosexual unions, but even that principle has been challenged by gays who wish to benefit from some of the legal guarantees extended to married couples and families. They have worked to redefine marriage legally to include the contractual mating of couples of the same sex with all the rights of heterosexual couples, including child adoption. Opposition to this goal, based on religious and moral grounds, remains strong.

John W. Fiero

FURTHER READING

Gies, Frances, and Joseph Gies. *Marriage and the Family in the Middle Ages.* New York: Harper & Row, 1987.

Harriss, John, ed. *The Family: A Social History of the Twentieth Century.* New York: Oxford University Press, 1991.

Henslin, James M., ed. *Marriage and Family in a Changing Society.* 3d ed. New York: Free Press, 1989.

Jeoffrey, V. H., and Zafar Nasir. *Marriage and Morals: Rebuttal to Bertrand Russell.* Karachi: Royal Book Company, 2001.

Macklin, Eleanor D., and Roger H. Rubin, eds. *Contemporary Families and Alternative Lifestyles.* Beverly Hills, Calif.: Sage, 1983.

Mintz, Steven, and Susan Kellog. *Domestic Revolutions: A Social History of American Family Life.* New York: Free Press, 1988.

Outhwaite, R. B., ed. *Marriage and Society: Studies in the Social History of Marriage.* New York: St. Martin's Press, 1982.

Russell, Bertrand. *Marriage and Morals.* 1929. Reprint. New York: H. Liveright, 1957.

Yalom, Marilyn. *A History of the Wife.* New York: HarperCollins, 2001.

SEE ALSO: Abuse; Adultery; Divorce; Family; Family values; Gay rights; Personal relationships; Premarital sex; Sexual revolution.

Marshall Plan

IDENTIFICATION: Program that transferred economic resources from the United States to Europe in order to restore European economies to prosperity
DATES: Proposed 1947; in effect 1948-1951
TYPE OF ETHICS: International relations
SIGNIFICANCE: The best-known example of foreign aid, the Marshall Plan advanced the principle that relieving economic distress promotes a peaceful world order.

The Marshall Plan, proposed in the spring of 1947 by General George C. Marshall, the American secretary of state, was intended to provide substantial economic aid to war-ravaged Europe. In order to prevent widespread economic collapse, the plan proposed to restore European economies to their prewar levels of production. Enacted by the Congress under the Truman administration, the plan provided more than $12 billion in economic aid to eleven Western European nations from 1948 to 1951. The amount equaled approximately 1.2 percent of the U.S. gross national product during each year of aid.

Essentially designed as government-to-government aid, the plan required each nation to formulate a list of needs and prescriptions for addressing them. Nations within the Soviet sphere of influence, unwilling to divulge their economic needs, quickly withdrew from consideration. After national programs had been approved, American aid, in the form of manufactured goods, machines, and raw materials, began to flow into the nations of Europe. American advisers supervised the program throughout to ensure that inflation did not destroy the gains. By 1951, the plan had succeeded in its goal of raising levels of productivity to prewar levels. The Marshall Plan brought benefits to both Europe and America by improving the economies on both sides of the Atlantic. It also laid the groundwork for future international cooperation in both commercial and military affairs.

Stanley Archer

SEE ALSO: Cold War; Economics; International Monetary Fund; Social justice and responsibility; Truman Doctrine.

Marx, Karl

IDENTIFICATION: German political philosopher
BORN: May 5, 1818, Trier, Prussia (now in Germany)
DIED: March 14, 1883, London, England
TYPE OF ETHICS: Politico-economic ethics
SIGNIFICANCE: The author of *Capital: A Critique of Political Economy* (*Das Kapital*, 3 volumes, 1867, 1885, 1894) and coauthor, with Friedrich Engels, of *The Communist Manifesto* (*Manifest der Kommunistischen Partei*, 1848), Karl Marx was perhaps the single most influential thinker of the nineteenth century. His theories of economics and of history formed the basis for revolutionary movements and socialist and communist governments during that century and the next. It has been said that, with the dissolution of the Soviet Union in 1989, historians were divided into two camps: those who believe that Marx's model of government failed, and those who believe that it was never attempted.

Karl Marx occupies a pivotal place in the history of the international socialist movement. A passionately committed revolutionary theorist and activist, he worked tirelessly to bring about the overthrow of capitalism and believed that he had discovered the historical laws that would inevitably produce its collapse. As an integral part of his philosophical system, he developed a materialistically based theory of ethics in which the prevailing moral principles of any historical period were seen as reflections of the underlying economic process and the interests and aspirations of the dominant social class. In presenting this view, he posed the question of capitalism's moral legitimacy more sharply than did any other philosopher of the nineteenth and twentieth centuries, and he offered a powerful alternative vision of a socialist society in which social classes would be abolished and all poverty and suffering would end.

HISTORICAL MATERIALISM

At the center of Marx's system lies his philosophy of dialectical materialism. His views on historical evolution, economics, society, and the theory of ethics all grow directly out of his materialist conception of the world. For Marx, it was not ideas that were the primary determinants of history, but material— particularly economic—facts. In the social world, in particular, the consciousness of human beings was determined by the conditions of their material existence and by the values and norms associated with the prevailing mode of economic production of the time.

All of history, Marx believed, moved through six distinct historical stages: primitive communism, the ancient slave state, feudalism, capitalism, socialism, and, ultimately, communism. At each stage in the process of historical development, the economic system created within it two antagonistic social classes, whose struggle for control of the productive property of the society was continuous and was reflected in their political and ethical ideas. In this struggle, the views of the dominant class—under feudalism, the landowning aristocracy, and under capitalism, the industrial bourgeoisie—tended to predominate. As Marx put it in *German Ideology* (1846): "The ideas of the ruling class are in every epoch the ruling ideas, i.e., the class which is the ruling *material* force of society is at the same time its ruling *intellectual* force."

Thus, for Marx, all ethical ideals—no matter how cleverly disguised—were class based and had their

Karl Marx. (Library of Congress)

903

origin in the conflicts generated by the underlying social and economic system. They were, in a real sense, ideological weapons used by the dominant and contending classes in their struggle for political hegemony, and thus were an ineluctable part of the class struggle itself. That struggle, Marx believed, was always resolved by revolution, and it unfolded naturally according to historical laws that were independent of the individual's will.

Rejection of Moral Absolutism

The materialist foundations of Marx's philosophy led logically to a categorical rejection of abstract moral idealism. To Marx, universal ethical principles such as those proposed by Immanuel Kant or by the Christian church were pure historical fictions. All ethical perspectives, he contended, were influenced by material interests and rooted in the economic conditions of a specific time and place. Abstract moral concepts such as "liberty," "equality," and "justice" were, in his view, illusions. Each social class tended to define such concepts in terms of its own historical experience, seeking to shape them in order to satisfy its ongoing material needs.

During the capitalist stage of development, for example, the bourgeoisie, the primary purchaser of labor in the society, and the working class, the seller of labor, naturally came to see such concepts as "liberty" and "equality" differently. This difference in perspective was based not on abstract moral reasoning but on contrasting positions of the classes in the productive process and the underlying economic relations of the age. In presenting their material demands, both classes made claims to absolute moral authority. No common moral ground in the class struggle existed, and the ultimate arbiter was always physical force.

Marx's belief that all morality was class morality took on a particular poignancy with regard to religion. The Church, he argued, like the state, was an institution that was dominated by the ruling class of any historical period. Therefore, it tended to espouse moral values that strengthened that class's political and social position. Specifically, the Church's promotion of the ideal of personal humility, scriptures against violence, and concentration on the afterlife were designed to teach the worker to be submissive to authority and to look to the next world for the ultimate reward. Religion, as Marx put it acidly, was "the opiate of the masses," and its destruction was an important step toward freeing the working class from the intellectual domination of the bourgeoisie.

Working-Class Morality

The vehemence with which Marx rejected the idea of universal ethical principles was accompanied by an equally disdainful attitude toward the more extreme forms of moral relativism. Since history, he argued, inevitably moved to materially "higher" and thus more potentially liberating stages, the ethical values of the ruling class of any historical period were inherently superior—in a developmental sense—to those of the ruling group that preceded it. Thus, the ethics of the bourgeoisie were "objectively" more progressive than those of the aristocracy and the slave-owning class before it, and those of the working class were the most liberating of all. Indeed, of all the classes that had appeared throughout history, the working class alone possessed a truly revolutionary morality. This was because its demands for human equality, an equitable distribution of property, and economic as well as political democracy grew directly out of its own material needs. It was this profoundly moral vision of the working class as a social carrier for a genuinely liberated society—even more than the purportedly scientific character of his historical analysis—that would account for much of Marx's influence after his death.

John Santore

Further Reading

Avineri, Shlomo. *The Social and Political Thought of Karl Marx*. London: Cambridge University Press, 1968.

Churchich, Nicholas. *Marxism and Morality: A Critical Examination of Marxist Ethics*. Cambridge, England: James Clark, 1994.

Cohen, G. A. *Karl Marx's Theory of History: A Defence*. Princeton, N.J.: Princeton University Press, 1978.

Cohen, Marshall, Thomas Nagel, and Thomas Scanlon, eds. *Marx, Justice, and History*. Princeton, N.J.: Princeton University Press, 1980.

Elster, Jon. *Making Sense of Marx*. Cambridge, England: Cambridge University Press, 1985.

Levine, Andrew. *A Future for Marxism? Althusser, the Analytical Turn, and the Revival of Socialist Theory*. London: Pluto, 2003.

Marx, Karl, and Friedrich Engels. *The Marx-Engels Reader.* Edited by Robert C. Tucker. 2d ed. New York: W. W. Norton, 1978.

Nielsen, Kai, and Stephen C. Patten, eds. *Marx and Morality.* Guelph, Ont.: Canadian Association for Publishing in Philosophy, 1981.

Sweet, Robert T. *Marx, Morality, and the Virtue of Beneficence.* 1991. Reprint. Lanham, Md.: University Press of America, 2002.

Wilde, Lawrence, ed. *Marxism's Ethical Thinkers.* New York: Palgrave, 2001.

SEE ALSO: Capitalism; Class struggle; Communism; *Communist Manifesto, The*; Economics; Hegel, Georg Wilhelm Friedrich; Ideology; Lenin, Vladimir Ilich; Marxism; Revolution.

Marxism

DEFINITION: Set of theories and practices espoused by, or associated with, Karl Marx, including historical materialism, the elimination of private property, and a commitment to bringing about a classless society

TYPE OF ETHICS: Modern history

SIGNIFICANCE: Classical Marxism was a revolutionary philosophy founded in a commitment to universal equality and justice. The actual governments that have come into being espousing Marxist principles, however, have often deviated from those ideals to such an extreme that the very meaning of the term has become a subject of significant controversy.

Implicit in Marxism is a unique variety of ethics that combines traditional theories of "might makes right" with the belief that under communism the wrongs of past injustices will be righted. Marxism as a theory has two distinct parts: Marx's interpretation of society as he perceived it and his image of society in the future. Marx can also be understood on two levels: as an economic theorist and as a moral theorist. He is more widely regarded, however, as an economic theorist with little regard for anything but economic justice. Some scholars of the last century have analyzed Marx as a moral theorist whose earlier writings in particular reflect values that are moral and perhaps even religious, although not in a traditional sense. These values were implicit in his theories of history and the revolutionary process.

Marx, in his early works, often spoke of the worker's alienation from society because of the division of labor and private property, which left the worker with little to show for his endeavors. Marx did not think that the situation could be corrected by invoking abstract theories of ethics and justice, since he believed that in every era ethics and values are imposed by the "ruling class." For example, Marx argued that in the Middle Ages, the feudal landowners who controlled the livelihood of others also set the norms of society. He believed that in the nineteenth century, capitalists (the bourgeoisie) controlled the means of production and therefore the political and social system. As part of their power, they set the standards of right and wrong. Although Marx criticized the ethical standards of his era, he accepted that the bourgeoisie had the right to set those standards.

ECONOMIC FORCES IN HISTORY

Marx believed that it was important to understand the economic forces that propel the evolution of history. His theory of historical materialism rejected traditional idealism and substituted for it a materialist interpretation, which defined the progression of history as the history of class struggle. Marx also predicted a fundamental revolution that would end class struggle and alienation in society.

Marx described a class struggle between the capitalists (the ruling class) and the proletariat (the workers) in his own era. The former controlled the means of production and therefore dominated society. The proletariat worked for the bourgeoisie in conditions of exploitation and hardship and were alienated from the products of their labor. Marx was concerned about the long hours the proletariat worked and low wages they received, about child labor, and about other social problems that were prevalent during the early stages of European capitalism, but he did not believe that those problems could be remedied.

Marx predicted that societal conditions would gradually worsen, as fewer and fewer people remained in the ruling class and more and more people joined the ranks of the proletariat. Eventually, Marx predicted, the proletariat would be so large and their conditions so terrible that they would rise up in spontaneous rebellion against the bourgeoisie. This revolution, born out of the dialectic and contradictions of history, would eventually provide the keys to ending exploitation. In the short run, the victorious proletariat would organize the dictatorship of the proletariat and begin to right the wrongs of history by removing privileges from the bourgeoisie—foremost among them, private property.

In the transitional era of the dictatorship of the proletariat, however, bourgeois values would still prevail. There would be a transitional period of undetermined length. Only in mature postcapitalist society, which Marx called communism, would people embrace new values and ethics, shed traditional acquisitiveness, and work for the good of society. Eventually, classes would disappear and a classless society would emerge in which people would work according to their abilities and receive compensation according to their needs. In the new society, people would no longer be alienated from their work and from society.

MARX'S ETHICS

Marx's theories of ethics were closely tied to his economic theories. He did not develop theories of ethics that were separate from his perception of economic reality. At the same time, the idea of transcending alienation and establishing new norms for society revealed an underlying idealism that was inconsistent with his conceptions of materialism.

Marx worked closely with Friedrich Engels from 1845 until his death. Their most famous publication, *The Communist Manifesto* (1848), contains guidelines for social norms and values that were to be followed after the proletarian revolution. Engels continued their work after Marx's death (1883). Engels's later writings on social issues, such as the family, and personal relations contain ethical overtones. In particular, Engels's writings on the family give evidence of the applications of the division of labor and "class struggle" within the family itself.

Although Marx would have bristled at the suggestion that he was an ethical thinker, an ethical undertone to his theory of history can be seen in his prediction that the injustices of the class struggle would be corrected on Earth, not in a distant heaven, when the revolutionary process led to the eventual emergence of communism.

Norma Corigliano Noonan

FURTHER READING

Avineri, Shlomo. *The Social and Political Thought of Karl Marx.* London: Cambridge University Press, 1968.

Churchich, Nicholas. *Marxism and Morality: A Critical Examination of Marxist Ethics.* Cambridge, England: James Clark, 1994.

Freedman, Robert. *The Marxist System: Economic, Political and Social Perspectives.* Chatham, N.J.: Chatham House, 1990.

Levine, Andrew. *A Future for Marxism?: Althusser, the Analytical Turn, and the Revival of Socialist Theory.* London: Pluto, 2003.

Lichtheim, George. *Marxism: An Historical and Critical Study.* 2d rev. ed. New York: Praeger, 1969. Reprint. New York: Columbia University Press, 1982.

Marx, Karl, and Friedrich Engels. *The Marx-Engels Reader.* Edited by Robert C. Tucker. 2d ed. New York: W. W. Norton, 1978.

Marx, Karl, Friedrich Engels, and Vladimir Lenin. *On Communist Society: A Collection.* 3d rev. ed. Moscow: Progress, 1978.

Renton, David. *Classical Marxism: Socialist Theory and the Second International.* Cheltenham, Gloucestershire, England: New Clarion, 2002.

Sweet, Robert T. *Marx, Morality, and the Virtue of Beneficence.* 1991. Reprint. Lanham, Md.: University Press of America, 2002.

Tucker, Robert C. *Philosophy and Myth in Karl Marx.* 3d ed. New Brunswick, N.J.: Transaction, 2001.

Wilde, Lawrence, ed. *Marxism's Ethical Thinkers.* New York: Palgrave, 2001.

SEE ALSO: Alienation; Capitalism; Class struggle; Communism; Dictatorship; Egalitarianism; Marx, Karl; Revolution; Socialism.

Maximal vs. minimal ethics

DEFINITION: Distinction between the least one must do to avoid transgression and the most one can do to accomplish good

TYPE OF ETHICS: Theory of ethics

SIGNIFICANCE: Minimal ethics are generally passive, since they involve one's obligations to refrain from evil acts, while maximal ethics require positive action to make either oneself or the world better conform with one's values and ideals.

The tension between maximal and minimal ethics arises in the attempt to relate what people *can* do to what they *ought* to do. How far and in what way should what is possible govern what is required?

WHO IS MY NEIGHBOR?

When ethical theories examine duties to others, tensions quickly emerge between consideration of what is owed to others and consideration of the effect upon one's own interests or well-being. The Christian scriptures highlight these tensions in such stories as that of Jesus' telling the young man to sell everything and give it to the poor (Mark 10) or telling the lawyer to imitate the Good Samaritan who risked everything to help a man who fell among thieves (Luke 10).

In the field of medical ethics, Tom L. Beauchamp and James F. Childress argue in *Principles of Biomedical Ethics* that a physician is "not morally obligated to emulate the Good Samaritan but rather to be what Judith Thomson calls 'a minimally decent Samaritan.'" They characterize the tension between maximal and minimal ethics in their discussion of the distinction between the duty of nonmaleficence ("do no harm") and the duty of beneficence ("do good"). "[T]he importance of the distinction is evident. The obligation of nonmaleficence is more independent of roles and relations, allows less discretion, and, in general, requires a higher level of risk assumption than the obligation of beneficence, which requires positive actions."

Some ethical theories simply make "do no harm" the duty and leave "doing good" to individual decision making. Other theories attempt to determine how far a person might be required to venture into doing good. Philosophers usually appeal to what it is "reasonable" to require, but no satisfactory agreement has been reached concerning how to define responsibilities that go beyond the minimum. Peter Singer, for example, in discussing duties to victims of famine, has argued that "if it is in our power to prevent something bad from happening, without thereby sacrificing anything of comparable moral importance, we ought, morally, to do it." Many people, however, believe that his principle is unreasonably

demanding. Michael Slote argues against Singer that it is not morally wrong to fail to prevent something bad from happening to someone else if preventing the evil "would seriously interfere with one's basic life style or with the fulfillment of one's basic life plans—as long as the life style or plans themselves involve no wrongs of commission."

In *Christian Faith, Health, and Medical Practice*, Hessel Bouma and others have provided a survey, from a religious perspective, of reasons that attempt to locate the source and motivation of a whole range of duties from the minimal to the maximal:

> [Picture ethical duties] on a spectrum, with minimal, legally enforceable ones at one end of the spectrum and, at the other end, those requiring heroic sacrifice for the sake of another's well-being. In the middle will be responsibilities such as truthfulness and civility that are morally mandated but not legally enforceable. . . . [A]t one end the state's sword power (its right and duty to use coercion, including its power to tax) provides added motivation, whereas at the other end the power of gratitude and the inspiring stories of good Samaritans and shepherds who lay down their lives for their sheep must be sufficient incentives.

BE ALL YOU CAN BE

Maximal vs. minimal ethics concerns more than the tension between duties to others and care for one's own interests. The tension between the minimal and the maximal can arise in the attempt to delineate the excellences that characterize a well-lived life. Immanuel Kant, for example, argued that people have a duty to develop their talents. How far does that duty extend? Is a modest cultivation of a particular talent sufficient? How much is enough? In *Beyond Good and Evil*, Nietzsche urges a maximal standard of human development in the application of purifying discipline to the "creature" in humanity in order to bring the "creator" element to greater perfection: "The discipline of suffering, of *great* suffering—do you not know that only *this* discipline has created all enhancements of man so far?"

CLASSIFYING THE MAXIMAL

Many ethical theories classify acts as forbidden, required, or simply permissible. In "Saints and

Heroes," J. Urmson argued that a further class of acts should be identified and that the old Christian concept of supererogation should be employed for this classification. Supererogatory acts, according to Urmson, are those that are not required by duty but go beyond duty in a way that merely permissible acts do not.

Urmson's arguments have led many people to agree that ethical theories should have a place for maximal expectations that are recommended but not required. His critics, however, question whether ethical theories can or should try to define a point at which one says, "We have done enough; everything else is beyond duty." They worry that the attempt to make a precise definition of what is strictly required leads theories to be narrow and legalistic in their account of human duties. They prefer an approach in which a "reasonable" account of how maximal duties are required can be given.

James V. Bachman

FURTHER READING

Beauchamp, Tom L., and James F. Childress. *Principles of Biomedical Ethics.* 5th ed. New York: Oxford University Press, 2001.

Bouma, Hessel, III, et al. *Christian Faith, Health, and Medical Practice.* Grand Rapids, Mich.: Eerdmans, 1989.

Goodin, Robert E. *Protecting the Vulnerable: A Reanalysis of our Social Responsibilities.* Chicago: University of Chicago Press, 1985.

Menssen, Sandra. "Maximal Wickedness vs. Maximal Goodness." In *Virtues and Virtue Theories*, edited by Michael Baur. Washington, D.C.: The Catholic University of America, 1998.

Nagel, Thomas. *The Possibility of Altruism.* Oxford, England: Clarendon Press, 1970.

New, Christopher. "Saints, Heroes, and Utilitarians." *Philosophy* 49 (1974): 179-189.

Singer, Peter. "Famine, Affluence, and Morality." In *Social Ethics*, edited by Thomas A. Mappes and Jane S. Zembaty. New York: McGraw-Hill, 1977.

Slote, Michael. "The Morality of Wealth." In *World Hunger and Moral Obligation*, edited by William Aiken and Hugh LaFollette. Englewood Cliffs, N.J.: Prentice-Hall, 1977.

Urmson, J. O. "Saints and Heroes." In *Moral Concepts*, edited by Joel Feinberg. Oxford, England: Oxford University Press, 1969.

SEE ALSO: Altruism; Benevolence; *Beyond Good and Evil*; Charity; Duty; Generosity; Ought/can implication; Perfectionism; Religion; Supererogation; Utilitarianism.

Mean/ends distinction

DEFINITION: Ethical distinction drawn between the goal being achieved and the method employed to achieve it

TYPE OF ETHICS: Theory of ethics

SIGNIFICANCE: The distinction between means and ends is the basis for hypothetical imperatives, which have the form "You should do x in order to accomplish y." Categorical imperatives presuppose that means and ends are one and the same: "You should always do x."

Theories of ethics vary widely in their philosophical perspectives. Nowhere is this chasm more broad than between the strict legalistic rules set forth by Kantian ethicists and the subjective interpretations favored by situationists. Immanuel Kant, as the father of the categorical imperative, believed that moral actions must hold up universally and unconditionally. Situational ethics, however, as developed by the consequential school, maintains that circumstances alter cases. Actions have no meaning or value in and of themselves; they become meaningful only in the light of the purpose they serve.

Situationists believe that any act—in fact, the same act—can be right or wrong, according to the situation. Such flexibility in moral reasoning lays the foundation for the popular maxim that the end justifies the means. Although unstated, the essential meaning of this philosophy is better represented by the clarification that a good end justifies a bad means. A good end achieved through good means needs no justification; a bad end, regardless of the quality of the means, deserves none.

The emphasis, then, is on the outcome, making the means/end distinction a favorite of consequential ethicists who argue that the moral act is the one that achieves the greatest good for the greatest number. With this reasoning, it is easy to extend the principle that an immoral act is justified if it is the vehicle by which a greater good is accomplished—telling a lie, for example, in order to save a life. Another school of thought, however, that of the situationists, places the rationale for this maxim not on the relative merits of the means and the end, but on the circumstances that define each individual situation.

Situationists believe that good and evil are not intrinsic properties belonging to a given act but are instead attributes that develop their character within the context in which the act occurs. The man who denies his financial problems as he provides comforting reassurance to his dying mother, for example, is acting in a compassionate and commendable way, not an immoral and deceitful one. The same subjectivity can be applied to other acts, too, including those conventionally considered good, such as self-sacrifice and philanthropy, and evil, such as thievery and murder. That the unscrupulous exploits of Robin Hood are hailed as heroic deeds by all but his villainous victims demonstrates the popularity of this notion. If acts are not intrinsically good or bad, then they must derive their merits from some other source. That source is the purpose that they serve or the intended outcome toward which they have been employed. Therefore, it is the end, and only the end, that justifies the means.

DEONTOLOGICAL VIEWS

Although strict deontologists believe that such a subjective philosophy foreshadows nothing short of moral anarchy, the means/end distinction has long been employed. Indeed, even the Bible contains numerous instances in which valued outcomes are achieved through violent or destructive means, such as the flooding of the earth in order to restore goodness, an action that is inconsistent with modern Judeo-Christian moral prescriptions. Despite the fears of legalistic ethicists, however, the means/end argument, when properly applied, is a stiff and rigorous test of ethical principles, demanding a careful examination of four individual elements: the end, the motive for desiring this end, the means by which the end will be accomplished, and, in true consequential fashion, the foreseeable consequences.

It is important to note that all consequences must be weighed, not only the intended ones. For example, the parent who successfully funds the family vacation by trimming household expenses must consider not only the financial effects of a debt-free summer

sojourn but also the physical and psychological effects of lowered nutritional standards and clothing stretched beyond its normal wearability. In addition, responsible implementation of the means/end distinction recognizes that because means are seen not only as benign tools used to negotiate an outcome but also as ingredients that lend their attributes and characteristics to the creation of the outcome, they must be carefully selected, fitting, and appropriate to the hoped-for end. The following list offers specific questions to help address these issues.

1. Is the end really good? Does it simply appear to be good because of its desirability? Real good is commonly recognized as that which contributes to the achievement of full human potential.

2. Is it probable that the means will achieve the end? Utilitarian ethicists refer to this concept as maximizing expected utility.

3. Is the same good possible to achieve using other means? Is the bad means simply the easiest? Combined with the question above, the lower the expectation that the means will achieve the expected result, the greater is the obligation to seek alternative means.

4. Is the good end clearly and overwhelmingly greater than the bad means that will be used to attain it?

5. Will the use of a bad means in order to achieve a good end withstand the test of publicity? Will others agree with the decision reached in the question above?

Although the means/end distinction provides a useful tool as well as a popular philosophy for weighing ethical choices, it is not without its handicaps. A primary shortcoming, consistent with all consequential theories, is the lack of precision with which outcomes can be predicted. Therefore, the distinction is a more accurate measure of moral correctness in hindsight rather than in the development of situations. Despite this weakness, however, the means/end argument remains a strong and practical one. Its simple and obvious logic offers an understandable formula by which to weigh and resolve challenging ethical questions.

Regina Howard Yaroch

FURTHER READING

Bovee, Warren G. "The End Can Justify the Means—But Rarely." *Journal of Mass Media Ethics* 6, no. 3 (1991): 135-145.

Fletcher, Joseph. *Situation Ethics: The New Morality*. Philadelphia: Westminster Press, 1966.

Kant, Immanuel. *Groundwork for the Metaphysics of Morals*. Edited and translated by Allen W. Wood. New Haven, Conn.: Yale University Press, 2002.

O'Neil, Shane. *Impartiality in Context: Grounding Justice in a Pluralist World*. Albany: State University of New York Press, 1997.

Smart, John Jamieson C. *Ethics, Persuasion, and Truth*. Boston: Routledge & Kegan Paul, 1984.

SEE ALSO: Consequentialism; Deontological ethics; Kant, Immanuel; Kantian ethics; Pragmatism; Situational ethics; Utilitarianism.

Media ownership

IDENTIFICATION: Owners and executive officers of print and broadcast media, such as newspapers, magazines, radio and television stations, and broadcast networks

TYPE OF ETHICS: Media ethics

SIGNIFICANCE: Ownership of multiple media outlets by single individuals or companies raises serious ethical concerns about the availability and fairness of news.

Media ownership raises a number of interesting ethical questions. Of particular important are questions relating to whether owners of the media conduct their operations in a fashion that is objective, comprehensive, and ultimately in the best interest of the general public. When large numbers of media outlets are concentrated in the hands of a few owners, especially when the outlets are of various kinds of media, then these ethical questions become particularly acute. Such situations periodically occur in Western society.

During the late nineteenth century, sizable numbers of newspapers in both the United States and Great Britain became concentrated in the hands of a few individuals, known in the United States as "press magnates" and in Britain as "press barons." By the 1880's, the American publisher Joseph Pulitzer—after whom Pulitzer Prizes are named—had assembled a number of newspapers under his control; these included the *New York World*. Meanwhile, his great rival, William Randolph Hearst, took over the *San Francisco Examiner* from his father in 1887 and in 1895 bought the *New York Morning Journal*. The following year, Hearst established the *New York Evening Journal*.

Low priced, easy to read, and filled with eye-catching sensational stories, the Pulitzer and Hearst papers soon had large circulations and enormous influence on public affairs—influence that Pulitzer and Hearst, in particular, were not shy about using. Perhaps the most striking example of their influence occurred during the Spanish-American War of 1898, which was actively pushed by the two newspaper chains, especially by the Hearst papers. At one point, before war had been declared, the famous artist Frederic Remington asked if he could return from his assignment as a war illustrator in Havana, since war between Spain and the United States appeared to be unlikely. Hearst is reported to have responded, "You provide the pictures and I'll furnish the war." Whether that story is literally true or not, Hearst's famous riposte accurately symbolized the considerable powers of media ownership and its ethical dilemmas.

At the same time that Pulitzer and Hearst were battling for media dominance in the United States, two brothers named Harmsworth were gathering a media empire in Great Britain. Better known as Lords Northcliffe and Rothermere, the brothers came to own a sizable portion of the British press, including the famous *Times of London* as well as such high-circulation papers as the *Daily Mail*, *Daily Mirror*, *Weekly/Sunday Dispatch*, *London Evening News*, and *Glasgow Evening News*. They also owned the magazine group Amalgamated Press. Although such acquisitions, the Harmsworths became the dominant media power in the United Kingdom, and Lord Northcliffe in particular was recognized as highly influential. In 1917, during the crisis of World War I, another press baron, Lord Beaverbook, was appointed minister of information by the British government, thus making him officially responsible for wartime propaganda both at home and, increasingly important, in neutral countries such as the United States. After this, there could be little doubt about the power of media ownership and control.

MODERN MEDIA CONSOLIDATION

The question of media consolidation in the hands of a relatively few individuals or corporations arose

Members of an organization called Code Pink march outside a Los Angeles radio station in May, 2003, to call attention to an impending Federal Communications Commission hearing on a proposal to deregulate media ownership which would allow large companies to increase their control over radio, television, and newspaper communications. (AP/Wide World Photos)

again toward the end of the twentieth century, as a handful of key players came to dominate the international media market. In addition to owning traditional newspapers, these new press barons also owned varieties of other media, most notably book publishing companies; film, radio, and television outlets; and new media channels, such as sites on the World Wide Web. They also introduced new forms of media, such as twenty-four-hour all-news networks, which operated in cooperation with their other holdings. Never before in history had such a variety of media been collected and controlled by so relatively few persons or companies.

Chief among these players were giant media corporations such as AOL-Time Warner, which was created by a merger early in 2000 and which operated Cable News Network, or CNN; Rupert Murdoch's News Corporation, which started in Australia and spread throughout the world and which started Fox Television as a challenge to CNN and the existing big three networks; and Finivest, an Italian multimedia group owned by Silvio Berlusconi, who went on to become prime minister of that nation. Of these groups, News Corporation and Finivest were known for espousing and spreading the conservative, sometimes extreme right-wing thoughts of their owners. Not since the days of Hearst and Colonel Robert McCormick, reactionary owner of the *Chicago Tribune*, had media owners been so blatant in allowing their personal viewpoints to shape the reporting of their organizations. The ethical problems created by such a situation, while obvious to many media observers and members of the general public, did not seem to trouble Murdoch and others.

At the same time, non-news corporations were purchasing media outlets, chief among them the major television networks in the United States. During the 1980's, the American Broadcasting Corporation (ABC) was bought by Capital Cities Communications, the National Broadcasting Corporation (NBC) by General Electric, and the Columbia Broadcasting System (CBS) by Loews Corporation. In addition to cutbacks in their news budgets, with possible negative impacts on coverage, diversity, and objectivity, the networks also faced the delicate situation of reporting potentially negative stories about their corporate owners that could lead to possible loss of value in the stock of the parent company. Such situations were clearly filled with potential ethical dilemmas, most of which could be traced back to the problem of media ownership that influences not only what stories are covered, but how and to what purpose as well.

Michael Witkoski

FURTHER READING

Christians, Clifford G., et al. *Media Ethics: Cases and Moral Reasoning.* 5th ed. New York: Longman, 1998.

Day, Louis A. *Ethics in Media Communications: Cases and Controversies.* Belmont, Calif.: Wadsworth, 1991.

Englehardt, Elaine E., and Ralph D. Barney. *Media and Ethics: Principles for Moral Decisions.* Belmont, Calif.: Wadsworth Thomson Learning, 2002.

Gorman, Lyn, and David McLean. *Media and Society in the Twentieth Century.* Oxford, England: Blackwell, 2003.

Kovach, Bill, and Tom Rosenstiel. *The Elements of Journalism.* New York: Crown, 2001.

Levy, Beth, and Denis M. Bonilla, eds. *The Power of the Press.* New York: H. W. Wilson, 1999.

Pavlik, John V. *Journalism and New Media.* New York: Columbia University Press, 2001.

Pritchard, David, ed. *Holding the Media Accountable: Citizens, Ethics, and the Law.* Bloomington: Indiana University Press, 2000.

SEE ALSO: Accuracy in Media; American Society of Newspaper Editors; Fairness and Accuracy in Reporting; Journalistic ethics; News sources; Public's right to know; Tabloid journalism.

Medical bills of rights

DEFINITION: Documents that explicitly list the rights of patients with regard to access to care, control over their care, privacy, or any other issues relevant to medical treatment

TYPE OF ETHICS: Bioethics

SIGNIFICANCE: Rights language shifts the focus of moral attention from the duty-bound caregiver to the patient to whom there is a duty—to the claims of the right holder.

Although the express use of rights language in medicine is an artifact of the late twentieth century, deontological (duty-based) conceptions of medical ethics trace back to the Hippocratic oath, which explicitly obligates physicians to "abstain from all intentional wrong-doing and harm"—particularly "from [sexual] abus[e]"—and from "divulging [information about patients] holding such things to be holy secrets." Correlative to these obligations (although unstatable at the time, since the language of rights had yet to be invented), patients have the right not to be intentionally harmed, not to be sexually abused, and not to have confidential information divulged.

Duty-based conceptions of the physician-patient relationship were dominated by the Hippocratic oath until three eighteenth century British writers—the Reverend Thomas Gisborne, Doctor John Gregory, and Thomas Percival—developed theories of obligation deriving from physicians' social responsibilities and from their sympathy with patients. In 1803, Percival published a syncretic version of all three theories in the form of a code of ethics; that code, in turn, became the basis of codes of medical ethics issued by nineteenth century regional and national medical associations throughout the world. Although these writers were familiar with rights language, their primary focus was stating the duties of physicians. Consequently, even though their theories on physicians' duties generate correlative rights, they eschew the language of rights—as do the codes of medical ethics they inspired.

The first document to focus primarily on patients' moral claims is the 1947 Nuremberg Code, a set of ten principles issued by the Nuremberg Tribunal to justify its finding that the medical experiments conducted by twelve German physicians and their assistants were "crimes against humanity." The first

Historical Table of Patients' Rights

Document	Date	Author	Rights
Hippocratic oath	400 B.C.E.	Unknown	Not to be harmed; not to be sexually abused; confidentiality.
Lecture on the Duties of Physicians	1772	John Gregory	Sympathetic and humane care.
On the Duties of Physicians	1794	Thomas Gisborne	Diligent attention; confidentiality; honesty; punctuality; steadiness and sympathy.
Medical Ethics	1803	Thomas Percival	Attention and steadiness; humanity; confidentiality; authority and condescension (to be treated as equals).
Code of Ethics	1847-1957*	AMA	Skill, attention, fidelity. Tenderness and firmness; authority and condescension (equal treatment); humanness and steadiness; confidentiality; not to be abandoned; treatment during epidemics (even if physician jeopardized).
Nuremberg Code	1947	Nuremberg Tribunal	To consent to, and to refuse to, be experimented upon; to be informed of experiments; to terminate experiments unilaterally.
Patient's Bill of Rights	Current	American Hospital Association	To considerate and respectful care; to know the name of one's physician; to be informed of diagnosis, prognosis, treatment plans, and alternatives; to consent to, and to refuse, treatment; to privacy and confidentiality; to be informed of conflicts of interest; to be informed of, and to refuse to participate in, research; to have continuity of care and appointments; to examine bills and have them explained; to be informed of hospital rules.
Accreditation Manual	Current	Joint Commission on Accreditation of Health Care Organization	Impartial access to treatment, regardless of race, creed, sex, or national origin, or sources of payment; to considerate and respectful care; to privacy and to wear personal clothing; to request a change of room; to know who is providing treatment; to refuse to be treated by trainees. to be clearly informed of diagnosis. to visitors, phone calls, and letters; to informed participation in health care decisions; to consent to, and to refuse, treatment; to be informed of, and to refuse to participate in, experiments; to consult with a specialist and to continuity of care; to receive itemized explanations of bills; to be informed of a hospital's rules and complaint procedures

* Most contemporary statements of medical and nursing ethics are formulated as standards or principles rather than duties or obligations, and thus do not generate correlative rights. In 1957, for example, the AMA replaced its *Code of Ethics* with *Principles of Medical Ethics*, the principles state standards of conduct rather than duties, but Principle IV of the current AMA *Principles* stipulates that a "physician shall respect the rights of patients."

Nuremberg principle opens by stating that for "moral, ethical, and legal [experimentation] . . . the voluntary consent of the human subject is essential." It closes by stating that "the duty . . . for ascertaining consent rests on each individual who initiates, directs, or engages in the experiment." The Nuremberg Code never uses the language of rights, yet most commentators treat it as the progenitor of patients' rights theory because its focus (exemplified in these quotations) is on the moral claims—the rights—of the subjects of research.

Rights language was first expressly used in major medical documents during the 1970's, when it surfaced in the American Hospital Association's 1972 *A Patient's Bill of Rights* and, concurrently, in the section "Rights and Responsibilities of Patients," in the *Accreditation Manual* of the JCAH(O), the Joint Commission on the Accreditation of Hospitals (later, Health Care Organizations)—the organization that accredits American medical hospitals, psychiatric hospitals, and nursing homes.

Robert Baker

FURTHER READING

Annas, George. *The Rights of Patients: The Basic ACLU Guide to Patients Rights*. 2d ed. Carbondale: Southern Illinois University Press, 1989.

Annas, George, and Michael Grodin, eds. *The Nazi Doctors and the Nuremberg Code: Human Rights in Human Experimentation*. New York: Oxford University Press, 1992.

Baker, Robert, Dorothy Porter, and Roy Porter, eds. *The Codification of Medical Morality: Historical and Philosophical Studies of the Formalization of Western Medical Morality in the Eighteenth and Nineteenth Centuries*. Dordrecht, Netherlands: Kluwer, 1993.

Edelstein, Ludwig. *Ancient Medicine: Selected Papers of Ludwig Edelstein*. Edited by Owsei Temkin and C. Lilian Temkin. Translated by C. Lilian Temkin. Baltimore: Johns Hopkins University Press, 1967.

Wood, Marie Robey. "Patients' Bill of Rights." *The National Voter* 49, no. 4 (June/July, 2000): 16-19.

SEE ALSO: American Medical Association; Health care allocation; Hippocrates; Medical ethics; Medical insurance; Medical research; Physician-patient relationship; *Principles of Medical Ethics*.

Medical ethics

DEFINITION: Formal, informal, institutional, and personal codes of conduct for health care professionals

TYPE OF ETHICS: Bioethics

SIGNIFICANCE: Because medical workers deal with matters of life and death, as well as the most intimate details of their patients' lives, the ethics governing their actions are both especially important and especially complex.

Health care professionals are faced with many situations that have moral significance. These situations are characterized by such questions as whether or when to proceed with treatment, which therapy to administer, which patient to see first, how to conduct research using human subjects, where to assign resources that are in short supply, and how to establish an equitable health care system. The discipline of medical ethics seeks to engage in a systematic and objective examination of these questions.

HISTORY

An ethical code of behavior is central to the writings collected in the *Corpus Hippocraticum*, attributed to an ancient physician known as Hippocrates and other writers of the fifth through third centuries B.C.E. Medicine, according to these writings, should relieve suffering, reduce the severity of an illness, and abstain from treating that which is beyond the practice of medicine; the physician is defined as a good person, skilled at healing. The notion of a morally good dimension inherent in the medical practitioner has survived to this day. The Hippocratic texts were expanded upon by medieval physicians in the West so that, by the fifteenth century, rules of conduct had been established in the medical schools of the time.

Eighteenth century physicians such as Benjamin Rush, Samuel Bard, John Gregory, and Thomas Percival stressed the need for primary moral rules of medical practice and began to wrestle with questions of truth-telling in the physician-patient relationship. Percival's writings would become the basis for the first American Medical Association Code of Ethics, issued in 1847.

Nineteenth century physicians such as Worthington Hooker, Austin Flint, Sr., and Sir William Osler continued to refine a primarily beneficence-based understanding of medical ethics (that is, a code based on taking action only for the patient's good). Osler argued that physicians should be broadly educated in the liberal arts so as to be able to practice medicine properly.

The enormous growth of medical research in the twentieth century led to remarkable advances in health care but also raised troubling ethical questions. In 1947, the Nuremberg Code established the first basic ethical requirements for the conduct of medical research. This document was a direct result of the Nuremberg Trials of Nazi war criminals who had engaged in human experimentation considered far outside the grounds of decency. The code was later expanded and revised to become the Declaration of Helsinki of the World Medical Association, originally issued in 1964.

During the 1950's, medical ethics began to move away from being primarily a set of internally generated rules of professional behavior. The writings of such nonphysicians as Joseph Fletcher and Paul Ramsey (both originally trained in theology) began to examine the impact of medicine and medical technology on the moral fabric of society.

The 1960's and 1970's brought an emphasis on patient autonomy to the consideration of biomedical ethics in the United States: Reverence for the wisdom of the medical doctor's decisions, which had been the rule during previous decades, was tempered by a growing respect for the patient's need to contribute to decisions affecting his or her future well-being. The ascendancy of autonomy parallels a rise in the technological capabilities of modern medicine, a time of unusually pronounced affluence in the West, and the appearance of what have since become paradigmatic legal challenges to the notion of the physician or medical institution as the sole participant in medical decision making.

Concurrent with these developments was the appearance of new institutions dedicated to the study of biomedical ethics, such as the Kennedy Institute of Ethics at Georgetown University and the Hastings Center in New York. At the same time, ethical theories developed by nineteenth century philosophers such as John Stuart Mill and Immanuel Kant began to be applied to situations arising out of medical practice by a number of individuals whose primary training was in philosophy and theology rather than clinical medicine.

With the 1980's and 1990's, the prospect of scarcity came to dominate ethical discussion in the United States, raising concern about such questions as health care rationing and public access to medical care. An emphasis on distributive justice began to temper the preceding two decades' concern with obligations of social justice to the individual.

ETHICAL PRINCIPLES

Ethical analysis consists of the application of primary principles to concrete clinical situations. It also employs comparative reasoning, whereby a particular problem is compared to other situations about which a moral consensus exists. Principled reasoning rests on four fundamental principles of biomedical ethics.

The principle of respect for autonomy requires that every person be free to take whatever autonomous action or make whatever autonomous decision he or she wishes, without constraint by other individuals. An example of respect for autonomy is the doctrine of informed consent, which requires that patients or research subjects be provided with adequate information that they clearly understand before voluntarily submitting to therapy or participating in a research trial.

The principle of nonmaleficence states that health care providers should not inflict evil or harm on a patient. Although straightforward in its enunciation, this principle may come into conflict with the principle of respect for autonomy in cases where a request for withdrawal of therapy is made. Similarly, the principle may come into conflict with obligations to promote the good of the patient, because many medical decisions involve the use of therapies or diagnostic procedures that have undesirable side effects.

The principle of double effect in the Roman Catholic moral tradition has attempted to resolve this latter conflict by stating that if the intent of an action is to effect an overriding good, the action is defensible even if unintended but foreseen harmful consequences ensue. Some commentators suggest, however, that intent is an artificial distinction, because all the consequences, both good and bad, are foreseen. As a result, the potential for harm should be weighed against the potential for benefit in deciding the best course of action. A formal evaluation of this kind is commonly referred to as a risk-benefit analysis.

Individual interpretation of the principle of non-maleficence lies at the heart of debates over abortion, euthanasia, and treatment withdrawal.

The principle of beneficence expresses an obligation to promote the patient's good. This can be construed as any action that prevents harm, supplants harm, or does active good to a person. As such, this principle provides the basis for all medical practice, be it preventive, epidemiologic, acute care, or chronic care. Not all actions can be considered uniformly beneficial. Certain kinds of therapy which may prove to be life-saving can leave a patient with what he or she finds to be an unacceptable quality of life. An examination of the positive and negative consequences of successful medical treatment is commonly called a benefit-burden analysis. In this context, the principle of beneficence most frequently comes into conflict with the principle of respect for autonomy. In such situations, the physician's appeal to beneficence is often considered paternalistic.

The principle of justice applies primarily to the distribution of health care resources in what can be considered a just and fair fashion. Because there are many competing theories of justice, there is no single, clear statement of this principle capable of being succinctly applied to all situations. However, the principle does require careful consideration of the means by which health care is allocated under conditions of scarcity. Scarce resources in the United States, for example, include transplantable organs, intensive care beds, expensive medical technologies in general, and in some circumstances basic medical care itself. Under conditions of scarcity, one's understanding of justice can easily come into conflict with the obligations to each of the three preceding principles. In general, the scarcer the resource, the more concerns about distributive justice influence the deployment of that resource.

ETHICAL ISSUES

Questions of medical ethics generally fall into two categories. A quandary is a moral question about which detailed ethical analysis yields a single undisputed answer. A dilemma, on the other hand, is a moral question to which there are at least two ethically defensible responses, with neither one taking clear precedence over the other.

Ethical issues in medicine can also be divided into macrocosmic (large-scale, societal) and microcos-

mic (small-scale, often individual) concerns. Macrocosmic issues are those that apply to a broad social constituency and therefore often involve both statutory and common law. Microcosmic concerns, on the other hand, are those that arise in the day-to-day practice of medicine, the discussion and resolution of which generally have less impact on society as a whole.

Primary among the macrocosmic ethical debates is the question of health care allocation, which centers largely on the development of health care delivery systems and health care financing. Proposals for reform of the U.S. health care system range from the creation of a single-payer national health insurance program, which would insure every citizen, to a series of proposals that would establish multiple requirements for private health insurance, often linking these requirements to employment. A problem common to all proposals for health care reform is the definition of what constitutes a basic minimum of health care to which each citizen is entitled. Even if consensus can be reached regarding a basic minimum, how and to whom scarce resources will be allocated remains to be determined. In both cases, solutions require an assessment of mechanisms for increasing supply and fairly distributing the resource in an ethically acceptable fashion.

PRIVACY

In medical ethics, respect for privacy stems both from the Hippocratic tradition and from the principle of respect for autonomy. Privacy also has been argued as a fundamental right of persons. All rights-based theories imply a correlative obligation on the part of others to respect these rights. Debate, therefore, centers on when an individual's unbridled right to privacy begins to abrogate the public good. For example, does an individual's right to choose privately to have an abortion or to request euthanasia place an unacceptable burden on society to comply with these requests? If a physician considers a patient to be a public menace, what levels of justification are required before confidentially obtained personal information is divulged? To whom is it appropriate to release this information? Concerns of this nature lie at the center of public discussions surrounding the rights of persons infected with the human immunodeficiency virus (HIV).

MEDICAL RESEARCH

Research ethics, as it applies to human subjects, deals primarily with two questions. First, does the proposed research appear to provide important information of substantial value to society at minimal risk to the research subject? Second, is the research subject completely aware of the personal risks and benefits of participation in the project so that consent is fully informed? In order to answer these questions, research involving human subjects must undergo ethical review at both the macrocosmic and the microcosmic levels. Nationally, it is regulated by agencies such as the U.S. Food and Drug Administration (FDA). At the microcosmic level, the FDA mandates and supervises the administration of institutional review boards (IRBs), which are charged with the responsibility of ensuring that human subjects are involved in creditable research, are treated in a humane manner, are not subjected to undue risks, and are fully cognizant both of the nature of the project in which they are participating and of any potential risks and benefits associated with it.

A third concern in biomedical research ethics, which does not directly apply to human subjects, is the question of what constitutes a conflict of interest on the part of the principal investigator or research institution. This becomes an increasing problem as more research is funded by private rather than public sources.

THE NATURE OF LIFE AND ETHICAL DECISION MAKING

This is perhaps the thorniest of all issues in that it revolves around definitional questions about which no consensus exists. Is human life consistently of greater value than all other forms of life? Is the value of human life defined primarily by consciousness? Is human life defined by genetic information, and if so, is alteration of this information a moral enterprise? If genetic engineering is in principle morally acceptable, are there circumstances under which it becomes unacceptable? When precisely does life begin and end? Each of these questions has a profound effect on an individual's opinion of issues such as abortion, the appropriate circumstances for treatment withdrawal, brain death, organ transplantation, euthanasia, animal research, and allocation of health care.

Although some commentators tend to assign primacy to one of the four principles of medical ethics—autonomy, nonmaleficence, beneficence, or justice—relegating others to subordinate roles, the prevailing approach to principled reasoning interprets each principle as being *prima facie* binding; that is, each principle confers a binding obligation upon the medical professional to the extent that it does not conflict with another, equally binding principle. When two *prima facie* principles require actions that are diametrically opposed, there is an appeal to proportionality that allows the requirements of each principle to be evaluated in the light of circumstances at hand. On a case-by-case basis, one principle may be judged to be more binding than another, depending on the context of the problem.

An alternative form of ethical analysis employs the technique of casuistry, or case-based analysis. Using this method, the circumstances of a particular ethical quandary or dilemma (the "reference case") are compared to those of a case about which it is abundantly clear what the correct moral decision should be (the "paradigm case"). The degree to which the reference case resembles or differs from the paradigm case provides guidance as to what the ethically appropriate course of action might be. This method of analysis has the advantage of being similar to the way in which conclusions are reached both in common law and in clinical medicine. Clinical decisions are regularly made in medical practice by comparing the facts of a particular case about which the treatment may be in question with those of similar cases in which the correct treatment is known.

A problem for those who favor casuistic analysis is the wedge argument, sometimes known as the "slippery slope." Detractors suggest that the use of a particular logical argument, such as the defense for withholding or withdrawing certain kinds of therapy, will drive a wedge further and further into the fabric of society until an undesirable consequence (for example, active nonvoluntary euthanasia) ensues. Proponents of casuistry respond that the undesirable consequence is far enough removed from the paradigm case to no longer resemble it.

Most clinical ethicists combine principle-based analysis with case-based reasoning to answer the specific ethical questions that arise in the practice of medicine. In addition, clinical ethicists benefit from training in law, sociology, and psychology, as well as the primary studies of medical science and philosophy.

PUBLIC POLICY

Macrocosmic, public issues are addressed publicly by a number of mechanisms. Blue-ribbon panels, such as the New York State Task Force on Life and the Law, can study a problem in depth, after which a consensus report with policy recommendations is issued. Such panels have the advantage of bringing together people who represent a wide range of opinion. Another avenue is the formation of grassroots organizations, such as Oregon Health Decisions, that attempt to generate a public consensus on ethically sensitive issues.

In one fashion or another, issues of public concern often are argued on the floors of both federal and state legislatures. Numerous state laws regulate the withholding and withdrawing of therapy; federal legislation, such as the Patient Self-Determination Act, also governs the disclosure of patients' rights to determine the course of their care when they cannot make decisions.

Even with legislative guidance, individual institutions often find themselves beset by microcosmic ethical questions such as when to terminate life-sustaining therapy or who should be admitted to intensive care units. Other common microcosmic dilemmas involve maternal-fetal conflict, wherein the autonomous requests or medical best interests of the mother do not coincide with the presumed best interests of her unborn child. In such situations, health care facilities often solicit the assistance of institutional ethics committees. Such committees are characteristically composed of individuals representing a broad spectrum of professional disciplines as well as community members not directly employed by the facility. In situations that require an institutional response, these committees will often assist in policy development. Ethics committees also serve as primary educational resources for both the institutional staff and members of the surrounding community.

Many committees have established mechanisms for case consultation or case review for patients whose care raises ethical questions. Consultations of this type involve review of the patient's clinical condition as well as pertinent social, religious, psychological, and family circumstances. Consultants investigate the ethical arguments that support alternative courses of action before issuing a final recommendation. In most cases, the recommendations are not binding; however, certain models do require that consultative recommendations determine the outcome in specific settings.

Although intervention by an ethics committee often allows for the resolution of ethical disputes within the walls of an institution, sometimes irreconcilable differences require judicial review by a court of law. Under these circumstances, the court's decision becomes a matter of public record, providing precedent for similar cases in the future. Microcosmic cases can thereby generate a body of common law that has profound effects at the macrocosmic level.

John A. McClung

FURTHER READING

Bandman, Bertram. *The Moral Development of Health Care Professionals: Rational Decision-making in Health Care Ethics*. Westport, Conn.: Praeger, 2003. Employs both classical and contemporary moral philosophy to construct a model of moral development based on rights and virtues and apply it to the medical professions.

Beauchamp, Tom L., and James F. Childress. *Principles of Biomedical Ethics*. 5th ed. New York: Oxford University Press, 2001. A lucidly written textbook. Although some commentators are critical of a primarily principle-based approach to bioethics, this remains the major introductory resource.

Beauchamp, Tom L., and Laurence B. McCullough. *Medical Ethics: The Moral Responsibilities of Physicians*. Englewood Cliffs, N.J.: Prentice-Hall, 1984. An excellent introduction to common problems encountered in clinical ethics. Each chapter opens with a case study that illustrates the focal topic. One of the best references for people completely new to the field.

Beauchamp, Tom L., and LeRoy Walters, eds. *Contemporary Issues in Bioethics*. 6th ed. Belmont, Calif.: Thomson/Wadsworth, 2003. A composite of readings culled from legal decisions, seminal legislation, ethical codes of conduct, and the writings of well-known ethicists. Readings are organized by topic and are preceded by a summary of ethical theory.

Jonsen, Albert R., Mark Siegler, and William J. Winslade. *Clinical Ethics: A Practical Approach to Ethical Decisions in Clinical Medicine*. 5th ed. New York: McGraw-Hill, 2002. A handbook of medical ethics aimed primarily at the physician in training. The authors present a method for evaluating the ethical dimensions of clinical cases, after which the book is organized lexically so that commonly encountered problems can be easily located. A concise reference that concentrates on practical rather than theoretical priorities.

Jonsen, Albert R., and Stephen Toulmin. *The Abuse of Casuistry: A History of Moral Reasoning*. Berkeley: University of California Press, 1988. A well-constructed history of the technique of case-based analysis that concludes with a practical description of how this approach can be used as an alternative to principle-based analysis in clinical situations.

Miles, Steven H. *The Hippocratic Oath and the Ethics of Medicine*. New York: Oxford University Press, 2004. A work of history and ethics; provides cultural analysis of the original meaning and context of the Hippocratic Oath and demonstrates its relevance and application to contemporary medical practice.

Post, Steven G., ed. *Encyclopedia of Bioethics*. 3d ed. 5 vols. New York: Macmillan Reference USA, 2004. A broad look at the entire field of bioethics and one of the most comprehensive collections of readings available under one title.

Veatch, Robert M. *Case Studies in Medical Ethics*. Cambridge, Mass.: Harvard University Press, 1977. A good survey of ethical issues, illustrated by 112 separate case presentations. Excellent for group discussions.

SEE ALSO: Bioethics; Diagnosis; Health care allocation; Hippocrates; Holistic medicine; Medical insurance; Medical research; Physician-patient relationship; *Principles of Medical Ethics*; Therapist-patient relationship.

Medical insurance

DEFINITION: Provision of or payment of costs incurred by health care services when needed, given to a particular group whose membership is limited by factors such as payment of premiums, employment, income, or citizenship

TYPE OF ETHICS: Bioethics

SIGNIFICANCE: Inequities in health insurance coverage are both indicative of, and contribute to, unjust and inequitable policies and practices for the poor.

At the beginning of the twenty-first century, health insurance was possibly the greatest cause of the rapidly escalating cost of medical care in the United States. The lack of regulation, the control of the industry by those who profit from it rather than those who purchase services, and the openness to abuse by both the insured and the providers of care combine to charge the insurance industry with helping have caused one of the most unfair aspects of modern American society: lack of access to needed care by a large portion of the population.

Access to health care has two major components: the patient's ability to pay and the availability of accessible and culturally acceptable facilities capable of providing appropriate care in a timely manner. Lack of health insurance is the greatest barrier to health care accessibility. In the absence of insurance coverage, people often postpone or forgo treatment. In 1980, 25 million Americans were uninsured; by 1999, over 42 million, or nearly one in six, people were uninsured according to the 2000 U.S. census. In 2002 the figure jumped to 43.6 million.

Generally employment-related and -financed, health insurance is a relatively recent development in the medical field. Only within the twentieth century did access to health care become of general concern, primarily because earlier systems of health care were for, the most part, ineffectual. Historically, the care of the sick was the responsibility of families and churches, and the costs of such care consisted mainly of lost wages, rather than payments to outside providers.

Skyrocketing costs and a shift in the workforce from the highly paid, largely unionized full-time manufacturing sector with employer-sponsored health insurance to a low-wage, increasingly part-time non-unionized service and clerical workforce whose employers are less likely to provide insurance account for the widespread lack of insurance. Many people who are not provided with employer-sponsored insurance plans choose not to seek health insurance. The recessionary cycles in the mid-1970's to mid-1990's resulting in massive layoffs also accounted for lack of insurance coverage or underinsurance (lack of insurance for catastrophic illness, preexisting illness, gaps in Medicare, lack of coverage for long-term care, deductibles, and co-payments).

In a survey conducted by the Commonwealth Fund, a private foundation supporting independent research in health and social issues, 26 percent of American adults aged nineteen to sixty-four (or an estimated 45.4 million people) experienced a period of time when they were uninsured in 2003. In addition to instability in insurance coverage, the survey found evidence of a decline in the quality of coverage among those who were insured. Premiums increased as cuts or new limits in benefits emerged. Instability in insurance coverage and declines in the quality of private health benefits appear to impede Americans' ability to obtain necessary health care. Health insurance premiums increased 13.9 percent in 2003, faster than the 8.5 percent growth in health care costs. Health care expenditures in 2002 were $1.6 trillion, or 14.9 percent of the nation's gross domestic product.

The United States has the highest health care spending of any country, yet it is the only major industrialized nation not to provide health insurance coverage for everyone. The uninsured generally have higher mortality rates. They are also three times more likely than the insured to experience adverse health outcomes and four times more likely to require avoidable hospitalizations and emergency hospital care.

HISTORY

In 1883, Germany enacted laws providing compulsory national health insurance to all workers. This was done to produce a more productive labor force and to enhance national defense rather than out of concern for the individual. Other countries in Western Europe quickly followed suit. In the United States, commercially provided insurance policies were available from the turn of the twentieth century, but it was not until the Great Depression that health insurance became a major industry. At that time, since few people had money to spend on anything but necessities, all but the most crucial medical treatments were neglected. Hospitals, finding themselves in increasingly difficult financial situations, banded together to form Blue Cross, an organization designed to elicit prepayment of hospital costs to insure against future need. Soon afterward, a similar organization was formed by local and state medical associations in order to collect funds to reimburse physicians for expenses incurred in service. This organization was known as Blue Shield.

The commercial insurance industry (as opposed to the "nonprofit" nature of Blue Cross and Blue Shield) expanded after World War II, with the increasing demands of labor unions to provide health insurance for all workers. The federal government got involved in 1965, when the plans for Medicare, which provides coverage for people over the age of sixty-five, and Medicaid, designed to give access to health care to the poor, were enacted as amendments to the Social Security Act. During the early 1990's Medicaid coverage expanded to include children and pregnant women.

HEALTH CARE IN THE TWENTY-FIRST CENTURY

During the first years of the twenty-first century, the United States was the only industrialized nation to provide total health care protection for less than 25 percent of its population. Only two other industrialized nations, Libya and Cyprus, provide for less than 90 percent of their populations. The majority of completely uninsured people in the United States are young people working at low-income jobs. Most are employed but work at jobs that do not provide group health coverage.

In most states, Medicaid does not provide care for employed persons, and the cutoff income for coverage is lower than the national poverty level; therefore, many people who are living in poverty do not have any form of medical insurance. Low-income Hispanic adults are particularly affected: 37 percent of this group were never insured with private coverage. As many as 80 percent of low-income Hispanics were uninsured sometime during 1996 through 1999 compared with 66 percent of low-income African Americans and 63 percent of low-income whites. Unstable work patterns and part-time employment increase the risk that families will experience gaps in coverage or periods of time without insurance. Gaps in coverage impede people's ability to obtain needed care and increase the risk of burdensome medical bills. The U.S. Department of Health and Human Services has said that closing the health gap for minorities is a key public policy priority.

BENEFITS OF INSURANCE

The greatest benefit derived from health insurance is security from financial risk in case of illness, security that health care will be available if needed. The other, more global benefit is ethical. Health insurance provides some equity by spreading the costs of undeserved illness between the sick and the healthy. While this does not compensate the ill person for the loss of health, it does allay some of the financial burden. Insurance also allows people the immediate gratification of providing for the possibility of bad times by spending a little less during the good. Health insurance is considered among life's most important commodities. In fact, significant numbers of employed individuals were reluctant to change jobs because they feared loss of health insurance. The Health Insurance Portability and Accountability Act (HIPAA) of 1996—which became effective on April 14, 2003—guaranteed "portability," or the ability of people with preexisting conditions to retain their insurance coverage when changing jobs.

COSTS OF INSURANCE

Aside from the actual premiums for insurance, there are several hidden costs. There are the administrative costs and risk of liability to the insurer. More ethically significant are the consequences of insurance. Insurance companies, as third-party payers, set limits as to the types of treatments or procedures that they will cover for a particular illness or condition. The medical community is obligated to respect the limits set forth by insurance companies, although the latter are not trained in medicine. Managed care is a system that strives to provide the cheapest option available for care, without regard to efficiency, quality, or cost-effectiveness. Financial incentives exist to undertreat, although the underlying framework of managed care is improving the health of the population, instead of focusing on an individual patient. Cost is the major concern.

In response to this decreased incentive, insurers have instituted cost-sharing plans including deductibles, coinsurance (in which the patient pays a certain percentage), and copayment (in which a flat fee is paid at the time of service). These cost-sharing means are much harder on the poor, because they take a larger portion of their income.

Medical insurance can be said to be an inherently unfair means of providing health care. If health care is considered to be a right, it cannot depend on individual ability to pay. Medical treatment for the uninsured is often more expensive than preventive, acute,

and chronic care of the insured, because the uninsured are more likely to receive medical care in the emergency department than in a physician's office. Those higher costs are passed on to the insured by cost shifting and higher premiums or to taxpayers through higher taxes to finance public hospitals and public insurance programs.

Improved access to health care is a vital and politically divisive issue. Presidential candidates, federal and state legislators, and health care industry leaders have all proposed ways to increase health insurance coverage, ranging from incremental expansions to various approaches that promise near-universal coverage.

Margaret Hawthorne
Updated by Marcia J. Weiss

FURTHER READING

Bodenheimer, Thomas S., and Kevin Grumbach. *Understanding Health Policy: A Clinical Approach.* 3d ed. New York: McGraw-Hill, 2002.

Daniels, Norman. "Accountability for Reasonableness in Private and Public Health Insurance." In *The Global Challenge of Health Care Rationing*, edited by Angela Coulter and Chris Ham. Philadelphia: Open Press University, 2000.

Daniels, Norman, and James E. Sabin. *Setting Limits Fairly: Can We Learn to Share Medical Resources?* New York: Oxford University Press, 2002.

Danis, Marion, Carolyn Clancy, and Larry R. Churchill, eds. *Ethical Dimensions of Health Policy.* New York: Oxford University Press, 2002.

Garrett, Thomas M., Harold W. Baillie, and Rosellen M. Garrett. *Health Care Ethics: Principles and Problems.* Englewood Cliffs, N.J.: Prentice-Hall, 1989.

Kovner, Anthony R., and Steven Jonas, eds. *Jonas and Kovner's Health Care Delivery in the United States.* 7th ed. New York: Springer, 2002.

Lee, Philip R., and Carroll L. Estes. *The Nation's Health.* 5th ed. Sudbury, Mass.: Jones and Bartlett, 1997.

Menzel, Paul T. *Medical Costs, Moral Choices.* New Haven, Conn.: Yale University Press, 1983.

Phelps, Charles E. *Health Economics.* New York: HarperCollins, 1992.

Roemer, Milton I. *National Health Systems of the World.* New York: Oxford University Press, 1991.

Medical research

DEFINITION: The application of bioethical principles to investigations whose goal is generalizable knowledge rather than individualized treatment
DATE: Fifth century B.C.E. to present
TYPE OF ETHICS: Bioethics
SIGNIFICANCE: Ethical medical research attempts to ensure that human subjects understand risks, while minimizing harm to them and distributing the benefits of research equitably within the context of social morality; it also promotes the humane treatment of animals.

Medical research, like other types of scientific inquiry, seeks either to discover patterns or to test proposed solutions (hypotheses) to problems. Broadly, the research entails observation and experimentation in accordance with the scientific method. Observation may be entirely passive—for example, an epidemiological study that tracks the spread of a disease through a population. Experiments depend upon intervention, that is, introducing some variable, such as a new drug or surgical procedure, in order to define that variable's effect on a disease.

Whether involving animal or human subjects, research poses complex ethical problems. In the case of human subjects, both the individual subject and the physician-researcher may face dilemmas if the social benefit of increased knowledge comes at the expense of the subject's health or societal moral principles. The trend in contemporary medicine has been to limit or eliminate ethical conflicts through defined principles, governmental regulation, and oversight panels.

THE NEED FOR RESEARCH

Every time physicians treat patients, some experimentation is involved, since however well tested a medicine or procedure may be, its use on the unique physiology of an individual patient amounts to a new test and carries some risk. In daily practice, however, physicians intend treatments to improve only the individual patient's health. By contrast, researchers hope to acquire generalized knowledge either to increase the basic understanding of the human psyche and soma or to treat all people who have a given disease. Accordingly, research has even broader social and scientific implications than does treatment.

The social implications of medical research become particularly important when such research contravenes a basic moral conviction held by the public in general or by a particular group. Beginning in the 1990's, advances in genetic engineering, stem cell research, and mammalian cloning provoked objections from diverse religious and humanitarian groups in the United States and prompted legislation by state and federal governments. To receive government funding and to protect their research from political pressures, scientists increasingly must accommodate research to extra-scientific moral issues.

HISTORY

In Western medicine, the Epidemics, traditionally attributed to the fourth century B.C.E. Greek philosopher Hippocrates, presented the first preserved general guidelines for physicians; its dictum to help patients or at least not harm them acquired pervasive moral authority. (Similar strictures appear in early Hindu and Chinese medical treatises.) The Hippocratic method stressed that physicians should observe patients and their surroundings and assist nature in restoring their health. The method was not innately experimental in the scientific sense.

Although Hippocrates' prestige was great, many early physicians approved of experimental procedures, and so the conflict between research and preserving patients from harm began early. The third century B.C.E. Alexandrian physicians Herophilus and Erasistratus believed that understanding the body's structures must precede effective treatment of diseases. Accordingly, they practiced vivisection on condemned prisoners to study anatomy, reasoning that the pain inflicted on them could lead to knowledge that would benefit humanity in general, which to them justified the vivisection. Later classical writers often disagreed. Celsus and the Christian philosopher Tertullian, for example, considered vivisection to be murder.

During the European Middle Ages, the teachings

of the second century Greek physician Galen dominated medicine. Galen taught that nature does nothing without a purpose and that the physician simply must discover that purpose. Medicine was primarily the application of the four-humors theory to specific cases, a method that was congenial to medieval Christian philosophy. Empirical experimentation was considered unnecessary and immoral.

After the Renaissance, when physicians began to abandon the humors theory and investigated the pathology of disease, biochemistry, and anatomy, the impetus to experiment grew. Little research was rigorous, and most of it involved experiments on patients, sometimes resulting in a public outcry. Such was the case in Boston during the smallpox epidemic of 1721-1722. Learning from England that small amounts of infected material stimulated immunity to the disease, Cotton Mather and Zebdeil Boylston inoculated 250 healthy Bostonians; 2 percent died, while 15 percent of plague victims died among the general population. However, the immunization experiment was decried. Not only did the procedure meddle with the workings of God, opponents claimed, but the 2 percent who died might not have contracted smallpox otherwise.

MODERN DEVELOPMENTS

The debate over the welfare of patients and the need for validated medical knowledge began to assume its modern shape during the second half of the nineteenth century. In 1865 Claude Bernard, a French physician, published his *Introduction to Experimental Medicine*, a fundamentally influential treatise. In it he argued that researchers must force nature to reveal itself; since experimental trials and procedures, including vivisection, are the surest means to produce verifiable knowledge, the physician has a duty to employ them. He added, however, that all research must benefit the test subjects. Those experiments that do only harm must be forbidden.

Bernard's book appeared as an antivivisection movement was spreading, intent upon exposing the cruelty of medical experiments on both animals and humans. Antivivisectionists criticized researchers for looking upon research subjects as objects rather than living, individual beings and for using subjects for the researchers' own ambitions with careless disregard of the pain and injury they may inflict. Such attitudes, according to the argument, are immoral be-

cause they conflict with the Christian principle of benevolence and the physicians' Hippocratic oath.

Efforts to codify ethical principles increased following World War II, mainly in reaction to grisly experiments performed in concentration camps by Nazi doctors. The post-World War II Nuremberg Code sought to prohibit experiments upon humans against their will or when death is the likely outcome; most subsequent codes were modeled upon it. The World Medical Association's Declaration of Helsinki (1964; revised 1975) suggested methods of protecting human subjects and urged researchers to respect animals' welfare and be cautious about the effect of experiments on the environment. In the United States, various federal agencies published regulations for experiments financed by public funds, especially the Food and Drug Administration (FDA) (1981) and the Department of Health and Human Services (1983), which required that institutional review boards (IRBs) approve research proposals before projects begin and monitor their execution.

In 1978, the National Commission for the Protection of Human Subjects of Biomedical and Behavioral Research released *The Belmont Report*, which proposed broad ethical principles to guide researchers in designing ethical studies. While widely influential, this brief document provided only a framework. Upon researchers and IRBs falls the task of interpreting and applying the principles to resolve ethical problems, sometimes in unprecedented contexts. For example, subsequent epidemics, such as acquired immunodeficiency syndrome (AIDS), challenged the ethics of clinical trials and research funding and raised concerns about public safety.

By 2000, IRBs in their traditional form were increasingly considered inadequate to handle ethical problems. With an estimated two million to twenty million people enrolled in clinical research projects, sometimes tens of thousands in a single drug trial, the case load for monitoring experiments threatened to be overwhelming. Additionally, the complexity of modern experiments and the potential effects on test subjects require understanding a broad range of research protocols and extensive scientific and technical expertise, difficult requirements for many local review boards to meet. At the same time, there was a trend for researchers or their academic institutions to seek profits in the research outcome, especially in patenting and licensing the applications of therapeutic innovations produced by genetic engineering. For these reasons, the Institute of Medicine recommended that IRBs be reconstituted to enhance protection of subjects, rigorously to exclude potential conflicts of interest, and to increase training in the ethics of human studies for board members and researchers.

Furthermore, although some government agencies regulate animal experiments, animal rights advocates condemn tests that harm animals for the benefit of humans, and groups such as the People for the Ethical Treatment of Animals (PETA) have sought legislative and judicial intervention to restrict the practice.

ETHICAL PRINCIPLES

The Belmont Report draws from assumptions about equity and autonomy that are common in modern cultures: Each human is to be treated as an individual, rather than as a component of a group; no individual is inherently superior; and no individual can be used primarily as the means to an end. The report's three *prima facie* principles—respect for persons, beneficence, and justice—assert these values' primacy when they conflict with the central value of scientific research, the acquisition of knowledge.

Respect for persons, also called autonomy, rests upon ensuring the self-determination of research subjects. Prospective subjects must not be enrolled in a study through coercion or deceit. Investigators must explain the nature of their study and its potential to harm subjects; then the subjects' formal, written consent must be obtained. For those subjects incapable of informed consent, such as children, the mentally impaired, and the brain dead, responsible guardians must consent to the enrollment. During the course of a study, researchers must protect the well-being and rights of subjects and permit them to end their participation at any time. In effect, researchers are to treat subjects as partners and collaborators, not as objects.

Beneficence obligates researchers to design a study protocol (the plans and rules for a study) so that the risk of harm to subjects is minimized and the potentiality for benefits is maximized. (Some ethicists divide this principle into beneficence, which assures the well-being of subjects, and nonmaleficence, which requires avoidance of harm. The division, they argue, reduces confusion and emphasizes the tenet in the Hippocratic oath against harming patients.) The

Department of Health and Human Services has defined minimal risk as the risk one runs in daily life or during routine physical or psychological tests. Beneficence entails a dual perspective: Not only should each subject expect benefits to health to be greater than harms, but there should also be a reasonable expectation that the study's findings will benefit society.

Because research risks the health of a few subjects, even if volunteers, in order to improve medicine for everyone, an innate inequity exists. The principle of justice seeks to moderate this inequity. No class of people, as defined by poverty, race, nationality, mentality, or condition of health, is to be exploited as research subjects so that they assume a disproportionate burden. The subjects are to be treated fairly; that is, their general human rights must be guarded. The benefits of research must be distributed equally among all groups in the society.

ETHICAL NORMS

Six norms, or standards, are widely used to verify that a study adheres to the principles of respect for persons, beneficence, and justice.

First, the design of the study should be rigorously defined and based upon the null hypothesis (also called equipoise). The null hypothesis assumes that none of the treatments involved in a study is known to be superior when the study begins; likewise, if a placebo (inert drug or innocuous procedure) is used, there must be no persuasive evidence beforehand that the treatment is superior to the placebo. This norm protects subjects, especially those with disease, from receiving treatments known to be inferior, and it helps physician-researchers overcome their central dilemma in medical research: withholding the best available treatment in order to test new treatments. Thereby, good research design supports respect for persons and beneficence.

Second, researchers must be competent, possessing adequate scientific knowledge and skill to conduct the study and to give subjects proper medical care. This norm also supports respect for persons and beneficence.

Third, the study should either balance possible benefits with harms or expect more benefits. Furthermore, if in the course of the study one treatment proves to be superior to another or to the placebo, researchers must terminate or modify the study so that all its subjects receive the better treatment. This norm incorporates all three ethical principles.

Fourth, researchers must obtain documented informed consent from each subject before a study begins, which assures respect for persons.

Fifth, to affirm the justice of a study, the selection of subjects must be equitable, drawing at random from the eligible population.

Sixth, again for the sake of justice, researchers should compensate subjects for any injuries incurred because of a study.

ETHICAL ISSUES

The most common form of medical research is the three-phase clinical trial, which usually tests new drugs. To eliminate possible biases toward the data and to provide equal treatment of subjects, researchers may incorporate one or more of the following four techniques. First, randomization assigns subjects by a lottery system, rather than on the basis of health, group affiliation, or economic condition. Second, one group of subjects receives the treatment under study, while a second, the control group, receives a placebo. When the first group reacts favorably to the treatment and there is no change to the control group, the researchers can conclude that the treatment causes the reaction, and it is not just an accident. Third, studies are blinded, which means that either the researchers, the subjects, or both (double-blinded) do not have access to documents recording which subjects are receiving treatment and which placebos. Fourth, the groups can exchange roles (crossover); that is, the first group changes from treatment to placebo and the second group from placebo to treatment. A study employing all these techniques is usually called a randomized, double-blinded, placebo-controlled clinical trial with crossover.

PHASE I AND PHASE II

Ethical issues trouble every step of such studies. For example, government regulation requires that a new drug be tested on animals before humans try it, and animal rights advocates have long denounced this procedure as cruel and exploitative. A phase I study determines the toxicity, side effects, and safe dosage of a drug on a small group of people in good health. Since an experimental drug can confer no health benefit on these "normals," the study lacks beneficence; however, the trend has been to conduct

phase I tests on subjects who have a disease for which a drug or procedure is a potential treatment, which obviates the ethical objection.

Phase II studies are controlled clinical trials on a small number of patients to determine whether a drug has a beneficial effect and is safe. Phase III trials, either with or without a control group, compare the effect of the new treatment with that of the standard treatment on a large group of subjects, while defining the medicinal properties and adverse effects as precisely as possible. When patients in a clinical trial are desperately ill, they may grasp at any new treatment with hope, so the use of randomization, blinded dispensation of treatment, and placebos can seem a deprivation of well-being.

Such was the case in the 1980's when azidothymidine (AZT) was tested on subjects carrying the human immunodeficiency virus (HIV) associated with AIDS; the phase I trial showed clinical improvements in some patients. Federal regulations called for a placebo-controlled phase II follow-up, yet scientists were sharply divided over the morality of withholding AZT from HIV-infected persons, because AIDS, once fully developed, was then thought to be universally fatal. A controlled study would be selective and would involve rationing of the drug, which they argued was unjust. Other scientists contended that only a thorough, controlled study could determine whether AZT had side effects more debilitating than the disease itself, and therefore the beneficence of the experimental treatment would remain in doubt.

When federal regulations made AZT the control drug for all further studies, concerns about confidentiality were raised. By selecting subjects for AIDS-related trials, researchers exposed the fact that these subjects were infected, and many subjects worried that they would face discrimination. Furthermore, the large amount of public funds devoted to AIDS research in the late 1980's brought complaints from scientists that other projects were left underfunded as a consequence. Some of these issues apply to studies of other widespread, deadly diseases, such as cancer and heart disease.

Ethical issues literally arise before subjects' births and continue after their deaths. For example, using the bodies of the brain-dead persons, even if legal wills explicitly grant permission, is potentially unethical if the family members object. Some right-to-life advocates, whose convictions demand that all human life is sacred, object to the use of fetuses or fetal tissue in research. Their beliefs come into direct conflict with stem cell research, one of the most promising lines of investigation at the beginning of the twenty-first century. Stem cells possess the capacity to self-renew and to differentiate into more than one type of cell. There are differing types of stems cells with disparate capacities, but the best for research and therapy are those human stem cells with the ability to become all types of cells, called pluripotent stem cells. They are harvested only from the embryo in an early stage of development. Such cells can be cultured indefinitely and hold great promise in testing pharmaceutical products, regenerating damaged organs, treating cancer, and investigating birth defects and fertility problems.

GENETIC RESEARCH

Because many religions accord full human status to embryos, harvesting embryonic cells following abortion is judged abhorrent, and the abortion itself is regarded as murder. Even the use of excess embryos from in vitro fertilization raises troubling questions about the moral and legal status of the human embryo to many observers. In 2001 President George W. Bush ordered that federal funding be restricted to embryonic stem cell research involving the cells lines already developed from sixty-four embryos.

Research into transgenic organ transplantation, genetic engineering, and the possibility of cloning humans raise even more basic ethical and moral questions than does embryonic stem cell research. By altering a basic natural process in some way, each challenges the nature of human identity and uniqueness. For example, scientists succeeded in introducing specially designed fragments of DNA into patients to treat genetic disorders. Transplanting a baboon's heart into a human baby can keep the child alive until a human organ can be found. Thus, cloning—making copies of embryos—promises to help elucidate basic cellular processes, simplify the testing of pharmaceuticals, create rejuvenation therapy, and provide treatments for infertility, genetic syndromes, and cancer.

Few dispute the potential benefits of such modern technologies. However, theologians, ethicists, and some scientists object to them for three basic reasons. The first is often characterized as the "playing god" accusation. Some religions find that the genetic engi-

A Biotechnological Conundrum

If a woman named Alice were to give birth to a daughter named Barbara, who was cloned from her, Alice might assume the role of Barbara's mother. However, Alice would, in fact, be Barbara's identical twin.

Relationship ambiguities such as this one raise difficult questions about human identity. For example, is the cloned person self and/or other? Are changes in these identities and roles beneficial or harmful? to what extent and to whom? Who should decide and on what basis should decisions about these changes be made?

neering of novel DNA and cloning (should it occur) are impious human attempts to replace the natural processes created by God and accordingly efface the complicated natural chain of events that makes each human unique. Scientists similarly worry that manufactured novelties, untested by the slow process of evolution through natural selection, may introduce counterproductive, even deadly, features into the human genome and accidentally eliminate some that are needed. The second objection comes from a general unease concerning the misuses of technology. The therapeutic effects, the argument runs, are admirable, but the power to intervene could escalate little by little into the power to dominate and change, a form of "technotyranny." So, genetic engineering and cloning, critics contend, might eventual produce designer children, eliminate politically unpopular traits, end diversity, and even create a new subspecies of *Homo sapiens*. This argument is sometimes called the "slippery slope" thesis. The third objection concerns matters of choice and justice. If it is possible to eliminate or replace human traits, who should decide which traits and on what basis? Moreover, since the technology involved is very expensive, there is the risk it will remain available only to a limited number of privileged persons. Although transgenic transplantation and genetic engineering weathered such critics for the most part, cloning research did not. By 2003, the United States, Great Britain, and many other countries considered partial or outright bans on human cloning.

Purely observational research may also be unethical when it withholds treatment and allows a disease to progress. For example, the Tuskegee Syphilis Study (1932-1972), designed to define the natural history of syphilis, illustrates harm by omission. The study followed four hundred black men with syphilis and about two hundred without it to determine the occurrence of untreated symptoms and mortality. The study continued even after penicillin, an effective treatment, became available during the late 1940's.

REGULATION

Scientists applying for public funding and pharmaceutical companies seeking FDA approval of a new drug must comply with federal regulations, many of which are designed to satisfy the ethical principles enunciated in *The Belmont Report*. The initial responsibility for compliance belongs to IRBs, which act on behalf of their parent institutions (mainly hospitals and universities), not as agents of the government. Composition of IRBs varies, but all must have doctors and scientists capable of reviewing the scientific merit of a proposed study; clergy, nurses, administrators, ethicists, and members of the public may also participate to safeguard the rights, well-being, and privacy of subjects. Even institutions that do not rely on public funds routinely convene IRBs to review research proposals.

Since federal agencies lack the resources to scrutinize every research project, medical research is largely self-regulated from a project's beginning, through IRBs, to its final product: publication. Medical journal standards call for editors to reject articles written by researchers who have not adhered to *The Belmont Report*'s principles, although some editors do publish such articles but follow them with editorials calling attention to ethical problems.

In the United States, the courts have also begun to provide ad hoc review of medical research as a result of litigation. Both individual and class-action civil suits seek redress, usually monetary awards, for injury sustained in research, but there have also been allegations of fraud or deception, which can involve punitive judgments as well. Researchers, institutions, and IRBs have been named as plaintiffs. As a result, research designers and IRBs must anticipate possible legal liabilities as part of their analysis of ethical issues.

Roger Smith

FURTHER READING

Beauchamp, Tom L., and James F. Childress. *Principles of Biomedical Ethics*. 5th ed. New York: Oxford University Press, 2001. General philosophical treatment of medical ethics, of which research ethics forms an appreciable part, and one of the most frequently cited investigations of the subject. Attempts to educe the ethical theory that best serves American health care.

Cohen, Carl. "The Case for the Use of Animals in Biomedical Research." *New England Journal of Medicine* 315 (October 2, 1986): 865-870. Argues that animal experimentation reduces risks to human subjects while accumulating much knowledge that is beneficial to human and veterinary medicine; urges also that animals be used humanely. While sympathetic to research, Cohen provides a good introduction to the animal rights controversy.

Espejo, Roman, ed. *Biomedical Ethics: Opposing Viewpoints*. Farmington Hills, Miss.: Greenhaven Press, 2003. The book offers reprinted articles that debate the ethics of human cloning, organ donations, reproductive technologies, and genetic research. It is well suited for readers unfamiliar with medical or bioethical terminology.

Holland, Suzanne, Karen Lebacqz, and Laurie Zoloth, eds. *The Human Embryonic Stem Cell Debate: Science, Ethics, and Public Policy*. Cambridge, Mass.: MIT Press, 2001. The reprinted and original articles in this collection provide sophisticated considerations of stem cell research in four parts. The first explains the science and its potential benefits to medicine. The second summarizes basic ethic issues. The third offers secular and religious perspectives on the controversy. The fourth discusses the role of public policy in the research. With a helpful glossary.

Kass, Leon R., ed. *Human Cloning and Human Dignity: The Report of the President's Council on Bioethics*. New York: Public Affairs, 2002. The President's Council on Bioethics provides this committee-generated report as an introduction to the moral significance of cloning and the ethical and policy questions raised by it in order to clarify its recommendations to President George W. Bush. It also supplies an explanation and history of cloning and a glossary.

Levine, Robert J. *Ethics and Regulation of Clinical Research*. 2d ed. Baltimore: Urban & Schwarzenberg, 1986. Levine, a consultant to the National Commission for the Protection of Human Subjects in Biomedical and Behavioral Research, interprets and expands upon the principals enunciated in *The Belmont Report*, drawing also upon such documents as the Nuremberg Code and the Declaration of Helsinki. A valuable, thorough discussion of specific issues as well as theory.

National Commission for the Protection of Human Subjects of Biomedical and Behavioral Research. *The Belmont Report.* Washington, D.C.: Government Printing Office, 1978. Brief document that has widely influenced research ethics in the United States. Far from exhaustive, it nevertheless describes the basic principles that underlie most subsequent discussions.

SEE ALSO: Animal research; Bioethics; Biotechnology; Cloning; Experimentation; Genetic engineering; Human Genome Project; Medical ethics; National Commission for the Protection of Human Subjects of Biomedical and Behavioral Research; Nazi science; Science; Stem cell research.

Mencius

IDENTIFICATION: Ancient Chinese philosopher
BORN: Meng Ke; c. 372 B.C.E., Zou, China
DIED: c. 289 B.C.E., China
TYPE OF ETHICS: Classical history
SIGNIFICANCE: A Confucian sage second only to Confucius, Mencius articulated, defended, and developed Confucianism; he held that human nature is inherently good and that the force of moral goodness is indefeatable.

In China, "Confucianism" is often referred to as "the way of Confucius and Mencius." Mencius (Chinese name, Mengzi) accepted Confucius's teachings without reservation, and his own teachings are largely elaborations of those of Confucius. He articulated Confucianism in an ingenious way, he defended Confucianism against rival ideologies such as Mohism and Yangism, and he combined Confucianism with his own theory of human nature. The book of *Mencius* is therefore regarded as one of the four central Confucian classics (the other three are the *Great Learning*,

the *Doctrine of the Mean*, and the *Analects of Confucius*). Mencius's moral courage and adherence to the practice of Confucianism exemplified the ideal personality of Confucianism.

REN AND YI

In Mencius's theory, as in that of Confucius, *ren* (benevolence, human-heartedness) and *yi* (righteousness) are central concepts. To be *ren* and to do whatever is in accordance with *yi* are essential to having a good life and a good society. According to Mencius, "*ren* is man's peaceful abode and *yi* his proper path." In other words, *ren* is the standing position of a moral agent, and *yi* is the character of moral acts. *Ren* is moral perfection that results in wisdom, courage, honor, and *yi*. Although *ren* and *yi* do not derive their justification from beneficial consequences, the power of *ren* and *yi* is so great that nothing can stop it. The "kingly way" defined by *ren* and *yi* can render *ba dao* (hegemonic force, the way of a despot) totally ineffective.

YANGISM AND MOHISM

To defend Confucianism against rival ideologies, Mencius focused his criticism on Yangism and Mohism. Yangzi advocated egoism. "He would not even pull out one hair to benefit the entire empire," because a hair is part of one's body, which is given by Heaven. This attitude is in direct opposition to Confucius's teaching that one has moral obligations to society; it is also, as Mencius put it, "a denial of one's ruler." Mozi, at the other extreme, advocated love without discrimination, which is not only unnatural but also amounts to a denial of one's father, for loving without discrimination will cause one's father to be treated in the same way as a stranger. "To deny one's ruler and one's father is to be no different from the beasts."

THEORY OF HUMAN NATURE

A fuller rejection of Yangism and Mohism requires a theory of human nature, a theory that answers the question, What is the decree of Heaven? According to Mencius, humans differ from other animals in that they have four hearts or incipient tendencies: The hearts of compassion (the germ of *ren*), of shame (of *yi*), of courtesy and modesty (of *li*, or rites), and of right and wrong (of wisdom). Their existence is indicated by the immediate impulses that one feels in certain situations. For example, when one suddenly sees a child on the verge of falling into a well, one would have an instantaneous feeling of compassion, although the feeling does not necessarily lead to an action. Since the feeling is spontaneous, it is the result of one's nature, which is given by Heaven; since it is disinterested, it is purely good; and since everyone has the feeling, no matter how faint and momentary, it is universal. Evil is a result of human failure to care for those tendencies and guard them against bad external influences.

"Man has these four tendencies just as he has his four limbs. When, having these four tendencies, he says of himself that he is incapable (of developing them), he is injuring himself," Mencius wrote. "Everyone is capable of becoming a Yao or a Shun" (ancient sage-kings of China). Since human nature is initially good, the way to be moral is to "retain the heart of a new-born babe."

HAO RAN ZHI QI

One can nourish one's good nature by accumulating righteous deeds. As one performs acts of righteousness, one will obtain and develop a *hao ran zhi qi*, a floodlike, vital, and refined energy. "As power, it is exceedingly great and strong"; "nourish it with integrity and place no obstacle in its path and it will fill the space between heaven and earth." This *qi* is both ontological (it actually exists) and moral. One cannot have the *qi* without being morally right. "If on self-examination I find that I am not right, I would tremble before a common fellow coarsely clad. But if on self-examination I find that I am right, I can go forward even against men in the thousands."

Mencius's theory gives clear answers to the following important questions that any adequate theory of ethics needs to answer: Why be moral? Who decides what is moral? How can one be moral? One should be moral because it is one's nature to be so. One need only look deep inside one's heart to find the answer about what is moral. To protect one's good nature from bad influences and to develop it by doing good deeds is the way to become a morally good person.

Peimin Ni

FURTHER READING

Chan, Wing-tsit. *A Source Book in Chinese Philosophy*. Princeton, N.J.: Princeton University Press, 1963.

Chang, Carsun. "The Significance of Mencius." *Philosophy East and West* 8 (1958): 37-48.

Fung Yu-lan. *A History of Chinese Philosophy*. Vol. 1. Translated by Derk Bodde. Princeton, N.J.: Princeton University Press, 1983.

_____. *A Short History of Chinese Philosophy*. Edited by Derk Bodde. New York: Macmillan, 1958.

Graham, Angus C. *Disputers of the Tao*. La Salle, Ill.: Open Court, 1989.

Ivanhoe, Philip J. *Confucian Moral Self Cultivation*. 2d ed. Indianapolis: Hackett, 2000.

_____. *Ethics in the Confucian Tradition: The Thought of Mengzi and Wang Yangming*. 2d ed. Indianapolis: Hackett, 2002.

Liu Xiusheng. *Mencius, Hume, and the Foundations of Ethics*. Burlington, Vt.: Ashgate, 2003.

Mencius. *Mencius*. Translated by David Hinton. Washington, D.C.: Counterpoint, 1998.

SEE ALSO: Confucian ethics; Confucius; Xunzi; Zhu Xi.

Men's movement

DEFINITION: Multifaceted, generally decentralized movement responding to changing conceptions of gender identity and gender politics from a masculine or a masculinist perspective

DATE: Late twentieth century

TYPE OF ETHICS: Sex and gender issues

SIGNIFICANCE: The men's movement was largely prompted by the second wave of feminism during the late 1960's and 1970's, but that prompting came in two different forms with very different consequences. For some members, feminism was perceived as accurately diagnosing problems with the construction of gender in patriarchy, and their response was to attempt to create a similar movement that would analyze and react to the patriarchal construction of masculinity. For others, the political and social activism of women was perceived as a threat which either victimized men or unfairly monopolized cultural attention with women's issues. This branch of the movement responded by creating advocacy groups to counteract what they saw as reverse or antimale sexism.

There actually have been several men's movements in North America, Europe, and other Westernized areas of the world. What is often taken to be a monolithic phenomenon is in fact composed of numerous groups that are sometimes in conflict with one another. Among these groups are profeminists, men's rights activists, spiritual revisionists, socialists, and African American and gay rights activists.

PROFEMINISM

Profeminism, as the name implies, is a positive male response to feminism. In the United States, profeminism is institutionally centered in the National Organization of Men Against Sexism (NOMAS), formerly the National Organization of Changing Men (NOCM) and the National Organization of Men (NOM). Similar groups exist in Europe and Australia (in Great Britain, for example, Men Against Sexism).

Profeminism developed during the late 1960's and early 1970's as groups of men began to take seriously the emerging body of feminist theory and began to consider ways to dismantle the male role in the maintenance of patriarchy, the institutionalization of male dominance. Drawing on the insights of feminist theory, profeminist men conducted critiques of male socialization and gender roles with an eye toward assisting women to gain political and economic parity with men; reducing male violence against women, children, and other men; and eliminating other expressions of sexism against females. The theoretical and critical work of profeminists is embodied in political activism directed at ending specific manifestations of sexism such as rape, pornography, and homophobia.

The men's rights movement is also politically active, but the focus of its activism is decidedly different from that of profeminism. Men's rights groups are concerned that modern constructions of the male gender unfairly limit men legally, socially, emotionally, and psychologically. Activists in this sector of the men's movement have called attention to numerous legal and social realities that place the male at a disadvantage, such as gender-based military conscription, the tendency of courts to favor mothers in child custody suits, and the much higher rates of suicide and violent crime (both perpetration and victimization) among men.

While not intrinsically antifeminist, men's rights groups often have been represented (and sometimes misrepresented) as such. To be sure, extremists within this group have reacted to what they regard as the excesses of feminism. In contrast to profeminists, some men's rights activists have argued that institutions and belief systems already overvalue the female. Principally, however, this movement is less a backlash against feminism than a utilization of feminist methods in the analysis of gender from the male point of view.

Spiritual revisionists share with men's rights activists a general dissatisfaction with traditional male roles, a ferment that may be rooted in countercultural tendencies of the 1950's, thus antedating the second wave of feminism. If this is true, the feminist movement that resurged during the late 1960's essentially provided a catalyst for the expression of a male discontent that was theretofore largely subterranean. Spiritual revisionism—or, as it is more commonly known, the mythopoetic men's movement—focuses primarily on the psychological and spiritual transformation of men. While there are certainly significant elements of political analysis and social activism in mythopoesis, spiritual revisionists usually focus attention on the individual self, maintaining that male malaise is fundamentally based on disorders of the soul.

Proponents believe that men need to overcome alienation from their bodies, their emotions, their work, other men, women, and the earth by recovering or creating myths and rituals, especially those that originate outside the industrialized Western world. This dimension of the men's movement has little or no organizational core; it is structured instead around small local support groups (akin to women's consciousness-raising groups), weekend retreats, and workshops. The mythopoetic movement has been influenced by the Jungian tradition in depth psychology and by recovery (twelve-step) programs. Many credit poet Robert Bly and psychologist James Hillman with inspiring this movement.

RELATED MOVEMENTS

Socialist, African American, and gay rights movements represent areas of overlap between the men's movement and other movements. Socialism has a broad political and philosophical perspective that involves more than gender analysis. Socialists in the men's movement view the construction of masculinities as part of larger economic conflicts, and hence they tend to be sensitive to the class differences between men. Profeminism, in particular, has ideological affinities with socialism.

The African American men's movement is especially concerned with the plight of the black male, who is faced both with the limitations and problems of the male sex role and with the injustices of racism. Many African American men have been comfortable in alliance with the spiritual revisionists, but others have criticized the men's movement for not making race a more prominent issue.

The gay rights movement intends to end social and political discrimination against homosexuals through political activity. Men who are involved in this movement are often allied with lesbians, profeminist men, and spiritual revisionists. Gay rights activists have called attention to the destructive effects of homophobia on all men, since the fear of homosexuality often leads to alienation between men and to insidious forms of self-hatred.

While the analyses and programs of these various groups differ considerably, they are all united in the conviction that traditional forms of masculinity require serious reevaluation and transformation for the greater well-being of both males and females.

Mark William Muesse

FURTHER READING

Brod, Harry, ed. *The Making of Masculinities: The New Men's Studies*. Boston: Allen & Unwin, 1987.

Clatterbaugh, Kenneth. *Contemporary Perspectives on Masculinity*. Boulder, Colo.: Westview Press, 1990.

Ehrenreich, Barbara. *The Hearts of Men*. Garden City, N.Y.: Anchor Press, 1983.

Jesser, Clinton J. *Fierce and Tender Men: Sociological Aspects of the Men's Movement*. Westport, Conn.: Praeger, 1996.

Messner, Michael A. *Politics of Masculinities: Men in Movements*. Walnut Creek, Calif.: AltaMira Press, 2000.

Seidler, Victor J. *Rediscovering Masculinity: Reason, Language, and Sexuality*. London: Routledge, 1989.

Stoltenberg, John. *Refusing to Be a Man: Essays on Sex and Justice*. Rev. ed. New York: UCL Press, 2000.

SEE ALSO: Gay rights; Homophobia; Pornography; Rape; Sexism; Sexuality and sexual ethics; Women's liberation movement.

Mental illness

DEFINITION: Nondevelopmental psychological or behavioral disorders

TYPE OF ETHICS: Psychological ethics

SIGNIFICANCE: Responses to mental illness by medical professionals, criminal justice systems, public policy experts, and society at large engage issues of paternalism, confidentiality, the right to privacy, individual autonomy, informed consent, the right to treatment, the right to refuse treatment, and the limits of criminal responsibility.

By conceptualizing mental disorders as illness, physicians are awarded primacy in regard to treatment decisions. Persons who suffer from mental illness may be viewed as requiring treatment, even when they do not desire such care. Under certain circumstances, persons who are mentally ill may be declared not responsible for their actions.

HISTORY

Historically, persons with mental disorders have been beaten, driven from their homes, subjected to inhumane treatments, and put to death. Early views of mental disorders were founded on a mixture of demonology and theories of organic causality. Demonology is founded on the idea that evil spirits or an angry god can dwell within or directly influence a person. Organic theories attribute the development of mental disorders to physical causes—injuries, imbalances in body fluids, or abnormal body structures.

Skulls dating back as far as 500,000 years show evidence of trephining, a technique using stone instruments to scrape away portions of skulls. It is assumed that these operations were performed to allow evil spirits to escape from the bodies of the people whose skulls were found. A modified form of trephining was revived in Europe in the Middle Ages. As late as the sixteenth century, some patients were subjected to surgical procedures in which a physician would bore holes in a patient's skull and an attending priest would remove stones that were assumed to be a cause of insanity.

An Egyptian papyrus of 3000 B.C.E. describes recommended treatments for war wounds and shows that the Egyptians recognized the relationship between organic injury and subsequent mental dysfunction. Another papyrus, of the sixteenth century B.C.E., shows that in regard to diseases not caused by obvious physical injuries, the Egyptians were likely to rely on magic for their explanations and incantations for their cures. Still, superstition was tempered with humane care—dream interpretation, quiet walks, and barge rides down the Nile.

The Hebrews viewed insanity as resulting from God's wrath or the withdrawal of his protection. Without God's protection, a person was subject to invasion by evil spirits, which could cause madness.

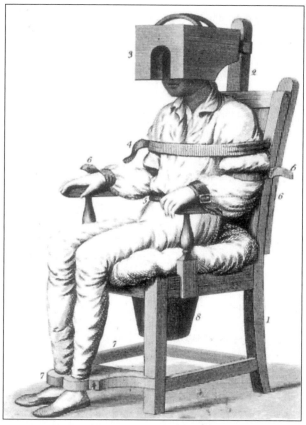

In 1811, Benjamin Rush, one of the founders of the American Psychiatric Association, invented what he called the "tranquillizing chair" to help calm patients with mental illness. (National Library of Medicine)

For the Hebrews, mental disease was a consequence of not living according to God's word.

Prior to the fifth century B.C.E. Greek beliefs concerning mental illness were founded on a mixture of religion and superstition. While the most typical responses to persons with mental abnormalities were banishment and stoning, some individuals received humane and supportive care. As did the Egyptians, the Greeks built temples devoted to healing and medicine. Baths, changes in diet, moderate exercise, and dream interpretation were aspects of the early Greek treatment regimen.

Subsequent to the fifth century B.C.E., Greek thought concerning diseases came under the influence of the physician Hippocrates. Hippocrates rejected the prevailing belief that attributed disease to possession. The writings of Hippocrates, nearly all of which were authored by his followers, are very clear in attributing diseases to natural processes. While many healthful remedies followed the Hippocratic idea that mental disorders could be traced to imbalances in body fluids, this same theory also led to many improper and inhumane interventions, such as bloodletting and the forced consumption of foul potions.

In addition to the deductions of Greek physicians, Greek philosophers also speculated concerning mental disturbances. The Greek philosopher Plato addressed the need to treat persons afflicted with mental disorders with compassion and argued that persons who commit a crime as a result of madness or disease should pay a fine but otherwise should be exempt from punishment.

The early Romans expanded upon and refined Greek ideas in regard to mental diseases. After the death in c. 199 C.E. of the Greek physician Galen, who practiced in Rome for most his lifetime, Roman medicine stagnated.

While Europeans abandoned scientific explanations for mental disorders, Islamic countries continued the inquiries initiated by the Greeks. In 792, the first hospital devoted exclusively to the care of mentally ill persons was opened in Baghdad. Humane treatment and a concern for the dignity of disturbed persons were key aspects of treatments recommended by Islamic physicians.

EUROPEAN TRADITIONS

In contrast to the Islamic tradition, Europeans routinely expelled, tortured, abused, and murdered the mentally disturbed. With the rise of Christianity, insanity was variously ascribed to demonic possession, hormonal imbalances, and folk superstitions. While some monasteries offered healing rituals based on incantations and prayer, it was far more common to view the mentally disturbed as abandoned by God or in league with Satan and in need of redemption rather than assistance.

During the mid-thirteenth century, the Church focused on the need to search out and identify witches and warlocks. Mentally ill persons were perfect targets for the papal inquisitors, although it is believed that many more sane than insane persons died as a result of the Inquisition. Commonly, the accused were tortured until they confessed, after which they were burned to death.

The fifteenth century also saw a major movement that was directed toward the confinement of the mentally ill. The institutions for the mentally disturbed were administered by physicians, and as a result, doctors assumed primacy in the care of the mentally disturbed. While the care of persons with mental disorders was transferred from the clergy to physicians, the quality of the patients' lives showed little improvement. Bloodletting, emetic potions, straitjackets, chains, dunking chairs, spinning devices, and terror were the most frequently prescribed treatments.

It was not until the late eighteenth century that positive changes occurred in regard to the treatment of the mentally ill. In 1793 a French physician, Philippe Pinel, was put in charge of a Paris asylum. Dismayed by the treatment that was provided the inmates, Pinel initiated a series of reforms that became the foundation for what was later called the Moral Treatment Revolution. The Moral Treatment Revolution was founded on the principles that mental patients should be treated with compassion, provided with supportive counseling, housed in comfortable surroundings, and given purposeful work.

While a number of existent asylums adopted the Moral Treatment approach and new hospitals were dedicated to its principles, it did not take long for economics and neglect to make a mockery of the stated principles. Over time, mental hospitals became little more than warehouses where the mentally ill were admitted, diagnosed, and forgotten.

THE MODERN ERA

While the late nineteenth century saw the development of new theories and techniques for the treatment of mental disorders that were based on free association and catharsis, only a few affluent persons with mental disorders received these treatments. Still, by the early twentieth century, bloodletting, purging, terror, and treatments designed to cause disorientation were being abandoned. These treatments were replaced by somatic therapies and pharmacological interventions. Major problems existed, however, in that the somatic therapies caused brain damage, and the drugs that were available prior to the 1950's were sedatives that caused extreme lethargy and sometimes death.

By the early 1930's, psychiatrists began experimenting with various types of somatic therapy. Insulin coma therapy involved administrations of toxic doses of insulin to nondiabetic patients. Electroconvulsive therapy (ECT) involved passing an electric current through a patient's brain, causing a seizure. Between the late 1930's and the 1960's, several hundred thousand mental patients were involuntarily treated with ECT.

During the mid-1930's, the Portuguese physician António Egas Moniz introduced a surgical procedure that evolved into the prefrontal lobotomy. Between 1935 and 1955, more than fifty thousand mental patients were subjected to lobotomies, in which healthy brain tissue was destroyed in a misdirected effort to treat mental illness.

By the mid-1950's, new pharmacological agents became available. The first of the drugs to be used was reserpine. Although the effects of reserpine on the behavior of psychotic patients were profound, the drug had dangerous side effects. Reserpine was soon replaced by the drug Thorazine. Over the next several years, hundreds of thousands of patients, some voluntarily and many involuntarily, were given Thorazine and other major tranquilizers. One side effect of Thorazine and other drugs of its class is tardive dyskinesia, a disfiguring disturbance that manifests as facial grimacing, palsy, and a staggering gait. For most patients, the tardive dyskinesia disappears when the drug is discontinued, but for some the symptoms are irreversible.

Partially as a result of the availability of psychotropic medications and as a result of changes in social policy, the 1960's saw the beginnings of the community mental health movement. The community mental health movement promoted the concepts of deinstitutionalization, treatment in the least restrictive environment, and treatment as close to the person's home community as possible. Deinstitutionalization involved discharging as many patients as possible from state hospitals and discouraging new admissions. As a result of deinstitutionalization, state hospital populations went from a peak of more than 500,000 during the mid-1950's to fewer than 130,000 during the late 1980's.

Clarification of Terms

Throughout the preceding narrative the terms "mental illness," "mental disease," "insanity," "madness," "mental abnormality," "mental disturbance," "mental dysfunction," and "mental disorder" have been used interchangeably. While this is a common practice, it can lead to misunderstandings.

While medical practitioners, legal documents, and the general public frequently refer to aberrant behavior and mental disorders as mental illness, this is a misuse of the term "illness." Illness implies that some underlying disease process exists. The American psychiatrist Thomas Szasz has argued that the complaints that are called symptoms of mental illness are simply communications concerning beliefs, discomfort, or desires that an individual experiences in regard to self or others. Labeling such communications as symptoms of mental illness is a sociopolitical process that vests authority in physicians to control and abuse persons whose communications make others uncomfortable or who are presumed to be dangerous.

While "insanity" is used interchangeably with "mental illness," it would be best if the term "insanity" were reserved to describe a mental state pertinent to legal proceedings. Most countries mitigate punishment if it is determined that a person was insane at the time of committing an illegal act. In fact, most states in the United States allow a finding of not guilty by reason of insanity. This means that a person who commits an illegal act while insane should be found not guilty of any criminal offense.

The terms "madness," "mental abnormality," "mental disturbance," and "mental dysfunction" are simply descriptive in nature. They have no particular standing in regard to the legal system or the medical establishment.

The term "mental disorder" is the official term adopted by the American Psychiatric Association and the American Psychological Association to describe abnormal behavioral or psychological states that cause personal distress, impaired functioning, or conflict with society. The Diagnostic and Statistical Manual of Mental Disorders catalogs the symptoms and behaviors of the various types of mental disorders. Only a minority of the several hundred disorders listed fit the criteria for identification as diseases. That is, it is not possible to identify infectious processes, biochemical imbalances, organ malfunctions, or physical trauma as causes of most disorders. Therefore, it is questionable to refer to them as illnesses.

Ethical Issues

The treatment of persons with mental disorders brings into consideration a number of ethical issues. Among the ethical issues that are of importance in regard to the treatment of persons identified as mentally ill are the following: paternalism, confidentiality, right to privacy, autonomy, informed consent, right to treatment, right to refuse treatment, and criminal responsibility.

In the United States, persons may be involuntarily confined in mental hospitals if they are "mentally ill" and a danger to self or others. Additionally, many states allow the commitment of "mentally ill" persons who are likely to deteriorate mentally or physically if they do not receive care. While at one time simply having a mental disorder could serve as grounds for loss of freedom, states now require an additional finding of dangerousness or probability of deterioration. The right of the state to confine selected citizens involuntarily is based on the concepts of paternalism and police power. Paternalism, or *parens patriae*, allows the state to protect citizens from themselves.

Confidentiality

Confidentiality is central to the practice of psychotherapy. Professional codes and legal procedures require that certain communications be held in confidence. Still, all states provide exceptions to confidentiality, which include the following: when criminal charges have been filed, in child custody cases, when a criminal offense is planned, when the client is a danger to self or others, and when the client has been informed that certain communications are not privileged.

While the right to privacy is a fundamental right that most citizens enjoy, it is frequently denied persons who have been diagnosed as mentally ill. If the mentally ill person does not cooperate with treatment, divulge personal secrets, and participate in routine hospital activities, he or she will be identified as an uncooperative patient and will find it very difficult to obtain his or her freedom.

Autonomy is the right to act in a manner that is consistent with one's personally held beliefs and to make decisions that affect one's fate and destiny. This is a right that is refused many mentally ill persons. Through involuntary commitment and forced treatment, persons deemed to be suffering from mental diseases are denied the right to make key decisions that affect their quality of life and their personal survival. Concerning personal survival, only two states have laws making suicide illegal. Furthermore, all states allow a competent adult to make decisions regarding the continuation of life-support devices. Most states either allow or are mute on the right of a competent person to terminate his or her life. Still, all states allow the forced incarceration of a mentally ill person who attempts suicide.

PATIENT RIGHTS

Informed consent requires that persons understand the nature of the procedures they are to experience, that their participation be voluntary, and that possible consequences be explained. Involuntary commitment, forced treatment, and failure to discuss side effects of psychotropic medications are examples of violations of informed consent in regard to mentally ill persons.

Right to treatment refers to the concept that persons involuntarily confined in mental institutions have a right to humane care and therapeutic treatment. During the 1971 Alabama case *Wyatt v. Stickney*, Judge Frank Johnson stated, "to deprive any citizen of his or her liberty upon an altruistic theory that the confinement is for humane and therapeutic reasons and then fail to provide adequate treatment violates the very fundamentals of due process."

During the 1975 case *O'Connor v. Donaldson*, the Supreme Court ruled that Donald Donaldson, who had been confined to a mental hospital in Florida

for fourteen years, deserved a periodic review of his mental status and could not be indefinitely confined if he was capable of caring for himself and was not a danger to himself or others. While not directly ruling on the issue of right to treatment, the court let stand an earlier decision that if Donaldson was not provided treatment, he should have been discharged from the hospital.

The right to refuse treatment is an issue that causes a great deal of controversy. Prior to the 1960's, it was common practice to force patients to undergo dangerous and disabling treatments. Involuntary sterilizations, electroconvulsive therapy, and psychosurgery were frequently prescribed for recalcitrant or difficult patients. While patients now have specific rights in regard to certain invasive treatments, their right to refuse unwanted medications was undefined as late as the early 1990's. During the 1979 case *Rogers v. Okin*, a patient who had been committed to the Boston State Hospital complained that he should not be required to take psychotropic medications against his will. While the initial court finding was that Rogers should have had a right to refuse medication, the case was appealed, and no clear precedent emerged from the case.

The issue of criminal responsibility is bound up with the concept of insanity. If a person, because of mental defect or state of mind, is unable to distinguish right from wrong, then most states would find the person exempt from criminal punishment. Beginning in 1975, however, Michigan adopted an alternate verdict of "guilty but mentally ill." As of 2000, twenty states had followed the Michigan example. The option of finding a person guilty but mentally ill increases the probability that incarceration will follow a crime committed by a person who previously would have been declared insane. Additionally, it allows for mitigation of the length of sentencing and provides for specialized treatment in a prison hospital.

Bruce E. Bailey

FURTHER READING

Bednar, Richard L., et al. *Psychotherapy with High-Risk Clients: Legal and Professional Standards.* Pacific Grove, Calif.: Brooks/Cole, 1991. Discusses legal and ethical issues related to the practice of psychotherapy. Topics related to client rights and therapist responsibilities are reviewed.

Foucault, Michel. *Madness and Civilization: A History of Insanity in the Age of Reason.* Translated by Richard Howard. 1965. Reprint. New York: Vintage Books, 1988. A seminal work on the cultural history of mental illness, detailing the origins of the category of madness and the uses to which that category has been put.

Goffman, Erving. *Asylums: Essays on the Social Situation of Mental Patients and Other Inmates.* Garden City, N.Y.: Anchor Books, 1961. Explores sociological and environmental influences within institutions that inappropriately shape and change behavior.

Medvedev, Zhores. *A Question of Madness.* Translated by Ellen de Kadt. New York: Knopf, 1971. Provides an account of the involuntary confinement and forced psychiatric treatment of the Russian biochemist Zhores Medvedev. Documents how Soviet psychiatrists collaborated with other agents of the state to silence his criticism of the government.

Roleff, Tamara L., and Laura K. Egendorf, eds. *Mental Illness: Opposing Viewpoints.* San Diego, Calif.: Greenhaven Press, 2000. An anthology of essays written on both sides of the central ethical issues facing contemporary mental health workers.

Szasz, Thomas S. *The Myth of Mental Illness: Foundations of a Theory of Personal Conduct.* Rev. ed. New York: Harper & Row, 1974. Explores issues and ethics related to the diagnosis and treatment of mental disorders. Promotes the concept that individuals and members of the medical establishment must assume responsibility for their behavior.

Valenstein, Elliot S. *Great and Desperate Cures.* New York: Basic Books, 1986. Examines the historical, social, scientific, and ethical issues that led to the development and use of psychosurgery as a cure for mental illness.

SEE ALSO: Child psychology; Confidentiality; Electroshock therapy; Hippocrates; Institutionalization of patients; Lobotomy; Psychology; Psychopharmacology; Soviet psychiatry; Suicide.

Mentoring

DEFINITION: Teaching or training relationship between a person acting as a counselor, or guide, to a person in a subordinate position

TYPE OF ETHICS: Theory of ethics

SIGNIFICANCE: Relationships between mentors and their charges, or mentees, must be founded on trust and devoted to increasing the skills, knowledge, and abilities of the mentees.

Mentors may be peers, colleagues, or friends and are usually persons with more experience than those whom they instruct. Mentoring may occur as the result of a planned, systematic process that is designed and supported by an organization or may develop as an unplanned process in which two parties naturally form a relationship and realize mutual benefits. Within organizations, mentors are usually selected because they exhibit positive character values, professional integrity, and high ethical standards in addition to their specialized knowledge, abilities, and skills.

In planned mentoring, mentors and their charges, known as mentees, are matched based on the charges' needs and what the mentors can provide to them. Regardless of the settings and the individuals involved in mentoring, however, there is an implicit understanding that mentoring is a special relationship whose success depends upon maintaining several ethical parameters.

The first parameter is confidentiality. Both the mentors and their charges must agree as to what issues are bound by limits of confidentiality and which are not. For example, in a situation within an organization in which a mentee expresses difficulty in resolving an issue that might negatively impact the organization, it must be clear to all parties whether or not the mentor is required to disclose that fact to someone else within the organization. Likewise, if the mentor discloses an issue as a teaching tool, the mentee must not betray trust by discussing the issue with anyone else. With that said, the limits of confidentiality should be discussed early in the relationship.

A second ethical issue involves maintaining the integrity of the relationship by not using it as a vehicle for self-promotion. That is, mentors should be never use information provided by their charges to advance their own interests. A third ethical issue involves not violating the trust of the relationship by making inappropriate advances, contact, or innuendo. Because of the frequent contact and close nature of mentor relationships, it is not unusual for one or both parties to feel a degree of emotional intimacy. Such intimacy must be confined to the professional relationships and not be allowed to drift into more personal intimacies.

A fourth ethical issue also deals with trust and integrity. Mentors must provide safe and supportive environments in which their charges can openly discuss and explore their concerns, weaknesses, and anxieties without fear of adverse occupational consequences or diminution of personal standing. A final ethical issue is that both mentors and their charges should be sensitive to the impact of cultural differences on each others' values, ideas, and viewpoints.

T. Steuart Watson
Tonya S. Butler

SEE ALSO: Confidentiality; Godparents; Moral education; Platonic ethics; Role models; Trustworthiness; Values clarification.

Mercenary soldiers

DEFINITION: Soldiers who serve in government or private military forces for money or adventure, rather than for reasons of patriotism or idealism

TYPE OF ETHICS: Military ethics

SIGNIFICANCE: By the end of the twentieth century, the use of mercenaries was rising throughout the world as the collapse of the Soviet Union made available large numbers of trained soldiers while at the same time the end of the Cold War led to increased instability that bred the kinds of small

One of the late twentieth century's most notorious mercenary leaders, Bob Denard (right) hands a surrender note to a Comorian policeman in October, 1995, one week after toppling the legal government of the Comoro Islands. Denard's short-lived coup was overturned by French forces invited in by the prime minister. Denard was later tried in France for the 1989 murder of an earlier Comorian prime minister. (AP/Wide World Photos)

wars that employ mercenaries. Additionally, the United States increasingly employed civilian contractors for duties traditionally performed by soldiers.

While the rise of nationalism in the nineteenth century seemed to doom large-scale use of mercenaries, such soldiers continued to be employed throughout the twentieth century, mostly in colonial and post-colonial regions. During the 1970's, the rebel government of Rhodesia, for example, depended heavily on mercenaries from North America and Europe in its attempt to remain in power. During the 1990's mercenaries were used by several factions in the conflicts that followed the collapse of Yugoslavia.

By its nature, mercenary service is generally seen as unethical behavior. To most military professionals, the very term "mercenary" is an insult. However, there exists among mercenaries themselves at least a theoretical code of conduct. Soldiers of fortune, as they often call themselves, are expected to provide professional and competent service to whomever or whatever pays for their services. However, those who employ mercenaries are aware that while mercenaries might form tight bonds with their fellow soldiers, their loyalty to the causes for which they fight depends largely on the amount of their pay, and the mercenaries might switch sides if the opposition offers them more money. Moreover, while mercenaries are usually willing to kill other people, they seldom are willing to die for the causes for which they fight.

BLURRING OF ROLES

Within the United States military, the line between mercenary and contractor blurred during the 1990's and into the twenty-first century as growing numbers of civilian employees—both U.S. nationals and local hires in foreign countries—performed many functions traditionally performed by soldiers. During the 1991 Persian Gulf War, for example, U.S. Army units in the Middle East theater of war contained about one civilian contractor for each one hundred soldiers. During the 2003 war against Iraq, the U.S. military had about one contractor for every ten soldiers. The tasks these civilians performed ranged from erecting tents to calibrating weapons systems. Their status under international law was uncertain. Although none of the civilian contractors served as riflemen, civilian technicians were involved in activi-

ties such as targeting and even firing land-based and sea-based missiles. Performing such activities makes them combatants, but they are not entitled to protections afforded soldiers under international laws. Although few contractors consider themselves to be mercenaries, the distinction was unclear.

Barry M. Stentiford

FURTHER READING

Baylor, Paul. *Manual of the Mercenary Soldier: Guide to Mercenary Warfare, Money, and Adventure.* Boulder, Colo.: Paladin Books, 1998.

David, James R., and James Davis. *Fortune's Warriors: Private Armies and the New World Order.* Toronto: Douglas and McIntyre, 2003.

Singer, P. W. *Corporate Warriors: The Rise of the Privatized Military Industries.* Ithaca, N.Y.: Cornell University Press, 2003.

SEE ALSO: Child soldiers; Geneva conventions; Land mines; Limited war; Military ethics; Patriotism; Prostitution; *Utopia*; War; War crimes trials.

Mercy

DEFINITION: Compassion and leniency toward someone over whom one has power

TYPE OF ETHICS: Personal and social ethics

SIGNIFICANCE: Mercy is generally thought of as a virtue on an individual level. On a social level it can be much more controversial, however, since by definition it entails either forgoing or lessening a punishment dictated by impersonal standards of justice.

Mercy originated as a theological term. Although it came into the English through the French and Latin, its meaning goes back to an ancient Israelite concept of how God acted toward people and how he expected people to act toward one another. Mercy most often is used to translate the word *hesed* in the Hebrew Bible, a word that is also often translated as "kindness," "loving kindness," and "steadfast love." In Jewish scripture, *hesed* denotes God's attitude toward people as pledged in a covenant relationship. If the people of Israel would be loyal to their agreement with God, then God's attitude would be one of mercy.

Hesed more often describes an activity than it does a disposition. Thus, after crossing the Red Sea and escaping from Egypt, Moses and the Israelites sang a song in which they called God's saving act *hesed*: "In your steadfast love [*hesed*] you led the people whom you redeemed; you guided them by your strength to your holy abode" (Exodus 15:13). *Hesed* is not used in the Hebrew Bible only to describe God's activity. It also denotes the mutual, right attitude that God expects of people in a covenant relationship. Thus, the trust and faithfulness that should characterize relations between relatives, friends, and other societal groups is *hesed*, and without *hesed*, society would be characterized by disorder. For example, the prophet Hosea (Hosea 4:1-3) claims that since the Israelites are living without *hesed*,

> Swearing, lying, and murder, and stealing and adultery break out; bloodshed follows bloodshed. Therefore the land mourns, and all who live in it languish; together with the wild animals and the birds of the air, even the fish of the sea are perishing.

In the Septuagint, which is the oldest surviving Greek version of the Old Testament, *hesed* was most often translated as *eleos*. *Eleos* also carried the connotations of the Hebrew *hesed* into the Christian New Testament. For example, Matthew's Gospel twice cites the announcement in Hosea that God desires mercy (*eleos*) rather than sacrifice (Hosea 6:6; Matt. 9:13, 12:7).

Eleos also carried with it other meanings, however, and it is from this Greek heritage that "mercy" received connotations of a sentiment. In prebiblical Greek literature, *eleos* denoted that feeling or emotion that occurs when witnessing suffering that is undeserved. Aristotle defined it "as a feeling of pain caused by the sight of some evil, destructive or painful, which befalls one who does not deserve it, and which we might expect to befall ourselves or some friend of ours, and moreover to befall us soon." The sentiment described here resembles pity more than mercy. Indeed, for Aristotle, *eleos* was not a virtue; it was an impediment, along with fear (*phobo*), to living a productive life. The importance of tragic art, according to Aristotle, lay in its ability to purge its audience of both pity and fear so that they could leave the theater and return to their lives free of such emotional baggage.

CHRISTIAN VIEWS

In the Christian New Testament, mercy is sometimes an activity and sometimes a sentiment. As in later Judaism, the merciful activity of God in the Christian scripture is sometimes connected to God's judgment at the end of time. In fact, the old French *merces* signified a payment or reward, and thus indicated the heavenly reward awaiting the compassionate person. Also, Christianity reinterpreted *eleos* in light of Jesus' death on the cross. Thus, there is more of a tendency in Christian literature than in the Hebrew Bible to think of God's mercy as preceding people's mercy and to relate mercy to suffering activity. For example, in the very influential parable of the Good Samaritan (Luke 10:29-37), the merciful Samaritan, following the model of Jesus, pays a price on behalf of the one who was assaulted. He is a good neighbor because he goes out of his way to care for another person who needs help.

In Jerome's *Vulgate*, the Hebrew *hesed* and the Greek *eleos* were often translated by *misericordia*, which combines the meanings of pity, compassion, kindness, and leniency. The Latin root emphasizes wretchedness and sorrow. Thomas Aquinas defines a merciful person as being sorrowful at heart (*miserum cor*); that is, as being affected with the sorrow or misery of another as if it were one's own. God's work of dispelling misery is the effect of his mercy. God's mercy, then, especially in medieval theology, connotes God's unmerited grace as he reaches down to wretched humans. Thus, Augustine can love and thank God "because Thou has forgiven me these so great and heinous deeds of mine. To thy grace I ascribe it, and to Thy mercy, that Thou hast melted away my sins as it were ice."

In modern usage, mercy retains elements of its earlier meanings, but it always connotes some form of leniency or restraint, whether from physical punishment or merely in the way one person judges another person's actions. Mercy always exists, then, within the context of an unequal power relationship. One could easily imagine, for example, that a subject would feel compassion for the troubles of a monarch, but that feeling would not under most circumstances be considered merciful. Normally, only compassion of the monarch for the subject could result in a show of mercy.

Although William Shakespeare claimed in *Titus Andronicus* that "Sweet Mercy is nobility's true badge" and wrote in the *Merchant of Venice* that "It [mercy] blesseth him that gives, and him that takes," mercy has not always been thought of as something good. For example, it was not included among Plato's cardinal virtues (justice, temperance, prudence, and fortitude), and because the Stoic philosophers thought that mercy was an emotion that might sway reason and misdirect justice, they did not trust it.

The tendency of mercy to resist justice was a trait that nineteenth century philosopher Friedrich Nietzsche found admirable. Nietzsche thought of mercy as one of the noblest of all virtues. He saw two things to admire in mercy. First, because of the power relationship within which it took place, the exercise of mercy was always the exercise of strength. For Nietzsche, this meant that mercy was a virtue based on the positive values one possessed, making it preferable to virtues like meekness that were based upon the negative values one lacked. Second, and more important, an act of mercy according to Nietzsche was based in the personal value system of the actor, and was performed solely for the actor's benefit. It was not based in supposedly universal values like justice which were meant to apply to everyone and which were meant to benefit society as a whole. For Nietzsche, this rendered mercy superior to justice, because he endorsed the development of distinctive, appropriate moral values for each individual and attacked universal systems of morality which expect everyone to share the same values. Mercy, Nietzsche said, is a virtue for the individual precisely because it is destructive to the general interests of society.

Likewise, the proponents of "lifeboat ethics" tend to think that the sentiment of mercy masks and makes it difficult for society to deal with the moral dilemma posed by a world population that is outstripping the available resources. Finally, from a different perspective, mercy's close association with power has led liberation theologians to associate human mercy with paternalism and imperialism. They call for solidarity with the poor rather than for mercy upon the poor.

James M. Dawsey
Updated by the editors

FURTHER READING

Aristotle. *On Rhetoric: A Theory of Civic Discourse.* Translated by George A. Kennedy. New York: Oxford University Press, 1991.

Buetow, Harold A. *The Scabbardless Sword: Criminal Justice and the Quality of Mercy.* Tarrytown, N.Y.: Associated Faculty Press, 1982.
Callahan, Sidney. *With All Our Heart and Mind: The Spiritual Works of Mercy in a Psychological Age.* New York: Crossroad, 1988.
Erasmus, Desiderius. *The Immense Mercy of God.* San Francisco: California State Library, 1940.
Murphy, Jeffrie G., and Jean Hampton. *Forgiveness and Mercy.* New York: Cambridge University Press, 1988.
Schimmel, Solomon. *Wounds Not Healed by Time: The Power of Repentance and Forgiveness.* New York: Oxford University Press, 2002.
Wilson, Matthew. *Mercy and Truth.* Menston, England: Scholar Press, 1973.

SEE ALSO: Aristotle; Christian ethics; Compassion; Forgiveness; Generosity; Jewish ethics; Lifeboat ethics; Nietzsche, Friedrich; Reconciliation; Religion.

Merit

DEFINITION: Character, performance, or skill that deserves or is worthy of recognition or reward
TYPE OF ETHICS: Theory of ethics
SIGNIFICANCE: Merit is the basis for systems of social justice that are based primarily on desert rather than on need.

As Wolfgang von Goethe said, "It never occurs to fools that merit and good fortune are closely united." Thus, types of justice can clash. Two main types of justice are meritocratic justice and distributive justice. Meritocratic justice requires that only the most qualified and worthy person be chosen for any position in question. Distributive justice requires people to minimize serious inequalities in well-being; for example, those arising from good or bad fortune.

Robert K. Fullinwider gives an example that undermines the decisiveness of meritocratic justice. He says that meritocracy is "too rigid and specific" and would condemn acts that "seem unobjectionable."

Suppose . . . an employer had two well-qualified applicants for a position, the slightly better qualified applicant already having a good, secure job, the other being unemployed. If the employer hired the unemployed applicant, would he have violated a . . . moral principle? To suggest [so] is . . . strongly counter-intuitive.

The distributive justice of hiring the unemployed seems to outweigh the problem with meritocratic justice. Moreover, Norman Daniels tries to show that the argument from meritocracy is not an argument from justice. Daniels considers the following example:

Jack and Jill both want jobs *A* and *B* and each much prefers *A* to *B*. Jill can do either *A* or *B* better than Jack. But the situation *S* in which Jill performs *B* and Jack *A* is more productive than Jack doing B and Jill *A* (*S´*), even when we include the effects on productivity of Jill's lesser satisfaction. [Meritocracy] selects *S*, not *S´*, because it is attuned to macroproductivity, not microproductivity. . . . It says, "Select people for jobs so that *overall* job performance is maximized."

Daniels anticipates the objection that meritocracy would select *S´*, not *S*, because meritocracy implies that "a person should get a job if he or she is the best available person for *that* job." He admits that this objection appears to be based on the point of justice "that it seems *unfair* to Jill that she gets the job she wants less even though she can do the job Jack gets better than he can." Daniels, however, thinks that the seeming unfairness derives from "inessential features of our economic system"; namely, that promoting microproductivity happens to be "the best rule of thumb" to follow to achieve macroproductivity. He says that favoring microproductivity (*S´*) over macroproductivity (*S*) because S seems unfair is relying on an intuition that is "just a by-product of our existing institutions" rather than based on justice. The happenstance that there is a mere rule of thumb in existing institutions is too superficial and arbitrary to be a fundamental consideration of justice. Once it is realized that the basis of meritocracy is macroproductivity, meritocracy will not support the intuition that Jill, in justice, deserves her favorite job *A* or the claim that justice requires *S´*. That the "inessential features of our economic system" are irrelevant to justice undermines that standing of meritocracy—

when conceived of as microproductivity—as a principle of justice. Meritocracy as macroproductivity survives.

Ronald Dworkin adds the following argument, which supports Daniels's claim that there is no merit abstracted from macroproductivity. Dworkin says,

There is no combination of abilities and skill and traits that constitutes "merit" in the abstract; if quick hands count as "merit" in the case of a prospective surgeon, this is because quick hands will enable him to serve the public better and for no other reason. If a black skin will, as a matter of regrettable fact [e.g., the need for black role models], enable another doctor to do a different medical job better, then that black skin is by the same token "merit" as well. That argument may strike some as dangerous; but only because they confuse its conclusion—that black skin may be a socially useful trait in particular circumstances—with the very different and despicable idea that one race may be *inherently* more worthy than another.

One may object that black skin cannot count as merit, since pigmentation is an inherited accident of birth rather than a matter of choice and achievement. As Dworkin argues, however,

it is also true that those who score low in aptitude or admissions tests do not choose their levels of intelligence. Nor do those denied admission because they are too old, or because they do not come from a part of the country underrepresented in the school, or because they cannot play basketball well, choose not to have the qualities that made the difference.

Tests allegedly measuring merit are often biased. Furthermore, a lower score under inferior conditions often indicates more ability than does a higher score under superior conditions. African Americans tend to take the tests under conditions (poverty, reduced parental supervision, reduced incentives, bleaker prospects caused by racism, and so forth) that are dramatically inferior to the conditions under which whites take such tests. For example, consider the dramatic differences between the best group and the worst group of American public high schools. The best group will generally give its students at least the following advantages over the students in the worst group: better teachers, better equipment, more programs (for example, extracurricular activities), better atmospheres in which to learn (atmospheres with less crime, noise, and disorder), better role models, and more peer pressure to achieve.

For example, Peter Singer notes, affirmative action programs "taking into account a student's race would merely be a way of correcting for the failure of standard tests to allow for the disadvantages that face blacks in competing with whites on such tests." Such disadvantages include less ability to afford preparation courses, which whites commonly take and which the free market has specifically designed to boost scores on standard tests (such as the SAT).

Similarly, Richard Wasserstrom argues,

> Most of what are regarded as the decisive characteristics for higher education have a great deal to do with things over which the individual has neither control nor responsibility: such things as home environment, socioeconomic class of parents, and of course, the quality of the primary and secondary schools attended. Since individuals do not deserve having had any of these things vis-à-vis other individuals, they do not, for the most part, deserve their qualifications.

In contrast, George Sher argues that society's conventions establish merit. He takes his view to extremes when he says, "We could even flog or torture in direct proportion to merit. . . . If the convention existed, our suggestion would imply that the meritorious deserved their beatings and abuse." Sher seems to be mistaken, since recognizing merit for what it is (good) implies that merit should be rewarded. If the convention were to punish merit, then the society would make the mistake of failing to recognize the value of merit, since its actions (punishment) speak louder than words (calling something merit).

Sterling Harwood

FURTHER READING

Adkins, Arthur W. H. *Merit and Responsibility: A Study in Greek Values*. New York: Oxford University Press, 1960. Reprint. Chicago: University of Chicago Press, 1975.

Daniels, Norman. "Merit and Meritocracy." *Philosophy and Public Affairs* 7 (1978): 206-223.

Fullinwider, Robert K. *The Reverse Discrimination Controversy: A Moral and Legal Analysis*. Totowa, N.J.: Rowman & Littlefield, 1980.

Furer-Haimendorf, Christoph von. *Morals and Merit: A Study of Values and Social Controls in South Asian Societies*. Chicago: University of Chicago Press, 1967.

Gould, Stephen Jay. *The Mismeasure of Man*. New York: W. W. Norton, 1981.

Harwood, Sterling, ed. *Business as Ethical and Business as Usual*. Boston: Jones & Bartlett, 1994.

Olsaretti, Serena, ed. *Desert and Justice*. New York: Oxford University Press, 2003.

Pojman, Louis P., and Owen McLeod, eds. *What Do We Deserve? A Reader on Justice and Desert*. New York: Oxford University Press, 1999.

Sher, George. *Desert*. Princeton, N.J.: Princeton University Press, 1987.

Young, Michael Dunlop. *The Rise of the Meritocracy*. New Brunswick, N.J.: Transaction, 1994.

SEE ALSO: Affirmative action; Discrimination; Egalitarianism; Elitism; Equality; Excellence; Fairness; Hiring practices.

Messianism

DEFINITION: Belief in a messiah, that is, a religious savior who will someday appear and lead humankind, or the followers of a particular religion, into an age of perfect justice, peace, and spiritual transcendence

TYPE OF ETHICS: Religious ethics

SIGNIFICANCE: Messianism provides believers with two models of moral perfection by which to judge reality: the messiah, who represents the ideal person, and the utopian social order the messiah will bring about. Messianism also often entails belief in an apocalyptic event that will precipitate the messianic age, and this may strongly affect believers' attitudes toward warfare, famine, and other similar events in the present.

Although the term "messiah" is rarely used in the Old Testament, the concept of an ideal ruler was expressed as early as the eighth century B.C.E. Isaiah 9 expressed hopes for a king who would give wonderful counsel (Isaiah 11 spoke of his wisdom), be god-like in battle, be continuous in fatherly care, and establish peace. Jeremiah 33:14-22 and Ezekiel 34:23-24 spoke of a future David who would administer the future golden age that God would usher in. The idea of a permanent Davidic dynasty (2 Samuel 7) developed the royal ideology of ancient Israel (see Psalms 2, 72, and 110). Other passages (for example, Isaiah 24:23 and Zechariah 14:9) looked toward a messianic age with God ruling directly.

The Dead Sea Scrolls, the Talmud, and subsequent Jewish sources reveal an ongoing, though not universal, hope among Jews for a messiah. In debates with Jews, early Christians claimed that Jesus was the messiah; indeed, the title "christ" is the Greek translation of the Hebrew title "messiah." Christians modified Jewish belief by identifying the messiah with the suffering servant (see Isaiah 52:13-53:12), claiming that he was divine, and looking forward to his return at the end of time. Certain rules of behavior (see, for example, Matthew 5:19, 6:1-6, 10:42, 16:27) tied gaining rewards to following the teachings of Jesus.

Paul L. Redditt

SEE ALSO: Christian ethics; Jesus Christ; Jewish ethics; Kabbala; Leadership; Nationalism; Religion; Talmud.

Metaethics

DEFINITION: Specialization within moral philosophy that is concerned with fundamental conceptual and epistemological questions in ethics
TYPE OF ETHICS: Theory of ethics
SIGNIFICANCE: Essentially the theory of the theory of ethics, metaethics attempts to ground moral philosophy by specifying what counts as a legitimate question for moral philosophers to answer and what counts as a legitimate method for answering that question.

First and foremost, metaethics seeks to answer the question What is the subject matter of ethics? Moral philosophy may be divided into three sets of concerns: metaethical theory, normative ethical theory,

and applied ethics. In applied ethics, philosophers reflect upon the significance of some general moral point of view for a particular problem of moral decision making. For example, a philosopher might consider whether, according to rule utilitarianism, the practice of euthanasia is morally permissible. Further distinctions (such as the distinction between active and passive euthanasia) might be made to help clarify the difficulty. In contrast to applied ethics, normative ethical theory focuses upon a comparative study of such general ethical theories as utilitarianism, egoism, Kantian formalism, virtue ethics, and so forth. The fundamental question in normative ethics is What makes an action, any action whatsoever, right or wrong?

It can be seen from these brief descriptions of normative ethical theory and applied ethics that both are interested in deciding what is right and what is wrong. Normative ethical theory attempts to develop a completely general account of what is right and what is wrong. Applied ethics investigates the moral quality of agents and their actions in specific moral contexts, usually by appealing to some normative ethical theory.

Metaethics differs from both normative and applied ethics in that it explores conceptual and epistemological questions that arise for those who use moral discourse and who devise and apply normative theories of right and wrong. Conceptual questions are posed for moral terms and statements; epistemological questions are raised about the possibility and character of moral reasoning.

CONCEPTUAL QUESTIONS

Metaethics did not emerge as a major preoccupation in philosophy until early in the twentieth century, when the problems of metaethics became insulated from the rest of moral philosophy primarily through the influence of Anglo-American linguistic philosophy. The change in path that led to the emergence of contemporary analytic philosophy has been called "the linguistic turn." In ethics, this change meant refined analysis of the terms used in moral discourse and of the structure and meaning of moral utterances. Thus, terms such as "good," "evil," "right," or "wrong" (called moral predicates) are examined directly. This sort of analysis is supposed to clarify what it means to use a moral predicate within a sentence of the form "*X* is right" or "*X* is wrong."

Locutions of the form "*X* is right" or "*X* is wrong" have the grammatical appearance of being simple judgments of fact. Many modern ethicists have suggested, however, that their grammatical appearance may be misleading. It is not obvious what facts one could point to to determine the truth value of a statement such as "Unrestricted abortion is morally wrong." Perhaps, then, such forms of discourse have no truth value at all; that is, perhaps they are neither true nor false. Perhaps they have a very different sort of meaning. Metaethicists who reach this conclusion about the general significance of moral utterances are called noncognitivists. They hold that normative ethics is impossible.

The cognitivists, those who believe that moral utterances are genuine statements with truth values, differ as to what sort of fact a moral fact is. Many have tried to analyze the good in terms of some more basic natural fact (such as pleasure or personal survival). They are called naturalists. G. E. Moore objected that all such attempts to define "good" commit the naturalistic fallacy. One cannot define "good" in terms of some natural property, since one can always ask without redundancy whether that property itself is good. Instead, he argued, the good should be regarded as a basic, indefinable, nonnatural property.

EPISTEMOLOGICAL QUESTIONS

If one adopts the cognitivist view that moral expressions are genuine judgments with truth values, a further question arises: How does one go about determining which moral judgments are true and which are false? Clearly, the possibility of genuine moral disagreement presupposes that moral utterances of the form "*X* is right" are either true or false, but how does one know which statements of that form are true? What sorts of reasons are relevant for adjudicating between conflicting moral judgments and between systems of normative ethics?

A related but even more fundamental question intrudes as well: Why adopt the moral point of view at all? This question demands the presentation of nonmoral reasons why one ought to be moral. Some have suggested that no nonmoral reasons can be given and that it is therefore not rational to adopt the moral point of view. Others agree that there are no nonmoral reasons for being moral but that this is unimportant since the question itself is mistaken. For them, moral philosophy begins with the observation that people do care about being moral. Still others have attempted to provide nonmoral reasons to justify taking the moral point of view.

SIGNIFICANCE OF METAETHICS

It is commonplace to assume that the questions of metaethics are logically prior to those of normative and applied ethics, and that there is no use proceeding with either normative or applied moral philosophy without coming to certain definite conclusions about matters of metaethical concern, but this assumption has also been disputed. For one may be right in regarding moral statements as cognitive and moral argument as possible without having any sort of elaborate metaethical theory to justify this view.

R. Douglass Geivett

FURTHER READING

Foot, Philippa. "Moral Arguments." *Mind* 67 (October, 1958): 502-513.

Hare, R. M. *The Language of Morals.* Oxford, England: Clarendon Press, 1952.

Jacobs, Jonathan. *Dimensions of Moral Theory: An Introduction to Metaethics and Moral Psychology.* Malden, Mass.: Blackwell, 2002.

Miller, Alexander. *An Introduction to Contemporary Metaethics.* Cambridge, England: Polity Press, 2003.

Moore, G. E. *Principia Ethica.* Rev. ed. New York: Cambridge University Press, 1996.

Snare, Francis. *The Nature of Moral Thinking.* London: Routledge, 1992.

Stevenson, Charles L. *Ethics and Language.* New Haven, Conn.: Yale University Press, 1960.

Taylor, Paul W., ed. *The Moral Judgement: Readings in Contemporary Meta-ethics.* Englewood Cliffs, N.J.: Prentice-Hall, 1963.

Timmons, Mark. *Morality Without Foundations: A Defense of Ethical Contextualism.* New York: Oxford University Press, 1999.

Toulmin, Stephen. *The Place of Reason in Ethics.* Chicago: University of Chicago Press, 1986.

SEE ALSO: Cognitivism; Epistemological ethics; Ethics; Fact/value distinction; Intuitionist ethics; Moore, G. E.; Naturalistic fallacy; Normative vs. descriptive ethics; Reason and rationality.

Milgram experiment

THE EVENT: Series of studies designed to determine the degree to which subjects would be willing to obey an authority's instructions to harm another person

DATE: Conducted in 1961-1962

TYPE OF ETHICS: Scientific ethics

SIGNIFICANCE: The Milgram investigations produced unexpected data regarding the willingness of people to violate their own moral values when instructed to do so by an authority figure. They also created extreme stress for their participants, leading to a reconsideration of the ethical guidelines governing such research.

Psychologist Stanley Milgram, horrified by the atrocities that had been committed by the Nazis during the Holocaust, conducted a program of research designed to explore the process of obedience to authority. The disturbing nature of his results and the ethical issues raised by his methods make this some of the most controversial and widely discussed research in the history of social science.

Recruited through a newspaper advertisement, a diverse group of adult subjects reported (individually) to Milgram's laboratory at Yale University expecting to participate in a study of memory and learning. Each participant was greeted by an experimenter dressed in a lab coat. Also present was a middle-aged gentleman, an accomplice who was ostensibly another participant in the session. The experimenter then described the research, which would investigate the effect of punishment on learning. Then, through a rigged drawing, the accomplice was assigned the role of "learner," while the actual subject became the "teacher."

THE EXPERIMENT

Next, the three went to an adjacent room, where the learner was strapped into an "electric chair" as the experimenter explained that shock would be used as punishment. The teacher was then escorted back to the first room and seated in front of a shock generator, the front panel of which consisted of a series of thirty switches that could be used to administer shock. Each was labeled with a voltage level, starting with 15 volts and increasing by 15-volt increments to 450 volts; several verbal labels below the switches also indicated the severity of the shock. After receiving instructions and a demonstration from the experimenter, the teacher presented a sequence of simple memory tests to the learner through an intercom. The learner made "errors" according to a script, and the teacher was instructed to respond to each error by pushing a switch, thus delivering a shock to the learner. The teacher started with 15 volts and was directed to use the next higher switch with each successive error.

The goal of this procedure was simply to determine how long the subject/teacher would continue to obey the order to administer shock. (The accomplice/learner never actually received any shock.) As the shocks grew stronger, the learner began protesting—eventually pleading to be let out, then screaming, and finally ceasing to respond at all. When the teacher balked, the experimenter provided one of several firm verbal "prods" to continue (for example, "you *must* go on"). The procedure was discontinued if the teacher refused to obey after four such prods for a given shock level.

Milgram and other experts felt that few if any participants would demonstrate obedience under these circumstances, particularly after the learner began protesting. Nearly two-thirds of them, however, obeyed the experimenter's orders all the way to the highest level of shock (450 volts). This result occurred with both men and women, even in a version of the study in which the learner was portrayed as having a heart condition.

The typical subject in these studies showed clear signs of distress over the plight of the learner. Subjects often perspired or trembled, and some exhibited nervous laughter or other indications of tension. Indeed, it is this aspect of the research that has been cited most frequently by those who consider the studies unethical. Critics argue that Milgram compromised the welfare of the participants in this research by subjecting them to inappropriately high levels of stress. Many of these same critics have also suggested that Milgram failed to provide his subjects with enough advance information to enable them to make a fully informed decision about whether to participate.

In his defense, Milgram points out that his procedure was not intended to cause stress for the participants. Furthermore, he and other experts did not anticipate the stress that did occur because they expected that subjects would be reluctant to obey these orders. It is also important to note that Milgram did take care to protect these subjects and their dignity, as indicated by the activities that followed the experimental sessions. These measures included a discussion of the experiment and its rationale, a meeting with the learner involving an explanation that he had not really been shocked, and reassurances that the subject's behavior (obedient or not) was entirely normal given the circumstances. Some three-fourths of all the participants indicated that they had learned something personally important as a result of being in the study, and additional follow-up by a psychiatrist a year later found no evidence of lasting psychological harm in any of those examined.

THE ETHICAL DILEMMA

More generally, this research illustrates a basic ethical dilemma faced frequently by experimental social psychologists. These researchers often need to create and manipulate powerful situations if they are to generate enough impact to observe something meaningful about social behavior, but doing so sometimes risks causing undue stress to subjects. This ethical issue is sometimes complicated still further by the need to deceive participants in order to preserve the authenticity of their behavior.

Few will deny that Milgram's research yielded significant insights into how obedience to an authority can prevent a subordinate from taking responsibility for inflicting harm on another person, but does the end justify the means employed to gain this knowledge? Ultimately, decisions of this sort must be made by carefully weighing the costs and benefits involved. Regardless of one's position on the ethics of the obedience studies, Milgram's work has done much to heighten sensitivity to ethical considerations in social research. Since Milgram's investigations were conducted, psychologists have adopted a more conservative set of principles governing research with people—guidelines that today would probably not allow the procedures he used.

Steve A. Nida

FURTHER READING

American Psychological Association. "Ethical Principles of Psychologists." *American Psychologist* 45 (March, 1990): 390-395.

Baumrind, Diana. "Some Thoughts on Ethics of Research: After Reading Milgram's 'Behavioral Study of Obedience.'" *American Psychologist* 19, no. 6 (1964): 421-423.

Blass, Thomas, ed. *Obedience to Authority: Current Perspectives on the Milgram Paradigm.* Mahwah, N.J.: Lawrence Erlbaum Associates, 2000.

Milgram, Stanley. *Obedience to Authority.* New York: Harper & Row, 1974.

Miller, Arthur G., ed. *The Social Psychology of Psychological Research.* New York: Free Press, 1972.

Myers, David G. *Social Psychology.* 7th ed. Boston: McGraw-Hill, 2002.

SEE ALSO: Collective guilt; Conscientious objection; Ethical Principles of Psychologists; Experimentation; Harm; Holocaust; Obedience; Psychology; Science.

Military ethics

DEFINITION: Codes of acceptable behavior in military situations, particularly those related to the conduct of war, that are unique to military cultures

TYPE OF ETHICS: Military ethics

SIGNIFICANCE: In most modern cultures, military ethics combine professional standards of conduct with more specific codes of conduct designed to regulate the behavior of military personnel in their dealings with their services, governments, enemies, and one another.

In Western culture, military ethics first arose as a field of ethics in ancient Greece. While other earlier cultures certainly had military subcultures that held values different from those of civil society, Greek philosophers began to explore more precisely the relationships between ethical conduct and war during and immediately after the Peloponnesian Wars of the early fifth century B.C.E. Greek conceptions of military ethics held sway, with some modification, through much of the Hellenistic and later Roman periods.

Military ethics underwent a profound shift by the fourth century C.E. The rise of Christianity in the

Mediterranean world replaced earlier concepts of ethical conduct in war with a philosophy based on forgiveness, brotherly love, and pacifism. With the triumph of Christianity over paganism as the official Roman religion, Christianity moved from its earlier position as a sometimes despised and persecuted sect to become the dominant cultural and political force of the Mediterranean world. Military ethics reappeared in the fifth century C.E. with St. Augustine's concept of just war. Augustine attempted to reconcile Christian notions of passivism with the need of societies to defend themselves. Although Augustine's complex work is often oversimplified, it provides much of the underlying moral justification for waging war in modern Western societies, for nations as well as for individual soldiers.

UNIQUENESS OF MILITARY ETHICS

Military ethics must of necessity differ from civilian ethics in that militaries at root use violence and threats of violence to achieve national aims. That violence can be against counterforce targets, which are the means of an enemy to wage war. These can be enemy soldiers as well as the economic infrastructures, such as factories, roads, and communication systems, that support them. Both types of targets are normally accepted as ethical targets in war. Less acceptable are so-called countervalue targets, such as large population centers, whose losses enemy nations cannot bear. Within that broad framework a varied concept of military ethics exists.

Most militaries around the world hold to codes of ethical military behavior, at least in theory. These codes typically set standards for differentiating between combatants and noncombatants in selecting targets for armed attack. Killing enemy soldiers in combat situations is universally seen as legitimate in military cultures. However, killing civilians and captured or wounded enemy soldiers is not considered ethical behavior in most modern militaries. Likewise, the destruction of factories producing military equipment, or military training centers, would be seen as ethical, whereas the destruction of schools, hospitals, and museums would not be.

ALTERNATIVES TO WESTERN THOUGHT

Western military ethics have come to dominate most of the militaries of the world to some extent, mainly as a result of Western military supremacy,

which began to assert itself around the beginning of the sixteenth century. However, other value systems have also had lasting impacts on what is considered ethical or moral in war. The most important of these in the Eastern world has been Confucianism.

Confucian philosophy was mostly concerned with maintaining stable order in society and saw war as the opposite of an orderly society. The unavoidable existence of war forced Confucianists to grapple with the ethical implications of their philosophy on war. In general, most Confucian concepts saw the necessity of separating combatants from noncombatants and the need for soldiers to obey their commanders. In these views, Confucian ethics were similar to later Western military ethics. The main difference came in the status of soldiers in Chinese society. Whereas soldiers in modern Western societies—especially officers—hold privileged positions, soldiers under Confucianism held much lower places in society—even lower than that of peasants.

The other philosophy to challenge Western domination of military ethics came from Marxism in the late nineteenth century. Fundamentally a political and economic philosophy of revolution, Marxism holds that traditional Western military ethics are unethical because they allow military and economic elites to maintain their control of society. Moreover, the societies that they control have perpetuated injustice and misery. Marxists have seen themselves as the vanguard of the final revolution to end human inequality and suffering. Thus any efforts to lessen the impact of wars have only prolonged the suffering of the masses. For these reasons, Marxist armies have tended to feel less restrained by more traditional Western military ethics.

THE MILITARY AND CIVILIAN GOVERNMENT

The militaries of most modern liberal democracies hold a firm ethos for civilian control of the military. In this view, the military exists to fight foreign wars under the orders of civilian authorities. In some nations, however, soldiers have seen their military organizations as the repositories of virtue and thus felt justified in seizing political power when their nations drift too far from what the military regards as government's proper values.

In nations whose militaries hold this value, typically those of developing nations, a central purpose of the military is typically to keep governments in power, with the fighting of foreign wars a secondary purpose. In such military systems, the involvement of the military in politics, including the seizure of power from civilian control, is not seen as unethical conduct for soldiers. Indeed, it is often seen as highly moral and patriotic.

INTERNATIONAL LAW

Most general modern military ethics, including special protections for wounded and surrendered enemy soldiers, avoidance of civilian casualties, and respect for cultural and historical artifacts in the area of military operations, became codified in international law during the twentieth century. However, only when the internal culture of the military organization of a given nation shares the same ethical standards do international laws of war have much impact.

By the early twenty-first century, wealthy industrialized nations were finding themselves fighting increasing numbers of wars against smaller and weaker nations or against nonstate military forces. Such nonstate forces often see international military ethics as a luxury they cannot afford. The established military sees itself fighting savages, while their opponents see themselves fighting for their very survival.

Barry M. Stentiford

FURTHER READING

Coker, Christopher. *Humane Warfare*. New York: Routledge, 2001.

Elshtain, Jean Bethke, ed. *Just War Theory: Readings in Social and Political Theory*. New York: New York University Press, 1991.

Gabrial, Richard A., and Paul L. Savage. *Crisis in Command*. New York: Hill & Wang, 1979.

Lacky, Douglas. *The Ethics of War and Peace*. Upper Saddle River, N.J.: Prentice Hall, 1988.

McKeogh, Colm. *Innocent Civilians: The Morality of Killing in War*. New York: Palgrave Macmillan, 2002.

Singer, P. W. *Corporate Warriors: The Rise of the Privatized Military Industries*. Ithaca, N.Y.: Cornell University Press, 2003.

SEE ALSO: Biochemical weapons; Chemical warfare; Child soldiers; Homeland defense; Just war theory; Limited war; Mercenary soldiers; Peacekeeping missions; Vietnam War; War; Weapons research.

Mill, John Stuart

IDENTIFICATION: English philosopher and economist
BORN: May 20, 1806, London, England
DIED: May 7, 1873, Avignon, France
TYPE OF ETHICS: Modern history
SIGNIFICANCE: The most famous modern proponent of utilitarianism, Mill revised and enhanced that philosophy by incorporating a discussion of intangible "spiritual" values. His most important works include *On Liberty* (1859), *Utilitarianism* (1863), and *The Subjection of Women* (1869).

Maintaining that a science of society was feasible, Mill focused his philosophic writings on four major issues: the methodology of the social sciences, the principle of utility, individual freedom, and the structure of government. While Mill supported Jeremy Bentham's corollary that moral problems could never be resolved through sentimental appeals to righteousness, he emphasized the importance of developing the spiritual aspects of humanity. Mill developed an "ethology" that consisted of the elements that were essential in the development of "character"—individual, societal, and national; he argued

John Stuart Mill. (Library of Congress)

that secular society must define and expand its ethical base so that happiness—freedom from pain—may be attained. Unlike Bentham, Mill maintained that an educated elite was necessary to guide society; Mill agreed with Alexis de Tocqueville's concern that democratic sentiments may lead to the "tyranny of the majority." Mill's fullest statement on ethics was advanced in *Utilitarianism.*

William T. Walker

SEE ALSO: Bentham, Jeremy; Freedom and liberty; Liberalism; *On Liberty*; Political liberty; Social contract theory; Utilitarianism.

Minimum-wage laws

DEFINITION: Laws requiring that workers' salaries fall no lower than specified hourly rates
TYPE OF ETHICS: Business and labor ethics
SIGNIFICANCE: The central ethical issue raised by minimum-wage laws is whether government has a duty to require employers to raise the wages of low-paid workers above what free market forces would dictate. In the background is the deeper problem of whether it is unjust for there to be unequal distribution of wealth.

In medieval Europe, local governments often fixed wages at customary levels for various kinds of work. However, they typically imposed maximum wage levels, rather than minimum levels. During the nineteenth century, classical economists strongly opposed the fixing of wages by government, and comparatively little such wage-fixing occurred. During that period, however, workers, especially those in factories, often labored for low pay under bad conditions. As public concern for their well-being gradually increased, laws setting minimum wages were proposed as one way to help workers. Such laws were enacted first in Australia and New Zealand during the 1890's. Many other countries soon followed suit.

Massachusetts was the first U.S. state to set a minimum wage, in 1912. Afterward, other states enacted laws setting minimum wages for women and children; however, these laws had little effect. Finally, the federal Fair Labor Standards Act of 1938, one component of Franklin D. Roosevelt's New Deal, established a uniform minimum wage for all workers who were directly or indirectly engaged in interstate commerce. Later, Congress repeatedly raised minimum wage levels and extended them to cover ever more types of employment. Democrats usually have been eager to raise the minimum wage, while Republicans have been less eager to do so. In 2003 the U.S. federal minimum wage stood at $5.15 per hour.

ARGUMENTS FOR MINIMUM-WAGE LAWS

Advocates of minimum-wage laws hold that without this form of government intervention the lowest-paid workers would be paid less than they need to live on, and this would be unfair, when others are living well. Setting minimum wages is thus seen as a move toward greater justice in the distribution of wealth.

Those who think this way tend to presuppose the view that society is more just when its wealth is more evenly distributed. Historically, one inspiration for this egalitarian view was the Judeo-Christian tradition that stressed the duty of the well-to-do to share with the poor. Another was criticism of the capitalistic system that came from socialists and communists; greedy employers, they said, exploited workers by taking, as profits, revenue that should rightly have belonged to the workers.

A modified version of egalitarianism, not based on religion or on communism, was formulated by the American philosopher John Rawls. He held that if a society is to be just, wealth and other advantages must be distributed equally, except when inequalities serve to raise the level of well-being of the least well-off group in the society. For example, paying physicians high salaries could be just, if that were the only way to ensure that health needs are met. Rawls's theory offers a rationale for minimum-wage laws, and for much else in the New Deal's program.

Advocates have often proposed as a guideline that minimum wage levels must be high enough to enable each worker to support a family of four.

ARGUMENTS AGAINST MINIMUM-WAGE LAWS

Opponents of the minimum wage argue that it has bad economic consequences for others in society, especially in that it increases unemployment. Those who fail to notice this are wrongly overlooking the fact that in a free market economy, wage levels affect how many job openings there will be. If minimum wage levels are high enough to have any effect, they must increase unemployment, because the labor of some would-be workers will have a market value less than the minimum wage, so employers will not hire them. The higher the minimum wage level, the more would-be workers will be excluded in this way.

If there were no minimum-wage law, these would-be workers could find jobs at wages proportionate to the market value of what they can do. Such workers probably would not earn enough to support families of four, but most of them do not have families, as many are adolescents. Those who work but earn too little to avoid poverty could be offered government welfare payments to supplement their low wages. This arrangement would be more efficient than having a minimum wage, since support would go only to those who need it, and the total cost to society of helping the least-well-off would decrease.

Opponents of the minimum wage generally agree with Adam Smith and later classical economists who argued that free market capitalism, functioning without government control over such economic variables as wages and prices, can unleash individual enterprise and make society much richer. Government intervention to set wages will introduce distortions in the allocation of resources, thereby reducing the national income. Instead of emphasizing equality, this way of thinking recommends that members of society tolerate inequality in the distribution of income, in order that total national income will be maximized. Here the idea is that a society is just in which owners who have acquired their property in noncriminal ways are protected in their possession of it, and wages that have been set through free market bargaining will not be altered by government edict. Robert Nozick was an American philosopher who defended this conception of justice.

Stephen F. Barker

FURTHER READING

Murray, Patrick. *Reflections on Commercial Life: An Anthology of Classic Texts*. New York: Routledge, 1997.

Nicholson, Walter. *Microeconomic Theory*. Cincinnati: South-Western/Thomson Learning, 2002.

Nozick, Robert. *Anarchy, State, and Utopia*. New York: Basic Books, 1974.

Rawls, John. *A Theory of Justice*. Rev. ed. Cambridge, Mass.: Belknap Press of Harvard University Press, 1999.

Smeeding, Timothy M., Michael O'Higgins, and Lee Rainwater, eds. *Poverty, Inequality, and Income Distribution in Comparative Perspective*. Washington, D.C.: Urban Institute Press, 1990.

Smith, Adam. *An Inquiry into the Nature and Causes of the Wealth of Nations: A Selected Edition*. Edited by Kathryn Sutherland. New York: Oxford University Press, 1998.

SEE ALSO: Child labor legislation; Corporate compensation; Cost-benefit analysis; Equal pay for equal work; Fair Labor Standards Act; Income distribution; Professional athlete incomes; *Theory of Justice, A*; Tipping; Wage discrimination.

Miranda v. Arizona

THE EVENT: U.S. Supreme Court decision mandating that all criminal suspects taken into police custody be informed of their constitutional rights prior to any questioning

DATE: Ruling made on June 13, 1966

TYPE OF ETHICS: Legal and judicial ethics

SIGNIFICANCE: The *Miranda* decision fundamentally altered basic police procedure and sought to ensure that accused citizens were aware of their rights under the Fifth and Sixth Amendments.

The manner in which Ernesto Miranda's rape confession was obtained—without coercion but without benefit of counsel—aroused the conscience of the nation. Despite the fact that he had not been informed of his right to an attorney prior to signing it, Miranda's written confession was admitted as evidence at his first trial, resulting in his conviction and imprisonment. His conviction was appealed to the Supreme Court, however, where Chief Justice Earl Warren, speaking for a divided Court, established guidelines for police interrogations: "Prior to any questioning, the person must be warned that he has a right to remain silent, that any statement he does make may be used as evidence against him, and that he has a right to the presence of an attorney, either retained or appointed."

This decision, denounced by presidents from Richard M. Nixon to Ronald Reagan, has served to

---

Miranda Warnings

Minimal warning, as outlined in the *Miranda v Arizona* case:

> You have the right to remain silent. Anything you say can and will be used against you in a court of law. You have the right to be speak to an attorney, and to have an attorney present during any questioning. If you cannot afford a lawyer, one will be provided for you at government expense.

Full warning:

> You have the right to remain silent and refuse to answer questions. Do you understand?
>
> Anything you do say may be used against you in a court of law. Do you understand?
>
> You have the right to consult an attorney before speaking to the police and to have an attorney present during questioning now or in the future. Do you understand?
>
> If you cannot afford an attorney, one will be appointed for you before any questioning if you wish. Do you understand?
>
> If you decide to answer questions now without an attorney present you will still have the right to stop answering at any time until you talk to an attorney. Do you understand?
>
> Knowing and understanding your rights as I have explained them to you, are you willing to answer my questions without an attorney present?

---

protect the ignorant and the indigent and has resulted in a profound change in police procedure, popularized in the media as the so-called Miranda Warning.

Lisa Paddock

SEE ALSO: Accused, rights of; Arrest records; Bill of Rights, U.S.; Civil rights and liberties; Due process; Police brutality; Supreme Court, U.S.

Monopoly

DEFINITION: Exclusive ownership or control of a good or service in a particular market
TYPE OF ETHICS: Business and labor ethics
SIGNIFICANCE: Monopolies are illegal in the major modern industrialized capitalist nations because

they are perceived as unfairly interfering with competition. They are thus said to infringe on the rights of companies to compete equitably in the marketplace, and on the rights of consumers to benefit from that competition.

In 1340, an English listing of the "evils of trade" included such things as forestalling (the physical obstruction of goods coming to market, or cornering the supply of goods, which deprived the owner of the market stall his rental), regrating (buying most or all the available goods at a fair for resale at a higher price), and engrossing (contracting for control of goods while they are still being grown or produced). These are all attempts at monopolization of a market, and such actions have been thought wrong since they began. The United States has had laws against monopoly since its founding, based on these terms taken from English common law and justified by reference to an abiding public interest in the maintenance of competition. Competition by ethical individuals results in the completion of mutually beneficial transactions, protects consumers from unreasonable price increases, and, according to Adam Smith (*An Inquiry Into the Nature and Causes of the Wealth of Nations*, 1776), leads to the greatest wealth for the nation.

Sandra L. Christensen

SEE ALSO: Antitrust legislation; Capitalism; Consumerism; Fairness; Price fixing; Profit economy; Smith, Adam.

Monroe Doctrine

IDENTIFICATION: American foreign policy conceived to confine the political spheres of influence of Europe and the United States to their respective hemispheres
DATE: Promulgated on December 2, 1823
TYPE OF ETHICS: International relations
SIGNIFICANCE: The Monroe Doctrine required the United States to refrain from interfering in the internal affairs of European powers or in ther intra-European wars. It also declared that any attempt

to interfere with the governance of a nation anywhere in the Western Hemisphere would be treated as a hostile act against the sovereignty of the United States. The Roosevelt Corollary of 1904 later made explicit an always implicit aspect of the Doctrine: that the U.S. was asserting its own rights to intervene in the Americas in whatever fashion it deemed appropriate.

After the defeat of Napoleon Bonaparte in 1815, the continental European leaders, led by Prince Klemens von Metternich of Austria, were concerned with keeping a lid on revolutionary disturbances. During the Napoleonic years, the New World colonies of Spain successfully gained their independence through revolution. Between 1815 and 1823, the European leaders discussed the idea of returning the colonies to Spain. These discussions inspired the Monroe Doctrine, put forward by president James Monroe in his annual address to Congress.

In essence, the Doctrine declared that the United States would keep out of the territories, wars, alliances, spheres of influence, and politics of the world outside the Western Hemisphere, and in return non-American powers would be expected to stay out of the political affairs of the Americas. Non-American countries with colonies in the Western Hemisphere could keep them, but they were to acquire no more colonies.

Bill Manikas

SEE ALSO: International law; Intervention; Isolationism; Manifest destiny; National security and sovereignty; Sovereignty.

Montesquieu

IDENTIFICATION: French political philosopher
BORN: January 18, 1689, La Brède, near Bordeaux, France
DIED: February 10, 1755, Paris, France
TYPE OF ETHICS: Enlightenment history
SIGNIFICANCE: As the leading *philosophe* during the early French Enlightenment, Montesquieu stimulated discussion on the nature of government, laws, and society with works such as *The Persian*

Montesquieu. (Library of Congress)

Letters (1721) and *The Spirit of the Laws* (*De l'ésprit des loix*, 1748).

Born Charles-Louis de Secondat, Montesquieu grew up in and around Bordeaux, where he studied law and sat in the French parliament. He disliked the tyrannical and warlike tendencies of the governments of Louis XIV and the Regency. Montesquieu became the most popular critic of the French government, Church, and social customs with his satirical *Persian Letters*. After being admitted to the French Academy, he traveled throughout Europe. He idealized England as a model of liberty, independent judiciary, and commerce.

Montesquieu's *Spirit of the Laws*, which influenced both the French and American revolutions, considers various types of constitutions and laws. He examined societies in terms of their customs and history, not as abstract types. The work's critical tone marks it as the foundation of modern political science. In addition to providing a detached analysis, the *Spirit* argues for personal freedom, toleration of opposing views, separation of church and state, intermediate bodies (particularly a hereditary aristocracy) to prevent royal despotism, sensible and equitable laws, a more rational and just criminal law system, and the separation of powers.

Thomas Renna

See also: Democracy; Enlightenment ethics; Freedom and liberty; Justice; Voltaire.

Moore, G. E.

Identification: English philosopher
Born: November 4, 1873, London, England
Died: October 24, 1958, Cambridge, England
Type of ethics: Modern history
Significance: In *Principia Ethica* (1903) and *Ethics* (1912), Moore propounded the view that "goodness" is an unanalyzable, indefinable property which is nevertheless discoverable through human intuition.

Moore was professor of mental philosophy and logic at Cambridge (1925-1939) and editor of the philosophical journal *Mind* (1921-1947). In ethics, he thought it quite important to distinguish two questions: "What ought to be?" (or "What is good in itself?") and "What ought we to do?" The first question can be subdivided: "What is the nature of goodness?" and "What things possess the property of goodness?" Regarding the nature of goodness, Moore was a nonnaturalist. He maintained that the term "good" stands for a basic or ultimate property that could not be defined in terms of anything else. Every attempt to define the good in terms of something else commits what Moore called "the naturalistic fallacy." Indeed, even to assume that "good" *must* denote some *real* property of things" is to make this same mistake.

With regard to the question "What things are good?" Moore was an intuitionist. The answer to this question is self-evident, but only in some defeasible sense. Finally, the question of morally obligatory conduct "can only be answered by considering what effects our actions will have." Thus, Moore was a consequentialist, though not of the egoistic or hedonistic utilitarian variety. For him, an action is right if it is, among all alternative actions, most productive of the nonnatural property "goodness." Moore was a se-

vere critic of all forms of ethical subjectivism, including emotivism.

R. Douglas Geivett

See also: Consequentialism; Emotivist ethics; Good, the; Hare, R. M.; Intuitionist ethics; Metaethics; Naturalistic fallacy; Perry, R. B.; Utilitarianism.

Moral education

Definition: Inculcation of children with moral values
Type of ethics: Beliefs and practices
Significance: Moral education is a key component of the process whereby individuals come to understand themselves as citizens of a given society, members of a given religion, and so on. It is in large part the source of shared moral systems and common languages for talking about moral issues.

Instruction in morality has traditionally been considered to be the province of the home or of the church. Parents are the child's first teachers and are obligated to communicate to their young what behaviors and attitudes are socially acceptable and what behaviors and attitudes will not be tolerated. "Listen, my son, to your father's instruction and do not forsake your mother's teaching" (Prov. 1:8), wrote King Solomon thousands of years ago. "Then you will understand what is right and just and fair—every good path" (Prov. 2:9). The approach used was didactic, unilateral, and passed down from generation to generation. Directly telling the child what is right and what is wrong has long been the most popular way of inculcating morality.

Indoctrination is also used by religious groups. The minister or rabbi or priest, being ordained of God, interprets the sacred writings of the faith in order to convey to the people what is good and what is evil. This interpretation is put in the context of what is pleasing to God. A moral person loves and fears the Lord, obeys God's commandments, and treats others in a way that makes for harmonious living. The question of whether a person can be morally educated without having religious faith has long been debated. The question "Why be moral?" has both philosophic and religious implications.

Moral Education in Schools

Provision must be made for those children who are not taught in the home or do not attend a place of worship where ethical instruction is given. The logical answer is the school. A few have argued that the school is even preferable because it introduces the child to a larger, more democratic community. Émile Durkheim, a French sociologist, maintained that the school frees the child from excessive dependency, from being a slavish copy of the family.

Jean Piaget, a Swiss philosopher, believed that the morality of cooperation (autonomy) encouraged by the school was more mature than the morality of unilateral constraint (heteronomy) taught in the home. Durkheim and Piaget differed, however, on the method to be used. Durkheim favored the direct teaching of moral values as essential for the child to become a fully functioning social being. Piaget opted for the use of moral dilemma stories to encourage the child's natural propensity to understand the good as a consequent of a maturing intellect.

During the last quarter of the twentieth century, moral education programs became part of the regular school day in many public and private institutions. This was done in one of two ways. Either the teacher would set aside a special period for a moral lesson or a discussion of an ethical problem would be incorporated into the regular academic curriculum. Which method is better has long been debated, and it is not expected that an agreement will be reached.

In England, the best-known program was designed by British philosopher of education John Wilson, who combined universally accepted principles with individual personal ideals. Wilson believed that the morally educated person has incorporated within the self the principles of a concern for others based on an understanding of the concept of "person," a sense of feeling for others as well as for oneself, basic knowledge and skill in knowing how to deal with moral situations, and acting upon that knowledge in real-life situations. There are sixteen subcategories within these four major areas, each one contributing to the formation of a rational, autonomous, morally educated person. Curricular materials have been developed but are not in a form that makes for ease in implementation in some educational settings. Wilson's desire to have in place a carefully developed philosophy of moral education before it was practiced in the classroom has contributed to the slow and deliberate pace with which it has been used.

In the United States, the two major programs are Lawrence Kohlberg's moral reasoning and Sidney Simon's values clarification. Both Kohlberg and Simon believe that indoctrination is unacceptable, that a person is not morally educated unless he or she has developed within the self an understanding of what is good and right. Morality by definition must come from within; it is never imposed by an outside source. This stance came in part from research that shows that only a minor portion of moral education occurs at the "facts" level. Simply knowing what society expects does not ensure that one will act in accordance with that knowledge. This idea of self-developed morality also came about because in a pluralistic society there is not always agreement among the groups that constitute a community regarding what is right and what is wrong.

Other Approaches

Borrowing from Piaget, Kohlberg made use of the moral dilemma story. Each child in the classroom states a position on the dilemma. Responses fall into one of six stages of moral understanding with two stages at each of three levels. At the first level (preconventional), the child makes statements that show an egocentric orientation: "It is good if it's good for me." At the second (conventional) level, the young person is concerned with pleasing others and winning their approval. Obeying the law and doing one's duty are also important: "A good person does what society expects of its members." At the third level, the adult wants justice for everyone alike: "Do unto others as you would have them do unto you." As students discuss the stories, they advance in moral understanding by listening to the reasoning of others within the classroom who are one stage or one level higher than their own.

The values-clarification approach used by Simon begins by asking students questions about the way they look at such topics as money, friendship, religion, prejudice, or love. The student must be able to state a position freely, consider alternatives as given by other students, make a choice after considering the possible consequences of each alternative, be happy with the choice made, tell others about the choice, act upon it, and incorporate the choice into his or her lifestyle. Curricular materials abound and are available for use not only in the school but also in the home and the church. According to Simon, the morally educated person is one who is given the freedom to choose, to affirm, and to act upon those values that make him or her a fully functioning individual.

Bonnidell Clouse

FURTHER READING

Chazan, Barry. *Contemporary Approaches to Moral Education: Analyzing Alternative Theories*. New York: Teachers College Press, 1985.

Durkheim, Émile. *Moral Education: A Study in the Theory and Application of the Sociology of Education*. Translated by Everett K. Wilson and Herman Schnurer. Edited by Everett K. Wilson. New York: Free Press, 1961.

Gilligan, Carol. *In a Different Voice: Psychological Theory and Women's Development*. Cambridge, Mass.: Harvard University Press, 1982.

Kohlberg, Lawrence. *The Psychology of Moral Development*. San Francisco: Harper & Row, 1984.

Macedo, Stephen, and Yael Tamir, eds. *Moral and Political Education*. New York: New York University Press, 2002.

Noddings, Nel. *Caring: A Feminine Approach to Ethics and Moral Education*. 2d ed. Berkeley: University of California Press, 2003.

_____. *Happiness and Education*. New York: Cambridge University Press, 2003.

Simon, Sidney B., and Sally W. Olds. *Helping Your Child Learn Right from Wrong: A Guide to Values Clarification*. New York: McGraw-Hill, 1977.

Wilson, John. *A New Introduction to Moral Education*. London: Cassell, 1990.

SEE ALSO: Aristotelian ethics; Children; Dilemmas, moral; Durkheim, Émile; Head Start; Kohlberg, Lawrence; Mentoring; Values clarification.

Moral equivalence

DEFINITION: Term commonly used to equate the morality and ethics of two entities that are not usually seen as comparable
TYPE OF ETHICS: Theory of ethics
SIGNIFICANCE: The term "moral equivalence" is typically employed to justify proposed courses of action that are controversial.

Social commentators, politicians, and other public officials often evoke the term "moral equivalence" in their pubic discourses. There are several reasons they do so. Whenever the word "morality" is used in reference to public policy, people tend to pay closer attention, and intellectual curiosity is aroused. The term is thus used as a means of gaining an audience. Also, its usage often refers back to events about which people feel strongly and for which they hold nearly consensual feelings, thus evoking a strong sense of emotional nostalgia. Using the expression is a way of trying to build popular and political support for new ideas, developments, or proposals by likening them to known and accepted past events.

The phrase seems first to have emerged during the mid-1960's in reference to American participation in the Vietnam War. Some commentators on the war saw the communist Viet Cong as "morally equivalent" to the American patriots of the Revolutionary War era. During the 1970's and 1980's, the term was used to stress the severity of the economic problems in the United States, by comparing them to the magnitude and severity of wartime conditions.

Critics might assert that evoking moral equivalence is senseless, worthless, and immaterial, arguing that it runs counter to the old adage that history does not repeat itself, and adding that any such comparisons are inherently futile. The claim of moral equivalence equates apples and oranges, doing credit to neither. Another ethical issue is that these comparisons are by nature subjective, as are the responses to them, and often are made only for political or partisan reasons, advancing no worthy goals.

Thomas W. Buchanan

SEE ALSO: Accountability; *Beyond Good and Evil*; Conscience; Ethics/morality distinction; Incommensurability; Moral-sense theories; Morality; Narrative ethics; Nussbaum, Martha; Vietnam War.

Moral luck

DEFINITION: Chance occurrences, beyond the control of an individual, which nevertheless affect the ethical character or culpability of that individual
TYPE OF ETHICS: Theory of ethics
SIGNIFICANCE: The concept of moral luck has been

used by some ethicists to refute several traditionally held views about morality. The most significant of these are the idea that people can be held morally responsible for all of their morally significant features and the assumption that morality is a trump value (that is, that given a choice between two alternatives, moral considerations are more important than all other considerations in determining which alternative to choose).

Before considering the possibility of moral luck and its implications for ways of thinking about people, it is important to explain the notion of moral luck in some detail.

First, consider the notion of a morally significant feature. People have many features, but only some of them are morally significant. For example, the following features are clearly not morally significant: being six feet tall, being born on a Monday, and having brown eyes. By contrast, the following features are morally significant: being cruel, having murdered someone, being loving, and having saved someone's life. These examples also illustrate the different kinds of morally significant features: some involve character traits, including beliefs and emotions, whereas others concern specific actions from one's personal history.

The notion of having control over a feature is also important for explaining the notion of moral luck. Roughly speaking, people have control over a feature only if there is something that they can do to acquire it or something that they can do to get rid of it. For example, it seems clear that nobody has control over the following features: having been born during the night, having a body that is mostly water, and being unable to run faster than the speed of sound. By contrast, it is typically believed that most people have control over the following features: being excessively selfish, being very generous, being rude to a stranger on a particular occasion, and being patient with a child in a specific instance. Given these notions, it is possible to explain the concept of moral luck with some precision: Moral luck involves people possessing morally significant features over which they have no control.

Is moral luck possible? Are there any actual cases of moral luck? These questions are controversial. Before considering an apparent case of moral luck, it will be helpful to explore the significance of moral luck for ways of thinking about people.

One often holds people responsible for the morally significant features that they possess. For example, if one learns that certain people are greedy and have been caught stealing, typically one thinks of them (rather automatically) as being blameworthy for having these features. Similarly, upon discovering that people are generous and regularly help less fortunate people, typically one thinks of them (rather automatically) as being praiseworthy for having these features. (Besides evaluating other people, one often evaluates oneself in these same ways.)

These nearly automatic reactions to the morally significant features that people possess are called into question by the possibility of moral luck. If moral luck is possible, then it could turn out that some people possess morally significant features over which they have no control; therefore, it would be completely inappropriate to hold them morally responsible for those features. (After all, typically, one does not hold people morally responsible for features over which they have no control, such as the fact that they are unable to jump over the moon.) Therefore, the possibility of moral luck suggests that people's relatively automatic practices of evaluating others may be hasty and superficial.

LUCK AND CHARACTER

Furthermore, the possibility of moral luck also seems to threaten people's conception of themselves as people who have control over their moral characters and actions. Although it is not surprising that there are some features over which one has no control, one's individual autonomy and self-determination seem to be undercut if one possesses morally significant features over which one has no control.

Given the significant implications of the possibility of moral luck, it is not surprising that questions concerning moral luck generate a great deal of controversy. Many people argue that moral luck is possible by appealing to the following kind of case: Imagine a truck driver who fails to stop at a stop sign and passes through an intersection without incident. Now imagine a second truck driver who does exactly what the first one does in similar circumstances but who also runs over and kills a small child who has darted into the street suddenly. This seems to be a case of moral luck, since it is a matter of luck that the second truck driver has a morally significant feature that the first truck driver lacks (namely, the feature of having killed a child).

Many people think that cases such as this demonstrate the possibility of moral luck. Some of them insist further that people's ways of evaluating others and their concepts of themselves as self-determining agents should be revised. Others simply deny the claim that a person must have control over a feature in order to be held morally responsible for possessing it. Still others, who are not persuaded by cases such as the one described above, reject the claim that moral luck is possible by restricting the notion of a morally significant feature in some way (for example, so that all such features are features over which persons have control). It is hard to say which approach to the question of the possibility of moral luck is best; reflective persons must decide themselves what to think.

Scott A. Davison

FURTHER READING

Card, Claudia. *The Unnatural Lottery: Character and Moral Luck*. Philadelphia: Temple University Press, 1996.

Dickenson, Donna. *Risk and Luck in Medical Ethics*. Malden, Mass.: Blackwell, 2003.

Feinberg, Joel. *Doing and Deserving*. Princeton, N.J.: Princeton University Press, 1970.

Fischer, John Martin, ed. *Moral Responsibility*. Ithaca, N.Y.: Cornell University Press, 1986.

Nagel, Thomas. *Mortal Questions*. Cambridge, England: Cambridge University Press, 1979.

Williams, Bernard. *Moral Luck: Philosophical Papers, 1973-1980*. New York: Cambridge University Press, 1990.

Wolf, Susan. "The Moral of Moral Luck." In *Setting the Moral Compass: Essays by Women Philosophers*, edited by Cheshire Calhoun. New York: Oxford University Press, 2004.

Zimmerman, Michael J. "Luck and Moral Responsibility." *Ethics* 97 (January, 1987): 374-386.

SEE ALSO: Accountability; Autonomy; Determinism and freedom; Equality; Fairness; Guilt and shame; Impartiality; Luck and chance; Merit; Moral responsibility; Ought/can implication.

Moral principles, rules, and imperatives

DEFINITION: Comprehensive, absolute, universalizable rules governing the judgment of right and wrong and the actions of those who desire to do right

TYPE OF ETHICS: Theory of ethics

SIGNIFICANCE: The principles, rules, and imperatives which together make up morality are taken by definition to apply universally to everyone and to be the proper basis for all human action. Moral philosophers who subscribe to this model of morality take the enumeration of these imperatives, rules, and principles to be their primary task. Exponents of systems such as pluralism which deny the existence of universal values eschew morality in favor of more modest or situated types of ethics.

All people have notions of right and wrong. These notions manifest themselves in a variety of ways. Some of these beliefs pertain to simple matters such as manners or taste, others pertain to more general matters such as customs and laws, and others guide the most fundamental aspects of human life: These are the beliefs that shape one's character and determine what others think about one as a human being. One's moral beliefs say more about one as an individual than does any other aspect of existence. Whether one is rich or poor, old or young, one's moral beliefs do more to define one's life than anything else.

The terms "morality" and "ethics" are often used interchangeably, but the distinction between the two is important to any serious study of ethical matters. The clearest distinction can be revealed by noting that there is a school of ethics called "situational ethics"; there is not, however, a moral school of thought that could be described as "situational." Morality can never be relative. What distinguishes morality from ethics is that morality is always universal and prescriptive. For this reason, the notions cited above about manners, taste, customs, and even laws may be considered ethical beliefs, but they are not part of a moral code. When ethical views and moral beliefs come into conflict, morality must prevail, because moral beliefs are universal and fundamental.

Looking at the negative connotations of these two terms is a helpful way to highlight their differences.

A person who cheats at cards may be considered unethical, but that does not necessarily mean that the person is immoral. Being immoral is a much graver character flaw than is being unethical. A person may behave unethically on occasions and in certain circumstances, but to be immoral is to possess fundamental—if not permanent—character flaws that render one untrustworthy in most situations.

It must be noted that some people are amoral. They have no broad system of beliefs that guide their behavior. This does not mean that they have no notion of dos and don'ts in life, only that their beliefs are not guided by a universal system that provides justification for human actions.

MORAL PRINCIPLES

The best example of moral principles continues to be the one articulated by Aristotle in his *Nicomachean Ethics*. Aristotle's moral principles were guided by a teleological concern. The teleological concern central to Aristotle was happiness. For Aristotle, morality meant doing what would provide a happy life as opposed to doing simply what one desired at the moment. Happiness, in this sense, has more to do with one's total lifestyle than it does with a few activities. It would be fair to say that Aristotle's understanding of happiness is more closely related to satisfaction or contentment than it is to simple pleasures. This is why reason plays such a large role in Aristotle's moral teachings.

Moral principles generally depend on reason. One must first understand the principle and then be able to apply it to different situations as they occur. Utilitarianism provides another good example of moral principles. The principle that guides utilitarianism is "the greatest good for the greatest number." One must understand this principle in order to exercise the judgment necessary to apply the principle.

The moral principles developed by Aristotle lead to a broad discussion of character. To him, morality is what determines who as well as what one is. Morality does much more than merely determine one's actions; it also determines one's thoughts and shapes one's soul.

MORAL RULES

The Ten Commandments listed in the Old Testament of the Bible represent a clear set of moral rules. The prescribed and prohibited forms of behavior cited in the Ten Commandments provide more specific guides to human actions than do abstract principles. Moral rules place less emphasis on reason and more on authority or obedience. The "thou shalts" and "thou shalt nots" of the Ten Commandments do not leave as much room for judgment as one usually finds in moral principles.

It is much easier to provide children with moral rules than it is to describe moral principles. Children are often told to share their toys or not to hit one another. These are good rules, and children are often expected to follow these rules because they have been told by their parents or other adults to behave that way. People often assume that any further explanation would be beyond the reach of very small children.

In a similar manner, religious rules are often presented as rules that should be accepted as an article of faith. While this is true to some extent of all moral guides, rules tend to provide fewer opportunities for individual judgment than do principles. Rules tend to be more rigidly prescriptive than principles. Like the parental rules cited above, they rely on the authority of the rule givers—authority that the rule receiver is in no position to question or challenge.

Moral rules function in much the same way as laws: They spell out, in the most direct and detailed manner, what one should or should not do, and those who fall under their jurisdiction are expected to be obedient. When Moses came down from the mountain with the Ten Commandments, he appeared in the capacity of a lawgiver, not that of a seminar leader. He appeared as a messenger from God with a strict set of specific orders that were intended to shape and guide the lives of the people. The only choice given to the people was obedience and salvation or disobedience and eternal damnation.

Moral rules are the simplest and most direct form of moral guide, but as people become more inquisitive about moral issues, certain moral rules may prove less clear and simple. Most often, moral rules are an effort to apply less tangible moral principles. When this occurs, the justification for the moral rules is found in the moral principles that guide them. When this is the justification for moral rules, it is important to remember that the rules are guided by the principles.

MORAL IMPERATIVES

Immanuel Kant established the most basic set of imperatives found in moral literature. Imperatives are commands or orders, so moral imperatives should be viewed as basic moral commandments or orders. Kant defines two distinct types of imperatives: hypothetical and categorical. Kant's hypothetical imperative is a means to some other end. If one desires a certain end, it is imperative that one employ a particular means. In contrast, a categorical imperative is an end with no reference to something beyond itself. Most ethical rules are hypothetical imperatives; morality, in contrast, consists of categorical imperatives. In the simplest terms, categorical imperatives are obeyed for their own sake.

Moral references to imperatives are generally considered to be references to what Kant defined as categorical imperatives, but it is important to keep the other alternative in mind when the general topic of moral imperatives arises. Kant further considered obligations and duties that accompany imperatives to be limited to rational creatures, for only rational beings can abide by such universal laws. If this is true, one might add that only rational beings are capable of moral considerations of any kind.

MORAL TENSIONS

Alexis de Tocqueville, the nineteenth century French philosopher and social historian, once made a distinction between what he called "instinctive patriotism" and "reflective patriotism." While either might produce the same behavior in a person, the former was akin to a reflex reaction that required little or no thought; the latter was the result of careful consideration and extensive reflection.

Morality would seem to have a similar distinction. There is the morality that is so deeply ingrained in one from an early age that it guides one's actions without one's ever giving it a moment's thought. There is also morality that is the result of extensive study and careful analysis. Generally, there is a link between the two, but not everyone is curious enough to want to examine the basic moral assumptions. Some people feel that a careful examination or questioning of their moral beliefs is heresy. For this reason, certain moral beliefs are caught in a tug-of-war between reason and revelation.

The conflict between reason and revelation can be explained in the light of the realization that some moral beliefs are the result of factors that claim to be beyond human comprehension, while others are considered the result of human comprehension. Faith in a superior being who reveals moral laws through a person, persons, writings, or acts provides the clearest example of rules that must be accepted yet might never be understood.

The quest to understand moral matters encompasses a wide range of competing notions about how one comes to such an understanding. Ancient philosophers considered understanding to be a matter of discovery. The laws that should guide human behavior were determined by nature and preceded human existence. The task of understanding is one of using intellectual ability to learn the truths over which one has no control. Many modern philosophers believe that people can understand only what they themselves create. Existentialism is the philosophical school most often associated with this belief.

HOW PEOPLE ACQUIRE MORAL BELIEFS

In *A Question of Values*, Hunter Lewis describes six ways of acquiring moral beliefs: authority, logic, sense experience, emotion, intuition, and science. This is a good representative sample of the different ways in which people develop moral beliefs. If one is taught to obey parental authority in one's early years, one will generally find it easier to accept other authorities in later years. For most people, parental authority is their first exposure to subordinating bodily desires to some other influence. If one learns to control one's desires, one can then substitute other influences for parental authority in later years. One's ability to respond to any kind of moral guidance is dependent upon one's ability to control one's own actions.

The factors that influence beliefs usually change as people mature emotionally and intellectually. For this reason, simple rules provide people's first exposure to moral codes. As people grow older, these rules become more complex, and as people develop greater intellectual abilities, they become more likely to look to broader principles for moral guidance. Eventually, an individual should reach the point at which he or she can understand the most compelling and imperative moral guides. This moral maturation should lead from acceptance of authority or emotional considerations to more sophisticated guidance via logic or science.

959

Moral development need not, however, be linear in nature. David Hume argued that there is a moral sentiment that directs human moral behavior; reason does not have the authority to do so. Moral philosophers have never agreed on the main source of morality or on its final justification; they agree only that moral theories and moral actions are a necessary part of being human.

Conclusion

Since the days of Socrates, morality has played a central role in the battle between passion and reason. How people temper their most basic desires and behave in a moral manner has been one of the truly great questions of moral philosophy. This concern has produced many competing theories over justification. How can one convince an individual or a community of individuals to behave in ways that appear to contradict the most basic instincts?

Reason, salvation, and self-interest have all been used to explain why one might choose to combat these most basic and primitive drives. A society's ability to convince its population to adhere to a set of moral rules, principles, or imperatives is what has determined whether that society is judged to be civilized or barbaric. The United Nation's Universal Declaration of Human Rights has become the global barometer that is used to determine which nations are civilized and which are not. In fact, it refers to violations of its moral code as "barbarous acts." The assumption behind this declaration is there are some common and universal moral principles that should guide the activities of any nation or state.

To use the terminology of the United States of America's Declaration of Independence, there are certain "unalienable rights" that human beings naturally possess. These "unalienable rights" constitute the moral imperative that should guide all civilized nations. The general principles called "human rights" are a direct result of this moral imperative.

Donald V. Weatherman

Further Reading

Ashmore, Robert. *Building a Moral System.* Englewood Cliffs, N.J.: Prentice-Hall, 1987. An excellent, short introduction to the basic principles and concepts necessary to understand general ethics. This well-written work makes the most critical moral issues accessible to general readers.

Foot, Philippa. *Virtues and Vices, and Other Essays in Moral Philosophy.* 1978. Reprint. New York: Oxford University Press, 2002. This classic collection of essays in virtue-ethics includes an essay on morality as a set of hypothetical imperatives and an essay on whether moral considerations always override all others.

Lewis, Hunter. *A Question of Values.* San Francisco: Harper & Row, 1990. A good introductory work that divides moral topics into a series of questions. Especially helpful is the way it breaks down the different approaches one can take in choosing a moral system. Contains a good mixture of theoretical issues and their behavioral applications.

Pojman, Louis, ed. *Ethical Theory: Classical and Contemporary Readings.* Belmont, Calif.: Wadsworth, 1989. As the title indicates, this volume contains both classical and contemporary writings on moral issues. A good reference work with very helpful reading lists at the end of each chapter.

Rachels, James. *The Elements of Moral Philosophy.* New York: Random House, 1986. One of the best topical introductions to morality in print. It examines religious and social approaches to moral theory in an objective manner. The suggestions for further reading are as good a guide to major writings on moral theory as can be found.

Solomon, Robert. *Ethics: A Short Introduction.* Dubuque, Iowa: Brown & Benchmark, 1993. This work is especially valuable because of the distinction it makes between ethics and morality. There is also a wonderful discussion on the tensions that can develop between community values and individual values.

_____. *Morality and the Good Life.* 2d ed. New York: McGraw-Hill, 1992. One of the best short anthologies of classical works on morality and ethics. This work has a helpful introductory chapter and provides a useful introduction to each of the readings. The readings are presented in chronological order, but the editor provides a convenient guide for a topical arrangement as well.

SEE ALSO: Absolutism; Ethics/morality distinction; Moral luck; Moral realism; Moral responsibility; Moral-sense theories; Morality; Pluralism; Universalizability.

Moral realism

DEFINITION: Theory that moral facts have an objective existence, independent of the individuals who may or may not come to know and recognize them

TYPE OF ETHICS: Theory of ethics

SIGNIFICANCE: Moral realism holds that morality exists as a set of objective facts in the world, rather than residing in the judgments of moral agents. Thus, a properly trained or intuitive person may be capable of determining moral truth, but someone lacking such training or sensitivity may spend his or her entire life transgressing moral law without ever knowing it.

Moral realism is a philosophical position that views moral facts such as good, right, and wrong in the same way that scientific realism views natural facts: that is, these facts are independent of and exist prior to their being thought, understood, and believed by individuals. G. E. Moore, in his book *Principia Ethica* (1903), was the first to formulate this position. Moore argues that beauty, goodness, right, wrong, and so forth are features of the world and actions that are true whether anyone recognizes them or not. When one claims that someone has done something good, for example, this does not reflect simply what one thinks of the action (as subjectivists argue), but reflects the intuition of a property that this action *really* has: goodness.

Moral properties, however, are not natural properties, or properties that one can recognize with one's natural faculties (senses). Moral properties are what Moore refers to instead as simple, unanalyzable, nonnatural properties. To clarify this idea, Moore compares the intuition of moral nonnatural properties to the intuition of mathematical axioms and proofs. One does not use one's senses to see that one step in a mathematical proof follows from another; likewise, one does not use one's senses to see that an act is good, but it is nevertheless seen to be good.

PROBLEMS WITH MOORE'S POSITION

There are some problems with Moore's position, however, and much of the work in moral realism since Moore has been an effort to resolve these difficulties. For example, since moral properties are nonnatural and are not perceived by the senses, Moore must account for people's intuition of these proper-ties by claiming that people have a moral intuition, a moral sense. The notion of a moral intuition or sense, however, is itself a rather mysterious notion that is left unexplained. Some proponents of moral realism, agreeing with Moore's claim that there are moral facts, have simply accepted this mystery. Philosophers such as William D. Ross, in *The Right and the Good* (1930), accept the notion of moral intuition as a commonsense given. Just as many people would accept the use of intuition in mathematics as a given, so do Moore and those who follow him accept the use of moral intuition in making moral claims.

A more troubling problem with moral realism involves explaining the ontological status of moral facts. If, as moral realists argue, moral facts have a reality that is independent of thinking, desiring subjects, and if these facts can give direction to and place constraints on actions, then the question of what this independent reality is arises. The reality of moral facts is not the same as that of natural facts, yet they have the power to motivate individuals to place constraints upon themselves. How do they do this? Critics argue that in answering this question, moral realists must argue for an extravagant and unnecessary ontology. In short, they must unjustifiably attribute rather strange attributes to an equally strange entity called a moral fact if these facts are to do what the moral realist says they do.

There have been many attempts to resolve this apparent problem, but two are of particular note. Richard Boyd, in "How to Be a Moral Realist" (1988), argues that moral properties can indeed be identified with physical properties, though in a sophisticated and peculiar way, and hence a moral realist need not be committed to the view that moral properties are nonnatural. The difficulty with Boyd's position lies in explaining this peculiar identification of moral properties with physical properties while avoiding what Moore calls the "naturalistic fallacy"—the fallacy of identifying simple, unanalyzable moral properties with identifiable natural properties. Boyd's response is to state that a moral realist can claim that moral properties are in some sense physical properties and also claim that these moral properties remain undefinable or unanalyzable. Precisely because moral properties are undefinable, the way in which the property of goodness is to be understood as physical will also always remain undefinable.

John McDowell, in "Values and Secondary Qualities" (1985), argues that moral properties are to be identified with physical properties (he avoids non-naturalism in this way) but are to be identified in the same way that secondary qualities such as color are identified with physical things. Thus, in the same way that red, a secondary quality, emanates from a physical object (which is a primary quality) by means of this object's reflection of light at a certain wavelength, so too are moral properties to be understood as an emanation from a primary quality such as a physical action or an event. Secondary qualities are inseparable from primary qualities, and therefore moral properties are inseparable from physical properties, but they are not strictly identical to primary qualities. For example, one can turn off the light in one's room at night and the objects (primary qualities) in the room will still be there, but the colors (secondary qualities) will not. Secondary qualities and moral properties are real, but they are not real in the same sense, or in the same way, that primary qualities and physical properties are real.

There are many variations among those who argue for moral realism, but they are all agreed, following Moore, that moral facts are independent, real, and distinct from the individuals who know and are motivated to act on the basis of such facts.

Jeff Bell

FURTHER READING

Boyd, Richard. "How to Be a Moral Realist." In *Essays on Moral Realism*, edited by Geoffrey Sayre-McCord. Ithaca, N.Y.: Cornell University Press, 1988.

Clark, David K. *Empirical Realism: Meaning and the Generative Foundation of Morality*. Lanham, Md.: Lexington Books, 2004.

Kaufman, Frederik. "Moral Realism and Moral Judgments." *Erkenntnis* 36, no. 1 (1992): 103-112.

McDowell, John. "Values and Secondary Qualities." In *Morality and Objectivity*, edited by Ted Honderich. Boston: Routledge & Kegan Paul, 1985.

Moore, G. E. *Principia Ethica*. Rev. ed. Reprint. New York: Cambridge University Press, 1996.

Shafer-Landau, Russ. *Moral Realism: A Defence*. New York: Clarendon Press, 2003.

Waller, Bruce. "Moral Conversion Without Moral Realism." *Southern Journal of Philosophy* 30, no. 3 (1992): 129-137.

SEE ALSO: Absolutism; Fact/value distinction; Good, the; Moore, G. E.; Moral principles, rules, and imperatives; Moral-sense theories; Morality; Nagel, Thomas; Naturalistic fallacy.

Moral responsibility

DEFINITION: Quality that renders one subject to ethical judgment, blame, or praise; accountability
TYPE OF ETHICS: Theory of ethics
SIGNIFICANCE: To determine the conditions under which one is morally responsible for a given action, ethicists must first determine the nature of the connection between people and their actions. Thus, theories of moral responsibility necessarily engage theories of mind and of free will versus determinism.

Many philosophers claim that determinism and moral responsibility are compatible. Austin Duncan-Jones claims that the statement, "He deserves blame for doing that wrong" simply means, "Blaming him for doing that wrong will favorably influence him and others." In that case, even if the man was causally determined to act as he did, blaming him could favorably influence him and others, and therefore determinism and moral responsibility are compatible.

Duncan-Jones's account cannot make good sense, however, of one person's being more blameworthy than another person. One person's deserving more blame than another person is not simply a matter of his being more favorably influenceable by blame. The person who is least blameworthy may be the person who is most favorably influenceable. Moreover, deserving blame and being overtly blamed to a good effect do not amount to the same thing. A wicked king on his deathbed may deserve blame for some wrong even if overtly blaming him for it will not favorably influence him or very many others.

P. H. Nowell-Smith defends the compatibility of determinism and desert as follows. "Finding the cause of a thing does not necessarily affect our evaluation of that thing. For example, finding that Wolfgang Amadeus Mozart's musical ability was due to his education, practice, and heredity would not diminish our admiration for his ability. Similarly, no matter how a person came to have his moral principles, they are his and he is judged for them. Explaining how one came to be as he is does not save the bad pianist who reveals his incompetence; nor does it save the bad man who reveals his wickedness."

Typically, people do ignore determinism when making judgments of praiseworthiness and blameworthiness. Yet if one cannot help being the way one is, can one really deserve credit or blame? This challenge to the typical approach is not adequately answered by merely redescribing that approach. Determinism would not rule out excellent qualities or the appreciation of them, but in spite of Nowell-Smith's argument, determinism might rule out the deserving of credit for such qualities.

In *Freedom and Resentment* (1977), P. F. Strawson argues as follows that determinism would not rule out the rationality of blame. "Because of our human nature and our membership in society, we have a certain way of looking at human relationships. For example, whether we feel grateful or resentful depends on what we think of other people's attitudes and behavior toward us. And we connect blame with wrongdoing. This way of looking at human relationships is part and parcel of being human and living in society. It is not something we choose or something that we can give up. It needs no further justification. But if we could give it up, our choice in this matter would not depend on whether determinism is true, but instead on whether giving up these attitudes would lead to an improved life in society. Therefore, whether we can give up blame or not, determinism would not rule out the rationality of blame."

Even if one cannot give up blame, however, that does not mean that blame is justified. If one cannot help feeling regret over something, it does not follow that one is adequately justified in having this feeling. If one had absolutely no control over what one did, it would make no sense to regret. It also might be possible to give up blame, since a society in which wrongs are viewed as illnesses beyond one's control is conceivable. If it is possible to give up blame, the question of whether it would be in the interests of society to do so is important. The main question at issue, however, is whether determinism would provide the kind of excuse that would rule out blame. It may be in the interests of society not to regard determinism as an excuse, even if, in all fairness, it is one.

OBJECTIONS TO DETERMINISM

In contrast to Strawson, Nowell-Smith, and Duncan-Jones, C. A. Campbell maintains that determinism is incompatible with moral responsibility. To support his position, Campbell cites the testimony of those he regards as being at an advanced stage of moral reflection. Such individuals are aware that everything may be causally determined and have wondered whether people really have a choice about what they do. They agree that one must have a choice in order to be morally responsible. For them, a person is blameworthy only if he or she could have chosen otherwise without being caused to do so. Campbell is making an appeal to moral authority. For it to succeed, there must be a consensus among the authorities. The problem for his argument is that such a consensus is lacking.

Even if the moral authorities agreed with Campbell, there would still be the following basis for maintaining the compatibility of determinism and moral responsibility. Making choices without being caused to do so would seem to be a matter of chance. If such choices are matters of chance, they seem to be things that simply happen to turn out well or ill and therefore are not things for which people deserve praise or blame. Thus, making choices without being caused to make them would seem to rule out moral responsibility. Also, if not being causally determined rules out being morally responsible, then being morally responsible requires being causally determined, in the same way that if being nonperfect rules out being God, then being God requires being perfect. Thus, it seems that moral responsibility is compatible with causal determination. A major question for this argument is, "Can making a choice without being caused to make it be plausibly construed as something besides a matter of chance?"

Gregory P. Rich

FURTHER READING

Cane, Peter. *Responsibility in Law and Morality.* Portland, Oreg.: Hart, 2002.

Dworkin, Gerald, ed. *Determinism, Free Will, and Moral Responsibility.* Englewood Cliffs, N.J.: Prentice-Hall, 1970.

Fischer, John Martin, ed. *Moral Responsibility.* Ithaca, N.Y.: Cornell University Press, 1986.

French, Peter A., ed. *The Spectrum of Responsibility.* New York: St. Martin's Press, 1991.

Glover, Jonathan. *Responsibility*. London: Routledge & Kegan Paul, 1970.

Widerker, David, and Michael McKenna, eds. *Moral Responsibility and Alternative Possibilities: Essays on the Importance of Alternative Possibilities*. Burlington, Vt.: Ashgate, 2003.

Young, Robert. *Freedom, Responsibility, and God*. New York: Barnes & Noble, 1975.

SEE ALSO: Accountability; Determinism and freedom; Hume, David; Moral principles, rules, and imperatives; Moral realism; Moral-sense theories; Morality; Private vs. public morality; Responsibility.

Moral-sense theories

DEFINITION: Set of theories locating morality within a human sense or faculty

DATE: Developed during the eighteenth century

TYPE OF ETHICS: Theory of ethics

SIGNIFICANCE: Moral-sense theories assert that humans are innately moral and that morality is a function of this innate faculty or capacity. They oppose attempts to locate moral codes in transhuman sources such as objective moral facts or divine revelation.

The best summary of moral-sense theory as a philosophical movement can be found in the Preface to James Bonar's book *Moral Sense* (1930):

> The subject [of this book] is the rise, progress, and decline of a theory of moral philosophy which prevailed in this country [England] for the greater part of the eighteenth century.
>
> Founded by Shaftesbury, and built up by Hutcheson, it derived our moral perceptions from a special Moral Sense, interpreted on the analogy of the Five Bodily Senses.
>
> The book attempts an account of these two leaders, and of their principal followers and critics. The followers include the doubtful supporter David Hume [and] the critics Adam Smith and Immanuel Kant.
>
> The movement had its origin in reaction, its growth in the positive statements of its principals, and its decline as much in changing fashions of explanation as in actual criticism.

ORIGINS

By the end of the seventeenth century in England, conventional religious morality, with its imposed standards of behavior, had come into serious question for a number of reasons. First, the rise of Protestantism had introduced an antiauthoritarian note into much of the discussion of the subject. The rationalist-materialist philosopher Thomas Hobbes argued that the human organism was a mechanical object whose principal motivation was avoidance of pain and death, and that what passed for social morality was the calculating surrender of certain rights to avoid these unpleasantnesses; no positive source of morality existed. Second, Isaac Newton's mathematical demonstrations loosened God's hold on the physical universe, so to speak, as the motions of stars and planets and of microscopic particles were explained without recourse to divine intervention.

The bodies of animals and humans had been found by Stephen Hales and William Harvey, among others, to be governed by mechanical principles; perhaps human spirit and morality might find a similar explanation. Finally, John Locke's relentless questioning of sources of knowledge—how can one truly know anything when the connection between the senses and brain impressions is so tenuous (a problem that continues to exist even in the present state of knowledge: Does translation of diverse stimuli into chemical-electrical impulses mean that one knows the world about one?)—suggested that new explanations were in order for morality and much else.

THE MORAL-SENSE ANSWER

The man who proposed and named the "moral-sense" was Anthony Ashley Cooper, the third earl of Shaftesbury. Principally in reaction to Hobbes's idea of the innate selfishness of man, Shaftesbury pointed out that, far from being selfish, humankind must necessarily possess a capacity for moral cooperation, or a successful society could not exist. Moral behavior, therefore, is that which works for the public interest, an argument later expanded by Hume. Francis Hutcheson developed the idea of the moral sense as a sense, explaining that good and bad actions arouse in people feelings of pleasure or revulsion, and feelings are the results of a sense like any other. The moral sense mediates between moral knowledge and moral behavior, and it is the motivation for the latter. It is also innate, not the result of moral education. One could not, in fact, be morally educated if one's moral sense were not present to identify virtuous and benevolent actions.

CRITICISM AND DECLINE

Moral-sense theory was not without its critics even as it was being developed. At the lowest level, equating it with sight, hearing, and so forth was derided because there was no moral sense organ comparable with the eyes or ears. Hume answered this objection by sidestepping it: People know their senses through their characteristic perceptions, and it is clear that people perceive the morality of behavior. Other objections had to do with the nonuniversality of moral standards and the lack of symmetry between pleasure and virtuous action—that is, one recognizes a virtuous action by one's feeling of pleasure at it, but a feeling of pleasure by itself does not imply a virtuous action. In these matters Hume, as already noted, strengthened the argument that human morality is largely societal and the greatest good for the greatest number is therefore a primary moral principle.

Other moral faculties were proposed: Samuel Clarke and others held that moral perception is the province of reason or understanding, not feeling. Adam Smith argued for "sympathy," which today people tend to call "empathy," the recognition of the passions or affections of others that leads to benevolent consideration of their welfare. The cleric Joseph Butler chose conscience as his implement of moral discrimination. Finally, Kant, in his monumental summation of the philosophy of reason at the end of the eighteenth century, rendered the question moot by stating that no logical or scientific demonstration was possible for God, freedom, or immortality, but that these were nevertheless logical necessities in a system that contained morality. Thus, a special moral sense or faculty was not necessary and efforts to demonstrate one gradually fell off.

AFTERMATH

Although identification of a moral faculty or sense is no longer considered a valid philosophical preoccupation, a number of the concerns of the moral-sense thinkers have persisted. Among these are the identification of morality as social in nature and the positions that feeling has a legitimate place in a system of morals, that there must be general rules for judging conduct, and that one of these rules should be the greatest good for the greatest number.

Robert M. Hawthorne, Jr.

FURTHER READING

Bell, Michael. *Sentimentalism, Ethics, and the Culture of Feeling*. New York: Palgrave, 2000.

Bonar, James. *Moral Sense*. London: G. Allen & Unwin, 1930. Reprint. Bristol, England: Thoemmes Press, 1992.

Cooper, Anthony Ashley, earl of Shaftesbury. *Characteristicks of Men, Manners, Opinions, Times*. Edited by Philip Ayres. 2 vols. New York: Oxford University Press, 1999.

Klein, Lawrence E. *Shaftesbury and the Culture of Politeness: Moral Discourse and Cultural Politics in Early Eighteenth-Century England*. New York: Cambridge University Press, 1994.

Raphael, David Daiches. *British Moralists, 1650-1800*. 2 vols. Oxford, England: Clarendon Press, 1969.

_____. *Moral Judgement*. London: George Allen & Unwin, 1955.

_____. *The Moral Sense*. London: Oxford University Press, 1947.

Selby-Bigge, L. A., ed. *British Moralists; Being Selections from Writers Principally of the Eighteenth Century*. 2 vols. 1897. Reprint. New York: Dover, 1965.

Sprague, Elmer. "Moral Sense." In *The Encyclopedia of Philosophy*, edited by Paul Edwards. Vol. 5. New York: Macmillan, 1972.

Willey, Basil. *The English Moralists*. New York: W. W. Norton, 1964.

SEE ALSO: Butler, Joseph; Hobbes, Thomas; Hume, David; Kant, Immanuel; Kantian ethics; Moral equivalence; Moral principles, rules, and imperatives; Moral realism; Morality; Shaftesbury, third earl of.

Moral status of animals

DEFINITION: Presence or absence of innate moral worth in animals

TYPE OF ETHICS: Animal rights

SIGNIFICANCE: One's moral obligations to other people may be seen as arising from people's innate moral worth. If animals possess a moral status similar to that of human beings, then one may have similar obligations to them.

In many respects, nonhuman animals are treated as morally irrelevant. Humans eat them, conduct painful experiments on them, and use them for entertainment and sport; animals are seen as a part of the material world to be manipulated for the benefit of humankind. This attitude has its roots deep in Western culture. In Genesis 1:28, God says: "Be fruitful, multiply, and replenish the earth, and subdue it; and have dominion over the fish of the sea, and over the fowl of the air, and over every living thing that moveth upon the earth," and philosophers including Saint Thomas Aquinas and Immanuel Kant have echoed this attitude. John Locke, whose ideas helped to shape capitalist democracies, regarded the dominion over nature given to humankind by God as the source of human rights to property.

A number of arguments have been put forward against this "dominion position." The indirect-value argument holds that, although humans are the only morally relevant beings, other animals are essential for human well-being and are valuable as means to that end. A sophisticated version of this argument merges the need for human well-being with a recognition of the need for biodiversity. This view, however, gives animals only the most tenuous grip on moral relevance. If people found that the eradication of crocodiles had no effect on the integration and stability of the ecosystem, then crocodiles would suddenly become morally irrelevant. Furthermore, the worth of the animal in question still depends on its contribution to human welfare, and this misses an important part of what it means to have moral worth. No one wishes to be regarded merely as a means to an end, and any morality that regarded people as such would be fundamentally impoverished.

The second counterargument to the dominion position is utilitarian. Utilitarianism holds that the only morally relevant feature in any situation is the presence or absence of pain and pleasure, and that in moral calculations everyone's pain or pleasure counts for one and no one's for more than one. Concerning animals, Jeremy Bentham argued: "The question is not 'Can they reason?' nor 'Can they talk?' but 'Can they suffer?'" (*Principles of Morals and Legislation*, 1789).

THE UTILITARIAN ARGUMENT

The utilitarian argument is powerful and for many people has proved decisive. Trips to a slaughterhouse, factory farm, or cosmetics testing laboratory, the utilitarian's visual aids, have often proved more powerful than a thousand academic discussions.

The third common route out of the dominion position is via a consideration of moral rights. A strong case for this approach is made by Tom Regan in *The Case for Animal Rights* (1983). Regan argues that, contrary to utilitarianism, in which value is attached simply to the pains and pleasures that people experience, individuals, as agents, have inherent value. This value is independent of gender, race, age, birthplace, or abilities and is founded on the fact that all people are "experiencing subjects of life." Each person is "a conscious creature having an individual welfare that has importance to us whatever our usefulness to others."

Regan then sets out to show that animals are just as much experiencing subjects of life as are humans and therefore also have inherent value, by showing that the differences postulated between humans and other animals are not significant. The primary supposed difference is reason—people are said to be the only rational animals. Regan argues that many animals have reasoning capacity and that although some humans don't have that capacity (infants, the comatose, and so forth), it is not assumed that they are less morally valuable than other humans.

In response to the utilitarian or rights argument, some people have tried to argue that animals do not feel pain or have interests. This argument is clearly vacuous. The question is really whether that pain and those interests count in the moral calculus in the same way that human pain and interests count. Someone who accepts that animals feel pain and have interests but claims that these features do not count in the same way that they do for humans may be immune to both the utilitarian and rights arguments. To argue that one should accept the moral significance of the pain of the animal on grounds of the pain of the animal, or the moral significance of its being an experiencing subject of life on the grounds of its being an experiencing subject of life, is clearly circular. Simply to argue on grounds of consistency and relevant similarity will not work, since the idea that those similarities are relevant in this case has already been rejected. This difficulty is experienced by all those who try to expand the circle of moral concern. It faced those who tried to abolish slavery and to extend full consideration to women and minorities.

Despite their difficulties, these three arguments have proved to be powerful and persuasive. International concern for the welfare of animals has led to the founding of groups campaigning for the ethical treatment of animals. The latter part of the twentieth century, in particular, has seen an intense focus on human attitudes toward animals and other elements of the natural world.

Robert Halliday

FURTHER READING

Fox, Michael A. *The Case for Animal Experimentation: An Evolutionary and Ethical Perspective.* Berkeley: University of California Press, 1986.

Midgley, Mary. *Animals and Why They Matter.* Harmondsworth, England: Penguin Books, 1983.

Regan, Tom. *The Case for Animal Rights.* Berkeley: University of California Press, 1983.

Rodd, Rosemary. *Biology, Ethics, and Animals.* Oxford, England: Clarendon Press, 1990.

Scully, Matthew. *Dominion: The Power of Man, the Suffering of Animals, and the Call to Mercy.* New York: St. Martin's Press, 2002.

Singer, Peter. *Animal Liberation.* New York: Ecco, 2002.

SEE ALSO: Animal consciousness; Animal research; Animal rights; Endangered species; Environmental ethics; Nature, rights of.

Morality

DEFINITION: Set of personal and social values, rules, beliefs, laws, emotions, and ideologies collectively governing and arbitrating the rightness and wrongness of human actions

TYPE OF ETHICS: Theory of ethics

SIGNIFICANCE: The nature, basis, and meaning of morality, and even assertions that morality has a nature, a basis, or a meaning, are all the subjects of enduring controversy.

Although less inclusive than ethics, morality encompasses a wide variety of areas related to the field of ethics. Many but not all ethical theories come within the sphere of morality. Theories that lack a primary notion of obligation or duty, concern for the noninstrumental good of other persons, the demand for responsibility, and the recognition of the distinction between moral and nonmoral reasons cannot be accounted moral theories.

Morality includes within its scope far more than ethical theories, however, for it accounts for (or attempts to account for) the human mechanisms for the choice between good and evil. In addition, since there is a social aspect to human moral adherence, the structures of religion, law, and society are often examined from the perspective of the roles they play in promoting morality.

VARIETIES OF MORALITY

Personal codes of morality and societal structures supportive of morality are an obvious reality in the world, but the theory of ethical nihilism (amoralism) holds that morality is based upon illusions and that moral enforcement by, and the supportive structures of, society serve other purposes.

Friedrich Nietzsche denied the legitimacy of any objective or totalizing theories of morality, claiming instead that different values were appropriate for different people. Whether familiar with the original or not, Nietzsche seemed to have divined the truth of Hume's is/ought dichotomy and its implications for objective morality. Nietzsche claimed that the question left unanswered by all systems of morality was "Why be moral?"

Additionally, Nietzsche's hard determinism led him to the same conclusions about the impossibility of any objective moral order, with its necessary dependence upon moral responsibility. Interestingly, Nietzsche ascribed the institution of a singular unified morality to the attempt of the weak and inferior members of the herd to restrain the strong and superior members. In doing so, the German philosopher was only elaborating and making more sophisticated the arguments put forward by Thrasymachus in Plato's *Republic*.

Immanuel Kant's critical philosophy was, in Nietzsche's view, an attempt of the class of the clerisy to retain its influence and power by mystification and mysticism, and this was especially true of the moral philosophy surrounding the doctrines of the categorical imperative. Nietzsche may be credited with further developing the sociological critique of morality, but Karl Marx, the father of communism, competed with him in that enterprise. The Marxian socioeconomic analysis of morality may be seen as the mirror image of the Nietzschean.

Karl Marx interpreted all history as the history of class conflict; particular forms of morality represented reflections of the economic orders out of which they arose. Thus, in the Marxian view, morality in general, along with religion, arose from the interests of the upper classes in controlling the proletariat—impeding both general uprisings and lesser depredation against property.

RELIGION AND MORALITY

For many people, religion is inextricably associated with morality, and the taboo systems of primitive mythic religions bear a distant but discernible relationship to the more elaborate and sophisticated systems of philosophy-based morality. Fear of vengeance by gods, demons, or animistic spirits for trespasses against sacred taboos may seem to be a long way from the Kantian categorical imperative or John Stuart Mill's act utilitarianism, but many moral systems—including many of great complexity—rely at least in part upon the fear of supernatural reprisals for violations against the moral law.

In Christian natural law ethics, acts done for the love of God, without fear of punishment and without desire for reward, are the most meritorious—the very embodiment of pure *caritas*. Despite this judgment, Saint Thomas Aquinas enthusiastically endorsed the biblical maxim that "Fear of God is the beginning of wisdom." Indeed, even Immanuel Kant declared posthumous rewards and punishments to be necessary so that the virtuous person not be proved a fool.

Historically, the notion of after-death rewards and punishments seems to have developed slowly. Taboo violations were usually punished here and now, as in Greek mythology, where various wrongdoers were cursed and punished in this life by the gods and Furies. Hades—the underworld abode of the dead—was a place of universal assignment of the shades of the departed, where the good and bad alike enjoyed a fleshless, tepid existence, as portrayed in the eleventh book of Homer's *Odyssey*. Tartarus was a place of special torture for those who, like Tantalus and Sisyphus, had directly offended the gods, while certain heroes, such as Hercules, underwent apotheosis, becoming divine. Such extraordinary positive and negative sanctions were rare, however, and the ordinary mortal could expect neither.

In like manner, the divine justice recorded in the early books of the Old Testament seemed to stop at the grave. In both the Hebrew and the classical traditions, this incomplete vision of justice may finally have culminated in the supreme artistry of the Greek tragedy and the Hebrew Book of Job. The unique tension in both forms arose from the development of full moral codes in the absence of a full theodic system at those times in those cultures.

In the *Republic* and elsewhere in the Platonic dialogues, Socrates spoke of souls that went before the lords of the underworld to be judged and suitably rewarded or punished for moral decisions made during their lives. Likewise, in Vergil's *Aeneid* (reflective of the ideas of the late Roman Republic and the early Roman Empire), the afterworld has become much more a place of reward, punishment, and purgation, and in Christianity, of course, the dogmas of Heaven, Hell, and purgatory combined with the doctrine of an all-loving, all-just God to provide a more thoroughgoing theodic system that served to reinforce the laws of morality.

CONSCIENCE AND MORALITY

In addition to promoting the idea of external reinforcement of the moral law, Christianity gave great prominence to the notion of *conscientia* ("conscience"), an interior faculty of the soul that aided the intellect in the recognition of the good. Medieval commentators attempted to relate the ancient Greek notion of *synderesis* to conscience, but although there were similarities between the two concepts, they were scarcely synonymous.

With the concept of conscience, late Judaism and early Christianity made the moral law an intimate and essential part of the individual person rather than a purely external constraint only. Natural law philosophers had to face the fact that many cultures did not conform to their moral teachings. If conscience were a natural faculty of soul, how could it be possible for diverse cultures to take such remarkably divergent positions regarding moral law? One society condemns cannibalism, while another condones it. In one nation, sexual libertinage is a punishable offense, while in another it is an unsanctioned common practice. In one land, slavery is an accepted practice; in another, it is the gravest of evils.

Natural law ethicians traditionally answered this problem by maintaining the position that although the conscience was a natural faculty of the soul that was not a social construct by one's culture, one's conscience could be perverted so that it would endorse evil. Such a perversion of conscience could be one of two kinds: Persons attracted to an evil action often indulge in elaborate self-deception in order to pervert conscience in a culpable manner. The most common form of nonculpable perversion of conscience is by an invincible ignorance of the good that blinds a person to certain moral truths, often because of the training, education, and orientation provided by the person's culture.

Morality is often enforced by the external constraints of society as well as the influences of conscience and reason. The training and instruction of society—in the family, in the church, in formal education, and in the structuring of life experiences—reinforces or undermines the official moral codes promulgated by society.

MORALITY AND LAW

In regard to the legal codes of society, as viewed by natural law analysis, a distinction may be made between two types of relations to the moral law. First, not all moral law needs to be enforced by positive law. Even the most theocratic of societies usually leaves a space between moral law and positive law— not every vice is punishable by the state. Few societies, for example, punish gluttony or private drunkenness (if they permit the drinking of alcohol) or simple lying (as opposed to fraud, perjury, or libel).

Within the law, however, another distinction applies—that between intrinsic and extrinsic morality. Acts forbidden or commanded by intrinsic morality are held to be obligatory or, alternatively, morally wrong in themselves (*malum in se*). When positive law commands or forbids acts under intrinsic morality, it is merely recapitulating and sanctioning the moral law. Divine law, ecclesiastical law, and civil law all have aspects of intrinsic morality. God commands humankind not to steal, but in the natural law view, stealing is wrong in itself, apart from being forbidden in the Decalogue. In Roman Catholic ecclesiastic law, priests are forbidden to perform the sacrament of matrimony in order to link a brother and a sister in marriage, but incest is wrong apart from this rule of canon law, and the positive law only recog-

nizes and articulates this inherent evil. Finally, the laws of New York State outlaw murder, but the willful killing of the innocent is a moral wrong that is independent of any statute law against it.

EXTRINSIC MORALITY

In the case of extrinsic morality, the act commanded or proscribed by the positive law is morally neutral in itself but is made morally wrong or morally obligatory by being commanded by just authority. In divine law, God commands the observance of the sabbath, but a day of rest, let alone a particular day of rest, is scarcely obligatory by virtue of the moral law written in human nature. It is obligatory only because it is commanded by just authority. In Catholic ecclesiastical law, priests in the Latin Rite are forbidden to marry. This is simply a rule of the Church that could be altered at any time. A priest who violates this rule does wrong not in the act itself, but because the Church is presumed to have the right to make that morally neutral act impermissible (*malum prohibitum*). Finally, residents of the United Kingdom are instructed to drive on the left-hand side of roadways. A British subject who drives to the right is not directly violating a moral law but is doing wrong because he is defying the Queen-in-Parliament.

Extrinsic morality, furthermore, is held to have three clear relations to intrinsic morality. First, extrinsic morality can never contradict intrinsic morality but may only supplement it. Second, the purposes served by extrinsic moral commands are ones that ultimately would be endorsed by values inherent in intrinsic morality. To take an example, most traffic regulations are in the sphere of extrinsic morality, but saving innocent persons from death and injury and facilitating commerce relate to values of the intrinsic moral order. Finally, obedience to just authority is itself a principle of intrinsic morality.

Many of the particular moral rules and structures of society are of the extrinsic moral order, although tradition and long usage may lend them sacrosanctity in the eyes of the people.

MORALITY AND PSYCHOLOGY

The psychological mechanisms of moral choice have also been a central concern of morality from the earliest days of ethical theory. In less-complex theories, such as hedonism, the mechanism of choice could be described simply. An individual instinctually pursues pleasure, and when he or she makes a choice that results in pain rather than pleasure, or in less pleasure than that which an alternative choice would have produced, that can be explained by ignorance. Even in the theory of the Cyrenaic (or irrationalist) school of hedonism, which clearly maintained the subjectivity of values, errors about consequences of actions or about one's own anticipated reaction to those consequences were still the source of "evil" actions.

In Immanuel Kant's deontology, there was, to a great extent, the assumption that freedom of the will, which itself was made central by the principle that "'Ought' implies 'can,'" explained the selection of evil. In the *Groundwork for the Metaphysics of Morals* and the *Critique of Practical Reason*, Kant spoke as if there could be such a thing as freely chosen evil, but by the time of his last work, *Religion Within the Limits of Reason Alone*, he had clearly abandoned that position as untenable. He took the Judeo-Christian story of the Fall in Eden and applied his own analysis. Did the tempter's wiles, or weakness of will, or the promptings of the first parents' lower natures cause the choice of evil? From the Kantian perspective, the problem in each of these explanations was that if they forced the will, then the will would not seem to be free. If the tempter's temptation was irresistible, then how could the Fall have been the moral fault of Adam and Eve, since they could not have acted otherwise, but if the serpent's seduction was resistible, why was it not resisted?

Given the full implications of Kant's moral psychology, there could be no such thing as freely chosen evil, and Kant ended by denying the possibility of "devilish minds"—that is, minds that freely and knowingly select evil over the good.

THOMISTIC ETHICS

It is, perhaps, in Thomistic ethics that the most detailed and complex explanation of the agathokakological (containing good and evil) paradox appears. Thomas Aquinas explained that all human action arises from a desire (*appetitus*) in the subject. This desire aims at obtaining a good (*bonum*) that the subject lacks, as a state of being (*ens*). All action, therefore, seeks self-perfection (*perfectio*), which is only completely achieved in the state of blessedness in Heaven (*beatitudo*). For Thomism, problems arise because every good can be a personally held value (*bonum proprium*), but such personally held values

may be truly good (*verum bonum*) or may be only an apparent good (*apparens bonum*). For Thomism, evil consists in the pursuit of a relative, apparent good in place of a true, absolute good.

Despite the sophistication of the Thomistic analysis of moral choice, serious questions remain unanswered: Why would the subject select an apparent good over a true good? If that choice had been made deliberately, how could the decision to pursue the apparent good over the true good have been made? If such a pursuit had not been deliberately chosen, how could the subject be morally responsible for that pursuit?

Another aspect of morality concerns the relationship of interior intentionality to exterior moral action. The subjective and objective elements in moral and immoral actions are necessarily related in all serious theories of moral philosophy. In the primitive taboo ethic, the simple act alone was sufficient. Speak the words, eat the substance, touch the object, and divine retribution followed, no matter what the motivation for the act, no matter what the subject's knowledge of the nature of the act.

Among libertarians and determinists alike, there is a recognition of the need for an interior disposition to the objective moral or immoral act for that act to make its perpetrator culpable. Habituation of vicious or virtuous actions eliminates the direct intentionality before particular acts of vice or virtue, but it is generally held to meet the standards for moral responsibility because the general intention in the course of habituating the action is held to replace the specific intention that would normally be present before each particular act.

MORALITY AND LAW

Although much of the relationship between interior disposition and external act has been explored in moral philosophy, it has not all been sufficiently explained. Why do moral philosophy and the law alike regard the actual accomplishment of external, objective acts of evil as crucial to the degree of immorality or of criminality in the intention? It is clear that without the intention, killing is not murder, but the justification of the greater immorality and the greater criminality in murder over attempted murder is not so easily justified. If one clearly intended to kill an innocent person without justification and carried out the attempt, but the attempt failed through some technical flaw, how might one be said to be less blamewor-thy than if one had succeeded?

From the point of view of human positive law alone, the sharp distinction between the criminal act that has been completed and that which has been merely attempted may, in fact, rest upon no more than accident or chance. One attempted to shoot a man, but one's aim proved faulty, and the bullet missed. One's intention has been precisely the same as that of a successful murderer, and it is only a matter of moral luck that one is not guilty of murder, but only of attempted murder. Why should the fact that one is a bad shot excuse a degree of guilt for what one has both intended and attempted?

Since the civil law deals with the needs of society as well as the moral values of its citizens and since the law can only very imperfectly scan the intentions of the human heart, it may well be understandable that the law of the state differentiates between crimes at-tempted and crimes completed, but why should the moral order make such a distinction? Intuitively, such a distinction seems to be reasonable, but no carefully articulated justification of such a distinc-tion has been successfully made.

Morality is at the core of the ethical sciences, and the most interesting problems in ethics are concen-trated in the sphere of morality. The nature of obliga-tion, the logic and mechanism of moral choice, and the relationship of intentionality to the objective fac-tor in the blameworthiness and praiseworthiness of moral actions are among the most challenging areas for further intellectual investigation.

Patrick M. O'Neil

FURTHER READING

Aristotle. *Nicomachean Ethics.* Translated and ed-ited by Roger Crisp. New York: Cambridge Uni-versity Press, 2000. The work demonstrates how all facets of human life relate to ethical choices.

Kant, Immanuel. *Groundwork for the Metaphysics of Morals.* Edited and translated by Allen W. Wood. New Haven, Conn.: Yale University Press, 2002. The good will (proper moral intention to obey the moral law) is seen as the source of all ethical good.

_____. *Religion Within the Limits of Reason Alone.* Translated by Theodore M. Greene and Hoyt H. Hudson. New York: Harper, 1960. Kant explores the possibility of freely chosen evil.

Katz, Leo. *Bad Acts and Guilty Minds: Conundrums of the Criminal Law.* Chicago: University of Chi-cago Press, 1987. The relation of interior inten-tion to outward action is explored.

Nietzsche, Friedrich. *On the Genealogy of Morals.* Edited and translated by Walter Kaufmann. New York: Vintage Books, 1967. Nietzsche argues against morality, understood as a universalizing system in which everyone must hold and abide by the same values. He defends more localized and nontotalizing sets of values. He traces the creation of a single totalizing morality back to the advent of the nation-state.

Plato. *The Collected Dialogues of Plato.* Edited by Edith Hamilton and Huntington Cairns. 1961. Reprint. Princeton, N.J.: Princeton University Press, 1984. The *Republic*, especially, deals with the role of social institutions in reinforcing moral values.

Thomas Aquinas, Saint. *The Summa Theologica.* Translated by Laurence Shapcote. 2d ed. 2 vols. Chicago: Encyclopaedia Britannica, 1990. Saint Thomas gives a detailed account of the moral psy-chology of the choice of good and evil.

SEE ALSO: Ethics/morality distinction; Good, the; In-trinsic good; Moral equivalence; Moral principles, rules, and imperatives; Moral realism; Moral respon-sibility; Natural law; Private vs. public morality; Right and wrong; Universalizability.

Moses

IDENTIFICATION: Ancient Hebrew leader
BORN: c. 1300 B.C.E., near Memphis, Egypt
DIED: c. 1200 B.C.E., place unknown
TYPE OF ETHICS: Religious ethics
SIGNIFICANCE: Moses delivered the Hebrews from Egyptian slavery, introduced the concept of ethi-cal monotheism, and created or transmitted the first legal code to be based on the idea of a divine covenant. He is traditionally regarded as the au-thor of the Torah.

Moses is best remembered for delivering the Hebrew people from Egyptian slavery and subsequently pro-viding them with a legal code that he claimed he received from God. Questions of authenticity, dates, and other issues raised by critical scholarship are beyond this article's scope. Rather, it is assumed here that the books of Genesis, Exodus, Leviticus, Numbers, and Deuteronomy, sometimes referred to as "The Laws of Moses," or simply the Torah (or Pentateuch), constitute a distinct body of literature. The latter four volumes contain specific directives that the ancient Hebrews believed to be a divinely sanctioned basis for their legal, political, religious, and social systems.

DIVISIONS WITHIN THE LAW

There are three primary divisions within the Hebrew law. The first division is the Decalogue, or Ten Commandments (Exod. 20:1-17; Deut. 5:1-21). The first four commandments define the proper attitude that one should exhibit toward God. Commandments five and ten establish the sanctity of the family, while commandments six through nine establish individual rights. Each commandment is a moral injunction aimed at establishing a code of right conduct.

Civil legislation marks the second division in Moses' law. These laws focus mainly on Hebrew interpersonal relationships. For example, between Exodus 20:18 and Exodus 23:33 there are more than seventy specific statements delineating between accidental and premeditated acts. Hebrew civil law usually determined the appropriate compensation that one should receive in the event of property loss.

The third division in Moses' law involved ceremony (Exod. 24-34; Lev.). This was perhaps the most far-reaching element of the Hebrew legal code. Whereas the civil law concerned individual relationships, the ceremonial law focused on the relationship between God and humanity. These laws outlined every facet of Hebrew worship, ranging from the construction of a suitable place of worship to the role that priests played both in religious ritual and society in general. The ceremonial law also outlined an elaborate system of offerings that Hebrews were commanded to offer to God. In some cases, these offerings were animal sacrifices; in others, grain offerings. In any event, the ceremonial law was designed to keep the Hebrews' religion pure and free from pagan influence. Moreover, since Moses described God both as holy and as expecting the Hebrews also to be holy, the ceremonial law provided a means whereby they could express a wide variety of spiritual needs, ranging from ceremonial cleansing from sin to joy and thanksgiving.

OLD TESTAMENT ETHICS

Ancient legal codes, most notably the Babylonian Code of Hammurabi, addressed legal issues on a case-by-case basis and emphasized retribution—"an eye for an eye." Certain features of the Mosaic code also called for retribution, but Moses' Law was more far-reaching. In *Toward Old Testament Ethics*, Walter C. Kaiser, Jr., enumerated characteristics of Old Testament ethics. First, they were personal. Since God used himself as the standard of absolute righteousness, he expected his people to obey the law. Second, Old Testament ethics were theistic. In addition to believing that God had given the law to Moses personally, the Hebrews also believed that the law reflected God's character. Third, Old Testament ethics were internal. Moses indicated that God's law was not merely an external checklist. Rather, God was concerned about the Hebrew's internal spiritual condition. Additionally, these ethics were future oriented.

Throughout the Old Testament, biblical writers indicate that a Messiah will ultimately fulfill the law perfectly. Hence, Old Testament ethics are rooted in hope. Jesus claimed to fulfill all requirements of the law (Matt. 5:17-18). Other New Testament writers likewise claimed that Jesus was the fulfillment of the law (Rom. 10:4; Gal. 3:24). Finally, Old Testament ethics are universal. Even though Moses delivered the law to the Hebrews, it is understood that God's standard of holiness was applicable to all nations (see Gen. 13:13, 18:25).

SIGNIFICANCE

Moses' significance to ethics is that he introduced ethical monotheism. If the Hebrews were to be God's people, Moses explained, they were obligated to obey God's commandments. Yet the Hebrews were not to keep Moses' law simply to win God's favor. Rather, Moses said that God was infinitely holy and, hence, the law was a standard of personal rectitude. Moreover, since the Hebrews saw God as infinitely good, the law was good because God himself had given it. Moses, therefore, revealed God as an ethicist. Additionally, Moses' law revealed a God who was genuinely interested in humanity. True, he could be offended, but he also provided forgiveness. He likewise promised to bless the Hebrews and go with them wherever they went. This concept of a holy God who placed just expectations upon people and cared about them personally laid the foundation for the ethics of the Western world.

Keith Harper

FURTHER READING

Freud, Sigmund. *Moses and Monotheism*. Translated and edited by James Strachey. Corr. ed. London: Hogarth Press, 1974.

Kaiser, Walter C., Jr. *Toward Old Testament Ethics*. Grand Rapids, Mich.: Zondervan, 1983.

Kirsch, Jonathan. *Moses: A Life*. New York: Ballantine Books, 1998.

Maston, Thomas Bufford. *Biblical Ethics: A Guide to the Ethical Message of Scriptures from Genesis through Revelation*. Macon, Ga.: Mercer University Press, 1982.

Muilenburg, James. *An Eye for an Eye: The Place of Old Testament Ethics Today*. Downers Grove, Ill.: InterVarsity Press, 1983.

_____. "Old Testament Ethics." In *A Dictionary of Christian Ethics*, edited by John Macquarrie. London: SCM Press, 1967.

Wright, Christopher J. H. *Living as the People of God: The Relevance of Old Testament Ethics*. Leicester, England: InterVarsity Press, 1983.

SEE ALSO: Christian ethics; Ethical monotheism; Hammurabi's code; Jewish ethics; Ten Commandments; Torah.

Motion picture ratings systems

DEFINITION: Formal systems for classifying films based on content which may be deemed inappropriate for children, detrimental to society, or objectionable on moral or religious grounds

TYPE OF ETHICS: Arts and censorship

SIGNIFICANCE: Ratings systems may be created by third-party organizations independently of film studios, or they may be self-regulatory systems instituted by the studios themselves. In the latter case, they raise issues regarding the boundaries between voluntary self-regulation and institutionally imposed censorship.

The motion picture industry of the United States of America has long attempted to forestall government controls by observing self-imposed regulations. Originally, those regulations were proscriptive, intended to make a preponderance of exhibited films palatable to general audiences, but subsequent policy, using ratings to influence public exposure, enabled a wider range of material to appear in major releases. Regulatory systems have been established elsewhere, but the varying U.S. approaches provide excellent studies in the application of standards.

State and local government attempts to censor film date back to a 1907 Chicago ordinance that was upheld by Illinois's supreme court in 1909. The potential impact of such rulings was evident in the proliferation of state and local censor boards as well as a 1915 U.S. Supreme Court determination that cinema was not protected under the First Amendment. With the goal of curtailing widespread government censorship, from 1909 to 1921 the National Board of Censorship assumed some responsibility for the prerelease evaluation of film content. This citizens' group, supported by the film industry, was the nation's first voluntary censorship body.

In 1922, the major Hollywood studios appointed Will Hays the head of their newly formed association, the Motion Picture Producers and Distributors of America (MPPDA). Created to maintain industry sovereignty, the MPPDA in 1934 enacted a code of ethics known as the Production Code, or "Hays Code." Arising out of the Mae West era, the code combined lofty statements of principle ("No picture shall be produced which will lower the moral standards of those who see it") with a battery of specific regulations (for example, "*Methods of Crime* should not be explicitly presented" and "The treatment of bedrooms must be governed by good taste and delicacy").

THE RATINGS

Two major ratings systems originated during this period. In 1933, the Film Board of National Organizations formulated the MPPDA-supported Green Sheet, which used age and educational criteria to classify films as *A* (Adult), *MY* (Mature Young People), *Y* (Young People), *GA* (General Audience), *C* (Children, unaccompanied), or a combination of those ratings. The following year, a committee of bishops formed the influential Legion of Decency, which rated movies on a scale from *A-I* (morally unobjectionable for general audiences) to *C* (condemned).

Movies without the Production Code Seal were effectively banned from theaters. Code stipulations were, however, periodically amended and perennially subject to administrative give and take (intense lobbying won a place for Rhett Butler's "forbidden" last word in 1939's *Gone with the Wind*). The Code remained in place during the 1940's, as Eric Johnston replaced Hays, the MPPDA became the Motion Picture Association of America (MPAA), and antitrust decisions forced studios to sell their theaters.

After the Supreme Court overturned its 1915 ruling in 1952, the newly opened theater market exhibited not only unapproved foreign features but also domestic productions such as *The Moon Is Blue* (1953),

Dustin Hoffman (left) and Jon Voight in Midnight Cowboy, *the first major motion picture to receive an X rating.* (Museum of Modern Art, Film Stills Archive)

which had been denied the Seal for its treatment of virginity. The commercial viability of such films, together with the precedent-setting releases of *Son of Sinbad* (1955) and *Baby Doll* (1956)—the first C films to receive the Seal—heralded further shifts in standard application. Additional Court decisions and jolting thrillers such as *Psycho* (1960) and *Cape Fear* (1962) built momentum for extensive Code revision in 1966, when Jack Valenti became the third MPAA president. Early frustrations with language in *Who's Afraid of Virginia Woolf* (1966) and nudity in *Blow-Up* (1966) influenced his replacement of proscription with a voluntary film rating system in 1968.

Officially intended to place responsibility for children's moviegoing with parents and guardians, the new system reflected contemporaneous rulings on children and obscenity. Overseen by the MPAA, the National Association of Theatre Owners (NATO), and the International Film Importers and Distributors of America, it classified submitted films according to their appropriateness for one of four possible audience groups. G for General Audiences, M for Mature Audiences (parental guidance suggested), and R for Restricted Audiences were trademarked; *X* (no one under 17 admitted), adopted at the urging of NATO, was not. M, which parents misinterpreted as being sterner than *R*, was initially replaced with *GP* (implying a "General Audience" film for which "Parental Guidance" was suggested) and later with *PG*. In 1984, the young audience categories were expanded to include *PG-13*.

ADULT FILMS

Adult film classification also changed. At first, some *X* features won significant mainstream interest. Soon, however, the rating became identified with pornography, to which it was frequently self-applied. Excluding the young audience market by definition, the rating also precluded advertising in most outlets, leading many major producers to edit movies from *X* to *R*. (Some features, such as *Midnight Cowboy*, 1969, eventually made that transition without cutting.) Ongoing debate over film tailoring and the need for another "adults only" category sparked the creation of the MPAA's federally registered certification mark, *NC-17*, first assigned to *Henry and June* (1990). During the early 1990's, the MPAA also began issuing explanations of specific ratings to theaters and critics.

Although criticized for representing an abandonment of moral and ethical responsibility, the shift from proscription to ratings has been praised for enabling major producers to exercise greater freedom of expression. Despite such increased license, the questions of the ratings system constituting a form of self-censorship remained.

Because ratings greatly influence a project's viability, films are not simply rated after completion; throughout the creative process there may be ratings-oriented interplay involving filmmakers, the Rating Board, and occasionally (after the code has been assigned) the Appeals Board. This process may receive wide public attention, often dwelling on potentially offensive material and sometimes leading to the creation of alternate versions aimed at different markets. Naturally, content not recognized as potentially offensive may be perceived as implicitly approved. The MPAA uses regular polling to establish that its standards represent the views of a majority of citizens.

Besides advising parents and guardians about film content, the ratings system, which encompasses trailers and film advertising, requires the cooperation of theater owners. At the box office, administrators discriminate according to age and appearance (sometimes requiring potential consumers to identify themselves by birth date), as well as geographic location. This approach reinforces and establishes taboos and hierarchies related to age, appearance, maturity, and media.

The ratings system has been endorsed by the Video Software Dealers Association. Similar systems of self-regulation have been adopted or proposed for recording, video games, and television programming.

David Marc Fischer

FURTHER READING

Bernstein, Matthew, ed. *Controlling Hollywood: Censorship and Regulation in the Studio Era*. New Brunswick, N.J.: Rutgers University Press, 1999.

De Grazia, Edward, and Roger K. Newman. *Banned Films*. New York: R. R. Bowker, 1982.

Farber, Stephen. *The Movie Rating Game*. Washington, D.C.: Public Affairs Press, 1972.

Leff, Leonard J., and Jerold L. Simmons. *The Dame in the Kimono*. New York: Grove Weidenfeld, 1990.

Randall, Richard S. *Censorship of the Movies*. Madison: University of Wisconsin Press, 1968.

Schumach, Murray. *The Face on the Cutting Room Floor*. New York: William Morrow, 1964.

SEE ALSO: Art; Art and public policy; Censorship; Children's television; Consistency; Family values; First Amendment; Freedom of expression; Language; Pornography; Self-regulation.

Motivation

DEFINITION: Purpose behind an action
TYPE OF ETHICS: Theory of ethics
SIGNIFICANCE: Motivation is important to virtue-based ethics and other systems that judge actions according to their intent. It is irrelevant to consequentialist theories, which attend only to the effects of one's actions. Some models of behavior hold that human action is overdetermined, that is, that there are so many separate motives behind an action that it is impossible to know or evaluate them all.

Ethics deals with determining what is good and bad and with moral principles and values. These are all aspects of behavior. In order for behavior to occur, a person must be motivated. Without motivation, the person would do virtually nothing. Driven to action by a motive, however, the person engages in behavior that persists until the motive is satisfied. The word "motive" derives from the Latin *movere*, meaning "to move."

One of the prevailing issues of motivation is the nature of human motives and thus the nature of human nature. As Charles N. Cofer and Mortimer H. Apley have stated the issue in *Motivation: Theory and Research* (1964):

Is man—unfettered and untarnished by the experiences and constraints of society—essentially good, altruistic, brotherly, creative, peace loving? Or, alternatively, is he essentially evil, egocentric, aggressive, competitive, warlike, requiring the constraints of society in order to keep him from destroying his fellows and himself?

EARLY CONCEPTIONS

In Aristotelian ethics, as in ethics generally, the issue concerned the appropriate direction of desire and action (that is, motivation). Good or right action was a product of reason and a strong will. Practicing performing good or just acts caused those acts to become pleasurable and habitual, and the will then chose freely that which knowledge determined to be good. Through the ensuing centuries, this belief that the will controlled the animal side of humanity and guided it toward right virtue and salvation persisted. The philosopher Immanuel Kant believed that good actions originated from a sense of duty or moral law. The will is motivated to choose a course of good action in the light of moral law.

A different view was elaborated during the mid-nineteenth century by the philosopher Arthur Schopenhauer. Will was viewed as a basic force or striving and was evil. The impulses of the will brought no pleasure, only pain. Gratification of the will's impulses did not produce happiness, only satiety.

These philosophical views have been carried into modern times by psychology. "Will" has been replaced by "motivation." The issue of whether human motivation is good or evil is addressed by three major theoretical systems, each of which provides a different answer: behavioral theory, psychodynamic theory, and humanistic theory.

BEHAVIORAL THEORY

Behaviorism was founded by John B. Watson in 1913. Behaviorists viewed motives as internal stimuli that persist and dominate behavior until the person reacts to satisfy the motive. Human motives are, however, neither good nor evil. Good and evil depend on conditioning provided by the environment. One of Watson's most famous (and outrageous) statements says: "Give me a dozen healthy infants, well formed, and my own specified world to bring them up in and I'll guarantee to take any one at random and train him to become any type of specialist I might select—doctor, lawyer, artist, merchant-chief and, yes, even beggar-man and thief, regardless of his talents, penchants, tendencies, abilities, vocations, and race of his ancestors." Although modern behaviorists are

no longer such extreme environmental determinists, they would agree with Watson that ethics is primarily a matter of environmental conditioning.

PSYCHODYNAMIC THEORY

To Sigmund Freud, the true purpose of life lay in the satisfaction of its innate motives. These motives derive from bodily needs, produce tension, and cause all activity. The two classes of motives are the life-sustaining motives (sex, hunger, and so forth) and the death or destructive motives (cruelty, sadism, violence, destruction, and murder).

The life and death motives arise from the oldest and most primitive part of the mutual apparatus: the id. The id is not conscious of reality; it is illogical and irrational, has no values and no concept of good or evil, has no morality, and continually seeks instant discharge and pleasure. In part, the functions of the other two divisions of the mental apparatus, the ego and the superego, are to control, regulate, and contain the id in a manner consistent with the demands of external reality. Acts of destruction and aggression, such as war, represent a failure to regulate and control the expression of the death motive.

The idea that the id knows no values and has no sense of good, evil, or morality is similar to the behavioral view of neutrality about the nature of human nature. Psychodynamic theory, however, is essentially a pessimistic view of human nature. The true purpose of life is not some lofty or idealistic state, but the satisfaction of the motives of the id in a manner consistent with maintaining civilized society. World War I and other widespread acts of death and destruction convinced Freud of the primacy of aggression and that the ego and superego often lose the battle to effectively control and regulate it.

HUMANISTIC THEORY

According to the clinical psychologist Carl Rogers, "The basic nature of human beings when functioning fully is constructive, trustworthy, forward-looking, good and capable of perfection." In 1956, John Adelson stated: "Man is born without sin, aspiring to goodness, and capable of perfection; human evil is exogenous, the betrayal of man's nature by cruel circumstance." This motive of full functioning or self-actualization is part of an inherent process called syntropy, a movement toward growth, expansion, and realization of the self.

That self-actualization is difficult to achieve is a result of societal constraints and the false goals set by society. Society often rejects, punishes, ridicules, or threatens nonactualized individuals, rather than helping them.

EVIDENCE

The nature of human nature has been debated since antiquity. Since humans are capable of both good and evil behaviors and amply exhibit both types, and since it is conceptually and ethically impossible to conduct an appropriate experiment to resolve the issue, the nature of human motivation will no doubt continue to be debated for many more centuries.

Laurence Miller

FURTHER READING

Care, Norman S. *Decent People*. Lanham, Md.: Rowman & Littlefield, 2000.

Cofer, Charles N., and Mortimer H. Appley. *Motivation: Theory and Research*. New York: Wiley, 1964.

Freud, Sigmund. *Beyond the Pleasure Principle*. Translated and edited by James Strachey. New York: Norton, 1989.

_____. *New Introductory Lectures on Psychoanalysis*. Translated and edited by James Strachey. New York: W. W. Norton, 1965.

Hampden-Turner, Charles. *Maps of the Mind*. New York: Macmillan, 1981.

Kant, Immanuel. *Groundwork for the Metaphysics of Morals*. Edited and translated by Allen W. Wood. New Haven, Conn.: Yale University Press, 2002.

Maslow, Abraham H. *Toward a Psychology of Being*. 2d ed. Princeton, N.J.: Van Nostrand, 1968.

Skinner, Burrhus F. *The Shaping of a Behaviorist*. New York: Knopf, 1979.

SEE ALSO: Behaviorism; Consequentialism; Freud, Sigmund; Intention; Mean/ends distinction; Motivation; Psychology.

Mozi

IDENTIFICATION: Ancient Chinese philosopher
BORN: c. 470 B.C.E., China
DIED: c. 391 B.C.E., China
TYPE OF ETHICS: Religious ethics
SIGNIFICANCE: The founder of the Mohist school of philosophy, Mozi (Mo Tzu in Wade-Giles spelling) maintained that wars, social disasters, and similar forms of chaos resulted because people did not love one another. He was alone among the Chinese philosophers of his day in not only condemning acts that were harmful to others but also calling on people to care for others as they cared for themselves and their own families.

Mozi lived during the fifth and fourth centuries B.C.E., an era of Chinese history known as the period of the "hundred philosophers" for its flowering of philosophical and religious thought. According to tradition, Mozi came from a declined noble family, served as an official of the kingdom of Sung, and studied the Chinese classics, including the writings of Confucius. Confucian thought maintained that social order could only be achieved if mutual responsibilities were fulfilled in a clearly defined hierarchical system.

Some sources say that although Mozi was born into a clan of the kingdom of Song, his family later emigrated to the kingdom of Lu, home of Confucius. It is said that here Mozi grew increasingly hostile to the Confucian classism and political conflicts of his day and abandoned Confucian thinking to establish the Mohist school, a system of thought based on principles described in the *Book of Mozi*. In this work, Mozi calls for a new, egalitarian society based on a sense of mutual aid and commitment to the common good.

THE BOOK OF MOZI

The collection of philosophical essays bearing Mozi's name was probably compiled by his disciples in the generations after his death. In this document, Mozi condemned the desires for profit, luxury, and wealth as the societal ills of his day. He also condemned the corresponding manifestations of these desires, including the practice of offensive warfare, the development of military power, the use of rituals, the pursuit of entertainment, and the cultivation of music. He considered offensive warfare to be mere thievery and supported strong defensive preparations only to prevent it. He deemed music, entertainment, and rituals to be costly activities of the wealthy that detracted from the material well-being of the poorer classes. As remedies for these desires and the conflicts they produced, Mozi championed frugality, strict respect for laws, advancement of people based on performance instead of class, and fear of the gods and spirits. The coordinating mechanism for these was the principle of universal love, of loving all others equally.

The religious characteristic of Mozi's thinking derived from his admonitions concerning the Will of Heaven and a belief in spirits. Mozi maintained that Heaven rewarded those who conducted themselves in a manner consistent with universal love—loving others as themselves and engaging in activities that benefited everyone. He believed that Heaven punished the evildoers—especially those who had been charged with the job of ruling others. He opposed fatalism, insisting that through work and honorable hardship, order could be achieved.

Mozi held that knowledge came through the experiences of the senses. In judging the validity of knowledge, he applied three criteria: the basis of the knowledge itself, its potential for verification, and its utility.

THE MOHISTS

During the last two hundred years before the unification of China (221 B.C.E.) Mohism attracted numerous converts. Its philosophy of defensive warfare, coupled with the belief that promotion should be based on merit rather than social status, led to the growth of a sect whose behavior was characterized by a soldierly discipline. Probably recruited from among the knights for hire or petty aristocrats, Mohists sold their services as specialists in defensive warfare. When a leader planned to invade or annex another territory, Mohists argued eloquently and passionately against it. If the leader could not be dissuaded, they joined the opposite side, defending the attacked kingdom. Hence, Mohists became known as both noteworthy orators and skillful defensive soldiers. Their obedience to the law and unswerving loyalty were also legendary, for they would even kill their own sons if they had committed crimes requiring the death penalty.

LEGACY OF MOHISM

The philosophy of Mozi lost ground after the onset of China's imperial period in the third century B.C.E. Mohism maintained that wars were unjust because they interfered with the survival of the agricultural classes by interrupting planting and harvesting as well as by destroying fields. Although the assessment of the impact of war on farmers was accurate, the conclusion that war was to be avoided was incompatible with the objectives of early imperial Chinese leaders, who saw territorial expansion as a means of obtaining more power and resources. Mozi's admonition against preferential treatment based on status was also distasteful to the increasingly hierarchical society that attended imperial rule. Consequently, the Mohist sect declined after the third century B.C.E. Its unique contribution to Chinese ethical thought lies in advocating universal love as the operative method for ordering society and avoiding chaos and harm.

Margaret B. Denning

FURTHER READING

Chan, Wing Tsit. *A Source Book in Chinese Philosophy.* Princeton, N.J.: Princeton University Press, 1973.

Fung Yu-lan. *A History of Chinese Philosophy.* Vol. 1. Translated by Derk Bodde. Princeton, N.J.: Princeton University Press, 1953.

Geaney, Jane. *On the Epistemology of the Senses in Early Chinese Thought.* Honolulu: University of Hawaii Press, 2002.

Gotshalk, Richard. *The Beginnings of Philosophy in China.* Lanham, Md.: University Press of America, 1999.

Lowe, Scott. *Mo Tzu's Religious Blueprint for a Chinese Utopia: The Will and the Way.* Lewiston, N.Y.: E. Mellen Press, 1992.

Mo Di. *Basic Writings.* Translated by Burton Watson. New York: Columbia University Press, 2003.

_____. *The Ethical and Political Works of Motse.* Translated by Yi-pao Mei. Westport, Conn.: Hyperion Press, 1973.

SEE ALSO: *Art of War, The*; Confucian ethics; Confucius; Egalitarianism; Fatalism; Military ethics; Pragmatism.

Muḥammad

IDENTIFICATION: Founder and Prophet of Islam and author of the Qurʾān

BORN: c. 570, Mecca, Arabia (now in Saudi Arabia)

DIED: June 8, 632, Medina, Arabia (now in Saudi Arabia)

TYPE OF ETHICS: Religious ethics

SIGNIFICANCE: Muslims believe that Muḥammad received the visions from Allah that constitute the Qurʾān, the scripture of Islam, and that his life served as a model for proper living.

Born in Mecca, Muḥammad was orphaned at age six. After being reared by his grandfather and an uncle, he became a caravan driver. At twenty-five he married Khadīja, a wealthy widow who bore him two sons who died in infancy and four daughters. Around the age of forty, Muḥammad received the first of the many revelations that would become the Qurʾān. The monotheism of Muḥammad's new religion created friction with the polytheistic Meccans, leading to his famous flight, or *hijra*, to Medina in 622.

Medina's citizens pledged to follow Muḥammad both politically and religiously, a connection between religion and the state that became the norm for traditional Muslims. Military conflicts between Medina and Mecca were fought from 624 to 630, ending in victory for Muḥammad. After becoming Mecca's political ruler, he cleansed Mecca of its idols to various gods and resumed his annual pilgrimages, making his final trip in 632.

The basic principles taught Muḥammad are largely contained in the Five Pillars, one of which directly concerns ethical behavior. Muḥammad taught that his followers should give alms of two types: obligatory assistance to the poor and charity beyond that. Such almsgiving was based on idea that the more one owns, the more one should give.

Muḥammad has occasionally been criticized, by Westerners especially, for taking several wives after the death of Khadīja, and allowing his followers to take as many as four. During his time, however, when women outnumbered men and had few rights, polygamy may have been the best way to ensure the care of widows and others who might otherwise have gone unmarried.

Accountability for ethical decisions may presuppose freedom to choose among more or less equal alternatives. Muslims have nevertheless often been deterministic and fatalistic. Muḥammad was less so, or not consistently so. He spoke on determinism in at least three different ways in the Qurʾān. Sura 18:28 says that God allows people to believe or disbelieve as they wish. By contrast, Sura 35:9 says that God leads astray or guides correctly whomever God wishes. Sura 2: 24-25, however, may mediate between these two views by saying that God leads astray only those who would go wrong anyway.

Much of Muḥammad's ethical teachings seems to have the pragmatic end of preserving and expanding his community and defending it from attack. Consequently, he permitted plunder, revenge, and war at the collective level and expected obedience to authority.

Paul L. Redditt

Muḥammad's Place in Islam

It is incorrect to say that Muḥammad is "worshipped" in Islam: Muslims worship only God (Allah). Muḥammad and his family are, however, deeply revered. Pilgrimage to Muḥammad's mausoleum in Medina is common, and the image of Muḥammad as merciful intercessor on behalf of the faithful emerged early in the history of Islam. Popular songs and poetry celebrate Muḥammad's life, and numerous stories of miracles have grown up around his biography. Intellectuals who are skeptical of many of the popular tales nevertheless have profound respect for the Prophet and his guidance of the Muslim community.

Muḥammad's life often has been interpreted in Sufism as having mystical and allegorical meaning. The *Isrāʾ* and *Miʿrāj* (the traditions of Muḥammad's nocturnal tours through Hell and through Paradise, respectively), in particular, have been fecund sources of Sufi literature, in which those journeys are seen as allegories representing the journey of the soul from worldly attachments, along the path of spiritual development, to the state of final mystical bliss. The Prophet is also seen by some philosophers, as having an eternal essence that exemplifies Divine Reason and is manifested in the Prophet's temporal life and teachings.

FURTHER READING

Armstrong, Karen. *Muhammad: A Biography of the Prophet.* San Francisco: HarperSanFrancisco, 1992.

Cragg, Kenneth. *Muhammad in the Qur'an: The Task and the Text.* London: Melisende, 2001.

Dashti, Ali. *Twenty Three Years: A Study of the Prophetic Career of Muhammad.* Translated by F. R. C. Bagley. London: Allen & Unwin, 1985.

Rogerson, Barnaby. *The Prophet Muhammad.* London: Little, Brown, 2003.

Schimmel, Annemarie. *And Muhammad Is His Messenger: The Veneration of the Prophet in Islamic Piety.* Chapel Hill: University of North Carolina Press, 1985.

SEE ALSO: ʿAlī ibn Abī Ṭālib; Fāṭima; *Ḥadīth*; Holy war; Islamic ethics; Qurʾān; Revelation; Sharīʿa; Sufism.

Muir, John

IDENTIFICATION: Scottish American naturalist
BORN: April 21, 1838, Dunbar, Scotland
DIED: December 24, 1914, Los Angeles, California
TYPE OF ETHICS: Environmental ethics
SIGNIFICANCE: Muir lobbied for the establishment of Yosemite, Sequoia, and General Grant National Parks; was a founder of the Sierra Club; and increased general public interest in preservationism.

John Muir moved to a Wisconsin homestead when he was eleven and attended the University of Wisconsin from 1858 to 1863. After a year of farming while waiting for a draft call, he decamped to stay in Canada from 1863 to 1864. In 1867, he began a full-time career in nature study, starting with a projected thousand-mile walk to the Gulf of Mexico on his way to South America. Frustrated by serious illness, he

John Muir. (Library of Congress)

went to California and lived in the Yosemite Valley for five years. In 1873, he began a full-time career as a nature writer and preservationist, spending summers hiking and observing natural phenomena in the mountains.

In 1889, Muir began writing and lobbying to preserve Yosemite Valley as a National Park. In 1896, as one of its founders, he became the first president of the Sierra Club; he remained in that position until 1914. He was preeminent in publicity and lobbying (1905-1913) against San Francisco's Hetch Hetchy water project. Although unsuccessful, this effort broadcast the preservationist ethic nationwide. Muir's contributions to glaciology and geomorphology give him minor scientific status. He published more than 500 articles and essays, many of which were based on his mountaineering journals. His books include *Mountains of California* (1894), *My First Summer in the Sierra* (1911), and *The Yosemite* (1912).

Ralph L. Langenheim, Jr.

SEE ALSO: Bioethics; Conservation; Endangered species; Environmental movement; Leopold, Aldo; National Park System, U.S.; Sierra Club.

Multiculturalism

DEFINITION: Position that education should reflect various cultures, ethnic backgrounds, and traditions, not merely the culture and traditions of the dominant segment of society

TYPE OF ETHICS: Race and ethnicity

SIGNIFICANCE: For educational traditionalists, multiculturalism represented an attack on the ethical core of modern society, because education was improperly politicized and universities were teaching ideology instead of timeless truths and core ethical values. Proponents of multiculturalism, on the other hand, asserted that education had always been political and that the truths and ethical values which traditionalists called "timeless" were merely the ones which embodied their own, dominant politics and ideologies.

Although the concept of multiculturalism is as old as the ancient Greeks and Hebrews, its advent as a ma-

jor issue in American education during the 1980's brought it into the mainstream of public debate. Questions about multiculturalism and the related "political correctness" movement were among the most widely discussed and divisive in the United States during the late 1980's and early 1990's. Particularly on college and university campuses, clashes over alleged sexism, racism, and insensitivity attracted extensive media attention. In public schools, where ethnic and racial diversity was a fact of life, parents, students, and public officials struggled with the complicated question of how to balance the broader community's interests with those of Native American, Mexican American, African American, and other minority groups.

The rights and dignity of women, homosexuals, and others not adequately represented, in the multiculturalist perspective, in American education or in the use of resources were basic concerns of the movement. Advocates of multiculturalism argued that traditional education ignored, and even distorted, the contributions of people outside the European American mainstream.

CONFLICTING ETHICAL VIEWS

Both advocates and critics of multiculturalism have appealed to ethical principles to justify their perspectives. Supporters have generally emphasized the need to correct the alleged harmful effects of traditional policies on the grounds that these policies have distorted the truth and have encouraged isolation and self-doubt. Growing evidence that many ethnic minority children were losing self-confidence and falling behind in their education seemed to substantiate the claims of multiculturalists that something was seriously wrong with the American educational process. As the proportion of minority children in American schools climbed from 21 percent in 1970 to more than 26 percent in 1984, public awareness of cultural diversity and related problems significantly increased. To many multiculturalists, it seemed obvious that inherent bias, especially in schools and colleges, was a major cause of inequality and its many socially harmful effects.

Critics, however, argued that the real causes of inequities lay elsewhere—in social history rather than the educational system and its support mechanisms—and that multiculturalism actually made matters worse by heightening tensions and group identity at the expense of community. Historian Arthur M. Schlesinger, Jr., wrote that multiculturalism encouraged the fragmentation of American society into "a quarrelsome spatter of enclaves, ghettos, tribes." Former secretary of education William J. Bennett dismissed multiculturalism as a symptom of the "disuniting of America."

POLITICAL CORRECTNESS AND CULTURAL PLURALISM

Complicating the quest for an ethical consensus on multiculturalism during the early 1990's was the "political correctness," or PC, movement, which sought to eradicate racist, sexist, and ethnocentric language from the classroom and public forums. When political correctness first appeared in public discussion around the turn of the twentieth century, it was a slogan among Marxists and certain other ideology-intensive groups indicating adherence to accepted party principles and interpretations. In the later environment of the multiculturalist movement, it was applied to the treatment of minorities, women, and ethnic groups. This added to the task of defining common ethical and political ground by subtly transforming the issue of community into one of words about community and symbolic behavior that might offend or discourage a particular group or individual within it.

Supporters of multiculturalism insisted that sensitivity to the feelings and positions of all people is not only ethically compelling but also politically and economically essential for the effective functioning of a democratic society. Without it, larger numbers of people drop out in one sense or another, to the detriment of the entire society. The art, historical contributions, and personal worth of all people, it is argued, augment the traditional culture with creative new elements that benefit all. If they are ignored, a potential enrichment of the culture is lost, and tragic consequences can result in regard to the ability of those left out to find a productive place in society.

IMPLICATIONS FOR ETHICS

In his *Civilization and Ethics* (1923), Albert Schweitzer observed that "ordinary ethics" seek accommodation and compromise. That is, "they try to dictate how much of my existence and of my happiness I must sacrifice, and how much I may preserve at the cost of the existence and happiness of other

lives." In essence, that is the pivotal issue in current multiculturalist theory. Its ethical norms are centered in the need to balance the individual's interests with those of the larger community.

For Schweitzer, the solution lay in envisioning a higher ethic that he called "reverence for life"; that is, an absolute regard for all life in a broadly inclusive ethic. The ethical challenge of multiculturalism is to find ways to avoid violating basic individual rights such as freedom of speech and conscience while protecting the rights of all segments of society and incorporating their identity and contributions into the whole. This thrusts it inevitably into the realm of politics, where moral vision is often blurred by considerations of resources, the need for competent personnel to lead multicultural educational programs in schools and elsewhere, and the development of cooperative undertakings that give substance to theory. In that sense, multiculturalism, to be meaningful, must defy the image that it is merely a buzzword or a new kind of oppression and ground itself in its most basic ethical principles of responsibility and cooperation to ensure both justice and respect for all.

Thomas R. Peake

FURTHER READING

Bain-Selbo, Eric. *Mediating the Culture Wars.* Cresskill, N.J.: Hampton Press, 2003.

Banks, J. A., and McGee Banks, eds. *Multicultural Education: Issues and Perspectives.* Boston: Allyn & Bacon, 1989.

D'Souza, Dinesh. *Illiberal Education: The Politics of Race and Sex on Campus.* New York: Vintage, 1992.

Gordon, Avery F., and Christopher Newfield, eds. *Mapping Multiculturalism.* Minneapolis: University of Minnesota Press, 1996.

Graff, Gerald. *Beyond the Culture Wars: How Teaching the Conflicts Can Revitalize American Education.* New York: W. W. Norton, 1992.

Hughes, Robert. *Culture of Complaint: The Fraying of America.* New York: Oxford University Press, 1993.

Sterba, James P. *Three Challenges to Ethics: Environmentalism, Feminism, and Multiculturalism.* New York: Oxford University Press, 2001.

_____, ed. *Ethics: Classical Western Texts in Feminist and Multicultural Perspectives.* New York: Oxford University Press, 2000.

Sykes, Charles J. *A Nation of Victims: The Decay of the American Character.* New York: St. Martin's Press, 1992.

Yates, Steven A. "Multiculturalism and Epistemology." *Public Affairs Quarterly* 6 (October, 1992): 435-456.

SEE ALSO: Bilingual education; Comparative ethics; Diversity; Ethnocentrism; Justice; Moral education; Pluralism; Political correctness; Postmodernism; Tolerance.

Multinational corporations

DEFINITION: Large commercial organizations that conduct business in more than a single nation
TYPE OF ETHICS: Business and labor ethics
SIGNIFICANCE: Ethical issues arise due to the very existence of multinational corporations in foreign countries, especially with respect to fundamental human rights and the problem of ethical relativism.

The single most important objective of any business enterprise is to create a monetary surplus, which, in turn, allows the business to reinvest in itself in order to continue to pursue the same fundamental objective. Should the business be a corporation with publicly held shares, its financial profits are also used to pay dividends to its shareholders. Should the corporation engage in any business activity with people in any country other than the one in which it is legally incorporated, it achieves the status of a multinational corporation. Such activities include, but are not limited to, the advertising and marketing of the corporation's products or services to people in other countries, the establishment of manufacturing plants in other countries, and the hiring of employees in other countries to work in such plants.

A variety of special ethical issues arises in the context of the normal business practices of any corporation. They concern workplace conditions, including health and safety issues; employee financial compensation issues; employee privacy issues; race, gender, and age discrimination issues; issues of due process when it comes to hiring and firing and the promotion and demotion of employees; product safety issues; issues concerning the environment; and many others. In addition to all these issues is the problem of ethical relativism.

ETHICAL RELATIVISM

Every culture has, to varying degrees, unique standards of morality that might conflict with those of other cultures; this is an empirical fact and is usually referred to as cultural relativism. Some people assume that, because cultural relativism is a fact, so too is ethical relativism. "Ethical relativism" is the belief that because people in various and different cultures do, in fact, adhere to different and sometimes conflicting standards of morality, there is (and can be) no objective standard of morality that applies equally to all people in every culture and throughout all of human history. In addition to the fact that the belief in the accuracy of ethical relativism does not logically follow from the empirical fact of cultural relativism, there are numerous beliefs that do logically follow from the belief in ethical relativism but that, typically, are found to be unacceptable even by proponents of ethical relativism. For example, to take seriously the belief in ethical relativism is to obligate one to accept the belief that there neither exists nor should exist any absolute moral prohibition of any type of human behavior, including murder.

EFFECTS OF ETHICAL RELATIVISM

Through the last four decades of the twentieth century, numerous Western-based multinational corporations attempting to start up business activities in foreign countries such as Indonesia, Nigeria, and Malaysia immediately faced threats of being prohibited from conducting any such business unless they paid what were, in effect, bribes to foreign officials. Despite the fact that most Western multinational corporate executives find such ultimatums to be morally offensive, they tend to attempt to justify compliance with such requirements on grounds of ethical relativism.

One of the most significant cultural distinctions to be found among various nations is the host of different positions of their respective governments on the question of fundamental human rights and the extent to which such rights are, and/or are allowed to be, abused. Historically, relationships between multinational corporations of industrialized Western nations and developing countries in South America, Africa, the Middle East, and the Far East are such that any of a variety of fundamental human rights are routinely neglected, if not abused outright. Again, executives of multinational corporations in such situations typically attempt to justify human rights abuses of foreign citizens on grounds of ethical relativism.

It is not uncommon for Western multinational corporations operating in poor foreign countries to hire children to work in unsafe and unhealthy conditions for long hours each day for the equivalent of only a few dollars per day. Despite the fact that such working conditions might be consistent with what is normally expected in the host countries and the fact that the wages that are paid might actually compare favorably to standard local wages, employing children raises serious ethical questions.

One might reasonably argue that children, in any country, have the right to at least a modicum of a formal education as well as the complementary right to not be coerced to work. Moreover, one could argue that employees (typically, as adults) have the right to reasonably safe and healthy workplace conditions as well as the right to financial compensation that is commensurate with work performance that is both of good quality and of whatever duration. Such rights are consistent with the Universal Declaration of Human Rights that was adopted by the United Nations in 1948. It was designed to be an objective standard by which to measure the extent to which any nation on Earth either respects or abuses the fundamental human rights of its citizens.

ABUSE OF THE PROFIT MOTIVE

Sometimes, attempts to justify, on grounds of ethical relativism, the business practices in each of the two types of examples as set out above, specifically, the bribery of government officials and the use of child labor (both in poor foreign countries), are really only veiled attempts to justify what is, arguably, the abuse of the profit motive. For multinational corporations, as for any businesses, the more that the executive decision makers are committed to the fundamental objective of creating profits, the more they are tempted to venture into business practices that may be morally suspect.

If bribing government officials is not the normal business practice within a foreign country, then such a practice cannot be justified on grounds of cultural, much less ethical, relativism. In such cases, the most reasonable explanation for bribes is greed on the part of the foreign government officials and abuse of the profit motive on the part of the multinational corporation's executives.

It is arguable that in the vast majority of cases of morally questionable business practices, from workplace conditions to issues concerning the environment, abuse of the profit motive is the most reasonable explanation.

Stephen C. Taylor

FURTHER READING

Berberoglu, Berch. *Globalization of Capital and the Nation-State: Imperialism, Class Struggle, and the State in the Age of Global Capitalism.* Lanham, Md.: Rowman & Littlefield, 2003.

Cavanagh, Gerald F. *American Business Values: With International Perspectives.* 4th ed. Upper Saddle River, N.J.: Prentice-Hall, 1998.

DeGeorge, Richard. *Competing with Integrity in International Business.* New York: Oxford University Press, 1993.

_____. "International Business Ethics." In *A Companion to Business Ethics*, edited by Robert Frederick. Oxford, England: Blackwell Publishers, 1999.

Donaldson, Thomas. *The Ethics of International Business.* New York: Oxford University Press, 1989.

_____. "International Business Ethics." In *Encyclopedic Dictionary of Business Ethics*, edited by Patricia Werhane and R. Edward Freeman. Oxford, England: Blackwell Publishers, 1997.

Dunning, John H., ed. *Making Globalization Good: The Moral Challenges of Global Capitalism.* New York: Oxford University Press, 2003.

SEE ALSO: Agribusiness; Antitrust legislation; Business ethics; Downsizing; Environmental ethics; Ethical codes of organizations; Globalization; Outsourcing; Telemarketing; World Trade Organization.

Mutually assured destruction

DEFINITION: Cold War doctrine in which nuclear powers are deterred from attacking each other by the fact that any resulting conflict would utterly destroy both nations

DATE: Term coined during the 1960's

TYPE OF ETHICS: Military ethics

SIGNIFICANCE: Mutually assured destruction (MAD) was, in retrospect, a successful doctrine, but it also created a pervasive, semiconscious fear that arguably colored the lives hundreds of millions of people for the duration of the Cold War. Moreover, the post-Cold War nuclear landscape contains new threats, such as nuclear terrorism, against which MAD is no longer a practical defense, and the nations which once relied upon MAD have been faced with the challenge of developing effective alternative strategies.

To protect and preserve values is the only justifying cause for the use of force that is admitted in civilized moral tradition. The defense and protection of the innocent is one of the cardinal points of those values. Counterpopulation destruction deterrence—that is, the threat to destroy civilian population as retaliation against a nuclear strike—is thus immoral, even when this threat is part of a strategy to prevent war. MAD defies one of the most fundamental traditional ethics of warfare, the principle of noncombatant immunity, which has been in operation since World War II and which requires that deliberate physical harm be limited to military targets. Others will argue, however, that even if it is morally wrong under any circumstances to deliberately kill innocent civilians, it is not necessarily wrong to threaten (or intend to risk) such killings, provided that such threats are necessary to deter greater evils. Nevertheless, it is virtually impossible to untangle the good and the evil elements in this concept; the good is an aspect of the evil, and the evil is both the source and the possible outcome of the good it seeks to achieve.

Olusoji A. Akomolafe

SEE ALSO: Atom bomb; Cold War; Deterrence; Hiroshima and Nagasaki bombings; National security and sovereignty; Nuclear arms race; Nuclear energy; SALT treaties; Unconditional surrender; Union of Concerned Scientists; War.

Mysticism

DEFINITION: Belief that there is a single objective reality beyond or in excess of the tangible world, and that this reality may be accessed or known through subjective experience

TYPE OF ETHICS: Religious ethics

SIGNIFICANCE: Controversy exists about the relationship of mysticism and ethics. Some claim that mystical experience supports ethical behavior, while others claim that it can lead to indifference to ethical issues.

Some religious thinkers and philosophers condemn mysticism because they view it as an attempt to escape from the duties and responsibilities of life. Ethical behavior presupposes a concern for self and others. Mystical experience occurs when a person directly perceives an undifferentiated unity that is beyond the deepest center of the individual self. While in the grip of mystical experience, one forgets everything else, including oneself and the world. Apologists for mysticism assert that although mystical experience involves a temporary withdrawal from the world and its problems, it is not intrinsically escapist. Mystical experience supports better ethical choices by expanding and sharpening awareness, making the person who has such an experience better able to assess the ethical ramifications of conduct.

DEFINITION OF MYSTICAL EXPERIENCE

Mystical experience is best defined first in terms of what it is not. Mysticism does not seek experience of the occult, such as that of ghosts or disembodied spirits. It does not include parapsychological phenomena, such as telepathy (communication at a distance), clairvoyance (perception beyond natural range of the senses), or precognition (knowledge of an event in advance of its occurrence). Mystical experience does not necessarily involve seeing visions or hearing voices. Individuals who are not mystics may possess supernormal powers or experience visions. Mystical experience is not necessarily associated with religion, although it is often sought for religious reasons and described in religious language.

The core of mystical experience involves an apprehension of an ultimate nonsensuous unity beyond all created things. Extrovertive mysticism finds the fundamental Unity manifesting itself in the diversity of the world, while introvertive mysticism finds the One beyond the deepest center of the individual self. The Upaniṣads of India, spiritual treatises that date from 800 to 400 B.C.E. and provide some of the oldest descriptions of mystical experience in the world, record experiences of both extrovertive and introvertive mysticism. The Upaniṣads claim that the Ultimate Reality is both inside and outside creation. The person who beholds all beings in the Ultimate Reality and the Ultimate Reality in all beings is truly wise and free.

The extrovertive mystic perceives the One by looking outward. While appreciating the diversity of the created world, the extrovertive mystic perceives the objects of perception in such a way that the One shines through them. The medieval German mystic Johann Eckhart described an experience in which he found the grass, wood, and stone that he observed to be distinct and yet One. The extrovertive mystic perceives the One in all things. It is a type of experience that tends toward pantheism, the view that God and creation are identical.

Extrovertive mysticism is not the predominant way of experiencing the Unity beyond the multiplicity of the created universe. Introvertive mysticism is the most common kind of mystical experience. The introvertive mystic finds the One beyond the deepest center of the self in an experience of pure consciousness. Conscious but not conscious *of* anything, the mystic is absorbed in a state of alertness that does not contain any concept, thought, or sensation. The mystic's individuality seems to melt away into infinity. This oneness, encountered beyond the deepest level of the self, is often identified with God because it is experienced as being eternal and infinite, beyond space and time. Saint John of the Cross, the sixteenth century Spanish poet and mystic, described pure consciousness as a state in which the person is so united to the simplicity and purity of God that the awareness is pure and simple, devoid of all objects of perception.

The actual experience of undifferentiated unity is said to be independent of the interpretation given to it. Religious people associate the experience with God. The Jewish tradition identifies pure consciousness with the apprehension of divine glory, not with God's being; while the Christian and Islamic traditions identify it as an experience of union with God. Other philosophies and religious traditions, such as

Hinduism, tend to view pure consciousness as an experience of the impersonal Absolute in which the individual self merges with the Ultimate Reality.

Evidence of mystical experience is found in religious and philosophical traditions all over the world and in all periods of history. Mystical experience is usually incorporated into a religious or philosophical tradition the purpose of which is to secure full knowledge, salvation, or liberation for the people who participate in it. Each tradition recommends ascetical practices to prepare a person for mystical experience. These include the practice of virtue and right action, the removal of sin and inclinations toward evil, and the renunciation of personal desires. Ascetical disciplines are practiced to remove obstacles between self and the Ultimate Reality and to prepare the person to enjoy direct contact with the One beyond all created things.

OBJECTIONS TO MYSTICISM ON MORAL GROUNDS

Although virtuous behavior is usually considered to be a prerequisite for mystical experience, some philosophers and religious thinkers have objected to mysticism on the basis of their belief that it undermines the basis for ethical decision making. The experience of a fundamental undifferentiated unity beyond perception causes the experiencer's awareness to transcend all distinctions, including the duality of good and evil. Mystical experience implies that the separation of the individual self, the created world, and the Absolute are illusions and that the eternal One is the only reality. All these ideas about the nature of mystical experience and the Ultimate Reality have implications for the mystic's approach to ethical issues.

The twentieth century theologian Paul Tillich objects on moral grounds to the experience of pure consciousness because individual identity seems to disappear when the mystic's awareness transcends all objects of perception. The experiencing individual, who is involved in relationships with self, others, and the wider environment, is necessary for morality. If all contents of consciousness disappear in mystical experience, the mystic steps outside both the positive and the negative elements of concrete experience. Those who transcend experience altogether allow themselves to forget about the existence of evil and problems in themselves and in the world. A truly moral person cannot withdraw from life, from relationships with others, or from involvement with the community. By retreating into oneself in search of a private experience of union with Ultimate Reality, the mystic neglects ethics and social obligations.

Another twentieth century theologian, Martin Buber, objects to mysticism because the loss of awareness of individuality in pure consciousness leaves open to doubt the reality of each individual self and each thing in the world of ordinary experience. Ethical values and obligations can be applied only to real selves and real things. In addition, a relationship between real selves and real things is a prerequisite for moral and ethical activity.

Mysticism is also attacked on the ground that morality has no basis if the phenomenal world is considered to be an expression of the infinite and eternal One beyond space and time. If individuals are not really separate beings, then the mystic might conclude that the wrong perpetrated by one person against another is an illusion. There is no reason to intervene to stop injustice if the person who is being wronged and the offender are two aspects of one reality. In transcending all differentiation in pure consciousness, the mystic also transcends the distinction between good and evil. A person who considers evil to be an illusion may be apathetic in the face of it, choosing to accept it rather than change it or fight it. Since the mystic makes no moral distinctions while united with the Ultimate Reality, one might conclude that mysticism is amoral at best.

In early Christianity contemplation of the divine essence was valued more highly than action. Since the ultimate goal of moral action in the world is salvation or the contemplation of God in Heaven, life's highest aspiration is to gain pure consciousness, which prefigures life in Heaven. When the would-be mystic is advised to reject all love and attraction for created things in order to direct all love toward God, he or she is encouraged to neglect social and moral obligations. The pursuit of mystical experience seems to undercut morality when it is considered to be superior to ethical action. Work in the world is downgraded to second-class status.

Hinduism and Buddhism are especially criticized on moral grounds for emphasizing contemplation of the Ultimate Reality over action. Both traditions define salvation as *mokṣa*, or liberation from ignorance about the true nature of the self. Enlightenment or salvation means the direct experiential knowledge that the individual self is in reality the Cosmic Self, the Ultimate Reality. The pursuit of *moksha* involves efforts to transform one's own state of consciousness and thereby change the quality of one's experience. The person is not primarily concerned with changing the world or fulfilling personal and social duties.

MYSTICISM'S CONTRIBUTION TO ETHICS

While apparently selfish reasons, such as the desire to escape personal suffering or gain eternal happiness, do inspire people to seek mystical experience; most mystics come to realize that mystical experience is not an end in itself. Supporters of mysticism on ethical grounds point out that the mystic prepares for mystical experience by concentrating on growing in virtue, developing self-discipline, and acting in accord with moral principles. In turn, mystical experience accelerates the growth of virtue and brings greater ethical effectiveness to the mystic's activity. Direct contact with the Ultimate Reality in pure consciousness has very direct and beneficial ethical consequences. Rather than a selfish and self-centered withdrawal from the world of action, the experience of pure consciousness is considered to be a most effective means of fostering right action.

The arguments against mysticism on moral grounds take the description of pure consciousness out of context. They disregard the ethical frameworks surrounding mystical experience, which demand moral conduct to prepare for it and consider moral conduct to be its fruition. They conclude that the experience of pure consciousness can have negative consequences for morality only in the sense that all distinctions are transcended within it. Although pure consciousness is an experience of undifferentiated unity, it does not necessarily lead the mystic to conclude that multiplicity and distinction are inconsequential. It does not make the mystic apathetic in the face of suffering and evil in the world. Mystics do not abandon ethical action because their enlightened state allows their awareness to go beyond distinctions between good and evil.

Such conclusions reflect a one-sided judgment of the impact of the experience of pure consciousness on the lives of the people who experience it. Advocates of mystical experience counter the objections to mystical experience on moral grounds by pointing to the descriptions of enlightened individuals found in different traditions and the testimony of the lives of great mystics. It is a paradox that the experience of pure consciousness in which individual identity seems to dissolve into absolute nothingness can improve the quality of the person's action. Critics of mysticism fail to recognize that the experience of unity can provide a basis for ethical decision making and conduct that is as good as or better than that provided by the experience of the separateness.

Mystics are described as friends of God whose extraordinary virtues follow from the powerful intimacy with God that union with God in pure consciousness creates. They are held up as models for others to emulate. In the Christian tradition, a person's spiritual attainment is found lacking if that person claims to enjoy mystical experience but does not lead a life of exemplary virtue. The Christian tradition considers charity or love of self and others because of God to be the most important virtue. Charity requires the mystic to tend to the needs of others and not only focus on mystical experience.

Gregory the Great, a sixth century pope and theologian, maintained that mystical experience reinforces morality. He advocated a lifestyle that combined the cultivation of mystical experience (the contemplative life) with active service to others. According to Richard of St. Victor, a twelfth century Scottish mystic, after enjoying the heights of mystical experience, the contemplative goes out on God's behalf in compassion to others.

The Advaita Vedānta tradition, founded by the ninth century Indian philosopher Śankara, maintains that *Brāhmin*, the Ultimate Reality, is all that exists. The person who views *Brāhmin* as the only Reality does not engage in immoral acts. The enlightened person works for the benefit of others.

BUDDHIST MYSTICISM

According to Buddhism, the goal of mystical experience is nirvana, the annihilation of desire in pure consciousness. Four virtues grace the person who experiences nirvana: friendliness toward all creatures, compassion for all sentient beings and the desire to remove their suffering, joy in the happiness of all creatures, and impartiality toward them all. Since an enlightened person is no longer governed by egocentric considerations, he or she acts for the benefit of others. The *bodhisattva* exemplifies the highest ex-

ample of virtue and enlightenment in the Buddhist tradition. Just as the Buddha worked in compassion to relieve the suffering in the world by making known the experience of nirvana, the *bodhisattva* renounces nirvana out of compassion for all created things, vowing not to step out of time into eternity until all other created things have entered nirvana first.

In Buddhism the emptiness of nirvana is said to manifest as infinite compassion toward all created beings. The goal of the *bodhisattva* is to lose all ego-consciousness through expanding in boundless giving to others. Separateness of individual persons and things from each other and from the Ultimate Reality is not necessary to motivate virtuous behavior. The compassionate conduct of the *bodhisattva* exemplifies this fact. Oneness can also serve as the basis for ethical conduct.

CHRISTIAN MYSTICISM

Christian mystics especially emphasize that mystical experience overflows into love for others and action for the benefit of others. Pure consciousness in the form of the secret infusion of God's love into the soul is the source of moral activity. When the person loses the awareness of the boundaries of the individual self in pure consciousness, the once-separate self is aligned with the Ultimate Reality. The love that flows out of mystical experience has its basis in the realization of the One, which eliminates the separation between one's neighbor and oneself. All selfishness, cruelty, and evil originate in alienation from self and others.

The relationship between mystical experience and ethics is also explained by the paradoxical assertion that absolute fullness and virtue is located in unmanifest form in the apparent nothingness of pure consciousness. Saint John of the Cross, a sixteenth century Spanish poet and perhaps the most important European mystic, describes pure consciousness as the nothingness (*nada*) that contains everything (*todo*). Every experience of pure consciousness infuses absolute divine attributes into its recipient.

The process of personal development through mystical experience involves the progressive infusion of these divine qualities. The infusion of divine attributes implies a corresponding process of purification, the removal of personal limitations that disallow that infusion to be complete. The Upaniṣads call the Ultimate Reality the source of all virtue and the destroyer of sin. The mystic's transformation through this dual process of illumination and purification improves his or her activity. The mystic performs action with a more finely tuned appreciation of right and virtue because contact with pure consciousness results in greater alertness and freedom from personal limitation.

Although initially a person might shun worldly concerns in order to concentrate on acquiring mystical experience, at some point, the mystic becomes concerned about moral issues. The life of Thomas Merton, the twentieth century writer and mystic, unfolded in this way. After seeking refuge from worldly life by entering a Trappist monastery near Louisville, Kentucky, he became increasingly concerned with the world he thought he had left behind. He called himself a guilty bystander who was implicated along with the rest of humanity in the crises and problems of society. His physical withdrawal from the world outside the monastery walls did not prevent him from trying to change the world. He attacked racism, the existence of nuclear weapons, and U.S. participation in the war in Vietnam. Merton exemplifies the contemplative who, by withdrawing from the world and devoting time to cultivating mystical experience, creates a certain distance between himself and the rest of the world that allows him to perceive evil more clearly. Merton became the prophet whose voice was heard in the wilderness, demanding the end to the madness of the nuclear threat and the injustice of racial discrimination. As prophet, the contemplative becomes involved and tries to communicate a vision of what God wants for society and for the world.

Personal limitations in the would-be mystic might initially motivate the person to seek mystical experiences in order to avoid problems or find personal salvation. Since mystical experience fosters increased awareness and removes personal limitations, however, at some point the mystic renounces such selfishness. The mystic's personal growth eventually translates itself into love and concern for others, two virtues that are fundamental for ethical decision making.

Mysticism does support ethics. The personal development that results from mystical experience provides the mystic with the means to reflect and to act in greater harmony with ethical and moral principles. Those who attack mysticism on moral grounds seem to disregard the evidence of the experience of the great mystics, who inspire others to emulate such high levels of personal integration and moral conduct that their admirers are tempted to proclaim them to be nothing less than perfect reflections of the divine on Earth.

Evelyn Toft

FURTHER READING

Barnard, G. William, and Jeffrey J. Kripal, eds. *Crossing Boundaries: Essays on the Ethical Status of Mysticism*. New York: Seven Bridges Press, 2002. Anthology of essays examining the relationship between mysticism and ethics in various Western and Eastern mystical traditions.

Horne, James R. *The Moral Mystic*. Waterloo, Ont.: Wilfrid Laurier University Press, 1983. A thorough exploration for the nonspecialist of the relationship among mysticism, religion, and morality.

Huxley, Aldous. *The Perennial Philosophy*. London: Triad Grafton, 1985. An anthology with commentary organized by topic that identifies the features common to mystical philosophy and experience in the world's major philosophical and religious traditions.

Wainwright, William J. *Mysticism: A Study of Its Nature, Cognitive Value, and Moral Implications*. Madison: University of Wisconsin Press, 1981. A philosophical critique of the various definitions and theoretical frameworks for understanding mystical experience. Includes an analysis of the relationship of mysticism and morality.

SEE ALSO: Asceticism; Bergson, Henri; Christian ethics; Existentialism; Ḥallāj, al-; Jain ethics; Kabbala; Rābiʿah al-ʿAdawīyah; Scientology; Sufism; Upaniṣads.

N

Nader, Ralph

IDENTIFICATION: Pioneer crusader for consumer rights

BORN: February 27, 1934, Winsted, Connecticut

TYPE OF ETHICS: Politico-economic ethics

SIGNIFICANCE: Noted for his advocacy of consumer rights, Ralph Nader merged his socioeconomic interests with a political agenda by running for president of the United States in four elections. Although his campaigns did not win, they succeeded in focusing debate on violation of citizen and consumer rights.

Born to Lebanese immigrants to the United States, Ralph Nader graduated from Princeton University and the Harvard Law School. While working in the federal Department of Labor during the Kennedy administration in the early 1960's, he began his crusade as a consumer advocate and published a scorching exposure of safety abuses in the auto industry, *Unsafe at Any Speed*, in 1965. By the end of the 1960's, Nader and his "Nader's Raiders" had effectively pressured Congress to pass legislation to improve the safety of automobiles, the quality of meat and air, and open access to government information. Founding organizations for responsive law and public interests, Nader argued that producers had responsibilities to paying consumers and that government officials had legal and ethical duties to monitor the producers' fidelity to these responsibilities.

Throughout his reform campaigns, Nader found a common political problem. Corporations and business interests protected themselves from regulatory legislation by financing the election of politicians and by funding lobbyists to mold the legislation and regulations. As such funding mushroomed during the 1980's, Nader decided that he had to enter the national political arena in order to address that threat directly.

Nader's first presidential campaign, as a write-in candidate in 1992, was weakly organized and overshadowed by the antilobbyist rhetoric and fortune of Reform Party candidate H. Ross Perot. At that time Nader published *The Concord Principles*, his statement of ethical conduct in government. The document suggested ten procedures and practices citizens and their elected representatives could pursue in order to regain and maintain control of government against a minority of corrupted political and economic power brokers. Nader's 1996 bid for the presi-

Ralph Nader speaking at a political rally in Portland, Oregon, in April, 2004. (AP/Wide World Photos)

dency attracted support from the Green Party, a political entity dedicated to protecting the environment from industry.

Nader's 2000 presidential campaign, again waged with Green Party support, proved controversial among his supporters. Many thought that he pulled away votes from the ecology-minded Democratic Party candidate, Al Gore. Nader divided the environmentalist vote against the Republican Party candidate, George W. Bush, allowing the latter's victory. To Nader the key issue was the financial corruption of the electoral system, in which he thought that both major parties were hopelessly mired. The Green Party needed to win 5 percent of the national vote to qualify for federal funding in the 2004 election and thereby obtain a sustaining political status to combat both political corruption and environmental pollution. Nader failed to obtain enough votes to achieve future federal campaign funds but nevertheless ran for president again in 2004.

In 2001 Nader founded Democracy Rising, a nonprofit organization, to continue the objectives of his campaign. Through its "People Have the Power" rallies in cities throughout the country, it alerted citizens to the need to combat public apathy and wrest civic interests from corporate manipulation.

Crucial to the support of Nader's efforts for consumer rights and responsible government has been the uniform recognition of his ethical integrity. Supporters and even foes of his efforts have repeatedly acknowledged the upright dedication of his work.

Edward A. Riedinger

FURTHER READING

Martin, Justin. *Nader: Crusader, Spoiler, Icon*. Cambridge, Mass.: Perseus, 2002.

Nader, Ralph. *Crashing the Party: Taking on the Corporate Government in an Age of Surrender*. New York: Thomas Dunne Books/St. Martin's Press, 2002.

_____. *The Ralph Nader Reader*. New York: Seven Stories Press, 2000

SEE ALSO: Business ethics; Consumerism; Green parties; Lobbying; Product safety and liability; Profit economy; Voting fraud; World Trade Organization.

Nāgārjuna

IDENTIFICATION: Indian Buddhist philosopher
BORN: c. 150, India
DIED: c. 250, India
TYPE OF ETHICS: Religious ethics
SIGNIFICANCE: Nāgārjuna founded the Mādhyamaka school of Mahāyāna Buddhism and developed the philosophy of *śūnyatā*, or "emptiness."

Nāgārjuna was an Indian Buddhist thinker central to the Mādhyamaka school of Mahāyāna Buddhism. He lived from approximately 150 to 250 and continued the classic Buddhist approach to liberation from suffering through mental discipline.

Nāgārjuna's innovation was the concept of "emptiness," or *śūnyatā*. This is a recognition that things have no meaning in themselves; instead, they derive significance from their relationship to other things. (For example, "day" has no meaning apart from "night.") This contextual understanding of meaning is called *pratītya-samutpāda*, or "dependent co-arising."

Despite the essential emptiness of the categories that people employ to understand the world, on a pragmatic level people have to use those categories in order to live. In terms of ethics, Nāgārjuna's contribution was to separate ultimate from conventional truths, because although people should live fully aware of the basic illusoriness of reality, they should also uphold a moral path in their daily lives. Rather than release from this world (*nirvāṇa*), Nāgārjuna believed the ideal to be that of the *bodhisattva*, or "enlightened being": living in the world but being aware of its insubstantiality and working for the benefit of all beings.

Nāgārjuna's thought has influenced Buddhism in Tibet, China, Korea, and Japan for the nearly two millennia since his death, particularly in the Zen tradition.

Cynthia Keppley Mahmood

SEE ALSO: Bodhisattva ideal; Buddha; Buddhist ethics; Zen.

Nagel, Thomas

IDENTIFICATION: American philosopher
BORN: July 4, 1937, Belgrade, Yugoslavia
TYPE OF ETHICS: Modern history
SIGNIFICANCE: Best known for his books *The Possibility of Altruism* (1970) and *The View from Nowhere* (1986), Nagel formulates a version of ethical realism that recognizes the existence of both objective and subjective reasons for action.

In his first book, *The Possibility of Altruism*, Thomas Nagel defends an extreme form of objectivism in ethics. He argues that objective reasons are the only legitimate kinds of reason. Thus, if someone has a reason to act in a way that will bring about some end, then everyone has a reason to bring about that end. Nagel's early view, then, was that there are only "agent-neutral" reasons, and thus there are no reasons that are simply "agent-relative."

SUBJECTIVE AND OBJECTIVE PERSPECTIVES

Nagel modified his view in *The View from Nowhere* by allowing for the possibility of agent-relative reasons. This change was, in part, due to his analysis of philosophical problems resulting from the human capacity to occupy increasingly objective perspectives. Nagel points out that transcending one's own subjective perspective is important in both science and ethics since new facts and values are revealed from the objective standpoint. However, it is a mistake to conclude from this that subjective perspectives are unreal or reducible to something more objective.

The recognition of irreducible subjective perspectives thus provides a metaphysical framework for acknowledging the reality of agent-relative reasons. These reasons stem from an agent's own desires and projects, deontological obligations not to mistreat others in certain ways, and special obligations to family members. However, such reasons cannot be explained in neutral terms making no reference to the agent, or in terms of the impersonal good.

ETHICAL REALISM

Nagel also employs the distinction between subjective and objective perspectives in his formulation of realism about values. The central claim of his version of ethical realism is that ethical propositions can be true or false independently of human judgment.

While Nagel's realism about science is based on the fact that there are mind-independent facts, his realism about ethics does not rest on an analogous view regarding the metaphysical status of values.

Many ethical realists are Platonists and thus believe that values are nonnatural entities or intrinsic properties of states of affairs. In contrast to this more metaphysical conception of ethical objectivity, Nagel's view is that people can transcend their own subjective perspectives and evaluate their reasons and motives from more objective standpoints. This process can lead them to reorder their motives in order to make them more acceptable from an external standpoint. Thus, they can discover motives and reasons for action that they did not have before. Nagel's later view thus endorses realism for both objective reasons that hold for everyone, independently of their individual perspectives, and subjective reasons that do depend on the specific standpoint of an agent.

David Haugen

FURTHER READING

Brink, David. *Moral Realism and the Foundations of Ethics*. Cambridge, England: Cambridge University Press, 1989.

Elster, Jon. "Selfishness and Altruism." In *Economics, Ethics, and Public Policy*, edited by Charles K. Wilber. Lanham, Md.: Rowman & Littlefield, 1998.

Post, Stephen G., et al., eds. *Altruism and Altruistic Love: Science, Philosophy, and Religion in Dialogue*. New York: Oxford University Press, 2002.

Rorty, Richard. *Objectivity, Relativism, and Truth*. New York: Cambridge University Press, 1991.

SEE ALSO: Epistemological ethics; Luck and chance; Moral luck; Moral realism; Plato; Practical reason; Reason and rationality; Values clarification.

Nānak

IDENTIFICATION: Indian religious leader
BORN: April 15, 1469, Rāi Bhoi dī Talvaṇḍī, Punjab (now Nankana Sahib, Pakistan)
DIED: 1539, Kartārpur, Punjab, Mughal Empire (now in Pakistan)
TYPE OF ETHICS: Religious ethics

Significance: The founder of the Sikh faith, Nānak put forward a religious code of ethics that emphasized the equality of all people.

Nānak, who was born in Punjab, in what is now Pakistan, founded the faith known as Sikhism. Nānak was called *guru*, or spiritual teacher, and his followers were called Sikhs, or disciples. The religious system established by Guru Nānak was firmly monotheistic, rejecting idolatry and ritualism of all kinds. The Sikh community, called the *Panth*, was egalitarian in its social life, emphasizing rejection of the Hindu caste system through its tradition of eating at community kitchens. Charity toward the poor and defense of the weak characterized the Sikhs.

After Guru Nānak's death, there were nine successor gurus who led the Sikh *Panth* in turn. Various innovations were introduced, most notably involving greater militancy in the face of persecution, but all of them continued to build on the ideals established by Guru Nānak. After the death of the last guru, Guru Gobind Singh, leadership passed to the holy book of the Sikhs, the *Guru Granth Sahib*. It is housed in *gurdwaras*, Sikh shrines where people gather to worship, eat together, and discuss community events. By the end of the twentieth century, there were about 16 million Sikhs in the world who claimed the heritage of Guru Nānak, most of them in the state of Punjab in India.

Cynthia Keppley Mahmood

See also: Golden rule; Hindu ethics; Sikh ethics.

Napster

Identification: Site on the World Wide Web through which computer users share digital recordings of music

Date: Began operation in early 1991

Type of ethics: Arts and censorship

Rapper Ludacris studies his song listings on the Napster Web site after the music-downloading site began offering downloads for fees in October, 2003. (AP/Wide World Photos)

SIGNIFICANCE: Napster's song-sharing software and Web site allowed Internet users to download songs to their own computers for free, prompting lawsuits from artists for copyright infringement, launching a major fight between the newest information technology and established copyright protections. Napster's eventual agreement not to violate copyright law saw the Internet partially brought under the control of the legal system.

The Napster Web site, with its song-sharing technology, prompted one of the earliest clashes between the Internet and some of the oldest laws in the United States. Users of Napster downloaded digital files of songs from the site and shared those songs with other users. Most of the songs distributed through Napster were protected under federal copyright law, which required the Web site to pay for their use and distribution. When Napster was sued by the copyright owners, ethical questions were raised about artistic freedom and property rights.

Copyrights are issued by the federal government, providing artists, writers and composers monopoly power over their creations for limited periods of time. Copyrights are given to provide incentives to creative persons, who earn money by selling access to their work. Eventually, all copyrighted works fall into the public domain and can be used by anyone without a fee. The Napster case presented a clash between those competing interests: artists wanting to protect their property and the public seeking to use technology to gain access to popular songs.

Public sharing of copyrighted songs raises ethical concerns about property rights and the right of artists to be rewarded for their efforts by selling their works, rather than having them traded freely. However, another ethical question arose when the artists sued for copyright infringement. Copyrights are intended to advance the creative arts by providing monetary incentives for artists to produce works. However, the protections granted to artists are to advance a general good—the furtherance of knowledge. Using copyright laws to restrict use of the Internet—one of the greatest tool for advancing knowledge ever developed—seems to defeat the purpose intended for issuing copyrights.

Internet users using Napster to download music were violating the copyright laws protecting artists.

Pious Pirates

When the Gospel Music Association conducted an online marketing study in early 2004, people within the Gospel music industry were dismayed to learn that avowedly Christian teenagers were pirating religious music from the Web at almost the same rate that other teenagers were pirating secular music. The study showed that many of the young Christian music pirates rationalized their illegal downloading of Christian music as an ethical way to help spread the Gospel. However, people in the industry thought that the practice violated the commandment, "Thou shalt not steal." Shawn C. Ames, a member of the Christian band Diligence agreed that downloading Christian songs was stealing, but called it "like stealing a Bible—why would someone have a problem with that?"

However, the reaction of the copyright owners, thousands of dollars of fines for people sharing music, was at times seemingly out of proportion to the damage being inflicted. Napster and its song sharing brought another technology under the partial control of government regulation. Napster's agreement to pay copyright owners and charge Internet users downloading songs may have marked a shift in the Internet from a freewheeling new technology to one that could become a center of profit-making activity.

Douglas Clouatre

FURTHER READING

Alderman, John. *Sonic Boom: Napster, MP3, and the New Pioneers of Music.* New York: Perseus Publishing, 2001.

Menn, Joseph. *All the Rave: The Rise and Fall of Shawn Fanning's Napster.* New York: Crown Business Publishing, 2003.

Merriden, Trevor. *Irresistible Forces: The Business Legacy of Napster and the Growth of the Underground Internet.* New York: Capstone, 2002.

SEE ALSO: Computer crime; Computer databases; Computer misuse; Computer technology; Copyright; Intellectual property; Internet piracy; Song lyrics.

Narcissism

DEFINITION: Excessive self-interest or self-love
TYPE OF ETHICS: Personal and social ethics
SIGNIFICANCE: The primary hallmark of narcissism is understanding everyone else in terms of one-self. Narcissists thus violate the ethical principle that one should treat others as ends in themselves rather than as means for one's own ends.

Narcissism is a complex vice and a neurotic complex. The narcissus complex, identified by Havelock Ellis and by Sigmund Freud, involves an inordinate fascination with one's self—one's body, one's mind, one's actions.

Narcissism was named for Narcissus, a beautiful youth in Greek mythology who spurned all lovers. Nemesis, the avenger of *hubris* (inordinate pride), punished Narcissus by causing him to fall in love with his own reflection in the water, rendering him unable to move away. He was transformed into a flower by the gods.

Selfishness and immoderate self-love may be a part of the effects of narcissism, but there is a core that is unique to the vice. In some ethical systems, only the effects of narcissism could be judged culpable, but in natural-law analysis, at least, narcissism would itself be blameworthy as an "occasion of sin" and as an orientation of will and intellect whereby one denies the appropriate concern owed to one's fellow humans and the appropriate worship owed to God.

The neurotic complex might seem to be outside the considerations of ethics, but to the extent to which the complex developed as the result of freely chosen actions and freely entertained dispositions, it is blameworthy. To the extent that the proclivities of the complex could be resisted but are not, the complex is subject to ethical analysis.

Finally, narcissism must be viewed not only as an endangerment to one's relationship to God and to fellow humans but also as a warping of the proper development of the self. Narcissism causes the aesthetic judgment, the intellectual faculty, and the power of the will to be perverted from their proper outward orientation, stunted, and turned inward.

Patrick M. O'Neil

SEE ALSO: Egoism; Egotist; Golden rule; Humility; Individualism; Love; Pride; Selfishness; Self-love.

Narrative ethics

DEFINITION: Ethics involving the use of literature to engage in ethical inquiry
TYPE OF ETHICS: Theory of ethics
SIGNIFICANCE: Literature can illuminate realms of human experience that may be otherwise inaccessible to abstract philosophical prose and thus can enrich ethical reflection.

Several genres of literature may be seen to have didactic potential in that they can teach moral virtue. For example, moral fables are often edifying in this way, providing moral instruction by illustrating the rewards of virtuous action and the ill consequences resulting from immoral deeds. Epic stories of moral heroism may also instruct by example.

There are also ways in which good literature can go beyond moral instruction and stimulate ethical reflection. Certain ethicists turn to literature—ranging from the ancient tragedies to the modern novel—as moral philosophy because, they argue, narratives offer a philosophical view that is unavailable in conventional philosophical discourse. Philosopher Martha Nussbaum has argued that literary narratives illumine the contexts in which moral deliberation and action take place in ways that abstract rational principles do not. She suggests that literature is attentive to particularity, to the complexities and ambiguities in human life that are often flattened or omitted in abstract ethical reasoning. Moreover, moral philosophy can and should be concerned with particulars, since human life, like literary experience, cannot be reduced entirely to abstract generalizations. In addition to philosophers, some novelists see in literature the potential for posing important moral inquiry. For example, South African writer J. M. Coetzee's *Elizabeth Costello* (2003) and *The Lives of Animals* (1999) explore the borders of literary aesthetics and moral philosophy.

Reading literature may itself be a moral practice; this can occur because reading literature requires the reader to take another person's point of view, to step outside of one's own world and imaginatively enter into another's, which is a crucial skill in developing a moral sense. Literature can expand one's horizons by cultivating empathy and sympathy toward those quite different from oneself, a capacity vital for moral agency.

Maria Heim

SEE ALSO: *Bhagavadgītā*; Heroism; Moral equivalence; Nussbaum, Martha; Personal relationships; Role models; Tragedy; *Uncle Tom's Cabin*.

Nation of Islam

IDENTIFICATION: African American religious and social movement that proclaims adherence to the Islamic faith and practices as the way to achieve equality, justice, and freedom in all spheres of life

DATE: Founded in 1931

TYPE OF ETHICS: Race and ethnicity

SIGNIFICANCE: The Nation of Islam's use of Islam to proclaim a millennium in which white racist supremacy would be supplanted by black supremacy was unprecedented. The group's advocacy of separatism has placed it at the center of continuing controversies over the ethics of segregation in the name of activism.

Variously referred to as Black Muslims, the Black Muslim Movement, the World Community of Al-Islam in the West, and the American Muslim Movement, the Nation of Islam is heir to the separatist and self-improvement ethics of Marcus Garvey's Universal Negro Improvement Association and the each-race-for-each-religion philosophy and strict ethical behavior of Noble Drew Ali's Moorish Science Temple. It is both a religious movement and a social movement. As part of the worldwide Islamic religion and as an African American expression of Islam, the Nation of Islam has evolved some uniquely radical ethics vis-à-vis the American racial problem.

HISTORY

The Great Depression of the 1930's was particularly difficult for African Americans. Living in overcrowded slums, laid off and displaced by white workers as jobs became scarce, culturally marginalized and insulted by welfare officials, most African American workers and their dependents resented the power and control wielded by white Americans. Noble Drew Ali had died and Marcus Garvey had been deported in 1927. A leadership vacuum among African Americans was thus created as the Great Depression arrived.

It was the destiny of Wallace D. Fard to fill this leadership role by shaping the frustrations, anger, and energy of marginalized African Americans into an Islamic redemptionist religious movement that taught Afro-Asiatic history in house-to-house meetings and fiercely proclaimed a divinely ordained future era in which black supremacy would replace white supremacy and blacks would rule the earth. Such was the beginning of the Nation of Islam in Detroit, where it built its first temple as African Americans became members in large numbers. Fard was succeeded by Elijah Muhammad, and under the latter the Nation of Islam moved its headquarters to Chicago and spread to other states, building temples, schools, farms, apartment complexes, restaurants, and grocery stores. It developed a security force called the Fruit of Islam (FOI) and began its own publications. As it grew, the movement experienced some internal problems, and in the course of its years has had prominent leaders such as Malcolm X, Warith Deen Muhammad, and Louis Farrakhan.

POLARITIES

Although changing social circumstances have resulted in its changing or modifying its views and beliefs, especially as it moves toward orthodox Islam, the Nation of Islam has tended to see things in racial polarities to counteract what it sees as the racist ideology of the dominant American culture. In place of the Magnolia myth (the stereotype of music-making servile African Americans "lounging peacefully under the sweet-scented magnolias behind the big house—happy and contented in their station" as loyal servants to the generous master), which is the foundation of the idea that the African American is naturally docile, inherently imbecilic, and instinctively servile, the Nation of Islam created the myth of Yakub, which states that the "original man" to whom Allah (God) gave the earth to rule was the black man and his race, and that a rebellious scientist named Yakub performed a genetic experiment from which an inferior white race emerged. White supremacy is thus counteracted by black supremacy, and in this polarity it is the unnaturally white devils versus naturally divine blacks, and the white religion (Christianity) versus the black religion (Islam). The black Zion is where the white man is absent. Thus, there seems to be a strong determination by the Nation of Islam to belie white myths and beliefs.

ETHICS

The Nation of Islam adheres to strict moral behavior in private and social life. Its religious practices include praying five times a day, facing east toward Mecca and making proper ablutions (for the Muslim must be clean inwardly and outwardly) before praying. It is morally binding on members to attend temple activities; defaulters are suspended. The religion forbids certain foods, such as pork, both for religious reasons and to denigrate white supremacy (because the hog is "dirty, brutal, quarrelsome, greedy, ugly, a scavenger which thrives on filth . . . [and] has all the characteristics of a white man!"); in addition, black-eyed peas, cornbread, and chitlins must be avoided because they are not easily digestible and are a "slave diet"—and there are "no slaves in Islam." Fresh lamb, chicken, fish, and beef are approved. Moderation in eating is encouraged. Members are also forbidden to gamble, use drugs, smoke, or consume alcohol.

Members of the Nation of Islam are encouraged to marry within the movement; those who marry outside the movement are pressured to bring their spouses to join it. Interracial marriages and liaisons may bring severe punishment, if not expulsion, and male members are expected constantly to watch and protect their women against the white man's alleged degrading sexual obsession. Divorce is discouraged, though not prohibited. Sexual morality is strictly enforced under the puritanical vigilance of FOI. The use of cosmetics and the wearing of revealing and provocative clothes are forbidden. It is unethical for a married woman to be alone in a room with a man other than her husband.

Long before social and governmental agencies in America took seriously the relationship between crime and drugs, the Nation of Islam had developed a method for ferreting out and rehabilitating drug addicts so that they could remain themselves and stay away from crimes. It introduced a six-point drug therapy: making the patient admit his drug addiction; making him realize why he is an addict; telling him how to overcome this by joining the Nation of Islam; exposing him to the religious and social habits of the clean and proud members of the movement; making him voluntarily initiate a break from drug addiction with the full support and charity of the Muslim fraternity during the agony of the withdrawal period; and, finally, sending him out, when cured, to seek out other drug addicts for rehabilitation. Under the watchful and caring eyes of the Nation of Islam, an ex-drug addict also becomes an ex-criminal, since the drug habit that requires stealing, killing, or engaging in prostitution to support it is eliminated.

The Nation of Islam believes that territorial, political, and economic separation of blacks and whites is necessary to the mutual progress, peace, and respect of the two races in North America; the alternative is for them to leave America—the blacks to Africa and the whites to Europe. It urges peace among brothers, including whites, but points out that peace with whites is impossible because the white man "can only be a brother to himself." Members should be willing to die for dignity and justice if that becomes necessary, and should never hesitate to defend themselves and retaliate when attacked. The movement warns that "an eye for an eye and a tooth for a tooth" is the most effective manner to resolve racism, and that members should "fight with those who fight against [them]."

While respecting the "original" Bible, the Nation of Islam teaches that the Bible dedicated to the white man called King James has been corrupted and used by the Christian religion to enslave African Americans. Christianity thus becomes a "slave religion" teaching the oppressed to love and pray for the oppressor and the enemy; it further teaches the oppressed to offer both cheeks to be repeatedly slapped by the oppressor without retaliation, even offering the oppressor the cloak after the oppressor has taken away the coat of the oppressed. Christianity in this view is a "religion organized and backed by the devils for the purpose of making slaves of black mankind."

The Nation of Islam encourages thrift and discourages buying on credit because "debt is slavery." Members are discouraged from living beyond their means and wasting money. Hard work is extolled, and honesty, competence, cleanliness, and respect for authority, self, and others are expected of all members. The movement operates numerous businesses and encourages members to buy goods made by African Americans.

CONCLUSION

The dynamism of the Nation of Islam is in its ability to modify some of its views to changing circumstances. Although it asks for a separate nation, it did not hesitate to support Jesse Jackson's attempt to run for the presidency of the Untied States in 1984. Keeping ethical behavior in perspective, Louis Farrakhan challenged Ronald Reagan's 1986 order that banned American citizens from visiting Libya and rebuked popsinger Michael Jackson for corrupting American youths by means of his effeminate behavior. Members of the movement have also castigated Michael Jackson for unethically disclaiming his blackness by bleaching his skin to a "leprous" color that is neither white nor black nor brown, and for destroying, through plastic surgery, the face that Allah gave him. The Nation of Islam makes strong demands on its adherents and draws attention to race relations in America.

I. Peter Ukpokodu

FURTHER READING

DeCaro, Louis A., Jr. *Malcolm and the Cross: The Nation of Islam, Malcolm X, and Christianity.* New York: New York University Press, 1998.

Kepel, Gilles. *Allah in the West: Islamic Movements in America and Europe.* Translated by Susan Milner. Stanford, Calif.: Stanford University Press, 1997.

Lee, Martha F. *The Nation of Islam: An American Millenarian Movement.* Lewiston, N.Y.: Edwin Mellen Press, 1988.

Lincoln, C. Eric. *The Black Muslims in America.* 3d ed. Grand Rapids, Mich.: W. B. Eerdmans, 1994.

Malcolm X. *The Autobiography of Malcolm X.* New York: Ballantine Books, 1992.

_____. *By Any Means Necessary: Speeches, Interviews, and a Letter by Malcolm X.* Edited by George Breitman. New York: Pathfinder, 1970.

_____. *Malcolm X: The Last Speeches.* Edited by Bruce Perry. New York: Pathfinder, 1989.

Marsh, Clifton E. *From Black Muslims to Muslims: The Transition from Separatism to Islam, 1930-1980.* Metuchen, N.J.: Scarecrow Press, 1984.

SEE ALSO: Civil Rights movement; Discrimination; Farrakhan, Louis; Islamic ethics; Malcolm X; Racial prejudice; Segregation.

National Anti-Vivisection Society

IDENTIFICATION: Organization established to abolish surgical experimentation on live animals

DATE: Founded in 1929

TYPE OF ETHICS: Animal rights

SIGNIFICANCE: The National Anti-Vivisection Society (NAVS) questions the validity of human domination over animals, believing in the fundamental equality of animals and humans.

As one of several national and international humanitarian organizations dedicated to the elimination of biomedical research using animals, The National Anti-Vivisection Society was formed as a reaction against more conservative animal welfare organizations such as the Humane Society of the United States and the American Society for the Prevention of Cruelty to Animals.

While these societies are dedicated to the prevention of cruelty and improvement of conditions for all animals, unlike the NAVS, they are not officially committed to the total elimination of animal experimentation for human gain. While vivisection narrowly refers to the surgical cutting of animals, with or without anesthesia, the term has been broadened to include any experimentation on animals. The antivivisection movement challenges the utilitarian notion that the sacrifice of animals for the greater good of humanity is acceptable and desirable, thereby condemning speciesism—the belief that humans have the right of domination over nature and are superior to animals. On a pragmatic level, the organization also challenges the usefulness and applicability of animal experimentation to human medical science.

Mary E. Virginia

SEE ALSO: Animal research; Animal rights; Dominion over nature, human; Moral status of animals; People for the Ethical Treatment of Animals; Sentience; Vivisection.

National Association for the Advancement of Colored People

IDENTIFICATION: Organization established to fight for legal rights for members of minority groups in the United States

DATE: Founded on February 12, 1909

TYPE OF ETHICS: Race and ethnicity

SIGNIFICANCE: The National Association for the Advancement of Colored People (NAACP) was the first major organization to seek legislation at the national, state, and local levels banning racial discrimination.

With more than 500,000 members and 1,600 local chapters at the turn of the twenty-first century, the NAACP promotes equality of rights for all Americans and continues to fight against racial discrimination in employment and education. It is an interracial organization seeking, through "litigation, legislation and education," a complete end to racial prejudice and discrimination. Its most important victory came in *Brown v. Board of Education* (1954), when Thurgood Marshall, chief counsel for the NAACP and a future Supreme Court justice, successfully argued that the "separate but equal" doctrine established by the Court in 1896 was unconstitutional. Segregation by law was declared illegal, and school districts that separated students by race would have to begin to desegregate "with all deliberate speed."

The National Negro Committee, out of which came the NAACP, was organized in 1909 in response to a bloody race riot in Springfield, Illinois, in 1908.

Roy Wilkins (second from right), who led the NAACP during the 1960's, confers with U.S. attorney general Robert F. Kennedy (left), Martin Luther King, Jr., and union leader A. Philip Randolph (right). (National Archives)

Two African Americans were murdered by a white mob and seventy more were injured. The state militia eventually restored order, but only after many homes in the black community were burned by a white mob and two thousand African Americans were forced to flee the city. No white rioters were punished.

William English Walling, a white southern journalist, was appalled by the death and destruction and called for "a large and powerful body of citizens" to come to the assistance of the African Americans in Springfield. At a national conference, the committee called for an end to "caste and race prejudice" and for "complete equality before the law." W. E. B. Du Bois, the famous black scholar and future editor of the NAACP's magazine *The Crisis*, along with Jane Addams, founder of Hull House in Chicago and a leading white advocate of equality, were among the early members.

Lawyers for the NAACP first appeared before the U.S. Supreme Court in 1915 and decided to seek out cases that violated the Constitution, especially the Fourteenth Amendment's protection of equal rights for all citizens of the United States. In their first successful case in 1927, NAACP lawyers convinced the court that a state law denying people the right to vote unless their grandfathers had been registered to vote was unconstitutional. Without the NAACP's litigation and successful pursuit of justice for all, equality of rights would have continued to be denied and segregation might still be the law of many states.

In 1915, the NAACP established a prize, the Spingarn Medal, to be given annually to the African American who had "reached the highest achievement in his field of activity." Named for Joel E. Spingarn, a white professor of literature at Columbia University and longtime chairman of the board of directors of the National Association, the medal became the group's highest tribute. Among the winners of the Spingarn Medal were Thurgood Marshall; W. E. B. Du Bois; George Washington Carver, the famous scientist; James Weldon Johnson, the poet; Carter Woodson, the historian; educator Mary McLeod Bethune; soprano Marian Anderson; novelist Richard Wright; labor leader A. Philip Randolph; chemist Percy Julian; U.N. diplomat Ralph J. Bunche; Jackie Robinson, the baseball player; poet Langston Hughes; and social scientist Kenneth Clark, for his work on the *Brown* decision.

Leslie V. Tischauser

SEE ALSO: *Brown v. Board of Education*; Civil Rights movement; Congress of Racial Equality; Discrimination; Du Bois, W. E. B.; Evers, Medgar; Segregation.

National Commission for the Protection of Human Subjects of Biomedical and Behavioral Research

IDENTIFICATION: Interdisciplinary body that formulated ethical guidelines governing the treatment of human subjects in federally funded research
DATE: Established in July, 1974
TYPE OF ETHICS: Bioethics
SIGNIFICANCE: The commission was the earliest and most successful government effort to establish a basic code of ethical conduct regulating scientific inquiry.

From 1966 through 1972, several revelations that reputable scientists had routinely risked the health and well-being of subjects without their knowledge eroded public confidence in science. Many incidents involved poor, institutionalized, old, military, or prison populations. Most notorious were the 1972 Tuskegee Syphilis Study revelations. For forty years, Public Health Service researchers had studied the natural course of syphilis in poor African American men from Tuskegee, Alabama; the researchers kept the men unaware of the study's purpose, failed to treat them, even when penicillin became available, and actively prevented outside treatment. In 1974, Congress established the commission and provided that its recommendations were to be accepted by the U.S. Department of Health, Education, and Welfare unless the reasons for rejecting them were made public.

The commission issued several reports, including the *Belmont Report: Ethical Principles and Guidelines for the Protection of Human Subjects of Research* (1978), which led to the establishment of comprehensive regulations. The basic regulations require that most federally funded researchers obtain informed consent, protect confidentiality, and minimize risks to subjects. Additional safeguards were implemented from other reports to govern research on children, pregnant women, prisoners, and other special populations. The commission's impact extends beyond directly funded research. Since institutions receiving federal funds must ensure that all research is conducted ethically, most institutions review all research under the same guidelines, which have become the accepted standard for ethical research.

Ileana Dominguez-Urban

SEE ALSO: Bioethics; Experimentation; Medical research.

(including AIDS-HIV concerns), and family issues (including domestic partnerships, foster and adoptive parenting, and child custody and visitation questions) and the impact of these problems on the gay community. The NGLTF lobby helped to secure the passage of the Federal Hate Crimes Statistics Act, the Americans with Disabilities Act, and AIDS emergency relief funding.

Mary Johnson

SEE ALSO: Acquired immunodeficiency syndrome (AIDS); Bigotry; Civil Rights movement; Gay rights; Homophobia; Homosexuality; Sexual stereotypes.

National Gay and Lesbian Task Force

IDENTIFICATION: Organization established to fight for full equality for gay, lesbian, bisexual, and transgender people
DATE: Founded in 1973
TYPE OF ETHICS: Sex and gender issues
SIGNIFICANCE: The National Gay and Lesbian Task Force (NGLTF) was the first national activist organization established on behalf of gay and lesbian rights. Its adjunct, the NGLTF Policy Institute, is the most significant national information clearinghouse and resource center dedicated to educating and organizing around gay and lesbian issues throughout the world.

The National Gay and Lesbian Task Force represents the estimated twenty-five million homosexual Americans and fights to secure full civil rights and equality for these citizens. Its activities involve strengthening and supporting grassroots groups; promoting research, education, and outreach; and providing activist leadership training to foster public policies to advance gay rights and end discrimination based on sexual orientation.

The NGLTF also compiles and publishes statistics on hate crimes (which increased 172 percent between 1988 and 1992), discrimination (the NGLTF has been working since 1975 to ensure passage of a federal civil rights bill that would end discrimination for reasons of sexual orientation in the areas of housing, employment, public accommodations, credit, and federally assisted programs), health care

National Labor Relations Act

IDENTIFICATION: Labor law outlawing unfair practices by employers and legalizing important labor practices, including collective bargaining and the closed shop
DATE: Enacted on July 5, 1935
TYPE OF ETHICS: Business and labor ethics
SIGNIFICANCE: The National Labor Relations Act represented at attempt by the federal government to promote harmony between labor and management and to avoid costly strikes in the midst of an already devastating Depression.

Within months of the U.S. Supreme Court's invalidation of the National Industrial Recovery Act of 1933, Congress, led by Senator Robert Wagner of New York, passed legislation to assist employees and at the same time attempt to cure industrial strife by eliminating its chief cause: strikes. The law (known as the Magna Carta of labor) would eradicate the underlying cause of strikes, unfair employer practices, by encouraging collective bargaining, thereby granting employees equal bargaining power with their employers. Using the National Labor Relations Board to administer its provisions, the act, which applies to all employers engaged in interstate commerce, provides governmental processes for the selection of employee bargaining representatives. The act prohibits employers from interfering with union formation, establishing a "company" union, discriminating against union workers, refusing collective bargaining, or retaliating against workers who file charges under this act. Congress amended the act in 1947 to forbid the closed shop and again in 1959 to monitor union officials' activities.

SEE ALSO: Arbitration; Congress; Executive Order 10988; Fair Labor Standards Act; Labor-Management Relations Act; National Labor Union; Work.

National Labor Union

IDENTIFICATION: National federation of trade unions organized to secure workers' rights
DATE: 1866-1873
TYPE OF ETHICS: Business and labor ethics
SIGNIFICANCE: The National Labor Union (NLU) represented an attempt to create a movement for economic equality which would parallel earlier national movements toward political and religious equality.

Fearing the widening economic gap between employer and worker, William H. Sylvis led the Molders' Union and other national labor (craft) unions to join forces to organize the NLU to lobby for the rights of labor. The platform of the highly political NLU provided a plan to maintain its laborers' freedom, equality, and stature in American life. The NLU advocated higher wages, an eight-hour day, cooperative stores, and government action to assist labor. Women and African Americans were encouraged to organize and participate in the NLU. Upon President Sylvis's death in 1869, the NLU split over such ethical issues as women's rights, labor party involvement, and monetary expansion. By 1872, the NLU had become essentially a labor party, and after its lack of success in the election of 1872, both the NLU and the labor party collapsed. The NLU established the first truly national association of labor unions and succeeded in lobbying Congress in 1868 to establish an eight-hour day for federal laborers and artisans.

Stephen D. Livesay

SEE ALSO: American Federation of Labor; Executive Order 10988; Fair Labor Standards Act; Knights of Labor; Labor-Management Relations Act.

National Organization for Women

IDENTIFICATION: Organization established to lobby for women's rights
DATE: Founded in 1966
TYPE OF ETHICS: Sex and gender issues
SIGNIFICANCE: The National Organization for Women (NOW) has become an organization of significant power in U.S. politics. It seeks statutory protection for what it believes to be fundamental moral rights.

NOW's activities are based on the assumption that women have been denied the opportunity for professional achievement because practices that discriminate against them are not illegal. Since the United States is committed to equality, NOW believes, its laws should prohibit practices that impede women's climb to success. The years of NOW's existence have been marked by controversy over what sorts of rights require legal protection if women are to advance. For example, most members of NOW believe that reproductive rights, including the right to abortion, must be protected by law if women are to be free to make career choices. Many antiabortionists support women's rights but criticize NOW for condoning killing.

Some members of NOW have argued that NOW should lobby to protect the rights of homosexuals and minorities if it is to help the advancement of women in those categories. Other members have responded that the organization can best serve the majority of women if it maintains a narrow focus on employment rights, as it did in its early years when it was headed by its founder, Betty Freidan, author of *The Feminine Mystique*.

Laura Duhan Kaplan

SEE ALSO: Equal pay for equal work; Equal Rights Amendment; *Feminine Mystique, The*; Feminist ethics; Lobbying; Wage discrimination.

National Park System, U.S.

IDENTIFICATION: Group of over 360 parcels of land owned, administered, and protected by the federal government

DATE: First park established in 1872

TYPE OF ETHICS: Environmental ethics

SIGNIFICANCE: The National Park System seeks to preserve environmental resources from industrial development, unregulated tourism, hunting, and other encroachments, on the theory that the nation's populace has an interest in, or benefits from, the conservation of wilderness. The creation of new parks may raise ethical issues regarding federal seizure of private or state land.

In 1870, members of the Washburn survey decided, around a campfire, to recommend public ownership and preservation of scenic features in the Yellowstone region rather than claim them for themselves.

The First U.S. National Parks

Date	Park	Location
1872	Yellowstone	Wyoming, Montana, and Idaho
1890	Kings Canyon	California
1890	Sequoia	California
1890	Yosemite	California
1899	Mount Ranier	Washington
1902	Crater Lake	Oregon
1903	Wind Cave	South Dakota
1906	Mesa Verde	Colorado
1914	Everglades	Florida
1915	Rocky Mountain	Colorado
1916	Hawaii Volcanoes	Hawaii
1916	Lassen Volcanic	California
1919	Acadia	Maine
1919	Grand Canyon	Arizona
1919	Zion	Utah

This led Ferdinand Vandiveer Hayden, director of the U.S. Geographical and Geological Survey of the Territories, to lobby Congress, which established Yellowstone National Park in 1872. In 1886, the park was organized under the Army. In 1916, the National Park Service was established in the Department of the Interior, with Stephen Mather as its first director.

Mather organized the system, emphasizing preservation and display. During the mid-1960's, Congress responded to the land ethic by directing the establishment of wilderness areas within existing parks. The park system also has broadened its scope from preserving spectacular scenic areas such as the Grand Canyon to include significant historical sites, outstanding recreational areas, and areas designed to preserve practical examples of important ecosystems, such as the Florida Everglades. National Parks are established by acts of Congress that define their areas and control their operation. Some national monuments, such as Death Valley National Monument, are of the same character as national parks but are established and controlled by Executive Order, a power granted to the president under the Antiquities Act of 1906.

Ralph L. Langenheim, Jr.

SEE ALSO: Conservation; Leopold, Aldo; Muir, John; Sierra Club; Wilderness Act of 1964.

National security and sovereignty

DEFINITION: Political concept concerned with preserving the identity of a state as such and with protecting its citizens from armed attack by other states or groups

TYPE OF ETHICS: International relations

SIGNIFICANCE: National security presents ethical challenges for liberal democracies seeking appropriate balances between security and freedom.

Because liberal democracies are fundamentally open societies, ensuring national security poses special problems for those governments. Unregulated government surveillance of citizens and other such tools of more repressive regimes are generally considered unacceptable within open societies. However, the September 11, 2001, terrorist attacks in New York and Washington, D.C., left Americans in shock from the devastation and carnage and predictably led to a rush of government actions aimed at increasing national security. These actions ranged from internal measures such as the passage of the Patriot Act of 2001 to external measures such as the NATO- and United Nations-sanctioned military attack against the Taliban government in Afghanistan, as well as the U.S.-led invasion of Iraq in 2003.

Although the U.S. Constitution places limits on government action, those limits are legal, not ethical, and in times of crises may be illusory. For example, during World War II, the federal government rounded up tens of thousands of American citizens of Japanese descent, confiscating their property and detaining them in "internment camps." The U.S. Supreme Court upheld the detainment as constitutional in the time of war in its 1943 *Korematsu v. United States* ruling.

The ethical challenge for a liberal democracy in the face of severe threats to national security is to resist the temptation to abandon traditional ideals in favor of short-term measures that trade away too much freedom for not enough security, particularly in situations in which costs are concentrated on discrete groups. An especially dangerous temptation is to use a consequentialist approach, or strict cost-benefit analysis, to resolve all national security concerns.

RACIAL PROFILING

Because all nineteen terrorists implicated in the September 11 hijackings were young men from Middle Eastern countries—primarily Saudi Arabia—the federal government engaged in a dragnet that snared hundreds of young Middle Easterners residing in the United States. Some were quickly released, others were prosecuted in Detroit, Michigan, and in Portland, Oregon, and many others were held on charges of immigration violations. In addition, in complying with Federal Aviation Administration directives to conduct "secondary screening" of passengers and carry-on luggage, commercial airlines were accused of engaging in "racial profiling"; that is, selecting men of supposed Middle Eastern appearance for disproportionate numbers of such searches. In one notable incident, American Airlines kicked a United States Secret Service agent named Walied Shater off

---

The Mathematics of Racial Profiling

The seductive appeal of a racial profile lies in the belief that if members of group X are disproportionately more likely to commit a particular crime than other people, it makes sense to focus attention on group X. However, if only a tiny percentage of group X members commit the crime, then such a focus may be ethically questionable, as it would burden the overwhelming majority of law-abiding members of group X. It is instructive to consider the mathematics of profiling.

If a particular crime that is committed by only 0.1 percent of the general population is committed by 1.0 percent of the members of group X, then any individual member of group X is ten times more likely to commit the crime than a member of the general population. However, 99 percent of the members of group X are law-abiding with respect to this crime. Moreover, if all the members of group X constitute less than 10 percent of the total population, then fewer than half of the people who commit the crime in question are actually members of group X.

---

a flight on Christmas Day in 2001 because of "inconsistencies in his paperwork."

Racial profiling was controversial even before the terrorist attacks. For example, a number of academic writers have long argued that the Drug Enforcement Agency's "drug courier profile" contains a racial component. At least one federal judge reached the same conclusion in 1992, labeling it "a racist practice . . . that openly targets African-Americans" in *United States v. Taylor*.

TORTURE AND OTHER EXTREME MEASURES

The threat that terrorism, particularly after the September 11 attacks, poses to society also poses a challenge to ethical conduct in law enforcement and antiterrorism actions. With terrorist groups such as al-Qaeda seeking weapons of mass destruction, including nuclear weapons, a successful terrorist attack could result in the deaths of hundreds of thousands, if not millions, of people.

Given such potentially catastrophic dangers, it is not easy to remain wedded to the principle that the ends do not justify the means. Indeed, the problem has been well known to philosophers and law professors as the "ticking time bomb" scenario, in which authorities capture a suspect who knows the location of a time bomb due to detonate at any time. Can the authorities torture the suspect in order to determine the location of the bomb, thereby saving hundreds of lives?

One familiar line of thought on this scenario is the consequentialist approach, a simple cost-benefit analysis: the harm of torturing one person is presumably outweighed significantly by the gain of saving hundreds of people. The problem with the consequentialist approach from an ethical perspective is that it has no readily apparent limits and might justify, for example, the killing of a healthy person to harvest that person's organs if doing so would save a large enough number of other sick persons.

Moreover, the ticking time bomb scenario offers comfort in the certainty that the suspect to be tortured is in fact the perpetrator, the bomb is real, and the only way to determine the bomb's location in time to stop it is to employ torture. In real life, it is doubtful that law enforcement authorities will have the luxury of such perfect information, making decisions to employ torture even more ethically difficult.

IMPLICATIONS FOR ETHICAL CONDUCT

Consequentialism is a seductively attractive principle in implementing national security, particularly during times of crises when the potential casualty toll from a terrorist attack or an armed attack by a foreign nation can be staggering. Because consequentialism knows no limits, however, it is not an attractive ethical guideline, even in the name of national security. This is not to say that one should not consider the potential consequences of failing to take a step in the name of national security; but rather that the ethics of ensuring national security require more than just balancing of numbers.

Tung Yin

FURTHER READING

Abrams, Norman. *Anti-Terrorism and Criminal Enforcement*. St. Paul: Thomson, 2003.

Cole, David. *Terrorism and the Constitution: Sacrificing Civil Liberties in the Name of National Security*. 2d ed. New York: New Press, 2002.

Dershowitz, Alan M. *Why Terrorism Works*. New Haven: Yale University Press, 2002.

Koh, Harold Hongju. *The National Security Constitution: Sharing Power After the Iran-Contra Affair*. New Haven: Yale University Press, 1990.

SEE ALSO: Homeland defense; International justice; Intervention; Monroe Doctrine; Mutually Assured Destruction; Patriotism; Peacekeeping missions; Refugees and stateless people; Sovereignty; United Nations Convention on the Prevention and Punishment of the Crime of Genocide; Zionism.

Nationalism

DEFINITION: Loyalty to a nation and devotion to that nation's interests over those of all other nations

TYPE OF ETHICS: Politico-economic ethics

SIGNIFICANCE: Nationalism is based, either consciously or unconsciously, upon the premise that one's nationality is the most important aspect of one's identity, overriding concerns of class, sex, race, religion, and so on. It may be seen as a vice, motivating unethical conduct, but it may also be seen as a virtue, in which case it is often called patriotism.

Nationalism is usually manifested in two forms: as a sentiment and as a movement. Nationalist sentiment is the feeling of anger aroused by the violation of the nationalist principle or the feeling of satisfaction aroused by its fulfillment. A nationalist movement is one that is actuated by a sentiment of this kind. There are various ways in which the nationalist principle can be violated. The political boundary of the state can fail to include all members of the nation or it can include them all but also be host to a substantial number of foreigners.

A nation may even exist in a multiplicity of states with no distinct political boundary, as in the case of the Jews before the creation of Israel in 1948. Another violation of the nationalist principle to which the nationalist sentiment is very sensitive and often hostile occurs when the political rulers of the nation belong to a nation other than that of the majority of people over whom they rule, a fact that explains the violent resistance encountered by some imperialist and colonial regimes.

HISTORICAL ORIGIN

The roots of modern nationalism have been traced to what was for perhaps a hundred thousand years the basic social institution of humankind: the tribe. Out of this institution grew a sentiment of union that was nurtured and reinforced by common traditions and customs, by legends and myths, and, most important, by a common language. Prior to the sixteenth century, military conquests, commercial activities, and certain religions overflowed tribal barriers and imposed "international" loyalty in place of tribal loyalties. Tribal nationalism was thus systematically replaced by a form of internationalism, which meant the subjection of local group feeling to the claims of a great empire or the demands of an inclusive church.

During the sixteenth and seventeenth centuries, this traditional internationalism would also crumble as the Roman Catholic Church was disrupted by the rise of the Protestant Reformation and empires fell one after the other. Out of the ruins of the empires and the wreckage of the church emerged a new system for Europe. This system involved an agglomeration of peoples with diverse languages, dialects, and traditions, whose purpose was more to increase the wealth, prestige, and power of reigning families than to build up homogeneous nationalities. In France and England, and later in Spain, Germany, Italy, and Russia, the strongest noble families won the territory and, with their supporters, created monarchical governments that by the early eighteenth century had started evolving steadily into modern-day national states.

EVOLUTION TO NATION STATES

The evolution from monarchical governments to national states was catalyzed in the eighteenth century by the advent of the philosophers of the Enlightenment, who did more than anybody else to convert people's loyalty from the royal families and the church to the service of the nation. Prior to the eighteenth century, wars were usually dynastic and religious in origin and had nothing to do with individual rights. European peoples were bartered from one reigning family to another, sometimes as a marriage dowry, sometimes as the booty of conquest. In the same manner, overseas peoples were exploited by rival sets of European tradesmen and soldiers, and there were great commercial wars to determine whether natives of America, Asia, and Africa should belong to Spain, France, Belgium, Holland, Germany, or England. The so-called national frontiers, which were referred to then as "natural," had been acquired by any means other than natural: force, guile, marriage, inheritance, purchase, diplomacy, and illegal confiscation, for example. Individuals (or subjects) could not choose to whom they wanted to give their loyalty.

Through the efforts of the Enlightenment philosophers, this status quo was challenged. Religion, which had hitherto been untouchable, was substantially demystified. The natural was substituted for the supernatural, and science for religion. The philosophers held that Christianity, be it Catholic or Protestant, was a tissue of myths and superstitions. In place of religion and the church, human reason was exalted and almost deified.

Perhaps the greatest contribution of the Enlightenment philosophers to modern nationalism was their insistence on the natural rights of the individual, and in particular the right of national self-determination, which allows the individual to choose the sovereign state to which to belong and the form of government under which to serve. Furthermore, they insisted that all governments should be for the good of the governed and that the prince should be the servant of the people. The first outbursts of modern nationalism (the French Revolution of 1789) were directly inspired and fanned by these principles.

THE SPREAD OF NATIONALISM

After the French Revolution, believing themselves to be the benefactors of the human race, the French were eager to impose their newly found liberty and their superior national institutions upon all of Europe and perhaps the world. That most of Europe and the world were not ready or willing to accept liberty *à la française* made little difference. French expansionism took precedence over its revolutionary messianism; what had been supposed to be a support for national liberation became a pretext for territorial expansion. Reacting to this turn of events, the rest of Europe became animated by the desire to resist the French. The name of France became not only feared but also hated. That fear and hate would later become fundamental in spreading the sentiment of modern nationalism, for it was in a bid to stop French expansionist aggression that the rest of Europe started appealing to national sentiment.

From that point on, nationalism was well on its way to becoming the dominant force. For many people, the nation became the chief object of allegiance. The loyalty and devotion once given to old dynasties and the church were now given to the fatherland. The defense of the fatherland had become the end of most people's endeavors and almost the sole object, other than immediate family, for which they would willingly die.

ETHICS VS. REALPOLITIK

In the same way that the realization of a common culture and destiny as well as the instinct to survive induced a group to believe itself a nation, so they also made that group aware of the differences that set it apart from other groups. As these differences sharpened, so did feelings of national exclusiveness and the national dislike of others.

Friedrich Hertz's *Nationality in History and Politics* (1957) identifies two aspects of the spirit of nationalism: its positive and constructive side, which promotes national solidarity and freedom; and its negative and destructive side, which promotes the mental seclusion of the nation, leading to mutual distrust and prejudice, and culminating in a striving for superiority and domination. In the latter case, nationalist sentiment is often accompanied by a show of national aggressiveness, in which, more often than not, the primary aim is the quest for national honor, which in turn is expressed in terms of power, superiority, a higher rank among nations, prestige, and domination. In other words (to echo the thoughts of Niccolò Machiavelli), the aims of politics in the national interest became ultimately centered on the acquisition of land, human energy and resources, and the relative weakening of other powers.

By the beginning of the nineteenth century, realpolitik nationalism had become the new religion of the people. Boyd C. Shafer, in *Nationalism: Myth and Reality* (1955), finds a number of parallels between the "new faith" and many of the distinguishing marks of the "old religions." According to him, like the traditional religions, nationalism developed a morality that had its own rewards and punishments, virtues and sins, and missionary zeal. There were many similarities, even in the fanaticism with which those of contrary opinions were persecuted in the

name of the new "divinities": liberty and fatherland. The similarity with religion did not end there.

Like the Christians, "good" nationalists were zealous in spreading their gospel, as indicated by the national imperialistic and colonial ventures of the nineteenth century, although behind the new national will for expansion, the motives were mixed and sometimes contradictory. Bourgeois entrepreneurs coveted trade and profit, politicians sought popularity, military men wanted glory, some hoped to propagate liberty and the Christian faith, and others were simply looking for adventure. That this might mean a denial of other people's right to a fatherland made no difference.

Nationalism became more and more violent and exclusive as people began to show an absolute faith in their superiority over other nationalities. National egoism, becoming more and more intensified, came to be accepted as moral and therefore desirable. Thus, most Western European powers, particularly France and Britain, acquired huge colonial empires to serve their national interests and bolster their national power. Germany, Italy, and Japan, all in the name of the nation, embarked on a series of expansionist aggressions that later culminated in World War II. After the war, in order to consolidate its national power, the Soviet Union pushed westward in Europe to absorb the Baltic states, making Poland, Czechoslovakia, Hungary, Romania, and Bulgaria into satellite nations. Finally, the United States, in an effort to propagate its own form of democracy abroad and thereby ensure its national security, "fought" the Cold War.

Nationalism also comes in other forms besides that of aggression against other nations. In some cases, it is manifested in the form of intolerance and aggression against internal opposition (totalitarian regimes), minorities (such as the Iraqi Kurds), or a racial segment of the population (as in apartheid-era South Africa). When this happens, more often than not, nationalism becomes a disruptive force, tending to destabilize rather than enhance social order. It may even come in a form of economic egotism, such as protectionism. During the early stages, political considerations dominated nationalism, but over the years, a tendency developed to regard the state as an economic as well as a political unit. Economic nationalism merged with imperialism to become one of the driving forces of modern history.

Thus, over time, nationalism had evolved from its original phase of liberalism as conceived by the Enlightenment philosophers, when reason, tolerance, and humanitarianism were the watchwords, and had become inevitably tied to the realpolitik that had begun with the rivalries of earlier tribal groups. In its process of transformation from a positive to negative force, liberal nationalism gradually deteriorated until it lost most, if not all, of its earlier moral character. Just as Machiavelli excluded morality from politics, so did Georg W. F. Hegel during the early nineteenth century place the nation-state above morality, a legacy that continued well into the twentieth century.

THE IMPERIALIST/COLONIAL LEGACY

In *Macro-Nationalisms: A History of the Pan-Movements* (1984), Louis L. Snyder identifies two lesser-known but important satellite movements running concurrently with established modern nationalisms.

The first movement involves the many mini-nationalisms that are seeking to break away from the established nation-states. The disadvantage of modern nationalism as it emerged from the European model in the eighteenth century is that it presupposes a common language and a reasonably homogeneous society. By the middle of the twentieth century, however, few states could claim to be "pure" nations with a completely homogeneous ethnic composition. Thus emerged the problem of minorities, their rights, their dubious loyalties, and their mistreatment by the majorities.

Expansionism, which was begun in the eighteenth and nineteenth centuries and which hitherto had been an attribute of national power, eventually became a Pandora's box for the imperialist powers, as problems of homogeneity and self-determination forced issues of nationalism into the forefront of global politics. This is particularly true of some Western European states, in which many mini-nationalisms inside the established nation-states seek to break away from larger units; for example, France (Corsica), Spain (Basque), and Britain (Catholic Ireland). Meanwhile, in the East, for similar reasons, the Soviet Union completely disintegrated, giving way to a multiplicity of new nations; Czechoslovakia gave birth to two autonomous states, while the former Yugoslavia, which is terribly divided along ethnic lines, engaged

in a bitter civil war to determine the fate of the newly created "nations."

The second movement involves the many macro-nationalisms that seek to expand the established nation-state to a supranational form. According to Snyder, macro-nationalisms, or pan-movements, seek to promote the solidarity of peoples united by common or kindred languages, group identification, traditions, or characteristics such as geographical proximity. Like established nationalisms, they reveal an aggressive impulse that seeks to control contiguous or noncontiguous territory. In addition to this power syndrome, they are also animated by specific elements: for Pan-Slavism, it was messianic zeal; for Pan-Germanism, territorial expansion; for Pan-Arabism, religious zeal; for Pan-Africanism, racial unity; for Pan-Asianism, anticolonialism; for Pan-Americanism hemispheric solidarity; and, finally, for Pan-Europeanism, economic unity.

The moral issues involved in the nationalism of Europe are different from those that operate in other parts of the world—especially in Asia and Africa—principally because, from the onset, the liberal values of the Enlightenment were not applied to the colonial possessions. Anticolonial nationalism was an intellectual response to this contradiction. Most of the peoples in these two continents were initially united in their struggle to gain national independence and to secure better standards of living for their people. Almost everywhere in the Third World, the ideology of nationalism was firmly linked to the ideology of development. Unfortunately, in some of these cases, nationalism and self-determination have had to be settled not by votes but by armed conflicts.

In Africa, the situation became particularly delicate when colonialism bestowed on the new states administrative structures that were anything but ethnically homogeneous. To preserve or attain national independence, African people have had to resort to civil wars (Belgian Congo, Nigeria, Sudan, Ethiopia), terrorism and guerrilla warfare (South Africa); or even full-scale war (Morocco).

THE MORAL LEGACY

In conclusion, it could be said that during the course of the twentieth century, the nationalist process matured into a real cult of superiority in which nationalism assumes the role of a "political religion," with prestige and power as its "supreme gods," as was the case in Nazi Germany and Benito Mussolini's Italy. Governments acted as they pleased, in their own national interest, and were limited only by superior strength, although in almost all cases elaborate efforts were made to cloak all acts of nationalism in moralism. Even the superpowers had to resort to the moral crusade to identify their own standards with general humanitarian principles to legitimize nationalistic endeavors. Thus, in the Cold War, the United States and the Soviet Union not only challenged each other along political and economic lines but also presented themselves as bearers of universal moral systems, proclaiming standards that they recommended for all nations.

Olusoji A. Akomolafe

FURTHER READING

Gellner, Ernest. *Nations and Nationalism*. Ithaca, N.Y.: Cornell University Press, 1983. Demonstrates how political units that do not conform to the principle "one state, one culture" feel the strain in the form of nationalistic activity. Although it is addressed to political scientists, sociologists, and historians, this book should appeal to anyone who is seriously concerned with human society.

Hertz, Friedrich O. *Nationality in History and Politics*. London: Routledge & Kegan Paul, 1957. A multidisciplinary study of nationalism that deals with the psychology, sociology, and politics of national sentiment. Provides an excellent analysis of the relationships among nationalism, religion, language, and race.

McKim, Robert, and Jeff McMahan, eds. *The Morality of Nationalism*. New York: Oxford University Press, 1997. A comprehensive anthology of essays by leading social and political philosophers, this volume confronts and engages the moral issues raised by contemporary nationalisms.

Moore, Margaret. *The Ethics of Nationalism*. New York: Oxford University Press, 2001. An ethical analysis of nationalism, with special attention to the nationalist aspirations of groups within nations. Includes discussions of secession, minority nationals, self-determination, nation-building, and multiculturalism.

Shafer, Boyd C. *Nationalism: Myth and Reality*. New York: Harcourt, Brace & World, 1955. This book offers the reader in nationalism a valuable starting point. It includes a chronological account of the history of nationalism.

Snyder, Louis L. *Macro-nationalisms: A History of the Pan-Movements*. Westport, Conn.: Greenwood Press, 1984. This is the second of two volumes that deal with two aspects of nationalism: mini-nationalism and macro-nationalism. Students of macro-nationalism will find it particularly useful, because it discusses in detail all the established pan-movements.

_____. *The New Nationalism*. Ithaca, N.Y.: Cornell University Press, 1968. A comprehensive account of post-1945 nationalism that includes detailed studies of Arab, African, Asian, and Latin American nationalisms.

SEE ALSO: Enlightenment ethics; Fascism; Loyalty; Nazism; Patriotism; Racial prejudice; Realpolitik; Sovereignty; Zionism.

Native American casinos

DEFINITION: Legal gambling establishments owned and operated by officially recognized Native American tribes

DATE: 1979 to the present

TYPE OF ETHICS: Politico-economic ethics

SIGNIFICANCE: By taking advantage of their special legal status as sovereign nations, many Native American tribes have opened highly profitable gambling centers that have raised a number of ethical questions about the fairness of their tax exemptions, the unequal distribution of benefits among impoverished tribes, and the morality of profiting from gambling, which many people regard as an inherently sinful activity.

Is gambling the answer to Native American impoverishment—the "new buffalo," as some Native Americans have called it? In some places, such as the Pequots' Foxwoods Resort Casino, in Connecticut, legalized gambling has been an economic boon, as members of small tribes have been enriched. For others, such as the New York Oneidas in upstate New York, gambling has provided an enriched upper class with the means to hire police to force dissident anti-gambling traditionalists from their homes.

The Foxwoods Money Machine

The Mashantucket Pequots' Foxwoods Resort Casino complex in Connecticut began as a small bingo parlor after roughly forty banks refused to lend the tribe money for a larger project. The bingo parlor began operating in 1986 and became wildly successful, drawing its clientele mainly from the urban corridor that stretches from Boston to New York City. With the profits from the bingo parlor, the Pequots opened a full-scale casino in 1992. By the year 2000, the resulting Foxwoods complex was drawing about fifty thousand gamblers on an average day. The surrounding complex included five casinos containing more than 300,000 square feet of gaming space, 5,842 slot machines, 370 gaming tables, a 3,000-seat high-stakes bingo parlor with $1,000,000 jackpots, a 200-seat Sportsbook, and a keno lounge. The Foxwoods casino complex also included four hotels, twenty-three shopping areas, twenty-four food services, and a movie-theater complex, as well as a museum.

Foxwoods quickly became a financial success for its sponsors, as well as the state government of Connecticut, to which the casino's management pledged a quarter of its profits. During the fiscal year spanning 1999 and 2000, Foxwoods' gross revenues on its slot and video machines alone totaled more than $9 billion. Foxwoods and a second casino, the Mohegan Sun, with thirteen thousand employees, paid the state of Connecticut more than $318 million in taxes during the 1999-2000 fiscal year.

Foxwoods Resort Casino. (AP/Wide World Photos)

Although many Native American cultures traditionally practiced forms of gambling as a form of sport—such as the Iroquois Peachstone game—there is no traditional Native American precedent for large-scale experience with gambling as a commercial enterprise. The history of reservation-based commercial gambling began during 1979, when the Seminole of Florida became the first Native nation to enter the bingo industry.

By the year 2000, Native American gaming revenue had grown to $10.6 billion—a figure representing 16 percent of the $64.9 billion generated by gaming in the United States as a whole. According to the National Indian Gaming Association, Indian gaming was contributing approximately $120 million in state and local tax receipts annually by 2002. Moreover, gaming patrons spent an estimated $237 million in local communities around Indian casinos.

Of the 562 federally recognized Native American governmental entities in the United States at that time, 201 participated in class II or class III gaming by 2001. Class II includes such games as bingo, pull-tabs, lotto, punch boards and certain card games permissible under individual state laws. Class III includes everything else, including casino-style table games, such as roulette and craps, and card games, such as poker and blackjack. Indian casinos operated in twenty-nine states under a total of 249 separate gaming compacts.

THE ONEIDA EXAMPLE

By the 1960's, the landholdings of New York's Oneida tribe had been reduced to a mere thirty-two acres, east of Syracuse, with almost no economic infrastructure. Three decades later, the New York Oneidas owned a large casino, the Turning Stone, which had incubated a number of other business ventures. Many of the roughly one thousand Oneida people who resided in the area were receiving substantial material benefits.

Despite the economic benefits, a substantial dissident movement arose among Oneidas who assert that Ray Halbritter, the "nation representative" of the New York Oneidas, had never been voted into his office. The dissident group was centered in the Shenandoah family, whose members include the notable singer Joanne Shenandoah and her husband, activist Doug George-Kanentiio. The dissidents argued that the New York Oneidas under Halbritter had merely established a commercial business, called it a "nation," and then acquired the requisite approvals from New York State and the federal governments to use their status to open the Turning Stone.

Under Halbritter's direction, the New York Oneidas appointed a "men's council"—an unheard-of body in traditional matrilineal Iroquois law or tradition—which issued a zoning code to "beautify" the Oneida Nation. That code enabled Halbritter's fifty-four-member police force to evict from their reservation homes Oneidas who opposed his role as leader of the tribe. Halbritter's control also was supported by the acquisition of *Indian Country Today*, a national Native American newspaper.

The experience of the Oneidas raised several ethi-cal questions, among them the question of whether the Oneida model might be a key to defining the future of Native American sovereignty. Critics wondered if the Oneidas' economic gains had been offset by an atmosphere of authoritarian rule and a devastating loss of traditional bearings, as many Oneida dissidents believe.

CULTURAL INTEGRITY

Writing in *Modern Tribal Development* in 2000, Dean Howard Smith erected a theoretical context in which he sought a model for Indian reservation development that would be consistent with "the cultural integrity and sovereignty of the Native American nations . . . leading to cultural integrity, self-determination, and self-sufficiency." Instead of being assimilated into an industrial capitalistic system, Smith believes that Native American traditions can be used to design "a new type of system that incorporates competitive behavior, social compatibility and adaptation, and environmental concerns."

Bruce E. Johansen

FURTHER READING

Chen, David W., and Charlie LeDuff. "Bad Blood in Battle Over Casinos; Issue Divides Tribes and Families as Expansion Looms." *The New York Times*, October 28, 2001, A-29.

Johansen, Bruce E. *Life and Death in Mohawk Country.* Golden, Colo.: North American Press/Fulcrum, 1993.

_____. "The New York Oneidas: A Case Study in the Mismatch of Cultural Tradition and Economic Development." *American Indian Culture and Research Journal* 26, no. 3 (2002): 25-46.

Johnson, Tim. "The Dealer's Edge: Gaming in the Path of Native America." *Native Americas* 12, no. 1 & 2 (Spring/Summer, 1995): 16-25.

Smith, Dean Howard. *Modern Tribal Development: Paths to Self-sufficiency and Cultural Integrity in Indian Country.* Walnut Creek, Calif.: AltaMira Press, 2000.

SEE ALSO: Betting on sports; Lotteries; Native American ethics; Taxes.

Native American ethics

DEFINITION: Diverse set of ethical systems and moral codes of North America's tribal peoples

TYPE OF ETHICS: Beliefs and practices

SIGNIFICANCE: Many Native American cultural traditions and worldviews differ significantly from those of Western traditions. The history of the interactions between Western colonizers and Native Americans, moreover, has imparted a unique status to the ethical systems of the latter group, which have been appropriated by many political dissidents and used as the basis for critiques of modern environmental and capitalist practices.

Several problems attend to any overview of Native American ethics. First, students of Native American cultural traditions have rarely focused on the topic of ethics, and therefore the amount of material available is minimal. Introductory texts on Native American religions typically fail to consider the topic. For example, Åke Hultkrantz's *The Study of American Indian Religions* (1983) and *Native Religions of North America* (1987), Sam D. Gill's *Native American Religions: An Introduction* (1982), and Lawrence E. Sullivan's *Native American Religions: North America* (1989) have no entries for "ethics" or "morality."

Second, the few scholars who did give some consideration to the manners, customs, and moral codes of Native American peoples generally had no formal training in ethics. Those who did tended to assume that the moral categories defined by the Western philosophic and religious traditions could be transferred to Native American cultures without any fear of misrepresentation. Thus, these scholars were preoccupied with questions of sexuality and general social structures, whether or not these were considered of prime importance by the natives.

Finally, the phrase "Native American ethics" suggests historical fiction. Only in the last four decades of the twentieth century did any pan-Indian identity emerge for Native Americans. The reality is that each tribal tradition considers itself to be a unique entity with a specific identity and cultural web.

TRAVELERS AND MISSIONARIES

Historically, Western discussions of the moral condition of Native American peoples date from the fifteenth century. For the next four centuries, materials relating to the ethics of Native American peoples primarily were recorded in the accounts of early travelers and missionaries. Typically, the debate centered on the question of the status of Native Americans as moral beings.

The earliest example dates from 1550, when Charles V of Spain summoned Juan Gines de Sepúlveda and Bartolomé de Las Casas to Valladolid to hear arguments on the nature of the beings discovered in the New World. Sepúlveda argued that the "Indians" were natural slaves. His evaluation provided justification for the Spanish system of *encomiendaro*. Las Casas, having spent four decades in the New World, provided broad evidence for a contrary view that the natives were highly developed and possessed natural virtues. New England Calvinists and romantics in the tradition of Jean-Jacques Rousseau carried forth the ignoble-noble savage debate into the twentieth century.

ANTHROPOLOGICAL AND ETHNOLOGICAL STUDIES

During the mid-nineteenth century, Max Müller, Edward Tylor, Herbert Spencer, and other evolutionary positivists used the existing materials on Native American cultures to serve their universal theories of human development. Spencer, for example, concluded that "savages" lacked the necessary mental capacities to make moral distinctions, while Tylor argued that primitive peoples had not risen to the stage of ethical development that is characteristic of higher religions. These ethnocentric appraisals of "primitive" peoples in general, and Native Americans specifically, continued to inform the study of Native American peoples through the first half of the twentieth century.

Led by Franz Boas and Clark Wissler, twentieth century anthropological and ethnological studies of Native American cultures tended to ignore religious topics except as they contributed to cultural or diffusionist theories. Discussions of social relations focused on kinship patterns and formal social organization. Boas's *Kwakiutl Ethnography* (1966), for example, contains no references to ethics, moral codes, or values. Paul Radin's *The Winnebago Tribe* (1923) and *The Trickster* (1956), Ruth Benedict's *Patterns of Culture* (1934), and Gladys Reichard's *Navaho Religion* (1950) use psychological approaches that reduce moral values to the satisfaction of human needs. Religion, when considered, focuses on topics such as the supernatural, sorcery, and witchcraft to the exclusion of ethical matters. Ruth Landes's *Ojibwa Religion and the Midéwiwin* (1968), for example, limits the term "ethics" to a distinction between "good" and "evil" in the context of sorcery and witchcraft, with no discussion of the ethical principles that might inform those evaluations.

PHILOSOPHICAL AND EMIC STUDIES

Richard Brandt's *Hopi Ethics* (1954) and John Ladd's *The Structure of a Moral Code* (1957) provide the only published formal theoretical studies of Native American ethics. Brandt and Ladd conclude that pragmatism best characterized Hopi and Navaho ethics. Brandt's methodology uses native interviews about ethical issues defined by Brandt rather than by the Hopi. Ladd's methodology is aimed at hypothetical reconstruction of Navaho ethics from the native point of view. Both Brandt and Ladd assume that ethics is concerned exclusively with social relations and therefore give little consideration to religious issues.

A. Irving Hallowell's *Ojib-wa Ontology, Behavior, and World View* (1960) marks a turning point in the study of the ethics of Native American peoples. Hallowell concluded that the key to Ojibwa behavior and worldview is found in a distinctive ontology that, on one hand, expands the category of person to include "other-than-human persons," and, on the other hand, defines moral behavior relationally. N. Scott Momaday's "The Man Made of Words" (1970) suggests that the idea of appropriation and the related concepts of appropriateness and propriety guide Native American relationships. Dorothy Lee's *Freedom and Culture* (1959), Howard Harrod's *Renewing the World* (1987), and Fritz Detwiler's "All My Relatives" (1992) further argue for the relational nature of the ethics of Native American peoples based on the expanded notion of "person." Harrod's work, in particular, grounds ethics in ritual experience. Through ritual, the ethical bonds that sustain a relational worldview are renewed and enhanced. If a relational ontology is fundamental to Native American worldviews, then further investigation of Native American ethics from a relational perspective is required.

Fritz Detwiler

FURTHER READING

Brandt, Richard B. *Hopi Ethics: A Theoretical Analysis*. Chicago: University of Chicago Press, 1954.

Detwiler, Fritz. "'All My Relatives': Persons in Oglala Religion." *Religion* 22 (July, 1992): 235-246.

Gill, Jerry H. *Native American Worldviews: An Introduction*. Amherst, N.Y.: Humanity Books, 2002.

Hallowell, A. Irving. *Ojibwa Ontology, Behavior, and World View*. Indianapolis: Bobbs-Merrill, 1960.

Harrod, Howard. *Renewing the World: Plains Indian Religion and Morality*. Tucson: University of Arizona Press, 1987.

Ladd, John. *The Structure of a Moral Code: A Philosophical Analysis of Ethical Discourse Applied to the Ethics of the Navaho Indians*. Cambridge, Mass.: Harvard University Press, 1957.

Momaday, N. Scott. "The Man Made of Words." In *The First Convocation of Indian Scholars*, edited by Rupert Costo. San Francisco: Indian Historian Press, 1970.

Tedlock, Dennis, and Barbara Tedlock, eds. *Teachings from the American Earth: Indian Religion and Philosophy*. New York: Liveright, 1975.

Waters, Anne, ed. *American Indian Thought: Philosophical Essays*. Malden, Mass.: Blackwell, 2004.

SEE ALSO: Environmental ethics; Native American casinos; Native American genocide.

Native American genocide

DEFINITION: Long, slow destruction of the indigenous peoples of the Americas and their ways of life

TYPE OF ETHICS: Race and ethnicity

SIGNIFICANCE: European Americans justified the extermination of millions of Native Americans by judging them to be less than human.

The European discovery of the New World had devastating consequences for the native population. Within a century of Christopher Columbus's landing in 1492, the number of people living in the Americas had declined from more than twenty-five million to a few million. Whole societies in Mexico and South

America died within weeks of initial contact with Spanish explorers and adventurers. The major cause of the devastation was disease. Native Americans had lived in total isolation from the rest of the world since first arriving in the New World from Central Asia around 20,000 B.C.E.; hence, they had escaped the devastating epidemics and diseases, such as smallpox and the plague, that had afflicted the rest of humankind for generations. Such diseases normally required human carriers to pass them on to others, and such conditions did not exist in the New World until after 1492.

Columbus and his crew made four separate voyages to the New World between 1492 and 1510, and on each of those voyages sailors brought new diseases with them. Even the common flu had devastating consequences for defenseless Native American babies and children. Other people of the world had built up immunities to these killers, but Native Americans had none, so they died in massive numbers. During the sixteenth century, most of the dying took place from Mexico south, since the Spanish appeared to be uninterested in colonizing North America. Only after the English settled Jamestown in 1607-1608

Indian Wars in the American West, 1840's-1890

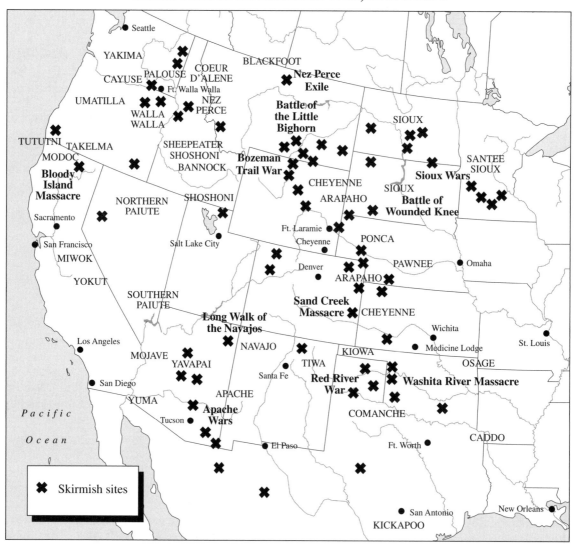

Examples of Native American Tribes That Were Exterminated

Date	Tribe	Region Inhabited	Cause
1513-1530	Calusa	Florida	Spanish warfare
1617-1633	Massachusetts	New England	Smallpox
1637-1638	Pequot	New England	English warfare
1637-1705	Powhatan	Virginia	English warfare
1675-1676	Narraganset	Rhode Island	English warfare
1675-1763	Susquehannock	New York	Disease and wars
1706-1717	Chitimacha	Louisiana	French warfare
1716-1731	Natchez	Mississippi	French warfare
1782-1853	Chinook	Columbia River region	Smallpox
1873-1905	Yavapai	Arizona	Tuberculosis

and Plymouth in Massachusetts in 1620 did the epidemics affect Native Americans in that region.

The first major tribe to be exterminated in North America was the Massachusetts of New England, whose population died out completely between 1619 and 1633 from a smallpox epidemic. Yet other things besides disease were killing Native Americans. Most Europeans believed that the people they came across in their explorations were not truly human at all, but instead savage, inferior beings who had no law and order, no cities, no wealth, and no idea of God or progress. When they died from "white man's diseases," this offered further proof of the weakness and helplessness of the population. They could not even make good slaves because they died so quickly from "minor" illnesses. That is why the Europeans turned to Africa for their supply of slave laborers; Africans, who had had a much longer history of contact with other peoples of the world, had built up immunities to the killing diseases. Native Americans were not so lucky.

U.S. GOVERNMENT POLICIES

As time passed, immunities were built up by native peoples, and fewer tribes were extinguished by diseases. Warfare, however, continued to take its toll. Thousands of Native Americans died defending their homelands from American settlers in the aftermath of the War for Independence. Native Americans were not made citizens by the Constitution of 1787 but were legally defined as residents of foreign nations living in the United States. Wars and conflicts over territory had devastated many tribes by 1830. In that year, President Andrew Jackson and Congress adopted a program, the Indian Removal Act, that they hoped would put an end to wars with the Native Americans. Under this new act, the American government would trade land west of the Mississippi River for land owned by the tribes in the east. Land in the west, acquired from France in 1803 as part of the Louisiana Purchase, was deemed unsuitable for farming by Europeans. Native Americans, on the other hand, would be able to survive on the Great Plains, called the "Great American Desert" by most whites, by hunting buffalo and other game.

Congress authorized the president to exchange land beginning in 1831. Three years later, a permanent Indian Country was created in the West and settlement by whites was declared illegal. By 1840, Indian Removal was complete, though it took the Black Hawk War in Illinois, the Seminole War in Florida, and the terrible march forcing the Cherokee from Georgia to the Indian Territory, to complete the process. At least three thousand Native American women and children died at the hands of the U.S. Army on the Cherokee "Trail of Tears." Indian Removal meant death and disaster for many eastern tribes.

Conflict was reduced by the program only until

whites began moving into the West during the 1860's. During the U.S. Civil War (1861-1865), several Indian Wars were fought in Minnesota and Iowa, and the infamous Chivington Massacre took place in Colorado in 1864. In this incident, 450 Native Americans were slaughtered without warning in a predawn raid by the Colorado militia. To prevent massacres in the West, Congress enacted a "reservation policy," setting aside several million acres of western lands for "permanent" Indian settlement. The Army had the job of keeping the tribes on their reservations. Frequent wars resulted as Great Plains tribes attempted to leave their reservations to hunt buffalo and the army drove them back.

Problems increased with the coming of railroads. The first transcontinental railroad began carrying passengers in 1869. Huge buffalo herds presented the railroads with a major problem, however, because they took hours and sometimes days to cross the tracks. To keep trains running on time, railroads hired hunters to kill the buffalo. By the late 1880's, they nearly accomplished their goal of killing off all the herds. Buffalo had once numbered 100 million, but by 1888, there were fewer than 1,000. With the destruction of the buffalo came the end of the Native American way of life.

The final war was fought in 1890 in the Black Hills of South Dakota on the Pine Ridge Reservation. An Indian holy man claimed that the whites would disappear and the buffalo would return if Native Americans danced a Ghost Dance. Magical shirts were given to the dancers that were supposed to protect them from white men's bullets. When the white Indian agent asked Washington for help to put down the Ghost Dancers, the Army responded by killing hundreds of the Native Americans, whose magical shirts did not work.

Native Americans did not become American citizens until 1924 and were required to live on reservations. Not until 1934 was self-government granted to the tribes, and by that time the reservations had become the poorest communities in the entire United States. The reservations continue to have the highest levels of unemployment, alcoholism, crime, and drug addiction found in U.S. communities. These signals of social disintegration and disruption are the final results of a policy of extermination that began in 1492.

Leslie V. Tischauser

FURTHER READING

Churchill, Ward. *A Little Matter of Genocide: Holocaust and Denial in the Americas, 1492 to the Present.* San Francisco: City Lights Books, 1997.

_____. *Struggle for the Land: Native North American Resistance to Genocide, Ecocide, and Colonization.* San Francisco: City Lights Books, 2002.

Debo, Angie. *A History of the Indians of the United States.* Norman: University of Oklahoma Press, 1970.

Deloria, Vine, Jr. *Custer Died for Your Sins: An Indian Manifesto.* New York: Macmillan, 1969.

Farb, Peter. *Man's Rise to Civilization as Shown by the Indians of North America from Primeval Times to the Coming of the Industrial State.* New York: Dutton, 1968.

Josephy, Alvin M., Jr. *The Indian Heritage of America.* New York: Alfred A. Knopf, 1968.

Washburn, Wilcomb E. *The Indian in America.* New York: Harper & Row, 1975.

SEE ALSO: Bigotry; Biochemical weapons; Genocide, cultural; Genocide and democide; Manifest destiny; Native American ethics; Racial prejudice; Racism.

Natural law

DEFINITION: Moral law existing in, or deriving from, nature rather than culture

TYPE OF ETHICS: Theory of ethics

SIGNIFICANCE: The many contradictory permutations of natural law theory share the notion of a universal law common to all humanity and derived in some fashion from nature or from the natural (pre-social) state of humanity. This notion is broad enough to have supported religious, secular, optimistic, pessimistic, human-centered, and non-human-centered versions of the theory.

The natural law theory of morality has its roots in classical Greek and Roman philosophy. Greek thinkers such as Aristotle emphasized the teleological nature of humanity. In other words, each human being has a fixed human nature and a certain "function"; namely, the capacity for rational thought. It is implied in Aristotle's philosophy that moral actions are those that fulfill one's nature as a rational human being. Furthermore, in the *Rhetoric* (c. 335 B.C.E.) Aristotle differentiates between positive or "particular" laws and laws "according to nature." Aristotle described the latter as a "common" law; that is, one that was common or natural to all humanity.

The notion of natural law is even more explicit in the writings of the ancient Roman philosopher and statesman Cicero, who is usually associated with the Stoic school of philosophy. Cicero argued in his essays for an eternal and immutable law that prevailed for all people at all times. Moreover, this law is grounded in human nature. According to Cicero, "Law is the highest reason, implanted in Nature, which commands what ought to be done and forbids the opposite." In general, this notion of a natural law *(ius naturale)* permeated the Stoic philosophy, which emphasized the equality of all persons according to the law of nature. Moreover, this idea of a natural law was not foreign to Roman jurists; hence, it affected the development and application of actual laws in Roman society.

One finds intimations of the presence of this natural law in several other classical writers, such as Saint Augustine and Boethius. Augustine, for example, contended that the only valid temporal laws were those that were consonant with the eternal and immutable law of God. Other laws were simply unjust and hence lacked any authority. Even Saint Paul concludes in one of his epistles that we find a morality that conscience discerns naturally inscribed in our hearts (Romans 2:14-16).

SAINT THOMAS AQUINAS

The philosopher who is most closely associated with the natural law ethic is Saint Thomas Aquinas. He developed an elaborate philosophical system based in large part on the philosophy of Aristotle. His most famous work is known as the *Summa Theologica* (1266-1273). The *Summa* is a lengthy treatise in which Thomas Aquinas presents and defends his complete philosophical system. In a major section of this work known as "The Treatise on Law," he articulated his conception of natural law morality. This brief work has been extremely influential in the history of moral and political philosophy.

Thomas Aquinas begins from what he calls the "eternal law," which is the law of God's creative work by which he directs everything to the fulfillment he

has in mind. All true laws are derived from and related to this eternal, unchanging law of God. According to Thomas Aquinas, the natural law that governs the lives of human beings is a participation in this eternal law. God created humans and gave them a definite nature that is subject to certain laws; specifically, the laws of its own development. Moreover, each nature is oriented intrinsically toward the goal of developing and realizing all of its vast potential. Hence, the primary obligation placed on humans by God is simply self-fulfillment. In other words, a human being's fundamental moral obligation is to fulfill his or her nature, to actualize his or her potentials, to develop in a fully human way. This obligation comes from God the creator but it is also written or inscribed ontologically into each human nature and clearly manifests itself to any intelligence that discerns this nature.

Given that human nature is oriented toward its own fulfillment, the first principle of morality is simple to deduce: "Good is to be done and promoted and evil is to be avoided." All other precepts of the natural law are based on this principle. It is important to note that the word "good" here refers to the final end of self-realization or self-fulfillment. Thus, the first precept of the natural law could be expressed as follows: "Fulfill your true nature as a person," or simply "Follow nature."

How exactly can one fulfill one's nature and actualize one's potential in order to become more fully human? In Thomas Aquinas's view, one must merely follow one's natural inclinations. These inclinations are a deep-seated and innate part of human nature, and they provide the general specifications of the first precept, "do good," as applied to human nature. The natural inclinations derive from three levels. As beings (or substances), humans are naturally inclined toward self-preservation; hence, whatever is a means of preserving life and avoiding death belongs to the natural law. As animals, humans are naturally inclined to take in food, to reproduce through sexual intercourse, and so forth. As rational human beings, humans are naturally inclined toward a life of reason (that is, the acquisition of knowledge), toward friendship and a social life, and toward a life of virtue and the love of God. Unfortunately, Thomas Aquinas does not provide a very extensive list of these inclinations, he lists only a few primary precepts of the natural law.

The main point, however, is clear: If one follows these natural inclinations, one will attain genuine self-fulfillment and happiness. Indeed, one is obliged to follow these inclinations and not to oppose one's own nature. The natural inclinations are not known by means of conceptual reasoning or logical analysis. Instead, they are known intuitively and naturally by anyone possessing a properly functioning practical reason. Hence, one's practical reason both knows these natural inclinations and directs their implementation in particular circumstances. In this sense then, reason—or what Thomas Aquinas calls "right reason" (*recta ratio*)—is indisputably the ultimate norm of morality.

Since, as Thomas Aquinas points out, people grasp as goods the fulfillments to which they are naturally inclined, it follows that there is a basic precept of the natural law that corresponds to each natural inclination. In other words, the natural inclinations as intuited or known by reason become the natural laws that bind one from within. They become the basic principles of morality—the so-called primary precepts of the natural law. These principles are immutable because they emanate from the fixed human nature. Also, these laws are universal, since all humans share a common nature. It becomes clear, therefore, that these primary precepts of the natural law, which are universal and immutable, serve as a fixed and unshakable basis for all morality and law.

Thomas Aquinas stresses that there are also secondary precepts of the natural law. These are derived from applying the primary precepts to more particular kinds of situations. Unlike the primary precepts, the secondary ones are not infallibly or intuitively known, may be disputed at times, and often hold only as a general rule or "for the most part." Many civil laws and other moral mandates fall into this category. Thomas Aquinas's treatment of these secondary precepts reveals that he does allow for some flexibility in the development of law and morality.

The final issue considered in Thomas Aquinas's discussion of natural law is the relationship between human law and the natural law. Human law, according to Thomas Aquinas, is a further application of the natural law in a particular community and historical epoch. The necessity of such laws emanates from the unwillingness of some people to follow their own natural aptitude for virtue. Thomas Aquinas insists that every genuine human law must be derived from

and based on the natural law. He argues that the force of law depends on its justice and rightness, which in turn depends on the rule of reason.

Since the first rule of reason is the law of nature, every law must be based on this law of nature. Many laws will be established by tyrannical or inept rulers and legislators that will depart from the natural law and will be neither right nor just. When such laws deviate from the natural law, they are a corruption of law and have no binding force. Thomas Aquinas maintains that laws can be unjust or illegitimate in two ways: They are opposed to either the human good or the divine good. Clearly, then, any law that violates the common good, that is not just and does not participate in the natural law, is no law at all. All human law must, therefore, yield to the higher law of nature. It should be pointed out that even laws passed by good and upright rulers, laws perhaps good in themselves, might be poorly adapted to a particular situation. Hence, one might be justified in not following such a law under such circumstances.

Thus, there is an explicit hierarchy in Thomas Aquinas's philosophy of law. The natural law participates in and derives from the eternal law, and human law is subservient to the natural law. Whenever it conflicts with that law, it is null and void. The natural law, then, should be the ultimate guide and moral compass for all legislators and leaders.

NATURAL LAW AND NATURAL RIGHTS THEORY

A related but conceptually different approach to morality is the natural rights theory, which was developed by English philosophers such as Thomas Hobbes and John Locke. Locke, for example, argues for various natural rights such as the right to life, liberty, and property. According to Locke, these natural rights should be the basis for the laws and rules of civil society. The similarity between this viewpoint and the natural law ethic of Thomas Aquinas is the grounding of morality in rights that emanate from the nature of human beings. Locke, however, detaches his limited natural law theory from the metaphysical and theological underpinnings used by Thomas Aquinas. He also rejects the idea of natural hierarchies. Like Thomas Aquinas and other natural law philosophers, however, he claims that there is something higher than civil laws. In other words, the ultimate standards of law and morality are the natural human rights of life, liberty, and property. Moreover, the state exists to secure and guarantee those fundamental rights. Thus, strictly speaking, Locke did not adopt a traditional view of morality based on natural law, but he did infer certain natural rights in the same manner as natural law philosophers such as Thomas Aquinas. Also, like traditional natural law theories, Locke's philosophy argues from the facts of human nature to the values that ground morality and law.

THE SCHOOL OF NATURAL LAW

During the seventeenth and eighteenth centuries, there were many further developments in the evolution of natural law theory. What came to be known as the school of natural law was dominated by thinkers such as Hugo Grotius and Samuel von Pufendorf, along with Johann Gottlieb Fichte and Immanuel Kant. These philosophers discussed natural law in purely secular terms; hence, they too disassociated natural law from its metaphysical and theological suppositions. They regarded the law of nature as manifest to anyone through the natural light of human reason. This school also focused on different types of associations that form in society—particularly those regulated by law. They developed theories of the state, society at large, and associations and their relation to the state. Grotius, for example, developed a natural law conception of the state. Beyond any doubt, even these obscure works have had a notable impact on the evolution of legal and political theory.

MODERN VERSIONS OF THE NATURAL LAW PHILOSOPHY

There are several insightful modern versions of natural law morality that for the most part have been inspired by the philosophy of Saint Thomas Aquinas. For example, legal philosophers such as John Finnis have attempted to build on and advance the work of Thomas Aquinas. In Finnis's version of natural law morality, there is a fuller and more elaborate articulation of human goods. Like Thomas Aquinas, Finnis contends that the end of each human being is self-fulfillment, or what he calls "human flourishing." In his seminal work *Natural Law and Natural Rights* (1980), Finnis argues for seven basic goods, or aspects of human well-being that contribute to this flourishing: life, knowledge, play, aesthetic experience, sociability and friendships, practicable reasonableness, and religion.

Human flourishing is realized by actualizing these basic goods. Finnis also contends that practical reasonableness directs and guides the way in which people actualize the other goods. It is a critical intermediate principle that guides the transition from human goods to judgments about right and wrong actions. According to Finnis, one is practically reasonable when one participates in all human goods *well*. Thus, the bedrock moral principle for Finnis can be summed up as follows: "Make one's choices open to human fulfillment; that is, avoid unnecessary limitations of human potentialities." In other words, the moral law holds that one should promote human flourishing by respecting these basic human goods in one's own actions and in the actions of others.

Finally, it is worth noting that the notion of a natural law grounded in human nature is implicit in the writings of many other modern thinkers. Consider, for example, the writings of Martin Luther King, Jr.; specifically, his famous "Letter from Birmingham Jail," which was written in 1963. In this letter, he explains his rationale for disobeying the law by claiming that an unjust law is not really a law at all. Citing Saint Augustine, King invoked a higher "natural" law as a standard for judging the unjust discriminatory laws that could be found in some states during the early 1960's. King's writings raise the question of how one is to judge the laws of civil society if one does not have this higher standard cited by Aristotle, Cicero, Augustine, Thomas Aquinas, and many others.

CRITICISMS

Critics have identified many problems associated with the natural law approach to morality. Some of the strongest criticism has been directed against Saint Thomas Aquinas, since he is regarded as the most noted systematizer of natural law theory. To begin with, the critics argue that Thomas Aquinas's discussion is seriously deficient in that he does not enumerate more primary precepts of natural law. Thomas Aquinas mentions only a few such precepts and should have given much more attention to the actual content of the natural law. Thus, the famous question 94 of the *Summa* in which these precepts are articulated under the form of natural inclinations is one of the most disappointing sections in the whole "Treatise on Law." It is difficult, then, to arrive at a comprehensive list of specific and definable duties that should be followed in the light of the natural law.

In addition, Thomas Aquinas and other natural

law advocates perhaps place too much emphasis on the immutability of human nature, which in turn accounts for the remarkable stability of the law. A more adequate moral theory must focus more explicitly on *possible* and future human fulfillment. In other words, more attention must be given to humanity's continual evolution and to possible forms of human fulfillment that have not yet been defined.

Still another criticism that is directed against Thomas Aquinas and his followers is the dependence of his natural law theory on the metaphysical assumptions of his philosophy. One such assumption is that the universe is organized in a teleological fashion and that all beings are ordained a certain end. Without this assumption, Thomas Aquinas's version of natural law becomes somewhat problematic, since it is predicated on the notion that human nature is oriented intrinsically toward self-realization. Science, however, specifically physics and biology, has rejected this teleological view of nature. For example, the biologist would argue that the development and growth of organisms is not caused by some inner teleology, but by the presence of genetic information that controls the process of growth. Thus, modern science and reason do not support the teleological assumptions of Aristotle and Thomas Aquinas. It is possible, of course, to revise the natural law framework so that it is not dependent on a foundation of teleology. In other words, the absence of a teleological assumption does not preclude a coherent natural law ethic.

RELEVANCE OF NATURAL LAW

The natural law tradition has had a significant influence on the development of law and political theory in Western civilization. First of all, it represents the viewpoint that there are objective moral principles that can be discerned by reason. It has also influenced the emphasis on natural rights that is expressed in constitutional laws. Natural law theory seeks to justify these rights and other moral requirements that should serve as the basis of any legal system. Unless a system adheres to this natural law, it cannot be considered legitimate or justified. Thus, the rules of any society are not valid if they come into conflict with the demands of the natural law. In short, a valid law must be a moral law; that is, one that is consistent with the natural law.

The natural law tradition stands in unequivocal opposition to the tradition of positivism that distinguishes between law and morality. In addition, legal positivists stress that an unjust law is still a law. They hold that natural law theory confuses what law is with what it ought to be. Obviously, the debate between positivists and natural law proponents is a spirited one that will not be resolved easily. It is also clear, however, that the framework of natural law, despite its flaws, has many merits, since it accounts for the authority of law and provides a general guideline for judging the worth and quality of diverse legal rules.

Richard A. Spinello

FURTHER READING

Biggar, Nigel, and Rufus Black, eds. *The Revival of Natural Law: Philosophical, Theological, and Ethical Responses to the Finnis-Grisez School.* Burlington, Vt.: Ashgate, 2000. An anthology of essays examining, critiquing, and applying the work of Finnis and Grisez in natural law ethics. Includes discussions of the relationship of natural law to theology and of its applicability to contemporary moral issues in bioethics and gender studies.

Finnis, John. *Natural Law and Natural Rights.* New York: Oxford University Press, 1980. A modern and comprehensive treatment of natural law in the tradition of Aristotle and Thomas Aquinas.

Grisez, Germain G., and Russell B. Shaw. *Beyond the New Morality: The Responsibilities of Freedom.* 3d ed. Notre Dame, Ind.: University of Notre Dame Press, 1988. A perceptive account of natural law theory that offers some practical guidance for implementing this theory in one's everyday moral decisions.

King, Martin Luther, Jr. "Letter from Birmingham Jail." In *Why We Can't Wait.* New York: New American Library, 1968. This letter was written to "My Dear Fellow Clergymen" during King's incarceration in Birmingham in the heyday of the Civil Rights movement. It is a clear and nontheoretical discussion of a "natural law" that governs all humanity.

O'Connor, D. J. *Aquinas and Natural Law.* London: Macmillan, 1967. This short book is a lucid account of Thomas Aquinas's ethical doctrines. It considers his philosophical presuppositions, along with the influence of Aristotle. The book also offers a critical assessment of Thomas Aquinas from the perspective of contemporary analytical philosophy.

Passerin d'Entreves, Alessandro. *Natural Law.* London: Hutchinson University Library, 1970. A brilliant and accessible discussion of the general spirit and aim of Thomas Aquinas's ethical thought and the entire natural law tradition.

Thomas Aquinas, Saint. *On Law, Morality, and Politics.* Edited by William P. Baumgarth and Richard J. Regan. Indianapolis: Hackett, 1988. Extended selections from Thomas Aquinas's writings on natural law and other areas of morality. Contains a useful introduction that helps to illuminate the main lines of Thomas Aquinas's complex writings.

SEE ALSO: Augustine, Saint; Cicero; Grotius, Hugo; Hobbes, Thomas; Kant, Immanuel; Locke, John; Natural rights; Stoic ethics; *Summa Theologica*; Thomas Aquinas.

Natural rights

DEFINITION: Inalienable rights of all people which exist in nature, prior to the institution of a social order, and which may be protected by governments but do not derive from governments

TYPE OF ETHICS: Human rights

SIGNIFICANCE: An influential doctrine during the Enlightenment, natural rights theory was used to justify the American and French revolutions of the eighteenth century. Moreover, a version of natural rights divorced from its original dependence on natural law became the basis in the twentieth century for discussions of universal human rights.

After World War II, the member nations of the United Nations were aghast at the systematic violations of human rights that had been committed during the war. Aware of the lack of enforcement mechanisms to hold persons accountable for such behavior, they initiated the process of developing legally binding international standards of conduct.

In 1948, the United Nations General Assembly adopted the Universal Declaration of Human Rights (UDHR), marking the introduction of a basic canon of civil, political, economic, social, and cultural rights into the international forum.

The Universal Declaration of Human Rights consists of thirty articles that declare, among others, the rights to life, liberty, property, nationality, education, thought, and religion, and freedom from torture, arbitrary arrest, and detention. Because of its ties with natural law, the UDHR has been criticized for being Eurocentric, giving rise to claims that its standards are not applicable to non-Western nations. Indeed, several pillars of the UDHR and subsequent international human rights instruments (the Covenant on Civil and Political Rights, the Covenant on Economic, Social and Cultural Rights, the Convention on the Elimination of All Forms of Racial Discrimination, and the Convention Against Torture) are rooted in the early ideas of justice that derive from Western civilization.

IDEAS OF JUSTICE IN ANCIENT GREECE

The Greek idea of justice was one that both guided individual behavior and served as a blueprint for the organization of society. The ethical beliefs of prominent Greek thinkers—Sophocles and Aristotle, in particular—were grounded in the belief that the higher laws of the gods transcended the obligations and duties dictated by the rulers of society. Like Plato and Socrates, Aristotle believed that adherence to ethics creates an ideal society, one in which hereditary class status does not determine one's social rank.

ROMAN AND CATHOLIC DOCTRINE OF THE MIDDLE AGES

Influenced by classical Greek philosophy, the Roman emperor Justinian (502-565) distinguished among Roman natural law (*jus civile*), the common law of all nations (*jus gentium*), and natural law (*jus naturale*). The Romans emphasized the necessity for a proper trial, the presentation of evidence and proof, and the illegality of bribery in judicial proceedings.

The ideas proposed by the Roman Marcus Tullius Cicero further cultivated a theory of natural law. Cicero's *Brotherhood of Man* made no distinction between what is legally right and morally right, and he promoted the idea that Roman law should be filled with "natural reason" (fair, equitable solutions) instead of reliance upon positive legal provisions. Natural law was God-given, eternal, and immutable, and it could be applied to all people at all times.

The emphasis on natural reason as the foundation of law continues with the Roman Catholic doctrine of the Middle Ages and the writings of Saint Thomas Aquinas. Hugo Grotius clearly breaks from the older doctrine of natural rights by maintaining that natural law originates in pure reason, not the scriptures. For Grotius, even nature and mathematics are unchangeable by God.

THE ENLIGHTENMENT

The basis of the Enlightenment was a belief in the perfectibility and decency of humankind. John Locke's essay on civil government (1689) contends that in the original state of nature all persons have the same rights and obligations and are entitled to defend their rights to life, freedom, and property. Jean-Jacques Rousseau's *Social Contract* (1712-1778) argued that the presence of evil cannot be blamed on humankind's natural tendencies, but must be ascribed to social injustice and inequality; like Locke, Rousseau believed in a natural state of existence in which all are equal. Voltaire, another eighteenth century natural law theoretician, advocated for the rights still demanded today, including the freedoms of person, press, and religion.

The basic documents of the American Revolution, which reveal the evolution of natural law theory during the Enlightenment, influenced the French struggle for freedom. The rights of man, the social contract, popular sovereignty, separation of government powers, right to property, religious freedom, and freedom of thought all are contained in the Declaration of Independence and the U.S. Bill of Rights.

Parallel to constitutional developments in America, the French Declaration of the Rights of Man and the Citizen (1789) recognized the rights to liberty, property, equality before the law, repudiation of all hereditary privilege, national sovereignty, accountability of public officials, freedom of speech and press, separation of government powers, personal safety, and the right to resist oppression. Subsequently, in 1793, a new French constitution was developed that went beyond the document of 1789 in providing for the rights to work, to mass education, and to rise in insurrection.

GENERATIONS OF HUMAN RIGHTS

France's development of the 1793 constitution is a historical example in which the dichotomy between civil, political rights, and economic, social, and cultural rights is visible. Just as the 1793 French document linked economic status and opportunity to the attainment of basic human rights, elements of current human rights discourse maintain that human

---

Human Rights That Evolved out of Natural Rights Concepts

Natural Rights Concept	Human Rights
Freedom	Self-determination: rights to food, shelter, education, medical care, and social security
Liberty: freedoms of expression and religion	Liberty: freedoms of assembly, expression, religion, thought, culture, nationality, and movement; right to asylum
Equality	Equality: equality before the law, equal education, equal employment
Property	Property: right to employment, equal pay
Self-government	Representative government: fair elections, participatory government, equal suffrage, equal access to public service.
Freedom from arbitrary arrest	Due process: presumption of innocence, right to fair trial; freedoms from torture, detention, and exile
Personal privacy	Right to privacy: domestic privacy, privacy of correspondence; rights to family, marriage, honor, reputation, and leisure

rights are indivisible. Poor nonwestern countries assert that civil and political rights (referred to as first-generation rights because they are readily attainable) cannot be given priority over economic, social, and cultural rights (second generation rights, inclusive of the rights to education, housing, employment, and social security). Amid diverse global conditions, the development of an international code of ethics, which began in ancient times, has been broadened by the demand for economic, social, and cultural justice.

NATURAL LAW AND APPLICABILITY OF HUMAN RIGHTS

The natural-law origins of the Universal Declaration of Human Rights fuel the conflict over the global application of human rights. Countries not rooted in the Western tradition of natural law agree that although human beings are born free and equal in dignity, the source of this higher order is dependent upon cultural protocol. Adherence to tradition and desire for its maintenance have given rise to the development of human rights documents that reflect differing social, cultural, and religious realities. Examples of such documents are the African (Banjul) Charter on Human and Peoples' Rights and the Islamic Declaration of Human Rights.

CONCLUSION

Since 1948, an extensive register of international human rights has been developed. For example, feminism has extended human rights arguments to the defense of women and their protection against male-biased social, religious, and legal norms. The continuous articulation of human rights is both an extension of natural-law doctrine and an effort to respond to varying cultural perceptions of human rights and differing global economies, religions, and political conditions. The 1948 Universal Declaration of Human Rights, with its mixture of first- and second-generation rights—civil and political rights with economic, social, and cultural rights—is testimony to the merging of tradition and modernity in the effort to develop an international collection of ethics. While the first twenty articles of the UDHR cover the rights to life, liberty, property, equality, and justice, subsequent articles proclaim the rights to education, equal pay, an adequate standard of living, nationality, and the cultural life of one's community.

The loss of natural rights as the major authority for human rights has led to two problematic results. The creation of seemingly unlimited and unattainable economic, social, and environmental rights, as well as the justification for the proliferation of many other rights; and the relativism of rights when each culture claims its own unique rights for itself and opposes any universal (natural rights) claim for human rights.

Richard C. Kagan
Kerrie Workman

FURTHER READING

Castberg, Frede. "Natural Law and Human Rights: An Idea-Historical Survey." In *International Protection of Human Rights*, edited by Asbjorn Eide and August Schou. New York: Interscience, 1968. Professor Eide is one of the great European (Norwegian) experts on human rights and natural rights law.

Maritain, Jacques. *Natural Law: Reflections on Theory and Practice*. Edited by William Sweet. South Bend, Ind.: St. Augustine's Press, 2001. A defense of natural rights and natural law which attempts to work through the challenges posed to those doctrines by diversity and pluralism.

Palumbo, Michael. *Human Rights: Meaning and History*. Malabar, Fla.: Robert E. Krieger, 1982. This basic reader on the history of human rights contains general readings from the works of philosophers and politicians. Provides a general overview of the development of human rights concepts.

Pollack, Ervin H. *Human Rights*. Buffalo, N.Y.: Jay Steuart, 1971. A collection of works by legal philosophers on such topics as the definition of human rights, the identification of human rights, and the relevance of international standards to morality.

Schwab, Peter, and Adamantia Pollis, eds. *Toward a Human Rights Framework*. New York: Praeger, 1982. The central theme of this volume is the universality of human rights. The work supports the idea that human rights are products of history and are dynamic. Argues for the indivisibility of human rights.

SEE ALSO: Aristotle; Cicero; Civil rights and liberties; Declaration of Independence; Enlightenment ethics; Grotius, Hugo; Human rights; Natural law; Rights and obligations; Thomas Aquinas; Universal Declaration of Human Rights.

Naturalistic fallacy

DEFINITION: Mistaken attempt to define a moral entity such as good in terms of a natural one such as pleasure

DATE: Term coined in 1903

TYPE OF ETHICS: Theory of ethics

SIGNIFICANCE: The argument against the naturalistic fallacy is meant to establish that the good is an irreducible quality, one which cannot be understood as a function of anything else. It therefore opposes any ethics that defines the good in terms of happiness, pleasure, enlightenment, or anything other than simple goodness.

G. E. Moore, a Cambridge philosopher, argued in his *Principia Ethica* (1903) that ethical naturalism should be rejected because it commits the naturalistic fallacy. Moore said that the naturalistic fallacy "consists in the contention that good *means* nothing but some simple or complex notion, that can be defined in terms of natural qualities." To the contrary, Moore maintained that good is simple and indefinable in any terms, natural or otherwise. Thus, he sometimes seemed to apply the "naturalistic fallacy" designation to *any* attempt to define good.

Moore did not object to saying that pleasure is good. In fact, it is the business of ethics to determine what things are good. His objection was against those who would claim that pleasure *means* good, that good and pleasure are the same thing. He would claim that people rightly say that a lemon is yellow, but they do not mean by that that lemon and yellow are the same.

"OPEN QUESTION ARGUMENT"

To support his claims about a fallacy, Moore offered what has been called the "open question argument." For any definition that might be proposed for "good," it can always be meaningfully asked whether that thing really is good; whereas, with a legitimate definition, such a question would not be meaningful. For example, if "mother" means "female parent," then these terms are interchangeable. It would make no sense to inquire whether your mother were really your female parent, since this would be asking whether your mother were really your mother. Moore maintained, however, that it will always make sense to ask whether pleasure (or any other proposed definition) is really good.

JOHN STUART MILL AND THE FALLACY

Moore stated that John Stuart "Mill has made as naive and artless a use of the naturalistic fallacy as anybody could desire." According to Moore, Mill claimed that good meant desirable and that what was desirable was to be discovered by looking at what was desired. Since pleasure is what is desired, it is the good. Moore accused Mill of slipping fallaciously from what *is* desired to what *ought* to be desired, from the *fact* of desired to the *value* of desirable.

In a summary of what he had said about Mill, Moore said, "if his contention that 'I ought to desire' means nothing but 'I do desire' were true, then he is only entitled to say, 'we do desire so and so because we do desire it'; and that is not an ethical proposition at all; it is a mere tautology." Thus, it can be seen that Moore was concerned not only with the naturalistic element of Mill's definition but also with his attempt at any sort of definition.

CRITICISM OF MOORE

There have been numerous critiques of Moore's fallacy claims. Some have pointed out that it is a misnomer, since the objection is to all definitions, not only naturalistic ones, and that it should perhaps be called the "definition fallacy." These critics have gone on to propose answers to the "open question argument." Some have suggested that perhaps "good" has several meanings and thus an examination of any one of these might seem to leave an open question. Perhaps, alternatively, the term is extremely difficult to define, as Socrates found with moral terms, but this difficulty does not prove that *no* definition is possible.

Other critics have denied that Mill and other naturalists were making any attempt at definition. In response to these critics, however, it has been argued that whether the naturalist appeals to a definition or to a principle, one always turns out to be grounded in the other, and in neither case can the moral element be logically deduced from the nature of things.

In further support of Moore, it has been said that if indeed a definition of "good" in some natural (or even metaphysical) term could be established, then this would rob moral judgments of their prescriptive force. That is, a judgment of "*X* is good" would become purely descriptive and would elicit a "so what?" response, just as might a judgment of "That apple is red." Put another way, although Moore's discussion of the naturalistic fallacy may be confusingly presented, it nevertheless testifies to the special character of moral terms as evaluative and action-guiding elements that cannot be captured by any descriptive substitution.

Ruth B. Heizer

FURTHER READING

Casebeer, William D. *Natural Ethical Facts: Evolution, Connectionism, and Moral Cognition.* Cambridge, Mass.: MIT Press, 2003.

Crosby, John F. "Response to Kendler's 'Psychology, Ethics, and the Naturalistic Fallacy.'" In *Moral Issues in Psychology: Personalist Contributions to Selected Problems,* edited by James M. Dubois. Lanham, Md.: University Press of America, 1997.

Harrison, Jonathan. "Ethical Naturalism." In *The Encyclopedia of Philosophy,* edited by Paul Edwards. New York: Macmillan, 1972.

Kendler, Howard H. "Psychology, Ethics, and the Naturalistic Fallacy." In *Moral Issues in Psychology: Personalist Contributions to Selected Problems,* edited by James M. Dubois. Lanham, Md.: University Press of America, 1997.

Moore, G. E. *Principia Ethica.* Rev. ed. New York: Cambridge University Press, 1996.

Schilpp, Paul Arthur, ed. *The Philosophy of G. E. Moore.* La Salle, Ill.: Open Court, 1968.

Simpson, Peter. *Goodness and Nature: A Defence of Ethical Naturalism.* Boston: M. Nijhoff, 1987.

Stratton-Lake, Philip, ed. *Ethical Intuitionism: Reevaluations.* New York: Oxford University Press, 2002.

Taylor, Paul. *Principles of Ethics: An Introduction.* Encino, Calif.: Dickenson, 1975.

Warnock, Mary. *Ethics Since 1900.* 3d ed. New York: Oxford University Press, 1978.

SEE ALSO: Fact/value distinction; Good, the; Intrinsic good; Intuitionist ethics; Is/ought distinction; Mill, John Stuart; Moore, G. E.; Utilitarianism.

Nature, rights of

DEFINITION: Rights which may be said to inhere in the natural world, including both organic life and inorganic aspects of the landscape

TYPE OF ETHICS: Environmental ethics

SIGNIFICANCE: Theories which ascribe rights to nature are generally attempts to construct a moral framework within which to reconcile the human ability to damage and manipulate the environment with the needs of other species and with the sense that lands and waters may themselves have qualitative worth. Such theories are anthropocentric, however, in the sense that they tend to ascribe moral worth to the environment by investing it with human moral characteristics.

Western thought, being greatly influenced by Christianity, has historically assumed the dominance of humans over all plant and animal species. The ability to destroy, domesticate, and alter other species has been seen as an inherent argument for human dominance of the natural world. Until the latter part of the twentieth century, little regard was given to the rights of nature to exist within a framework beneficial to species other than humans. The development of environmental crises such as global warming, extinctions, and the depletion of natural resources has led philosophers to consider the rights of nature.

When Thomas Jefferson wrote the Declaration of Independence, he declared that all men were created with unalienable rights that allowed them to be treated with equality. Jefferson's ideal, while extended to all humans, was not at the time the reality for all humans.

DARWINISM

Approximately one hundred years after Jefferson wrote the Declaration of Independence, Charles Darwin presented the idea of the evolution of species. Darwin's idea suggested that those species that currently exist do so because they were best able to adapt to the changing environment in which they live. It is important to note that Darwin did not put forth the idea that the strongest species survived, but rather that the most adaptable species survived. Darwin's theory was slightly distorted and generally believed to be survival of the fittest or strongest. This distortion of Darwin's theory, coupled with Jefferson's emphasis on the unalienable rights of humankind, led to a popular belief that humans had the right to regard nature as simply a resource to use and dominate without regard for any rights that nature might possess.

As a result of the idea of dispensable natural resources, be they inanimate or animate, human technological development and industrialization led to several ecological problems during the latter half of the twentieth century. Global warming, depletion of the earth's protective ozone layer, increases in harmful gases in the atmosphere, and the extinctions of plant and animal species are a few of these problems. The burgeoning ecological crisis began to illustrate the intricate and dependent relationship of humans with the natural world. As a result, philosophers and other thinkers began to reevaluate the rights of nature and the role of humans. It became clear that all species on the planet were interconnected and that the environment had forced all species into a subtle compact for survival.

Initially, nature was not viewed as possessing inalienable rights. Instead, the argument was made to protect nature for the benefit of human existence. Nature was important only insofar as it provided what was needful for human existence; if a human activity infringed upon nature in a way that was not viewed as destructive to human existence, then the activity was morally acceptable. Indeed, this view is still held; however, a deeper view of nature began to develop from this perspective. This deeper view argued that humans are only a percentage of an ecological whole, and that each part of this whole is dependent upon the other parts. The interdependence of the parts means that the rights of any one part are not greater than the rights of other parts of the ecological whole. Each species acts upon the society of other species and is acted upon by this society. This fact is commonly illustrated by such concepts as the food chain. In fact, all species, as a result of their existence in the environment, are involved in a social contract with one another. Those who argue from this perspective point out that humans as well as other animals perceive and react to the environment; therefore, humans and other animals have equal value in an environmental context.

Interdependence of Species

The interdependence of species is the cornerstone for the rights-of-nature argument. The theory of evo-

lution supports the idea that all species are created equal because all species have evolved from common ancestors. The species currently residing on the planet are not historically the strongest or most fit but the descendants of the most adaptable species. It is an error to use one species' ability to manipulate the environment as a sanction to disregard the rights of other species. Furthermore, the fact that humans are able to know many of the details about how nature works as a result of biological science does not mean that humans have the right to disregard the rights of nature. Jefferson's unalienable rights for men do not discriminate upon the basis of intelligence; thus, the argument is applied to nature and humans. Humans are capable of knowing the workings of other species, but this should not justify disregard for these species' rights.

If it is held that nature has rights and that human rights are rights that should be accorded to the entire community of species, then how should actions be judged to be right or wrong? Perhaps the best definition is that of Aldo Leopold, who defines an action as being right when it preserves the integrity, stability, and beauty of the biotic community. If nature is accorded an ethical status that is equal to human ethical status, a benchmark such as Leopold's will be needed to make judgments about the actions that humans take.

Tod Murphy

Further Reading

Attfield, Robin. *Environmental Ethics: An Overview for the Twenty-First Century.* Malden, Mass.: Blackwell, 2003.

_____. *The Ethics of Environmental Concern.* New York: Columbia University Press, 1983.

Brennan, Andrew. *Thinking About Nature: An Investigation of Nature, Value, and Ecology.* Athens: University of Georgia Press, 1988.

Day, David. *The Eco Wars: A Layman's Guide to the Ecology Movement.* London: Harrap, 1989.

Light, Andrew, and Holmes Rolston III, eds. *Environmental Ethics: An Anthology.* Malden, Mass.: Blackwell, 2003.

Miller, G. Tyler, Jr. *Living in the Environment: Principles, Connections, and Solutions.* 12th ed. Belmont, Calif.: Brooks/Cole, 2002.

Pimm, Stuart. *The Balance of Nature? Ecological Issues in the Conservation of Species and Com-*

munities. Chicago: University of Chicago Press, 1991.

Spellerberg, Ian. *Evaluation and Assessment for Conservation: Ecological Guidelines for Determining Priorities for Nature Conservation*. London: Chapman & Hall, 1992.

SEE ALSO: Animal rights; Dominion over nature, human; Environmental ethics; Global warming; Leopold, Aldo; Moral status of animals; *Silent Spring*.

Nature Conservancy Council

IDENTIFICATION: British agency established to promote the conservation of natural environments

DATE: Chartered as Nature Conservancy in 1949; Council established 1973 by an act of Parliament; dissolved December 21, 1991

TYPE OF ETHICS: Environmental ethics

SIGNIFICANCE: The Nature Conservancy Council (NCC) established national nature reserves and conducted research within them, simultaneously preserving wildlife and increasing the scientific community's understanding of the importance of such preservation.

The Nature Conservancy Council was established "to provide scientific advice on the conservation and control of the natural flora and fauna of Great Britain; to establish, maintain and manage nature reserves in Great Britain; and to organize and develop the research and scientific services related thereto." While the NCC was not the only conservation organization in the United Kingdom, its mission of scientific research combined with conservation was unique. Some national nature reserves were owned by the conservancy; others were privately or publicly owned lands that were subject to reserve agreements.

The conservancy was given the power to acquire land compulsorily when necessary. Through its land acquisition activities, it provided an alternative to development and played an important role in habitat preservation. The NCC worked with voluntary organizations, universities, and other government organizations in its conservation and scientific efforts. It increased public awareness of ecological processes and support for conservation. The British Nature Conser-

vancy provided a model for the United States organization of the same name, established in 1951. The latter is a private nonprofit organization that conserves critical habitats by acquiring land through purchases or gifts, manages the sanctuaries, and supports research. In 1991, the NCC was divided into three smaller entities: English Nature, Scottish Natural Heritage, and the Countryside Council for Wales.

Marguerite McKnight
Updated by the editors

SEE ALSO: Biodiversity; Conservation; Endangered species.

Nazi science

DEFINITION: Experiments conducted by the German scientific establishment during the period when Adolf Hitler and the Nazi Party dominated Germany

DATE: 1933-1945

TYPE OF ETHICS: Scientific ethics

SIGNIFICANCE: The experiments conducted on Jews and other unwilling subjects by Nazi scientists have been used to symbolize the convergence of logic and moral atrocity in the Holocaust and the rationalist, dispassionate evil of the "final solution."

For more than twelve years (January 31, 1933-May 2, 1945), Germany was dominated by a political movement called the *Nationalsozialistische Deutsche Arbeiterpartei* (NSDAP or Nazis, for short). Upon becoming the chancellor of Germany, Nazi leader Adolf Hitler launched the twin programs of *Machtergreifung* and *Gleichschaltung* (the former term meaning "seizure of power" and the latter meaning "coordination"). The Nazis first installed members of their own party or party sympathizers into positions of authority in every government organization in Germany—schools and universities, scientific research institutes, medical facilities, youth groups, women's organizations, museums, philharmonic orchestras, art galleries, and virtually everything else in Germany.

Nazis or Nazi sympathizers in those organizations then "coordinated" the activities of the people they controlled with Hitler's view of what all Germans should do and think. German scientists also had to coordinate their experiments with Hitler's own peculiar view of the universe and humanity's place in it. The ultimate result was the destruction of human lives on a scale so massive as to defy understanding.

EUGENICS THEORIES

Hitler's understanding of human society represented a vulgarized form of ideas that evolved from scientific experiments and theories in Western Europe and the United States during the nineteenth century. Evolutionists, geneticists, and eugenicists from the so-called "hard" sciences, along with psychologists and Social Darwinists from the "soft" sciences, contributed to the construction in the minds of Hitler and many other people of an essentially racial interpretation of human history.

Evolutionists taught that all members of a species of living organisms are involved in a constant struggle for survival. Those organisms that have inherited characteristics from their ancestors that are best suited for survival will outcompete their less genetically blessed rivals and thus pass along those beneficial traits to their offspring. When scientists rediscovered Mendelian genetics immediately after 1900, many of them began to realize that breeding a superior stock of human beings poses no more of a scientific problem than does the selective breeding of plants and animals. A program of selective human breeding would assure that only desirable characteristics would pass from one generation to the next.

Social Darwinists argued that human races (or nations) are engaged in a struggle for survival, as are the members of individual species. If a nation or race does not possess or adopt the physical and intellectual qualities necessary to allow it to outcompete its rivals, it will be swept into the dustbin of history and become extinct or its members will become subservient to superior nations or races. Social Darwinists combined with advocates of selective human breeding to form the international eugenics movement.

Eugenicists included scientists from every discipline, but especially anthropology, medi-

cine, and psychology. They argued that governments should adopt regulations to assure that future generations would enjoy the best physical and intellectual constitutions that their gene pools could supply. Eugenicists advocated that individuals with congenital diseases of the mind or body should undergo mandatory sterilization to prevent their disabilities from being passed along to future generations. During the 1920's and 1930's, governments in many Western European countries and several state legislatures in the United States adopted laws mandating sterilization for persons with inheritable infirmities.

Some of the eugenicists advocated that enlightened governments should adopt euthanasia programs to eliminate persons with mental or physical disabilities that were of a terminal nature or that rendered

---

Examples of Nazi Science

Field	Research and Experiments
Physics	Research program to produce a nuclear bomb
Optics	Research program to establish a giant mirror in low earth orbit that would focus the Sun's energy on enemy targets on Earth and incinerate them
Chemistry	Experiments that succeeded in producing synthetic rubber and synthetic gasoline; development of several new types of poison gases, including nerve gas
Aeronautics	Development of aircraft powered by jet and rocket engines; development of ballistic missiles
Medicine	Experiments on unwilling human subjects, including mass sterilization utilizing X rays, experiments in reviving persons subjected to extremely low temperatures, and experiments in the medical killing of terminally ill and incurably insane patients
Biology	Selective breeding of human beings (the *Lebensborn* program); biological warfare experiments

them incapable of enjoying an ill-defined "quality of life" acceptable to the euthanasists. The euthanasists tried to convince governments that the inmates of medical clinics, hospitals, and insane asylums should be screened by qualified physicians who would determine whether their lives were of any further value to themselves or to society. Those inmates deemed by screening physicians to be incurably ill (mentally or physically) or as "useless eaters" should, according to the euthanasists, be granted "mercy deaths." Only in Nazi Germany did the government adopt euthanasia. The German euthanasia program led directly to mass murders in Nazi concentration camps.

WEAPONS

The Nazi government also coopted all the other sciences in Germany to advance its own view of how Germany and the world should be organized. The sciences of aeronautical engineering, chemistry, and physics in particular became integral parts of a huge military-industrial complex designed to make advanced weapons of war. In Hitler's Social Darwinistic worldview, war was a natural and necessary condition of human evolution. In his semiautobiographical *Mein Kampf* (1926), Hitler clearly expressed his intent to conquer territory in the Soviet Union into which the German race could expand. As one of his earliest actions after attaining dictatorial power in Germany, Hitler began a massive expansion of the German armed forces. German scientists from every discipline began to devote their research to areas that would further Hitler's military intentions.

Some German scientists began programs that led to the development of the world's first operational jet fighter aircraft. Others began developing experiments in rocketry that culminated in the V-2, a ballistic missile that wreaked great havoc among civilians in Britain. German chemists developed toxic gases (never used) that were more deadly than any that had been used in World War I. Chemists also discovered how to make synthetic rubber as well as synthetic gasoline derived from coal, in an effort to assure that the German war machine could continue to function even if it were cut off from supplies of petroleum and rubber by an enemy blockade. German physicists began research designed to produce revolutionary new weapons of war, including a program that almost produced a nuclear bomb. Other exotic weapons-

systems research included plans for a giant mirror that, when placed in low Earth orbit, could focus the sun's rays on any spot on Earth with devastating results.

MEDICAL RESEARCH

Perhaps the most flagrant violations of accepted scientific ethical principles in Germany during the Nazi era occurred in medical science. Medical researchers in some concentration camps routinely used unwilling human subjects in macabre experiments that often resulted in the death or disfigurement of the subjects. Physicians in concentration camps, medical clinics, and insane asylums willingly participated in "selections" (determining whether individuals were fit for work or should be summarily executed). In the case of some of the concentration camps, physicians made these selections without conducting even cursory medical examinations. The physicians also extracted organs from the cadavers of those who had been killed and sent them to medical research institutes throughout Germany for experimentation. Physicians perpetrated this dismemberment without the knowledge or approval of the victims or the victims' families.

Many scientists presently condemn the atrocities that were committed in the name of science in Germany during the Nazi era. They believe that German scientists of the period abandoned all accepted ethical principles while they were caught up in a national madness brought on by extraordinary circumstances. A number of the German scientists involved, however, maintained that their actions were entirely ethical, because they were all intended to serve the highest good—the improvement of the human condition. In the long view of history, they maintained, the human race will benefit enormously from their actions—materially, physically, and intellectually. The Nazi scientists adopted the position that, in science, the end justifies the means. Many scientists in all countries today accept that position, at least to some degree. Perhaps more than any other event in history, the Nazi era underscores the absolute necessity of a universally accepted code of scientific ethics if any semblance of humanity is to be maintained in the wake of an increasingly technological and scientific society.

Paul Madden

FURTHER READING

Beyerchen, Alan D. *Scientists Under Hitler: Politics and the Physics Community in the Third Reich.* New Haven, Conn.: Yale University Press, 1977.

Bracher, Karl Dietrich. *The German Dictatorship: The Origins, Structure, and Effects of National Socialism.* Translated by Jean Steinberg. New York: Praeger, 1970.

Cecil, Robert. *The Myth of the Master Race: Alfred Rosenberg and Nazi Ideology.* New York: Dodd, Mead, 1972.

Lifton, Robert Jay. *The Nazi Doctors: Medical Killing and the Psychology of Genocide.* New York: Basic Books, 1986.

Muller-Hill, Benno. *Murderous Science: Elimination by Scientific Selection of Jews, Gypsies, and Others, Germany 1933-1945.* New York: Oxford University Press, 1988.

Szöllösi-Janze, Margit, ed. *Science in the Third Reich.* New York: Berg, 2001.

Weale, Adrian. *Science and the Swastika.* London: Channel 4 Books, 2001.

SEE ALSO: Atom bomb; Concentration camps; Eugenics; Experimentation; Hitler, Adolf; Holocaust; Medical research; Nazism; Nuremberg Trials; "Playing god" in medical decision making.

Nazism

DEFINITION: German political movement that advocated racial nationalism, including anti-Semitism, dictatorial government, and expansion into eastern Europe by means of war

DATE: Party organized in 1919, dissolved in 1945

TYPE OF ETHICS: Modern history

SIGNIFICANCE: By far the most famous example of a fascist movement in modern history, the rise of Nazism in Germany began with the suppression of democracy and civil rights and led ultimately to World War II and the Holocaust.

Nazism, a contraction of the term "National Socialism," was a German political movement that emerged in the aftermath of World War I with Adolf Hitler as its leader. From the very start, it espoused ideas that rejected Western values of humanitarianism, rationalism, liberalism, democracy, and socialism in favor of extreme nationalism, racism, and a political system of single-party dictatorship. Nazi policies and practices violated human and civil rights, first in Germany and later in conquered Europe, and resorted to violent power politics in international affairs.

The forerunner of Nazism as a political party was the German Workers' Party, which was organized in Munich early in 1919. Adolf Hitler, a lower-middle-class Austrian by birth and a corporal in the German army during World War I, joined the German Workers' Party later in the year. It soon was renamed the National Socialist German Workers' Party, and Hitler, showing oratorical and organizational talent, became its undisputed leader in 1921.

The main tenets of Nazism were drawn from the party program of 1920, Hitler's speeches and writings (especially his ponderous two-volume *Mein Kampf* [*My Struggle*], published in 1925 and 1926), and other Nazi publications. They attacked liberalism and parliamentarianism, including democracy, as inherently weak political systems and branded the early leaders of the Weimar Republic, liberals, socialists, and Jews as "November criminals" of 1918, who had overthrown the imperial government. In place of the failed parliamentary democracy, Nazism offered authoritarian rule rooted in a solid hierarchical system of leaders and followers. At the head would be a *Führer*, or "leader," who, with the support of the Nazi Party, would exercise total control over the society and mobilize it for the achievement of the political and social goals that he postulated.

Nazism, above all, extolled racial nationalism, which was derived from the nineteenth century racial theories of the Frenchman Joseph-Arthur de Gobineau, the Germanized Englishman Houston Chamberlain, and the German Paul de Lagarde. Proponents of Nazism contended that human races were divided into culture-creating and culture-destroying groups, which were engaged in a Social Darwinian struggle of survival of the fittest. At the top of the culture-creating races stood the Nordic-Aryan-Germanic group, the "master race," which was destined to dominate inferior races.

At Hitler's instigation, Nazism singled out the Jews as the greatest threat to the pure Aryans because the Jews, the leading culture-destroying race, were conspiring to gain domination over the world. In

Adolf Hitler (left) in 1935 with his top military commanders, including air force commander Hermann Göring (second from left), and Schutzstaffel (SS) chief Heinrich Himmler (center). (Library of Congress)

Nazi foreign policy, the idea of the primacy of the Aryan race was combined with a Great German nationalism or imperialism, whose aim it was to create a Great German empire far beyond the borders of the German nation. Such an expansion was to give the German people the *Lebensraum*, or "living space," that it needed to ensure its security and economic independence.

EXERCISE OF POWER

The Nazis did not conceal that they would attain power legally, but once in office they would destroy the constitutional system. Within one month after Hitler was appointed chancellor early in 1933, he had communists and many socialists confined to quickly established concentration camps and suspended civil rights. Through cajolery, pressure, and terror, he prevailed upon the Reichstag (parliament) to give him dictatorial powers, which he used to eliminate trade unions and all political parties except the Nazi Party. In 1934, he murdered the top leadership of the Storm Troopers, or S.A., and some non-Nazis, when he felt threatened by a rival from within his own ranks. He justified these acts of criminality by declaring: "I was

responsible for the fate of the German people and thereby I became the Supreme Judge of the German people."

The Nazi practices of eliminating opponents by sending them to concentration camps or murdering them, persecuting Jews purely on racial grounds, maintaining a police state, and pursuing an aggressive foreign policy left no room for the observance of ethical principles in politics. It is important to realize, however, that liberal democratic governments also generally do not feel bound by ethical constraints if the national interest is at stake. Although idealists among philosophers and scholars argue that, for example, foreign policy must be based on prudence and ethical principle, realists on the order of George Kennan (and they are a majority) maintain that in world politics moral or ethical concerns must be subordinated to national interest. Given the absence of accepted international standards of morality and effective bodies of enforcement when violations occur, each government, being concerned with military security, the integrity of its political life, and the wellbeing of its citizens, must act on its own to protect its national interests. Implied in this stance, however, is a sense of moderation and responsibility when pursuing the national interest in international relations.

EXPANSIONISM

The Nazi regime under Hitler's direction defined national interest in the most expansive terms. Hitler once characterized Germany's foreign policy by declaring: "Germany will become a world power or it will not exist at all." During the early years of Nazi dictatorship, he and his associates constantly proclaimed the German Reich's "sincere desire for peace," while unilaterally abrogating the restrictions of the Treaty of Versailles, rearming Germany, and then, in 1938, annexing Austria and the German-speaking Sudetenland of Czechoslovakia. In 1939, Nazi Germany unleashed World War II through aggression against Poland, followed by campaigns into France and other European countries in 1940. One year later, Hitler attacked the Soviet Union, waging an unparalleled brutal ideological war in the quest for *Lebensraum* in the East.

While worldwide violence was raging as a result of war, the Nazi regime also prepared for the elimination of "racially inferior" populaces and "those of lesser value" in society. The persecution of German Jews culminated in the violence against Jewish property and people of the *Kristallnacht* of 1938. With the outbreak of the war in 1939, a euthanasia program was begun, resulting in the killing by injection or by gassing of almost 100,000 mentally and physically disabled persons, most of whom were German. Finally, the plan to liquidate all European Jews in Nazi hands—the Final Solution—was implemented by Hitler and some of his immediate associates in 1941. It claimed the lives of almost six million people. In addition, Nazi actions led to the murder of millions of Gypsies, Slavs, homosexuals, and other racial and political "enemies." This unprecedented mechanized genocide was only stopped by the defeat of Nazi Germany and the suicide of Adolf Hitler in 1945.

COLLAPSE OF HITLER'S REGIME

After the total defeat of Germany and the inglorious death of Hitler, Nazism never revived as a significant force. Following the establishment of the Federal Republic of Germany in 1949, its Federal Constitutional Court outlawed the noisy but unim-

portant Socialist Reich Party in 1952 as a neo-Nazi organization. During the 1960's and 1980's, two right-wing parties were formed: the National Democratic Party and the Republicans. Both have shown some neo-Nazi features but have achieved little influence. More noteworthy have been a number of small neo-Nazi groups formed since the 1970's, whose racist hate propaganda and violence, directed not primarily against Jews but against foreigners, especially Turks, have aroused consternation since the unification of Germany in 1990. These groups cannot, however, be viewed as the forerunners of an organized neo-Nazi movement.

George P. Blum

FURTHER READING

Bracher, K. D. *The German Dictatorship: The Origins, Structure, and Effects of National Socialism.* Translated by Jean Steinberg. New York: Praeger, 1970.

Bullock, Alan. *Hitler: A Study in Tyranny.* Rev. ed. New York: Harper & Row, 1962.

Donahue, Anne Marie, ed. *Ethics in Politics and Government.* New York: H. W. Wilson, 1989.

Fleming, Gerald. *Hitler and the Final Solution.* Berkeley: University of California Press, 1984.

Hitler, Adolf. *Mein Kampf.* Translated by Ralph Manheim. Boston: Houghton Mifflin, 1999.

Jackel, Eberhard. *Hitler's Weltanschauung: A Blueprint for Power.* Translated by Herbert Arnold. Middletown, Conn.: Wesleyan University Press, 1972.

LeBor, Adam, and Roger Boyes. *Seduced by Hitler: The Choices of a Nation and the Ethics of Survival.* Naperville, Ill.: Sourcebooks, 2001.

Spielvogel, Jackson J. *Hitler and Nazi Germany: A History.* 2d ed. Englewood Cliffs, N.J.: Prentice-Hall, 1992.

Steinweis, Alan E., and Daniel E. Rogers, eds. *The Impact of Nazism: New Perspectives on the Third Reich and Its Legacy.* Lincoln: University of Nebraska Press, 2003.

SEE ALSO: Anti-Semitism; Concentration camps; Fascism; Genocide and democide; Hitler, Adolf; Holocaust; Nazi science; Nuremberg Trials; Schindler, Oskar.

Needs and wants

DEFINITION: Needs are generally understood to be whatever is necessary to enable human beings to continue to be human, and not merely what is necessary for survival; wants are things that enhance human life but are not necessary to it.

TYPE OF ETHICS: Personal and social ethics

SIGNIFICANCE: A principal challenge in any theory and practice of distributive justice is the construction of a system of claims and desert related to a defensible index of human needs and wants.

An index of human needs is never completely exhausted by speaking of food, clothing, and shelter. Nobody dies from a lack of music or good books, but this does not mean that such things do not constitute human needs. Indeed, needs may even arguably include such basic liberties as freedom of speech, movement, thought, and choice.

The distribution of what one needs is related to questions of fairness, equality, and justice. However, to distribute goods in proportion to basic needs is equivalent to neither equality nor justice, because there must first be some grounds for saying whether distribution should be independent of the question of desert.

One may ask whether it is the case that to say that *S* needs *X* is to say that if *S* does not have *X*, he or she will be harmed. If *X*'s absence is a crucial or fundamental harm to *S*, then a moral ought arises apart from desert. This is different from saying that the fact that *S* needs *X* means that without *X* that person cannot achieve some goal or purpose he or she wants to achieve.

A person wants a certain thing if when a certain desire occurs, there is an increase in one's inclination to perform an act to satisfy it. Wants are thus related to desire, and among desires the ethicist may ask which are rational and which are not, and whether some are derivative and some final. After all, there may be no limit to what human beings can want, but there are limits on what can be done or provided. For example, men cannot give birth to babies, no matter how much they may want to do so.

If an index of needs and wants can be established, one may still wonder whether these are natural, or whether they vary according to human condition and technological achievement. Generally speaking, the more abundant a society's material goods, the more previously thought of wants become seen as needs. This means that if needs are determined by nature and wants are circumstantial, then an ethicist's task is of one sort. Whereas, if both are circumstantial, culturally and technologically contingent, then the work of ethics is different because the line between need and want is fixed by human decision.

FURTHER READING

Pojman, Louis, and Robert Westmoreland, eds. *Equality: Selected Readings.* Oxford, England: Oxford University Press, 1997.

Rescher, Nicholas. *Fairness: Theory and Practice of Distributive Justice.* New Brunswick, N.J.: Transaction Publishers, 2002.

Sen, Amartya. *Inequality Reexamined.* Cambridge, Mass.: Harvard University Press, 1995.

Ronnie Littlejohn

SEE ALSO: Desire; Greed; Incommensurability; Inequality; Justice; Poverty; Profit economy; *Walden*.

Negligence

DEFINITION: Failure to maintain due standards of care in one's actions, thereby causing or potentially causing harm to another

TYPE OF ETHICS: Business and labor ethics

SIGNIFICANCE: Negligence raises interesting and unique questions about the relationship of intentionality to guilt. Virtually all moral relations have a potential for negligence.

Negligence has long been an important concept in both ethics and law. In ethics, the notion of negligence arises out of the conception that one owes a duty of a degree of care toward one's fellow humans in all one's activities and that under given circumstances, one may owe even greater degrees of care arising out of special duties that one takes upon oneself in virtue of the public office or profession one has assumed.

Law and morality both recognize a distinction between advertent negligence, which involves the wrongdoer's proceeding with acts after recognizing the dangerous nature of those actions or omissions, and inadvertent negligence, which involves the wrongdoer's undertaking dangerous acts (or omissions) without having recognized the risk that they impose upon others. The former, which is often called recklessness, is generally regarded as the more culpable form, while the latter raises complex theoretical difficulties for ethicians and legal scholars.

The primary problem with inadvertent negligence both in ethics and in law arises from the seeming contradiction between the nature of such negligence and the deliberate intentionality requisite for an act to be culpable. In moral theory, the problem is easily resolved by linking the inadvertent negligence to the idea of culpable ignorance.

The wrongdoer behaved unsafely because he did not know the potential consequences of his actions, but this ignorance does not exculpate him because he should have known. At some time in his past, he failed to acquire the knowledge necessary to recognize the character of his acts. If this failure resulted from deliberate neglect on the part of the wrongdoer—for example, skipping sessions of his job training—then this was culpable ignorance and the wrongs which flowed from it were blameworthy.

In the case of legal negligence, both civil and criminal, more difficult problems seem to present themselves. Criminal guilt usually involves both an *actus reus*, or guilty act, and a *mens rea*, or guilty mind (criminal intention). H. L. A. Hart, the noted British legal philosopher, wrestled with this problem without reaching a conclusive solution: How can inadvertent negligence have a *mens rea*? If one were to recognize the nature and potential consequences of one's act(s), would one not be guilty of advertent negligence, or worse?

The answer to this puzzle may lie in a non-proximate *mens rea* that the law may be seen as assuming to exist in the absence of plausible proof to the contrary. Take, for example, the case of a roofer who has been carefully dropping waste materials from a roof into a dumpster several floors below. Suddenly, after such care, he hurls a bucket off the roof without checking its trajectory and injures a pedestrian below.

The roofer testifies at his trial that he does not know why he threw the bucket as he did and that he gave no thought to the dangers involved in such an act. If he is believed, he will be convicted of an offense connected with inadvertent negligence. If the roofer could provide a plausible explanation of his action that could trace its origins to a cause ultimately outside the roofer's control, however, he might expect acquittal.

Assume that the roofer produces proof that the tar he employed—a new variety on the market—emitted hallucinogenic fumes and that he was working with that tar just before the allegedly negligent incident. If his proofs were accepted, he would doubtlessly be exonerated, because he had indicated a cause for his actions that lay outside his control.

In the absence of such proof, however, the unstated assumption of the law must be that at some earlier time—perhaps even years before—the defendant developed (by omission or commission) habits of mind that were likely ultimately to lead to negligent actions in the future and that in the acquisition of these habits lay the culpability.

The acceptance of those habits of mind constitutes a nonproximate *mens rea* for any negligent acts that might later be done as a result. This interpretation demonstrates that the law of negligence is not a strict liability statute—that is, one enforced without regard to intentionality—as some have maintained.

OTHER DIFFICULTIES

Another difficulty that has perplexed legal theorists involves whether the standard of negligence should be objective or subjective. H. L. A. Hart stated that the objective standard attributes fault to an agent who failed "to take those precautions which any reasonable man with normal capacities would in the circumstances have taken." A subjective standard would give greater weight to the particular circumstances and capacities of the subject.

Finally, there is the question of the relationship of the degree of blameworthiness in negligent acts to the actual results that flow from them. A negligent driver (for example, one using excessive speed) might injure somebody or might not. Under one theory, his or her blameworthiness remains the same despite the external circumstances, but others have asserted that effects in the extramental world are a factor in guilt, as a result of so-called "moral luck."

Patrick M. O'Neil

FURTHER READING

Cane, Peter, and Jane Stapelton, eds. *The Law of Obligations: Essays in Celebration of John Fleming.* New York: Oxford University Press, 1998.

Feinberg, Joel. *Doing and Deserving*. Princeton, N.J.: Princeton University Press, 1970.

Hart, Herbert L. *Punishment and Responsibility: Essays in the Philosophy of Law*. New York: Oxford University Press, 1968.

Milo, Ronald D. *Immorality*. Princeton, N.J.: Princeton University Press, 1984.

Morris, Herbert. *Freedom and Responsibility*. Stanford, Calif.: Stanford University Press, 1961.

Smith, Holly. "Culpable Ignorance." *Philosophical Review* 92 (October, 1983): 543-572.

SEE ALSO: Accountability; Business ethics; Duty; Employee safety and treatment; Hart, H. L. A.; Intention; Moral luck; Professional ethics; Prudence; Responsibility.

New York Times Co. v. Sullivan

THE EVENT: U.S. Supreme Court decision that limited states' authority to award libel damages and established "actual malice" as the standard for cases involving public officials, later expanded to include "public figures"

DATE: Ruling made on March 9, 1964

TYPE OF ETHICS: Media ethics

SIGNIFICANCE: The Supreme Court's opinion in *Sullivan* significantly expanded the First Amendment protection of the press's right to engage in social criticism and political commentary by specifying that nothing printed about a public official could be deemed libelous unless it was the specific intent of the author to defame the official. Thus, even untrue stories are protected in the absence of malicious intent to do harm.

New York Times Co. v. Sullivan was sparked by an advertisement placed in *The New York Times* in 1960 by the Committee to Defend Martin Luther King and the Struggle for Freedom in the South. The advertisement, which was meant to raise support for King's Civil Rights movement, criticized several southern jurisdictions, including Montgomery, Alabama, although it did not name any individuals. In response, Montgomery city commissioner L. B. Sullivan sued the *Times* for libel in circuit court, which found the newspaper guilty under Alabama law. After the Ala-

bama Supreme Court affirmed this judgment, the *Times* appealed to the Supreme Court, claiming violations of its rights of free speech and due process under the First and Fourteenth Amendments to the Constitution. The Court held unanimously that Alabama law failed to protect adequately freedom of speech and of the press, and that "actual malice" would henceforth be the national standard for determining libel actions involving public officials.

Lisa Paddock

SEE ALSO: Due process; First Amendment; Libel; Supreme Court, U.S.

News sources

DEFINITION: Individuals who provide information to reporters for mass media dissemination

TYPE OF ETHICS: Media ethics

SIGNIFICANCE: Journalistic codes of ethics require reporters objectively to evaluate information provided by sources, to verify important information with multiple independent sources, and to protect the privacy of confidential sources by withholding their names and other identifying details from the public.

The information conveyed through the mass media is of fundamental importance to American society. On the basis of this information, public opinion is formed, votes are cast, and democracy is enacted. Media professionals, therefore, are obligated to seek out and make use of information sources that are reliable, credible, and well-intentioned. Too often, however, such exemplary sources do not exist, and journalists are left to struggle with questions of conduct and concerns about the ethical treatment of their sources.

JOURNALISTIC ETHICS

The National Society of Professional Journalists attempts to address the issue by assessing both the journalist's principles and the consequences of his or her actions. Truth-telling is a fundamental governor in a free society and becomes, therefore, an activity that journalists are both morally and socially obligated to pursue. Developing and maintaining reliable news sources is an essential part of this journalistic mission, for without credible sources, reporters may never gain access to the type of information that their "watchdog" role requires.

The U.S. Constitution, through the broad protections offered by the First Amendment, recognizes the unique nature of the press's responsibilities and grants generous latitude in the cultivation and protection of source-reporter relationships. Strict, absolute rules of conduct are incompatible with this intentionally unrestricted domain, leaving questions of ethics up for examination on a case-by-case basis.

The three main ethical considerations regarding sources of information are anonymity, confidentiality, and the source-reporter relationship. The use of anonymous sources is a fairly common media practice despite industry concerns about both its practical and ethical value. Practically, media professionals agree that the custom detracts from the press's integrity and engenders suspicion about the veracity of the report. Ethically, related considerations range from the erosion of the public trust to the publication of stolen or purchased information and the potential for furthering someone else's purpose by disseminating information that is politically or financially expedient to the source.

ANONYMITY

Anonymity undermines the journalistic mission of truth-telling because the source is an important part of the story. Failure to disclose the name of the source results in an incomplete or distorted version of truth. Once an anonymous source has been used, the issue of confidentiality arises. Various ethical questions surround this issue. How far is a news organization obligated to go in order to protect the identity of its source? How binding is a reporter's promise of anonymity?

A 1991 Supreme Court decision ruled that the Minneapolis *Star Tribune* violated an implied contract created by the promise of anonymity when the paper publicly revealed a source's identity. The decision reinforced the mutually dependent nature of the source-reporter relationship, one that has long been the subject of controversy. While general opinion agrees that the relationship is frequently characterized by betrayal and manipulation, industry members differ regarding whether it is the reporter or the source who is guilty of malevolence. The debate

sparks the question of intention and the ethical implications of using people as a means to further an individual's purpose, journalistic or otherwise.

In general, a liberalized deontological approach is employed to resolve these ethical quandaries. That is, media professionals are expected to adhere to general industry guidelines unless there is a compelling reason not to do so. For example, most news organizations have policies that reflect a cautionary stance regarding the granting of anonymity. Reporters are encouraged to try to get the source to agree to attribution and/or to find alternative ways to verify the information. Many news organizations require that journalists receive authorization from a superior before quoting from anonymous sources. Typically, editorial approval for anonymity is granted when that anonymity is supported by duty-based principles: when the information is of vital public interest and consistent with the truth-telling ethic; when the justification of minimizing grievous harm is clearly served, such as in the protection of a whistleblower or the victim of abuse; or when a concern for social justice is at stake, as in governmental corruption cases. In addition, industry guidelines seek to mitigate further the negative effects of anonymous sources by requiring identification as fully as possible, such as by position or title, and by explaining the reason for the use of anonymity.

Because anonymity is zealously guarded, once granted, the promise of confidentiality becomes supreme. The reputation of the press rests on the integrity with which sources are protected, and even the threat of legal action is not justification for exposing a confidential source. Confidentiality may be broken, however, if the news organization discovers that the source has provided false or misleading information. Malicious intent by a source, as was the case in the Minneapolis *Star Tribune* case, is not an acceptable reason to breach the confidential relationship. Rather, the responsibility lies with journalists not only to examine their own motives for publishing certain information but also to explore the possible motives of their sources. These actions act as safeguards against the likelihood that media professionals will fall prey to sources who are using the press in an effort to damage another's reputation, and reinforce a basic Judeo-Christian principle: Reporters should not treat others or allow themselves to be treated, as a means to someone else's end.

The use of anonymous sources raises a number of ethical considerations in itself, as well as the potential for confidentiality and source-reporter relationship abuses. Therefore, journalists should pursue such a course of action only after thoughtful and deliberate consideration.

Regina Howard Yaroch

FURTHER READING

Black, Jay, Bob Steele, and Ralph Barney. *Doing Ethics in Journalism: A Handbook with Case Studies*. Greencastle, Ind.: Sigma Delta Chi Foundation and the Society of Professional Journalists, 1993.

Boeyink, David E. "Anonymous Sources in News Stories: Justifying Exceptions and Limiting Abuses." *Journal of Mass Media Ethics* 5, no. 4 (1990): 233-246.

Christians, Clifford G., et al. *Media Ethics: Cases and Moral Reasoning*. 5th ed. New York: Longman, 1998.

Day, Louis A. *Ethics in Media Communications: Cases and Controversies*. Belmont, Calif.: Wadsworth, 1991.

Meyer, Philip. *Ethical Journalism*. New York: Longman, 1987.

Smith, Rod F. *Groping for Ethics in Journalism*. 5th ed. Ames: Iowa State Press, 2003.

SEE ALSO: Accuracy in Media; American Society of Newspaper Editors; Confidentiality; Fairness and Accuracy in Reporting; International Covenant on Civil and Political Rights; Journalistic entrapment; Journalistic ethics; Tabloid journalism.

Nicomachean Ethics

IDENTIFICATION: Book based on Aristotle's lectures, recorded by his son Nicomachus
DATE: *Ethica Nicomachea*, wr. c. 335-323 B.C.E. (English translation, 1797)
TYPE OF ETHICS: Classical history
SIGNIFICANCE: The *Nicomachean Ethics* is arguably the first text in Western philosophy to treat ethics as a coherent philosophical system. It defines a virtuous person as one who desires the good that the intellect discerns. Such a good is usually a mean between the extremes of too much and too little.

Aristotle assumes that all things, human beings included, have a good, a purpose or end, which it is their nature to fulfill. To understand the virtue of human nature, one must discover the specific good that is its purpose. Human nature, in Aristotle's analysis, has two levels: the nonrational and the rational. Each level has its good and corresponding virtue.

The virtue of the rational level is to recognize and contemplate truth. This purely intellectual virtue has value in itself but is not sufficient for morality. Morality is only possible when both levels of human nature work together.

The nonrational level of human nature includes vegetative functions, such as biological growth, over which reason has no control, and appetitive functions, such as hunger and sexual desire, which can be guided by reason. The virtue of this level of human nature occurs when the "appetite" comes to desire the good that the intellect discerns. This is moral virtue. It requires not only insight but also practice that cultivates moral behavior into habit.

In most cases, Aristotle says, the good is a mean between two extremes. Courage, for example, is the good that lies between rashness (too much) and cowardice (too little).

Ted William Dreier

SEE ALSO: Aristotelian ethics; Aristotle; Golden mean; Good, the; Teleological ethics.

Niebuhr, H. Richard

IDENTIFICATION: American theologian
BORN: September 3, 1894, Wright City, Missouri
DIED: July 5, 1962, Greenfield, Massachusetts
TYPE OF ETHICS: Religious ethics
SIGNIFICANCE: In works such as *The Meaning of Revelation* (1941) and *Christ and Culture* (1951), Niebuhr used insights from history, sociology, psychology, and philosophy to explore ways in which the Christian faith could help to transform and redeem the world. He became one of the leading Christian ethicists of the twentieth century.

H. Richard Niebuhr taught and wrote in the heyday of Christian theology in the twentieth century. Karl Barth, Paul Tillich, and his own brother Reinhold were his contemporaries. Niebuhr's ethics emphasized perpetual reformation. His evaluation of Christianity in the United States convinced him that Christian faith everywhere had to keep attuned to the God who could free it from cultural enslavement. To the degree that Christian communities made the "fitting response," they could spark a transformation that would bring the world closer to the kingdom of God.

Niebuhr's greatest contribution may be his way of engaging in ethical reflection. His thought moved back and forth between society and human encounters with the ultimate. His ethics aimed at turning rigidity into openness, misplaced absoluteness into creative relativity, and the difficulties of history into movements of responsible faith. Thus, if adjectives such as existential, relativistic, and cultural are necessary to describe Niebuhr's ethics, no less accurate are terms such as theocentric, communal, and universalistic.

SEE ALSO: Christian ethics; Hartshorne, Charles; Niebuhr, Reinhold; Tillich, Paul.

Theological Seminary in New York; Niebuhr remained there until his retirement in 1960.

Although Niebuhr continued his social activism while at Union, he also became famous as a writer and as a professor of Applied Christianity. He wrote more than twenty books and 1,500 articles, reviews, and editorials. Among his important topics were liberalism and fundamentalism, and the nature of faith in the light of history and science. Perhaps his most significant contribution to American social ethics was in his rethinking of the social gospel, a religious movement prevalent in early twentieth century American theology that optimistically held that people, through their efforts to reform society, could help God bring his kingdom to Earth in the near future.

Niebuhr did not think that the problems of society could be easily solved, for to him, social decisions presented themselves as choices between relative evils. In his writings, he focused on the limitations imposed by evil. Niebuhr argued that, although individuals were capable of moral behavior and development, nations, corporations, labor unions, and other such collective entities were not, because pride more easily manifested itself in groups.

James M. Dawsey

SEE ALSO: Christian ethics; Niebuhr, H. Richard.

Niebuhr, Reinhold

IDENTIFICATION: American theologian
BORN: June 21, 1892, Wright City, Missouri
DIED: June 1, 1971, Stockbridge, Massachusetts
TYPE OF ETHICS: Religious ethics
SIGNIFICANCE: An important leader in, and critic of, the social gospel movement of the early twentieth century, Niebuhr worked to demonstrate that his brand of Christianity was relevant to the practical issues of his day.

Reinhold Niebuhr, the son of an immigrant minister, was born in Wright City, Missouri, in 1892. After studying at Eden Theological Seminary and Yale Divinity School, he became in 1915 the pastor of the Bethel Evangelical Church in Detroit, where he took an active role combating racial prejudice and supporting labor's right to strike. In 1928, Henry Sloane Coffin offered Niebuhr a teaching position at Union

Nietzsche, Friedrich

IDENTIFICATION: German philosopher
BORN: October 15, 1844, Röcken, Saxony, Prussia (now in Germany)
DIED: August 25, 1900, Weimar, Germany
TYPE OF ETHICS: Modern history
SIGNIFICANCE: One of the most influential thinkers of the nineteenth century, Nietzsche created a critique of traditional ethics in *Beyond Good and Evil* (*Jenseits von Gut und Böse: Vorspiel einer Philosophie der Zukunft*, 1886), and *On the Genealogy of Morals* (*Zur Genealogie der Moral*, 1887) profoundly impacted the intellectual landscape of the twentieth century. The precise nature of his critique remains a subject of controversy, however, as there is little or no consensus as to the "authentic" meaning of his texts.

Friedrich Nietzsche. (Library of Congress)

Nietzsche attacked traditional ethical theories, especially those rooted in religion. He did so because he believed that human life has no moral purpose except for the meaning that human beings give it. His outlook encouraged moral perspectivism or pluralism, but he also advocated a demanding personal ethical perspective of his own. It emphasized the individual will, excellence, and discipline. In both its critical and its affirmative dimensions, Nietzsche's philosophy continues to have profound effects on moral theory and practice.

THE WILL TO POWER

"We are unknown to ourselves, we men of knowledge—and with good reason." Thus begins Nietzsche's *On the Genealogy of Morals*. His theme was that even though people may regard themselves as well informed, sophisticated, and knowledgeable, their lack of courage keeps them from uncovering what is happening in human existence and morality. Nietzsche tried to check this plague of self-delusion.

Nietzsche contended that it is self-deception not to admit honestly that "life simply *is* will to power." He was no advocate of the democratic ideal of human equality. Such a doctrine, he thought, only levels the quality of life toward mediocrity. Individuals vary greatly in their talents and abilities, and there are basic qualitative differences that leave us unequal as persons. Nevertheless, each individual, according to Nietzsche, will do what he or she can do to assert power.

As Nietzsche interpreted the course of human history, Western culture had been dominated by an unfortunate distinction between "good" and "evil," a distinction that the Christian religion in particular has done much to encourage. Spurred by a deep hatred of aristocratic ways they could not emulate, the masses of humanity, often supported by religious leaders, indulged in a revenge-motivated negation of the qualities of an aristocratic life. As Nietzsche saw things, the "good" of the good-evil distinction had emphasized equality, selflessness, meekness, humility, sympathy, pity, and other qualities of weakness. It had castigated the noble, aristocratic qualities—self-assertion, daring creativity, passion, and desire for conquest—by calling them evil. The prevalence of this concept of evil, Nietzsche contended, is responsible for weakness and mediocrity among those in dominant positions. It has annihilated the qualities that are essential for excellence in life.

Human existence, however, need not end on this dismal note. If Nietzsche sometimes regarded himself as a voice crying in the wilderness, he also thought human life could redeem itself by going "beyond good and evil": "Must not the ancient fire some day flare up much more terribly, after much longer preparation?" he wrote. "More: must one not desire it with all one's might? even will it? even promote it?" The spirit of nobility—affirmation of life, struggle, conquest, and a passionate desire to excel—these characteristics need to be uplifted. Nietzsche's aim, however, was not to duplicate the past but to put these essential qualities back into modern life.

GOD IS DEAD

Nietzsche's proclamation of the death of God was a fundamental ingredient in the revaluation of all values Nietzsche advocated. This proclamation emerged from his conviction that the morality of mediocrity and affirmations of God's existence, especially as the latter are understood in Christianity, stand inextricably tied together. Nothing, argued Nietzsche, has done more than Christianity to entrench the morality of mediocrity in human consciousness. In Nietzsche's view, for example, the Christian emphasis on love extols qualities of weakness. Christianity urges that it is our responsibility to cultivate those attributes, not because of an abstract concept of duty but because it is God's will that we do so. As this conception developed, Nietzsche argued, it bound people in debilitating guilt. It also led them to an escapist tendency to seek for fulfillment beyond this world.

Arguably one-sided, Nietzsche's critique was loud and clear: Christianity, with its conception of a transcendent, omnipotent, omniscient, just, and loving God, denies and negates too much that is valuable in this world. Nietzsche did not deny that the long dominance of the Christian faith is a real manifestation of the will to power and that certain individuals have revealed unusual qualities of strength in establishing Christianity's authority. He was convinced, however, that the result has been to place an inferior breed in control of life. Nietzsche believed that, by proclaiming that God is dead, he would eliminate the underpinning of Christian morality, thus making it less difficult to move beyond the conventional understanding of good and evil.

The issue of God's existence, believed Nietzsche, is more psychological than metaphysical. That is, Nietzsche thought that belief in God is an additional tool used to distort the facts of life and to attack and to bring to submission individuals of noble character. His aim was not so much to prove or disprove the existence of God as to show that belief in God can create a sickness. He wanted to convince people that the highest achievements in human life depend on the elimination of this belief.

IMPLICATIONS FOR ETHICAL CONDUCT

Nietzsche's philosophy places strong demands on those who would live by it. He urged such people to consider that life is an eternal recurrence. Therefore, one ought to choose so there is no need for regret. The goal is to act so that, if confronted by an identical situation an infinite number of times, one could honestly say that one would do nothing differently.

John K. Roth

FURTHER READING

Froese, Katrin. *Rousseau and Nietzsche: Toward an Aesthetic Morality.* Lanham, Md.: Lexington Books, 2001.

Hales, Steven D., and Rex Welshon. *Nietzsche's Perspectivism.* Urbana: University of Illinois, 2000.

Heller, Erich. *The Importance of Nietzsche: Ten Essays.* Chicago: University of Chicago Press, 1988.

Kaufmann, Walter. *Nietzsche: Philosopher, Psychologist, Antichrist.* Princeton, N.J.: Princeton University Press, 1974.

May, Simon. *Nietzsche's Ethics and His War on "Morality."* New York: Oxford University Press, 1999.

Nehamas, Alexander. *Nietzsche: Life as Literature.* Cambridge, Mass.: Harvard University Press, 1985.

Nietzsche, Friedrich. *Beyond Good and Evil.* Translated by Walter Kaufmann. New York: Vintage, 1989.

_____. *On the Genealogy of Morals.* Edited and translated by Walter Kaufmann. New York: Vintage Books, 1967.

Schacht, Richard, ed. *Nietzsche's Postmoralism: Essays on Nietzsche's Prelude to Philosophy's Future.* New York: Cambridge University Press, 2001.

Solomon, Robert C. *Living with Nietzsche: What the Great "Immoralist" Has to Teach Us.* New York: Oxford University Press, 2003.

SEE ALSO: *Beyond Good and Evil*; Cruelty; Derrida, Jacques; Egoism; Individualism; Pluralism; Power; Relativism; Selfishness; Weakness of will; Will.

Nihilism

DEFINITION: Doctrine holding that there is no rational foundation for truth and that existence is without meaning

TYPE OF ETHICS: Modern history

SIGNIFICANCE: Nihilism may refer to the ultimate lack of conviction, that is, an inability to believe in anything at all. It may also refer to the active embrace of nothingness—either through ascetic self-denial or through antisocial violence, destruction, or anarchy—as a positive goal. The distinction is elucidated in Nietzsche's famous diagnosis: "Man would rather will nothingness than have nothing to will."

Nihilism in general refers to the view that the world is without meaning. It is often used as a term of criticism, for if a philosophical position can be shown to result in nihilism, its assumptions may warrant reexamination. Other thinkers maintain that nihilism is a tenable position to hold.

FRIEDRICH JACOBI

The term "nihilism" was first used by the German philosopher Friedrich Jacobi. Jacobi criticized modern philosophy's faith in reason as the foundation of all knowledge. The rationalist doubts everything but what the mind can discover by itself. For Jacobi, this skeptical approach must culminate in the belief that nothing exists, for there is no rational foundation for belief in anything outside one's own mind. For Jacobi, reason affirmed nothing, and he called the belief in nothing "nihilism," from the Latin word *nihil*, meaning "nothing."

In his *David Hume on Belief: Or, Idealism and Realism* (1787), Jacobi argues that the radical skepticism of Hume is in fact nihilism. The nihilist, as epitomized for Jacobi by Hume, sees no justification for belief in the existence of the external world, other people, God, or even a self.

Nihilism, then, is primarily a problem with the theory of knowledge for Jacobi. The reliance of modern philosophy on reason as the source of all knowledge leads to an unacceptable outcome, and therefore the reliance on reason alone must be misguided.

Nihilism also has unacceptable ethical implications, according to Jacobi. If nothing exists outside one's own mind, there can be no ethical obligations to other beings. The nihilist is free to decide what is right or wrong. Whatever the nihilist wills is good, because there is no standard for goodness other than what the mind itself wills.

RUSSIAN NIHILISM

Nihilism first came into popular use in Russia during the mid-nineteenth century, as both a literary and a political term. In Ivan Turgenev's novel *Fathers and Sons* (1862), the character Bazarov proudly declares himself a nihilist. For Turgenev, nihilism entails rejecting tradition in favor of scientific rationalism and materialism.

As a political movement in Russia, nihilism was associated with belief in radical freedom, a questioning of all social conventions and authority. The nihilists saw themselves as the vanguard of social change, exposing tyranny and hypocrisy in the name of reason. Factions of the movement degenerated into advocating anarchism and terrorism.

For Fyodor Dostoevski, nihilism is associated with atheism. In *The Brothers Karamazov* (1880), Ivan Karamazov declares, "If God does not exist, then everything is permitted," exemplifying the destructive ethical consequences of nihilism. There is no basis on which to call any act right or wrong. The individual has complete freedom to follow all desires and impulses and to declare these desires good.

FRIEDRICH NIETZSCHE

The figure in philosophy with whom nihilism is most closely associated is the German philosopher Friedrich Nietzsche. He uses the term in both a negative and positive sense. As a term of criticism, he uses it to describe the result of Western culture's search for truth. In Nietzsche's view, this search began with Socrates' dialectic method as seen in the dialogues of Plato. He sees the reliance on rational inquiry as undermining the healthy, noble, and artistic instincts typified by the ancient Greek tragedians.

In *The Will to Power* (1887), Nietzsche asks: "What does nihilism mean? That the highest values devaluate themselves." Western culture values truth most highly, but the very search for truth is destined for failure at the outset because, according to Nietzsche, there is in fact no truth to be discovered. He sees himself as the first person to fully grasp this insight, but he believes that the history of modern thought has increasingly moved toward the same realization and thus toward nihilism. The entire enterprise of truth-seeking is in fact nihilistic because it avoids the reality that there is no truth.

In *Thus Spoke Zarathustra* (1884), Nietzsche prophesies that Western civilization will culminate in the "last men," who are aware that there is no foundation for values or truth, but who are indifferent to this lack. The last men will live a life of pleasure, relieved of the burden of seeking truth and of any moral duties that an objective right or wrong might require. Nietzsche calls this attitude "passive nihilism."

Out of the last men will emerge an "overman," one who fully recognizes that there is no independent meaning or value in the world. The overman in this sense is a nihilist also. In contrast to the last men, however, he sees that the lack of independent meaning gives him the power to create his own truth. This realization enables him to create a world of significance in his own image, breaking free of the passive nihilism of the last men. Nietzsche calls the overman's creative response to nihilism "active nihilism," and sees this creation of meaning out of nothing as the highest, noblest task for humans.

THE TWENTIETH CENTURY

A number of twentieth century philosophers argue that it is impossible to justify moral judgments rationally. Nihilism is sometimes used as a critical term to describe these views. For example, the emotivist Charles Stevenson argues that moral judgments are merely aesthetic expressions of approval or disapproval and cannot be proved or disproved. Similarly, the existentialism of Jean-Paul Sartre and Albert Camus asserts that moral judgments are always simply the arbitrary decisions of individuals.

Paul Gallagher

FURTHER READING

Allison, David, ed. *The New Nietzsche.* Cambridge, Mass.: MIT Press, 1985.

Banham, Gary, and Charlie Blake, eds. *Evil Spirits: Nihilism and the Fate of Modernity.* New York: St. Martin's Press, 2000.

Beiser, Frederick. *The Fate of Reason: German Philosophy from Kant to Fichte.* Cambridge, Mass.: Harvard University Press, 1987.

Edwards, James C. *The Plain Sense of Things: The Fate of Religion in an Age of Normal Nihilism.* University Park: Pennsylvania State University Press, 1997.

Gillespie, Michael Allen. *Nihilism Before Nietzsche.* Chicago: University of Chicago Press, 1995.

Heidegger, Martin. *Nietzsche.* Translated by David F. Krell. San Francisco: Harper & Row, 1979-1987.

Nietzsche, Friedrich. *On the Genealogy of Morals.* Edited and translated by Walter Kaufmann. New York: Vintage Books, 1967.

Rosen, Stanley. *Nihilism.* New Haven, Conn.: Yale University Press, 1969.

Yarmolinsky, Avrahm. *Road to Revolution.* Princeton, N.J.: Princeton University Press, 1986.

SEE ALSO: Anarchy; *Being and Nothingness*; *Beyond Good and Evil*; Camus, Albert; Dostoevski, Fyodor; Existentialism; Sartre, Jean-Paul.

Nirvana

DEFINITION: Eastern concept of the final transcendent state of being achieved by the virtuous and enlightened when they extinguish desire and individual consciousness, enabling them to end the cycle of reincarnation

TYPE OF ETHICS: Religious ethics

SIGNIFICANCE: Most closely associated with Buddhism, nirvana provides an ethical teleology similar in some respects to the Christian heaven. Rather than simply representing a reward for virtue, however, nirvana also provides Buddhists with a model of virtue.

The term "nirvana" (Sanskrit, *nirvāna*) is used to designate the ultimate reality in Buddhist traditions. While the Hindu and Jain traditions also employ this concept, nirvana has received its most distinctive formulations in the many varieties of Buddhism.

EARLY INTERPRETATIONS

According to Buddhist tradition, Siddhārtha Gautama, the Buddha, achieved enlightenment more than 2,500 years ago and came to see the true nature of existence. The Pali scriptures relate that in that moment Gautama, now referred to as the Buddha, or awakened one, realized both the fundamental problem of existence and its solution. The Buddha's message, based on this moment of insight, was that the basic quality of existence is *duḥkha*, which connotes suffering, illness, emptiness, unsatisfactoriness, and insubstantiality. In his analysis of this situation, the Buddha stated that the pervasive reality of *duḥkha* is predicated on a false understanding of the nature of the self. People suffer anguish because they believe in a permanent, substantial self or soul, a belief that generates obsessive craving (*tṛṣṇa*) for objects, experiences, ideals, or persons that will provide comfort, security, and enrichment for the "self." Transient reality, however, is unable to fulfill human desires. Those things that people expect to satisfy their cravings for permanence and happiness are unable to do so because they are insubstantial and evanescent. The more people grasp, the more they suffer and, according to Buddhist teaching, the more they are reborn into the world of *saṃsāra*. (The Buddhist traditions accept many of the Hindu assumptions about the nature of reincarnation.)

The Buddha then offered a practical solution to the problem of *duḥkha*. If the cause of anguish is a mistaken belief, then its resolution lies in gaining wisdom, or enlightenment. Enlightenment reveals the insubstantiality of the self (*anātman*) and shows that what is called "self" (Buddhists often use the term "ego" to designate this construction) is merely a constantly changing constellation of energies (aggregates of being). The deep existential appropriation of this insight has profound behavioral and moral consequences, beginning with the cessation of craving. The *arhat* (one who has achieved enlightenment) has realized nirvana, the absolute state of perfect wisdom and release from the cycle of rebirth.

Nirvana is most often described in negative terms, not because it designates a negative state, but because it names a reality that is beyond ordinary experience and hence beyond the limitations of language. Nirvana is "the eradication of ignorance," "the elimination of suffering," and the "end of desire." Translated literally, nirvana is "extinction." Unfortunately, this meaning has often conveyed to the Western mind the misleading impression that Buddhism is a nihilistic religious tradition. Nirvana does not mean extinction of the self—since in Buddhism there is no real self—but rather the extinction of the illusion of self. Referred to in more positive terms, nirvana is bliss, absolute happiness, and unconditioned tranquillity.

Tradition distinguishes between two modes of nirvana: nirvana with substrate (*sopadhiśeṣa nirvāṇa*) and nirvana without substrate (*nirupadhiśeṣa nirvāṇa*). The distinction names the difference between the arhat who lives and the one who is dead, or the difference between nirvana and final nirvana (*parinirvāṇa*). As a living person, the arhat may still experience physical pain and other forms of karmic fruition (the consequences of previous actions). At *parinirvāṇa*, however, all karmic energies are dissipated and the arhat is released from rebirth. The Buddha refused to answer his disciples' questions about the nature of final nirvana. At most, he would say that final nirvana is neither nothingness nor not-nothingness, a paradoxical way of stating that the unconditional is beyond ordinary comprehension.

Nirvana is intrinsically related to the ethical outlook of Buddhism. The path to nirvana is in great measure an ethical one. The Buddha prescribed for his followers a regimen that included study, meditation practice, and moral behavior (the eightfold noble path). He encouraged his followers to live by specific precepts, which were to be accepted not as commandments but as principles for striving to live a compassionate and egoless existence. Among these precepts were abstaining from false speech, not harming sentient beings (*ahiṃsā*), not taking that which is not offered, abstaining from sexual misconduct, not consuming alcohol or other drugs, and earning one's living in a way that helps rather than harms other beings. The Buddha also counseled the cultivation of wholesome characteristics such as friendliness, patience, and compassion. Each aspect of the Buddhist path is intended to enable the individual to overcome the ego's tendency to become attached (or addicted) to things, persons, and ideas. The path fosters nonattachment and egolessness, which advances one's progress toward enlightenment. Wisdom and morality therefore are inextricably connected. To behave in a purely selfless way, one must grasp the truth about the nature of existence, especially the nonexistence of the self; and to realize this truth, one must follow the precepts that help remove the obstacles that hinder awareness.

LATER INTERPRETATIONS

In subsequent development of the Buddhist traditions (particularly in the Mahāyāna and Vajrayāna), greater emphasis was placed on the element of compassion, and nirvana came to be interpreted in more corporate terms. Because of his compassionate and selfless nature, the Buddha, it was believed, would not abandon those who had not yet attained nirvana. Spurred by his conviction, the Mahāyāna Buddhist communities began to venerate the ideal of the *bodhisattva*. The bodhisattva was regarded as a great being who postponed final nirvana to assist all beings in the alleviation of suffering and the realization of nirvana. Since Buddhahood was now considered an ontological reality attainable in principle by anyone, the Buddhist universe came to be populated by countless bodhisattvas, all working to bring about the simultaneous nirvana of all beings.

Mark William Muesse

Further Reading

Collins, Steven. *Nirvana and Other Buddhist Felicities: Utopias of the Pali Imaginaire.* New York: Cambridge University Press, 1998.

Corless, Roger J. *The Vision of Buddhism: The Space Under the Tree.* New York: Paragon House, 1989.

Harvey, Peter. *An Introduction to Buddhism: Teachings, History and Practices.* New York: Cambridge University Press, 1990.

Kalupahana, David J. *Buddhist Philosophy: A Historical Analysis.* Honolulu: University of Hawaii Press, 1976.

Nyanaponika Mahathera. *The Road to Inner Freedom.* Kandy, Sri Lanka: Buddhist Publication Society, 1982.

Rahula, Walpola. *What the Buddha Taught.* Rev. ed. New York: Grove Press, 1974.

See also: Ahiṁsā; Bodhisattva ideal; Buddha; Buddhist ethics; Four noble truths; Hindu ethics; Jain ethics; Karma.

Nobel Peace Prizes

Definition: Annual prizes awarded to individuals or organizations that have done the most to promote world peace during the previous year

Date: First award made in 1901

Type of ethics: Human rights

Significance: By honoring those people who have furthered the causes of human rights and world peace, the Nobel Peace Prize has served to publicize and promote good works.

Alfred Bernhard Nobel, a Swedish chemist and industrialist, was initially noted for his invention of dynamite, for which he received a patent in 1867. Although the explosive properties of his invention were later associated with military weapons, the only applications that Nobel had in mind were for peaceful purposes such as the construction of railroad systems and highways. His industrial research also contributed toward the production of a variety of materials, including artificial textiles and rubber. As a consequence, Nobel had amassed a considerable fortune by the time of his death in 1896.

Establishment of the Nobel awards was based on Nobel's will, which was written in November, 1895.

Nobel directed that the major portion of his fortune—which was then worth the equivalent of nine million U.S. dollars, should be set aside for a fund, invested in safe securities, whose interest would be distributed in the form of annual prizes to people who had done the most for humanity during the previous year. The awards were initially to be given in the fields of chemistry, literature, physics, physiology or medicine, and peace. Economics was added later. The Peace Prize was to be administered by a committee of five persons elected by the Norwegian parliament. The Nobel Foundation, which was to supervise the investments, was established and approved by King Oscar II of Sweden, in June, 1900.

Nobel's attitude toward peace evolved from his interest in literature. In 1887, he began conducting a regular correspondence with the Austrian writer Bertha von Suttner. The wife of an Austrian baron, von Suttner was among the first notable women writers to establish a pacifist view. Her 1889 novel *Die Waffen nieder!* (1889; *Lay Down Your Arms*, 1892) was a denunciation of war and its consequences, and its title became the slogan for the peace movement. In 1905 von Suttner herself became the seventh recipient of the Nobel Peace Prize.

Although the extent to which Nobel was directly influenced by the baroness is in dispute, there is no question that Nobel admired both her writings and her work on behalf of pacifism. Nobel had few illusions about the attitude of the peace movements toward immediate disarmament and compulsory arbitration. It was his view that movement toward those worthy goals could only proceed gradually. For example, he believed that governments should develop agreements for the peaceful settlement of disputes but that those agreements should be limited to a single year.

Supporting Peace

During the early 1890's, Nobel evolved the idea of an economic support for peace. Several concepts contributed to this idea. In a letter that he wrote to von Suttner in 1892, he argued that if nations would establish mutual military agreements, the "atmosphere of security" would ease the transition to disarmament. In addition, the very horror of war itself, particularly in the light of the development of new and more destructive weapons, would cause "all civilized nations . . . to recoil from war and discharge their troops."

It remains unclear why Nobel rejected Swedish

Iranian attorney Shirin Ebadi receives the 2003 Nobel Peace Prize for her human rights work among Muslim women. Other recent winners include United Nations secretary general Kofi Annan (2001) and former U. S. president Jimmy Carter (2002). (AP/Wide World Photos)

academies for the Peace Prize Committee in favor of the Norwegian parliament. The Swedish press were, in fact, indignant when Nobel's "rejection" became known. Several theories for Nobel's decision have been proposed. The explanation that seems most credible reflects on the Norwegian parliament's strong support for international cooperation and arbitration. In addition, during the period in which Nobel was clarifying his will, the Norwegian poet Bjørnstjerne Bjørnson was playing a major role in the peace movement. Another explanation that seems equally likely is that Nobel had hoped the rivalry between Norway and Sweden would be eased if the final prize were presented in Oslo, rather than in Sweden.

Nobel's original idea was that each year's prize should be awarded to persons who have done the most to promote the concept of peace during the previous year. However, by the end of the twentieth century most of the awards were going to organizations. The most obvious example is that of the United Nations. Controversy has also been associated with certain choices, though this in itself is nothing new. For example, the 1973 awards made to Henry Kissinger of the United States and Le Duc Tho of Vietnam for their efforts to end the Vietnam War achieved little. Much the same might be said about the 1994 awards to Palestinian spokesman Yasir Arafat and Israeli representatives Shimon Peres and Yitzhak Rabin, and their futile efforts to end the Middle East conflict.

Despite such controversies, the award has brought recognition to organizations and issues about which the international public is often unaware. For example, the 1997 award on behalf of attempts to eliminate land mines raised hopes that their use in the future might at least be limited. Likewise, the 1999 award to Médecins Sans Frontières (Doctors Without Borders) brought attention to an apolitical organization that had been largely unknown throughout the world.

SELECTION PROCEDURES

The procedure for selecting recipients of the Nobel Peace Prize is similar to that established for awarding the other prizes. Nominations are requested in September of the year preceding the award, and the deadline is the end of January in the year of the award. Individuals eligible to tender nominations include both current and former members of Norway's parliament, their advisers, members of international committees relevant to the peace process.

Final decisions on recipients are made by the Norwegian Nobel Committee. Committee members are picked by the Norwegian parliament and are chosen on the basis of their expertise in at least one of three areas: international law, political history, and political economy. The field of nominees is narrowed between February and September, and the final decision is usually announced in early October.

The first recipients of the award in 1901 were Jean Henri Dunant and Frédéric Passy. Dunant had spent his life in the pursuit of morality and peace; it was his vision that led to the establishment of the International Red Cross in 1863. During the Franco-Prussian War in the 1870's, Dunant pushed for an international court of arbitration through his association with Alliance Universelle de l'Ordre et de la Civilisation. Among the speakers before the alliance was Passy. Dunant also worked for more humane treatment for prisoners of war, views that eventually came to a measure of fruition. Passy, too, was a strong advocate for peace societies. As a member of the French Chamber of Deputies, he was instrumental in creating a variety of treaties of arbitration.

During the more than one hundred years since the first awards were made, a wide variety of both individuals and institutions have been honored with the prize. Winners have been international, from the Americas and Europe, but also from Asia and Africa. During the first five decades of the award, the basis for the honor was generally international in scope. For example, beginning in 1902, individuals associated with the International Peace Bureau were hon-

ored several times. After World War II, however, honorees tended to be more parochial, in that awards were based on initiatives for changes in more localized areas. In 1952, for example, Albert Schweitzer was honored for his humanitarian work in Africa. In 1960, Albert Lutuli received the prize for his peaceful campaign to end apartheid in South Africa. Lutuli's award represented a watershed for the prize committee in that it was the first time a black African was so honored. Other Africans later honored included Desmond Tutu (1984) and Nelson Mandela (1993), also of South Africa, and Kofi Annan (2001), the Ghanaian secretary-general of the United Nations. In 2004, Wangari Muta Maathai of Kenya became the first African woman to receive the award. She was honored primarily for her environmental work—a reflection of the Nobel Committee's broadening interpretation of Alfred Nobel's intent.

Richard Adler

FURTHER READING

Abrams, Irwin. *The Nobel Peace Prize and the Laureates: An Illustrated Biographical History, 1901-2001*. Canton, Mass.: Science History Publications, 2001.

Chatfield, Charles, and Peter van den Dungen, eds. *Peace Movements and Political Cultures*. Knoxville: University of Tennessee Press, 1988.

Cobban, Helena. *The Moral Architecture of World Peace: Nobel Laureates Discuss Our Global Future*. Charlottesville: University of Virginia Press, 2000.

Evianoff, Michael, and Marjorie Fluor. *Alfred Nobel: The Loneliest Millionaire*. Los Angeles: Ward Ritchie Press, 1969.

Gray, Tony. *Champions of Peace: The Story of Alfred Nobel, the Peace Prize, and the Laureates*. New York: Paddington Press, 1976.

Lipsky, Mortimer. *The Quest for Peace: The Story of the Nobel Award*. South Brunswick, N.J.: A. S. Barnes, 1966.

Pauli, Hertha. *Toward Peace: The Nobel Prize and Man's Struggle for Peace*. New York: Ives Washburn, 1969.

SEE ALSO: Amnesty International; Dalai Lama; Human Rights Watch; International Red Cross; King, Martin Luther, Jr.; Mandela, Nelson; Peace studies; Schweitzer, Albert; Tutu, Desmond; Wiesel, Elie.

Nonviolence

DEFINITION: Refusal to use violence to resolve conflict and/or the use of nonviolent forms of power to resist oppression or promote social change

TYPE OF ETHICS: Politico-economic ethics

SIGNIFICANCE: Although based for some practitioners in a belief that nonviolent resistance is in fact more effective than violent resistance in attaining social justice, nonviolence is often an anticonsequentialist practice based in the belief that even just ends cannot justify violent means.

Nonviolence, as Robert L. Holmes has documented, has roots in a variety of cultures and historical documents, including the Bible, the Talmud, the *Bhagavadgītā, Laozi,* and Sophocles' *Antigone* (c. 441 B.C.E.). In certain periods and traditions, such as early Christianity (pre-fourth century) and Jainism (a religion related to Hinduism), the prohibition against violence takes an absolute form. Based on the recognition of the sacredness of all human life, nonviolence stands as a continuing protest to the wanton destruction of life evidenced in the collective histories of warfare, crime and punishment, and economic and political oppression.

HISTORY

Throughout most of its history, nonviolence has been expressed as nonresistance, the refusal to use violence to combat evil even for purposes of self-defense. In the nineteenth century, in the work of persons such as Henry David Thoreau and Leo Tolstoy, strategies of passive resistance were developed whose purpose was to point out social injustice with the hope of generating a consensus for positive social change. Such theorists advocated noncompliance with unjust laws and resistance against unjust social policies.

The practice of nonviolence was further developed in the twentieth century, particularly in the work of Mohandas K. Gandhi in freeing India from British rule and that of Martin Luther King, Jr., in struggling to end racial inequality in the United States. Both developed strategies of nonviolent resistance that emphasized the active confrontation of injustice for purposes of social transformation. Both emphasized that true nonviolence is not passivity in the face of evil, but the active confrontation of evil

and injustice wherever they exist. Central to these religious philosophies is the belief in personal as well as social transformation. The practitioner of nonviolence must, as Gandhi notes, renounce the "internal violence of the spirit" and truly love the opponent. Also central is the recognition of the ineffectiveness of violence, which only creates more hatred and more violence in a never-ending spiral. Only nonviolent suffering acting as witness to truth and justice can break the spiral. Nonviolentists must, then, according to Gandhi, learn "the art of dying" just as violentists have learned the "art of killing."

Following the partial success of Gandhi's and King's movements, political theorists began to analyze nonviolence as a political rather than a religious strategy. Here the emphasis is placed on organizing nonviolent forms of power as a means of forcing social change rather than upon personal transformation and the use of the power of love. As analysts recognized, the exercise of power requires the consent of the governed. Organized withdrawal of that consent on a large scale can lead to the collapse or transformation of social systems (such as the collapse of communism in Eastern Europe). Such theorists explore the use of various forms of nonviolent power in such areas as labor (strikes and slowdowns), buying (boycotts), noncompliance with laws, and moral suasion. Much analysis has focused on situations in which nonviolent strategies have been employed.

Theorists have unearthed a rich tradition of historical applications of nonviolence. Although nonviolence is often viewed as a tool for oppressed, powerless groups, advocates have developed plans for the total nonviolent civilian defense of nations against external aggression. Confronted with nuclear weapons, against which military defense may mean self-annihilation, nonviolent civilian defense is presented as the only sane alternative.

As a theory and a practice, nonviolence continues to develop and be refined. Important developments include an expansion of the concept of violence that is to be transformed by nonviolent means to include psychological violence (for example, racism, sexism, terrorism), institutional violence, the violence caused by the structure of existing social institutions (such as hunger, poverty, political oppression), and violence against the natural environment. Feminists have developed connections between feminist theory and nonviolence pertaining to women's issues and

1047

the development of nonhierarchical social structures. Nonviolence continues as an important strategy in a variety of Third World settings in which the resort to violence by oppressed groups is regarded as futile.

ETHICAL ARGUMENTS EMPLOYED

(1) All human life is sacred and all persons have equal worth. People do not have the right to take a life, not even in self-defense. (2) The recognition of the sacredness of persons requires people to intervene nonviolently wherever people suffer from war, political oppression, poverty, or discrimination. (3) Violence breeds more violence and does not provide lasting solutions to conflicts. One must, then, love one's opponent, accept the opponent's violence, and return love. Love, however, requires that one recognize truth and injustice, demanding change. Only such love can break the cycle of violence and create just social structures and renewed relationships. (4) There are many nonviolent means that may be employed. Moral action requires the development of an effective strategy for social change. (5) Although the practice of nonviolence may lead to suffering and death for its practitioners and will sometimes fail, the suffering caused will be much less than it would have been if violent means had been employed. In addition, the likelihood of lasting success is much greater.

Charles L. Kammer III

FURTHER READING

Cooney, Robert, and Helen Michalowski, eds. *The Power of the People: Active Nonviolence in the United States.* Philadelphia: New Society, 1987.

Holmes, Robert L., ed. *Nonviolence in Theory and Practice.* Belmont, Calif.: Wadsworth, 1990.

Lampen, John, ed. *No Alternative? Nonviolent Responses to Repressive Regimes.* York, England: W. Sessions, 2000.

McAllister, Pam, ed. *Reweaving the Web of Life: Feminism and Nonviolence.* Philadelphia: New Society, 1982.

Merton, Thomas. *The Nonviolent Alternative.* Edited by Gordon Zahn. New York: Farrar, Straus and Giroux, 1980.

Sharp, Gene. *The Politics of Nonviolent Action.* 3 vols. Boston: Porter Sargent, 1973.

Steger, Manfred B. *Judging Nonviolence: The Dispute Between Realists and Idealists.* New York: Routledge, 2003.

SEE ALSO: Ahiṁsā; Civil disobedience; Gandhi, Mohandas K.; King, Martin Luther, Jr.; Pacifism; Religion and violence; Thoreau, Henry David; Violence.

Normative vs. descriptive ethics

DEFINITION: Distinction between moral philosophies that tell people what they should do (normative ethics) and moral philosophies that merely describe what people already believe they should do (descriptive ethics).

TYPE OF ETHICS: Theory of ethics

SIGNIFICANCE: Descriptive ethical statements are generally taken to be judgments of fact which may be shown to be true or false. Normative ethical statements are much more difficult to prove, and for some moral philosophers, are statements of value which are neither true nor false.

Normative ethics deals with the formulation of ethical codes of behavior and moral models of evaluative decision making. Normative ethics prescribes moral principles defining the good, the right, duty, obligation, law, and justice. A normative approach assumes the universality of its ethical principles and attempts to justify them on a rational basis.

Christian ethics is a classic example of normative ethics. The following are normative moral utterances: "All promises ought to be kept." "Killing another human being is wrong." "Capital punishment is just because it deters crime." "A father has a duty to provide physical support for his children." In all these examples, the common element is the prescription of a certain course of action or its evaluation. The most famous example of normative ethics is found in the Ten Commandments.

DESCRIPTIVE ETHICS

Descriptive ethics is ethics shorn free of prescriptive or evaluative elements. Descriptive ethics deals with the meanings of moral utterances, the relationships between them and moral actors, and the nature of moral argumentation. Descriptive ethics may take a sociological, psychological, ethnographic, or philosophic approach. A sociological analysis of ethics may concern itself with the relationship between moral behavior and social coercion. Psychology may deal with the relationships between moral behavior and the different stages of human growth and development. Ethnography may study the relationships between ethical beliefs and culture and tradition. Philosophical analysis will tend to concern itself with the semantic meaning of moral utterances, their sense and pragmatic context.

Thomas Hobbes treated ethics as a descriptive science of the aversions and appetites of the human organism. The good, according to Hobbes, is any object of human desire and appetite. Human behavior, in this view, is motivated by aversion to fear and want and appetites for security and gain. Hobbes's descriptive approach is made possible by his mechanistic view of the universe and human nature.

NATURALISM

The descriptive approach that finds a natural cause for moral behavior is known as naturalism. One famous advocate of naturalism was David Hume, who, more than any other philosopher, thoroughly modernized and secularized ethics and philosophy. In *A Treatise of Human Nature* and *An Enquiry Concerning the Principles of Morals*, Hume attempts to answer the metaethical questions of the meanings of ethical terms such as "good," "right," "justice," "virtue," and "vice." Hume concludes that ethical terms are not qualities of a special moral sense or predicates of ethical objects. Instead, they only convey sentiments of approbation or approval; therefore, ethical judgments are entirely subjective. Whenever an object is judged to be good, it means that it is either pleasant or useful. Thus, moral judgments are really judgments of taste.

Naturalistic analysis claims that the good and the right are determined by human appetites. Naturalism holds that an object is valued as good because it is desirable. The proposition "*X* is good" means "I desire *X*." One form of naturalism is emotivism, which holds that ethical judgments are only expressions of personal feelings of approval or distaste. This could lead to subjectivism and ethical relativism. In fact, there can be no real ethical disagreements. Ethical judgments only express the attitudes of speakers.

Hedonism is another form of naturalism. Hedonism equates good and evil with pleasure and pain. Whatever produces pleasure is equivalent to the good. Utilitarianism in the hands of Jeremy Bentham maintained a vulgar view that overvalued the quantitative aspects of pleasure. John Stuart Mill, in *Utilitarian-*

ism, distinguished between good and bad pleasures. Intellectual and cultural pleasures are superior to mere physical pleasures. As Mill put it, "I would rather be Socrates dissatisfied than a pig satisfied." One of the most formidable challenges to naturalism came from G. E. Moore. Moore's critique of naturalism is known as the naturalistic fallacy. This fallacy involves defining good in terms of something else, such as pleasure. For Moore, good was an indefinable quality.

As Karl-Otto Apel points out, normative ethics seems to have been made obsolete by Hume's distinction—norms cannot be derived from facts; an "ought" statement cannot be derived from an "is" statement. The scientific grounding of ethics is impossible. Science deals only with facts. In effect, Hume relegated moral norms to the subjective domain. As a result, modern science will accept objectivity only in the mathematical and empirical sciences—not in morality. Morality is purely subjective, from the point of view of modern science. Since Hume and Max Weber, science has claimed to be value free, only positing technological goals, but one can only ask with Apel: What about the criteria for and desirability of technological goals? Can science really free itself from ethics?

As Apel claims, scientific claims involve arguments. Arguments occur in speech situations, in contexts of communication in which certain ethical norms are, in fact, presupposed. Other persons are recognized as genuine subjects of communication. Involvement in argumentation implies ethical claims such as truthfulness and sincerity. Thus, if Apel is correct, science is not value free and there cannot ever be a purely descriptive ethics.

Michael R. Candelaria

FURTHER READING

Apel, Karl-Otto. *Towards a Transformation of Philosophy.* Translated by Glyn Adey and David Frisby. London: Routledge & Kegan Paul, 1980.

Ayer, A. J. *Language, Truth, and Logic.* London: V. Gollancz, 1936. Reprint. Introduction by Ben Rogers. London: Penguin, 2001.

Dancy, Jonathan, ed. *Normativity.* Malden, Mass.: Blackwell, 2000.

Hume, David. *A Treatise of Human Nature.* London: Everyman, 2003.

Moore, G. E. *Principia Ethica.* Rev. ed. New York: Cambridge University Press, 1996.

North Atlantic Treaty Organization

IDENTIFICATION: International alliance initially formed to provide security to Western European nations against a perceived Soviet threat

DATE: Founded on April 4, 1949

TYPE OF ETHICS: International relations

SIGNIFICANCE: During the Cold War, North Atlantic Treaty Organization's (NATO) status as a true alliance of equals, rather than a mere instrument of the United States, was sometimes questioned, raising issues about imperialism and the self-determination of European members. In the post-Cold War era, NATO remains one of the most important organs of military power on the world stage, albeit one with a less coherent sense of purpose.

The North Atlantic Treaty Organization is a defensive and political alliance among twenty-six nations. The alliance was created when twelve nations (Belgium, Canada, Denmark, France, Iceland, Italy, Luxembourg, Netherlands, Norway, Portugal, the United Kingdom, and the United States) signed the North Atlantic Treaty in Washington, D.C., on April 4, 1949. It was later joined by Greece and Turkey (February, 1952), West Germany (later Germany; May, 1955), Spain (May, 1982), the Czech Republic, Hungary, and Poland (March, 1999), and Bulgaria, Estonia, Latvia, Lithuania, Romania, Slovakia, and Slovenia (March, 2004). The treaty is a military alliance designed to prevent aggression or to repel it should it occur. It also provides for continuous consultation and cooperation among member nations in political and economic matters.

The United States was instrumental in creating NATO and has enjoyed hegemonic status within the alliance; the alliance's commitments consume about 50 percent of the U.S. defense budget each year. American commitment to NATO marked a fundamental transformation of the guiding principles of U.S. foreign policy; it caused the United States to depart from its traditional policy against entanglement in permanent alliances and from its isolationist foreign policy.

HISTORICAL BACKGROUND

NATO has provided the basic framework for the political and military structure of the West during the postwar period. The idea of a permanent peacetime alliance among North Atlantic nations was conceived when "Cold War" conflict was developing between the United States and the Soviet Union. The Truman Doctrine of March, 1947, for example, acknowledged the disharmony of interests with the Soviet Union and underlined the need to contain the expansion of Soviet communism. The events of 1948—the communist coup in Prague in the spring of 1948 and the Soviet blockade of Berlin in June, 1948—further convinced the United States and its allies that the Soviet Union was an expansionist power and that it was willing to use force and subversion to become involved in the affairs of Western Europe.

NATO, which was a response to the perceived Soviet threat to Western Europe, became the keystone of American security commitments. NATO had two main goals. Its short-term goal was to rehabilitate the war-shattered economies of Western European nations and to maintain their political stability by countering communist-inspired subversions in Europe. NATO's long-term goal was to re-create a European balance of power against the Soviet Union by making Europe strong militarily as well as politically and economically. NATO has succeeded in accomplishing both goals.

STRUCTURE OF NATO

The North Atlantic Council, which is composed of ministerial representatives of member countries, is the chief policy-making body of NATO; it meets at least twice a year. The Council is assisted by several committees. The Military Committee is the highest military authority in NATO. It is composed of the chiefs of staff of all member countries except France (Iceland, having no military forces, is represented by a civilian), and it makes recommendations to the Council and to the Defense Planning Committee on military matters. NATO forces are divided into three commands: Allied Command Europe, the Atlantic Ocean Command, and the Channel Command.

NATO's First Half Century

Although the alliance has survived for more than a generation, NATO's solidarity has varied over time. During the early 1950's, West Germany's participation in NATO became an issue and was settled in the Paris Agreements of 1954; West Germany joined the alliance in 1955. The withdrawal of the French forces from the integrated military command structure of NATO in 1966 weakened the alliance (France remains a member of the North Atlantic alliance). As a result of the French action, NATO headquarters had to be moved from Paris to Brussels. In 1974, Greece withdrew (until 1980) from the NATO military command because of Turkish military actions in Cyprus. Yet the political cohesion of NATO has been quite remarkable.

NATO members agreed from the beginning that the primary purpose of the alliance was to be prepared militarily to counter Soviet attack. Their strategy rested in credible deterrence of threats to Western security. For protection against possible Soviet attack on Europe, NATO has relied on the U.S. nuclear umbrella. American nuclear weapons have been deployed in Western Europe, though they have always remained under U.S. command. The deployment of intermediate-range nuclear weapons (Cruise and Pershing II missiles) in 1983 and 1984, however, brought strong opposition from intellectuals, political leaders, and peace activists who feared that the presence of the intermediate-range nuclear weapons in Europe would increase the likelihood of a nuclear confrontation with the Soviet Union.

NATO's strategy of deterrence has also been questioned on moral and ethical grounds, since it uses civilian populations as potential nuclear targets. Yet, the developments of the late 1980's—the 1987 Soviet-American INF treaty (supported by all NATO members) on the elimination of a class of intermediate- and short-range nuclear missiles based in Europe, the breaking down of the Berlin Wall in 1989 followed by the reunification of two Germanys in 1990, and the disintegration of the Soviet Union and of the Warsaw Pact (NATO's communist counterpart)—have radically transformed the political and strategical environment in which NATO operates.

Sunil K. Sahu

Further Reading

Carpenter, Ted Galen, ed. *NATO at Forty: Confronting a Changing World.* Lexington, Mass.: Lexington Books, 1990.

Cerutti, Furio, and Rodolfo Ragionieri, eds. *Rethinking European Security.* New York: Crane Russak, 1990.

Golden, James, ed. *NATO at Forty: Change, Continuity, and Prospects.* Boulder, Colo.: Westview Press, 1989.

Hyde-Price, Adrian. *European Security Beyond the Cold War.* Newbury Park, Calif.: Sage, 1991.

Ireland, Timothy P. *Creating the Entangling Alliance: The Origins of the North Atlantic Treaty Organization.* Westport, Conn.: Greenwood Press, 1981.

Kaplan, Lawrence S. *NATO and the United States: The Enduring Alliance.* Boston: Twayne, 1988.

Moens, Alexander, Leonard J. Cohen, and Allen G. Sens, eds. *NATO and European Security: Alliance Politics from the End of the Cold War to the Age of Terrorism.* Westport, Conn.: Praeger, 2003.

Sloan, Stanley R., ed. *NATO During the 1990s.* Washington, D.C.: Pergamon-Brassey's, 1989.

Steinbruner, John D., and Leon V. Sigal, eds. *Alliance Security: NATO and the No-First-Use Question.* Washington, D.C.: Brookings Institution, 1983.

Trachtenberg, Marc, ed. *Between Empire and Alliance: America and Europe During the Cold War.* Lanham, Md.: Rowman & Littlefield, 2003.

See also: Bosnia; Cold War; International law; Peacekeeping missions; Truman Doctrine; United Nations.

"Not in my backyard"

DEFINITION: Popular objection to the establishment of socially necessary but unattractive or troublesome facilities, such as landfills, prisons, and group homes

DATE: Term first used during the 1980's

TYPE OF ETHICS: Environmental ethics

SIGNIFICANCE: Both proponents and opponents of unpopular projects utilize moral arguments to support their positions.

"Not-in-my-backyard" (often represented by the acronym NIMBY) objections are often raised to the introduction of an unwanted facility to an area, particularly one in or near a residential area. Almost all members of the society may recognize the need for the facility and support it in principle, while at the same time not wanting it in their own neighborhoods or communities. Citizen groups may form and noisily oppose projects such as prisons, nuclear waste sites, and low-income housing projects. In acrimonious NIMBY debates among project developers and members of the public, all sides may raise ethical arguments. As in other aspects of life, multiple ethical principles often apply and create conflict of moral rules.

ETHICAL ARGUMENTS IN FAVOR OF PROJECTS

The first argument in favor of an unpopular project is that it will serve the common good of society. The project's utilitarian consequences, it may be argued, will bring health, happiness, and general well-being to the greatest number. Indeed, a community would have a difficult time surviving without facilities to dispose of its wastes, create its energy, and provide its human services. The question is: Where are the facilities necessary to perform these functions to be located?

Abhorrent consequences may follow if NIMBY advocates succeed. The blocked project will simply be relocated elsewhere, to the detriment of another community. Furthermore, there is a possibility that the alternative site may not be as safe or effective as the site initially selected by scientific planners.

Human beings are ethically required not to cause real harm to others. However, they also are not obligated to abstain from conduct that is erroneously perceived as harmful. Protesters are often ill-informed about plans they oppose. For example, many people do not distinguish between hazardous and nonhazardous types of waste, or they may believe false stereotypes about the dangers of people with mental disabilities. The fact that members of a community are psychologically uncomfortable with a plan does not constitute a morally relevant reason for disallowing it.

ETHICAL RULES IN OPPOSITION

In an ideal society, the costs imposed by essential services should be shared equally by all. Unpopular projects, such as waste dumps and prisons, unfairly burden their closest neighbors. While the community as a whole may be served by having such facilities, the facilities' nearest neighbors receive no compensation for the extra noise, unpleasant odors, extra dangers, inconvenient traffic, and fall in the value of their properties. Furthermore, a basic rule of fairness requires that all members of a community should clean up their own messes. NIMBY neighbors are blameless; they are not any more responsible for community problems such as nuclear wastes, energy shortages, highway congestion, or prison populations that the unpopular facilities are designed to fix.

In a fair contest, the better competitor should win without cheating. Some NIMBY opposition arguments focus on unethical project planning and marketing. Public land uses should be determined in consultation with the public, as community members should have a say in events affecting their own neighborhoods. However, in NIMBY situations, proposals are typically imposed and implemented by outside bodies. Such bodies may promote projects unethically, break their promises, conceal the truth, and intimidate opponents.

TWO TYPES OF NIMBY PROJECTS

One class of NIMBY projects poses some type of environmental threat, while at the same time providing a needed service. A large subclass is disposal site proposals, including facilities for nuclear wastes and regular landfills. There are also environment-altering NIMBY proposals that do not deal with waste, such as airports, oil refineries, windmill farms, cellular phone towers, and ballparks.

A second major class of projects provides needed human services such as new prisons, group homes for people with drug or alcohol problems or mental disabilities, and nursing homes that admit AIDS patients. Babies and children are not exempt from NIMBY opposition. Even small day-care facilities have been opposed in some residential neighborhoods. The ethical issues raised about these two project types include the points already discussed, as well as variants for each type of project.

ENVIRONMENTAL PROJECTS

When waste disposal sites and polluting farms or factories are planned, the neighbors who are affected are typically poor and nonwhite. The concept of "environmental racism" critiques burdening society's

Examples of NIMBY Projects
Airports
Day-care facilities
Drug rehab centers
Garbage dumps and landfills
Group homes for troubled youths
Halfway houses for alcoholics
Low-income housing
Mental hospitals
Nursing homes
Oil refineries
Power plants
Prisons and jails
Recycling centers
Schools
Sports arenas and other venues that draw crowds
Windmill farms

least powerful groups, unable to defend themselves, with exposure to unsafe and unpleasant substances. To add insult to injury, the employment opportunities promised to the poor in return for acceptance of the new facilities often do not materialize.

Some ardent environmental activists contend that all the world's neighborhoods deserve protection from exposure. They argue that it is immoral to export toxins to developing countries. Rich nations should not dump their trash on the world's poor. This viewpoint has been nicknamed NOPE, an acronym for "Not on Planet Earth." Activists urge fundamental changes in materialistic societies such as the United States. They argue that Americans need fewer landfills, not more, and suggest that recycling and less wasteful lifestyles are the answers. According to this view, landfills are the evil products of pollution and materialism.

Proponents of new waste sites contend that they will improve public health and safety, especially in communities whose existing dumps are overburdened and leaky. Without larger, leakproof facilities, a town's dumps may remain, and dangerous practices such as late-night dumping of wastes by unscrupulous haulers will continue. Furthermore, it is argued, it is morally unfair to put off permanent solutions to waste problems, leaving them for future generations to solve.

HUMAN SERVICE PROJECTS

A moral community is responsive to the needs of all its members. It is compassionate toward its weakest and most needy. All people should be treated humanely, and in ways that allow them to thrive and develop their abilities. Additionally, both law and morality require that people be treated equally unless there are valid reasons for doing otherwise. There is no morally relevant reason to exclude people with mental disabilities from middle-class neighborhoods. Similar arguments are made by advocates for placing small, moderate-income housing within such neighborhoods. Research has shown that both subgroups are harmed by being segregated off by themselves. Moreover, society as a whole can benefit in that intergroup contact often leads to decreases in intergroup prejudices.

Nancy Conn Terjesen

FURTHER READING

Bullard, Robert D. *Dumping in Dixie: Race, Class and Environmental Quality.* Boulder, Colo.: Westview Press, 1990.

Gerrard, Michael B. *Whose Backyard, Whose Risk.* Cambridge, Mass.: MIT Press, 1994.

Hornblower, Margot. "Not in My Backyard, You Don't." *Time* 131 (June 27, 1988): 44, 45.

Inhaber, Herbert. *Slaying the NIMBY Dragon.* New Brunswick, N.J.: Transaction Publishers, 1998.

Morris, Jane Anne. *Not in My Backyard: The Handbook.* San Diego, Calif.: Silvercat Publications, 1994.

SEE ALSO: Ecology; Environmental ethics; Environmental Protection Agency; Nuclear Regulatory Commission; Toxic waste.

Nozick, Robert

IDENTIFICATION: American philosopher
BORN: November 16, 1938, Brooklyn, New York
DIED: January 23, 2002, Cambridge, Massachusetts
TYPE OF ETHICS: Politico-economic ethics
SIGNIFICANCE: Robert Nozick made significant contributions to political ethics, epistemology, rational choice theory, and other areas of philosophy. He also provided philosophical justifications for

questioning redistribution of wealth and income in the modern welfare state.

Robert Nozick is best known for his book *Anarchy, State, and Utopia* (1974), which he wrote partly in response to *A Theory of Justice* (1971) by his fellow Harvard professor, John Rawls. Rawls's book had provided a philosophical justification for the welfare state by asking what kind of society rational persons would want if they did not know what their own positions in that society would be. Rawls maintained that this would be a society that provided the most possible resources to its least fortunate members. The ethical implication of this argument was that inequality among people could be accepted as just only to the extent that it was in the interest of those at the bottom.

Nozick responded to Rawls's thesis by arguing that justice requires recognition of the rights of individuals to self-ownership and to ownership of the products of their own labor. Resources, he argued, are created by the things that individuals do, and they are exchanged among individuals. So long as people acquire their possessions through their own work and exchange, they have just and ethical claims to their own property. Redistribution involves taking from some individuals and giving to others. Unless it is redistribution of goods acquired unjustly, through force, this is equivalent to making some people work unwillingly for other people, taking away the right to self-ownership.

The ethical positions of both Rawls and Nozick rejected utilitarianism, the argument that social ethics should be based on the greatest good of the largest number of people. Both philosophers founded ethical principles on individuals. For Rawls, however, this entailed creating the kind of society that would maximize the well-being of an abstract and hypothetical individual who might be placed at the bottom. For Nozick, it entailed as little interference as possible in the lives of individuals.

After publishing *Anarchy, State, and Utopia*, Nozick wrote several books that explored other philosophical questions. His last book, *Invariances: The Structure of the Objective World* (2001), examined issues of the nature of objective truth. While his first book relied on traditional philosophical reasoning, his final book attempted to take into consideration scientific evidence from economics, evolutionary biology, and cognitive neuroscience. Among other considerations, Nozick attempted to root ethics in the evolution of human consciousness. Arguing that ethics stem from cooperation for the sake of mutual benefit, he described a series of levels of ethics, from the most minimal sorts needed for cooperation, to aid and caring for other people. However, he did not entirely desert his earlier libertarianism, since he argued that the highest levels of ethics must be voluntary and cannot be created by the force of a government or other social agency.

Carl L. Bankston III

FURTHER READING

Schmidtz, David, ed. *Robert Nozick*. New York: Cambridge University Press, 2002.

Wolff, Jonathan. *Robert Nozick: Property, Justice and the Minimal State*. Stanford, Calif.: Stanford University Press, 1991.

SEE ALSO: Consent; Corporate compensation; Distributive justice; Entitlements; Income distribution; Libertarianism; Poverty; Rawls, John; *Theory of Justice, A*; Utilitarianism.

Nuclear arms race

DEFINITION: Rapid competitive expansion of nuclear weapons among rival nations in order to gain military and political superiority

DATE: Began in August, 1949

TYPE OF ETHICS: International relations

SIGNIFICANCE: The increasing numbers of progressively more destructive nuclear weapons in the world has intensified the possibility for human misery and threatens the very existence of the planet.

Arms races have been a major factor in prompting war in modern times, especially since World War I (1914-1918). Demobilization immediately after the end of World War II was quickly followed by rearmament as the Cold War era unfolded. The nuclear arms race began on August 29, 1949, when the Soviet Union tested its first atom bomb, and it intensified when the United States and the Soviet Union first tested hydrogen bombs in November, 1952, and August, 1953, respectively. This led to the strengthening of military alli-

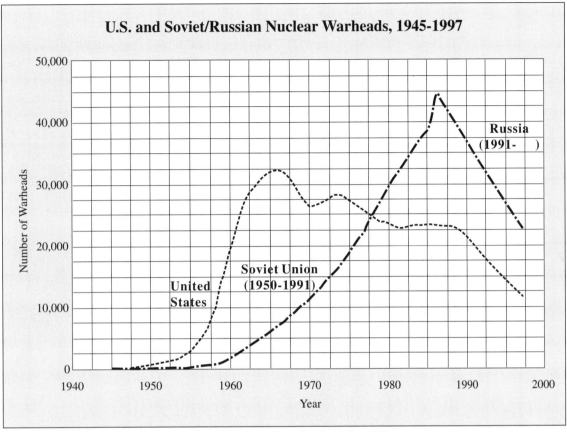

U.S. and Soviet/Russian Nuclear Warheads, 1945-1997

Source: Data adapted from *The Bulletin of the Atomic Scientists* (November-December, 1997).

Note: For the years following 1987, approximately 50 percent of the Russian warheads and 75 percent of the U.S. warheads shown were operational. The remaining warheads were held in reserve or had been retired but not yet destroyed.

ances (the North Atlantic Treaty Organization, or NATO, and the Warsaw Pact) and the escalation of threats. In January, 1954, the United States warned that it would meet communist aggression with "massive retaliation" using nuclear weapons.

During the late 1950's, the Soviet Union improved its ability to produce and deliver nuclear weapons, thus causing the Western bloc to fear a "missile gap" and motivating the Western nations to produce more missiles. Questions regarding the morality of pursuing such a course have received widely varying answers over time, ranging from the rightness of attempting to deter aggression to the position that the arms race is inherently wrong because it protects the power and wealth of the privileged. Nuclear tests aroused worldwide concern about radioactive fallout, but test bans were ignored by France and China, which acquired hydrogen bombs by 1968.

After this occurrence, the nuclear arms race between the United States and the Soviet Union surged ahead. American officials announced in 1974 that the United States was capable of dropping thirty-six bombs on each of the 218 Soviet cities with populations of 100,000 or more.

The arms race between the United States and the Soviet Union slowed somewhat during the 1970's and 1980's as a result of arms limitation and reduction treaties. It ended altogether when the Cold War came to an end in 1989. The conclusion of the arms race between super powers did not end the danger posed by nuclear build-up and proliferation, however. When the Soviet Union fragmented, the fate of the weapons which had been under its centralized control was uncertain. Several newly formed states found themselves with nuclear arms they were ill-equipped to maintain or even secure. Moreover, after

Pakistanis demonstrating in support of their nation's successful nuclear weapons tests in 1998. (AP/Wide World Photos)

the 1980's, the focus of nuclear proliferation shifted to the smaller, sometimes less-industrialized countries that regarded nuclear weapons as simply another tool in the struggle for power and survival. North Korea admitted in 2003 that it possessed a limited cache of nuclear weapons, but it subsequently withdrew that admission. India, which had had nuclear capabilities since 1974, officially declared itself to be a nuclear state in 1998 following the underground detonation of five atomic devices. Pakistan responded with its own nuclear tests less than a month later.

These developments pose two separate problems. First, India and Pakistan were still bitter enemies during the early twenty-first century with religious differences at least as deep-seated as the political and economic differences that drove the Cold War. As a result, the brinksmanship between them was potentially even more volatile than that between the United States and the Soviet Union had been. Additionally, the breakup of the Soviet Union and the development of nuclear technology by Pakistan and possibly North Korea have led to a new and unprecedented concern: that a nuclear power might sell devastating weapons to terrorists or other private individuals. Because such individuals do not necessarily represent, or even reside in, any particular nation, they are unlikely to be concerned about retaliation. Since the threat of retaliation has been the primary deterrent to the use of nuclear weapons since their creation, nuclear combatants who do not fear retaliation are a matter of grave concern.

Andrew C. Skinner
Updated by the editors

SEE ALSO: Atom bomb; Cold War; Military ethics; Mutually Assured Destruction; SALT treaties; Weapons research.

Nuclear energy

DEFINITION: Production of energy via processes that affect the nucleus of the atom

DATE: Developed during the mid-twentieth century

TYPE OF ETHICS: Environmental ethics

SIGNIFICANCE: The use of nuclear science to generate power raises ethical issues, because it is unclear whether the significant benefits of atomic power outweigh the actual and potential damage to humans and the environment caused by radioactive materials and nuclear accidents.

The invention and utilization of devices to convert energy from natural forms into readily accessible forms has accompanied the technological progress of humans. Humans are continuously searching for methods that efficiently meet their rapidly increasing energy demands.

The "nuclear age" began in 1938 with the discovery by Otto Hahn and Fritz Strassmann that substantial amounts of energy are released when heavy atoms such as uranium are broken into smaller atomic fragments. This process of nuclear fission is one of three types of nuclear reaction that release substantial amounts of energy. The fission of one gram of uranium 235 can keep a 100-watt light bulb continuously lit for twenty-three years, whereas only eight minutes of light can be generated by burning one gram of gasoline. When controlled, the fission process can be used to generate electric power; uncontrolled, it becomes the destructive power of atom bombs.

PEACEFUL VS. MILITARY USES

Although the peaceful uses of nuclear power cannot be morally equated with the military uses, events such as the accidents at Three Mile Island and Chernobyl demonstrate the conflict between basic ecological priorities and technological accomplishments. Ethical considerations in the past have focused mainly on human beings. People tend to regard themselves as the only beings of inherent value, with the remainder of the natural world being a resource valued only for its usefulness to humans. While the limitations of past technologies have allowed the survival of the natural biosphere, modern technology, with its potential for impact on future generations, requires an ethics of long-range responsibility.

When Hiroshima was bombed, little was known about radioactive fallout. During the 1950's, it was discovered that the above-ground testing of nuclear weapons introduced radioactive materials into the upper atmosphere to be transported by the winds for deposition in distant places. The strontium 90 produced in these explosions became a concern in 1954. Chemically, it behaves like calcium and is incorporated into the food chain via plants, cows, and milk, ultimately ending up in children's bones. Another radioactive by-product, iodine 131, incorporates itself into the thyroid gland. The radioactive emissions from these incorporated elements can lead to the development of cancer.

Humans can thrive only in the particular environmental niche to which they are adapted. The fact that human bodies cannot discriminate between species such as radioactive iodine and safe iodine shows that damaging the environment jeopardizes the survival of the human race. Radioactive pollutants are particularly insidious because they remain in the environment for long periods of time—it takes almost four hundred years for the radioactivity of a sample of strontium 90 to degrade to a negligible level. These problems led the United States and the Soviet Union to prohibit the atmospheric testing of nuclear weapons in 1963.

On December 2, 1942, a team of scientists at the University of Chicago produced the first controlled nuclear chain reaction, the experiment that led to the harnessing of the atom for peaceful purposes. Nuclear reactors have since been used to generate electricity, to power ships and rockets, and to power water desalination plants.

SAFETY ISSUES

Although a modern nuclear reactor is not a bomb, because its concentration of radioactive fuel is too low, environmental safety is still an issue. Major accidents, such as the 1957 Windscale, England, disaster in which the reactor core overheated and a significant amount of radiation was released into the atmosphere and the 1986 Chernobyl catastrophe in which ninety thousand people had to be evacuated from a nineteen-mile danger zone and a large amount of radioactive material was ejected into the atmosphere, are examples of the destructive potential of nuclear energy production. Although absolute safety at nuclear reactors cannot be guaranteed, modern

Location of Chernobyl Accident

safeguards have decreased the likelihood of such disasters.

Little attention was paid to the disposal of nuclear wastes during the early days of nuclear power generation. Nuclear waste includes all by-products generated in either routine operations or accidents at any point along the nuclear fuel trail (uranium mining, enrichment, fuel fabrication, spent fuel, and so forth). Since these wastes cannot be detoxified, they must be completely isolated from human contact until they have decayed to negligible levels. For plutonium, the most dangerous species in nuclear waste, this time period is at least 240,000 years.

Is it possible to store such materials in isolation for thousands of centuries? Historically, nuclear waste has not been adequately contained. While scientists predicted that the plutonium stored at Maxey Flats, Kentucky, the world's largest plutonium waste facility, would migrate only one-half inch on-site over a 24,000-year period, it actually migrated two miles off-site within ten years. More than 500,000 gallons of waste stored at Hanford, Washington, leaked into the soil, introducing radioactive pollutants into the Columbia River and the Pacific Ocean. The worst example of breached storage occurred in the Ural Mountains of the Soviet Union during the late 1950's, when an unexpected and uncontrolled nuclear reaction occurred in stored waste, rendering more than twenty square miles uninhabitable to humans and other species. Thus, the ethics of using nuclear energy until the technology exists for safe storage repositories must be questioned.

Even if safe storage technology can be developed, storing waste for thousands of centuries remains a gamble. Disposal sites must remain undisturbed by acts of war, terrorism, and natural processes such as ice sheets and geological folding, while storage conditions must not allow the waste to become reactive. History discounts the ability of humans to protect their "treasures" for extended periods of time; for example, the tombs of Egypt were left undisturbed for less than four thousand years.

How humanity generates the energy needed by its technology is a complex issue. The elimination of nuclear energy generation without a concomitant reduction in humanity's energy requirements would only result in the burning of more fossil fuel. Although this occurrence would avoid future nuclear disasters and end the accumulation of radioactive waste, it would also exacerbate the "greenhouse effect" and the resultant global warming, which also puts the biosphere at risk for future generations. Ultimately, the chance of disaster in the present and the legacy of toxic waste that humans neither have the knowledge to make safe nor the ability to contain must be compared to the risks posed by alternative methods of energy production to present and future generations.

Arlene R. Courtney

FURTHER READING

Barlett, Donald L., and James B. Steele. *Forevermore: Nuclear Waste in America.* New York: W. W. Norton, 1985.

Cohen, Bernard L. *Nuclear Science and Society.* Garden City, N.Y.: Anchor Press, 1974.

Irwin, Michael. *Nuclear Energy: Good or Bad?* New York: Public Affairs Committee, 1984.

Medvedev, Zhores A. *Nuclear Disaster in the Urals.* New York: W. W. Norton, 1979.

Nye, Joseph S. *Nuclear Ethics.* New York: Free Press, 1986.

Welsh, Ian. *Mobilising Modernity: The Nuclear Moment.* New York: Routledge, 2000.

Williams, David R. *What Is Safe? The Risks of Living in a Nuclear Age.* Cambridge, England: Royal Society of Chemistry, Information Services, 1998.

SEE ALSO: Atomic Energy Commission; Global warming; Greenhouse effect; "Not in my backyard"; Nuclear arms race; Nuclear Regulatory Commission; Science; Toxic waste; Union of Concerned Scientists.

Nuclear Regulatory Commission

IDENTIFICATION: Independent agency of the U.S. government that licenses and regulates the civilian uses of nuclear energy and materials

DATE: Established on October 11, 1974

TYPE OF ETHICS: Environmental ethics

SIGNIFICANCE: The Nuclear Regulatory Commission (NRC) is responsible for protecting the environment from damage caused by nuclear materials.

The Energy Reorganization Act of 1974 established the Energy Research and Development Administration (ERDA) and the Nuclear Regulatory Commission (NRC) and abolished the Atomic Energy Commission (AEC). One purpose of the act was "to enhance the goals of restoring, protecting, and enhancing environmental quality." The act separated the licensing and regulation of civilian nuclear energy and materials from their development and promotion. These functions had been joined under the AEC. The act directed the NRC to identify possible nuclear-energy sites and to evaluate potential environmental impacts from their construction and operation. In 1977, the ERDA was abolished and its responsibilities were transferred to the Department of Energy.

The NRC regulates the processing, transport, handling, and disposal of nuclear materials and is responsible for protecting public health and safety and the environment. It licenses and oversees the construction and operation of nuclear reactors that generate electricity. Before licensing reactors, the NRC holds hearings to enable public participation in the process. It also inspects facilities for violations of safety standards and investigates nuclear accidents.

Marguerite McKnight

SEE ALSO: Atomic Energy Commission; Nuclear energy; Toxic waste; Union of Concerned Scientists.

Nuremberg Trials

THE EVENT: Series of trials in which Nazi officials were prosecuted for war crimes

DATE: 1945 to 1949

TYPE OF ETHICS: International relations

SIGNIFICANCE: The Nuremberg Trials were a significant milestone in the development of international laws capable of enforcing human rights. They were based upon the principle that a soldier's duty to the state is superceded by the soldier's duty to humanity and to moral laws, even in times of war.

Following the end of World War II, twenty-four Nazi leaders were brought before the International Military Tribunal as war criminals on charges of conspiracy; crimes against peace—planning or waging a war of aggression; war crimes—"violations of the laws or customs of war," including murder or ill-treatment of civilians and prisoners of war, killing hostages, plundering property, wanton destruction of cities, and "devastation not justified by military necessity"; and crimes against humanity—"murder, extermination, enslavement, deportation, and other inhumane acts committed against any civilian population, before or during the war, or persecutions on political, racial, or religious grounds in execution of or in connection with any crime within the jurisdiction of the tribunal, whether or not in violation of domestic law of the country where perpetrated."

THE DEFENDANTS

The tribunal tried twenty-two of the indicted. Hermann Göring, first the head of the Gestapo and later the commander-in-chief of the Luftwaffe, was

Former high-ranking Nazi officials listen to testimony at Nuremberg. The most prominent of the defendants, Hermann Göring (in left front corner of the box) committed suicide before his ordered execution could be carried out. Seated next to him is Rudolf Hess, who became the last convicted Nazi leader to die in prison, in 1987. (National Archives)

considered the major defendant. Rudolf Hess had been deputy leader; in 1941, he flew to Scotland and was imprisoned. Joachim von Ribbentrop served as foreign minister. Wilhelm Keitel took over as the chief of staff of the High Command of the Armed Forces after Adolf Hitler abolished the War Ministry in 1938. Ernst Kaltenbrunner headed the Reich Security Police, including the Gestapo and the security service of the SS. Alfred Rosenberg was the minister for the Occupied Eastern Territories.

Hans Frank, a Nazi Party lawyer, was the governor-general of occupied Poland. Wilhelm Frick was the minister of the interior. Julius Streicher was the leading anti-Semite propagandist. Walter Funk was president of the Reichbank. Hjalmar Schacht headed the Reichbank prior to Funk and the Ministry of Economics prior to the war, where he piloted the financing of war production. Karl Doenitz, as admiral, directed the U-boat battle in the Atlantic and succeeded Erich Raeder as commander-in-chief of the Navy. Raeder was commander-in-chief of the Navy until 1943, when he resigned in a disagreement with Hitler.

Baldur von Schirach built the Hitler Youth organization and later was made governor of Vienna. Fritz Sauckel headed the forced-labor mobilization. Alfred Jodl was chief of the Operations Staff of the Armed Forces. Franz van Papen served as vice chancellor after Hitler came to power. Arthur Seyss-Inquart, an Austrian who assisted in the Nazi takeover of Austria, was Reich governor of Austria, assisted in the Nazi takeover of Czechoslovakia and Poland, and was Reich commissioner for the Netherlands. Albert Speer was Hitler's architect and minister of armaments. Constantin von Neurath, a diplomat, was made the Reich protector of occupied Czechoslovakia. Hans Fritzsche headed the radio division of the Propaganda Ministry. Martin Bormann, Hitler's secretary and head of the party chancellery after Hess fled, had not been captured but was tried in absentia. Robert Ley, leader of the Labor Front, committed suicide before the trial began, and industrialist Gustav Krupp was found to be too senile to stand trial.

The charter (articles 9, 10, and 11) provided that

Summary of Nuremberg Verdicts

Defendant	*Verdicts*
Hermann Göring	Guilty on all four counts
Alfred Jodl	Guilty on all four counts
Wilhelm Keitel	Guilty on all four counts
Constantin von Neurath	Guilty on all four counts
Joachim von Ribbentrop	Guilty on all four counts
Alfred Rosenberg	Guilty on all four counts
Wilhelm Frick	Guilty on three of four counts
Walter Funk	Guilty on three of four counts
Erich Raeder	Guilty on all three counts
Arthur Seyss-Inquart	Guilty on three of four counts
Martin Bormann (*in absentia*)	Guilty on two of three counts
Karl Doenitz	Guilty on two of three counts
Hans Frank	Guilty on two of three counts
Rudolf Hess	Guilty on two of four counts
Ernst Kaltenbrunner	Guilty on two of three counts
Fritz Sauckel	Guilty on two of four counts
Albert Speer	Guilty on two of four counts
Baldur von Schirach	Guilty on one of two counts
Julius Streicher	Guilty on one of two counts
Hans Fritzsche	Not Guilty on three counts
Franz von Papen	Not Guilty on two counts
Hjalmar Schacht	Not Guilty on two counts

---

the tribunal could declare organizations criminal and that individuals could be tried before national, military, or occupation courts of the four Allied powers for membership in such organizations. The indictment charged that the following organizations were criminal in character: the Reich cabinet, the leadership corps of the Nazi Party, the SS (*Schutzstaffeln*, or Black Shirts), the SD (*Sicherheitsdienst*), the SA (*Sturmabteilungen*, or Stormtroopers), the Gestapo (secret state police), and the General Staff and High Command of the Armed Forces.

THE TRIALS

Each of the four Allied powers named a judge and an alternate judge to the International Military Tribunal: Lord Justice Geoffrey Lawrence and Justice Norman Birkett (Great Britain); Attorney General

Francis Biddle and Judge John J. Parker (United States); Professor Henri Donnedieu de Vabres and Conseiller Robert Falco (France); and Major General I. T. Nikitchenko and Lieutenant Colonel A. F. Volchkov (Soviet Union).

The trial began on November 20, 1945, and, after 216 trial days, concluded on October 1, 1946, when the tribunal delivered its judgment. Justice Robert Jackson of the Supreme Court led the prosecution counsel for the United States; Attorney General Hartley Shawcross and David Maxwell-Fyfe for Great Britain; François del Menthon, Auguste Champetier de Ribes, Charles Dubost, and Edgar Fauré for France; and General R. A. Rudenko and Colonel Y. V. Pokrovsky for the Soviet Union. Each defendant was represented by the counsel of his choice.

The tribunal acquitted three defendants (Schacht, von Papen, and Fritzsche). Twelve were sentenced to death by hanging (Göring, von Ribbentrop, Keitel, Kaltenbrunner, Rosenberg, Frank, Frick, Streicher, Sauckel, Jodl, Bormann, and Seyss-Inquart) and were hanged on October 16, 1946. Three were sentenced to life imprisonment (Hess, Funk, and Raeder); two to twenty-year terms (von Schirach and Speer), one to fifteen years (von Neurath), and one to ten years (Doenitz). Göring committed suicide the evening before the scheduled executions. Four Nazi organizations were declared criminal: the leadership corps of the Nazi Party, the SS, the SD, and the Gestapo.

Between October, 1946, and April, 1949, twelve subsequent trials, conducted by American judges primarily from state supreme courts, were held at Nuremberg. In the Doctors' Trial, twenty-three physicians were tried; all but seven were found guilty of experiments on human subjects. Other trials involved judges who were SS members, SS officers who operated concentration camps and committed mass murders, industrialists—including Alfred Krupp (son of Gustav) and the directors of I. G. Farben—who used slave labor, and army leaders who took hostages, destroyed villages, and shot prisoners.

Ron Christenson

FURTHER READING

Conot, Robert E. *Justice at Nuremberg*. New York: Harper & Row, 1983.

Lifton, Robert Jay. *The Nazi Doctors: Medical Killing and the Psychology of Genocide*. New York: Basic Books, 1986.

Smith, Bradley F. *Reaching Judgment at Nuremberg*. New York: Basic Books, 1977.

Sprecher, Drexel A. *Inside the Nuremberg Trial: A Prosecutor's Comprehensive Account*. 2 vols. Lanham, Md.: University Press of America, 1999.

Taylor, Telford. *The Anatomy of the Nuremberg Trials*. New York: Knopf, 1992.

Tusa, Ann, and John Tusa. *The Nuremberg Trial*. London: Macmillan, 1983.

SEE ALSO: Concentration camps; Geneva conventions; Genocide and democide; Holocaust; International Criminal Court; International justice; International law; Nazi science; Nazism; War crimes trials.

Nussbaum, Martha

DEFINITION: American legal scholar
BORN: May 6, 1947, New York, New York
TYPE OF ETHICS: International relations
SIGNIFICANCE: Nussbaum believes in a universal world morality among nations that controls and binds their actions and argues that a shared sense of ethics should be the driving force behind international dealings, not expediency or force.

International affairs, the evolving nature of education, and the conflict between national culture and world morality are among the subjects that Martha Nussbaum has addressed in voluminous writings and speeches. She has been inspired by the philosophers and political scientists of the late Renaissance and Enlightenment eras, such as John Locke and Jean-Jacques Rousseau. Hugo Grotius, in particular, has powerfully influenced her views. Locke's view that individuals possess inalienable, basic rights (life, liberty, and property, as he defined them) is one of Nussbaum's core beliefs, as is Rousseau's contention that a truly functioning democracy is possible and pragmatic. Grotius, who is Nussbaum's most important philosophical influence, is widely considered to be the first author to deal persuasively with issues such as human rights, the ethical conduct of war, and world peace. Nussbaum has embraced all of these ideas while adding her own thoughts and findings in support of an anticipated rebirth of international moralism.

While fully embracing the right of people to be free and make free choices, Nussbaum accepts the necessity of the sovereign state and its primacy in foreign affairs. This support of state power exists only to the degree that the state governs its citizens justly in accordance with natural rights and conducts itself in a proper, ethical fashion in its dealings with other nations. She further postulates that all nations are immutably tied to one another by a set of moral responsibilities, and these ethical and moral concerns are what should always determine the course of international relationships. Moreover, nation states have the ethical obligation to protect the natural rights of their citizens and to provide them with the basic necessities of life, and the international community has the responsibility of aiding each state in achieving these goals.

Nussbaum firmly opposes cultural relativism, believing that many traditional group beliefs—such as those inspired by religion, race, ethnicity, and class—oppress women. Moreover, such oppression is downplayed or ignored by liberal cultural relativists and supporters of situational ethics. Nussbaum argues that many progressives are quick to point out the injustices inflicted by governments, and rightly so, but far fewer speak out against the wrongs inflicted by tradition and culture. In Nussbaum's view, the degradation of women leads to a new demand for international morality to establish and protect the natural rights of all. International relations based on consensus building, and not unilateralism, will help create a more just world.

Thomas W. Buchanan

FURTHER READING

Nussbaum, Martha C. *Love's Knowledge: Essays on Philosophy and Literature.* New York: Oxford University Press, 1990.

_____. *Sex and Social Justice.* New York: Oxford University Press, 1999.

_____. *The Therapy of Desire: Theory and Practice in Hellenistic Ethics.* Princeton, N.J.: Princeton University Press, 1994.

_____. *Upheavals of Thought: The Intelligence of Emotions.* New York: Cambridge University Press, 2001.

SEE ALSO: Altruism; Diversity; Grotius, Hugo; Locke, John; Moral equivalence; Narrative ethics; Relativism.

O

Obedience

DEFINITION: Submission to or compliance with the will of someone in authority

TYPE OF ETHICS: Personal and social ethics

SIGNIFICANCE: The ethical import of obedience is generally judged by the values of the authority figure to whom one is obedient. It is a virtue when the authority, or the ideals represented by the authority, seem virtuous; it is a serious moral transgression when the authority's commands are deemed immoral.

Obedience is not necessarily bad or good. A sinister example of obedience occurred in World War II, when more than six million innocent people were tortured and killed by Nazis who claimed that they were only following the orders of their superiors. A positive example of obedience is a three-year-old who obeys her parents' commands to play in the yard rather than the road. A sinister example of disobedience is a criminal who disobeys laws. A positive example of disobedience is Rosa Parks, who was arrested in 1955 for disobeying laws that segregated seats on public buses in Montgomery, Alabama. Her disobedience of the law was a landmark in the civil rights revolution in the United States. Whether obedience is right or wrong is determined by the individual, the situation, and others' or history's evaluation of the obedience or disobedience.

Some obedience is necessary. Social groups of any size depend on a reasonable amount of obedience to function smoothly. Society would be chaotic if orders from police, parents, physicians, bosses, generals, and presidents were routinely ignored or disobeyed. The division of labor in a society requires that individuals have the capacity to subordinate and coordinate their own independent actions to serve the goals and purposes of the larger social organization.

Obedience results because people do not feel responsible for the actions they perform under orders from an authority figure. They believe that the person giving the orders has the responsibility for the results of the actions. At the Nuremberg Trials after World War II, many of the Nazi war criminals stated that they believed their actions were wrong but did not feel personally responsible for them, because they were merely following orders.

The feeling of not being responsible, however, is insufficient to explain why people so readily follow orders, especially in cases in which the behavior far exceeds the scope of the order. For example, the cruelty and savagery of some of the soldiers in the infamous My Lai incident (in which U.S. soldiers killed innocent Vietnamese villagers) was not necessarily demanded in their orders to "pacify the village."

A personal factor that may underlie the willingness to follow orders is ideological zeal, the belief that the required actions are right or in support of a good cause. Another personal factor is gratification; people feel powerful and free upon carrying out the orders. Furthermore, individuals sometimes believe that they will reap material gain or personal advancement by following the specified orders. Another personal factor that influences whether people obey is the role that they are filling. Roles often include rules that people obey the orders of certain others.

SITUATIONAL FACTORS

Situational factors that influence obedience are prestige, proximity, the presence of others who disobey, and reminders of personal responsibility. Prestige means that it is easier to obey the commands of a high-ranking (prestigious) officer than those of a low-ranking officer. Proximity has to do with both the person giving the orders and the victim. Thus, it is easier for soldiers to follow orders given in person rather than over the phone, and it is easier to follow orders to kill others by high-altitude bombing than to follow orders to kill others by stabbing. Also, it is easier to disobey when others present are disobeying than it is if others are obeying. Finally, obedience diminishes when a person is reminded that he or she will be held personally responsible for any harm that results from his or her actions.

Several other factors may affect disobedience. First, embarrassment hinders disobedience. Many people do not want to rock the boat, make a scene, or be rude. Second, lacking a language of protest hinders disobedience. Many people literally have no words with which to disobey. Third, people may be entrapped into obedience. The first steps of entrapment pose no difficult choices. One step leads to another, however, and the person is ultimately committed to a course of obedience.

Obedience can result from five types of power that individuals and groups can exercise over others. First, coercive power arises from the potential to deliver punishment to force another to change his or her behavior. For example, parents who punish their children for putting their hands into cookie jars are exercising coercive power to induce their children to obey their directives to stay out of the cookie jar. Second, reward power arises from the potential to deliver positive reinforcement to induce another to change his or her behavior. For example, parents who give their children cookies for doing their homework are exercising reward power to induce their children to obey their directives to do their homework. Third, legitimate power arises from being in a particular role or position. Generals, for example, have the authority to give orders to underlings because of their rank. Fourth, expert power arises because others see the person as particularly knowledgeable. Physicians, for example, induce others to obey their directives to quit smoking because they are seen as health care experts. Fifth, reverent power arises because others admire the person giving the orders. For example, Mother Teresa could probably get others to obey her commands because she was greatly admired.

Lillian M. Range

FURTHER READING

Blass, Thomas, ed. *Obedience to Authority: Current Perspectives on the Milgram Paradigm*. Mahwah, N.J.: Lawrence Erlbaum Associates, 2000.

Hamilton, V. Lee. "Obedience and Responsibility: A Jury Simulation." *Journal of Personality and Social Psychology* 36, no. 2 (February, 1978): 126-146.

Kelman, Herbert C., and V. Lee Hamilton. *Crimes of Obedience*. New Haven, Conn.: Yale University Press, 1989.

Milgram, Stanley. *Obedience to Authority*. New York: Harper & Row, 1974.

Plato. *Crito*. Edited by Chris Emlyn-Jones. London: Bristol Classical Press, 1999.

Sabini, Jon, and Maury Silver. "Critical Thinking and Obedience to Authority." In *Thinking Critically*, edited by John Chaffee. 2d ed. Boston: Houghton Mifflin, 1988.

Weiss, Roslyn. *Socrates Unsatisfied: An Analysis of Plato's "Crito."* New York: Oxford University Press, 1998.

SEE ALSO: Civil disobedience; Conscientious objection; Divine command theory; Leadership; Milgram experiment; Nuremberg Trials; Psychology; Whistleblowing.

Objectivism

DEFINITION: Philosophical system developed by Ayn Rand that claims that there are objective facts about the world and human beings that should be the basis for philosophical speculations

TYPE OF ETHICS: Theory of ethics

SIGNIFICANCE: Randian objectivism posits that each individual human being has intrinsic value and incomparable worth, and is therefore obligated to act only in his or her own interest. It rejects altruism, communitarianism, and socialism in the name of liberal individualism and egoism.

There is an initial problem with explaining objectivism. Its major developer and proponent, Ayn Rand, did not write a well-reasoned philosophical treatise on her worldview, but used objectivism as a backdrop for the characters in her novels and offered glimpses of it in her frequent lectures. One must be a bit of a detective to piece together her position. Compounding the problem is the fact that a significant segment of the philosophical community does not take her work seriously, because she was not a professional philosopher. It should be said at the outset that objectivism is not only an ethical theory but also an overarch-

Ayn Rand. (Library of Congress)

ing integrated worldview with ethical, metaphysical, epistemological, political, social, and aesthetic elements. What follows is an account of the ethical component of her thought.

REJECTION OF ALTRUISM

Ayn Rand begins by rejecting traditional ethical theory, which she labels "the ethics of altruism." Whether utilitarian or deontological in nature, the ethics of altruism requires a moral agent sometimes to set her or his interests aside and act for the interests of others. It is even possible, in this view, to be obligated to give up one's life for the sake of others. To put it another way, the ethics of altruism may require a moral agent to think of herself or himself as without value as compared to others. Individuals can become merely means to others' ends. Rand finds this result absolutely abhorrent. At the core of her theory is the fact of the absolute moral worth of the individual. Each human being has intrinsic value, and any theory that requires someone to negate that value is wrong.

Egoism, on the other hand, embraces the intrinsic worth of the individual and places the individual's in-terests at the heart of the ethical theory. Because it claims that a right action is one that is in the best interest of the individual who is acting, it will never require that an agent sacrifice her or his interests for the interests of others. The worth of the individual is intact.

RAND'S VERSION OF EGOISM

Egoism as an ethical theory has been around at least since the time of Plato. Rand takes the basic framework of the egoistic principle and reworks it in the light of certain moral facts about human beings that she takes as fundamental. These facts can be ascertained by reflecting on the answers to the following questions. What is the end for which a human should live? On what principle shall a human act to achieve this end? Who should benefit from the actions? In other words, what is the ultimate value? What is the ultimate virtue? Who is the primary beneficiary?

According to Rand, life itself is the goal of life. People live in order to live. This is why she says that human life has intrinsic value. A human life is always an end in itself. The principle on which to act is rationality. It is that aspect of human nature that distinguishes humans from other living things. Therefore, it must be the primary virtue. One lives life to the fullest by being rational. Finally, the only beneficiary of an agent's actions that would meet the criterion of rationality would be the agent. It is this last condition that permits the marriage of these moral facts with egoism. It follows, then, that for a human being to achieve an end, she or he must live according to the ethical principle of rational self-interest. Human beings are under an ethical obligation to do whatever would promote the interests of that individual.

REACTION

Needless to say, objectivism caused a stir. Critics were quick to point out that Rand's ethical claims were tantamount to selfishness and, since selfishness is not a desirable character trait, ought to be dismissed summarily. Rand did little to dispel this association with selfishness and, in fact, tried to exploit this identification (and controversy) for her own gain. Witness the title of her 1964 book: *The Virtue of Selfishness.*

In point of fact, however, though Rand did use the word "selfishness" often, her theory is much more sophisticated than her critics allow. She gives selfishness a precise definition, which turns out to be nothing like the imprecise understanding of the term in common usage. For Rand, selfishness is merely the rational pursuit of self-interest. Certainly, it would be in one's rational self-interest to take into consideration, sometimes, the interests of others. The common understanding of selfishness embodies the idea of pursuit of one's interests exclusively without regard to the interests of others. Therefore, Rand's use of the term is different from the common usage. Rand admits that she chose the term "selfishness" deliberately for its shock value and uses the above equivocation for the twofold purpose of undermining the ethics of altruism and championing her brand of ethical egoism.

This ethical component of objectivism, then, stands or falls with ethical egoism. There is nothing inherently wrong with Rand's version. The other components of objectivism, however, do not stand up well to philosophical criticism, and this is another reason objectivism is held in low regard.

John H. Serembus

FURTHER READING

Kelley, David. *The Contested Legacy of Ayn Rand: Truth and Toleration in Objectivism.* 2d ed. New Brunswick, N.J.: Transaction, 2000.

Machan, Tibor R. *Ayn Rand.* New York: P. Lang, 1999.

Peikoff, Leonard. *Objectivism: The Philosophy of Ayn Rand.* New York: Dutton, 1991.

Rand, Ayn. *Atlas Shrugged.* 35th anniversary ed. New York: Dutton, 1992.

_____. *For the New Intellectual.* New York: Random House, 1961.

_____. *The Fountainhead.* New York: Scribner Classics, 2000.

_____. *The Virtue of Selfishness: A New Concept of Egoism.* New York: New American Library, 1964.

SEE ALSO: Altruism; Cognitivism; Egoism; Fact/value distinction; Rand, Ayn; Self-interest; Selfishness.

On Liberty

IDENTIFICATION: Book by John Stuart Mill (1806-1873)

DATE: Published in 1859

TYPE OF ETHICS: Modern history

SIGNIFICANCE: *On Liberty* has been a central focus of liberal ethics and philosophy for well over a century, and it continues to be a major work for those interested in questions of individual freedom.

In *On Liberty*, John Stuart Mill provided a powerful defense of individual freedom of thought and action. Mill's ideas have been a source of inspiration for those concerned with civil liberty and individual freedom for more than one hundred years, but his assertions in this volume were not in accord with the rest of his substantial body of work. The popularity of *On Liberty* was the result of a combination of Mill's substantial reputation and the work's contents, which, while popular with the general reader, have been frequently criticized by professional scholars and reviewers.

MILL'S BACKGROUND

John Stuart Mill was the son of Scottish philosopher James Mill, who, under the influence of Jeremy Bentham, reared the boy to be a prodigy. At the age of three, the young Mill was studying Greek, and throughout his youth, childish pleasures were denied him in favor of intellectual activities. At twenty, he fell into clinical depression, apparently caused by the lack of emotional support in his upbringing, but he recovered and ultimately had a successful career as a bureaucrat in the India Office and as a philosopher. Among his important works are *System of Logic* (1843), *Principles of Political Economy* (1848), and *The Subjection of Women* (1869). In 1830 he met Harriet Taylor. They conducted an intense though, according to themselves, chaste courtship until 1851, when, Taylor's husband being two years dead, they married. Harriet Taylor proved to be an important influence on Mill's thought. It was thanks to his wife that Mill came to regard "the woman question"—that is, women's social, political, and economic equality—as one of the most important issues of the mid-nineteenth century. This attitude appears to have been decisive in the development of *On Liberty* (1859), Mill's most popular work.

ON LIBERTY

Mill opened his consideration of the question of liberty by asserting that he was making one simple, straightforward proposition: Society had no warrant by legal sanction or moral suasion to limit the individual's freedom of thought or action for any reason except to prevent harm to another person or property. Even should an action be clearly shown to be harmful to the individual, Mill insisted, any restriction other than fair warning was wrong.

In the realm of ideas, Mill believed that free discussion was necessary if the truth was to be determined. To deny any idea currency was to deny the possibility, however faint, that it might be true and to deny it the opportunity of challenging other ideas to test their truthfulness. To set standards of logic or taste or scholarship or of any kind was to set up a censor. Who was to set the standard and enforce it? One of Mill's great fears was that the community might attempt to do so, thus establishing a tyranny of the majority.

While certainly extreme, Mill's position concerning freedom of expression was far from unprecedented, though he did not take the case so far in any of his other writings. His argument that action too should be unfettered as long as it posed no threat to anyone but the actor, however, was quite unusual. In *On Liberty*, it is clear, though not really explicit, that Mill was concerned much more with physical and material harm than with moral or spiritual harm when he asserted that society might restrain the individual from harming others. As truth emerged from the forum of free debate, the development of truly individualistic character in a person arose from the process of choosing types of conduct. For many of Mill's contemporaries, this was little more than advocacy of anarchy. Within the liberal tradition, freedom of action was regarded as good but not without limits. Free speech would lead to changes in those limits (laws, custom, and so forth) so that acceptable behaviors might be enlarged. Mill's emphasis on diversity and individual, unfettered, development was one of his significant contributions to liberalism.

The absolute nature of Mill's view of liberty left him with a number of difficult questions to confront. For example, what about indirect harm such as that caused by drunks to their dependents? Does experience ever establish a moral truth so clearly that society should insist that it be observed? Mill insisted that

beyond teaching rationality to children (the principle of liberty did not apply until an individual reached maturity), society had no right to require a standard of conduct. When society tried to do so, it usually simply insisted on the standard of the majority. Unfortunately, the examples provided in *On Liberty* tend to be issues such as religious beliefs, which had already been largely agreed upon as inappropriate for society to impose.

Another problem for Mill was the source of individual morality. He had long since rejected the possibility that humankind's moral sense was intuitive or innate. In the end, he asserted that moral sense was "natural" in that it was a "natural outgrowth" of human nature. Although this conclusion was not very satisfactory, Mill went further with the question.

Not only did the ideas in *On Liberty* not coincide with those contained in Mill's other work, but there were two issues that Mill was unwilling to leave to the workings of the principle of liberty: education and population control. He was willing to insist that parents be required to educate their children and that the growth of population be restrained. These matters were too critical for the welfare of humankind to be left to be developed, like truth, from debate; therefore, the state should intervene. This lack of consistency within his complete oeuvre and even within *On Liberty* itself seems to have been a result of the influence of Harriet Taylor Mill. Not only was she more inclined toward single-issue, simplistic thought than was Mill, but she also pressed Mill to pursue the issue of women's equality ever more vigorously. *On Liberty* reads as if it came from an extremely repressive society, but aside from what was called the "woman question," nineteenth century England was not such a society. Part of the purpose of *On Liberty* seems to have been to universalize the issue of feminine equality so that men had a stake in it and would take it seriously. This purpose apparently led Mill into a position more extreme than the one that he generally took.

IMPLICATIONS FOR ETHICAL CONDUCT

Mill's established reputation meant that *On Liberty* had an immediate and large audience. Although many reviewers and scholars took issue with some of its ideas, the book was enormously popular with undergraduates and the general reading public. Not only did it broaden the liberal attitude about freedom of speech, but it also led to a much greater support for freedom of action. Its influence continued to be strong during the early twenty-first century.

Fred R. van Hartesveldt

FURTHER READING

Cowling, Maurice. *Mill and Liberalism.* Cambridge, England: Cambridge University Press, 1963.

Dworkin, Gerald, ed. *Mill's "On Liberty": Critical Essays.* Lanham, Md.: Rowman & Littlefield, 1997.

Hamburger, Joseph. *Intellectuals in Politics: John Stuart Mill and the Philosophic Radicals.* New Haven, Conn.: Yale University Press, 1965.

Himmelfarb, Gertrude. *On Liberty and Liberalism: The Case of John Stuart Mill.* New York: Alfred A. Knopf, 1974.

Packe, Michael St. John. *The Life of John Stuart Mill.* London: Secker & Warburg, 1954.

Riley, Jonathan. *Routledge Philosophy Guidebook to Mill "On Liberty."* New York: Routledge, 1998.

SEE ALSO: Democracy; Freedom and liberty; Freedom of expression; Liberalism; Mill, John Stuart; Political liberty; Privacy; Social justice and responsibility; Utilitarianism; Value.

On War

IDENTIFICATION: Book by Carl von Clausewitz (1780-1831)

DATE: *Vom Kriege*, 1832-1834 (English translation, 1873)

TYPE OF ETHICS: Military ethics

SIGNIFICANCE: In *On War*, Carl von Clausewitz argued that war is not an end in itself but always a means to the achievement of a political end, and it must therefore be understood through the lens of politics and conducted by political rather than solely military leaders. He also advocated a policy of total war, in which all available resources are used to attack and destroy all resources available to the enemy. Only total war, von Clausewitz argued, can achieve total victory.

Carl von Clausewitz's purpose in analyzing war is purely theoretical and not prescriptive. To the question "What is war?" he answers: "War is an act of violence to compel our opponent to fulfill our will." War is not an isolated act; it is an extension of *Politik*—a blatant instrument of such policy. The decision to go to war and the proposed goal beyond victory are political, not military. Theory must, however, be analyzed in the context of real events. A paper war is not a real war; a real war is subject to influence by chance and circumstance. Real war is dangerous for its participants and is a test of their exertion.

War is not only "an elaborate duel" ("*ein erweiterter Zweikampf*"), a vast drama—a comedy for the victor, a tragedy for the loser. From another point of view, war is a game ("*ein Spiel*") and a "gamble" ("*ein Glücksspiel*"), both objectively and subjectively. A theory of war must be an analytical investigation that later might prove beneficial to reason and judgment. It must consider the ends and means of warfare, which consist of strategy and tactics. Tactics are the uses to which the army is put to achieve victory. Strategy has to do with the plan for achieving victory. The real activity of war lies in the tactical aspect of battle, since tactics govern fighting. The immediate object of battle is to destroy or overcome the enemy, but the ultimate object is to subject the enemy to one's will in a political sense. Toward this end a combatant may desire to enforce whatever peace it pleases; it may occupy the enemy's frontier districts and use them to make satisfactory bargains at the peace settlements.

Richard P. Benton

SEE ALSO: *Art of War, The*; Geneva conventions; Just war theory; Military ethics; War.

Oppression

DEFINITION: Systematic subjugation or domination of a relatively disempowered social group by a group with more access to social power

TYPE OF ETHICS: Human rights

SIGNIFICANCE: Oppression is a function of collective, social, and structural configurations of power. Therefore, those who seek to resist perceived patterns of oppression often have trouble communicating about it effectively within the context of a liberal individualist society which insists that individual actions and individual choices are the only proper objects of moral judgment.

Within a given society or subculture, groups are often either accorded or denied access to rights and privileges, relative to other groups, based on specific socially constructed categories. This system is based on a belief in the inherent superiority of one group over all others and its right to dominate. While it is true that one individual can harass, intimidate, violate, molest, and brutalize another, in the broadest sense, "oppression" as a concept is generally discussed within a larger historical, social, and political context.

Oppression is composed of two key elements: prejudice and social power. "Prejudice"—from the Latin *praejudicium* ("previous judgment")—involves holding an adverse opinion or belief without just ground or before acquiring sufficient valid information. "Social power" can be defined as the ability to get what one wants and to influence others. "Target group" is the term given to those oppressed groups that are denied access to the rights and privileges enjoyed by other groups. Group members are oppressed simply on the basis of their target group status. (Synonyms for "target group" include "minority group," "oppressed group," "disenfranchised group," "subordinate group," and "stigmatized group," among others.)

Examples of target groups in the United States are people of color—African Americans, Asian Americans, Latinos, Native Americans or "Indians" (race); immigrants (ethnicity or national origin); Jews, Muslims, atheists (religion); women (biological sex); gay, lesbian, and bisexual people (sexual orientation or identity); transgenderists (gender identity); working class and poor people (class); the very old and the very young (age); people with mental and physical disabilities (ability); and fat people (appearance). "Dominant group" is the term given to groups with access to rights and privileges that are denied to target groups. (Synonyms for "dominant group" include "majority group" and "oppressor group.")

Examples of dominant groups in the United States are white people or "Caucasians" (race); people of European, especially Anglo-Saxon, ancestry (race, ethnicity, national origin); Christians, and especially Protestant sects (religion); males (biological sex); heterosexuals (sexual orientation or identity); middle

and "owning" class (class); people generally between the ages of twenty-one and fifty (age); and people considered "able bodied" physically and mentally (ability, appearance).

Most people find themselves both in groups targeted for oppression and in those dominant groups that are granted relatively higher degrees of power and prestige. Some examples of such situations are a white middle-class woman, a Jewish man, an African American Christian man, a white lesbian, and a blind thirty-five-year-old white man.

FORMS OF OPPRESSION

There are as many names for the varieties of oppression as there are for the categories of target and dominant groups based, for example, on race (racism), ethnicity or patriotism (ethnocentrism, chauvinism, imperialism, xenophobia), religious affiliation (religious prejudice, anti-Semitism), biological sex (sexism, misogyny), sexual orientation or identity (homophobia, biphobia, heterosexism), economic status (classism), age (ageism), and mental and physical ability (ableism).

This does not mean that all groups experience forms of oppression similarly. The experiences of victims of racism, for example, are not identical to those of the victims of homophobia. The forms of oppression, however, run parallel and at points intersect. All involve negative prejudgments whose purpose is to maintain control or power over others. Oppression can be the result of a deliberate, conscious act, or it may be unconscious and unintentional yet still have oppressive consequences.

Oppression involves negative beliefs (that may or may not be expressed), exclusion, denial of civil and legal protections, and, in some cases, overt acts of violence directed against target groups. The many forms of oppression can be said to operate on four distinct but interrelated levels: the personal, the interpersonal, the institutional, and the societal (or cultural). The personal level refers to an individual's belief (bias or prejudice) that members of target groups are inferior psychologically or physically.

The interpersonal level is manifested when a bias affects relations among individuals, transforming prejudice into its active component—discrimination. The institutional level refers to the ways in which governmental agencies; businesses; and educational, religious, and professional organizations systematically discriminate against target groups. Sometimes laws, codes, or policies actually enforce discrimination. The societal (or cultural) level refers to social norms or codes of behavior that, although not expressly written into law or policy, nevertheless work within a society to legitimize prejudice and discrimination. This often involves epithets and stereotypes directed against target groups. Oppression is said to be "internalized" when target group members take on the shame that is associated with their target group status.

FUNCTIONS OF OPPRESSION

Dominant groups maintain oppression over target groups for a number of reasons: to gain or enhance economic, political, or personal rewards or to avoid the potential loss of such; to protect self-esteem against psychological doubts or conflicts; to promote and enhance dominant group value systems; to better comprehend a complex world by categorizing or stereotyping others.

Although oppression clearly serves many functions, it can also be said to hurt members of the dominant group. Frederick Douglass, a former slave and an abolitionist, said at a civil rights meeting in Washington, D.C., on October 22, 1883, that no person "can put a chain about the ankle of [another person] without at last finding the other end fastened about his neck." His words remain relevant, for everyone is diminished when anyone is demeaned.

Warren J. Blumenfeld

FURTHER READING

Bishop, Anne. *Becoming an Ally: Breaking the Cycle of Oppression in People.* 2d ed. New York: Palgrave, 2002.

Blumenfeld, Warren J., ed. *Homophobia: How We All Pay the Price.* Boston: Beacon Press, 1992.

Daly, Mary. *Gynecology: The Metaethics of Radical Feminism.* Boston: Beacon Press, 1978.

Goffman, Erving. *Stigma: Notes on the Management of Spoiled Identity.* New York: Simon & Schuster, 1963.

Kovel, Joel. *White Racism.* New York: Columbia University Press, 1984.

O'Connor, Peg. *Oppression and Responsibility: A Wittgensteinian Approach to Social Practices and Moral Theory.* University Park: Pennsylvania State University, 2002.

Smith, Barbara, ed. *Home Girls: A Black Feminist Anthology.* New York: Kitchen Table Press, 1983.

Wilson, Catherine, ed. *Civilization and Oppression.* Calgary, Alta.: University of Calgary Press, 1999.

Wistrich, Robert S. *Anti-Semitism: The Longest Hatred.* New York: Pantheon Books, 1991.

Zinn, Howard. *A People's History of the United States.* New York: Harper & Row, 1980.

SEE ALSO: Ageism; Anti-Semitism; Bigotry; Disability rights; Discrimination; Ethnocentrism; Exploitation; Homophobia; Racial prejudice; Racism; Segregation.

Organ transplants

DEFINITION: Replacement of worn-out, diseased, or injured organs and tissues with healthy substitutes

DATE: Begun in early twentieth century

TYPE OF ETHICS: Bioethics

SIGNIFICANCE: Organ transplantation and substitution raises ethical issues regarding the definition of death, the equitable distribution of scarce resources (including the ethics of selling body parts), and the quality of life of the transplant patient.

For centuries, humans have longed to be able to replace the diseased or injured parts of the body with healthy organs. Stories abound from ancient civilizations of attempts at organ and tissue transplantation, but until recently these seem to have been mostly dreams. Finally, during the early nineteenth century, there were successful skin grafts. These were autografts in which a patient's own tissue was used, and thus there was little danger of rejection. When material was taken from one member of a species and placed in another (an allograft), however, it was rejected by the recipient.

This was not the only problem faced by these early medical pioneers. Before organ transplantation could be done on a routine basis, it was necessary to develop better methods of tying up weakened arteries, aseptic surgery, anesthesia, and tissue typing. By 1913, the French physician Alexis Carrel transplanted a kidney from one cat to another and later developed a profusion machine that drenched a removed organ in blood, thus sustaining its life.

However, a major obstacle remained; namely, the rejection of the transplanted organ. The mechanics of this little-understood process were discovered by Peter Medawar at Oxford University during the 1940's. He found that this process was caused by the immune system's rejection of the body's lymphoid organs. Thus, the recipient's system recognized the donor tissue as foreign and responded by destroying the transplant. The amount of genetic disparity of the two individuals determines the degree and speed of this rejection. Attempts to limit the activity of the immune system eventually led to the use of a combination of a

corticosteroid (prednisone) with the antileukemia drug (azathioprine). A third medicine, cyclosporine, discovered in 1972, was particularly important because it took less of a scattergun approach than the others. Rather than suppressing the entire immune response, cyclosporine targets the T cells, the particular parts of the system that attack alien tissues. The most effective treatment of transplant patients includes daily doses of these three drugs.

TYPES OF ORGAN TRANSPLANTS

The human body contains twenty-one different transplantable organs and tissues, including the heart, liver, kidneys, lungs, pancreas, cornea, bone marrow, and blood vessels. In 1954, a team of Boston physicians led by Joseph E. Murray successfully transplanted a kidney from one twin brother to another. Cardiac transplantation began in 1967, when Christiaan Barnard performed a human-to-human operation, but the first fully successful heart transplant was done by Norman Shumway in the United States. Although lung transplants were attempted as early as 1964, because of problems with infection that are peculiar to this organ it was not until the 1980's that John D. Cooper of Toronto made the process feasible. The work of Thomas E. Starzl led in 1967 to successful transplanting of the liver. Also during the decade of the 1960's, the pancreas, bone marrow, cornea, and blood vessels were transplanted with increasing frequency.

By the turn of the twenty-first century, more than 16,000 kidney, liver, pancreas, heart, heart-lung, and lung transplants were being performed each year in the United States alone. These operations seem to be the only treatment that can transform individuals from a near-death condition to a relatively normal life in a matter of days.

A doctor prepares a human heart for transplant at the Cleveland Clinic in Cleveland, Ohio, in July, 2003. (AP/Wide World Photos)

ETHICAL CONCERNS

Such procedures raise a number of ethical and moral problems. Those that concern organ donation often result from worry that individuals will not receive adequate treatment if they sign donor agreements.

An understanding of the modern definition of death can deal with much of this confusion. Until the 1960's, cessation of brain function inevitably followed cessation of cardiopulmonary function. Individuals did not live for extended periods with the heart and other organs functioning after the brain activity ceased. New medical techniques such as the use of respirators made this condition possible. Machines could maintain blood and oxygen circulation even when the body could never again operate on its own.

The notion of "brain death" was therefore proposed. In 1966, Pope Pius XII defined death as the departure of the spirit from the body through the cessation of brain function rather than the loss of pumping action of the heart. The United States and other countries have passed laws that have given legal sanction to this definition. Patients who are brain dead may be kept alive for a few days, but not permanently. A physician can confirm this situation beyond a doubt through neurological examination. Public support for this position has gained wide acceptance, and currently very few people oppose organ donation.

More difficult problems remain that involve the recipient. Some of these concern the selection of those who are to receive transplants. Despite the thousands of operations performed in 1991, there were still more than 30,000 individuals listed by the United Network for Organ Sharing (UNOS) who needed one or more of the major organs. In an attempt to alleviate this shortage, UNOS, an organization of transplant centers, was founded. It has established a national waiting list to ensure equitable organ allocation according to policies that forbid favoritism based on race, sex, financial status, or political influence. The only considerations are the medically determined conditions of the patients. This organization has been quite successful in raising awareness of the need for donor organs.

Even if a person receives a transplant, there is a continuing need for a more healthy lifestyle and the constant cost and bother of daily medication. Finally, the entire situation of the expense and availability of transplants is a microcosm of the macrocosm of health care for everyone. How can scarce resources be allocated? Who is wise or caring enough to decide who will die and who will have a chance at a new life? Such questions must be addressed by the general field of medical ethics.

Robert G. Clouse

FURTHER READING

Fox, Renee, and Judith P. Swazey. *The Courage to Fail: A Social View of Organ Transplants and Dialysis.* 2d rev. ed. Chicago: University of Chicago Press, 1978.

Price, David. *Legal and Ethical Aspects of Organ Transplantation.* New York: Cambridge University Press, 2000.

Sheil, A. G., and Felix T. Rapapport. *World Transplantation.* 3 vols. East Norwalk, Conn.: Appleton & Lange, 1989.

Shelton, Wayne, ed. *The Ethics of Organ Transplantation.* New York: Elsevier Science, 2001.

Starzl, Thomas E. *The Puzzle People: Memoirs of a Transplant Surgeon.* Pittsburgh: University of Pittsburgh Press, 1992.

Veatch, Robert M. *Transplantation Ethics.* Washington, D.C.: Georgetown University Press, 2000.

Warshofsky, Fred. *The Rebuilt Man.* New York: Thomas Y. Crowell, 1965.

SEE ALSO: Bioethics; Health care allocation; Life and death; Medical ethics; *Principles of Medical Ethics.*

Ortega y Gasset, José

IDENTIFICATION: Spanish philosopher
BORN: May 9, 1883, Madrid, Spain
DIED: October 18, 1955, Madrid, Spain
TYPE OF ETHICS: Modern history
SIGNIFICANCE: A metaphysics professor and existentialist, Ortega y Gasset helped to bring Spain into contact with the thought and culture of the rest of Europe. He was the author of *The Revolt of the Masses* (1929).

José Ortega y Gasset was a professor of metaphysics at the University of Madrid from 1910 until 1936. He had traveled and studied in Europe, especially in Germany, and when he returned, he brought European philosophy and political thought that had been ignored in Spain for centuries. An excellent and prolific writer, he wrote scores of newspaper and magazine essays and articles on philosophy and on general cultural topics. He studied and taught metaphysics, because he was interested in questions about the fundamental nature of reality.

Ortega y Gasset's quest for an ultimate reality led him to questions about the nature of knowledge and the nature of society. Ortega y Gasset's social theories made him an international figure. In *The Revolt of the Masses*, he argued that society is always ready to topple and that humankind is always ready to slip back into barbarism. Only by bowing to an elite class can people keep their societies going. This small, elite group thinks and plans and holds the power—it gets things done. So long as everyone else is willing to accept this leadership, human societies can stand firm.

Cynthia A. Bily

SEE ALSO: Elitism; Existentialism; Unamuno y Jugo, Miguel de.

Orwell, George

IDENTIFICATION: British novelist and essayist
BORN: Eric Blair; June 25, 1903, Motihari, Bengal, India
DIED: January 21, 1950, London, England
TYPE OF ETHICS: Modern history
SIGNIFICANCE: Despite his belief that states could never be restrained from tyranny by ethical or religious codes, Orwell remained committed to the belief in an essentially socialist state, based on democratic principles, under which individuals enjoyed equality and justice under the law.

Best known for the political fable *Animal Farm* (1945), a satirical examination of the Russian Revolution, and the dystopian novel *Nineteen Eighty-Four* (1949), which provides a broader indictment of totalitarianism, George Orwell infused all of his writing with a keen moral sense. Spurning the traditional morality of religious institutions, he championed humanistic values rooted in the fundamental decency of human beings.

Orwell's essay "Reflections on Gandhi" (1949) evaluates the Indian nationalist leader Mohandas K.

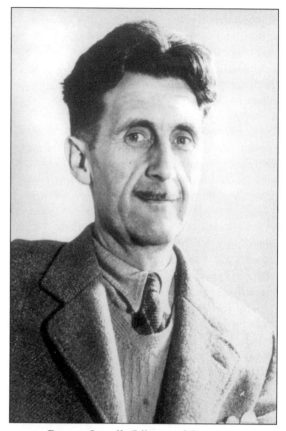

George Orwell. (Library of Congress)

Gandhi's appeal to Western leftist movements, despite what Orwell calls the "otherworldly, antihumanist tendency of his doctrines." He argues that groups as varied as anarchists and pacifists fail to recognize that "Gandhi's teachings cannot be squared with the belief that Man is the measure of all things, and that our job is to make life worth living on this earth, which is the only earth we have." It is the power of the average person, working toward a common good with honesty and integrity, that Orwell identified as the principal hope of humanity.

Orwell's abhorrence of totalitarianism, expressed in varying degrees in all of his major works of fiction, nonfiction, and journalism, stemmed chiefly from the tendencies of governments to suppress individual liberties. In "Literature and Totalitarianism" (1941), Orwell wrote, "We live in an age in which the autonomous individual is ceasing to exist—or perhaps one ought to say, in which the individual is ceasing to have the illusion of being autonomous." The physical suppression of individual liberty is no less dangerous in Orwell's view than the suppression of personal opinion or will. Totalitarianism seeks the submission of the individual to the state. Troublesome people could be removed, as Winston Smith discovers in *Nineteen Eighty-Four*; but more dangerous still, troublesome ideas or facts could also disappear by revising or simply erasing them. In such a world, the nature of truth becomes subservient to the state, the power of individuals to effect change is eliminated, and the equality of all people becomes impossible.

Perhaps the closest thing to an ethical or religious maxim in Orwell's thought is the concept of decency. In "The English People" (1944), Orwell tries to provide a sense of the typical morality of the English. "They have the virtues and the vices of an old-fashioned people. To twentieth-century political theories they oppose not another theory of their own, but a moral quality which must be vaguely described as decency." Orwell's idea of decency covers a multitude of social and political qualities, from a strict code of honesty in words and actions to the preservation of basic human freedoms by the state. It is this old-fashioned idea of decency that embodies Orwell's love of all things English, from a simple cup of tea to the beauty of the common toad, and that sustains his belief in the ability of common individuals to make life worth living.

Philip Bader

FURTHER READING

Bal, Sant Singh. *George Orwell: The Ethical Imagination*. New Delhi, India: Arnold-Heinemann Publishers, 1981.

Bowker, George. *Inside George Orwell*. New York: Palgrave Macmillan, 2003.

Orwell, George. *Essays*. New York: Alfred A. Knopf, 2002.

SEE ALSO: Arendt, Hannah; Communism; Dictatorship; Fascism; Gandhi, Mohandas K.; Honesty; Stalin, Joseph.

The Other

DEFINITION: Term used to signify a negative object for the sake of positive identification

TYPE OF ETHICS: Theory of ethics

SIGNIFICANCE: In its function as negative object used for positive identification, the concept of the other serves as a conceptual placeholder to elicit ethical responsibility.

Using the "other" as a term to orient discourses on ethics is a relatively recent development. However, as an ethical issue, the general concept of the "other" has been in play as long as humans have tried to account for the strangeness of existing in the world and as a way to control their particular environments.

Specifically, in assigning orientations for individuals' ethical relations, the issue of the other has evolved from signifying relationships of negative identification to that of ordering relationships of supporting the continued existence of the other, as other. In the former mode, human beings have traditionally taught themselves to identify all that is other as that which does not belong to the same kind, group, or set grounded on the propositional claims made by authoritative (or authoring) subjects. The result has historically been politically and socially to attempt to eliminate each other, indeed all others, in efforts to substantiate one's own identity claims or to secure material possessions for the sake of survival.

To judge the prevalence of this need to control or destroy the other to secure and maintain individual and group self-identity, one can find evidence in social narratives. People create grand narratives to justify the accounting methods they use to educate their young into forms of society that replicate earlier patterns of survival over others. Accordingly, modernity can be understood as chronicling the emergence of humans from the dark ages of authoritarian control, maintained by the exercise of violent force by some beings over others, to a process of rediscovering the other and reassessing institutional patterns based on structural relationships of dominance and subjection.

This new relationship with other beings of the world resulted in hundreds of years of progressive enlightenment and liberation, marked by revolutionary upheavals and forms of transforming social and environmental relationships. However, such transformations were accompanied by the application of historical patterns of hegemonic control with newly developed instruments of industrialization that also resulted in the highly efficient and logically ordered business of efficiently eliminating other human beings. This trend culminated in the Holocaust of World War II, in which tens of millions of "other" human beings were killed.

Three modern French intellectuals whose writings have explored this phenomenon are Albert Camus, Simone de Beauvoir, and Emmanuel Levinas. Camus wrote popular stories about modern alienation. Beauvoir defied the historical "othering" of women as inferior by men in her famous book, *The Second Sex* (1953), and Levinas reversed ideas about the other, claiming that "the other is that one for whom I am most responsible."

Julius Simon

FURTHER READING

Arp, Kristana. *The Bonds of Freedom: Simone de Beauvoir's Existentialist Ethics.* Chicago: Open Court, 2001.

Beauvoir, Simone de. *The Second Sex.* Edited and translated by H. M. Parshley. 1953. Reprint. New York: Alfred A. Knopf, 1993.

Camus, Albert. *The Stranger.* New York: Vintage Books, 1989.

Levinas, Emmanuel. *Ethics and Infinity.* Pittsburgh: Duquesne University Press, 1985.

SEE ALSO: Beauvoir, Simone de; *Being and Nothingness*; Camus, Albert; Hate crime and hate speech; Levinas, Emmanuel; Love; *Second Sex, The.*

Ought/can implication

DEFINITION: Philosophical principle which states that anything one is morally obligated to do, one is necessarily capable of doing

TYPE OF ETHICS: Theory of ethics

SIGNIFICANCE: If the ought/can implication is valid, then one's inability to do something stands as proof that one was not required to do it, or that one is not morally accountable for failing to do it. The principle presupposes that the world makes sense, and it arguably contradicts the Christian doctrine of Original Sin.

The "ought-implies-can" principle has practical and theoretical importance in ethics. In particular cases, it provides a defense against the charge of wrongdoing, not by providing an excuse for the wrong, but by denying that any wrong was committed. Assuming the principle to be true, if one can never act otherwise, then any time one thinks that one did not act in such a way as to fulfill an obligation is really a time when one did not have that obligation. In other words, assuming the truth of the principle and that one can never act otherwise, one can never do wrong.

The root idea of the moral "ought" seems to be that something is morally necessary or morally owed. "Ought" is supposed to imply "can" in the sense that if it is not true that one can do x, then it is not true that one is obligated to do it. Some people think that the principle is, like the statement "Bachelors are males," true simply because of the meanings of the words. It is self-contradictory, however, to say "Bachelors are not males," and it is not self-contradictory to say "I know what I ought to do, but I cannot do it." Therefore, the principle does not seem to be a conceptual truth.

R. M. Hare, in chapter 4 of his *Freedom and Reason* (1963), claims that people use "ought" in moral contexts to prescribe or advise, and that it makes no sense to advise one to do something that is impossible. Even if such advice is pointless, however, it does not follow that the principle is true. One does not show that "believing X" implies that "X is true" by pointing out that in certain contexts it makes no sense to advise one to believe something that is false.

A defender of the principle may say that people do not blame a person for failing to do something once they realize that it was impossible for that person to do it. The suggestion is that people do not blame in such cases because the person's inability to do something meant that the person was not, after all, obligated to do it. It seems, however, that people might not blame in such a case because they accept the person's inability as an excuse for failing to fulfill the obligation, not because they accept the inability as a reason for saying that the person was not obligated.

CULPABLE POWERLESSNESS

A person may have inappropriate feelings and be unable to control them. Even then, it may be reasonable to say that that person ought to feel ashamed, grateful, disturbed, or remorseful, and that there is something wrong with anyone who cannot have these feelings. One may say that the "ought" in such cases expresses an ideal, as does the "ought" in the statement "Everyone ought to be able to live like a king." An "ought" that expresses an ideal does not imply "can," but not every case in which "ought" does not imply "can" seems to involve an ideal "ought."

Consider, for example, cases of culpable powerlessness. Imagine that Smith promises to meet Jones in two hours, then changes his mind and takes a powerful sedative. At the time of the promised meeting, Smith cannot be there, but it still seems that he ought to be there. Defenders of the principle may say that Smith's obligation to be there ceased once he could not be there, but that he did wrong in making it impossible for himself to be there. If people should be blamed for failing to fulfill an obligation, however, then Smith was obligated to be there, since one would blame him for not being there as well as for making it impossible for himself to be there. To hold to the principle in cases of culpable powerlessness seems to make it too easy for people to cancel their obligations.

Alvin I. Goldman, in chapter 7 of his *A Theory of Human Action* (1970), considers rewriting the principle as follows to avoid such cases: If a person ought to do x at time t, then there is some time, at or before t, at which he or she is able to do x at t. In that case, there is no reason to say that Smith is not obligated to keep his appointment, since before he took the sedative he was able to keep the appointment he had made for time t.

Now, however, cases of powerlessness that should rule out obligation will not do so. For example, if before Smith could take the sedative he was struck with complete paralysis while alone in his apartment, his obligation should terminate. It will not terminate given the revised principle, however, since according to it, he *can* still keep his appointment.

There is, however, the following basis for believing that at least one interpretation of the principle is true. If a person ought to do x, he is properly subject to moral judgment if he fails to do it. If he is properly subject to moral judgment if he fails to do x, then it is physically possible for him to do it. (Something is physically possible if it is consistent with the laws of nature. Being able to fly is inconsistent with those

laws, and that is why not being able to fly is not properly subject to moral judgment.) Therefore, if a person ought to do x, it is physically possible for him to do it. If "ought" also implies a sense of "can" that rules out causal determination, the principle provides some reason for believing that determinism is incompatible with freedom and moral responsibility.

Gregory P. Rich

FURTHER READING

Goldman, Alvin I. *A Theory of Human Action*. Englewood Cliffs, N.J.: Prentice-Hall, 1970.

Henderson, G. P. "'Ought' Implies 'Can.'" *Philosophy* 41 (April, 1966): 101-112.

Montefiore, Alan. "'Ought' and 'Can.'" *Philosophical Quarterly* 8 (January, 1958): 24-40.

O'Connor, D. J. *Free Will*. Garden City, N.Y.: Anchor Books, 1971.

Stocker, Michael. "'Ought' and 'Can.'" *Australasian Journal of Philosophy* 49, no. 3 (December, 1971): 303-317.

White, Alan R. *Modal Thinking*. Ithaca, N.Y.: Cornell University Press, 1975.

Widerker, David, and Michael McKenna, eds. *Moral Responsibility and Alternative Possibilities: Essays on the Importance of Alternative Possibilities*. Burlington, Vt.: Ashgate, 2003.

SEE ALSO: Determinism and freedom; Hare, R. M.; Kant, Immanuel; Maximal vs. minimal ethics; Moral luck; Moral responsibility; Responsibility; Thomas Aquinas.

Outsourcing

DEFINITION: Business practice of having important company services performed by other companies or individual persons outside the firm

TYPE OF ETHICS: Business and labor ethics

SIGNIFICANCE: Changing conceptions of corporate efficiency have reconfigured divisions between in-house functions and those that are subcontracted to external agencies, raising new ethical questions about the treatment of employees.

Corporations were once largely self-contained and comprehensive collections of functions, some of which might be outsourced, that is, subcontracted to other companies or to individual freelance workers. Keeping functions in-house removed the need to generate profits, and therefore generally saved money; however, costs could easily outweigh savings. Moreover, units of a company that are not expected to generate profits have less reason to use resources effectively. Thus, the same considerations supporting competition in the marketplace would seem to favor competition within the corporation.

In effect, extensive outsourcing brings the competitiveness of the marketplace inside individual corporations, as functions are contracted out to more specialized companies or individual workers. The decade of the 1990's witnessed dramatic developments in this direction, as corporations downsized and otherwise re-engineered their way to being more cost-effective and thus more profitable. Automobile manufacturers do not need to do their own landscaping or package delivery, so one might legitimately ask what other functions such companies could outsource—design, production, sales, accounting, perhaps even management.

One logical result of this line of thought is a distributed, or networked, organization, which has been called the "virtual" corporation. The enterprise becomes a kind of dormant network that can be brought to full life when the need arises, much as a Hollywood film-production company expands its activities when it launches a new film.

GLOBALIZATION AND ITS DISCONTENTS

Increasingly easy, cheap, and reliable communications and transportation systems make a distributed approach to business possible for corporations. In the government sphere, the same approach is known as privatization. As American manufacturing jobs have moved overseas in search of cheaper labor, other functions, such as software design and financial services, can be imported as needed. An ethically positive consequence of this new globalized flexibility is increased possibilities of productive, synergistic linkages among people, resources, and opportunities. This can mean a constant stream of better and cheaper products and services. Ethically negative consequences include destabilization of companies, greater insecurity for employees whose jobs are being reconfigured or eliminated, and the domination of everyday life by the ceaseless scramble for continuous quality improvement in a world in which everything is new and improved, but nothing is ever good enough.

Edward Johnson

FURTHER READING

Breslin, David A. "On the Ethics of Outsourcing: A Philosophical Look at A-76." *Program Manager Magazine* (November-December, 1999): 24-26.

Petzinger, Thomas, Jr. *The New Pioneers: The Men and Women Who Are Transforming the Workplace and Marketplace.* New York: Simon & Schuster, 1999.

Wolman, William, and Anne Colamosca. *The Judas Economy: The Triumph of Capital and the Betrayal of Work.* Reading, Mass.: Addison-Wesley, 1997.

SEE ALSO: Business ethics; Corporate responsibility; Corporate scandal; Cost-benefit analysis; Downsizing; Globalization; Multinational corporations.

P

Pacifism

DEFINITION: Moral opposition to war or to violence in general

TYPE OF ETHICS: Politico-economic ethics

SIGNIFICANCE: Pacifism is often seen as a virtue, especially in discussions of famous pacifists such as Jesus Christ or Mohandas K. Gandhi. It may also be judged immoral, however, when it involves the refusal to take up arms against evil or terror.

One of the most ethically troubling aspects of human existence is the problem of war, because of its connection with killing. Given the moral aversion to killing found in most ethical theories, war has been the subject of much ethical reflection and analysis in an attempt to provide either a justification for or a critique of war. Pacifism results from the belief that war can never be justified and is always immoral. Although pacifism may take different forms, moral opposition to war is a common theme. One of the questions that pacifists have tried to answer is whether pacifism also implies opposition to all forms of violence in addition to war.

HISTORY AND SOURCES

While pacifism has a philosophical grounding, its main source is religion. The Jain tradition in India practices pacifism by avoiding killing even insects. Buddhism also has a pacifist dimension. The dominant source for pacifism in Western culture, however, has been the Christian tradition.

Employing elements of the Hebrew scriptures, such as peace, righteousness, and compassion, along with an image of Jesus as nonviolent, early Christians began to raise ethical questions about war and participation in the military. The basis for these concerns centered on two factors. First, the Roman army had its own gods and religious rituals that contradicted both the Christian emphasis on one God and Christian forms of worship. Participation in the Roman army for a Christian would therefore be equivalent to idolatry or false worship. The second factor was based on more explicit ethical concerns about the morality of killing. Using the statements of Jesus, especially those taken from the Sermon on the Mount, some early Christians developed a moral framework that opposed the shedding of blood and, by extension, participation in war. Warfare was seen as a denial of the message of Jesus regarding love of enemies as well as a rejection of the kind of life that Jesus demanded of his disciples. The question thus arose whether a person could be both a Christian and a warrior.

This ethical issue of Christian participation in war increased as Christianity came more and more to be the established religion of the state following the proclamation of toleration by Constantine in the year 313 C.E.. Christians faced the dual changes of subsiding persecution and more direct involvement in the affairs of state, including war.

The ethical concern over war turned on the conflict between two principles: not harming others and protecting the innocent. Sometimes protecting the innocent might entail harming others, even killing them. War also became a matter of loyalty to the state. Moral qualms about killing were often resolved by means of a separation between public and private ethics. Christians could kill and participate in war as a consequence of the public duty of being soldiers, but not as private individuals. In addition, the development of the just war theory began to be the dominant ethical perspective on war in Christianity. There was still a strong pacifist element within the Christian tradition, however, and it surfaced most dramatically in the Protestant Reformation during the sixteenth century.

The Radical Reformation, or the Anabaptists, viewed war as directly antithetical to the Christian message. The Anabaptists sought a return to what was described as the New Testament Church, which they understood to be completely opposed to war and violence. One of the major documents of the Anabaptist movement, the Schleitheim Confession of 1527, holds that the use of the sword is outside the perfection of Christ. The Anabaptists thus rejected the distinction between public and private ethics and the justification that it provided for war. As a consequence, they also sought to limit the demands of the state and to call into question the claims of value made on behalf of the state. The Anabaptists are the ancestors of the Historic Peace Churches, such as those of the Mennonites, Quakers, and Amish. Pacifism is a central component of their views of Christian ethics.

Pacifism was also defended on humanistic and philosophical grounds. Desiderius Erasmus, the sixteenth century Christian humanist, argued that war was wasteful and impractical. It offered nothing from which humanity could benefit and only revealed the horrors that human beings could visit upon one another. The eighteenth century philosopher Immanuel Kant emphasized the impracticality and irrationality of war. His famous dictum to treat people as ends and never as means also created a strong argument against the morality of war, since it seemed that war did treat people as a means. These religious and philosophical views have combined to give pacifism its focus and variety. John Howard Yoder lists eighteen types of pacifism in his book *Nevertheless* (1976).

MORAL FOUNDATIONS

The moral basis of pacifism usually has several dimensions: a view of God, a normative understanding of humanity, and the importance of love. A philosophically based pacifism may not fully develop a view of God. If God is part of the pacifist ethic, God is seen as underlying creation, which imparts a moral structure to the world in the direction of sustaining creation. War, which is destructive, denies the divine relationship to creation and becomes immoral. Humanity is characterized by a fundamental unity.

Beneath the differences that qualify human existence is an explicit humanness that extends beyond differences such as race, religion, or ethnic origin. Pacifism seeks to uphold the basic unity by refusing

to allow the differences to become justifications for war and killing. As a result, love is often the central moral feature of pacifism in a practical sense. A pacifist would claim that love, as the basis for human actions, entails the rejection of war and possibly even all forms of violence. For this reason, the goals of pacifism are more than simple opposition to war; they involve finding alternatives to the use of violence to resolve conflicts and an emphasis on peace research and education.

Ron Large

FURTHER READING

Brock, Peter. *Freedom from Violence: Sectarian Nonresistance from the Middle Ages to the Great War.* Toronto: University of Toronto Press, 1991.

Cady, Duane. *From Warism to Pacifism: A Moral Continuum.* Philadelphia: Temple University Press, 1989.

Early, Frances H. *A World Without War: How U.S. Feminists and Pacifists Resisted World War I.* Syracuse, N.Y.: Syracuse University Press, 1997.

Hauerwas, Stanley. *The Peaceable Kingdom: A Primer in Christian Ethics.* Notre Dame, Ind.: University of Notre Dame Press, 1983.

Helgeland, John, R. J. Daly, and J. Patout Burns. *Christians and the Military: The Early Experience.* Edited by R. J. Daly. Philadelphia: Fortress Press, 1985.

Lampen, John, ed. *No Alternative? Nonviolent Responses to Repressive Regimes.* York, England: W. Sessions, 2000.

Mayer, Peter, ed. *The Pacifist Conscience.* Chicago: Regnery, 1967.

Miller, Richard. *Interpretations of Conflict: Ethics, Pacifism, and the Just-War Tradition.* Chicago: University of Chicago Press, 1991.

Teichman, Jenny. *Pacifism and the Just War.* New York: Basil Blackwell, 1986.

Yoder, John Howard. *Nevertheless: The Varieties and Shortcomings of Religious Pacifism.* Scottdale, Pa.: Herald Press, 1976.

SEE ALSO: Ahiṁsā; Buddhist ethics; Conscientious objection; Gandhi, Mohandas K.; Jain ethics; Jesus Christ; King, Martin Luther, Jr.; Nonviolence; Peace studies; Religion and violence.

Pain

DEFINITION: Fundamentally unpleasant physical or emotional sensation; suffering

TYPE OF ETHICS: Bioethics

SIGNIFICANCE: Pain names the broad class of experience which all sentient beings are conditioned to avoid. It is the most primal negative influence on behavior, as pleasure is the most primal positive influence. In many ethical systems, to intentionally cause pain in another is among the most serious moral transgressions, and to alleviate the pain of another is among the most morally admirable acts.

The treatment and relief of pain is often considered to be a central goal of the medical profession, at least by those who seek care. People usually think of pain as a warning sign that something has gone wrong in the body's systems; however, not all pain serves this function, and not all pain is indicative of physical malfunction.

PHYSIOLOGY

Pain is usually separated (somewhat arbitrarily) into two diagnoses: acute and chronic. While chronic pain is often defined clinically as acute pain persisting longer than six months, there are differences in perception and meaning that go beyond merely temporal distinctions.

Acute pain is also of two types, classified by the speed with which the actual nerve impulses reach the brain. When an event, such as a burn, triggers signals to be sent to the brain, one set of signals travels much faster. These are the initial impulses, "fast" pain, that travel on myelinated (sheathed in a protein-lipid layer) A delta fibers. These impulses reach the brain in a fraction of a second, while the "slow" pain, which travels on unmyelinated C fibers, takes up to a couple of seconds to register in a person's consciousness. The further the site of stimulus is from the brain, the greater the difference in the times these signals register. Fast pain is sharp and bright. Slow pain is dull and aching, and ultimately more unpleasant.

In addition to the nerve impulses sent to the brain, for which the chemical neurotransmitter seems to be substance P (for pain), chemicals are released at the site of stimulus. Prostaglandins draw blood to the area to gain the healing and infection-fighting power of white blood cells. Prostaglandins also increase the sensitivity of the nerves in the immediate vicinity of the injury, as do bradykinins and leukotrienes, which are also released.

PSYCHOLOGICAL COMPONENTS OF PAIN

Pain cannot, however, be relegated to mere physical perception. The knowledge of the consequences of pain is inextricably entwined with the feeling and assessment of pain. In a now-famous study published in 1946, Henry K. Beecher found that men who were severely wounded in battle reported far less pain (and some no pain at all) than did civilian patients with comparable wounds caused by surgery. The reason for this seems clear: For men in battle, severe wounds are the ticket home. Pain cannot be separated from the personal and social consequences of its presence.

Many people take pain and suffering to be synonymous, yet they are different and distinct. Pain can occur without causing suffering, as does the pain that athletes endure during competition. There can certainly be suffering without pain, either physical, such as severe itching, or mental, as in grief. (Some authorities do not distinguish between physical and mental suffering, believing them to be so linked as to be inseparable.) Pain is usually taken to be a physical perception, while suffering is psychological distress. Intrinsic to suffering is a threat to the integrity of a person as a whole. The anticipation of pain and loss can cause as much suffering as the actuality thereof.

MEANINGS OF PAIN

Pain has had different interpretations in different cultures and periods of history. While today Western culture ostensibly reaches toward the eradication of pain, this has by no means always been the case. Aside from medical inability to eliminate pain in the past, pain and suffering have themselves been considered valuable in many cultures. The Christian religion, in particular, has traditionally deemed experiencing pain, in some circumstances, a virtue.

Suffering, especially suffering for others, is considered one of the highest forms of sanctity, as can be seen from the litany of saints by martyrdom throughout the ages. In other religious traditions, pain and suffering are, or can be, due punishment for sins or wrong actions committed either in this life, as in Judaism and Islam, or in past lives, as in Hinduism and

Buddhism. The word "pain" in English is derived from the Latin word *poena*, meaning "punishment." The English word for one who seeks medical care, "patient," also comes from the Latin. Its root, *pati*, means "the one who suffers." Underlying these derivations, and extending beyond the words themselves, is the cultural acceptance that pain and suffering are an inevitable part of life and as such are not intrinsically evil. This attitude is the basis for medical hesitancy to consider pain a problem to be treated in and of itself, rather than simply as a symptom of other disease or injury.

TREATMENT OF PAIN

Because of these deep-rooted cultural attitudes toward pain and those who suffer, only recently has aggressive treatment of pain become an issue in medical ethics. Studies have shown surprising underutilization of pain-relieving medication for sufferers of severe pain, especially among terminal cancer patients. This seems to be because of fears of addiction to narcotics and a lack of knowledge of proper use. The use of heroin for terminal patients has long been accepted in Great Britain but continues to be prohibited in the United States.

Alternative forms of treatment are becoming more acceptable, although the efficacy of some remains to be substantiated. Biofeedback techniques, chiropractic, hypnosis, and TENS (transcutaneous electrical nerve stimulation) are generally accepted to be of value for many patients. Acupuncture is gaining ground in the United States. For millions of people, however, effective pain relief still lies in the future.

Margaret Hawthorne

FURTHER READING

Bendelow, Gillian. *Pain and Gender.* New York: Prentice Hall, 2000.

Bowker, John W. "Pain and Suffering: Religious Perspectives." In *Encyclopedia of Bioethics*, edited by Warren T. Reich. Rev. ed. Vol. 4. New York: Macmillan, 1995.

Care, Norman S. *Living with One's Past: Personal Fates and Moral Pain.* Lanham, Md.: Rowman & Littlefield, 1996.

Ganong, William F. *Review of Medical Physiology.* 21st ed. New York: Lange Medical Books/ McGraw-Hill, 2003.

Hardcastle, Valerie Gray. *The Myth of Pain.* Cambridge, Mass.: MIT Press, 1999.

Morris, David B. *The Culture of Pain.* Berkeley: University of California Press, 1991.

SEE ALSO: Biofeedback; Cruelty; Harm; Hypnosis; Illness; Sentience.

Pan-Africanism

DEFINITION: Global nationalist movement aimed at uniting peoples of African descent

DATE: Term coined in 1900

TYPE OF ETHICS: Race and ethnicity

SIGNIFICANCE: Pan-Africanism seeks through racial unity to find solutions to the problems of flagrant injustice, economic deprivation, and discrimination based on skin color. Despite operating across existing political boundaries, it raises many of the ethical issues raised by nationalism generally, and it has been both celebrated and vilified as a species of nationalism.

The European discovery and partitioning of Africa was a classic story of gold, glory, and God, compounded by greed, adventure, and missionary zeal. In the process, imperialist invaders squeezed the continent of its wealth, while announcing to the world that they were bringing the benefits of civilization to backward peoples. Pan-Africanism awakened a new spirit that rejected patience and the acceptance of suffering and inferiority. The emotional impetus for its concepts flowed from the experience of a widely dispersed people—those of African descent—who believed themselves either physically, through dispossession or slavery, or socially, economically, politically, and mentally, through colonialism, to have lost their homeland. With this loss came enslavement, persecution, inferiority, discrimination, and dependency. It involved a loss of freedom and dignity. This realization, bolstered by an awareness of their common heritage, led to a desire among black people for some link with their African origins. It became a vehicle for the struggle of black people to regain their wealth, pride, strength, and independence as emotions were converted into ideas and ideas into slogans. Above all, however, the ideals of

Pan-Africanism grew from the desire to regain dignity and equality for all black people.

GROWTH IN DIASPORA

Originally, Pan-Africanism was dominated by the leadership of black people residing in the United States and the West Indies. During the late 1870's, following the era of Reconstruction, African Americans in the United States were alienated by growing racism and economic depression. Some among them began to think in terms of returning to Africa. Marcus Garvey, who was of Jamaican origin, would later ex-

ploit this discontent by preaching a back-to-Africa message to the black people of the New World during the early 1920's. His idea of exodus to Africa was embedded in the prospective creation of an exclusively black race, an idea that earned him the endorsement and eventually the open support of the Ku Klux Klan, who, although for different reasons, welcomed his desire to expatriate all blacks to Africa.

Another pioneer spokesman for Pan-Africanism in the diaspora was W. E. B. Du Bois. His main concern was achieving absolute equality for the entire black race, an idea that had been born out of his con-

---

Pan-Africanism Time Line

Date	Place	Event
1900	London	Henry Sylvester Williams calls first Pan-African Conference.
1920	New York	Declaration of the Rights of the Negro Peoples of the World is read at a conference held in New York. During the conference, Marcus Garvey is elected provisional president of Africa.
1919-1927	Europe and the United States	W. E. B. Du Bois calls four Pan-African Congresses.
1945	Manchester, England	Fifth Pan-African Congress is the first organized by Africans.
1958	Accra, Ghana	First conference of Independent African States is held.
1959	Ghana	Ghana-Guinea Union is declared by its signatories to be the beginning of a Union of Independent African States.
1960	Addis Ababa, Ethiopia	At Second conference of Independent African States, Pan-African movement splits into two factions over ideological rifts.
1960	Brazzaville, Congo	Brazzaville Group (also known as the Union of African States and Madagascar) convenes and makes public its moderate views on African unity and related issues.
January 3-7, 1961	Casablanca, Morocco	Casablanca Conference announces that it favors a political union that will eventually lead to a "United States of Africa."
May 8-12, 1961	Monrovia, Liberia	Taking its cue from the Brazzaville Group, the Monrovia Conference announces that it favors a form of unity that allows for the preservation of national sovereignty.
July 1, 1961	Accra, Ghana	In response to the Brazzaville Group, Ghana, Guinea, and Mali issue the Charter for the Union of African States.
May 25, 1963	Addis Ababa, Ethiopia	Organization for African Unity, which unites the two camps, is founded.

viction that the "favored few" had no moral right to prosper at the expense of the toil of the "tortured many."

THE NATIONALIST DIMENSION

The second stage of Pan-Africanism began with the gradual decolonization of Africa after World War II, when the character and leadership of the movement became more Africanized. Educated Africans who had come to study in universities in Europe and America had come to know firsthand about racial intolerance and the economic subjugation of blacks. Three of those students, Kwame Nkrumah of the Gold Coast (later Ghana), Nnamdi Azikiwe of Nigeria, and Hastings Banda of Nyasaland (Malawi), all of whom had been exposed to the Pan-Africanist movement of the diaspora, would later become presidents of their respective countries at independence.

The African nationalist leaders gave a new meaning to Pan-Africanism—African solidarity and unity—for it was believed then (and now) that the process of political and economic emancipation that had begun during the nationalist days could be consolidated only through a cohesive and united continental Africa. The dreams of African unity that they had so nurtured and cherished would run into all kinds of problems, however, and by 1960, ideological differences had sharply divided the newly independent nations into rival camps, a division that was further aggravated by superpower rivalry. While some insisted on a political union that would require giving up some sovereignty, others favored a simple association of states. This proved to be harmful for the continent's much-needed economic development and political stability, and it was not until 1963 that they finally found a common ground with the establishment of the Organization of African Unity (OAU).

The OAU's charter sought to "promote unity and solidarity of African states" through "political, economic and scientific cooperation." Ever since, the continent has been plagued by a series of problems ranging from political instability to outright economic disasters. Allegations of human rights abuse are widespread, and in many cases, the prospects for majority rule have been dampened by the installation of military regimes, which usually are corrupt and morally bankrupt. Civil wars and cases of mass starvation are rampant, while the whole continent continues to be haunted by the discriminatory policies of South Africa. Many of these problems have been blamed on, among other things, the lack of a sound guiding philosophy for development as well as the absence of a leadership code of ethics.

Olusoji Akomolafe

FURTHER READING

Ackah, William B. *Pan-Africanism, Exploring the Contradictions: Politics, Identity, and Development in Africa and the African Diaspora*. Brookfield, Vt.: Ashgate, 1999.

Ajala, Adekunle. *Pan-Africanism: Evolution, Progress, and Prospects*. London: A. Deutsch, 1973.

Genge, Manelisi, Francis Kornegay, and Stephen Rule. *African Union and a Pan-African Parliament: Working Papers*. Pretoria: Africa Institute of South Africa, 2000.

Mathurin, Owen Charles. *Henry Sylvester Williams and the Origins of the Pan-African Movement, 1869-1911*. Westport, Conn.: Greenwood Press, 1976.

Poe, D. Zizwe. *Kwame Nkrumah's Contribution to Pan-Africanism: An Afrocentric Analysis*. New York: Routledge, 2003.

Rimmer, Douglas, ed. *Africa Thirty Years On*. Portsmouth, N.H.: Heinemann, 1992.

Tokareva, Zinaida. *Organization of African Unity: Twenty-Five Years of Struggle*. Translated by Clance Nsiah Jaybex. Moscow: Progress, 1989.

SEE ALSO: African ethics; Du Bois, W. E. B.; Integration; Nationalism.

Panentheism

DEFINITION: Belief that all reality is a subset of the being of God

TYPE OF ETHICS: Beliefs and practices

SIGNIFICANCE: Panentheism attempts to reconcile the belief that God is everything and the belief that God transcends reality by positing that both statements are true.

To understand panentheism, one must also become familiar with pantheism, for both philosophies consider God, this world, and the universe, and both try to explain how the three are related. The older of the two is pantheism, which posits that God and the universe are one and the same. Despite apparent diversity and disorder in the cosmos, the universe is ordered and unified, and that order and that unification are expressions of God. Because pantheists give no place to the transcendence of God, however, that philosophical position eventually gave rise to panentheism, whose advocates hold that all reality is part of the being of God and that God transcends all reality. God is the universe, but he is also much more. Although the philosopher who first coined and defined the term "panentheism" was the German Karl Christian Friederich Krause, various early Greek philosophers (such as Thales, Xenophanes, and Parmenides) held many views that were consistent with panentheism.

PANENTHEISM

In developing their philosophical "system," modern panentheists usually follow Krause, who attempted to mediate between theism and pantheism. Panentheists believe that God (absolute being) is primordial, a being without contrariety who is one with the universe but is not exhausted by it (God is bigger than the universe). All individuals are part of a spiritual whole, a league of humanity. For the human being, self-consciousness provides the starting point of panentheism, for it allowed, Krause held, the ego to learn that it was both mind and body and also to learn that it was part of God.

Because God is good, humankind should share in the goodness, and humankind's inner union with God becomes the foundation of ethics, with ethics becoming the heart of religion. Just as a living cell has certain freedom within a living body, however, so, too, do humans have a degree of freedom. Krause viewed all individuals as part of the divine, and he became a crusading reformer who, for example, argued against capital punishment; he also believed that republican government was the only political system that was worthy of the divine. Regarding all "organized" religion as oppressive, he criticized theocracy, religious censorship, and religionists' disdain for the world.

Closely related to both pantheism and panentheism is the doctrine of "emanation," which asserts that an overflowing superabundance of the divine God resulted in the production of the universe. All reality, then, flows from a perfect and transcendent principle. The first gift of the divine overflow was intelligence, which allowed humans to understand their world, their reality. Opposed to evolutionism, emanationism is timeless, and its source (God) remains undiminished.

PANENTHEISM: ITS CRITICS AND ITS SUPPORTERS

Most critics hold that both pantheism and panentheism fail to account for the individuality, the personality, and the freedom of each human being. Likewise, both beliefs fail to account for evil, ignorance, and error on the part of some people. Thus, negatives exist in the world and the universe—negatives that could not emanate from a perfectly good God. Using acquired knowledge and the powers of observation, critics also deny that the universe contains total unity. Indeed, the idea of a unified universe is actually devoid of content, because diversity obviously exists. Likewise, modern scientific progress is not in accord with a unity theory. Charles Darwin's evolutionary theory, for example, stands opposed to both pantheism and panentheism. Organized religion also remained most critical of both pantheism and panentheism; one religionist called both beliefs "worms" of heretical "perversity" and inventions of the devil.

Some critics of panentheism attack the philosophic reputation of Krause, who gave the doctrine its most complete explanation. During his lifetime, for example, his ideas were so suspect that he was denied professorships at such prestigious universities as Göttingen and Munich. Furthermore, he coined many words that had meaning only for him (and that confused later scholars). Likewise, he also produced bizarre neologisms that were too much for the German language, as well as being untranslatable.

Over time, supporters of panentheism—such as Krause's disciples Julian Sanz del Rio of Spain, Heinrich Ahrens of Belgium, and Hermann von Leohardi of Germany—attempted to answer the critics, but in doing so they raised more questions. For example, while grappling with the problem of evil, some supporters argued that evil resulted only when an individual organism—because of ego—tried to tear itself away from the harmony of the whole (which is part of God). Yet such a defense actually raises the question about the goodness of God. Why would God create organisms that ultimately try to tear away?

Although panentheism has shown a remarkable ability to survive, such survival is no indication that—especially in view of the criticisms—it has any basis in fact.

James Smallwood

FURTHER READING

Aiken, Alfred. *That Which Is: A Book on the Absolute*. 1955. Rev. ed. New York: Hillier Press, 1971.

Hegel, G. W. F. *Lectures on the Philosophy of Religion*. Edited by Peter C. Hodgson. Translated by R. F. Brown et al. 3 vols. Berkeley: University of California Press, 1984-1987.

Jacob, Margaret C. *The Radical Enlightenment: Pantheists, Freemasons, and Republicans*. London: Allen & Unwin, 1981.

Nikkel, David H. *Panentheism in Hartshorne and Tillich: A Creative Synthesis*. New York: P. Lang, 1995.

Piper, H. W. *The Active Universe*. London: University of London Press, 1962.

Spinoza, Benedictus de. *The Collected Works of Spinoza*. Edited and translated by Edwin Curley. Princeton, N.J.: Princeton University Press, 1985- .

Wolfson, Harry A. *The Philosophy of Spinoza*. Cambridge, Mass.: Harvard University Press, 1983.

SEE ALSO: Ethical monotheism; God; Pantheism.

Pantheism

DEFINITION: Belief that God and reality are coextensive

TYPE OF ETHICS: Beliefs and practices

SIGNIFICANCE: Pantheism holds that God is everything and everything is God. Its effects upon ethics are paradoxical and potentially controversial, since it would seem to require respect for all life and nature, but it also raises difficult questions about how suffering, evil, and injustice can be part, not merely of God's plan, but of God himself.

Pantheism is older than civilization. Some see its origins in animism, the primal religious conviction that everything has a soul or spirit. Popularized during the Enlightenment, the English word "pantheism" is from two Greek roots, *pan* ("all") and *theos* ("god"), meaning that "God is everything." This term suggests that God is the totality of all things—real and imagined, actual or potential. As a being "apart" or "separate" from nature, God does not "exist." Within the Western tradition, Pantheism was a powerful moral force for the Stoics, the Neoplatonists, and such modern thinkers as Baruch Spinoza. Within the Eastern traditions, Pantheism is evident in Islamic mysticism (Sufism), certain types of Daoism (urging conformity to the *Dao*, or "rhythm of the world"), and Hinduism.

C. George Fry

SEE ALSO: Daoist ethics; Ethical monotheism; Ethics; God; Marcus Aurelius; Mysticism; Panentheism; Spinoza, Baruch; Stoic ethics; Sufism.

Paradoxes in ethics

DEFINITION: Formal arguments that prove the truth of contradictory propositions

TYPE OF ETHICS: Theory of ethics

SIGNIFICANCE: The existence of paradoxes in ethics may demonstrate that reason and rationality alone are insufficient tools for making ethical decisions.

Ethical questions deal with the correct values one should use in making individual and collective decisions. The dilemma for recent ethical thinkers has been to agree upon a set of values that may form the basis for collective decisions, given the increasing pluralism of many societies and the global environment. A common response has been that even though all individuals may not agree on value issues, if all individuals agree to behave rationally—that is, to act in a consistent manner in pursuing their individual self-interests—then collective goals can be reached and collective decisions can be made. Unfortunately, two problems show that ethical paradoxes arise even when the only assumption one makes about individual motivations is that all individuals are acting to maximize their own utilities. These paradoxes cast doubt on the idea that rationality is a sufficient means of reaching collective decisions or goals.

LOGIC OF COLLECTIVE ACTION

Two political theorists, Brian Barry and Russell Hardin, define a paradox as a set of conflicting or contradictory conclusions to which one is led by apparently sound arguments. The first paradox of rationality to be discussed is the problem of collective action. This problem states that a self-interested individual may not be able to work with others toward a collective good even when all individuals involved realize that their individual interests would be served if all cooperated in the venture. A "collective good" is defined as a benefit in which all in a group may share, even if all do not contribute to its creation or maintenance. Examples of collective goods include clean air, which all may breathe even if all individuals did not help clean up the environment, or public television, which all may watch even if all did not send in contributions during a pledge drive.

It has been generally assumed in the social sciences that self-interested individuals will contribute to collective goods if they feel that they receive more in benefits than the cost of contribution; hence, the common appeal from public television that "if you feel the entertainment on PBS is worth more than $100 a year, please pledge this amount to the station." The logic of collective action, however, disputes this claim.

Assume that one individual does believe that the benefits received will outweigh the costs of contributing. If the individual contributes to the goal and the goal is reached, that individual's profit is the worth of a share of the collective good minus the cost of contribution. If the individual does not contribute to the goal, however, and the goal is reached, that individual's profit is the worth of his share of the collective good with no deductions. Under these circumstances, the self-interested individual should "free-ride" on the work of others and not contribute. If the individual contributes to the goal and the goal is not reached, the individual's profit is negative and is equal to the cost of contribution, since there is no collective good to share. If the individual does not contribute to the goal and the goal is not reached, the individual's profit is zero.

Under these circumstances, the self-interested individual should once again not contribute. Hence, the individual should not contribute regardless of whether the goal is reached; the only exception to this rule occurs when one individual's contribution will make the difference between success or failure in the venture. Given that the chances of such a situation are very small in large groups, no large-scale collective action should be possible. One may ask, of course, "what if all persons acted that way?" The sting of the problem is that all self-interested persons should be expected to act this way, so that goods such as clean air, public television, and others should not be created by voluntary contributions.

ALTRUISM

Some people have argued that a sense of altruism might lead individuals to contribute to a collective good. There are two problems with this argument. First, even if one is motivated by humanitarian concerns, it still might not be reasonable to contribute to a large-scale collective effort if that effort might not succeed because of the logic of collective action; one would be better off giving the money to a homeless person. Second, there remains a great deal of behavior that humanitarian motives cannot explain. Individuals do not join interest groups such as the National Organization for Women or the National Rifle Association out of altruism; they join out of self-interest. It is there that the paradox of collective action arises: An individual's self-interest may prevent him or her from participating in collective action that would serve his or her self-interest if all individuals participated in it. Furthermore, all persons involved may realize that this situation exists and still be unable to do anything about it.

CYCLICAL VOTING PATTERNS

The second paradox involves cyclical voting patterns. It shows how three individuals, ranking three alternative choices, may not be able to assemble a transitive ranking for the whole group. Consider three individuals, *A*, *B*, and *C*, and three policy choices, *X*, *Y*, and *Z*. Assume that the three individuals rank these choices in the following manner.

	A	B	C
First preference	x	y	z
Second preference	y	z	x
Third preference	z	x	y

Note that all individuals' preference orderings are transitive—that is, if X is preferred to Y, and Y is preferred to Z, then X is preferred to Z. How does the group rank these preferences, using majority rule? Since A and C prefer X to Y, the group prefers X to Y by majority rule. Since A and B prefer Y to Z, the group prefers Y to Z by majority rule. Since the group prefers X to Y and Y to Z, one would assume that the group prefers X to Z. B and C prefer Z to X, however, so by majority rule, the group prefers Z to X. One arrives at two results, one in which the group prefers X to Z, and another in which the group prefers Z to X.

PROPOSED SOLUTIONS

Several solutions to this problem have been advanced, but none is entirely satisfactory. One answer states that all three choices are equally preferred by the group, but that is not true; in fact, any given choice may be beaten by another choice as the top preference. Another answer suggests changing the voting rules so that more than a majority is needed to reach a group preference. Kenneth Arrow has shown in a general proof, however, that *any* decision rule based upon individual choices may fall victim to this problem, if three or more choices and three or more individuals are involved. Another answer suggests that one should merely use the first result derived, but this solution leaves the result dependent upon the order in which alternatives are considered. For example, if the group considers X and Y first, X is preferred to Y; if the group then considers Y and Z, Y is preferred to Z, and hence, the group prefers X to Y and Y to Z. If the group considers Z and X first, however, Z is preferred to X; if the group then considers X and Y, X is preferred to Y, and hence, the group prefers Z to X and X to Y.

The ordering of these alternatives has been changed entirely simply by changing the sequence in which the alternatives were considered. For those who value majority rule as an ethical means of reaching decisions, this problem gives dictatorial power over voting results to the individuals who decide the sequence for voting on alternatives.

Finally, one may simply say that it is impossible to reach a decision. One may then, however, define this as alternative W and rank it as the least preferred alternative for all three members. Hence, all three persons would wind up with gridlock, their last choice. Majority rule thus may prevent individuals

from reaching a majority decision; indeed, if one goes back to the original three-person problem, any given ordering of X, Y, and Z would mean that one of the three individuals (A, B, or C) will get his or her way despite the disapproval of a majority of the other group members.

PROBLEMS AS "PARADOXES"

The paradox in both of these problems is evident. In the first case, self-interested action prevents the creation of collective goods that would serve all individuals' self-interests. In the second case, majority rule may result in decisions that violate the majority will or in gridlock, which is the alternative least preferred by all. By pursuing self-interest or majority rule, one arrives at conclusions in both cases that contradict one's original rules. The ethical problem here is evident: In both cases, individuals follow the rational pursuit of their own self-interests and discover that rationality alone is insufficient grounds for taking group action or reaching a group decision. These paradoxes illustrate that rationality alone cannot bear the burden of generating an ethical consensus about the correct forms of action or decisions in a society.

Frank Louis Rusciano

FURTHER READING

Abrams, Robert. *Foundations of Political Analysis: An Introduction to the Theory of Collective Choice.* New York: Columbia University Press, 1980.

Arrow, Kenneth J. *Social Choice and Individual Values.* New York: John Wiley & Sons, 1963.

Barry, Brian. *Economics, Sociologists, and Democracy.* Chicago: University of Chicago Press, 1978.

Barry, Brian, and Russell Hardin, eds. *Rational Man and Irrational Society?* Beverly Hills, Calif.: Sage, 1982.

Downs, Anthony. *An Economic Theory of Democracy.* New York: Harper & Row, 1957.

Falletta, Nicholas. *The Paradoxicon.* New York: John Wiley & Sons, 1990.

Hofstadter, Douglas R. *Gödel, Escher, Bach: An Eternal Golden Braid.* New York: Random House, 1983.

Rusciano, Frank Louis. *Isolation and Paradox: Defining "the Public" in Modern Political Analysis.* Westport, Conn.: Greenwood Press, 1989.

Schelling, Thomas. *Micromotives and Macrobehavior.* New York: W. W. Norton, 1977.

Sorensen, Roy. *A Brief History of the Paradox: Philosophy and the Labyrinths of the Mind.* New York: Oxford University Press, 2003.

SEE ALSO: Jesus Christ; Mysticism; Platonic ethics; Politics; Prisoner's dilemma; Reason and rationality; Socrates; Temptation; Tolerance; Truth.

Parenting

DEFINITION: Legal and moral obligations that parents have with respect to their own children

TYPE OF ETHICS: Children's rights

SIGNIFICANCE: Several important ethical issues concern the moral dimensions of parent-child relationships, including the amount of control parents should exercise over their children, the amount of state and social intervention into the parent-child relationship that is permissible, and what special rights and obligations parents possess.

Explorations of the moral dimensions of parent-child relationships are motivated, in part, by the widespread physical and emotional abuse of children. Some philosophers, such as Jan Narveson, hold the view that children are the property of their parents. This sort of view has an affinity with the belief that parents should be able do nearly anything to their children, free from the intervention of others.

Some of the modern philosophical interest in exploring the parent-child relationship is also motivated by the value of parenthood for those adults who are or who want to become parents. At the beginning of the twenty-first century, several debates were going on among philosophers and other professionals involved with children and family life concerning the justification of the paternalistic treatment of children, the level of permissible intrusions into parent-child relationships, and what it is that makes for good parents.

PATERNALISM

The most prevalent view on parenting, voiced by philosophers such as John Locke and John Stuart Mill, is that parents must treat their children in paternalistic ways. That is, parents must often make choices on behalf of their children that go against their children's wishes or limit their freedom, but which are intended to benefit them. Paternalistic treatment of children is said to be justified by the children's lack of knowledge, experience, and moral development.

In contrast, some authorities, such as Richard Farson, believe that children should be granted the same legal and moral status that adults possess. That is, children should have the same freedoms and responsibilities as adults.

PRIVACY AND FAMILY LIFE

Family relationships are like other relationships, insofar as part of what makes them valuable is that they are intimate interpersonal relationships in which individuals share themselves with those who are close to them. Parents and children can greatly benefit from the goods that arise within family life. In order to secure these goods, some level of freedom from outside interference may be required. Some amount of privacy may be necessary so that families can enjoy the intimacy and meaning that family relationships are able to provide.

The state may have an interest in allowing for diverse parenting styles and creating a social system in which families can flourish. Difficulties arise, however, when respect for family privacy allows parents to engage in physical and emotional abuse or neglect, leaving many children at risk of being harmed, often in very serious ways. Much controversy surrounds the issue of how best to respect the privacy of families while also minimizing possible risks to children. Some, such as Narveson, argue that the state should generally refrain from intervening in the lives of families. In contrast to this view, William Irvine argues that parents should be required to obtain parenting licenses before being allowed to raise children. David Archard argues that closer monitoring of families by state and local agencies is desirable.

THE RIGHTS AND OBLIGATIONS OF PARENTS

Most parents believe that they have obligations to protect and provide for their children by giving them basic care and providing for their basic needs. Parents who abuse or neglect their children arguably fail to fulfill their obligations as parents. Irvine is representative of many philosophers in his belief that parents should see themselves as stewards of their children, and that parents who see themselves this way are altruistic with respect to their children, as they place their children's interests before their own. They thus tend to see themselves as having many parental duties but few parental rights.

According to Irvine, parents are morally obliged to help their children develop their talents, skills, and abilities; to prevent harm from coming to them; to educate them; to help them develop into autonomous beings; and to provide them with as much freedom as possible regarding their future lives.

Many psychologists say that parents who love their children should pursue intimate and honest relationships with them and seek to impart to them some vision of a good life. Children, at least at a young age, need this sort of care and guidance. It may include encouraging children to understand and adopt the political, moral, and religious beliefs of their parents. One limit that is often imposed on this aspect of the parent-child relationship is that parents must not indoctrinate their children. That is, it is wrong for parents to force their beliefs on their children. Instead, parents will ideally explain and perhaps even advocate their own political, moral, and religious views, while at the same time respecting the rights of their children to choose different paths. This is generally thought to be important because parents must respect the autonomy of their children, accepting the possibility that their children may adopt and pursue a different view of the good life. However, when this occurs, the general view of psychologists is that parents should continue to pursue loving relationships with their children, given the fact that most children need such a relationship with their parents.

Michael W. Austin

FURTHER READING

Aiken, William, and Hugh LaFollette, eds. *Whose Child? Children's Rights, Parental Authority, and State Power.* Totowa, N.J.: Littlefield, Adams, 1980.

Archard, David. *Children: Rights and Childhood.* New York: Routledge, 1993.

Blustein, Jeffrey. *Parents and Children.* New York: Oxford University Press, 1982.

Farson, Richard. *Birthrights.* New York: Macmillan, 1974.

Irvine, William. *Doing Right by Children: Reflections on the Nature of Childhood and the Obligations of Parenting.* St. Paul, Minn.: Paragon House, 2001.

_____. *The Politics of Parenting.* St. Paul, Minn.: Paragon House, 2003.

Ladd, Rosalind Ekman, ed. *Children's Rights Re-Visioned.* Belmont, Calif.: Wadsworth, 1996.

Purdy, Laura M. *In Their Best Interest? The Case Against Equal Rights for Children.* Ithaca, N.Y.: Cornell University Press, 1992.

SEE ALSO: Birth control; Child abuse; Child support; Children; Children's Bureau; Children's television; Divorce; Family; Godparents; Women's ethics.

Parole of convicted prisoners

DEFINITION: Conditional release of prisoners who are serving indeterminate or unexpired sentences, usually based upon their good behavior during their incarceration

TYPE OF ETHICS: Legal and judicial ethics

SIGNIFICANCE: The early release of convicted criminals back into society presents a variety of ethical problems relating to the rights of both members of society and the parolees themselves.

Convicts who are let out of prison before serving their full sentences may pose dangers to society, and they themselves may believe that they will not be held fully accountable for their actions because of their early release. Moreover, the victims of their crimes and their relatives may feel that justice is not being served when the convicts are released early and may also feel endangered by the convicts' freedom.

Public concerns about dangers posed by paroled convicts are not without foundation. Studies of former convicts indicate that parolees released from prison have a high probability of ending up in prison again. Recidivism rates toward the end of the twentieth century were close to 80 percent—in other words, four out of every five prisoners released from prison either violate the terms of their paroles or commit new crimes and are returned to prison.

At least three factors contribute to the high rates of recidivism. First, prisons are mislabeled as correctional institutes, when in fact they are often breeding grounds for crime. New prisoners learn more about crime from veteran convicts inside prison walls. Secondly, parolees often cannot find satisfactory employment after they are released from prison. As a result, they tend to return to criminal activity, which in turn returns them to prison. Finally, some parolees simply cannot adapt to society, in which they are stigmatized and stereotyped.

TOUGHENED LAWS

As a result of growing public weariness with increasing crime rates during the last decades of the twentieth century, a number of states took tougher stances against crime. Some states adopted "three-strikes" laws, which impose mandatory twenty-five-year-to-life sentences on persons convicted of their third felony offense. Other states have adopted "truth in sentencing" laws that require convicts to serve most of their full sentences, regardless of whether they are model prisoners or not.

These tougher laws have led to significant increases in U.S. prison populations, which totaled more than one million inmates in 2003. In the midst of the "get tough" climate, a number of federal courts have begun ordering early-release programs because of prison overcrowding. These court interventions have combined with economic downturns in state economies to lead to early-release programs.

The growing numbers of parolees have focused increasing attention on the question of whether it is ethical to release prisoners who have not served their full terms, especially when their victims and their relatives believe that justice is not being fully carried out. At the same time, equally valid questions may be asked as to whether it is ethical to keep convicts in prison indefinitely when they have been model prisoners and might become productive members of society outside prison.

Mfanya D. Tryman

FURTHER READING

Champion, Dean J. *Probation, Parole, and Community Corrections.* Upper Saddle River, N.J.: Prentice Hall, 2002.

Lamm, Richard D., and Richard A. Caldwell. *Hard Choices.* Denver: Center for Public Policy and Contemporary Issues, 1991.

Petersilia, Joan. *When Prisoners Come Home: Pa-role and Prisoner Reentry.* New York: Oxford University Press, 2003.

Sykes, Charles. *A Nation of Victims.* New York: St. Martin's Press, 1992.

SEE ALSO: Capital punishment; Criminal punishment; Deterrence; Erroneous convictions; Forgiveness; Punishment; Reconciliation; Three-strikes laws.

Pascal, Blaise

IDENTIFICATION: French philosopher
BORN: June 19, 1623, Clermont-Ferrand, France
DIED: August 19, 1662, Paris, France
TYPE OF ETHICS: Renaissance and Restoration history
SIGNIFICANCE: The author of *The Provincial Letters* (*Lettres provinciales*, 1656-1657) and *Pensées* (1670), Pascal developed persuasive arguments against compromising one's moral values in order to attain political or social influence.

Although Blaise Pascal was an important mathematician and physicist, he has remained famous above all for his eloquent writings on the moral obligations that accompany a commitment to Christianity. Pascal believed that an acceptance of divine authority enables people to develop an objective foundation for moral values. The problem of ethical subjectivity disappears once one accepts the revealed and liberating truths to be found in the Bible and in the exegetical works of respected church fathers such as Saint Jerome and Saint Augustine. Because of the clarity and the depth of his analysis of ethical questions, Pascal has remained one of the most influential and controversial French writers, even several centuries after his death in 1662.

THE PROVINCIAL LETTERS

Beginning in 1646, Pascal and his sister Jacqueline Périer became very interested in the Catholic religious movement associated with the monastery, convent, and school at Port-Royal. The priests and nuns at Port-Royal were referred to as Jansenists because a major influence on their view of Christian spirituality had been a 1640 book on Saint Augustine by a Dutch theologian named Cornelius Jansen. The

Blaise Pascal. (Library of Congress)

Jansenists encouraged personal spiritual development and denounced all attempts to allow worldly values to interfere with the purity of a total commitment to Christian values.

Books by such important Jansenist theologians as Antoine Arnauld and Pierre Nicole provoked an intense controversy with French Jesuits, who were then very influential at the court of King Louis XIV and with French bishops and priests. The basic disagreements between the Jesuits and the Jansenists dealt with the theological concept of grace and the use of casuistry, which is the practice by which a priest applies general moral standards to individual cases in order to determine if a specific action was sinful or if a repentance was sincere.

Between January, 1656, and March, 1657, Pascal published eighteen anonymous letters that were addressed "to a Jesuit provincial by one of his friends." Ever since its creation during the 1540's by Saint Ignatius Loyola, the Jesuit order has been administratively divided into broad geographical areas called provinces whose spiritual leaders are called provincials. The eighteen *Provincial Letters* are masterpieces of polemic rhetoric. Pascal sought to diminish the growing influence of French Jesuits by attribut-

ing to the entire order rather extreme positions taken by certain Jesuit theologians such as Antonio Escobar y Mendoza and Luis de Molina, who had argued that specific actions that most Christians would consider to be patently wrong would not be considered sinful if the motivations of the people who did those things were taken into account.

Pascal believed that such an approach to ethics was very dangerous because it could lead people to justify actions that were clearly incompatible with God's teachings. In his seventh Provincial Letter, for example, Pascal denounced efforts by Escobar y Mendoza and Molina to justify dueling. A duelist might well claim that his intention was not to kill his adversary but to defend his own honor, but Pascal ridiculed such convenient and insincere excuses designed to disregard God's straightforward commandment: "Thou shalt not kill." Although Pascal was clearly unfair in associating all Jesuits with the radical positions of such theologians, his *Provincial Letters* did denounce very effectively the danger of moral laxism and the pernicious belief that "the end justifies the means."

THOUGHTS

During the last few years of his life, Pascal was writing "an apology for the Christian religion," but extremely poor health required him to rest frequently and this prevented him from writing for extended periods of time. He was, however, able to compose eight hundred fragments that were discovered and edited after his death by his nephew Étienne Périer, who called these fragments *Thoughts* (*Pensées*). Despite the uncompleted nature of *Thoughts*, it contains profound insights into the myriad relationships between ethical and religious problems. Unlike his fellow mathematician and philosopher René Descartes, who had argued in his 1637 book *Discourse on Method* that logic alone sufficed to explore moral problems, Pascal was convinced that only an acceptance of the revealed truths of Christianity could enable him to recognize the moral foundation for a just society.

Pascal stated that there were basically two ways of dealing with moral problems. By means of "the spirit of geometry" ("*l'esprit de géométrie*") one examines in a purely logical manner the many steps that are involved in resolving ethical questions. "The spirit of insight" ("*l'esprit de finesse*") helps one to recognize intuitively that certain actions are morally wrong whereas others are morally correct. Although he did not deny the importance of logical reasoning for discussions of ethical problems, Pascal sensed that most moral decisions are inspired by intuitive feelings that are formed by one's religious training and by the diversity of one's experiences. In *Thoughts*, Pascal appealed to the deep emotional and psychological reactions of his readers in order to persuade them that an acceptance of "the grandeur of man with God" and "the misery of man without God" will lead people to embrace those religious and ethical values that are presented in the Bible.

Edmund J. Campion

FURTHER READING

Davidson, Hugh. *Blaise Pascal*. Boston: Twayne, 1983.

Hammond, Nicholas, ed. *The Cambridge Companion to Pascal*. New York: Cambridge University Press, 2003.

Krailsheimer, A. J. *Pascal*. New York: Hill & Wang, 1980.

MacKenzie, Charles. *Pascal's Anguish and Joy*. New York: Philosophical Library, 1973.

Mortimer, Ernest. *Blaise Pascal*. New York: Harper, 1959.

Nelson, Robert. *Pascal: Adversary and Advocate*. Cambridge, Mass.: Harvard University Press, 1981.

Pascal, Blaise. *"The Provincial Letters"; "Pensées"; and "Scientific Treatises."* Translated by W. F. Trotter, Thomas M'Crie, and Richard Scofield. 2d ed. Chicago: Encyclopedia Britannica, 1990.

Topliss, Patricia. *The Rhetoric of Pascal*. Leicester, England: Leicester University Press, 1966.

SEE ALSO: Calvin, John; Casuistry; Christian ethics; God; Justice; Revelation; Ten Commandments.

Passions and emotions

DEFINITION: Irrational, subjective, deeply felt, partly mental, and partly physical sentiments or sensations; feelings

TYPE OF ETHICS: Personal and social ethics

SIGNIFICANCE: The passions and emotions are often contrasted with reason and rationality as the two forces influencing moral decisions. Their ethical import is a matter of controversy: For some, the emotions are deceptive, and dispassionate reasoning is the only way to discern moral truth. For others, passion constitutes moral truth and the denial of emotion in the name of reason is a dehumanizing and immoral act.

Emotions add color to the world of experience. They motivate people to approach or avoid something, generally in an energetic way. They are made up of four components: conscious or subjective experience, bodily or physiological arousal, characteristics or overt behavior, and changes in thoughts or cognitions.

On the feeling or subjective level, emotions have elements of pleasure (or displeasure), intensity, and complexity. Pleasant or positive emotions tend to enhance an individual's sense of well-being and promote constructive relationships with others. Unpleasant or negative emotions, in contrast, tend to decrease an individual's sense of well-being and create disturbed relationships with others. Intensity is often reflected in the words used to describe emotions; for example, uneasy, fretful, tense, apprehensive, tremulous, agitated, panicky, and terrified. The complexity of emotions means that one person's sense of joy is different from another's. Thus, emotions have a private, personal, and unique component. They are complex subjective feelings.

On the physiological level, emotions are accompanied by bodily sensations or physiological arousal. The physiological arousal occurs mainly through the actions of the autonomic nervous system, which regulates the activity of glands, smooth muscles, and blood vessels. The autonomic responses that accompany emotions are ultimately controlled in the brain by the hypothalamus, the amygdala, and the adjacent structures in the limbic system.

PHYSIOLOGICAL AND BEHAVIORAL CHANGES

There are several different types of physiological changes that accompany emotions. One change is in galvanic skin response, the electrical conductivity of the skin that occurs when sweat glands increase their activity. A second change is in the pulse rate. When a person is very angry or afraid, for example, his or her heart may accelerate from about 72 beats per minute to as many as 180 beats per minute. A third change is in the blood pressure, which may rise alarmingly when a person is angry or afraid. A fourth change is in the breathing rate, which typically becomes rapid and uneven when a person is experiencing strong emotion. A fifth change is in muscular tension, which is particularly prominent when the emotion is intense fear or anger.

Other changes that accompany emotions include inhibition of salivation, pupil dilation, and inhibition of digestive processes. The physiological changes that accompany love, joy, or other emotions may be smaller and more subtle than those accompanying anger and fear.

On the behavioral level, people reveal their emotions through characteristic overt expressions, such as smiles, frowns, furrowed brows, clenched fists, slumped shoulders, and changes in posture and tone of voice. When people are sad, for example, they tend to slouch and to speak in a lower, less variable pitch than the one they use when they are angry or afraid. People reveal their emotions in their body language, or nonverbal behavior. Some researchers argue that no body movement is accidental or meaningless. Rather, one communicates something in the slightest movement, even though one may be unaware of it.

On the cognitive level, emotions are accompanied by changes in thoughts, beliefs, and expectations. When happy, people become more optimistic; when sad, they are likely to see the negative sides of situations. In general, people's thoughts are guided by and consistent with their emotions.

THE BASIC EMOTIONS

Like colors, emotions cover a wide spectrum. There are six basic emotions: love, joy, surprise, anger, sadness, and fear. Three dimensions on which these basic emotions vary are evaluation (positive or negative), potency (strong or weak), and activity (relatively high or low in arousal). Some theorists include disgust and contempt as primary emotions. Others add shame, contempt, interest, guilt, anticipation, acceptance, and distress as primary emotions. Still other theorists reject the concept of basic emotions altogether. People experience many different emotions. Some theorists propose that many emotions are produced by blends and variations in intensity of primary emotions, like colors on a color wheel.

What causes emotions? Several theories have been developed to answer this question. One theory is that they result from specific physiological changes, with each emotion having a different physiological basis. Proposed independently during the late nineteenth century by William James and Carl Lange, this theory stood common sense on its head. Everyday logic suggests that when a person stumbles onto a rattlesnake in the woods, the conscious experience of fear leads to visceral arousal (the fight-or-flight response). This theory, in contrast, asserts the opposite: The perception of visceral arousal leads to the conscious experience of fear. Thus, this theory asserts that the person becomes afraid because the sight of the rattlesnake causes muscles, skin, and internal organs to undergo changes. Fear is simply the awareness of these changes. The James-Lange theory of emotions emphasizes the physiological determinants of emotion.

The James-Lange theory of emotions has two overall criticisms. First, anger, fear, and sadness seem to share similar physiological patterns of arousal, although recent research has detected some subtle differences in the patterns of visceral arousal that accompany basic emotions. Second, people with severe spinal cord injuries are deprived of most feedback from their autonomic nervous systems, yet they still experience emotions. Physiologists generally agree that physiological arousal influences the intensity of emotions, but not the emotions themselves.

A second theory of emotions asserts that when a person is emotional, two areas of the brain, the thalamus and the cerebral cortex, are stimulated simultaneously. Stimulation of the cortex produces the emotional component of the experience, whereas stimulation of the thalamus produces physiological changes in the sympathetic nervous system. Accordingly, emotional feelings accompany physiological changes; they do not produce them. This theory of emotions holds that they are physiologically similar to, and occur sooner than, changes in the internal organs.

Proposed by physiologists Walter Cannon and Philip Bard during the 1920's, this theory has two criticisms. First, physiological changes in the brain do not happen exactly simultaneously. Second, people often report that they have an experience and then later have physiological and emotional reactions to it. For example, they have a near-accident in a car, and only later become very frightened.

FACIAL FEEDBACK

A third theory of emotions is that they are caused by facial feedback. The idea is that sensations from the movement of facial muscles and skin are interpreted by the brain and result in emotion. According to this somatic view, smiles, frowns, and furrowed brows help to create the subjective experience of various emotions. Consistent with this view, research shows that if people are induced to frown, they tend to report that they feel angry. Furthermore, people who have been blind since birth smile and frown much like everyone else, even though they have never seen a smile or frown. Also, infants only a few hours old show distinct expressions of emotions that closely match those of adults, and infants recognize facial expressions in others at a very young age. Thus, infant and cross-cultural similarities in emotional expression support the facial feedback or evolutionary theory of emotions.

Originally proposed by Charles Darwin, this theory asserts that emotions developed because they have adaptive value. They signal an intent to act and prepare the individual to act. Fear, for example, would help an organism avoid danger and thus would aid in survival. This view of emotions is that they are a product of the evolution of facial expressions, which were our ancestors' primary mode of communication before language developed.

This facial feedback theory of emotions suffers from the criticism that there is little evidence that specific facial feedback initiates specific emotions. Researchers generally agree that facial feedback and physiological arousal influence the intensity of emotions, but not the emotions themselves.

OTHER THEORIES

A fourth theory of emotions is that interpreting or appraising a situation as having a positive or negative impact on one's life results in a subjective feeling that is called emotion. The idea is that a stimulus causes physiological arousal. The arousal creates a need for an explanation of some kind, which the person makes from the situational cues available and from his or her cognitive processes, such as thoughts, interpretations, and appraisals. This explanation results in emotion. This theory of emotion stresses that there are two components to emotions: a cognitive component and a situational component.

This theory of emotion, which can be traced to psychologists Stanley Schachter and Jerome Singer during the early 1960's, was revised by Arnold Lazarus in 1991 to recognize the fact that emotions may initially occur without physiological arousal. Lazarus also believed that each emotion has its own specific relational theme, or person-environment relation, which involves benefit in the case of positive emotions and harm in the case of negative ones.

To test this theory of emotion, Schachter and Singer conducted an experiment in which they told volunteers that they were testing the effects of a vitamin supplement. Instead, these volunteers were injected with epinephrine, a powerful stimulant that increases physiological arousal. The volunteer students were unaware of the typical bodily effects of the adrenaline. To see if the setting in which the volunteers experienced their arousal influenced how they interpreted their emotions, Schachter and Singer hired undergraduates and paid them to act either happy and relaxed or sad, depressed, and angry. These hired students, called stooges, pretended that they were volunteers in the same drug study. Instead, they were given injections of saltwater, not epinephrine. Their emotional behavior was strictly an act.

The happy stooges shot wads of paper into a wastepaper basket and flew airplanes around the room. The unhappy stooges complained about the questionnaire they had to fill out and voiced their dissatisfaction with the experiment. All the volunteers showed increased physiological arousal. Those with happy stooges reported that the drug made them feel good; those with the sad, angry stooges reported that the drug made them feel anger. Schachter and Singer concluded that the physiological feelings that accompanied both joy and anger were the same, but the label attached to the emotion depended on the person's situation.

These theories of emotions may all be partly right, but no one theory fits all the data. Physiological and cognitive influences interact in complex ways to produce emotional experiences.

FUNCTIONS OF EMOTIONS

Emotions have three main functions. One function of emotions is that they help people adapt and survive. For example, crying alerts others that one is in pain or discomfort, and being in love fosters social interactions. A second function of emotions is that they signal that something important is happening and rouse one to action. In an evolutionary sense, some emotions are part of an emergency arousal system that increases the chances of survival by energizing, directing, and sustaining adaptive behaviors. For example, being afraid may motivate one to run away from a dangerous bear that is running toward one, and being angry may cause one to work harder to reach one's goals. Other emotions, such as sadness, relief, and contentment, may involve an integrated pattern that includes a decrease in arousal and behavioral intensity.

Although rousing people to action may be positive, it may also be negative, so that emotions may disrupt behavior. The relationship between physiological arousal that accompanies an emotion and task performance is known as the Yerkes-Dodson law, which states that performance on a task depends on the amount of physiological arousal and the difficulty of the task. In general, for many tasks, moderate arousal helps performance. For new or difficult tasks, low arousal facilitates performance; for easy or well-learned tasks, high arousal facilitates performance. For example, high arousal would interfere with performance on a difficult test, but it facilitates signing one's own name legibly. In contrast, low to medium arousal would result in better performance on a difficult test, but it might lead one to sign one's name illegibly.

Emotions rouse people to action in another sense as well: The expectation of pleasant emotions serves as an incentive. Many purposeful, motivated behaviors are designed to induce feelings of happiness, joy, excitement, or pride.

A third function of emotions is to help people communicate by sending social signals. They inform others about one's internal state and intentions. Many facial expressions, such as happiness, anger, sadness, fear, disgust, and surprise, are recognized as emotional expressions by people in widely varying cultures. In fact, emotional facial expressions are strikingly similar in different cultures. Yet different cultures encourage or discourage the expression of some emotions more than others. Adults in all societies learn to suppress some of their emotional responses or to mask them with voluntary control of facial muscles. This masking is never perfect, and other facial muscles can give away true feelings.

Influences on Emotions

Different factors influence emotion. Personality and motivational factors affect emotion by influencing what situations people expose themselves to and how they think about those situations, as well as physiological and behavioral responses. Therefore, personality variables can predispose people to experience certain kinds of emotions. For example, extroverted people are likely to experience strong positive emotions in response to positive events but less-intense reactions to negative events. In contrast, people who are high in neuroticism experience weak positive emotional responses to positive events but strong negative responses to negative events.

Learning also influences emotion. Cultures have different standards for defining the good, the bad, and the ugly. For example, physical features that provoke sexual arousal and feelings of infatuation in one culture (such as scars) may elicit feelings of disgust in another culture.

Biological factors also influence emotion. The concept of preparedness suggests that people may be biologically primed to experience fear in response to certain stimuli, such as heights or snakes.

Intrapsychic factors may also predispose people to certain emotions. For example, anger that has been stored up since childhood may be released if a situation reminds one of that internal conflict. Also, psychological defenses sometimes predispose people to transform one emotional response into another, more acceptable one. Thus, anger may be transformed into sadness, or sexual feelings into fear.

Emotions do not occur in a vacuum. Rather, they always have objects. People are not simply angry, afraid, proud, or in love. They are angry at something or someone, afraid of something or someone, and so forth. Furthermore, the stimuli that trigger emotional responses are not always external. Sometimes they are internal, occurring in the form of images and memories. Usually, people can identify the eliciting stimuli, but not always.

Emotions are shaped by one's biological and psychological predispositions, by what one learns in one's environment, and by one's personality and motivations. One experiences them in response to internal or external objects. They give life color.

Lillian M. Range

FURTHER READING

Carlson, John G., and Elaine Hatfield. *Psychology of Emotion*. Fort Worth, Tex.: Harcourt Brace Jovanovich, 1992. This text is an outstanding summary of theory and research on emotion. It has a readable and informative description of the biology and psychology of emotion. Contains many interesting examples and practical applications.

Cottingham, John. *Philosophy and the Good Life: Reason and the Passions in Greek, Cartesian, and Psychoanalytic Ethics*. New York: Cambridge University Press, 1998. An analysis of the attempts of three different schools of thought to reconcile the tension between reason and passion in human experience. Cottingham discusses the place of passion in classical Greek thought, modern philosophy, and psychoanalysis—the latter two of which are usually portrayed as either dismissive or contemptuous of emotion. An important rereading of canonical sources.

Ekman, P. *Telling Lies: Clues to Deceit in the Marketplace, Politics, and Marriage*. New York: W. W. Norton, 1985. Describes the evidence on complex nonverbal patterns that reveal emotions that are different from what people may be saying. Attempts to explain how to accomplish the very difficult task of detecting deceit in business and in life.

Izard, C. E. "The Structure and Functions of Emotions: Implications for Cognition, Motivation, and Personality." In *The G. Stanley Hall Lecture Series*, edited by I. S. Cohen. Washington, D.C.: American Psychological Association, 1989. Provides an overview of current issues in research on emotions, including Izard's theory, facial feedback theory, and the development of emotions in children.

Lazarus, R. S. *Emotion and Adaptation*. New York: Oxford University Press, 1991. This monumental work contains reviews and distillations of Lazarus's work and that of others. It arrives at a new statement of cognitive appraisal theory.

McNaughton, N. *Biology and Emotion*. Cambridge, England: Cambridge University Press, 1989. A thoughtful, highly readable, up-to-date integration of evolutionary and physiological approaches to the understanding of emotion.

Nussbaum, Martha C. *Upheavals of Thought: The Intelligence of Emotions*. New York: Cambridge University Press, 2001. An extensive and meticulously argued work by one of the most important modern philosophers of law, emotion, and ethics. Nussbaum argues that emotion rather than reason is the most important register through which we understand and engage with the world, and through which we make ethical decisions.

Plutchik, R., and H. Kellerman, eds. *Emotion: Theory, Research, and Experience*. Vol. 1. San Diego, Calif.: Academic Press, 1990. Offers up-to-date and comprehensive reviews of the scientific literature for the field of emotion.

Prokhovnik, Raia. *Rational Woman: A Feminist Critique of Dichotomy*. New York: Routledge, 1999. An attack upon the classical mind/body dualism, and upon the traditional mapping of reason onto mind and emotion onto body. Demonstrates the ways in which gender hierarchies have been perpetuated by assigning the body to woman and the mind to man. Argues for a unification of these categories, rather than seeing them in terms of hierarchy.

Strongman, K. T. *The Psychology of Emotion: Theories of Emotion in Perspective*. 4th ed. New York: John Wiley & Sons, 1996. Offers a historical overview of theories of emotion, written at a level appropriate for advanced undergraduates. Also includes information on the role of cognition in emotion.

SEE ALSO: Anger; Compassion; Desire; Intuitionist ethics; James, William; Love; Moral-sense theories; Psychology; Reason and rationality; Self-control.

Paternalism

DEFINITION: Use of coercion or deception to interfere with or frustrate the choices and actions of underlings for their own good

TYPE OF ETHICS: Personal and social ethics

SIGNIFICANCE: Although aimed at protecting or promoting someone else's own good, acting paternalistically may compromise the individual's moral autonomy.

The word "paternalism" connotes attitudes that are fatherly or parental, combining the element of looking out for the interests of a child with the further element of doing so over the wishes of the child. Paternalism is the extension of such paternal concern toward children to other relationships, usually involving those in some position of authority. Paternalism may appear in the relation of government officials to citizens but can also extend to employer-employee and doctor-patient relationships.

John Stuart Mill provided the classic discussion of the issue of paternalism between society and the individual in *On Liberty* (1859). Mill argued that the only sound reason for society to coerce an adult to do or refrain from some action is to prevent harm to others. The person's own good is not a good reason to justify societal interference with a person's liberty of action. Mill stated that individuals should be "sovereign" over their own bodies and minds.

Mill was ready to accept the implications of his antipaternalist position. He thought that adults should be free to engage in conduct that endangered themselves, such as drunkenness or using addictive drugs such as opium. Society may warn individuals of the harm and even seek to persuade them to refrain from such dangerous activities, but should never resort to force. By extension, a strict opponent of paternalism would oppose such safety measures as laws requiring people to wear seat belts while riding in automobiles or safety helmets while riding motorcycles.

Opponents of paternalism use a variety of arguments. Mill thought that a free society that left individuals to decide matters relating to their own good would lead to greater social progress and individual well-being. Some have argued that human freedom and autonomy are importantly valuable in themselves, and that undue interference involves a kind of disrespect to human dignity, similar to treating adults as children. Most defenders of paternalism counter that at least limited forms of paternalistic interference are both reasonable and beneficial. It is difficult to confine the costs of dangerous and self-harmful behavior to the individuals involved. Also, even adults can use guidance and pressure from society in order to avoid the sometimes serious and irreversible harms that may follow lapses in judgment and the taking of foolish risks.

Although most discussion of paternalism takes place within the context of interference with liberty, it can be an important issue in other contexts as well. In medical practice, for example, a dominant model for the physician-patient relationship was historically paternalistic, with the implication that doctors might withhold information or even deceive patients for their own good. The paternalistic model in medicine, in the workplace, and in colleges and universities has waned due to increased autonomy concerns on the part of patients, employees, and students.

Mario Morelli

FURTHER READING

Kleinig, John. *Paternalism*. Totowa, N.J.: Rowman & Allanheld, 1984.

Mill, John Stuart. *On Liberty, and Other Essays.* Edited by John Gray. New York: Oxford University Press, 1998.

Sartorius, Rolf, ed. *Paternalism*. Minneapolis: University of Minnesota Press, 1983.

SEE ALSO: Elitism; Libertarianism; Mill, John Stuart; Parenting; Physician-patient relationship.

Patriotism

DEFINITION: Love of, or loyalty to, one's own country

TYPE OF ETHICS: Personal and social ethics

SIGNIFICANCE: Patriotism's moral status is a matter of controversy on two levels. First, its traditional theoretical status as a virtue has been questioned by modern philosophers. Second, there is significant debate over what genuine or authentic patriotism actually entails in practice.

The moral significance of patriotism may be approached in the first instance by asking this question: Is patriotism the positive form of an emotion or ideology whose negative form is nationalism? Or is patriotism simply a euphemism for nationalism? If patriotism is merely a polite term for nationalism, then it is difficult to defend as anything other than an unreasoning prejudice. If, on the other hand, nationalism is actually the corrupted form of the properly noble emotion of genuine patriotism, then it may be appropriate to think of patriotism not only as a virtue, but as a socially vital value.

What, then, would constitute a noble and virtuous form of nationalism? Patriotism is most often defined as love of country. Such a definition is deceptively simple, however. Indeed, it is quite ambiguous. What kind of love should one feel for a nation? Is it the same sort of love that one feels for a sports team one supports, or a food one likes to eat? Is it the sort of love that one feels for a friend? A family member? Whatever explicit answer one may give to this question upon considered reflection, it is too often the case that the implicit and unconsidered answer evident in the behavior of professed patriots is that a country is like a sports team. Sports fans know the faults of their teams better than anyone, and they are perfectly happy to list them in private, among like-minded fans. If confronted by external criticism, however, everything changes. Suddenly, the team can do no wrong, and even minor criticisms, however accurate, become unjustified attacks upon the honor and dignity of the team and all its true supporters. Loyalty to a team is measured by the loudness of one's cheering and the staunchness with which one refutes the team's critics, whatever the merits of their criticism.

Now consider the sort of love one feels for a friend. It is intimate, based on a genuine interaction between both participants in the relationship, and because of that, it comes over time to be quite nuanced. Interpersonal love and loyalty are difficult values to negotiate. They do not admit of the simple formulas of fandom. One might say of an errant friend, as a patriot would of a nation, "He's my friend, right or wrong." That statement, however, would be the beginning of a conversation, not the end of one. It would be an expression of reassurance to prepare the way for the hard work of friendship, for the rigors of determining and then fulfilling the specific and complex obligations imposed by one's loyalty.

It is unclear whether patriotism can ever be accounted a virtue. It certainly seems necessarily to entail treating one's fellow citizens as superior to other people. It seems, moreover, almost always to involve the foreclosure of at least some avenues of national reform and improvement, such as just distribution of resources in a capitalist nation, or separation of church and state in a theocracy. If there is moral value in patriotism, however, it is to be found in the analogy to friendship. If one could take one's patriotism as an impetus to explore one's relationship to one's nation, rather than as itself constituting a given and immutable relationship, patriotism could provide a basis for moral practice, thereby acquiring moral worth.

Andy Perry

FURTHER READING

Levi, Margaret. *Consent, Dissent, and Patriotism*. New York: Cambridge University Press, 1997.

MacIntyre, Alasdair. "Is Patriotism a Virtue?" In *Theorizing Citizenship*, edited by Ronald Beiner. Albany: State University of New York Press, 1995.

Nathanson, Stephen. *Patriotism, Morality, and Peace*. Lanham, Md.: Rowman & Littlefield, 1993.

Nussbaum, Martha C. *For Love of Country? Debating the Limits of Patriotism*. Edited by Joshua Cohen. Reprint. Boston: Beacon Press, 2002.

Primoratz, Igor, ed. *Patriotism*. Amherst, N.Y.: Humanity Books, 2002.

Vincent, Andrew. *Nationalism and Particularity*. New York: Cambridge University Press, 2002.

Viroli, Maruizio. *For Love of Country: An Essay on Patriotism and Nationalism*. New York: Clarendon Press, 1995.

SEE ALSO: Citizenship; Fascism; Loyalty; Loyalty oaths; Moral principles, rules, and imperatives; National security and sovereignty.

Peace Corps

IDENTIFICATION: Independent federal agency that promotes international friendship by supplying trained personnel to other countries

DATE: Founded in 1961

TYPE OF ETHICS: Human rights

SIGNIFICANCE: While the theory behind the Peace Corps seems morally unobjectionable, and even laudatory, the organization's practical actions in the service of its goals have at times been controversial.

The Peace Corps of the United States is an independent agency of the federal government that sends volunteers to countries throughout the world to help staff schools and hospitals, and to share agricultural and technical knowledge. The Peace Corps was founded in 1961 while John F. Kennedy was president. He asked young people to volunteer for two-year terms, and many recent college graduates seeking adventure and a chance to serve accepted the offer. At first, anyone who was willing to volunteer was accepted and given something to do.

President John F. Kennedy (right) greets some of the first Peace Corps volunteers at a White House reception. (Library of Congress)

By the 1980's, Peace Corps volunteers tended to be older and more highly trained in technical areas. In the wake of the Vietnam War and Watergate, a growing cynicism about the government caused fewer volunteers to join. In 1983, the Ronald Reagan administration revived the program, hoping to use the volunteers to spread conservative ideas worldwide. By the 1990's, opinion about the Peace Corps was divided. Many people believed that the Peace Corps was primarily a means for a wealthy nation to share its prosperity, and to promote world harmony. Others saw an insidious form of interventionism in the program.

Nevertheless, in 2004, more than seventy nations were hosting more than 7,500 Peace Corps volunteers. These nations included nine former Soviet republics and four other Eastern European nations. Between 1993 and 2004, even the People's Republic of China hosted more than 230 Peace Corps volunteers.

Cynthia A. Bily

SEE ALSO: Altruism; Developing world; Idealist ethics; Intervention; Poverty and wealth; Service to others.

Peace studies

DEFINITION: Interdisciplinary course of academic study that explores alternatives to war while promoting a progressive agenda including national and international social justice, human rights, conflict resolution, and activism

TYPE OF ETHICS: Theory of ethics

SIGNIFICANCE: Frankly and unapologetically political in orientation, peace studies attempt to educate future thinkers, activists, and leaders to create a more just and less violent world.

Peace studies is an emerging discipline that affirms that peace is more than the absence of war; peace is harmony among people and countries based on respect for oneself and others. The study of peace weaves together three major threads. Peace studies as an academic discipline examines war, relations among nations, conflicts and their resolution, and proposals for peace; peace education identifies effective methods used to teach peace in a family, a classroom, or a community setting in order to develop civic and global citizenship and world peace; and peacemaking focuses on the values by which one lives one's life and cares for others in the family, for the community, and for the planet. Unless these three threads are woven together in theory and practice, the goal and meaning of peace studies are lost.

Desire for peace and the elimination of war can be traced to the ancient oral and written histories and literature of diverse peoples from all continents. A modern study of peace can be traced to the establishment of the World Peace Foundation in 1910. The advent of atomic warfare in World War II increased the demand for the study of foreign policy, development, international conflict, and alternatives to war. Early in U.S. history, George Washington called for the establishment of a United States Academy for Peace, a proposal that was reconsidered by every Congress until 1986, when the United States Institute for Peace was established.

ACADEMIC PROGRAMS

Peace studies emerged slowly as an academic discipline. During the 1960's, there were few courses in higher education that addressed peace issues, although peace studies formed the basis of education in several colleges run by the historic Peace Churches, notably the Brethren, Quaker, and Mennonite churches. Peace studies received an impetus during the Vietnam War, when growing numbers of war protesters raised issues of war and alternatives to war in classrooms and institutions of higher learning around the world.

The Institute for World Order (now the World Policy Institute) was among the first organizations (1966) to link and address issues of war, development, gender and racial inequality, human rights, and ecological balance with issues of world peace. As terrorist activities and the nuclear threat escalated during the late 1970's, the leaders of most of the world's religions added their voices to the call for the study of peace and justice issues. By 1983, at the peak of the International Nuclear Freeze Campaign, public and private campuses worldwide began including one or more courses related to the study of war, the nuclear threat, conflict management, global cooperation, and world peace in their curriculums. Ten years later, hundreds of campuses worldwide offered peace studies programs. Students can now receive a minor or major at the undergraduate level, a master's degree, and, at several universities, a doctoral degree in peace studies.

Academic programs in higher education, which often focus on the historical or theoretical, hold an important place in peace studies, for it is in the academy that the various disciplines provide for the examination of diverse topics that are related to war and peace. Two acknowledged dangers in the academy include the failure to study issues of peace from a cross-cultural or interdisciplinary perspective and the failure to link the theoretical and historical perspectives of peace with personal, family, and community lifestyle choices. A growing number of scholars have suggested that peace studies must move beyond theory; it must be values based, address domestic and global issues, be relevant to all age groups, and lead to education for responsible global citizenship.

Peace education programs at the elementary and secondary levels, developed during the Vietnam era, do promote values, as well as attitudes and skills related to affirmation, communication, cooperation, respect for diversity, nonviolent resolution of conflict, and skills for critical thinking and decision making. Three of the most notable in the United States are the Children and Non-Violence, Children's Creative Response to Conflict, and Peacemaking for Children: Alternatives to Violence programs. The Nuclear Freeze Campaign of 1982 expanded international awareness of the nuclear threat and generated new calls for peace education. Milwaukee's public schools became the first major school system in the United States to respond to this call, implementing a K-12 peace education curriculum in 1985.

PEACEMAKING

Peacemaking for Families educational programs, developed in 1976 by Jacqueline Haessly, evolved from a belief that the values, attitudes, and skills of peacemaking are first shaped in the home. Five years later, the National Parenting for Peace and Justice Education Network was established by James and Kathleen McGinnis. Family Life Education for Peace, initiated by Nona and Carroll Cannon, is an emerging field in the academy. All three programs link peace with values education.

Peacemaking as a way of life occurs when individuals and societies make the link between the personal and the political. Julia Sweig and Sharon Boggs are among those who remind peace educators that issues of domestic and community violence must be addressed and skills for community building must be taught if peace is to be achieved in a community and the world.

Organizations that promote peace studies in the United States include Children's Creative Responses to Conflict; Council for Peace and Conflict Studies; Consortium for Peace Education, Research, and Development; Educators for Social Responsibility; Fellowship of Reconciliation; Global Education Associates; Jane Addams Peace Association; the Milwaukee Peace Education Resource Center; Parenting for Peace and Justice Network; the United Nations University for Peace—San Diego; the United States Institute for Peace; and the World Policy Institute (formerly the Institute for World Order). Many of these organizations also have international affiliations.

Jacqueline Haessly

FURTHER READING

Duhon-Sells, Rose, ed. *Exploring Self Science Through Peace Education and Conflict Resolution*. Lewiston, N.Y.: E. Mellen Press, 1997.

Freire, Paulo. *Education for Critical Consciousness*. New York: Seabury Press, 1973.

Haessly, Jacqueline. *Peacemaking: Family Activities for Justice and Peace*. New York: Paulist Press, 1980.

Klare, Michael T., ed. *Peace and World Security Studies: A Curriculum Guide*. 6th ed. Boulder, Colo.: L. Riennen, 1994.

McGinnis, James, and Kathleen McGinnis. *Parenting for Peace and Justice*. Maryknoll, N.Y.: Orbis Books, 1981.

Mendlovitz, Saul, ed. *On the Creation of a Just World Order*. New York: Free Press, 1975.

Mische, Gerald, and Patricia Mische. *Toward a Human World Order*. New York: Paulist Press, 1977.

Montessori, Maria. *Education and Peace*. Chicago: Regnery, 1972.

Reardon, Betty. *Comprehensive Peace Education: Educating for Global Responsibility*. New York: Teachers College Press, 1988.

_____. *Education for a Culture of Peace in a Gender Perspective*. Paris: UNESCO, 2001.

Salomon, Gavriel, and Baruch Nevo, eds. *Peace Education: The Concept, Principles, and Practices Around the World*. Mahwah, N.J.: Lawrence Erlbaum Associates, 2002.

SEE ALSO: Conflict resolution; International justice; International law; Moral education; Multiculturalism; Nobel Peace Prizes; Pacifism.

Peacekeeping missions

DEFINITION: International military interventions, usually authorized by the United Nations

DATE: First mission launched in 1956

TYPE OF ETHICS: Military ethics

SIGNIFICANCE: Increasingly utilized tools of preventive diplomacy aimed at managing conflict and preventing wars from starting or spreading, peacekeeping missions are typically justified on humanitarian grounds, even when they are at odds with the deeply entrenched principle of state sovereignty.

Although individual countries have historically intervened in the affairs of others, unilateral military intervention became a highly dangerous means of addressing conflicts in the bipolar world that emerged after World War II. With each alliance headed by a superpower armed with a growing nuclear capability, the avoidance of both war and superpower confrontation became ever more important. Alternative means of managing international hot spots were needed.

United Nations (U.N.) peacekeeping missions became one of the more effective alternatives developed to prevent conflicts from escalating during the Cold War years (1947-1992). Simultaneously a code of conduct developed to ensure the neutrality of these operations and improve their effectiveness. After the collapse of communism in the Soviet Union and Eastern Europe, peacekeeping missions became a more common means of managing communal violence, defusing civil wars, and containing other forms of conflict in an increasingly turbulent world.

The first United Nations peacekeeping mission was launched in 1956 to defuse an awkward military and diplomatic situation. Without consulting Washington, France and Great Britain had joined Israel in a military operation that left them in control of Egypt's Suez Canal but on the receiving end of criticism from the United States and the Soviet Union for their invasion of Egypt. Although it initially pitted both superpowers against two of the closest allies of the United States, it also threatened to expand into a broader Arab-Israeli conflict that would have placed the United States and the Soviet Union on opposite sides.

Into this morass stepped U.N. secretary-general Dag Hammarskjöld with a proposal designed to let every faction down gently. In return for Egypt's agreeing to guarantee international access to the Suez Canal, its occupiers agreed to withdraw. To prevent a recurrence of hostilities, Egypt also agreed to allow the deployment of a U.N. peacekeeping contingent in the Sinai Peninsula, between Israel and Egypt's army. The force soon became the model for the deployment of peacekeeping missions elsewhere during the Cold War years—a human shield placed between potential combatants to prevent conflicts from occurring, expanding, or rekindling where cease-fires have been achieved.

ENSURING NEUTRALITY

For peacekeeping missions to succeed, it is imperative that the peacekeepers be perceived as neutral by the parties involved in the conflicts. During the Cold War, it was also important to keep the superpowers out of the conflicts as far as possible. The rules of deployment that evolved out of U.N. peacekeeping missions prior to the end of the Cold War were intended to do both. They emphasized the multilateral nature of peacekeeping, the inclusion of forces from Third World states, and the exclusion of troops from either superpower or their military allies. Also, peacekeeping troops themselves were to engage in combat only to defend themselves when fired upon. Finally, mindful of the admonition in the U.N. Charter against interfering in the domestic affairs of any member state, U.N. troops were to be deployed only with the consent of the host governments.

POST-COLD WAR CONFLICTS

Within this framework U.N. peacekeeping missions were highly successful during the Cold War years. Out of the approximately twenty missions launched between 1956 and 1990, the United Nations failed only once to maintain order—during the civil war that erupted in the Congo in 1960-1961. That failure was due largely to superpower involvement and the fact that there was no peace to keep when the mission began.

Beginning in the 1990's, however, internal civil wars became a greater source of instability in the international system than international conflicts, such as the Arab-Israeli conflict. Clan warfare in Somalia, genocide in Rwanda, and wars in the former Yugoslavia, with their atrocities, high casualty figures, and discharges of numerous of refugees into adjacent states, far more resembled the challenges faced by U.N. peacekeepers in the Congo than in those arenas where the U.N. peacekeepers successfully deployed during the Cold War. The existing U.N. peacekeeping model had to be modified in two important ways to adapt to this changing world setting.

First, because in the more recent conflicts it was often necessary to establish a peace for the peacekeepers to keep, peacekeeping missions came to depend on the exercise of substantial military assets. In the post-Cold War world, that has meant assigning a major role to the United States or the North Atlantic Treaty Organization (NATO) in the peace-making and peacekeeping process, and using military forces to end ongoing conflicts. These departures from the original model have frequently made it difficult for peacekeeping missions to retain the image of neutrality.

Second, in many conflicts there has been either no government in sufficient control of a country to request peacekeeping assistance or no government willing to do so. Politicians opposed to peacekeeping missions have normally cited the concept of state sovereignty and the internal nature of their civil wars as placing them beyond U.N. jurisdiction. Hence, the legal basis for peacekeeping operations has had to be found elsewhere.

1103

PEACEKEEPING MISSIONS AND "JUST WARS"

That justification has been found in the concept of the just war, largely as articulated by Michael Walzer in his *Just and Unjust Wars* (1977). According to his thesis, in order to maintain a secure environment in which human rights can be guarded and people protected, it may become necessary to intervene in a state's affairs, especially when the action of the state's leaders violates prevailing international law or when the conflict sends so many refugees into neighboring states that it loses its domestic nature. In such instances, intervention becomes an ethical imperative, so long as it conforms to the rules designed to ensure its neutrality in establishing and keeping the peace and focuses on the humanitarian goals of the mission rather than on having an impact on the distribution of power in the area to which the forces are dispatched.

Joseph R. Rudolph, Jr.

FURTHER READING

Carnegie Commission on Preventing Deadly Conflict. *Preventing Deadly Conflict: Final Report.* New York: Carnegie Corporation, 1997.

Hoffmann, Stanley. *World Disorders: Troubled Peace in the Post Cold War Era.* Lanham, Md.: Rowman & Littlefield, 2000.

Phillips, Robert L., and Duane L. Cady. *Humanitarian Intervention: Just War vs. Pacifism.* Lanham, Md.: Rowman & Littlefield, 1996.

Regan, Richard, J. *Just War: Principles and Cases.* Washington, D.C.: Catholic University of America Press, 1996.

Rudolph, Joseph R., Jr. "Intervention in Communal Conflicts." *Orbis* 39, no. 2 (Spring, 1995): 259-274.

Traub, James. "Making Sense of the Mission." *New York Times Magazine.* April 11, 2004, 32-37, 55, 58, 62-63.

Walzer, Michael. *Just and Unjust Wars.* New York: Basic Books, 1977.

SEE ALSO: Bosnia; Cold War; Dallaire, Roméo; Intervention; Just war theory; Kosovo; Limited war; Military ethics; North Atlantic Treaty Organization; Rwanda genocide; United Nations.

Peirce, Charles Sanders

IDENTIFICATION: American philosopher
BORN: September 10, 1839, Cambridge, Massachusetts
DIED: April 19, 1914, near Milford, Pennsylvania
TYPE OF ETHICS: Modern history
SIGNIFICANCE: One of the founders of pragmatism and one of the most original philosophers of the nineteenth century, Peirce attacked traditional conceptions of truth and knowledge and made significant contributions to the fields of logic, semiotics, and epistemology.

From 1864 to 1907, Peirce served as an occasional lecturer at Harvard and Johns Hopkins University on the topics of logic and pragmatism. His genius and potential on pragmatic theory were never fully realized or publicly appreciated, however, because of his personal difficulties, eccentricity, and opposition to traditional philosophical thought. Peirce believed that it was a mistake to accept a priori reasoning, or absolute truth, without first examining its results.

In an article published in *Popular Science Monthly* in 1878, Peirce attempted to answer the question "How to Make Our Ideas Clear" by stating that an idea's utility and results or effects give it meaning, not some inherent absolute truth or a priori reasoning. One's conception of these effects becomes one's conception of the object. Peirce interpreted every subject, including philosophy, almost entirely from a logical (pragmatic) perspective. Peirce emphasized that pragmatism is a principle of method—not of metaphysics. Using this principle, he claimed that scientific laws were statements of probabilities only and subject to evolutionary change. Unlike his disciple and benefactor William James, however, Peirce never discarded his beliefs in an Absolute or in universals. Scholars consider Peirce's work an important intellectual foundation for twentieth century progressivism.

Stephen D. Livesay

SEE ALSO: Dewey, John; Intersubjectivity; James, William; Pragmatism; Progressivism.

Peltier conviction

THE EVENT: Criminal conviction of Leonard Peltier (1944-　) during the 1975 shooting deaths of two Federal Bureau of Investigation (FBI) agents

DATE: Convicted April 18, 1977; sentenced June 1, 1977

TYPE OF ETHICS: Race and ethnicity; legal and judicial ethics

SIGNIFICANCE: Peltier's conviction is a source of bitter disagreement between law enforcement advocates and agents—who see Peltier as nothing more than a common murderer—and Peltier's followers and sympathizers—who see him as nothing less than a political prisoner punished for his beliefs by a tyrannical and unjust government.

On June 26, 1975, two FBI agents were killed in a shoot-out on the Lakota Indian Reservation in Pine Ridge, South Dakota. Leonard Peltier, a member of the American Indian Movement (AIM), was found guilty of the killings. Peltier declared himself innocent and appealed his conviction many times. During the appeals, the court found that the government had acted improperly in arresting and trying him. Federal authorities admitted to falsifying affidavits used to extradite Peltier from Canada. Witnesses in the original trial had been coerced, and evidence supporting Peltier's claims was suppressed.

In spite of the irregularities, the courts refused to overturn Peltier's conviction. Peltier's case became known throughout the world. Many people believed that, even if he were guilty, he had not been granted a fair trial. Amnesty International declared him a political prisoner, and important religious leaders spoke out on his behalf. A book and three films were made about the case.

In 1992, a "Mr. X" confessed to the killings.

Marchers use the occasion of Thanksgiving Day in 2001 to proclaim a "National Day of Mourning" and call for the release of Leonard Peltier in a demonstration in Plymouth, Massachusetts—a place of special symbolic significance as the site of the first Thanksgiving celebrated by settlers and Native Americans. (AP/Wide World Photos)

Peltier's supporters continued to hope that they could win him a new trial, or at the very least a parole hearing. The United States Parole Commission, however, repeatedly refused to grant Peltier such a hearing until December, 2008, at the earliest. Peltier's supporters claimed that he was being required to wait twice as long as the average convict in his situation before being considered for parole.

Cynthia A. Bily
Updated by the editors

SEE ALSO: Amnesty International; Arrest records; Due process; Erroneous convictions; Native American ethics.

Pentagon Papers

IDENTIFICATION: Classified documents at issue in *United States v. New York Times Company*, which the U.S. Supreme Court held the federal government could not restrain *The New York Times* from publishing

DATE: Court ruling made on June 30, 1971

TYPE OF ETHICS: Media ethics

SIGNIFICANCE: The Pentagon Papers case dealt with the issue of prior restraint, that is, censorship before the fact which prevents the censored material from ever seeing the light of day. Prior restraint is the most extreme form of censorship, and the Supreme Court ruled that the government must meet a heavy burden of justification before it can prevent the press from publishing even top secret information.

Popular sentiment against the Vietnam War was on the rise in the spring of 1971, when Daniel Ellsberg, a former U.S. Department of Defense employee, and his friend, Anthony Russo, Jr., stole copies of two massive volumes that have come to be known as the Pentagon Papers. These volumes, "History of U.S. Decision-Making Process on Vietnam Policy" and "Command and Control Study of the Gulf of Tonkin Incident"—which were classified "Top Secret-Sensitive" and "Top Secret," respectively—together constituted a history of American involvement in Vietnam since World War II.

Ellsberg and Russo passed the filched documents on to *The New York Times* and *The Washington Post.* In its June 13, 1971, edition, the *Times* began publishing a series of excerpts from the government studies.

GOVERNMENT ATTEMPTS PRIOR RESTRAINT

After the *Times* had published two more excerpts on June 14 and 15, 1971, the federal government filed a motion in the U.S. District Court for the Southern District of New York requesting that the court restrain the *Times* from publishing more passages from the Pentagon Papers. Although the court refused to issue an injunction against the paper, it did grant the government a temporary restraining order, which prevented the *Times* from publishing portions of the Pentagon Papers while the government prepared its case. On June 18, *The Washington Post* also began publishing excerpts from the Pentagon Papers, and the government moved to restrain it, too, in federal court in the District of Columbia. The legal action in the case, however, remained focused on New York City.

On June 18, the district court in New York heard the case, in which the government claimed that the publication of the documents in question would compromise the nation's war effort. Nevertheless, the government's request for an injunction was denied, although the temporary restraining order was extended until the government's appeal to a higher court could be heard. This appeal also was rejected, and on June 24, the government filed a petition with the Supreme Court.

SUPREME COURT REJECTS GOVERNMENT CASE

The parties appeared before the Court on June 26, 1971, and the Court delivered its opinion on June 30: The entire litigation had lasted slightly longer than two weeks. Like the lower courts, the Supreme Court rejected the government's attempts to rationalize prior restraint of the press by appealing to national security, dismissing the cases against both the *Times* and the *Post.* The Court was not unanimous in its decision, voting six to three, but writing for the majority, Justice Hugo L. Black delivered a stinging rebuke to the administration of President Richard M. Nixon: "the Solicitor General argues . . . that the general powers of the Government adopted in the original Constitution should be interpreted to limit and restrict the specific and emphatic guarantees of the Bill of Rights. . . . I can imagine no greater perversion of history."

Although the dissenters, Chief Justice Warren E. Burger, Justice Harry A. Blackmun, and Justice John M. Harlan II, argued that the Court should defer to the executive branch's concerns, Justice Black's opinion reaffirmed the Court's role as interpreter of the Constitution and guardian of individual rights: "Madison and the other Framers of the First Amendment . . . wrote in language they earnestly believed could never be misunderstood: 'Congress shall make no law . . . abridging the freedom . . . of the press. . . .'"

CONTINUED PROSECUTION

The government continued, nevertheless, to prosecute Ellsberg and Russo, gaining indictments against them for theft of federal property and violations of the federal Espionage Act. The two defendants were tried in the U.S. District Court for the Central District of California, where the Pentagon Papers were allegedly stolen. Unlike the original Pentagon Papers litigation, the Ellsberg and Russo prosecution dragged on for many months. Although the government had first obtained a preliminary indictment against Ellsberg in June, 1971, the trial of the two defendants did not commence until more than a year later.

The trial was halted almost immediately after it began, however, when it was revealed that the government had been secretly taping the defendants' confidential communications. After the parties had gone through the process of selecting a new jury, the trial recommenced in January, 1973. Shortly thereafter, however, the entire Pentagon Papers case was colored by news of the Watergate imbroglio, which began with the September, 1971, government-sponsored burglary of the offices of Lewis Fielding, Ellsberg's psychoanalyst, committed in an effort to uncover other Ellsberg accomplices. When further revelations of the government's continuing illegal wiretaps of Ellsberg's conversations reached the court, the entire criminal prosecution of Ellsberg and Russo was dismissed. The Nixon administration had not only undermined its reputation and its case against the defendants but had also ensured that future administrative attempts to restrain the press from exercising its First Amendment rights would be more difficult.

Lisa Paddock

FURTHER READING

Ellsberg, Daniel. *Secrets: A Memoir of Vietnam and the Pentagon Papers*. New York: Viking, 2002.

French, Peter A. *Conscientious Actions: The Revelation of the Pentagon Papers*. Cambridge, Mass.: Schenkman, 1974.

Meiklejohn Civil Liberties Institute. *Pentagon Papers Case Collection: Annotated Procedural Guide and Index*. Berkeley, Calif.: Author, 1975.

Rudenstine, David. *The Day the Presses Stopped: A History of the Pentagon Papers Case*. Berkeley: University of California Press, 1996.

Salter, Kenneth W. *The Pentagon Papers Trial*. Berkeley, Calif.: Editorial Justa, 1975.

Schrag, Peter. *Test of Loyalty: Daniel Ellsberg and the Rituals of Secret Government*. New York: Simon & Schuster, 1974.

Ungar, Sanford J. *The Papers and the Papers: An Account of the Legal and Political Battle Over the Pentagon Papers*. New York: Columbia University Press, 1989.

SEE ALSO: Censorship; First Amendment; Invasion of privacy; Journalistic ethics; Public's right to know; Supreme Court, U.S.; Watergate scandal.

People for the Ethical Treatment of Animals

IDENTIFICATION: Animal rights organization

DATE: Founded in 1980

TYPE OF ETHICS: Animal rights

SIGNIFICANCE: Known for using controversial tactics to draw attention to the view that animals do not exist to serve humans, People for the Ethical Treatment of Animals (PETA) is an aggressive organization that follows the principle that animals are not for humans to eat, wear, experiment on, or use for entertainment.

PETA was founded in 1980 by Ingrid Newkirk, an animal-control officer in the District of Columbia, and Alex Pacheco, a student at George Washington University. Both men were influenced by Peter Singer's book *Animal Liberation* (1975), which argued that animals should have the same basic rights as humans. In 1981, Pacheco recorded an incident of

PETA members demonstrating against leather goods near the White House in Washington, D.C., in late 2001. (AP/Wide World Photos)

cruelty to animals in a Silver Springs, Maryland, research laboratory. PETA's investigation led to the first police raid, the first arrest, and the first conviction of a researcher for animal cruelty. The incident afterward became known as the Silver Springs Monkeys case. PETA also documented cases of animal cruelty in university laboratories and publicized the harsh living conditions of ducks that were being raised to make liver pâté and chinchillas that were being electrocuted to harvest their fur.

In addition to documenting and publicizing cases of animal cruelty, PETA is well known for publicity campaigns involving celebrities who have posed for advertisements in its "I'd Rather Go Naked than Wear Fur" campaign. In 1994, three PETA members dressed in rabbit suits and chained themselves to a flagpole in front of the Gillette headquarters in Boston, Massachusetts, to protest the company's use of testing of animals.

Many PETA actions have been designed to win publicity by attracting controversy. For example, the organization targeted college students in "Got Beer?" advertisements in college newspapers that were modeled on the milk industry's "Got Milk?" advertising slogan. PETA took the position that beer was healthier for humans to drink than milk and that cows should not be imprisoned in order to benefit human beings. Critics of PETA have charged that the organization has ties with more violent animal rights groups, such as the Animal Liberation Front. That charge has gained apparent credence when self-described PETA members have poured red paint, symbolizing blood, on women wearing animal furs.

John David Rausch, Jr.

SEE ALSO: Advertising; Animal research; Animal rights; Cruelty to animals; Endangered species; Humane Society of the United States; Moral status of animals; National Anti-Vivisection Society; Singer, Peter; Society for the Prevention of Cruelty to Animals; Vegetarianism; Vivisection.

Perfectionism

DEFINITION: Tendency to set unrealistically high standards for oneself or others

TYPE OF ETHICS: Theory of ethics

SIGNIFICANCE: Perfectionism may affect the way in which one views and responds to one's own moral transgressions, as well as the transgressions of others. To the extent that it can cause emotional pain, or result in the achievement of excellence, perfectionism may itself become the object of ethical judgments.

Although originally believed to be a unidimensional concept involving only the self, perfectionism is now thought to be a multidimensional construct that has three components: self-oriented perfectionism, other-oriented perfectionism, and socially prescribed perfectionism. Self-oriented perfectionism is intrapersonal (within the self) and involves being strongly motivated to be perfect, setting and holding unrealistically high goals for oneself, striving compulsively, thinking in an all-or-nothing manner in which only total success or total failure exist as outcomes, focusing on flaws and past failures, and generalizing unrealistic self-standards across behavioral domains. For example, self-oriented perfectionism is expecting oneself to be Atlas and hold up the world without dropping anything, and thinking of oneself as a failure if one errs in any way.

Other-oriented perfectionism is interpersonal and involves beliefs and expectations about significant others. It entails setting unrealistically high standards for others, placing great importance on whether they attain these standards, and rewarding them only if they meet these standards. For example, other-oriented perfectionism is expecting a significant other to be Atlas and hold up the world and giving no positive reinforcement if anything at all is dropped.

Socially prescribed perfectionism is also interpersonal and involves the need to meet the standards and expectations that are perceived by significant others. Its essence is the belief that significant others have unrealistic standards and perfectionistic motives for their behaviors, and that they will be satisfied only when these standards are met. For example, socially prescribed perfectionism is thinking that significant others expect one to be Atlas and hold up the world and believing that they will be utterly disappointed if one fails in any way. Self-oriented, other-oriented, and socially prescribed perfectionism are three separate but related aspects of perfectionism.

POSITIVE AND NEGATIVE ASPECTS

Perfectionism may be positive or negative. On the positive side, most employers would rather have employees who take pride in their work, who consistently work to the best of their ability, and who try to make their results as perfect as possible. Likewise, most teachers would rather have students who are exact and precise in their work, who do all their assignments as instructed, and who consistently operate at their maximum capacity. In other life situations as well, perfectionism can be a very positive quality. On the negative side, there are intrapersonal and interpersonal costs associated with perfectionism.

Intrapersonally, perfectionists are never satisfied with their efforts, no matter how hard they try. They consistently fail to meet their goals, so their lives can be quite frustrating and their self-esteem quite low. They can fail to produce a whole picture of the forest because they are so thoroughly examining the trees. They fail to understand that there are times when an adequate job is all that is required. Interpersonally, perfectionists can be difficult persons with whom to live, work, and interact. Their exacting standards can lead to rigidity and make interpersonal relationships fraught with disappointments and recriminations. Therefore, perfectionism may be a positive or negative personal characteristic.

THE PERFECTIONISM SCALE

During the late 1980's and early 1990's, Paul Hewitt and Gordon Flett and colleagues in Winnipeg, Canada, developed the Multidimensional Perfectionism Scale (MPS), a forty-five-item measure of self-oriented, other-oriented, and socially prescribed perfectionism. Respondents rate such statements as "When I am working on something, I cannot relax until it is perfect" (self-oriented perfectionism), "I have high expectations for the people who are important to me" (other-oriented perfectionism), and "People expect nothing less than perfection from me" (socially prescribed perfectionism) on a seven-point Likert scale from 1 = Strongly Disagree to 7 = Strongly Agree. Respondents receive scores for all three dimensions of perfectionism.

1109

The MPS is a strong instrument. In terms of reliability, the MPS is internally consistent as well as consistent over time. In terms of validity, the MPS is correlated with related concepts such as high self-standards, self-criticism, fear of negative evaluation, and social importance goals. In terms of multidimensionality, factor analysis has produced results that are consistent with the three dimensions of the MPS. Furthermore, it is not substantially influenced by response biases. Thus, the MPS is an experimentally sound instrument.

Using the MPS, researchers have shown that perfectionism is correlated with anxiety, suicide, alcoholism, eating disorders, and personality disorders. It is also correlated with feelings of failure, guilt, indecisiveness, procrastination, shame, and low self-esteem. Thus, perfectionism is associated with psychopathology. General research on perfectionism has adopted a diathesis-stress approach that highlights the role of mediators between perfectionism and adjustment. According to this approach, problems of adjustment are elevated considerably when self-oriented perfectionism is combined with such mediating variables as negative life stressors, an internal attributional style, emotion-focused coping, and ego-involving conditions.

Lillian M. Range

FURTHER READING

Basco, Monica Ramirez. *Never Good Enough: How to Use Perfectionism to Your Advantage Without Letting It Ruin Your Life*. New York: Simon & Schuster, 2000.

Hewitt, Paul L., and Gordon L. Flett. "Perfectionism in the Self and Social Contexts: Conceptualization, Assessment, and Association with Psychopathology." *Journal of Personality and Social Psychology* 60 (March, 1991): 456-470.

_____, eds. *Perfectionism: Theory, Research, and Treatment*. Washington, D.C.: American Psychological Association, 2002.

Hewitt, Paul L., Gordon L. Flett, and Samuel F. Mikail. "The Multidimensional Perfectionism Scale: Reliability, Validity, and Psychometric Properties in Psychiatric Samples." *Psychological Assessment: A Journal of Consulting and Clinical Psychology* 3 (September, 1991): 464-480.

Mosher, Shawn W. "Perfectionism, Self-Actualization, and Personal Adjustment." *Journal of Social Behavior and Personality* 6, no. 5 (1991): 147-160.

SEE ALSO: Maximal vs. minimal ethics; Psychology; Self-control; Self-respect; Suicide.

Perjury

DEFINITION: Crime of testifying falsely while under oath
TYPE OF ETHICS: Legal and judicial ethics
SIGNIFICANCE: Perjury interferes with the ability of judicial systems to ascertain the truth and mete out justice. It is therefore commonly thought to be a violation of the general interests of a given society. Perjury, rather than lying in general, is a violation of the Ninth Commandment.

The essence of the crime of perjury is giving false testimony under oath regarding a matter that is being considered by a court or other tribunal. "False" does not mean mistaken, however great the error; it means that the witness believes his or her own testimony to be false and makes false statements willfully in spite of taking an oath to tell the truth.

Perjury is a serious crime. It was punishable by death in England in ancient times; later, the punishment became banishment or mutilation of the tongue. Penalties are still severe; in the United States during the 1990's, perjury was still punishable by life imprisonment in a few states and by a long term of years in all the others. However, there are few perjury prosecutions. It is a difficult crime to prove, because the prosecution has to show that the witness knew the testimony to be false. In the United States a person who has been acquitted of a criminal offense is now protected by the double-jeopardy clause from being charged with perjury for testimony given in his or her own defense.

Robert Jacobs

SEE ALSO: Accused, rights of; Adversary system; Clinton, Bill; Jury system; Lying; Morality; Professional ethics.

Permissible acts

DEFINITION: Actions whose performance does not constitute a moral transgression

TYPE OF ETHICS: Theory of ethics

SIGNIFICANCE: One way to conceive of the goal of ethics is as dividing all human actions into permissible and impermissible acts. Such a conception leads to the portrayal of duty as a negative rather than a positive concept.

The concept of a permissible act is one that is typically learned very early in life. One learns that there are certain requirements that are binding upon one's behavior, and permissible acts are recognized as those acts that do not violate any of these requirements. Because most of these requirements are actually requirements to refrain from certain types of acts, one quickly identifies certain courses of action as being impermissible. Permissible acts, then, are acts one knows one can perform without violating these requirements.

More precisely, the relation between permissibility and duty is the following: If one has a moral duty to perform a particular act, then it is permissible for one to perform the act but not permissible for one to refrain from performing the act. If one has a moral duty to refrain from a particular act, then it is permissible for one to refrain from the act but not permissible for one to perform the act. If one does not have a moral duty either to perform or refrain from a particular act, then it is permissible for one to perform the act and permissible for one to refrain from the act.

Ethicists have distinguished four different categories of morally permissible acts. First, some morally permissible acts are neither morally praiseworthy nor morally blameworthy. These acts tend to be somewhat inconsequential as far as morality is concerned. For example, raising one's hand in the air or clearing one's throat is a morally neutral act (under most circumstances). It is neither praiseworthy nor blameworthy, and hence it cannot be the violation of duty.

Second, there are morally permissible acts that one has a moral duty to perform. Indeed, all instances of carrying out one's moral duty are permissible; it can never be impermissible to carry out one's duty.

Third, some morally permissible acts are morally praiseworthy but not the fulfillment of duty. That is, it is sometimes possible to act in a way that goes beyond moral duty, and it is always permissible to perform such acts. This category includes so-called acts of supererogation, acts whose performance is praiseworthy but not obligatory and whose omission is not blameworthy.

Fourth, some morally permissible acts are morally blameworthy. These acts, known as acts of offense, are blameworthy without constituting a violation of duty. They are bad enough to warrant blame but not bad enough to be classified as forbidden. Of all the acts that are permissible, these are the only ones whose performance has a negative ethical status. A significant number of moralists are skeptical as to whether acts of this type are possible.

ABSOLUTISM VS. RELATIVISM

There is considerable disagreement in ethics between those who defend an absolutist approach and those who defend a relativist approach. The concept of permissibility is thought of quite differently by the defenders of these two approaches.

Defenders of an absolutist approach follow Plato in thinking that there are standards of morality that are eternal, absolute, and unchanging. They are the same for everyone and are discovered, not made. From this it follows that what is morally permissible is also the same for everyone in relevantly similar circumstances. What is permissible does not depend upon one's culture or the period of history in which one lives.

Defenders of a relativist approach believe that people draw up standards of morality to govern their lives; before there were any people, there were no standards of morality. Different cultures have different conceptions of what is permissible, and that is exactly what one should expect. Someone from one culture might become quite alarmed at discovering that adultery, for example, is considered permissible in a different culture. That is not to say, however, that one culture is right and another is wrong, for in this view there are no moral absolutes. All that one can say is that different things are permissible in different cultures, and there is no question of one culture's being better or more correct than another.

Some ethical traditions place such emphasis upon duty as to virtually eliminate the possibility of permissible acts other than those that consist in doing one's duty. For example, in certain theological traditions, the demands of God or of other deities are so all-encompassing as to leave few occasions in which, with respect to the same act, it is both permissible to perform it and permissible to omit it. One is virtually always in a position of having a duty either to perform an act or to refrain from performing it, depending upon the will of God.

Another example is act utilitarianism. Roughly speaking, act utilitarianism is the view that one ought always act in such a way as to bring about the greatest benefits for the greatest number of persons. Thus, at any given time, one has a duty to choose the act that maximizes benefits and a corresponding duty not to choose any act that does not. In this view, it is hard to see how there can ever be an act that is both permissible to perform and permissible to omit.

Other ethical traditions place a high premium on the possibility of permissible acts and of the importance of learning how to choose between two or more permissible acts. Learning to make such choices is not possible within the confines of act utilitarianism. There is good reason to believe, however, that people attain moral maturity in situations in which decision making is more than following the stark demands of duty. Sooner or later, people must learn how to make wise decisions regarding courses of action that are permissible but not uniformly prudent from a moral point of view. This is especially true with respect to acts that are blameworthy but permissible; moral maturity will teach one to avoid these when possible, even though they violate no moral duties.

Gregory F. Mellema

FURTHER READING

Baier, Kurt. *The Moral Point of View.* Ithaca, N.Y.: Cornell University Press, 1958.

Donagan, Alan. *The Theory of Morality.* Chicago: University of Chicago Press, 1977.

Kovesi, Julius. *Moral Notions.* London: Routledge & Kegan Paul, 1967.

Singer, Marcus. *Generalization in Ethics.* New York: Russell & Russell, 1971.

Stob, Henry. *Ethical Reflections.* Grand Rapids, Mich.: Wm. B. Eerdmans, 1978.

Williams, Gerald J. *A Short Introduction to Ethics.* Lanham, Md.: University Press of America, 1999.

SEE ALSO: Absolutism; Cannibalism; Consistency; Drug abuse; Duty; Professional ethics; Relativism; War.

Perry, R. B.

IDENTIFICATION: American philosopher
BORN: July 3, 1876, Poultney, Vermont
DIED: January 22, 1957, Cambridge, Massachusetts
TYPE OF ETHICS: Modern history
SIGNIFICANCE: The author of *General Theory of Value* (1926) and *Realms of Value* (1954), Perry developed a general, systematic theory of value.

Ralph Barton Perry enjoyed a distinguished career as a professor of philosophy at Harvard from 1902 to 1946. He was the leading authority of his time on psychologist-philosopher William James, and his book *The Thought and Character of William James* (1935) earned him the 1936 Pulitzer Prize. Perry is best known, however, for his value theory, which he saw as an extension of modern science to human life.

Perry's definition of value was "any object of any interest." The word "interest" captured that aspect of human psychology of being for some things and against others and included desire, feeling, and will. Thus, objects acquire value when someone seeks or favors them. Perry notes his affinity with the Dutch philosopher Baruch Spinoza, who had said in his book *Ethics* (1677) that human beings never strive for anything because they deem it to be good but deem something to be good because they strive for it. This view contrasts with that of the Greek philosopher Aristotle, that because something is good it is an object of rational desire.

For Perry, the central aim of morality is the harmonizing and integration of interests. A morally good object is one the interest of which meets the requirement of harmony, by aiming at another person's interest or at harmony itself. Perry's theory about right action is consequentialist; namely, an action is right if it is conducive to moral good.

Perry's theory is a type of ethical naturalism and cognitivism. He analyzes value and moral terms into naturalistic ones, employing the psychological concept of interest. He thereby rejects the nonnaturalism of English philosopher G. E. Moore. For Perry, moral judgments are empirical and cognitive, contrasting with the emotivism of English philosopher A. J. Ayer and the American philosopher Charles L. Stevenson.

Mario Morelli

SEE ALSO: Ayer, A. J.; Emotivist ethics; Is/ought distinction; Journalistic ethics; Moore, G. E.; Spinoza, Baruch; Value; Values clarification.

Personal injury attorneys

DEFINITION: Lawyers who specialize in representing persons who have been injured against those responsible for the injuries

TYPE OF ETHICS: Legal and judicial ethics

SIGNIFICANCE: Considered outlaws within the legal profession, personal injury attorneys contribute to negative public perceptions of the ethics of attorneys generally.

Among the least flattering images of unscrupulous lawyers is that of the ambulance chaser, the lawyer who arrives shortly after an accident to find among the injured and bleeding a new client. In fact, ambulance chasers are outlaws among attorneys, subject to disbarment for their unethical solicitation of clients. However, people who have been injured in some way nevertheless frequently need legal representation, and personal injury attorneys specialize in such cases. Personal injury lawyers may handle cases as varied as those involving relatively minor traffic accidents and those involving the injuries and deaths produced by an airliner crash.

Personal injury lawyers usually rely on a particular kind of fee arrangement, called a contingency fee agreement. This agreement provides that the personal injury attorney will not recover a fee in a case unless the attorney obtains some recovery for the client. In addition, personal injury attorneys generally pay the expenses needed to prepare a case for trial and deduct these from any ultimate recovery. These expenses, which include the fees of expert witnesses and the cost of pretrial discovery of facts about the case, can be very substantial and would be beyond the means of most individuals. However, by setting aside money from prior successful cases, personal injury attorneys are able to keep a reserve of cash for use on the expenses of subsequent cases. Consequently, by using the contingency fee agreement and by paying litigation expenses up front, personal injury attorneys are able to provide representation to individuals regardless of their financial standing.

But these financial aspects of personal injury practice are also controversial. The first and perhaps most important element of a successful personal injury practice is obtaining cases involving personal injury plaintiffs. This need to find clients causes some personal injury lawyers to engage in television or radio advertising, which is viewed as demeaning to the profession by more conservative lawyers. Furthermore, the need to find clients also tempts some personal injury lawyers to violate established rules against soliciting clients: in short, to engage in ambulance chasing.

Even after personal injury attorneys find their clients, they may be tempted to provide funds to these clients to cover medical and living expenses prior to trial or settlement. Personal injury clients are sometimes lured into accepting artificially low settlements for their injuries because they lack the financial resources to survive the lengthy period of time it normally takes to win a verdict at trial and sustain it on appeal. However, the law has long disfavored allowing persons to encourage litigation by offering support or other encouragements to litigating parties. The legal doctrines of champerty and maintenance, for example, make it a crime in many jurisdictions for persons to offer such support. Furthermore, rules of legal ethics prohibit attorneys from providing medical or living expenses to their clients.

Timothy L. Hall

SEE ALSO: Advertising; Attorney-client privilege; Exploitation; Law; Legal ethics; Medical insurance; Professional ethics.

Personal relationships

DEFINITION: Intimate associations or bonds among two or more persons

TYPE OF ETHICS: Personal and social ethics

SIGNIFICANCE: Philosophers since antiquity have posited that humans are fundamentally social beings and that without interpersonal relationships they cannot be considered fully human. Close personal relationships, moreover, are often considered to create ethical obligations between people, but they may also enable one person to coerce another into committing immoral acts.

The Old Testament tale of Adam and Eve's expulsion from the Garden of Eden opens the theme of a personal relationship that leads to disaster for both parties. Philosophy, religion, law, and social institutions have sought to structure personal relationships in marriage and the family to bring the conduct of individuals in line with the good of others and social stability. Monogamous marriage and a nuclear family are believed to have conferred an evolutionary advantage on the human race by increasing the probability of survival for children born and reared in such unions.

The family is not only a biological survival unit, a haven, and a refuge. It is also a school for moral sentiments: Parents experience moral growth and socialize children according to community norms, and natural affection among family members generates altruistic emotions. The traditional duties of a husband and father were to furnish security and economic support and to exercise moral authority within the family. The wife and mother managed the household, nurtured children, and owed her husband fidelity. Children were to obey and respect parents and elders, and to help and be loyal to one another.

ANCIENT GREECE AND CHRISTIANITY

Plato questioned the ethical value of marriage and the family and championed other forms of personal relationships. Athenian women were often uneducated and did not move in society, even in the company of their husbands. Wealthy aristocrats enjoyed the company of cultivated women prostitutes, and some courted male adolescents as protégés. In the *Symposium*, Plato maintains that an erotic relationship between a mature and a younger man, when inspired by philosophy, enables each to progress to the highest levels of human moral and intellectual development and creativity. Since the first step in moral progress is to admire another for qualities of mind and character, rather than physical attractiveness, "Platonic love" has come to mean nonsexual friendship between any two persons with shared ideals of beauty, truth, and goodness. This nonsexual Platonic ideal enriches many teacher-student relationships and associations between those who dedicate themselves to science, art, and philanthropic activities.

In *Republic*, Plato's ideal state abolishes marriage and the family because they constitute "exclusive centers of private joys and sorrows" that distract citizens from the common good and prevent women from developing their talents and serving the whole community. Plato proposes eugenic matches between men and women of reproductive age and the communal rearing of children, so that neither parents nor children know their biological relationships. By law, all children call one another brother or sister and all adults father or mother; adults call each child son or daughter. In this way, Plato theorized, each person would develop for others in the community the bonds of affection and loyalty ordinarily limited to a few.

Aristotle (fourth century B.C.E.) claimed that *Republic*'s personal ties would be "watery" and morally ineffectual. He insisted that the friendly relationships of private life should promote both individual happiness and communal harmony. There is friendship when two persons mutually desire the good of the other for the other's own sake and each does some kind of good for the other. He distinguishes more transient "imperfect" friendships, in which the good achieved is pleasure or utility, from permanent "perfect" friendships based on appreciation of each other's character, in which the two join in pursuing noble goals, as in Platonic love. By maintaining that perfect friendship may exist between husband and wife, Aristotle defended the moral potential of marriage, whose family life combines daily virtuous activities, pleasure, and utility.

Christianity introduced new moral elements into personal relationships: It demanded love for those without attractive or useful qualities and love for those who do wrong or offend one. Being modeled on divine love, Christian love is generous, compassionate, and forgiving; it chastises but does not abandon a wrongdoer, seeking instead the person's moral regeneration.

Viewing sexual appetite as a source of evil, Christian ethics required fidelity of both husband and wife and prohibited both premarital and extramarital sex. The relationship of Dante Alighieri to Beatrice in Dante's *Divine Comedy* reflects the medieval ideal of noble love, a model for the Christian relationship of man and woman. Dante's vision of the beautiful young Beatrice draws him heavenward: She personifies divine, loving concern for his weakness and inspires him to transcend carnal desires in order to achieve a loving union with her.

ROMANTIC LOVE AND THE SEXUAL REVOLUTION

The plays of William Shakespeare portray the popular modern ideal of romantic love. In them, a man and a woman feel erotic passion for each other and believe that they are perfectly suited for life together. Shakespeare is realistic in depicting the ambivalent potential of romantic love for happiness or misery: In the comedies, the lovers' ingenuity and constancy enable them to overcome obstacles, including the objections of kin, and they end in socially approved marriages. Impulsiveness, jealousy, or imprudence, however, lead to tragedy for the naïve adolescent lovers of *Romeo and Juliet* (pr. c. 1595-1596), the military hero of *Othello* (pr. 1604) and his bride Desdemona, and the sophisticated older lovers of *Antony and Cleopatra* (pr. c. 1606-1607).

The romantic ideal of marriage based on mutual attraction prevails in American society. When romance fails or attends a third party, divorce is a resort. In the case of a couple with young children, remarriage and custody arrangements alter the tenor of family life and complicate parent-child and sibling relationships. The sexual revolution of the 1960's and 1970's liberalized sexual morality and legitimated various consensual forms of personal relationships.

Premarital and extramarital sex, children born out of wedlock, homosexuality, lesbianism, and abortion no longer have the social stigma that once was attached to them. In common speech, a "relationship" connotes two unmarried persons who engage in consensual sex and are constant companions. The social norms of "recreational sex" are mutual consent and avoidance of pregnancy and sexually transmitted diseases. These limited norms do not address romantic feelings, which may exist on one side but not the other, and the consequent dangers of misunderstanding, deception, and exploitation of one by the other.

MALE BONDING

Films such as *The Deer Hunter* (1978) celebrate the phenomenon of "male bonding." Men who come together in often arduous activities of war, sports, work, leisure, or even crime develop comradeship that leads them to undertake dangerous tasks for the sake of one or more of their number. Male bonding is a source of strength and mutual support; it is ennobling and useful to society when it inspires men to behave courageously and selflessly. In the absence of moralizing influences such as the family, however, male bonding in urban gangs incites violent behavior and often is destructive to the individuals themselves. Gang members rely on money, power, and intimidation in relationships with outsiders and sometimes with intimates as well.

Some feminists consider male bonding, marriage, the family, and romantic love stratagems as elements of a patriarchal social organization that is designed to keep men in positions of power and women in subordination. Feminism has profoundly affected all forms of personal relationships by attacking the ideal of feminine submissiveness: Instead, feminism promotes self-assertion and independence for women both within and outside marriage and the family; it has opposed male domination in sexual harassment and employment practices. Some feminists condemn pornography on the grounds that it leads men to view and treat women as sex objects.

MODERN ETHICS

Modern "justice" ethics, represented by John Rawls's *Justice and Fairness* (1971), confers on consensual personal relationships equal legitimacy with marriage and family ties. Rawls does not accord marriage and family their traditional status of objective values to be endorsed by the moral principles of a just society; he categorizes them as subjective preferences, optional elements in an individual's life plan. Family partiality for the economic security of its members impedes a more egalitarian distribution of wealth. The assignment of special moral weight to the needs and well-being of family members is improper, for the moral attitude in justice ethics is one of rational impartiality toward individuals.

The morality of personal relationships in justice ethics is rights-based and contractual: Since autonomy, the power of the individual to act in accordance with his or her life plan without interference from others, is an objective value, intimates may not intrude upon it. One is obliged to respect the autonomy of all others and not to violate their basic human rights; other ideals or duties are matters of mutual agreement or subjective preference. Impartiality requires one to translate legal bans against racial, ethnic, and sexist discrimination into personal conduct by not showing bias in personal relationships with others.

Psychologist Carol Gilligan, in *In a Different*

Voice (1977), theorizes that justice ethics embodies a masculine ethical perspective: Men value autonomy for the freedom it affords them to pursue power and prestige in the social organization without the burden of personal relationships. Women articulate a different ethical voice that reflects the nurturing functions that they fulfill in human life and that values "relatedness." In ethical dilemmas, men apply universal moral principles impartially in order to secure justice in society; women seek a detailed narrative of the situation in order to resolve it without impairing valued relationships.

CRITICS OF JUSTICE ETHICS

Other philosophical critics of justice ethics say that it overlooks the moral power of friendship and family ties. They formulate a "care" ethic in which the well-being of particular persons has independent moral weight. Their ethical attitude is one of attentive solicitude to particular persons. A person's moral responsibility is to be sensitive to the needs of intimates and anticipate threats to their well-being, to be receptive to their interpretation of a situation, and through dialogue to seek resolutions that respect each person's integrity. Some feminists hear the feminine ethical voice as calling them to lives of self-abnegation and devotion to others, threatening the gains of women's liberation.

Existentialist philosophers Martin Heidegger and Jean-Paul Sartre see personal relationships as being inextricably connected with personal identity and social structure. One's personal identity depends on what one is to others and what they are to one; these interpretations of self and other in turn are determined by how each plays his or her social role, which is defined by the social organization.

According to Heidegger's *Being and Time* (1927), one's everyday mentality is so task-oriented that one tends to lose sight of the particular human beings for whose sake one does the work. Individuals relate to others in three different ways: The prevalent way is to distance oneself from others, hiding oneself or putting on a disguise in order to get along smoothly with them and get on with one's work. When another's affairs demand attention, one steps into the other's life, managing matters for the other so as to "remove" the other's own care. This way makes one dominant and the other dependent; both lose their freedom. In authentic solicitude, one stands by the other, looks to what the future has in store for both, and helps the other to understand the shared situation and to be resolute in making his or her own place in the world. In this way, each gains authentic selfhood without losing freedom.

According to Sartre's *Being and Nothingness* (1943), sexual relationships model all personal relationships in a capitalist society, which values power and promotes competition among individuals. The "battle of the sexes" reflects the battle of egos in all forms of personal relationships. One seeks to inveigle or force the other to surrender freedom and acknowledge one's own superiority. This incessant struggle for domination is self-defeating and turns into masochism and sadism. Personal relationships cannot be self-affirming, Sartre suggests, until a restructuring of society enables each to will the freedom of all others.

Heidegger's and Sartre's theories point out undesirable ways of caring for others, which render personal relationships mutually self-destructive. Personal sexual relationships involve power, not only pleasure. Evils in personal relationships are the short-sighted, callous, or cruel exercise of power and authority, and the manipulation and exploitation of another for personal advantage. Modern ethics stresses the evils of sexual harassment and the violation of another's rights, autonomy, and dignity.

It is agreed that each person in a relationship should be honest, sincere, and compassionate toward the other, respecting the other's individuality and integrity. Although a relationship should foster moral development, there is debate regarding whether one should be "the conscience of others," in Heidegger's phrase, or withhold forgiveness from an intimate on moral grounds. Most controversial is the primacy of autonomy, especially in close personal relationships. Joint decision making by spouses, for example, on matters of common interest is desirable yet may compromise autonomy; on occasion, one's own good, the good of another, or the preservation of the relationship itself may involve some yielding of autonomy. Because autonomy honors commitments based on rational choice and can change according to circumstances, it does not support biological family ties, and every personal loyalty, including marriage, is revocable. Yet constancy amid changing circumstances is the ethical and emotional heart of enduring personal relationships.

UNFINISHED BUSINESS

Anglo-American ethics, with its emphasis on individual rights and autonomy, has largely neglected the philosophy of personal relationships. Social changes since World War I—such as the entry of women of childbearing age into the work force, the liberalization of sexual relationships, divorce and remarriage of those with young children, increase in life span, and government social programs—have altered traditional forms of personal relationships and created new ones. The dynamics of intimacy and personal moral character for traditional relationships in these changed social conditions and for newer forms of relationships require further study.

A major issue is the reevaluation of the social importance of the family. The disintegration of the family contributes to, or makes intractable, social problems of drug addiction, child abuse and neglect, learning and educational deficiencies, juvenile crime, and homelessness. It is estimated that 40 percent of violent crimes take place between persons who know each other—often, between family members or persons with consensual relationships. Training and support in family life help an individual to deal with anger and frustration toward intimates and to develop the self-discipline needed to succeed in education and employment.

A second issue is the reexamination of ideals and standards of conduct in marriage, the family, and consensual relationships. Family life needs not only to embody justice but also to be fulfilling to adults and attentive to the well-being and moral development of children. Although fear of AIDS has led to more circumspection in sexual relationships and negative features of the "single-parent" family prompt measures to prevent pregnancy among teenagers, attention should go beyond health to the impact of consensual personal relationships on the characters and overall well-being of the individuals concerned and others caught in their relationships.

Gender differences in personal relationships make a difference. Whether women and men have divergent ethical perspectives is still being debated, but there is agreement that the goals and expectations of men and women differ in heterosexual relationships: Women usually look for trust, security, and companionship, while men more often seek immediate pleasure and are content with less emotional involvement. Gender differences also operate in problems of sexual harassment in and out of the workplace.

Finally, there are ethical differences between parity and nonparity personal relationships. In relationships between friends, spouses, coworkers, and siblings, there is rough parity between two persons in terms of power, knowledge, talents, and moral authority. In contrast, parent-child, employer-employee, doctor-patient, and teacher-student relationships involve an imbalance so that the obligations, ideals, and goals of one are in some respects not the same or commensurate with those of the other. Achieving the ideals of the relationship and the avoidance of manipulation and destructive dependency may take different forms in parity and nonparity relationships.

The physician-patient relationship provides a model of how modern ethics has changed ideals in interpersonal relationships. In traditional medical paternalism, a doctor made decisions about how to treat and what to tell a patient and often withheld from a patient knowledge of the seriousness of his or her medical condition. Biomedical ethics has modified this nonparity relationship: A physician is now required by law to obtain informed consent for treatment from a competent patient; a patient has the moral obligation to participate in decision making and to take into account interests of his or her intimates. A patient needs to know the truth about his or her future prospects, in part because they affect the lives of his or her intimates. By extending and applying the insights and ideals of justice and care ethics, the philosophy of personal relationships may analyze and reform more intimate one-on-one intercourse.

Evelyn M. Barker

FURTHER READING

Badinter, Elisabeth. *The Unopposite Sex: The End of the Gender Battle.* Translated by Barbara Wright. New York: Harper & Row, 1989. A lively anthropological account of heterosexual relationships from prehistory onward, with speculation on the impact of new reproductive technologies.

Blum, Lawrence A. *Friendship, Altruism, and Morality.* London: Routledge & Kegan Paul, 1980. Argues the reliability of altruistic emotions for moral motivation and the consistency of friendship with ethical impartiality.

Gilligan, Carol. *The Birth of Pleasure.* New York: Alfred A. Knopf, 2002. At once a critique of the negative effects of patriarchy upon loving relationships and a hopeful manifesto for a better way of life, this book examines children's play, adult couples' therapy, and literary representations to reach conclusions about the way we can, should, and do interact with one another.

_____. *In a Different Voice: Psychological Theory and Women's Development*. Cambridge, Mass.: Harvard University Press, 1982. An eloquent description of psychological studies supporting the theory of two different courses of moral development in men and women.

Murphy, Jeffrie G., and Jean Hampton. *Forgiveness and Mercy*. New York: Cambridge University Press, 1988. A revealing debate on the justice ethics proposition that forgiveness is sometimes morally wrong.

Noddings, Nel. *Caring: A Feminine Approach to Ethics and Moral Education*. Berkeley: University of California Press, 1984. A readable exposition of an ethics based on caring rather than on principles, showing how ethical care develops from natural care experienced in childhood.

Thomas, Laurence. *Living Morally: A Psychology of Moral Character*. Philadelphia: Temple University Press, 1989. An insightful analysis of parental love that compares it to friendship and romantic love.

SEE ALSO: *Being and Nothingness*; Family; Family values; Friendship; Heidegger, Martin; *I and Thou*; Internet chat rooms; Marriage.

Pessimism and optimism

DEFINITION: Pessimism: tendency to expect the worst or to favor the grimmest possible interpretation of events; optimism: tendency to expect the best or to favor the most positive possible interpretation of events

TYPE OF ETHICS: Theory of ethics

SIGNIFICANCE: To outside observers, both pessimism and optimism may seem to pervert a person's ability to see the world clearly. To the pessimist or optimist, failure to see the world as they do may constitute a failure to see the world clearly. In either case, pessimism and optimism may have significant ethical consequences, since they either represent or interfere with the ability to understand the true ethical significance of a given state of affairs.

Pessimism and optimism are cognitive explanatory styles (stable tendencies to make particular kinds of attributions concerning positive and negative events). A pessimistic explanatory style looks at uncontrollable events as internal ("It is my fault"), stable ("I will always be this way"), and global ("This is an overall characteristic of mine"). An optimistic explanatory style looks at uncontrollable events as external ("It is someone else's fault"), unstable ("It will be different in the future"), and specific ("Other aspects of myself are different"). When confronted with stressful situations, pessimists believe that they can never gain control, whereas optimists believe that they can maintain control.

Pessimism and optimism are typically measured by means of either self-report scales or content analysis of written or verbal materials. Scales that measure pessimism and optimism are the Life Orientation Test and the Coping Orientations to Problems Experienced (COPE). The COPE has thirteen subscales in three general categories: problem-focused (active coping, planning, suppressing competing activities, restraint, and seeking instrumental social support), emotion-focused (seeking emotional social support, positive reinterpretation and growth, acceptance, turning to religion, and denial), and maladaptive (focusing and venting emotions, behavioral disengagement, and mental disengagement).

HUMAN NATURE

Pessimism and optimism carry differing views of basic human nature. Pessimists view humans as basically selfish, aggressive, and cruel. They believe that people are governed by aggressive, even death-seeking instincts. Optimists view humans as basically good, helpful, and cooperative. They believe that people are basically decent and life-affirming. Pessimists assume that nothing will work out, because people cannot be trusted; optimists assume that everything will work out, because people will ultimately behave well.

Pessimism and optimism are related to psychopathology. Pessimism is associated with depression, suicidal ideas and actions, hopelessness about the future, helplessness about the present, feelings of alienation, anxiety, neuroticism, irrational beliefs, and hostility. In contrast, optimism is related to high self-esteem, achievement, and internal locus of control. Thus, pessimism is linked to psychological illness and optimism is linked to psychological health.

Pessimism and optimism are associated with different coping strategies. Pessimists are more likely to cope with stress by focusing on and venting emotion, giving up, disengaging, or denying the stress. Furthermore, pessimists are at relatively greater risk for helplessness and depression when they confront stressful events.

Optimists are more likely to cope with stress by acting, focusing on problems, and seeking social support. Furthermore, optimists are more likely to emphasize the positive in their appraisals of stressful events. For example, when faced with a problem such as a risky operation or a serious continuing struggle with a competitor, they focus on what they can do rather than on how they feel. They have a relatively higher expectation of being successful, so they do not give up at the first sign of setback. They keep their sense of humor, plan for the future, and reinterpret the situation in a positive light. They acknowledge their problems and illnesses but have confidence that they will overcome them.

PRACTICAL IMPLICATIONS

These coping differences have practical implications. For example, optimistic beginning insurance agents sold 37 percent more insurance than did pessimistic agents in their first two years on the job and were more likely to persist through the difficulties of the job and stay with the company.

Pessimists are at increased risk for illness, suicide attempts and completions, and other types of death. For example, in one 1987 study by Christopher Peterson and Martin Seligman, pessimists had twice as many illnesses and made about twice as many visits to doctors as did optimists. In another study of recent heart bypass surgery patients, optimists employed more adaptive coping strategies, recovered faster, returned to normal activities sooner, and attained a higher quality of life than pessimists did. Longitudinal studies suggest that pessimists may suffer more illnesses over their lifetimes and die younger than optimists.

Optimists are relatively more likely to be physically healthy and to live longer. For example, in one

study by Sandra Levy and colleagues, women who came to the National Cancer Institute for treatment of breast cancer were followed for five years. On the average, optimists died later than pessimists did, even when the physical severity of the disease was the same at the beginning of the five-year period. In another study, baseball Hall-of-Famers who had played between 1900 and 1950 were rated on their cognitive explanatory style. Optimists were significantly more likely to have lived well into old age than were pessimists. Perhaps pessimists are more likely to become ill because they stir up negative emotions rather than acting constructively, they have passive rather than active coping efforts, and they have relatively poor health habits.

Optimism and pessimism are learned or developed early in life. In one study it was found that third-graders had already developed a habitual explanatory style. Furthermore, third-graders with a more pessimistic explanatory style were more prone to depression and performed more poorly on achievement tests compared with those with a more optimistic style.

Pessimistic explanatory styles may be altered—at least optimists think so. Cognitive therapy has been successful in teaching depressed, pessimistic people new explanatory styles. This therapeutic approach involves teaching people to replace pessimistic thoughts with more realistic ones. Following this kind of therapy, Aaron Beck and colleagues found that changes in explanatory style were still evident after one year. Thus, a pessimistic explanatory style may be learned at an early age but can be changed with long-lasting results.

Lillian M. Range

FURTHER READING

Beck, Aaron T., et al. *Cognitive Therapy of Depression*. New York: Guilford Press, 1979.

Chang, Edward C., ed. *Optimism and Pessimism: Implications for Theory, Research, and Practice*. Washington, D.C.: American Psychological Association, 2001.

Folkman, Susan, and Richard S. Lazarus. "Coping as a Mediator of Emotion." *Journal of Personality and Social Psychology* 54, no. 3 (March, 1988): 466-475.

Levy, S. M., et al. "Survival Hazards Analysis in First Recurrent Breast Cancer Patients: Seven-Year

Follow-Up." *Psychosomatic Medicine* 50, no. 5 (September-October, 1988): 520-528.

Peterson, Christopher, Martin E. Seligman, and George E. Vaillant. "Pessimistic Explanatory Style Is a Risk Factor for Physical Illness: A Thirty-Five-Year Longitudinal Study." *Journal of Personality and Social Psychology* 55, no. 1 (July, 1988): 23-27.

Ruprecht, Louis A., Jr. *Tragic Posture and Tragic Vision: Against the Modern Failure of Nerve.* New York: Continuum, 1994.

Scheier, Michael F., Jagdish K. Weintraub, and Charles S. Carver. "Coping With Stress: Divergent Strategies of Optimists and Pessimists." *Journal of Personality and Social Psychology* 51, no. 6 (December, 1978): 1257-1264.

SEE ALSO: Psychology; Santayana, George; Schopenhauer, Arthur; Self-love; Self-respect.

Phenomenology of Spirit

IDENTIFICATION: Book by Georg Wilhelm Friedrich Hegel (1770-1831)

DATE: *Die Phänomenologie des Geistes*, 1807 (*The Phenomenology of Spirit*, 1868; also known as *The Phenomenology of Mind*, 1910)

TYPE OF ETHICS: Modern history

SIGNIFICANCE: Hegel's *Phenomenology* represented his attempt to complete what he saw as Immanuel Kant's incomplete philosophical system. It portrayed the teleological development of consciousness into self-consciousness, self-consciousness into social consciousness, social consciousness's incarnation in a social and ethical community, the historical evolution of different forms of community, and finally, the perfection of consciousness, society, and reality and the realization of the ideal ethical community at the end of history. The structure of Hegel's argument and his philosophy of history were crucial influences upon Karl Marx and the development of Marxism.

Phenomenology of Spirit occupies a crucial place in the development of Hegel's thought. It marks his maturation as a philosopher of the highest rank and anticipates within its own unique format every aspect of his later work. Hence, it is important to understand the overarching themes of the book before turning to its examination of ethics.

A major aim of Hegel in *Phenomenology* is to renew classical Platonic and Aristotelian philosophy from within the modern philosophical tradition. It was only through examination and critique of everything that had been thought since the Greeks that a worldview modeled on theirs could become a practical framework from within which modern people could think and act. In striving to fulfill that aim, Hegel developed a view of the subject who experiences, knows, and acts, which was in conscious opposition to any and all views of subjectivity that were empirical (for example, John Locke), naturalistic (for example, much of the thought of the Enlightenment), or transcendental (for example, Immanuel Kant). His view was that the acting and experiencing subject is both self-transforming over time (hence, historical) and fundamentally social (in opposition to any and all individualist models).

Thus, in the book's first major section, "Consciousness," Hegel demonstrates that consideration of even the apparently most basic forms of knowing, such as sense perception, produces in the knowing subject an awareness of both itself as knowing and of other knowing subjects. Out of these experiences arises self-consciousness. In Hegel's famous examination of the master-servant relationship in the section "Self-Consciousness," he graphically describes the social yet divided character of human experience.

In the remainder of *Phenomenology*, Hegel depicts the experiences of this divided human self. In doing so, he examines what are for him the key movements in the development of consciousness in Western culture from the Greeks to Hegel's own time. Stoicism, skepticism, the unhappy consciousness of religion, the development of modern philosophy from René Descartes to Kant, the opportunities and perils of freedom in the era of the French Revolution, the phases of religious development in human history—all these are subsumed into Hegel's story of the development of *Geist*, or "spirit." *Geist* is the larger rational plan of which all phases of the development of human consciousness are instances. Each phase is therefore a partial revelation of *Geist*.

RELEVANCE TO ETHICS

Chapter 6 of *Phenomenology*, in which Hegel examines the development of *Geist* from the Greeks down to his own time, is the section of the book that is germane to ethics. It is structured around a distinction crucial to Hegel's thought, that between morality (*Moralität*) and ethical community (*Sittlichkeit*). Morality is that arena of human life in which the individual is thought of as a subject who is responsible for his or her actions. For Hegel, however, moral life attains its highest realization only within the larger life of a society; this is the realm of ethical community. To be truly morally free therefore requires a society within which that freedom can be expressed.

Here, Hegel's historical reconstruction of Western consciousness becomes crucial. Once there *was* a historically existing ethical community—that of the ancient Greeks—in which the city-state provided for its citizens the essential meaning of their lives. This primal *Sittlichkeit* was lost forever in its original form, however, because of developments within Greek culture itself. Hegel's profound discussion of the tensions between divine law and human law in Sophocles' play *Antigone* (c. 441 B.C.E.) exemplifies his view that the Greek ethical world had within it the seeds of its own destruction.

Such a natural ethical system, arising spontaneously out of the early developments of Greek cultural life, was inevitably going to be destroyed, Hegel thought, because the ongoing development of *Geist* toward greater self-consciousness would show such a system to be restricted. Socrates' inquiries initiate the transformation of this first natural *Sittlichkeit*: its original unity was shattered by developments within it as Greek thinkers restlessly searched for universal standards of reason and morality—that is, standards greater than the framework of polis life.

Hegel then went on to describe the standpoint of morality as characteristic of the modern spirit. It is crucial to emphasize that the moral standpoint is, for Hegel, an individualist model of human action. Even when this modern individualist morality is developed to its highest point, at which the individual moral self is seen as identical with the universal law of reason, as in the philosophy of Kant, it is still partial or one-sided in Hegel's view.

Thus, *Phenomenology* contains a tension in Hegel's ethical thought as it had developed to this point: From a historical point of view, modern morality was superior to Greek ethical community because it was a later, higher stage of *Geist*'s ongoing self-revelation; if modern morality is an advance, however, it is nevertheless a one-sided and partial one, doing scant justice to the social aspects of human communal life. What Hegel would later attempt in *Philosophy of Right* (*Grundlinien der Philosophie des Rechts*, 1821) was the construction of a modern notion of ethical community that would be historically as well as philosophically superior to both Greek ethical life and modern individualist moralities. The reader of *Phenomenology of Spirit* thus catches the development of Hegel's ethical thought in process and will be led to turn to *Philosophy of Right* to encounter his resolution of the tension that so provocatively animates the discussion of ethics in *Phenomenology*.

Michael W. Messmer

FURTHER READING

Beiser, Frederick C., ed. *The Cambridge Companion to Hegel*. Cambridge, England: Cambridge University Press, 1993.

Heidegger, Martin. *Hegel's Phenomenology of the Spirit*. Bloomington: Indiana University Press, 1988.

Pippin, Robert B. *Hegel's Idealism: The Satisfactions of Self-Consciousness*. New York: Cambridge University Press, 1989.

Shklar, Judith N. *Freedom and Independence: A Study of the Political Ideas of Hegel's "Phenomenology of Mind."* Cambridge, England: Cambridge University Press, 1976.

Solomon, Robert C. *In the Spirit of Hegel: A Study of G. W. F. Hegel's "Phenomenology of Spirit."* New York: Oxford University Press, 1983.

Stern, Robert. *Routledge Philosophy Guidebook to Hegel and the "Phenomenology of Spirit."* New York: Routledge, 2002.

Taylor, Charles. *Hegel*. Cambridge, England: Cambridge University Press, 1975.

_____. *Hegel and Modern Society*. Cambridge, England: Cambridge University Press, 1979.

Wood, Allen W. *Hegel's Ethical Thought*. Cambridge, England: Cambridge University Press, 1990.

SEE ALSO: Ethics/morality distinction; Hegel, Georg Wilhelm Friedrich; Idealist ethics; Intersubjectivity; Kant, Immanuel; Kantian ethics; Marx, Karl; Teleological ethics; Transcendentalism.

Philo of Alexandria

IDENTIFICATION: Early Egyptian philosopher
BORN: c. 20 B.C.E., Alexandria (now in Egypt)
DIED: c. 45 C.E., Alexandria (now in Egypt)
TYPE OF ETHICS: Religious ethics
SIGNIFICANCE: The author of *The Creation of the World*, *That God Is Immutable*, and *On the Ten Commandments* (all early first century C.E.), Philo combined Old Testament theology with Greek philosophy, especially that of Plato and the Stoics.

Philo of Alexandria, also known as Philo Judaeus, is best remembered as an allegorist who attempted to bridge the gap between Greek philosophy and Hebrew Scripture. For example, he harmonized Plato's *Timaeus* with the scriptural account of creation by articulating a view that the Logos, or the world of intelligible ideas, existed first as God's thoughts and then as the way in which God leads creatures to know him. Philo wished to reconcile natural knowledge and prophetic knowledge, laws of nature and miracles, and causality and free will.

Philo's attempt to blend Greek and Jewish ideas affected his moral philosophy. On one hand, his writings are filled with expressions of Jewish piety. In his personal life, he practiced renunciation of the self and sought immediate communion with God through the Logos. On the other hand, much of Philo's teaching shows clear signs of Stoic origins; for example, in the attention that he gives to virtue.

Philo differed from the Stoics in that he did not believe that emotions needed to be rooted out. Again harmonizing Greek philosophy with Hebrew Scripture, Philo held that most people were neither completely virtuous nor completely wicked. God's grace led people to improve. Also, based upon his reading of Scripture, Philo included faith; *philanthropia*, or giving help to those in need; and repentance in his list of virtues. Moreover, he held that God would reward virtuous acts in the spiritual hereafter.

James M. Dawsey

SEE ALSO: Jewish ethics; Plato; Platonic ethics; Stoic ethics; Torah.

Photojournalism

DEFINITION: Profession of news photographers
TYPE OF ETHICS: Media ethics
SIGNIFICANCE: As the tellers of visual stories in the news, photojournalists have special ethical and legal responsibilities to create pictures that are honest reflections of reality.

Photojournalism is the journalistic side of photography that visually captures and documents moments in time. Photographers create still-life documentaries that tell stories about politics, sports, disasters, wars, crime, and other situations that involve human emotions, and supplement the written stories of the news. The profession dates back to the mid-1800's, when photographs began being used as the bases for engraved illustrations in news publications. By the end of the century, the halftone process, a technique that enabled printing something closer to true photographs, alongside text, was used worldwide. During the 1930's, candid photography was brought to the masses and photojournalism, as it later became known, was born. During that decade, many picture magazines flourished, most notably *Life*, which then set the world standard for photojournalism. As the profession grew, so did the need for ethical standards.

THE RIGHT OF PRIVACY

During the mid-nineteenth century, the journalism profession underwent a major change after two lawyers, Samuel D. Warren and Louis D. Brandeis, argued for the right for privacy in an article published in the *Harvard Law Review*. Their article stemmed from the insensitive coverage by Boston newspapers of a woman's private social life. As a result of the law review article, privacy doctrines were established in journalism that set standards for both writers and photojournalists.

The first principle, called appropriation, forbade the unauthorized commercial use of private individuals' names or identities. This principle protected the property interests people have in their own names and images. Examples of forbidden behavior included photographing formally staged creative performances without permission, photographing images for editorial purposes and then using them for advertising without obtaining written permission, and manipulating and deliberately distorting photographic images without labeling them as "photo illustrations."

The second principle, intrusion and trespass, pertains to the offensive physical, electronic, or mechanical invasion of other people's solitude or seclusion. Historically, this principle has been frequently violated by aggressive photojournalists, who trespass on private property to get their pictures, and photographers of celebrities known as "paparazzi," who are notorious for their intrusiveness and disrespect for the privacy of their subjects.

The second principle is closely related to the third, the prohibition against public disclosure of private information that is offensive or that is of not legitimate concern to the public. Examples include photographing undressed celebrities sunbathing on their private yachts, eavesdropping with telephoto lenses, and shooting pictures with hidden cameras. Another prohibition is falsely portraying, distorting, or fictionalizing a subject's characteristics, conduct, or beliefs, in reckless disregard of the subject's privacy and reputation.

Although all persons are protected under these principles, violations by photojournalists have been common. The subjects of photojournalists who receive the least respect for their privacy are criminals, followed by public officials (both elected and appointed), other public figures, celebrities, short-term heroes in news stories, innocent victims of tragedies, and relatives of prominent people. Photojournalists who adhere to their profession's ethical standards respect the principles of privacy and try to get signed releases from subjects not considered public figures before publishing their pictures.

PROFESSIONAL CODE OF ETHICS

The National Press Photographers Association, a professional society of photojournalists, has created a code of ethics for its members. The foundation of the ethical code is built on truthfulness, honesty, and objectivity. The code also calls for photojournalists to maintain sympathy for humanity and to remember their duty to society. The code advises photojournalists to use common sense and good judgment in situations not covered in the code.

A policy on handling electronic images issued by the Associated Press in 1990 states that photographs should not be manipulated or changed in any way, so that journalistic pictures always tell the truth. The

O. J. Simpson's unretouched police mug shot. (AP/Wide World Photos)

Doctored Photos

In 1994, *Time* magazine used a manipulated police mug shot of murder suspect O. J. Simpson on its cover. The fact that the photograph had been altered was immediately evident to anyone who compared it to the cover of *Newsweek* magazine, which used an unaltered version of the same shot. *Time* had altered its cover photograph to such a degree that it made Simpson's face look darker, blurry, and unshaven, thus making him appear to be more sinister. The person who altered the photograph justified his manipulation, saying that he had wanted to make the picture "more artful, more compelling."

photojournalists' code of ethics does not answer all the questions faced by photojournalists. For example, some of the most frequently occurring issues, including publication of graphic images of nudity, obscene behavior, severe injuries, dead people, and other forms of human suffering, are the focus of many newsroom debates. Even ostensibly innocent photographs of children playing under sprinklers on hot summer days might result in ethical and legal problems.

Betty Attaway-Fink

FURTHER READING

Clark, Roy P., and Cole C. Campbell, eds. *The Values and Craft of American Journalism.* Gainesville: University Press of Florida, 2002.

Day, Louis A. *Ethics in Media Communications: Cases and Controversies.* 4th ed. Belmont, Calif.: Wadsworth, 2002.

Kovach, Bill, and Tom Rosenstiel. *The Elements of Journalism: What Newspeople Should Know and the Public Should Expect.* New York: Crown Publishers, 2001.

Parrish, Fred S. *Photojournalism: An Introduction.* Belmont, Calif.: Wadsworth, 2002.

Pavlik, John V. *Journalism and New Media.* New York: Columbia University Press, 2001.

Pritchard, David, ed. *Holding the Media Accountable: Citizens, Ethics, and the Law.* Bloomington: Indiana University Press, 2000.

Sloan, David W., and Lisa M. Parcell. *American Journalism: History, Principles, Practices.* Jefferson, N.C.: McFarland, 2002.

SEE ALSO: Accuracy in Media; American Society of Newspaper Editors; Electronic surveillance; Fairness and Accuracy in Reporting; Invasion of privacy; Journalistic entrapment; Journalistic ethics; Media ownership; News sources; Professional ethics; Tabloid journalism.

Physician-patient relationship

DEFINITION: Association between a doctor and client
TYPE OF ETHICS: Personal and social ethics
SIGNIFICANCE: Ethical aspects of the physician-patient relationship are governed both by codes of professional conduct and by statutory law. The relationship raises issues involving paternalism, autonomy, confidentiality, and informed consent.

The two parties to any physician-patient relationship are polarized in numerous respects, which normally include (but are not limited to) educational status, economic status, social status, and health status. The presence of any combination of these differences in status, and the extent to which they prevail, in any particular physician-patient relationship has a decided effect on the relationship itself. This is so be-

cause it is precisely these kinds of differences in status that translate into differences in the interests, goals, values, and expectations of the patient and of the physician. Ultimately, these latter differences all too often serve to undermine the success of the physician-patient relationship.

While physician-patient relationships can involve anything from preventive medical examinations of patients whose health status is not noticeably diminished to the treatment of terminally ill patients who are suffering from a significantly diminished health status, Western medical orthodoxy has evolved in such a way as to treat disease and illness after the fact rather than to promote measures and practices that might prevent the onset of disease or illness. Consequently, the vast majority of people in Western cultures who find themselves in a physician-patient relationship as the patient do so only after recognition of their own diminished health status. This, too, has a decided effect on the relationship in question. This is true because the severity of the symptoms of the patient's disease, illness, or injury determines the extent to which the patient has also fallen victim to physiological and/or emotional pain, impairment of the cognitive and reasoning abilities, fear of the unknown, and a perceived loss of control over oneself, one's body, and one's world as one knows it.

For all these reasons, it is not atypical for the physician-patient relationship to engender a very one-sided imbalance of power, and it is precisely this imbalance of power that raises the following fundamental ethical issues that are inherent in the physician-patient relationship: paternalism, autonomy, and informed consent.

PATIENT'S RIGHT TO CHOOSE

Whenever a physician restricts or otherwise impedes a patient's freedom to determine what is done by way of therapeutic measures to herself or himself and attempts to justify such an intrusion by reasons exclusively related to the welfare or needs of the patient, the physician can be construed to have acted paternalistically. To the extent that a physician engages in such paternalistic practices with respect to a patient, the physician is failing to respect that patient's autonomy; that is, the patient's moral right to self-determination.

In spite of the fact that the primary goal of both the physician and the patient should be the restoration of the patient's optimal health status, any differences between the interests, other goals, values, and expectations of the patient as compared to those of the physician within the context of the very same therapeutic relationship set the stage for paternalistic practices on the part of the physician at the expense of the patient's autonomy. Furthermore, the very presence of any or all of the aforementioned by-products of the symptoms of disease, illness, or injury serve only to exacerbate the problem.

For example, an old patient with several major medical problems, the combined effects of which indicate that she has only a couple of weeks to live, decides that she wants her kidney dialysis (which is her lifeline because of chronic renal failure) discontinued. Any additional week or so of her life that may be gained by continuing the dialysis is, in her mind, far outweighed both by her own poor quality of life and by the emotional trauma being caused to her loved ones. The attending physician, however, who is committed to a profession that is dedicated to healing and to the sustaining of life, believes firmly that any means of prolonging the life of this patient is justified and should be pursued.

In this case, there would appear to be a conflict of values, if not of expectations and interests, between the physician and the patient, the result of which is paternalistic practices on the part of the physician at the expense of the patient's autonomy. When asked to justify his position, the physician might argue that the patient's cognitive and reasoning abilities have been impaired by the combined symptoms of her many and varied medical problems to the extent that her capacity for effective deliberation concerning her own medical treatment is significantly compromised and that, consequently, the patient is no longer capable of autonomous decision making.

The central question in such a case is whether the patient's decision is consistent with the types of values, interests, and goals that she has expressed throughout her life, or, failing that, whether the patient's decision is the reasonable outcome of a prudent reassessment of her own values, interests, and goals in the light of her present circumstances. The answer to this question should determine whether the patient is any longer capable of autonomous decision making, and consequently, whether questions concerning the transgression of the patient's autonomy should even arise.

> ## When Physicians May Breach Patient Confidentiality
>
> Whether physicians or genetic counselors should breach patient confidentiality in order to inform at-risk relatives of their risks of developing genetic diseases is an area of great controversy. The American Society of Human Genetics has argued that professional disclosure of familial genetic information to at-risk relatives, against a patient's expressed wishes, is permitted when all these criteria are met:
>
> - the physicians cannot persuade the patients to disclose the information
>
> - the harm of not disclosing the information is serious and foreseeable
>
> - the patients' at-risk relatives are known
>
> - the diseases are preventable or treatable, or early monitoring will reduce genetic risks
>
> - the harm of not disclosing the genetic information is greater than the harm of disclosure

Informed consent is intended to be both a moral and a legal safeguard to respect the patient's autonomy and to promote the welfare of the patient. In the medical context, "informed consent" refers to a patient's agreement to and approval of, upon obtaining an understanding of all relevant information, a recommended treatment or procedure that is intended to be of therapeutic value to the patient. The very concept of informed consent raises the following ethical questions.

Given the previously mentioned by-products of the symptoms of disease, illness, or injury (up to and including the impairment of cognitive and reasoning abilities), what percentage of patients, either in the physician's office or in the medical institution, are truly competent to provide their *informed* consent? Given the various respects, already mentioned, in which physicians and their patients are polarized, what constitutes the proper quantity and quality of information necessary for a patient's consent to be truly informed? Given the imbalance of power that normally exists in the physician-patient relationship and the extreme authority status typically afforded physicians, which together pose a serious threat of manipulation of the patient, when, if ever, is a patient's informed consent truly voluntary?

In response to these and other ethical questions that arise within the context of the physician-patient relationship, various models of the relationship have been proposed; however, each of these models has been shown to be flawed (some more than others). Suffice it to say that any model that is proposed for any personal relationship, including that of physician and patient, will fail to the extent that it does not adequately appreciate the singular importance of the individual character of both parties to the relationship. In the final analysis, any attempt to legislate morality is doomed to fail.

Stephen C. Taylor

FURTHER READING

Brody, Howard. "The Physician-Patient Relationship." In *Medical Ethics*, edited by Robert M. Veatch. Boston: Jones & Bartlett, 1989.

Childress, James F. *Who Should Decide? Paternalism in Health Care*. New York: Oxford University Press, 1982.

Jackson, Jennifer. *Truth, Trust, and Medicine*. New York: Routledge, 2001.

Ramsey, Paul. *The Patient as Person*. New Haven, Conn.: Yale University Press, 1970.

Shelp, Earl E., ed. *Virtue and Medicine*. Dordrecht, Netherlands: D. Reidel, 1985.

Tauber, Alfred I. *Confessions of a Medicine Man: An Essay in Popular Philosophy*. Cambridge, Mass.: MIT Press, 1999.

U.S. President's Commission for the Study of Ethical Problems in Medicine and Biomedical and Behavioral Research. *Making Health Care Decisions*. Vols. 1 and 3. Washington, D.C.: Government Printing Office, 1982.

SEE ALSO: Confidentiality; Consent; Death and dying; Diagnosis; Hippocrates; Illness; Institutionalization of patients; Medical bills of rights; Medical ethics; "Playing god" in medical decision making; *Principles of Medical Ethics*; Therapist-patient relationship.

Plagiarism

DEFINITION: Unauthorized and unacknowledged appropriation of other persons' work in work that one presents as one's own; usually takes the form of writing but may also occur in such other forms as music, art, computer programming, and even data collection

TYPE OF ETHICS: Media ethics

SIGNIFICANCE: Plagiarism can call into question the unspoken contract between writer and reader, rob original producers of the credit they deserve, and fundamentally disrupt academic integrity and the learning processes. Nonetheless, because definitions of, and reactions to, plagiarism vary across time and cultures and even among academics themselves, its ethical ramifications are often disputed.

The word "plagiarism" derives from *plagiarius*, a Latin word for kidnapper. Despite plagiarism's violent etymology and the fact that plagiarism itself is often regarded as theft, plagiarism is a practice that robs its victims of nothing material. It is related to copyright violation and fraud but should not be confused with those practices, which differ from plagiarism in being offenses that are punishable under legal statutes. For professional writers, journalists, and scholars found guilty of plagiarism, however, the practice can be grounds for dismissal and public disgrace. Most universities have policies warning students that if they plagiarize in their course work, they will fail their courses. Repeat plagiarism violations usually result in expulsion from universities.

Around the turn of the twenty-first century, plagiarism was receiving considerable attention, both in the mainstream media and among educators. Famous—and sometimes controversial—cases included accusations of plagiarism against Martin Luther King, Jr., historian and scholar Doris Kearns Goodwin, and *New York Times* reporter Jayson Blair.

Plagiarism was becoming increasingly recognized as a widespread and growing problem, made easier by such new information technologies as the Internet, that allow for both easy research and source retrieval and easy ways to cut and paste without attribution.

PROBLEMS WITH DEFINING PLAGIARISM

Statistics about the pervasiveness of plagiarism have revealed certain contradictions. For example, some reports have suggested that anywhere from 45 percent to 80 percent of high school students have admitted to "cheating," while some 15 percent to 54 percent say that have plagiarized from sites on the Internet's World Wide Web. These wide variations in statistics, and the evident discrepancies between cheating and plagiarism rates, may suggest that some students do not consider plagiarism to be "cheating" or that they do not consider what they do to be plagiarism. Indeed, in a 2003 survey conducted by Rutgers University professor Donald L. McCabe, approximately half the students surveyed declared that they did not think it was cheating to copy up to an entire paragraph of text from the Web.

Most of those students' teachers would disagree, although they, too, vary in how they define this problem. Any sort of blatant fraud—such as downloading or purchasing entire term papers or articles and presenting them as one's own work—is generally reviled as an extreme form of dishonesty. It is also usually considered plagiarism to include in one's paper literal word-for-word copies of substantial portions of others' work when the original sources are not acknowledged.

Plagiaristic practices can also include the failure to credit sources when presenting other writers' ideas, even when they are merely paraphrased or summarized. However, this view is complicated by the fact that what people consider to be "common knowledge"—which usually does not need to be cited—varies from discipline to discipline and among student levels within a discipline. Sometimes, using quotation marks but not citations, or listing sources only at the end of a paper, without providing appropriate footnotes within the text, may be considered plagiarism, though this might more accurately be called improper citation.

IMPORTANCE OF CITATION

Because plagiarism involves a failure to provide acknowledgment, it is useful to understand why academics consider citation important. As with the definition of plagiarism, there are multiple rationales. Many people focus on the moral issues, believing that citing is the fair or ethical thing to do because it gives recognition to others whose ideas are important to one's own work. They believe that to deny credit is tantamount to stealing another person's ideas.

Other people focus on the social ethics involved, explaining that citations work to build a community of scholars. They believe that all knowledge is ulti-

After it was revealed that the New York Times' *rising star reporter Jayson Blair had filled his news stories with plagiarized material and pure fiction, he was fired, and there was a shakeup in the newspaper's top editorial staff. Afterward, Blair published a memoir,* Burning Down My Master's House: My Life at "The New York Times" *(2004), that was filled with revelations about shoddy practices at the newspaper but which failed to justify his own actions. (AP/ Wide World Photos)*

mately collaborative and want all persons involved in its creation to be recognized as contributors to the process. Such a rationale, like the first, relies on notions of fairness to earlier producers.

Citations also serve an intellectual purpose, showing the history of ideas and how they have developed over time. At the same time, they also help ensure the accuracy of one's work, as the listed sources can be tracked, traced, and corroborated. Of little ethical significance, though important rhetorically, citations help bolster a writer's authority. Through citation, writers exhibit knowledge of the field on which they are writing and show the supporting evidence for their ideas, thus giving their work as a whole more credibility and legitimacy in the eyes of their readers.

Finally, there is what may be called the amoral rationale, which considers citations one of many social and genre-specific conventions that writers must emulate in order to demonstrate proficiency in their particular realm of writing. For example, while academic essays demand extensive attribution, a magazine article may rely on paraphrasing or summarizing with few or no references listed. Some workplace writing, especially anonymous or bureaucratic forms, use no citations at all, and even the direct transcription of sources may be acceptable.

Even among educators, however, the understanding of the ethical issues surrounding plagiarism may vary according to one's academic, theoretical, or methodological framework.

APPROACHES TO PLAGIARISM

The traditional approach calls on universal moral standards in casting all sorts of plagiarism as cheating. It decries plagiarism as fundamentally immoral, equivalent to theft or lying, because it violates tenets of authorial originality. It may place the blame for plagiarism on permissive social values or moral relativism. There are concerns that this sort of cheating is becoming an acceptable part of the student culture of high schools and colleges. Illustrated in most university policies, this approach fails to distinguish between types of plagiarism or the differing conventions governing writing tasks. It also may not factor in intentionality—whether or not writers purposely set out to deceive their teachers—or deficiencies in understanding the norms of citation use.

In the historical approach, those studying the his-

tory of plagiarism view the concept—and its ethical ramifications—as developing in specific and disparate cultural contexts. They assert that plagiarism is not a universally despised example of "theft" or "dishonesty." Instead, they see it as a set of practices that carries diverse moral inflections and receives various ethical treatments. Unacknowledged copying, in other words, may be normative in one era and decried in another. For example, Renaissance writers esteemed imitation, seeing it as a way of exhibiting one's learning and expressing one's debt to earlier writers. Knowledge was believed to be shared, and inspiration was seen as a gift from God.

With the rise of the print marketplace in the eighteenth century, however, the financial stakes were raised. The first copyright law was passed in 1709 at the urging of booksellers; the notion of individual artistic originality developed over the next half century. With a vested interested in seeing their writing as property, a new class of professional writers begin representing plagiarism as a pressing moral and artistic concern.

Literary historians are thus careful, when discussing plagiarism, not to present it as a concept that is "naturally" or "normally" understood as a timeless social ill, but one that bears the imprint of the cultural expectations of specific times and places. Practitioners of this approach have been charged with conveying a dangerous moral relativism, though most do not condone cheating, copying, or fraudulent authorship in an academic environment.

IMPACT OF TECHNOLOGY

As the World Wide Web has increasingly become many students' primary research tool, new technology-based forms of plagiarism have proliferated. Not only can students easily download or cut and paste from a variety of legitimate information sites, but digital "paper mills"—online businesses that sell completed student papers—make the most egregious forms of plagiarism easier than ever. Some observers believe that the only way to combat the increased opportunities for "cyber-plagiarism" provided by these new opportunities is to turn to technology itself. Web-based search engines such as Google can often track down, in seconds, the Web sources copied into student papers.

Furthermore, services have been created that provide online plagiarism-detection software; Turnitin

.com is one of the most widely used. Many universities or their individual departments subscribe to such services, knowing that their doing so deters student cheating, even when individual teachers do not use these services themselves. Nonetheless, ethical questions have been raised about possible violations of student privacy—every paper submitted becomes part of the business's database—and the propriety of responding to all student work with suspicion.

Another way of understanding Internet-specific plagiarism, however, suggests that these may be futile—or even reactionary—responses. They see the ease with which students can copy from the Internet not as a temptation, but a new way of thinking about creating texts. Much information on the Web, after all, is collective or anonymous. Web pages often contain chunks of other pages, and graphics freely circulate—mostly without attribution. The Web's ephemeral nature is thought to be fundamentally incompatible with the fixity of text required for "real" plagiarism. Supporters of these ideas draw on historical studies to highlight the different practices of writing supported by modern communication technologies in contrast to those based in market- and property-driven print forms. They believe that new media bring with them a new ethos, and that popular notions of the morality of plagiarism are outdated. Others, however, decry what has been termed the "Napsterization of knowledge" and urge a continuation of print-based ways of understanding and regulating the copying of texts.

PEDAGOGICAL APPROACH

Many of those concerned about student plagiarism—whether they draw on conservative, historical, or technological approaches to understand it—assert that a large part of the ethical responsibility for the problem lies with educators themselves. Many composition instructors, for example, believe that while academic dishonesty should be condemned, proper research methodology, source use, and citation practices should be more rigorously taught to students. Indeed, many believe that "patchwriting," as Rebecca Howard terms the linking together of several paraphrases from unacknowledged sources, is an important stage in the evolution of student knowledge and rhetorical skill.

Such critics may also view plagiarism as a problem in the development of "voice," a reflection of a student's lack of confidence in his or her own opinions and authority, or a misunderstanding of the very purposes of academic writing. Because they see plagiarism as a complex learning issue, these educators question the morality of "prosecuting" students for their ignorance or lack of ability, and they resent the negative effects that the "policing" of plagiarism has on teacher-student relations. Many policy statements written by this camp thus classify plagiarism into two tiers, distinguishing purposeful fraud from accidental source misuse.

The pedagogical approach goes beyond the teaching of writing skills, however. It also focuses on ways instructors can structure classrooms actively to prevent plagiarism. Some insist that academic integrity itself not be taken for granted, but should be routinely explained to, and discussed with, students. Others suggest that teachers should develop more assignments that are difficult to plagiarize because of their specificity, their reliance on course materials, or their relevance to student lives and individual opinions.

ETHICAL IMPLICATIONS

Clearly, plagiarism is a complex issue with a rich history. There are a variety of ways to define and respond to it. Perhaps the most urgent ethical responsibility of students and educators alike, then, is that they continue to explore together the complicated questions engendered by these multiple approaches.

Lisa Maruca

FURTHER READING

Boynton, Robert S. "Is Honor Up for Grabs? Education Isn't About Surveillance." *Washington Post*, May 27, 2001, p. B1. Claims that although the "Napsterization of knowledge" has altered student views of intellectual property, teachers should trust their students instead of policing plagiarism.

Howard, Rebecca Moore. "Plagiarisms, Authorships, and the Academic Death Penalty." *College English* 57, no. 7 (1995): 788-806. This article by an expert in the field of plagiarism and composition uses the history of authorship to argue for a more enlightened view of student patchwriting.

Kewes, Paulina, ed. *Plagiarism in Early Modern England*. New York: Palgrave Macmillan, 2003. Collection of scholarly essays that illustrate the diverse practices and attitudes toward literary borrowing during the sixteenth and seventeenth centuries.

Lathrop, Ann, and Kathleen Foss. *Student Cheating and Plagiarism in the Internet Era: A Wake Up Call.* Westport, Conn.: Greenwood Press, 2000. Guide for educators that discusses the extent of student "high-tech cheating" and provides solutions.

Mallon, Thomas. *Stolen Words.* Rev ed. New York: Harcourt, 2001. Traditionalist approach to plagiarism that covers several case studies. An updated afterword discusses the special problems posed by the Internet.

Vaidhyanathan, Siva. *Copyrights and Copywrongs: The Rise of Intellectual Property and How It Threatens Creativity.* New York: New York University Press, 2003. Broad survey of copyright issues that considers special problems of modern digital resources

Wherry, Timothy Lee. *The Librarian's Guide to Intellectual Property in the Digital Age: Copyright, Patents, Trademarks.* Chicago: American Library Association, 2002. Handbook designed to give librarians practical advice.

Woodmansee, Martha. "Genius and the Copyright." In *The Author, Art and the Market: Rereading the History of Aesthetics.* New York: Columbia University Press, 1994. This historical study of authorship, copyright, and the concept of originality in the eighteenth century provides important background for understanding historical approaches to plagiarism.

SEE ALSO: Art; Computer crime; Computer misuse; Copyright; Intellectual property; Internet piracy; Science.

Plato

IDENTIFICATION: Ancient Greek philosopher
BORN: Aristocles; c. 427 B.C.E., Athens, Greece
DIED: 347 B.C.E., Athens, Greece
TYPE OF ETHICS: Classical history
SIGNIFICANCE: One of the most significant figures in the history of philosophy, Plato wrote numerous dialogues which either preserved the words of Socrates or employed Socrates as a fictional character. In *Republic* (*Politeia*, 388-368 B.C.E.) and other writings, Plato developed a theory of justice based upon a division of the soul in which each part performs a distinctive function.

Plato's writings are in a dialogue format. He discusses philosophical topics through question-and-answer sessions conducted by Socrates. The Socrates of the Platonic dialogues is very closely modeled after the historical Socrates, whose life and death had a tremendous influence upon Plato. The Socrates of the dialogues is, however, at least in part, a fictional character used to impart Platonic themes.

Plato's dialogues are divided into three groups: the early, or Socratic, dialogues; the dialogues of middle age; and the dialogues of old age. The early dialogues employ a particularly rigorous dialectic form. These dialogues frequently deal with ethical topics. In *Protagoras* (399-390 B.C.E.) and *Meno* (388-368 B.C.E.), Plato asks whether virtue can be taught. In *Protagoras* and *Euthydemus* (388-368 B.C.E.), he argues both for and against the supposed Socratic doctrine that virtue and knowledge are identical. In *Gorgias* (399-390 B.C.E.), Plato considers whether it is better to do a wrong than to suffer one. In *Protagoras*, he accepts the hedonistic position that one ought to seek pleasure, but in *Gorgias*, he argues against it. Plato also considers definitions of major ethical terms. He questions the nature of courage, justice, temperance, and piety.

THEORY OF FORMS AND IMPORTANCE OF KNOWLEDGE FOR ETHICS

Plato is perhaps best known for the theory that true reality belongs to eternal, immutable forms. All other things are poor copies of these realities. According to Plato, there are two "worlds": the world of being and that of becoming. Physical objects and copies of these objects (for example, a horse and the shadow of a horse) belong to the two levels of the world of becoming. These things change, come into being, and perish. Forms (such as beauty and justice) and mathematical concepts belong to the world of being. These entities are eternal and possess more reality than do mutable objects. Everything is made possible by the form of the good.

The theory that more knowledge can be had at higher levels is central to Plato's epistemology and ethics. One important aspect of Platonic ethical theory is that the moral individual strives to obtain more knowledge and thus to come closer to the good.

Two important points are illuminated through this discussion of the moral individual's movement toward the good. The first of these is the Platonic/Socratic doctrine that "to know the good is to do the good." Plato argues that a failure to do good is simply a lack of knowledge. Ignorance causes one to behave wrongly.

Plato also argues that reason is more important for ethics than is pleasure. Reason is primary because one must determine which things bring more or less pleasure. Again, the moral individual is the knowledgeable individual.

DEFINITION OF JUSTICE

In *Republic*, Plato puts forward his conception of the ideal state. In book 1, Socrates is concerned with the definition of justice. He believes that justice is preferable to injustice but needs support for this conviction. He moves the discussion to a different level. If one can discern justice in the larger context of a state, then one should be able to understand the meaning of justice at the level of the individual. Plato thus develops a political model for his theory of justice.

In the same way that the just state is the state in which each individual is doing what he or she does best, so the just soul is the soul in which each "part" is performing its unique function. The soul, according to Plato, has three parts: reason, spirit, and appetites. It is, as he explains in *Phaedrus* (388-368 B.C.E.), like a charioteer (reason) trying to control two horses, a wayward one (the appetites) and one that can take orders (the spirited one). The charioteer can reach his goal only when the horses are in control. Likewise, the soul is in harmony only when reason controls and sets the goals, the spirited element moves toward the goals, and the appetites are in control.

Plato explains that there is a virtue that corresponds to each division of the soul. Properly functioning reason has wisdom. The spirit that moves in accordance with reason has courage. The appetites, which are under the control of reason, have temperance. All three parts of the soul working in harmony exhibit the virtue of justice. These four cardinal virtues are an important part of Plato's ethical theory. His concern is more with what kind of person one

should be than with what kinds of things one should do. Again, to *be* wise is to *do* good.

PLACE IN HISTORY

Plato develops an absolutist ethical theory. There is a "right" and a "good" toward which to aspire. He develops this theory to respond to the skepticism and the relativism of the Sophists. One person may be more or less just than another, but each is just in that he or she copies or participates in the form of justice. This form is eternal and unchanging—an absolute.

Alfred North Whitehead claimed that all philosophy after Plato is a series of footnotes to Plato. This is especially true with regard to ethics. Aristotle (384-322 B.C.E.) developed a virtue-based theory of ethics similar to that described above and yet with its own peculiarly Aristotelian slant. Other ethical theories are patterned after that of Aristotle and, thus, that of Plato. Furthermore, any ethical theory insisting upon absolutes is Platonic.

Rita C. Hinton

FURTHER READING

Annas, Julia. *An Introduction to Plato's "Republic."* Oxford, England: Clarendon Press, 1981.

_____. *Platonic Ethics, Old and New.* Ithaca, N.Y.: Cornell University Press, 1999.

Bobonich, Christopher. *Plato's Utopia Recast: His Later Ethics and Politics*. New York: Oxford University Press, 2002.

Gould, John. *The Development of Plato's Ethics.* New York: Russell & Russell, 1972.

Heinaman, Robert, ed. *Plato and Aristotle's Ethics.* Burlington, Vt.: Ashgate, 2003.

Plato. *The Collected Dialogues of Plato.* Edited by Edith Hamilton and Huntington Cairns. 1961. Reprint. Princeton, N.J.: Princeton University Press, 1984.

_____. *The Republic.* Translated by Desmond Lee. 2d ed. New York: Penguin Books, 2003.

Taylor, A. E. *Plato: The Man and His Work.* New York: Dover, 2001.

SEE ALSO: Absolutism; *Apology*; Aristotle; Idealist ethics; Intuitionist ethics; Platonic ethics; *Republic*; Social justice and responsibility; Socrates; Sophists; Virtue ethics.

Platonic ethics

DEFINITION: Moral system put forward by, or modeled on that of, Plato, primarily concerned with ideal ethical forms and with the most ethically beneficial form of government

TYPE OF ETHICS: Classical history; theory of ethics

SIGNIFICANCE: Plato's ethics have influenced moral philosophy for millennia by framing the questions that have occupied ethicists and by securing the place of reason in the resolution of ethical issues.

The key ethical topics of Plato's dialogues may be listed as follows: the definition of the virtues, most prominently justice, moderation, courage, wisdom, and piety; the so-called Socratic paradoxes (first, that no one sins knowingly, and second, that virtue is knowledge); the inseparability of virtue and happiness (*eudaimonia*); the relation of the virtues to political life; the virtues as subspecies of the idea of the good; and the denunciation of hedonism—that is, the rejection of the popular notion that pleasure is that which produces happiness.

Beyond these topics, which are explicitly identified by Plato, the dialogues address numerous areas of ethical import. These include the existence of the soul, immortality, and life after death (in the dialogue *Phaedo*); rewards and punishments; education; the value of the fine arts; men's duties to the gods, to other men, to their cities, to their families, and to themselves; the rights and duties of women; and in the story of Gyges and his invisibility ring (*Republic*), the question of whether the moral status of one's conduct should depend on the consequences of that conduct.

HISTORY

The event that more than any other turned Plato from politics to philosophy was the trial and condemnation of his teacher, Socrates, in the year 399 B.C.E. In his *Phaedo*, written while he was still in his twenties and poignantly close to the memory of Socrates, Plato described Socrates as the best, most intelligent, and most moral man of his time. After that, Plato determined to take no active part in the radically democratic Athenian judicial or governmental system, which he came to define as the government of those least qualified by temperament and intelligence to rule.

Plato's antidote to what he felt to be the rule of the mob was his concept of government by philosopher-kings, people prepared by lifelong education to be good rulers. In his most famous dialogue, *Republic*, he stated that "Unless philosophers become kings of states or else those who are now kings and rulers become real and adequate philosophers . . . there can be no respite from evil for states or, I believe, for the human race."

This idea antedated by many years the appearance of *Republic*. According to Plato's "Seventh Letter," the search for a king whom he might train in philosophy led him in about 389 B.C.E. to Syracuse, Sicily. Having failed in this attempt to turn the Syracusan tyrant Dionysius I into a philosopher-king, Plato returned to Athens in 387 and in the latter 380's founded his Academy, which J. E. Raven called "a training ground for future statesmen." *Republic* was most likely produced soon afterward, during the early 370's.

Any study of Plato's ethical thought must begin with Socrates' attempts to refute the moral relativism of the sophists. Plato's ethics seems to have evolved beyond his master's, for Plato continued to explore the field in his mature and in his latest dialogues, including *Republic*, *Philebos*, and *Laws*.

The sophists had said that the only ethical standards that were morally binding on an individual's behavior were those that all people agreed to or that followed the laws of nature (*physis*). Most of the rules people live by are, they said, really only local norms or customs (*nomos*) that hold little or no moral force. In most cases, therefore, each person is the judge of what is good for himself or herself, and ethics (the ethical measure of *physis*) does not really come into play. Where it is simply a matter of *nomos*, the operative rule was "man is the measure"; that is, what seemed to each individual to be good was, for him, good.

A prime example of a natural law (*physis*) prevalent universally in the world and thus binding on humanity was that of the sophist Thrasymachus, who in *Republic* argued that "might makes right." In the *Gorgias*, Plato makes Callicles of Acharnae articulate the corollary sophist view that local laws were artificial and conventional (mere *nomos*) and framed by the many weak men as a means of keeping the strong under their control.

DEFINITION OF THE VIRTUES

Socrates responded (as is known from Plato's earlier, or Socratic, dialogues) that individual virtues such as courage (discussed in *Laches*), moderation (*Charmides*), piety (*Euthyphro*), and justice (*Republic*) could be defined for all to understand, so as to place most or all ethical activity under the umbrella of universally accepted standards. The realm in which each person was to be judge of the ethical quality of his own actions was much reduced; sophist ethics was defeated.

The Socratic contribution to ethical thought—essential in Plato's system—was identified by Aristotle, who credited Socrates with laying down the principles of "universal definition and inductive reasoning"; that is, arriving at the universal definition of each virtue by means of a discussion and analysis of particular actions (inductive reasoning).

THE SOCRATIC PARADOXES

In developing his own ethical program, Plato took his point of departure from the so-called Socratic paradoxes. The first paradox argues that all men naturally seek to do good but often act wrongly because they mistake evil for good. Men thus commit sin involuntarily and out of ignorance (*Protagoras*). This paradox allows Plato, with Socrates, to define all sin or evil as ignorance and, conversely, to assert that all virtue is knowledge or wisdom: the second paradox.

This knowledge is available to men in general, but ordinary men occasionally err. It thus behooves the best men to acquire knowledge about the virtues, understand their nature, and act on a foundation of knowledge. This is no easy matter and requires a lifelong pursuit of wisdom (*Republic*). Thus, philosophers (seekers of wisdom) will be the wisest and, seeking the good (as all men do), will be less likely to err.

John Gould, in *The Development of Plato's Ethics* (1955), strongly asserts that the goal of Plato's ethical system (virtue, or *areté*) was always to lead to virtuous activity or behavior—for example, justice in the soul will express itself in just action—not merely to arrive at a valid ethical theory. This too was inspired by Socrates, as Plato dramatically demonstrated in the *Crito*, in which his teacher put his ethics into action by accepting the sentence of death as legally binding, refusing to escape from prison when he had the opportunity to do so, and refusing to disobey the state's command that he take poison.

THE TEACHABILITY OF VIRTUE

Since virtue is knowledge and all men possess an innate capacity for knowledge, then virtue can be taught, and teaching and guidance may direct an individual toward good. On this point Plato seems initially to have wavered, for in the *Meno* Plato has Socrates say that virtue comes rather by chance, while in the *Protagoras* he suggests its teachability. Thus, the moral and political education of youths depends on the identity of virtue with knowledge and therefore on the teachability of virtue.

PLATO'S THEORY OF IDEAS OR FORMS AS RELATED TO ETHICS

When one comes really to know the virtues, it is the immutable, stable, and abiding idea, form, or universal definition of the virtue that one comes to know. In the *Gorgias*, Plato has Socrates make the point that belief or opinion (which Gorgias, as a sophist, teaches) is not a sufficient standard for guiding moral and political life. The idea (or definition) of a virtue is learned by induction from particular case studies of the virtue in action.

In *Republic*, Plato lays out the course of lifelong study whose goal is the attainment of knowledge of the ideas and of the highest of the ideas, which Plato variously calls the idea of beauty, truth, or the good. Intimate knowledge of the ideas of the different virtues allows the guardians of the state to recognize the virtues and their opposites in every action in which they are present.

After a primary education (to age eighteen), the citizens, especially those who will emerge as guardians of the republic, are made to dwell in beautiful surroundings so as to attain a love of the idea of the beautiful-in-itself. They next serve two years of military service. This is followed by the citizens' higher education, which consists of ten years in "propaedeutic" (preparatory) studies for those who will become the guardians or philosopher-kings of the state. The subjects studied in this phase are arithmetic, geometry, astronomy, and harmonics (music). The purpose of this scientific quadrivium is to lead the mind away from material and changing objects of the realm of opinion (for example, two apples, two cubes) to immaterial and immutable realities (for example, the concept of "two" and "cubeness").

Plato had derived from Pythagoras a respect for abstract numbers as unchanging realities. Numbers are akin to the unchanging ideas of the virtues, and this training in correct thinking about numbers, Plato thought, prepared the mind to recognize virtue and vice in action. Many aspiring guardians would be left behind during this phase of education.

The final level of higher education consisted of five years of training in dialectic, also known as the Socratic *elenchos*. Dialectic is the process of repeatedly proposing hypotheses and drawing out consequences, used by Socrates in his conversations with his pupils. By this means of interlocution, the pupils were drawn ever closer to the irrefutable and true hypothesis that it had always been the purpose of the session to achieve. Thus, the pupils, future guardians, were trained to brainstorm, together or privately, in the quest for the form or idea that defined and produced knowledge about the virtue in question. This knowledge enabled the guardians to know which human actions claiming to share in the virtue in question were virtuous and which were not. No doubt, other citizens would, at this final plateau, fail to qualify for the ranks of the guardians. Completion of training in dialectic brought the guardians to age thirty-five.

THE OVERRIDING IDEA OF THE GOOD

Some Plato scholars are troubled that in the minor dialogues (*Laches*, among others), the definitions of the virtues sometimes break down when Socrates tests them for their production of happiness in an individual or city. That Plato may have done this deliberately in these early dialogues is indicated by the hints of dramatic purpose as opposed to an air of tentative inquiry in their structure and logic.

In *Republic*, Plato himself warns that these early definitions of virtues are not final. The utility of virtue must be related to an ultimate standard or ideal of the good. He devotes much of *Republic* and *Symposium* to achieving this.

For Plato, the forms of the virtues are themselves subcategories of the idea of the good. In reality, moderation, justice, and all the other virtues, including knowledge, are virtues because they participate in goodness. Plato is clear about this in *Republic*, where he calls the good the ultimate aim of life, the final ob-

ject of desire, and the sustaining cause of everything else. The virtues, whether severally or united under the paradox that all virtue is knowledge, themselves aim at the good.

It is the guardians' vision of the good that enables them to inculcate right opinion, teach virtue, and mold character and institutions in the light of a reasoned concept of goodness in private and public life.

The *Symposium* and other dialogues provide parallels to the idea of the good as final cause by looking, for example, at a hierarchy of friendship, passion, and love culminating in the apprehension of the idea of beauty, which is depicted by Plato as practically identical to the good.

THE RELATIONSHIP OF UTILITY AND PLEASURE TO ETHICS

Plato is clear in rejecting Protagoras's dictum that pleasure is to be identified with the good. He denies as well the notion that utility is the source and goal of morality. In *Lysis* and *Symposium*, Plato rejects the theory that the good is desired as a remedy against evil because that would make the good merely a means to an end. For the same reason, he explicitly rejects the hope of immortality as the origin of and reasons for people's morality. In *Republic*, he strenuously opposes the view of Thrasymachus and Callicles that justice is an artificial convention devised by the weak in their conspiracy to neutralize the strong.

In his article "Plato's Ethics," Paul Shorey believes Plato's whole ethical thrust to be a polemic against hedonism: "This doctrine of the negativity of what men call pleasure is the fundamental basis of Plato's ethics." On this basis, Shorey continues, rests Plato's demonstration that virtue and happiness are one. Moreover, pleasures are never pure but always mixed with desire or pain. Finally, Shorey adds, "Pleasure and pain, like confidence and fear, are foolish counselors."

The dialogues devote much space to analyzing the concept of pleasure, which arises in some form in more dialogues than does any other issue. The *Gorgias* and *Philebos* directly oppose the sophist doctrine that defines the good as pleasure and that asserts that true happiness comes from gratifying the sensual appetites. This repudiation of hedonism also appears in *Phaedo* and *Republic*. In *Republic*, where Plato presents the idea of man's tripartite soul, pleasures are ranked as intellectual, energetic, and sensual. Plato allowed the thesis of the *Protagoras* that a surplus of pleasure is good, but only when the pleasure is kept in perspective and is free from all evil consequences. Only in the sense that it suited his ethical system to argue that the virtuous life is the most pleasurable did Plato make Socrates identify pleasure and the good at the end of *Protagoras*. Rather, it is wisdom (*sophia*) that delivers happiness, for wisdom always achieves its object, wisdom never acts in error, and absence of error entails happiness.

FINAL DEVELOPMENTS IN PLATO'S ETHICS

In Plato's last years, his ethical approach underwent a change little noticed in discussions of mainstream Platonism. John Gould remarks that in his last work, *Laws*, "Plato the aristocrat, Plato the constructor of systems, Plato the lover of the aesthetic are all represented in their final and most convincing forms, while the ghost of Socrates . . . is no longer present even in the *dramatis personae*."

In *Laws*, the thrust is still the perfection of the individual, but now no longer through the personal acquisition of virtue. Instead, the individual is to be improved by means of ideal legislation whose explicit goal is the control and obliteration of nonvirtuous behavior in the interest of the perfection of society. In this last dialogue of Plato's corpus, the primary virtues are given their own separate existence as *sōphrosynī* (moderation or temperance), *dikaiosyne* (justice), *phronesis* (wisdom), and *andreia* (courage), and possession of only one of them is not sufficient.

Plato's thinking has, in fact, undergone a change from that of his Socratic period. In his new ideal state, the legislator will guide his people to virtue by manipulating the distribution of honor and dishonor and by using the pleasures, desires, and passions that motivate people: a kind of nascent behaviorist theory. By using a system of repetitive propaganda to work on popular emotions, he will steer them to virtue (*areté*). Plato's goal was ever the same. What changed in his latter years was his attitude toward human nature, which became more pessimistic. The mistakes of Athenian democracy, rule by the masses, had convinced him that a more thoroughgoing system of controls had to prevail, and this he intended to provide in his new "second-best" state, governed not by philosophers but by law.

Daniel C. Scavone

FURTHER READING

Annas, Julia. *Platonic Ethics, Old and New.* Ithaca, N.Y.: Cornell University Press, 1999. Reads Plato through the lens of the Middle Platonists. Argues for a reinterpretation of Plato that treats each of his dialogues as an autonomous text, rather than reading each as a mere evolutionary step toward the ethics expressed in the *Republic*.

Bobonich, Christopher. *Plato's Utopia Recast: His Later Ethics and Politics.* New York: Oxford University Press, 2002. A major reconsideration of Plato's late works, especially *Laws*, examining his changing attitudes toward ethics in general and the life of the nonphilosopher in particular.

Crombie, I. M. *An Examination of Plato's Doctrines.* London: Routledge & Kegan Paul, 1963. A general work on all aspects of Plato's philosophy, with ninety pages on ethics. Especially useful in tracing Plato's ideas through the early minor dialogues: *Euthyphro*, *Charmides*, *Laches*, *Meno*, and *Euthydemus*.

Gould, John. *The Development of Plato's Ethics.* New York: Russell & Russell, 1972. An excellent survey of the evolution of Plato's ethical views from his youthful days under the influence of Socrates to the fully mature thought of his last dialogues, chiefly *Philebos* and *Laws*.

Grube, G. M. A. *Plato's Thought.* Indianapolis: Hackett, 1980. Perhaps the best introduction to the entire philosophical system of Plato.

Raven, J. E. *Plato's Thought in the Making.* Cambridge, England: Cambridge University Press, 1965. A highly readable discussion of Plato's life and thought, featuring a generous treatment of his ethics and especially a critique of the views of other premier Plato scholars on important issues.

Rowe, Christopher. *An Introduction to Greek Ethics.* London: Hutchinson, 1976. A short introduction to the field that ranges from Homer to the Epicureans and Stoics.

Shorey, Paul. "Plato's Ethics." In *Plato: A Collection of Critical Essays*, edited by Gregory Vlastos. Vol. 2. Garden City, N.Y.: Anchor Books, 1971. A concise introduction to the major ethical issues considered by Plato from the pen of an important Plato scholar.

_____. *What Plato Said.* Chicago: University of Chicago Press, 1978. A highly acclaimed résumé and analysis of Plato's writings with synopses of and critical commentary on twenty-eight dialogues. Treats ethics in appropriate contexts.

Taylor, A. E. *Plato: The Man and His Work*. New York: Dover, 2001. An indispensable book for any study of Plato's philosophy in English. Provides a thorough discussion of every aspect of Platonism.

SEE ALSO: *Apology*; Aristotelian ethics; Aristotle; Boethius; Cynicism; *Nicomachean Ethics*; Plato; *Republic*; Socrates; Sophists; Stoic ethics; *Utopia*.

"Playing god" in medical decision making

DEFINITION: Concept based on the idea that in making decisions—particularly those relating to matters of life and death—medical practitioners and researchers exercise godlike powers

TYPE OF ETHICS: Bioethics

SIGNIFICANCE: The idea of "playing god" may arouse opposition from some individuals and groups who do not believe that human beings should intervene in what they see as a divine plan—either to save life, to allow death, or to engage in research that violates what is perceived as the natural order of things, thus making such activities unethical.

In 1982, theological representatives of three major religions advised the President's Commission for the Study of Ethical Problems in Medicine and Biomedical and Behavioral Research. They concluded that the abilities to carry out treatment and research and to make related decisions raise issues of responsibility, rather than simple prohibition based on purely moral grounds. In fact, they asserted that human beings may actually have a responsibility to pursue that which can improve and benefit human life, and to refuse to do so may be unethical in itself.

Theologically, human beings, having God-given powers, can be seen as co-creators with the Supreme Creator. Many religions therefore respect and support the acquisition of knowledge about nature that has great potential both for improving human life or endangering it and thus stresses responsibility for its use. The ability to "play God" may then reflect not an objection to action, but an expression of awe and concern not only from religious institutions, but from secular institutions as well.

Martha O. Loustaunau

SEE ALSO: Brain death; Experimentation; Infanticide; Life and death; Medical ethics; Medical research; Nazi science; Physician-patient relationship; "Slippery-slope" arguments; Stem cell research; Triage.

Plessy v. Ferguson

THE EVENT: U.S. Supreme Court decision that gave legal sanction to racial segregation in the United States by affirming that separate-but-equal accommodations for blacks and whites were constitutional

DATE: Ruling made on May 18, 1896

TYPE OF ETHICS: Race and ethnicity

SIGNIFICANCE: The Court's decision in *Plessy* rendered racial segregation legal in the United States for almost sixty years, until it was overturned by a much more progressive Court.

Plessy v. Ferguson was provoked by an African American challenge that argued that an act of Louisiana's legislature was unconstitutional because it violated the Thirteenth and Fourteenth Amendments to the U.S. Constitution. The act in question required all railroads to provide "equal but separate" accommodations for blacks and whites and also forbade intermingling between the two groups.

The Supreme Court's majority opinion concentrated on the Fourteenth Amendment. The Court acknowledged that "the object of the amendment was undoubtedly to enforce the absolute equality of the two races before the law," but the majority opinion also underscored that "in the nature of things, it could not have been intended to abolish distinctions based upon color, or to enforce social, as distinguished from political equality." The effect of this decision was to give legal sanction to segregation in the United States.

Significantly, the Court's decision was not unanimous. There was a lone dissenter, Justice John M. Harlan, whose minority opinion argued that the U.S.

Constitution is "color-blind, and neither knows nor tolerates classes among citizens. In respect of civil rights, all citizens are equal before the law." Justice Harlan's opinion later became the unanimous opinion of the Court in *Brown v. Board of Education*, which overturned the separate-but-equal principle.

SEE ALSO: *Brown v. Board of Education*; Civil Rights movement; Racial prejudice; Racism; Segregation; Supreme Court, U.S.

Pluralism

DEFINITION: Theory that there is not only one valid set of values and principles, but rather a plurality of such sets

TYPE OF ETHICS: Theory of ethics; beliefs and practices

SIGNIFICANCE: Pluralism takes a middle path between moral relativism on one hand and moral absolutism on the other. Absolutism holds that there is a single, universal moral law that applies to everyone in all situations, and all other moral values are invalid. Relativism holds that all moral systems are equally valid and no set of values is better than any other set of values. Pluralism, or perspectivism, holds that some value systems are indeed superior to other value systems, but there will always be at least two different, mutually exclusive systems which are equally valid.

Pluralism as it is associated with ethics has had a long history. One can find a precedent in Aristotle for the view that there is no master principle, no moral principle that applies unequivocally to all concrete situations and circumstances. A rule that might apply in one situation might not apply in another. For example, although it may ordinarily be wrong to lie, it could be right to lie if doing so will save someone's life. The moral principle that determines the right thing to do, therefore, is dependent upon the circumstances, and since there are many concrete situations and circumstances, there is a plurality of ways of doing the right thing. As Aristotle would put this, there is a plurality of ways to achieve the good life, and each of these ways entails the actualization of different values and moral principles.

Pluralism is to be distinguished from both monism and relativism. A monist argues that there is an overarching moral principle that unambiguously prescribes what to do in any and every circumstance. An example of such a principle is the utilitarian greatest-happiness principle, which holds that, in every action, one ought to act so as to create the greatest amount of happiness for the greatest number of people. The relativist, however, although agreeing with the pluralist that values depend upon circumstances, claims that there is no objective reason for what is right or wrong other than simply what the people in a given culture or circumstance do.

The pluralist believes that there is such an objective reason; thus, even though there is a plurality of ways to achieve the good life, Aristotle nevertheless argues that each way is objectively right precisely because it does achieve the good life. The pluralist, therefore, agrees with the monist that there is to be an objective criterion whereby moral values are to be judged but disagrees with the monist in that the pluralist argues that there is no unique set or system of values that is the only one that satisfies the criteria. Likewise, the pluralist agrees with the relativist that there is a plurality of values but disagrees with the relativist's claim that such values are not legitimated by an objective criterion.

Amélie Rorty, in her essay "The Advantages of Moral Diversity" (1992), argues for a version of Aristotelian pluralism. Like Aristotle, she claims that there is no unique and single conception of what everyone ought to do to achieve the good life. Furthermore, Rorty argues that learning to live and cooperate with others who have different values from our own is beneficial to achieving the good life. A deontologist, who argues that the consequences of an action are not to be considered when determining the moral worth of an action, and a utilitarian, who claims that the consequences are to be considered, will, Rorty believes, when living and cooperating together, keep each other in line; and this keeping each other in line is precisely what Rorty believes to be beneficial for the attainment of the good life.

John Kekes, in his book *The Morality of Pluralism* (1993), holds a position similar to those of Rorty and Aristotle. He also argues that there is a plurality of ways to achieve the good life and that each way requires the realization of often radically different types of values. He also claims that having radically different values present in a society is, as Rorty argued, beneficial both to society and to individuals.

VARIATIONS

Pluralism is not, however, without its variations. Peter Wenz, for example, in "Minimal, Moderate, and Extreme Moral Pluralism" (1993), accuses the pluralist who argues for the advantages of having radically different, if not contradictory, values coexisting together of promoting incoherence and inconsistency in ethics. This brand of pluralism he labels "extreme pluralism." Rorty and Kekes, however, although calling for the coexistence of radically different values in society, do not call for an individual to hold contradictory values. An individual, they maintain, should sustain a consistent and coherent system of values, whereas society ought to maintain a plurality of values. For this reason, Rorty and Kekes are not to be seen as pluralists of the type that Wenz criticizes.

Christopher Stone, an environmental ethicist who argues for moral pluralism, does hold that an individual ought to maintain radically different values. A father, for example, could be a utilitarian at work but a Kantian deontologist at home with his family. It is this view that, referring explicitly to Stone, Wenz criticizes in his article. Stone's pluralism does promote inconsistency and incoherence and is, by Wenz's definition, "extreme pluralism."

A less-extreme pluralism, or moderate pluralism, as Wenz defines it, is roughly the view that Aristotle, Rorty, and Kekes hold; that is, there is a plurality of ways of achieving the good life, yet each way is in itself consistent and coherent. Minimal pluralism, Wenz believes, is true of every ethical theory. In other words, there is no true monistic theory, for monistic theories (such as utilitarianism) do not give a uniquely correct and unambiguous answer in every situation to the question of what one ought to do. There is always a plurality of possible answers, and hence these theories are minimally pluralistic. All ethical theories, Wenz concludes, are to some degree pluralistic.

There are other important philosophers with whom pluralism is associated—most notably, the pragmatists. William James, in *A Pluralistic Universe* (1909), and Richard Rorty, in *Philosophy and the Mirror of Nature* (1979), argue, for example, that what is considered true is simply what is necessary to survive. Truth does not express a relationship of correspondence to reality; instead, truth is determined by the particular goals and needs associated with survival, and because there is a plurality of ways to satisfy these needs, there is a plurality of truths. Truth, like morality, is not one; it is plural.

Jeff Bell

FURTHER READING

Aristotle. *Nicomachean Ethics*. Translated and edited by Roger Crisp. New York: Cambridge University Press, 2000.

Hales, Steven D., and Rex Welshon. *Nietzsche's Perspectivism*. Urbana: University of Illinois, 2000.

James, William. *A Pluralistic Universe*. New York: Library of America, 1987.

Kekes, John. *The Morality of Pluralism*. Princeton, N.J.: Princeton University Press, 1993.

_____. *Pluralism in Philosophy: Changing the Subject*. Ithaca, N.Y.: Cornell University Press, 2000.

Nehamas, Alexander. *Nietzsche: Life as Literature*. Cambridge, Mass.: Harvard University Press, 1985.

Rorty, Amélie. "The Advantages of Moral Diversity." *Social Philosophy and Policy* 9, no. 2 (1992): 38-62.

Wenz, Peter. "Minimal, Moderate, and Extreme Moral Pluralism." *Environmental Ethics* 15 (Spring, 1993): 61-74.

SEE ALSO: Absolutism; Aristotle; James, William; *Nicomachean Ethics*; Nietzsche, Friedrich; Pragmatism; Relativism; Situational ethics; Teleological ethics.

Pogroms

DEFINITION: Organized massacres of Jews and destruction of their property by Russian mobs, acting with the tacit approval of political authorities

TYPE OF ETHICS: Race and ethnicity

SIGNIFICANCE: The Russian pogroms represented an example of racial violence bordering on ethnic cleansing. While elimination of Jews from Russian soil was not their primary purpose, they did result in the emigration of many thousands of Russian Jews around the turn of the twentieth century.

In modern Russian history, pogrom-like attacks were initially leveled against the Armenians, Tatars, and the Russian intelligentsia. As it is employed in many languages specifically to describe the pillage, murder, and rape of Russian Jews, however, the term "pogrom" denotes three large-scale waves of devastation between 1881 and 1921. Each of these pogroms surpassed the preceding one in scope and savagery and occurred during periods of severe social and political upheaval in Russia. For example, the first pogroms of the 1880's followed the assassination of Czar Alexander II as a result of false rumors about widespread Jewish involvement in the assassination plot. Mobs from more than two hundred towns, inspired by local leaders acting with official support, took part.

Pogroms greatly influenced Russian Jewry and history. In their wake, the Russian government adopted systematic policies of discrimination, harassment, and persecution of the Jews. The murder of innocent individuals and whole families was commonplace. This led numerous European anti-Semites to conclude that violence was legitimate and thus helped to pave the way for pogroms to be carried out later in Poland and Germany.

Andrew C. Skinner

SEE ALSO: Anti-Semitism; Genocide and democide; Hitler, Adolf; Nazism; Oppression; Racism; Rape and political domination; Religion and violence.

Police brutality

DEFINITION: Police misconduct involving the unnecessary use of force or the excessive use of force, up to and including fatal force

TYPE OF ETHICS: Civil rights

SIGNIFICANCE: Consistent patterns of police brutality tend to cause fear and distrust of the police among the very segments of the population most in need of police protection. Thus, beyond representing individual instances of injustice, they can lead to the spread of injustice in society as crimes go unreported and potential victims go unprotected.

From the beginning, Americans have never fully trusted their government or its officials, even though they must rely upon both. The Fifty-first Federalist Paper argued, "If men were angels no government would be necessary." Human beings are definitely not angels, and they succumb to both good and bad activities. Although checks and balances were written into the U.S. Constitution to limit the "abuse of power" by distributing it between competing branches of government and among federal, state, and local authorities, no comparable safeguards exist to protect citizens against police misconduct. Perhaps this is because the first official U.S. police force was formed in New York in 1844, long after the government was established.

A national police force that would prevent local police misconduct has never been established, because of the fear that a U.S. president could use it as a private army or to spy on citizens. Almost all of the twelve thousand police forces in the United States are local. Their power is virtually absolute and often goes unchallenged. This situation creates a police culture that believes that it is above the law, an attitude that fosters abuse. Therefore, although citizens rely upon the police, they also mistrust them in the belief that informed criticism is the best way to correct misconduct, incompetence, and arbitrariness as well as to encourage a healthy police culture to do its job fairly.

NIETZSCHE, THE WILL TO POWER, AND THE POLICE

Friedrich Nietzsche argued that the human "will to power" makes people seek power and control over others. Those who succeed in this struggle become the master class. They value courage, strength, pride, risk-taking, directness, and sports. Morality, or what is correct in their opinion, becomes associated with the traits possessed by the ruling elite. Morality, for the master class, is not a set of abstract principles.

There is also a slave morality that is based upon values such as humility, justice, self-denial, prudence, and altruism. The slave's morality is reactive; that is, whatever the master class values as good the slave defines as bad. Slaves reject the morality of the master class because they associate it with oppression, evil, and injustice, and they resent the power of the master class. From the slave morality comes not only the concept of justice but also those of guilt and conscience.

POLICE CULTURE AND BRUTALITY

Police have a unique culture that has its own internal values. When young officers go through training at a police academy, they typically have every intention of becoming exemplary officers. Seasoned officers consider such young officers naïve. They are ritually introduced to "real police work" by their field training officer. By custom, the training officer's first words to the rookie must be, "Forget everything they taught you at the Academy. This is the real world."

Police culture glorifies the visible symbol of police power: the gun. Target practice becomes a fetish for many officers. Citizens are dehumanized and may become viewed as targets or potential targets rather than human beings. Peer pressure encourages police to socialize together. This isolates them from average civilians and creates an insulated mentality. Most officers ride in patrol cars and ride from one distress call to another over a large area. This gives them a jaundiced view of citizens, because for eight hours a day many of the citizens with whom they interact are either criminals or suspected criminals. In time, some officers begin to view most citizens as either criminals or suspects. They see themselves as besieged, beleaguered, and misunderstood.

Out of this view develops the idea that it is "us" against "them." Some sadistic officers use this attitude to divert attention away from their misconduct and to increase group morale. A sense of common identity forms that is based on the degrading of outsiders. Police especially devalue outsiders whom they consider hostile. These people are considered more "them" than others. When stress develops between insiders and outsiders, violence is more likely to occur.

The police believe, understandably, that they are abused and called names often yet receive little money or status from society, despite the danger of their job. This resentment can lead to feelings of anger and powerlessness. One way to regain a sense of power is by exercising elemental power over other human beings. When making arrests, the desire for power may lead police to force suspects to restrict their movement or to stand where they are told to stand. Failure to obey may be swiftly met with violence in an effort to gain power and control. Once such violence starts, it can easily escalate out of control.

Some police view themselves as a tight-knit, elite "thin blue line" that protects society from criminal chaos and lawlessness. Such police fear that they are losing the battle against crime and that a nationwide breakdown of ethical standards and morals forces them to close ranks with fellow officers by developing a cult of secrecy that they call the "code of silence." Confrontational attitudes develop, they claim, in self-defense. Whistle-blowers are rare in this culture. Virtually everyone tries to be a "stand-up cop." In addition, in some departments, if an officer reports witnessing brutality carried out by a fellow officer, both officers are suspended without pay. This practice discourages officers from informing the department of misconduct and strengthens the code of silence.

Police chiefs who make it clear that they respect the code of silence and ignore charges of brutality leveled against police, so long as there is peace and order on the street, reinforce this culture and invite brutality. Officers

During the trial of four New York City police officers charged with brutality, demonstrators outside the Albany courtroom dramatized their protest by carrying a door on which they had painted a human body and numerous bullet holes to symbolize what they regarded as the officers' use of excessive force. (AP/Wide World Photos)

are reluctant to arrest or even fine fellow police. For many police officers, "good" is whatever makes their jobs less dangerous and easier, even if it involves the unjust violation of others' rights.

THE RODNEY KING CASE

Thousands of cases of police brutality are filed annually, but the King case is unique because some of the events were captured on videotape. On March 3, 1991, the Los Angeles police stopped a twenty-four-year-old black male motorist named Rodney Glen King after a difficult and dangerous high speed (115 m.p.h.) car chase. Police ordered King to get out of his car, then several officers brutally assaulted King. Four officers in particular took turns clubbing, kicking, and shocking the unarmed King with Taser stun guns, while other officers watched. The officers clubbed King at least fifty-six times, breaking his skull in nine places, breaking his leg, and inflicting many other injuries. Any one of the officers who stood by and watched this beating could have stepped in and stopped it, but none did. Each conformed to group norms and police culture by observing the code of silence.

In such a situation, normal judgment, reasoning, and critical thinking are abandoned. This is made possible by the anonymity of the individual in the crowd. The notion of individual responsibility that normally restrains behavior is gone. Members of the group act rapidly on impulse. In a crowd, behavior gravitates to the lowest common level. Members focus upon what is different—"them." Nothing else matters, and the members attack the outsider. Bystanders who observe such violence and do nothing are in pain but often deny it and cover it up by justifying the violent behavior.

Each act such as the King beating changes all who participate in it or witness it. Those who do the beating tend to grow more aggressive. The officers appear to have become prisoners of the master mentality.

In most cases, an officer's word carries more weight than does a civilian's, as is indicated by the fact that in 1990 the Los Angeles Police Department received more than 2,500 complaints of police brutality, but fewer than fifty cases—less than one-half of one percent—went before a grand jury. In 1987, more than eight thousand complaints of police brutality were filed, yet not one officer broke the code of silence by offering incriminating evidence about an-

other officer. In almost all cases, the victims of police brutality have previously violated some law that has brought them to the attention of the police. Therefore, their credibility is not easy to establish. King was a convicted felon, even though that should not have mattered in the beating case. In reality, police who engage in misconduct have little to fear under the current system. Police can cover up misconduct by alleging that a suspect was "resisting arrest." King did not plan to press charges, for fear that it would be difficult to prove his case.

Little did either side know that George Holliday had captured more than seven minutes of the savage beating on videotape from his balcony. He sold the tape to television stations, and the beating was seen in millions of homes worldwide. There was definite evidence of police misconduct in this case. Because the arresting officers were white and King was African American, the case became very volatile, and attorney Warren Christopher was asked to head a commission that was established to investigate this case.

The Christopher Commission listened to computerized tapes of police transmissions on the night that King was beaten and discovered that the officers were so confident that police culture would protect them that they recorded messages saying, "Capture him, beat him, and treat him like dirt," and "What, did you beat another guy?" Christopher was troubled by the officers' flagrant confidence that "nothing would be done" and that such brutality would be tolerated.

Other messages recorded by the commission betrayed open contempt for racial and ethnic minorities and homosexuals. One message recorded during the King incident made reference to "gorillas in the mist," an obvious racial slur. Hospital nurses who treated King stated that the officers who beat him followed him to the hospital to threaten and tease him.

In the face of irrefutable evidence of police misconduct and brutality, the Christopher Commission sided with the slave morality and called for justice. It noted that, although the problem of police brutality is widespread, a handful of "problem officers" create most incidents. To settle police brutality claims against the city of Los Angeles between 1970 and 1980, the city paid more than $65 million in damages, and the tension created within communities by these cases caused even greater damage. Riots erupted following the trials of the officers who beat Rodney King. These riots destroyed billions of dollars worth of property and cost dozens of people their lives.

Immanuel Kant would have appreciated this appeal to principle, even though Nietzsche would have been appalled. Unless or until the values cherished by police culture and those embraced by civilian culture are more closely aligned by establishing civilian review boards for police departments and rewarding police for preventing crimes through community service programs, then these two value systems will clash, and the result may too often be police brutality.

Dallas L. Browne

FURTHER READING

Barker, Thomas, and David L. Carter. *Police Deviance*. 2d ed. Cincinnati, Ohio: Anderson, 1991.

Brenner, Robert N., and Marjorie Kravitz, eds. *A Community Concern: Police Use of Deadly Force*. Washington, D.C.: United States Department of Justice, 1979.

Burns, Ronald G., and Charles E. Crawford. *Policing and Violence*. Upper Saddle River, N.J.: Prentice Hall, 2002.

Donner, Frank. *Protectors of Privilege: Red Squads and Police Repression in Urban America*. Berkeley: University of California Press, 1990.

Dudley, William, ed. *Police Brutality*. San Diego, Calif.: D. L. Bender, 1991.

Elliston, Frederick, and Michael Feldberg, eds. *Moral Issues in Police Work*. Totowa, N.J.: Rowman & Allen, 1985.

Lawrence, Regina G. *The Politics of Force: Media and the Construction of Police Brutality*. Berkeley: University of California Press, 2000.

Lundman, Richard J., ed. *Police Behavior: A Sociological Perspective*. New York: Oxford University Press, 1980.

Skolnick, Jerome H., and James J. Fyfe. *Above the Law: Police and the Excessive Use of Force*. New York: Free Press, 1993.

Stratton, John G. *Police Passages*. Manhattan Beach, Calif.: Glennon, 1984.

SEE ALSO: Abuse; Arrest records; *Beyond Good and Evil*; Bystanders; Criminal punishment; Justice; *Miranda v. Arizona*; Professional ethics; Stonewall Inn riots; Violence.

Political correctness

DEFINITION: Attitude that language and ideas that offend political sensibilities should be avoided

DATE: Term coined during the late 1980's

TYPE OF ETHICS: Politico-economic ethics

SIGNIFICANCE: Initially a self-deprecating term used by the Left to poke fun at its own orthodoxies, political correctness became a label employed by the Right to vilify an informal set of attitudes about what sorts of language and ideas are appropriate—particularly in an academic setting.

During the early 1990's, colleges and universities became politically polarized places. Multiculturalism, identity politics, feminism, and other progressive movements seeking academic reform brought about significant changes in curricula and in academic life generally. These changes were met with dismay and anger by conservatives, and many institutions of higher learning became intellectual battlegrounds. Discussions of race, class, gender, sexuality, and other categories of identity took place frequently, and the divergent values of participants in those discussions formed barriers to effective communication.

Often, both progressives and conservatives demonstrated utter contempt for those whose viewpoints differed from their own. As a result, each side developed key words that it would use to dismiss speakers from opposing camps as wrongheaded and unworthy of attention, thus bringing discussions to abrupt conclusions. For example, a progressive wishing to silence a conservative might call the conservative a "racist," and a conservative wishing to silence a progressive might call that person "politically correct." Each term indicated that the person in question was hopelessly blind to his or her own prejudices and was simply beyond the reach of rational argument.

THE LEFT VS. THE RIGHT

The term "political correctness" first developed as a result of intolerant attitudes on the part of the Left toward perceived insensitivity on the part of the Right. Members of the Right often spoke of political correctness, or "PC," as though it were a formal code of conduct. However, with rare exceptions, no such codes existed on any college campuses. Rather, it was often the case that people whose speech was perceived to be racially insensitive or homophobic, for example, would be harshly criticized by their interlocutors. Because the values dominant on college campuses were often radically different from the values dominant in public life as a whole, such strong negative reactions greatly surprised those who expressed traditional, mainstream ideas. Conservative students who were criticized by progressive students would often respond by censoring themselves in the future to avoid further criticism. They would then claim that they had been censored by others. Thus the myth of political correctness as a formal orthodoxy rather than the de facto result of informal attitudes began to emerge. Peer pressure was thus interpreted as policy.

The ethical import of a value system as controversial as political correctness is obviously very much in dispute. Those who support political correctness tend to favor self-determination, arguing, for example, that members of minorities should have the right to choose their own labels, rather than having names imposed upon them by others. They also argue that speech is a form of power that should be respected and perhaps even regulated, just as are physical forms of power.

Those who oppose political correctness argue that names and other forms of speech are, in themselves, harmless, do not admit of ethical evaluation, and therefore should not be regulated. They advocate free speech and claim the right to say whatever they want, free from any negative consequences that would inhibit the open exchange of ideas. Orthodoxies of judgment, they say, whether formal, or informal, amount to nothing less than censorship.

Their opponents respond that anti-PC people *are* allowed to say whatever they want but must accept the fact that their utterances will be judged morally by those who hear them. Speech should be free, progressives argue, but that does not mean that it should be free from consequences. It is unrealistic to demand, in effect, the right to express controversial ideas and yet to remain free from controversy. Indeed, no matter what one believes, it will always be dangerous to speak one's mind, because *anything worth saying* is going to be controversial to someone—a fact about which people on both sides of the PC issue can agree.

Andy Perry

Examples of Politically Incorrect Terms

Politically Incorrect	Politically Correct
Negro, black	African American
Indian	Native American, American Indian
Oriental	Asian American
Mexican American	Chicano/Chicana, Latino/Latina
colored people	people of color
homosexual	gay or lesbian
disabled	differently abled
handicapped	physically challenged
reverse racism	ethnocentric revitalization
reverse discrimination	affirmative action

FURTHER READING

Detmer, David. *Challenging Postmodernism: Philosophy and the Politics of Truth.* Amherst, N.Y.: Humanity Books, 2003.

D'Souza, Dinesh. *Illiberal Education: The Politics of Race and Sex on Campus.* New York: Vintage Books, 1992.

Feldstein, Richard. *Political Correctness: A Response from the Cultural Left.* Minneapolis: University of Minnesota Press, 1997.

Friedman, Marilyn, and Jan Narveson. *Political Correctness: For and Against.* Lanham, Md.: Rowman & Littlefield, 1995.

Graff, Gerald. *Beyond the Culture Wars: How Teaching the Conflicts Can Revitalize American Education.* New York: W. W. Norton, 1992.

Levitt, Cyril, Scott Davies, and Neil McLaughlin, eds. *Mistaken Identities: The Second Wave of Controversy over "Political Correctness."* New York: P. Lang, 1999.

Noonan, Jeff. *Critical Humanism and the Politics of Difference.* Ithaca, N.Y.: McGill-Queen's University Press, 2003.

Weissberg, Robert. *Political Tolerance: Balancing Community and Diversity.* Thousand Oaks, Calif.: Sage, 1998.

SEE ALSO: Academic freedom; Affirmative action; Censorship; Communitarianism; Conservatism; Diversity; Hate crime and hate speech; Multiculturalism; Progressivism.

Political liberty

DEFINITION: Freedom from coercion or constraint by government or its agents

TYPE OF ETHICS: Politico-economic ethics

SIGNIFICANCE: In liberal democracies, political liberty is generally understood to include civil rights and liberties such as freedom of expression, as well as the right to vote and otherwise participate in representative government.

As defined above, "political liberty" is to be conceived of as a negative freedom—that is, a freedom *from* external coercion or constraint. It is this conception of political liberty that has been fundamental to the tradition of such Western ideas as individualism and liberalism in both political philosophy and political theory. The classic expression of this conception of political liberty is John Stuart Mill's *On Liberty* (1859).

In practice, however, political liberty almost always refers to a positive freedom—that is, a freedom *of* some specific kind of good or some specific type of activity. Examples of the latter include some of the basic democratic liberties: freedom of thought, freedom of expression, freedom of assembly, freedom of religious pursuits, freedom of political participation, and so forth; freedom of property acquisition and disposal is an example of the former. Although this second conception of political liberty is dependent on the initial one, every particular freedom that can be associated with this positive conception involves some form of individual or social activity with respect to which the right to *choose on one's own* is acknowledged as both socially and morally significant.

It is important not to confuse the two very different ideas of human abilities and political liberties. To conflate what one *can* do with what one is *at liberty* to do makes little or no sense. The fact that a member of a particular society is unable to vote on election day because of, for example, major medical surgery is irrelevant to whether that same individual, as a member of that society who satisfies all voting eligibility requirements, is at liberty to vote. In other words, just because this individual was unable to vote and, in fact, did not vote does not in any way mean that this individual was not free to vote.

This same irrelevancy between what one can do and what one is at liberty to do also holds true for a member of a particular society who is, in fact, able to vote, but who is not allowed to vote merely because this individual happens to be a member of a particular segment of the society each of the members of which is systematically prohibited from voting. That is, just because this individual was not at liberty to vote— that is, not allowed to vote—does not in any way mean that this individual was not able to vote. In neither of these cases does one's ability (or lack thereof) to vote have anything to do with one's freedom (or lack thereof) to vote.

LIBERTY VS. AUTHORITY

Fundamentally, political liberty must be construed as a balance between the exercise of authority of the society over its members, on one hand, and the liberty of choice and of effectual action that individual members of the society are allowed to exercise, on the other. That is, individual liberty and governmental authority are the two sides of the same political coin; the more there is of either one, the less there must be of the other. Within this framework, questions of conflict concerning the political liberties of the individual, justice, and the well-being of the society as a whole naturally arise.

In political theory, both the kinds of particular political liberties and the degree to which each ought to be acknowledged by the government to be granted to individuals depend upon a whole host of factors, such as one's conception of both human nature and human rationality, one's conception of the relationship between an individual's right to autonomy and a sense of the appropriate degree of latitude to be granted to governmental authority, and one's conception of what ought to be the purpose of both the government itself and its social and political institutions (for example, whether the fundamental reason for the very existence of government and its social and political institutions is to promote human happiness or satisfaction; to provide for the peace, security, and any or all associated rights of each member of the society; or to provide for the development in each member of the society of some particular conception of human excellence).

In practice, too, both the kinds of particular political liberties and the degree of which each ought to be acknowledged by the government to be granted to individuals depend upon a vast array of circumstances, not the least of which is the form of government that has been established. For example, the differences between both the number and the extent of political liberties granted to individuals under a totalitarian regime as compared to a democracy are usually obvious.

POLITICAL LIBERTY IN THE REAL WORLD

Even in representative democracies according to which individual members of the society are allowed a wide latitude of autonomy, however, it is possible for political leaders to engage in a more insidious type of political coercion than that typically found in totalitarian societies. In order for a democracy to be effective, its individuals need access to more, rather than less, and accurate, rather than inaccurate, information relevant to political decision making.

To the extent that those in positions of political power, presumably for reasons of self-interest, deny to members of the society the quantity and quality of information necessary to well-informed political decision making (for example, through manipulation of the media of communication and distortion or denial of relevant information), however, to precisely that extent is that democracy being undermined and to precisely that extent are the members of such a society being denied their political liberties. In the final analysis, political liberty means liberty of choice and of effectual action; consequently, to the extent that this insidious type of political coercion is perpetrated against the members of such a society, the menu of practical options available to them is artificially diminished, which, in turn, diminishes their freedom both of choice and of effectual action, and ultimately denies them at least some of their political liberties.

Stephen C. Taylor

FURTHER READING

Berlin, Isaiah. *Two Concepts of Liberty*. Oxford, England: Clarendon Press, 1958. Reprinted in *Four Essays on Liberty*. Oxford, England: Oxford University Press, 1969.

Dumm, Thomas L. *Michel Foucault and the Politics of Freedom*. Lanham, Md.: Rowman & Littlefield, 2002.

Gregg, Samuel. *On Ordered Liberty: A Treatise on the Free Society*. Lanham, Md.: Lexington Books, 2003.

Griffiths, A. Phillips, ed. *Of Liberty*. Cambridge, England: Cambridge University Press, 1983.

Hirschmann, Nancy J. *The Subject of Liberty: Toward a Feminist Theory of Freedom*. Princeton, N.J.: Princeton University Press, 2003.

Mill, John Stuart. *On Liberty, and Other Essays*. Edited by John Gray. New York: Oxford University Press, 1998.

Pelczynski, Z. B., and John Gray, eds. *Conceptions of Liberty in Political Philosophy*. London: Athlone Press, 1984.

Raphael, D. D. *Problems of Political Philosophy*. 2d rev. ed. London: Macmillan Education, 1990.

Ryan, Alan, ed. *The Idea of Freedom*. Oxford, England: Oxford University Press, 1979.

SEE ALSO: Choice; Constitution, U.S.; Democracy; Freedom and liberty; Liberalism; Libertarianism; Mill, John Stuart; *On Liberty*; Politics; Power.

Political realism

DEFINITION: View that leaders of nations should disregard considerations of morality and should instead act in their own best interests in order to gain and maintain power

TYPE OF ETHICS: Politico-economic ethics

SIGNIFICANCE: Political realism rests upon the assumption that there is a contradiction between reality and ethics. In other words, it implies that it is unrealistic to expect those in positions of power to behave morally, that reality and morality are in some sense mutually exclusive. It therefore portrays ethical conduct as a luxury which political leaders simply cannot afford.

Critics of political realism say that a leader who is a political realist is likely to be a tyrant who is uninterested in the welfare of the citizens of her or his own nation and other nations. Such a leader is also likely to gain support by using political rhetoric to trick others into believing that her or his actions do serve their interests. Such a leader abdicates the responsibilities of considering the interests of others and telling them the truth. Defenders of political realism say that a realistic reading of history shows that practicality rather than ethics is the principle guiding the behavior of governments and leaders. For example, leaders have always used cruelty in order to make people fear and obey them. Some defenders of political realism say that ethics are simply not relevant to government and that behaving ethically would hamper a leader's ability to get things done. Other defenders say that political realists follow a competitive ethic, wherein those who are best at the games of power are the most successful leaders.

Laura Duhan Kaplan

SEE ALSO: Machiavelli, Niccolò; Politics; Power; Realpolitik.

Politics

DEFINITION: Art of governing
TYPE OF ETHICS: Politico-economic ethics
SIGNIFICANCE: Politics is the practical attainment and exercise of power over other people. As such, it may be seen theoretically as the realm of human behavior most in need of ethical regulation, and it appears to many people empirically to be the realm least subject to actual moral constraint.

The standard view of politics' relation to ethics is captured in H. B. Acton's famous aphorism: "Power tends to corrupt, and absolute power corrupts absolutely." The first part of Lord Acton's aphorism identifies a danger inherent in the political process. Since political ends can be achieved only by the exercise of power, power is concentrated in the hands of politicians. Unfortunately, as much of history illustrates, politicians have often diverted power away from its proper use, despite the institution of checks and balances to prevent abuses.

The second part of Acton's aphorism makes the more cynical claim that the political process is inherently immoral. Since power is the ability to do work,

however, it follows from that claim that the ability to do work is immoral. From this conclusion follows the odd conclusion that only the completely impotent are moral. The conclusion is odd because it creates a paradox: While most people think that governments do perform valuable functions, Acton's aphorism would lead one to believe that governments are immoral to the extent they are able to perform those functions.

This paradox indicates that the relationship between ethics and the political process involves more than simply the existence or nonexistence of power. Power is central to government, but the questions of exactly how much and what types of power governments should have and to what ends that power should be put have generated a number of political theories. Many of those theories have been put into practice, and although the political arena contains many instances of hypocrisy, lying, disloyalty, and thievery, there is evidence that in both theory and practice politics has been and continues to be influenced greatly by ethics.

THE INFLUENCE OF ETHICS

Aside from the amount of corruption that exists in governments, part of the difficulty in seeing the influence of ethics is the diversity of opinions about what in fact is ethical. Debates exist about whether morality is essentially religious or secular, relative or universal, altruistic or egoistic. Such differences of opinion make it easy for those on one side of a debate to see those on the other as immoral. Another part of the difficulty is that even those who agree about what is ethical may disagree about the proper methods to be used to achieve it. Some may believe that the end justifies the means—that is, that it is justifiable to lie about a political rival if doing so achieves a good goal—while other advocates of the same end may reject that premise.

The complex relationship between ethics and politics can be captured in three pairs of related questions: questions of ends (What is good? What does this politician think is good?), questions of means (Does the end justify the means? Does this politician think the end justifies the means?), and questions of integrity (Is this politician or system practicing what is good? Is this politician or system practicing what he, she, or it thinks is good?). A judgment about the influence of ethics on politics is a result of answers to these questions.

ETHICS AND GOVERNMENT

Government is a social institution that formulates and enforces rules. In both the content of its rules and its method of enforcing them, government is unique. Other social institutions formulate rules, but the rules that they formulate apply only to those who participate in that institution. For example, a baseball league is a social institution that formulates rules, but its rules apply only to those who play in the baseball league. A government's rules, by contrast, apply to all members of the society. Other social institutions also enforce their rules, but the maximum penalty for violating a rule is to be disassociated from the institution. If, for example, one violates the rules of baseball, one may be kicked off the team. A government, by contrast, is the only social institution that enforces its rule by the use of physical force. If one violates a government's rules, it may confiscate one's property, restrict one's liberty, or even kill one.

Since government is the only social institution that makes universal rules that are backed up by the use of physical force, the content of those rules is of special importance. What rules are so important that everyone should follow them? What rules are so important that if they are violated the drastic resort of physical force is appropriate?

The only way to answer these questions is by appealing to ethics. Politics, accordingly, is an institutionalization of an ethics. This fact is easier to recognize in political theories: Plato, Thomas Hobbes, and John Locke, for example, appeal to (conflicting) ethical principles and moral evaluations of human nature in defending their political theories. Despite corruption, however, most political practice also illustrates the application of ethics.

THREE HISTORICAL EXAMPLES

The influence of ethics on political practice can be seen in the three systems that dominated the twentieth century: Marxism (or international socialism), fascism (or National Socialism), and capitalism (or constitutional democracy). Each system has had enormous practical influence on political theory and practice, and each puts into practice a set of explicit principles that its advocates believe to be moral.

COLLECTIVISM

Marxism and fascism are versions of collectivism. Collectivism defines morality socially, holding that the welfare of the group is primary and, accordingly, that individual interests are subordinate to those of the group. Collectivists admonish individuals not to be self-interested; that is, not to put their personal interests above group interests but to sacrifice their interests for the welfare of the group.

Depending on how the group is defined, versions of collectivism arise. Some versions hold that the family is the proper group and that individuals should devote their lives to serving their families. Other versions hold that the group to which individuals should sacrifice is the tribe, the nation, the race, the working class, or the ecosystem. The common denominator in all these versions of collectivism is that individuals are not ends in themselves.

Largely through the influence of Georg Wilhelm Friedrich Hegel, collectivism dominated nineteenth century German philosophy. The two most prominent versions of collectivism to arise after Hegel were Marxism and fascism.

MARXISM

"From each according to his ability, to each according to his need." Karl Marx's slogan, from his *Critique of the Gotha Program* (written 1875; published 1891), is the clearest statement of the fundamental ethical principle of his version of collectivism. According to the principle, individuals are not ends in themselves. They should see themselves as servants of the needs of others, and they should devote their lives to serving others' needs to the best of their ability. As long as someone has an unfulfilled need and I, for example, have the ability to fill it, I have a duty to sacrifice my personal interests and devote myself to fulfilling that need. To the extent that I shirk my duty, I am acting unethically. To the extent that the society I live in allows me to shirk my duty, the society is unethical.

Marx noted that Western societies often pay lip service to altruistic principles; in practice, however, they encourage the pursuit of self-interest, the profit motive, and capitalism. What is needed to make society ethical, Marx argued, is a radical shift away from the individual to the collective, from the private to the social.

In defining "social," Marx takes the broadest possible view. Society, he argued, should not be conceived along familial, racial, religious, or ethnic lines. If, for example, I define the moral society racially, then I will see myself as a servant of my race; if service to my race is of the highest moral significance, then I will view members of other races as having less moral significance. Such attitudes can only foster racial conflict. If I define myself as an individual, then I will hold my own interests to be of the highest significance, but this will lead me into conflict with other individuals and will lead to a competitive society. To prevent these conflicts, Marx argued, individuals must learn not only to define themselves primarily as social, not individual, beings but also to conceive of society as including the entire human race. Only then, Marx believed, would socialism be realized. Marxism, accordingly, defends socialism by appealing to collectivist ethical principles, which it hopes to apply internationally.

Fascism

During the twentieth century, "fascism" was the name adopted by a group of Italians to designate their new version of socialism. The leader of this group, Benito Mussolini, had for many years been a Marxist socialist before deciding that substituting "the Italian people" for "the working class" would give socialist ideas a better chance of success in Italy, for then they would be able to draw upon the nationalistic loyalty of most Italians. "Fascism" also labels the political system of Germany during the 1930's and 1940's, under Adolf Hitler's National Socialism. In both countries, fascists applied collectivist ethical principles to politics.

The core doctrine was expressed clearly by Alfred Rocco, a leading Italian fascist. Fascism stresses, he said, "the necessity, for which the older doctrines make little allowance, of sacrifice, even up to the total immolation of individuals, in behalf of society. . . . For Liberalism [i.e., individualism], the individual is the end and society the means; nor is it conceivable that the individual, considered in the dignity of an ultimate finality, be lowered to mere instrumentality. For Fascism, society is the end, individuals the means, and its whole life consists in using individuals as instruments for its social ends."

In their insistence upon the morality of collectivism, the fascists agreed with the Marxists. "There is more that binds us to Bolshevism [the dominant Russian version of Marxism] than separates us from it," declared Hitler. Like the Marxists, the Italian and German fascists believed that capitalism was evil be-

cause of its individualism, its tolerance of the profit motive, and its emphasis on pursuing private interests. Hitler defined National Socialism as "idealism," as the system in which each individual "willingly subordinates his own ego to the life of the community and, if the hour demands it, even sacrifices it."

The fascists disagreed with the Marxists about some important points. While the Marxists defined the moral community internationally and economically, the fascists defined it nationally and racially. While the Marxists attacked all religions, the fascists focused their attacks almost exclusively on Judaism. Despite these differences, the fundamental thesis of Marxism and fascism is the same: Both have the same collectivist view of the relationship between the individual and the society. Both Marxists and fascists could accept the following statement from *Mein Kampf*: "each activity and each need of the individual will be regulated by the party as the representative of the general good."

Italian leader Benito Mussolini is credited with coining the term "fascist." (National Archives)

NATIONAL SOCIALISM

By the mid-1930's, years before the beginning of World War II, the National Socialists had put into practice many standard socialist economic policies. Medicine was socialized, a modern welfare system was instituted, and the goal of complete equality of income was being sought. German industrial production was regulated and directed by the central government; while owners maintained legal possession of their enterprises, government bureaucrats set production goals and controlled wages, prices, and interest rates. Additionally, since private interests were not to be trusted to serve the public good, the Reichskulturkammer instituted a sweeping censorship covering what was taught in schools, what books were published, and what appeared on radio and in films, plays, and newspapers. The important point is that all these policies were instituted by appealing to collectivist ethical principles: *Gemeinnutz vor Eigennutz!* ("The common interest before self-interest") was the standard slogan justifying Nazi policies.

Since socialism requires that individuals subordinate their private interests to the good of the group, and since under Hitler the designated group was the German nation, "National Socialism" was an appropriate name for Hitler's political program.

It is sometimes argued that dictators such as V. I. Lenin and Joseph Stalin in the Soviet Union and Hitler and Mussolini in Germany and Italy were simply cynical power seekers who mouthed collectivist and socialist slogans without really believing them, but this idea is not plausible. If one is young, cynical, and seeking power, the most likely route to power is by infiltrating the established, already-powerful political parties (or the military). The least likely route to power is to join a fringe political group, since fringe groups rarely have any influence. Fringe groups attract only people who are committed to the causes for which the group stands. Yet the Communist and National Socialist Parties were, when Lenin, Stalin, and Hitler joined them, tiny and far from power. Therefore, it is likely that these men believed in the principles that they preached.

While collectivist ideas were most influential in eastern Europe, in Italy, and later in Asia, they also had an impact in the West. During the late nineteenth and early twentieth centuries, it was common for intelligent American and English students to spend some time studying in Germany, which was at the time the world's leading intellectual nation. While in Germany, the students were naturally exposed to the latest collectivist theories. As Friedrich Hayek noted, "Many a university teacher during the 1930's has seen English and American students return from the Continent uncertain whether they were communists or Nazis and certain only that they hated Western liberal civilization."

INDIVIDUALISM AND CAPITALISM

In the West, however, classical liberal ideas had retained a strong hold. Classical liberalism emphasizes the importance of the individual and tends to see social institutions as valuable to the extent that they leave individuals free to pursue their values. Individuals are ends in themselves, according to this view, and not means to the ends of other individuals or to groups.

By deemphasizing or rejecting collectivism, individualists tend to reject or at least be suspicious of any claims upon the individual to sacrifice life, liberty, or well-being. In politics, this individualist ethic leads to the view that the role of the government is not to exact sacrifices from individuals to serve a collective good, but to protect the lives and liberties of individuals as they pursue their personal conceptions of the good life. In economics, individualists tend to advocate a free market, since a free market decentralizes political power, leaving investment, buying, and selling decisions in the hands of private individuals. In this way, advocates of capitalism's limited government and free markets have tended to appeal to individualist ethical principles in support of their political policies.

CONCLUSION

Ethics has had a broad influence in the history of modern and contemporary politics. Many conflicting ethical theories have contributed to that influence, but in terms of their influence on modern and contemporary political affairs those ethical theories fall into two major categories: individualist and collectivist. The moral slogan of individualism, "Every individual is an end in himself," stands in contrast to the moral slogan of collectivism, "From each according to his ability, to each according to his need." The principle of individualism provides moral support for capitalism; the principle of collectivism provides moral support for socialism.

Historically, it can be seen that to the extent that the politicians in power were committed to an ethic that holds individual interests to be immoral or at least subordinate to collective interests, they believed it to be improper to leave economic and political power in private hands. Accordingly, their ethics dictated that power must be concentrated in public hands, and therefore a centralization of political and economic power resulted.

By contrast, to the extent that the politicians in power were committed to an ethic that holds individuals' pursuits of their own interests to be moral, then the politicians believed it to be proper to leave power in hands of those private individuals and to see their role as politicians as secondary and supportive. Accordingly, their ethics dictated that power must not be concentrated in public hands, and therefore a decentralization of political and economic power resulted.

Stephen R. C. Hicks

FURTHER READING

Althusser, Louis. "Ideology and Ideological State Apparatuses." In *Lenin and Philosophy, and Other Essays*, translated by Ben Brewster. New York: Monthly Review Press, 2001. An extremely influential Marxist account of the covert political functions of overtly nonpolitical institutions, such as the family, the church, and the school.

Hitler, Adolf. *Mein Kampf*. Translated by Ralph Manheim. Boston: Houghton Mifflin, 1999. The original manifesto of National Socialism. Hitler is very explicit about the collectivist principles of ethics upon which National Socialism depends.

Machiavelli, Niccolò. *The Prince*. Edited and translated by Angelo M. Codevilla. New Haven, Conn.: Yale University Press, 1997. A classic work in the "cynical" tradition of ethics and politics. The author provides practical guidance to politicians by advocating the use of immoral methods to achieve and maintain power.

Marx, Karl, and Friedrich Engels. *The Communist Manifesto*. New York: Bantam, 1992. A clear and brief survey of the principles of communism, with special emphasis on what Marx and Engels see as the moral failings of capitalism.

Peikoff, Leonard. *The Ominous Parallels*. New York: Stein & Day, 1982. A clear and detailed exposition of the philosophical and historical roots of German National Socialism.

Rand, Ayn. "What Is Capitalism?" In *Capitalism: The Unknown Ideal*. New York: New American Library, 1966. A defense of capitalism on moral grounds.

Roberts, Robert North. *Ethics in U.S. Government: An Encyclopedia of Scandals, Reforms, and Legislation*. Westport, Conn.: Greenwood Press, 2001. Encyclopedic treatment of ethical issues relating to misconduct throughout the full history of American government.

Sterba, James P. *How to Make People Just: A Practical Reconciliation of Alternative Conceptions of Justice*. Totowa, N.J.: Rowman & Littlefield, 1988. An introductory survey of a broad range of political theories, showing the ethical presuppositions of each. The author also defends a moderate version of socialism.

SEE ALSO: Campaign finance reform; Capitalism; Congress; Ethics in Government Act; Political liberty; Political realism; Power; Realpolitik.

Poll taxes

DEFINITION: Form of capitation, or head tax, which people must pay before being allowed to vote
DATE: Abolished in the United States in 1964
TYPE OF ETHICS: Civil rights
SIGNIFICANCE: Poll taxes raise the ethical questions of whether it is proper to make people pay for the right of voting and whether such taxes disfranchise the poor.

Poll taxes existed in the United States from the earliest colonial times. They were usually quite small and did not act to discourage many people from voting. In the years following the U.S. Civil War, the poll tax system was refined in the southern states for the purpose of disfranchising black voters. The tax remained small, but it had to be paid for every election in which the potential voter might have voted. This tax effectively disfranchised nearly all black voters. Because the election laws in the United States are made by state governments, a constitutional amendment was needed to do away with poll taxes. In 1964, the Twenty-fourth Amendment abolished the payment of such taxes as a condition for voting in federal elections.

Robert Jacobs

SEE ALSO: Constitution, U.S.; Discrimination; Suffrage; Voting fraud.

Pollution

DEFINITION: Environmental contamination with human-made waste
TYPE OF ETHICS: Environmental ethics
SIGNIFICANCE: Pollution has effects on many different levels, from causing people minor inconvenience and aesthetic displeasure up to and including mass human illness and death, and the extinctions of other species.

Pollution must be viewed in the light of natural versus human-based events. A natural event is part of the fundamental cycle of Earth processes that maintain a balance of building up and wearing down, of destruction and recovery. A volcano may spew tons of ash into the atmosphere and darken the sky so much that weather patterns are changed. Mudflows precipitated by loose debris and rapidly melting glaciers clog waterways on which nearby ecosystems rely. Lava kills everything in its path. Despite these drastic, destructive changes, natural processes will clear the air to reestablish customary weather patterns, will create more glaciers whose runoff will establish new river ecosystems, and will produce fertile soils to support life in areas where it was destroyed.

Pollution is the introduction of agents by humans into the environment in quantities that disrupt the balance of natural processes. Its possible detrimental effect on human life is not part of pollution's definition. Neither are human ignorance or lack of foresight, which may greatly influence the course and severity of pollution.

Ethics is a dimension specific to pollution that is not characteristic of natural processes. Humankind has the intellectual capacity to affect its course, and is itself affected morally by pollution's existence.

Pollution started when humans began manipulating the environment. Although pollution is usually characterized as chemicals or by-products of synthetic processes, this characterization is not entirely accurate. Waste from herds of domestic animals, for example, is a natural product, but it causes many environmental problems. Introducing aggressive nonnative species into an established ecosystem is also pollution, since such species frequently overwhelm the natural system's balance and displace native species. It has even been asserted that the human species itself is a pollutant, since it is both an aggressive species and nonnative to many habitats that it occupies and exploits.

In considering pollution created by manufacturing and daily human activities, there is no uncontaminated ecosystem. Even beyond Earth's known biosphere, humankind sends objects into outer space, and those that become defunct or were never intended to return are dubbed "space junk." Invisible pollutants cannot be overlooked. Various types of synthesized and concentrated radiation—from ultra-low-frequency sound waves to sonic booms; from artificial lighting in classrooms, offices, and along highways to nuclear radioactivity—bombard and vibrate the molecules of the land, the air, and the inhabitants. As a result of all these different contaminants, plant and animal species suffer from aborted embryos, deformed offspring, poor health, shortened lives, and death. Among those suffering is the human species.

HISTORY

Since pollution has an ethical dimension, why has humanity not exercised its moral strength in preventing or halting it? Part of the answer is ignorance. It is not until environmental damage is recognized—usually by detecting injury to some species of plant or animal—that humankind realizes that pollution has occurred.

When gasoline-powered cars were introduced, it never occurred to proponents of modern transportation that the admittedly malodorous exhaust could possibly place large numbers of people in dire respiratory straits, let alone cause Earth to face global warming. Even when auto exhaust was recognized as a major contributor to the unsightly haze of smog, scientists had not yet developed sensing and testing equipment that would give them knowledge of the scope of the air pollution problem.

Another reason that humankind's moral capacity has not been a force in preventing pollution is lack of foresight. This issue illustrates two kinds of humanity's arrogance. Many people assume that humankind has the power and intelligence to solve every problem it recognizes. Many people also have the unrealistic, erroneous belief that there are segments of society that cannot be affected by the dangers that everyone else faces.

When nuclear power plants were developed, the designers were aware that lethal by-products would be generated, and planners incorporated holding ponds and other storage areas in the building complexes. They had not yet developed any means for the safe disposal of nuclear waste, assuming that they would be able to do so as necessary at some future date. Since these designers recognized most of the possible problems of such facilities, did they assume that they were invulnerable to those problems?

Another factor in the pollution situation is the human population's exponential growth. The relationship between technological development and increased human survival has so far been linked in an endless circle. If the human population was only one percent of what it is now, with a corresponding ratio of contaminants in the environment, pollution would be no less real, though it might not seem as serious.

DISCUSSION

The ethics of the survival of life on Earth are shaped by the immediate danger presented by environmental pollution. Most people presume that the survival of the human species is the most important issue. Some reject this conclusion as blatant homocentric speciesism and argue that the survival of human life is inherently no more urgent or legitimate than the survival of any other species. Many people realize, without making claims for the necessity of human survival, that it is dependent on uncountable plant and animal species surviving and upon an environment unsullied enough to support them. All these considerations are based on human acceptance of responsibility for the future. Is humankind responsible for the future? Should humankind assume any responsibility for it?

Perhaps human arrogance causes humankind to presume that such a responsibility exists. Could it be that human history is merely a natural part of evolution on Earth? Are humankind's effects on the environment part of the natural scheme of things to which the environment will eventually adapt? Will that adaptation include mass extinctions and the subsequent development of other life-forms capable of tolerating the changes that humankind has wrought?

Is humankind responsible for all future generations of life? Is humankind morally liable for the future of Earth itself? If humankind does accept any of these responsibilities, what are the exigent considerations?

Given the history of discovering pollution by hindsight, it would seem logical that humankind should not introduce any further agents, unknown or known, into the environment. If additional contamination by known pollutants is to be stopped, it cannot be done without accepting the moral consequences of the human misery and death that will follow as a result of the loss of jobs and the decreased availability and less efficient distribution of food and other human necessities.

As with most moral issues, the pollution dilemma has no easy answers. Yet if humankind is to persist, there can be no avoiding the ethical considerations involved in a possible solution to the problems of pollution.

Marcella T. Joy

FURTHER READING

Allsopp, Bruce. *Ecological Morality.* London: Frederick Muller, 1972.

Attfield, Robin. *Environmental Ethics: An Overview for the Twenty-First Century.* Malden, Mass.: Blackwell, 2003.

Light, Andrew, and Holmes Rolston III, eds. *Environmental Ethics: An Anthology.* Malden, Mass.: Blackwell, 2003.

Partride, Ernest, ed. *Responsibilities to Future Generations: Environmental Ethics.* Buffalo, N.Y.: Prometheus Books, 1981.

Rolston, Holmes, III. *Environmental Ethics: Duties to and Values in the Natural World.* Philadelphia: Temple University Press, 1988.

Scherer, Donald, ed. *Upstream/Downstream: Issues in Environmental Ethics.* Philadelphia: Temple University Press, 1990.

Silver, Cheryl Simon, with Ruth DeFries. *One Earth, One Future: Our Changing Global Environment.* Washington, D.C.: National Academy Press, 1990.

Pollution permits

DEFINITION: Governmental exemptions that grant industries the right to release defined amounts of pollution into the environment

TYPE OF ETHICS: Environmental ethics

SIGNIFICANCE: Although pollution permits have proven to be an effective means of controlling and reducing pollution, thus benefiting society, their critics argue that it is ethically wrong to give any industry the right to cause pollution.

Pollution is a problem of the common resources that are used by all members of society. Such "commons" include air, water, and the oceans. The problem in protecting these resources is how to deal with the external costs, including environmental degradation and injury to human health. The external costs of pollution are borne by those using the common resources and not by the polluters.

Early proposals to control pollution included taxation, which was favored by economists, and command and control, which was favored by politicians. In the latter method, regulatory agencies determine acceptable levels of pollution and impose the implementation of new technologies to reduce it. Both solutions have difficulties, however. Another mechanism for reducing pollution has been the issuance of marketable or tradable pollution permits, a system that relies on free market forces and economic efficiency. The use of pollution permits has resulted in the elimination of lead additives in petroleum refining, in major reductions of sulfur dioxide (which are responsible for acid rain) and particulate emissions, and in lesser reductions of chlorofluorocarbons and nitrogen oxides. The U.S. Congress incorporated pollution permits in the provisions of its 1990 Clean Air Act.

How Pollution Permits Work

Employing cost-benefit analysis, a regulatory agency determines a permissible level of pollution and allocates permits to the industries producing the pollution. Those able to reduce emissions inexpensively may then sell their unused permits to those less able to afford reductions of their emissions. Unlike the command-and-control approach, the pollution permits system allows polluters to determine how best to reduce pollution.

Many economists prefer the pollution permit system because it allows free market forces to act, while environmentalists like it because it does reduce pollution. However, the system presents ethical difficulties. First, the common resources, such as air and water, belong to all members of society but appear to be treated as private property under the pollution permit system. Defenders respond that the permits only authorize use of the commons, not ownership of some part of it.

Critics also argue that polluting is morally wrong and that the pollution permit systems allows favorites—the permit holders—to do something that no one should be permitted to do. Sellers transfer the right to pollute and thus cause harm, something no one should have the right to sell. Others assert that holders of permits should have no right to sell them, as permits should be given away. Defenders of the system responding to these criticisms argue that the goal of the permits is the benefit of humanity, and that studies of health and the environment determine permissible levels of pollution. In addition, the permissible levels should gradually be lowered until pollutants such as leaded gasoline are eliminated or further reductions in pollution cost more than the benefits accrued from the total elimination of the pollution.

Finally, critics argue that pollution permit practices that produce "hot spots"—areas where higher concentrations of pollution develop—often in economically poorer neighborhoods, must be banned.

Kristen L. Zacharias

FURTHER READING

Girdner, Eddie J., and Jack Smith. *Killing Me Softly: Toxic Waste, Corporate Profit, and the Struggle for Environmental Justice*. New York: Monthly Review Press, 2002.

Steidlmeier, Paul. "The Morality of Pollution Permits." *Environmental Ethics* 15 (1993): 133-150.

Tietenberg, T. H. "Ethical Influences on the Evolution of the U.S. Tradable Permit Approach to Pollution Control." *Ecological Economics* 24 (1998): 241-257.

SEE ALSO: Bioethics; Clean Air Act; Clean Water Act; Cost-benefit analysis; Environmental Protection Agency; Pollution; *Silent Spring*; Sustainability of resources; Toxic waste.

Poona Pact

IDENTIFICATION: Agreement guaranteeing members of the casteless untouchables joint legal representation with the general population of colonial India

DATE: Announced on September 25, 1932

TYPE OF ETHICS: Civil rights

SIGNIFICANCE: The Poona Pact drew attention to the plight of the untouchables, whose lives were severely circumscribed by the strictures of the Hindu caste system.

The independence movement in India accelerated when Mohandas K. Gandhi returned from South Africa to India in 1915 and brought with him the weapon of *satyagraha*, or "truth force." He had developed *satyagraha* to protest nonviolently the Boers' refusal to recognize the validity of traditional Indian marriages. He also used moral force to attempt to end the oppression of East Indians by the South African white minority government.

Gandhi joined the Indian National Congress, a Hindu-dominated independence movement, and persuaded others in that organization to join forces with Mohammed Ali Jinnah, whose Muslim League also wanted independence for all of India under a policy that Jinnah labeled *khilafat*. Gandhi persuaded both groups to boycott British-made products, to strike, and to engage in a general policy of noncooperation with Britain. The British initially responded with force to suppress this movement. In 1932, when this response failed, British prime minister Ramsay MacDonald announced constitutional proposals known as the Communal Award, which were viewed as conciliatory measures.

The Communal Award provided for separate electorates for Muslims, Europeans, Anglo-Indians, Sikhs, Christians, upper-caste Hindu Indians, and untouchables. For several thousand years Hindus have been divided into four major castes. Each caste performs specific jobs that its members monopolize.

Members of a caste tend to marry within their caste. The *Brāhmins*, who are considered the highest caste, tend to be priests, rulers, landowners, and intellectuals. At the very bottom of this social hierarchy are the untouchables. They are outcastes who are considered so low and vile that to touch them pollutes a person. They are stigmatized, held in contempt, discriminated against, and assigned the least desirable work, housing, and food.

Gandhi believed that the British were using the classic strategy of "divide and rule," viewing the attempt to segregate untouchable voters in the Communal Award as a bid to divide the Hindu community and to grant power to either the Muslim or the European minority. Either scenario would have fragmented the independence movement and delayed independence. Gandhi believed that communal separatism could be avoided if a secular government were created. Gandhi vowed to fast until he died unless the Communal Award's establishment of separate electorates for various classes of Indian society was rescinded.

GANDHI'S CHALLENGE

Gandhi was a *Vaiśya* (a member of the merchant caste); therefore, his vow to resist, with his life if necessary, segregating untouchables on a separate election roll was revolutionary. No member of a privileged caste had ever proposed such an act. Gandhi's action threatened the caste-based system of segregation, discrimination, and exclusive privilege. He fasted until separate representation for untouchables was rescinded. The key to the victory was Indian unity, which Gandhi forged through the Poona Pact. By means of this pact, the entire Hindu community voted on each candidate. As a result, untouchables were also guaranteed their fair share of seats in schools and representation throughout Indian society.

For decades, Britain had denied colonial subjects the right of self-determination on the grounds that they were racially and mentally inferior, and thus incapable of enlightened self-rule. Gandhi's Poona Pact, coupled with his noncompliance campaign, constituted a direct challenge to the colonial order. Both assumed that all people had certain basic rights, and that assumption defied the British notion of native inferiority. Gandhi was able to unite Muslims and Hindus by appealing to the Hindu doctrine that each individual must find his or her own path to God. Gandhi also effectively utilized the Muslim tradition of tolerance for neighbors who practiced different religions, as long as peace was maintained. This appealed to Jinnah and the Muslim community, who wanted Pan-Indian unity. Although Gandhi did not wish to abolish the caste system entirely, because it had so thoroughly permeated Indian society, his efforts on behalf of the untouchables pointed out the unfairness of the concept of untouchability.

Dallas L. Browne

SEE ALSO: Bigotry; Caste system, Hindu; Colonialism and imperialism; Gandhi, Mohandas K.; Hindu ethics; Human rights.

Population Connection

IDENTIFICATION: Organization established to fight for social and economic stability by advocating that population growth be limited to accord with available resources
DATE: Founded in 1968; renamed on May 1, 2002
TYPE OF ETHICS: Environmental ethics
SIGNIFICANCE: Population Connection not only focuses on encouraging individuals to do their part to improve living conditions for all peoples of the world but also mounts political campaigns intended to change national policy in order to limit population growth and destruction of the environment.

With a membership during the 1990's of more than forty thousand and an annual budget of more than two million dollars, Population Connection (originally known as Zero Population Growth) promotes protection of the environment through reduction of population growth. Because 1990 figures reflect an increase of 95 million people per year worldwide, scientists fear that the ability of the earth's resources to support the population will be seriously undermined. Population Connection works in several ways, both within the United States and internationally, to educate legislators, organizations, teachers, and individuals regarding the massive negative impact of the burgeoning population and its consequent demands upon the earth's resources because of in-

creasing food and energy demands, as well as lifestyle choices that result in the wasting of resources and pollution. Among the organization's activities are political action to ensure reproductive rights, including making available safe, reliable family planning information and services and legal abortion when contraception fails; enhancing the economic and social status of women worldwide through both governmental and private efforts; and, most important, educating people regarding the crucial link between continued population growth and environmental degradation, pollution, poverty, and political and social unrest.

Mary Johnson

SEE ALSO: Abortion; Birth control; Conservation; Ecology; Population control.

Population control

DEFINITION: Attempt to limit human population by various means
TYPE OF ETHICS: Environmental ethics
SIGNIFICANCE: Population control is generally driven by ethical concerns about the effects of human overpopulation upon both the environment and the quality of life of individual members of the human race. Some methods of population control raise ethical concerns of their own, however, about paternalism, the right to privacy, and basic human rights.

The human population, like that of other creatures, is limited in growth by its biotic potential, the maximum rate at which a species can produce offspring given unlimited resources and ideal environmental conditions. At this rate of growth, the population would at first grow slowly only to increase rapidly to produce an exponential curve. Neither humans nor any other species in a given ecosystem can indefinitely grow at their biotic potential, since one or more factors always act as limiting agents. The maximum population size an ecosystem can support indefinitely under a given set of environmental conditions is called that ecosystem's carrying capacity.

1155

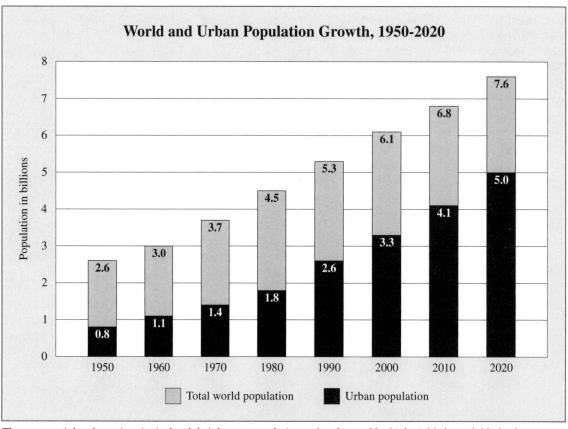

World and Urban Population Growth, 1950-2020

The exponential and ongoing rise in the globe's human population makes the need for high-yield, dependable food crops ever more compelling.

Source: Data are from U.S. Bureau of the Census International Data Base and John Clarke, "Population and the Environment: Complex Interrelationships," in *Population and the Environment* (Oxford, England: Oxford University Press, 1995), edited by Bryan Cartledge.

GROWTH POTENTIAL

Human population has continued to grow as Earth's carrying capacity for humans has been extended as a result of human cleverness, technological and social adaptations, and other forms of cultural evolution. People have altered their ecological niche by increasing food production, controlling disease, and using large amounts of energy and material resources to make habitable those parts of the world that are normally not so.

Observers believe a wide range of populations is possible. Some observers believe that people have already gone beyond the carrying capacity point at which all the earth's inhabitants can be fed, sheltered, and supported. Estimates on the low end of population are that only 1.2 billion people can be supported to U.S. dietary standards and only 600 million at the U.S. rate of energy consumption. These numbers are likely low, since the U.S. rate of food and energy use is high. The higher estimate for human carrying capacity is 45 billion people on a diet similar to U.S. dietary standards, made possible by cultivating all available land, using nuclear power for energy, and mining much of the earth's crust to a depth of 1.6 kilometers for resources. An even higher estimate for human carrying capacity is 157 billion if diets are based solely on grains.

The human population continues to grow, regardless of what the carrying capacity may be. The world population doubles every thirty-five years at growth rates of the 1970's and 1980's. If the population were controlled to zero population growth, the world population would continue to grow for several generations because of decreasing death rates.

ETHICAL CONCERNS

Ethically, most nations favor stabilized or low population growth, because problems of peace, poverty, racism, disease, pollution, urbanization, ecosystem simplification, and resource depletion become harder to solve as the population increases. At the same time, many less-developed nations feel that population control, coupled with the continued status quo of international economic order, poses a dire threat to already oppressed people. These nations insist that for population control to become accepted, there must be a reorganization of economic and political power. These nations argue that people are the most vital of the world's resources and that problems of resource depletion and pollution can be solved by human ingenuity and technology. It is argued that the more people there are, the more likely it is that these problems will be solved. Economic growth would be stimulated because with more people there would be more production.

In contrast, others argue that, ethically, the world population should be limited because most people would be added to the least-developed countries, where education, health, and nutrition levels are so low that continued rapid population growth would condemn millions to an early death. Although technological advances do not come only from people who are well educated or well paid, nations that favor limited population growth feel that encouraging rapid birth rates in the hope that someone may be born to solve the world's pollution and resource problems is an inhumane way to preserve the lives of people who already exist. Nations that encourage better education, nutrition, health care, and work opportunities for a smaller population feel that, ethically, that approach has a greater chance of making needed technological breakthroughs without adding to human suffering.

METHODS OF POPULATION CONTROL

Most nations favor limiting population growth by controlling birth rates. Two approaches to controlling birth rates are economic development and family planning. It is argued that economic development may not be able to help the least-developed countries lower their birth rates, since economic development for these nations is more difficult than it is for those nations that developed in the nineteenth century. In these least-developed countries, expanded family planning programs may bring a more rapid decrease in the birth rate than can economic development alone.

Family planning is a purely voluntary approach whereby information and contraceptives are provided to help couples have the number of children they want when they want to have them. Between 1965 and 1985, family planning was claimed to be a major factor in reducing the birth rates of China, Mexico, and Indonesia. In the same period, moderate to poor results of family planning occurred in the least-developed countries, such as India, Brazil, Bangladesh, and many countries in Africa and Latin America. India started the world's first national family planning program in 1952. Its population then was 400 million; by 1985, it had grown to 765 million, and it topped 1 billion during 2000.

Many people believe that effective population control must include a combination of economic development and the use of methods that go beyond voluntary family planning. Among these methods are voluntary abortion and increased rights, education, and work opportunities for women.

David R. Teske

FURTHER READING

Attfield, Robin. *Environmental Ethics: An Overview for the Twenty-First Century.* Malden, Mass.: Blackwell, 2003.

Ehrlich, Anne H., and Paul R. Ehrlich. "Needed: An Endangered Humanity Act?" In *Balancing on the Brink of Extinction*, edited by Kathryn A. Kohm. Washington, D.C.: Island Press, 1991.

Fritsch, Albert J., et al. *Environmental Ethics: Choices for Concerned Citizens.* Garden City, N.Y.: Anchor Press, 1980.

Hardin, Garrett. *Naked Emperors: Essays of a Taboo-Stalker.* Los Altos, Calif.: William Kaufmann, 1982.

Miller, G. Tyler, Jr. *Environmental Science: Working with the Earth.* 9th ed. Pacific Grove, Calif.: Brooks/Cole, 2003.

Newland, Kathleen. *Women and Population Growth: Choice Beyond Childbearing.* Washington, D.C.: Worldwatch Institute, 1977.

SEE ALSO: Birth control; Environmental ethics; Future-oriented ethics; Immigration; Lifeboat ethics; Malthus, Thomas; Population Connection; Zero-base ethics.

Pornography

DEFINITION: Explicit representations of sexuality intended to cause arousal

TYPE OF ETHICS: Arts and censorship

SIGNIFICANCE: The moral status of pornography is a source of considerable controversy not only between ideological movements, but also within them. Some feminists, for example, attack pornography as a tool of women's oppression, while other feminists embrace it, or even produce it, as a celebration of female sexuality. In the legal arena, U.S. law distinguishes between indecent material—which may be regulated, but is still protected by the First Amendment—and obscene material, which has no constitutional protection and may be banned altogether.

Supreme Court Justice Potter Stewart made the comment in *Jacobellis v. Ohio* (1964) about obscenity that "I know it when I see it." While many scholars and laypersons have made light of the statement, his famous words encapsulate the problematic nature of the debate about pornography. Since pornography eludes common definition, its impact on society and individuals is also passionately debated.

Conflicting perspectives on pornography from conservative, libertarian, and feminist standpoints reflect in condensed form broader societal, political, and legal debates on modern-day issues relating to morality, censorship, and women's rights.

In the United States, where the First Amendment to the U.S. Constitution assumes preeminent status to expression as a "preferred freedom," the pornography debate is strongly tied to jurisprudential arguments about the limits of free expression. Jurisprudence in this area raises questions about the correct "balance" between freedom and equality and the appropriate emphasis on individual rights versus community values and morality.

The terms "pornography" and "obscenity" are sometimes used interchangeably. Some scholars, however, distinguish between obscenity, which is the legal term, and pornography, which is a broader term. Obscenity refers to nonwholesome sexually explicit materials that contradict societal norms. Pornography may include both socially unacceptable, lewd material and sexually explicit erotica consisting of materials that are sexually explicit but not necessarily "offensive" to societal values.

HISTORY OF REGULATION

Excavations of ancient Greek artifacts reveal art depicting sexually explicit and even violent sexual acts. In Greek and Roman times and in England until the seventeenth century, censorship was practiced primarily to control objectionable religious (blasphemous) and political (heretical) writings. While norms in most societies have shunned open displays of sexuality, written materials of any kind have been largely unavailable to the masses except in the last several centuries.

The English case *King v. Sedley* (1663) is often cited as a precursor of modern obscenity law. While the case did not deal directly with the distribution of obscene materials, it provided the legal and theoretical basis for modern obscenity law. Sir Charles Sedley was penalized by the court for standing nude and drunk on a tavern balcony. He spoke to a crowd below, using profane language, and poured urine on the bystanders beneath him. For offending public morality, he was fined and jailed.

Obscenity regulation was rare until the beginning of the nineteenth century, when government regulation of sexual morality became more common. By one estimate, there were approximately three obscenity prosecutions yearly in England between 1802 and 1857. By the mid-1850's, urbanization, expansion of the market for popular books, and Victorian moral standards combined to explain increased interest in and dissemination of sexually explicit materials. The regulation of such materials likewise increased. In 1857, for example, Lord Campbell's Act, which banned the dissemination of obscene works, was enacted.

DEFINING "OBSCENITY"

In the English case of *Regina v. Hicklin* (1868), the court provided a definition of obscenity that shaped English, Canadian, and American law in this area well into the 1950's. The obscene publication *The Confessional Unmasked* was invidiously anti-Roman Catholic, purporting to describe the sexual depravity of Catholic priests. Chief Justice Alexander Cockburn's obscenity test in this case struck at any materials, including those devoid of religious or political assault, that "deprave and corrupt those whose minds are open to such immoral influences, and into whose hands a publication of this sort may fall." This test is generally viewed as extremely restrictive, since it regulates materials that "corrupt" even the most susceptible members of society, as opposed to restricting materials that corrupt the mythical "average" person used in later tests.

An 1815 Pennsylvania case was the first obscenity case decided in the United States. Generally, very little obscenity regulation occurred in the United States until passage of the Comstock Act in 1868 by the New York legislature, which prohibited the dissemination of obscene literature. A federal law regulating mailing of obscene works was passed in 1873, and most states passed antidissemination laws during the late nineteenth century.

Judges applied the Hicklin test until about 1933, when most U.S. jurisdictions relied upon a modified test devised by federal court judges in the case of *United States v. One Book called Ulysses*. Judges in the *Ulysses* case, which did not reach the Supreme Court level, declared obscene only those sexually explicit works that, on the whole, had a prurient effect on average readers. This less-restrictive definition protected some sexually explicit works with literary merit.

LANDMARK COURT CASES

Two major Supreme Court decisions have shaped obscenity law. In 1957, the landmark case of *Roth v. United States* established that obscene materials are outside of limits of First Amendment protection. Since the First Amendment holds that "Congress shall make no law . . . abridging freedom of speech or of the press," *Roth* constituted an important ruling on the issue, suggesting the limits of protected content. The decision defined obscenity in terms of "whether to the average person, applying modern community standards, the dominant theme of the material taken as a whole appeals to the prurient interest."

In 1973, the Supreme Court refined its definition in *Miller v. California*. Regulation of hard-core pornography was the primary aim of the decision, which specified "patently offensive representations or descriptions of ultimate sexual acts, normal or perverted, actual or simulated," and "patently offensive representations or descriptions of masturbation, excretory functions, and lewd exhibition of the genitals."

The Court's guidelines for judging obscene work,

set down in *Miller*, are: "(a) whether 'the average person, applying modern community standards' would find that the work, taken as a whole, appeals to the prurient interest (Roth), (b) whether the work depicts or describes, in a patently offensive way, sexual conduct specifically defined by the applicable state law, and (c) whether the work, taken as a whole, lacks serious literary, artistic, political or scientific value."

The *Miller* case raised questions about why government should be able to decide which material has value. Some scholars argue that such decisions about value should be left to the marketplace and to individual consumers. Critics, including dissenting justices, also expressed concern about *Miller*'s definition of obscenity, which they viewed as insufficiently precise and clear.

In contradistinction, the regulation of child pornography is almost universally accepted. Because of the special vulnerability of children, the legal system has allowed greater protection for children from the harms of pornography. In *New York v. Ferber* (1982), the Supreme Court upheld a statute banning pornography in which children are used as models or actors. The Court accepted broader regulation of child pornography in comparison with other forms, permitting government prohibition of works that only in incidental part (not as a whole) are graphic as well as materials that may possess "serious artistic, literary, scientific or educational value," and works that may not arouse "prurient" thoughts in average individuals.

CONSERVATIVE VIEWS ON PORNOGRAPHY

Clear justifications for allowing government regulation of obscenity are often lacking in Supreme Court decisions on the subject. Stated definitions and rationales for obscenity regulation, however, suggest underpinnings in conservative thought.

Conservatives, who support strong regulation and enforcement of obscenity law, seek to preserve societal values and morals in the interest of the general welfare. From the 1960's through the 1980's, support by conservatives for obscenity regulation was grounded in a commitment to traditional family roles and values. From the conservative standpoint, pornography threatens those values, since it depicts, and may arguably promote, sexual relationships outside of marriage as well as unusual and societally condemned sexual practices depicted in pornography.

For example, the 1986 *Final Report of the At-*

torney General's Commission on Pornography suggested that "it is far from implausible to hypothesize that materials depicting sexual activity without marriage, love, commitment, or affection bear some causal relationship to sexual activity without marriage, love, commitment or affection."

Thus, obscenity, in the conservative view, compromises the integrity of the community by precipitating a decline in religious and moral values among its members.

Support for pornography regulation by conservatives also rests on the assertion that pornography degrades human relationships and depreciates the individuals depicted by the pornography. Sexual acts in pornography are reduced to their purely physical dimensions; they are depicted as animalistic rather than presented in the context of consensual and loving human relationships.

Pornography regulation is also justifiable when expression harms individuals, according to the conservative view. The 1986 *Attorney General's Report*, for example, documents many cases in which individuals, usually women, were adversely affected by pornography—as participants in its production or victims of its effects. Possible links between pornography and violence against women and children have been investigated by social scientists, who have reached mixed conclusions in experimental studies.

LIBERALS' SUPPORT FOR FREE EXPRESSION

Conservatives' support for obscenity regulation in the interests of society and community often conflicts with liberals' support for individual freedom of consenting adults to self-expression and choice in what they read or see.

Generous free speech rights are also defined within the framework of the "marketplace of ideas" wherein ideas compete for acceptance. Theoretically, weak or harmful ideas will falter within the marketplace and lose acceptance. The theory places faith in individual citizens to judge astutely the merits of the ideas presented.

Free speech rights may also be justified by democratic aims. Free speech and expression are particularly valued in democratic societies, such as the United States, in order to promote effective citizenship and participation in government. Confidence in the ability of individuals to make wise choices is an essential part of democratic society.

Some scholars also support maximum expression rights as a function of the need for tolerance in a democracy, particularly one with a diverse, pluralistic, and multicultural population. Unusual, unpopular, and abhorrent ideas should be tolerated with the expectation that tolerance will be reciprocated. Thus, from this perspective, citizens must tolerate some obnoxious, even harmful, expression.

Obscenity regulation is sometimes defended on the basis that, unlike vilified, objectionable speech with political significance, obscenity is "low value" expression, outside the ambit of the political and intellectual expression intended to be protected by the First Amendment.

Others justify pornography on the basis of overlooked positive functions that it might provide, including a possible sexually therapeutic effect for inhibited or sexually dysfunctional individuals or couples. Pornography may also provide informational benefits. The norm of sexual privacy impedes dissemination of information about sexuality, which may hamper self-expression and understanding of sexuality.

While mindful of the potential harms of pornography, liberals contend that the harms must reach a high threshold to justify regulation. Liberals are, therefore, skeptical of social scientific evidence suggesting harms of pornography. They support regulation only when nearly definitive proof of harm can be mustered.

The National Commission on Obscenity and Pornography (1970) embraced libertarian views that pornography's harms are relatively limited. At that time, available social scientific evidence suggested the absence of a connection between pornography usage and violence. This finding has been modified by subsequent studies.

ANTI-PORNOGRAPHY FEMINIST POSITION

While in virtual agreement that pornography degrades women, feminists are divided in their views about the regulation of pornography.

During the 1980's, feminist scholars reconceptualized pornography as a civil rights issue, thus juxtaposing the values of equality for women against the free expression rights of individuals. Feminists such as Catharine MacKinnon, who, with Andrea Dworkin, wrote a civil rights ordinance that addressed the pornography issue, contend that liberals' preoccupation with free speech rights is myopic in that it underestimates the harms of such expression to women. In 1986, the MacKinnon-Dworkin ordinance was declared unconstitutional in federal courts.

Defining pornography in terms of its harms to women, feminists, such as MacKinnon, have also pointed out that while the analogy of the marketplace of ideas with regard to free expression might be appropriate if all citizens had equal access to and voice in the marketplace, the analogy fails when the distribution of power in society is unequal. Socially, politically, legally, and economically, according to this argument, women have less power and voice than do men within a patriarchy, and therefore their arguments are less likely to be viewed as credible.

In feminist "dominance" theory, MacKinnon argues that because men have defined social reality and legal theory, issues such as pornography, sexual assault, and sexual harassment may be defined and viewed differently by women and men, yet the male perspective on these issues is more frequently the preferred one.

Furthermore, concepts such as neutrality and objectivity, which are integral tools in legal interpretation, have been characterized in feminist and postmodern theory as, in practice, upholding the views of the socially powerful. For example, the "contemporary community standards" guideline in *Miller* is rejected by MacKinnon as irrelevant to feminist concerns because women are pervasively devalued and dehumanized as sex objects, making such subordination of women an accepted part of the culture—befitting "contemporary community standards."

Specific harms attributable to pornography are cited in the civil rights ordinance as well as in feminist literature. The cited harms primarily affect women. For example, the ordinance recognizes the potential for women and children to be coerced into performing in pornography productions as well as abused, beaten, threatened, and tortured. Linda Marchiano, who appeared in the pornographic film *Deep Throat*, contends that she performed in the film under duress and that she was severely beaten and abused while making the film.

The 1986 *Attorney General's Report* also contains numerous examples of victim testimony citing the use of coercive and misleading tactics to force women and children to perform in the production of pornographic materials.

Feminists have also rekindled the argument that pornography use is linked with sexual assault. Such causal connections are supported by anecdotal evidence that some assailants model their crimes on ideas found in pornographic materials. In addition, certain findings by social scientists suggest that pornography exposure can affect attitudes toward women and that, in laboratory settings, exposure to sexually violent pornography is correlated with increased aggression toward women.

The most pervasive harm of pornography to women, as presented in feminist theory, is that it reinforces the subordination of women by men. In pornography, women are depicted as sexual objects whose purpose is to provide pleasure to men. MacKinnon and Dworkin argue that pornography asserts that women desire to be battered, humiliated, and beaten. It eroticizes male domination of women, including violence against women. A common theme of pornography involves a woman who is raped and at first resists, but later enjoys it. Social science research cited in the 1986 *Attorney General's Report* shows that nonoffender college males, who were not generally aroused by sexually aggressive pornography, were aroused by rapes in which the victim appeared to enjoy the assault. Furthermore, such arousal was shown to be correlated with acceptance of rape myths.

The objectification of women in pornography mirrors societal attitudes about women, whose importance is judged on the basis of sexual attractiveness and availability. From this standpoint, pornography is symptomatic of women's situation, limiting women's opportunities and making it difficult for women's full capabilities to be equally recognized.

SUMMARY

Divergent perspectives on pornography derive from different emphases on the values of community, individual freedom, and equality. The conservative perspective places primary emphasis on morality and the general welfare, while increasingly demonstrating additional concern for the harms to individuals correlated with exposure to pornography or its users. The concern over harm is shared by feminists, who place strong emphasis upon the need for equality and women's rights. Liberals stress the value of individual free expression rights, which are central to a democratic society, suggesting that these rights be cautiously balanced against the claims of harms to individuals or the general welfare.

Mary A. Hendrickson

FURTHER READING

Clor, Harry M. *Obscenity and Public Morality: Censorship in a Liberal Society.* Chicago: University of Chicago Press, 1969. While somewhat dated, this volume supplies a lucid and comprehensive argument in support of obscenity regulation.

Cornell, Drucilla, ed. *Feminism and Pornography.* New York: Oxford University Press, 2000. Although overweighted with antipornography essays, this valuable anthology attempts to bring together in dialogue many of the different feminist points of view on pornography. Includes pro- and anticensorship arguments, as well as several essays by or about sex workers and their views on pornography.

Donnerstein, Edward, Daniel Linz, and Steven Penrod. *The Question of Pornography: Research Findings and Policy Implications.* New York: Free Press, 1987. This volume is useful for its summary and analysis of social science "effects" studies that consider possible links between pornography and violence.

Downs, Donald Alexander. *The New Politics of Pornography.* Chicago: University of Chicago Press, 1989. Downs explores the new challenges of feminist and conservative analyses of pornography to obscenity doctrine.

Dworkin, Andrea. *Letters from a War Zone: Writings, 1976-1989.* New York: E. P. Dutton, 1988. Essays written during the period indicated, including several on the topic of pornography from law journals and speeches. Written from a feminist perspective.

Juffer, Jane. *At Home with Pornography: Women, Sex, and Everyday Life.* New York: New York University Press, 1998. An exploration of contemporary pornography from the point of view of the female consumer. Focuses on the domestication of pornography, arguing that women can be simultaneously empowered and subjugated by their use of pornography for their own pleasure.

Lederer, Laura, ed. *Take Back the Night: Women on Pornography.* New York: William Morrow, 1980. A collection of essays exploring various aspects of the pornography issue as it affects women.

MacKinnon, Catharine A. *Feminism Unmodified: Discourses on Life and Law.* Cambridge, Mass.: Harvard University Press, 1987. A series of essays from the perspective of feminist jurisprudence, several of which explicate feminist views of current obscenity doctrine. An exegesis in support of a civil rights approach to pornography regulation that recognizes pornography's harms to women.

United States Attorney General's Commission on Pornography. *Final Report of the Attorney General's Commission on Pornography.* Nashville, Tenn.: Rutledge Hill Press, 1986. The conclusions of this commission conflict with those of the 1970 presidential commission's report. This report highlights the harms of pornography and suggests stronger enforcement and regulation.

Williams, Linda. *Hard Core: Power, Pleasure, and the "Frenzy of the Visible."* Expanded ed. Berkeley: University of California Press, 1999. An expanded version of a seminal text in the study of pornography. Traces the historical and cultural forms and meanings of pornographic images from the 19th century to the present, from a rigorously feminist and anticensorship point of view.

SEE ALSO: Art; Art and public policy; Bill of Rights, U.S.; Censorship; Freedom and liberty; Freedom of expression; Rape; Sexuality and sexual ethics; Song lyrics; Supreme Court, U.S.

Post-Enlightenment ethics

DEFINITION: Ethics influenced by or following in the tradition of the Enlightenment of the eighteenth century

TYPE OF ETHICS: Modern history

SIGNIFICANCE: In a very real sense, all formal scholarly ethics written in Europe and the United States after 1800 could be said to be post-Enlightenment ethics. The terms and methods created by Enlightenment philosophers, especially by Immanuel Kant, have constituted the basic parameters of the field ever since, and any contemporary work of moral philosophy must either accept those terms and methods, or argue directly and explicitly against them.

The term "Enlightenment" took its place in the English language in the seventeenth century. Its frequent employment did not occur, however, until the twilight of the movement to which it is applied. Immanuel Kant's 1784 essay *What Is Enlightenment?* made the term applicable to the philosophical movement that was centered in France and Germany from the middle of the seventeenth century to the dawn of the nineteenth century.

The Enlightenment has bequeathed to succeeding ages the methodical study of human relations. The social sciences became the offspring of the Enlightenment. Although these disciplines were not a part of the movement proper, they were spawned by the Enlightenment *philosophes*' struggle to improve society.

The Enlightenment was a sharp break with the dominant view of life that was prevalent during the Middle Ages. In medieval society, belief was the chief means by which humanity operated. Thus, both the church and superstition held unquestioned authority in most circles. The Enlightenment, however, introduced a rejection of traditional doctrines, whose validity largely rested upon their longevity. The Enlightenment's questioning and probing method was conducive to the growth of science and its application to the political and social realms.

Generally, the Enlightenment tended to reject the restraints that had been placed on medieval thinking. The movement's free thinking not only expanded beyond metaphysical constraints but also dismissed them as being irrelevant and incomprehensible in determining what is ethical. The narrow focus of medieval Scholasticism was replaced by an interdisciplinary pursuit of knowledge. Philosophy became the medium through which Enlightenment thinkers examined history, politics, science, and other fields.

CHIEF TENETS

The Enlightenment set forth the employment of free reason, which involved the analysis and evaluation of existing institutions and doctrines. This movement subjected traditional authority to examination and interrogation. The motive behind the probing was a belief in progress. Unlike the thinkers of the *ancien régime*, thinkers of the post-Enlightenment era believed that human effort was the chief contribution to progress. Some *philosophes* believed in it so fervently that they conceived of a heaven on Earth that was a product of humanity's designs.

Immanuel Kant called the statement *sapere aude* ("dare to know") the Enlightenment's motto. Indeed, a chief objective of the movement was self-knowledge. The way to knowledge, according to the *philosophes*, was through experience. Since humanity was a part of nature, experience through that medium was possible. Hence, for Enlightenment thinkers, nature became the great teacher. This belief in experiential knowledge became known as empiricism.

The focus on the knowledge of humankind put a new emphasis on humankind's motivation and nature. Instead of taking the medieval view of humankind's preoccupation with otherworldly rewards, the *philosophes* conceived of humanity as being motivated by such temporal concerns as appetite, fear, and pride. This view ushered in the era of rational scientific materialism.

Thus, post-Enlightenment ethics have sought to reform society. It is believed that societal redemption will improve individuals who are influenced by the social environment in which they live. Hence, the Enlightenment and its following generations have focused their attention on life in the present rather than a life to come.

There is a temptation to dismiss the Enlightenment as being atheistic, but to do so would be inaccurate. Only in a few extreme cases were attempts made by Enlightenment thinkers to disprove the existence of a Supreme Being.

Instead, the *philosophes* were areligious. Although religion did not hold sway over them as it had over the medievalists, most of the Enlightenment's leaders did ascribe to various elements of religious teachings in their personal faith. For example, many of them were Deists and therefore believed in God as creator but not in divine immanence in history.

INFLUENCE ON RELIGION

Many post-Enlightenment Protestant theologians have synthesized this movement with orthodoxy to form a theology that is at odds with John Calvin's doctrine of predestination and Martin Luther's bondage of the will. Modern Protestantism accentuates personal accountability. The individual is believed to be able to exercise choice regarding his or her eternal destiny. Such a view was readily accepted by Puritan New England. The American colonists were rebelling against the authority of the Church of England. Their belief in the freedom of conscience was confirmation of a crucial link with an important tenet of the Enlightenment.

New England continued to abide by Calvinism's belief in hard work and thrift. The region also, however, came to incorporate the Enlightenment's teachings. As a result, American Protestantism, so far as salvation was concerned, moved toward an Arminian theology in which human individual freedom of choice was stressed.

The Enlightenment's view of humanity called for something other than a metaphysical solution to the problem of bringing into being a moral society. The *philosophes* devised a system that emphasized human choice. Providing a quasi-link with the rigidity of medieval theology, however, the Enlightenment did believe that laws could be found in nature. They believed that the laws that brought order to the physical environment could be studied and used in the social arena to form a moral society.

Thus, although the Enlightenment did emphasize individual freedom, it did not advocate anarchy. Natural law was believed to contain principles that would ensure societal advantages that included the recognition of the equality of human beings and the right to pursue happiness. While it was individualistic in its accentuation of freedoms, it was at the same time a submission to natural laws that called for order and continuity in both the physical and the social environment.

The *philosophes* believed that it was possible and even desirable that society should exist without religious supervision. They did not, however, advocate the abolition of religion as a necessity. Instead, they called for religious tolerance. Arguments in favor of this position particularly were characteristic of the English Protestants. Consequently, the post-Enlightenment United States (a former English colony) has adopted an official stance of separation of state and church. By not having a state religion, the country attempts to tolerate all faiths and to ensure personal freedom of religion.

INFLUENCE ON SCIENCE

With its probing nature, the Enlightenment was conducive to scientific investigations. Its rejection of unquestioned authority created a climate for scientific explorations, experiments, and resulting discoveries and inventions. This ushered in the Industrial Revolution, which has not only transformed but also expanded the world's economies. Out of this technological growth came the belief that human

beings were capable of shaping life's conditions. The optimistic view of progress swayed the post-Enlightenment world away from a reliance upon fate.

The post-Enlightenment world has come to depend more on human ingenuity to explain the causes of phenomena, including explanations for destructive storms, floods, and other natural disasters. The modern world is not inclined to attribute such events to acts of divine justice or the inevitable. Instead, it looks for causative factors and preventive measures that will deter or minimize future damages. Thus, the post-Enlightenment world depends on human effort rather than on religion or superstition to explain the unknown.

Unfortunately, post-Enlightenment manipulators have applied some of the *philosophes'* scientific cataloging to justify classism, racism, and ethnocentrism. By classifying humanity into various segments, these individuals have used the *philosophes'* efforts to bring about order to create disunity among human beings. By going beyond the species of *Homo sapiens* and classifying humans into races and classes, the post-Enlightenment manipulation introduced a stratified chain of being for humanity. This doctrine subverted the Enlightenment's attempt to recognize the equality that nature had decreed. Hence, scientific racism became a perverted use of the Enlightenment's doctrines.

INFLUENCE ON PHILOSOPHY

During the Middle Ages, philosophy and theology were one. Because of the Church's domination, it was considered sacrilegious to conduct speculative thinking that was independent of religious dogma. The few medievalists, such as Peter Abelard, who exercised some degree of free thought were ostracized and persecuted. The Enlightenment's philosophy, however, exemplified human reason as the avenue to truth. In fact, the Enlightenment's *philosophes* were also scientists; that is, they studied nature in the belief that it contained laws that brought order to the universe. This concept led them to classify and organize information into a system. As a result, the *philosophes'* most important form of publication was the encyclopedia, in which they cataloged scientific and philosophical knowledge. Natural law was perceived as governing not only the physical environment but also society.

This was a clear divorcement from medieval thinking. The *philosophes* did not believe that ethics could be mastered by studying metaphysics or religion. Thus, for ethics to be comprehended, it was believed that the student had to abandon metaphysics and religion. The Enlightenment viewed these disciplines as explanations for the imponderable.

The *philosophes*, again unlike the medievalists, did not concern themselves with otherworldly rewards and punishments. Instead, their focus was humanity's present situation. Thus, they attempted to discover natural laws that spoke to human behavior, government, and individual freedoms.

Because of this emphasis, the post-Enlightenment world has turned its attention toward the improvement of society. Disciplines such as sociology and psychology came of age because of the Enlightenment's scrutiny of humanity's problematic situation. The systematic study of these problems was a fundamental component of the development of the social sciences. The post-Enlightenment world has been much more understanding and helpful in treating mental disease. While the medievalist was prone simply to dismiss a disturbed person as one possessed by a demon, modern science has searched for the physical and psychological causes of mental disturbance. The net result of the advent of such social sciences has been the emergence of a more humane way of dealing with such patients.

The *philosophes*' views were widely dispersed. Their philosophy reached far beyond western Europe. The United States was particularly receptive to the positions expostulated by Montesquieu, Voltaire, Locke, and others. These Enlightenment thinkers came to have a basic and profound impact upon the American Revolution and the democratic government that was formed in the aftermath.

INFLUENCE ON POLITICS

The Enlightenment had a tremendous impact in the governmental sphere. Its philosophy of natural law became the basic argument for individual freedom, including the pursuit of happiness. Thus, the Enlightenment declared that the governed did not exist for the benefit of the governor. Jean-Jacques Rousseau espoused the view that government was really a contract between the governed and the governor, who had reciprocal responsibilities. Opposing arbitrary authority and the divine right doctrine, the *philosophes* held that a citizen had rights that included expectations of the government.

Furthermore, the Enlightenment gave credence to the doctrine of the right to revolt. Whenever the government infringed upon citizens' individual freedoms, the citizens were justified in overthrowing that government.

While this doctrine legitimated the American and French revolutions in the eighteenth century, it was paradoxical to its contemporary practices of slavery and colonialism. Thus, while the Enlightenment ushered in a new era that was characterized by emphasis upon individual freedoms, it did not provide a clean break with the despotic past. Many of the violations that subverted the human being's pursuit of happiness would continue for many years, even in lands where the Enlightenment's principles had been formally adopted as the basis for government. These continued violations illustrated that many of the *philosophes* were overoptimistic. Their hope for an earthly utopia has continued to elude humanity even though reforms and democratic ideals have become diffused throughout the post-Enlightenment world.

INFLUENCE ON SOCIAL STRATIFICATION

Among the doctrines set forth by the Enlightenment was the equality of human beings. This idea was a radical departure from the medieval practice of feudalism. Under the *ancien régime*, a vassal would swear his fealty to a nobleman. The vassal was subservient to the nobleman in every way imaginable. His major assignment was to render service and obeisance unto his lord (the nobleman). In no way did the serf consider himself to be on an equal basis with his master.

The Enlightenment was an integral part of the modernization of the Western world. As the growth of the middle class occurred, feudalism's structure of nobility and serfdom was challenged. Thus, the Enlightenment challenged this archaic stratification and at the same time served as an apologetic mechanism for the emerging middle class. In this way, the Enlightenment helped to pave the way for the spread of both democracy and capitalism. The Enlightenment's teachings regarding natural law and equality undermined the feudal structure. Thus, socially, post-Enlightenment society tended to be fluid. In modern democratic society it is reasonable to expect social and economic mobility. American optimism espe-

1165

cially made the modern citizen believe that economic and social improvement is a reasonable expectation and perhaps even a right.

Yet despite the post-Enlightenment world's optimistic expectations, social stratification continues. Certainly, modern stratification in the industrialized countries is not as drastic as the plight of the medieval serf as contrasted with the comfortable life of the aristocratic nobility. Yet the dream of a classless society has proved to be an unrealistic aspiration. Even communism's imposition of a uniform dress code (as in the case of China) has not proved to be successful in producing a totally egalitarian society. Thus, the unattainable goal of a utopia free of classism again demonstrates the unrealistic expectations of some of the *philosophes*.

In fact, the post-Enlightenment world has not completely obliterated feudalism. The remains of this medieval institution can certainly still be found in the military and in the business world's corporate culture. Despite this structure, however, the Enlightenment has influenced these modern organizations. There are rules that the rulers are expected to follow, and if they do not, they can be replaced. Thus, despite the military and corporate hierarchy, the post-Enlightenment world does demand personal accountability from all.

CONTRIBUTION

Post-Enlightenment ethics are characterized by an appreciation for individual freedoms, democratic government, and an optimistic belief in human progress. As a result, society has become less staid and evasive of human accountability. Post-Enlightenment ethics do not ascribe blame for accidents and disasters to God or fate. Instead, human ingenuity and negligence are cited as factors in bringing about either success or failure. Such thinking has given birth to two opposing positions. Fatalists have used aspects of the Enlightenment to classify humanity into groups that range from the primitive to the most advanced. By doing so, they have maintained the inequities that were part of the *ancien régime*. Such misuse of the Enlightenment has subverted its aspiration for a totally reformed society. Yet the Enlightenment has also helped to inspire democratic ideals and universal fraternity. Since these noble ideals are not fully attained, it might be said that the Enlightenment is still in progress.

Randolph Meade Walker

FURTHER READING

Capaldi, Nicholas. *The Enlightenment: The Proper Study of Mankind*. New York: G. P. Putnam's Sons, 1967. This work provides a comprehensive overview of the dominant themes of the Enlightenment and the ways in which they differed from those of the *ancien régime* against which they were set.

Cassirer, Ernst. *The Philosophy of the Enlightenment*. Translated by Fritz C. A. Koelln and James P. Pettegrove. Boston: Beacon Press, 1955. This specialized study examines the Enlightenment's thinking. The prominent concepts of the movement are explained in a clear and understandable manner. Defends the new thinking in the light of the Romantic movement's characterization of it as "shallow Enlightenment."

Commager, Henry Steele. *The Empire of Reason: How Europe Imagined and America Realized the Enlightenment*. Garden City, N.Y.: Anchor Press/ Doubleday, 1977. The contention of this book is that the Enlightenment originated in Europe but did not reach its fruition until it was incorporated in Anglo-America.

Crocker, Lester G. *Nature and Culture: Ethical Thought in the French Enlightenment*. Baltimore: Johns Hopkins University Press, 1963. A valuable specialized study of the place of ethics in the Enlightenment's teachings. It contends that a homogeneity of thought on human nature and morals disappeared with the breakup of medieval Christian metaphysical teachings.

Gay, Peter. *The Enlightenment: An Interpretation*. 2 vols. New York: Knopf, 1966-1969. Reprint. New York: Norton, 1977. This is the definitive text on the Enlightenment. It examines the *philosophes'* world and explains why their demands and expectations were made.

Horkheimer, Max, and Theodor W. Adorno. *Dialectic of Enlightenment: Philosophical Fragments*. Translated by Edmund Jephcott. Edited by Gunzelin Schmid Noerr. Stanford, Calif.: Stanford University Press, 2002. The most famous and influential of the Frankfurt School critiques of the Enlightenment and its legacy. Details the failures of reason in the West, and relates Enlightenment rationality directly to the rise of fascism.

Hyland, Paul, Olga Gomez, and Francesca Greensides, eds. *The Enlightenment: A Sourcebook and Reader*. New York: Routledge, 2003. Anthology collecting both important source texts by Enlightenment thinkers and contemporary criticism on the subject. The source texts are organized by topic; sections include "Moral Principles and Punishments," "Political Rights and Responsibilities," and "The Development of Civil Society."

Koch, Adrienne, ed. *The American Enlightenment: The Shaping of the American Experiment and a Free Society.* New York: George Braziller, 1965. Complete with an introduction that gives a comprehensive interpretation of the American Enlightenment, this work is a collection of primary sources. It includes letters, autobiographies, and other writings of some of America's key Enlightenment figures, such as Benjamin Franklin and Thomas Jefferson.

Palmer, R. R. *The Age of the Democratic Revolution: A Political History of Europe and America, 1760-1800.* Princeton, N.J.: Princeton University Press, 1959-1964. This volume offers a synthesis of political history on both sides of the Atlantic. It provides an important connective understanding of the various movements for democratic reform that were staged in Europe as well as America, demonstrating that the birth of democracy was not an isolated event.

SEE ALSO: Enlightenment ethics; Kantian ethics; Natural rights; Postmodernism.

Postmodernism

DEFINITION: Group of aesthetic and theoretical responses to late twentieth century political, economic, and social life

TYPE OF ETHICS: Modern history

SIGNIFICANCE: Postmodernism is a largely celebratory movement, advocating and enjoying the chaos, fragmentation, and commodification endemic to contemporary capitalist society. Its embrace of ethical ambiguity has been criticized both by those who advocate a return to traditional ethical values and by those who see it as inappropriately upholding traditional capitalist values such as individual choice and personal preference.

In 1907, Pope Pius X wrote an official letter condemning what he called "modernism." His letter charged that modernists were denying the Church's ancient traditions. In fact, modernism often implies the sense of an antitradition, and the pope feared that modernist ideas would necessitate a devaluation of papal authority and historical legitimacy.

Modernity, that is, the era beginning with the Industrial Revolution and ending some time in the second half of the twentieth century, was a time of rapid scientific, technological, and economic development in much of the world. The values both of tradition and of progress were constantly at issue and constantly questioned. There were two responses to this movement, one positive and one negative. On the positive side, during the modern period, there was a general feeling of impatience with the past and a popular optimism toward the future. There was a sense that perfection is possible for human society. Science, technology, and human reason could create a utopia for the world in which people would live good lives in peace and harmony. Ancient traditions no longer provided the means of future progress and advancement, and so had to be left behind.

On the negative side, however, many writers, artists, and intellectuals responded to this conception of technology and reason with skepticism. Their work decried the mechanization and rationalization of human society. They saw humans being replaced by machines and, even worse, a tendency to see the human as a type of machine. These "modernists" believed that the problem with modernity lay in the invention of a new sort of culture, mass culture, which produced artworks, as well as electronic, automotive, and other products, on a mass scale. Mass culture was seen as a culture of technology and the rational marketplace, rather than a culture beauty and artistic value. Modernism was a largely pessimistic reaction against modern mass culture, an attempt to "rescue" the category of high art from the "degradations" of the masses.

POSTMODERN SKEPTICISM

The modernist skepticism toward traditional models of progress that had led to the creation of mechanized, mass culture was amplified in the late twentieth century. As capitalism developed and became global, modernity developed into postmodernity. The general public began to believe that their earlier optimism had been unwarranted. Science and technology did have good effects, but there was a dark side for every advance. With new technology came pollution, for example, and more advanced means for conducting war.

At the same time, the globalization of mass culture brought radically different value systems into intimate contact with one another. The result was a heightened awareness that not all races and nationalities thought the same way. Knowledge which once had seemed objective and universal was revealed to be the perspective of one particular group. Postmodernity, then, brought about a popular acceptance of the skepticism that had been expressed only by individual intellectuals in modernity. The notion of a universal ethics that would apply to all people came to seem implausible.

Ironically, some creators of art and literature in postmodernity began to celebrate the very fragmentation of traditions and values that had seemed so foreboding to the modernists. New kinds of aesthetic movements developed which, far from "rescuing" art from mass degradation, celebrated mass culture and denied that there was any difference between high art and popular culture. These movements were identified as examples of "postmodernism." Modernism and postmodernism thus tended to agree as to the nature of reality, identity, and values—but where modernism resisted the death of tradition, postmodernism reveled in it.

Examples of Postmodern Ethics

Postmodernism views ethics as something which has to be decided by the individual or group. Various races and cultures, for example, have diverse ways of living and speaking, thus making it difficult to state uniformly what is right and wrong. In postmodernity, there is an explosion of diversity in all aspects of life, and postmodernism celebrates that diversity. From one point of view, heterosexuality is normal, whereas from another, homosexuality seems right. The American desire to bring democracy to the world seems to some to be a lofty and honest goal. But a postmodernist view states that this is merely one story that can be told about the role of the United States in the world, and others may be equally valid.

Changing roles for men and women provide another example of diversity. In modernity, women were the housekeepers and men were the breadwinners. Role reversals have brought about confusion and disorientation as to what vocational choices to

make. In postmodernity, it is not possible to state, in principles that hold for all people, what is right and wrong, ethical or unethical.

Winifred Whelan

Further Reading

Foster, Hal, ed. *The Anti-aesthetic: Essays on Postmodern Culture.* New York: New Press, 1998.

Gibson, Andrew. *Postmodernity, Ethics, and the Novel: From Leavis to Levinas.* New York: Routledge, 1999.

Harvey, David. *The Condition of Postmodernity: An Enquiry into the Origins of Cultural Change.* Cambridge, Mass.: Blackwell, 1990.

Hoffmann, Gerhard, and Alfred Hornung, eds. *Ethics and Aesthetics: The Moral Turn of Postmodernism.* Heidelberg, Germany: C. Winter, 1996.

Jameson, Fredric. *Postmodernism: Or, The Cultural Logic of Late Capitalism.* Durham, N.C.: Duke University Press, 1991.

Lyotard, Jean François. *The Postmodern Condition: A Report on Knowledge.* Translated by Geoff Bennington and Brian Massumi. Foreword by Fredric Jameson. Minneapolis: University of Minnesota Press, 1984.

_____. *Postmodern Fables.* Translated by Georges Van Den Abbeele. Minneapolis: University of Minnesota Press, 1997.

Madison, Gary B., and Marty Fairbairn, eds. *The Ethics of Postmodernity: Current Trends in Continental Thought.* Evanston, Ill.: Northwestern University Press, 1999.

Marchitello, Howard, ed. *What Happens to History: The Renewal of Ethics in Contemporary Thought.* New York: Routledge, 2001.

Whelan, Winifred. "Postmodernism in the Work of Julia Kristeva." In *Religious Education: An Interfaith Journal of Spirituality, Growth, and Transformation* 94, no. 3 (Summer 1999): 289-298.

Ziarek, Ewa Płonowska. *An Ethics of Dissensus: Postmodernity, Feminism, and the Politics of Radical Democracy.* Stanford, Calif.: Stanford University Press, 2001.

See also: Absolutism; Art; Critical theory; Deconstruction; Derrida, Jacques; Foucault, Michel; Language; Pluralism; Post-Enlightenment ethics; Relativism; Skepticism.

Winston S. Churchill (left), Harry S. Truman (center), and Joseph Stalin at Potsdam. (National Archives)

naïve idealist who believed implicitly in his country's innate goodness, had faith in the principle of international cooperation. Great Britain sided with Truman, who demanded that free elections be held in eastern European countries that, it was charged, had unfairly been made satellites of the Soviet orbit of control. Stalin refused.

War damages, or reparations, were another crucial issue. The Soviets wanted to rebuild their war-torn economy with German industry; the United States feared that it would be saddled with the entire cost of caring for defeated Germans. Each side ended up taking reparations from its zone of occupation, and Germany was divided in two without input. The growing antagonism between the United States and the Soviet Union resulted in the Cold War.

Andrew C. Skinner

SEE ALSO: Cold War; Stalin, Joseph; Truman Doctrine.

Potsdam Conference

THE EVENT: Final meeting of the Allied leaders of Great Britain, the Soviet Union, and the United States during World War II

DATE: July 17 to August 2, 1945

TYPE OF ETHICS: Modern history

SIGNIFICANCE: Over the course of the Potsdam Conference, long-standing ideological and ethical differences between the United States and the Soviet Union emerged to solidify the territorial and economic dismantling of Germany and lay the foundations of the Cold War.

In the Berlin suburb of Potsdam, the Allied powers met from July 17 to August 2, 1945, to strengthen their resolve to defeat Japan and to decide how to put the world back together after the shattering experience of World War II had ended. Joseph Stalin, who had been cunning and brutal in securing control at home, was bent on exploiting the Soviet Union's victory after the war. President Harry S. Truman, the

Poverty

DEFINITION: Condition of having insufficient resources or income to meet such basic human needs as nutrition, clothing, shelter, and health care

TYPE OF ETHICS: Politico-economic ethics

SIGNIFICANCE: Political philosophers and social activists often appeal to competing moral bases to ground their arguments about alleviating poverty. Arguments and rationales include individual rights to life and property, mutual and intergenerational obligations of citizens, legitimacy of the state, and obligations of affluent nations to poverty-stricken nations.

Welfare provision as a matter of charity is based on the notion that individuals have no moral right to what they receive because no one has a right to another's charity. People have a right to acquire and retain goods and resources by initial acquisition or by voluntary agreement. Welfare provision as a strict obligation for those with resources implies that those in need have moral claim on more affluent persons. One's right to life means more than the right not to be killed unjustly. It implies a moral claim compelling more affluent persons to relinquish part of their surplus wealth on behalf of poor persons. However, the principle generally assumes that poor persons do all they legitimately can to meet basic needs.

In the absence of strict moral claims, poor persons are dependent on others' beneficence, which may or may not be forthcoming. A duty to be benevolent, based on welfare as charity, obligates those with resources only to assist people whom they choose to assist. It cannot be enforced under equal rules for all, and it favors private, nonstate forms of provision. The role of the state is residual. Government acts as a safety net when private sector welfare is inadequate. Conversely, the strict obligation view of welfare implies that individuals have a right to such provisions. The state not only must ensure that such rights are protected and applied equally, but it also should be instrumental in welfare provision. The state's legitimacy in part derives from its welfare providing functions.

ETHICS OF RELIEF

The ethics of relief obligate charitable organizations and governments to assist those who cannot meet their own basic needs. Political philosopher James Sterba argues that poor persons have a moral claim on the surplus resources of the more affluent. Sterba's argument that the needs of the poor take priority over the liberty of the affluent persons to meet luxury needs conflicts with the views of libertarian and liberal political philosophers. For example, Robert Nozick maintains that the only claims to welfare help that can be justified are from those whose poverty has resulted from some form of social injustice, such as discrimination.

ETHICS OF PREVENTION

The ethics of prevention concern what must be done to reduce future poverty. Economist Gordon Tullock has suggested that if income were redistributed to alleviate poverty in the United States, one of the effects would be to slow the rate of economic growth by approximately 2 percent annually. After about fifteen years, the consequent reduced economic growth would leave people at the lower end of the income scale worse off than if no transfer of income had taken place. Likewise, if affluent countries were to redistribute wealth to the poorest counties, the consequent reduction in the rate of economic growth in the United States would reduce the rate of growth in the recipient countries because the United States would be consuming less of the world's goods. Over time the cumulative effects would worsen poverty in the poor countries.

The ethics of relief and of prevention are affected by the closeness of the relationship between providers and receivers. There is much less moral ambiguity around alleviating poverty among more immediate family members, other relatives, or close friends. More distant family members, acquaintances, or strangers are more ethically problematic. As Sterba notes, however, no one is morally required to do either what is beyond their power to do or what would entail too great a sacrifice. Setting limits on efforts to alleviate poverty is permissible to the extent such efforts result in immense personal or social sacrifice on those who are not poor.

Richard K. Caputo

FURTHER READING

Nozick, Robert. *Anarchy, State, and Utopia*. Oxford, England: Blackwell, 1974.

Plant, Raymond, Harry Lesser, and Peter Taylor-Gooby. *Political Philosophy and Social Welfare: Essays on the Normative Basis for Welfare Provision*. London: Routledge & Kegan Paul, 1980.

Rawls, John. *A Theory of Justice*. Cambridge, Mass.: Harvard University Press, 1971.

Sterba, James P. *Justice: Alternative Political Perspectives*. 3d ed. Belmont, Calif.: Wadsworth, 1999.

Tullock, Gordon. "The Reality of Redistribution." In *Poverty and Inequality: The Political Economy of Redistribution*, edited by Jon Neill. Kalamazoo, Mich.: W. E. Upjohn Institute for Employment Research, 1997.

Van Parjis, Philippe. *Real Freedom for All: What (if Anything) Can Justify Capitalism?* Oxford, England: Oxford University Press, 1995.

Poverty and wealth

DEFINITION: Poverty: lack of sufficient material resources to sustain oneself, or of extraneous or luxury possessions; wealth: abundance of material resources and riches

TYPE OF ETHICS: Politico-economic ethics

SIGNIFICANCE: The extreme disparity of wealth levels between industrialized and developing nations may raise significant ethical issues relating to social and distributive justice, especially since the wealth of industrialized nations is largely maintained and increased at the direct expense of developing nations. Many members of the industrialized world, however, would disagree with this statement, arguing that the poverty of others creates no obligation on the part of the wealthy and that global free markets are in the long-term interests of all people.

Nonindustrialized, or developing, nations cover 60 percent of the world's land surface and include 70 percent of the world's population. They form a much less homogeneous group than do the major industrialized nations, since they represent a wide variety of social, economic, cultural, political, and geographical environments. Unfortunately, what developing nations do have in common is a marked socioeconomic disadvantage that manifests itself in weak economies, overpopulation, and widespread poverty.

In developing nations, poverty is pervasive both relative to industrialized nations and on an absolute level. State welfare systems are either inadequate or nonexistent, and for that reason millions of people are malnourished and die in periodic famines. Housing and shelter are often inadequate.

Developing nations are characterized by weak economic systems; low agricultural productivity; an undeveloped industrial base; limited technology; limited purchasing power; overreliance on a small number of export products, making their economies particularly vulnerable to fluctuations in supply and demand; and reliance on foreign investments and the importation of industrial equipment.

Developing nations also have demographic deficiencies, such as low life expectancy at birth, high rates of infant mortality, large families, rampant disease, and high rates of infection. These countries also tend to have incompetent governments that are characterized by poor administration, widespread corruption, lack of opportunity and high unemployment, glaring inequities between social classes, a disproportionate concentration of wealth and power in the hands of a ruling elite, and insufficient resources devoted to social programs and education (impoverished sub-Saharan countries continue to spend two to three times as much on armaments as on education). Because of such inequities, the best-educated segment of the population may leave; for example, during the 1980's, one-third of Africans with a postsecondary education emigrated to Europe.

It is obvious that there is an enormous disparity between the developed and the underdeveloped world in terms of the distribution of wealth and power, and this disparity appears to be growing according to reports of the United Nations Development Program. Income disparities between the richest and the poorest 20 percent of countries more than doubled between 1960 and 1990. As of 1992, the average income gap was more than 140 to 1 ($22,808 to $163). In terms of control over economic activity, in 1989, the richest 20 percent of nations controlled between 80 and 95 percent of total gross national product, world trade, commercial lending, domestic savings, and domestic investment. The poorest 20 percent of countries controlled between 0.2 and 1.4 percent of economic activity.

ETHICS AND THE WEALTH OF NATIONS

Most developing nations are in a relationship of unequal exchange with the countries of the developed world. One theory maintains that the way to decrease this inequality is to redistribute wealth. Central to this strategy is the belief that economic interaction is a zero-sum game; that is, that as one nation acquires more wealth and becomes richer, another nation loses wealth and becomes poorer. As Marjorie Kelly put it: "Wealth is made on the backs of the poor." Therefore, if the developed countries are hoarding all the wealth and this wealth is generating poverty in the undeveloped nations, poverty can be wiped out by redistributing the wealth from developed to undeveloped nations. Examples of this theory being put into practice include the Peace Corps, foreign aid, and low-interest loans or grants that are provided by the World Bank and the International Monetary Fund.

The concept of redistribution may be ethically laudable, but it has not worked in practice, as is indicated by the growing disparity between developed and undeveloped nations. The zero-sum theory says that significant improvement in the well-being of nonindustrialized countries can occur only if a significant decline in the well-being of industrialized countries occurs simultaneously. A similar rationale works on a smaller scale for the powerful interest and economic groups within nonindustrialized countries that have monopolized the wealth of those countries. Clearly, these nations and groups have not been willing to undertake such a level of redistribution. In fact, the data suggest that they are accumulating an even greater share of the wealth. According to Jacob Needleman, "The outward expenditure of mankind's energy now takes place in and through money." Marjorie Kelly observed that one of the consequences of this single-minded accumulation of money is that "we have come to lack a sense of financial obesity: a cultural consensus that enough is enough and too much is grotesque . . . we lack any . . . revulsion to vast sums of money."

Kelly argues that a solution to this problem may be to recognize that equality of wealth is impossible to achieve. Kelly suggests that one solution might be to encourage the creation of wealth that does not cause poverty, creating a win-win situation, an ethically earned prosperity that also makes others prosperous. For example, a product is sold by a company to customers who become prosperous by using the product. Kelly's idea is interesting, but it is not clear on what scale a win-win situation could operate globally. In addition, the success of such a strategy hinges on—as Kelly noted—a duty on the part of the wealthy to care for those who do not have wealth. The fact that affluent nations are becoming wealthier while developing nations sink deeper into poverty suggests that Kelly's sense of duty has not yet achieved recognition or high priority.

Laurence Miller
Updated by the editors

FURTHER READING

Bello, Walden, Shea Cunningham, and Bill Rau. *Dark Victory: The United States, Structural Adjustment, and Global Poverty*. London: Pluto Press, 1994.

Berberoglu, Berch. *The Political Economy of Development*. Albany: State University of New York Press, 1992.

Kelly, Marjorie, et al. "Are You Too Rich if Others Are Too Poor?" *The Utne Reader*, no. 53 (September-October, 1992): 67-70.

Little, Daniel. *The Paradox of Wealth and Poverty: Mapping the Ethical Dilemmas of Global Development*. Boulder, Colo.: Westview Press, 2003.

Osterfield, David. *Prosperity Versus Planning*. New York: Oxford University Press, 1992.

Pacione, Michael, ed. *The Geography of the Third World: Progress and Prospect*. New York: Routledge, 1988.

Pogge, Thomas W., ed. *Global Justice*. Malden, Mass.: Blackwell, 2001.

Smeeding, Timothy M., Michael O'Higgins, and Lee Rainwater, eds. *Poverty, Inequality, and Income Distribution in Comparative Perspective*. Washington, D.C.: Urban Institute Press, 1990.

SEE ALSO: Capitalism; Class struggle; Communism; Distributive justice; Economic analysis; Famine; Income distribution; Poverty; Profit economy; World Trade Organization.

Power

DEFINITION: Ability to produce effects
TYPE OF ETHICS: Theory of ethics
SIGNIFICANCE: Power is arguably the thing which ethics is designed to regulate: One's actions and even one's existence are morally significant only to the extent that one has recognizable effects upon oneself and others. For philosophers like Michel Foucault and Friedrich Nietzsche, power—that is, the sum total of one's effects—is synonymous with existence.

Power is often confused with authority, but power is distinct from authority. In general, power implies an ability or capacity of some sort. More particularly, power implies an ability or capacity to exercise influence, control, or dominion over others. Authority is the legitimate right to use power. Not everyone, however, believes in the separation between power and authority. Despots, tyrants, and dictators eschew legitimacy and wield authority like a sword. Vladimir Ilich Lenin viewed the rule of the Communist Party, the dictatorship of the proletariat, as being based on brutal force, unlimited by any laws or rules. Mao Zedong identified power with authority. One has authority because one has power to rule. "Political power grows out of the barrel of a gun," said Mao. This article will focus on the sources and nature of power.

POWER AS KNOWLEDGE

Power has been identified with knowledge, freedom, justice, and political authority. In Plato's allegory of the cave, knowledge is likened to the power that emancipates slaves of sensory perception from the darkness of ignorance to the bright light of intellectual knowledge. Francis Bacon claimed that knowledge is power. In the *Advancement of Learning* (1605), he wrote, "For there is no power on Earth which setteth up a throne or chair of estate in the spirits and souls of men, and in their cogitations, opinions, and beliefs, but knowledge and learning."

POWER AS FREEDOM

Thomas Hobbes, Baruch Spinoza, Immanuel Kant, and Jean-Paul Sartre understood freedom to be the source of power. Hobbes argued that the social contract came about by means of the surrender or alienation of natural freedom to society. Hobbes wanted to place all power in the hands of the sovereign. Spinoza identified freedom as power—power to act, power for self-preservation. Spinoza defined power as *conatus*, the special propensity or capacity of a thing to perform; in short, the freedom of self-preservation. Kant postulated that human beings have free will to impose laws upon themselves; that is, human beings have moral autonomy or freedom, which is the source of power. Sartre believed that freedom was the power of self-determination.

POWER AS POLITICAL AUTHORITY

The Greek Sophist Cratylus, a skeptic and relativist, claimed that the law of right is the law of the strongest; in other words, power is right, power is jus-

tice. This ethic was taken over by the argumentative Sophist Thrasymachus. Plato's *Republic* opens with a discussion between Socrates and the aged Cephalus over the meaning of life, which leads to the question of the just life. Having asked for a definition of justice, Socrates receives a reply from Polemarchus, son of Cephalus, who argues on the authority of the Greek poet Simonides that justice is to give to each what is owed. In the course of the discussion, a frustrated and impatient Thrasymachus charges into the debate. Justice, he argues, is whatever brings advantage to the stronger or to established rule. At the end of the argument, Thrasymachus winds up defending injustice as being more valuable than justice, because injustice can be used to the advantage of the stronger. In effect, Thrasymachus defines justice as power.

JOHN LOCKE AND KARL MARX

John Locke identified political power with legitimate authority. In the *Second Treatise of Government* (1690), Locke differentiated political power and despotical power. The difference consisted in the fact that political power is legitimate authority, whereas despotical power is arbitrary. Political power is founded on the social contract, in which self-rule is willfully handed over to society for the common good and for protection. Despotical power is simply arbitrary power over other persons.

Karl Marx claimed that political power can be explained in terms of economic relations of property ownership; therefore, he viewed power in capitalist society as exploitation. For Marx, private property is the source of social power. Marx believed that private property ownership patterns created asymmetrical relations of power resulting in the development of two classes: the exploiting class and the exploited class. The property-owning classes are the exploiting classes because they exploit the labor power of the non-owning classes. Workers must enjoy freedom from servitude and must be propertyless. The reason that capitalist power is exploitative is that capitalist society must constantly renew its conditions of existence by ensuring that a sizable percentage of the population remains propertyless and therefore subordinate to the dominant class. The worker has no choice, if he or she wants to survive, but to appear on the labor market as a commodity to be bought and sold. Power over others, therefore, grows out of unequal property relations.

Max Weber, unlike Marx, found sources of power outside the economic realm. Power may flow from the possession of economic or political resources. High positions may also confer power.

MACHIAVELLI

Niccolò Machiavelli wrote *The Prince* (1513) and dedicated it to Lorenzo de Medici, hoping to attract the attention of the Medicis. *The Prince* has been called a grammar of power, and for good reasons. The book was written about the acquisition of absolute power. *The Prince* was taken from the *Discourses*, which set forth several principles: the superiority of the democratic republic, reliance upon mass consent, organic unity, the role of leadership in achieving cohesiveness, the imperative of military power, the use of national religion to unify the masses and to cement morale, the will to survive and ruthless measures, and the cyclical rise and fall caused by the decadence of the old and reinvigoration of the new. Although *The Prince* can be studied in the context of the Mirror of Princes Literature, a genre that flourished during the Middle Ages and depicted princely virtues, it signified a revolutionary turn in political thinking by rejecting ethics and metaphysics and espousing political realism.

Machiavelli refused to imagine human beings as they ought to be; instead, he employed as his starting point the realistic acknowledgment of human beings as they are. Machiavelli believed that ideals and ethics were ineffective in government. Chapters 15 through 19 of *The Prince* are the most radical. These chapters deal with the qualities that a prince ought to possess. The prince is advised to disregard the question of whether his actions should be called virtuous or vicious. The choice of action, Machiavelli claims, depends not upon ethics but upon circumstances. Machiavelli was not concerned with good or evil, but with effective government; not with virtues, but with *virtù*, or vitality. Chapter 14 stresses the primacy and necessity of brute power being employed for strategic ends—in other words, war. For Machiavelli, the prince has no other aim but war. The prince is counseled to learn war through action and study and to know and defend even in peacetime.

THOMAS HOBBES

Thomas Hobbes defined the nature of political power in *Leviathan* (1651), which contains a power-ful argument on behalf of strong government. Hobbes wrote *Leviathan* while exiled in Paris from the English Civil wars. Hobbes's aim was to unite Church and state into one powerful structure. Holding to a mechanical view of the universe, he naturally constructed his theory of human nature on the basis of mechanistic principles. For example, he depicted the human mind as a function of the nervous system. Chapter 13 contains the famous passage called the "Naturall Condition of Mankind." Hobbes claimed that the state of nature is a state of war because of human equality (for example, a small man could kill a big man with a rock). Human life in this natural state is "solitary, poore, nasty, brutish, and short." Power is socially and equitably distributed. In order to gain mutual protection, and because human beings enjoyed a natural rational propensity to seek peace, a commonwealth was in order. Such a commonwealth would be formed by a compact in which each individual agreed to allow as much liberty to others as he or she would expect to enjoy. By forming a compact and mutually renouncing individual freedom and power, the members of society would grant absolute power to the sovereign. Only the government, then, could assign rights and determine justice.

FRIEDRICH NIETZSCHE

Friedrich Nietzsche, in *The Dawn* (1881), *The Gay Science* (1882), *Beyond Good and Evil* (1886), *The Will to Power* (1901), and *Thus Spoke Zarathustra* (1883), made power an interpretative principle of human behavior and morality. The will to power is at the heart of his philosophy. He pointed out a dualistic morality—a slave morality, or herd morality, versus a master morality. The slave morality was guided by resentment against the successful, wealthy, and powerful. The superman (*Übermensch*) appears as the Nietzschean hero who affirms life and recalls Wolfgang von Goethe's Faust, who symbolized the ever-striving, never satisfied power of the human spirit. "Dead are all gods; now we will that superman live." Superman is the goal of history. In *The Antichrist* (1895), Nietzsche defined the good as power. "What is good? Everything that heightens the feeling of power in man, the will to power, power itself."

MICHEL FOUCAULT

Foucault was one of the brightest luminaries to grace the French firmament of intellectual thought in the twentieth century, and his influence can be felt throughout the academic world of the West. His major contribution to social thought was the stimulation of new thinking about power. This concept is central to his social and political critique. In it, he thinks he has found the Archimedean point with which to understand the systems and structures of rationality, political authority, and science. However one may conceive of Foucault's use of the concept of power, there is no way to interpret his project of contemporary historical analysis without tackling the ineluctable idea of power.

Power for Foucault is not some kind of substance. It is neither an essence composed of definable qualities nor an ontological category representing some real entity. Instead, power is an abstract configuration, an abstract possibility of relations of force. Foucault conceives of power in essentially nominalistic terms. "Power in the substantive sense, *le pouvoir*, doesn't exist. . . . In reality power means relations, a more-or-less organized, hierarchical coordinated cluster of relations." Relations within the social body make the presence of power ubiquitous. This is the case because Foucault views power coterminously with the conditions of social relations. What is revolutionary about Foucault is his localization of the mechanisms of power in the apparatuses outside the state. He locates power, or "micro-powers," on the mundane, quotidian level of familial relationships, kinship systems, local administrations, and so forth. He cautions, therefore, that unless the mechanisms of power that function outside the state are changed, nothing in society will be changed. Foucault then locates power at every point of society. In fact, he contends that the functioning of the state depends on concrete power relations diffused throughout the social body. Power functions at myriad points of social contact and has myriad effects.

Foucault thinks of power as having "capillary" forms of existence—the capillaries being the points at which power enters and invests itself in individuals. It is at this level that power becomes productive of social knowledge.

The functioning of power creates new bodies of knowledge. Power and knowledge are inexorably connected. One cannot exist without the other. Power is constrained to produce knowledge, and knowledge cannot escape engendering more power. Foucault does not mean the same thing by power/knowledge that members of the Frankfurt School meant by reason/domination. Foucault is not trying to unmask the oppressive systems of the dominant classes. Instead, he is attempting to locate the points of intersection of power and knowledge as they are dispersed strategically throughout the social body.

THE INDIVIDUAL IN SOCIETY

What part does the individual play in the process of the determination of power within the social body? Foucault seems rather ambiguous concerning the individual subject and the problem of subjectivity. On one hand, he says that it is the position of the subject that exercises power, not the individual; on the other, he says that power is exercised in the very bodies of individuals. The effects of power invest themselves in the bodies of individuals. Biopower (also called political technology) and biopolitics refer to the control of species and the control of the body. Political technology leads to the categorization of human species and converts the human body into an object to be manipulated (disciplinary power). The aim is to create a docile and productive body. Biopolitics depicts the individual as an object of political concern for the purpose of normalization.

In *Discipline and Punish* (1979), Foucault presents power as the force of normalization and the formation of knowledge. Normalization and knowledge invest the body, the individual, the masses, and the body politic. "The soul is the effect and the instrument of a political anatomy; the soul is the prison of the body." Through knowledge, power moves to a new level. Knowledge is power over people that ends up normalizing people and standardizing them in the factory, school, prison, hospital, or military.

Power is not built up of individual wills. Individuals and subjects are not particular powers, they do not possess power, and power does not emanate from them. Yet all individuals are subjects in a universal struggle in which everyone fights everyone else. There is, for Foucault, no such thing as an oppressor/oppressed polarity such as the Marxist class struggle between the proletariat and the bourgeoisie. Forms of rationality other than the economic enmesh themselves in the institutions and domains of society, engendering effects such as sexism and racism.

At his inaugural address at the Collège de France, France's most distinguished academic institution, Foucault presented a discourse about discourse entitled "L'Ordre du discours." In it, Foucault argues that the production of discourse is controlled by procedures of exclusion, sexual and political prohibition, taboo, ritual, and the right to speak. The will to knowledge leads to a system of exclusion that relies on institutional support. Procedures arise for the control of discourse, systems of restriction, conditions, and rules of access. The number of those allowed to participate is small. Ritual defines qualifications, gestures, behavior, and circumstances. Societies of discourse preserve discourse within a restricted group.

For Foucault, then, power is a heuristic principle, or explanatory rule, for understanding social practices. He corrected the too-long-held view that power is exclusively repressive or constraining. In fact, what Foucault demonstrated was the insidious way in which power produces conformity, legitimizes political power, and creates exclusionary forms of knowledge.

Michael Candelaria

FURTHER READING

Allen, Amy. *The Power of Feminist Theory: Domination, Resistance, Solidarity.* Boulder, Colo.: Westview Press, 1999. A feminist critique and theorization of power, focusing on the work of Foucault, Judith Butler, and Hannah Arendt.

Foucault, Michel. *Discipline and Punish: The Birth of the Prison.* Translated by Alan Sheridan. New York: Vintage Books, 1979. This work concerns itself with the expression of power in penal institutions and the development of disciplinary techniques that can convert the body into a docile instrument.

_____. *Power/Knowledge: Selected Interviews and Other Writings, 1972-1977.* Edited by Colin Gordon. Translated by Colin Gordon et al. New York: Pantheon Books, 1980. Essays and interviews that concentrate mostly on the issue of power and its pervasive presence in every area of human life, especially in human bodies. It also deals with penal institutions, the Panopticon of Jeremy Bentham, health institutions, and the history of sexuality.

Hobbes, Thomas. *Leviathan.* Edited by Richard Tuck. Rev. student ed. New York: Cambridge University Press, 1996. This masterpiece of political literature contains a powerful argument for a strong authoritarian government. Its subjects include social contract theory, the state of nature, the mechanistic view of human nature, naturalistic ethics, and the unity of Church and state.

Kaplan, Laura Duhan, and Laurence F. Bove, eds. *Philosophical Perspectives on Power and Domination: Theories and Practices.* Atlanta: Rodopi, 1997. An anthology of essays on power written from a wide variety of perspectives. Explores such issues as the relationship of individual identity to global networks of power, and the relationship of theory to practice.

Machiavelli, Niccolò. *The Prince.* Edited and translated by Angelo M. Codevilla. New Haven, Conn.: Yale University Press, 1997. This masterly analysis of power was written during a time when there was a growing need for the centralization of the Italian city-states, an increasingly nationalistic ethos, and a restoration of the Medicis to power in Florence. Although *The Prince* was written to gain favor with the Medicis, its aim was to describe how principalities are won, held, and lost.

Nehamas, Alexander. *Nietzsche: Life as Literature.* Cambridge, Mass.: Harvard University Press, 1985. A superb explication of Nietzsche's philosophy. Chapter 3 is one of the best readings extant of Nietzsche's doctrine of the "will to power."

Nietzsche, Friedrich. *The Portable Nietzsche.* Edited and translated by Walter Kaufmann. New York: Viking Press, 1984. Most of the works contained here are new translations by Kaufmann. Included are the entire text of *Thus Spoke Zarathustra* and selections from works such as *Beyond Good and Evil.* Also includes letters and notes.

SEE ALSO: *Beyond Good and Evil*; Dirty hands; Foucault, Michel; Freedom and liberty; Hobbes, Thomas; *Leviathan*; Locke, John; Machiavelli, Niccolò; Marxism; Nietzsche, Friedrich; Politics.